P9-AGL-411

We're the brightest name in movies...

...because we're the only production payroll service in town open 24 hours a day

...because we provide complete casting services and celebrity look-alikes

...because we provide 24 hour telephone answering for producers and entertainment professionals

PRODUCERS' & ARTISTS' SERVICES   **(213) 656-440**
8235 Santa Monica Boulevard, Suite 311, West Hollywood, CA 900

ORDER FORM
Prices are for current editions only.
Call 1-800-FILMBKS or 213/471-8066 for more information.

YES! PLEASE SEND THE FOLLOWING BOOKS:

QTY.	ANNUAL DIRECTORIES	PRICE	CA. TAX	TOTAL
____	FILM DIRECTORS—8th Ed.	$59.95	$4.05	$____
____	PRODS/STUDIOS/AGENTS			
	CASTING			
	DIRECTORS - 2nd Ed.	29.95	2.02	$____
____	CINEMATOGRAPHERS			
	PRODUCTION DESIGNERS			
	COSTUME DESIGNERS &			
	FILM EDITORS - 2nd Ed.	29.95	2.02	$____
____	FILM WRITERS - 2nd Ed.	29.95	2.02	$____
____	TELEVISION WRITERS - 1st Ed.	39.95	2.70	$____
____	SPECIAL EFFECTS &			
	STUNTS -1st Ed.	24.95	1.68	$____
____	TV DIRECTORS - 1st Ed.	29.95	2.02	$____

SUBTOTAL $_____
ADD IN SHIPPING $_____
TOTAL ORDER $_____

UPS SHIPPING CHARGES		
	CONT. USA	CANADA
First Book	$5.50	$10.00
Add'l. Books	$3.00	$5.00

SHIPPING CHARGES (Overseas)		
	AIRMAIL	SURFACE
Film Directors	$45.00	$12.50
Other Directories	$30.00	$10.00

For Faster Service
Call 213/471-8066 (CA) or
1/800-FILMBKS (except CA)

FAX ORDERS ACCEPTED: 213/471-4969

PAYMENT IS BY:
Check ____ Money Order____ Visa ____ MC ____ AMEX_____
Card No._____ Exp. Date_____
Signature_____
(exactly as it appears on your card)
SHIP BOOKS TO:
NAME_____
COMPANY_____ PHONE (very imp't.!)_____
ADDRESS _____
CITY/STATE/ZIP_____

ORDER FORM
Prices are for current editions only.
Call 1-800-FILMBKS or 213/471-8066 for more information.

YES! PLEASE SEND THE FOLLOWING BOOKS:

QTY.	ANNUAL DIRECTORIES	PRICE	CA. TAX	TOTAL
____	FILM DIRECTORS—8th Ed.	$59.95	$4.05	$____
____	PRODS/STUDIOS/AGENTS			
	CASTING			
	DIRECTORS - 2nd Ed.	29.95	2.02	$____
____	CINEMATOGRAPHERS			
	PRODUCTION DESIGNERS			
	COSTUME DESIGNERS &			
	FILM EDITORS - 2nd Ed.	29.95	2.02	$____
____	FILM WRITERS - 2nd Ed.	29.95	2.02	$____
____	TELEVISION WRITERS - 1st Ed.	39.95	2.70	$____
____	SPECIAL EFFECTS &			
	STUNTS -1st Ed.	24.95	1.68	$____
____	TV DIRECTORS - 1st Ed.	29.95	1.35	$____

SUBTOTAL $_____
ADD IN SHIPPING $_____
TOTAL ORDER $_____

UPS SHIPPING CHARGES		
	CONT. USA	CANADA
First Book	$5.50	$10.00
Add'l. Books	$3.00	$5.00

SHIPPING CHARGES (Overseas)		
	AIRMAIL	SURFACE
Film Directors	$45.00	$12.50
Other Directories	$30.00	$10.00

For Faster Service
Call 213/471-8066 (CA) or
1/800-FILMBKS (except CA)

FAX ORDERS ACCEPTED: 213/471-4969

PAYMENT IS BY:
Check ____ Money Order____ Visa ____ MC ____ AMEX_____
Card No._____ Exp. Date_____
Signature_____
(exactly as it appears on your card)
SHIP BOOKS TO:
NAME_____
COMPANY_____ PHONE (very imp't.!)_____
ADDRESS _____
CITY/STATE/ZIP_____

ORDER FORM
Prices are for current editions only.
Call 1-800-FILMBKS or 213/471-8066 for more information.

YES! PLEASE SEND THE FOLLOWING BOOKS:

QTY.	ANNUAL DIRECTORIES	PRICE	CA. TAX	TOTAL
____	FILM DIRECTORS—8th Ed.	$59.95	$4.05	$____
____	PRODS/STUDIOS/AGENTS			
	CASTING			
	DIRECTORS - 2nd Ed.	29.95	2.02	$____
____	CINEMATOGRAPHERS			
	PRODUCTION DESIGNERS			
	COSTUME DESIGNERS &			
	FILM EDITORS - 2nd Ed.	29.95	2.02	$____
____	FILM WRITERS - 2nd Ed.	29.95	2.02	$____
____	TELEVISION WRITERS - 1st Ed.	39.95	2.70	$____
____	SPECIAL EFFECTS &			
	STUNTS - 1st Ed.	24.95	1.68	$____
____	TV DIRECTORS - 1st Ed.	29.95	2.02	

SUBTOTAL $_____
ADD IN SHIPPING $_____
TOTAL ORDER $_____

UPS SHIPPING CHARGES		
	CONT. USA	CANADA
First Book	$5.50	$10.00
Add'l. Books	$3.00	$5.00

SHIPPING CHARGES (Overseas)		
	AIRMAIL	SURFACE
Film Directors	$45.00	$12.50
Other Directories	$30.00	$10.00

For Faster Service
Call 213/471-8066 (CA) or
1/800-FILMBKS (except CA)

FAX ORDERS ACCEPTED: 213/471-4969

PAYMENT IS BY:
Check ____ Money Order____ Visa ____ MC ____ AMEX_____
Card No._____ Exp. Date_____
Signature_____
(exactly as it appears on your card)
SHIP BOOKS TO:
NAME_____
COMPANY_____ PHONE (very imp't.!)_____
ADDRESS _____
CITY/STATE/ZIP_____

ORDER FORM
Prices are for current editions only.
Call 1-800-FILMBKS or 213/471-8066 for more information.

YES! PLEASE SEND THE FOLLOWING BOOKS:

QTY.	ANNUAL DIRECTORIES	PRICE	CA. TAX	TOTAL
____	FILM DIRECTORS—8th Ed.	$59.95	$4.05	$____
____	PRODS/STUDIOS/AGENTS			
	CASTING			
	DIRECTORS - 2nd Ed.	29.95	2.02	$____
____	CINEMATOGRAPHERS			
	PRODUCTION DESIGNERS			
	COSTUME DESIGNERS &			
	FILM EDITORS - 2nd Ed.	29.95	2.02	$____
____	FILM WRITERS - 2nd Ed.	29.95	2.02	$____
____	TELEVISION WRITERS - 1st Ed.	39.95	2.70	$____
____	SPECIAL EFFECTS &			
	STUNTS -1st Ed.	24.95	1.68	$____
____	TV DIRECTORS - 1st Ed.	24.95	2.02	$____

SUBTOTAL $_____
ADD IN SHIPPING $_____
TOTAL ORDER $_____

UPS SHIPPING CHARGES		
	CONT. USA	CANADA
First Book	$5.50	$10.00
Add'l. Books	$3.00	$5.00

SHIPPING CHARGES (Overseas)		
	AIRMAIL	SURFACE
Film Directors	$45.00	$12.50
Other Directories	$30.00	$10.00

For Faster Service
Call 213/471-8066 (CA) or
1/800-FILMBKS (except CA)

FAX ORDERS ACCEPTED: 213/471-4969

PAYMENT IS BY:
Check ____ Money Order____ Visa ____ MC ____ AMEX_____
Card No._____ Exp. Date_____
Signature_____
(exactly as it appears on your card)
SHIP BOOKS TO:
NAME_____
COMPANY_____ PHONE (very imp't.!)_____
ADDRESS _____
CITY/STATE/ZIP_____

NO POSTAGE
NECESSARY IF
MAILED IN THE
UNITED STATES

BUSINESS REPLY CARD

FIRST CLASS PERMIT NO. 4842, BEVERLY HILLS, CA.

POSTAGE WILL BE PAID BY:

LONE EAGLE PUBLISHING CO.
9903 Santa Monica Blvd. #204
Beverly Hills, CA 90212-9942

NO POSTAGE
NECESSARY IF
MAILED IN THE
UNITED STATES

BUSINESS REPLY CARD

FIRST CLASS PERMIT NO. 4842, BEVERLY HILLS, CA.

POSTAGE WILL BE PAID BY:

LONE EAGLE PUBLISHING CO.
9903 Santa Monica Blvd. #204
Beverly Hills, CA 90212-9942

NO POSTAGE
NECESSARY IF
MAILED IN THE
UNITED STATES

BUSINESS REPLY CARD

FIRST CLASS PERMIT NO. 4842, BEVERLY HILLS, CA.

POSTAGE WILL BE PAID BY:

LONE EAGLE PUBLISHING CO.
9903 Santa Monica Blvd. #204
Beverly Hills, CA 90212-9942

NO POSTAGE
NECESSARY IF
MAILED IN THE
UNITED STATES

BUSINESS REPLY CARD

FIRST CLASS PERMIT NO. 4842, BEVERLY HILLS, CA.

POSTAGE WILL BE PAID BY:

LONE EAGLE PUBLISHING CO.
9903 Santa Monica Blvd. #204
Beverly Hills, CA 90212-9942

MICHAEL SINGER'S

FILM DIRECTORS

A COMPLETE GUIDE

Eighth Annual International Edition

Compiled and Edited by Michael Singer

This book is lovingly dedicated to
a loving father
LOUIS SINGER

SOME THINGS ARE LEFT OUT OF THE PICTURE WHEN YOU FILM IN BRITISH COLUMBIA.

MEMBER OF
AFC
INTERNATIONAL
ASSOCIATION OF
FILM COMMISSIONERS

For fast acting relief from shooting pains,
send us your script or plop us a line.

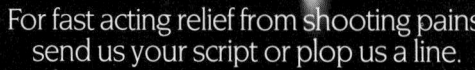
Hot Property

B.C. Film Commission, 3rd Floor, B.C. Enterprise Centre, 750 Pacific Blvd. South, Vancouver, B.C., Canada V6B 5E7 (604) 660-2732

Photography by Toris Von Wolfe except for photo of Walter Hill and Steven Soderbergh.
Black and white photos printed by Isgo Lepejian, Custom Black & White Photo Lab, Burbank, CA

Michael Singer's FILM DIRECTORS: A Complete Guide — Eighth Annual International Edition

Copyright © 1990 by Michael Singer

All rights reserved. No part of this book may be reproduced or utilized in any form or by any means, electronic or mechanical, including photocopying, recording or by any information storage and retrieval system, without permission in writing from the publisher. Inquiries should be addressed to:

LONE EAGLE PUBLISHING CO.
9903 Santa Monica Blvd.
Beverly Hills, CA 90212
213/471-8066

Printed in the United States of America

Book designed by Liz Ridenour

This book was entirely typeset using an Apple Macintosh Plus, Apple Macintosh Two, LaserwriterPlus, Microsoft Word and Aldus Pagemaker.

Printed by McNaughton & Gunn, Saline, Michigan 48176

ISBN: 0-943728-35-5
ISSN: 0740-2872

NOTE: We have made every reasonable effort to ensure that the information contained herein is as accurate as possible. However, errors and omissions are sure to occur. We would appreciate your notifying us of any which you may find.

* Lone Eagle Publishing is a division of Lone Eagle Productions, Inc.

LETTER FROM THE PUBLISHER

This **Eighth Annual International Edition of FILM DIRECTORS: A Complete Guide** brings with it some interesting changes and additions: We have combined the indices for the main listing and for Notable Directors of the Past. (We have still kept the two listing sections separate as the main focus of this book is for *active* directors, and we didn't feel the reader wanted to leaf through pages of listings for D. W. Griffith or Alfred Hitchcock while looking for the director of his or her next project.) For those of you trying to find a particular location, we have listed film commissions in the United States and Canada, as well as some of the major ones around the world.

     Michael Singer has, once again, outdone himself in putting this book together. However, as always, contacts for directors are the hardest to pin down. Please do us (and yourselves a favor) and keep us informed of any changes in your representation.

     For those eagle-eyes reader, you will notice that Ralph Singleton's name does not appear on this letter. That is simply because you will be able to read several pages of his thoughts as one of the directors Michael chose to interview this year. I think you will find all the interviews full of fascinating details about working in the *business*.

See you at the movies!

Joan V. Singleton

Joan V. Singleton
Publisher

FILM
DIRECTORS
GUIDE

The U.S. Virgin Islands Film Office

Charlie's Angels

Four Seasons

Dreams of Gold

The Island of Dr. Moreau

TEL: (809) 775-1444   FAX : (809) 774-4390

Contact: Win deLugo, Director or Eric Matthews, Asst. Director, Film Promotion Office, Dept. ED&A, Box 6400, St. Thomas, U.S. Virgin Islands 00804.

We're No Virgins to Filmmaking.

St. Thomas · St. John · St. Croix

V

ALBUQUERQUE

NEW MEXICO'S ONLY MAJOR METROPOLITAN AREA OFFERS EVERYTHING...

FROM *Lasso's*

TO LASERS

...TO MEET YOUR PRODUCTION AND LOCATION NEEDS.

ALBUQUERQUE • FILM • AND TELEVISION • COMMISSION

MEMBER OF

AFC
INTERNATIONAL
ASSOCIATION OF FILM COMMISSIONERS

PATRICIA TORN • DIRECTOR
P.O. BOX 1293 ALBUQUERQUE, NEW MEXICO 87103 • (505) 768-4512

TABLE OF CONTENTS

INTRODUCTION

It's an expanding universe, and motion pictures are no exception. Keeping up with the bewildering array of films and filmmakers from around the world grows ever more challenging, especially since more productions than ever seem to go before the cameras from one week to the next. Home video and cable television have opened new territories for enterprising directors, resulting in a stupendous number of feature-length films specifically aimed at those markets. Distribution agreements allow movies to be played in theatres for a mere week or so before heading straight to the racks in your neighborhood videocassette parlor. Often, they completely bypass theatrical distribution. A new development has seen feature films previously shelved by their respective studios resurrected as "premiere" movies on cable or network TV. How does all this affect the latest edition of FILM DIRECTORS: A COMPLETE GUIDE? To be perfectly honest, tracking this frenzy of filmmaking—and the directors who specialize in these latter-day equivalents of "quota quickies"—can be quite tough. Directors like David A. Prior, Fred Olen Ray and Cirio H. Santiago (Roger Corman's man in Manila) turn 'em out so fast and furious— and with so many title changes—that the editor's head sometimes imitates Linda Blair's in *THE EXORCIST*! Take heart, B-movie fans...they've returned...with a vengeance!

As in the past, the main intention of this book is to provide an easy, practical and comprehensive reference to selected international film directors and their work. We have no desire to editorialize or pontificate on the careers of these filmmakers. Their credits speak for themselves.

Among our features are:

- An alphabetical listing of directors by name and a concise rundown of their credits by year.

- *FROM THE DIRECTOR'S CHAIR*, a special section highlighting six filmmakers, each representing different styles and approaches to moviemaking. These interviews are conducted by the editor especially for this book.

- A cross-referenced index to over 30,000 film titles in alphabetical order followed by the names of their directors. This will help those who remember the name of a film, but not its director.

- Academy and Emmy Award nominees and winners among the directors listed in the book.

- *NOTABLE DIRECTORS OF THE PAST*, highlighting the careers of selected filmmakers since the end of the 19th century.

Some words of explanation (the same old story) about the listings:

DIRECTORS: The listings herein are selective by necessity, as the inclusion of every living person who ever directed a full-length feature film would inflate the guide to encyclopedic proportions. Selecting is not an easy task, and we are—as always—open to suggestions and submissions. In fact, a justifiable request for inclusion is always honored. Although the listed directors are primarily active, also included are some retired greats out of sheer respect for their place in film history. Foreign directors included herein represent those whose films have had some distribution and recognition in the United States, or those who have gained the most prominence in their own countries. We continue to make an effort to recognize independent filmmakers working outside the studio system, as they often give the industry a needed shot in the arm with their freshness and occasional impertinence.

The reader should be reminded that because we list only full-length features and telefeatures, a director whose last credit in the book is ten years old could be one of the many who is consistently employed in short-form episodic television. Birthdates, birthplaces and contacts have been provided whenever possible, but it's well known that all three are subject to change without notice.

(Note on the alphabetizing of Asian directors' names: In China, Hong Kong, Taiwan, Korea, Japan and other parts of Asia, tradition dictates that when writing one's name, the family name precedes the given name, i.e. Kurosawa Akira or Lee Jang-Ho rather than Akira Kurosawa or Jang-Ho Lee. However, through the years, the Japanese have followed the western custom of first name first, family name last, when writing or speaking their names for non-Japanese. Therefore, we all know the director of *SEVEN SAMURAI* as Akira Kurosawa. In China, Taiwan and Korea, however, the original tradition remains. [The exceptions are those Asian directors who have "westernized" their names, such as Edward Yang, Ann Hui and Johnny Mak.] Although we would address Xie Jin as "Mr. Xie," it would be unthinkable to list him in the book as "Jin Xie." However, that is exactly what we have been doing in a misguided attempt to keep the alphabetizing consistent. Therefore, we will begin to keep Asian tradition intact, and break our own, by now listing those Asian filmmakers as they are known in their own countries— Zhang Yimou rather than Yimou Zhang, Lee Doo-Yong rather than Doo-Yong Lee, etc. Of course, they are now alphabetized by their first, rather than family names, but it's the best we can do to facilitate readers trying to locate these filmmakers' credits.)

FILMS: While we make every effort to insure that credits are as complete as possible, the now famous "Spanish/Bulgarian Syndrome" (also known as the "Icelandic/Moroccan Syndrome") continues to plague the editor. This refers to the inevitable discovery, usually in the wee hours of the morning whilst staring blankly at a flickering television screen, of an obscure film heretofore not included in a director's *oeuvre*, a Spanish/Bulgarian co-production released theatrically only in Sofia, not in Madrid, and definitely not in the United States. God knows how these films are discovered and aired by the local networks, but they do help us complete our task at hand.

The criteria for listed films, in terms of running times, are as follows:
Features: A running time of 60 minutes or longer. Although it pains us to exclude short subjects of fine quality, including such films would legitimately mean that we should also accept episodic TV programs as well, which usually run from 22 to 45 minutes in length without commercials.
Telefeatures: On commercial television, an air time of 90 minutes to 4-1/2 hours. This is not as eccentric as it might seem—without commercials, a 90 minute television program still runs approximately 72 minutes—the length of a short feature—and a 4-1/2 hour "mini-series" clocks in at about 3 hours and 45 minutes, which is the length of such long features as *GONE WITH THE WIND* and *HEAVEN'S GATE*. On non-commercial television, air times of 60 minutes to 4 hours are acceptable because of the elimination of any commercial interruptions.
Television Mini-Series: On commercial television, an air time of 4-1/2 hours or longer, or 4 hours or more on non-commercial television.
Videotaped television dramas—some of which are now called "movies" by the networks— are *not* included. Although truly impressive work has been done on video, such as Edward Zwick's *SPECIAL BULLETIN* and Anthony Page's *THE MISSILES OF OCTOBER*, we feel obliged to live up to the *film* in our book's title.

TITLES: Films are often known by a multiplicity of titles in the course of international distribution. Since this is a U.S.-based book, American release titles are utilized with alternate titles following in *italics*, e.g.,

BUTCHER, BAKER, NIGHTMARE MAKER *NIGHT WARNING/MOMMA'S BOY*
    Royal American, 1981

In the case of films from England, Australia or other English-speaking foreign countries, a title in italics usually represents the original title in that country if different from its American release title, e.g.,

THE ROAD WARRIOR *MAD MAX II* Warner Bros., 1982, Australian

For foreign films which were distributed in the United States, the American title is listed first, followed by the original foreign-language title, only if its meaning is substantially different from the English, e.g.,

ALL SCREWED UP *TUTTO A POSTE E NIENTE IN ORDINE* New Line Cinema, 1974, Italian

Films that did not receive American distribution are generally listed under their original foreign-language titles, as are films which were actually released in the U.S. under those original titles, e.g.,

LA BELLA DI ROMA Lux Film, 1955, Italian

or:

LA VIE CONTINUE Triumph/Columbia, 1982, French

DISTRIBUTORS AND PRODUCTION COMPANIES: Original American distributors of feature films are listed, although movies often change their distributors through the course of time. For foreign films that received no US distribution, the original distributors or production companies in their respective countries are included whenever possible.

Telefeatures and television mini-series are identified with the names of their production companies rather than the networks on which they aired.

Production companies are also listed for features which have not yet found distributors.

YEAR OF RELEASE: This is often extremely hard to determine. Usually, a foreign film is released to the United States a year or two (sometimes more) after its initial appearance in its own country. Therefore, for the sake of accuracy, the *original* year of release is provided rather than the American release date. Also, there are many U.S. films which are completed in one year and released in another. We generally utilize the year in which a film is reviewed in *Daily Variety* or other trade publications. Needless to say, there are often differences of opinion as to when certain films, domestic *and* foreign, were first exhibited. The dates herein may be at variance with other sources. Also release dates for films not yet released are projections.

COUNTRY OF ORIGIN: These are the years of incredibly complex international co-production and tax shelter deals. How does one explain that a film made in England with an American director, French producer and international cast, but registered in Panama for tax purposes is, therefore, a Panamanian film? We have opted for realism based upon the nationalities of production personnel and geographic locations of companies with financial participation.

As always, thanks to the superb staffs of the UCLA Theatre Arts Library and Academy of Motion Pictures Arts and Sciences Margaret Herrick Library. Once again, the esteemed Italian film scholar Lorenzo Codelli donated virtually all of the information herein concerning his country's filmmakers. His special contribution to this book can never be underestimated. And gratitude to all my friends and acquaintances around the world who made contributions to this book and to my life...they know who they are!

Joan Singleton and the terrific staff at Lone Eagle—Bethann Wetzel, Mike Green and Lori Copeland—are to be congratulated for their expertise, advice, phenomenal support and perhaps most of all, patience. Bethann, in particular, provided herculean efforts that were nothing short of miraculous, and nothing less than extraordinary. And a tip of the hat to all the other Lone Eagle authors, my supportive comrades-in-reference.

Michael Singer
Los Angeles, California
August 1990

DIRECTOR'S

CHAIR

Courtesy of The Lone Wolf Company

WALTER HILL

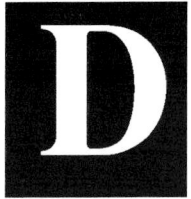**D**ELIGHTING MANY, outraging others, Walter Hill has never been a shrinking violet of the movies. Although primarily known as a smooth, kinetic action director, Hill's work has also exhibited exciting tendencies toward *noir* surrealism, thick atmospherics and a stubborn streak of stylistic individuality.

Before taking hold of directing reins, Hill wrote or co-wrote such films as *HICKEY AND BOGGS, THE GETAWAY* and *THE DROWNING POOL*. His own work as a filmmaker includes a number of projects that range from the overtly commercial to the downright personal, among them *HARD TIMES, THE DRIVER, THE WARRIORS, THE LONG RIDERS, SOUTHERN COMFORT, 48 HRS., STREETS OF FIRE, CROSSROADS, RED HEAT, JOHNNY HANDSOME* and the recent *ANOTHER 48 HRS.*

MICHAEL SINGER: It seems to me that the reasons people become directors now are different than what they were 30 or 40 years ago.

WALTER HILL: I think there are a lot of people now who become directors because they're very committed to bringing certain projects to fruition rather than going into it as a career. If someone became a director in the old days, it was a craft, a profession, and if you didn't get into it at a fairly early age, chances were you weren't going to become a director at all. Now there are a lot of people who become directors when they are in their forties. That didn't happen very much back then.

It seems that now, if you're only a screenwriter rather than a hyphenate, you only have half a career.

That's unfortunate. I think screenwriting is a craft, a profession. The idea that you have somehow fallen short of the mark if you don't become a director seems silly to me, because an awful lot of people by temperament or talent are not cut out to be directors. The fact that you write doesn't guarantee that you can direct, any more than the fact that you can direct means you can write. There are people that are good at both, of course.

When you segued from writing to directing, had that been the goal all along or did an opportunity just present itself to you?

I had a rather strange beginning in that my first real work was as a writer and then I became an assistant director and then I became a writer again and then I became a director. But I think I always really wanted to become a director. My own writing was pointed in that direction. I don't mean that to contradict my first remarks, but I think in my case it was true. I never really thought of myself, in that sense, as a writer. I think of myself as a director who writes. And early on I thought of myself as someone who probably was going to be a director but was writing to make a living. One of the reasons I like to work with writers is that I think they help you test your ideas. I don't like to write alone and then direct what I write, although I've done that. People often ask me, "Don't you want to write originals and then direct them?" I've done that and I don't want to anymore. I'd much rather work with other writers. It's a lot more fun. You have the excitement of being part of a conspiracy.

I understand that you like to do a lot of writing on the set during production.

Yeah, I rewrite as I go, constantly. I think I know the film and the characters better as the picture goes on. I'm not one to think that if you write it, it's the same truth three or six months later. Making pictures is a process, at least the way I do it. You get the script and then you shoot the film and then you cut the film. In a sense, it's all writing. In another sense, it's all filmmaking. And the old joke is the truth—the final rewrites are in the editing room. Movies are always looking for something that plays, which is not necessarily the same thing as literary truth. You can construct something that is quite right on the page, but doesn't play. And filmmakers are always going to be pushing everything toward what plays.

You have a great feeling for rural America in movies like *HARD TIMES, SOUTHERN COMFORT* and *THE LONG RIDERS*. On the other hand, you're known for urban actioners like *48 HRS., THE DRIVER* and *RED HEAT*. Do you like spending a lot of time in places outside Los Angeles to soak up atmosphere and ideas?

I've traveled a lot...and I'm sick of traveling. Basically, I like to sit home and read. I don't like going out very much at all. I don't mind going out on a picture. But I think that atmosphere you mention comes out of your dream life. I grew up in the sticks, and I think I approached urban living with a sense of wonder. I like things with rural settings, but I think that generally those pictures aren't very commercial anymore. One has to adapt.

Do you feel that you've been forced to adapt as a filmmaker in any way?

I think I'm a good example of somebody who would have been very happy in the studio system 30, 40, 50 years ago. I'd have probably made westerns. They don't make those very much anymore.

You made *THE LONG RIDERS*, which was a "real" western, and *EXTREME PREJUDICE*, which was a contemporary western. Some have suggested that most of your films have a western sensibility.

It's interesting to speculate on the decline of the western. I think the single biggest factor is that Americans are no longer in touch or care a lot about their agrarian past, which is a way of saying that they've lost a sense of their own history. I think it's also true that westerns were done to death on television, which exhausted the genre.

I think TV is still doing them to death with those "hunks-in-buckskin" sort of shows.

I haven't seen them. The other thing you have to say about the westerns is that of all the motion picture genres, they were the most subject to parody. Once that begins to happen, it's a lot more difficult for the audience to take them seriously. The large audiences want very much to believe in the drama. Parody appeals to intellectuals, but on the whole

3

it doesn't appeal to larger audiences. However, I don't think westerns are irreversibly gone. They'll never be what they were as an industry staple, but I think occasionally somebody will make one and have no better or worse a chance for success than any other period movie. If you've got one with the right story and cast, it could work very well. I think one of the sad things is that we've not only lost westerns, but period movies as well.

Period movies are still a staple in Eastern Europe, or at least were until the recent developments.

I think a lot of that has to do with the social conditions in those countries. I think there's a greater nostalgia for the past over there than we have in America, and for good reason. I think the great majority of Americans are not imbued with a sense of nostalgia for their own history. Again, we're talking in very big generalities. The truth is, if you write a good book about some aspect of America's past, there's a great chance for commercial success. But to make a commercially successful motion picture, you have to get a much larger audience than you need to get a best-seller.

If you had your druthers, would you be working a lot more on period pieces than contemporary, urban action films?

I don't know. You want to do a variety of films. I don't want to sound like I'm unhappy with my lot. I'm really mainly interested in the characters of the stories I have done. Therefore, I'd rather do a contemporary drama with characters I'm interested in than I would a nostalgic rural piece with characters that don't particularly interest me.

Your newest film, *ANOTHER 48 HRS.*, is a follow-up to a smash hit you made a few years ago. One of your stars, Eddie Murphy, is in very different circumstances now than when you worked with him the first time. He's achieved superstardom, and has also directed as well. Has the dynamic changed between you on this shoot?

People ask me, "How has Eddie changed?" I find Eddie to be exactly the same...except he's a lot more so. Whatever tendencies he had in the past, he's just more so now. But working with him has been exactly the same. We get in,

rehearse the scene, work until we decide we like it, and we shoot it. We worked out the character of Reggie Hammond in the last one. The biggest difference between shooting the last one and this one is that Eddie, Nick Nolte and myself feel that we know the characters this time. We're more confident about how the characters would react to the situation. So in that sense, it's changed a bit. I've never made a sequel before. I suppose the nicest thing about a sequel is that you know the characters already. The most difficult thing about this sequel...I don't think it's unfair to say that *48 HRS.* has been a much imitated movie. I wonder occasionally how much ground is left. Some of the imitations are good films, but you wonder how much ground they've used up. There's only so much land to stand on.

How do you find that additional square foot of ground that hasn't been covered yet?

I don't know that we have. You'd better ask me that next year. I think it's a good story. But what the film is really about is an exploration of the personalities of the two main characters—set in a bizarre, comic, violent world. It's certainly not realistic, but it's informed by a certain kind of street truth. That's the basis of the humor. I think the characters are necessarily softer in this one than they were in the original. A lot of the antagonism in the first movie worked at a very direct racial level. To put them back in that framework would mean that each character had learned nothing from the first experience. It would be a denial of the first movie, which I think would be unfair. So as I've uncharitably put it, a lot of this movie is like a husband and wife fighting with each other. They fight like they mean it, but at the same time you know they're going to kiss and make up.

Were you at all reluctant to take *ANOTHER 48 HRS.* on, because it *is* a sequel?

Yeah, I was. Paramount had asked me a number of times over the years to get into it. It didn't appeal to me. But Eddie called me and said he'd very much like to do another one, and thought there was room to do another one, could we sit down and talk about it? Then he called Nick and Nick called me, and said we ought to do it. Eddie and I worked out a story which I liked, and thought, what the

hell. I also like working with my friends, and I count both Eddie and Nick as my friends. I think having fun while you make a motion picture is important.

You said before that you would have been happy in the old studio system, and you're the first director I've ever interviewed who ever said that...except for George Sidney and Gene Kelly, who *did* work in that system and seemed to enjoy it.

Well, I think I felt that a little stronger a few years ago than I do now, to be frank. I'll tell you why. I like the work, to stage and shoot for a living. I have a good time making motion pictures on the whole, even with all the problems that go with it. I think the most frustrating thing about the business—less so now than a few years ago—is the *business*, the negotiating, the deals. You're always going to meetings. What I like about my understanding of the old studio system is that they made lots of movies, and you just went to work. Nowadays, so often you spend more time getting a deal on a movie set up than you do on the movie itself. I think that was truer five years ago and certainly truer 10 years ago than now. There's a more positive attitude now about making films, and what underlies it is their profitability. I think it's much easier to be a young director now than 10 or 15 years ago when I was first starting, because there's more product.

Here's the Walter Hill stereotype: two-fisted action director in the classic mode. Are you comfortable with that?

I just say oh shit, throw me in the briar patch. I don't think anyone wants to be thought of as just an action director, but I also think there's a long and honorable tradition in Hollywood with action directors. You hope you can make your own contribution. Historically, action directors in Hollywood have been thought of as being on the back porch. But listen, that's not exactly the fate of the Boat People. There are a lot of things in the world that are a lot tougher. I like doing action films. The definitions are always a little funny because what is violent to one person is action to someone else. If you say, "You wanna go out and see a violent movie?," most people would say no. If you say, "You wanna go out and see an action movie?," most people say yes. In dealing with physical

violence, sometimes I've presented it in a very tough and harsh way. At times I've presented it in a way that's palatable for general entertainment. What I find remarkable is that if you film violence in a way that's totally light and doesn't really deal with physical consequences, everybody's quite happy with you. If you actually show how tough and hard it can be, everybody gets mad at you. The moralists jump all over you, when I would have thought they would be unhappy about the reverse. These are among the many things about the world that puzzle me.

What else puzzles you?

When somebody transcends the genre, they're no longer considered action directors. Among many other things, *SEVEN SAMURAI* is an action movie. The fact that it is a very great film doesn't mean that it is not an action film. I find it a little off-putting that when somebody does it very well, there's a perception that it's no longer an action movie. The problem isn't making action films...it's whether or not you make good movies or bad movies.

People assume I like action movies. I don't particularly like them. If anything, I'm probably a harsher critic of action films than other genres. I like romantic comedies very much, dramas as well. George Cukor was one of my favorite directors. He was an admirable director not because of the kind of films he made, but because he made them so well. That's what directing is all about, not selecting high-toned subjects. I think that in Hollywood and in film criticism, movies are quite often judged by their intentions rather than their execution and the ability of the filmmaker to execute them. If noble intentions were what made a good film, then it would be very easy to get to heaven. It's not that simple.

JOHNNY HANDSOME **was probably the most controversial of all your films. It won its avid supporters and incredible detractors, dividing people very strongly. Were you glad that it did?**

I think that's always a pretty good sign that something's going on. I didn't think it was a safe film to make when I was shooting it. The foreign reception has been quite good, but I think that's not unexpected. Whether it would work for

an American audience was always problematic. I frankly never thought it would, given what it was, because it was a film that was certainly not a feel-good movie. I liked it as a piece of work.

How do reviews affect you?

I did a film many years ago called *THE DRIVER*. It got a very poor critical reception in New York. It got good reviews in London, Rome, Tokyo, Stockholm. Then people say "Too bad the critics didn't like your movie." I never quite know what to say. The critics in New York didn't like it, but the world's a bigger place than that. Still, as an American, it probably is more important what's coming out of New York. I had a movie a few years ago, *RED HEAT*. It did pretty well at the domestic box-office, but not as well as we hoped it was going to do. It was big foreign. It was a very big seller on cassette. Did the movie do poorly, medium or well? We're into a much less parochial market now than we were 15 years ago. The idea that you're going to judge a film's success or failure on its domestic box-office revenue or its reception by New York film critics is simply wrong.

Why do you think that grip has loosened?

Most of it is economics. The world is a lot closer, whether it's the electronic revolution or the intellectual-political currents in Europe, America or Asia. We're all holding hands and standing next to each other in closer ways than before. I think, to a tremendous degree, the events in Eastern Europe last year had to do with the communications revolution and the fact that you can't hide the truth of how life is in the West. It created enormous dissatisfaction. It's hard to have a system work when nobody wants to live there.

Are there any films you would choose from your body of work that stands as the quintessential Walter Hill picture?

Every film you do is an aspect of your personality. I don't analyze my movies. I don't see them after I'm done with them. I think that's counter productive. It's much better to go on to the next story.

What about the critics and reviews?

There's a quote from Samuel Johnson—which I'll probably get wrong—"The author comes unasked into the arena seeking his fortune at the hazard of disgrace." The idea that you weren't rolling the dice when you took the job is simply naïve. I've gotten a lot of good reviews in my life and I've had my share of scorchers. No complaints. I've had a good ride. I think I'm about halfway there. I'm going to keep doing it. Criticism is quite important to keep you honest. It's unfortunate that so much of it is written by second-raters, but an awful lot of films are made by second-raters, so what the hell. First and foremost, one should be a good professional. I think that there inevitably comes a time when they take away your uniform. Directors are a lot like ballplayers. But very few of them go gracefully.

Toris Von Wolfe

ROBERT M. YOUNG

I N THE KNOCKABOUT WORLD of commercial filmmaking, Robert M. Young has always presented a refreshing alternative voice. Firmly rooted in a traditional humanist tradition, Young has nevertheless turned a clear eye to humanity's more ferocious instincts in such films as *SHORT EYES, THE BALLAD OF GREGORIO CORTEZ, EXTREMITIES* and *TRIUMPH OF THE SPIRIT*.

Entering feature filmmaking in the mid-1960s from a distinguished documentary career, Young's movies have ranged from the starkly dramatic to the light and comedic: including the groundbreaking "minority" films *NOTHING BUT A MAN* and *ALAMBRISTA!,* as well as RICH *KIDS, ONE-TRICK PONY, DOMINICK AND EUGENE* and the forthcoming *TALENT FOR THE GAME*, his third collaboration with actor Edward James Olmos.

MICHAEL SINGER: You are one of the few filmmakers working today working from a staunchly humanist tradition. There seems to be a determined effort on your part to avoid becoming involved with any projects which in any way would be antithetical to what must be a strong personal code.

ROBERT M. YOUNG: I suppose that's true. At the time we are infants in the crib and learning things from our mother's face, we begin to read things about life. And these are things that really inform us. We have to try and pay attention to the things that we think are true about life. So I think that film, of course, is based on that. We look at behavior on the screen and we in the audience are reading something and get insights. I think that it's wrong to be misinforming people and putting their values askew. I think that with such a powerful medium, we have a great influence on people. So it's not that I'm some kind of goody-goody. I'm the same as anyone else. It's just that I believe things have to be psychologically true. It's just that simple.

Do you feel that you're ever held suspect by, say, the critical establishment for making films that take—as much as possible—a positive view of the human condition?

Well, sometimes I feel a little bit discouraged when I see things that are false so widely accepted, or even hailed. I think that I'll never be that successful.

But when I hear myself say that, I think, "What, are you feeling sorry for yourself? You don't have to be judged by somebody else's standards. You just have to be judged by your own." But the danger in this area is that I don't take myself that seriously. When I sound that sober, I have to make fun of myself. To me, when I make a film, I'm making it for myself in some deep way. Not in the sense that I don't care what anyone else thinks. It's not that at all. I'm really interested in communicating with other people. What I mean is that the lessons or experimental things in the film are things that I'm trying to understand and explore in a personal way.

You began as a documentary filmmaker, and many of your dramatic films have a sense of documentary-like realism. What was it in your background that encouraged you to take this approach to moviemaking?

I don't know how to do it any other way. As a filmmaker, you have to operate from inside yourself. How do you, in fact, judge whether something is true or false? How do you look at a performance and how do you reflect back to the actor what you see and possibly make some suggestions as to how something might be changed? It's your own reaction. If I have to do something and I can't trust myself, then how can I direct? I don't do it according to some kind of formula. I don't know how to be a director operationally. In other words, I don't do masters. I don't have that kind of approach. I try to put the camera where I think the story is. That's a difficult thing. I want to put the audience in a certain place where they should be experiencing the situation. And what is the situation that they are to be experiencing? What is the nature of it? Is it true? Am I taking them into a process or is this just telling them a result, because I don't like things that are result-oriented. I'm not a political filmmaker in the sense that I'm making any statements. I don't like to make statements. I like taking you into an experience so that you are put in a position where this experience is seen and made new again. I want to take people on some kind of a journey. I think every story is some kind of a journey, just as I think our lives are journeys. The process for me, hopefully, is to have more understanding as I get older so I can bring to bear whatever kind of insights I have.

Your films have a visual and dramatic immediacy which seems to be a direct outgrowth of your experience as a documentarian.

The outgrowth of that background, I suppose, is my feeling that the camera should be in the place where the camera should be and should only see what you are supposed to see. That doesn't mean the eye shouldn't have the kind of freedom inside the frame to move around. But it's not as if it's just to cover something. That's just too formalist for me. It's not where the story is. When I started making documentary films—and I continued to do it for a number of years—I was a cameraman, but I always took the responsibility for the material. In other words, I never worked as a cameraman where somebody else told me what to do. Strange, but I couldn't shoot that way. I'd ask difficult questions like "Who is this guy?," and someone would say "Just shoot him, it's not your job to ask questions."

I always wanted to know why I was shooting a particular person. That influenced the way I'd shoot him and the way the light would be on his face, what I would emphasize in the shot. To me it was about seeing. It was about knowing, not about just reproducing an image. The next thing I had to understand in making documentaries was what was going on. I'd move in on a situation. What was

happening? What is the relationship between these two people? As soon as I find the situation, the situation has the dynamics of the relationship. Then I learned very quickly to capture the pieces, the surfaces of the reality, that when they're cut together are going to give you the dynamics of the situation. So for me, the aesthetic was to understand what are the facts, who are these people, what is the situation, what are the facts of the situation and what is the situation I'm going to be using.

The situation was what was tremendously important, but I would try never to indicate, never try to tell about it, but rather allow it to unfold and let the audience really come inside and decide for themselves. There's negative space in film, just as there is in architecture. You're making a film that's two hours long. It's a construct. It can't be everything. So I want it to be alive and for it to be alive, it has to have this negative space. It has to have the room for the audience to come inside. As soon as you try and tell something completely, you've told a lie. I think it has much more verisimilitude to life if you capture the fragments that pull the audience into this negative space by suggestion.

Your camera seems to be a participant or an observer, rather than an intruder. I've never see a sequence in any of your films where one is studying the camera movement rather than what's happening dramatically.

I don't want to draw any attention to the camera, yet the camera may be moving tremendously. In *EXTREMITIES*, for example, I didn't want to allow the audience to be in a safe place to watch what's happening, which is an attempted rape. That would be obscene. So I explored the space between the people in the film, and it's all choreographed so that it's one shot against another shot. I don't want the audience to sit back and watch. I want them to participate.

SHORT EYES **was one of the most difficult films I've ever seen in terms of the intensity and realism of its violence. I actually had a lot of trouble sitting through it.**

Some of the critics couldn't even watch it. But if you compare *SHORT EYES* with other films about men in similar situations, I think you'll see that it has much less violence in it. There's a great deal of psychological violence, and that's what I think it should be about. I think that is what film is tremendously effective at accomplishing. Film is a psychological medium. When Charlie Chaplin is about to sit down on a chair, and there's a hypodermic needle on that chair, your body tightens up. But as wonderful as *LAWRENCE OF ARABIA* is, you don't get heat prostration by watching it. You're not affected by those things. That's not what works in film. You can tell people about cold, but you don't make them feel cold. You can turn up the air conditioning...that's more effective.

In *TRIUMPH OF THE SPIRIT* **you were walking a very thin line, because you were making a film about a subject which some people, like Elie Wiesel, feel is inevitably trivialized in the movies...the Holocaust.**

I felt that we approached *TRIUMPH OF THE SPIRIT* in the spirit of Wiesel's book *Night*, and in the spirit of Primo Levi and Frankel's books as well. I feel that we had avoided obscene images in the film, like naked bodies being thrown into furnaces. I don't want to put those kinds of images into people's heads. That's not what the film was about, and I thought it would just push people away. And as I said, I'm interested in taking people into something, not showing them or telling them. We showed Elie Wiesel the film and he was very affected by it. He thought it was elegant, done with delicacy and was the finest movie that had been done on the Holocaust.

Now, nobody knew that he saw it. Some of the negative reviews that we've gotten even quoted Elie Wiesel, without knowing that he admired the film!

We've had curious reviews. On the one hand we've gotten fantastically good notices, and then we have some that I cannot understand. Siskel and Ebert complained that we didn't show bodies being put into the ovens and so we weren't being horrific enough. Another critic said the movie was unfeeling and cold. Actual survivors have put their arms around us and said that the film is real and they're glad it was made so that people won't forget. This is a good lesson for me to find out how vulnerable I am. You do still want to be praised and have people like your work and say what a good boy you are. I'm putting it in those terms because I have a certain amount of contempt for my own vulnerability about that. That doesn't mean that what I've done is right, because I know I'm very small and insignificant and see things from a very limited point of view. But I believe very deeply that we were very much in touch with our subject matter in *TRIUMPH OF THE SPIRIT,* and operated out of our deepest feelings and sensitivities. We always tried to solve our problems in the most honest way we could. There was a collaboration of actors and myself on the film which was really at the highest level. Willem Dafoe, Edward James Olmos and the others were rooted in their characters. When you somehow bring things to that level, I can take some kind of credit and responsibility in helping to make it happen.

There are a lot of wonderful performances in your films. What kind of atmosphere do you create on the set to allow that to happen?

There is a back and forth, but it is the actor who ultimately does it. It's about an honesty, not violating the truth. We're trying not to violate your sensibilities of what really is true. The ones that you started out with when you were in the crib and you get so that you know by that look on your mother's face just what she's thinking and feeling. I call up my wife and I hear the first word she says and I know from the timbre of the voice what kind of day she's had. That's what I'm interested in, that kind of truth. I think we have to build on truth and not subvert it. You need escape when going to the movies, sure. I love seeing something funny. But I also think it's like going and plugging in your charger and coming out feeling more alive and in touch with the world and yourself. And I think that's the function of art, quite honestly. It's to center you. If you've had a hectic day and you need some good laughs and you go to a movie that's funny, you come out and now you have another perspective. What is laughter? Laughter helps you put things back into perspective. When you see how ridiculous we are, it's a very healthy anecdote to the pomposity and self-importance that we tend to fall into. By the same token, drama that takes you into being in

for your next location —

TAMPA

has . . . crews, weather, right-to-work, locations and cooperation!

Contact:
Patricia Y. Hoyt
Director for Motion Picture
and Television Development
1 City Hall Plaza, 7E
Tampa, Florida 33602
813/223-8419
Fax 813/227-7176

MEMBER OF
AFC
INTERNATIONAL
ASSOCIATION OF
FILM COMMISSIONERS

FLORIDA
CAMERA READY

Tampa. . .On Florida's Beautiful West Coast!

FROM THE DIRECTORS CHAIR   ROBERT M. YOUNG

touch with how things really are, with the truth and the best of our ability to render it, is to make us more in touch with being alive.

In other words, you won't be directing *RAMBO IV*?

I wouldn't be the right director to try and make something which is built on conceits. If it's a conceit, I'm not interested in it. If it could be funny—if you prick the balloon and see that it's a conceit—yes, then I'm interested. I'd love to do a comedy. I enjoyed making *RICH KIDS*. It did have some very funny things in it. I hope this new film, *TALENT FOR THE GAME*, will have some funny things in it, too. God knows, I'm dying to do something funny after movies like *TRIUMPH OF THE SPIRIT*, *DOMINICK AND EUGENE* and *SHORT EYES*.

TALENT FOR THE GAME **is set against the backdrop of professional baseball, which is something of a change of pace for you. Have you been a fan of the sport?**

I've never been a baseball fan. Forgive me, but I've been so oriented toward work or doing something "meaningful." I always thought that watching a baseball game would be a waste of time, and what's been exciting for me is that I found that I've been wrong. As I learned about the game, as I've been reading about it and talking to players and seeing baseball, I'm watching it now with new eyes and learning a fantastic amount. The game is really a metaphor for life, what our values are.

Much of the film will have a humorous edge, but it will also ask questions about business practices and ethics in baseball. I'm really excited.

★ ★ ★

9

Toris Von Wolfe

PHILLIP NOYCE

A SELF-DESCRIBED DIRECTORIAL "chameleon," Australian director Phillip Noyce has stubbornly refused to allow his body of work to be defined. His films have crossed a number of genre and stylistic borders, from the period drama of *NEWSFRONT* and the exotic eroticism of *ECHOES TO PARADISE* to the chilling suspense of *DEAD CALM* and tongue-in-cheek action of *BLIND FURY*. They all seem to have been made by different directors...and that's just the way Noyce wants it.

A native of Griffith, a small town in New South Wales, Noyce studied at the Australian National Film School in the first year of its existence, and helped pioneer the renaissance of his country's movie industry in its mid-1970s heyday.

MICHAEL SINGER: What do you want out of movies?

PHILLIP NOYCE: Movies are for me a piece of life. It isn't a job, it's everything. You can't make them unless you're obsessed. They tend to take you over, like a spell. Even when you're on holiday you're not really on holiday, because the characters and story you're dealing with chases and catches you. Even when you're asleep, the tensions that are running through the film you're making are the tensions that enter your mind like spirits and trap you. They guide your dreams as much as they guide your waking. There's no escaping movies, and as I get older I realize I have a limited number of films that I can actually make. Ten years ago, I thought I was immortal and my total potential film output could be counted in the hundreds. Now I know that I might only make ten more films in my whole life. So given the limit on how many films you can make, and the fact that films are your life, and the fact that I want to continually be challenged as a life goal and as a film goal, I guess I want to keep making different kinds of movies. Each film I make...I hope...will be very different from the last one. If anyone ever writes a summary of my work, I hope they call me a chameleon, because they'd find it totally impossible to categorize me, at least stylistically. Obviously, in the end—because a film director is just a person in the end and even though they think they're god—certain obsessions come through even when you're trying to be different.

It's true that *NEWSFRONT*, *HEATWAVE*, *ECHOES OF PARADISE*, *DEAD CALM*, and *BLIND FURY* are all completely different. Some directors need to impress a very personal and recognizable style onto their films, but you seem to quite intentionally avoid that.

Yes, I do. To make films, you can't escape the movie-making process. Therefore, it is your life. Each film, for the duration of a year or two or three, just takes you over. Everything else is subordinated to making the movie. So what you realize is that you want to keep having as many different life experiences as possible. I would just go crazy if I had to remake *DEAD CALM* over and over again, or *NEWSFRONT*, or any of them. I guess I'd like to be a cat, and in the ten more films that I will make have ten more lives, rather than the same life ten times over.

Some directors seem to keep making the same film, even if the subject matter is different.

I feel that the subject of each movie dictates the style, the approach. There's not a technique or approach that you then adapt. The movie dictates how you treat it.

Do you get upset when you see films that put the story in the service of style, rather than the other way around, which is how you seem to work?

Absolutely. Finally, what I'd say in answer to your first question—what do I hope to get out of movies—is pre-eminently, a good time. I want to have fun.

As long as I can keep doing that and people keep paying me to have fun, then I won't change the way I make movies. Eventually, maybe I'll run out of benefactors.

Has it mostly been fun so far?

Always it's been fun. It's tough, but it's always fun. In part it comes from being an Australian and growing up in a country that had absolutely no film industry, where almost all films were imported. You would have been considered a madman to say that you were going to make a career as a film director. It wasn't something you could do even if you had the talent, because no one was making movies, and there were no potential opportunities to make them. I still feel it's some sort of incredible privilege to have the chance to direct films.

If there is a consistent thread in your films, it's atmosphere and the importance of the physical setting. Is that conscious?

The only answer I can give is that I just respond to the material and the situation.

I suppose it's your response to the place where you happen to be shooting—whether it's the ocean in *DEAD CALM* or Thailand in *ECHOES OF PARADISE*.

For me, sound plays a very important part in any film that I make. Atmosphere or sense of place is often created more strongly for the audience by the soundtrack than by the images. Sound goes directly from the ear to the heart. Images go from the eye, then they're decoded by the brain. Sound is the most piercing and direct emotional connection you can have with your audience. More than an image of heat, for example, the sound of cicadas can suggest you're in a tropical or very hot place. More than the lighting even, the right musical note or the right natural sound elements can suggest tension. My images have always been okay, but I don't see myself as an imagist. However, I've always been obsessed with soundtrack. I probably spend more time on sound than I do on image.

Were you always a sound fanatic, or was this something that began to develop when you started making

11

films and discovered how important sound could be when matched with image? You started making experimental films when you were very young.

It comes from an experimental film weekend conducted in Canberra, Australia's national capital. Two Australian experimental filmmakers, Arthur and Corinne Cantrill, were conducting the weekend. They had a lot of found footage, newsreel footage, offcuts from TV stations, that type of thing. They were encouraging us to take these bits, cut them together, then go and find a soundtrack and play the two on a double-head projector. They also gave us some clear film and encouraged us to draw on it. So here we had a random image and clear film with some marks on it and sound elements. What I observed was that the same image could be altered to produce the absolute opposite emotional response from the audience just by changing the sound. It's sort of like that old theory of shot A plus shot B equals C, but shot B followed by shot A equals something else. There we had 80 people just fooling around with film, and there was a real naïvete and sense of experimentation about what we were doing. We had nothing to lose, and just tried anything. I guess that's when I first became aware of the power of sound in movies.

You were raised in a small town called Griffith. Did you fall in love with the movies there, or did you have to venture to Sydney?

Falling in love with the idea of making movies was a two-stage process. First of all, it was falling in love with show business. That resulted from a fascination with the tent shows that came to town before television. In a small country town, the special day of the year for us was the show. It started as an agricultural show, where farmers used to show their produce, but vaudevillians would also come to town on that day. Eventually there would be 100 or more tent shows that would perform on the showgrounds of each country town. You would have the Roaring Twenties, the boxing troupe, the magicians, the two-headed lady, the pygmies from Africa and so on. There was something about these traveling shows that caught my

imagination. Every year my parents would give me one Australian pound, and my brother and I would put it underneath our pillows. The night before the show we would amuse each other with stories of which performances we were going to see based on what was there last year. Of course, they were always different. There were 100 shows, and a pound could only get you into ten of them. So once you ran out of money, there were only two ways to get in. One was to sneak under the tent, which I did a lot of. The other was to present yourself as a stooge. A stooge took part in the greatest show of all, which was outside of the tent—getting the people to pay their money to go inside. And the stooge had to be a local person who was known and could basically be made a fool of. I tried to get them to choose me as often as possible, which was a little easier than the others because I was taller than the rest.

I understand that you became quite an entrepreneur, raising money for your first short film by selling roles to your friends.

It was a completely fallible idea. Unfortunately, the guy who had the most money...he was a doctor's son...was a rotten actor. He played the lead in that film, and he was terrible. But that taught me a director is very much dependent on his actors. A good performance is largely due to the right casting. The socialist bookshop owner was a bit of a capitalist, and he gave us the top floor of his shop for the cinema. So the people who came to the filmmakers' cinema had to pass through his bookshop, and inevitably they'd spend more money on books than admission to the cinema. This cinema ran every Sunday and people like Bruce Beresford, Peter Weir, George Miller, Paul Cox, Gillian Armstrong, myself and others would personally show their films there. None of us were making features yet, but would collect a program of films that were linked thematically or at least stylistically—or else a filmmaker would show his life work— and then we would talk after each film. There was a lot of interplay with the audience and the filmmakers in the audience. About 120 people would fit up there.

What happened in Australia during the early 1970s that allowed all of you to start making features?

It was government intervention, purely and simply. The fertilizer that allowed us to bear flowers was much more complex. It was a time of great change, just like the flowering in the Spanish cinema since the overthrow of Franco. Australia had been ruled from 1949 to 1972 by one government, an extremely conservative government. And Australia was one of the most censored countries in the world, in terms of literature, film and art. In 1972, we elected a socialist democratic government, the Labour Party, the first non-conservative government for 23 years. With that government came the aspirations of a whole generation. The second factor was the Vietnam War. Our involvement ended in 1972 with Labour's election. The war had been for Australia, as it was for America, a traumatic experience. It taught us that we needed to think more independently about politics. There was also the factor of the post-war baby boomers, the first generation whose parents encouraged them to be frivolous and gave them the opportunity to do whatever they wanted. For Australians, this was perhaps the first generation which was given leisure time to devote to cultural activities. The result was an overnight film industry.

What's inevitably happened, of course, is that good Australian directors—having been discovered by the rest of the world, particularly Hollywood—have to some degree left their country to make films elsewhere. There was a fear that the Australian film industry was going to be destroyed by the success of its own filmmakers. Do you feel a need to keep a connection with Australia, while at the same time pursuing your career in the U.S?

I can't think of an Australian director who actually maintains his principal home here in America. I don't know anyone who lives here full-time. When they come here, they come as outsiders. Obviously, their Australian identity is very important to them.

Is the Australian government still supportive of the film industry, or have things changed from the early 1970s?

The government is still supportive, but one of the problems there is that you get sick of the system and want to break out of it. You see, every time a bureaucrat looks at the film industry, they want to change the rules by which the subsidy is administered. If you have to make films because of the government handout, you're subject to the whims of whoever is controlling that government. The only way out of that is to get real, and within our orbit the only reality is here in Hollywood. Hollywood is the most successful colonizer in the history of mankind. More successful than the Romans, because Hollywood has colonized the hearts and minds of all the world. Hollywood has developed such an amazing distribution system around the world that it always needs product to feed that system. The only way out of the whims of government control is to somehow take advantage of this machine, this octopus that has its tentacles stretched all over the world. Let this octopus sell your film—because it does it better than anyone else—and let the octopus finance your movie. That way, as long as you can keep supplying that machine with whatever it wants, it will keep allowing you to make movies. The only real criteria is the criteria of economics, ordinary supply and demand. This is a difficult mine field to negotiate, but it's a lot better and you know the rules, because unlike bureaucratic rules, they're consistent from generation to generation.

Do you feel that the compromises you might have to make under the Hollywood system are less disturbing than those you make under the Australian system?

The thing I've learned—and I guess you'd have to be incredibly thick-skinned if it didn't impress itself upon you—is the way Hollywood is connected to the audience. You can almost feel the connection when you talk to some of the people in Hollywood. I feel grateful that I have relative artistic independence in Australia, and that as an outsider I can look at what Hollywood has to teach a filmmaker about contact with an audience. For me, if I'm not in contact with that audience, then forget it. I may as well not be doing it. I'm not making films for me. I'm making films for them, wherever they are.

When did the audience become more important to you than your own aesthetics in the transition from experimental to more commercial filmmaking?

It was actually through making films for television and experiencing the audience reaction to my feature *HEATWAVE*, which was a film that I made for myself. I remember sitting night after night in cinemas in Sydney when *HEATWAVE* opened, and I realized that I hadn't pressed the buttons with the audience. I hadn't connected with them. I'd mingle with the audience, and they didn't have the buzz that I meant them to have. It wasn't working. After that, I spent several years making television films, working with the Kennedy-Miller organization. And the turning point for me was a 10-hour mini-series which I co-wrote and co-directed called *THE COWRA BREAKOUT*. It has to do with the nature of the television medium and its relationships to the audience, which is so different from cinema. In the cinema, once you get them into the theatre, they're there. They're not going to leave unless you really upset them. In television, they've got multiple choice. Unless you reach out of the screen and grab hold of them in their seat and bolt them down, they'll leave you. So you have to involve a TV audience more and more as time goes on. Here I was, faced with writing and directing a 10-hour mini-series, which is like five feature films. We started out at a certain level of ratings, and we increased every half-hour over the 10 hours. I spent two-and-a-half years on that project, and I thought "Now I've graduated. Now I know something about making a movie. Now I know something about telling a story." And even though it was television, we never thought of it as TV. TV was only the means by which we were delivering it to the audience. We were just telling a story. It's not TV, it's not cinema, it's just a story.

Television as a training ground for feature filmmaking is hotly debated in this country, because the networks tend to ground down any individuality of style on the part of the director.

But this was a different sort of television. This was television where the sponsor and the network had bought the project from Kennedy-Miller on an idea and the next time they were involved was when they saw the finished project. We had total creative freedom to do anything in the world that we wanted to do. The network had no involvement in casting, scripting, editing or anything.

Is this system still working in Australia?

Certainly at Kennedy-Miller, because that's the kind of deal they've had on every project they've done.

Does Kennedy-Miller use TV as a training ground for young directors?

I think TV is used as an investigation into the nature of storytelling, as I've said before. As it happens, certain directors have then gone on to make feature films with Kennedy-Miller. Chris Noonan is now working on a feature. On the other hand, Ken Cameron made features and then went on to do TV with them. It's not so much a conscious decision to provide a training ground as it is something that grows out of working together.

There's no stigma in Australia of going from features to TV? Here that seems to be a problem for directors.

No. We go from commercials to theatre to cinema to television.

Toris Von Wolfe

RALPH S. SINGLETON

N THE INTERESTS OF COMPLETE honesty and integrity, let's make one thing perfectly clear. Ralph S. Singleton is indeed—along with Joan V. Singleton—the publisher of this book. He's also the author of four other Lone Eagle books: *Film Scheduling, Filmmaker's Dictionary, Film Scheduling/Film Budgeting Workbook* and *Movie Production and Budget Forms...Instantly!*

And those titles give first indication of what makes Ralph Singleton such a worthy subject for this section—in 21 years of motion picture experience, he rose through the ranks to the head of his class in production knowledge and experience. Beginning as a production assistant, he segued on an upward scale to assistant location manager, location manager, DGA trainee, second assistant director, first assistant director, production manager, associate producer, producer, executive producer and now (the real reason why he's interviewed) director of *Stephen King's GRAVEYARD SHIFT* for Paramount Pictures.

This is not the route most first-time filmmakers are taking these days in America, but Singleton had ample opportunity to learn the director's craft while working side-by-side during the 1970s with such experts as William Friedkin on *THE FRENCH CONNECTION*, Alan J. Pakula on *KLUTE,* Sidney Lumet on *NETWORK* and Martin Scorsese on *TAXI DRIVER*. Singleton devoted much of the '80s to the mammoth Dan Curtis mini-series *THE WINDS OF WAR*, working with Francis Coppola at Zoetrope Studios, and then the popular *CAGNEY AND LACEY*—producing 98 episodes and winning an Emmy in the process. Returning to features, he co-produced *HARLEM NIGHTS* and co-executive produced *ANOTHER 48 HRS.* before gaining his first motion picture directing assignment with *Stephen King's GRAVEYARD SHIFT*.

MICHAEL SINGER: You worked your way into directing in much the way they did in the old Hollywood and English systems, but not so much the way it happens today. Why don't more directors emerge from the production ranks?

RALPH S. SINGLETON: The American system for assistant directors, location managers and production managers is a nuts-and-bolts approach to filmmaking. A good production manager or assistant director is a logistics expert, not a creative expert. They don't deal with cast and they don't deal with story, and from that you realize that the chance to get involved with the creative end of the story is limited at best. Whereas in the European or English system you would be more involved in those things.

So have you, in fact, been limited in your aspirations to direct by your success in the production end of filmmaking?

I would have to say yes. And that was a chosen thing. When I got into the film business 21 years ago I told someone that I wanted to be a film director, and she said "That's very nice, and that's the xerox machine over there." And I said "Thank you very much." That was my first lesson in how to say all the wrong things. You know, they say that you shouldn't ever tell anyone you want to be a director, because it's the kiss of death. I think that you really have to decide what you want in this business,

and then focus on it. Eventually, you might get there. In my case, I chose the production route, which is not the most direct route. In fact, most of the people I know chose the production route. Some chose the DGA Trainee Program. They eventually became successful producers, and as a result managed to direct. A lot of this business is opportunity. A month before *GRAVEYARD SHIFT* became a reality, I turned the job down as director. I was already the producer of the film with Bill Dunn, and was listening to a lot of people telling me that it was the wrong picture for me to start with. And then a writer/director friend of mine who specializes in horror films said to me, "There is never the right opportunity." And I realized that what I've said to people for a long time—if you want to be a director, then *direct*—may be rather sophomoric but is also the reality. I've now directed my first feature, and I'm very happy about what's happened. Five pictures from now—if I'm hired after this one, God willing—then I'll have a better understanding of what a director really has to go through as far as the process is concerned.

Didn't you get to know that in 21 years of film production?

Even though I've worked for a lot of directors in a production capacity, until you actually step into the position, you never really understand it. The crew around you doesn't understand it, because they're not doing it. They give everything they can, as good crews will, but they still don't understand the responsibility you have. I'll tell you something...there are days you walk in as prepared as you think you are, and things just don't work out. And there are other days you walk in not as prepared as you'd like to be, and things work out quite well. You can't predict it. In production you try to lay it out, and it's a mechanical thing. But the big question mark is what the director will do. I mean, you can sit back like I do before I take a job on the production end and analyze what the director's done, you can talk to other production people who have worked with that director, you can find what their schedule is like, you can find out how many set-ups they do per day. You can analyze all that stuff, but then when you

15

find yourself in that position, you find that you can't do 20 set-ups a day on a feature. You might be able to do four or five on a good day. So a lot of things you learn in production you realize that you can't utilize as a director, except for the logistical end of it. So it helps you in some respects to understand the production process, but it can also hinder you if you try to apply all those production principles because you can end up a mechanic rather than a creator.

Or you can strike a balance...get what you need creatively while keeping the logistics in check.

I walked into a situation with *GRAVEYARD SHIFT* in which I gave myself 40 days to do an incredibly complicated picture. I was dealing with animals, state-of-the-art special effects, locations.

A good production person would never put himself in that position, but there was no choice. We finished the picture in 41 days instead of the scheduled 40. We checked everything we were doing on video. Some of the second unit stuff took five hours to set up, but I didn't have that luxury.

What about your relationship to the actors? As you said earlier, production personnel rarely get involved with the creative end of moviemaking.

I knew that the audience had to care about the characters in the movie, and that I would need good relationships with the actors who were playing them.

Did you ever find the "mechanic" part of you at war with the creator?

Yes I did. And I would try to sit back and weigh the overview of the film, because to me, the story is the most important aspect. I think the reason Spielberg and Lucas are so successful is because they're great storytellers. In spite of my experience as a production animal, I recognized that the creative aspect was more important than the nuts-and-bolts. There is a meeting of minds between the mechanic and the creator, and you have to find that. The production roots definitely benefited me, because if nothing else, I had the respect of the people around me who felt that I knew what the hell I was doing. If I wanted to spend more time on something, they figured that I could balance it out. Well, we went

in with a 40 day schedule and finished in 41. That's not too bad. Not in this day and age, when a movie takes 60 to 70 days to shoot, which I don't understand. We didn't take 60 to 70 days on *KLUTE*, *THE FRENCH CONNECTION* and *NETWORK*. First of all, we didn't have the money. Second of all, we didn't have the time. Yet, shooting on 70, 80, 90 day schedules and spending $30-, $40-, $50 million dollars seems to be more of a standard than an exception...which I think is insane.

Why do you think that's happened?

Because studios have accepted the fact that it takes that amount of time to make a film...and I think that's crazy. A lot of movies aren't planned enough. There's not enough pre-production in films, because nobody wants to spend the time. They think you're going to work it out as you go along, or in the cutting room. It's the wrong approach. If a movie costs $50 million, how are you going to make back your money? The movie has to make in excess of $100 million to break even. So from the economic standpoint, making a $50 million movie—unless it's the Russian version of *WAR AND PEACE*—doesn't make any sense, and never has. I'm not saying that every picture should cost $5-million, but they shouldn't cost $50 million either. Money is often badly spent on films. Why? Beats the hell out of me. It's totally wrong.

What made you want to direct? Did you wake up one morning and realize that you wanted to make a change?

I wish that were true, but it's not. I was 13 years old, my father had a 16mm camera, and I made a western and a horror film. That's when I wanted to direct. I went off, finished college, became an intelligence agent in the Middle East, went into the publishing business with a large company, and eventually got into the movie business as a production assistant. I knew then that if I stuck with it, I would eventually direct a movie. To be perfectly honest, what always stuck with me was that my mother said to me a long time ago, "Ralph, if you're going to dig ditches, dig the best ditch." So I tried to be the best of whatever I was doing in

production, both in New York and then in L.A. It didn't happen overnight, but it always in the back of my mind that once it all came together and there was enough confidence, I would direct. It was a matter of getting into the position to do it. And hopefully, this epic horror film that we've done will work. I mean, we only steal from the very best! I looked at every horror film I've ever known. You take these various films, put them together and try to figure out what made them work and what can work for you...and what can you do in your film to make it different and unique? The greatest horror and suspense director of all time was probably Hitchcock, so for our film, out came Albert Whitlock to do storyboards and mattes, and out came Harold Michelson as visual consultant. Both of them worked with Hitchcock for years. For *GRAVEYARD SHIFT*, we have suspense and comedy and gore...to give the audience what they're looking for. It was probably the most fun I've had in this business for a long time.

How did you get along with your crew?

I had wonderful people around me who made it happen. I mean, the director is the orchestrator. You cannot make a picture without collaborators. Directors don't pick every shot. They never have, to my knowledge. You have to end up with a true collaboration between the director and the cinematographer, editor, production designer, costume designer. We only had three days of rehearsal with the actors. On day one, we had a read-through of the script. On day two, I took them out to the locations so we could smell the turf and walk the track.

How well equipped did you think you were to handle the actors? Were you reading Stanislavsky? Taking acting classes on the side?

I think that was the biggest fear. I was gratified that a couple of the leading actors told me afterward that I was capable of sitting down and listening to their point of view and always being open whether I ultimately used their ideas or not. I never closed them out. There was a true collaboration. I was able to deal with actors as human beings, but had a solid point of view of what I wanted from them. There was real trust between

The Maine Attraction

Fresh locations • Low costs
Skilled crews • Few permits
Lobsters • Cooperation
3,500 mile coast • 1 hr to New York

Call or write for
Maine Production Guide

Maine Film Office
State House Station #59
Augusta, Maine 04333

Phone   (207) 289•5711   24-hrs   (207) 289•5705   FAX   (207) 289•2861

FROM THE DIRECTORS CHAIR   RALPH S. SINGLETON

us, and we felt our way through.

I enjoyed being challenged by them, but everything they did had to be totally justified. That's where the director has to sit down and interpret the material, and orchestrate everything for both the actors and the crew. Most production people I know do not like actors—they don't have the time or the tolerance. You have to have a lot of tolerance to be a director, at least a successful one. I mean, you can be a pirate and get your point across real quick. Or you can be a collaborator. It takes a lot more time—your time—but you end up with a better piece. The actors eventually trust you. If you're a first-time director with limited experience, they have no idea where you're coming from. They will constantly test you, see how far they can go or not go. They tested me every day. But the magic of directing is that actors take their lives and put it in your hands. You have to determine where their characters begin and end. I also had to deal with a mechanical creature which was a character in itself.

Because of your vast production experience, did you ever feel the inclination to do everybody else's job for them?

I was conscious of other people's jobs, but not in the sense of wanting to step in. Because I had been there, I appreciated those jobs. I knew the hours they had to put in, how hard it was. I knew that when I suddenly changed the schedule on any given day, I would drive the first assistant director nuts. I know how hard it is to be a dolly grip. It wasn't a matter of competition...just appreciating what the other person does.

May I assume that at this point in your career, directing is the road you want to continue pursuing?

I think that if *GRAVEYARD SHIFT* is at all successful, then I'll direct again. I like producing. I like directing. I like the combination of the production background that I have and the creative end. But I'll tell you, anyone who thinks they can fully produce and fully direct at the same time, just can't. It's too demand-

ing. To negotiate a contract and worry about an actor's motivation at the same time is pure hell!

17

Toris Von Wolfe

E D W A R D Z W I C K

HEN THE 1989 CIVIL WAR spectacle *GLORY* won critical praise, success at the box-office and a slew of Oscar nominations, a lot of heads turned in Hollywood. Not only are historical epics out of fashion in today'sbusiness, but *GLORY*'s director—Edward Zwick—had until then been known as a prime explicator of the way we live *now*, not *then*.

The co-creator and co-executive producer (with Marshall Herskovitz)of TV's primetime sensation *THIRTYSOMETHING*, Zwick's only previous feature directing credit was the contemporary comedy-drama *ABOUT LAST NIGHT*..., about romantic commitment (or lack of same) in America today. But with *GLORY*, Zwick pulled the rug out from under conventional industry analysts, demonstrating a strong grip on historical accuracy and a fine flair for poetic visual action.

Zwick's next feature project will return him to modern times, directing Ed Solomon's bittersweet original screenplay *LEAVING NORMAL.*

MICHAEL SINGER:What gave you the confidence to approach a film on such a huge scale as GLORY, considering the fact that your previous work in both film and television has been on a much more intimate scale?

EDWARD ZWICK: I would never presume to suggest that I would be able to accomplish anything in the same league as people like David Lean, John Ford, Akira Kurosawa and so many others, but I've always been taught that directing is about overreaching. All that I want to do is to challenge myself in order to grow. If I had made a choice that in some sense was in the same arena in which I've been working, not only would others have presumed that's all I wanted to do, but I would have been in danger of somehow limiting myself and inhibiting growth at what is still a very early moment in my career. Also, I would say that these last couple of years doing *THIRTYSOMETHING* have created an extraordinary opportunity, because I have shot hours and hours of film. What directors have no opportunity to do these days is to direct. They do one film and a couple of years go by, and the stakes immediately rise so high that the second film they do is based on having shot only two hours. But as a director of television, or executive producer of a show like this, I've had the sense of having the growth I

may have made as an artist between the first and second films with the number of hours and thousands of feet of film having been shot.

Would you say that in some way television—whether episodic or TV movies—has become the contemporary equivalent of the way two-reelers functioned in the old days, as a training ground for directors?

I would say absolutely. I think there are other equivalents. I think there are certain kinds of low-budget films that accomplish the same thing. But I'm about to direct another episode of *THIRTYSOMETHING* tomorrow. It may be another year before I do another film. But a director directs, just as a writer writes.

In America—but not in England or Europe—there seems to be something of a professional stigma attached to making a successful feature and then returning to direct TV.

Less and less, though. Jim Brooks is doing it. So have Dick Donner, Joe Dante, Steven Spielberg and others.

Do you think we're finally growing up?

Right. I think the English model is a much more legitimate one. Those guys go back and forth from television to films to the theatre to commercials with impunity. It's about a difference in form, and

there are virtues and liabilities in each of the forms. Television is limited by time and money. It is also, however, visceral and intuitive and often it is anonymous, which promotes risk-taking and growth. The subject matters allowed on television are either immediate or intimate in a way films can't be. Conversely, the scale and canvas of a film are unlike any you can approach in television. Everything has its merits. It's just a difference in form.

The stereotyping of directors is probably even more prevalent than the stereotyping of actors. Is this something you specifically fought against when you chose to make GLORY?

I just think it's something that everyone is aware of. I don't think that I've cynically chosen this film to avoid stereotyping. I chose *GLORY* based on the power and the wonder of the story, how compelling it was to me that I could presume to recapitulate that for an audience. But I am aware of stereotyping, and I think it's a real and destructive thing. It's for those who are too busy to think, or are unwilling or lazy. They want things made knowable, and artists are much more complex than that.

Do you think that some directors actually fall prey to that stereotyping, and can't break their own molds?

I don't presume to know what goes on in other artists' heads, but I suppose there are those who fall prey to a stereotype and then there are those who have such a singularity of vision that it makes them wonderful as artists. I don't think that David Lynch thinks of himself in any stereotypical way, yet his sensibility is so unique as to insist that the work he does is distinctive. I think it's also true of people like Brian De Palma and Martin Scorsese.

Your background was more theatrical than cinematic, wasn't it?

I was trained in repertory theatre, and that meant you would do Strindberg one night and Sam Shepard the next and Shakespeare the one after that.

What compelled you to eventually go into film?

I learned very early that if you have a vision and the ability to articulate it to

19

those around you, then you can indeed realize those things. But why does one artist begin with pastels and end up with oils? I don't know. I can't even speculate.

In discussing some filmmakers who influenced you, the names of Hawks, Ford and Kurosawa are mentioned. But would you say that their movies or techniques have had direct impact on your work?

I don't know. I have to say that there's a promiscuity of influence in my life, and not just having to do with film. I do know that at a very young age I saw a lot of European cinema and was affected by the humanist traditions of Truffaut and Bergman. On the other hand, I know that paintings had a lot to do with *GLORY*. I kept looking at Goya, for example. And the Pulitzer Prize-winning novel *Killer Angels* by Michael Shaara was somehow very important to me in making the movie. It brought you inside an historical moment and let you understand the personal context of the larger canvas. That was an extraordinary accomplishment.

You used the great Freddie Francis as your cinematographer on *GLORY*, a man who's worked with a lot of other greats in the past...including David Lean, perhaps the most famous of all living directors who specialize in historical epics. What kind of working relationship did you have with him? Were you intimidated by his vast experience?

Well, I obviously wanted somebody who had been through everything and would be undaunted by the scale and the demands made on us. He really has been everywhere and done everything. Our collaboration, however, was very typical of any I've had with other cinematographers. We'd talk about an idea...I'd tell him very specifically what I had in mind...and then he'd go and do exactly what he wanted to do!

In the look of *GLORY*, you and Francis chose a very clear palette rather than a muted "period" sepia tone.

I felt that sepia would be a cliche and distract the viewer from the story. We felt that we could use smoke from fires,

smokestacks and oil burners, which would be a natural diffusing element. And we also very carefully art-directed the palette to be monochromatic with the blues and browns and greens.

The white protagonist in *GLORY*, Robert Gould Shaw, writes a letter to his mother in which he expresses some feeling of distance from the black men under his command. Did you, as a white director working with a mostly black cast, share any of those emotions?

I have to say that I don't subscribe to that kind of thinking in general. I do believe that a director's function is interpretive, that a director has to be able to project himself into Shakespearean England, or outer space. Those things are what distinguishes a director in terms of his ability to recognize the commonality of experience, or the humanity in everyone, and to project himself firmly into that. As far as the issue of race, I'm a third generation American Jew—not the child immigrant—but it's easy for me to lapse into a kind of fond Yiddish inflection and emulation of that culture in a way that is done without baggage and trying, amidst the humor, to find the dignity in that. For Denzel Washington, Morgan Freeman, Andre Braugher and the other actors in GLORY, I suspect they did that with extraordinary ease. Not to say they weren't grappling with some of the pain of remembrance of the real indignity of slavery...but they did it, as far as I was concerned, with a real generosity of spirit. There was never any baggage. They read the script, knew my purpose for being there, and made themselves vulnerable to me in the process. I also, in turn, opened myself to their contributions in order to get it right. I didn't presume to tell them things that they knew much better and more profoundly than I. I also believe that their performances in *GLORY* had to do with a sense of purpose. I was humbled by that, and knew that sometimes the best thing to do was to get out of the way and let those performances unfold and have their moment. I think there are some parts of *GLORY* that are indeed inspired.

You've said that *GLORY* is not so much a film about the Civil War as it is a film about passion.

I think there was a certain fervor of the Utopian ideal, the abolitionist zeal that had a legacy, and some of that legacy was unexpected. It was contradictory, too. But it was also about an extraordinary opportunity of men being given the occasion to fight for something they believed in. To have that occasion, to strike a blow against that which has oppressed one, is quite rare. The fight to be in that situation is very beautiful. And certainly, young people now don't quite understand the context of political passions. I think to tell a story about a nation seized by passion, good and bad, was very contemporary to me.

How do you answer charges that the film actually glorifies war?

The title *GLORY* is deliberately ironic. It does suggest that there are moments in which the only response against oppression is to fight it...there is a certain dignity in risking everything for that which one believes. But on the other hand, we went to such extraordinary lengths to try and portray the savagery and horror of what war is. My interest was to do anything *but* glorify war.

The battle scenes in *GLORY* really do portray a terrible beauty.

I guess if the first battle in the movie was somehow narrative, and the second very subjective—to try and capture the inside feeling of combat—then the third and final battle was trying to address what that terrible beauty is. And I suppose that certain elevated tone that it takes on is what I was going for...the myth after the fact.

James Horner's music was very important in that mythical elevation. Was he involved with the film from inception?

From the very beginning, James and I knew that the sound of The Boys Choir of Harlem had to be heard in the film. We felt that boys are always fighting wars, and we wanted to somehow juxtapose the sound of those beautiful voices against some of the atrocities that are depicted in the film.

GLORY was refreshingly free of cliches that one usually finds in historical films, such as extraneous romantic subplots. Was there any pres-

Canada's Yukon.

Your location search isn't complete until you set your sites on the Yukon.

Discover our unique locations, historic towns,
and authentic Yukon hospitality.
Come and experience a hassle-free production.
That's our commitment.
Call or write now for more information.

The Yukon Film Promotion Office
P.O. Box 2703
Whitehorse, Yukon,
Canada. Y1A 2C6
Phone (403) 667-5400
Fax (403) 667-2634

Yukon
The Magic and the Mystery...

MEMBER OF
AFC
INTERNATIONAL
ASSOCIATION OF
FILM COMMISSIONERS

sure from the studio to include some of those more conventional elements?

Remarkably, no. We did begin to film some sequences between Robert Gould Shaw and a woman who, in historical fact, did have a friendship and possibly a romance with him. But the scenes just weren't working in the context of the story we were telling, so they were cut.

ABOUT LAST NIGHT... **and** *GLORY* **are totally different from each other in both setting and tone. Is either one closer to the kind of film you really want to make?**

To answer that question, I'll tell you my favorite joke. Mrs. Feingold wants her Miami Beach apartment re-decorated. So she calls the decorator, who asks "What would you like?" Mrs. Feingold answers, "I want it should be done period." And he asks, "Well, what kind of period? Louis the Fourteenth? Second Empire? Restoration?" And she responds, "No, no, no! It should be so beautiful that when my friends come, they take one look at it and drop dead...*period!*"

Your next feature project is *LEAVING NORMAL,* **which is based on an original screenplay by Ed Solomon. What attracted you to the script?**

It's very rare for me to come to a script that I wasn't personally involved in creating, but when I found *LEAVING NORMAL*, I was very struck by the one thing that I look for in any film...a *voice*. I think every film re-invents the universe, and those that do it best create behavior and rules for their characters to observe. And what this script did was present a whole world view that was slightly pixillated, eccentric to be sure. And it was aggressively a reaction against what I see around me now—films in which people have stated goals which they strive for and win. Films in which people overcome all odds. Here is a story that says the opposite...that the journey you take is not the journey you expect, and indeed, while you think nothing may happen, in the end *everything* might happen. I was also very moved by Ed's presentation of women in *LEAVING NORMAL*, which does not neces-

sarily involve men, or rape, or chases or any other elements of genre other than the effect of one character upon the other.

Do you feel once again, as with *GLORY,* **that you're swimming against the tide? And do you enjoy that?**

Well, I don't know, but I've always subscribed to Casey Stengel's theory..."Hit it where they ain't!"

★ ★ ★

Courtesy of Miramax Films

STEVEN SODERBERGH

HEN *sex lies, and videotape* became an international film festival favorite (winning, among other awards, the Grand Prix at Cannes) and a major critical and box-office success in the U.S., no one could have been more surprised than its young creator. The remarkably gifted Steven Soderbergh wrote *sex, lies, and videotape* as an act of personal expiation rather than as a determined commercial venture. He never dreamed that millions of filmgoers would so readily and willingly hook into his moving, funny and poetic vision of alienation and salvation.

Sharpening his filmmaking skills with a series of self-financed shorts, Soderbergh brought the craft of a talented veteran to *sex, lies, and videotape*, his first feature. Quickly heralded as Hollywood's latest "flavor of the month," Soderbergh nonetheless combines a healthy regard for studio filmmaking with an uncompromising personal agenda—which includes living in Virginia rather than Los Angeles.

MICHAEL SINGER: Have you been truly surprised by the commercial success of *sex, lies, and videotape*?

STEVEN SODERBERGH: Well, when I finished the screenplay, I certainly felt it was the most aggressively non-commercial thing I had ever written. I had other pieces of original material, five other screenplays, that I felt were much more accessible and palatable. Of course, they hadn't gone anywhere either, but for different reasons. All of them were on a bigger scale, and people were reluctant to drop four or five million dollars on a first-time director. *sex, lies, and videotape* was written so much as an act of expulsion—I just had to get it out of my system—that I didn't really expect anybody to want to do it. I thought I would have to raise some money from friends and make it on the cheap for about $60,000.

How was the film financed?

What happened was, Robert Newmyer, Nancy Tenenbaum and Morgan Mason [the producers of the film] all had connections that we ended up following. Bob Newmyer knew a gentleman named Larry Estes at RCA/Columbia, and he is the man who got the film made. He liked the script very much and just pushed it through. Nancy and Morgan, meanwhile, pursued connections that they had with Virgin Vision in the U.K. for foreign financing. RCA/Columbia came in for $1.2 million, and Virgin bought foreign rights for about half

that figure. But our actual production budget was $1.2 million.

It went a long way on-screen.

It did. The irony is that most of the money—even though the actors accepted well under what they normally got—went to actor's salaries. Which is why, when people say "Couldn't you have used more money?," I think the film would not have been any better with more money, and it may even have been worse. I don't know if the film that I originally thought about making for $60,000 in black and white and 16-millimeter would have been any worse. I think it would just have been very different.

Although $1.2 million is a lot grander than $60,000, it's still a very small budget by feature standards. Do you think the budgetary restrictions helped to make *sex, lies* the film that it turned out to be?

Absolutely. I think that the film could have been harmed by attempts at opening it up, saying, "Well, we got more money, so let's try to stage more of it outside." I think ultimately that would have diluted it. In this case, the enforced restrictions were helpful.

I assume that going the independent route, the film didn't have to go through the usual development hell.

Well, you're right in the sense that it didn't have to go through that kind of creation-by-committee process, which is rarely successful. Most of the changes that did occur were discussed with Nancy Tenenbaum over a period of months, and

then of course, once the actors got involved. We had a week's worth of rehearsals before we started filming, and I made a lot of changes in the dialogue and incorporated ideas from the actors. The changes were very consistent, and always along the same lines.

There was such a sense of the actors completely inhabiting their roles in the film.

I thought so, too. Obviously, in a film like this, rehearsal time is mandatory. I knew that we needed time, and I knew that ultimately it was important for the performances to be good, that each actor be able to bring something to their part. That was more important than them speaking every word that I wrote. I also think it's important, when you're directing your own script, to have a healthy disrespect for your own material. Ultimately, you have to sit there and make decisions while you're shooting, and I believe that actors have to sound natural. And if you're objective about it, if you have good actors and can tell them, "Look, if you're having trouble with the lines, just make them your own," then they will. It's idiotic not to take advantage of actors who have really good ideas.

It was a revelation to discover what a wonderful actress Andie MacDowell is.

I felt lucky for the two of us, actually, when she came in to read. I felt lucky for me because I was going to look like a hero. I got to look smart simply because I recognized her talent. I felt the same way about Laura San Giacomo, who had never done any films. I'm so happy for Andie, because she had been getting a bum rap after they dubbed her voice in *GREYSTOKE*. Like a lot of actors, Andie needs to be comfortable. When she is comfortable, she can be amazingly unselfconscious. I did everything in my power to make sure she was comfortable, and I got everything I wanted from her performance.

The film struck an amazing chord in the public, almost as if a lot of us saw pieces of ourselves in not one, but all four of the protagonists. I don't know if that was your intention, because you often speak of how personal the film was to you.

That's exactly why I've been so surprised by the success of the film. It did seem to me, in many ways, very fragmented, very internal, and reflected things that only I

23

thought about at any great length. I may have just overestimated how unique I am. It turned out that *everybody* has these thoughts.

I recall reading that you wrote *sex, lies, and videotape* almost as an act of contrition.

Yes, I was trying to get this thing out of my system. I'd been through a relationship that I really screwed up, and I thought for a long time...why did this happen...how did this happen? I guess my therapy was to turn it into art. So in many ways, once it was written, it had served its purpose. And since it had, in this odd way, there was less of a burning desire to get this film made than some of my other unproduced scripts.

Was there ever a point where you were almost afraid to put something so personal on film?

There were a couple of times when I knew that the line was very, very fine, in the sense that it was either going to be very good or unbearably pretentious.

Do you feel that the film is, as so many critics have suggested, more European than American in style?

Yes and no. I do things that seem more European than American in execution only because the film is paced in a way that many American films aren't. But the films that I kept in mind—like *FIVE EASY PIECES* and *THE LAST PICTURE SHOW*—are films that I felt were incredibly well directed, that had the consistency of conception and execution. If you were looking at these films as a director, you saw that they were very wonderfully made, yet not flashy, and never called attention to themselves. It just always seemed like the camera was in the right place. That's the kind of thing I tried to keep in mind, and certainly those are two very American films.

One thing that impressed me about *sex, lies, and videotape* was that it seemed to at the same time have an improvisational quality, and yet the camerawork was very careful and meticulous. I know that you were open to changes from the actors, but how prepared would you be with mapping out camera placement?

I really went seat-of-the-pants, because I knew that this was a performance movie. We'd come onto the set, block the scene—making whatever changes or improvements that we had made through all the various processes of rehearsal—and then I would decide where to put the camera. The camera always followed the actor, and so in that way we were able to easily accommodate any improvisation. At that point, the improvisation going on was extremely minor and would not really affect camera placement. It was really a matter of watching the actors go through a scene and finding the right tone.

But the film never seemed static, even though most of it was shot indoors.

That was a tough one. I knew that I was going to have to keep the camera moving a decent amount to keep things going, but I didn't want it to move in a way that called attention to itself. I really wanted this feeling, or impression, of the camera floating toward something, both emotionally and visually.

The film was shot far away from Hollywood, in Baton Rouge, Louisiana. Is that where you're from?

Mostly. I lived there longer than anyplace else, and that's where I started making films.

Can you talk about your background in films? Where did you acquire the assurance you demonstrated in *sex, lies, and videotape*?

Well, I think the most important thing to address—and especially people reading interviews with directors who are themselves aspiring directors—is that I've made a lot of short films, and have essentially done a lot of odd jobs, both in and out of the film business, to finance them—in the belief that they are the only real proving ground for feature filmmaking. On the other hand—and this is the key—they were never resume pieces. In my case, they were never shown, except to people who were interested to see my work. They were all very legitimate, very personal acts of expression. I was trying to develop my craft as a filmmaker and getting ideas onto the screen. The last three shorts that I made are every bit as complex, technically and conceptually, as *sex, lies, and videotape*— which is kind of distressing, because it makes me feel like I haven't really come that far since I got out of high school! The other important thing about financing your own short films is that you get a very clear understanding of what things cost. I did the budget for *sex, lies* with John Hardy, one of the producers. I did the first version, he did the second, and then we went back and forth adjusting every dollar in the budget so that we could get bang for our buck. I think it's going to be interesting to see if I'm able to apply the same "guerilla filmmaking" mentality to a film that costs $5 or 10 million. In theory, if I made a film for $1.2 million that looks like $2 -1/2 or 3 million, then I should be able to make a film for $9 or 10 million that looks like $15 million. I can't stand waste on a film.

Some people suggest that you can learn how to direct by *watching* films.

Well, I think that's like a woman watching another woman giving birth—it's just not the same thing. There's only one exception that I can think of off-hand, and that's Lawrence Kasdan, who hadn't directed anything before *BODY HEAT*. But if you're an inexperienced, insecure director, things can get bad quickly. If you've never directed anything before, you'll be up against a lot of things that will be confusing, frustrating and nerve-wracking. If you don't know what's important to deal with and what to let slide down your back, it's going to drive you nuts. It's not something I would wish on just anybody.

When you walked onto the *sex, lies, and videotape* set that first day, did you have that confidence?

It was no big deal. I had a few more people on the crew than I was accustomed to, but not that many more. I knew the process, and it's the process of making a film that excites me, not the reward. So that's why, when people ask me if I'm afraid of getting swallowed up by Hollywood, I just answer that basically, the process is the same. It may involve more money, but you still have to tell a story in a series of images, and you have to shoot them one by one whether it's in Super 8-millimeter or 35-millimeter.

You indicated before that you had some scripts that were more commercial than *sex, lies, and videotape*. Does this mean that you're not necessarily committed to alternative cinema?

Although I have an appreciation for specialty films, I don't want to make them for the rest of my life. There may be other films that I'll make that will fall into that category, but certainly not all of them. It just worked out with *sex, lies* that this particular script, this particular budget and these particular people came together. But I like a lot of different kinds of films, and I'll make a lot of different kinds of films if I'm able to.

★ ★ ★

DIRECTORS

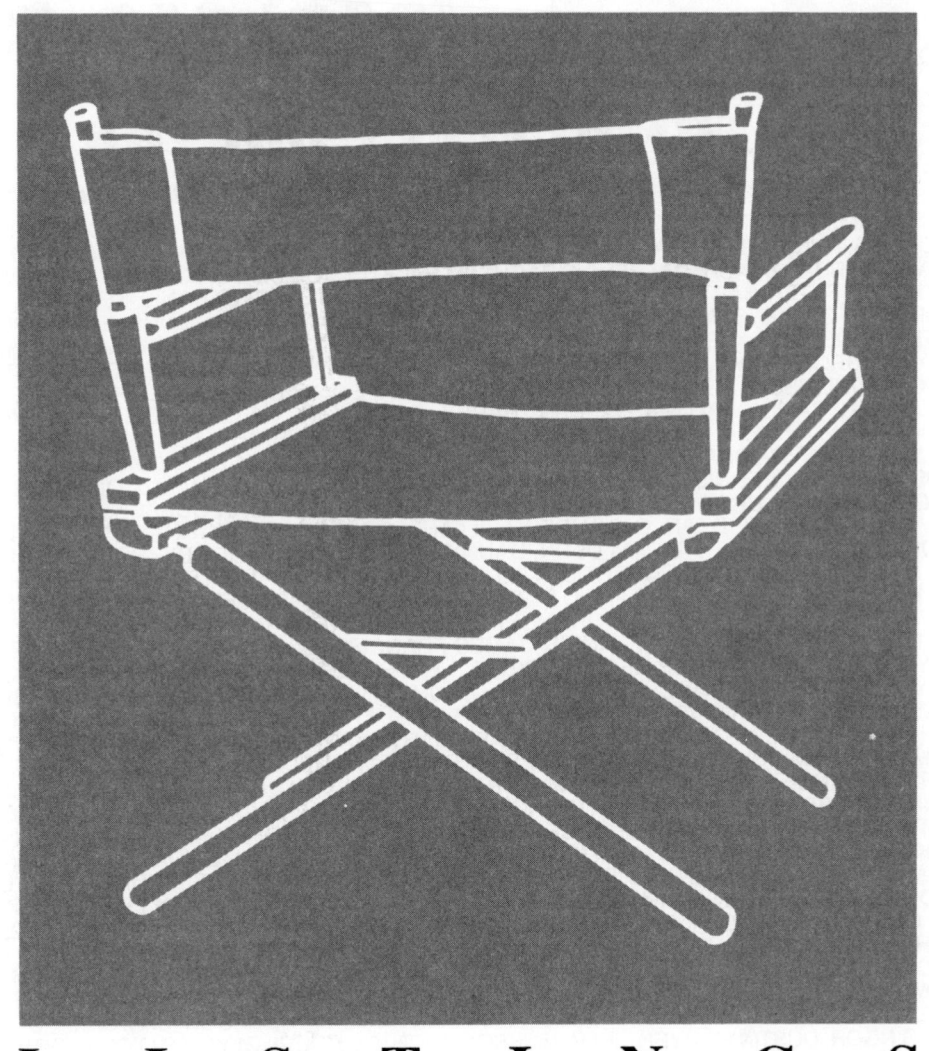

LISTINGS

THE HENRY HIGGINS OF HOLLYWOOD, INC.

ROBERT EASTON

(213) 463-4811

THE DIALECT DOCTOR
Accents Cured – Dialects Strengthened

has taught: DON ADAMS, JENNY AGUTTER, ANA ALICIA, STEVE ALLEN, FERNANDO ALLENDE, MARIA CONCHITA ALONSO, ANTHONY ANDREWS, ANN-MARGRET, ADAM ANT, ANNE ARCHER, EVE ARDEN, JEAN-PIERRE AUMONT, MARGARET AVERY, CANDICE AZZARA, BARBARA BACH, CATHERINE BACH, JIM BACKUS, JOE DON BAKER, IAN BANNEN, ADRIENNE BARBEAU, DREW BARRYMORE, PETER BARTON, BELINDA BAUER, STEVE BAUER, STEPHANIE BEACHAM, BONNIE BEDELIA, JIM BELUSHI, BARBI BENTON, CRYSTAL BERNARD, KEN BERRY, BIJAN, BARBARA BILLINGSLEY, JACQUELINE BISSET, SUSAN BLAKELY, PETER BONERZ, KLAUS MARIA BRANDAUER, EILEEN BRENNAN, BEAU BRIDGES, LLOYD BRIDGES, DANIELLE BRISEBOIS, JAMES BRODERICK, JAMES BROLIN, PIERCE BROSNAN, BRYAN BROWN, GEORG STANFORD BROWN, IAN BUCHANAN, TOM BURLINSON, DELTA BURKE, RAYMOND BURR, LeVAR BURTON, RUTH BUZZI, CORINNE CALVET, KIRK CAMERON, COLLEEN CAMP, VIRGINIA CAPERS, HARRY CAREY, JR., GEORGE CARLIN, DAVID CARRADINE, KEITH CARRADINE, BARBARA CARRERA, THOMAS CARTER, VERONICA CARTWRIGHT, SHAUN CASSIDY, MAXWELL CAULFIELD, RICHARD CHAMBERLAIN, STOCKARD CHANNING, LORRAINE CHASE, JOAN CHEN, LOIS CHILES, CANDY CLARK, JAMES COBURN, IMOGENE COCA, DENNIS COLE, DABNEY COLEMAN, DIDI CONN, MICHAEL CONRAD, ROBERT CONRAD, ALEX CORD, BUD CORT, MICHAEL CRAWFORD, MARY CROSBY, TOM CRUISE, JOAN CUSACK, JIM DALE, TONY DANZA, PATTI DAVIS, PAM DAWBER, FELICITY DEAN, OLIVIA DE HAVILLAND, REBECCA DE MORNAY, PATRICK DEMPSEY, ROBERT DE NIRO, BRIAN DENNEHY, BO DEREK, LAURA DERN, DANNY DE VITO, ALISON DOODY, ROBYN DOUGLASS, BRAD DOURIF, LESLEY-ANNE DOWN, DAVID DUKES, ROBERT DUVALL, SHEENA EASTON, ANITA EKBERG, HECTOR ELIZONDO, STEPHEN ELLIOTT, RON ELY, LINDA EVANS, PETER FALK, STEPHANIE FARACY, TOVAH FELDSHUH, LUPITA FERRER, SHIRLEY ANN FIELD, LINDA FIORENTINO, PETER FIRTH, FIONNULA FLANAGAN, LOUISE FLETCHER, NINA FOCH, JANE FONDA, ROBERT FOXWORTH, TONY FRANCIOSA, GENIE FRANCIS, JAMES FRANCISCUS, KATHLEEN FREEMAN, TERESA GANZEL, TERRI GARBER, ANDY GARCIA, CHRISTOPHER GEORGE, LYNDA DAY GEORGE, RICHARD GERE, MEL GIBSON, SIR JOHN GIELGUD, ROBERT GINTY, ALEXANDER GODUNOV, TRACEY GOLD, JOHN GOODMAN, MARJOE GORTNER, GERRITT GRAHAM, ERIN GRAY, LINDA GRAY, MELANIE GRIFFITH, MOSES GUNN, STEVE GUTTENBERG, SHELLEY HACK, GENE HACKMAN, VERONICA HAMEL, MARK HAMILL, NICHOLAS HAMMOND, TOM HANKS, DARYL HANNAH, ED HARRIS, RUTGER HAUER, PATRICIA HAYES, GINA HECHT, MARIEL HEMINGWAY, LANCE HENRIKSEN, PAMELA HENSLEY, BARBARA HERSHEY, HOWARD HESSEMAN, CHARLTON HESTON, ANNE HEYWOOD, JOHN HILLERMAN, POLLY HOLLIDAY, EARL HOLLIMAN, ANTHONY HOPKINS, BO HOPKINS, DENNIS HOPPER, BOB HOSKINS, JOAN HOTCHKIS, BETH HOWLAND, SEASON HUBLEY, FINOLA HUGHES, GARY IMHOFF, JILL IRELAND, KATE JACKSON, HERB JEFFERSON JR., GLYNIS JOHNS, ELAINE JOYCE, KATY JURADO, WILLIAM KATT, JAMES KEACH, HARVEY KEITEL, MARTHE KELLER, SALLY KELLERMAN, LINDA KELSEY, LANCE KERWIN, MARGOT KIDDER, RICHARD KIEL, VAL KILMER, PERRY KING, NASTASSJA KINSKI, SWOOSIE KURTZ, RON LACEY, CHRISTOPHER LAMBERT, TED LANGE, CLORIS LEACHMAN, EVA LeGALLIENNE, ANNIE LENNOX, JAY LENO, FIONA LEWIS, SHARI LEWIS, EMILY LLOYD, GARY LOCKWOOD, ROBERT LOGGIA, LYNN LORING, DOLPH LUNDGREN, KARL MALDEN, NICK MANCUSO, MONTE MARKHAM, ANDREW McCARTHY, PEGGY McCAY, RODDY McDOWALL, DOROTHY McGUIRE, DOUG McKEON, FRANK McRAE, JAYNE MEADOWS, HEATHER MENZIES, BETTE MIDLER, JULIET MILLS, LYNNE MOODY, DEMI MOORE, MARY TYLER MOORE, TERRY MOORE, MICHAEL MORIARTY, DONNY MOST, PATRICIA NEAL, LIAM NEESON, SAM NEILL, CRAIG T. NELSON, BARRY NEWMAN, HAING NGOR, DUSTIN NGUYEN, JULIA NICKSON, MICHAEL NOURI, GLYNNIS O'CONNOR, SIR LAURENCE OLIVIER, EDWARD JAMES OLMOS, JENNIFER O'NEILL, CATHERINE OXENBERG, AL PACINO, JOANNA PACULA, JAMESON PARKER, BARBARA PARKINS, MANDY PATINKIN, GREGORY PECK, LISA PELIKAN, JOHN BENNETT PERRY, MARIA PERSCHY, PENNY PEYSER, MICHELLE PFEIFFER, DONALD PLEASENCE, JOAN PLOWRIGHT, AMANDA PLUMMER, STEFANIE POWERS, LAWRENCE PRESSMAN, LEE PURCELL, RANDY QUAID, KATHLEEN QUINLAN, BEULAH QUO, DEBORAH RAFFIN, STEVE RAILSBACK, JOHN RAITT, DAVID RASCHE, JOHN RATZENBERGER, ALYSON REED, LEE REMICK, ALEJANDRO REY, CYNTHIA RHODES, NATASHA RICHARDSON, JACK RILEY, MOLLY RINGWALD, JOHN RITTER, TANYA ROBERTS, PAUL RODRIGUEZ, TRISTAN ROGERS, JOHN RUBINSTEIN, JOHN RUSSELL, EVA MARIE SAINT, EMMA SAMMS, JOHN SAXON, GRETA SCACCHI, JACK SCALIA, ANNE SCHEDEEN, AVERY SCHREIBER, RICKY SCHRODER, ARNOLD SCHWARZENEGGER, JEAN BRUCE SCOTT, MARTHA SCOTT, CONNIE SELLECCA, CAROLINE SEYMOUR, JANE SEYMOUR, YOKO SHIMADA, WIL SHRINER, DWIGHT SHULTZ, GREGORY SIERRA, JONATHAN SILVERMAN, JEAN SIMMONS, MADGE SINCLAIR, JACLYN SMITH, JIMMY SMITS, ANN SOTHERN, DAVID SOUL, SISSY SPACEK, SYLVESTER STALLONE, ANDREW STEVENS, CONNIE STEVENS, FISHER STEVENS, PARKER STEVENSON, DEAN STOCKWELL, MADELYN STOWE, PETER STRAUSS, GAIL STRICKLAND, DONALD SUTHERLAND, PATRICK SWAYZE, JACK THOMPSON, SIGRID THORNTON, CHARLENE TILTON, LILY TOMLIN, LIZ TORRES, CONSTANCE TOWERS, TOMMY TUNE, TWIGGY, SUSAN TYRRELL, CICELY TYSON, ROBERT URICH, PAVLA USTINOV, MONIQUE VAN DE VEN, MERETE VAN KAMP, DICK VAN PATTEN, JOYCE VAN PATTEN, ROBERT VAUGHN, CHICK VENNERA, SAL VISCUSO, LINDSAY WAGNER, ROBERT WAGNER, DEE WALLACE, SHANI WALLIS, RAY WALSTON, JESSICA WALTER, RACHEL WARD, LESLEY ANN WARREN, DENZEL WASHINGTON, CARLENE WATKINS, DENNIS WEAVER, LISA WHELCHEL, FORREST WHITAKER, CINDY WILLIAMS, BRUCE WILLIS, FLIP WILSON, MARIE WINDSOR, JAMES WOODS, JANE WYATT, JANE WYMAN, RICHARD YNIGUEZ, MICHAEL YORK, SUSANNAH YORK, ALAN YOUNG, JOHNNY YUNE, DAPHNE ZUNIGA

. . . and over two thousand others.

KEY TO ABBREVIATIONS

(TF)   =   TELEFEATURE
             Motion pictures made for television with an on-air
             running time of 1-1/2 hours to 4-1/2 hours on
             commercial television; or 1 hour to 4 hours on
             non-commercial television.

(CTF)   =   CABLE TELEFEATURE
             Motion pictures made for cable television with an on-air
             running time of 1 hour to 4 hours.

(MS)   =   MINISERIES
             Motion pictures made for television with an on-air
             running time of 4-1/2 hours and more on commercial
             television; or 4 hours or more on non-commercial television.

(CMS)   =   CABLE MINISERIES
             Motion pictures made for cable television with an
             on-air running time of 4 hours or more.

(FD)   =   FEATURE DOCUMENTARY
             Documentary films made for theatrical distribution or
             feature length (1 or more hours.)

(TD)   =   TELEVISION DOCUMENTARY
             Documentary films made for television of feature
             length (1-1/2 hours or more on commercial television,
             1 or more hours on non-commercial television.)

(CTD)   =   CABLE TELEVISION DOCUMENTARY
             Documentary films made for cable television of
             feature length (1 or more hours.)

(AF)   =   ANIMATED FEATURE

(ATF)   =   ANIMATED TELEFEATURE

(HVF)   =   HOME VIDEO FEATURE
             Motion picutres made especially for the home video
             market of feature length (1 or more hours.)

(HVD)   =   HOME VIDEO DOCUMENTARY
             Documentary film made especially for the home video
             market of feature length (1 or more hours.)

KEY TO SYMBOLS

*   after a director's name denotes membership in the Directors
       Guild of America.

★   after a film title denotes a directorial Academy Award nomination.

★★   after a film title denotes a directorial Academy Award win.

☆   after a film title denotes a directorial Emmy Award nomination.

☆☆   after a film title denotes a directorial Emmy Award win.

DIRECTORS
ACADEMY AWARDS AND NOMINATIONS
1977-1989

★★ = winner in category

**F
I
L
M**

**D
I
R
E
C
T
O
R
S**

1977
ANNIE HALL ....Woody Allen★★
STAR WARS .... George Lucas
THE TURNING POINT ....Herbert Ross
CLOSE ENCOUNTERS OF
    THE THIRD KIND .... Steven Spielberg
JULIA .... Fred Zinnemann

1978
INTERIORS .... Woody Allen
COMING HOME .... Hal Ashby
HEAVEN CAN WAIT ....Warren Beatty
THE DEER HUNTER .... Michael Cimino★★
HEAVEN CAN WAIT .... Buck Henry
MIDNIGHT EXPRESS .... Alan Parker

1979
ALL THAT JAZZ .... Bob Fosse
APOCALYPSE NOW .... Francis Coppola
BREAKING AWAY .... Peter Yates
KRAMER VS. KRAMER .... Robert Benton★★
LA CAGE AUX FOLLES .... Edouard Molinaro

1980
THE ELEPHANT MAN .... David Lynch
ORDINARY PEOPLE .... Robert Redford★★
RAGING BULL .... Martin Scorsese
THE STUNT MAN .... Richard Rush
TESS .... Roman Polanski

1981
ATLANTIC CITY .... Louis Malle
CHARIOTS OF FIRE .... Hugh Hudson
ON GOLDEN POND .... Mark Rydell
RAIDERS OF THE LOST ARK .... Steven Spielberg
REDS .... Warren Beatty★★

1982
DAS BOOT ....Wolfgang Peterson
E.T. THE EXTRA-TERRESTRIAL ....Steven Spielberg
GANDHI ....Richard Attenborough★★
TOOTSIE .... Sydney Pollack
THE VERDICT .... Sidney Lumet

1983
THE DRESSER.................................Peter Yates
FANNY & ALEXANDER ....Ingmar Bergman
SILKWOOD .... Mike Nichols
TENDER MERCIES .... Bruce Beresford
TERMS OF ENDEARMENT ....James L. Brooks★★

1984
AMADEUS ....Milos Forman★★
BROADWAY DANNY ROSE ....Woody Allen
THE KILLING FIELDS ....Roland Joffe
A PASSAGE TO INDIA ....David Lean
PLACES IN THE HEART .... Robert Benton

1985
KISS OF THE SPIDER WOMAN ....Hector Babenco
OUT OF AFRICA .... Sydney Pollack★★
PRIZZI'S HONOR ....John Huston
RAN .... Akira Kurosawa
WITNESS .... Peter Weir

1986
BLUE VELVET .... David Lynch
HANNAH AND HER SISTERS ....Woody Allen
THE MISSION .... Roland Joffe
PLATOON .... Oliver Stone★★
A ROOM WITH A VIEW .... James Ivory

1987
THE LAST EMPEROR ....Bernardo Bertolucci★★
HOPE AND GLORY ....John Boorman
MY LIFE AS A DOG ....Lasse Hallstrom
MOONSTRUCK ....Norman Jewison
FATAL ATTRACTION .... Adrian Lyne

1988
MISSISSIPPI BURNING ....Alan Parker
A FISH CALLED WANDA ....Charles Chrichton
THE LAST TEMPTATION
    OF CHRIST .... Martin Scorsese
RAIN MAN .... Barry Levinson★★
WORKING GIRL ....Mike Nichols

1989
BORN ON THE FOURTH OF JULY ...Oliver Stone★★
CRIMES AND MISDEMEANORS ....Woody Allen
DEAD POETS SOCIETY ....Peter Weir
HENRY V .... Kenneth Branagh
MY LEFT FOOT .... Jim Sheridan

A

PAUL AARON *
Agent: CAA - Beverly Hills, 213/288-4545

A DIFFERENT STORY   Avco Embassy, 1978
A FORCE OF ONE   American Cinema, 1979
THE MIRACLE WORKER (TF)   Katz-Gallin Productions/
     Half-Pint Productions, 1979
THIN ICE (TF)   CBS Entertainment, 1981
MAID IN AMERICA (TF)   CBS Entertainment, 1982
DEADLY FORCE   Embassy, 1983
WHEN SHE SAYS NO (TF)   I&C Productions/Jozak-
     Decade Enterprises, 1984
MAXIE   Orion, 1985
MORGAN STEWART'S COMING HOME   co-director with
     Terry Winsor, both directed under pseudonym of Alan
     Smithee, New Century/Vista, 1987
IN LOVE AND WAR (TF)   Carol Schreder Productions/
     Tisch-Avnet Productions, 1987

GEORGE ABBOTT
b. June 25, 1887 - Forestville, New York
Business: 1270 Avenue of the Americas, New York, NY
     10022

WHY BRING THAT UP?   Paramount, 1929
HALF-WAY TO HEAVEN   Paramount, 1929
MANSLAUGHTER   Paramount, 1930
THE SEA GOD   Paramount, 1930
STOLEN HEAVEN   Paramount, 1931
SECRETS OF A SECRETARY   Paramount, 1931
MY SIN   Paramount, 1931
THE CHEAT   Paramount, 1931
TOO MANY GIRLS   RKO Radio, 1940
THE PAJAMA GAME   co-director with Stanley Donen,
     Warner Bros., 1957
DAMN YANKEES   co-director with Stanley Donen,
     Warner Bros., 1958

ROBERT J. ABEL *
b. March 10, 1937 - Cleveland, Ohio
Address: 1616 N. Queens Road, Los Angeles, CA 90069
Attorney: Sam Halper, Halper, Lebe & Finer, 1880 Century
     Park East - Suite 1015, Los Angeles, CA 90067,
     213/552-1093

ELVIS ON TOUR (FD)   co-director with Pierre Adidge,
     MGM, 1972
LET THE GOOD TIMES ROLL (FD)   co-director with
     Sidney Levin, Columbia, 1973

JIM ABRAHAMS *
b. May 10, 1944 - Milwaukee, Wisconsin
Agent: ICM - Los Angeles, 213/550-4000
Business Manager: Abrahams Boy, Inc., 11777 San
     Vicente Blvd. - Suite 600, Los Angeles, CA 90049,
     213/820-1942

AIRPLANE!   co-director with David Zucker & Jerry Zucker,
     Paramount, 1980
TOP SECRET!   co-director with David Zucker & Jerry
     Zucker, Paramount, 1984

RUTHLESS PEOPLE   co-director with David Zucker &
     Jerry Zucker, Buena Vista, 1986
BIG BUSINESS   Buena Vista, 1988
WELCOME HOME, ROXY CARMICHAEL   Paramount,
     1990

EDWARD ABROMS *
Home: 1866 Marlowe Street, Thousand Oaks, CA 91360,
     805/495-0701
Agent: Larry Mirisch, Triad Artists, Inc. - Los Angeles,
     213/556-2727

SULTAN AND THE ROCK STAR (TF)   Walt Disney
     Productions, 1978
THE IMPOSTER (TF)   Warner Bros. TV, 1985

TENGIZ ABULADZE
b. January 31, 1924 - Georgia, U.S.S.R.
Contact: Union of Soviet Filmmakers, Vassilievskaya 13,
     Moscow, U.S.S.R., tel.: 250-4114

MAGDAN'S DONKEY   Gruziafilm, 1955, Soviet
SOMEONE ELSE'S CHILDREN   Gruziafilm, 1958, Soviet
ME, GRANDMA, ILIKO AND HILLARION   Gruziafilm, 1963,
     Soviet
THE ENTREATY   Gruziafilm, 1969, Soviet
A NECKLACE FOR MY BELOVED   Gruziafilm, 1972,
     Soviet
THE MIRACLE TREE   Gruziafilm, 1977, Soviet
REPENTANCE   Cannon, 1984, Soviet, originally made
     for television

JOVAN ACIN
b. 1941 - Belgrade, Yugoslavia
Contact: Yugoslavia Film, Knez Mihailova 19, 11000
     Belgrade, Yugoslavia, 011/625-860

THE CONCRETE ROSE   1975, Yugoslavian
HEY BABU RIBA   *DANCING ON WATER*   Orion Classics,
     1986, Yugoslavian

DAVID ACOMBA *
Address: 80 Front Street - Suite 607, Toronto, Ontario
     M5E IT4, Canada, 416/364-6063

SLIPSTREAM   1973, Canadian
HANK WILLIAMS: THE SHOW HE NEVER GAVE
     Simcom/Film Consortium of Canada, 1982, Canadian
NIGHT LIFE   Wild Night Productions, 1989

CATLIN ADAMS *
b. October 11, 1950 - Los Angeles, California
Address: 210 West 70th Street - Apt. 1503, New York,
     NY 10023
Agent: Caitlin Buchman, Triad Artists, Inc. - Los Angeles,
     213/556-2727

STICKY FINGERS   Spectrafilm, 1988
STOLEN: ONE HUSBAND (TF)   King Phoenix
     Entertainment, 1990

DANIEL ADAMS
RELIGION, INC.   Blossom Pictures, 1989
PRIMARY MOTIVE   Ascension Films, 1990

DOUG ADAMS
BLACKOUT   Magnum Entertainment, 1988

AL ADAMSON

Business: Independent-International Pictures, 223 State
  Highway 18, East Brunswick, NJ, 201/249-8982

TWO TICKETS TO TERROR   Victor Adamson, 1964
GUN RIDERS   1969
BLOOD OF DRACULA'S CASTLE   Crown International,
  1969
SATAN'S SADISTS   Independent-International, 1970
HELL'S BLOODY DEVILS   *THE FAKERS*   Independent-
  International, 1970
FIVE BLOODY GRAVES   Independent-International, 1971
HORROR OF THE BLOOD MONSTERS   Dalia, 1971
THE FEMALE BUNCH   Dalia, 1971
LAST OF THE COMANCHEROS   Independent-
  International, 1971
BLOOD OF GHASTLY HORROR   Independent-
  International, 1972
THE BRAIN OF BLOOD   Hemisphere, 1972
DOOMSDAY VOYAGE   Futurama International, 1972
DRACULA VS. FRANKENSTEIN   Independent-
  International, 1973
THE DYNAMITE BROTHERS   Cinemation, 1974
GIRLS FOR RENT   Independent-International, 1974
THE NAUGHTY STEWARDESSES   Independent-
  International, 1975
STUD BROWN   Cinemation, 1975
BLAZING STEWARDESSES   Independent-International,
  1975
JESSIE'S GIRL   Manson International, 1976
BLACK HEAT   Independent-International, 1976
CINDERELLA 2000   Independent-International, 1977
BLACK SUMURAI   BLLJ International, 1977
SUNSET COVE   Cal-Am Artists, 1978
DEATH DIMENSION   *FREEZE BOMB*   Movietime, 1978
NURSE SHERRI   Independent-International, 1978
CARNIVAL MAGIC   Krypton Corporation, 1982

LOU ADLER*

b. Los Angeles, California
Business Manager: Dick DeBlois, Ernst & Whinney,
  1875 Century Park East, Los Angeles, CA 90067,
  213/553-2800

UP IN SMOKE   Paramount, 1978
LADIES AND GENTLEMEN...THE FABULOUS STAINS
  Paramount, 1982

PERCY ADLON

b. 1935 - Munich, Germany
Contact: German Film & TV Academy, Pommernallee 1,
  1 Berlin 19, 0311/302-6096

THE GUARDIAN AND HIS POET (TF)   1978,
  West German
CELESTE   New Yorker, 1981, West German
FIVE LAST DAYS   1982, West German
THE SWING   1983, West German
SUGARBABY   Kino International, 1985, West German
HERSCHEL AND THE MUSIC OF THE STARS (TF)
  Bayerischer Rundfunk, 1985, West German
BAGDAD CAFE   *OUT OF ROSENHEIM*   Island Pictures,
  1987, West German-U.S.
ROSALIE GOES SHOPPING   Four Seasons
  Entertainment, 1989, West German-U.S.

JOSE LUIS GARCIA AGRAZ

(John Agras / Joseph Louis Agraz)
b. November 1952 - Mexico City, Mexico
Contact: Azteca Films, 555 N. La Brea Avenue, P.O. Box
  36095, Hollywood, CA 90036, 213/938-2413

NOCOUT   Azteca Films, 1984, Mexican
LAS NOCHES DEL CALIFAS   American General Films,
  1986, Mexican
TREASURE OF THE MOON GODDESS   *DREAMS OF
  GOLD*   Ascot Entertainment Group, 1987

CHARLIE AHEARN

Agent: William Morris Agency - Beverly Hills, 213/274-7451

WILD STYLE   First Run Features, 1983

CHANTAL AKERMAN

b. June 1950 - Brussels, Belgium
Home: Rue de Florence 13, 1050 Brussels, Belgium,
  02/537-0811
Contact: National Tourist Office, 61 Rue de Marche Aux
  Herbes, B1000 Brussels, Belgium, 02/513-8940

SAUTE MA VILLE   1968, Belgian
L'ENFANT AIME   1971, Belgian
LA CHAMBRE   1972, Belgian
HOTEL MONTEREY   1972, Belgian
LE 15/18   co-director, 1973, Belgian
HANGING OUT - YONKERS   1974
JE, TU, IL, ELLES   1974, Belgian
JEANNE DIELMAN, 23 QUAI DE COMMERCE, 1080
  BRUXELLES   1975, Belgian
NEWS FROM HOME   1976, Belgian
LES RENDEZVOUS D'ANNA   Gaumont, 1979, French
DIS MOI   1980, Belgian
TOUTE UN NUITE   Paradise Films/Avidia Films,
  1982, Belgian
LES ANNEES 80S   Paradise Films, 1983, Belgian
L'HOMME A LA VALISE   1983, Belgian
SEVEN WOMEN, SEVEN SINS   co-director, ASA
  Communications, 1987, West German-French-U.S.-
  Austrian-Belgian
HISTOIRES D'AMERIQUE   Mallia Films/Paradise Films/
  La Sept/The Pompidou Center/R.T.D.F./French Ministry
  of Culture/ Belgian Ministry of French Culture, 1989,
  French-Belgian
NIGHT AND DAY   Paradise Films/GRP, 1990,
  Belgian-West Germany

MOUSTAPHA AKKAD

b. Syria
Business: Trancas International Films, Inc., 9229 Sunset
  Blvd. - Suite 415, Los Angeles, CA 90069, 213/657-7670

MOHAMMAD, MESSENGER OF GOD   *THE MESSAGE*
  Tarik, 1977, Lebanese-British
LION OF THE DESERT   United Film Distribution, 1981,
  Libyan-British

LUIS ALCORIZA

b. 1920 - Badajoz, Spain
Contact: Azteca Films, 555 N. La Brea Avenue, P.O. Box
  36095, Hollywood, CA 90036, 213/938-2413

LOS JOVENES   Azteca Films, 1960, Mexican
TLAYUCAN   Azteca Films, 1961, Mexican
TIBURONEROS   Azteca Films, 1962, Mexican

TARAHUMARA   Azteca Films, 1964, Mexican
MECANICA NACIONAL   Azteca Films, 1971, Mexican
FE, ESPERANZA & CARIDAD   co-director, Azteca Films,
     1973, Mexican
PRESAGIO   Azteca Films, 1974, Mexican
TAC-TAC   Peliculas Trio/Alcion Films, 1981, Spanish-
     Mexican
TERROR Y ENCAJES NEGRO   Conacite II, 1986,
     Mexican
LO QUE IMPORTA ES VIVIR   Peliculas Mexicanas, 1989,
     Mexican
DIA DE DIFUNTO   Televicine, 1989, Mexican

ALAN ALDA*
b. January 28, 1936 - New York, New York
Agent: Martin Bauer, Bauer Benedek Agency -
     Beverly Hills, 213/275-2421

THE FOUR SEASONS   Universal, 1981
SWEET LIBERTY   Universal, 1986
A NEW LIFE   Paramount, 1988
BETSY'S WEDDING   Buena Vista, 1990

WILL ALDIS
Agent: William Morris Agency - Beverly Hills, 213/274-7451

STEALING HOME   co-director with Steven Kampmann,
     Warner Bros., 1988

ADELL ALDRICH*
b. June 11, 1943 - Los Angeles, California
Home: 556 S. Norton Avenue, Los Angeles, CA 90020,
     213/487-4870

DADDY, I DON'T LIKE IT LIKE THIS (TF)   CBS
     Entertainment, 1978
THE KID FROM LEFT FIELD (TF)   Gary Coleman
     Productions/Deena Silver-Kramer's Movie
     Company, 1979

TOMAS GUTIERREZ ALEA
(See Tomas GUTIERREZ ALEA)

A.K. ALLEN
(See Janet GREEK)

COREY ALLEN*
b. June 29, 1934 - Cleveland, Ohio
Agent: Ronald Leif, Contemporary Artists - Beverly Hills,
     213/278-8250

PINOCCHIO   EUE, 1971
SEE THE MAN RUN (TF)   Universal TV, 1971
CRY RAPE! (TF)   Leonard Freeman Productions, 1973
YESTERDAY'S CHILD (TF)   co-director with Bob
     Rosenbaum, Paramount TV, 1977
THUNDER AND LIGHTNING   20th Century-Fox, 1978
AVALANCHE   New World, 1979
STONE (TF)   Stephen J. Cannell Productions/
     Universal TV, 1979
THE MAN IN THE SANTA CLAUS SUIT (TF)   Dick Clark
     Productions, 1979
THE RETURN OF FRANK CANNON (TF)   QM
     Productions, 1980
MURDER, SHE WROTE: THE MURDER OF SHERLOCK
     HOLMES (TF)   Universal TV, 1984
CODENAME: FIREFOX (TF)   Universal TV, 1985
BRASS (TF)   Carnan Productions/Jaygee Productions/
     Orion TV, 1985

BEVERLY HILLS COWGIRL BLUES (TF)   The Leonard
     Goldberg Company, 1985
I-MAN (TF)   Mark H. Ovitz Productions/Walt Disney
     Productions, 1986
THE LAST FLING (TF)   Leonard Hill Films, 1987
DESTINATION AMERICA (TF)   Stephen J. Cannell
     Productions, 1987
J.J. STARBUCK (TF)   Stephen J. Cannell Productions,
     1987
STAR TREK: THE NEXT GENERATION (TF)   Paramount
     TV, 1987
THE ANN JILLIAN STORY (TF)   NBC, 1988

DAVID ALLEN
THE DUNGEONMASTER   co-director, Empire Pictures,
     1985
PUPPETMASTER II   Full Moon Entertainment, 1990

DEBBIE ALLEN*
Agent: William Morris Agency - Beverly Hills, 213/274-7451

POLLY (TF)   Echo Cove Productions/Walt Disney TV, 1989

IRWIN ALLEN*
b. June 12, 1916 - New York, New York
Agent: William Morris Agency - Beverly Hills, 213/274-7451

THE SEA AROUND US (FD)   RKO Radio, 1951
THE ANIMAL WORLD (FD)   Warner Bros., 1956
THE STORY OF MANKIND   Warner Bros., 1957
THE LOST WORLD   20th Century-Fox, 1960
VOYAGE TO THE BOTTOM OF THE SEA   20th Century-
     Fox, 1961
FIVE WEEKS IN A BALLOON   20th Century-Fox, 1962
CITY BENEATH THE SEA (TF)   20th Century-Fox TV/
     Motion Pictures International, 1971
THE TOWERING INFERNO   action sequences only, 20th
     Century-Fox, 1974
THE SWARM   Warner Bros., 1978
BEYOND THE POSEIDON ADVENTURE   Warner Bros.,
     1979

WOODY ALLEN*
(Allen Stewart Konigsberg)
b. December 1, 1935 - Brooklyn, New York
Agent: Sam Cohn, ICM - New York City, 212/556-6810
Personal Manager: Jack Rollins/Charles Joffe, 130 West
     57th Street, New York, NY, 212/582-1940

WHAT'S UP, TIGER LILY?   American International, 1966
TAKE THE MONEY AND RUN   Cinerama Releasing
     Corporation, 1969
BANANAS   United Artists, 1971
EVERYTHING YOU ALWAYS WANTED TO KNOW
     ABOUT SEX* (*BUT WERE AFRAID TO ASK)
     United Artists, 1972
SLEEPER   United Artists, 1973
LOVE AND DEATH   United Artists, 1975
ANNIE HALL ★★   United Artists, 1977
INTERIORS ★   United Artists, 1978
MANHATTAN   United Artists, 1979
STARDUST MEMORIES   United Artists, 1980
A MIDSUMMER NIGHT'S SEX COMEDY   Orion/Warner
     Bros., 1982
ZELIG   Orion/Warner Bros., 1983
BROADWAY DANNY ROSE ★   Orion, 1983
THE PURPLE ROSE OF CAIRO   Orion, 1985
HANNAH AND HER SISTERS ★   Orion, 1986
RADIO DAYS   Orion, 1987

SEPTEMBER   Orion, 1987
ANOTHER WOMAN   Orion, 1988
NEW YORK STORIES   co-director with Francis Ford
   Coppola & Martin Scorsese, Buena Vista, 1989
CRIMES AND MISDEMEANORS ★ Orion, 1989
ALICE   Orion, 1990

NESTOR ALMENDROS
b. 1930 - Barcelona, Spain

IMPROPER CONDUCT (FD)   co-director with Orlando
   Jimenez-Leal, Cinevista/Promovision International,
   1984, French
NOBODY LISTENED (FD)   co-director with Jorge Ulla,
   The Cuban Human Rights Film Project, 1988

MICHAEL ALMEREYDA
Agent: William Morris Agency - Beverly Hills, 213/274-7451

TWISTER   Vestron, 1990

PEDRO ALMODOVAR
Agent: ICM - Los Angeles, 213/550-4000

PEPI, LUCI, BOM AND OTHER GIRLS ON THE HEAP
   Figaro, 1981, Spanish
LABERINTO DE PASIONES   Musidora, 1982, Spanish
DARK HABITS   Cinevista, 1984, Spanish
WHAT HAVE I DONE TO DESERVE THIS?   Cinevista,
   1985, Spanish
MATADOR   Cinevista, 1986, Spanish
LAW OF DESIRE   Cinevista/Promovision International,
   1987, Spanish
WOMEN ON THE VERGE OF A NERVOUS BREAKDOWN
   Orion Classics, 1988, Spanish
TIE ME UP! TIE ME DOWN! ATAME   Miramax Films,
   1990, Spanish

PAUL ALMOND*
b. April 26, 1931 - Montreal, Quebec, Canada
Home: 54 Malibu Colony, Malibu, CA 90265, 213/456-3089
Attorney: Eric Weissmann, 9665 Wilshire Blvd. - Suite 900,
   Beverly Hills, CA 90212, 213/858-7888

BACKFIRE   Anglo Amalgamated, 1962, British
THE DARK DID NOT CONQUER (TF)   CBC, 1963,
   Canadian
JOURNEY TO THE CENTRE (TF)   CBC, 1963, Canadian
ISABEL   Paramount, 1968, Canadian
ACT OF THE HEART   Universal, 1970, Canadian
JOURNEY   EPOH, 1972, Canadian
FELLOWSHIP (TF)   CBC, 1976, Canadian
EVERY PERSON IS CRAZY (TF)   CBC, 1979, Canadian
FOR THE RECORD (TF)   1980, Canadian
FINAL ASSIGNMENT   Almi Cinema 5, 1980, Canadian
UPS AND DOWNS   JAD International, 1983, Canadian
CAPTIVE HEARTS   MGM/UA, 1987, Canadian

JOHN A. ALONZO*
b. 1934 - Dallas, Texas
Agent: Scott Harris, Harris & Goldberg - Los Angeles,
   213/553-5200

FM   Universal, 1978
CHAMPIONS...A LOVE STORY (TF)   Warner Bros. TV,
   1979

PORTRAIT OF A STRIPPER (TF)   Moonlight Productions/
   Filmways, 1979
BELLE STARR (TF)   Entheos Unlimited Productions/
   Hanna-Barbera Productions, 1980
BLINDED BY THE LIGHT (TF)   Time-Life Films, 1980

EMMETT ALSTON
NEW YEAR'S EVIL   Cannon, 1981
NINE DEATHS OF THE NINJA   Crown International, 1985
DEMONWARP   Vidmark, 1988
TIGER SHARK   Chappell Productions, 1989, U.S. -Filipino
ACROSS MANILA BAY   Kelday International, 1989,
   Filipino

ROBERT ALTMAN*
b. February 20, 1925 - Kansas City, Missouri
Business: Sandcastle 5 Productions, 502 Park Avenue -
   Suite 156, New York, NY 10022

THE DELINQUENTS   United Artists, 1957
THE JAMES DEAN STORY (FD)   co-director with George
   W. George, Warner Bros., 1957
NIGHTMARE IN CHICAGO (TF)   MCA-TV, 1964
COUNTDOWN   Warner Bros., 1968
THAT COLD DAY IN THE PARK   Commonwealth United,
   1969, Canadian-U.S.
M*A*S*H ★   20th Century-Fox, 1970
BREWSTER McCLOUD   MGM, 1970
McCABE & MRS. MILLER   Warner Bros., 1971
IMAGES   Columbia, 1972, Irish
THE LONG GOODBYE   United Artists, 1973
THIEVES LIKE US   United Artists, 1974
CALIFORNIA SPLIT   Columbia, 1974
NASHVILLE ★   Paramount, 1976
BUFFALO BILL AND THE INDIANS or SITTING BULL'S
   HISTORY LESSON   United Artists, 1976
3 WOMEN   20th Century-Fox, 1977
A WEDDING   20th Century-Fox, 1978
A PERFECT COUPLE   20th Century-Fox, 1979
QUINTET   20th Century-Fox, 1979
HEALTH   20th Century-Fox, 1980
POPEYE   Paramount, 1980
COME BACK TO THE 5 & DIME JIMMY DEAN, JIMMY
   DEAN   Cinecom, 1982
STREAMERS   United Artists Classics, 1983
SECRET HONOR   Sandcastle 5, 1984
THE LAUNDROMAT (CTF)   Byck-Lancaster Productions/
   Sandcastle 5 Productions, 1985
FOOL FOR LOVE   Cannon, 1985
BEYOND THERAPY   New World, 1987
O.C. AND STIGGS   MGM/UA, 1987, filmed in 1983
THE DUMB WAITER (TF)   Secret Castle Productions, 1987
ARIA   co-director, Miramax Films, 1987, British
THE ROOM (TF)   Sandcastle 5 Productions/Secret Castle
   Productions, 1987
THE CAINE MUTINY COURT MARTIAL (TF)   CBS
   Entertainment, 1988
VINCENT AND THEO   Hemdale, 1990, British-French

JOE ALVES*
b. May 21, 1938 - San Leandro, California
Home: 4176 Rosario Road, Woodland Hills, CA 91364,
   818/346-4624
Agent: Christopher Nassif, C.N.A. - Los Angeles,
   213/657-2063

JAWS 3-D   Universal, 1983

DENIS AMAR

Contact: French Film Office, 745 Fifth Avenue, New York,
   NY 10151 212/832-8860

ASPHALTE   1981, French
L'ADDITION   New World, 1985, French
INSTANT JUSTICE   Warner Bros., 1987, Gibralter,
   uncredited
ENNEMIS INTIMES   Les Films Ariane, 1987, French
WINTER OF '54   HIVER 54, L'ABBE PIERRE   Circle
   Releasing, 1990, French

SUZANA AMARAL

b. Brazil
Contact: Concine/National Cinema Council, Rua Mayrink
   Veiga 28, Rio de Janeiro, Brazil, 2/233-8329

THE HOUR OF THE STAR   Kino International, 1986,
   Brazilian

ROD AMATEAU*

b. December 20, 1923 - New York, New York
Agent: CAA - Beverly Hills, 213/288-4545
Home: 133-1/2 S. Linden Drive, Beverly Hills, CA 90212,
   213/274-3865

THE BUSHWHACKERS   Realart, 1951
MONSOON   United Artists, 1952
PUSSYCAT, PUSSYCAT, I LOVE YOU   United Artists,
   1970, British
THE STATUE   Cinerama Releasing Corporation, 1971,
   British
WHERE DOES IT HURT?   American International,
   1972, British
DRIVE IN   Columbia, 1976
THE SENIORS   Cinema Shares International, 1978
HITLER'S SON   1978, British
UNCOMMON VALOR (TF)   Brademan-Self Productions/
   Sunn Classic, 1983
HIGH SCHOOL U.S.A. (TF)   Hill-Mandelker Films, 1983
LOVELINES   Tri-Star, 1984
THE GARBAGE PAIL KIDS MOVIE   Atlantic Releasing
   Corporation, 1987

JON AMIEL

Address: 30 Wolseley Road, London N8 8RP, England,
   71/341-1690
Agent: Judy Daish, 83 Eastbourne Mews, London W2 6IQ,
   England, 71/262-1101

A SUDDEN WRENCH (TF)   BBC, 1983, British
BUSTED (TF)   BBC, 1984, British
GATES OF GOLD (TF)   BBC Belfast, 1984,
   Northern Irish
TANDOORI NIGHTS (TF)   Channel Four, 1985, British
THE SILENT TWINS (TF)   BBC, 1985, British
THE SINGING DETECTIVE (TF)   BBC/ABC Australia,
   1986, British-Australian
QUEEN OF HEARTS   Cinecom, 1989, British
AUNT JULIA AND THE SCRIPTWRITER   Cinecom, 1990

GIDEON AMIR

Contact: Writers Guild of America, West - Los Angeles,
   213/550-1000

P.O.W. THE ESCAPE   Cannon, 1986

ROBERT AMRAM

b. June 12, 1930 - Budapest, Hungary
Business: Amram Films, 8741 Shoreham Drive, Los
   Angeles, CA 90069, 213/657-3692

SENTINELS OF SILENCE (FD)   1972
SKY HIGH! (FD)   1975
PACIFIC CHALLENGE (FD)   1975
THE LATE GREAT PLANET EARTH (FD)   1980

FRANCO AMURRI*

b. September 12, 1958 - Rome, Italy
Business: Effe Films Inc., 328 So. Beverly Drive - Suite A,
   Beverly Hills, CA 902l2, 213/876-0899 or 213/277-7351
Agent: William Morris Agency - Beverly Hills, 2l3/859-4251
Attorney: Walter S. Teller, Hansen, Jacobson & Teller, 335
   No. Maple Drive - Suite 270, Beverly Hills, CA 90210,
   213/271-8777

IL RAGAZZO DEL PONY EXPRESS   Numero Uno,
   1986, Italian
DA GRANDE   Gruppo BEMA, 1986, Italian
FLASHBACK   Paramount, 1990

TORGNY ANDERBERG

TRAIN TO HEAVEN   Filmstallet/Exat/Condor Film/
   Cinemateca Ecuador, 1989, Swedish-Ecuadorian

ANDY ANDERSON

Agent: Triad Artists, Inc. - Los Angeles, 213/556-2727
Business: 817/461-1228

POSITIVE I.D.   Universal, 1987

LAURIE ANDERSON

HOME OF THE BRAVE   Cinecom, 1986

LINDSAY ANDERSON

b. April 17, 1923 - Bangalore, India
Address: 9 Stirling Mansions, Canfield Gardens, London
   NW6, England
Agent: Triad Artists, Inc. - Los Angeles, 213/556-2727

THIS SPORTING LIFE   Continental, 1962, British
IF...   Paramount, 1969, British
O LUCKY MAN!   Warner Bros., 1973, British
IN CELEBRATION   American Film Theatre, 1975, British-
   Canadian
BRITTANIA HOSPITAL   United Artists Classics, 1982,
   British
THE WHALES OF AUGUST   Alive Films, 1987
GLORY! GLORY! (CTF)   HBO Pictures/Atlantis Films Ltd./
   Orion TV/Stan Daniels Productions/Greif-Dore Company,
   1989

MICHAEL ANDERSON*

b. January 30, 1920 - London, England
Contact: Directors Guild of Canada, 3 Church Street - Suite
   202, Toronto, Ontario M5E 1M2, Canada, 416/364-0122

PRIVATE ANGELO   co-director with Peter Ustinov,
   Associated British Picture Corporation, 1949, British
WATERFRONT WOMEN   WATERFRONT   Rank, 1950,
   British
HELL IS SOLD OUT   Eros, 1951, British
NIGHT WAS OUR FRIEND   Monarch, 1951, British

WILL ANY GENTLEMAN?   Associated British Picture
  Corporation, 1953, British
THE HOUSE OF THE ARROW   Associated British Picture
  Corporation, 1953, British
THE DAM BUSTERS   Warner Bros., 1955, British
1984   Columbia, 1956, British
AROUND THE WORLD IN 80 DAYS ★   United Artists,
  1956
BATTLE HELL   *YANGTSE INCIDENT*   DCA,
  1957, British
CHASE A CROOKED SHADOW   Warner Bros.,
  1958, British
SHAKE HANDS WITH THE DEVIL   United Artists,
  1959, British
THE WRECK OF THE MARY DEARE   MGM, 1959
ALL THE FINE YOUNG CANNIBALS   MGM, 1960
THE NAKED EDGE   United Artists, 1961
FLIGHT FROM ASHIYA   United Artists, 1964
WILD AND WONDERFUL   Universal, 1964
OPERATION CROSSBOW   MGM, 1965, British-Italian
THE QUILLER MEMORANDUM   Paramount,
  1966, British
THE SHOES OF THE FISHERMAN   MGM, 1968
POPE JOAN   Columbia, 1972, British
DOC SAVAGE, THE MAN OF BRONZE   Warner Bros.,
  1975
CONDUCT UNBECOMING   Allied Artists, 1975, British
LOGAN'S RUN   MGM/United Artists, 1975
ORCA   Paramount, 1976
DOMINIQUE   Sword And Sworcery Productions,
  1979, British
THE MARTIAN CHRONICLES (TF)   Charles Fries
  Productions/Stonehenge Productions, 1980
MURDER BY PHONE   New World, 1983, Canadian
SECOND TIME LUCKY   United International Pictures,
  1984, New Zealand- Australian
SEPARATE VACATIONS   RSL Entertainment, 1986,
  Canadian
SWORD OF GIDEON (CTF)   Alliance Entertainment/
  Les Films Ariane/HBO Premiere Films/CTV/Telefilm
  Canada/Rogers Cablesystems/Radio- Canada, 1986,
  Canadian-French
THE JEWELLER'S SHOP   PAC/RAI-1/Alliance
  Entertainment/International Movies Productions,
  1988, Italian-French-Canadian
MILLENNIUM   20th Century Fox, 1989, Canadian-U.S.
YOUNG CATHERINE (CMS)   Consolidated Productions/
  Turner Network TV, 1990

THEO ANGELOPOULOS

b. 1936 - Athens, Greece
Contact: Greek Film Centre, 10 Panepistimiou Street,
  Athens 134, Greece, 01/618924

RECONSTRUCTION   1970, Greek
DAYS OF 36   1973, Greek
THE TRAVELLING PLAYERS   1975, Greek
THE HUNTERS   1978, Greek
MEGALEXANDROS   1980, Greek
JOURNEY TO CYTHERA   Greek Film Centre,
  1984, Greek
O MELISSOKOMOS   Greek Film Centre/Theo
  Angelopoulos Productions/Marin Karmitz Productions/
  ICC/RAI/RAITRE/ERT-1, 1986, Greek-French-Italian
LANDSCAPE IN THE MIST   New Yorker , 1988,
  Greek-French-Italian

JEFF ANGELUCCI

THE ACTOR   The Blum Group, 1989

KEN ANNAKIN*

b. August 10, 1914 - Beverley, England
Home: 3510 Sweetwater Mesa Road, Malibu, CA 90265,
  213/456-2352
Agent: William Morris Agency - Beverly Hills, 213/274-7451

HOLIDAY CAMP   Universal, 1947, British
MIRANDA   Eagle-Lion, 1948, British
BROKEN JOURNEY   Eagle-Lion, 1948, British
HERE COME THE HUGGETTS   General Film Distributors,
  1948, British
QUARTET   co-director with Ralph Smart, Harold French &
  Arthur Crabtree, Eagle-Lion, 1948, British
VOTE FOR HUGGETT   General Film Distributors, 1949,
  British
THE HUGGETTS ABROAD   General Film Distributors,
  1949, British
LANDFALL   Associated British Picture Corporation,
  1949, British
TRIO   co-director with Harold French, Paramount,
  1950, British
HOTEL SAHARA   United Artists, 1951, British
THE STORY OF ROBIN HOOD   co-director with
  Alex Bryce, RKO Radio, 1952, U.S.-British
OUTPOST IN MALAYA   *THE PLANTER'S WIFE*   United
  Artists, 1952, British
THE SWORD AND THE ROSE   RKO Radio, 1953,
  U.S.-British
DOUBLE CONFESSION   Stratford, 1953, British
YOU KNOW WHAT SAILORS ARE   United Artists, 1954,
  British
LAND OF FURY   *THE SEEKERS*   Universal, 1955, British
LOSER TAKES ALL   British Lion, 1956, British
VALUE FOR MONEY   Rank, 1957, British
THREE MEN IN A BOAT   DCA, 1958, British
ACROSS THE BRIDGE   Rank, 1958, British
THIRD MAN ON THE MOUNTAIN   Buena Vista, 1959,
  U.S.-British
ELEPHANT GUN   *NOR THE MOON BY NIGHT*   Lopert,
  1959, British
SWISS FAMILY ROBINSON   Buena Vista, 1960
THE HELLIONS   Columbia, 1962, British
A COMING-OUT PARTY   *VERY IMPORTANT PERSON*
  Union, 1962, British
THE FAST LADY   Rank, 1962, British
CROOKS ANONYMOUS   Allied Artists, 1962, British
THE LONGEST DAY   co-director with Andrew Marton &
  Bernhard Wicki, 20th Century-Fox, 1962
THOSE MAGNIFICENT MEN IN THEIR FLYING MACHINES
  20th Century- Fox, 1965, British
BATTLE OF THE BULGE   Warner Bros., 1965
UNDERWORLD INFORMERS   *THE INFORMERS*
  Continental, 1966, British
THE LONG DUEL   Paramount, 1967, British
THE BIGGEST BUNDLE OF THEM ALL   MGM, 1968,
  U.S.-Italian
THOSE DARING YOUNG MEN IN THEIR JAUNTY
  JALOPIES   Paramount, 1969, British-Italian-French
CALL OF THE WILD   Constantin, 1975,
  West German-Spanish
PAPER TIGER   Joseph E. Levine Presents, 1976, British
MURDER AT THE MARDI GRAS (TF)   The Jozak
  Company/Paramount TV, 1978
HAROLD ROBBINS' THE PIRATE (TF)   Howard W. Koch
  Productions/Warner Bros. TV, 1978
THE 5TH MUSKETEER   Columbia, 1979, Austrian
INSTITUTE FOR REVENGE (TF)   Gold-Driskill Productions/
  Columbia TV, 1979
CHEAPER TO KEEP HER   American Cinema, 1980
THE PIRATE MOVIE   20th Century-Fox, 1982, Australian

THE NEW ADVENTURES OF PIPPI LONGSTOCKING
    Columbia, 1988
JOSEPH AND EMMA   Independent, 1990

JEAN-JACQUES ANNAUD
b. October 1, 1943 - Jurisy, France
Agent: Jeff Berg, ICM - Los Angeles, 213/550-4000

BLACK AND WHITE IN COLOR LA VICTOIRE EN
    CHANTANT   Allied Artists, 1978, French-Ivory
    Coast-Swiss
COUP DE TETE HOTHEAD   Quartet, 1980, French
QUEST FOR FIRE   20th Century-Fox, 1982,
    Canadian-French
THE NAME OF THE ROSE   20th Century Fox, 1986,
    West German-Italian- French
THE BEAR   Tri-Star, 1988, French

DAVID ANSPAUGH*
Contact: Directors Guild of America - Los Angeles,
    213/274-7451

HOOSIERS   Orion, 1986
DEADLY CARE (TF)   Universal TV, 1987
FRESH HORSES   Columbia/WEG, 1988

JOSEPH ANTHONY
b. May 24, 1912 - Milwaukee, Wisconsin

THE RAINMAKER   Paramount, 1956
THE MATCHMAKER   Paramount, 1958
CAREER   Paramount, 1959
ALL IN A NIGHT'S WORK   Paramount, 1961
CONQUERED CITY   American International, 1966, Italian
TOMORROW   Filmgroup, 1972

GREG ANTONACCI*
Agent: Irv Schechter Company - Beverly Hills, 213/278-8070

SPLASH, TOO (TF)   Mark H. Ovitz Productions/Walt
    Disney TV, 1988

LOU ANTONIO*
b. Oklahoma City, Oklahoma
Contact: Directors Guild of America - Los Angeles,
    213/289-2000
Agent: InterTalent - Los Angeles, 213/271-0600

SOMEONE I TOUCHED (TF)   Charles Fries Productions,
    1975
LANIGAN'S RABBI (TF)   Universal TV, 1976
RICH MAN, POOR MAN - BOOK II (TF)   Universal TV,
    1976
THE GIRL IN THE EMPTY GRAVE (TF)   NBC-TV, 1977
SOMETHING FOR JOEY (TF) ☆   MTM Productions, 1977
THE CRITICAL LIST (TF)   MTM Productions, 1978
A REAL AMERICAN HERO (TF)   Bing Crosby Productions,
    1978
BREAKING UP IS HARD TO DO (TF)   Green-Epstein
    Productions/Columbia TV, 1979
SILENT VICTORY: THE KITTY O'NEILL STORY (TF) ☆
    Channing-Debin- Locke Company, 1979
THE CONTENDER (TF)   co-director with Harry Falk,
    Universal TV, 1980
WE'RE FIGHTING BACK (TF)   Highgate Pictures, 1981
THE STAR MAKER (TF)   Channing-Debin-Locke Company/
    Carson Productions, 1981
SOMETHING SO RIGHT (TF)   List-Estrin Productions/Tisch-
    Avnet Television, 1982

BETWEEN FRIENDS (CTF)   HBO Premiere Films/Marian
    Rees Associates/Robert Cooper Films III/List-Estrin
    Productions, 1983, U.S.-Canadian
A GOOD SPORT (TF)   Ralph Waite Productions/Warner
    Bros. TV, 1984
THREESOME (TF)   CBS Entertainment, 1984
REARVIEW MIRROR (TF)   Simon-Asher Entertainment/
    Sunn Classic Pictures, 1984
AGATHA CHRISTIE'S 'THIRTEEN AT DINNER' (TF)
    Warner Bros. TV, 1985
ONE TERRIFIC GUY (TF)   CBS Entertainment, 1986
PALS (TF)   Robert Halmi, Inc., 1987
MAYFLOWER MADAM (TF)   Robert Halmi, Inc., 1987
THE OUTSIDE WOMAN (TF)   Green-Epstein Productions,
    1989
DARK HOLIDAY (TF)   Peter Nelson-Lou Antonio
    Productions/The Finnegan- Pinchuk Company/
    Orion TV, 1989
FACE TO FACE (TF)   Robert Halmi, Inc., 1990

MICHELANGELO ANTONIONI
b. September 29, 1912 - Ferrara, Italy
Home: via Vincenzo Tiberio 18, Rome, Italy, 06/399598

STORY OF A LOVE AFFAIR   New Yorker, 1950, Italian
I VINTI   Film Costellazione, 1953, Italian
LA SIGNORA SENZA CAMELIE   1953, Italian
LOVE IN THE CITY   co-director with Federico Fellini,
    Alberto Lattuada, Carlo Lizzani, Francesco Maselli &
    Dino Risi, Italian Films Export, 1953, Italian
LE AMICHE   Trion Falcine/Titanus, 1955, Italian
IL GRIDO   Astor, 1957, Italian
L'AVVENTURA   Janus, 1961, Italian
LA NOTTE   Lopert, 1961, Italian-French
L'ECLISSE   Times, 1962, Italian-French
RED DESERT   Rizzoli, 1965, Italian-French
I TRE VOLTI   co-director with Mauro Bolognini & Franco
    Indovina, De Laurentiis, 1964, Italian
BLOW-UP ★   Premier, 1966, British-Italian
ZABRISKIE POINT   MGM, 1970
CHUNG KUO (FD)   Golan Productions, 1972, Italian
THE PASSENGER PROFESSIONE: REPORTER
    MGM/United Artists, 1975, Italian-French-Spanish-U.S.
THE MYSTERY OF OBERWALD   RAI/Polytel International,
    1980, Italian
IDENTIFICATION OF A WOMAN   Iter Film/Gaumont, 1982,
    Italian-French

MICHAEL APTED*
b. February 10, 1941 - Aylesbury, England
Agent: CAA - Beverly Hills, 213/288-4545

NUMBER 10 (TF)   Granada TV, 1968, British
YOUR NAME'S NOT GOD, IT'S EDGAR (TF)   Granada TV,
    1968, British
BIG BREADWINNER HOG (TF)   Granada TV, 1968, British
IN A COTTAGE HOSPITAL (TF)   Granada TV, 1969,
    British
DON'T TOUCH HIM, HE MIGHT RESENT IT (TF)
    Granada TV, 1970, British
SLATTERY'S MOUNTED FOOT (TF)   London Weekend TV/
    Kestrel Films, 1970, British
THE DAY THEY BURIED CLEAVER (TF)   Granada TV,
    1970, British
BIG SOFT NELLIE (TF)   Granada TV, 1971, British
THE MOSEDALE HORSESHOE (TF)   Granada TV, 1971,
    British
ONE THOUSAND POUNDS FOR ROSEBUD (TF)
    Granada TV, 1971, British

ANOTHER SUNDAY AND SWEET F.A. (TF)   Granada TV,
    1972, British
JOY (TF)   BBC, 1972, British
SAID THE PREACHER (TF)   BBC, 1972, British
THE STYLE OF THE COUNTESS (TF)   Granada TV,
    1972
THE REPORTERS (TF)   BBC, 1972, British
BUGGINS' ERMINE (TF)   Granada TV, 1972, British
KISSES AT FIFTY (TF)   BBC, 1973, British
HIGH KAMPF (TF)   BBC, 1973, British
JACK POINT (TF)   BBC, 1973, British
THE TRIPLE ECHO   Altura, 1973, British
POOR GIRL (TF)   Granada TV, 1974, British
A GREAT DAY FOR BONZO (TF)   Granada TV,
    1974, British
STARDUST   Columbia, 1975, British
WEDNESDAY LOVE (TF)   BBC, 1975, British
THE COLLECTION (TF) ☆☆   Granada TV, 1976,
    British
STRONGER THAN THE SUN (TF)   BBC, 1977, British
THE SQUEEZE   Warner Bros., 1977, British
AGATHA   Warner Bros., 1979, British
COAL MINER'S DAUGHTER   Universal, 1980
CONTINENTAL DIVIDE   Universal, 1981
KIPPERBANG   *P'TANG YANG, KIPPERBANG*
    MGM/UA Classics, 1983, British
GORKY PARK   Orion, 1983
FIRSTBORN   Paramount, 1984
28 UP (FD)   First Run Features, 1984, British,
    originally made for television
BRING ON THE NIGHT (FD)   Samuel Goldwyn
    Company, 1985
CRITICAL CONDITION   Paramount, 1987
GORILLAS IN THE MIST   Universal, 1988
THE LONG WAY HOME (TD)   Yerosha Productions/
    Granada TV/CBS Music Video Enterprises,
    1989, British
CLASS ACTION   Buena Vista, 1990

MANUEL GUTIERREZ ARAGON
b. Spain
Contact: Ministry of Culture, Motion Picture Division,
    Avenida de Burgos 5, 28036 Madrid, Spain,
    91/202-5351

HABLA, MUDITA   1973, Spanish
CAMADA NEGRA   1977, Spanish
SONAMBULOS   1977, Spanish
EL CORAZON DEL BOSQUE   1978, Spanish
DEMONIOS EN EL JARDIN   1982, Spanish
FEROZ   1983, Spanish
LA NOCHE MAS HERMOSA   1984, Spanish
HALF OF HEAVEN   *LA MITAD DEL CIELO*   Skouras
    Pictures, 1986, Spanish
MALAVENTURA   CB FILM, 1988, Spanish

ALFONSO ARAU
Business: Productions AA, S.A., Privada Rafael Oliva 8,
    Coyoacan 04120, Mexico City, Mexico, 905/689-3989
Agent: The Lantz Office - Los Angeles, 213/858-1144

THE BAREFOOT EAGLE   Televicine International
    Distribution Corporation, 1967, Mexican
CALZONZIN INSPECTOR   Azteca Films, 1974, Mexican
MOJADO POWER   Producciones AA, 1980, Mexican
CHIDO GUAN   General International, 1984, Mexican

DENYS ARCAND
b. June 25, 1941 - Deschambault, Quebec, Canada
Address: 4921 Coronet - Suite 12, Montreal, Quebec,
    Canada, 514/341-6139

SEUL OU AVEC D'AUTRES (FD)   co-director with Denis
    Heroux and Stephane Venne,   Association Generale des
    Etudiants de l'Universite de Montreal, 1962, Canadian
ON EST AU COTON (FD)   National Film Board of Canada,
    1970, Canadian
QUEBEC: DUPLESSIS ET APRES... (FD)   National Film
    Board of Canada, 1972, Canadian
LA MAUDITE GALETTE   France Film, 1972, Canada
REJEANNE PADOVANI   Cinak, 1972, Canadian
GINA   1975, Canadian
LE CONFORT ET L'INDIFFERENCE (FD)   Canadian
    Empire Inc., 1982, Canadian
THE CRIME OF OVIDE PLOUFFE   co-director with Gilles
    Carle,   Cine Plouffe II/CBC/National Film Board of
    Canada, 1984, Canadian
MURDER IN THE FAMILY (MS)   co-director with Gilles
    Carles,   ICC/Filmax/ Antenne-21 Films A2, 1985,
    Canadian-French
THE DECLINE OF THE AMERICAN EMPIRE   Cineplex
    Odeon, 1986, Canadian
JESUS OF MONTREAL   Orion Classics, 1990, Canadian

EMILE ARDOLINO*
Address: 24 Fifth Avenue, New York, NY 10011,
    212/254-0349
Agent: Robert Hohman, Triad Artists, Inc. - Los Angeles,
    213/556-2727

HE MAKES ME FEEL LIKE DANCIN' (FD)   NBC, 1983
DIRTY DANCING   Vestron, 1987
CHANCES ARE   Tri-Star, 1989
THREE MEN AND A LITTLE LADY   Buena Vista, 1990

DARIO ARGENTO
b. 1943 - Italy
Home: via G. Devoti 16, Rome, Italy, 06/438-5341

THE BIRD WITH THE CRYSTAL PLUMAGE   UMC, 1970,
    Italian-West German
CAT O'NINE TAILS   National General, 1971, Italian-West
    German-French
FOUR FLIES ON GREY VELVET   Paramount, 1972,
    Italian-French
LE CINQUE GIORNATE   Seda Spettacoli, 1973, Italian
DEEP RED   Howard Mahler Films, 1976, Italian
SUSPIRIA   International Classics, 1977, Italian
INFERNO   20th Century-Fox
UNSANE   *TENEBRAE*   Bedford Entertainment/Film
    Gallery, 1982, Italian
CREEPERS   *PHENOMENA*   New Line Cinema,
    1985, Italian
OPERA   Dacfilm/RAI, 1987, Italian
TWO EVIL EYES   co-director with George A. Romero,
    Taurus Entertainment, 1990, Italian

ADOLFO ARISTARAIN
b. 1943 - Buenos Aires, Argentina
Contact: Instituto Nacional de Cinematografica, Lima 319,
    1073 Buenos Aires, Argentina, 370028

LA PARTE DEL LEON   1978, Argentine
LA PLAYA DEL AMOR   1979, Argentine
LA DISCOTECA DEL AMOR   1980, Argentine
TIEMPO DE REVANCHA   Aries Films, 1981, Argentine

ULTIMOS DIAS DE LA VICTIMA   Aries Films, 1982,
   Argentine
THE STRANGER   Columbia, 1987, Argentine-U.S.

A L A N   A R K I N *
b. March 26, 1934 - New York, New York
Agent: ICM - Los Angeles, 213/550-4000

LITTLE MURDERS   20th Century-Fox, 1970
FIRE SALE   20th Century-Fox, 1977

A L L A N   A R K U S H *
b. April 30, 1948 - New York, New York
Home: 10851 Willow Crest, Studio City, CA 91604,
   818/508-7024
Agent: Alan Greenspan, ICM - Los Angeles,
   213/550-4428

HOLLYWOOD BOULEVARD   co-director with Joe Dante,
   New World, 1976
DEATHSPORT   co-director with Henry Suso,
   New World, 1978
ROCK 'N' ROLL HIGH SCHOOL   New World, 1979
HEARTBEEPS   Universal, 1981
GET CRAZY   Embassy, 1983
CADDYSHACK II   Warner Bros., 1988

G E O R G E   A R M I T A G E *
Home: 1113 N. Beverly Glen Blvd., Los Angeles, CA
   90077, 213/475-5014
Agent: Mickey Freiberg, The Artists Agency - Los Angeles,
   213/277-7779

PRIVATE DUTY NURSES   New World, 1972
HIT MAN   MGM, 1973
VIGILANTE FORCE   United Artists, 1976
HOT ROD (TF)   ABC Circle Films, 1979
MIAMI BLUES   Orion, 1990

G I L L I A N   A R M S T R O N G *
b. December 18, 1950 - Melbourne, Australia
Agent: William Morris Agency - Beverly Hills,
   213/274-7451

THE SINGER AND THE DANCER   Gillian Armstrong
   Productions, 1976, Australian
MY BRILLIANT CAREER   Analysis, 1980, Australian
STARSTRUCK   Cinecom International, 1982, Australian
MRS. SOFFEL   MGM/UA, 1984
HARD TO HANDLE: BOB DYLAN WITH TOM PETTY
   AND THE HEARTBREAKERS (HVD)   CBS/Fox
   Video Music, 1986
HIGH TIDE   Tri-Star, 1987, Australian
BINGO, BRIDESMAIDS AND BRACES (FD)   Film
   Australia/The Big Picture Co., 1988, Australian
FIRES WITHIN   Pathe Entertainment, 1991

M I C H A E L   A R M S T R O N G
b. July 24, 1944 - Bolton, Lancashire, England
Home: 114 N. Doheny Drive, Los Angeles, CA 90048

HORROR HOUSE   *THE HAUNTED HOUSE OF HORROR*
   American International, 1970, British-U.S.
MARK OF THE DEVIL   Hallmark Releasing Corporation,
   1970, West German- British

G W E N   A R N E R *
Contact: Directors Guild of America - Los Angeles,
   213/289-2000

MY CHAMPION   Shochiku, 1981, Japanese-U.S.

MOTHER'S DAY ON WALTON'S MOUNTAIN (TF)   Lorimar
   Productions/Amanda Productions, 1982
A MATTER OF PRINCIPLE (TF)   Rubicon Film Productions,
   1984
NECESSARY PARTIES (TF)   The Corelli Co./
   WonderWorks, 1988

J A C K   A R N O L D *
b. October 14, 1916 - New Haven, Connecticut
Home: 4860 Nomad Drive, Woodland Hills, CA 91364,
   818/703-8324

GIRLS IN THE NIGHT   Universal, 1953
IT CAME FROM OUTER SPACE   Universal, 1953
THE GLASS WEB   Universal, 1953
THE CREATURE FROM THE BLACK LAGOON
   Universal, 1954
REVENGE OF THE CREATURE   Universal, 1955
THE MAN FROM BITTER RIDGE   Universal, 1955
TARANTULA   Universal, 1955
OUTSIDE THE LAW   Universal, 1956
RED SUNDOWN   Universal, 1956
THE INCREDIBLE SHRINKING MAN   Universal, 1957
THE TATTERED DRESS   Universal, 1957
MAN IN THE SHADOW   Universal, 1958
THE LADY TAKES A FLYER   Universal, 1958
THE SPACE CHILDREN   Paramount, 1958
MONSTER ON THE CAMPUS   Universal, 1958
THE MOUSE THAT ROARED   Columbia, 1959, British
NO NAME ON THE BULLET   Universal, 1959
BACHELOR IN PARADISE   MGM, 1961
THE LIVELY SET   Universal, 1964
A GLOBAL AFFAIR   MGM, 1964
HELLO DOWN THERE   Paramount, 1969
BLACK EYE   Warner Bros., 1974
THE GAMES GIRLS PLAY   General Films, 1975
BOSS NIGGER   Dimension, 1975
THE SWISS CONSPIRACY   SJ International, 1977
SEX AND THE MARRIED WOMAN (TF)   Universal TV,
   1977
MARILYN: THE UNTOLD STORY (TF)   co-director with
   John Flynn & Lawrence Schiller, Lawrence Schiller
   Productions, 1980

N E W T   A R N O L D *
Home: 16996 Strawberry Drive, Encino, CA 91436,
   818/907-6398
Business Manager: Gary Osheroff, Jonevan Productions,
   Inc., 929 East 2nd Street - Suite 201, Los Angeles, CA
   90012, 213/687-3107

BLOODSPORT   Cannon, 1987

I S A A C   A R T E N S T E I N
b. Mexico

BREAK OF DAWN   Platform Releasing, 1988

K A R E N   A R T H U R *
b. August 24, 1941, Omaha, Nebraska
Agent: Ken Gross, Robinson, Weintraub, Gross &
   Associates - Los Angeles, 213/653-5802

LEGACY   Kino International, 1976
THE MAFU CAGE   Clouds Productions, 1979
CHARLESTON (TF)   Robert Stigwood Productions/
   RSO, Inc., 1979
RETURN TO EDEN (MS)   McElroy & McElroy/
   Hanna-Barbera Australia Productions, 1983, Australian

F
I
L
M

D
I
R
E
C
T
O
R
S

VICTIMS FOR VICTIMS (TF)   Daniel L. Paulson - Loehr Spivey Productions/ Orion TV, 1984
A BUNNY'S TALE (TF)   Stan Margulies Company/ABC Circle Films, 1985
THE RAPE OF RICHARD BECK (TF)   Robert Papazian Productions/Henerson- Hirsch Productions, 1985
CROSSINGS (MS)   Aaron Spelling Productions, 1986
LADY BEWARE   Scotti Brothers, 1987
CRACKED UP (TF)   Aaron Spelling Productions, 1987
EVIL IN CLEAR RIVER (TF)   The Steve Tisch Company/ Lionel Chetwynd Productions/Phoenix Entertainment Group, 1988
BRIDGE TO SILENCE (TF)   Fries Entertainment/Briggle, Hennessy, Carrothers & Associates, 1989
BLUE BAYOU (TF)   Fisher Entertainment/Touchstone TV, 1990
FALL FROM GRACE (TF)   NBC Productions, 1990

WILLIAM ASHER*

b. 1919
Agent: Jim Berkus, Leading Artists - Beverly Hills, 213/858-1999

LEATHER GLOVES   co-director with Richard Quine, Columbia, 1948
THE SHADOW ON THE WINDOW   Columbia, 1956
THE 27TH DAY   Columbia, 1956
BEACH PARTY   American International, 1963
JOHNNY COOL   United Artists, 1963
MUSCLE BEACH PARTY   American International, 1963
BIKINI BEACH   American International, 1964
BEACH BLANKET BINGO   American International, 1965
HOW TO STUFF A WILD BIKINI   American International, 1965
FIREBALL 500   American International, 1966
BUTCHER, BAKER, NIGHTMARE MAKER *NIGHT WARNING/MOMMA'S BOY*   Comworld, 1981
MOVERS & SHAKERS   MGM/UA, 1985
I DREAM OF JEANNIE: 15 YEARS LATER (TF)   Can't Sing Can't Dance Productions/Columbia TV, 1985
RETURN TO GREEN ACRES (TF)   JaYgee Productions/ Orion TV, 1990

DAVID ASHWELL*

Agent: William Morris Agency - Beverly Hills, 213/274-7451

YOU RUINED MY LIFE (TF)   Lantana-Kosberg Productions/Mark H. Ovitz Productions/Walt Disney TV, 1987

SAMSON ASLANIAN

TORMENT   co-director with John Hopkins, New World, 1986

OLIVIER ASSAYAS

Contact: French Film Office, 745 Fifth Avenue, New York, NY 10151, 212/832-8860

DESORDRE   Forum Distribution, 1986, French
L'ENFANT D'HIVER   Gemini Films/GPFI, 1989, French

JOHN ASTIN*

b. March 30, 1930 - Baltimore, Maryland
Contact: Directors Guild of America - Los Angeles, 213/289-2000

OPERATION PETTICOAT (TF)   Universal TV, 1977
ROSSETTI AND RYAN: MEN WHO LOVE WOMEN (TF)   Universal TV, 1977

RICHARD ATTENBOROUGH*

b. August 29, 1923 - Cambridge, England
Agent: CAA - Beverly Hills, 213/288-4545 or: Derek Webster/David Booth, John Redway and Associates Ltd., 5 Denmark Street, London WC2H 8LP, England, 71/836-2001

OH! WHAT A LOVELY WAR   Paramount, 1969, British
YOUNG WINSTON   Columbia, 1972, British
A BRIDGE TOO FAR   United Artists, 1977, British
MAGIC   20th Century-Fox, 1978
GANDHI ★★   Columbia, 1982, British-Indian
A CHORUS LINE   Columbia, 1985
CRY FREEDOM   Universal, 1987, British-U.S.

DANIEL ATTIAS*

Agent: Martin Shapiro, Shapiro-Lichtman Agency - Los Angeles, 213/859-8877

SILVER BULLET   Paramount, 1985

BILLE AUGUST

b. 1948 - Denmark
Agent: ICM - Los Angeles, 213/550-4000

IN MY LIFE   1978, Danish
ZAPPA   1983, Danish
TWIST AND SHOUT   Miramax Films, 1984, Danish
BUSTER'S WORLD   1985, Danish, originally made for television
PELLE THE CONQUEROR   Miramax Films, 1988, Danish-Swedish

RAY AUSTIN*

b. December 5, 1932 - London, England
Agent: Gary Salt, Paul Kohner, Inc. - Los Angeles, 213/550-1060

IT'S THE ONLY WAY TO GO   Hallelujah, 1970, British
FUN AND GAMES   1971, British
THE VIRGIN WITCH   Joseph Brenner Associates, 1972, British
HOUSE OF THE LIVING DEAD   1973, British
TALES OF THE GOLD MONKEY (TF)   Universal TV/ Belisarius Productions, 1982
THE RETURN OF THE MAN FROM U.N.C.L.E. (TF)   Michael Sloan Productions/Viacom Productions, 1983
THE ZANY ADVENTURES OF ROBIN HOOD (TF)   Bobka Productions/ Charles Fries Entertainment, 1984
LIME STREET (TF)   R.J. Productions/Bloodworth-Thomason-Mozark Productions/ Columbia TV, 1985
RETURN OF THE SIX MILLION DOLLAR MAN AND THE BIONIC WOMAN (TF)   Michael Sloan Productions/ Universal TV, 1987

IGOR AUZINS

Agent: The Gersh Agency - Beverly Hills, 213/274-6611

ALL AT SEA (TF)   1977, Australian
HIGH ROLLING   Hexagon Productions, 1977, Australian
THE NIGHT NURSE (TF)   Reg Grundy Organization, 1978, Australian
WATER UNDER THE BRIDGE (TF)   Shotton Productions, 1980, Australian
TAURUS RISING (MS)   1982, Australian
WE OF THE NEVER NEVER   Triumph/Columbia, 1983, Australian
THE COOLANGATTA GOLD   Film Gallery, 1984, Australian

PUPI AVATI
(Giuseppe Avati)
b. November 3, 1938 - Bologna, Italy
Home: via del Babuino 135, Rome, Italy, 06/678-0735

BALSAMUS L'UOMO DI SATANA   Magic Film,
   1968, Italian
THOMAS...GLI INDEMONIATI   Cidierre Cinematografica,
   1969, Italian
LA MAZURKA DEL BARONE DELLA SANTA E DEL FICO
   FIORONE   Euro International Films, 1974, Italian
BORDELLA   Euro International Films, 1975, Italian
LA CASA DALLE FINESTRE CHE RIDONO   AMA Film,
   1976, Italian
TUTTI DEFUNTI TRANNE I MORTI   AMA Film,
   1977, Italian
JAZZ BAND (TF)   AMA Film, 1978, Italian
LE STRELLE NEL FOSSO   AMA Film, 1978, Italian
CINEMA!!! (TF)   AMA Film/RAI, 1979, Italian
AIUTAMI A SOGNARE   AMA Film/RAI, 1981, Italian
DANCING PARADISE (TF)   AMA Film/RAI, 1981, Italian
UNA GITA SCOLASTICA   AMA Film/RAI, 1983, Italian
ZEDER   AMA Film, 1983, Italian
NOI TRE   Istituto Luce/RAI/Due A Film, 1984, Italian
IMPIEGATI   Due A Film/Dania Film/National
   Cinematografica/Filmes International, 1984, Italian
FESTA DI LAUREA   Due A Film/Dania Film/Filmes
   International/National Cinematografica, 1985, Italian
REGALO DI NATALE   Due A Film, 1986, Italian
THE LAST MINUTE   International Film Exchange,
   1987, Italian
SPOSI   co-director, Due A Film, 1988, Italian
STORIA DI RAGAZZI E DI RAGAZZE   Due A Film/RAI/
   Unione Cinematografica, 1989, Italian

HOWARD (HIKMET) AVEDIS
Business: Hickmar Productions, The Burbank Studios,
   4000 Warner Blvd., Burbank, CA 91522, 818/954-5104
Attorney: Jerome E. Weinstein, Weinstein & Hart, 433
   N. Camden Drive - Suite 600, Beverly Hills, CA 90210,
   213/274-7157

THE STEPMOTHER   Crown International, 1973
THE TEACHER   Crown International, 1974
DR. MINX   Dimension, 1975
THE SPECIALIST   Crown International, 1975
SCORCHY   American International, 1976
TEXAS DETOUR   Cinema Shares International, 1978
THE FIFTH FLOOR   Film Ventures International, 1980
SEPARATE WAYS   Crown International, 1981
MORTUARY   Artists Releasing Corporation/Film Ventures
   International, 1983
THEY'RE PLAYING WITH FIRE   New World, 1984
KIDNAPPED   Virgin Vision, 1987

HY AVERBACK*
b. 1925
Agent: CAA - Beverly Hills, 213/288-4545

CHAMBER OF HORRORS   Warner Bros., 1966
WHERE WERE YOU WHEN THE LIGHTS WENT OUT?
   MGM, 1968
I LOVE YOU, ALICE B. TOKLAS   Warner Bros., 1968
THE GREAT BANK ROBBERY   Warner Bros., 1969
SUPPOSE THEY GAVE A WAR AND NOBODY CAME?
   Cinerama Releasing Corporation, 1970
RICHIE BROCKELMAN: MISSING 24 HOURS (TF)
   Universal TV, 1976

THE LOVE BOAT II (TF)   Aaron Spelling Productions, 1977
MAGNIFICENT MAGNET OF SANTA MESA (TF)
   Columbia TV, 1977
THE NEW MAVERICK (TF)   Cherokee Productions/
   Warner Bros. TV, 1978
A GUIDE FOR THE MARRIED WOMAN (TF)   20th Century-
   Fox TV, 1978
PEARL (TF)   Silliphant-Konigsberg Productions/Warner
   Bros. TV, 1978
THE NIGHT RIDER (TF)   Stephen J. Cannell Productions/
   Universal TV, 1979
SHE'S IN THE ARMY NOW (TF)   ABC Circle Films, 1981
THE GIRL, THE GOLD WATCH AND DYNAMITE (TF)
   Fellows-Keegan Company/Paramount TV, 1981
WHERE THE BOYS ARE   Tri-Star, 1984
THE LAST PRECINCT (TF)   Stephen J. Cannell
   Productions, 1986

JAC AVILA
b. 1952 - Bolivia
Business: Mountain Top Films, 48 East Broadway - Suite 3,
   New York, NY 10002, 212/741-1814

KRIK? KRAK! TALES OF A NIGHTMARE   co-director with
   Vanyoska Gee, Mountain Top Films, 1988, Haitian-U.S.-
   Canadian

JOHN G. AVILDSEN*
b. 1937 - Chicago, Illinois
Home: 45 East 89th Street - Suite 37A, New York, NY
   10028, 212/534-5891
Agent: Martin Bauer, Bauer Benedek Agency - Los Angeles,
   213/275-2421

TURN ON TO LOVE   Haven International, 1969
GUESS WHAT WE LEARNED IN SCHOOL TODAY?
   Cannon, 1970
JOE   Cannon, 1970
CRY UNCLE!   Cambist, 1971
OKAY BILL   Four Star Excelsior, 1971
THE STOOLIE   Jama, 1972
SAVE THE TIGER   Paramount, 1973
FORE PLAY   co-director with Bruce Malmuth & Robert
   McCarty, Cinema National, 1975
W.W. AND THE DIXIE DANCEKINGS   20th Century-Fox,
   1975
ROCKY ★★   United Artists, 1976
SLOW DANCING IN THE BIG CITY   United Artists, 1978
THE FORMULA   MGM/United Artists, 1980
NEIGHBORS   Columbia, 1982
A NIGHT IN HEAVEN   20th Century-Fox, 1983
THE KARATE KID   Columbia, 1984
THE KARATE KID PART II   Columbia, 1986
HAPPY NEW YEAR   Columbia, 1987
FOR KEEPS   Tri-Star, 1988
LEAN ON ME   Warner Bros., 1989
THE KARATE KID PART III   Columbia, 1989
ROCKY V   MGM/UA, 1990

TOM AVILDSEN*
Home: S. 2709 Post, Spokane, WA 99203, 509/838-8010

THINGS ARE TOUGH ALL OVER   Columbia, 1982

MEIERT AVIS
Agent: William Morris Agency - Beverly Hills, 213/274-7451

FAR FROM HOME   Vestron, 1989

JON AVNET*
b. Brooklyn, New York
Business: The Avnet-Kerner Company, 505 N. Robertson
  Blvd., Los Angeles, CA 90048, 213/271-7408
Agent: CAA - Beverly Hills, 213/288-4545

BETWEEN TWO WOMEN (TF)   The Jon Avnet Company,
  1986

GABRIEL AXEL
Agent: Lou Pitt, ICM - Los Angeles, 213/550-4000

(The following is an incomplete list of Mr. Axel's credits)

HAGBARD AND SIGNE   *THE RED MANTLE*   Prentoulis
  Films, 1967, Danish-Swedish-Icelandic
BELOVED TOY   1968, Danish
AMOUR   1970, Danish
THE CRIME OF OUR TIME (TF)   French
THE NIGHT WATCH (TF)   French
THE VICAR OF TOURS (TF)   French
THE COLUMNS OF HEAVEN (MS)   1986, French
BABETTE'S FEAST   Orion Classics, 1987,
  Danish-French
CHRISTIAN   Chrysalide Films/Victoria Films/Ellepi Film/
  Dania Film/ DMV Distribuzione/Reteitalia, 1989,
  Danish-French-Italian

GEORGE AXELROD
b. June 9, 1922 - New York, New York
Agent: Camden Artists - Los Angeles, 213/556-5600

LORD LOVE A DUCK   United Artists, 1966
THE SECRET LIFE OF AN AMERICAN WIFE   20th
  Century-Fox, 1968

DAN AYKROYD
b. July 1, 1952 - Ottawa, Canada
Contact: Screen Actors Guild - Hollywood, 213/465-4600

VALKENVANIA   Warner Bros., 1990

MARIO AZZOPARDI
b. 1950 - Malta
Address: 378 Armadale, Toronto, Ontario M6S 3X8,
  Canada, 416/762-5960

DEADLINE   The Horror Film Production Inc./Henry Less &
  Associates, 1980, Canadian
STATE OF SURVIVAL   1986, Canadian
NOWHERE TO HIDE   New Century/Vista, 1987,
  U.S.-Canadian

B

BETH B
VORTEX   co-director with Scott B, 1983
SALVATION!   Circle Films, 1987

SCOTT B
VORTEX   co-director with Beth B, 1983

HECTOR BABENCO*
b. Argentina
Agent: ICM - Los Angeles, 213/550-4000

KING OF THE NIGHT   1975, Brazilian
LUCIO FLAVIO   Unifilm/Embrafilme, 1978, Brazilian
PIXOTE   Unifilm/Embrafilme, 1981, Brazilian
KISS OF THE SPIDER WOMAN ★   Island Alive/FilmDallas,
  1985, Brazilian-U.S.
IRONWEED   Tri-Star, 1987
AT PLAY IN THE FIELDS OF THE LORD   Saul Zaentz
  Company, 1991

RANDALL BADAT
Contact: Writers Guild of America - Los Angeles,
  213/550-1000

SURF II   Arista, 1983

PHIL BADGER
THE FORGOTTEN ONE   Spirited Productions, 1990

JOHN BADHAM*
b. 1939 - England
Business: Badham/Cohen/Group, l00 Universal City Plaza -
  Suite l27, Universal City, CA 9l608, 8l8/777-8226
Agent: Lee Rosenberg, Triad Artists, Inc. - Los Angeles,
  213/556-2727

THE IMPATIENT HEART (TF)   Universal TV, 1971
ISN'T IT SHOCKING? (TF)   ABC Circle Films, 1973
THE LAW (TF)   Universal TV, 1974
THE GUN (TF)   Universal TV, 1974
REFLECTIONS OF MURDER (TF)   ABC Circle Films, 1974
THE GODCHILD (TF)   MGM TV, 1974
THE KEEGANS (TF)   Universal TV, 1976
THE BINGO LONG TRAVELING ALL STARS AND MOTOR
  KINGS   Universal, 1976
SATURDAY NIGHT FEVER   Paramount, 1977
DRACULA   Universal, 1979
WHOSE LIFE IS IT ANYWAY?   MGM/United Artists, 1981
BLUE THUNDER   Columbia, 1983
WARGAMES   MGM/UA, 1983
AMERICAN FLYERS   Warner Bros., 1985
SHORT CIRCUIT   Tri-Star, 1986
STAKEOUT   Buena Vista, 1987
BIRD ON A WIRE   Universal, 1990
THE HARD WAY   Universal, 1991

REZA BADIYI*
b. April 17, 1936 - Iran
Home: 3300 Wonderview Drive, Los Angeles, CA 90068,
  213/851-8955
Agent: Ronald Leif, Contemporary Artists - Beverly Hills,
  213/278-8250

DEATH OF A STRANGER   Delta Commerz, 1972, West
  German-Israeli
THE EYES OF CHARLES SAND (TF)   Warner Bros. TV,
  1972
TRADER HORN   MGM, 1973
THE BIG BLACK PILL (TF)   Filmways/NBC
  Entertainment, 1981
OF MICE AND MEN (TF)   Of Mice and Men
  Productions, 1981
WHITE WATER REBELS (TF)   CBS Entertainment, 1983
MURDER ONE, DANCER 0 (TF)   Mickey Productions,
  1983

POLICEWOMAN CENTERFOLD (TF)   Moonlight
   Productions, 1983
BLADE IN HONG KONG (TF)   Terry Becker Productions,
   1985

MAX BAER, JR.*
b. December 4, 1937 - Oakland, California
Contact: Directors Guild of America - Los Angeles,
   213/289-2000

THE WILD McCULLOCHS   American International, 1975
ODE TO BILLY JOE   Warner Bros., 1976
HOMETOWN, U.S.A.   Film Ventures International, 1979

TED BAFALOUKOS
b. May 18, 1946 - Athens, Greece
Home: P.O. Box 400, Canal Street Station, New York,
   NY 10013
Agent: Arnold Rifkin/Caitlin Buchman, Triad Artists, Inc. -
   Los Angeles or New York, 213/556-2727 or
   212/489-8100

ROCKERS   New Yorker, 1979

CHUCK BAIL*
Contact: Directors Guild of America - Los Angeles,
   213/289-2000

BLACK SAMSON   Warner Bros., 1974
CLEOPATRA JONES AND THE CASINO OF GOLD
   Warner Bros., 1975
GUMBALL RALLY   Warner Bros., 1976
CHOKE CANYON   United Film Distribution, 1986

PATRICK BAILEY*
b. April 17, 1947 - Crawfordsville, Indiana
Home: 14401 Villa Woods Place, Pacific Palisades, CA
   90272, 213/454-4713
Agent: Susan Smith & Associates - Los Angeles,
   213/852-4777

DOOR TO DOOR   Castle Hill Productions, 1984

FRED BAKER
LENNY BRUCE WITHOUT TEARS (FD)   Video Tape
   Network, 1972
MURDER SHE SINGS   92 Releasing Organization, 1986

GRAHAM BAKER*
Agent: Leading Artists - Beverly Hills, 213/858-1999

THE FINAL CONFLICT   20th Century-Fox, 1981
IMPULSE   20th Century Fox, 1984
ALIEN NATION   20th Century Fox, 1988
THE RECRUIT   Warner Bros., 1991

ROY WARD BAKER
b. 1916 - London, England
Agent: Michael Whitehall, 125 Gloucester Road, London
   SW7 4TE, England, 71/244-8466

THE OCTOBER MAN   Eagle-Lion, 1947, British
THE WEAKER SEX   Eagle-Lion, 1948, British
PAPER ORCHID   1949, British

OPERATION DISASTER   MORNING DEPARTURE
   Universal, 1950, British
HIGHLY DANGEROUS   Lippert, 1951, British
I'LL NEVER FORGET YOU   THE HOUSE IN THE SQUARE
   20th Century-Fox, 1951, British
DON'T BOTHER TO KNOCK   20th Century-Fox, 1952
NIGHT WITHOUT SLEEP   20th Century-Fox, 1952
INFERNO   20th Century-Fox, 1953
PASSAGE HOME   1955, British
JACQUELINE   Rank, 1956, British
TIGER IN SMOKE   1956, British
THE ONE THAT GOT AWAY   Rank, 1958, British
A NIGHT TO REMEMBER   Rank, 1958, British
THE SINGER NOT THE SONG   Warner Bros., 1962,
   British
FLAME IN THE STREETS   Atlantic Pictures, 1962, British
THE VALIANT   co-director with Giorgio Capitani, United
   Artists, 1962, British-Italian
TWO LEFT FEET   1963, British
FIVE MILLION YEARS TO EARTH   QUATERMASS AND
   THE PIT   20th Century-Fox, 1968, British
THE ANNIVERSARY   20th Century-Fox, 1968, British
THE SPY KILLER (TF)   Halsan Productions, 1969
FOREIGN EXCHANGE (TF)   Halsan Productions, 1970
MOON ZERO TWO   Warner Bros., 1970, British
THE VAMPIRE LOVERS   American International,
   1970, British
THE SCARS OF DRACULA   American Continental,
   1971, British
DR. JEKYLL AND SISTER HYDE   American International,
   1972, British
ASYLUM   Cinerama Releasing Corporation, 1972, British
THE VAULT OF HORROR   Cinerama Releasing
   Corporation, 1973, British
AND NOW THE SCREAMING STARTS   Cinerama
   Releasing Corporation, 1973, British
THE 7 BROTHERS MEET DRACULA   THE LEGEND OF
   THE SEVEN GOLDEN VAMPIRES   Dynamite
   Entertainment, 1979, British
MINDER (TF)   1979, British
THE FLAME TREES OF THIKA (MS)   London Films Ltd./
   Consolidated Productions Ltd., 1980, British
THE MONSTER CLUB   ITC, 1981, British
THE MASKS OF DEATH (TF)   Tyburn Productions,
   1984, British
FAIRLY SECRET ARMY II (MS)   Video Arts Television/
   Channel Four, 1985, British
THE IRISH R.M. II (MS)   Channel Four, 1985, British
MINDER VI (MS)   co-director with Francis Megahy, Terry
   Green & Bill Brayne, Euston Films, 1988, British

RALPH BAKSHI*
b. October 26, 1938 - Haifa, Palestine
Agent: Directors Guild of America - Los Angeles,
   213/289-2000

FRITZ THE CAT (AF)   American International, 1972
HEAVY TRAFFIC (AF)   American International, 1973
COONSKIN (AF)   Bryanston, 1974
WIZARDS (AF)   20th Century-Fox, 1977
THE LORD OF THE RINGS (AF)   United Artists, 1978
AMERICAN POP (AF)   Paramount, 1981
HEY GOOD LOOKIN' (AF)   Warner Bros., 1982
FIRE AND ICE (AF)   20th Century-Fox, 1983
IMAGINING AMERICA (TF)   co-director with Matt Mahurin,
   Mustapha Khan & Ed Lachman, Vanguard Films, 1989

BOB BALABAN*
b. August 16, 1945 - Chicago, Illinois
Address: 390 West End Avenue, New York, NY 10024,
212/362-3114
Agent: Triad Artists, Inc. - Los Angeles, 213/556-2727

PARENTS   Vestron, 1989

FERDINANDO BALDI
Home: via Fratelli Bandiera 6, Rome, Italy, 06/5804895
or 06/5896448

THE TARTARS   co-director with Richard Thorpe, MGM,
1960, Italian
DAVID AND GOLIATH   co-director with Richard Pottier,
Allied Artists, 1960, Italian
DUEL OF CHAMPIONS   co-director with Terence Young,
Medallion, 1961, Italian-Spanish
IL PISTOLERO DELL'AVE MARIA   BRCSRL, 1970,
Italian-Spanish
BLINDMAN   20th Century-Fox, 1972, Italian
CARAMBOLA   B.R.C./Aetoscin, 1974, Italian
GET MEAN   Cee Note, 1976, Italian
NOVE OSPITI PER UN DELITTO   Overseas, 1976, Italian
MY NAME IS TRINITY   1976, Italian
THE SICILIAN CONNECTION   Joseph Green Pictures,
1977, Italian
L'INQUILINA DEL PIANO DI SOPRA   Fair Film, 1977,
Italian
LA SELVAGGIA   *GEOMETRA PRINETTI SEL
VAGGIAMENTEOSVALDO*   Interfilm, 1978, Italian
LA RAGAZZA DEL VAGONE LETTO   1979, Italian
COMIN' AT YA   Filmways, 1981, U.S.-Spanish
TREASURE OF THE FOUR CROWNS   Cannon, 1983,
U.S.-Spanish

PETER BALDWIN*
Agent: Irv Schechter Company - Beverly Hills,
213/278-8070

THE HARLEM GLOBETROTTERS ON GILLIGAN'S ISLAND
(TF)   Sherwood Schwartz Productions, 1981
THE BRADY GIRLS GET MARRIED (TF)   Sherwood
Schwartz Productions, 1981
LOTS OF LUCK (CTF)   Tomorrow Entertainment, 1985
A VERY BRADY CHRISTMAS (TF)   Sherwood Schwartz
Productions/ Paramount TV, 1988

MURRAY BALL
Contact: New Zealand Film Commission, P.O. Box 11546,
Wellington, New Zealand, 4/859-754

FOOTROT FLATS (AF)   Magpie Productions, 1986,
New Zealand

CARROLL BALLARD*
b. October 14, 1937 - Los Angeles, California
Agent: Leading Artists - Beverly Hills, 213/858-1999

THE BLACK STALLION   United Artists, 1979
NEVER CRY WOLF   Buena Vista, 1983
NUTCRACKER: THE MOTION PICTURE   Atlantic
Releasing Corporation, 1986

JOHN BANAS
EMMA, QUEEN OF THE SOUTH SEAS (TF)   Anro
Productions, 1988, Australian

ANNE BANCROFT*
(Anna Maria Louise Italiano)
b. September 17, 1931 - Bronx, New York
Business: Brooksfilms Limited, 20th Century Fox, P.O.
Box 900, Beverly Hills, CA 90213, 213-203-1375

FATSO   20th Century-Fox, 1980

ALBERT BAND*
(Alfredo Antonini)
b. May 7, 1924 - Paris, France
Business: BandCompany, 9200 Sunset Blvd. - Suite 530,
Los Angeles, CA 90069, 213/859-1040 or: BandCompany
S.R.L., via Zebio 43, Rome, Italy, 06/361-0036

THE YOUNG GUNS   Allied Artists, 1956
I BURY THE LIVING   United Artists, 1958
FACE OF FIRE   Allied Artists, 1959
THE AVENGER   Medallion, 1962, Italian-French
MASSACRO AL GRANDE CANYON   Metra Film,
1965, Italian
THE TRAMPLERS   Embassy, 1966, Italian
DRACULA'S DOG   Crown International, 1978
SHE CAME TO THE VALLEY   RGV Pictures, 1979
GHOULIES II   Empire Pictures, 1988

CHARLES BAND
b. 1952 - Los Angeles, California
Business: BandCompany, 9200 Sunset Blvd. - Suite 530,
Los Angeles, CA 90069, 213/859-1040 or: BandCompany
S.R.L., via Zebio 43, Rome, Italy, 06/361-0036

CRASH   Group 1, 1977
PARASITE   Embassy, 1982
METALSTORM: THE DESTRUCTION OF JARED-SYN
Universal, 1983
THE DUNGEONMASTER   co-director, Empire
Pictures, 1985
FUTURE COP   Empire Pictures, 1985
PULSEPOUNDERS   Empire Pictures, 1988
MERIDIAN   JGM Enterprises, 1990
CRASH AND BURN   Full Moon Entertainment, 1990

MIRRA BANK
ENORMOUS CHANGES AT THE LAST MINUTE
co-director with Ellen Hovde, TC Films International, 1985

URI BARBASH
b. Israel
Agent: Leading Artists - Beverly Hills, 213/858-1999

STIGMA   1983, Israeli
BEYOND THE WALLS   Warner Bros., 1984, Israeli
UNSETTLED LAND   *ONCE WE WERE DREAMERS*
Hemdale, 1987, U.S.-Israeli
ONE OF US   Nachshon Films, 1989, Israeli
LAST MOMENTS   Nachshon Films, 1990, Israeli

BARRY BARCLAY
b. 1944 - Wairarapa, New Zealand
Business: Pacific Film Productions Ltd., P.O. Box 2040,
Wellington, New Zealand, 4/872-191

NGATI   Pacific Film Productions/New Zealand Film
Commission, 1987, New Zealand
TE RUA   Pacific Film Productions, 1990, New Zealand

RICHARD L. BARE*
Home: 700 Harbor Island Drive, Newport Beach, CA 92660,
    714/675-6269

SMART GIRLS DON'T TALK   Warner Bros., 1948
FLAXY MARTIN   Warner Bros., 1949
THE HOUSE ACROSS THE STREET   Warner Bros., 1949
THIS SIDE OF THE LAW   Warner Bros., 1950
RETURN OF THE FRONTIERSMAN   Warner Bros., 1950
PRISONERS OF THE CASBAH   Columbia, 1953
THE OUTLANDERS   Warner Bros., 1956
THE STORM RIDERS   Warner Bros., 1956
BORDER SHOWDOWN   Warner Bros., 1956
THE TRAVELLERS   Warner Bros., 1957
SHOOT-OUT AT MEDICINE BEND   Warner Bros., 1957
GIRL ON THE RUN   Warner Bros., 1958
THIS REBEL BREED   Warner Bros., 1960
WICKED, WICKED   MGM, 1973

CLIVE BARKER
Agent: CAA - Beverly Hills, 213/288-4545

HELLRAISER   New World, 1987, British
TRANSMUTATIONS   Empire Pictures, 1988, British
NIGHTBREED   20th Century Fox, 1990

MICHAEL BARNARD
SHOPPING MALL   The Gustafson Group/D.H.B. Films,
    1985
NIGHTS IN WHITE SATIN   Mediacom Productions, 1987

STEVE BARNETT
RETURN TO HOLLYWOOD BOULEVARD   Concorde,
    1990

ALLEN BARON*
b. 1935 - New York, New York
Home: 407 S. Spalding, Beverly Hills, CA 90212,
    213/553-4050
Agent: Don Kopaloff, The Kopaloff Company, Inc. -
    Los Angeles, 213/203-8430

BLAST OF SILENCE   Universal, 1961
PIE IN THE SKY   Allied Artists, 1964
RED, WHITE AND BLUE   George Edwards Productions,
    1970
FOX FIRE LIGHT   Ramblin International, 1981

BRUNO BARRETO
Business: Producoes Cinematograficas L.C. Barreto Ltda.,
    Rua Visconde De Caravelas, 28-Botafogos, Rio de
    Janeiro, Brazil, 021/286-7186
Agent: Jane Sindell, ICM - Los Angeles, 213/550-4000

DONA FLOR AND HER TWO HUSBANDS   New Yorker,
    1977, Brazilian
AMADA AMANTE   1979, Brazilian
AMOR BANDIDO   Analysis Releasing Corporation,
    1982, Brazilian
GABRIELA   MGM/UA Classics, 1983, Brazilian-Italian
O BEIJO NO ASPHALTO   1984, Brazilian
HAPPILY EVER AFTER   European Classics, 1985,
    Brazilian
ROMANCE DA EMPREGADA   Embrafilme, 1988,
    Brazilian
A SHOW OF FORCE   Paramount, 1990

LEZLI-AN BARRETT
Contact: British Academy of Film & Television Arts,
    195 Piccadilly, London W1, England, 71/734-0022

BUSINESS AS USUAL   Cannon, 1987, British

CHUCK BARRIS*
b. June 3 - Philadelphia, Pennsylvania
Home: 9100 Wilshire Blvd. - Suite 411 E, Beverly Hills, CA
    90212, 213/278-9550

THE GONG SHOW MOVIE   Universal, 1980

ARTHUR BARRON
Contact: Writers Guild of America, West - Los Angeles,
    213/550-1000

THE WRIGHT BROTHERS (TF)   PBS-TV, 1971
JEREMY   United Artists, 1973
BROTHERS   Warner Bros., 1977
CRIMES OF VIOLENCE (TD)   Arnold Shapiro Productions/
    KTLA-TV, 1988

STEVE BARRON
b. May 4, 1956 - Dublin, Ireland
Business: Limelight Films, l724 N. Whitley Avenue,
    Los Angeles, CA 90028, 213/464-3109
Agent: William Morris Agency - Beverly Hills, 213/274-7451

ELECTRIC DREAMS   MGM/UA, 1984, British
TEENAGE MUTANT NINJA TURTLES   New Line Cinema,
    1990

ZELDA BARRON
b. England
Business: Limelight Films, l724 N. Whitley Avenue,
    Los Angeles, CA 90028, 213/464-3109
Agent: Merrily Kane, The Artists Agency - Los Angeles,
    213/277-7779

SECRET PLACES   TLC Films/20th Century-Fox,
    1984, British
SHAG   Hemdale, 1988
FORBIDDEN SUN   Filmscreen/Marlborough Films,
    1989, British

PAUL BARTEL*
b. August 6, 1938 - Brooklyn, New York
Agent: Peter Rawley, ICM - Los Angeles, 213/550-4165

PRIVATE PARTS   MGM, 1972
DEATH RACE 2000   New World, 1975
CANNONBALL   New World, 1976
EATING RAOUL   20th Century Fox International
    Classics, 1982
NOT FOR PUBLICATION   Samuel Goldwyn
    Company, 1984
LUST IN THE DUST   New World, 1985
THE LONGSHOT   Orion, 1986
SCENES FROM THE CLASS STRUGGLE IN BEVERLY
    HILLS   Cinecom, 1989

DICK BARTLETT
OLLIE HOPNOODLE'S HAVEN OF BLISS (CTF)
    The Disney Channel/Creative Television Associates/
    Pholly Inc., 1988

HALL BARTLETT*
b. November 27, 1922 - Kansas City, Missouri
Home: 861 Stone Canyon Road, Los Angeles, CA 90024,
    213/476-3916
Business: Hall Bartlett Films, Inc., 9200 Sunset Blvd. -
    Suite 908, Los Angeles, CA 90069, 213/278-8883

UNCHAINED   Warner Bros., 1955
DRANGO   co-director with Jules Bricken, United
    Artists, 1957
ZERO HOUR   Paramount, 1957
ALL THE YOUNG MEN   Columbia, 1960
THE CARETAKERS   United Artists, 1963
CHANGES   Cinerama Releasing Corporation, 1969
THE WILD PACK   *THE SANDPIT GENERALS/THE
    DEFIANT*   American International, 1972
JONATHAN LIVINGSTON SEAGULL   Paramount, 1973
THE CHILDREN OF SANCHEZ   Lone Star, 1978, U.S.-
    Mexican
LOVE IS FOREVER (TF)   Michael Landon-Hall Bartlett
    Films/NBC-TV/20th Century-Fox TV, 1983
LEAVING HOME   Hall Bartlett Films, 1986

WILLIAM S. BARTMAN*
Agent: Tom Klassen, 73 Market Street, Venice, CA
    90291, 213/396-5937

O'HARA'S WIFE   Davis-Panzer Productions, 1982

JAHNU BARUA
b. India
Contact: Films Division, Ministry of Information &
    Broadcasting, 24 Dr G Beshmukh Marg, Bombay
    40026, India, 36-1461

APAROOPA   1982, Indian
APEKSHA   1984, Indian
PAPORI   1986, Indian
HALODHIA CHORAYE BAODHAN KHAI   1988, Indian
BANANI   Purbanchal Film Cooperative Society,
    1990, Indian

HAL BARWOOD*
b. Hanover, New Hampshire
Agent: ICM - Los Angeles, 213/550-4000

WARNING SIGN   20th Century Fox, 1985

FRED BARZYK*
Business: Creative Television Association, 90 Windom
    Street, Boston, MA 02134, 617/783-2103

BETWEEN TIME & TIMBUKTU (TF)   PBS, 1974
THE PHANTOM OF THE OPEN HEARTH (TF)   co-director
    with David R. Loxton, WNET-13 Television Laboratory/
    WGBH New Television Workshop, 1976
CHARLIE SMITH AND THE FRITTER TREE (TF)
    co-director with David R. Loxton, WNET-13 Television
    Laboratory/WGBH New Television Workshop, 1978
THE LATHE OF HEAVEN (TF)   co-director with David R.
    Loxton, WNET-13 Television Laboratory/Taurus
    Film, 1980
COUNTDOWN TO LOOKING GLASS (CTF)   L & B
    Productions/Primedia Productions, 1984
THE STAR-CROSSED ROMANCE OF JOSEPHINE
    COSNOWSKI (TF) WGBH New TV Workshop/
    Creative TV Associates, 1985
JENNY'S SONG (TF)   Westinghouse Broadcasting, 1988
THE MAD HOUSERS (TF)   WBZ-TV/Group W, 1990

RICHARD BASKIN*
Agent: CAA - Beverly Hills, 213/288-4545

SING   Tri-Star, 1989

JULES BASS
Business: Rankin-Bass Productions, Inc., 1 East 53rd Street,
    New York, NY 10022, 212/759-7721

MAD MONSTER PARTY (AF)   Embassy, 1967
THE WACKY WORLD OF MOTHER GOOSE (AF)   1968
THE HOBBIT (ATF)   co-director with Arthur Rankin, Jr.,
    Rankin-Bass Productions, 1977
RUDOLPH AND FROSTY (ATF)   co-director with Arthur
    Rankin, Jr., Rankin-Bass Productions, 1979
THE RETURN OF THE KING (ATF)   co-director with Arthur
    Rankin, Jr., Rankin- Bass Productions, 1979
THE LAST UNICORN (AF)   co-director with Arthur Rankin,
    Jr., Jensen Farley Pictures, 1982
THE FLIGHT OF DRAGONS (ATF)   co-director with Arthur
    Rankin, Jr., Rankin- Bass Productions, 1986
THE WIND IN THE WILLOWS (ATF)   co-director with
    Arthur Rankin, Jr., Rankin-Bass Productions, 1987,
    filmed in 1985

SAUL BASS*
b. May 8, 1920 - New York, New York
Business: Saul Bass/Herb Yager & Associates, 7039 Sunset
    Blvd., Los Angeles, CA 90028, 213/466-9701

PHASE IV   Paramount, 1974

LAWRENCE BASSOFF
Business: Dauntless Director, 228 Main Street - Suite D,
    Venice, CA 90291, 213/553-5380

WEEKEND PASS   Crown International, 1984
HUNK   Crown International, 1987

MICHAL BAT-ADAM
Contact: Israel Film Centre, Ministry of Industry & Trade,
    30 Agron Street, P.O. Box 299, Jerusalem 94190, Israel,
    02/210297

EACH OTHER   *MOMENTS*   Franklin Media, 1979,
    Israeli-French
THE THIN LINE   New Yorker, 1980, Israeli
YOUNG LOVE   GUY Film Productions Ltd., 1983, Israeli
THE LOVER   Cannon, 1986, Israeli
A THOUSAND WIVES   *THE THOUSAND WIVES OF
    NAFTALI*   Angelika Films, 1989, Israeli

KENT BATEMAN*
Agent: Scott Schwartz, ICM - Los Angeles, 213/550-4221

SNOWMAN   International Picture Show, 1973

ROY BATTERSBY
Agent: Peters, Fraser & Dunlop, The Chambers, Chelsea
    Harbour, Lots Road, London SW10 OXF,
    71/376-7676

THE BODY   MGM, 1970, British
ROLL ON FOUR O'CLOCK (TF)   Granada TV,
    1971, British
LEEDS UNITED (TF)   BBC, 1973, British
THE PALESTINIAN (TD)   1978, British

WINTER FLIGHT   Cinecom, 1984, British, originally
   made for television
MR. LOVE (TF)   Enigma/Goldcrest Films & TV,
   1986, British
EUROCOPS: FIRING THE BULLETS (TF)   Picture Palace
   Productions/ Channel Four/European Co-Production
   Associates, 1988, British

GIACOMO BATTIATO
b. 1943 - Verona, Italy
Agent: William Morris Agency - Rome, 06/486961

IL MARSIGLIESE (TF)   RAI, 1975, Italian
UN DELITTO PERBENE (TF)   RAI, 1976, Italian
IL GIORNO DEI CRISTALLI (TF)   RAI, 1977, Italian
MARTIN EDEN (TF)   RAI, 1979, Italian
COLOMBA (TF)   RAI, 1981, Italian
I PALADINI   Vides Produzione, 1983, Italian
BLOOD TIES   IL CUGINO AMERICANO (CTF)
   RAI/Racing Pictures/Showtime, 1986, Italian-U.S.
STRADIVARIUS   Titanus, 1988, Italian
UNA VITA SCELLERATA   RAI/Cinemax/Taurus Film,
   1990, Italian- West German-French

LAMBERTO BAVA
(John Old, Jr.)
b. 1944 - Rome, Italy
Home: via della Camilluccia 535, Rome, Italy, 06/327-0240

LA VENERE D'ILLE (TF)   co-director with Mario Bava,
   RAI, 1978, Italian
MACABRO   A.M.A. Film/Medusa Distribuzione,
   1980, Italian
LA CASA CON LA SCALA NEL BUIO   National
   Cinematografica/ Nuova Dania Cinematografica,
   1983, Italian
BLASTFIGHTER   National Cinematografica/Nuova Dania
   Cinematografica, 1984, Italian
MONSTER SHARK   SHARK ROSSO NELL'OCEANO
   Cinema Shares International, 1984, Italian
DEMONI   Dac Film, 1985, Italian
DEMONI 2   Dac Film, 1986, Italian
MORIRAI A MEZZANOTTE   Dania Film/Reteitalia,
   1986, Italian
LE FOTO DI GIOIA   Devon Film/Dania Film/Medusa
   Distribuzione/Filmes International, 1987, Italian
L'UOMO CHE NON VOLEVA MORIRE   1989, Italian
IL MAESTRO DEL TERRORE (TF)   1989, Italian
IL GIOCO (TF)   ANFRI/Reteitalia/Hamster Productions,
   1989, Italian
SABBAH, LA MASCHERA DEL DEMONIO   Anfri/
   Reteitalia, 1990, Italian

CRAIG R. BAXLEY*
Agent: Leading Artists - Beverly Hills, 213/858-1999

ACTION JACKSON   Lorimar, 1988
DARK ANGEL   Vision p.d.g., 1990

STEPHEN BAYLY
b. July 7, 1942 - Baltimore, Maryland
Home: 11-13 Macklin Street, London WC2, England
Business: Red Rooster Films, 11-13 Macklin Street,
   London WC2B 5NH, England, 71/405-8147

JONI JONES (MS)   1982, British
AND PIGS MIGHT FLY (TF)   1983, British
THE DREAM FACTORY (TD)   1984, British
THE WORKS (TF)   S4C, 1984, Welsh

COMING UP ROSES   Skouras Pictures, 1986, Welsh
JUST ASK FOR DIAMOND   Kings Road, 1988, British

DAVID BEAIRD*
Home: 4169 Greenbush Avenue, Sherman Oaks, CA
   91423, 818/905-0221
Agent: CAA - Beverly Hills, 213/288-4545

OCTAVIA   International Film Marketing, 1984
THE PARTY ANIMAL   International Film Marketing, 1984
MY CHAUFFEUR   Crown International, 1985
PASS THE AMMO   New Century/Vista, 1988
IT TAKES TWO   MGM/UA, 1988
SCORCHERS   Goldcrest Films, 1990, U.S.-British

ROBERT B. BEAN*
Home: 8 Hilltop Road, Norwalk, CT 06854, 203/853-1352

MADE FOR EACH OTHER   20th Century-Fox, 1971

CHRIS BEARDE*
Home: 2220 Avenue of the Stars, Suite 506, Los Angeles,
   CA 90067, 213/277-0800
Agent: William Morris Agency - Beverly Hills, 213/274-7451

HYSTERICAL   Embassy, 1983

ALAN BEATTIE
DELUSION   New Line Cinema, 1981
THE HOUSE WHERE DEATH LIVES   New American, 1984
STAND ALONE   New World, 1985

WARREN BEATTY*
b. March 30, 1937 - Richmond, Virginia
Agent: CAA - Beverly Hills, 213/288-4545

HEAVEN CAN WAIT★   co-director with Buck Henry,
   Paramount, 1978
REDS★★   Paramount, 1981
DICK TRACY   Buena Vista, 1990

GABRIELLE BEAUMONT*
Agent: Alan Greenspan, ICM - Los Angeles, 213/550-4428
Business Manager: Burton Merrill, Individual Productions,
   Inc., 4260 Arcola Avenue, Toluca Lake, CA 91602,
   818/763-6903

VELVET HOUSE   Cannon, 1969, British
THE JOHNSTOWN MONSTER   Sebastian Films, Ltd.,
   1971, British
THE GODSEND   Cannon, 1980, British
DEATH OF A CENTERFOLD: THE DOROTHY STRATTEN
   STORY (TF)   Wilcox Productions/MGM TV, 1981
SECRETS OF A MOTHER AND DAUGHTER (TF)
   The Shpetner Company, 1983
GONE ARE THE DAYES (CTF)   Walt Disney
   Productions, 1984
THE CORVINI INHERITANCE (TF)   Fox-Hammer, 1984
HE'S MY GIRL   Scotti Brothers, 1987
CARMILLA (CTF)   Think Entertainment, 1989

GORMAN BECHARD
b. March 15, 1959 - Waterbury, Connecticut
Business: Generic Films, Inc., P.O. Box 2715, Waterbury,
   CT 06723, 203/756-3017

DISCONNECTED   Generic Films/Reel Movies
   International, 1984
AND THEN?   Generic Films, 1985

PSYCHOS IN LOVE   Generic Films, 1986
PANDEVIL   Empire Pictures, 1988
TWENTY QUESTIONS   Generic Films, 1988
TEENAGE SLASHER SLUTS   Empire Pictures, 1988
GALACTIC GIGOLO   Urban Classics, 1988
PSYCHOS ON PARADE   Generic Films, 1989
CEMETERY HIGH   Titan Productions/Generic Films, 1989

HAROLD BECKER*
Agent: CAA - Beverly Hills, 213/288-4545

THE RAGMAN'S DAUGHTER   Penelope Films,
   1972, British
THE ONION FIELD   Avco Embassy, 1979
THE BLACK MARBLE   Avco Embassy, 1980
TAPS   20th Century-Fox, 1981
VISION QUEST   Warner Bros., 1985
THE BOOST   Hemdale, 1988
SEA OF LOVE   Universal, 1989

MICHAEL BECKHAM
Contact: British Academy of Film & Television Arts,
   195 Piccadilly, London W1, England, 71/734-0022

TINY REVOLUTIONS (TF)   Granada TV, 1981, British

TERRY BEDFORD*
(Terrence L. Bedford)
b. 1943 - London, England
Business: Jennie & Co., 3 Duck Lane, London W1,
   England, 71/437-0600
Agent: ICM - Los Angeles, 213/550-4000

FREEDOM OF THE DIG (TF)   BBC, 1976, British
SLAYGROUND   Universal/AFD, 1983, British

GREG BEEMAN*
Agent: Daniel Ostroff, The Daniel Ostroff Agency -
   Los Angeles, 213/278-2020

THE RICHEST CAT IN THE WORLD (TF)   Les Alexander
   Productions/Walt Disney, TV, 1986
LITTLE SPIES (TF)   Walt Disney TV, 1986
LICENSE TO DRIVE   20th Century Fox, 1988
MOM AND DAD SAVE THE WORLD   Warner Bros., 1991

JEAN-JACQUES BEINEIX
b. 1946 - Paris, France
Agent: William Morris Agency - Beverly Hills, 213/274-7451
Contact: French Film Office, 745 Fifth Avenue, New York,
   NY 10151, 212/832-8860

DIVA   United Artists Classics, 1982, French
THE MOON IN THE GUTTER   Triumph/Columbia, 1983,
   French-Italian
BETTY BLUE   *37.2 DEGREES LE MATIN*   Alive Films,
   1986, French
ROSELYNE ET LES LIONS   Cargo Films/Gaumont, 1989,
   French

MARTIN BELL*
Agent: William Morris Agency - Beverly Hills, 213/274-7451

STREETWISE (FD)   Angelika Films, 1984
A MATTER OF TRUST: BILLY JOEL IN THE U.S.S.R. (TD)
   Rick London Productions/Martin Bell Productions/Robert
   Dalrymple Films, 1988

EARL BELLAMY*
b. March 11, 1917 - Minneapolis, Minnesota
Agent: Sanford-Beckett-Skouras & Associates - Los Angeles,
   213/208-2100

SEMINOLE UPRISING   Columbia, 1955
BLACKJACK KETCHUM, DESPERADO   Columbia, 1956
TOUGHEST GUN IN TOMBSTONE   United Artists, 1958
STAGECOACH TO DANCERS' ROCK   Universal, 1962
FLUFFY   Universal, 1965
INCIDENT AT PHANTOM HILL   Universal, 1966
GUNPOINT   Universal, 1966
MUNSTER, GO HOME   Universal, 1966
THREE GUNS FOR TEXAS   co-director with David Lowell
   Rich & Paul Stanley, Universal, 1968
BACKTRACK   Universal, 1969
THE PIGEON (TF)   Thomas-Spelling Productions, 1969
DESPERATE MISSION (TF)   20th Century-Fox TV, 1971
THE TRACKERS (TF)   Aaron Spelling Productions, 1971
SEVEN ALONE   Doty-Dayton, 1975
SIDECAR RACERS   Universal, 1975, Australian
PART 2 WALKING TALL   American International, 1975
AGAINST A CROOKED SKY   Doty-Dayton, 1975
FLOOD! (TF)   Irwin Allen Productions/20th Century-
   Fox TV, 1976
FIRE! (TF)   Irwin Allen Productions/20th Century-
   Fox TV, 1977
SIDEWINDER ONE   Avco Embassy, 1977
SPEEDTRAP   First Artists, 1978
DESPERATE WOMEN (TF)   Lorimar Productions, 1978
THE CASTAWAYS OF GILLIGAN'S ISLAND (TF)
   Sherwood Schwartz Productions, 1979
VALENTINE MAGIC ON LOVE ISLAND (TF)   Dick Clark
   Productions/PKO/Osmond Television, 1980
MAGNUM THRUST   Shenandoah Films, 1981

DONALD BELLISARIO*
Agent: Norman Kurland, Broder-Kurland-Webb-Uffner
   Agency - Los Angeles, 213/656-9262

AIRWOLF (TF)   Belisarius Productions/Universal TV, 1984
THREE ON A MATCH (TF)   Belisarius Productions/
   Tri-Star TV, 1987
LAST RITES   MGM/UA, 1988

MARCO BELLOCCHIO
b. November 9, 1939 - Piacenza, Italy
Home: Viale Angelico 36/B, Rome, Italy

FIST IN HIS POCKET   Peppercorn-Wormser, 1965, Italian
CHINA IS NEAR   Royal Films International, 1967, Italian
AMORE E RABBIA   co-director, 1969, Italian
NEL NOME DEL PADRE   1972, Italian
SBATTI IL MOSTRO IN PRIMA PAGINA   1972, Italian
MATTA DA SLEGARE (FD)   11 Marzo Cinematografica,
   1975, Italian
VICTORY MARCH   Summit Features, 1976, Italian-French
LES YEUX FERTILES   1977, French-Italian
IL GABBIANO (TF)   RAI, 1977, Italian
LA MACCHINA CINEMA (TD)   RAI, 1978, Italian
LEAP INTO THE VOID   Summit Features, 1979, Italian
THE EYES, THE MOUTH   Triumph/Columbia, 1983,
   Italian-French
HENRY IV   Orion Classics, 1984, Italian
DEVIL IN THE FLESH   Istituto Luce/Italnoleggio, 1986,
   Italian-French
LA VISIONE DEL SABBA   Bema/Reteitalia, 1987, Italian
LA CODANNA   Cinema Europa 92/Istituto Luce/Banfilm,
   1990, Italian-French

VERA BELMONT
Contact: French Film Office, 745 Fifth Avenue, New York, NY 10151, 212/832-8860

LOVER   Shapiro Glickenhaus Entertainment, 1990, French-West German

JERRY BELSON*
Agent: CAA - Beverly Hills, 213/288-4545

JEKYLL AND HYDE...TOGETHER AGAIN   Paramount, 1982
SURRENDER   Warner Bros., 1987

MARIA LUISA BEMBERG
Agent: Lauri Apelian, The Chasin Agency - Beverly Hills, 213/278-7505

MOMENTOS   GEA Cinematografica, 1981, Argentine
SENORA DE NADIE   1982, Argentine
CAMILA   European Classics, 1985, Argentine-Spanish
MISS MARY   New World, 1986, Argentine
I, THE WORSE OF ALL   GEA Producciones SRL, 1990, Argentine

JACK BENDER*
Agent: Arnold Rifkin, Triad Artists, Inc. - Los Angeles, 213/556-2727

IN LOVE WITH AN OLDER WOMAN (TF)   Pound Ridge Productions/Charles Fries Productions, 1982
TWO KINDS OF LOVE (TF)   CBS Entertainment, 1983
SHATTERED VOWS (TF)   Bertinelli-Pequod Productions, 1984
DEADLY MESSAGES (TF)   Columbia TV, 1985
LETTING GO (TF)   Adam Productions/ITC Productions, 1985
THE MIDNIGHT HOUR (TF)   ABC Circle Films, 1985
THE BLACKBOARD JUNGLE (TF)   MGM-UA TV, 1987
SIDE BY SIDE (TF)   Avnet-Kerner Productions, 1988
TRICKS OF THE TRADE (TF)   Leonard Hill Films, 1988
MY BROTHER'S WIFE (TF)   Robert Greenwald Productions/ Adam Productions, 1989
THE DREAMER OF OZ (TF)   Bedrock Productions/Adam Productions, 1990

JOEL BENDER
RICH GIRL   Film West Inc., 1990

LASLO BENEDEK*
b. March 5, 1907 - Budapest, Hungary
Home: 70 Bank Street, New York, NY 10014, 212/924-4161

THE KISSING BANDIT   MGM, 1948
PORT OF NEW YORK   Eagle-Lion, 1949
DEATH OF A SALESMAN   Columbia, 1951
THE WILD ONE   Columbia, 1954
BENGAL BRIGADE   Columbia, 1954
KINDER, MUTTER UND EIN GENERAL   1955, West German
AFFAIR IN HAVANA   Allied Artists, 1957
MALAGA   *MOMENT OF DANGER*   Warner Bros., 1959, British
RECOURSE EN GRACE   1960, French
NAMU, THE KILLER WHALE   United Artists, 1966
DARING GAME   Paramount, 1968
THE NIGHT VISITOR   UMC, 1971
ASSAULT ON AGATHON   Nine Network, 1976

ROBERTO BENIGNI
b. 1952 - Florence, Italy
Home: via Sant'Anselmo 29, Rome, Italy, 06/575-8856

TU MI TURBI   Best International Films, 1982, Italian
NON CI RESTA CHE PIANGERE   co-director with Massimo Troisi, Yarno Cinematografica/Best International Films, 1984, Italian
IL PICCOLO DIAVOLO   Warner Bros. Italia, 1988, Italian

RICHARD BENJAMIN*
b. May 22, 1938 - New York, New York
Agent: Phil Gersh, The Gersh Agency - Beverly Hills, 213/274-6611

MY FAVORITE YEAR   MGM/UA, 1982
RACING WITH THE MOON   Paramount, 1984
CITY HEAT   Warner Bros., 1984
THE MONEY PIT   Universal, 1986
LITTLE NIKITA   Columbia, 1988
MY STEPMOTHER IS AN ALIEN   Columbia/WEG, 1988
DOWNTOWN   20th Century Fox, 1990
MERMAIDS   Orion, 1990

RICHARD (DICK) BENNER
b. 1946 - Sterling, Illinois
Home: 184 Seaton Street, Toronto, Ontario M5A 2T4, Canada, 416/967-5371 or: 228 West 4th Street, New York, NY 10014, 212/620-5983
Agent: The Colbert Agency, 303 Davenport Road, Toronto, Ontario M5R 1K5, Canada, 416/964-3302
Business Manager: Tom Selz, Frankfurt, Garbus, Klein & Selz, 485 Madison Avenue, New York, NY 10022, 212/980-0120

LONDON DRAG   1969
OUTRAGEOUS!   Cinema 5, 1977, Canadian
HAPPY BIRTHDAY GEMINI   United Artists, 1980, U.S.-Canadian
TOO OUTRAGEOUS!   Spectrafilm, 1987, Canadian-U.S.

BILL BENNETT
Agent: William Morris Agency - Beverly Hills, 213/274-7451
Contact: Australian Film Commission, 9229 Sunset Blvd., Los Angeles, CA, 90069, 213/275-7074

A STREET TO DIE   Mermaid Beach Productions, 1986, Australian
BACKLASH   Samuel Goldwyn Company, 1986, Australian
DEAR CARDHOLDER   Mermaid Beach Productions/ Multifilms, 1987, Australian
JILTED   J.C. Williamson/Mermaid Beach Productions, 1987, Australian
MALPRACTICE   Film Australia, 1989, Australian
MORTGAGE   Film Australia, 1990, Australian

RICHARD C. BENNETT*
Home: 17136 Index Street, Granada Hills, CA 91344, 818/363-3381
Agent: Glennis Liberty, The Liberty Agency - Los Angeles, 213/824-7937

HARPER VALLEY PTA   April Fools, 1978
THE ESCAPE OF A ONE-TON PET (TF)   Tomorrow Entertainment, 1978
A STATE OF EMERGENCY   Esstar Productions, 1986

RODNEY BENNETT
Agent: London Management, 235 Regent Street, London
    W1A 2JT, England, 71/491-4400

EDWIN (TF)   Anglia, 1983
LOVE SONG (TF)   Anglia, 1984
MONSIGNOR QUIXOTE (TF)   Thames TV, 1985, British
THE VERGER (TF)   Anglia, 1986

JACQUES W. BENOIT
b. 1941
Address: 4139 Avenue Old Orchard, Montreal, Quebec
    H4A 3B3, Canada, 514/484-3952

HOW TO MAKE LOVE TO A NEGRO WITHOUT GETTING
    TIRED   Angelika Films, 1989, Canadian-French

ROBBY BENSON
(Robby Segal)
b. January 21, 1956 - Dallas, Texas
Agent: CAA - Los Angeles, 213/288-4545

WHITE HOT   *CRACK IN THE MIRROR*   Triax
    Entertainment Group, 1988
MODERN LOVE   Triumph Releasing Corporation, 1990

ROBERT BENTON*
b. September 29, 1932 - Waxahachie, Texas
Business: 110 West 57th Street - 5th Floor, New York, NY
    10019, 212/247-5652
Agent: Sam Cohn, ICM - New York City, 212/556-6810

BAD COMPANY   Paramount, 1972
THE LATE SHOW   Warner Bros., 1976
KRAMER VS. KRAMER★★   Columbia, 1979
STILL OF THE NIGHT   MGM/UA, 1982
PLACES IN THE HEART★   Tri-Star, 1984
NADINE   Tri-Star, 1987

OBIE BENZ
HEAVY PETTING (FD)   Skouras Pictures, 1989

LUCA BERCOVICI*
Agent: The Gage Group - Los Angeles, 213/859-8777

GHOULIES   Empire Pictures, 1985
ROCKULA   Cannon, 1990

BRUCE BERESFORD*
b. 1940 - Australia
Agent: William Morris Agency - Beverly Hills, 213/274-7451

THE ADVENTURES OF BARRY McKENZIE   Double Head
    Productions, 1972, Australian
BARRY McKENZIE HOLDS HIS OWN   Satori, 1974,
    Australian
DON'S PARTY   Satori, 1976, Australian
THE GETTING OF WISDOM   Atlantic Releasing
    Corporation, 1977, Australian
MONEY MOVERS   South Australian Film Corporation,
    1978, Australian
BREAKER MORANT   New World/Quartet, 1980,
    Australian
THE CLUB   South Australian Film Corporation, 1981,
    Australian
PUBERTY BLUES   Universal Classics, 1982, Australian
TENDER MERCIES★   Universal/AFD, 1983

KING DAVID   Paramount, 1985, U.S.-British
THE FRINGE DWELLERS   Atlantic Releasing Corporation,
    1986, Australian
CRIMES OF THE HEART   DEG, 1986
ARIA   co-director, Miramax Films, 1987, British
HER ALIBI   Warner Bros., 1989
DRIVING MISS DAISY   Warner Bros., 1989
MISTER JOHNSON   Avenue Pictures, 1991

PAMELA BERGER
THE IMPORTED BRIDEGROOM   Lara Classics, 1989

ANDREW BERGMAN*
b. February 20, 1945 - New York, New York
Agent: Sam Cohn, ICM - New York City, 212/556-5600

SO FINE   Warner Bros., 1981
THE FRESHMAN   Tri-Star, 1990

INGMAR BERGMAN
(Ernst Ingmar Bergman)
b. July 14, 1918 - Uppsala, Sweden
Agent: Paul Kohner, Inc. - Los Angeles, 213/550-1060

CRISIS   Svensk Filmindustri, 1945, Swedish
IT RAINS ON OUR LOVE   Sveriges Folkbiografer,
    1946, Swedish
THE LAND OF DESIRE   Sveriges Folkbiografer,
    1947, Swedish
NIGHT IS MY FUTURE   Terrafilm, 1948, Swedish
PORT OF CALL   Janus, 1948, Swedish
THE DEVIL'S WANTON   Terrafilm, 1949, Swedish
THREE STRANGE LOVES   *THIRST*   Janus, 1949,
    Swedish
TO JOY   Janus, 1950, Swedish
THIS CAN'T HAPPEN HERE   Svensk Filmindustri,
    1951, Swedish
ILLICIT INTERLUDE   *SOMMARLEK*   Janus, 1951,
    Swedish
SECRETS OF WOMEN   Janus, 1952, Swedish
MONIKA   Janus, 1953, Swedish
SAWDUST AND TINSEL   *THE NAKED NIGHT*   Janus,
    1953, Swedish
A LESSON IN LOVE   Janus, 1954, Swedish
DREAMS   Janus, 1955, Swedish
SMILES OF A SUMMER NIGHT   Janus, 1955, Swedish
THE SEVENTH SEAL   Janus, 1957, Swedish
WILD STRAWBERRIES   Janus, 1957, Swedish
SO CLOSE TO LIFE   Janus, 1958, Swedish
THE MAGICIAN   Janus, 1958, Swedish
THE VIRGIN SPRING   Janus, 1960, Swedish
THE DEVIL'S EYE   Janus, 1960, Swedish
THROUGH A GLASS DARKLY   Janus, 1961, Swedish
WINTER LIGHT   Janus, 1962, Swedish
THE SILENCE   Janus, 1963, Swedish
ALL THESE WOMEN   Janus, 1964, Swedish
PERSONA   United Artists, 1966, Swedish
HOUR OF THE WOLF   United Artists, 1968, Swedish
SHAME   United Artists, 1968, Swedish
FARO DOCUMENT (TD)   1969, Swedish
THE RITUAL   Janus, 1969, Swedish, originally made
    for television
THE PASSION OF ANNA   United Artists, 1969, Swedish
THE TOUCH   Cinerama Releasing Corporation, 1971,
    Swedish, originally made for television
CRIES AND WHISPERS★   New World, 1972, Swedish
SCENES FROM A MARRIAGE   Cinema 5, 1973, Swedish,
    originally made for television

THE MAGIC FLUTE   Surrogate, 1975, Swedish,
     originally made for television
FACE TO FACE★   Paramount, 1976, Swedish
THE SERPENT'S EGG   Paramount, 1978, West German
AUTUMN SONATA   New World, 1978, West German
FROM THE LIFE OF THE MARIONETTES   Universal/AFD,
     1980, West German
FARO DOCUMENT 1979 (TD)   Cinematograph, 1979,
     Swedish
FANNY AND ALEXANDER★   Embassy, 1983,
     Swedish-French-West German
AFTER THE REHEARSAL   Triumph/Columbia, 1983,
     Swedish-West German, originally made for television
DOCUMENT FANNY AND ALEXANDER (FD)   Swedish
     Film Institute, 1986, Swedish
THE BLESSED ONES (TF)   STV2, 1986, Swedish

ALAN BERGMANN*
Home: 6330 Allott Avenue, Van Nuys, CA 91401,
     818/764-0404
Agent: APA - Los Angeles, 213/273-0744

THE HITCH-HIKERS   The Hitch-Hikers Company, 1990

LUIS GARCIA BERLANGA
b. July 12, 1921 - Valencia, Spain
Contact: Ministry of Culture, Motion Picture Division,
     Avenida de Burgos, 5, 28036 Madrid, Spain, 91/202-5351

ESA PAREJA FELIZ   1951, Spanish
BIENVENIDO SR. MARSHALL   1953, Spanish
NOVIO A LA VISTA   1953, Spanish
CALABUCH   1956, Spanish
LOS JUEVES, MILAGRO   1957, Spanish
PLACIDO   1961, Spanish
LAS CUATRO VERDADES   co-director, 1962, Spanish
EL VERDUGO   1963, Spanish
LA BOUTIQUE   1967, Spanish
VIVAN LOS NOVIOS   1971, Spanish
TAMANO NATURAL   1973, Spanish
ESCOPETA NACIONAL   Jet Films, 1978, Spanish
PATRIMONIO NACIONAL   Jet Films/Incine, 1980, Spanish
NACIONAL III   Kaktus, 1983, Spanish
LA VAQUILLA   1985, Spanish
MOROS Y CRISTIANOS   Estela Films, 1987, Spanish

DAVID BERLATSKY*
Home: 8261 W. Norton - Apt. 4, Los Angeles, CA 90046,
     213/656-0714

THE FARMER   Columbia, 1977

TED BERMAN
THE FOX AND THE HOUND (AF)   co-director with Art
     Stevens & Richard Rich, Buena Vista, 1981
THE BLACK CAULDRON (AF)   co-director with Richard
     Rich, Buena Vista, 1985

CHRIS BERNARD
Contact: British Academy of Film & Television Arts,
     195 Piccadilly, London W1, England, 71/734-0022

LETTER TO BREZHNEV   Circle Releasing, 1985, British
CONSPIRACY   Target International, 1990, British

EDWARD BERNDS
BLONDIE'S SECRET   Columbia, 1948
BLONDIE'S BIG DEAL   Columbia, 1949
BLONDIE HITS THE JACKPOT   Columbia, 1949

FEUDIN' RHYTHM   Columbia, 1949
BEWARE OF BLONDIE   Columbia, 1950
BLONDIE'S HERO   Columbia, 1950
GASOLINE ALLEY   Columbia, 1951
CORKY OF GASOLINE ALLEY   Columbia, 1951
GOLD RAIDERS   United Artists, 1951
HAREM GIRL   Columbia, 1952
ACE LUCKY   Columbia, 1952
WHITE LIGHTNING   Allied Artists, 1953
PRIVATE EYES   Allied Artists, 1953
LOOSE IN LONDON   Allied Artists, 1953
HOT NEWS   Allied Artists, 1953
THE BOWERY BOYS MEET THE MONSTERS   Allied
     Artists, 1954
JUNGLE GENTS   Allied Artists, 1954
BOWERY TO BAGDAD   Allied Artists, 1955
SPY CHASERS   Allied Artists, 1955
WORLD WITHOUT END   Allied Artists, 1956
NAVY WIFE   Allied Artists, 1956
DIG THAT URANIUM   Allied Artists, 1956
CALLING HOMICIDE   Allied Artists, 1956
THE STORM RIDER   20th Century-Fox, 1957
REFORM SCHOOL GIRL   American International, 1957
ESCAPE FROM RED ROCK   20th Century-Fox, 1958
QUANTRILL'S RAIDERS   20th Century-Fox, 1958
SPACE MASTER X-7   20th Century-Fox, 1958
QUEEN OF OUTER SPACE   Allied Artists, 1958
JOY RIDE   Allied Artists, 1958
ALASKA PASSAGE   20th Century-Fox, 1959
THE RETURN OF THE FLY   20th Century-Fox, 1959
VALLEY OF THE DRAGONS   Columbia, 1961
THE THREE STOOGES MEET HERCULES
     Columbia, 1962
THE THREE STOOGES IN ORBIT   Columbia, 1962
PREHISTORIC VALLEY   ZRB Productions, 1966

ARMYAN BERNSTEIN*
Agent: CAA - Beverly Hills, 213/288-4545

WINDY CITY   Warner Bros., 1984
CROSS MY HEART   Universal, 1987

WALTER BERNSTEIN*
b. August 29, 1929 - Chicago, Illinois
Home: 320 Central Park West, New York, NY 10025,
     212/724-1821
Agent: Sam Cohn, ICM - New York City, 212/556-6810

LITTLE MISS MARKER   Universal, 1980

CLAUDE BERRI
(Claude Langmann)
b. July 1, 1934 - Paris, France
Business: Renn Productions, 10 rue Lincoln, 75008 Paris,
     France, 04/256-2590
Agent: Artmedia, 10 Avenue Georges V, 75008 Paris,
     France, 04/723-7860

LE BAISERS   co-director, 1964, French
LE CHANCE ET L'AMOUR   co-director, 1964, French
THE TWO OF US   *LE VIEL HOMME ET L'ENFANT*
     Cinema 5, 1968, French
MARRY ME! MARRY ME!   *MAZEL TOV OU LE MARIAGE*
     Allied Artists, 1969, French
THE MAN WITH CONNECTIONS   *LE PISTONNE*   Colum-
     bia, 1970, French
LE CINEMA DU PAPA   Columbia, 1971, French
LE SEX SHOP   Peppercorn-Wormser, 1973, French
MALE OF THE CENTURY   Joseph Green Pictures, 1975,
     French

Be

**FILM
DIRECTORS
GUIDE**

**F
I
L
M

D
I
R
E
C
T
O
R
S**

THE FIRST TIME   EDP, 1976, French
ONE WILD MOMENT   Quartet/Films Incorporated, 1978, French
A NOUS DEUX   AMLF, 1979, French
JE VOUS AIME   Renn Films/FR3/Cinevog, 1980, French
LE MAITRE D'ECOLE   AMLF, 1981, French
TCHAO PANTIN   European Classics, 1983, French
JEAN DE FLORETTE   Orion Classics, 1987, French
MANON OF THE SPRING   Orion Classics, 1987, French
URANUS   Renn Productions, 1990, French

BILL BERRY
Contact: Writers Guild of America, West - Los Angeles, 213/550-1000

OFF THE MARK   Fries Entertainment, 1987

JOHN BERRY*
b. 1917 - New York, New York
Address: 109 Avenue de la Payt, Issy Les Molineaux 92130, France

MISS SUSIE SLAGLE'S   Paramount, 1945
FROM THIS DAY FORWARD   RKO Radio, 1946
CROSS MY HEART   Paramount, 1946
CASBAH   Universal, 1948
TENSION   MGM, 1949
HE RAN ALL THE WAY   United Artists, 1951
C'EST ARRIVE A PARIS   1952, French
CA VA BARDER   1954, French
JE SUIS UN SENTIMENTAL   1955, French
PANTALOONS DON JUAN   United Motion Picture Organizations, 1956, French-Spanish
OH, QUE MAMBO   1958, French
TAMANGO   Valiant, 1959, French
MAYA   MGM, 1966
A TOUT CASSER   1967, French
CLAUDINE   20th Century-Fox, 1974
THIEVES   Paramount, 1977
SPARROW (TF)   1978
THE BAD NEWS BEARS GO TO JAPAN   Paramount, 1978
ANGEL ON MY SHOULDER (TF)   Mace Neufeld Productions/Barney Rosenzweig Productions/Beowulf Productions, 1980
SISTER, SISTER (TF)   20th Century-Fox TV, 1982
HONEYBOY (TF)   Fan Fares Inc. Productions/Estrada Productions, 1982
LE VOYAGE A PAIMPOL   Jomy Productions/FR3/AFC, 1985, French
MALDONNE   Cannon France, 1987, French-Belgian
A CAPTIVE IN THE LAND   Gloria Productions/Gorky Film Studios/Soyuzfilmservice, 1990, U.S.-Soviet

TOM BERRY
BLIND FEAR   Malofilm Group, 1989, Canadian
THE AMITYVILLE CURSE   Vidmark, 1990

BERNARDO BERTOLUCCI*
b. March 16, 1940 - Parma, Italy
Home: via della Lungara 3, Rome, Italy 00165, 06/580-0071
Agent: Jeff Berg, ICM - Los Angeles, 213/550-4000

LA COMMARE SECCA   1962, Italian
BEFORE THE REVOLUTION   New Yorker, 1964, Italian
PARTNER   New Yorker, 1968, Italian
AMORE E RABBIA   co-director, 1969, Italian
THE SPIDER'S STRATAGEM   New Yorker, 1970, Italian
THE CONFORMIST   Paramount, 1971, Italian-French-West German

LAST TANGO IN PARIS★   United Artists, 1973, Italian-French
1900   Paramount, 1977, Italian
LUNA   20th Century-Fox, 1979, Italian-U.S.
TRAGEDY OF A RIDICULOUS MAN   The Ladd Company/Warner Bros., 1982, Italian
THE LAST EMPEROR★★   Columbia, 1987, British-Chinese
THE SHELTERING SKY   Warner Bros., 1990, British

MICHAEL BERZ
SNOW WHITE   Cannon, 1987, U.S.-Israeli

JAMES BESHEARS
HOMEWORK   Jensen-Farley Pictures, 1982

DAN BESSIE
HARD TRAVELING   New World, 1986

LUC BESSON
Business: Films Du Loup, 22 rue Drouot, 75009 Paris, France, 04/359-8413
Contact: French Film Office, 745 Fifth Avenue, New York, NY 10151, 212/832-8860

LE DERNIER COMBAT   Gaumont/Les Films du Loup/Constantin Alexandrof Productions, 1983, French
SUBWAY   Island Pictures, 1985, French
KAMIKAZE   co-director with Didier Grousset, Gaumont, 1987, French
THE BIG BLUE   Columbia/WEG, 1988, French
ATLANTIS (FD)   Gaumont, 1989, French
NIKITA   Samuel Goldwyn Company, 1990, French

GILL BETTMAN*
Home: 10521 Selkirk Lane, Los Angeles, CA 90077, 213/475-3906
Agent: Richard Shepherd, The Artists Agency - Los Angeles, 213/277-7779

CRYSTAL HEART   Izaro Films/Eagle Films Corporation, 1985
NEVER TOO YOUNG TO DIE   Paul Releasing, 1986

JONATHAN BETUEL*
Agent: Bauer Benedek Agency - Los Angeles, 213/275-2421

MY SCIENCE PROJECT   Buena Vista, 1985

EDWARD BIANCHI*
b. April 24, 1942
Home: 36 Gramercy Park East, New York, NY 10010, 212/228-3668
Business: Bianchi Films, 141 Fifth Avenue, New York, NY 11415, 212/505-0670
Agent: Scott Yoselow, The Gersh Agency - New York City, 212/997-1818

THE FAN   Paramount, 1981
MOON OVER MIAMI   Orion, 1990

ROBERT BIERMAN
Address: 14/18 Ham Yard, London W1V 7PD, England, 71/836-3903
Agent: William Morris Agency - Beverly Hills, 213/274-7451

APOLOGY (CTF)   Roger Gimbel Productions/Peregrine Entertainment/ASAP Productions/HBO, 1986, U.S.-Canadian
VAMPIRE'S KISS   Hemdale, 1988

50

JEAN-CLAUDE BIETTE

Contact: French Film Office, 745 Fifth Avenue, New York, NY 10151, 212/832-8860

LE THEATRE DES MATIERES   1978, French
LOIN DE MANHATTAN   1981, French
CHAISSE GARDE   Films de Loup, 1986, French
LES CHAMPIGNON DES CARPATHES   Films du Losange, 1990, French

KATHRYN BIGELOW*

Agent: CAA - Beverly Hills, 213/288-4545

THE LOVELESS   co-director with Monty Montgomery, Atlantic Releasing Corporation, 1981
NEAR DARK   DEG, 1987
BLUE STEEL   MGM/UA, 1990
RIDERS ON THE STORM   20th Century Fox, 1991

ERIN BIGNAM

LOON   One World Productions, 1989

TONY BILL*

b. August 23, 1940 - San Diego, California
Business: Tony Bill Productions, 73 Market Street, Venice, CA 90291, 213/396-5937
Agent: Alan Greenspan, ICM - Los Angeles, 213/550-4428

MY BODYGUARD   20th Century-Fox, 1980
SIX WEEKS   Universal, 1982
LOVE THY NEIGHBOR (TF)   Patricia Nardo Productions/ 20th Century Fox TV, 1984
FIVE CORNERS   Cineplex Odeon, 1987
CRAZY PEOPLE   Paramount, 1990

KEVIN BILLINGTON

b. 1933 - England
Agent: Merrily Kane, The Artists Agency - Los Angeles, 213/277-7779
Business: Court House Films, 52 Tottenham Street, London W1, England, 71/636-1275

INTERLUDE   Columbia, 1968, British
THE RISE AND RISE OF MICHAEL RIMMER   Warner Bros., 1970, British
THE LIGHT AT THE EDGE OF THE WORLD   National General, 1971, U.S.- Spanish
VOICES   Hemdale, 1973, British
AND NO ONE COULD SAVE HER (TF)   Associated London Films, 1973, British
ECHOES OF THE SIXTIES (TD)   ALA Productions, 1979
THE GOOD SOLDIER (TF)   Granada TV, 1981, British
THE OUTSIDE EDGE (TF)   London Weekend TV, 1982, British
REFLECTIONS (TF)   Court House Films/Film Four International, 1984, British
FACE OF THE EARTH (TF)   BBC Wales, 1988, Welsh

BRUCE BILSON*

b. May 19, 1928 - Brooklyn, New York
Home: 12505 Sarah Street, Studio City, CA 91604, 818/985-5121
Agent: The Cooper Agency - Los Angeles, 213/277-8422

THE GIRL WHO CAME GIFT-WRAPPED (TF)   Spelling-Goldberg Productions, 1974
DEAD MAN ON THE RUN (TF)   Sweeney-Finnegan Productions, 1975

THE NEW DAUGHTERS OF JOSHUA CABE (TF)   Spelling-Goldberg Productions, 1976
BJ & THE BEAR (TF)   Universal TV, 1978
THE NORTH AVENUE IRREGULARS   Buena Vista, 1979
DALLAS COWBOYS CHEERLEADERS (TF)   Aubrey-Hammer Productions, 1979
PLEASURE COVE (TF)   Lou Shaw Productions/David Gerber Company/Columbia TV, 1979
THE GHOSTS OF BUXLEY HALL (TF)   Walt Disney Productions, 1980
CHATTANOOGA CHOO CHOO   April Fools, 1984
FINDER OF LOST LOVES (TF)   Aaron Spelling Productions, 1984
GIDGET'S SUMMER REUNION (TF)   Ackerman-Riskin Productions/Columbia TV, 1985
THE BRADYS (TF)   Brady Productions/Paramount TV, 1990

DANNY BILSON

Agent: Bauer Benedek Agency - Los Angeles, 213/255-2421

ZONE TROOPERS   Empire Pictures, 1986
THE WRONG GUYS   New World, 1988

JOHN BINDER*

Agent: Bauer Bendek Agency - Los Angeles, 213/255-2421

UFORIA   Universal, 1984

WILLIAM BINDLEY

Agent: William Morris Agency - Beverly Hills, 213/274-7451

THE HOMEROOM NEWS   Creative Edge Films, 1989

MACK BING*

Address: P.O. Box 11382, Beverly Hills, CA 90213, 213/656-1804
Agent: Phil Gersh, The Gersh Agency - Beverly Hills, 213/274-6611

ALL THE LOVING COUPLES   U-M, 1969
THE CLASS OF '74   co-director with Arthur Marks, Crest, 1972
GABRIELLA   1974

PATRICIA BIRCH*

Agent: Ron Bernstein, The Gersh Agency - Beverly Hills, 213/274-6611
Attorney: Marsha Brooks, Colton/Hartwick/Yamin/Sheresky, 79 Madison Avenue, New York, NY 10016, 212/532-5100

GREASE 2   Paramount, 1982

STEWART BIRD

Contact: Writers Guild of America, East - New York City, 212/245-6180

HOME FREE ALL   Almi Classics, 1984

ANDREW BIRKIN

Agent: ICM - Los Angeles, 213/550-4000

BURNING SECRET   Vestron, 1988, U.S.-British-West German

ALAN BIRKINSHAW
Contact: British Academy of Film & Television Arts,
195 Piccadilly, London W1, England, 71/734-0022

TEN LITTLE INDIANS   Cannon, 1989, British
THE FALL OF THE HOUSE OF USHER   21st Century
    Distribution, 1990, British
THE MASQUE OF THE RED DEATH   21st Century
    Distribution, 1990, British

LOREN BIVENS
Contact: Texas Film Commission, P.O. Box 12728,
    201 East 5th Street - Suite B-6, Austin, TX 78711,
    512/469-9111

TRESPASSES   co-director with Adam Roarke, Shapiro
    Entertainment, 1987

BILL BIXBY*
b. January 22, 1934 - San Francisco, California
Personal Manager: Paul Brandon, Brandon-Dworski &
    Associates - Los Angeles, 213/273-6173

THE BARBARY COAST (TF)   Paramount TV, 1975
THREE ON A DATE (TF)   ABC Circle Films, 1978
THE INCREDIBLE HULK RETURNS (TF)   B&B
    Productions/New World TV, 1988
THE TRIAL OF THE INCREDIBLE HULK (TF)
    Bixby-Brandon Productions/New World TV, 1989
THE DEATH OF THE INCREDIBLE HULK (TF)
    Bixby-Brandon Productions/New World TV, 1990

NOEL BLACK*
b. 1937 - Chicago, Illinois
Home: 126 Wadsworth Avenue, Santa Monica, CA 90405,
    213/392-6050
Agent: The Chasin Agency - Beverly Hills, 213/278-7505

TRILOGY: THE AMERICAN BOY (TF)   ABC Stage 67,
    1968
PRETTY POISON   20th Century-Fox, 1968
COVER ME BABE   20th Century-Fox, 1970
JENNIFER ON MY MIND   United Artists, 1971
MULLIGAN'S STEW (TF)   Paramount TV, 1977
MIRRORS   First American, 1978
A MAN, A WOMAN AND A BANK   Avco Embassy,
    1979, Canadian
THE GOLDEN HONEYMOON (TF)   Learning in Focus,
    1980
THE OTHER VICTIM (TF)   Shpetner Company, 1981
PRIME SUSPECT (TV)   Tisch-Avnet Television, 1982
THE ELECTRIC GRANDMOTHER (TF)   Highgate
    Pictures, 1982
HAPPY ENDINGS (TF)   Motown Productions, 1983
PRIVATE SCHOOL   Universal, 1983
QUARTERBACK PRINCESS (TF)   CBS Entertainment,
    1983
DEADLY INTENTIONS (TF)   Green-Epstein
    Productions, 1985
PROMISES TO KEEP (TF)   Sandra Harmon Productions/
    Green-Epstein Productions/Telepictures, 1985
A TIME TO TRIUMPH (TF)   Billos-Kauffman Productions/
    Phoenix Entertainment Group, 1986
MY TWO LOVES (TF)   Alvin Cooperman Productions/Taft
    Entertainment TV, 1986
CONSPIRACY OF LOVE (TF)   New World TV, 1987
DOCTORS WILDE (TF)   Columbia TV, 1987
THE TOWN BULLY (TF)   Dick Clark Productions, 1988
THE EYES OF THE PANTHER (CTF)   Think
    Entertainment, 1989

CHRISTIAN BLACKWOOD
Business: Christian Blackwood Productions, Inc., 115 Bank
    Street, New York, NY 10014, 212/242-6260

SPOLETO: FESTIVAL OF TWO WORLDS (FD)   Christian
    Blackwood Productions, 1967
HARLEM THEATER (FD)   Christian Blackwood
    Productions, 1968
SUMMER IN THE CITY (FD)   Christian Blackwood
    Productions, 1968
SAN DOMINGO   co-director with Hans-Jurgen Syberberg,
    1970, West German
ELIOT FELD: ARTISTIC DIRECTOR (FD)   Christian
    Blackwood Productions, 1970
JUILLIARD (FD)   Christian Blackwood Productions, 1971
KENTUCKY KITH AND KIN (FD)   Christian Blackwood
    Productions, 1972
BLACK HARVEST   Christian Blackwood Productions, 1973
YESTERDAY'S WITNESS: A TRIBUTE TO THE
    AMERICAN NEWSREEL (FD)   Christian Blackwood
    Productions, 1974
LIVING WITH FEAR (FD)   Christian Blackwood
    Productions, 1974
TO BE A MAN (FD)   Christian Blackwood Productions, 1977
ROGER CORMAN: HOLLYWOOD'S WILD ANGEL (FD)
    Christian Blackwood Productions, 1978
COUSINS (FD)   Christian Blackwood Productions, 1979
TAPDANCIN' (FD)   Christian Blackwood Productions, 1980
ALL BY MYSELF (FD)   Christian Blackwood
    Productions, 1982
CHARLES AZNAVOUR: BREAKING AMERICA (FD)
    Christian Blackwood Productions, 1983
OBSERVATIONS UNDER THE VOLCANO (FD)   Christian
    Blackwood Productions, 1984
MY LIFE FOR ZARAH LEANDER (FD)   Christian Blackwood
    Productions, 1985
PRIVATE CONVERSATIONS (FD)   Christian Blackwood
    Productions, 1985
NIK AND MURRAY (FD)   Christian Blackwood
    Productions, 1986
SIGNED: LINO BROCKA (FD)   Christian Blackwood
    Productions, 1987
TWO HOTELS IN OUR TROUBLED MIDDLE EAST (FD)
    Christian Blackwood Productions, 1988
MOTEL (FD)   Christian Blackwood Productions, 1989

LES BLAIR
b. October 23, 1941 - Manchester, England
Home: 63 Oakfield Road, London N4 4LD, England,
    71/340-8261
Agent: Elaine Steel, 21 Brookfield Mansions, 5 Highgate
    Hill West, London N6 6AS, England, 71/633-0333

BLOOMING YOUTH (TF)   BBC, 1971, British
LAW AND ORDER (TF)   BBC, 1978, British
BEYOND THE PALE (TF)   BBC, 1980, British
THE NATION'S HEALTH (TF)   Euston Films/Channel Four,
    1983, British
NUMBER ONE   Mark Forstater Productions/Stageforum
    Productions, 1984, British
HONEST, DECENT AND TRUE (TF)   BBC, 1985, British
LONDON'S BURNING (TF)   London Weekend TV,
    1986, British
LEAVE TO REMAIN   Spellbound Productions/Film Four
    International, 1988, British

MICHAEL BLAKEMORE
b. June 18, 1928 - Sydney, Australia
Agent: The Lantz Office - Los Angeles, 213/858-1144

A PERSONAL HISTORY OF THE AUSTRALIAN SURF (FD)
Adams-Parker Films, 1982, Australian
PRIVATES ON PARADE   Orion Classics, 1983, British
TALES FROM THE HOLLYWOOD HILLS: THE OLD
RELIABLE (TF)   WNET-NY/Zenith Productions, 1988

RONEE BLAKLEY
b. 1946 - Caldwell, Idaho
Agent: The Lantz Office - Los Angeles, 213/858-1144

I PLAYED IT FOR YOU (FD)   Ronee Blakley
Productions, 1985

KEN BLANCATO*
Address: 178 S. Victory Blvd. - Suite 208, Burbank, CA
91502, 818/841-0596
Business Manager: Peter Grossman, 9665 Wilshire Blvd. -
Suite 900, Beverly Hills, CA 90212, 213/858-7888

STEWARDESS SCHOOL   Columbia, 1986

LES BLANK
b. November 27, 1935 - Tampa, Florida
Business: Flower Films, 10341 San Pablo Avenue,
El Cerrito, CA 94530, 415/525-0942

DRY WOOD AND HOT PEPPER (FD)   Flower Films, 1973
A POEM IS A NAKED PERSON (FD)   Skyhill Films/
Flower Films, 1974
CHULAS FRONTERAS (FD)   Brazos Films, 1976
ALWAYS FOR PLEASURE (FD)   Flower Films, 1978
GARLIC IS AS GOOD AS 10 MOTHERS (FD)   Flower
Films, 1980
BURDEN OF DREAMS (FD)   Flower Films, 1982
IN HEAVEN THERE IS NO BEER? (FD)   Flower
Films, 1984
ZIVELI: MEDICINE FOR THE HEART (FD)   Flower
Films, 1987
J'AI ETE AU BAL (I WENT TO THE DANCE)   co-director
with Chris Strachwitz, Brazos Films/Flower Films, 1989

WILLIAM PETER BLATTY*
b. 1928 - New York, New York
Agent: William Morris Agency - Beverly Hills, 213/274-7451

THE NINTH CONFIGURATION   Warner Bros., 1979,
re-released under title TWINKLE, TWINKLE 'KILLER'
KANE by United Film Distribution in 1980
THE EXORCIST III: LEGION   20th Century Fox, 1990

COREY BLECHMAN*
Agent: CAA - Los Angeles, 213/277-4545

THE THREE WISHES OF BILLY GRIER (TF)   I & C
Productions, 1984

JEFF BLECKNER*
b. August 12, 1943 - Brooklyn, New York
Home: 4701 Natoma Avenue, Woodland Hills, CA 91364
Agent: Bauer Benedek Agency - Los Angeles, 213/275-2421

RYAN'S FOUR (TF)   Fair Dinkum Inc./Groverton
Productions/Paramount TV, 1983
WHEN YOUR LOVER LEAVES (TF)   Major H
Productions, 1983

CONCEALED ENEMIES (TF)☆☆   WGBH-Boston/Goldcrest
Films and Television/Comworld Productions, 1984,
U.S.-British
DO YOU REMEMBER LOVE (TF)☆   Dave Bell
Productions, 1985
BROTHERLY LOVE (TF)   CBS Entertainment, 1985
FRESNO (MS)   MTM Productions, 1986
WHITE WATER SUMMER   Columbia, 1987
TERRORIST ON TRIAL: THE UNITED STATES VS. SALIM
AJAMI (TF)   George Englund Productions/Robert
Papazian Productions, 1988
MY FATHER, MY SON (TF)   Fred Weintraub Productions/
John J. McMahon Productions, 1988
FAVORITE SON (MS)   NBC Productions, 1988

BERTRAND BLIER
b. March 11, 1939 - Paris, France
Contact: French Film Office, 745 Fifth Avenue, New York,
NY 10151, 212/832-8860

HITLER? CONNAIS PAS!   1963, French
SI J'ETAIS UN ESPION   1967, French
GOING PLACES   LES VALSEUSES   Cinema 5,
1974, French
FEMMES FATALES   CALMOS   New Line Cinema,
1976, French
GET OUT YOUR HANDKERCHIEFS   New Line Cinema,
1978, French
BUFFET FROID   Parafrance, 1979, French
BEAU PERE   New Line Cinema, 1981, French
MY BEST FRIEND'S GIRL   European International,
1983, French
SEPARATE ROOMS   NOTRE HISTOIRE   Spectrafilm,
1984, French
MENAGE   TENUE DE SOIREE   Cinecom, 1986, French
TOO BEAUTIFUL FOR YOU   Orion Classics, 1989, French

BRUCE BLOCK*
Contact: Directors Guild of America - Los Angeles,
213/289-2000

PRINCESS ACADEMY   Empire Pictures, 1987,
Yugoslavian-French

JEFFREY BLOOM*
Agent: William Morris Agency - Beverly Hills, 213/274-7451

DOGPOUND SHUFFLE   Paramount, 1974, Canadian
THE STICK UP   Trident-Barber, 1978, British
BLOOD BEACH   Jerry Gross Organization, 1981
JEALOUSY (TF)   Charles Fries Productions/Alan Sacks
Productions, 1983
STARCROSSED (TF)   Fries Entertainment, 1985
THE RIGHT OF THE PEOPLE (TF)   Big Name Films/Fries
Entertainment, 1986
FLOWERS IN THE ATTIC   New World, 1987

GEORGE BLOOMFIELD*
b. 1930 - Montreal, Quebec, Canada
Home: 50 Admiral Road, Toronto, Ontario M5R 2LF,
Canada, 416/967-0826

JENNY   Cinerama Releasing Corporation, 1970
TO KILL A CLOWN   20th Century-Fox, 1972
CHILD UNDER A LEAF   Cinema National, 1974, Canadian
LOVE ON THE NOSE (TF)   CBC, 1974, Canadian
NELLIE McCLUNG (TF)   CBC, 1978, Canadian
RIEL   CBC/Green River Productions, 1979, Canadian
NOTHING PERSONAL   American International, 1980,
Canadian

DOUBLE NEGATIVE   Best Film and Video, 1981,
   Canadian
THE CAMPBELLS (MS)   John Delmage/CTV/Settler Film
   Productions/ Scottish TV/Fremantle International/Telefilm
   Canada, 1986, Canadian-Scottish
AFRICAN JOURNEY (TF)   The Film Works, 1990,
   Canadian

CHRIS BLUM
BIG TIME (FD)   Island Pictures, 1988

ANDY BLUMENTHAL
Contact: Concorde Pictures, 11600 San Vicente Blvd.,
   Los Angeles, CA 90049, 213/826-0978

BLOODFIST II   Concorde, 1990

DON BLUTH
Business: Sullivan/Bluth Studios, 3800 W. Alameda
   Avenue - Suite 1120, Burbank, CA 91505,
   818/840-9446 or: Sullivan/Bluth Studios, Phoenix
   House, Conyngham Road, Dublin 8, Ireland,
   011/353-I795-099

BANJO, THE WOODPILE CAT (AF)   Aurora
   Productions, 1980
THE SECRET OF NIMH (AF)   MGM/UA, 1982
AN AMERICAN TAIL (AF)   Universal, 1986
THE LAND BEFORE TIME (AF)   Universal, 1988
ALL DOGS GO TO HEAVEN (AF)   MGM/UA, 1989
ROCK-A-DOODLE (AF)   MGM/UA, 1990
A TROLL IN CENTRAL PARK (AF)   Sullivan-Bluth
   Studios Ireland Ltd., 1990

DAVID BLYTH
b. New Zealand

DEATH WARMED UP   1984, New Zealand
RED BLOODED AMERICAN GIRL   SC Entertainment,
   1990, Canadian

JEFF BLYTH*
Home: 802 Foxkirk, Glendale, CA 91206, 818/244-9202
Agent: Nancy Roberts, The Roberts Company -
   Beverly Hills, 213/275-9384

CHEETAH   Buena Vista, 1989

BUDD BOETTICHER*
(Oscar Boetticher, Jr.)
b. July 29, 1916 - Chicago, Illinois
Contact: Directors Guild of America - Los Angeles,
   213/289-2000

ONE MYSTERIOUS NIGHT   Columbia, 1944
THE MISSING JUROR   Columbia, 1944
A GUY, A GAL AND A PAL   Columbia, 1945
ESCAPE IN THE FOG   Columbia, 1945
YOUTH ON TRIAL   Columbia, 1945
THE FLEET THAT CAME TO STAY   Paramount, 1946
ASSIGNED TO DANGER   Eagle-Lion, 1948
BEHIND LOCKED DOORS   Eagle-Lion, 1948
THE WOLF HUNTERS   Monogram, 1949
BLACK MIDNIGHT   Monogram, 1949
KILLER SHARK   Monogram, 1950
THE BULLFIGHTER AND THE LADY   Republic, 1951
THE SWORD OF D'ARTAGNAN   Universal, 1951
THE CIMARRON KID   Universal, 1951
RED BALL EXPRESS   Universal, 1952

BRONCO BUSTER   Universal, 1952
HORIZONS WEST   Universal, 1952
CITY BENEATH THE SEA   Universal, 1953
SEMINOLE   Universal, 1953
THE MAN FROM THE ALAMO   Universal, 1953
EAST OF SUMATRA   Universal, 1953
WINGS OF THE HAWK   Universal, 1953
THE MAGNIFICENT MATADOR   20th Century-Fox, 1955
THE KILLER IS LOOSE   United Artists, 1956
SEVEN MEN FROM NOW   Warner Bros., 1956
THE TALL T   Columbia, 1957
DECISION AT SUNDOWN   Columbia, 1958
BUCHANAN RIDES ALONE   Columbia, 1958
RIDE LONESOME   Columbia, 1959
WESTBOUND   Warner Bros., 1959
COMANCHE STATION   Columbia, 1960
THE RISE AND FALL OF LEGS DIAMOND   Warner
   Bros., 1960
A TIME FOR DYING   Etoile, 1971
ARRUZA (FD)   Avco Embassy, 1972
MY KINGDOM FOR... (FD)   Lusitano Productions, 1985

PAUL BOGART*
b. November 21, 1919 - New York, New York
Agent: William Morris Agency - Beverly Hills, 213/274-7451

A MEMORY OF TWO MONDAYS (TF)   WNET, 1969
MARLOWE   MGM, 1969
HALLS OF ANGER   United Artists, 1970
SKIN GAME   Warner Bros., 1971
IN SEARCH OF AMERICA (TF)   Four Star Productions,
   1971
CLASS OF '44   Warner Bros., 1973
CANCEL MY RESERVATION   Warner Bros., 1974
TELL ME WHERE IT HURTS (TF)   Tomorrow
   Entertainment, 1974
MR. RICCO   MGM, 1975
WINNER TAKE ALL (TF)   The Jozak Company, 1975
THE THREE SISTERS   NTA, 1977
FUN AND GAMES (TF)   Kanin-Gallo Productions/
   Warner Bros. TV, 1980, directed under pseudonym of
   Alan Smithee
OH, GOD! YOU DEVIL   Warner Bros., 1984
THE CANTERVILLE GHOST (TF)   Pound Ridge
   Productions/Inter-Hemisphere Productions/HTV/
   Columbia TV, 1986, U.S.-British
NUTCRACKER: MONEY, MADNESS AND MURDER (MS)
   Green Arrow Productions/Warner Bros. TV, 1987
TALES FROM THE HOLLYWOOD HILLS: NATICA
   JACKSON (TF)   WNET/ Zenith Productions/KCET, 1987
TORCH SONG TRILOGY   New Line Cinema, 1988

YUREK BOGAYEVICZ
b. Poland
Agent: CAA - Beverly Hills, 213/288-4545

ANNA   Vestron, 1987

PETER BOGDANOVICH*
b. July 30, 1939 - Kingston, New York
Agent: CAA - Beverly Hills, 213/288-4545

TARGETS   Paramount, 1968
DIRECTED BY JOHN FORD (FD)   American Film Institute,
   1971
THE LAST PICTURE SHOW★   Columbia, 1971
WHAT'S UP, DOC?   Warner Bros., 1972
PAPER MOON   Paramount, 1973
DAISY MILLER   Paramount, 1974
AT LONG LAST LOVE   20th Century-Fox, 1975

NICKELODEON   Columbia, 1976
SAINT JACK   New World, 1979
THEY ALL LAUGHED   United Artists Classics, 1982
MASK   Universal, 1985
ILLEGALLY YOURS   MGM/UA, 1988
TEXASVILLE   Columbia, 1990
ANOTHER YOU   Tri-Star, 1991

WILLY BOGNER
FIRE AND ICE   Concorde, 1987

CLIFFORD BOLE*
Agent: Shapiro-Lichtman Agency - Los Angeles,
   213/859-8877
Business Manager: Brad Marer & Associates - Los Angeles,
   213/278-6690

T.J. HOOKER (TF)   Spelling-Goldberg Productions, 1982
PARADISE (TF)   co-director with Michael Lange,
   CBS, 1989

JOSEPH BOLOGNA*
b. December 30, 1936
Contact: Flora Lasky - New York City, 212/897-2030

IT HAD TO BE YOU   co-director with Renee Taylor,
   Limelite Studios, 1989

MAURO BOLOGNINI
b. June 28, 1922 - Pistoia, Italy
Home: Piazza di Spagna 6, Rome, Italy, 06/679-8369

CI TROVIAMO IN GALLERIA   Athena Cinematografica,
   1953, Italian
I CAVALIERI DELLA REGINA   Thetis Film, 1954, Italian
LA VENA D'ORO   Athena Cinematografica, 1955, Italian
GLI INNAMORATI   Jacovoni, 1955, Italian
GUARDIA, GUARDIA SCELTA, BRIGADIERE E
   MARESCIALLO   Imperial Film, 1956, Italian
MARISA LA CIVETTA   Ponti/Balcazar, 1957,
   Italian-Spanish
GIOVANI MARITI   Nepi Film, 1957, Italian
ARRANGIATEVI   Cineriz, 1959, Italian
LA NOTTE BRAVA   *ON ANY STREET/BAD GIRLS DON'T
   CRY*   Ajace Film/Franco London Film, 1959,
   Italian-French
IL BELL'ANTONIO   Cino Del Duca/Arco Film/Lyre
   Cinematographique, 1960, Italian-French
FROM A ROMAN BALCONY   *LA GIORNATA BALORDA/
   LOVE IS A DAY'S WORK/ PICKUP IN ROME*
   Continental, 1960, Italian-French
LA VIACCIA   Embassy, 1960, Italian
SENILITA'   Zebra Film/Aera Film, 1961, Italian-French
AGOSTINO   Baltea Film, 1962, Italian
LA CORRUZIONE   Arco Film/SOPAC/Burgundia Films,
   1963, Italian French
LA DONNA E' UNA COSA MERAVIGLIOSA   Zebra Film/
   Aera Film, 1964, Italian-French
LA MIA SIGNORA   co-director with Tinto Brass & Luigi
   Comencini, De Laurentiis, 1964, Italian-French
BAMBOLE!   *LE BAMBOLE*   co-director with Dino Risi,
   Luigi Comencini & Franco Rossi, Royal Films
   International, 1964, Italian-French
I TRE VOLTI   co-director with Michelangelo Antonioni &
   Franco Indovina, De Laurentiis, 1964, Italian
MADEMOISELLE DE MAUPIN   Jolly Film/Consortium
   Pathe/Tecisa, 1965, Italian-French-Spanish
THE QUEENS   co-director with Luciano Salce, Mario
   Monicelli & Antonio Pietrangeli, Royal Films
   International, 1966, Italian-French

THE WITCHES   co-director with Luchino Visconti, Pier Paolo
   Pasolini, Franco Rossi & Vittorio De Sica, Lopert, 1967,
   Italian-French
ARABELLA   Cram Film, 1967, Italian
THE OLDEST PROFESSION   *LE PLUX VIEUX METIER DU
   MONDE*   co- director with Franco Indovina, Philippe De
   Broca, Claude Autant-Lara, Jean-Luc Godard & Michael
   Pfleghar, Goldstone, 1968, French-Italian- West German
THAT SPLENDID NOVEMBER   *UN BELLISSIMO
   NOVEMBRE*   United Artists, 1968, Italian
CAPRICCIO ALL'ITALIANA   co-director with Pier Paolo
   Pasolini, Mario Monicelli & Steno, De Laurentiis,
   1968, Italian
L'ASSOLUTO NATURALE   Tirrenia Studios, 1969, Italian
METELLO   Documento Film, 1969, Italian
BUBU'   BRC, 1970, Italian
IMPUTAZIONE DI OMICIDIO PER UNO STUDENTE
   Documento Film, 1971, Italian
LIBERA AMORE MIO   Roberto Loyolo Cinematografica,
   1973, Italian
FATTI DI GENTE PER BENE   Filmarpa/Lira Film,
   1974, Italian
DOWN THE ANCIENT STAIRS   20th Century-Fox, 1976,
   Italian-French
L'EREDITA' FERRAMONTI   Flag Production, 1976, Italian
GRAN BOLLITO   Triangolo Film, 1977, Italian
DOVE VAI IN VACANZA?   co-director with Luciano Salce &
   Alberto Sordi, Rizzoli, 1978, Italian
LA VERA STORIA DELLA SIGNORA DELLE CAMELIE
   Opera Film Produzione/ Les Films du Losange, 1980,
   Italian-French
LA CERTOSA DI PARMA (TF)   RAI, 1984, Italian
LA VENEXIANA   Lux International, 1985, Italian
MOSCA ADDIO   Istituto Luce/Italnoleggio, 1987, Italian
A TIME OF INDIFFERENCE (MS)   Consorzio Europeo/
   Titanus, 1988, Italian

BEN BOLT*
(Benedict L. Bolt)
b. May 9, 1952 - England
Agent: Alan Greenspan, ICM - Los Angeles, 213/550-4428

(The following is an incomplete list of Mr. Bolt's credits)

RAINY DAY WOMEN (TF)   BBC, 1986, British
THE BIG TOWN   Columbia, 1987

ROBERT BOLT
b. August 15, 1924 - Sale, England
Contact: British Academy of Film & Television Arts, 195
   Piccadilly, London W1, England, 71/734-0022

LADY CAROLINE LAMB   United Artists, 1973, British

JAMES BOND III
Contact: Screen Actors Guild - Hollywood, 213/465-4600

DEF BY TEMPTATION   Troma, 1990

TIMOTHY BOND
b. 1942 - Ottawa, Ontario, Canada
Home: 44 Palmerston Gardens, Toronto, Ontario M6G 1V9,
   Canada, 416/535-3870
Agent: Scott Yoselow, The Gersh Agency - New York City,
   212/997-1818

DEADLY HARVEST (TF)   Ambassador Film Distributors,
   1976, Canadian
TILL DEATH DO US PART (TF)   CTV, 1982, Canadian

ONE NIGHT ONLY (TF)   RSL Films, 1983, Canadian
OAKMOUNT HIGH (TF)   1985, Canadian

SERGEI BONDARCHUK
b. September 25, 1920 - Belozersk, Ukraine, U.S.S.R.
Contact: Union of Soviet Filmmakers, Vassilievskaya 13,
   Moscow, U.S.S.R., tel.: 250-4114

FATE OF A MAN   Lopert, 1961, Soviet
WAR AND PEACE   Continental, 1968, Soviet
WATERLOO   Paramount, 1971, Italian-Soviet
THEY FOUGHT FOR THEIR MOTHERLAND   Mosfilm,
   1974, Soviet
THE STEPPE   IFEX Film/Sovexport film, 1977, Soviet
RED BELLS: MEXICO IN FLAMES   Mosfilm/Conacite-2/
   RAI/Vides International/Cinefin, 1982, Soviet-
   Mexican-Italian
RED BELLS: I'VE SEEN THE BIRTH OF THE
   NEW WORLD   Mosfilm/Conacite-2/ Vides International,
   1983, Soviet-Mexican-Italian
BORIS GODOUNOV   Sovfilm/Barrandov Studio, 1986,
   Soviet-Czechoslovakian

PETER BONERZ*
b. August 6, 1938 - Portsmouth, New Hampshire
Agent: CAA - Beverly Hills, 213/288-4545

NOBODY'S PERFEKT   Columbia, 1981
SHARING RICHARD (TF)   Houston Motion Picture
   Entertainment/CBS Entertainment, 1988
POLICE ACADEMY 6: CITY UNDER SIEGE   Warner
   Bros., 1989

JOHN BOORMAN*
b. January 18, 1933 - Shepperton, Middlesex, England
Home: "The Glebe," Annamoe, County Wicklow, Ireland
Agent: Jeff Berg, ICM - Los Angeles, 213/550-4000
Business Manager: Edgar F. Gross, International Business
   Management - Los Angeles, 213/277-4455

HAVING A WILD WEEKEND   CATCH US IF YOU CAN
   Warner Bros., 1965, British
POINT BLANK   MGM, 1967
HELL IN THE PACIFIC   Cinerama Releasing Corporation,
   1968
LEO THE LAST   United Artists, 1970, British
DELIVERANCE★   Warner Bros., 1972
ZARDOZ   20th Century Fox, 1974, British
THE HERETIC: EXORCIST II   Warner Bros., 1977
EXCALIBUR   Orion/Warner Bros., 1981, British-Irish
THE EMERALD FOREST   Embassy, 1985, British
HOPE AND GLORY★   Columbia, 1987, British
WHERE THE HEART IS   Buena Vista, 1990

H. GORDON BOOS*
Home: 6106 Graciosa Drive - Apt. 9, Los Angeles, CA
   90068, 213/466-0729

RED SURF   Arrowhead Entertainment, 1990

JOSÉ LUIS BORAU
b. August 8, 1929 - Zaragoza, Spain
Home: 3491 Shernoll Place, Sherman Oaks, CA 91403,
   818/788-3291
Business: El Iman S.A., Alberto Alcocer 42, Madrid 16,
   Spain, 250-5534

BRANDY, EL SHERIFF DE LOSATUMBA   1963, Spanish
CRIMEN DE DOBLE FILO   1964, Spanish

HAY QUE MATAR A B   1974, Spanish
FURTIVOS   El Iman, 1975, Spanish
LA SABINA   El Iman/Svensk Filminstitut, 1979,
   Spanish-Swedish
ON THE LINE   Miramax, 1984, Spanish
TATA MIA   Profilmar/El Iman, 1986, Spanish

LIZZIE BORDEN
(Linda Borden)
b. Detroit, Michigan

BORN IN FLAMES   1986
WORKING GIRLS   Miramax Films, 1987
LOVE CRIMES   Sovereign Pictures, 1991

ROBERT BORIS
Agent: Leading Artists - Beverly Hills, 213/858-1999

OXFORD BLUES   MGM/UA, 1984, British
STEELE JUSTICE   Atlantic Releasing Corporation, 1987
BUY AND CELL   Trans World Entertainment, 1989

CLAY BORRIS
b. 1950 - New Brunswick, Canada
Home: 914 Venezia Avenue, Venice, CA 90291,
   213/827-5304
Agent: Mike Simpson, William Morris Agency - Beverly Hills,
   213/274-7451

ROSE'S HOUSE   1977, Canadian
ALLIGATOR SHOES   New Cinema, 1981, Canadian
QUIET COOL   New Line Cinema, 1986
THE GUNFIGHTERS (TF)   Grosso-Jacobson Productions/
   Alliance Entertainment/Tribune Entertainment, 1987,
   U.S.-Canadian

PHILLIP BORSOS*
b. 1953 - Tasmania, Australia
Address: The Radio-Telegraphic Company, 240 Indian Road,
   Toronto, Ontario M6R 2W9, Canada, 416/769-7508
Agent: Bauer Benedek Agency - Los Angeles, 213/275-2421

THE GREY FOX   United Artists Classics, 1983, Canadian
THE MEAN SEASON   Orion, 1985
ONE MAGIC CHRISTMAS   Buena Vista, 1985,
   U.S.-Canadian
BETHUNE: THE MAKING OF A HERO   Hemdale, 1990,
   Canadian-Chinese- French

JOHN BOSKOVICH
Agent: William Morris Agency - Beverly Hills, 213/274-7451

WITHOUT YOU I'M NOTHING   MCEG, 1990

ROY BOULTING
b. November 21, 1913 - Bray, Buckinghamshire, England
Agent: Derek Webster/David Booth, John Redway and
   Associates Ltd., 5 Denmark Street, London WC2H 8LP,
   England, 71/836-2001

TRUNK CRIME   Angelo, 1939, British
INQUEST   Grand National, 1939, British
PASTOR HALL   United Artists, 1940, British
THUNDER ROCK   English Films, 1942, British
DESERT VICTORY (FD)   Army Film Unit, 1943, British
TUNISIAN VICTORY (FD)   co-director with Frank Capra,
   Army Film Unit, 1943, British
BURMA VICTORY (FD)   Army Film Unit, 1945, British

THE OUTSIDER *THE GUINEA PIG* Pathe, 1948, British
FAME IS THE SPUR Two Cities, 1949, British
HIGH TREASON Rank, 1951, British
SAILOR OF THE KING *SINGLE-HANDED* 20th Century-Fox, 1953, British
CREST OF THE WAVE *SEAGULLS OVER SORRENTO* co-director with John Boulting, MGM, 1954
JOSEPHINE AND MEN 1955, British
RUN FOR THE SUN United Artists, 1956, British
BROTHERS IN LAW British Llon, 1957, British
HAPPY IS THE BRIDE Kassler, 1959, British
MAN IN A COCKED HAT *CARLTON-BROWNE OF THE F.O.* co-director with Jeffrey Dell, Show Corporation, 1960, British
A FRENCH MISTRESS Films Around the World, 1960, British
THE RISK *SUSPECT* co-director with John Boulting, Kingsley International, 1961, British
THE FAMILY WAY Warner Bros., 1967, British
TWISTED NERVE National General, 1969, British
THERE'S A GIRL IN MY SOUP Columbia, 1970, British
UNDERCOVERS HERO *SOFT BEDS AND HARD BATTLES* United Artists, 1975, British
THE LAST WORD Samuel Goldwyn Company, 1979
THE MOVING FINGER (TF) BBC, 1984, British

SERGE BOURGUIGNON*
b. 1928 - France
Contact: Directors Guild of America - Los Angeles, 213/289-2000

SUNDAYS AND CYBELE *LES DIMANCHES DE VILLE D'AVRAY* Davis- Royal, 1962, French
THE REWARD 20th Century-Fox, 1965
TWO WEEKS IN SEPTEMBER *A COEUR JOIE* Paramount, 1967, French
THE PICASSO SUMMER Warner Bros., 1969
MY KINGDOM FOR A HORSE (FD) Cheval Magazine, 1986, French
THE FASCINATION Samurai Productions, 1987, Japanese

JENNY BOWEN
b. San Francisco, California
Agent: Dave Wirtschafter, ICM - Los Angeles, 213/550-4000

STREET MUSIC Specialty, 1982
THE WIZARD OF LONELINESS Skouras Pictures, 1988
ANIMAL BEHAVIOR co-director with Kjehl Rasmussen, both directed under pseudonym of H. Anne Riley, Millimeter Films, 1989, filmed in 1985

GEORGE BOWERS*
Home: 6417 Maryland Drive, Los Angeles, CA 90048, 213/931-2363
Agent: Lee Dinstman, Contemporary Artists - Beverly Hills, 213/278-8250

THE HEARSE Crown International, 1980
BODY AND SOUL Cannon, 1982
MY TUTOR Crown International, 1983
PRIVATE RESORT Tri-Star, 1985

JOHN R. BOWEY
b. January 4, 1958 - Sussex, England
Contact: A Cut Above Productions, Inc.,11816 Chandler Blvd. - Suite 8, No. Hollywood, CA 9l606, 818/985-2105

TIME OF THE BEAST A Cut Above Productions, 1989

KENNETH BOWSER
Business: Barking Dog Productions, Inc., 1619 Broadway - Suite 705, New York, NY 10019
Agent: Lucy Kroll Agency - New York City, 212/877-0627

IN A SHALLOW GRAVE Skouras Pictures, 1988
PRESTON STURGES: THE RISE AND FALL OF AN AMERICAN DREAMER (TD) Barking Dog Productions/ American Masters, 1990

DANIEL BOYD
b. September 14, 1956 - Martinsburg, West Virginia
Home: Big Pictures, Inc., 1115 Hollyberry Lane, South Charleston, West Virginia 25309, 304/340-1492
Attorney: Benjamin L. Bailey, Bowles, Rice, McDavid, Graff & Love, P.O. Box 1386, Charleston, West Virginia 25325, 304/347-1178

CHILLERS Big Pictures, 1988
STRANGEST DREAMS: INVASION OF THE SPACE PREACHERS Troma, Inc., 1990

GIANNI BOZZACCHI*
Home: 112 West 56th Street, New York, NY 10019, 212/245-3980
Agent: Ben Benjamin, ICM - New York, 212/556-5600

I LOVE N.Y. directed under pseudonym of Alan Smithee, Manhattan Films, 1988

SAMUEL BRADFORD
TEEN VAMP New World, 1989

RANDY BRADSHAW
Contact: Academy of Canadian Cinema and Television, 653 Yonge Street - Second Floor, Toronto, Ontario M4Y 1Z9, Canada, 416/967-0315

LAST TRAIN HOME (CTF) Atlantis Films Ltd./Great North Productions/ CBC, 1990, Canadian

ROBERT (BOB) BRALVER*
Home: 17589 Camino De Yatasto, Pacific Palisades, CA 90272, 213/462-2301

RUSH WEEK Noble Entertainment, 1988
MIDNIGHT RIDE Cannon, 1990

BILL BRAME*
b. June 28, 1928
Home: 1111 Heatherside Drive, Pasadena, CA 91105, 818/795-6389

CYCLE SAVAGES Trans American, 1970
JIVE TURKEY Goldstone, 1976

KENNETH BRANAGH
b. Belfast, Northern Ireland
Contact: British Academy of Film & Television Arts, 195 Piccadilly, London W1, England, 71/734-0022

HENRY V ★ Samuel Goldwyn Company, 1989, British

LARRY BRAND
Agent: Robert Eisenbach, Inc. - Los Angeles, 213/982-5809

THE DRIFTER Concorde, 1988
THE MASQUE OF THE RED DEATH Concorde, 1989
OVEREXPOSED Concorde, 1990

KLAUS MARIA BRANDAUER
Agent: Paul Kohner, Inc. - Los Angeles, 213/550-1060

GEORG ELSER   Deutscher Verleigh/Senator Film, 1990,
   West German-U.S.

MARLON BRANDO*
b. April 3, 1924 - Omaha, Nebraska
Contact: Directors Guild of America - Los Angeles,
   213/289-2000

ONE-EYED JACKS   Paramount, 1961

CHARLOTTE BRANDSTROM
b. May 30, 1959 - Paris, France
Agent: Jeff Berg, ICM - Los Angeles, 213/550-4205

UN ETE D'ORAGES   AAA, 1989, French
SWEET REVENGE   The Movie Group, 1990, French-U.S.

TINTO BRASS
(Giovanni Tinto Brass)
b. March 26, 1933 - Milan, Italy
Home: Casale Tronconi, via Ferraioli, Isola Farnese, Rome,
   Italy, 06/360-3707

CHI LAVORA E' PERDUTO   *IN CAPO AL MONDO*
   Zebra Film/Franco London Film, 1963, Italian-French
LA MIA SIGNORA   co-director with Luigi Comencini &
   Mauro Bolognini, De Laurentiis, 1964, Italian
IL DISCO VOLANTE   De Laurentiis, 1964, Italian
CA IRA, IL FIUME DELLA RIVOLTA   Zebra Film,
   1965, Italian
YANKEE   Tigielle, 1966, Italian
COL CUORE IN GOLA   Panda/Les Films Corona, 1967,
   Italian-French
NEROSUBIANCO   Lion Film, 1969, Italian
DROPOUT   Medusa/Lion Film, 1972, Italian
LA VACANZA   Lion Film, 1972, Italian
L'URLO   Lion Film, 1972, Italian
SALON KITTY   American International, 1976, Italian
CALIGULA   Analysis Film Releasing, 1977, Italian-U.S.
ACTION   Attori Registri Solidali, 1979, Italian
LA CHIAVE   San Francisco Film, 1985, Italian
MIRANDA   San Francisco Film, 1985, Italian
REMEMBERING CAPRI   *CAPRICCIO*   DEG,
   1987, Italian
SNACK BAR BUDAPEST   Medusa, 1988, Italian

MARY ANN BRAUBACH
b. San Antonio, Texas
Attorney: Frank Gruber, 9601 Wilshire Blvd., Beverly Hills,
   CA 90210, 213/274-5638

A GREAT BUNCH OF GIRLS (FD)   co-director with Tracy
   Tynan, Cowgirl Productions, 1978

CHARLES BRAVERMAN*
b. March 3, 1944 - Los Angeles, California
Business: Braverman Productions, 1861 S. Bundy Drive,
   Los Angeles, CA 90025, 213/826-6466
Agent: Ken Gross, Robinson, Weintraub, Gross &
   Associates - Los Angeles, 213/653-5802

HIT AND RUN   *REVENGE SQUAD*   Comworld, 1982
PRINCE OF BEL AIR (TF)   Leonard Hill Films, 1986
BROTHERHOOD OF JUSTICE (TF)   Guber-Peters
   Productions/Phoenix Entertainment Group, 1986

VALERIE BREIMAN
THE UNSINKABLE SHECKY MOSKOWITZ   TTI, 1990

ROBERT BRESSON
b. September 25, 1907 - Bromont-Lamothe, France
Contact: French Film Office, 745 Fifth Avenue, New York,
   NY 10151, 212/832-8860

LES AFFAIRES PUBLIQUE   Arc Films, 1934, French
LES ANGES DU PECHE   Synops/Roland Tual,
   1943, French
THE LADIES OF THE PARK   Brandon, 1945, French
DIARY OF A COUNTRY PRIEST   Brandon, 1950, French
A MAN ESCAPED   Continental, 1956, French
PICKPOCKET   New Yorker, 1959, French
THE TRIAL OF JOAN OF ARC   Pathe Contemporary,
   1962, French
AU HASARD, BALTHAZAR   Cinema Ventures,
   1966, French
MOUCHETTE   1967, French
UNE FEMME DOUCE   New Yorker, 1969, French
FOUR NIGHTS OF A DREAMER   New Yorker,
   1972, French
LANCELOT OF THE LAKE   New Yorker, 1975,
   French-Italian
LE DIABLE PROBABLEMENT   Gaumont, 1977, French
L'ARGENT (MONEY)   Cinecom, 1983, French-Swiss

MARTIN BREST*
b. 1951 - New York, New York
Home: 831 Paseo Miramar, Pacific Palisades, CA 90272,
   213/315-2145
Agent: CAA - Beverly Hills, 213/288-4545

HOT TOMORROWS   American Film Institute, 1977
GOING IN STYLE   Warner Bros., 1979
BEVERLY HILLS COP   Paramount, 1984
MIDNIGHT RUN   Universal, 1988

MARSHALL BRICKMAN*
Agent: ICM - Los Angeles, 213/550-4000

SIMON   Orion/Warner Bros., 1980
LOVESICK   The Ladd Company/Warner Bros., 1983
THE MANHATTAN PROJECT   20th Century Fox, 1986

PAUL BRICKMAN*
b. Chicago, Illinois
Agent: CAA - Beverly Hills, 213/288-4545

RISKY BUSINESS   The Geffen Company/Warner
   Bros., 1983
MEN DON'T LEAVE   The Geffen Company/Warner
   Bros., 1990

ALAN BRIDGES*
b. September 28, 1928 - Liverpool, England
Home: The Old Manor Farm, Church Street, Sunbury-on-
   Thames, Middlesex TW16 6RG, England, 093/278-0166
Agent: Ames Cushing, William Morris Agency - Beverly Hills,
   213/274-7451 or: Derek Webster/David Booth, John
   Redway and Associates Ltd., 5 Denmark Street, London
   WC2H 8LP, England, 71/836-2001

ACT OF MURDER   Warner-Pathe/Anglo-Amalgamated,
   1964, British
INVASION   Warner-Pathe/Anglo-Amalgamated,
   1966, British
THE LIE   BBC, 1970, British

THE HIRELING   Columbia, 1973, British
BRIEF ENCOUNTER (TF)   Carlo Ponti Productions/Cecil
    Clarke Productions, 1974, British
OUT OF SEASON   Athenaeum, 1975, British
SATURDAY, SUNDAY, MONDAY (TF)   Granada TV,
    1977, British
AGE OF INNOCENCE   Rank, 1977, British-Canadian
LA PETITE FILLE EN VELOURS BLEU   Warner-Columbia,
    1978, French
RAIN ON THE ROOF (TF)   London Weekend TV,
    1980, British
VERY LIKE A WHALE   Black Lion, 1981, British
THE RETURN OF THE SOLDIER   European Classics,
    1982, British
PUDDN'HEAD WILSON (TF)   The Great Amwell Company/
    Nebraska ETY Network/Taurus Film, 1984,
    U.S.-West German
THE SHOOTING PARTY   European Classics,
    1984, British
DISPLACED PERSON (TF)   1985, British
FIRE PRINCESS   Eagle/Zalon Entertainment, 1990

BEAU BRIDGES*
(Lloyd Vernet Bridges III)
b. December 9, 1941 - Los Angeles, California
Agent: CAA - Beverly Hills, 213/288-4545

THE KID FROM NOWHERE (TF)   Cates-Bridges
    Company, 1982
THE THANKSGIVING PROMISE (TF)   Mark H. Ovitz
    Productions/Walt Disney TV, 1986
THE WILD PAIR   Trans World Entertainment, 1987
SEVEN HOURS TO JUDGMENT   Trans World
    Entertainment, 1988

JAMES BRIDGES*
b. February 3, 1936 - Paris, Arkansas
Agent: CAA - Beverly Hills, 213/288-4545

THE BABY MAKER   National General, 1970
THE PAPER CHASE   20th Century-Fox, 1973
9/30/55   SEPTEMBER 30, 1955   Universal, 1977
THE CHINA SYNDROME   Columbia, 1979
URBAN COWBOY   Paramount, 1980
MIKE'S MURDER   The Ladd Company/Warner
    Bros., 1984
PERFECT!   Columbia, 1985
BRIGHT LIGHTS, BIG CITY   MGM/UA, 1988

BURT BRINCKERHOFF*
b. October 25, 1936
Contact: Directors Guild of America - Los Angeles,
    213/289-2000

TWO BROTHERS (TF)   KCET-TV, 1976
DOGS   R.C. Riddell, 1977
ACAPULCO GOLD   R.C. Riddell, 1978
THE CRACKER FACTORY (TF)   Roger Gimbel
    Productions/EMI TV, 1979
CAN YOU HEAR THE LAUGHTER? THE STORY OF
    FREDDIE PRINZE (TF)   Roger Gimbel Productions/
    EMI TV, 1979
MOTHER AND DAUGHTER - THE LOVING WAR (TF)
    Edgar J. Scherick Associates, 1980
BRAVE NEW WORLD (TF)   Universal TV, 1980
THE DAY THE WOMEN GOT EVEN (TF)   Otto Salaman
    Productions/PKO, 1980
BORN TO BE SOLD (TF)   Ron Samuels Productions, 1981

DEBORAH BROCK
Business: Concorde Pictures, 11600 San Vicente Blvd.,
    Los Angeles, CA 90049, 213/826-0978

SLUMBER PARTY MASSACRE II   Concorde, 1987
ANDY COLBY'S INCREDIBLE ADVENTURE
    Concorde, 1988
ROCK 'N' ROLL HIGH SCHOOL FOREVER   Four Seasons
    Entertainment, 1990

LINO BROCKA
b. 1940 - San Jose, Nueva Ecija, Philippines
Contact: Manila Film Center, CCP Complex, Rexas Blvd.,
    Manila, Philippines, 832-1125

WANTED: PERFECT MOTHER   1970, Filipino
SANTIAGO   1970, Filipino
TUBOG SA GINTO   1970, Filipino
NOW   1971, Filipino
LUMUHA PATI MGA ANGHEL   1971, Filipino
CADENA DE AMOR   1971, Filipino
STARDOOM   1971, Filipino
CHERRY BLOSSOMS   1972, Filipino
VILLA MIRANDA   1972, Filipino
YOU ARE WEIGHED IN THE BALANCE BUT ARE FOUND
    LACKING   1974, Filipino
TATLO, DALAWA, ISA   1974, Filipino
DUNG-AW   1975, Filipino
MANILA IN THE CLAWS OF LIGHT   1975, Filipino
LUNES, MARTES, MYERKOLES...   1976, Filipino
INSIANG   1976, Filipino
TAHAN NA EMPOY, TAHAN   1977, Filipino
INAY   1977, Filipino
LAHING PILIPINO   1977, Filipino
GUMISING KA, MARUJA   1978, Filipino
HAYOP SA HAYOP   1978, Filipino
INIT   1978, Filipino
RUBIA SERVIOS   1978, Filipino
INA, KAPATID, ANAK   1979, Filipino
INA KA NG ANAK MO   1979, Filipino
JAGUAR   1979, Filipino
BONA   1980, Filipino
NAKAW NA PAG-IBIG   1980, Filipino
ANGELA MARKADO   1980, Filipino
BORGIS   1981, Filipino
HELLO, YOUNG LOVERS   1981, Filipino
BINATA SI MISTER, BALAGA SI MISIS   1981, Filipino
LAMENTATIONS (TF)   1981, Filipino
CAIN AT ABEL   1982, Filipino
P.X.   1982, Filipino
KONTROBERSYAL   1982, Filipino
IN THIS CORNER   1982, Filipino
CAUGHT IN THE ACT   1982, Filipino
PALIPAT-LIPAT, PAPALIT-PALIT   1982, Filipino
MOTHER DEAR   1982, Filipino
EXPERIENCE   1983, Filipino
STRANGERS IN PARADISE   1983, Filipino
HOT PROPERTY   1984, Filipino
MY COUNTRY: IN DESPERATE STRAITS   BAYAN-KO
    1984, Filipino
MISQUELITO   1984, Filipino
ANO ANG KULAY NG MUKHA NG DIYOS?   LEA
    Productions, 1985, Filipino
HINUGOT SA LANGIT   1986, Filipino
MACHO DANCER   Special People Productions,
    1988, Filipino
I CARRY THE WORLD   1988, Filipino
FIGHT FOR US   Cannon, 1989, French-Filipino

F
I
L
M

D
I
R
E
C
T
O
R
S

AL BRODAX
STRAWBERRY FIELDS (AF)   ITC Productions, 1990

JOHN BRODERICK*
Home: 881 El Capitan, Millbrae, CA 94030, 213/461-1879
Agent: Associated Talent International - Beverly Hills,
   213/271-4662

BAD GEORGIA ROAD   Dimension, 1976
THE WARRIOR AND THE SORCERESS   New
   Horizons, 1984

KEVIN BRODIE*
Agent: Ronald Leif, Contemporary Artists - Beverly Hills,
   213/278-8250

MUGSY'S GIRLS   Shapiro Entertainment/Spectrum
   Cinema/ICE Corporation, 1984

HUGH BRODY
Contact: British Academy of Film & Television Arts,
   195 Piccadilly, London W1, England, 71/734-0022

1919   Spectrafilm, 1985, British

REX BROMFIELD
Address: 1034 Princess Avenue, Victoria, British Columbia
   V8T 1L1, Canada, 604/383-9583
Agent: Daniel Ostroff Agency - Los Angeles, 213/278-2020

LOVE AT FIRST SIGHT   Movietown, 1977, Canadian
TULIPS   co-director with Mark Warren & Al Waxman
   under the collective pseudonym of Stan Ferris,
   Avco Embassy, 1981, Canadian
MELANIE   Jensen Farley Pictures, 1983, Canadian
HOME IS WHERE THE HART IS   Atlantic Releasing
   Corporation, 1987, Canadian

PETER BROOK
b. March 21, 1925 - London, England
Address: c/o C.I.C.T., 9 Rue du Cirque, Paris 8, France

THE BEGGAR'S OPERA   Warner Bros., 1953, British
MODERATO CANTABILE   Royal International, 1963,
   French-Italian
LORD OF THE FLIES   Continental, 1963, British
THE PERSECUTION AND ASSASINATION OF
   JEAN-PAUL MARAT AS PERFORMED BY THE
   INMATES OF THE ASYLUM OF CHARENTON
   UNDER THE DIRECTION OF THE MARQUIS
   DE SADE   United Artists, 1967, British
TELL ME LIES   Continental, 1968, British
KING LEAR   Altura, 1971, British-Danish
MEETINGS WITH REMARKABLE MEN   Libra, 1979,
   British
LA TRAGEDIE DE CARMEN   MK2/Alby Films/Antenne-2,
   1983, French
THE MAHABHARATA   MK2 USA, 1989, French-
   British-U.S.

ADAM BROOKS
b. September 3, 1956 - Toronto, Ontario, Canada
Home: 144 Franklin Street, New York, NY 10013,
   212/925-8064
Agent: Caitlin Buchman, Triad Artists, Inc. - New York,
   212/489-8100

ALMOST YOU   TLC Films/20th Century Fox, 1984
RED RIDING HOOD   Cannon, 1987, U.S.-Israeli

ALBERT BROOKS*
b. July 22, 1947 - Los Angeles, California
Personal Manager: Herb Nanas, Moress Nanas
   Entertainment, 2128 Pico Blvd., Santa Monica, CA 90405,
   213/450-9797

REAL LIFE   Paramount, 1979
MODERN ROMANCE   Columbia, 1981
LOST IN AMERICA   The Geffen Company/Warner
   Bros., 1985
DEFENDING YOUR LIFE   The Geffen Company/Warner
   Bros., 1991

BOB BROOKS*
b. 1927 - Philadelphia, Pennsylvania
Home: BFCS, 59 N. Wharf Road, London W2, England,
   71/402-5561
Agent: Anthony Jones, Peters, Fraser & Dunlop,
   The Chambers, Chelsea Harbour, Lots Road, London
   SW10 OXF, England, 71/376-7676

THE KNOWLEDGE (TF)   1979, British
TATTOO   20th Century-Fox, 1981

JAMES L. BROOKS*
b. May 9, 1940 - Brooklyn, New York
Business: Gracie Films, P.O. Box 900, Beverly Hills, CA
   91403, 213/203-3771
Agent: Jeff Berg, ICM - Los Angeles, 213/550-4000

TERMS OF ENDEARMENT★★   Paramount, 1983
BROADCAST NEWS   20th Century Fox, 1987

JOSEPH BROOKS*
Business: Chancery Lane Films, Inc., 41-A East 74th Street,
   New York, NY 10021, 212/759-8720

YOU LIGHT UP MY LIFE   Columbia, 1977
IF EVER I SEE YOU AGAIN   Columbia, 1978
HEADIN' FOR BROADWAY   20th Century-Fox, 1980
INVITATION TO THE WEDDING   Chancery Lane Films,
   1984, British

MEL BROOKS*
(Melvin Kaminsky)
b. 1926 - New York, New York
Agent: CAA - Beverly Hills, 213/288-4545
Business: Brooksfilms Limited, 20th Century Fox, P.O. Box
   900, Beverly Hills, CA 90213, 213/203-1375

THE PRODUCERS   Avco Embassy, 1968
THE TWELVE CHAIRS   UMC, 1970
BLAZING SADDLES   Warner Bros., 1973
YOUNG FRANKENSTEIN   20th Century-Fox, 1974
SILENT MOVIE   20th Century-Fox, 1976
HIGH ANXIETY   20th Century-Fox, 1977
HISTORY OF THE WORLD, PART I   20th Century-
   Fox, 1981
SPACEBALLS   MGM/UA, 1987
LIFE STINKS   Pathe Entertainment, 1991

RICHARD BROOKS*
b. May 18, 1912 - Philadelphia, Pennsylvania
Attorney: Gerald Lipsky, 190 N. Canon Drive, Beverly Hills,
   CA 90210, 213/878-4100

CRISIS   MGM, 1950
THE LIGHT TOUCH   MGM, 1951
DEADLINE - U.S.A.   MGM, 1952

BATTLE CIRCUS   MGM, 1953
TAKE THE HIGH GROUND   MGM, 1953
FLAME AND THE FLESH   MGM, 1954
THE LAST TIME I SAW PARIS   MGM, 1954
THE BLACKBOARD JUNGLE   MGM, 1955
THE LAST HUNT   MGM, 1956
THE CATERED AFFAIR   MGM, 1956
SOMETHING OF VALUE   MGM, 1957
CAT ON A HOT TIN ROOF★   MGM, 1958
THE BROTHERS KARAMAZOV   MGM, 1958
ELMER GANTRY   United Artists, 1960
SWEET BIRD OF YOUTH   MGM, 1962
LORD JIM   Columbia, 1964
THE PROFESSIONALS★   Columbia, 1966
IN COLD BLOOD★   Columbia, 1967
THE HAPPY ENDING   United Artists, 1969
$ DOLLARS   Columbia, 1971
BITE THE BULLET   Columbia, 1975
LOOKING FOR MR. GOODBAR   Paramount, 1977
WRONG IS RIGHT   Columbia, 1982
FEVER PITCH   MGM/UA, 1985

NICHOLAS BROOMFIELD

Contact: British Academy of Film & Television Arts,
   195 Piccadilly, London W1, England, 71/734-0022

DRIVING ME CRAZY   First Run Features, 1988, British
DARK SECRETS   DIAMOND SKULLS   Circle Releasing,
   1989, British

BARRY BROWN*

Home: 770 Amalfi Drive, Pacific Palisades, CA 90272,
   213/459-4455

THE WAY WE LIVE NOW   United Artists, 1970
CLOUD DANCER   Blossom, 1980

GEORG STANFORD BROWN*

b. June 24 - Havana, Cuba
Agent: Alan Greenspan, ICM - Los Angeles, 213/550-4428
Business: Nexus Productions, Inc., 4049C Radford Avenue,
   Studio City, CA 91604, 818/760-4651

ROOTS: THE NEXT GENERATIONS (MS)   co-director
   with John Erman, Charles Dubin & Lloyd Richards,
   Wolper Productions, 1979
GRAMBLING'S WHITE TIGER (TF)   Jenner-Wallach
   Productions/Inter Planetary Productions, 1981
MIRACLE OF THE HEART: A BOYS TOWN STORY (TF)
   Larry White Productions/Columbia TV, 1986
VIETNAM WAR STORY (CTF)   co-director with Ray
   Danton & Kevin Hooks, Nexus Productions, 1987
KIDS LIKE THESE (TF)   Taft Entertainment TV/Nexus
   Productions, 1987
ALONE IN THE NEON JUNGLE (TF)   Robert Halmi, Inc.,
   1988
STUCK WITH EACH OTHER (TF)   Nexus Productions,
   1989

GREGORY BROWN

DEAD MAN WALKING   Metropolis Productions/
   Hit Films, 1988
STREET ASYLUM   Metropolis Productions, 1989

JIM BROWN

WASN'T THAT A TIME! (FD)   United Artists Classics, 1982
HARD TRAVELIN' (TD)   Ginger Group/Harold Leventhal
   Management, 1984
MUSICAL PASSAGE (FD)   Films Inc., 1984

WE SHALL OVERCOME (TD)   PBS, 1988
A TRIBUTE TO WOODY GUTHRIE AND LEADBELLY (CTD)
   Showtime, 1988

TONY BROWN

Business: Tony Brown Productions, Inc., 1501 Broadway -
   Suite 2014, New York, NY 10036, 212/575-0876

THE WHITE GIRL   Tony Brown Productions, 1988

KIRK BROWNING*

b. May 28, 1921 - New York, New York
Home: 80 Central Park West, New York, NY 10023,
   212/595-6474

BIG BLONDE (TF)   PBS-TV, 1980

JAMES BRUCE

THE SUICIDE CLUB   Angelika Films, 1988

FRANCO BRUSATI

b. August 4, 1922 - Milan, Italy
Home: via San Filippo Martire 51, Rome, Italy, 06/803386

IL PADRONE SONO ME   Rizzoli Film, 1956, Italian
IL DISORDINE   Titanus/Societe Nouvelle Pathe, 1962,
   Italian-French
TENDERLY   Italnoleggio, 1968, Italian
I TULIPANI DI HAARLEM   Ultra Film, 1970, Italian
BREAD AND CHOCOLATE   World Northal, 1978, Italian
TO FORGET VENICE   Quartet, 1980, Italian-French
THE GOOD SOLDIER   Gaumont, 1982, Italian
LO ZIO INDEGNO   Ellepi/Dania/DMV/Reteitalia,
   1989, Italian

JAMES BRYAN

DON'T GO IN THE WOODS   Seymour Borde &
   Associates, 1983
THE EXECUTIONER PART II   21st Century
   Distribution, 1984
HELL RIDERS   21st Century Distribution, 1985

BILL BRYDEN

b. April 12, 1942 - Greenock, Scotland
Agent: William Morris Agency - Beverly Hills, 213/274-7451
Business: National Theatre, South Bank, London SE1 9PX,
   England, 71/928-2033

ILL FARES THE LAND   Channel Four, 1982, British
THE HOLY CITY (TF)   BBC, 1986
ARIA   co-director, Miramax Films, 1987, British

TONY BUBA

Business: Tony Buba Productions, 219 Fifth Street,
   Braddock, PA 15104

LIGHTNING OVER BRADDOCK: A RUST BOWL
   FANTASY (FD)   Zeitgeist Films, 1989

LARRY BUCHANAN*

Home: 27575 Loma del Rey, Carmel, CA 93923,
   408/626-0110

FREE, WHITE AND 21   American International, 1963
UNDER AGE   Falcon International, 1964
THE TRIAL OF LEE HARVEY OSWALD   Falcon
   International, 1964
ZONTAR - THE THING FROM VENUS   American
   International, 1966

CREATURE OF DESTRUCTION   American
   International, 1967
HELL RAIDERS   American International, 1968
MARS NEEDS WOMEN   American International, 1968
STRAWBERRIES NEED RAIN   1970
A BULLET FOR PRETTY BOY   American International,
   1970
GOODBYE, NORMA JEAN   Stirling Gold, 1976
HUGHES AND HARLOW: ANGELS IN HELL   Pro
   International, 1978
THE LOCH NESS HORROR   Omni-Leisure International,
   1982
GOODNIGHT, SWEET MARILYN   Studio Entertainment,
   1989
BEYOND THE DOORS   Omni-Leisure International,
   1989, filmed in 1983

COLIN BUCKSEY*
Agent: Leading Artists - Beverly Hills, 213/858-1999

BLUE MONEY (TF)   London Weekend TV, 1984, British
THE McGUFFIN (TF)   BBC, 1985, British
CALL ME MISTER (TF)   BBC/Australian Broadcasting
   Corporation, 1987, British-Australian
DEALERS   Skouras Pictures, 1989, British
CURIOSITY KILLS (CTF)   Dutch Productions, 1990

JOHN CARL BUECHLER
Business: Imageries Entertainment, Inc., 12031 Vose -Suites
   19-21, North Hollywood, CA 91605, 818/765-6150

THE DUNGEONMASTER   co-director, Empire
   Pictures, 1985
TROLL   Empire Pictures, 1986
CELLAR DWELLAR   Empire Pictures, 1988
FRIDAY THE 13TH PART VII - THE NEW BLOOD
   Paramount, 1988
GHOULIES GO TO COLLEGE   Taurus Entertainment, 1990

ALAN BUNCE
BABAR: THE MOVIE (AF)   New Line Cinema, 1989,
   Canadian-French

MARK BUNTZMAN
EXTERMINATOR 2   Cannon, 1984

JUAN BUÑUEL
b. November 9, 1934 - Paris, France
Home: 6, Rue Leneveux, Paris 75014, France,
   Tel.: 540 53 94
Agent: Anne Alvarez Correa, 18, Rue Troyon, Paris
   75017, France, Tel.: 755 80 85

AU RENDEZ-VOUS DE LA MORT JOYEUSE   United
   Artists, 1972, French
LA FEMME AUX BOTTES ROUGES   UGC/CFDC, 1974,
   French-Spanish
LEONOR   CIC, 1975, French-Italian-Spanish
THE ISLAND OF PASSION   1984, French
LA REBELION DE LOS COLGADOS   Sociedad
   Cooperativa Rio Mixcoac, 1987, West German-Italian-
   French-British-Austrian-Mexican

DEREK BURBIDGE
Agent: Zoetrope Ltd., Zoetrope House, 93 Union Road,
   London SW4 6JD, England, 71/720-8513

URGH! A MUSIC WAR (FD)   Filmway, 1982
MEN WITHOUT WOMEN (FD)   1983
GOIN' HOME: TEN YEARS AFTER (HVD)   Jem Music
   Video, 1986, British

ROBERT A. BURGE
VASECTOMY, A DELICATE MATTER   Seymour Borde &
   Associates, 1986
KEATON'S COP   Cannon, 1990

STUART BURGE
b. January 15, 1918 - Brentwood, England
Agent: Harriet Cruickshank, 97 Old South Lambeth Road,
   London SW8, England

THERE WAS A CROOKED MAN   United Artists,
   1962, British
UNCLE VANYA   Arthur Cantor, 1963, British
OTHELLO   Warner Bros., 1967, British
THE MIKADO   Warner Bros., 1967, British
JULIUS CAESAR   American International, 1971, British
BREAKING UP (TF)   BBC, 1986, British
NAMING THE NAMES (TF)   BBC, 1987, British
THE RAINBOW (TF)   BBC, 1989, British

MARTYN BURKE
b. Canada
Agent: CAA - Beverly Hills, 213/288-4545

THE CLOWN MURDERS   Canadian
POWER PLAY   Magnum International Pictures/Cowry Film
   Productions, 1978, Canadian-British
THE LAST CHASE   Crown International, 1981, Canadian
WITNESSES (FD)   Stornoway Productions, 1988,
   Canadian

TOM BURMAN
MEET THE HOLLOWHEADS   Moviestore
   Entertainment, 1989

CHARLES BURNETT
Agent: Triad Artists, Inc. - Los Angeles, 213/556-2727

SEVERAL FRIENDS   1969
THE HORSE   1973
KILLER OF SHEEP   1974
MY BROTHER'S WEDDING   1984
TO SLEEP WITH ANGER   Edward R. Pressman
   Productions/SVS Films, 1990

ALLAN BURNS*
b. Baltimore, Maryland
Agent: CAA - Beverly Hills, 213/288-4545

JUST BETWEEN FRIENDS   Orion, 1986

JEFF BURR
Business: Conquest Entertainment, 9417 Wexford Drive,
   Tujunga, CA 91042, 818/352-4316
Personal Manager: Eli Johnson, Keith Addis & Associates,
   8444 Wilshire Blvd., Beverly Hills, CA, 213/653-8867
Agent: William Morris Agency - Beverly Hills, 213/274-7451

DIVIDED WE FALL   co-director, Conquest Entertainment/
   Pegasus Productions, 1982
THE OFFSPRING   FROM A WHISPER TO A SCREAM
   TMS Pictures, 1987
THE VAULT   Empire Pictures, 1988
STEPFATHER II   Millimeter Films, 1989
LEATHERFACE: THE TEXAS CHAINSAW MASSACRE III
   New Line Cinema, 1990

CHRISTINE BURRILL
MARICELA (TF)   KCET/Richard Soto Productions, 1986

GEOFF BURROWES
Agent: InterTalent - Los Angeles, 213/271-0600

RETURN TO SNOWY RIVER   Buena Vista, 1988,
   Australian
RUN   Buena Vista, 1991

JAMES BURROWS*
b. December 30, 1940 - Los Angeles, California
Agent: Bob Broder, Broder-Kurland-Webb-Uffner Agency -
   Los Angeles, 213/656-9262

MORE THAN FRIENDS (TF)   Reiner-Mishkin Productions/
   Columbia TV, 1978
PARTNERS   Paramount, 1982

TIM BURSTALL
b. April 20, 1929 - England
Home: 148 Nichols Street, Fitzroy, Victoria 3065, Australia
Agent: Peter Rawley, ICM - Los Angeles, 213/550-4000

TWO THOUSAND WEEKS   Eltham Film Productions/
   Senior Film Productions, 1968, Australian
STORK   Tim Burstall & Associates/Bilcock & Copping Film
   Productions, 1971
LIBIDO   co-director with John B. Murray, Fred Schepisi &
   David Baker, Producers and Directors Guild of Australia,
   1973, Australian
ALVIN PURPLE   Hexagon Productions, 1974, Australian
PETERSEN   Hexagon Productions, 1974, Australian
END PLAY   Hexagon Productions, 1975, Australian
ELIZA FRASER   Hexagon Productions, 1976, Australian
THE LAST OF THE KNUCKLEMEN   1978, Australian
ATTACK FORCE Z   John McCallum Productions/
   Central Motion Picture Corporation, 1980,
   Australian-Taiwanese
DUET FOR FOUR   Greater Union, 1981, Australian
A DESCANT FOR GOSSIPS (MS)   1983, Australian
THE NAKED COUNTRY   Naked Country Productions,
   1984, Australian
KANGAROO   Cineplex Odeon, 1986, Australian
GREAT EXPECTATIONS - THE UNTOLD STORY
   Hemdale, 1987, Australian
NIGHTMARE AT BITTER CREEK (TF)   Swanton Films/
   Guber-Peters Entertainment Company/Phoenix
   Entertainment Group, 1988

TIM BURTON*
Agent: William Morris Agency - Beverly Hills, 213/274-7451

PEE-WEE'S BIG ADVENTURE   Warner Bros., 1985
BEETLEJUICE   The Geffen Company/Warner Bros., 1988
BATMAN   Warner Bros., 1989
EDWARD SCISSORHANDS   20th Century Fox, 1990

JOHN A. BUSHELMAN*
Home: 11972 Sunshine Terrace, Studio City, CA 91604,
   818/760-7575

SNIPERS RIDGE   20th Century-Fox, 1961
THE SILENT CALL   20th Century-Fox, 1961
BROKEN LAND   20th Century-Fox, 1962
DAY OF THE NITEMARE   Governor, 1965
CRUISIN' HIGH   Gamma III, 1975
HIGH SEAS HIJACK   Toho/Pine-Thomas Productions,
   1976, Japanese-U.S.

WILLIAM BUSHNELL, JR.*
Home: 2751 Pelham Place, Los Angeles, CA 90068,
   213/469-1517
Business: Los Angeles Theatre Center, 514 S. Spring Street,
   Los Angeles, CA, 213/221-4916
Personal Manager: Harvey Shotz, The Shotz Group -
   Los Angeles, 213/659-4030

PRISONERS   1973
THE FOUR DEUCES   Avco Embassy, 1974

GEORGE BUTLER
Business: White Mountain Films, 165 East 80th Street,
   New York, NY 10021
Agent: William Morris Agency - Beverly Hills, 213/274-7451

PUMPING IRON (FD)   co-director with Robert Fiore,
   Cinema 5, 1977
PUMPING IRON II: THE WOMEN (FD)   Cinecom, 1985
IN THE BLOOD (FD)   White Mountain Films, 1989

ROBERT BUTLER*
b. November 17, 1927 - Los Angeles, California
Agent: Alan Berger, ICM - Los Angeles, 213/550-4311

THE COMPUTER WORE TENNIS SHOES   Buena Vista,
   1970
THE BAREFOOT EXECUTIVE   Buena Vista, 1971
SCANDALOUS JOHN   Buena Vista, 1971
DEATH TAKES A HOLIDAY (TF)   Universal TV, 1971
NOW YOU SEE HIM, NOW YOU DON'T   Buena
   Vista, 1972
THE BLUE KNIGHT (TF)☆   Lorimar Productions, 1973
THE ULTIMATE THRILL   General Cinema, 1974
STRANGE NEW WORLD (TF)   Warner Brothers TV, 1975
DARK VICTORY (TF)   Universal TV, 1976
JAMES DEAN (TF)   The Jozak Company, 1976
MAYDAY AT 40,000 FEET (TF)   Andrew J. Fenady
   Associates/Warner Brothers TV, 1976
IN THE GLITTER PALACE (TF)   The Writer's Company/
   Columbia TV, 1977
HOT LEAD AND COLD FEET   Buena Vista, 1978
A QUESTION OF GUILT (TF)   Lorimar Productions, 1978
LACY AND THE MISSISSIPPI QUEEN (TF)   Lawrence
   Gordon Productions/ Paramount TV, 1978
NIGHT OF THE JUGGLER   Columbia, 1980
UNDERGROUND ACES   Filmways, 1981
UP THE CREEK   Orion, 1983
CONCRETE BEAT (TF)   Picturemaker Productions/
   Viacom, 1984
MOONLIGHTING (TF)   Picturemaker Productions/ABC
   Circle Films, 1985
OUR FAMILY HONOR (TF)   Lawrence Gordon-Charles
   Gordon Productions/ Lorimar Productions, 1985
LONG TIME GONE (TF)   Picturemaker Productions/ABC
   Circle Films, 1986
OUT ON A LIMB (MS)   Stan Margulies Company/ABC
   Circle Films, 1987
OUT OF TIME (TF)   Columbia TV, 1988

HENDEL BUTOY
Business: Walt Disney Productions, 500 S. Buena Vista
   Street, Burbank, CA 91521, 818/560-1000

THE RESCUERS DOWN UNDER (AF)   co-director with
   Michael Gabriel, Buena Vista, 1990

Z A N E   B U Z B Y *
Home: 3446 Troy Drive, Los Angeles, CA 90068,
213/876-5566

LAST RESORT   Concorde/Cinema Group, 1986

D A V I D   B Y R N E
b. Dumbarton, Scotland
Agent: CAA - Beverly Hills, 213/288-4545

TRUE STORIES   Warner Bros., 1986

J O H N   B Y R U M *
b. March 14, 1947 - Evanston, Illinois
Agent: CAA - Beverly Hills, 213/288-4545

INSERTS   United Artists, 1976, British
HEART BEAT   Orion/Warner Bros, 1980
THE RAZOR'S EDGE   Columbia, 1984
THE WHOOPEE BOYS   Paramount, 1986

C

J A M E S   C A A N *
b. March 26, 1939 - Bronx, New York
Agent: Arnold Rifkin, Triad Artists, Inc. - Los Angeles,
213/556-2727

HIDE IN PLAIN SIGHT   MGM/United Artists, 1980

E L L E N   C A B O T
DEADLY EMBRACE   Gerardfilm Ltd., 1989
MURDER WEAPON   Cinema Home Video, 1990

M I C H A E L   C A C O Y A N N I S
b. June 11, 1922 - Cyprus
Contact: Greek Film Centre, Panepistimiou Street,
Athens 134, Greece, 01/618924

WINDFALL IN ATHENS   Audio Brandon, 1953, Greek
STELLA   Milas Films, 1955, Greek
THE FINAL LIE   Finos Films, 1958, Greek
OUR LAST SPRING   Cacoyannis, 1959, Greek
A GIRL IN BLACK   Kingsley International, 1959, Greek
THE WASTREL   Lux/Tiberia, 1960, Italian
ELECTRA   Lopert, 1962, Greek
ZORBA THE GREEK ★   International Classics, 1964,
Greek
THE DAY THE FISH CAME OUT   20th Century-Fox,
1967, British-Greek
THE TROJAN WOMEN   Cinerama Releasing Corporation,
1971, U.S.-Greek
THE STORY OF JACOB AND JOSEPH (TF)   Screen
Gems/Columbia TV, 1974
ATTILA '74 (FD)   1975, Greek
IPHIGENIA   Cinema 5, 1977, Greek
SWEET COUNTRY   Cinema Group, 1987, Greek

M I C H A E L   C A F F E Y *
Agent: Shapiro-Lichtman Agency - Los Angeles,
213/859-8877

SEVEN IN DARKNESS (TF)   Paramount TV, 1969
THE SILENT GUN (TF)   Paramount TV, 1969
THE DEVIL AND MISS SARAH (TF)   Universal TV, 1971
THE HANGED MAN (TF)   Fenady Associates/Bing Crosby
Productions, 1974
MacGYVER: LEGEND OF THE HOLY ROSE (TF)
co-director with Charles Correll, Henry Winkler-John Rich
Productions/Paramount TV, 1989

C H R I S T O P H E R   C A I N *
b. October 29, 1943 - Sioux Falls, South Dakota
Agent: William Morris Agency - Beverly Hills, 213/274-7451

BROTHER, MY SONG   Eagle International, 1976
GRAND JURY   CCF, 1976
THE BUZZARD   CCF, 1976
SIXTH AND MAIN   National Cinema, 1977
THE STONE BOY   TLC Films/20th Century Fox, 1984
THAT WAS THEN...THIS IS NOW   Paramount, 1985
WHERE THE RIVER RUNS BLACK   MGM/UA, 1986
THE PRINCIPAL   Tri-Star, 1987
YOUNG GUNS   20th Century Fox, 1988
WHEELS OF TERROR (CTF)   Once Upon A Time
Productions/Wilshire Court Productions, 1990

J A M E S   C A M E R O N *
b. August 16, 1954 - Kapuskasing, Ontario, Canada
Agent: Jeff Berg, ICM - Los Angeles, 213/550-4000

PIRANHA II - THE SPAWNING   Saturn International,
1983, Italian-U.S.
THE TERMINATOR   Orion, 1984
ALIENS   20th Century Fox, 1986
THE ABYSS   20th Century Fox, 1989

J U L I A   C A M E R O N
Contact: Writers Guild of America - Los Angeles,
213/550-1000

GOD'S WILL   Power and Light Productions, 1989

K E N   C A M E R O N
Business: Pavilion Films, 117 Blues Point Road, McMahons
Point, NSW, Australia 2060, 02/92-8358

MONKEY GRIP   Cinecom, 1982, Australian
CRIME OF THE DECADE (TF)   1984, Australian
FAST TALKING   Cinecom, 1985, Australian
THE GOOD WIFE   Atlantic Releasing Corporation,
1986, Australian
STRINGER (TF)   co-director with Chris Thomson & Kathy
Mueller, Australian Broadcasting Corporation/Televenture
Film Productions, 1988, Australian-British
THE CLEAN MACHINE (TF)   Kennedy Miller Productions,
1988, Australian

D O N A L D   C A M M E L L *
Home: 9 Rue Delambre, Paris 14, France
Agent: William Morris Agency - Beverly Hills, 213/274-7451

PERFORMANCE   co-director with Nicolas Roeg, Warner
Bros., 1970, British
DEMON SEED   MGM/United Artists, 1977
WHITE OF THE EYE   Palisades Entertainment,
1987, British

JOE CAMP*
b. April 20, 1939 - St. Louis, Missouri
Business: Mulberry Square Productions, One Glen Lakes,
8140 Walnut Hill Lane - Suite 301, Dallas, TX 75231,
214/369-2430

BENJI   Mulberry Square, 1974
HAWMPS   Mulberry Square, 1976
FOR THE LOVE OF BENJI   Mulberry Square, 1978
THE DOUBLE McGUFFIN   Mulberry Square, 1979
OH HEAVENLY DOG   20th Century-Fox, 1980
BENJI THE HUNTED   Buena Vista, 1987

ROY CAMPANELLA II*
Address: 256 S. Robertson Blvd., Beverly Hills, CA 90211,
213/652-6452
Agent: William Morris Agency - Beverly Hills, 213/274-7451

PASSION AND MEMORY (TD)   Morningstar Productions,
1986
BODY OF EVIDENCE (TF)   CBS Entertainment, 1988
QUIET VICTORY: THE CHARLIE WEDEMEYER STORY
(TF) The Landsburg Company, 1988

DOUG CAMPBELL
Agent: Carl Belfor Entertainment Management Company -
Sherman Oaks, 818/994-8095

SEASON OF FEAR   MGM/UA, 1989
ZAPPED AGAIN   ITC Entertainment Group, 1990

GRAEME CAMPBELL
Contact: Academy of Canadian Cinema and Television,
633 Yonge Street - 2nd Floor, Toronto, Ontario
M4Y 1Z9, Canada, 416/967-0315

MURDER ONE   Miramax Films, 1988, Canadian
INTO THE FIRE   Moviestore Entertainment, 1987,
Canadian
BLOOD RELATIONS   Miramax Films, 1988, Canadian
STILL LIFE   SC Entertainment, 1989

MARTIN CAMPBELL
Agent: Alan Greenspan, ICM - Los Angeles, 213/550-4428

MUCK & BRASS (TF)   Central TV, 1979
REILLY - ACE OF SPIES (MS)   co-director with Jim
Goddard, Euston Films Ltd., 1981, British
CHARLIE (MS)   Central TV, 1983, British
EDGE OF DARKNESS (MS)   BBC/Lionheart Television
International, 1985, British
FRANKIE & JOHNNY (TF)   BBC, 1985, British
CRIMINAL LAW   Hemdale, 1988
DEFENSELESS   New Century/Vista, 1989

NORMAN CAMPBELL*
b. 1924 - Los Angeles, California
Address: 20 George Henry Blvd., Willowdale, Ontario
M2J 1E2, Canada, 416/979-3244

THE MAGIC SHOW   Producers Distributing Company,
1983, Canadian

JANE CAMPION
b. Wellington, New Zealand
Contact: New Zealand Film Commission, P.O. Box 11546,
Wellington, New Zealand, 4/859-754

SWEETIE   Avenue Pictures, 1988, Australian
AN ANGEL AT MY TABLE   Circle Releasing, 1990,
New Zealand,   originally made for television

MICHAEL CAMPUS*
Home: 2121 Kress Street, Los Angeles, CA 90046,
213/656-2648
Agent: Mickey Freiberg, The Artists Agency - Los Angeles,
213/277-7779

Z.P.G.   Paramount, 1972
THE MACK   Cinerama Releasing Corporation, 1973
THE EDUCATION OF SONNY CARSON   Paramount, 1974
THE PASSOVER PLOT   Atlas, 1977, U.S.-Israeli

MARIO CAMUS
Contact: Ministry of Culture, Motion Picture Division,
Avenida de Burgos, 5, 28036 Madrid, Spain, 91/202-5351

CON EL VIENTO SOLANO   1965, Spanish
LOS PAJAROS DE BADEN-BADEN   1974, Spanish
LA COLMENA   Agata Films, 1982, Spanish
GUERILLA - LOS DESASTRES DE LA GUERRA
1983, Spanish
THE HOLY INNOCENTS   Samuel Goldwyn Company,
1986, Spanish
LA CASA DE BERNALOA ALBA   1987, Spanish
LA RUSA   Pedro Maso Productions, 1988, Spanish
LA FORJA DE UN REBELDE (MS)   RTVE/Beta Film, 1990,
Spanish-West German

DYAN CANNON*
(Samille Diane Friesen)
b. January 4, 1937 - Tacoma, Washington
Contact: Directors Guild of America - Los Angeles,
213/289-2000

ONE POINT OF VIEW   O.P.V. Productions, 1990

BERNT CAPRA
Contact: Swiss Film Center, Munstergasse 18, 8001 Zurich,
Switzerland, 01/472860

MINDWALK   Mindwalk Productions, 1990, Swiss

FRANK CAPRA*
b. May 18, 1897 - Palermo, Sicily
Home: P.O. Box 98, La Quinta, CA 92253

THE STRONG MAN   First National, 1926
LONG PANTS   First National, 1927
FOR THE LOVE OF MIKE   First National, 1927
THAT CERTAIN THING   Columbia, 1928
SO THIS IS LOVE   Columbia, 1928
THE MATINEE IDOL   Columbia, 1928
THE WAY OF THE STRONG   Columbia, 1928
SAY IT WITH SABLES   Columbia, 1928
SUBMARINE   Columbia, 1928
THE POWER OF THE PRESS   Columbia, 1928
THE YOUNGER GENERATION   Columbia, 1929
THE DONOVAN AFFAIR   Columbia, 1929
FLIGHT   Columbia, 1929
LADIES OF LEISURE   Columbia, 1930

RAIN OR SHINE   Columbia, 1930
DIRIGIBLE   Columbia, 1931
THE MIRACLE WOMAN   Columbia, 1931
PLATINUM BLONDE   Columbia, 1931
FORBIDDEN   Columbia, 1932
AMERICAN MADNESS   Columbia, 1932
THE BITTER TEA OF GENERAL YEN   Columbia, 1933
LADY FOR A DAY ★   Columbia, 1933
IT HAPPENED ONE NIGHT ★★   Columbia, 1934
BROADWAY BILL   Columbia, 1934
MR. DEEDS GOES TO TOWN ★★   Columbia, 1936
LOST HORIZON   Columbia, 1937
YOU CAN'T TAKE IT WITH YOU ★★   Columbia, 1938
MR. SMITH GOES TO WASHINGTON ★   Columbia, 1939
MEET JOHN DOE   Warner Bros., 1941
PRELUDE TO WAR (FD)   U.S. Army, 1942
THE NAZIS STRIKE (FD)   co-director with Anatole Litvak,
    U.S. Army, 1942
DIVIDE AND CONQUER (FD)   co-director with Anatole
    Litvak, U.S. Army, 1943
BATTLE OF BRITAIN (FD)   co-director, U.S. Army, 1943
BATTLE OF CHINA (FD)   co-director with Anatole Litvak,
    U.S. Army, 1943
THE NEGRO SOLDIER (FD)   U.S. Army, 1944
TUNISIAN VICTORY (FD)   co-director with Roy Boulting,
    Army Film Unit, 1944, British
ARSENIC AND OLD LACE   Warner Bros., 1944
KNOW YOUR ENEMY: JAPAN (FD)   co-director with
    Joris Ivens, 1945
TWO DOWN AND ONE TO GO (FD)   1945
IT'S A WONDERFUL LIFE ★   RKO Radio, 1946
STATE OF THE UNION   MGM, 1948
RIDING HIGH   Paramount, 1950
HERE COMES THE GROOM   Paramount, 1951
A HOLE IN THE HEAD   United Artists, 1959
POCKETFUL OF MIRACLES   United Artists, 1961

LEOS CARAX

b. 1961 - Suresnes, France
Contact: French Film Office, 745 Fifth Avenue, New York,
    NY 10151, 212/832-8860

BOY MEETS GIRL   Cinecom/M&R, 1984, French
MAUVAIS SANG   AAA, 1986, French
LES AMANT DU PONT NEUF   FPC/Unite 3/Gaumont,
    1988, French

LAMAR CARD*

b. September 8, 1942 - Lookout Mountain, Tennessee
Business: 7318 Woodrow Wilson Drive, Los Angeles, CA
    90046, 213/851-1128
Agent: Jeff Melnick, Artists and Agents Agency -
    Los Angeles, 213/278-7972

THE CLONES   Premiere International, 1977
SUPERVAN   New World, 1980
DISCO FEVER   Group 1, 1982

JACK CARDIFF

b. September 18, 1914 - Yarmouth, England
Home: 32 Woodland Rise, London N10, England
Agent: Eric L'Epine Smith, 10 Wyndham Place,
    London W1, England, 71/724-0739

WEB OF EVIDENCE   *BEYOND THIS PLACE*   Allied
    Artists, 1959, British
INTENT TO KILL   20th Century-Fox, 1959, British
HOLIDAY IN SPAIN   1960, British
SCENT OF MYSTERY   Todd, 1960, British
SONS AND LOVERS ★   20th Century-Fox, 1960, British

MY GEISHA   Paramount, 1962
THE LION   20th Century-Fox, 1962, British
THE LONG SHIPS   Columbia, 1964, British-Yugoslavian
YOUNG CASSIDY   MGM, 1965, British
THE LIQUIDATOR   MGM, 1966, British
DARK OF THE SUN   *THE MERCENARIES*   MGM, 1968,
    British
THE GIRL ON A MOTORCYCLE   *NAKED UNDER
    LEATHER*   Claridge, 1968, British-French
PENNY GOLD   Scotia-Barber, 1973, British
THE MUTATIONS   Columbia, 1974, British

J. S. CARDONE

Agent: Circle Talent Associates - Beverly Hills, 213/281-3765

THE SLAYER   21st Century Distribution, 1982
THUNDER ALLEY   Cannon, 1985
SHADOWZONE   JGM Enterprises, 1990
A ROW OF CROWS   Propaganda Films, 1991

JOHN (BUD) CARDOS*

Agent: Gerald K. Smith Associates - Burbank, 818/849-5388

SOUL SOLDIER   *THE RED, WHITE AND BLACK*
    Fanfare, 1972
DRAG RACER   Robert Glenn Productions, 1974
KINGDOM OF THE SPIDERS   Dimension, 1977
THE DARK   Film Ventures International, 1979
THE DAY TIME ENDED   Compass International, 1979
OTHER REALMS   CKE International, 1983
NIGHT SHADOWS   *MUTANT*   Artists Releasing
    Corporation/Film Ventures International, 1984
SKELETON COAST   Silvertree Pictures/Walanar Group/
    Breton Film Productions, 1988, British
OUTLAW OF GOR   Cannon, 1989, U.S.-British
ACT OF PIRACY   Blossom Pictures, 1990,
    U.S.-South African

TOPPER CAREW*
(Colin Anthony Carew)

b. July 16, 1943 - Boston, Massachusetts
Contact: Directors Guild of America - Los Angeles,
    213/289-2000

BREAKIN' & ENTERIN'   Rainbow TV Works, 1985

GILLES CARLE

b. 1929 - Maniwaki, Quebec, Canada
Address: 318 Carre St.-Louis, Montreal, Quebec, Canada,
    514/282-1326

LA VIE HEUREUSE DE LEOPOLD Z   NFB, 1965,
    Canadian
PLACE A OLIVIER GUIMOND   Onyx Films, 1966,
    Canadian
PLACE AUX JEROLAS   Onyx Films, 1967, Canadian
LE VIOL D'UNE JEUNE FILLE DOUCE   Onyx-Fournier,
    1968, Canadian
RED   Onyx Films/SMA, 1970, Canadian
LES MALES   Onyx Films/France Films, 1970, Canadian
LES CHEVALIERS   COFCI/ORTF, 1972, Canadian
LE VRAIE NATURE DE BERNADETTE   Les Productions
    Carle-Lamy, 1972, Canadian
LES CORPS CELESTES   Les Productions Carle-Lamy,
    1973, Canadian
LA MORT D'UN BUCHERON   Les Productions Carle-Lamy,
    1973, Canadian
LA TETE DE NORMANDE ST. ONGE   Les Productions
    Carle-Lamy, 1975, Canadian

THE ANGEL AND THE WOMAN   RSL Productions, 1977,
    Canadian
NORMANDE   Fred Baker Films, 1979, Canadian
FANTASTICA   Les Productions du Verseau/El Productions,
    1980, Canadian- French
THE PLOUFFE FAMILY   ICC/Cine-London Productions,
    1981, Canadian
THE GREAT CHESS MOVIE (FD)   co-director with Camille
    Coudari, 1982, Canadian
MARIA CHAPDELAINE   The Movie Store, 1983,
    Canadian-French
THE CRIME OF OVIDE PLOUFFE   co-director with Denys
    Arcand, ICC/Filmax/ Antenne-2/Films A2, 1985,
    Canadian-French
MURDER IN THE FAMILY (MS)   co-director with Denys
    Arcand, ICC/Filmax/ Antenne-2/Films A2, 1985,
    Canadian-French
O PICASSO (TD)   Films Transit, 1985, Canadian
SCALP   Via Le Monde Gilles Carle, 1985, Canadian
LA GUEPE   Via Le Monde Francois Floquet, 1986,
    Canadian
QUEBEC, UN VILLE (FD)   Les Productions Dix-Huit/Films
    Francois Brault, 1988, Canadian

LEWIS JOHN CARLINO*
b. January 1, 1932 - New York, New York
Agent: CAA - Beverly Hills, 213/288-4545

THE SAILOR WHO FELL FROM GRACE WITH THE SEA
    Avco Embassy, 1976, British
THE GREAT SANTINI   *THE ACE*   Orion/Warner Bros.,
    1980
CLASS   Orion, 1983

HENNING CARLSEN
b. June 4, 1927 - Aalborg, Denmark
Address: Puggaardsgade 15, DK-1573, Copenhagen V,
    Denmark, 45/33939291
Contact: Danish Film Institute, St. Soendervoldstraede,
    1419 Copenhagen K, Denmark, 01/576-500

A WORLD OF STRANGERS   Minerva Film/Bent
    Christensen Filmproduktion, 1962, Danish
EPILOGUE   Bent Christensen Filmproduktion/Constantin
    Films, 1963, Danish
THE CATS   National Showmanship, 1964, Swedish
HUNGER   Sigma III, 1966, Danish-Norwegian-Swedish
PEOPLE MEET AND SWEET MUSIC FILLS THE HEART
    Trans-Lux, 1967, Danish-Swedish
WE ARE ALL DEMONS   Nordisk Film/Sandrews/
    Teamfilm/Henning Carlsen Film, 1969, Danish-
    Swedish-Norwegian
ARE YOU AFRAID? OF WHAT?   Henning Carlsen Film,
    1971, Danish
OH TO BE ON THE BANDWAGON!   Henning Carlsen
    Film/Nordisk, 1972, Danish
A HAPPY DIVORCE   CFDC, 1975, French-Danish
WHEN SVANTE DISAPPEARED   Dagmar Filmproduktion,
    1976, Danish
DID SOMEBODY LAUGH?   Dagmar Filmproduktion/
    Sam-Film, 1978, Danish
YOUR MONEY OR YOUR LIFE   Dagmar Filmproduktion,
    1982, Danish
THE WOLF AT THE DOOR   *OVIRI*   International Film
    Marketing, 1986, Danish-French

MARCEL CARNE
b. August 18, 1909 - Paris, France
Contact: French Film Office, 745 Fifth Avenue, New York, NY
    10151, 212/832-8860

NOGENT - ELDORADO DU DIMANCHE (FD)   co-director
    with Michel Sanvoisin, 1929, French
JENNY   1936, French
BIZARRE BIZARRE   *DROLE DE DRAME*   1937, French
PORT OF SHADOWS   Film Alliance, 1938, French
HOTEL DU NORD   1938, French
DAYBREAK   *LE JOUR SE LEVE*   Vog, 1939, French
THE DEVIL'S ENVOYS   *LES VISITEURS DU SOIR*   1942,
    French
CHILDREN OF PARADISE   Tricolore, 1945, French
LES PORTES DE LA NUIT   1946, French
LA MARIE DU PORT   1950, French
JULIETTE OU LA CLE DES SONGES   1951, French
THE ADULTRESS   *THERESE RAQUIN*   Times Film
    Corporation, 1953, French
L'AIR DE PARIS   1954, French
LE PAYS D'OU JE VIENS   1956, French
THE CHEATERS   Continental, 1958, French-Italian
TERRAIN VAGUE   1960, French
DU MOURON POUR LES PETITS OISEAUX   1963, French
TROIS CHAMBRES A MANHATTAN   1965, French
LES JEUNES LOUPS   1968, French
LES ASSASSINS DE L'ORDRE   1971, French
LA MARVEILLEUSE VISITE   1974, French
LA BIBLE (FD)   1976, French

GLENN GORDON CARON*
Agent: CAA - Beverly Hills, 213/288-4545

CLEAN AND SOBER   Warner Bros., 1988

JOHN CARPENTER*
b. January 16, 1948 - Carthage, New York
Agent: Jim Wiatt, ICM - Los Angeles, 213/550-4000

DARK STAR   Jack H. Harris Enterprises, 1974
ASSAULT ON PRECINCT 13   Turtle Releasing
    Corporation, 1976
HALLOWEEN   Compass International, 1978
SOMEONE IS WATCHING ME (TF)   Warner Bros. TV,
    1978
ELVIS (TF)   Dick Clark Productions, 1979
THE FOG   Avco Embassy, 1981
ESCAPE FROM NEW YORK   Avco Embassy, 1981
THE THING   Universal, 1982
CHRISTINE   Columbia, 1983
STARMAN   Columbia, 1984
BIG TROUBLE IN LITTLE CHINA   20th Century Fox, 1986
PRINCE OF DARKNESS   Universal, 1987
THEY LIVE   Universal, 1988

STEPHEN CARPENTER
Agent: Dodie Gold, William Morris Agency - Beverly Hills,
    213/274-7451

THE DORM THAT DRIPPED BLOOD   *PRANKS*   co-director
    with Jeffrey Obrow, Artists Releasing Corporation/Film
    Ventures International, 1982
THE POWER   co-director with Jeffrey Obrow, Artists
    Releasing Corporation/Film Ventures International, 1983
THE KINDRED   co-director with Jeffrey Obrow, FM
    Entertainment, 1987

Ca

T E R R Y   C A R R *
Address: 12424 Wilshire Blvd. - Suite 1000, Los Angeles,
CA 90025, 213/820-8872
Agent: CAA - Los Angeles, 213/277-4545

WELCOME TO 18   American Distribution Group, 1986

D A V I D   C A R R A D I N E *
b. December 8, 1936 - Hollywood, California
Agent: Peter Rawley, ICM - Los Angeles, 213/550-4000

YOU AND ME   Filmmakers International, 1975
AMERICANA   Crown International, 1983

M I C H A E L   C A R R E R A S
b. 1927 - London, England
Contact: British Academy of Film & Television Arts,
195 Piccadilly, London W1, England, 71/734-0022

THE STEEL BAYONET   United Artists, 1958, British
PASSPORT TO CHINA   *VISA TO CANTON*   Columbia,
1961, British
THE SAVAGE GUNS   MGM, 1962, Spanish-U.S.
MANIAC   Columbia, 1963, British
WHAT A CRAZY WORLD   Warner-Pathe, 1963, British
THE CURSE OF THE MUMMY'S TOMB   Columbia,
1965, British
PREHISTORIC WOMEN   *SLAVE GIRLS*   20th Century-
Fox, 1967, British
THE LOST CONTINENT   20th Century-Fox, 1968, British
CALL HIM MR. SHATTER   Avco Embassy, 1975,
British-Hong Kong

J .   L A R R Y   C A R R O L L
b. October 7, 1946

GHOST WARRIOR   *SWORDKILL*   Empire Pictures, 1986

R O B E R T   M A R T I N   C A R R O L L
SONNY BOY   Trans World Entertainment, 1988

W I L L A R D   C A R R O L L
THE RUNESTONE   Runestone Corp., 1990

T H O M A S   C A R T E R *
Agent: CAA - Beverly Hills, 213/288-4545

TRAUMA CENTER (TF)   Glen A. Larson Productions/
Jeremac Productions/20th Century-Fox TV, 1983
CALL TO GLORY (TF)   Tisch-Avnet Productions/
Paramount TV, 1984
MIAMI VICE (TF)   The Michael Mann Company/
Universal TV, 1984
HEART OF THE CITY (TF)   American Flyer TV Ltd./20th
Century Fox TV, 1986
UNDER THE INFLUENCE (TF)   CBS Entertainment, 1986
A YEAR IN THE LIFE (MS)   Universal TV, 1986
EQUAL JUSTICE (TF)   The Thomas Carter Company/
Orion TV, 1990

S T E V E   C A R V E R *
b. April 5, 1945 - Brooklyn, New York
Address: 1010 Pacific Avenue, Venice, CA 90291,
213/396-9905
Agent: Tom Chasin, The Chasin Agency - Beverly Hills,
213/278-7505

THE ARENA   New World, 1974
BIG BAD MAMA   New World, 1974

CAPONE   20th Century-Fox, 1975
DRUM   United Artists, 1976
FAST CHARLIE...THE MOONBEAM RIDER
Universal, 1979
STEEL   *LOOK DOWN AND DIE*   World Northal, 1980
AN EYE FOR AN EYE   Avco Embassy, 1981
LONE WOLF McQUADE   Orion, 1983
OCEANS OF FIRE (TF)   Catalina Production Group, 1986
JOCKS   Crown International, 1987
BULLETPROOF   CineTel Films, 1987
RIVER OF DEATH   Cannon, 1989, British

R O N   C A S D E N *
Agent: Laura Sutton, The Agency - Los Angeles,
213/551-3000

CAMPUS MAN   Paramount, 1987

N I C K   C A S T L E *
b. September 21, 1947 - Los Angeles, California
Address: 760 N. La Cienega Blvd., Los Angeles, CA 90069,
213/652-0222
Agent: CAA - Beverly Hills, 213/288-4545

TAG   New World, 1982
THE LAST STARFIGHTER   Universal, 1984
THE BOY WHO COULD FLY   20th Century Fox, 1986
TAP   Tri-Star, 1989

H O I T E   C A S T O N *
Home: 3589 Multiview Drive, Los Angeles, CA 90068,
213/851-0606
Agent: Tim Stone, Stone Manners Agency - Los Angeles,
213/275-9599

THE DIRT BIKE KID   Concorde/Cinema Group, 1986

G I L B E R T   C A T E S *
b. June 6, 1934 - New York, New York
Business: Film-Jamel Productions, 195 S. Beverly Drive -
Suite 412, Beverly Hills CA 90212, 213/273-7773
Agent: William Morris Agency - Beverly Hills, 213/274-7451

RINGS AROUND THE WORLD (FD)   Columbia, 1967
I NEVER SANG FOR MY FATHER   Columbia, 1970
TO ALL MY FRIENDS ON SHORE (TF)   Jemmin & Jamel
Productions, 1972
SUMMER WISHES, WINTER DREAMS   Columbia, 1973
THE AFFAIR (TF)   Spelling-Goldberg Productions, 1973
ONE SUMMER LOVE   *DRAGONFLY*   American
International, 1976
JOHNNY, WE HARDLY KNEW YE (TF)   Talent Associates/
Jamel Productions, 1977
THE PROMISE   Universal, 1979
THE LAST MARRIED COUPLE IN AMERICA
Universal, 1980
OH, GOD! BOOK II   Warner Bros., 1980
COUNTRY GOLD (TF)   CBS Entertainment, 1982
HOBSON'S CHOICE (TF)   CBS Entertainment, 1983
BURNING RAGE (TF)   Gilbert Cates Productions, 1984
CONSENTING ADULT (TF) ☆   Starger Company/David
Lawrence and Ray Aghayan Productions, 1985
CHILD'S CRY (TF)   Shoot the Moon Enterprises/Phoenix
Entertainment Group, 1986
BACKFIRE   New Century/Vista, 1987
FATAL JUDGMENT (TF)   Jack Farren Productions/Group W
Productions, 1988
MY FIRST LOVE (TF)   The Avnet-Kerner Company, 1988
DO YOU KNOW THE MUFFIN MAN? (TF) ☆   The
Avnet-Kerner Company, 1989

JOSEPH CATES*

b. 1924
Business: Cates Films, 57 East 74th Street, New York, NY
    10021, 212/517-7100

GIRL OF THE NIGHT   Warner Bros., 1960
WHO KILLED TEDDY BEAR?   Magna, 1965
FAT SPY   Magna, 1966

DON CATO

DIXIE LANES   SC Entertainment, 1987

MICHAEL CATON-JONES

b. Broxburn, Scotland
Agent: CAA - Beverly Hills, 213/288-4545

SCANDAL   Miramax Films, 1989, British
MEMPHIS BELLE   Warner Bros., 1990, U.S.-British

LILIANA CAVANI

b. January 12, 1937 - Carpi, Italy
Home: via Filangeri, 4, Rome, Italy, 06/360-1832

FRANCESCO D'ASSISI (TF)   1966, Italian
GALILEO   Fenice Cinematografica/Rizzoli Film/Kinozenter,
    1968, Italian-Bulgarian
THE YEAR OF THE CANNIBALS   I CANNIBALI
    American International, 1969, Italian
L'OSPITE   1971, Italian
THE NIGHT PORTER   Avco Embassy, 1974, Italian
MILAREPA   Lotar Film, 1974, Italian
BEYOND GOOD AND EVIL   International Showcase,
    1977, Italian-French-West German
LA PELLE   Triumph/Columbia, 1981, Italian-French
THE SECRET BEYOND THE DOOR   Gaumont,
    1982, Italian
THE BERLIN AFFAIR   Cannon, 1985,
    Italian-West German
FRANCESCO   Karol Film/RAI/Royal Film, 1989,
    Italian-West German

FELIPE CAZALS

b. 1937 - Mexico City, Mexico
Contact: Azteca Films, 555 N. La Brea Avenue, P.O. Box
    36095, Hollywood, CA 90036, 213/938-2413

LA MANZANA DE LA DISCORDIA   Azteca Films,
    1968, Mexican
FAMILIARIDADES   Azteca Films, 1969, Mexican
EMILIANO ZAPATA   Azteca Films, 1970, Mexican
EL JARDIN DE LA TIA ISABEL   Azteca Films, 1971,
    Mexican
AQUELLOS ANOS   Azteca Films, 1972, Mexican
LOS QUE VIVEN DONDE SOPLA EL VIENTO SUAVE
    Azteca Films, 1973, Mexican
CANOA   Azteca Films, 1975, Mexican
EL APANDO   Azteca Films, 1975, Mexican
LAS POQUIANCHIS   Azteca Films, 1976, Mexican
LA GUERA RODRIGUEZ   Azteca Films, 1977, Mexican
EL ANO DE LA PESTE   Azteca Films, 1978, Mexican
BAJO LA METRALLA   Azteca Films, 1983, Mexican
LOS MOTIVOS DE LUZ   Producciones Chimalistac,
    1985, Mexican
CUENTOS DE LA MADRUGATA   Producciones
    Chimalistac, 1985, Mexican
EL TRES DE COPAS   Casablanca Films/Conacine,
    1987, Mexican
LO DEL CESAR   Casablanca Films/Television Espanola,
    1987, Mexican

JAMES CELLAN-JONES*

b. July 13, 1931 - Swansea, Wales
Home: 19 Cumberland Road, Kew, Surrey TW9 3HJ,
    England, 71/940-8742
Agent: William Morris Agency - Beverly Hills, 213/274-7451

THE NELSON AFFAIR   A BEQUEST TO THE NATION
    Universal, 1973, British
CAESAR AND CLEOPATRA (TF)   NBC-TV, 1976,
    U.S.-British
SCHOOL PLAY (TF)   BBC, 1979, British
THE DAY CHRIST DIED (TF)   Martin Manulis Productions/
    20th Century-Fox TV, 1980
THE KINGFISHER (TF)   1982, British
A FINE ROMANCE (TF)   1982, British
SLEEPS SIX (TF)   BBC, 1984, British
OXBRIDGE BLUES (TF)   BBC, 1985, British
SLIP-UP (TF)   BBC/Polymuse, 1986, British
FORTUNES OF WAR (MS)   BBC/WGBH-TV/Primetime TV,
    1987, British-U.S.

CLAUDE CHABROL

b. June 24, 1930 - Paris, France
Agent: Cineart, 31 Avenue Champs Elysees, 75008 Paris,
    France, 4/256-3574
Contact: French Film Office, 745 Fifth Avenue, New York,
    NY 10151, 212/832-8860

LE BEAU SERGE   United Motion Picture Organization,
    1958, French
THE COUSINS   Films Around the World, 1959, French
LEDA   WEB OF PASSION/A DOUBLE TOUR   Times,
    1959, French
LES BONNES FEMMES   Robert Hakim, 1960,
    French-Italian
LES GODELUREAUX   Cocinor-Marceau, 1961,
    French-Italian
SEVEN CAPITAL SINS   co-director with Jean-Luc Godard,
    Roger Vadim, Sylvaine Dhomme, Edouard Molinaro,
    Philippe De Broca, Jacques Demy, Marie-Jose Nat,
    Dominique Paturel, Jean-Marc Tennberg & Perrette
    Pradier, Embassy, 1962, French-Italian
L'OEIL DU MALIN   Lux Film, 1962, French-Italian
OPHELIA   New Line Cinema, 1962, French-Italian
LANDRU   Embassy, 1963, French-Italian
LES PLUS BELLES ESCROQUERIES DU MONDE
    co-director, 1964, French-Italian-Japanese
LE TIGRE AIME LA CHAIR FRAICHE   Gaumont, 1964,
    French-Italian
PARIS VU PAR...   co-director, 1965, French
MARIE-CHANTAL CONTRE LE DOCTEUR KHA   SNC,
    1965, French-Italian- Moroccan
LE TIGRE SE PARFUME À LA DYNAMITE   Gaumont,
    1965, French-Spanish-Italian
LA LIGNE DE DEMARCATION   CCFC, 1966, French
THE CHAMPAGNE MURDERS   LE SCANDALE   Universal,
    1967, French
LA ROUTE DE CORINTHE   CCFC, 1967, French-Italian-
    West German
LES BICHES   VGC, 1968, French-Italian
LA FEMME INFIDELE   Allied Artists, 1968, French-Italian
THIS MAN MUST DIE   Allied Artists, 1969, French-Italian
LE BOUCHER   Cinerama Releasing Corporation, 1969,
    French-Italian
LA RUPTURE   New Line Cinema, 1970,
    French-Italian-Belgian
JUST BEFORE NIGHTFALL   Libra, 1971, French-Italian
TEN DAYS' WONDER   Levitt-Pickman, 1971, French
HIGH HEELS   DOCTEUR POPAUL   Les Films La Boetie,
    1972, French-Italian

WEDDING IN BLOOD   New Line Cinema, 1973,
    French-Italian
DE GREY - LE BANC DE DESOLATION (TF)
    1973, French
THE NADA GANG   *NADA*   New Line Cinema, 1974,
    French-Italian
UNE PARTIE DE PLAISIR   Joseph Green Pictures,
    1975, French
DIRTY HANDS   *LES INNOCENTS AUX MAIN SALES*
    New Line Cinema, 1975, French-Italian-West German
LES MAGICIENS   1975, French
FOLIES BOURGEOISES   FFCM, 1976, French-Italian-
    West German
ALICE OU LA DERNIERE FUGUE   Filmel-PHPG, 1977,
    French
LES LIENS DE SANG   Filmcorp, 1978, Canadian-French
VIOLETTE   *VIOLETTE NOZIERE*   New Yorker,
    1978, French
FANTOMAS (TF)   1979, French
LE CHEVAL D'ORGEUIL   Planfilm, 1980, French
MADAME LE JUGE (TF)   1980, French
LE SYSTEME DU DOCTEUR GOUDRON ET DU
    PROFESSEUR PLUME (TF) FR3/Films du Triangle/
    TCV, 1981, French-Mexican
LES AFFINITES ELECTIVES (TF)   FR3/Telecip/Galaxy
    Film Produktion, 1982, French-West German
LA DANSE DE MORT (TF)   FR3/Technisonor/SFP,
    1982, French
LES FANTOMES DU CHAPELIER   Gaumont,
    1982, French
THE BLOOD OF OTHERS (CMS)   HBO Premiere Films/
    ICC/Filmax Productions, 1984, Canadian-French
POULET AU VINAIGRE   MK2 Difussion, 1985, French
INSPECTEUR LAVARDIN   MK Difussion, 1986, French
MASQUES   MK2/Films A2, 1987, French
LE CRI DU HIBOU   UIP, 1988, French-Italian
STORY OF WOMEN   MK2 Productions USA/New Yorker,
    1988, French
QUIET DAYS IN CLICHY   AZ Films Produzione/Italfrance/
    Direkt Films, 1990, Italian-French-West German
DR. M   N.E.F./Anthea/Ellepi, 1990, French-
    West German-Italian

DON CHAFFEY*
b. August 5, 1917 - England
Home: 7020 La Presa Drive, Los Angeles, CA 90068,
    213/851-0391
Agent: Ronald Leif, Contemporary Artists - Beverly Hills,
    213/278-8250

THE MYSTERIOUS POACHER   General Film Distributors,
    1954, British
THE CASE OF THE MISSING SCENE   General Film
    Distributors, 1951, British
SKID KIDS   Associated British Film Distributors/Children's
    Film Foundation, 1953, British
TIME IS MY ENEMY   Independent Film Distributors,
    1954, British
THE SECRET TENT   British Lion, 1956, British
THE GIRL IN THE PICTURE   Eros, 1957, British
THE FLESH IS WEAK   DCA, 1957, British
A QUESTION OF ADULTERY   Eros, 1958, British
THE MAN UPSTAIRS   Kingsley International, 1958, British
DANGER WITHIN   British Lion, 1959, British
DENTIST IN THE CHAIR   Ajay, 1960, British
LIES MY FATHER TOLD ME   Eire, 1960, British
NEARLY A NASTY ACCIDENT   Universal, 1961, British
GREYFRIARS BOBBY   Buena Vista, 1961, U.S.-British
A MATTER OF WHO   Herts Lion, 1962, British
THE PRINCE AND THE PAUPER   Buena Vista, 1962,
    U.S.-British

THE WEBSTER BOY   RFI, 1963, British
THE HORSE WITHOUT A HEAD   Buena Vista, 1963,
    British
JASON AND THE ARGONAUTS   Columbia, 1963, British
THEY ALL DIED LAUGHING   *A JOLLY BAD FELLOW*
    Continental, 1963, British
THE THREE LIVES OF THOMASINA   Buena Vista, 1963,
    British-U.S.
THE CROOKED ROAD   7 Arts, 1965, British-Yugoslavian
ONE MILLION YEARS B.C.   20th Century-Fox,
    1967, British
THE VIKING QUEEN   American International, 1967, British
A TWIST OF SAND   United Artists, 1968, British
CREATURES THE WORLD FORGOT   Columbia,
    1971, British
CLINIC XCLUSIVE   Doverton, 1972, British
CHARLEY-ONE-EYE   Paramount, 1973, British
THE TERROR OF SHEBA   *PERSECUTION*   Blueberry Hill,
    1974, British
THE FOURTH WISH   South Australian Film Corporation,
    1975, Australian
HARNESS FEVER   Walt Disney Productions, 1976,
    Australian
RIDE A WILD PONY   *BORN TO RUN*   Buena Vista, 1976,
    U.S.-Australian
SURF   Trans-Atlantic Enterprises, 1977
PETE'S DRAGON   Buena Vista, 1977
SHIMMERING LIGHT (TF)   Australian Broadcasting
    Commission/Trans-Atlantic Enterprises, 1978, Australian
THE MAGIC OF LASSIE   International Picture Show, 1978
THE GIFT OF LOVE (TF)   Osmond Productions, 1978
C.H.O.M.P.S.   American International, 1979
CASINO (TF)   Trellis Productions/Aaron Spelling
    Productions, 1980
INTERNATIONAL AIRPORT (TF)   co-director with Charles
    S. Dubin, Aaron Spelling Productions, 1985
MISSION IMPOSSIBLE - THE GOLDEN SERPENT (TF)
    Paramount TV, 1989

EVERETT CHAMBERS*
b. August 19, 1926 - Montrose, California
Agent: David Shapira & Associates - Sherman Oaks,
    818/906-0322

RUN ACROSS THE RIVER   Omat Corporation, 1959
THE LOLLIPOP COVER   Continental, 1964

GREGG CHAMPION*
Agent: ICM - Los Angeles, 213/550-4000

SHORT TIME   20th Century Fox, 1990

JACKIE CHAN
(Chen Yuan-Long)
b. 1954 - Hong Kong
Business: c/o Golden Harvest (HK) Ltd., 8 Hammer Hill
    Road, Hong Kong

THE FEARLESS HYENA   1979, Hong Kong
YOUNG MASTER   Golden Harvest, 1980, Hong Kong
DRAGON LORD   Golden Harvest, 1982, Hong Kong
PROJECT A   Golden Harvest, 1983, Hong Kong
POLICE STORY   Golden Harvest, 1985, Hong Kong
THE ARMOUR OF GOD   Golden Harvest, 1986,
    Hong Kong
PROJECT A (PART II)   Golden Harvest/Golden Way
    Productions, 1987, Hong Kong
THE BROTHERS   Golden Way Productions, 1987,
    Hong Kong

POLICE STORY - PART II   Golden Harvest, 1988,
   Hong Kong
MR. CANTON AND LADY ROSE   Golden Harvest, 1989,
   Hong Kong

BAE CHANG-HO
b. May 10, 1953 - Taegu, Korea

PEOPLE IN SLUM AREA   1982, South Korean
THE IRON MEN   1982, South Korean
TROPICAL FLOWER   1983, South Korean
WHALE HUNTER   1984, South Korean
WARM IT WAS THAT WINTER   1984, South Korean
DEEP BLUE NIGHT   1984, South Korean
WHALE HUNTER II   1985, South Korean
HWANG JIN-I   1986, South Korean
OUR SWEET DAYS OF YOUTH   1987, South Korean

MATTHEW CHAPMAN*
b. September 2, 1950
Home: 8003 Jovenita Canyon Road, Los Angeles, CA
   90046, 213/650-5372
Agent: CAA - Beverly Hills, 213/288-4545

HUSSY   Watchgrove Ltd., 1980, British
STRANGERS KISS   Orion Classics, 1984
SLOW BURN (CTF)   Joel Schumacher Productions/
   Universal Pay TV, 1986
HEART OF MIDNIGHT   Virgin Vision, 1988

MICHAEL CHAPMAN*
b. November 21, 1935 - Maine
Agent: Leading Artists - Beverly Hills, 213/858-1999

ALL THE RIGHT MOVES   20th Century-Fox, 1983
THE CLAN OF THE CAVE BEAR   Warner Bros., 1986
THE ANNIHILATOR (TF)   Universal TV, 1986

AMIN Q. CHAUDHRI
Business: Continental Film Group, 330 West 42nd Street,
   New York, NY 10036, 212/564-1828

ONCE AGAIN   Continental Film Group, 1986
TIGER WARSAW   Sony Pictures, 1988
AN UNREMARKABLE LIFE   SVS Films, 1989

MEHDI CHAREF
b. 1952 - Algeria
Contact: French Film Office, 745 Fifth Avenue, New York,
   NY 10151, 212/832-8860

TEA IN THE HAREM   *LE THE AU HAREM D'ARCHIMEDE*
   M&R Films/Cinecom, 1985, French
MISS MONA   AAA, 1987, French
CAMOMILLE   K.G. Productions, 1988, French

DAVID CHASE*
Agent: InterTalent - Los Angeles, 213/556-2727

ALMOST GROWN (TF)   Universal TV/Atlantis Films, 1988

JEREMIAH S. CHECHIK*
b. Montreal, Quebec, Canada
Contact: Directors Guild of America - Los Angeles,
   213/289-2000

NATIONAL LAMPOON'S CHRISTMAS VACATION   Warner
   Bros., 1989

DOUGLAS CHEEK*
Home: 454 West 25th Street, New York, NY 10001,
   213/989-6257

C.H.U.D.   New World, 1984

KAIGE CHEN
(See Chen KAIGE)

ROBERT CHENAULT*
Address: P.O. Box 750, San Pedro, CA 90233,
   213/548-4239
Agent: Barry Perelman Agency - Los Angeles, 213/274-5999

DECEPTIONS (TF)   co-director with Melville Shavelson,
   Louis Rudolph Productions/ Consolidated Productions/
   Columbia TV, 1985, U.S.-British

JOHN R. CHERRY, III
DR. OTTO AND THE RIDDLE OF THE GLOOM BEAM
   1985
ERNEST GOES TO CAMP   Buena Vista, 1987
ERNEST SAVES CHRISTMAS   Buena Vista, 1988
ERNEST GOES TO JAIL   Buena Vista, 1990

STANLEY Z. CHERRY*
Address: 11222 Ventura Blvd., Studio City, CA 91604,
   818/760-2804
Business Manager: Steven Kattleman, Cooper, Epstein,
   Hurewitz, 9465 Wilshire Blvd., Beverly Hills, CA 90212,
   213/278-1111

BRING ME THE HEAD OF DOBIE GILLIS (TF)   20th
   Century Fox TV, 1988

LIONEL CHETWYND
b. 1940 - London, England
Agent: Alan Berger, ICM - Los Angeles, 213/550-4000

MORNING COMES   1975, Canadian
TWO SOLITUDES   New World-Mutual, 1978, Canadian
THE HANOI HILTON   Cannon, 1987
SO PROUDLY WE HAIL (TF)   Lionel Chetwynd Productions/
   CBS Entertainment, 1990

COLIN CHILVERS*
b. 1945 - England
Home: P.O. Box 135, Ridgeway, Ontario L0S 1NO, Canada,
   416/894-2963
Agent: William Morris Agency - Beverly Hills, 213/274-7451

WAR OF THE WORLDS (TF)   Triumph Entertainment
   Corporation of Canada/Ten-Four Productions/Paramount
   TV, 1988, Canadian-U.S.
MOONWALKER   co-director with Jerry Kramer, Warner
   Bros., 1988

STEPHEN CHIODO*
Home: 425 S. Flower Street, Burbank, CA 91502,
   818/842-5656

KILLER KLOWNS FROM OUTER SPACE   Trans World
   Entertainment, 1988

PARK CHOI-SU
b. November 20, 1947 - Chongdo, Kyongsangbukdo, Korea

THE RAIN ONLY WHEN AT NIGHT   1979, South Korean

THE PAINFUL MATURITY   1980, South Korean
THE WILD DOG   1982, South Korean
THE BELL OF NIRVANA   1983, South Korean
MOTHER   1985, South Korean
THE PILLAR OF MIST   1986, South Korean

MARVIN J. CHOMSKY*
b. May 23, 1929 - New York, New York
Agent: The David B. Cohen Talent Agency, Inc.,
   2049 Century Park East - Suite 3700, Los Angeles, CA
   90067, 213/201-8779

ASSAULT ON THE WAYNE (TF)   Paramount TV, 1971
MONGO'S BACK IN TOWN (TF)   Bob Banner
   Associates, 1971
EVEL KNIEVEL   Fanfare, 1972
FIREBALL FORWARD (TF)   20th Century-Fox TV, 1972
FAMILY FLIGHT (TF)   Universal TV, 1973
FEMALE ARTILLERY (TF)   Universal TV, 1973
THE MAGICIAN (TF)   Paramount TV, 1973
MRS. SUNDANCE (TF)   20th Century-Fox TV, 1974
THE FBI STORY: THE FBI VERSUS ALVIN KARPIS,
   PUBLIC ENEMY NUMBER ONE (TF)   QM Productions/
   Warner Bros. TV, 1974
ATTACK ON TERROR: THE FBI VS. THE KU KLUX
   KLAN (TF)   QM Productions, 1975
MACKINTOSH AND T.J.   Penland, 1975
LIVE A LITTLE, STEAL A LOT   MURPH THE SURF
   American International, 1975
KATE McSHANE (TF)   Paramount TV, 1975
BRINK'S: THE GREAT ROBBERY (TF)   QM Productions/
   Warner Bros. TV, 1976
A MATTER OF WIFE...AND DEATH (TF)   Columbia TV,
   1976
LAW AND ORDER (TF)   Paramount TV, 1976
ROOTS (MS) ☆   co-director with David Greene, John
   Erman & Gilbert Moses, Wolper Productions, 1977
LITTLE LADIES OF THE NIGHT (TF)   Spelling-Goldberg
   Productions, 1977
DANGER IN PARADISE (TF)   Filmways, 1977
HOLOCAUST (MS) ☆☆   Titus Productions, 1978
GOOD LUCK, MISS WYCKOFF   Bel Air/Gradison, 1979
HOLLOW IMAGE (TF)   Titus Productions, 1979
DOCTOR FRANKEN (TF)   co-director with Jeff Lieberman,
   Titus Productions/Janus Productions, 1980
ATTICA (TF) ☆☆   ABC Circle Films, 1980
KING CRAB (TF)   Titus Productions, 1980
EVITA PERON (TF)   Hartwest Productions/Zephyr
   Productions, 1981
MY BODY, MY CHILD (TF)   Titus Productions, 1982
INSIDE THE THIRD REICH (TF) ☆☆   ABC Circle
   Films, 1982
I WAS A MAIL ORDER BRIDE (TF)   Jaffe Productions/
   Tuxedo Limited Productions/MGM TV, 1982
TANK   Universal, 1984
NAIROBI AFFAIR (TF)   Robert Halmi, Inc., 1984
ROBERT KENNEDY AND HIS TIMES (MS)   Chris-Rose
   Productions/Columbia TV, 1985
PETER THE GREAT (MS)   co-director with Lawrence
   Schiller, PTG Productions/ NBC Productions, 1986
THE DELIBERATE STRANGER (TF)   Stuart Phoenix
   Productions/Lorimar-Telepictures, 1986
ANASTASIA: THE MYSTERY OF ANNA (TF)   Telecom
   Entertainment/ Consolidated Productions/Reteitalia,
   1986, U.S.-Italian
ANGEL IN GREEN (TF)   Aligre Productions/Taft Hardy
   Group, 1987, U.S.-New Zealand
BILLIONAIRE BOYS CLUB (TF) ☆   Donald March/
   Gross-Weston Productions/ ITC Productions, 1987

BROTHERHOOD OF THE ROSE (TF)   NBC
   Productions, 1989
STRAUSS DYNASTY (MS)   MR TV-Film/ORF/ECA, 1990,
   Austrian-West German

THOMAS CHONG*
b. May 24, 1938 - Edmonton, Canada
Business Manager: Joseph Mannis, Mannis & Barbakow,
   11661 San Vicente Blvd. - Suite 1010, Los Angeles, CA
   90049, 213/476-7311

THE NEXT CHEECH & CHONG MOVIE   Universal, 1980
CHEECH & CHONG'S NICE DREAMS   Columbia, 1981
CHEECH & CHONG: STILL SMOKIN   Paramount, 1983
CHEECH & CHONG'S THE CORSICAN BROTHERS
   Orion, 1984
FAR OUT MAN   New Line Cinema, 1990

JOYCE CHOPRA*
Home: 7 North, Kent, CT 06757
Agent: Alan Greenspan, ICM - Los Angeles, 213/550-4428

SMOOTH TALK   Spectrafilm, 1985
THE LEMON SISTERS   Miramax Films, 1989

MOHAMED CHOUIKH
b. Algeria

RUPTURE   1982, Algerian
EL KALAA   CAAIC, 1988, Algerian

ELIE CHOURAQUI
b. 1950 - Paris, France
Contact: French Film Office, 745 Fifth Avenue, New York,
   NY 10151, 212/832-8860

MON PREMIER AMOUR   1978, French
QU'EST-CE QUI FAIT COURIR DAVID?   1982, French
LOVE SONGS   PAROLES ET MUSIQUE   Spectrafilm,
   1984, Canadian-French
MAN ON FIRE   Tri-Star, 1987, Italian-French
MISS MISSOURI   AAA, 1990, French

CHRISTINE CHOY
b. New York, New York

FROM SPIKES TO SPINDLES (FD)   1976
TO LOVE, HONOR AND OBEY (FD)   1980
BITTER SWEET SURVIVAL (FD)   1981
MISSISSIPPI TRIANGLE (FD)   1983
WHO KILLED VINCENT CHIN? (FD)   co-director with
   Renee Tajima, 1988
BEST HOTEL ON SKID ROW (FD)   co-director with
   Renee Tajima, 1990

NAT CHRISTIAN
CALIFORNIA CASANOVA   Rumar Films, 1990
CLUB FED   Rumar Productions, 1990

ROGER CHRISTIAN
b. February 25, 1944 - London, England
Address: 24 Bloemfontein Avenue, London W12, England
Agent: Duncan Heath & Associates, 162 Wardour Street,
   London W1, England, 71/439-1471

THE SENDER   Paramount, 1982, U.S.-British
STARSHIP   LORCA AND THE OUTLAWS   Cinema Group,
   1985, British-Australian

BYRON CHUDNOW*
Home: 918 S. Westgate Avenue - Suite 4, Los Angeles, CA
    90049, 213/820-1066

THE DOBERMAN GANG   Dimension, 1973
THE DARING DOBERMANS   Dimension, 1973
THE AMAZING DOBERMANS   Golden, 1976

VERA CHYTILOVA
b. 1929 - Ostava, Czechoslovakia
Contact: Czechoslovak Filmexport, Department of
    Coproductions & Service Facilities, Vaclavske
    Namesti 28, 111-45 Prague 1, Czechoslovakia,
    tel.: 268-412

ANOTHER WAY OF LIFE   1963, Czech
PEARLS AT THE BOTTOM   co-director, 1965, Czech
DAISIES   1966, Czech
THE APPLE GAME   1976, Czech
PANEL STORY   1979, Czech
CALAMITY   1980, Czech
CHYTILOVA VERSUS FORMAN (FD)   1981, Czech
THE VERY LATE AFTERNOON OF A FAUN   1984, Czech
WOLF'S LAIR   1986, Czech
THE JESTER AND THE QUEEN   Barrandov Film Studio,
    1988, Czech
SNOWBALL REACTION   Barrandov Film Studio,
    1989, Czech

GERARD CICCORITTI
b. August 5, 1956 - Canada
Business: Lightshow Communications, Inc., 19 Tennis
    Crescent - Suite 8, Toronto, Ontario M4K 1J4, Canada,
    416/465-6465

PSYCHO GIRLS   Cannon, 1985, Canadian
GRAVEYARD SHIFT   Shapiro/Virgin, 1986, Canadian
LOVE AND DIE   Cinema Ventures, 1988, Canadian
GRAVEYARD SHIFT II   Virgin Vision, 1989, Canadian
A WHISPER TO A SCREAM   Distant Horizon/Lighthouse
    Communications, 1989, Canadian

MATT CIMBER
(Matteo Ottaviano)
SINGLE ROOM FURNISHED   Crown International, 1968
MAN AND WIFE   1970
CALLIOPE   Moonstone, 1971
THE BLACK SIX   Cinemation, 1974
THE CANDY TANGERINE MAN   Moonstone, 1975
GEMINI AFFAIR   Moonstone, 1975
LADY COCOA   Dimension, 1975
THE WITCH WHO CAME FROM THE SEA
    Moonstone, 1976
BUTTERFLY   Analysis, 1981
FAKE OUT   Analysis, 1983
A TIME TO DIE   Almi Films, 1983
HUNDRA   Film Ventures International, 1984, Spanish
YELLOW HAIR AND THE FORTRESS OF GOLD   Crown
    International, 1984, Spanish
G.L.O.W.   Film Ventures International, 1987

MICHAEL CIMINO*
b. 1943
Agent: Jeff Berg, ICM - Los Angeles, 213/550-4000
Attorney: Barry Hirsch, Armstrong & Hirsch, 1888 Century
    Park East, Los Angeles, CA 90067, 213/553-0305

THUNDERBOLT AND LIGHTFOOT   United Artists, 1974
THE DEER HUNTER ★★   Universal, 1978

HEAVEN'S GATE   United Artists, 1980
YEAR OF THE DRAGON   MGM/UA, 1985
THE SICILIAN   20th Century Fox, 1987
DESPERATE HOURS   MGM/UA, 1990

SOULEYMANE CISSÉ
b. April 21, 1940 - Bamako, Mali

DEN MUSO   1975, Malian
BAARA   1979, Malian
THE WIND   1982, Malian
BRIGHTNESS   Island Pictures, 1987, Malian

RICHARD CIUPKA
b. 1950 - Liege, Belgium
Address: 71 Cornwall Street, Montreal, Quebec H3P 1M6,
    Canada, 514/738-9996

CURTAINS   directed under pseudonym of Jonathan
    Stryker, Jensen Farley Pictures, 1983, Canadian

BOB CLARK*
b. 1941 - New Orleans, Louisiana
Home: 1040 Country Club Lane, Escondido, CA 92026,
    619/741-5501
Agent: CAA - Beverly Hills, 213/288-4545
Business Manager: Harold D. Cohen, Associated
    Management Company, 9200 Sunset Blvd., Los Angeles,
    CA, 213/550-0570

DEATHDREAM   1972, Canadian
CHILDREN SHOULDN'T PLAY WITH DEAD THINGS
    Gemini Film, 1972, Canadian
DEATH OF NIGHT   Europix International, 1974, Canadian
BLACK CHRISTMAS   *SILENT NIGHT, EVIL NIGHT/
    STRANGER IN THE HOUSE*   Warner Bros.,
    1975, Canadian
BREAKING POINT   20th Century-Fox, 1976, Canadian
MURDER BY DECREE   Avco Embassy, 1979,
    Canadian-British
TRIBUTE   20th Century-Fox, 1980, U.S.-Canadian
PORKY'S   20th Century-Fox, 1982, U.S.-Canadian
PORKY'S II: THE NEXT DAY   20th Century-Fox, 1983,
    U.S.-Canadian
A CHRISTMAS STORY   MGM/UA, 1983, Canadian
RHINESTONE   20th Century Fox, 1984
TURK 182   20th Century Fox, 1985
FROM THE HIP   DEG, 1987
LOOSE CANNONS   Tri-Star, 1990

BRUCE CLARK
NAKED ANGELS   Favorite, 1969
THE SKI BUM   Avco Embassy, 1971
HAMMER   United Artists, 1972
GALAXY OF TERROR   New World, 1981

FRANK C. CLARK
BEYOND THE REEF   Universal, 1981

GREYDON CLARK
TOM   Four Star International, 1973
BLACK SHAMPOO   Dimension, 1976
THE BAD BUNCH   Dimension, 1976
SATAN'S CHEERLEADERS   World Amusement, 1977
HI-RIDERS   Dimension, 1978
ANGELS BRIGADE   Arista, 1980
WITHOUT WARNING   Filmways, 1980
THE RETURN   1981
JOYSTICKS   Jensen Farley Pictures, 1982

WACKO   Jensen Farley Pictures, 1983
FINAL JUSTICE   Arista, 1985
UNINVITED   Amazing Movies, 1988
SKINHEADS   Amazing Movies, 1989
OUT OF SIGHT, OUT OF MIND   Spectrum
   Entertainment, 1990
THE FORBIDDEN DANCE   Columbia, 1990

JAMES B. CLARK*
Home: 10051-5 Valley Circle Blvd., Chatsworth, CA
   91311, 818/998-0962

UNDER FIRE   20th Century-Fox, 1957
SIERRA BARON   20th Century-Fox, 1958
VILLA!   20th Century-Fox, 1958
THE SAD HORSE   20th Century-Fox, 1959
A DOG OF FLANDERS   20th Century-Fox, 1960
ONE FOOT IN HELL   20th Century-Fox, 1960
THE BIG SHOW   20th Century-Fox, 1961,
   U.S.-West German
MISTY   20th Century-Fox, 1961
FLIPPER   MGM, 1963
DRUMS OF AFRICA   MGM, 1963
ISLAND OF THE BLUE DOLPHINS   20th Century-
   Fox, 1964
AND NOW MIGUEL   Paramount, 1966
MY SIDE OF THE MOUNTAIN   Paramount, 1969
THE LITTLE ARK   National General, 1972

LAWRENCE GORDON CLARK
Contact: British Academy of Film & Television Arts, 195
   Piccadilly, London W1, England, 71/734-0022

ROMANCE ON THE ORIENT EXPRESS (TF)   Frank von
   Zerneck Productions/ Yorkshire TV, 1985, U.S.-British
JAMAICA INN (TF)   HTV/Metromedia Producers
   Corporation/United Media Ltd./ Jamaica Inn Productions,
   1985, British-U.S.
MURDER BY THE BOOK (TF)   TVS Ltd./Benton Evans
   Productions, 1986, British
CAPTAIN JAMES COOK (MS)   Australian Broadcasting
   Corporation/Revcom, 1987, Australian
ACT OF BETRAYAL (TF)   Griffin Productions/TVS/
   Australian Broadcasting Corporation/RTE/Strongbow,
   1988, British-Australian
MAGIC MOMENTS (TF)   Arena Films/Yorkshire TV/Atlantic
   Videoventures, 1988, British
JUST ANOTHER SECRET (CTF)   F.F.S. Productions/
   Taurusfilm/Blair Communications/USA Network, 1989,
   U.S.-British
MURDER BY THE BOOK (CTF)   TVS Productions/Benbow
   Evans Productions, 1990, British-U.S.

MATT CLARK*
Agent: Paul Kohner, Inc. - Los Angeles, 213/550-1060

DA   FilmDallas, 1988

RICHARD CLARK
DR. HACKENSTEIN   Vista Street Productions, 1988

RON CLARK
Agent: Mark Harris, David Shapira & Associates -
   Sherman Oaks, 818/906-0322

THE FUNNY FARM   New World, 1983, Canadian

ALAN CLARKE
b. October 28, 1935 - Liverpool, England
Address: 123 Harley Street, London W1, England
Agent: William Morris Agency - Beverly Hills, 213/274-7451

SCUM   Berwick Street Films, 1979, British, originally
   made for television
CONTACT (TF)   BBC, 1985, British
MADE IN BRITAIN (TF)   1985, British
BILLY THE KID AND THE GREEN BAIZE VAMPIRE   Zenith
   Productions/ITC, 1985, British
RITA, SUE AND BOB, TOO   Orion Classics, 1987, British

JAMES KENELM CLARKE
b. 1941 - Gloucestershire, England
Personal Manager: Hamish Gibson, Norfolk International
   Pictures, 2706 La Cuesta Drive, Los Angeles, CA 90046,
   213/876-4953

GOT IT MADE   Target International, 1973, British
EXPOSE   Target International, 1975, British
LET'S GET LAID   1977, British
FUNNY MONEY   Cannon, 1982, British
LOVE TRAP   1982, British
GOING UNDERCOVER   Miramax Films, 1985
THE HOUSE ON STRAW HILL   Norfolk International, 1988

SHIRLEY CLARKE
b. 1925 - New York, New York
Home: 1301 N. Harper Avenue, Los Angeles, CA 90046
Business: UCLA Theatre Arts Department, 405 Hilgard
   Avenue, Los Angeles, CA 90024, 213/825-5761

DANCE IN THE SUN   1953
IN PARIS PARKS   1954
BULLFIGHT   1955
A MOMENT OF LOVE   1957
THE SKYSCRAPER   co-director with Willard
   Van Dyke, 1958
LOOPS   1958
BRIDGES-GO-ROUND   1959
A SCARY TIME   1960
THE CONNECTION   Films Around the World, 1962
THE COOL WORLD   Cinema 5, 1964
PORTRAIT OF JASON (FD)   Film-Makers, 1967
ORNETTE: MADE IN AMERICA (FD)   Caravan of Dreams
   Productions, 1985

JAMES CLAVELL*
b. October 10, 1924 - Sydney, Australia
Agent: CAA - Beverly Hills, 213/288-4545

FIVE GATES TO HELL   20th Century-Fox, 1959
WALK LIKE A DRAGON   Paramount, 1960
TO SIR, WITH LOVE   Columbia, 1967, British
THE SWEET AND THE BITTER   Monarch, 1968, British
WHERE'S JACK?   Paramount, 1969, British
THE LAST VALLEY   Cinerama Releasing Corporation,
   1971, British

WILLIAM F. CLAXTON*
b. October 22, 1914 - California
Home: 1065 Napoli Drive, Pacific Palisades, CA 90272,
   213/454-3246
Agent: Ronald Leif, Contemporary Artists - Beverly Hills,
   213/278-8250

HALF PAST MIDNIGHT   20th Century-Fox, 1948
TUCSON   20th Century-Fox, 1949
ALL THAT I HAVE   Family Films, 1951

STAGECOACH TO FURY   20th Century-Fox, 1956
THE QUIET GUN   20th Century-Fox, 1957
YOUNG AND DANGEROUS   20th Century-Fox, 1957
ROCKABILLY BABY   20th Century-Fox, 1957
GOD IS MY PARTNER   20th Century-Fox, 1957
DESIRE IN THE DUST   20th Century-Fox, 1960
YOUNG JESSE JAMES   20th Century-Fox, 1960
LAW OF THE LAWLESS   Paramount, 1963
STAGE TO THUNDER ROCK   Paramount, 1964
NIGHT OF THE LEPUS   MGM, 1972
BONANZA: THE NEXT GENERATION (TF)   Gaylord
   Production Company/ LBS Communications/Bonanza
   Ventures, 1988

JACK CLAYTON*
b. 1921 - Brighton, England
Home: Heron's Flight, Highfield Park, Marlow,
   Buckinghamshire, England
Agent: Douglas Rae Management, 28 Charing Cross
   Road, London WC2H 0DB, England, 01/836-3903

ROOM AT THE TOP ★   Continental, 1959, British
THE INNOCENTS   20th Century-Fox, 1962, British
THE PUMPKIN EATER   Royal International, 1964, British
OUR MOTHER'S HOUSE   MGM, 1967, British
THE GREAT GATSBY   Paramount, 1974
SOMETHING WICKED THIS WAY COMES   Buena
   Vista, 1983
THE LONELY PASSION OF JUDITH HEARNE   Island
   Films, 1987, British

TOM CLEGG
Contact: British Academy of Film & Television Arts, 195
   Piccadilly, London W1, England, 71/734-0022

LOVE IS A SPLENDID ILLUSION   Schulman,
   1970, British
SWEENEY 2   EMI, 1978, British
McVICAR   Crown International, 1981, British
G'OLE! (FD)   Warner Bros., 1983, British
THE INSIDE MAN   Producers Enterprises/Nordisk
   Tonefilm/Terra Film International, 1984,
   British-Swedish
LORD MOUNTBATTEN - THE LAST VICEROY (MS)
   George Walker TV Productions/Mobil Corporation,
   1986, British
ANY MAN'S DEATH   International Entertainment
   Corporation, 1990, British
A CASUALTY OF WAR (CTF)   F.F.S. Productions/
   Taurusfilm/Blair Communications, 1990, British
IF THE SHOE FITS   The Movie Group, 1991, U.S.-French

DICK CLEMENT*
b. September 5, 1937 - West Cliff-on-Sea, England
Agent: Elliot Webb, Broder-Kurland-Webb-Uffner Agency -
   Los Angeles, 213/656-9262

OTLEY   Columbia, 1969, British
A SEVERED HEAD   Columbia, 1971, British
CATCH ME A SPY   Rank, 1971, British
PORRIDGE   ITC, 1979, British
BULLSHOT!   Island Alive, 1983, British
WATER   Atlantic Releasing Corporation, 1984, British

RENÉ CLEMENT
b. March 18, 1913 - Bordeaux, France
Contact: French Film Office, 745 Fifth Avenue, New York,
   NY 10151, 212/832-8860

LA BATAILLE DU RAIL   1946, French

LE PERE TRANQUILLE   1946, French
LES MAUDITS   1947, French
THE WALLS OF MALAPAGA   Films International of
   America, 1949, Italian-French
LE CHATEAU DE VERRE   1950, French-Italian
FORBIDDEN GAMES   Times, 1952, French
LOVERS, HAPPY LOVERS!   MONSIEUR RIPOIS/KNAVE
   OF HEARTS   20th Century-Fox, 1954, French-British
GERVAISE   Continental, 1956, French
THIS ANGRY AGE   Columbia, 1958, Italian-French
PURPLE NOON   TImes, 1960, French-Italian
QUELLE JOIE DE VIVRE   1961, French-Italian
THE DAY AND THE HOUR   MGM, 1962, French-Italian
JOY HOUSE   LES FELINS   MGM, 1964, French
IS PARIS BURNING?   Paramount, 1966, French-U.S.
RIDER ON THE RAIN   Avco Embassy, 1970,
   French-Italian
THE DEADLY TRAP   LA MAISON SOUS LES ARBRES
   National General, 1971, French-Italian
...AND HOPE TO DIE   LA COURSE DU LIEVRE A
   TRAVERS LES CHAMPS   20th Century-Fox,
   1972, French
LA BABY-SITTER   Titanus, 1975, Italian-French-Monacan

RON CLEMENTS
Business: Walt Disney Productions, 500 S. Buena Vista
   Street, Burbank, CA 91521, 818/560-1000

THE GREAT MOUSE DETECTIVE (AF)   co-director with
   John Musker, Dave Michener & Burny Mattinson, Buena
   Vista, 1986
THE LITTLE MERMAID (AF)   co-director with John Musker,
   Buena Vista, 1989

GRAEME CLIFFORD*
Agent: Lou Pitt, ICM - Los Angeles, 213/550-4000

FRANCES   Universal/AFD, 1982
BURKE AND WILLS   Hemdale, 1985, Australian
GLEAMING THE CUBE   20th Century Fox, 1989
THE TURN OF THE SCREW (CTF)   Think Entertainment,
   1989

PETER CLIFTON
Contact: British Academy of Film & Television Arts,
   195 Piccadilly, London W1, England, 71/734-0022

POPCORN (FD)   Sherpix, 1969, U.S.-Australian
SUPERSTARS IN FILM CONCERT (FD)   National Cinema,
   1971, British
THE SONG REMAINS THE SAME (FD)   co-director with
   Joe Massot, Warner Bros., 1976, British
SWEET SOUL MUSIC (FD)   1977, British
THE LONDON ROCK & ROLL SHOW (FD)   1978, British
ROCK CITY   SOUND OF THE CITY: LONDON
   1964-73 (FD)   Columbia, 1981, British

ROBERT CLOUSE
Home: 70 Water Street, Ashland, OR 97520, 503/488-0131
Agent: ICM - Los Angeles, 213/550-4000

DARKER THAN AMBER   National General, 1970
DREAMS OF GLASS   Universal, 1970
ENTER THE DRAGON   Warner Bros., 1973,
   U.S.-Hong Kong
BLACK BELT JONES   Warner Bros., 1974
GOLDEN NEEDLES   American International, 1974
THE ULTIMATE WARRIOR   Warner Bros., 1976
THE AMSTERDAM KILL   Columbia, 1978,
   U.S.-Hong Kong

THE PACK   Warner Bros., 1978
GAME OF DEATH   Columbia, 1979, U.S.-Hong Kong
THE OMEGA CONNECTION (TF)   NBC-TV, 1979
THE KIDS WHO KNEW TOO MUCH (TF)   Walt Disney
   Productions, 1980
THE BIG BRAWL   Warner Bros., 1980
FORCE: FIVE   American Cinema, 1981
NIGHT EYES *THE RATS*   Warner Bros., 1983, Canadian
DARK WARRIOR   Arista, 1984
GYMKATA   MGM/UA, 1985
CHINA O'BRIEN   Golden Harvest, 1990, U.S.-Hong Kong

LEWIS COATES
(Luigi Cozzi)
Home: via Cassia 834, pal.F, Rome, Italy, 06/366-8116

LA PORTIERA NUDA   CIA Cinematografica, 1975, Italian
L'ASSASSINO E COSTRETTO AD UCCIDERE ANCORA
   Albione Cinematografica/GIT International, 1976, Italian
DEDICATO A UNA STELLA   Euro, 1978, Italian
STARCRASH   New World, 1979, Italian
ALIEN CONTAMINATION   Cannon, 1980,
   Italian-West German
HERCULES   MGM/UA/Cannon, 1983, Italian
HERCULES II   Cannon, 1983, Italian
WITCHCRAFT   Film Mirage, 1988, Italian
PAGANINI HORROR   Fulvia Film, 1989, Italian
THE BLACK CAT   21st Century Film Corporation,
   1989, Italian

JOEL COEN
Agent: Leading Artists - Beverly Hills, 213/858-1999

BLOOD SIMPLE   Circle Releasing Corporation, 1984
RAISING ARIZONA   20th Century Fox, 1987
MILLER'S CROSSING   20th Century Fox, 1990
BARTON FINK   20th Century Fox, 1991

ANNETTE COHEN
Address: 25 Imperial Street, Toronto, Ontario M5P 1C1,
   Canada, 416/483-8018

LOVE   co-director with Nancy Dowd, Liv Ullmann & Mai
   Zetterling, Velvet Films, 1982, Canadian

ELI COHEN
Contact: Israel Film Centre, Ministry of Industry and Trade,
   30 Agron Street, P.O. Box 299, Jerusalem, Israel,
   02/210-297

RICOCHETS   Marathon Pictures, 1986, Israeli
AVIA'S SUMMER   Shapira Films, 1988, Israeli

HOWARD R. COHEN
SATURDAY THE 14TH   New World, 1981
SPACE RAIDERS   New World, 1983
SATURDAY THE 14TH STRIKES BACK   Concorde, 1988
TIME TRACKERS   Concorde, 1989
SPACE CASE   Lunar Bynne Limited Productions, 1990
DEATHSTALKER IV   Concorde, 1990

LARRY COHEN*
b. July 15, 1941 - New York, New York
Home: 2111 Coldwater Canyon Blvd., Beverly Hills, CA
   90210, 213/550-7942

ONE SHOCKING MOMENT   1965
BONE   Jack H. Harris Enterprises, 1972
BLACK CAESAR   American International, 1973

HELL UP IN HARLEM   American International, 1973
IT'S ALIVE   Warner Bros., 1974
DEMON *GOD TOLD ME TO*   New World, 1977
IT LIVES AGAIN   Warner Bros., 1978
THE PRIVATE FILES OF J. EDGAR HOOVER   American
   International, 1978
SEE CHINA AND DIE (TF)   CBS, 1981
FULL MOON HIGH   Filmways, 1981
Q   United Film Distribution, 1982
SPECIAL EFFECTS   New Line Cinema, 1985
PERFECT STRANGERS   New Line Cinema, 1985
THE STUFF   New World, 1985
IT'S ALIVE III: ISLAND OF THE ALIVE   Warner
   Bros., 1987
RETURN TO SALEM'S LOT   Warner Bros., 1987
DEADLY ILLUSION   co-director with William Tannen,
   CineTel Films, 1987
WICKED STEPMOTHER   MGM/UA, 1989
AMBULANCE   Triumph Releasing Corporation, 1990

MARTIN COHEN
Business: Amblin Entertainment, 100 Universal City Plaza -
   Bungalow 477, Universal City, CA 91608, 818/777-1000

ONCE IN A BLUE MOON   Lunelife Productions, 1990

NEIL COHEN
Agent: William Morris Agency - Beverly Hills, 213/274-7451

RICH BOYS *CHIEF ZABU*   co-director with Howard Zuker
   (Zack Norman),   International Film Marketing, 1988

ROB COHEN*
b. April 12, 1949 - Cornwall-on-the-Hudson, New York
Agent: Jim Berkus, Leading Artists - Beverly Hills,
   213/858-1999

A SMALL CIRCLE OF FRIENDS   United Artists, 1980
SCANDALOUS   Orion, 1984

HARLEY COKLISS
b. February 11, 1945 - San Diego, California
Agent: Leading Artists - Beverly Hills, 213/858-1999

THAT SUMMER   Columbia, 1979, British
BATTLETRUCK *WARLORDS OF THE 21ST CENTURY*
   New World, 1982, U.S.-New Zealand
BLACK MOON RISING   New World, 1986
MALONE   Orion, 1987
DREAM DEMON   Spectrafilm, 1988, British

JOHN DAVID COLES*
Home: 789 West End Avenue, New York, NY 10025,
   212/749-2900
Agent: Rob Scheidlinger, ICM - New York City, 213/556-5600

SIGNS OF LIFE   Avenue Pictures, 1989
RISING SON (CTF)   Turner Network TV, 1990

RICHARD A. COLLA*
Home: 2533 Greenvalley Road, Los Angeles, CA 90046,
   213/656-8178
Agent: Alan Greenspan, ICM - Los Angeles, 213/550-4000

THE WORLD IS WATCHING (TF)   Universal TV, 1969
ZIGZAG   MGM, 1970
McCLOUD: WHO KILLED MISS U.S.A.? (TF)   Universal
   TV, 1970
THE OTHER MAN (TF)   Universal TV, 1970

SARGE: THE BADGE OR THE CROSS (TF)   Universal
   TV, 1971
THE PRIEST KILLER (TF)   Universal TV, 1971
FUZZ   United Artists, 1972
TENAFLY (TF)   Universal TV, 1973
THE QUESTOR TAPES (TF)   Universal TV, 1974
LIVE AGAIN, DIE AGAIN (TF)   Universal TV, 1974
THE TRIBE (TF)   Universal TV, 1974
THE UFO INCIDENT (TF)   Universal TV, 1975
OLLY OLLY OXEN FREE   Sanrio, 1978
BATTLESTAR GALACTICA   Universal, 1979
DON'T LOOK BACK (TF)   TBA Productions/Satie
   Productions/TRISEME, 1981
STINGRAY (TF)   Stephen J. Cannell Productions, 1985
THAT SECRET SUNDAY (TF)   CBS Entertainment, 1986
SOMETHING IS OUT THERE (TF)   Columbia TV, 1988
NAKED LIE (TF)   Shadowplay Films/Phoenix
   Entertainment Group, 1989
ROXANNE: THE PRIZE PULITZER (TF)   Qintex
   Entertainment, 1989
SPARKS: THE PRICE OF PASSION (TF)   Shadowplay
   Films/Victoria Principal Productions/King Phoenix
   Entertainment, 1990
STORM AND SORROW (CTF)   King Phoenix
   Entertainment/Lifetime, 1990

ROBERT COLLECTOR

Agent: William Morris Agency - Beverly Hills, 213/274-7451

RED HEAT   TAT Filmproductions/Aida United GMBH/
   International Screen, 1984, West German-U.S.
NIGHTFLYERS   directed under pseudonym of T.C. Blake,
   New Century/Vista, 1987

JAMES F. COLLIER*

Home: 9410 Huer Huero Drive, Creston, CA 93432

FOR PETE'S SAKE!   World Wide, 1966
HIS LAND   World Wide, 1967
TWO A PENNY   World Wide, 1970, British
CATCH A PEBBLE   World Wide, 1971, British
TIME TO RUN   World Wide, 1972
THE HIDING PLACE   World Wide, 1975
JONI   World Wide, 1980
THE PRODIGAL   World Wide, 1984
CRY FROM THE MOUNTAIN   World Wide, 1986
CAUGHT   World Wide, 1987
CHINA CRY   Parakletos Productions, 1990

ROBERT COLLINS*

Home: 3998 Sunswept Drive, Studio City, CA 91604,
   818/980-6246
Agent: Robert Stein, Leading Artists - Los Angeles,
   213/858-1999

SERPICO: THE DEADLY GAME (TF)   Dino De Laurentiis
   Productions/ Paramount TV, 1976
THE LIFE AND ASSASSINATION OF THE KINGFISH (TF)
   Tomorrow Entertainment, 1977
WALK PROUD   Universal, 1979
GIDEON'S TRUMPET (TF)   Gideon Productions, 1980
SAVAGE HARVEST   20th Century-Fox, 1981
OUR FAMILY BUSINESS (TF)   Lorimar Productions, 1981
MONEY ON THE SIDE (TF)   Green-Epstein Productions/
   Hal Landers Productions/Columbia TV, 1982
MAFIA PRINCESS (TF)   Jack Farren Productions/
   Group W Productions, 1985
J. EDGAR HOOVER (CTF)   RLC Productions/The
   Finnegan Company/ Showtime, 1987

THE HIJACKING OF THE ACHILLE LAURO (TF)
   Spectator Films/ Tamara Asseyev Productions/New
   World TV, 1989
PRIME TARGET (TF)   RLC Productions/The
   Finnegan-Pinchuk Company/ MGM-UA TV, 1989
JOHNNY RYAN (TF)   Dan Curtis TV Productions/
   MGM-UA TV/NBC Productions, 1990

CHRIS COLUMBUS*

Agent: CAA - Beverly Hills, 213/288-4545

ADVENTURES IN BABYSITTING   Buena Vista, 1987
HEARTBREAK HOTEL   Buena Vista, 1988
HOME ALONE   20th Century Fox, 1990

LUIGI COMENCINI

b. June 8, 1916 - Salo, Brescia, Italy
Home: via Savoia 82, Rome, Italy, 06/865851

PROIBITO RUBARE   Lux Film, 1948, Italian
L'IMPERATORE DI CAPRI   Lux Film, 1949, Italian
PERSIANE CHIUSE   Rovere Film, 1951, Italian
HEIDI   United Artists, 1952, Swiss
LA TRATTA DELLA BIANCHE   Excelsa/Ponti/Dino De
   Laurentiis Cinematografica, 1952, Italian
BREAD, LOVE AND DREAMS   Italian Film Export,
   1953, Italian
LA VALIGIA DEI SOGNI   Mambretti, 1954, Italian
FRISKY   PANE, AMORE E GELOSIA   DCA, 1954, Italian
LA BELLA DI ROMA   Lux Film, 1955, Italian
LA FINESTRA SUL LUNA PARK   Noria Film, 1957, Italian
MARITI IN CITTA   Oscar Film/Morino Film, 1957, Italian
MOGLI PERICOLOSE   Morino/Tempo Film, 1958, Italian
UND DAS AM MONTAGMORGEN   1959, West German
LE SORPRESE DELL'AMORE   Morino/Tempo Film,
   1959, Italian
EVERYBODY GO HOME!   Royal Films International, 1960,
   Italian-French
A CAVALLO DELLA TIGRE   Alfredo Bini, 1961, Italian
IL COMMISSARIO   Dino De Laurentiis Cinematografica,
   1962, Italian
BEBO'S GIRL   Continental, 1963, Italian-French
TRE NOTTI D'AMORE   co-director with Renato Costellani &
   Franco Rossi, Jolly Film/Cormoran FIlm, 1964,
   Italian-French
LA MIA SIGNORA   co-director with Mauro Bolognini & Tinto
   Brass, Dino De Laurentiis Cinematografica, 1964, Italian
BAMBOLE!   co-director with Dino Risi, Franco Rossi &
   Mauro Bolognini, Royal Films International, 1965, Italian
IL COMPAGNO DON CAMILLO   Rizzoli Film/Francoriz/
   Omnia Film, 1965, Italian-West German
LA BUGIARDA   Ultra Film/Consortium Pathe/Tecisa, 1965,
   Italian-French-Spanish
INCOMPRESO   1966, Italian
ITALIAN SECRET SERVICE   1968, Italian
INFANZIA, VOCAZIONE E PRIME ESPERIENZE DI
   GIACOMO CASANOVA - VENEZIANO   1969, Italian
SENZA SAPERE NULLA DI LEI   Rizzoli Film, 1969, Italian
LO SCOPONE SCIENTIFICO   De Laurentiis, 1972, Italian
LE AVVENTURE DI PINOCCHIO   RAI/ORTF/Bavaria Film,
   1972, Italian-French- West German
DELITTO D'AMORE   Documento Film, 1974, Italian
MIO DIO COME SONO CADUTA IN BASSO   Dean Film,
   1974, Italian
LA DONNA DELLA DOMENICA   Prinex Italiana/Fox-Lira,
   1975, Italian
SUNDAY WOMAN   20th Century-Fox, 1976, Italian-French
BASTA CHE NON SI SAPPIA IN GIRO   co-director with
   Nanni Loy & Luigi Magni, Medusa, 1976, Italian

F
I
L
M

D
I
R
E
C
T
O
R
S

SIGNORE E SIGNORI BUONANOTTE   co-director, Titanus,
   1976, Italian
QUELLE STRANE OCCASIONI   co-director, Cineriz,
   1977, Italian
TILL MARRIAGE US DO PART   Franklin Media,
   1977, Italian
L'AMORE IN ITALIA (TF)   1978, Italian
IL GATTO   United Artists, 1978, Italian
TRAFFIC JAM   *L'INGORGO*   New Image, 1979,
   Italian-French-Spanish
THEY ALL LOVED HIM   Medusa, 1980, Italian
VOLTATI EUGENIO   Gaumont, 1981, Italian-French
CERCASI GESU   Intercontinental/Nouvelle Cinevog,
   1982, Italian-French
IL MATRIMONIO DI CATERINA (TF)   1982, Italian
CUORE (MS)   RAI/Difilm/Antenne-2, 1984, Italian-French
LA STORIA (MS)   RAI/Antenne-2/Ypsilon Cinematografica/
   Maran Film/TVE, 1986, Italian-French
THE BOY FROM CALABRIA   International Film Exchange,
   1987, Italian-French
LA BOHEME   New Yorker, 1988, French
BUON NATALE, BUON ANNO JOYEUX   AFMD, 1990,
   Italian-French

RICHARD COMPTON*
Home: 161 West 15th Street - Apt. 2H, New York, NY
   10011, 212/315-5098
Agent: Shapiro-Lichtman Agency - Los Angeles,
   213/859-8877

ANGELS DIE HARD   New World, 1970
WELCOME HOME, SOLDIER BOYS   20th Century-
   Fox, 1972
MACON COUNTY LINE   American International, 1974
RETURN TO MACON COUNTY   American
   International, 1975
MANIAC   New World, 1977
DEADMAN'S CURVE (TF)   Roger Gimbel Productions/
   EMi TV, 1978
RAVAGES   Columbia, 1979
WILD TIMES (TF)   Metromedia Producers Corporation/
   Rattlesnake Productions, 1980
DESPERADO: AVALANCHE AT DEVIL'S RIDGE (TF)
   Walter Mirisch Productions/Charles E. Sellier, Jr.
   Productions/Universal TV, 1988
BAYWATCH: PANIC AT MALIBU PIER (TF)   GTG
   Entertainment, 1989

WILLIAM CONDON
Agent: CAA - Beverly Hills, 213/288-4545

SISTER, SISTER   New World, 1987

KEVIN CONNOR*
b. July 14, 1940 - London, England
Home: 7954 Woodrow Wilson Drive, Los Angeles, CA
   90046, 213/650-4033
Agent: Larry Becsey, The Agency - Los Angeles,
   213/551-3000

FROM BEYOND THE GRAVE   Howard Mahler Films,
   1975, British
THE LAND THAT TIME FORGOT   American International,
   1975, British
AT THE EARTH'S CORE   American International,
   1976, British
DIRTY KNIGHT'S WORK   *A CHOICE OF WEAPONS*
   Gamma III, 1976, British
THE PEOPLE THAT TIME FORGOT   American
   International, 1977, British
WARLORDS OF ATLANTIS   Columbia, 1978, British
ARABIAN ADVENTURE   AFD, 1979, British

MOTEL HELL   United Artists, 1980
GOLIATH AWAITS (TF)   Larry White Productions/Hugh
   Benson Productions/Columbia TV, 1981
THE HOUSE WHERE EVIL DWELLS   MGM/UA, 1982,
   U.S.-Japanese
MASTER OF THE GAME (MS)   co-director with Harvey
   Hart, Rosemont Productions, 1984
MISTRAL'S DAUGHTER (MS)   co-director with Douglas
   Hickox, Steve Krantz Productions/R.T.L. Productions/
   Antenne-2, 1984, U.S.-French
NORTH AND SOUTH, BOOK II (MS)   Wolper Productions/
   Robert A. Papazian Productions/Warner Bros. TV, 1986
THE RETURN OF SHERLOCK HOLMES (TF)   CBS
   Entertainment, 1987, British
THE LION OF AFRICA (CTF)   HBO Pictures/Lois Luger
   Productions, 1987
WHAT PRICE VICTORY (TF)   Wolper Productions/Warner
   Bros. TV, 1988
DIRTY DOZEN: DANKO'S DOZEN (TF)   MGM-UA TV/
   Jadran Films/TV Espanola, 1988, U.S.-Yugoslavian
GREAT EXPECTATIONS (CTF)   The Disney Channel/
   Primetime TV/HTV/ Tesauro TV, 1989, U.S.-British-
   Spanish
THE HOLLYWOOD DETECTIVE (CTF)   Casiano-Riggs
   Productions/ MCA TV/USA Network, 1989
THE MYSTERIES OF THE DARK JUNGLE (MS)   RCS-TV/
   RAI/Beta Film/ZDF/ ORF/TF1/TVE, 1990, Italian-West
   German-French

ROBERT CONRAD*
(Conrad Robert Falk)
b. March 1, 1935 - Chicago, Illinois
Address: 21355 Pacific Coast Highway - Suite 200, Malibu,
   CA 90265, 213/456-5655
Agent: David Shapira & Associates - Sherman Oaks,
   818/906-0322

HIGH MOUNTAIN RANGERS (TF)   A. Shane
   Company, 1987
GLORY DAYS (TF)   A. Shane Company/Sibling
   Rivalries, 1988
JESSE HAWKES (TF)   A. Shane Company, 1989

WILLIAM CONRAD*
b. September 27, 1920 - Louisville, Kentucky
Home: P.O. Box 5289, Sherman Oaks, CA 91413,
   818/343-5638

THE MAN FROM GALVESTON   Warner Bros., 1964
TWO ON A GUILLOTINE   Warner Bros., 1965
MY BLOOD RUNS COLD   Warner Bros., 1965
BRAINSTORM   Warner Bros., 1965
SIDE SHOW (TF)   Krofft Entertainment, 1981

BERT CONVY
b. July 23, 1933 - St. Louis, Missouri
Agent: The Chasin Agency - Beverly Hills, 213/278-7505
Personal Manager: Howard Hinderstein - Los Angeles, 213/
   462-7140

WEEKEND WARRIORS   The Movie Store, 1986

JAMES L. CONWAY*
b. October 27, 1950 - New York, New York
Home: 4300 Coquette Place, Tarzana, CA 91356,
   818/342-8155
Agent: CAA - Beverly Hills, 213/288-4545

IN SEARCH OF NOAH'S ARK   Sunn Classic, 1976
THE LINCOLN CONSPIRACY   Sunn Classic, 1977

THE INCREDIBLE ROCKY MOUNTAIN RACE (TF)   Sunn
   Classic Productions, 1977
THE LAST OF THE MOHICANS (TF)   Sunn Classic
   Productions, 1977
BEYOND AND BACK   Sunn Classic, 1978
DONNER PASS: THE ROAD TO SURVIVAL (TF)   Sunn
   Classic Productions, 1978
GREATEST HEROES OF THE BIBLE (MS)   Sunn Classic
   Productions, 1978
THE FALL OF THE HOUSE OF USHER   Sunn Classic,
   1979
HANGAR 18   Sunn Classic, 1980
THE LEGEND OF SLEEPY HOLLOW (TF)   Sunn
   Classic, 1980
EARTHBOUND   Taft International, 1981
NASHVILLE GRAB (TF)   Taft International, 1981
THE BOOGENS   Jensen Farley Pictures, 1981
THE PRESIDENT MUST DIE   Jensen Farley
   Pictures, 1981

KEVIN CONWAY
b. May 29, 1942 - New York, New York
Contact: Screen Actors Guild - Los Angeles, 213/856-6600

THE SUN AND THE MOON   *THE VIOLINS CAME WITH
   THE AMERICANS*   Double Helix, 1987

BRUCE COOK
Address: 425 N. Chappell - Unit D, Alhambra, CA 91801,
   818/300-8419

THE CENSUS TAKER   Argentum Productions, 1984
LINE OF FIRE   Shapiro Glickenhaus Entertainment, 1988
NIGHTWISH   Vidmark, 1988

FIELDER COOK*
b. March 9, 1923 - Atlanta, Georgia
Address: 180 Central Park South, New York, NY 10019,
   212/247-5100
Agent: CAA - Beverly Hills, 213/288-4545

PATTERNS   United Artists, 1956
HOME IS THE HERO   Showcorporation, 1961, Irish
A BIG HAND FOR THE LITTLE LADY   Warner Bros., 1966
HOW TO SAVE A MARRIAGE AND RUIN YOUR LIFE
   Columbia, 1968
PRUDENCE AND THE PILL   20th Century-Fox,
   1968, British
TEACHER, TEACHER (TF) ☆   NBC, 1969
SAM HILL: WHO KILLED THE MYSTERIOUS MR.
   FOSTER? (TF)   Universal TV, 1971
GOODBYE, RAGGEDY ANN (TF)   Metromedia Producers
   Corporation, 1971
THE HOMECOMING (TF) ☆   Lorimar Productions, 1971
THE HANDS OF CORMAC JOYCE (TF)   Crawford
   Productions/Foote, Cone & Belding, 1972
EAGLE IN A CAGE   National General, 1972,
   British-Yugoslavian
MIRACLE ON 34TH STREET (TF)   20th Century-Fox
   TV, 1973
FROM THE MIXED-UP FILES OF MRS. BASIL E
   FRANKWEILER   *THE HIDEAWAYS*   Cinema 5, 1973
THAT WAS THE WEST THAT WAS (TF)   Universal
   TV, 1974
MILES TO GO BEFORE I SLEEP (TF)   Tomorrow
   Entertainment, 1975
THE RIVALRY (TF)   NBC-TV, 1975
VALLEY FORGE (TF)   Clarion Productions/
   Columbia TV, 1975

BEAUTY AND THE BEAST (TF)   Palms Films Ltd.,
   1976, British
JUDGE HORTON AND THE SCOTTSBORO BOYS (TF) ☆
   Tomorrow Entertainment, 1976
A LOVE AFFAIR: THE ELEANOR AND LOU GEHRIG
   STORY (TF)   Charles Fries Productions/Stonehenge
   Productions, 1977
TOO FAR TO GO (TF)   Sea Cliff Productions, 1979
I KNOW WHY THE CAGED BIRD SINGS (TF)   Tomorrow
   Entertainment, 1979
GAUGUIN THE SAVAGE (TF)   Nephi Productions, 1980
FAMILY REUNION (TF)   Creative Projects Inc./Columbia
   TV, 1981
WILL THERE REALLY BE A MORNING? (TF)   Jaffe-Blakely
   Films/Sama Productions/Orion TV, 1983
WHY ME? (TF)   Lorimar Productions, 1984
EVERGREEN (MS)   Edgar J. Scherick Associates/
   Metromedia Producers Corporation, 1985
SEIZE THE DAY (TF)   Learning in Focus, 1986
A SPECIAL FRIENDSHIP (TF)   Entertainment
   Partners, 1987

ALAN COOKE*
b. April 29, 1935 - London, England
Home: 1997 Lucile Avenue, Los Angeles, CA 90039,
   213/666-4840
Agent: Tim Stone, Stone Manners Agency - Los Angeles,
   213/275-9599

FLAT TWO   Anglo-Amalgamated, 1962, British
THE MIND OF MR. SOAMES   Columbia, 1970, British
THE RIGHT PROSPECTUS (TF)   BBC-TV, 1972, British
BLODWYN HOME FROM RACHEL'S MARRIAGE (TF)
   BBC-TV, 1972, British
A PICTURE OF KATHERINE MANSFIELD (MS)   BBC,
   1973, British
SHADES OF GREENE (MS)   Thames TV, 1976, British
THE HUNCHBACK OF NOTRE DAME (TF)   BBC-TV,
   1978, British
RENOIR, MY FATHER (TF)   BBC-TV, 1979, British
COVER (MS)   ITC, 1980, British
NADIA (TF)   Dave Bell Productions/Tribune Entertainment
   Company/Jadran Film, 1984, U.S.-Yugoslavian

TONY COOKSON
Agent: William Morris Agency - Beverly Hills, 213/274-7451

NEWMAN   Panorama Film International, 1990

MARTHA COOLIDGE*
b. August 17, 1946 - New Haven, Connecticut
Agent: The Gersh Agency - Beverly Hills, 213/274-6611

NOT A PRETTY PICTURE   Films Incorporated, 1976
VALLEY GIRL   Atlantic Releasing Corporation, 1983
JOY OF SEX   Paramount, 1984
THE CITY GIRL   Moon Pictures, 1984
REAL GENIUS   Tri-Star, 1985
PLAIN CLOTHES   Paramount, 1988
TRENCHCOAT IN PARADISE (TF)   Ogiens-Kate Company
   Productions/ The Finnegan-Pinchuk Company, 1989

HAL COOPER*
b. February 23, 1923 - New York, New York
Home: 2651 Hutton Drive, Beverly Hills, CA 90210,
   213/271-8602
Agent: Barrett, Benson, McCartt & Weston - Los Angeles,
   213/277-4998

MILLION DOLLAR INFIELD (TF)   CBS Entertainment, 1982

JACKIE COOPER*
September 15, 1922 - Los Angeles, California
Agent: Ronald Leif, Contemporary Artists - Beverly Hills,
    213/278-8250

STAND UP AND BE COUNTED   Columbia, 1971
HAVING BABIES III (TF)   The Jozak Company/Paramount
    TV, 1978
PERFECT GENTLEMEN (TF)   Paramount TV, 1978
RAINBOW (TF)   Ten-Four Productions, 1978
SEX AND THE SINGLE PARENT (TF)   TIme-Life
    Productions, 1979
MARATHON (TF)   Alan Landsburg Productions, 1980
WHITE MAMA (TF)   Tomorrow Entertainment, 1980
RODEO GIRL (TF)   Steckler Productions/Marble Arch
    Productions, 1980
LEAVE 'EM LAUGHING (TF)   Julian Fowles Productions/
    Charles Fries Productions, 1981
ROSIE: THE ROSEMARY CLOONY STORY (TF)   Charles
    Fries Productions/Alan Sacks Productions, 1982
MOONLIGHT (TF)   co-director with Rod Holcomb,
    Universal TV, 1982, both directed under pseudonym of
    Alan Smithee
GO FOR THE GOLD   Go for the Gold Productions, 1984
GLITTER (TF)   Aaron Spelling Productions, 1984
THE NIGHT THEY SAVED CHRISTMAS (TF)   Robert
    Halmi Inc., 1984
IZZY AND MOE (TF)   Robert Halmi Inc., 1985
THE LADIES (TF)   NBC, 1987, filmed in 1983

PETER H. COOPER*
Business: Moir Productions, 220 East 23rd Street,
    New York, NY, 212/213-9797

ORDINARY HEROES   Crow Productions/Ira Barmak
    Productions, 1986

STUART COOPER
b. 1942 - Hoboken, New Jersey
Agent: Jim Wiatt, ICM - Los Angeles, 213/550-4000

LITTLE MALCOLM AND HIS STRUGGLE AGAINST THE
    EUNUCHS   Multicetera Investments, 1974, British
OVERLORD   1975, British
THE DISAPPEARANCE   Levitt-Pickman,
    1977, Canadian
A.D. - ANNO DOMINI (MS)   Procter & Gamble
    Productions/International Film Productions, 1985,
    U.S.-Italian
THE LONG HOT SUMMER (TF)   Leonard Hill
    Productions, 1985
CHRISTMAS EVE (TF)   NBC Productions, 1986
MARIO PUZO'S THE FORTUNATE PILGRIM   THE
    FORTUNATE PILGRIM   (MS)   NBC Productions, 1988

CHRISTOPHER COPPOLA
DRACULA'S WIDOW   DEG, 1988

FRANCIS FORD COPPOLA*
b. April 7, 1939 - Detroit, Michigan
Business: Zoetrope Studios, Sentinel Building, 916 Kearny
    Street, San Francisco, CA 94133, 415/788-7500

TONIGHT FOR SURE   Premier Pictures, 1961
DEMENTIA 13   American International, 1963
YOU'RE A BIG BOY NOW   7 Arts, 1966
FINIAN'S RAINBOW   Warner Bros., 1968
THE RAIN PEOPLE   Warner Bros., 1969
THE GODFATHER ★   Paramount, 1972

THE CONVERSATION   Paramount, 1974
THE GODFATHER, PART II ★★   Paramount, 1974
APOCALYPSE NOW ★   United Artists, 1979
ONE FROM THE HEART   Columbia, 1982
THE OUTSIDERS   Warner Bros., 1983
RUMBLE FISH   Universal, 1983
THE COTTON CLUB   Orion, 1984
PEGGY SUE GOT MARRIED   Tri-Star, 1986
GARDENS OF STONE   Tri-Star, 1987
TUCKER: THE MAN AND HIS DREAM   Paramount, 1988
NEW YORK STORIES   co-director with Woody Allen &
    Martin Scorsese, Buena Vista, 1989
THE GODFATHER, PART III   Paramount, 1990

GERARD CORBIAU
Contact: National Tourist Office, 61 Rue de Marche Aux
    Herbes, B1000 Brussels, Belgium, 02/513-8940

THE MUSIC TEACHER   Orion Classics, 1988, Belgian

SERGIO CORBUCCI
b. December 6, 1927 - Rome, Italy
Home: via Donatello 15, Rome, Italy, 06/360-7610

SALVATE MIA FIGLIA   Lauro, 1951, Italian
LA PECCATRICE DELL'ISOLA   Audax Film, 1953, Italian
TWO COLONELS   Comet, 1961, Italian
DUEL OF THE TITANS   ROMOLO E REMO   Paramount,
    1961, Italian
GOLIATH AND THE VAMPIRES   MACISTE CONTROL IL
    VAMPIRO   co-director with Giacomo Gentilomo,   American
    International, 1961, Italian
THE SLAVE   IL FIGLIO DI SPARTACUS   MGM, 1962,
    Italian
IL GIORNO PIU' CORTO   Titanus, 1963, Italian
MINNESOTA CLAY   Harlequin International, 1965, Italian-
    Spanish-French
DJANGO   BRC, 1966, Italian
NAVAJO JOE   UN DOLLARO A TESTA   United Artists,
    1966, Italian-Spanish
JOHNNY ORO   Sanson, 1966, Italian
THE HELLBENDERS   Embassy, 1966, Italian-Spanish
BERSAGLIO MOBILE   Rizzoli Film, 1967, Italian
IL GRANDE SILENZIO   Adelphia Cinematografica,
    1967, Italian
THE MERCENARY   United Artists, 1969, Italian-Spanish
GLI SPECIALISTI   Adelphia Cinematografica, 1969, Italian
COMPAÑEROS   VAMOS A MATAR COMPAÑEROS
    Cinerama Releasing Corporation, 1971, Spanish-Italian-
    West German
VIVA LA MUERTE...TUA!   Tritone Filmind, 1971, Italian
CHE C'ENTRIAMO NOI CON LA RIVOLUZIONE?
    Fair Film, 1972, Italian
LA BANDA J & S - CRONACA CRIMINALE DEL FAR-WEST
    Roberto Loyola Cinematografica/Orfeo/Terra Film Kunst,
    1973, Italian- Spanish-Monacan
IL BESTIONE   C.C. Champion, Inc., 1974, Italian-French
BLUFF - STORIE DI TRUFFE E DI IMBRAGLIONE   Cineriz,
    1975, Italian
UN GENIO, DUE COMPARI, UN POLLO   Titanus, 1975,
    Italian-French-West German
DI CHE SEGNO SEI?   PIC, 1976, Italian
IL SIGNOR ROBINSON - MOSTRUOSA STORIA D'AMORE
    E D'AVVENTURE   United Artists, 1976, Italian
TRE TIGRI CONTRO TRE TIGRI   Italian International Film,
    1977, Italian
ECCO NOI PER ESEMPIO   CIDIF, 1977, Italian
LA MAZZETTA   United Artists, 1978, Italian
GIALLO NAPOLETANO   CIDIF, 1979, Italian
PARI E DISPARI   CIDIF, 1979, Italian

I DON'T UNDERSTAND YOU ANYMORE   Capital,
   1980, Italian
I'M GETTING MYSELF A YACHT   Capital, 1981, Italian
CHI TROVO UN AMICO, TROVA UN TESORO   CEIAD,
   1981, Italian
SUPER FUZZ   Avco Embassy, 1981, Italian
MY DARLING, MY DEAREST   PLM Film, 1982, Italian
THREE WISE KINGS   PLM Film, 1982, Italian
COUNT TACCHIA   DAC/Adige, 1982, Italian
SING SING   Columbia, 1983, Italian
QUESTO E QUELLO   CIDIF, 1983, Italian
A TU PER TU   DAC, 1984, Italian
SONO UN FENOMENO PARANORMALE   Columbia,
   1986, Italian
RIMINI RIMINI   Medusa, 1987, Italian
ROBA DA RICCHI   Scena Film, 1987, Italian
I GIORNI DEL COMMISSARIO AMBROSIO   Numero Uno
   International/ Reteitalia, 1988, Italian
NIGHT CLUB   Reteitalia, 1989, Italian
WOMEN IN ARMS (TF)   Sacis, 1990, Italian

NICHOLAS COREA*
b. April 7, 1943 - St. Louis, Missouri
Agent: Dan Richland, Richland/Wunsch Agency -
   Los Angeles, 213/278-1955

THE ARCHER: FUGITIVE FROM THE EMPIRE (TF)
   Mad-Dog Productions/ Universal TV, 1981

RAFAEL CORKIDI
b. 1930 - Puebla, Mexico
Contact: Azteca Films, 555 N. La Brea Avenue, P.O. Box
   36095, Hollywood, CA 90036, 213/938-2413

ANGELES & QUERUBINES   Azteca Films,
   1971, Mexican
AUANDAR ANAPU   Azteca Films, 1974, Mexican
PAFNUCIO SANTO   Azteca Films, 1976, Mexican
DESEOS   Azteca Films, 1977

ROGER CORMAN
b. April 5, 1926 - Los Angeles, California
Business: Concorde Pictures, 11600 San Vicente Blvd.,
   Los Angeles, CA 90049, 213/826-0978

FIVE GUNS WEST   American International, 1955
THE APACHE WOMAN   American International, 1955
THE DAY THE WORLD ENDED   American
   International, 1956
SWAMP WOMAN   Woolner Brothers, 1956
THE OKLAHOMA WOMAN   American International, 1956
THE GUNSLINGER   ARC, 1956
IT CONQUERED THE WORLD   American
   International, 1956
NOT OF THIS EARTH   Allied Artists, 1957
THE UNDEAD   American International, 1957
NAKED PARADISE   American International, 1957
ATTACK OF THE CRAB MONSTERS   Allied Artists, 1957
ROCK ALL NIGHT   American International, 1957
TEENAGE DOLL   Allied Artists, 1957
CARNIVAL ROCK   Howco, 1957
SORORITY GIRL   American International, 1957
THE VIKING WOMEN AND THE SEA SERPENT
   American International, 1957
WAR OF THE SATELLITES   Allied Artists, 1958
THE SHE GODS OF SHARK REEF   American
   International, 1958
MACHINE GUN KELLY   American International, 1958
TEENAGE CAVEMAN   American International, 1958
I, MOBSTER   20th Century-Fox, 1959

A BUCKET OF BLOOD   American International, 1959
THE WASP WOMAN   American International, 1959
SKI TROOP ATTACK   Filmgroup, 1960
THE HOUSE OF USHER   American International, 1960
THE LITTLE SHOP OF HORRORS   Filmgroup, 1960
THE LAST WOMAN ON EARTH   Filmgroup, 1960
CREATURE FROM THE HAUNTED SEA   Filmgroup, 1961
ATLAS   Filmgroup, 1961
THE PIT AND THE PENDULUM   American
   International, 1961
THE INTRUDER   *I HATE YOUR GUTS*   Pathe
   American, 1962
THE PREMATURE BURIAL   American International, 1962
TALES OF TERROR   American International, 1962
TOWER OF LONDON   American International, 1962
THE RAVEN   American International, 1963
THE TERROR   American International, 1963
"X" - THE MAN WITH THE X-RAY EYES   American
   International, 1963
THE HAUNTED PALACE   American International, 1963
THE YOUNG RACERS   American International, 1963
THE SECRET INVASION   United Artists, 1964
THE MASQUE OF THE RED DEATH   American
   International, 1964, British-U.S.
THE TOMB OF LIGEIA   American International, 1965
THE WILD ANGELS   American International, 1966
THE ST. VALENTINE'S DAY MASSACRE   20th Century-
   Fox, 1967
THE TRIP   American International, 1967
TARGET: HARRY   directed under pseudonym of Harry
   Neill, ABC Pictures International, 1968
BLOODY MAMA   American International, 1970
GAS-S-S-S!...OR IT BECAME NECESSARY TO DESTROY
   THE WORLD IN ORDER TO SAVE IT!   American
   International, 1970
VON RICHTOFEN AND BROWN   United Artists, 1971
ROGER CORMAN'S FRANKENSTEIN UNBOUND
   FRANKENSTEIN UNBOUND   20th Century Fox, 1990

JOHN CORNELL
b. 1941 - Kalgoorlie, Australia
Contact: Australian Film Commission, 9229 Sunset Blvd.,
   Los Angeles, CA 90069, 213/275-7074

"CROCODILE" DUNDEE II   Paramount, 1988, Australian
ALMOST AN ANGEL   Paramount, 1990, Australian-U.S.

HUBERT CORNFIELD
b. February 9, 1929 - Istanbul, Turkey

SUDDEN DANGER   United Artists, 1955
LURE OF THE SWAMP   20th Century-Fox, 1957
PLUNDER ROAD   20th Century-Fox, 1957
THE THIRD VOICE   20th Century-Fox, 1959
ANGEL BABY   co-director with Paul Wendkos, Allied
   Artists, 1961
PRESSURE POINT   United Artists, 1962
THE NIGHT OF THE FOLLOWING DAY   Universal, 1969
LES GRAND MOYENS   Fox, 1976, French

EUGENE CORR*
Home: 40 Park Terrace, Mill Valley, CA 94941,
   415/388-4819
Agent: CAA - Beverly Hills, 213/288-4545

OVER-UNDER, SIDEWAYS-DOWN   co-director with Steve
   Wax & Peter Gessner, Steve Wax/Cine-Manifest
   Productions, 1977
DESERT BLOOM   Columbia, 1986

Co

FILM
DIRECTORS
GUIDE

F
I
L
M

D
I
R
E
C
T
O
R
S

81

CHARLES CORRELL*
Agent: Richard Weston, Barrett, Benson, McCartt &
  Weston - Los Angeles, 213/277-4998

MacGYVER: LEGEND OF THE HOLY ROSE (TF)
  co-director with Michael Caffey, Henry Winkler-John
  Rich Productions/Paramount TV, 1989
GUNSMOKE: THE LAST APACHE (TF)   CBS
  Entertainment/Galatea Productions, 1990

RICHARD CORRELL*
Contact: Directors Guild of America - Los Angeles,
  213/289-2000

SKI PATROL   Triumph Releasing Corporation, 1990

AXEL CORTI
b. 1933 - Paris, France
Contact: Directors Guild of Austria, Museumstrasse 5/17,
  A-1070, Vienna, Austria, 0222/938380

GOD DOES NOT BELIEVE IN US ANYMORE   Roxie
  Releasing, 1981, Austrian-West German-Swiss
SANTA FE   Roxie Releasing, 1985, Austrian
WELCOME IN VIENNA   Roxie Releasing, 1986, Austrian
A WOMAN'S PALE BLUE HANDKERCHIEF (TF)
  ORF/RAI, 1988, Austrian-Italian
THE KING'S WHORE   Cinema & Cinema/AFC France,
  1990, French-Italian

**WILLIAM H. (BILL)
COSBY, JR.***
b. July 12, 1937 - Philadelphia, Pennsylvania
Agent: Norman Brokaw, William Morris Agency - Beverly
  Hills, 213/274-7451
Business Manager: Mary E. Waller, SAH Enterprises, Inc.,
  205 Hill Street, Santa Monica, CA 90405, 213/457-8023

BILL COSBY, HIMSELF   20th Century-Fox International
  Classics, 1983

DON COSCARELLI*
b. February 17, 1954 - Tripoli, Libya
Business: Starway International, 8033 Sunset Blvd. -
  Suite 405, Los Angeles, CA 90046, 213/650-6995

JIM - THE WORLD'S GREATEST   Universal, 1976
KENNY AND COMPANY   20th Century-Fox, 1976
PHANTASM   Avco Embassy, 1979
THE BEASTMASTER   MGM/UA, 1982
PHANTASM II   Universal, 1988
SURVIVAL QUEST   MGM/UA, 1989

GEORGE PAN COSMATOS*
b. January 4, 1941
Agent: ICM - Los Angeles, 213/550-4000

MASSACRE IN ROME   *RAPPRESAGLIA*   National
  General, 1973, Italian-French
THE CASSANDRA CROSSING   Avco Embassy, 1977,
  British-Italian-West German
RESTLESS   Joseph Brenner Associates, 1978
ESCAPE TO ATHENA   AFD, 1979, British
OF UNKNOWN ORIGIN   Warner Bros., 1983, Canadian
RAMBO: FIRST BLOOD PART II   Tri-Star, 1985
COBRA   Warner Bros., 1986
LEVIATHAN   MGM/UA, 1989, U.S.-Italian

THOMAS COST
Contact: Writers Guild of America, West - Los Angeles,
  213/550-1000

PRIME SUSPECT   Premier Pictures/Silver-Regan
  Productions, 1989

COSTA-GAVRAS
(See Costa GAVRAS)

KEVIN COSTNER*
b. January 18, 1955 - Los Angeles, California
Agent: CAA - Beverly Hills, 213/288-4545

DANCES WITH WOLVES   Orion, 1990

JACK COUFFER*
Agent: Ben Benjamin, ICM - Los Angeles, 213/550-4153

NIKKI, WILD DOG OF THE NORTH   co-director with Don
  Haldane, Buena Vista, 1961, U.S.-Canadian
RING OF BRIGHT WATER   Cinerama Releasing
  Corporation, 1969, British
LIVING FREE   Columbia, 1972, British
THE DARWIN ADVENTURE   20th Century-Fox,
  1972, British
THE LAST GIRAFFE (TF)   Westfall Productions, 1979

JEROME COURTLAND*
b. December 27, 1926 - Knoxville, Tennessee
Agent: Christine Foster, The Agency - Los Angeles,
  213/551-3000

RUN, COUGAR, RUN   Buena Vista, 1972
DIAMONDS ON WHEELS   Buena Vista, 1972, U.S.-British
THE SKY TRAP (TF)   Walt Disney Productions, 1979

RAOUL COUTARD
b. September 16, 1924 - Paris, France
Address: 138 Boulevard Murat, 75016 Paris, France,
  04/525-7630
Contact: French Film Office, 745 Fifth Avenue, New York,
  NY 10151, 212/832-8860

HOA-BINH   Transvue, 1971, French
LA LEGION SAUTE SUR KOLWEZI   Bela Productions/FR3,
  1980, French
S.A.S. A SAN SALVADOR   UGC, 1982,
  French-West German

BILL COUTURIE
Agent: CAA - Beverly Hills, 213/288-4545

DEAR AMERICA: LETTERS HOME FROM VIETNAM (FD)
  Taurus Entertainment, 1987

ALEX COX
b. December 15, 1954 - Liverpool, England
Home: P.O. Box 1002, Venice, CA 90291
Agent: Stephanie Mann & Associates - Los Angeles,
  213/653-7130

REPO MAN   Universal, 1984
SID AND NANCY   Samuel Goldwyn Company,
  1986, British
STRAIGHT TO HELL   Island Films, 1987, British-Spanish
WALKER   Universal, 1987, U.S.-Nicaraguan

NELL COX*
Home: 9015 Burroughs Road, Los Angeles, CA 90046,
    213/654-9543
Agent: David Gersh, The Gersh Agency - Beverly Hills,
    213/274-6611

LIZA'S PIONEER DIARY (TF)   Nell Cox Films, 1976
THE ROOMMATE   Rubicon Film Productions, 1985
KONRAD (TF)   Sunn Classics Pictures, 1985
TRAITOR IN MY HOUSE (TF)   Educational Film Center/
    American Film Works Inc./WonderWorks, 1990

PAUL COX
b. April 16, 1940 - Venlo, Netherlands
Agent: Robert Kent, S.T.E. Representation - Los Angeles,
    213/550-3982 or Cameron's Management, 120 Victoria
    Street, Kings Cross, NSW, 2011, Australia, 02/358-6433

ILLUMINATIONS   Illumination Film Productions,
    1976, Australian
INSIDE LOOKING OUT   Illumination Film Productions,
    1977, Australian
KOSTAS   Illumination Film Productions, 1979, Australian
LONELY HEARTS   Samuel Goldwyn Company,
    1982, Australian
MAN OF FLOWERS   Spectrafilm, 1983, Australian
MY FIRST WIFE   Spectrafilm, 1984, Australian
CACTUS   Spectrafilm, 1986, Australian
HANDLE WITH CARE (TF)   Alsof Productions,
    1986, Australian
VINCENT - THE LIFE AND DEATH OF VINCENT VAN
    GOGH   Roxie Releasing, 1987, Australian-Dutch
THE PAPER BOY (TF)   Australian Children's Television
    Foundation/ITC, 1987, Australian
ISLAND   Illumination Films/Atlantis Releasing/Film
    Victoria, 1989, Australian
GOLDEN BRAID   Australian Film Commission/Film
    Victoria/Illumination Films, 1990, Australian

LUIGI COZZI
(See Lewis COATES)

WILLIAM CRAIN*
b. June 20, 1949
Business: Raindance Entertainment Company, P.O. Box
    744, Beverly Hills, CA 90213, 213/874-8978
Agent: Jerry Adler, The Sy Fischer Company - Los Angeles,
    213/969-2900

BLACULA   American International, 1972
DR. BLACK, MR. HYDE   Dimension, 1976
THE WATTS MONSTER   Dimension, 1979
THE KID FROM NOT-SO-BIG   1982
STANDING IN THE SHADOWS OF LOVE   Brandenberg-
    Crain Productions, 1984

PETER CRANE*
Business: Alpha Centauri, Ltd., 6061 Galahad Drive,
    Malibu, CA 90265, 213/457-4821
Agent: Alan Greenspan, ICM - Los Angeles, 213/550-4428

HUNTED   Warner/Columbia, 1972, British
ASSASSIN   Warner/Columbia, 1973, British
MOMENTS   Warner/Columbia, 1974, British
COVER UP (TF)   Glen A. Larson Productions/20th
    Century Fox TV, 1984
THE LAW AND HARRY McGRAW: DEAD MEN DON'T
    MAKE PHONE CALLS (TF)   Universal TV, 1987

WES CRAVEN*
b. August 2, 1949 - Cleveland, Ohio
Agent: ICM - Los Angeles, 213/550-4000

LAST HOUSE ON THE LEFT   Hallmark Releasing
    Corporation, 1973
THE HILLS HAVE EYES   Vanguard, 1977
STRANGER IN OUR HOUSE (TF)   Inter Planetary Pictures/
    Finnegan Associates, 1978
DEADLY BLESSING   United Artists, 1981
SWAMP THING   Avco Embassy, 1982
INVITATION TO HELL (TF)   Moonlight Productions II, 1984
A NIGHTMARE ON ELM STREET   New Line Cinema, 1984
CHILLER (TF)   Polar Film Corporation/J.D. Feigleson
    Productions, 1985
THE HILLS HAVE EYES PART II   Castle Hill
    Productions, 1986
DEADLY FRIEND   Warner Bros., 1986
THE SERPENT AND THE RAINBOW   Universal, 1988
SHOCKER   Universal, 1989

WAYNE CRAWFORD
Business: Crawford/Lane Prods., 14101 Valleyheart Drive -
    Suite 205, Sherman Oaks, CA 91423, 818/501-2076
Agent: Paul Kohner, Inc. - Los Angeles, 213/550-1060

CRIME LORDS   Crawford/Lane Productions/
    Rainboworld, 1990

RICHARD CRENNA*
b. November 30, 1926 - Los Angeles, California
Agent: CAA - Beverly Hills, 213/288-4545

BETTER LATE THAN NEVER (TF)   Ten-Four
    Productions, 1979

CHARLES CRICHTON
b. August 6, 1910 - Wallasey, England
Agent: MLR Representation Ltd., 200 Fulham Road, London
    SW10, England

FOR THOSE IN PERIL   1944, British
PAINTED BOATS   1945, British
DEAD OF NIGHT   co-director with Alberto Cavalcanti, Basil
    Dearden & Robert Hamer, Universal, 1945, British
HUE AND CRY   Fine Arts, 1947, British
AGAINST THE WIND   Eagle Lion, 1948, British
ANOTHER SHORE   Rank, 1948, British
TRAIN OF EVENTS   co-director with Basil Dearden &
    Sidney Cole, Rank, 1949, British
DANCE HALL   Rank, 1950, British
THE LAVENDER HILL MOB   Universal, 1951, British
THE STRANGER IN BETWEEN   *HUNTED*   Universal,
    1952, British
THE TITFIELD THUNDERBOLT   Universal, 1953, British
THE LOVER LOTTERY   Continental, 1953, British
THE DIVIDED HEART   Republic, 1954, British
DECISION AGAINST TIME   *THE MAN IN THE SKY*   MGM,
    1956, British
LAW AND DISORDER   co-director with Henry Cornelius,
    Continental, 1958, British
FLOODS OF FEAR   Universal, 1958, British
THE BATTLE OF THE SEXES   Continental, 1959, British
THE BOY WHO STOLE A MILLION   Paramount,
    1960, British
THE THIRD SECRET   20th Century-Fox, 1964, British
HE WHO RIDES A TIGER   Sigma III, 1966, British
A FISH CALLED WANDA ★   MGM/UA, 1988, British

MICHAEL CRICHTON*

b. October 23, 1942 - Chicago, Illinois
Address: 1750 14th Street - Suite C, Santa Monica, CA
90404, 213/452-6200
Agent: CAA - Beverly Hills, 213/288-4545

PURSUIT (TF)   ABC Circle Films, 1972
WESTWORLD   MGM, 1973
COMA   MGM/United Artists, 1978
THE GREAT TRAIN ROBBERY   United Artists,
1979, British
LOOKER   The Ladd Company/Warner Bros., 1981
RUNAWAY   Tri-Star, 1984
PHYSICAL EVIDENCE   Columbia, 1989

DONALD CROMBIE

b. Australia
Business: Forest Home Films, 141 Penhurst Street,
Willoughby, NSW, 2068, Australia, 02/411-4972

WHO KILLED JENNY LANGBY? (TF)   1974, Australian
DO I HAVE TO KILL MY CHILD? (TF)   1976, Australian
CADDIE   Atlantic Releasing Corporation, 1976, Australian
THE IRISHMAN   Forest Home Films, 1978, Australian
CATHY'S CHILD   CB Productions, 1979, Australian
THE KILLING OF ANGEL STREET   Forest Home Films,
1981, Australian
KITTY AND THE BAGMAN   Quartet/Films Incorporated,
1982, Australian
ROBBERY UNDER ARMS   co-director with Ken Hannam,
ITC Productions, 1985, Australian
PLAYING BEATIE BOW   CEL, 1986, Australian
CYCLONE TRACY (MS)   co-director with Kathy Mueller,
PBL Productions, 1986, Australian
THE ALIEN YEARS (MS)   Resulution/Australian
Broadcasting Corporation/Revcom TV, 1988, Australian
THE HEROES (TF)   TVS/Network Ten, 1988,
British-Australian
THE SAINT IN AUSTRALIA (TF)   Templar Productions/
Taffner Ramsay Productions, 1989, U.S.-Australian

DAVID CRONENBERG

b. March 15, 1943 - Toronto, Ontario, Canada
Business: 217 Avenue Road, Toronto, Ontario M5R 2J3,
Canada, 416/961-3432
Agent: CAA - Beverly Hills, 213/288-4545

STEREO   Emergent Films, 1969, Canadian
CRIMES OF THE FUTURE   Emergent Films,
1970, Canadian
THEY CAME FROM WITHIN   *SHIVERS*   Trans-America,
1976, Canadian
RABID   New World, 1977, Canadian
THE BROOD   New World, 1979, Canadian
FAST COMPANY   Topar, 1979, Canadian
SCANNERS   Avco Embassy, 1981, Canadian
VIDEODROME   Universal, 1983, Canadian
THE DEAD ZONE   Paramount, 1983, Canadian
THE FLY   20th Century Fox, 1986, U.S-Canadian
DEAD RINGERS   20th Century Fox, 1988, Canadian

AVERY CROUNSE

Business: Elysian Pictures - Los Angeles, 213/871-8689

EYES OF FIRE   Aquarius/Clark Films, 1984
THE INVISIBLE KID   Taurus Entertainment, 1988

CAMERON CROWE*

b. July 13, 1957 - Palm Springs, California
Agent: William Morris Agency - Beverly Hills, 213/274-7451

SAY ANYTHING   20th Century-Fox, 1989

CHRISTOPHER CROWE*

Agent: Bauer Benedek Agency - Los Angeles, 213/275-2421

STREETS OF JUSTICE (TF)   Universal TV, 1985
OFF LIMITS   20th Century Fox, 1988

DICK CROY

b. January 30, 1943 - Greensberg, Pennsylvania
Agent: Jim Heacock, Heacock Literary Agency, 1523 Sixth
Street, Santa Monica, CA 90405, 213/393-6227

THE UNKNOWN FORCE (TF)   International Television
Films, 1977

MARK CULLINGHAM*

b. September 14, 1941 - Windsor, England
Home: 2571 Glen Green, Los Angeles, CA 90068,
213/650-6555
Agent: Robinson, Weintraub, Gross & Associates -
Los Angeles, 213/653-5802

SUNDAY DRIVE (TF)   Walt Disney TV, 1986
GRYPHON (TF)   Max Mambru Films Ltd., 1988

ROBERT CULP*

b. August 16, 1930 - Berkeley, California
Personal Manager: Hillard Elkins, 1420 N. Laurel Avenue,
Los Angeles, CA 90046, 213/650-3806
Agent: David Wardlow, Camden Artists - Los Angeles,
213/556-2022

HICKEY AND BOGGS   United Artists, 1972

HOWARD CUMMINGS

STORY OF A MARRIAGE - EPISODE ONE:
COURTSHIP (MS)   Indian Falls Corporation/American
Playhouse/WGBH-Boston, 1987
BIG TIME (TF)   co-director with Jan Egleson, Advocated
Productions/ WGBH-Boston, 1989

SEAN S. CUNNINGHAM*

b. December 31, 1941 - New York, New York
Agent: Peter Rawley, ICM - Los Angeles, 213/550-4000

TOGETHER   Hallmark Releasing Corporation, 1971
CASE OF THE FULL MOON MURDERS   *CASE OF THE
SMILING STIFFS/SEX ON THE GROOVE TUBE*
co-director with Brad Talbot, Seaberg, 1974
HERE COME THE TIGERS   American International, 1978
MANNY'S ORPHANS   United Artists, 1979
FRIDAY THE 13TH   Paramount, 1980
A STRANGER IS WATCHING   MGM/United Artists, 1982
SPRING BREAK   Columbia, 1983
THE NEW KIDS   Columbia, 1985
DEEPSTAR SIX   Tri-Star, 1989

DAN CURTIS*

b. August 12, 1928 - Bridgeport, Connecticut
Agent: ICM - Los Angeles, 213/550-4000
Business Manager: Michael Rutman, Breslauer, Jacobson &
Rutman, 10345 Olympic Blvd., Los Angeles, CA 90064,
213/282-0477

HOUSE OF DARK SHADOWS   MGM, 1970
NIGHT OF DARK SHADOWS   MGM, 1971
THE NIGHT STRANGLER (TF)   ABC Circle Films, 1973
THE NORLISS TAPES (TF)   Metromedia Producers
Corporation, 1973

SCREAM OF THE WOLF (TF)   Metromedia Producers
   Corporation, 1974
DRACULA (TF)   Universal TV/Dan Curtis
   Productions, 1974
MELVIN PURVIS: G-MAN (TF)   American International
   TV, 1974
THE GREAT ICE RIP-OFF (TF)   ABC Circle Films, 1974
TRILOGY OF TERROR (TF)   ABC Circle Films, 1975
THE KANSAS CITY MASSACRE (TF)   ABC Circle
   Films, 1975
BURNT OFFERINGS   United Artists, 1976
CURSE OF THE BLACK WIDOW (TF)   Dan Curtis
   Productions/ABC Circle Films, 1977
WHEN EVERY DAY WAS THE FOURTH OF JULY (TF)
   Dan Curtis Productions, 1978
THE LAST RIDE OF THE DALTON GANG (TF)   NBC
   Productions/Dan Curtis Productions, 1979
MRS. R'S DAUGHTER (TF)   NBC Productions/Dan Curtis
   Productions, 1979
THE LONG DAYS OF SUMMER (TF)   Dan Curtis
   Productions, 1980
THE WINDS OF WAR (MS) ☆   Paramount TV/Dan Curtis
   Productions, 1983
WAR AND REMEMBRANCE (MS) ☆ Dan Curtis
   Productions/ABC Circle Films, 1988-89
DARK SHADOWS (TF)   Dan Curtis Productions/MGM-UA
   TV, 1990

DOUGLAS CURTIS

THE SLEEPING CAR   Triax Entertainment, 1990

D

RENEE DAALDER
b. Netherlands

DE BLANKE SLAVIN   1969, Dutch
MASSACRE AT CENTRAL HIGH   Brian Distributing, 1976
POPULATION: ONE   American Scenes, 1986

JOHN DAHL
Agent: Bauer Benedek Agency - Los Angeles, 213/275-2421

KILL ME AGAIN   MGM/UA,   1989

BOB DAHLIN*
Home: 828 Pine Street, Santa Monica, CA 90405,
   213/450-6206

MONSTER IN THE CLOSET   Troma, 1987

ZALE DALEN
b. 1947 - Iloilo, Philippines
Address: Site 1, Comp. 23, R.R. #1, 546 Marine Drive,
   Gibsons, British Columbia V0N 1V0, Canada,
   604/886-8029
Agent: Triad Artists, Inc. - Los Angeles, 213/556-2727

SKIP TRACER   Highlight Productions Ltd.,
   1977, Canadian
THE HOUNDS OF NOTRE DAME   Pan-Canadian Film
   Distributors, 1980, Canadian

HOLLYWOOD NORTH   Independent Pictures,
   1987, Canadian
ANYTHING TO SURVIVE (TF) ATL Productions/B.C. Films,
   1990, U.S.-Canadian
TERMINAL CITY RICOCHET   Festival Films,
   1990, Canadian

TOM DALEY
b. December 28, 1947 - Newark, New Jersey
Business: Pegasus Pictures, 821 Cooke Street, Honolulu,
   Hawaii 96813, 808/533-1805

THE OUTING   THE LAMP   TMS Pictures, 1987
BREAKDANCERS FROM MARS II: DOIN' THE LAMBADA
   Pegasus/Shoji Productions, 1990

ROBERT DALVA*
b. April 14, 1942 - New York, New York
Home: 33 Walnut Avenue, Larkspur, CA 94939,
   415/924-0164
Agent: Larry Becsey, The Agency - Los Angeles,
   213/551-3000

THE BLACK STALLION RETURNS   MGM/UA, 1983

DAMIANO DAMIANI
b. July 23, 1922 - Pasiano, Italy
Home: via delle Terme Deciane 2, Rome, Italy, 06/571841

IL ROSSETTO   Europa Cinematografica/Explorer Film/
   EFPC, 1960, Italian-French
IL SICARIO   Europa Cinematografica/Galatea, 1961, Italian
ARTURO'S ISLAND   MGM, 1962, Italian
LA RIMPATRIATA   Galatea/22 Dicembre/Coronet, 1963,
   Italian-French
THE EMPTY CANVAS   Embassy, 1964, Italian
LA STREGA IN AMORE   Arco Film, 1966, Italian
MAFIA   IL GIORNO DELLA CIVETTA   American
   International, 1968, Italian
A BULLET FOR THE GENERAL   QUIEN SABE?   Avco
   Embassy, 1968, Italian-Spanish
UNA RAGAZZA PIUTTOSTO COMPLICATA   Produzioni
   Filmena/Fono Roma, 1969, Italian
CONFESSIONS OF A POLICE CAPTAIN   CONFESSIONE
   DI UN COMMISSARIO   1970, Italian
LA MOGLIE PIU BELLA   Explorer '58, 1970, Italian
L'ISTRUTTORIA E CHIUSA DIMENTICHI   Fair Film,
   1971, Italian
IL SORRISO DEL GRANDE TENTATORE   Euro,
   1972, Italian
GIROLIMONI - IL MOSTRO DI ROMA   Dino De Laurentiis
   Cinematografica, 1972, Italian
THE DEVIL IS A WOMAN   20th Century-Fox, 1975,
   British-Italian
UN GENIO, DUE COMPARI, UN POLLO   Rafran
   Cinematografica, 1975, Italian
I AM AFRAID   Auro Cinematografica, 1977, Italian
GOODBYE AND AMEN   Cineriz, 1978, Italian-French
UN UOMO IN GINOCCHIO   Cineriz, 1979, Italian
TIME OF THE JACKALS   Capital, 1980, Italian
AMITYVILLE II: THE POSSESSION   Orion, 1982
LA PIOVRA (MS)   SACIS, 1984, Italian
ATTACCO ALLA PIOVRA   Columbia, 1985, Italian
PIZZA CONNECTION   C.G. Silver/Alexandre, 1985, Italian
L'INCHIESTA   Italian International, 1987, Italian
IL TRENO DI LENIN (TF)   RAI/Beta Taurus/TFI, 1988,
   Italian-West German-French
GIOCO AL MASSACRO   1989, Italian
THE PERFORMANCE   Sacis, 1989, Italian
THE DARK SUN   Cecchi Gori/Tiger/Reteitalia, 1990, Italian
LA VENDETTA, IL RITRATTO DI UNA DONNA   PAC/Atlas,
   1990, Italian

MEL DAMSKI*
b. July 21, 1946 - New York, New York
Agent: William Morris Agency - Beverly Hills, 213/274-7451

LONG JOURNEY BACK (TF)   Lorimar Productions, 1978
THE CHILD STEALER (TF)   The Production Company/
   Columbia TV, 1979
A PERFECT MATCH (TF)   Lorimar Productions, 1980
WORD OF HONOR (TF)   Georgia Bay Productions, 1981
AMERICAN DREAM (TF)   Mace Neufeld Productions/
   Viacom, 1981
FOR LADIES ONLY (TF)   The Catalina Production Group/
   Viacom, 1981
THE LEGEND OF WALKS FAR WOMAN (TF)   Roger
   Gimbel Productions/EMI TV/Raquel Welch Productions/
   Lee Levinson Productions, 1982
AN INVASION OF PRIVACY (TF)   Dick Berg-Stonehenge
   Productions/Embassy TV, 1983
YELLOWBEARD   Orion, 1983, British
ATTACK ON FEAR (TF)   Tomorrow Entertainment, 1984
MISCHIEF   20th Century Fox, 1985
BADGE OF THE ASSASSIN (TF)   Blatt-Singer
   Productions/Columbia TV, 1985
A WINNER NEVER QUITS (TF)   Blatt-Singer Productions/
   Columbia TV, 1985
HERO IN THE FAMILY (TF)   Barry & Enright Productions/
   Alexander Productions/Walt Disney Productions, 1986
MURDER BY THE BOOK   Nelson Productions/
   Orion TV, 1987
THE THREE KINGS (TF)   Aaron Spelling
   Productions, 1987
EVERYBODY'S BABY: THE RESCUE OF JESSICA
   McCLURE (TF) Dick Berg-Stonehenge Productions/The
   Campbell Soup Company/Interscope Productions, 1989
A CONNECTICUT YANKEE IN KING ARTHUR'S COURT
   (TF)   Schaefer-Karpf Productions/Consolidated
   Productions, 1989
THE GIRL WHO CAME BETWEEN THEM (TF)
   Saban-Scherick Productions, 1990
HAPPY TOGETHER   Borde Releasing Corporation, 1990

LAWRENCE DANE
b. 1937 - Masson, Quebec, Canada
Address: P.O. Box 310, Station F, Toronto MHY 2L7,
   Canada, 416/923-6000

HEAVENLY BODIES   MGM/UA, 1985, Canadian

CLAUDE D'ANNA
b. March 31, 1945
Contact: French Film Office, 745 Fifth Avenue, New York,
   NY 10151, 212/832-8860

LA MORT TROUBLE   1969, French
LA PENT DOUCE   1971, French
TROMP L'OEIL   1974, French
L'ORDRE ET LA SECURITE DU MONDE   1977, French
LE CERCLE DES PASSIONS   1982, French
PARTENAIRES   Dedalus/FR3, 1985, French
SALOME   Cannon, 1986, Italian-French
MACBETH   Dedalus/Unitel/SFPC/Atlantic Consolidated
   Enterprises, 1987, French-West German-U.S.
EQUIPE DE NUIT   Capital Cinema, 1988, French

ROD DANIEL*
Home: 619 Euclid Street, Santa Monica, CA 90402,
   213/394-1750
Agent: CAA - Beverly Hills, 213/288-4545

TEEN WOLF   Atlantic Releasing Corporation, 1985

STRANDED (TF)   Tim Flack Productions/Columbia TV,
   1986
LIKE FATHER LIKE SON   Tri-Star, 1987
K-9   Universal, 1989

HERBERT DANSKA*
Home: 711 Amsterdam Avenue, New York, NY 10025,
   212/666-4735

SWEET LOVE, BITTER   IT WON'T RUB OFF, BABY
   Peppercorn-Wormser, 1967
RIGHT ON!   Leacock-Pennebaker, 1970

JOE DANTE*
Agent: David Gersh, The Gersh Agency - Beverly Hills,
   213/274-6611

HOLLYWOOD BOULEVARD   co-director with Allan Arkush,
   New World, 1976
PIRANHA   New World, 1978
THE HOWLING   Avco Embassy, 1980
TWILIGHT ZONE - THE MOVIE   co-director with John
   Landis, Steven Spielberg & George Miller, Warner
   Bros., 1983
GREMLINS   Warner Bros., 1984
EXPLORERS   Paramount, 1985
AMAZON WOMEN ON THE MOON   co-director with John
   Landis, Carl Gottlieb, Robert K. Weiss & Peter Horton,
   Universal, 1987
INNERSPACE   Warner Bros., 1987
THE 'BURBS   Universal, 1989
GREMLINS 2 THE NEW BATCH   Warner Bros., 1990

RAY DANTON*
b. September 19, 1931 - New York, New York
Home: 25218-1/2 Malibu Road, Malibu, CA 90265,
   213/456-3558

THE DEATHMASTER   American International, 1972
CRYPT OF THE LIVING DEAD   Atlas, 1973
PSYCHIC KILLER   Avco Embassy, 1975
THE RETURN OF MICKEY SPILLANE'S MIKE HAMMER
   (TF)   Jay Bernstein Productions/Columbia TV, 1986
VIETNAM WAR STORY (CTF)   co-director with Georg
   Stanford Brown & Kevin Hooks, Nexus Productions,
   1987

PHILIP D'ANTONI*
b. February 19, 1929 - New York, New York
Contact: Directors Guild of America - Los Angeles,
   213/289-2000

THE SEVEN UPS   20th Century-Fox, 1973

FRANK DARABONT
Agent: Writers and Artists Agency - Los Angeles,
   213/820-2240

TILL DEATH DO US PART (CTF)   Niki Marvin Productions/
   USA Network, 1990
BURIED ALIVE(CTF)   Niki Marvin Productions/MCA
   Entertainment, 1990

JOAN DARLING*
b. April 14, 1935 - Boston, Massachusetts
Home: P.O. Box 6700, Tesuque, NM 87574, 505/983-1690
Agent: Naomi Gurian, The Gurian Agency - Los Angeles,
   213/550-0400

FIRST LOVE   Paramount, 1977

WILLA (TF)   co-director with Claudio Guzman, GJL
   Productions/Dove, Inc., 1979
THE CHECK IS IN THE MAIL   Ascot Entertainment
   Group, 1984
HIROSHIMA MAIDEN (TF)   Arnold Shapiro
   Productions, 1988

DAVID DARLOW
TAILSPIN: BEHIND THE KOREAN AIRLINE TRAGEDY
   (CTF)   Darlow Smithson Productions/HBO Showcase/
   Granada TV, 1989, U.S.-British

JAMES DARREN*
b. June 8, 1936 - Philadelphia, Pennsylvania
Agent: Larry Becsey, The Agency - Los Angeles,
   213/551-3000

POLICE STORY: GLADIATOR SCHOOL (TF)   Columbia
   TV, 1988

JULIE DASH
DAUGHTERS OF THE DUST   Geechee Girls Productions/
   American Playhouse Theatrical Films, 1990

JULES DASSIN
b. December 12, 1911 - Middletown, Connecticut
Home: Athinaeon Efivon 8, Athens, Greece 11521,
   tel.: 721-1616
Business Manager: Leon Kaplan, Mitchell, Silberberg &
   Knapp, 11377 W. Olympic Blvd., Los Angeles, CA
   90064, 213/312-3187

NAZI AGENT   MGM, 1942
THE AFFAIRS OF MARTHA   MGM, 1942
REUNION IN FRANCE   MGM, 1942
YOUNG IDEAS   MGM, 1943
THE CANTERVILLE GHOST   MGM, 1944
A LETTER FOR EVIE   MGM, 1945
TWO SMART PEOPLE   MGM, 1946
BRUTE FORCE   Warner Bros., 1947
THE NAKED CITY   Universal, 1948
THIEVES' HIGHWAY   RKO Radio, 1949
NIGHT AND THE CITY   20th Century-Fox, 1950, British
RIFIFI   Pathe, 1954, French
WHERE THE HOT WIND BLOWS   LA LOI   MGM, 1960,
   French-Italian
NEVER ON SUNDAY ★   Lopert, 1960, Greek
PHAEDRA   Lopert, 1962, Greek-U.S.-French
TOPKAPI   United Artists, 1964
10:30 P.M. SUMMER   Lopert, 1966, U.S.-Spanish
SURVIVAL '67 (FD)   United, 1968, U.S.-Israeli
UP TIGHT   Paramount, 1968
PROMISE AT DAWN   Avco Embassy, 1970, French-U.S.
A DREAM OF PASSION   Avco Embassy, 1978,
   Greek-U.S.
CIRCLE OF TWO   World Northal, 1981, Canadian

HERSCHEL DAUGHERTY*
Home: 925 Santa Fe Drive, Encinitas, CA 92024
Messages: 914/753-6470

THE LIGHT IN THE FOREST   Buena Vista, 1958
THE RAIDERS   Universal, 1963
WINCHESTER '73 (TF)   Universal TV, 1967
THE VICTIM (TF)   Universal TV, 1972
SHE CRIED "MURDER" (TF)   Universal TV, 1973
TWICE IN A LIFETIME (TF)   Martin Rackin
   Productions, 1974

BOAZ DAVIDSON*
b. August 11, 1943 - Tel Aviv, Palestine
Contact: Directors Guild of America - Los Angeles,
   213/289-2000

AZIT THE PARATROOPER DOG   Liran Corporation,
   1972, Israeli
CHARLIE AND A HALF   Filmonde, 1973, Israeli
LUPO GOES TO NEW YORK   Noah Films, 1977, Israeli
THE TZANANI FAMILY   Noah Films, 1978, Israeli
LEMON POPSICLE   Noah Films, 1981, Israeli
GOING STEADY (LEMON POPSICLE II)   Noah Film,
   1981, Israeli
SEED OF INNOCENCE   TEEN MOTHERS   Cannon, 1981
X-RAY   HOSPITAL MASSACRE   Cannon, 1981
HOT BUBBLEGUM (LEMON POPSICLE III)   Noah Films,
   1981, Israeli
THE LAST AMERICAN VIRGIN   Cannon, 1982
PRIVATE POPSICLE (LEMON POPSICLE IV)   Noah Films,
   1982, Israeli-West German
ALEX FALLS IN LOVE   Berkey Pathe, 1986, Israeli
DUTCH TREAT   Cannon, 1986
GOING BANANAS   Cannon, 1987
SALSA   Cannon, 1988

GORDON DAVIDSON*
b. May 7, 1933 - New York, New York
Business: Center Theatre Group, 135 N. Grand Avenue,
   Los Angeles, CA 90012, 213/972-7388
Agent: Michael Peretzian, William Morris Agency - Beverly
   Hills, 213/274-7451

WHO'S HAPPY NOW? (TF)   WNET-TV, 1968
THE TRIAL OF THE CATONSVILLE NINE   Cinema 5, 1972
IT'S THE WILLINGNESS (TF)   PBS, 1979

MARTIN DAVIDSON*
b. November 7, 1939 - New York, New York
Agent: Major Clients Agency - Los Angeles, 213/277-4998

THE LORDS OF FLATBUSH   co-director with Stephen
   Verona, Columbia, 1974
ALMOST SUMMER   Universal, 1978
HERO AT LARGE   MGM/United Artists, 1980
EDDIE AND THE CRUISERS   Embassy, 1983
LONG GONE (CTF)   HBO Pictures/The Landsburg
   Company, 1987
HEART OF DIXIE   Orion, 1989

JOHN DAVIES
b. August 20, 1934 - Birmingham, England
Home: 45 Leamington Road, London W11, England,
   71/221-7313

KIM (TF)   London Films, 1984, British

JOHN DAVIES
Business: Frontroom Productions, 79 Wardour Street,
   London W1, England, 71/743-4603

MY FAVOURITE FROM THE SOUTH   1978, British
CITY FARM   1979, British
MAEVE   1981, British
ACCEPTABLE LEVELS (TF)   Frontroom Productions/
   Channel Four, 1983, British
URSULA & GLENYS (TF)   Frontroom Productions,
   1985, British

RAY DAVIES
Contact: British Film & Television Academy, 195 Piccadilly,
London W1, England, 71/734-0022

RETURN TO WATERLOO   New Line Cinema,
1985, British

TERENCE DAVIES
Contact: British Academy of Film & Television Arts, 195
Piccadilly, London W1, England, 71/734-0022

DISTANT VOICES, STILL LIVES   Alive Films,
1988, British

ANDREW DAVIS*
Agent: Larry Becsey, The Agency - Los Angeles,
213/551-3000

STONY ISLAND   World Northal, 1980
THE FINAL TERROR   Comworld, 1983
CODE OF SILENCE   Orion, 1985
ABOVE THE LAW   Warner Bros., 1988
THE PACKAGE   Orion, 1989

BARRY DAVIS
Contact: British Academy of Film & Television Arts,
195 Piccadilly, London W1, England, 71/734-0022

TELFORD'S CHANGE (TF)   BBC Enterprises,
1979, British
OPPENHEIMER (MS)   BBC-TV/WGBH-Boston, 1982,
British-U.S.

BJ DAVIS*
Agent: Richard Shepherd, The Artists Agency -
Los Angeles, 213/277-7779
Business: 712 Wilshire Blvd. - Suite 50, Santa Monica, CA
90401, 213/462-2301

WHITE GHOST   Trans World Entertainment, 1988
LASER MISSION   Interfilm, 1990

DESMOND DAVIS
b. 1928 - London, England
Agent: Martin, Shapiro, Shapiro-Lichtman Agency -
Los Angeles, 213/859-8877

THE GIRL WITH GREEN EYES   United Artists,
1964, British
TIME LOST AND TIME REMEMBERED   I WAS HAPPY
HERE   Continental, 1966, British
THE UNCLE   Lennart, 1966, British
SMASHING TIME   Paramount, 1967, British
A NICE GIRL LIKE ME   Avco Embassy, 1969, British
CLASH OF THE TITANS   MGM/United Artists,
1981, British
THE SIGN OF FOUR   Mapleton Films Ltd., 1983, British
THE COUNTRY GIRLS   London Films Ltd./Channel Four,
1983, British
ORDEAL BY INNOCENCE   Cannon, 1984, British
CAMILLE (TF)   Rosemont Productions, 1984, U.S.-British
FREEDOM FIGHTER (TF)   HTV/Columbia TV/Embassy
TV, 1988, U.S.-British
THE MAN WHO LIVED AT THE RITZ (TF)   Harmony
Gold, 1988

OSSIE DAVIS
b. December 18, 1917 - Cogdell, Georgia
Agent: The Artists Agency - Los Angeles, 213/277-7779

COTTON COMES TO HARLEM   United Artists, 1970
BLACK GIRL   Cinerama Releasing Corporation, 1972
KONGI'S HARVEST   Tan Communications, 1973
GORDON'S WAR   20th Century-Fox, 1973
COUNTDOWN AT KUSINI   Columbia, 1976, U.S.-Nigerian

PETER DAVIS
Contact: Writers Guild of America, East - New York City,
212/245-6180

HEARTS AND MINDS (FD)   Warner Bros., 1975
THE RISE AND FALL OF THE BORSCHT BELT (FD)   1986
WINNIE/NELSON (FD)   1986

ANTHONY M. DAWSON
(Antonio Margheriti)
b. September 19, 1930 - Rome, Italy
Home: via Appia Antica 184, Rome Italy, 06/782-2367

SPACE-MEN   ASSIGNMENT OUTER SPACE   Ultra Film/
Titanus, 1960, Italian
THE OUTSIDER   Ultra Film/Lux Film, 1961, Italian
THE GOLDEN ARROW   MGM, 1962, Italian-U.S.
IL CROLLO DI ROMA   Atlantica Film, 1963, Italian
DANZA MACABRA   Addessi, 1963, Italian
ANTHAR L'INVINCIBILE   Antares Cinematografica,
1964, Italian
I LINGHI CAPELLI DELLA MORTE   Cinegay, 1964, Italian
LA VERGINE DI NORIMBERGA   Atlantica Cinematografica,
1964, Italian
I GIGANTI DI ROMA   Devon/Radius, 1964, Italian-French
URSUS IL TERRORE DEI KIRGHISI   Adelphia,
1964, Italian
IL PELO NEL MONDO   co-director with Marco Vicario,
Atlantica Cinematografica, 1964, Italian
LIGHTNING BOLT   OPERAZIONE GOLDMAN   Woolner
Brothers, 1965, Italian-Spanish
WILD, WILD PLANET   I CRIMINALI DELLA GELASSIA
MGM, 1966, Italian
WAR BETWEEN THE PLANETS   MISSIONE PIANETA
ERRANTE   Fanfare, 1966, Italian
PLANET ON THE PROWL   Mercury, 1966, Italian
SNOW MAN   Mercury, 1966, Italian
A 077 SFIDA AI KILLERS   Aenit/Flora/Regina, 1967, Italian
JOE L'IMPLACABILE   Seven/Hispamer, 1967,
Italian-Spanish
NUDE...SI MUORE   Super International Pictures,
1968, Italian
JOKO INVOCA DIO...E MUORI!   Super International
Pictures, 1968, Italian
IO TI AMO   Genesio, 1968, Italian
THE YOUNG, THE EVIL AND THE SAVAGE   SETTE
VERGINI PER IL DIAVOLO   American International,
1968, Italian
THE INNATURALS   SIP/EDO/CCC, 1969,
Italian-West German
...E DIO DISSE A CAINO   DC7, 1970, Italian
L'INAFFERABILE INVINCIBILE   MR. INVISIBILE   EDO/
Carsten, 1970, Italian- West German
NELLA STRETTA MORSA DEL RAGNO   DC7/Terra
Filmkunst/Paris-Cannes Productions, 1971, Italian-West
German-French
NOVELE GALEOTTE D'AMORE   Seven Film, 1972, Italian

FINALMENTE...LE MILLE E UNA NOTTE   Pink Medusa,
   1972, Italian
LA MORTE NEGLI OCCHI DEL GATTO   Starkis/Falcon/
   Roxy/Capitol, 1973, Italian-West German-French
MING, RAGAZZI!   Champion, 1973, Italian
DECAMERON 3   Starkis, 1973, Italian
MANONE IL LADRONE   Laser Film, 1974, Italian
WHISKY E FANTASMI   Champion/Cipi, 1974,
   Italian-Spanish
LES DIABLESSES   Planfilm, 1974, French-Italian-
   West German
BLOOD MONEY   Champion/Midega, 1974, Italian-Spanish
TAKE A HARD RIDE   20th Century-Fox, 1974
DEATH RAGE   *CON LA RABBIA AGLI OCCHI*   S.J.
   International, 1977, Italian
THE STRANGER AND THE GUNFIGHTER   Columbia,
   1976, Italian-Hong Kong
THE SQUEEZE   *THE RIP-OFF*   Maverick International,
   1976, Italian-U.S.
HOUSE OF 1,000 PLEASURES   Group 1, 1977, Italian
KILLER FISH   Associated Film Distribution, 1978,
   British-Brazilian-French
CANNIBALS IN THE STREETS   Almi Cinema 5, 1980,
   Italian-Spanish
THE LAST HUNTER   *HUNTER OF THE APOCALYPSE*
   World Northal, 1980, Italian
CAR CRASH   Cleminternational Cinematografica,
   1981, Italian
FUGA DALL'ARCIPELAGO MALEDETTO   Flora/Gico
   Cinematografica, 1982, Italian
THE HUNTERS OF THE GOLDEN COBRA   *THE
   RAIDERS OF THE GOLDEN COBRA*   World Northal,
   1982, Italian
YOR, THE HUNTER FROM THE FUTURE   Columbia,
   1983, Italian-Turkish-U.S.
TORNADO   Gico Cinematografica, 1983, Italian
ARK OF THE SUN GOD   Trans World Entertainment,
   1984, Italian-Turkish
I SOPRAVVISSUTI DELLA CITTA' MORTA   Flora Film,
   1984, Italian
CODENAME: WILDGEESE   New World, 1984, Italian-
   West German
LA LEGGENDA DEL RUBINO MALESE   L'Immagine,
   1985, Italian
COMMANDO LEOPARD   Ascot Distribution, 1985,
   West German-Italian
L'ISOLA DEL TESORO (MS)   RAI/TFI/Bavaria Film,
   1987, Italian-French- West German
THE COMMANDER   Prestige Film/Ascot Film, 1988,
   Italian-West German
INDIO   Filmauro/RPA/Reteitalia, 1989, Italian

ERNEST DAY*
Home: 9 The Ridings, Cobham, Surrey KT11 2PT,
   England, 37/284-3276
Agent: Sanford-Beckett-Skouras & Associates -
   Los Angeles, 213/208-2100

GREEN ICE   Universal/AFD, 1981, British
WALTZ ACROSS TEXAS   Atlantic Releasing
   Corporation, 1983

ROBERT DAY*
b. September 11, 1922 - Sheen, England
Agent: CAA - Beverly Hills, 213/288-4545

THE GREEN MAN   DCA, 1957, British
STRANGERS' MEETING   Rank, 1957, British
THE HAUNTED STRANGLER   *GRIP OF THE
   STRANGLER*   MGM, 1958, British
CORRIDORS OF BLOOD   MGM, 1958, British

FIRST MAN INTO SPACE   MGM, 1959, British
LIFE IN EMERGENCY WARD 10   Eros, 1959, British
BOBBIKINS   20th Century-Fox, 1960, British
TWO-WAY STRETCH   Showcorporation, 1960, British
TARZAN THE MAGNIFICENT   Paramount, 1960, British
CALL ME GENIUS   *THE REBEL*   Continental,
   1961, British
OPERATION SNATCH   Continental, 1962, British
TARZAN'S THREE CHALLENGES   MGM, 1963, British
SHE   MGM, 1965, British
TARZAN AND THE VALLEY OF GOLD   American
   International, 1966, U.S.-Swiss
TARZAN AND THE GREAT RIVER   Paramount, 1967
I THINK WE'RE BEING FOLLOWED   1967, British
THE HOUSE ON GREENAPPLE ROAD (TF)   QM
   Productions, 1970
RITUAL OF EVIL (TF)   Universal TV, 1970
BANYON (TF)   Warner Bros. TV, 1971
IN BROAD DAYLIGHT (TF)   Aaron Spelling
   Productions, 1971
MR. AND MRS. BO JO JONES (TF)   20th Century-
   Fox TV, 1971
THE RELUCTANT HEROES (TF)   Aaron Spelling
   Productions, 1971
THE GREAT AMERICAN BEAUTY CONTEST (TF)   ABC
   Circle Films, 1973
DEATH STALK (TF)   Wolper Productions, 1975
THE TRIAL OF CHAPLAIN JENSEN (TF)   20th Century-
   Fox TV, 1975
SWITCH (TF)   Universal TV, 1975
A HOME OF OUR OWN (TF)   QM Productions, 1975
TWIN DETECTIVES (TF)   Charles Fries Productions, 1976
KINGSTON: THE POWER PLAY (TF)   Universal TV, 1976
HAVING BABIES (TF)   The Jozak Company, 1976
BLACK MARKET BABY (TF)   Brut Productions, 1977
LOGAN'S RUN (TF)   Goff-Roberts-Steiner Productions/
   MGM TV, 1977
THE INITIATION OF SARAH (TF)   Charles Fries
   Productions, 1978
THE GRASS IS ALWAYS GREENER OVER THE SEPTIC
   TANK (TF)   Joe Hamilton Productions, 1978
MURDER BY NATURAL CAUSES (TF)   Richard
   Levinson-William Link Productions, 1979
WALKING THROUGH THE FIRE (TF)   Time-Life
   Films, 1979
THE MAN WITH BOGART'S FACE   *SAM MARLOW,
   PRIVATE EYE*   20th Century-Fox, 1980
PETER AND PAUL (TF)   Universal TV, 1981 .
SCRUPLES (TF)   Lou-Step Productions/Warner Brothers
   TV, 1981
MARIAN ROSE WHITE (TF)   Gerald Abrams Productions/
   Cypress Point Productions, 1982
RUNNING OUT (TF)   CBS Entertainment, 1983
YOUR PLACE OR MINE (TF)   Poolhouse Productions/
   Finnegan Associates, 1983
CHINA ROSE (TF)   Robert Halmi Inc., 1983
COOK & PEARY: THE RACE TO THE POLE (TF)
   Robert Halmi Inc., 1983
HOLLYWOOD WIVES (MS)   Aaron Spelling
   Productions, 1985
THE LADY FROM YESTERDAY (TF)   Barry Weitz Films/
   Comworld Productions, 1985
LOVE, MARY (TF)   CBS Entertainment, 1985
DIARY OF A PERFECT MURDER (TF)   Viacom
   Productions, 1986
THE QUICK AND THE DEAD (CTF)   HBO Pictures/Joseph
   Cates Company, 1987
CELEBRATION FAMILY (TF)   Frank von Zerneck
   Films, 1987
HIGHER GROUND (TF)   Green-Epstein Productions/
   Columbia TV, 1988

F
I
L
M

D
I
R
E
C
T
O
R
S

NISSIM DAYAN
b. 1946 - Tel Aviv, Palestine
Contact: Israel Film Centre, Ministry of Industry & Trade,
30 Agron Street, P.O. Box 299, Jerusalem, Israel,
02/210297

LIGHT FROM DARKNESS   1972, Israeli
THE END OF MILTON LEVY   1980, Israeli
CHILDREN OF VILLA EMMA (FD)   1983, Israeli
MICHAEL EZRA SAFRA AND SONS (MS)   1983, Israeli
ON A NARROW BRIDGE   Gesher Productions,
1985, Israeli

LYMAN DAYTON*
Home: 1021 Valley View Drive, St. George, UT 84770,
801/628-1534

BAKER'S HAWK   Doty-Dayton, 1976
RIVALS   World Entertainment, 1979
THE STRANGER AT JEFFERSON HIGH (TF)   Lyman
Dayton Productions, 1981
THE AVENGING   Comworld, 1981
SOLO   Dayton-Stewart Organization, 1984
THE RED FURY   Dayton-Stewart Organization, 1985
THE DREAM MACHINE   International Creative
Exchange, 1990

WILLIAM DEAR*
Agent: InterTalent - Los Angeles, 213/271-0600

TIMERIDER   Jensen Farley Pictures 1983
HARRY AND THE HENDERSONS   Universal, 1987
IF LOOKS COULD KILL   Warner Bros., 1991

JAMES DEARDEN
b. September 14, 1949 - London, England
Home: 7 Chesilton Road, London SW6 5AA, England,
71/736-6509
Agent: ICM - Los Angeles, 213/550-4000

THE COLD ROOM (TF)   Jethro Films/Mark Forstater
Productions, 1984, British
PASCALI'S ISLAND   Avenue Pictures, 1988, British-U.S.
A KISS BEFORE DYING   Universal, 1991

FRANK DEASY
THE COURIER   co-director with Joe Lee, Vestron, 1988,
Irish-British

JOHN DE BELLO
ATTACK OF THE KILLER TOMATOES   1980
HAPPY HOUR   TMS Pictures, 1987
RETURN OF THE KILLER TOMATOES   New World, 1988
KILLER TOMATOES STRIKE BACK   Four Square
Productions, 1990

GIANFRANCO de BOSIO
b. September 16, 1924 - Verona, Italy
Home: via Monti 57, Milan, Italy, 02/4985823

IL TERRORISTA   22 Dicembre/Galatea, 1964, Italian
LA BETIA   Titanus, 1972, Italian-Yugoslavian
MOSES THE LAWGIVER (MS)   ATV, Ltd./ITC/RAI, 1975,
British-Italian
MOSES   Avco Embassy, 1976, British-Italian, feature
film version of MOSES THE LAWGIVER

PHILIPPE de BROCA
b. March 15, 1933 - Paris, France
Contact: French Film Office, 745 Fifth Avenue, New York,
NY 10151, 212/832-8860

LES JEUX DE L'AMOUR   1960, French
THE JOKER   Lopert, 1961, French
THE FIVE DAY LOVER   Kinglsey International, 1961,
French-Italian
SEVEN CAPITAL SINS   co-director with Jean-Luc Godard,
Roger Vadim, Sylvaine Dhomme, Edouard Molinaro,
Claude Chabrol, Jacques Demy, Marie-Jose Nat,
Dominique Paturel, Jean-Marc Tennberg & Perrette
Pradier, Embassy, 1962, French-Italian
CARTOUCHE   Embassy, 1962, French-Italian
LES VEINARDS   co-director, 1962, French
THAT MAN FROM RIO   Lopert, 1964, French-Italian
MALE COMPANION   International Classics, 1966,
French-Italian
UP TO HIS EARS   *LES TRIBULATIONS D'UN CHINOIS
EN CHINE*   Lopert, 1966, French-Italian
THE KING OF HEARTS   Lopert, 1967, French-Italian
THE OLDEST PROFESSION   *LES PLUX VIEUX METIER
DU MONDE*   co-director with Franco Indovina, Mauro
Bolognini, Michael Pfleghar, Claude Autant-Lara & Jean-
Luc Godard, Goldstone, 1968, French- Italian-
West German
THE DEVIL BY THE TAIL   Lopert, 1969, French-Italian
GIVE HER THE MOON   *LES CAPRICES DE MARIE*
United Artists, 1970, French-Italian
TOUCH AND GO   *LA ROUTE AU SOLEIL*   Libra,
1971, French
LA POUDRE D'ESCAMPETTE   Columbia, 1971,
French-Italian
CHERE LOUISE   Warner-Columbia, 1972, French-Italian
LE MAGNIFIQUE   Cine III, 1973, French
INCORRIGIBLE   EDP, 1975, French
JULIE-POT-DE-COLLE   Prodis, 1977, French
DEAR DETECTIVE   *DEAR INSPECTOR*   Cinema 5, 1978,
French
LE CAVALEUR   CCFC, 1979, French
PRACTICE MAKES PERFECT   Quartet/Films Incorporation,
1980, French
JUPITER'S THIGH   *ON A VOLE LA CRUISSE DE JUPITER*
Quartet/Films Inc., 1980, French
PSY   Ariane Films/Antenne-2, 1981, French
L'AFRICAIN   Renn Productions, 1982, French
LOUISIANA (CTF)   ICC/Antenne-2/Superchannel/CTV/
Societe de Development de L'Industrie Cinematogra-
phique Canadienne, 1983, Canadian-French
PIRANHA D'AMOUR   AAA, 1985, French
LE CROCODILE   AMLF, 1985, French
LA GITANE   AMLF, 1986, French
CHOUANS   UGC, 1988, French
LES 1,001 NUITS   UGC, 1990, French-Italian

DAVID DeCOTEAU
CREEPOZOIDS   Urban Classics, 1987
LADY AVENGER   Filmtrust, 1987
SORORITY BABES IN THE SLIMEBALL BOWL-A-RAMA
Urban Classics, 1988
AMERICAN RAMPAGE   Amazing Movies, 1988
DEADLY EMBRACE   Cinema Home Video, 1988
DR. ALIEN   Phantom Productions, 1989
LADY AVENGER   South Gate Entertainment, 1989
NIGHTMARE SISTERS   Trans World Entertainment, 1989
TAN-TALIZER   Phillips & Mora Entertainment, 1990

FRANK de FELITTA*
b. August 3, 1921 - New York, New York
Home: 3008 Paulcrest Drive, Los Angeles, CA 90046,
    213/654-1310
Agent: Mickey Freiberg, The Artists Agency - Los Angeles,
    213/277-7779

TRAPPED (TF)   Universal TV, 1973
THE TWO WORLDS OF JENNY LOGAN (TF)   Joe Wizan
    TV Productions/ Charles Fries Productions, 1979
DARK NIGHT OF THE SCARECROW (TF)   Joe Wizan TV
    Productions, 1981
KILLER IN THE MIRROR (TF)   Litke-Grossbart
    Productions/Warner Bros. TV, 1986
SCISSORS   DDM Film Corporation, 1990

PHILIP DeGUERE*
Agent: CAA - Beverly Hills, 213/288-4545

DR. STRANGE (TF)   Universal TV, 1978

ROLF DE HEER
Contact: Australian Film Commission, 9229 Sunset Blvd.,
    Los Angeles, CA 90069, 213/275-7074

TAIL OF A TIGER   Producers Circle, 1986, Australian
INCIDENT AT RAVEN'S GATE   Hemdale,
    1988, Australian
DINGO - DOG OF THE DESERT   Gevest Productions,
    1990, Australian

MARK DEIMEL
PERFECT MATCH   Airtight Productions, 1987
DEUCE COUPE   Airtight Filmworks/Deuce Coupe
    Partners, 1990

DONNA DEITCH
b. June 8, 1945 - San Francisco, California
Agent: Martha Luttrell, ICM - Los Angeles, 213/550-4000
Business: Desert Heart Productions, 685 Venice Blvd.,
    Venice, CA 90291, 213/827-1515

DESERT HEARTS   Samuel Goldwyn Company, 1985
THE WOMEN OF BREWSTER PLACE (TF)   Harpo
    Productions/Phoenix Entertainment Group, 1989

STEVE DeJARNATT*
Agent: Bauer Benedek Agency - Los Angeles, 213/275-2421

ALFRED HITCHCOCK PRESENTS (TF)   co-director with
    Randa Haines, Joel Oliansky & Fred Walton, Universal
    TV, 1985
CHERRY 2000   Orion, 1986
MIRACLE MILE   Hemdale, 1988

ATE DE JONG*
Agent: The Lantz Office - Los Angeles, 213/858-1144

BLIND SPOT   Dutch
THE INHERITANCE   Dutch
KNOWN FACES, MIXED FEELINGS   Dutch
A FLIGHT OF RAINBIRDS   Dutch
BURNING LOVE   Dutch
SHADOW OF VICTORY   Dutch
HIGHWAY TO HELL   Hemdale, 1990

FRED DEKKER*
b. April 9, 1959 - San Francisco, California
Agent: InterTalent - Los Angeles, 213/271-0600

NIGHT OF THE CREEPS   Tri-Star, 1986
THE MONSTER SQUAD   Tri-Star, 1987

JEAN DELANNOY
b. January 12, 1908 - Noisy-le-Sec, France
Contact: French Film Office, 745 Fifth Avenue, New York,
    NY 10151, 212/832-8860

PARIS - DEAUVILLE   1935, French
LA VENUS DE L'OR   1938, French
LE DIAMANT NOIR   1940, French
MACAO L'ENFER DE JEU   1940, French
FIEVRES   1941, French
L'ASSASSIN A PEUR LA NUIT   1942, French
PONTACARRAL COLONEL D'EMPIRE   1942, French
L'ETERNEL RETOUR   1943, French
LE BOSSU   1944, French
LA PART DE L'OMBRE   1945, French
LA SYMPHONIE PASTORALE   1946, French
LES JEUX SONT FAITS   1947, French
AUX YEUX DU SOUVENIR   1949, French
LE SECRET DE MAYERLING   1949, French
DIEUX A BESOIN DES HOMMES   1950, French
LE GARCON SAUVAGE   1951, French
THE MOMENT OF TRUTH   Arlan Pictures, 1952, French
DAUGHTERS OF DESTINY   *DESTINEES*   co-director with
    Marcel Pagliero, Arlan Pictures, 1953, French-Italian
THE BED   *SECRETS D'ALCOVE*   co-director,
    Getz-Kingsley, 1953, French- Italian
LA ROUTE NAPOLEON   1953, French
OBSESSION   Gibe Films, 1954, French-Italian
CHIENS PERDUS SANS COLLIER   1955, French
MARIE ANTOINETTE   Rizzoli, 1956, French-Italian
THE HUNCHBACK OF NOTRE DAME   *NOTRE DAME DE
    PARIS*   RKO Radio, 1956, French
INSPECTOR MAIGRET   *MAIGRET TEND UN PIEGE*
    Lopert, 1958, French- Italian
GUINGUETTE   1959, French
MAIGRET ET L'AFFAIRE SAINT-FIACRE   1959, French
LE BARON DE L'ECLUSE   1960, French
LOVE AND THE FRENCHWOMAN   co-director with Michel
    Boisrond, Rene Clair, Christian-Jaque & Jean-Paul
    Lechannois, Kingsley International, 1960, French
LA PRINCESSE DE CLEVES   1961, French
LE RENDEZ-VOUS   1961, French
VENUS IMPERIALE   1962, French
THIS SPECIAL FRIENDSHIP   *LES AMITIES
    PARTICULIERES*   Pathe Contemporary, 1964, French
LE LIT A DEUX PLACES   1965, French
LE MAJORDOME   1965, French
LES SULTANS   1966, French
THE ACTION MAN   *LE SOLEIL DES VOYOUS*   H.K. Film
    Distribution, 1967, French
LE PEAU DE TORPEDO   1970, French
PAS FOLLE LA GUEPE   1972, French
BERNADETTE   Cannon, 1988, French
THE PASSION OF BERNADETTE   Rachel Productions,
    1990, French

BILL D'ELIA
Business: 212/532-7428

THE FEUD   Castle Hill Productions, 1990

FRANCIS DELIA*
Home: 9901 Edmore Place, Sun Valley, CA

FREEWAY   New World, 1988

JEFFREY S. DELMAN
Contact: 1918 Canal Street, # 2, Venice, CA 90291,
   213/306-3325
Manager: Matt Kenner, Kenner Organization -
   Santa Monica, 213/450-9497

DEAD TIME STORIES   Cinema Group, 1986

PETER DEL MONTE
b. 1943 - San Francisco, California
Home: via Poerio 59/D, Rome, Italy, 06/585451

FUORI CAMPO   Centro Sperimentale di Cinematografia,
   1969, Italian
LA PAROLE A VENIRE   RAI, 1970, Italian
IRENE IRENE   Cooperative Artea, 1975, Italian
L'ALTRA DONNA   RAI/ITF/Polytel International Film,
   1980, Italian
PISO PISELLO   RAI/Clesi Cinematografica, 1981, Italian
INVITATION AU VOYAGE   Mel Difussion/Filmalpha,
   1982, French-Italian
PICCOLI FUOCHI   Intersound, 1985, Italian
JULIA AND JULIA   Cinecom, 1987, Italian
ETOILE   Gruppo BEMA/Reteitalia, 1989, Italian

NATHALIE DELON
Contact: French Film Office, 745 Fifth Avenue, New York,
   NY 10151, 212/832-8860

SWEET LIES   Island Pictures, 1989, French-U.S.

DEBORAH DEL PRETE
SIMPLE JUSTICE   Panorama Entertainment, 1989

RUDY DeLUCA*
Agent: The Gersh Agency - Beverly Hills, 213/274-6611

TRANSYLVANIA 6-5000   New World, 1985

DOM DE LUISE*
b. August 1, 1933 - Brooklyn, New York
Home: 1186 Corsica Drive, Pacific Palisades, CA 90272,
   213/459-2911
Business Manager: Executive Business Management,
   132 S. Rodeo Drive, Beverly Hills, CA 90212,
   213/858-2000

HOT STUFF   Columbia, 1979

RICHARD DEMBO
b. 1948 - France
Contact: Swiss Film Center, Munstergasse 18, 8001 Zurich,
   Switzerland, 01/472860

DANGEROUS MOVES   Arthur Cohn Productions,
   1984, Swiss

BOB DEMCHUK*
Business: Scene East Productions, Ltd., 229 West 97th
   Street - Apt. 3B, New York, NY 10025, 212/749-2399

WHATEVER IT TAKES   Aquarius, 1986

JONATHAN DEMME*
b. 1944 - Rockville Centre, New York
Address: 225 Central Park West, New York, NY 10024,
   212/496-8810
Agent: CAA - Beverly Hills, 213/288-4545

CAGED HEAT   New World, 1974
CRAZY MAMA   New World, 1975
FIGHTING MAD   20th Century-Fox, 1976
CITIZENS BAND   *HANDLE WITH CARE*   Paramount, 1977
LAST EMBRACE   United Artists, 1979
MELVIN AND HOWARD   Universal, 1980
WHO AM I THIS TIME? (TF)   Rubicon Film
   Productions, 1982
SWING SHIFT   Warner Bros., 1983
STOP MAKING SENSE (FD)   Cinecom International/Island
   Alive, 1984
SOMETHING WILD   Orion, 1986
SWIMMING TO CAMBODIA   Cinecom, 1987
MARRIED TO THE MOB   Orion, 1988
SILENCE OF THE LAMBS   Orion, 1990

PIERRE De MORO
b. Corsica
Home: 16816 Charmel Lane, Pacific Palisades, CA 90272,
   213/454-0558 or 213/459-4197

DEVIL'S IVY   1973
CHRISTMAS MOUNTAIN   Christmas Mountain
   Productions, 1980
SAVANNAH SMILES   Embassy, 1983
HELL HOLE   Arkoff International Pictures, 1985
MICHELANGELO AND ME   Grand Marquee Films/Polivideo,
   1990, U.S.-Swiss

JACQUES DEMY*
b. June 5, 1931 - Pont-Chateau, France
Home: 86 Rue Daguerre, Paris 75014, France, 43/223-236
Agent: The Lantz Office - Los Angeles, 213/858-1144

LOLA   Films Around the World, 1961, French
SEVEN CAPITAL SINS   co-director with Jean-Luc Godard,
   Roger Vadim, Sylvaine Dhomme, Edouard Molinaro,
   Philippe de Broca, Claude Chabrol, Marie-Jose Nat,
   Dominique Paturel, Jean-Marc Tennberg & Perrette
   Pradier, Embassy, 1962, French-Italian
BAY OF THE ANGELS   Pathe Contemporary,
   1964, French
THE UMBRELLAS OF CHERBOURG   Landau, 1964,
   French-West German
THE YOUNG GIRLS OF ROCHEFORT   Warner Bros.,
   1968, French
MODEL SHOP   Columbia, 1969
DONKEY SKIN   Janus, 1971, French
THE PIED PIPER   Paramount, 1972, British-West German
L'EVENEMENT LE PLUS IMPORTANT DEPUIS QUE
   L'HOMME A MARCHE SUR LA LUNE   Lira Films/Roas
   Production, 1973, French-Italian
A SLIGHTLY PREGNANT MAN   SJ International,
   1977, French
LADY OSCAR   Toho, 1978, Japanese-French
UN CHAMBRE EN VILLE   UGC, 1982, French
PARKING   A.M. Films, 1985, French
LA TABLE TOURNANTE   Films Paul Grimault,
   1987, French
TROIS PLACES POUR LE 26   AMLF, 1988, French

CLAIRE DENIS

Contact: French Film Office, 745 Fifth Avenue, New York,
    NY 10151, 212/832-8860

CHOCOLAT   Orion Classics, 1988, French
S'EN FOUT LA MORT   Cinea/Pyramide/Camera One,
    1990, French

JEAN-PIERRE DENIS

Contact: French Film Office, 745 Fifth Avenue, New York,
    NY 10151, 212/832-8860

FIELD OF HONOR (CHAMP D'HONNEUR)   Orion
    Classics, 1987, French

PEN DENSHAM*

b. 1947 - England
Agent: WIlliam Morris Agency - Beverly Hills, 213/274-7451

THE ZOO GANG   co-director with John Watson, New
    World, 1985
THE KISS   Tri-Star, 1988, U.S.-Canadian

RUGGERO DEODATO
(Roger Rockefeller)

Home: via Caroncini 52, Rome, Italy, 06/870712

DONNE...BOTTE E BERSAGLIERI   Fida, 1968, Italian
FENOMENAL E IL TESORI DI TUTANKAMEN   Ikar,
    1968, Italian
GUNGALA LA PANTERA NUDA   Summa Cinematografica,
    1968, Italian
VACANZE SULLA COSTA SMERALDA   Fida,
    1969, Italian
I QUATTRO DEL PATER NOSTER   S.P.E.D. Film,
    1969, Italian
ZENABEL   Italiana Cinematografica Artisti Riuniti,
    1969, Italian
UNA ONDATA DI PIACERE   Tdl Cinematografica,
    1975, Italian
UOMINI SI NASCE POLIZIOTTI SI MUORE   C.P.C.
    Citta di Milano/ Tdl Cinematografica, 1976, Italian
ULTIMO MONDO CANNIBALE   Erre Cinematografica,
    1977, Italian
L'ULTIMO SAPORE DELL'ARIA   Tritone Cinematografica,
    1978, Italian
CONCORDE AFFAIRE '79   Dania Film/National
    Cinematografica, 1979, Italian
CANNIBAL HOLOCAUST   F.D. Cinematografica,
    1980, Italian
LA CASA SPERDUTA NEL PARCO   F.D.
    Cinematografica, 1980, Italian
I PREDATORI DI ATLANTIDE   Regency Productions,
    1983, Italian
INFERNO IN DIRETTA   Racing Pictures, 1985, Italian
THE BARBARIANS   Cannon, 1987, Italian
THE LONE RUNNER   Trans World Entertainment,
    1988, Italian
UN DELITTO POCO COMUNE   1988, Italian
CASABLANCA EXPRESS   1988, Italian
PHANTOM OF DEATH   Globe Films/Tandem
    Cinematografica/ Reteitalia, 1988, Italian
DIAL: HELP   Metro Film/San Francisco Film, 1989, Italian
OCEAN   San Francisco Film/Cristaldi Film/Cinecitta,
    1990, Italian

MANOEL DE OLIVEIRA

b. December 10, 1908 - Oporto, Portugal
Contact: Instituto Portugues de Cinema, Rua de S. Pedro
    de Alcantara 45, 1200 Lisbon, Portugal, 36-66-34

ESTATUAS DE LISBOA   1931, Portuguese
FAMILICAO   1940, Portuguese
ANIKI-BOBO   1942, Portuguese
ACTO DA PRIMAVERA   1963, Portuguese
O PASSADO E O PRESENTE   1972, Portuguese
BENILDE OU A VIRGEM   1975, Portuguese
AMOR DE PERDICAO   1978, Portuguese
FRANCISCA   1981, Portuguese
MEMORIAS E CONFISSOES   1982, Portuguese
LISBOA CULTURAL (TF)   1983, Portuguese
A PROPOS DE VIGO (TD)   1984, French
THE SATIN SLIPPER   Cannon, 1985, French
MON CAS   Les Films du Passage/La Sept/Filmargen,
    1986, French-Portuguese
OS CANIBAIS   Filmargem/Gemini Films/AB Cinema/Light
    Night/Pandora Films/Portugese Film Institute/Portuguese
    Radio and Television Company/Calouste Gulbenkian
    Foundation, 1988, Portuguese-French-Italian-Swiss-
    West German
NON OU A VA GLORIA DE MANDAR   Madragoa Filmes/
    Tornasol Filmes/Gemini Films/SGGC/RTP/Secretaria de
    Estado Da Cultura/Instituto Portugues de Cinema/
    Camara Municipal de Lisboa/Fundacao Calouste
    Gulbenkian/Fundacao Do Oriente/RTVE/Ministerio de la
    Cultura/CNC/Ministere de la Culture/Eurimages, 1990,
    Portuguese-Spanish-French

BRIAN DE PALMA*

b. September 11, 1940 - Newark, New Jersey
Agent: Bauer Benedek Agency - Los Angeles, 213/275-2421

MURDER A LA MOD   Aries, 1968
GREETINGS   Sigma III, 1968
THE WEDDING PARTY   co-director with Wilford Leach &
    Cynthia Munroe, Powell Productions Plus/Ondine, 1969
DIONYSUS IN '69   co-director with Robert Fiore & Bruce
    Rubin, Sigma III, 1970
HI, MOM!   Sigma III, 1970
GET TO KNOW YOUR RABBIT   Warner Bros., 1972
SISTERS   American International, 1973
PHANTOM OF THE PARADISE   20th Century-Fox, 1974
OBSESSION   Columbia, 1976
CARRIE   United Artists, 1976
THE FURY   20th Century-Fox, 1978
HOME MOVIES   United Artists Classics, 1980
DRESSED TO KILL   Filmways, 1980
BLOW OUT   Filmways, 1981
SCARFACE   Universal, 1983
BODY DOUBLE   Columbia, 1984
WISE GUYS   MGM/UA, 1986
THE UNTOUCHABLES   Paramount, 1987
CASUALTIES OF WAR   Columbia, 1989
THE BONFIRE OF THE VANITIES   Warner Bros., 1990

FRANK DE PALMA

b. May 3, 1957 - Compton, California
Telephone: 213/650-1146

FUTURE TENSE (CTF)   Walt Disney Productions, 1983
PRIVATE WAR   Smart Egg Releasing, 1989

JACQUES DERAY
(Jacques Deray Desrayaud)
b. February 19, 1929 - Lyons, France
Contact: French Film Office, 745 Fifth Avenue, New York,
   NY 10151, 212/832-8860

LE GIGOLO   1960, French
RIFIFI IN TOKYO   MGM, 1961, French-Italian
PAR UN BEAU MATIN D'ETE   1964, French
SYMPHONY FOR A MASSACRE   7 Arts, 1965,
   French-Italian
THAT MAN GEORGE!   L'HOMME DE MARRAKECH
   Allied Artists, 1966, French-Italian-Spanish
AVEC LA PEAU AUTRES   1967, French
THE SWIMMING POOL   Avco Embassy, 1970,
   French-Italian
BORSALINO   Paramount, 1970, French-Italian
DOUCEMENT LES BASSES!   CIC, 1971, French
UN PEU DE SOLEIL DANS L'EAU FROIDE   SNC,
   1971, French
THE OUTSIDE MAN   UN HOMME EST MORT   United
   Artists, 1973, French-Italian
BORSALINO AND CO.   Medusa, 1974, French-Italian
FLIC STORY   Adel Productions/Lira Films/Mondial,
   1975, French
LE GANG   Warner-Columbia, 1977, French
UN PAPILLON SUR L'EPAULE   Action Films,
   1978, French
TROIS HOMMES A ABBATRE   Adel Production/Films A2,
   1980, French
LE MARGINAL   Gaumont/Cerito Rene Chateau,
   1983, French
ON NE MEURT QUE DEUX FOIS   UGC, 1985, French
REGLEMENTS DE COMPTES   AMLF, 1986, French
MALADIE D'AMOUR   AMLF, 1987, French
LE SOLITAIRE   AMLF/Cerito, 1987, French
LES BOIS NOIRS   BAC Films, 1989, French

JOHN DEREK*
(Derek Harris)
b. August 12, 1926 - Hollywood, California
Agent: CAA - Beverly Hills, 213/288-4545

ONCE BEFORE I DIE   7 Arts, 1967, U.S.-Filipino
A BOY...A GIRL   Jack Hanson, 1968
CHILDISH THINGS   Filmworld, 1969
AND ONCE UPON A TIME   FANTASIES   Joseph Brenner
   Associates, 1973
LOVE YOU   1978
TARZAN, THE APE MAN   MGM/United Artists, 1981
BOLERO   Cannon, 1984
GHOSTS CAN'T DO IT   Triumph Releasing
   Corporation, 1990

DOMINIQUE DERUDDERE
Contact: Scott Yoselow, The Gersh Agency - New York
   City, 212/997-1818

LOVE IS A DOG FROM HELL   CRAZY LOVE
   1987, Belgian
WAIT UNTIL SPRING, BANDINI   Orion Classics, 1989,
   Belgian-French-Italian-U.S.

CALEB DESCHANEL*
b. September 21, 1944 - Philadelphia, Pennsylvania
Business: 73 Market Street, Venice, CA 90291,
   213/396-5937
Agent: Ronda Gomez-Quinones, Triad Artists, Inc.-
   Los Angeles, 213/556-2727

THE ESCAPE ARTIST   Orion/Warner Bros., 1982
CRUSOE   Island Pictures, 1988, U.S.-British

TOM DeSIMONE*
Agent: APA - Los Angeles, 213/273-0744

CHATTER-BOX   American International, 1977
HELL NIGHT   Compass International, 1981
THE CONCRETE JUNGLE   Pentagon, 1982
REFORM SCHOOL GIRLS   New World, 1986
ANGEL III: THE FINAL CHAPTER   New World, 1988

ANDRE DE TOTH*
(Sasvrai Farkasfawi Tothfalusi Toth Endre
Antai Mihaly)
b. 1910 - Mako, Hungary
Home: 3690 Barham Blvd., Burbank, CA 90068,
   818/874-3548

TOPRINI NASZ   BALALAIKA   1939, Hungarian
OT ORA 40   5:40 P.M.   1939, Hungarian
KET LANY AZ UTCAN   THE GIRLS ON THE STREET
   1939, Hungarian
SEMMELWEIS   1939, Hungarian
HAT HET BOLDOGSAG   SIX WEEKS OF HAPPINESS
   1939, Hungarian
PASSPORT TO SUEZ   Columbia, 1943
NONE SHALL ESCAPE   Columbia, 1944
DARK WATERS   United Artists, 1944
RAMROD   United Artists, 1947
THE OTHER LOVER   United Artists, 1947
PITFALL   United Artists, 1948
SLATTERY'S HURRICANE   20th Century-Fox, 1949
MAN IN THE SADDLE   Columbia, 1951
CARSON CITY   Warner Bros., 1952
SPRINGFIELD RIFLE   Warner Bros., 1952
LAST OF THE COMANCHES   Columbia, 1952
HOUSE OF WAX   Warner Bros., 1953
THE STRANGER WORE A GUN   Columbia, 1953
THUNDER OVER THE PLAINS   Warner Bros., 1953
RIDING SHOTGUN   Warner Bros., 1954
THE CITY IS DARK   Warner Bros., 1954
THE BOUNTY HUNTER   Warner Bros., 1954
TANGANYIKA   Universal, 1954
THE INDIAN FIGHTER   United Artists, 1955
MONKEY ON MY BACK   United Artists, 1957
HIDDEN FEAR   United Artists, 1957
THE TWO-HEADED SPY   Columbia, 1959
DAY OF THE OUTLAW   United Artists, 1959
MAN ON A STRING   Columbia, 1960
MORGAN THE PIRATE   MGM, 1960, British
THE MONGOLS   co-director with Leopoldo Savina,
   Colorama, 1960, Italian
GOLD FOR THE CAESARS   co-director with Sabatino
   Ciuffini, Colorama, 1962, Italian-French
PLAY DIRTY   United Artists, 1968, British

HOWARD DEUTCH*
Agent: CAA - Beverly Hills, 213/288-4545

PRETTY IN PINK   Paramount, 1986
SOME KIND OF WONDERFUL   Paramount, 1987
THE GREAT OUTDOORS   Universal, 1988

ROSS DEVENISH
b. South Africa
Agent: Peter Murphy, Curtis Brown, 162-168 Regent
    Street, London W1R 57B, England, 71/437-9700

BOESMAN AND LENA   Bluewater, 1974, South African
THE GUEST AT STEENKAMPSKRAAL   Guest
    Productions, 1977, South African
MARIGOLDS IN AUGUST   Southern Serpent Productions/
    RM Productions, 1980, South African
CHIP OF GLASS RUBY (TF)   Channel Four, 1983, British
BLEAK HOUSE (MS)   BBC, 1985, British
THE HAPPY VALLEY (TF)   BBC, 1986, British
ASINAMALI (TF)   Porterhouse Productions/BBC,
    1986, British
DEATH OF A SON (TF)   Centre Films/BBC, 1988, British

MICHEL DEVILLE
b. April 13, 1931 - Boulogne-sur-Seine, France
Contact: French Film Office, 745 Fifth Avenue, New
    York, NY 10151, 212/832-8860

UNE BALLE DANS LE CANON   co-director with Charles
    Gerard, 1958
CE SOIR OU JAMAIS   1960, French
ADORABLE MENTEUSE   1961, French
A CAUSE A CAUSE D'UNE FEMME   1962, French
L'APPARTEMENT DES VOLE LA JACONDE
    1965, French
MARTIN SOLDAT   1966, French
TENDRE REQUINS   1967, French
BENJAMIN   *BENJAMIN OU LES MEMOIRES D'UN
    PUCEAU*   Paramount, 1968, French
BYE BYE BARBARA   1969, French
THE BEAR AND THE DOLL   Paramount, 1970, French
RAPHAEL OU LE DEBAUCHE   Columbia, 1971, French
LA FEMME EN BLEU   Les Films La Boetie, 1973,
    French-Italian
THE FRENCH WAY   *LE MOUTON ENRAGE*
    Peppercorn-Wormser, 1974, French
L'APPRENTI SALAUD   Prodis, 1977, French
LE DOSSIER 51   1978, French
VOYAGE EN DOUCE   1980, French
EAUX PROFONDES   1982, French
LA PETITE BANDE   1983, French
PERIL   *PERIL EN LA DEMEURE*   Triumph/Columbia,
    1985, French
DEATH IN A FRENCH GARDEN   1986, French
LE PALTOQUET   AAA, 1986, French
LA LECTRICE (THE READER)   Orion Classics,
    1988, French
NUIT D'ETE EN VILLE   AAA, 1990, French

DANNY DeVITO*
b. November 17, 1944 - Asbury Park, New Jersey
Agent: CAA - Beverly Hills, 213/288-4545

THE RATINGS GAME (CTF)   Imagination-New Street
    Productions, 1984
THROW MOMMA FROM THE TRAIN   Orion, 1987
THE WAR OF THE ROSES   20th Century Fox, 1989

DAVID deVRIES*
Business: David deVries Films, 100 Riverside Drive,
    New York, NY 10024, 212/580-2888

HOME AT LAST (TF)   deVries Films, 1988

MAURY DEXTER*
b. 1927
Business Manager: Hank Tani, 1384 Camino Magenta,
    Thousand Oaks, 805/498-0540

THE HIGH POWERED RIFLE   20th Century-Fox, 1960
WALK TALL   20th Century-Fox, 1960
THE PURPLE HILLS   20th Century-Fox, 1961
WOMAN HUNT   20th Century-Fox, 1961
THE FIREBRAND   20th Century-Fox, 1962
AIR PATROL   20th Century-Fox, 1962
THE DAY MARS INVADED EARTH   20th Century-
    Fox, 1962
HOUSE OF THE DAMNED   20th Century-Fox, 1962
HARBOR LIGHTS   20th Century-Fox, 1963,
    U.S.-Puerto Rican
THE YOUNG SWINGERS   20th Century-Fox, 1963
POLICE NURSE   20th Century-Fox, 1963
YOUNG GUNS OF TEXAS   20th Century-Fox, 1963
SURF PARTY   20th Century-Fox, 1963
RAIDERS FROM BENEATH THE SEA   20th Century-
    Fox, 1964
WILD ON THE BEACH   20th Century-Fox, 1965
THE NAKED BRIGADE   Universal, 1965
MARYJANE   American International, 1968
THE MINI-SKIRT MOB   American International, 1968
BORN WILD   American International, 1968
HELL'S BELLES   American International, 1969

NIGEL DICK
Agent: The Gersh Agency - Beverly Hills, 213/274-6611

PRIVATE INVESTIGATIONS   MGM/UA, 1987
DEADLY INTENT   Fries Entertainment, 1988

CARLOS DIEGUES
b. 1940 - Maceio, Alagoas, Brazil
Contact: Concine/National Cinema Council, Rua Mayrink
    Veiga 28, Rio de Janeiro, Brazil, 2/233-8329

GANGA ZUMBA   1963, Brazilian
O GRANDE CIDADE   1966, Brazilian
OS HERDEIROS   1969, Brazilian
QUANDO O CARNAVAL CHEGAR   1972, Brazilian
JOANA FRANCESCA   1973, Brazilian
XICA   XICA DA SILVA   New Yorker, 1976, Brazilian
CHUVAS DE VERAO   1978, Brazilian
BYE BYE BRAZIL   Carnaval/Unifilm, 1980, Brazilian
QUILOMBO   New Yorker, 1984, Brazilian
SUBWAY TO THE STARS   FilmDallas, 1987,
    Brazilian-French
DIAS MELHORES VIRAO   Embrafilme, 1990, Brazilian

MARIO DI LEO*
Business: Di Leo Enterprises, 2100 N. Topanga
    Canyon Blvd., Topanga, CA 90290, 213/455-1323
Agent: Barry Perelman, Barry Perelman Agency -
    Los Angeles, 213/274-5999

FINAL ALLIANCE   Trans World Entertainment, 1989

MICHAEL DINNER*
Agent: William Morris Agency - Beverly Hills, 213/274-7451
Business Manager: Victor Meschures, Jamner, Pariser &
  Meschures, 760 N. La Cienega Blvd., Los Angeles, CA
  90069, 213/652-0222

MISS LONELYHEARTS   H. Jay Holman Productions/
  American Film Institute, 1983
HEAVEN HELP US   Tri-Star, 1985
OFF BEAT   Buena Vista, 1986
HOT TO TROT   Warner Bros., 1988

VINCENT DiPERSIO*
Contact: Directors Guild of America - Los Angeles,
  213/289-2000

FLYING BLIND   Columbia, 1989

MARK DiSALLE
KICKBOXER   co-director with David Worth,
  Cannon, 1989

IVAN DIXON*
b. April 6, 1931 - New York, New York
Contact: Directors Guild of America - Los Angeles,
  213/289-2000

TROUBLE MAN   20th Century-Fox, 1972
THE SPOOK WHO SAT BY THE DOOR   United
  Artists, 1973
LOVE IS NOT ENOUGH (TF)   Universal TV, 1978

KEN DIXON
SLAVE GIRLS FROM BEYOND INFINITY   Urban
  Classics, 1987

WHEELER DIXON
b. March 12, 1950 - New Brunswick, New Jersey
Attorney: Mark Brown, Muffly, Oglesby & Brown, 414 S.
  11th Street, Lincoln, NE 68508, 402/479-3397

THE GAMMA CHRONICLES (MS)   Gold Key
  Entertainment, 1980
THE GALAXY COLLECTION (TF)   Deliniator Films, 1985

EDWARD DMYTRYK*
b. September 4, 1908 - Grand Forks, Canada
Agent: Kurt Frings Agency - Beverly Hills, 213/274-8883

THE HAWK   Herman Wohl, 1935
TELEVISION SPY   Paramount, 1939
EMERGENCY SQUAD   Paramount, 1940
MYSTERY SEA RAIDERS   Paramount, 1940
GOLDEN GLOVES   Paramount, 1940
HER FIRST ROMANCE   Monogram, 1940
THE DEVIL COMMANDS   Columbia, 1941
UNDER AGE   Columbia, 1941
SWEETHEART OF THE CAMPUS   Columbia, 1941
THE BLONDE FROM SINGAPORE   Columbia, 1941
CONFESSIONS OF BOSTON BLACKIE   Columbia, 1941
SECRETS OF THE LONE WOLF   Columbia, 1941
COUNTER ESPIONAGE   Columbia, 1942
SEVEN MILES FROM ALCATRAZ   RKO Radio, 1942
THE FALCON STRIKES BACK   RKO Radio, 1943
HITLER'S CHILDREN   RKO Radio, 1943
CAPTIVE WILD WOMAN   Universal, 1943
BEHIND THE RISING SUN   RKO Radio, 1943

TENDER COMRADE   RKO Radio, 1943
MURDER MY SWEET   RKO Radio, 1945
BACK TO BATAAN   RKO Radio, 1945
TILL THE END OF TIME   RKO Radio, 1945
CROSSFIRE ★   RKO Radio, 1947
SO WELL REMEMBERED   RKO Radio, 1947
THE HIDDEN ROOM   *OBSESSION*   British Lion,
  1949, British
GIVE US THIS DAY   *SALT TO THE DEVIL*   Eagle Lion,
  1949, British
MUTINY   Universal, 1952
THE SNIPER   Columbia, 1952
EIGHT IRON MEN   Columbia, 1952
THE JUGGLER   Columbia, 1953
THE CAINE MUTINY   Columbia, 1954
BROKEN LANCE   20th Century-Fox, 1954
THE END OF THE AFFAIR   Columbia, 1954
SOLDIER OF FORTUNE   20th Century-Fox, 1955
THE LEFT HAND OF GOD   20th Century-Fox, 1955
THE MOUNTAIN   Paramount, 1956
RAINTREE COUNTY   MGM, 1957
THE YOUNG LIONS   20th Century-Fox, 1958
WARLOCK   20th Century-Fox, 1959
THE BLUE ANGEL   20th Century-Fox, 1959
WALK ON THE WILD SIDE   Columbia, 1962
THE RELUCTANT SAINT   Davis-Royal, 1962, Italian-U.S.
THE CARPETBAGGERS   Paramount, 1963
WHERE LOVE HAS GONE   Paramount, 1964
MIRAGE   Universal, 1965
ALVAREZ KELLY   Columbia, 1966
ANZIO   Columbia, 1968, Italian
SHALAKO!   Cinerama Releasing Corporation, 1968, British
BLUEBEARD   Cinerama Releasing Corporation, 1972,
  Italian-French-West German
THE HUMAN FACTOR   Bryanston, 1974, British-U.S.
HE IS MY BROTHER   Atlantic Releasing Corporation, 1976

FRANK Q. DOBBS*
Agent: Ronald Leif, Contemporary Artists - Beverly Hills,
  213/278-8250

UPHILL ALL THE WAY   New World, 1985

JERZY DOMARADZKI
Contact: Ministry of Culture and Arts, Cinematography
  Authority, Krakowskie Przedmiecie 21/23, 00071 Warsaw,
  Poland, tel.: 268072

THE BIG RACE   Film Unit X/Poltel/Perspektyva Unit,
  1981, Polish
THE TAILOR'S PLANET   Film Unit X, 1983, Polish
WHITE DRAGON   Legend Productions/Perspektyva, 1986,
  U.S.-Poland
CUPID'S BOW   Perspektyva Unit, 1987, Polish
RIDERS ON THE STORM   Beyond International,
  1990, Australian

ROGER DONALDSON*
b. November 15, 1945 - Ballarat, Australia
Agent: CAA - Beverly Hills, 213/288-4545

SLEEPING DOGS   Aardvark Films, 1977, New Zealand
SMASH PALACE   Atlantic Releasing Corporation, 1981,
  New Zealand
THE BOUNTY   Orion, 1984, British
MARIE   MGM/UA, 1985
NO WAY OUT   Orion, 1987
COCKTAIL   Buena Vista, 1988
CADILLAC MAN   Orion, 1990

STANLEY DONEN*

b. April 13, 1924 - Columbia, South Carolina
Agent: Sam Cohn, ICM - New York City, 212/556-5600

ON THE TOWN   co-director with Gene Kelly, MGM, 1949
ROYAL WEDDING   MGM, 1951
SINGIN' IN THE RAIN   co-director with Gene Kelly,
   MGM, 1952
LOVE IS BETTER THAN NONE   MGM, 1952
FEARLESS FAGAN   MGM, 1952
GIVE A GIRL A BREAK   MGM, 1953
SEVEN BRIDES FOR SEVEN BROTHERS   MGM, 1954
DEEP IN MY HEART   MGM, 1954
IT'S ALWAYS FAIR WEATHER   co-director with
   Gene Kelly, MGM, 1955
FUNNY FACE   Paramount, 1957
THE PAJAMA GAME   co-director with George Abbott,
   Warner Bros., 1957
KISS THEM FOR ME   20th Century-Fox, 1957
INDISCREET   Warner Bros., 1958, British
DAMN YANKEES   co-director with George Abbott,
   Warner Bros., 1958
ONCE MORE, WITH FEELING   Columbia, 1960
SURPRISE PACKAGE   Columbia, 1960
THE GRASS IS GREENER   Universal, 1961
CHARADE   Universal, 1964
ARABESQUE   Universal, 1966, British-U.S.
TWO FOR THE ROAD   20th Century-Fox, 1967,
   British-U.S.
BEDAZZLED   20th Century-Fox, 1967, British
STAIRCASE   20th Century-Fox, 1969, British
THE LITTLE PRINCE   Paramount, 1974, British
LUCKY LADY   20th Century-Fox, 1975
MOVIE MOVIE   Warner Bros., 1978
SATURN 3   AFD, 1980
BLAME IT ON RIO   20th Century Fox, 1984

WALTER DONIGER*

b. July 1, 1917 - New York, New York
Home: 555 Huntley Drive, Los Angeles, CA 90048,
   213/659-2787

DUFFY OF SAN QUENTIN   Warner Bros., 1953
THE STEEL CAGE   United Artists, 1954
THE STEEL JUNGLE   Warner Bros., 1955
UNWED MOTHER   Allied Artists, 1958
HOUSE OF WOMEN   Warner Bros., 1960
SAFE AT HOME!   Columbia, 1962
MAD BULL   co-director with Len Steckler, Steckler
   Productions/Filmways, 1977
KENTUCKY WOMAN   Walter Doniger Productions/20th
   Century-Fox TV, 1983

TOM DONNELLY*

Agent: Bauer Benedek Agency - Los Angeles,
   213/275-2421

QUICKSILVER   Columbia, 1986

CLIVE DONNER*

b. January 21, 1926 - London, England
Contact: Directors Guild of America - Los Angeles,
   213/289-2000

THE SECRET PLACE   Rank, 1957, British
HEART OF A CHILD   Rank, 1958, British
MARRIAGE OF CONVENIENCE   Allied Artists,
   1961, British
THE SINISTER MAN   Allied Artists, 1961, British
SOME PEOPLE   American International, 1962, British

THE GUEST   *THE CARETAKER*   Janus, 1963, British
NOTHING BUT THE BEST   Royal Films International,
   1964, British
WHAT'S NEW PUSSYCAT?   United Artists, 1965, British
LUV   Columbia, 1967
HERE WE GO ROUND THE MULBERRY BUSH   Lopert,
   1968, British
ALFRED THE GREAT   MGM, 1969, British
OLD DRACULA   *VAMPIRA*   American International,
   1975, British
ROGUE MALE (TF)   BBC, 1976, British
SPECTRE (TF)   20th Century-Fox TV, 1977
THE THIEF OF BAGHDAD (TF)   Palm Films Ltd.,
   1979, British
THE NUDE BOMB   Universal, 1980
CHARLIE CHAN AND THE CURSE OF THE DRAGON
   QUEEN   American Cinema, 1980
OLIVER TWIST (TF)   Claridge Group Ltd./Grafton Films,
   1982, British
THE SCARLET PIMPERNEL (TF)   London Films Ltd.,
   1982, British
TO CATCH A KING (CTF)   HBO Premiere Films/
   Entertainment Partners/Gaylord Productions, 1984
A CHRISTMAS CAROL (TF)   Entertainment Partners Ltd.,
   1984, U.S.-British
ARTHUR THE KING (TF)   Martin Poll Productions/Comworld
   Productions/Jadran Film, 1985, U.S.-Yugoslavian
AGATHA CHRISTIE'S 'DEAD MAN'S FOLLY' (TF)   Warner
   Bros. TV, 1986, U.S.-British
BABES IN TOYLAND (TF)   Orion TV/Finnegan Associates/
   Bavaria Atelier, 1986
STEALING HEAVEN   Scotti Bros., 1988, U.S.-Yugoslavian
NOT A PENNY MORE, NOT A PENNY LESS (TF)   BBC/
   Paramount TV/Revcom, 1990, British-U.S.

JÖRN DONNER

b. February 5, 1933 - Helsinki, Finland
Business: Jörn Donner Productions, Pohjoisranta 12,
   SF-00170 Helsinki, Finland, 0/66-12-12

A SUNDAY IN SEPTEMBER   1963, Swedish
TO LOVE   1964, Swedish
ADVENTURE STARTS HERE   1965, Swedish
STIMULANTIA   co-director, 1967, Swedish
ROOFTREE   1967, Swedish
BLACK ON WHITE   1968, Finnish
SIXTYNINE   1969, Finnish
PORTRAITS OF WOMEN   1970, Finnish
ANNA   1970, Finnish
FUCK OFF! IMAGES OF FINLAND (FD)   1971, Finnish
TENDERNESS   1972, Finnish
THE WORLD OF INGMAR BERGMAN (FD)   1975, Swedish
MAN CANNOT BE RAPED   1978, Finnish
9 WAYS TO APPROACH HELSINKI (TD)   1982, Finnish

RICHARD DONNER*

Agent: CAA - Beverly Hills, 213/288-4545
Business Manager: Gerald Breslauer, Breslauer, Jacobson &
   Rutman - Los Angeles, 213/282-0477

X-15   United Artists, 1961
SALT AND PEPPER   United Artists, 1968, British
LOLA   *TWINKY*   American International, 1970,
   British-Italian
LUCAS TANNER (TF)   Universal TV, 1974
SENIOR YEAR (TF)   Universal TV, 1974
A SHADOW IN THE STREETS (TF)   Playboy
   Productions, 1975
SARAH T. - PORTRAIT OF A TEENAGE ALCOHOLIC (TF)
   Universal TV, 1975

THE OMEN   20th Century-Fox, 1976
SUPERMAN   Warner Bros., 1978, U.S.-British
INSIDE MOVES   AFD, 1980
THE TOY   Columbia, 1982
LADYHAWKE   Warner Bros., 1985
THE GOONIES   Warner Bros., 1985
LETHAL WEAPON   Warner Bros., 1987
SCROOGED   Paramount, 1988
LETHAL WEAPON 2   Warner Bros., 1989
RADIO FLYER   Columbia, 1991

MARTIN DONOVAN
b. Argentina
Agent: Bauer Benedek Agency - Los Angeles, 213/275-2421

APARTMENT ZERO   Skouras Pictures, 1988,
   British-Argentine

PAUL DONOVAN
b. 1954 - Canada
Address: P.O. Box 2261, Station M, Halifax, Nova
   Scotia B3J 3L8, Canada, 902/420-1577

TORPEDOED   *SOUTH PACIFIC 1942*   Surfacing Film
   Productions, 1980, Canadian
SELF DEFENSE   *SIEGE*   co-director with Maura
   O'Connell, New Line Cinema, 1983, Canadian
DEF-CON 4   New World, 1985, Canadian
CARIBE   Shapiro Entertainment, 1987, Canadian
THE SQUAMISH FIVE   CBC, 1988, Canadian
GEORGE'S ISLAND   Astral Films, 1989, Canadian
NORMAN'S AWESOME EXPERIENCE   Norstar
   Entertainment, 1989, Canadian, filmed in 1987

TOM DONOVAN*
Business: Director's Service, Inc., 650 Park Avenue,
   New York, NY 10021, 212/737-6910
Attorney: Thomas H. Ryan - New York City, 212/355-7003

THE LAST BRIDE OF SALEM (TF)   20th Century-Fox
   TV, 1974
TRISTAN AND ISOLT   *LOVESPELL*   Clar Productions,
   1981, British

LEE DOO-YONG
b. December 24, 1942 - Seoul, Korea

(The following is an incomplete list of Mr. Lee's credits)

LOST WEDDING VEIL   1970, South Korean
YOUR DADDY LIKE THIS?   1971, South Korean
THE GENERAL IN RED ROBE   1973, South Korean
CHOBUN   1977, South Korean
POLICE STORY   1978, South Korean
MULDORI VILLAGE   1979, South Korean
PIMAK   1980, South Korean
SPINNING WHEEL   1983, South Korean
FIRST SON   1984, South Korean
PONG   1985, South Korean
EUNUCH   1986, South Korean

ROBERT DORNHELM
THE CHILDREN OF THEATRE STREET (FD)
   Peppercorn-Wormser, 1977
SHE DANCES ALONE   Continental, 1982, U.S.-Austrian
DIGITAL DREAMS   Ripple Productions Ltd., 1983
ECHO PARK   Atlantic Releasing Corporation, 1985,
   U.S.-Austrian
COLD FEET   Avenue Pictures, 1989

DORIS DÖRRIE
(Doris Doerrie)
b. 1955 - Hanover, West Germany
Agent: William Morris Agency - Beverly Hills, 213/274-7451

STRAIGHT THROUGH THE HEART   1983, West German
IN THE BELLY OF THE WHALE   1984, West German
MEN...   New Yorker, 1985, West German
PARADIES   Delta Film/H.J. Seybusch/WDR, 1986,
   West German
ME AND HIM   Columbia, 1988, West German-U.S.
GELD   Olga Film/ZDF, 1990, West German

SHIMON DOTAN
b. December 23, 1949 - Ajud, Romania
Agent: Shapiro-Lichtman Agency - Los Angeles,
   213/859-8877

REPEAT DIVE   Original Cinema, 1982, Israeli
83 (FD)   co-director, Tzavta, 1983
THE SMILE OF THE LAMB   Original Cinema, 1986, Israeli

BILL DOUGLAS
b. Scotland
Home: Flat 3, 3-4 Archer Street, London W1V 7HE, England
Contact: British Film Institute, 81 Dean Street, London W1,
   England

MY CHILDHOOD   British Film Institute, 1972, British
MY AIN FOLK   British Film Institute, 1973, British
MY WAY HOME   British Film Institute, 1978, British
COMRADES   British Film Institute, 1986, British-Australian

GORDON DOUGLAS*
b. December 5, 1909 - New York, New York
Home: 6600 West 6th Street, Los Angeles, CA 90048
Business Manager: Robert Stilwell, Ryder, Stilwell, Inc., P.O.
   Box 92920, Los Angeles, CA 90009, 213/937-5500

GENERAL SPANKY   co-director with Fred Newmayer,
   MGM, 1936
ZENOBIA   United Artists, 1939
SAPS AT SEA   United Artists, 1940
ROAD SHOW   co-director with Hal Roach & Hal Roach, Jr.,
   United Artists, 1941
BROADWAY LIMITED   United Artists, 1941
NIAGARA FALLS   United Artists, 1941
THE DEVIL WITH HITLER   RKO Radio, 1942
THE GREAT GILDERSLEEVE   RKO Radio, 1942
GILDERSLEEVE'S BAD DAY   RKO Radio, 1943
GILDERSLEEVE ON BROADWAY   RKO Radio, 1943
GILDERSLEEVE'S GHOST   RKO Radio, 1944
A NIGHT OF ADVENTURE   RKO Radio, 1944
GIRL RUSH   RKO Radio, 1944
THE FALCON IN HOLLYWOOD   RKO Radio, 1944
ZOMBIES ON BROADWAY   RKO Radio, 1945
FIRST YANK INTO TOKYO   RKO Radio, 1945
DICK TRACY VS. CUEBALL   RKO Radio, 1946
SAN QUENTIN   RKO Radio, 1946
IF YOU KNEW SUSIE   RKO Radio, 1948
THE BLACK ARROW   Columbia, 1948
WALK A CROOKED MILE   Columbia, 1948
MR. SOFT TOUCH   co-director with Henry Levin,
   Columbia, 1949
THE DOOLINS OF OKLAHOMA   Columbia, 1949
THE NEVADAN   Columbia, 1950
FORTUNES OF CAPTAIN BLOOD   Columbia, 1950
ROGUES OF SHERWOOD FOREST   Columbia, 1950
KISS TOMORROW GOODBYE   United Artists, 1950

BETWEEN MIDNIGHT AND DAWN   Columbia, 1950
THE GREAT MISSOURI RAID   Paramount, 1951
ONLY THE VALIANT   Warner Bros., 1951
I WAS A COMMUNIST FOR THE FBI   Warner Bros., 1951
COME FILL THE CUP   Warner Bros., 1951
MARU MARU   Warner Bros., 1952
THE IRON MISTRESS   Warner Bros., 1952
SHE'S BACK ON BROADWAY   Warner Bros., 1953
THE CHARGE AT FEATHER CREEK   Warner Bros., 1953
SO THIS IS LOVE   Warner Bros., 1953
THEM   Warner Bros., 1954
YOUNG AT HEART   Warner Bros., 1954
THE McCONNELL STORY   Warner Bros., 1955
SINCERELY YOURS   Warner Bros., 1955
SANTIAGO   Warner Bros., 1956
THE BIG LAND   Warner Bros., 1957
BOMBERS B-52   Warner Bros., 1957
FORT DOBBS   Warner Bros., 1958
THE FIEND WHO WALKED THE WEST   20th Century-
   Fox, 1958
UP PERISCOPE   Warner Bros., 1959
YELLOWSTONE KELLY   Warner Bros., 1959
GOLD OF THE SEVEN SAINTS   Warner Bros., 1961
THE SINS OF RACHEL CADE   Warner Bros., 1961
CLAUDELLE INGLISH   Warner Bros., 1961
FOLLOW THAT DREAM   United Artists, 1962
CALL ME BWANA   United Artists, 1963
ROBIN AND THE SEVEN HOODS   Warner Bros., 1964
RIO CONCHOS   20th Century-Fox, 1964
SYLVIA   Paramount, 1965
HARLOW   Paramount, 1965
STAGECOACH   20th Century-Fox, 1966
WAY...WAY OUT!   20th Century-Fox, 1966
IN LIKE FLINT   20th Century-Fox, 1967
CHUKA   Paramount, 1967
TONY ROME   20th Century-Fox, 1967
THE DETECTIVE   20th Century-Fox, 1968
LADY IN CEMENT   20th Century-Fox, 1968
SKULLDUGGERY   Universal, 1970
BARQUERO   United Artists, 1970
THEY CALL ME MISTER TIBBS!   United Artists, 1970
SLAUGHTER'S BIG RIP-OFF   American
   International, 1973
NEVADA SMITH (TF)   Rackin-Hayes Productions/
   Paramount TV, 1975
VIVA KNIEVEL!   Warner Bros., 1978

KIRK DOUGLAS*

(Issur Danielovitch)
b. December 9, 1916 - Amsterdam, New York
Business: The Bryna Company, 141 El Camino Drive,
   Beverly Hills, CA 90212, 213/274-5294
Agent: CAA - Beverly Hills, 213/288-4545

SCALAWAG   Paramount, 1973, U.S.-Italian
POSSE   Paramount, 1975

PETER DOUGLAS*
Agent: CAA - Beverly Hills, 213/288-4545

A TIGER'S TALE   Atlantic Releasing Corporation, 1987

NANCY DOWD
b. Framingham, Massachusetts
Agent: Leading Artists - Beverly Hills, 213/858-1999

LOVE   co-director with Annette Cohen, Liv Ullmann & Mai
   Zetterling, Velvet Films, 1982, Canadian

KATHLEEN DOWDEY
b. November 13, 1949 - Washington, D.C.
Business: Five Point Films, Inc., 915 Highland View N.E. -
   Suite B, Atlanta, GA 30306, 404/875-6076
Attorney: Peter Nichols, 9601 Wilshire Blvd. - Suite 825,
   Beverly Hills, CA 90210, 213/858-7888

A CELTIC TRILOGY (FD)   First Run Features, 1979
BLUE HEAVEN   Vestron/Shapiro Entertainment, 1984
DAWN'S EARLY LIGHT: RALPH McGILL AND THE
   SEGREGATED SOUTH (TD)   South Carolina
   Educational TV Network, 1989

ROBERT DOWNEY*
b. June, 1936
Agent: ICM - Los Angeles, 213/550-4000

BABO 73   1963
CHAFED ELBOWS   Grove Press, 1965
NO MORE EXCUSES   Rogosin, 1968
PUTNEY SWOPE   Cinema 5, 1969
POUND   United Artists, 1970
GREASER'S PALACE   Greaser's Palace, 1972
MAD MAGAZINE PRESENTS UP THE ACADEMY   Warner
   Bros., 1980
AMERICA   ASA Communications, 1986
RENTED LIPS   Cineworld, 1988
TOO MUCH SUN   New Line Cinema, 1990

BERT L. DRAGIN
Agent: The Wallerstein Company - Beverly Hills,
   213/859-4804

SUMMER CAMP NIGHTMARE   Concorde, 1987
TWICE DEAD   Concorde, 1988

STAN DRAGOTI*
b. October 4, 1932 - New York, New York
Agent: CAA - Beverly Hills, 213/288-4545

DIRTY LITTLE BILLY   Columbia, 1972
LOVE AT FIRST BITE   American International, 1979
MR. MOM   20th Century-Fox, 1983
THE MAN WITH ONE RED SHOE   20th Century Fox, 1985
SHE'S OUT OF CONTROL   WEG/Columbia, 1989

JAMES R. (JIM) DRAKE*
Agent: Bob Broder, Broder-Kurland-Webb-Uffner Agency -
   Los Angeles, 213-656-9262
Business: Brijim Productions, Inc., 5145 Calvin Drive,
   Tarzana, CA 91356, 818/344-6548

THIS WIFE FOR HIRE (TF)   The Belle Company/Guillaume-
   Margo Productions/Comworld Productions, 1985
POLICE ACADEMY 4: CITIZENS ON PATROL   Warner
   Bros., 1987
GODDESS OF LOVE (TF)   Phil Margo Enterprises/New
   World TV/Phoenix Entertainment Group, 1988
SPEED ZONE   Orion, 1989, U.S.-Canadian

ARTHUR DREIFUSS*
b. March 25, 1908 - Frankfurt am Main, Germany
Home: 11407 Valley Spring Lane, Apt. 7, Studio City, CA
   91604, 818/762-2070
Business Manager: Stephany Courtney, 12214 Viewcrest
   Road, Studio City, CA 91604

DOUBLE DEAL   International Road Shows, 1939
MYSTERY IN SWING   International Road Shows, 1940

MURDER ON LENOX AVENUE   International Road
   Shows, 1941
SUNDAY SINNERS   International Road Shows, 1941
REG'LAR FELLERS   Producers Releasing
   Corporation, 1941
BABY FACE MORGAN   Producers Releasing
   Corporation, 1942
THE BOSS OF BIG TOWN   Producers Releasing
   Corporation, 1942
THE PAY-OFF   Producers Releasing Corporation, 1942
SARONG GIRL   Monogram, 1943
MELODY PARADE   Monogram, 1943
CAMPUS RHYTHM   Monogram, 1943
NEARLY EIGHTEEN   Monogram, 1943
THE SULTAN'S DAUGHTER   Monogram, 1944
EVER SINCE VENUS   Columbia, 1944
EDDIE WAS A LADY   Columbia, 1945
BOSTON BLACKIE BOOKED ON SUSPICION
   Columbia, 1945
BOSTON BLACKIE'S RENDEZVOUS   Columbia, 1945
THE GAY SENORITA   Columbia, 1945
PRISON SHIP   Columbia, 1945
JUNIOR PROM   Monogram, 1946
FREDDIE STEPS OUT   Monogram, 1946
HIGH SCHOOL HERO   Monogram, 1946
VACATION DAYS   Monogram, 1947
BETTY CO-ED   Columbia, 1947
LITTLE MISS BROADWAY   Columbia, 1947
TWO BLONDES AND A REDHEAD   Columbia, 1947
SWEET GENEVIEVE   Columbia, 1947
GLAMOUR GIRL   Columbia, 1948
MARY LOU   Columbia, 1948
I SURRENDER DEAR   Columbia, 1948
AN OLD-FASHIONED GIRL   Eagle Lion, 1948
MANHATTAN ANGEL   Columbia, 1948
ALL AMERICAN PRO   Columbia, 1948
SHAMROCK HILL   Eagle Lion, 1949
THERE'S A GIRL IN MY HEART   Allied Artists, 1949
SECRET FILE   Triangle, 1955, British-Dutch
ASSIGNMENT ABROAD   Triangle, 1956, British-Dutch
LIFE BEGINS AT 17   Columbia, 1958
THE LAST BLITZKRIEG   Columbia, 1959
JUKE BOX RHYTHM   Columbia, 1959
THE QUARE FELLOW   Astor, 1962, Irish-British
RIOT ON SUNSET STRIP   American International, 1967
THE LOVE-INS   Columbia, 1967
FOR SINGLES ONLY   Columbia, 1968
A TIME TO SING   MGM, 1968
THE YOUNG RUNAWAYS   MGM, 1968

DI DREW
Contact: Australian Film Commission, 9229 Sunset Blvd.,
   Los Angeles, CA 90069, 213/275-7074

THE RIGHT HAND MAN   FilmDallas, 1987, Australian
TROUBLE IN PARADISE (TF)   Qintex Entertainment,
   1989, U.S.- Australian

SARA DRIVER
b. 1956 - New York, New York

SLEEPWALK   Ottoskop Filmproduktion/Driver Films,
   1986, West German-U.S.

DAVID DRURY*
Agent: Alan Greenspan, ICM - Los Angeles, 213/550-4428

CITY (TF)   Granada TV, 1981, British
MINTER (TF)   Granada TV, 1981, British

CITIZEN BULL (TF)   Granada TV, 1982, British
FOREVER YOUNG   Cinecom, 1984, British, originally
   made for television
HOME AND AWAY (TF)   Granada TV, 1984, British
DEFENSE OF THE REALM   Hemdale, 1985, British
TERRA ROXA   Filmefekt, 1986, British
SPLIT DECISIONS   New Century/Vista, 1988
INTRIGUE (TF)   Crew Neck Productions/Linnea
   Productions/ Columbia TV, 1988

CHARLES S. DUBIN*
b. February 1, 1919 - New York, New York
Home: 651 Lorna Lane, Los Angeles, CA 90049
Agent: Ronald Leif, Contemporary Artists - Beverly Hills,
   213/278-8250

MISTER ROCK & ROLL   Paramount, 1957
TO DIE IN PARIS (TF)   co-director with Allen Reisner,
   Universal TV, 1968
MURDER ONCE REMOVED (TF)   Metromedia
   Productions, 1971
MURDOCK'S GANG (TF)   Don Fedderson
   Productions, 1973
MOVING VIOLATION   20th Century-Fox, 1976
THE TENTH LEVEL (TF)   CBS, Inc., 1976
THE DEADLY TRIANGLE (TF)   Columbia TV, 1977
TOPPER (TF)   Cosmo Productions/Robert A. Papazian
   Productions, 1979
ROOTS: THE NEXT GENERATIONS (MS)   co-director with
   John Erman, Lloyd Richards & Georg Stanford Brown,
   Wolper Productions, 1979
THE GATHERING, PART II (TF)   Hanna-Barbera
   Productions, 1979
THE MANIONS OF AMERICA (MS)   co-director with Joseph
   Sargent, Roger Gimbel Productions/EMI TV/Argonaut
   Films Ltd., 1981
MY PALIKARI (TF)   Center for TV in the Humanities, 1982
INTERNATIONAL AIRPORT (TF)   co-director with Don
   Chaffey, Aaron Spelling Productions, 1985
A MASTERPIECE OF MURDER (TF)   20th Century
   Fox TV, 1986
DROP-OUT MOTHER (TF)   Fries Entertainment/Comco
   Productions, 1988

JAY DUBIN*
Address: 260 W. Broadway, New York, NY 10013,
   212/226-2044
Agent: Rob Scheidlinger, ICM - New York City,
   212/556-5690

THE ANDREW DICE CLAY CONCERT MOVIE (HVD)
   20th Century Fox, 1990

DANIELE DUBROUX
Contact: French Film Office, 745 Fifth Avenue, New York,
   NY 10151, 212/832-8860

LES AMANTS TERRIBLES   Citevox, 1984, French
LA PETITE ALLUMEUSE   Cannon France, 1987, French

ROGER DUCHOWNY*
Home: P.O. Box 302, Crest Park, CA 92326,
   213/457-2404
Agent: Martin Shapiro, Shapiro-Lichtman Agency -
   Los Angeles, 213/859-8877

MURDER CAN HURT YOU!   Aaron Spelling
   Productions, 1970

PETER JOHN DUFFELL
Home: 13 Stratford Grove, Putney, London, SW15 1NV,
    England, 71/785-9512
Agent: Merrily Kane, The Artists Agency - Los Angeles,
    213/277-7779

PARTNERS IN CRIME   Allied Artists, 1961, British
THE HOUSE THAT DRIPPED BLOOD   Cinerama
    Releasing Corporation, 1971, British
ENGLAND MADE ME   Cine Globe, 1973, British
INSIDE OUT   Warner Bros., 1976, British
THE RACING GAME (TF)   Yorkshire TV, 1978, British
DAISY (TF)   BBC, 1979, British
MURDER TAP (TF)   BBC, 1979, British
CAUGHT ON A TRAIN (TF)   BBC, 1980
THE WATERFALL (TF)   BBC, 1980, British
BRIGHT EYES (TF)   BBC, 1981, British
EXPERIENCE PREFERRED, BUT NOT ESSENTIAL
    Samuel Goldwyn Company, 1983, British
THE FAR PAVILIONS (CMS)   Geoff Reeve & Associates/
    Goldcrest, 1984, British
LETTERS TO AN UNKNOWN LOVER (TF)   Portman
    Productions/Channel Four/Antenne-2, 1985,
    British-French
INSPECTOR MORSE   Zenith Productions, 1988, British
KING OF THE WIND   Davis-Panzer Productions/HTV
    International, 1989, British

DENNIS DUGAN*
Agent: Bob Gersh, The Gersh Agency - Beverly Hills,
    213/274-6611

PROBLEM CHILD   Universal, 1990

MICHAEL DUGAN*
Home: 3822 E. First Street, Long Beach, CA 90803,
    213/439-3370

MAUSOLEUM   MPM, 1983

JOHN DUIGAN*
Home: 10 Bruce Street, Rozelle, N.S.W., Australia 2039,
    2/810-5651
Agent: William Morris Agency - Beverly Hills, 213/274-7451

THE FIRM MAN   John Duigan Productions, 1975,
    Australian
THE TRESPASSERS   Vega Film Productions, 1976,
    Australian
MOUTH TO MOUTH   Vega Film Productions, 1978,
    Australian
DIMBOOLA   Ko-An Productions, 1979, Australian
WINTER OF OUR DREAMS   Satori, 1981, Australian
FAR EAST   Filmco Australia, 1983, Australian
ONE NIGHT STAND   Astra Film Productions/
    Hoyts-Edgely, 1984, Australian
STOP WATCH (TF)   ACTF Productions, 1985, Australian
VIETNAM (MS)   co-director with Chris Noonan, Kennedy
    Miller Productions, 1987, Australian
ROOM TO MOVE (TF)   Australian Children's Television
    Foundation/ITC Entertainment, 1987, Australian
THE YEAR MY VOICE BROKE   Avenue Pictures,
    1987, Australian
ROMERO   Four Seasons Entertainment, 1989
FLIRTING   Kennedy Miller Productions, 1990, Australian

BILL DUKE*
Home: 2200 Broadview Terrace, Los Angeles, CA 90068,
    213/851-3904
Agent: Jeremy Zimmer, Bauer Benedek Agency -
    Los Angeles, 213/275-2421

THE KILLING FLOOR (TF)   Public Forum Productions/
    KERA-Dallas-Ft. Worth, 1984
JOHNNIE MAE GIBSON: FBI (TF)   Fool's Cap
    Productions, 1986
A RAGE IN HARLEM   Miramax Films, 1991, U.S.-British

DARYL DUKE*
b. Vancouver, Canada
Address: 180 West 2nd Avenue, Vancouver, British
    Columbia V5Y 3T9, Canada, 604/876-1344

THE SASKATCHEWAN (TF)   CBC, 1965, Canadian
THE PSYCHIATRIST: GOD BLESS THE CHILDREN (TF)
    Universal TV, 1970
PAYDAY   Cinerama Releasing Corporation, 1972
HAPPINESS IS A WARM CLUE (TF)   Universal TV, 1973
THE PRESIDENT'S PLANE IS MISSING (TF)   ABC Circle
    Films, 1973
I HEARD THE OWL CALL MY NAME (TF)   Tomorrow
    Entertainment, 1973
A CRY FOR HELP (TF)   Universal TV, 1975
THEY ONLY COME OUT AT NIGHT (TF)   MGM TV, 1975
GRIFFIN AND PHOENIX (TF)   ABC Circle Films, 1976
THE SILENT PARTNER   EMC Film/Aurora, 1979,
    Canadian
THE THORN BIRDS (MS)   David L. Wolper-Stan Margulies
    Productions/ Edward Lewis Productions/Warner
    Bros. TV, 1983
FLORENCE NIGHTINGALE (TF)   Cypress Point
    Productions, 1985
TAI-PAN   DEG, 1986
WHEN WE WERE YOUNG (TF)   Richard & Esther Shapiro
    Entertainment, 1989
HANG TOUGH   Moviestore Entertainment, 1990,
    Canadian, filmed in 1980

PATRICK DUNCAN
Agent: Patrick Strull, Preferred Artists - Encino,
    818/990-0305

84 CHARLIE MOPIC   New Century/Vista, 1989

RUDY DURAND*
Business: Koala Productions, Ltd., 9606 Santa Monica Blvd.,
    Beverly Hills, CA 90210, 213/476-1949
Business Manager: Gary Dohner, Financial Management
    International, 9200 Sunset Blvd., Los Angeles, CA 90069,
    213/859-0655

TILT   Warner Bros., 1979

MARGUERITE DURAS
b. 1914 - Giadinh, French Indochina
Contact: French Film Office, 745 Fifth Avenue, New York,
    NY 10151, 212/832-8860

LA MUSICA   co-director, 1966, French
DESTROY, SHE SAID   1969, French
JAUNE DE SOLEIL   1971, French
NATHALIE GRANGER   Films Moliere, 1973, French
LA FEMMES DU GANGES   Sunchild Productions,
    1974, French

INDIA SONG   Sunchild Productions/Films Armorial,
   1975, French
DES JOURNEES ENTIERES DANS LES ARBRES
   Theatre D'Orsay-Duras Films, 1976, French
SON NOM DE VENISE DANS CALCUTTA DESERT (FD)
   Cinema 9, 1976, French
BAXTER, VERA BAXTER   Sunchild Productions,
   1977, French
LE CAMION   Films Moliere, 1977, French
LE NAVIRE NIGHT   MK2/Gaumont/Les Films du Losange,
   1979, French
AURELIA STEINER   Hors Champ Diffusion,
   1979, French
AGATHA ET LES LECTURES ILLIMITEES   Hors Champ
   Diffusion, 1981, French
IL DIALOGO DI ROMA (FD)   RAI/Lunga Cooperative,
   1983, Italian
LES ENFANTS   co-director with Jean-Marc Turine & Jean
   Mascolo, French Ministry of Culture/Les Productions
   Berthemont, 1985, French

TODD DURHAM

Business: Living Hell Productions, P.O. Box 1627,
   Beverly Hills, CA 90213, 213/851-8540
Agent: William Morris Agency - Beverly Hills,
   213/274-7451

VISIONS OF SUGAR-PLUMS   Regency
   Entertainment, 1984
HYPERSPACE   Regency Entertainment, 1986

ROBERT DUVALL

b. January 5, 1931 - San Diego, California
Agent: Bill Robinson, ICM - Beverly Hills, 213/550-4000

WE'RE NOT THE JET SET (FD)   1975
ANGELO, MY LOVE   Cinecom, 1983

JOHN DWYER

Business: Epic Productions, 1203 West 44th Street,
   Austin, TX 78756, 512/452-9461
Agent: William Morris Agency - Beverly Hills,
   213/274-7451
Attorney: Frank Arnold, Arnold & Booker, 300 West 15th
   Street, Austin, TX 78701, 512/320-5200

CONFESSIONS OF A SERIAL KILLER   Concorde, 1990

ROBERT DYKE

MOONTRAP   Shapiro Glickenhaus Entertainment, 1989

BOB DYLAN
(Robert Zimmerman)

b. May 24, 1941 - Hibbing, Minnesota
Agent: William Morris Agency - Beverly Hills,
   213/274-7451

RENALDO AND CLARA   Circuit, 1978

E

ALLAN EASTMAN

b. 1950 - Manitoba, Canada
Business: Labyrinth Film & Videoworks, 159 Westminster
   Avenue, Toronto, Ontario M6R 1N8, Canada,
   416/537-7455
Agent: William Morris Agency - Beverly Hills, 213/274-7451
Representative: Ronald Cohen, 1155 Dorchester Blvd. West
   - Suite 4103, Montreal, Quebec H3B 3V6, 514/397-1511

DEUX EX MACHINA (TF)   1974, Canadian-British
FOREIGNERS (TF)   1975, Canadian-British-French
SNAP SHOT   A SWEETER SONG   Epoh, 1976, Canadian
THE WAR BOY   Norstar Releasing, 1984, Canadian
CRAZY MOON   Miramax, 1985, Canadian
RACE FOR THE BOMB (MS)   1986, Canadian-French
FORD: THE MAN AND THE MACHINE (TF)   Lantana
   Productions/Filmline International Productions/Robert
   Halmi, Inc., 1987, Canadian-U.S.
CHAMPAGNE CHARLIE (TF)   Action Media Group/Telefilm
   Canada/CTV/ FR3/La Sept, 1989, Canadian-French

CHARLES EASTMAN*

Home: 113B 27th Street, Manhattan Beach, CA 90266,
   213/543-4212
Agent: Merrily Kane, The Artists Agency - Beverly Hills,
   213/277-7779

THE ALL-AMERICAN BOY   Warner Bros., 1973

CLINT EASTWOOD*

b. May 31, 1930 - San Francisco, California
Business: Malpaso Productions, 4000 Warner Blvd.,
   Burbank, CA 91522, 818/954-1228
Agent: William Morris Agency - Beverly Hills, 213/274-7451

PLAY MISTY FOR ME   Universal, 1971
HIGH PLAINS DRIFTER   Universal, 1972
BREEZY   Universal, 1973
THE EIGER SANCTION   Universal, 1974
THE OUTLAW JOSEY WALES   Warner Bros., 1976
THE GAUNTLET   Warner Bros., 1977
BRONCO BILLY   Warner Bros., 1980
FIREFOX   Warner Bros., 1982
HONKYTONK MAN   Warner Bros., 1982
SUDDEN IMPACT   Warner Bros., 1983
PALE RIDER   Warner Bros., 1985
HEARTBREAK RIDGE   Warner Bros., 1986
BIRD   Warner Bros., 1988
WHITE HUNTER, BLACK HEART   Warner Bros., 1990
THE ROOKIE   Warner Bros., 1990

THOM EBERHARDT

Agent: Daniel Ostroff, The Daniel Ostroff Agency -
   Los Angeles, 213/278-2020

SOLE SURVIVOR   International Film Marketing, 1984
NIGHT OF THE COMET   Atlantic Releasing
   Corporation, 1984
THE NIGHT BEFORE   Kings Road Productions, 1987
WITHOUT A CLUE   Orion, 1988

GROSS ANATOMY   Buena Vista, 1989
PARKER LEWIS CAN'T LOSE (TF)   Fox Broadcasting, 1990

DESIRE ECARÉ
b. April 15, 1939 - Treicheville, Ivory Coast
Contact: Ministry of Information, BP 138, Abidjan, Ivory Coast, tel.: 442585

FACES OF WOMEN   New Yorker, 1985, Ivory Coast

ULI EDEL*
Agent: CAA - Beverly Hills, 213/288-4545

CHRISTIANE F.   1981, West German
LAST EXIT TO BROOKLYN   Cinecom, 1989, West German-U.S.

DON EDMONDS
BARE KNUCKLES   Intercontinental, 1978
TERROR ON TOUR   World Distributing/Four Features Partners, 1983

BLAKE EDWARDS*
b. July 26, 1922 - Tulsa, Oklahoma
Agent: Triad Artists, Inc. - Los Angeles, 213/556-2727
Business: Blake Edwards Entertainment, 1888 Century Park East - Suite 1616, Los Angeles, CA 90067, 213/553-6741

BRING YOUR SMILE ALONG   Columbia, 1955
HE LAUGHED LAST   Columbia, 1956
MISTER CORY   MGM, 1957
THIS HAPPY FEELING   Universal, 1958
THE PERFECT FURLOUGH   Universal, 1959
OPERATION PETTICOAT   Universal, 1959
HIGH TIME   20th Century-Fox, 1960
BREAKFAST AT TIFFANY'S   Paramount, 1961
EXPERIMENT IN TERROR   Warner Bros., 1962
DAYS OF WINE AND ROSES   Warner Bros., 1962
THE PINK PANTHER   United Artists, 1964
A SHOT IN THE DARK   United Artists, 1964
THE GREAT RACE   Warner Bros., 1965
WHAT DID YOU DO IN THE WAR, DADDY?   United Artists, 1966
GUNN   Warner Bros., 1967
THE PARTY   United Artists, 1968
DARLING LILI   Paramount, 1970
WILD ROVERS   MGM, 1971
THE CAREY TREATMENT   MGM, 1972
THE TAMARIND SEED   Avco Embassy, 1974
RETURN OF THE PINK PANTHER   United Artists, 1975, British
THE PINK PANTHER STRIKES AGAIN   United Artists, 1976, British
REVENGE OF THE PINK PANTHER   United Artists, 1978, British
10   Orion/Warner Bros., 1979
S.O.B.   Paramount, 1981
VICTOR/VICTORIA   MGM/United Artists, 1982
TRAIL OF THE PINK PANTHER   MGM/UA, 1982
CURSE OF THE PINK PANTHER   MGM/UA, 1983
THE MAN WHO LOVED WOMEN   Columbia, 1983
MICKI & MAUDE   Columbia, 1984
A FINE MESS   Columbia, 1986
THAT'S LIFE!   Columbia, 1986
BLIND DATE   Tri-Star, 1987
SUNSET   Tri-Star, 1988
JUSTIN CASE (TF)   The Blake Edwards Company/Walt Disney TV, 1988

SKIN DEEP   20th Century Fox, 1989
PETER GUNN (TF)   The Blake Edwards Company/New World TV, 1990
SWITCH   Warner Bros., 1991

GEORGE EDWARDS
Agent: Artists Group, Ltd. - Los Angeles, 213/552-1100

THE ATTIC   Atlantic Releasing Corporation, 1984

VINCENT EDWARDS*
(Vincent Edward Zoimo)
b. July 9, 1928 - New York, New York
Contact: Directors Guild of America - Los Angeles, 213/289-2000

MANEATER   Universal TV, 1973

CHRISTINE EDZARD
b. France
Address: Grices Wharf, 119 Rotherhithe Street, London SE16 4NF, England

STORIES FROM A FLYING TRUNK   EMI, 1979, British
BIDDY   Sands Films Ltd., 1983, British
LITTLE DORRIT, PART I: NOBODY'S FAULT   Cannon, 1987, British
LITTLE DORRIT, PART II: LITTLE DORRIT'S STORY   Cannon, 1987, British
THE FOOL   Sands Films Ltd., 1990, British

JAN EGLESON*
Home: 139 Larch Road, Cambridge, MA 02138, 617/492-2521
Agent: William Morris Agency - Beverly Hills, 213/274-7451

BILLY IN THE LOWLANDS   Theatre Company of Boston, 1979
THE DARK END OF THE STREET   First Run Features, 1981
THE LITTLE SISTER (TF)   Shefida Features/American Playhouse/Christina Associates, 1986
ROANOAK (TF)   South Carolina ETV Network/First Contact Films/National Video Corporation, 1986
LEMON SKY   American Playhouse Theatrical Films, 1988
BIG TIME (TF)   co-director with Howard Cummings, Advocated Productions/ WGBH-Boston, 1989
A SHOCK TO THE SYSTEM   Corsair Pictures, 1990

ATOM EGOYAN
b. 1960 - Cairo, Egypt
Business: Ego Film Arts, 490 Adelaide Street West - Suite 102, Toronto, Ontario M5V 1T3, 416/365-2137

NEXT OF KIN   Ego Film Arts, 1985, Canadian
FAMILY VIEWING   Ego Film Arts, 1987, Canadian
SPEAKING PARTS   Channel Four/Academy Pictures/ Telefilm Canada/Ontario Film Development, 1989, Canadian-British-Italian

ROBERT ELFSTROM
THE NASHVILLE SOUND (FD)   co-director with David Hoffman, 1970
JOHNNY CASH! THE MAN, HIS WORLD, HIS MUSIC (FD)   Continental, 1970
PETE SEEGER...A SONG AND A STONE (FD)   Theatre Exchange, 1972
THE GOSPEL ROAD   20th Century-Fox, 1973

MYSTERIES OF THE SEA (FD)   co-director with Al
    Giddings, Polygram Pictures/Ocean Films Ltd., 1980
MOSES PENDLETON PRESENTS MOSES
    PENDLETON (FD)   ABC Video Enterprises, 1982

LAWRENCE (LARRY) ELIKANN*

b. July 4, 1923 - New York, New York
Agent: William Morris Agency - Beverly Hills, 213/274-7451

JOEY AND REDHAWK (TF)   Daniel Wilson
    Productions, 1978
THE GREAT WALLENDAS (TF)   Daniel Wilson
    Productions, 1978
CHARLIE AND THE GREAT BALLOON CHASE (TF)
    Daniel Wilson Productions, 1981
SPRAGGUE (TF)   MF Productions/Lorimar
    Productions, 1984
POISON IVY (TF)   NBC Productions, 1985
BERRENGER'S (TF)   co-director with Nicholas Sgarro,
    Roundelay Productions/ Lorimar Productions, 1985
PEYTON PLACE: THE NEXT GENERATION (TF)
    Michael Filerman Productions/ 20th Century
    Fox TV, 1985
A LETTER TO THREE WIVES (TF)   20th Century
    Fox TV, 1985
DALLAS: THE EARLY WIVES (TF)   Roundelay
    Productions/Lorimar- Telepictures, 1986
STRANGER IN MY BED (TF)   Taft Entertainment TV/
    Edgar J. Scherick Productions, 1986
THE HIGH PRICE OF PASSION (TF)   Edgar J. Scherick
    Productions, 1986
HANDS OF A STRANGER (TF)   Taft Entertainment
    TV, 1987
DANGEROUS AFFECTION (TF)   Freyda Rothstein
    Productions/Litke-Grossbart Productions/New
    World TV, 1987
GOD BLESS THE CHILD (TF)   Indieprod Company/
    Phoenix Entertainment Group, 1988
DISASTER AT SILO 7 (TF)   Mark Carliner
    Productions, 1988
A STONING IN FULHAM COUNTY (TF)   The Landsburg
    Company, 1988
I KNOW MY FIRST NAME IS STEVEN (TF)☆   Andrew
    Adelson Company/ Lorimar TV, 1989
TURN BACK THE CLOCK (TF)   Michael Filerman
    Productions/Republic Pictures Corporation/NBC
    Productions, 1989
LAST FLIGHT OUT   The Mannheim Company/Co-Star
    Entertainment/NBC Productions, 1990

HARRISON ELLENSHAW

STARDUMB   Curb/Esquire Films, 1990

LANG ELLIOTT*

b. 1950 - Los Angeles, California
Address: P.O. Box 7419, Thousand Oaks, CA 91359,
    818/707-9797 or 818/548-0111

THE PRIVATE EYES   New World, 1980
CAGE   New Century/Vista, 1989

JOSEPH ELLISON

DON'T GO IN THE HOUSE   Film Ventures
    International, 1980
JOEY   Satori Entertainment, 1985

IAN EMES

b. December 17, 1949 - Birmingham, England
Agent: ICM - Los Angeles, 213/550-4000

KNIGHTS AND EMERALDS   Warner Bros., 1986, British
THE YOB (TF)   Comic Strip Productions/Channel Four,
    1988, British

ROLAND EMMERICH

Agent: William Morris Agency - Beverly Hills, 213/274-7451

THE NOAH'S ARK PRINCIPLE   MGM/UA Classics, 1984,
    West German
MAKING CONTACT   JOEY   New World, 1985,
    West German
HOLLYWOOD MONSTER   Centropolis Film Production/
    Futura Filmverlag, 1987, West German
MOON 44   INTRUDER   Centropolis Film Production, 1989,
    West German

ROBERT ENDERS

Agent: Peter Crouch Associates, 59 Frith Street, London W1,
    England, 71/734-2167

STEVIE   First Artists, 1978, British

CY ENDFIELD

b. November, 1914 - South Africa
Contact: British Academy of Film & Television Arts, 195
    Piccadilly, London W1, England, 71/734-0022

GENTLEMAN JOE PALOOKA   Monogram, 1946
STORK BITES MAN   United Artists, 1947, British
THE ARGYLE SECRETS   Film Classics, 1948, British
JOE PALOOKA IN THE BIG FIGHT   Monogram, 1949
THE UNDERWORLD STORY   United Artists, 1950
THE SOUND OF FURY   United Artists, 1950
TARZAN'S SAVAGE FURY   RKO Radio, 1952
COLONEL MARCH INVESTIGATES   Criterion,
    1953, British
THE MASTER PLAN   directed under pseudonym of Hugh
    Raker, Astor, 1954, British
THE SECRET   Eros, 1955, British
CHILD IN THE HOUSE   Eros, 1956, British
HELL DRIVERS   Rank, 1957, British
SEA FURY   Lopert, 1958, British
JET STORM   United Producers Organization, 1959, British
MYSTERIOUS ISLAND   Columbia, 1961, British
HIDE AND SEEK   Universal, 1964, British
ZULU   Embassy, 1964, British
SANDS OF THE KALAHARI   Paramount, 1965, British
DE SADE   American International, 1969,
    U.S.-West German
UNIVERSAL SOLDIER   Hemdale, 1971, British

ANDI ENGEL

Contact: German Film & TV Academy, Pommernallee 1,
    1 Berlin 19, West Germany, 0311/302-6096

MELANCHOLIA   British Film Institute/Lichtblick Film
    produktion/Channel Four/NDR/Film Fonds Hamburg/
    Hamburger Filmbuero, 1989, British-West German

DAVID ENGELBACH*
b. September 20, 1946 - Philadelphia, Pennsylvania
Agent: The Rosen/Turtle Group, Inc. - Sherman Oaks, CA,
   818/907-9891

AMERICA 3000   Cannon, 1986

GEORGE ENGLUND*
b. June 22, 1926 - Washington, D.C.
Agent: CAA - Beverly Hills, 213/288-4545

THE UGLY AMERICAN   Universal, 1963
SIGNPOST TO MURDER   MGM, 1965
ZACHARIAH   Cinerama Releasing Corporation, 1970
SNOW JOB   Warner Bros., 1972
A CHRISTMAS TO REMEMBER (TF)   George Englund
   Productions, 1978
DIXIE: CHANGING HABITS (TF)   George Englund
   Productions, 1983
THE VEGAS STRIP WAR (TF)   George Englund
   Productions, 1984

ROBERT ENGLUND
Contact: Screen Actors Guild - Los Angeles, 213/465-6600

976-EVIL   New Line Cinema, 1988

ROBERT ENRICO
b. April 13, 1931 - Lievin, France
Agent: Artmedia, 10 Avenue Georges V, 75008 Paris,
   France, 04/723-7860
Contact: French Film Office, 745 Fifth Avenue, New York,
   NY 10151 212/832-8860

AU COEUR DE LA VIE   1962, French
LA BELLE VIE   1963, French
THE WISE GUYS   Universal, 1965, French
THE LAST ADVENTURE   I TRE AVVENTURIERI
   Universal, 1969, Italian- French
ZITA   Regional, 1968, French
HO!   1968, French
UN PEU, BEAUCOUP, PASSIONEMENT   CFDC,
   1971, French
BOULEVARD DU RHUM   Gaumont, 1971,
   French-Italian-West German
LES CAIDS   Parafrance, 1972, French
LE COMPAGNON INDESIRABLE   1973, French
LE SECRET   Cinema National, 1974, French
THE OLD GUN   Surrogate, 1976, French-West German
COUP DE FOUDRE   1978, French
UN NEVEU SILENCIEUX   MK2, 1979, French
L'EMPREINTE DES GEANTS   Filmel/SNC/FR3/Rialto
   Film, 1979, French-West German
HEADS OR TAILS   Castle Hill, 1980, French
FOR THOSE I LOVED   20th Century-Fox, 1983,
   Canadian-French
ZONE ROUGE   AAA/Revcom Films, 1986, French
DE GUERRE LASSE   Sara Films/TFI, 1987, French
LA REVOLUTION FRANCAISE: LES ANNEES LUMIERE
   Ariane Films/ Films A2/Laura Films/Antea/Les
   Productions Alliance/Alcor Films, 1989, French-
   West German-Italian-Canadian

MARCELO EPSTEIN
BODY ROCK   New World, 1984

ROBERT EPSTEIN
Agent: Curtis Brown, Ltd. - Los Angeles, 213/461-0148

WORD IS OUT   New York Films, 1977
THE TIMES OF HARVEY MILK (FD)   1984
COMMON THREADS: STORIES FROM THE
   QUILT (CTD)   co-director with Jeffrey Friedman, Telling
   Pictures/The Couturie Company, 1989

VICTOR ERICE
b. 1940 - Carranza, Spain
Contact: Ministry of Culture, Motion Picture Division, Avenida
   de Burgos, 5, 28036, Madrid, Spain, 91/202-5351

LOS DESAFIOS   co-director with Claudio Guerin Hill &
   Jose Luis Egea, 1968, Spanish
THE SPIRIT OF THE BEEHIVE   Janus, 1973, Spanish
EL SUR   New Yorker, 1983, Spanish-French

GORDON ERIKSEN
Home: 116 Prospect Place - Apt. 3, Brooklyn, NY 11217

THE BIG DIS   co-director with John O'Brien, Pyramid
   Films, 1989

JOHN ERMAN*
b. Chicago, Illinois
Agent: CAA - Beverly Hills, 213/288-4545

MAKING IT   20th Century-Fox, 1971
ACE ELI AND RODGER OF THE SKIES   directed under
   pseudonym of Bill Sampson, 20th Century-Fox, 1973
LETTERS FROM THREE LOVERS (TF)   Spelling-Goldberg
   Productions, 1973
GREEN EYES (TF)   ABC, 1977
ROOTS (MS)☆   co-director with David Greene, Marvin J.
   Chomsky & Gilbert Moses, Wolper Productions, 1977
ALEXANDER: THE OTHER SIDE OF DAWN (TF)   Douglas
   Cramer Productions, 1977
JUST ME & YOU (TF)   Roger Gimbel Productions/
   EMI, 1978
ROOTS: THE NEXT GENERATIONS (MS)   co-director with
   Charles S. Dubin, Lloyd Richards & Georg Stanford
   Brown, Wolper Productions, 1979
MY OLD MAN (TF)   Zeitman-McNichol-Halmi
   Productions, 1979
MOVIOLA (MS)☆   David L. Wolper-Stan Margulies
   Productions/Warner Bros. TV, 1980
THE LETTER (TF)   Hajeno Productions/Warner
   Bros. TV, 1982
ELEANOR, FIRST LADY OF THE WORLD (TF)   Murbill
   Productions/Embassy TV, 1982
ANOTHER WOMAN'S CHILD (TF)   CBS
   Entertainment, 1983
WHO WILL LOVE MY CHILDREN? (TF) ☆☆   ABC
   Circle Films, 1983
A STREETCAR NAMED DESIRE (TF)☆   Keith Barish
   Productions, 1984
THE ATLANTA CHILD MURDERS (TF)   Mann-Rafshoon
   Productions/Finnegan Associates, 1985
RIGHT TO KILL? (TF)   Wrye-Konigsberg Productions/Taper
   Media Enterprises/ Telepictures Productions, 1985
AN EARLY FROST (TF)☆   NBC Productions, 1985
THE TWO MRS. GRENVILLES (TF)   Lorimar-
   Telepictures, 1987
WHEN THE TIME COMES (TF)   Jaffe-Lansing Productions/
   Republic Pictures, 1987
THE ATTIC: THE HIDING OF ANNE FRANK (TF)☆
   Telecom Entertainment/Yorkshire TV, 1988, U.S.-British
DAVID (TF)   Tough Boys Inc./Donald March Productions/
   ITC Entertainment Group, 1988
STELLA   Buena Vista, 1990

EMILIO ESTEVEZ*
b. 1963 - Los Angeles, California
Agent: InterTalent - Los Angeles, 213/271-0600

WISDOM   20th Century Fox, 1987
MEN AT WORK   Triumph Releasing Corporation, 1990

RICHARD EYRE
Home: 4 St. Martin's Road, London, SW9, England,
    71/733-6207
Agent: Judy Daish , 83 Eastbourne Mews, London W2 6LQ,
    England, 71/262-1101

THE PLOUGHMAN'S LUNCH   Samuel Goldwyn
    Company, 1983, British
LOOSE CONNECTIONS   Orion Classics, 1983, British
LAUGHTER HOUSE (TF)   Film Four International,
    1984, British
PAST CARING (TF)   BBC, 1985, British
THE INSURANCE MAN (TF)   BBC, 1985, British
SINGLETON'S PLUCK (TF)   Greenpoint Films,
    1987, British
TUMBLEDOWN (TF)   BBC, 1988, British

CHRISTIAN FABER
BAIL JUMPER   Angelika Films, 1990

PETER FAIMAN
Agent: CAA - Beverly Hills, 213/288-4545

"CROCODILE" DUNDEE   Paramount, 1986, Australian

FERDINAND FAIRFAX*
b. August 1, 1944 - London, England
Address: 6 Clapham Common, Northside, London SW4
    0QW, England, 71/627-5702
Agent: Alan Greenspan, ICM - Los Angeles, 213/550-4000

THE SPEED KING (TF)   BBC, British
DANGER UXB (MS)   Thames TV, 1979, British
WINSTON CHURCHILL - THE WILDERNESS YEARS (MS)
    Southern Pictures Productions, 1983, British
NATE AND HAYES SAVAGE ISLANDS   Paramount,
    1983, New Zealand
THE LAST PLACE ON EARTH (MS)   Central Productions/
    Renegade Films, 1985, British
A FIGHTING CHOICE (TF)   Walt Disney
    Productions, 1986
THE RESCUE   Buena Vista, 1988
THE SECRET LIFE OF IAN FLEMING (CTF)
    Saban-Scherick Productions, 1990, U.S.-British

HARRY FALK*
Contact: Directors Guild of America - Los Angeles,
    213/289-2000

THREE'S A CROWD (TF)   Screen Gems/Columbia
    TV, 1969
THE DEATH SQUAD (TF)   Spelling-Goldberg
    Productions, 1974

MEN OF THE DRAGON (TF)   Wolper Productions, 1974
THE ABDUCTION OF SAINT ANNE (TF)   QM
    Productions, 1975
MANDRAKE (TF)   Universal TV, 1979
CENTENNIAL (MS)   co-director with Paul Krasny, Bernard
    McEveety & Virgil Vogel, Universal TV, 1980
THE NIGHT THE CITY SCREAMED (TF)   David Gerber
    Company, 1980
THE CONTENDER (TF)   co-director with Lou Antonio,
    Universal TV, 1980
THE SOPHISTICATED GENTS (TF)   Daniel Wilson
    Productions, 1981
ADVICE TO THE LOVELORN (TF)   Universal TV, 1981
HEAR NO EVIL (TF)   Paul Pompian Productions/
    MGM TV, 1982
EMERALD POINT, N.A.S. (TF)   Richard and Esther Shapiro
    Productions/20th Century-Fox TV, 1983
NORTH BEACH & RAWHIDE (TF)   CBS
    Entertainment, 1985
HIGH DESERT KILL (CTF)   Lehigh Productions/
    MCA TV, 1989

JAMAA FANAKA
Business Manager: Saul Rihenberg, Loeb & Loeb, 10100
    Santa Monca Blvd. - Suite 2200, Los Angeles, CA 90067

WELCOME HOME, BROTHER CHARLES   Crown
    International, 1975
EMMA MAE   Pro-International, 1977
PENITENTIARY   Jerry Gross Organization, 1980
PENITENTIARY II   MGM/UA, 1982
PENITENTIARY III   Cannon, 1987

CLAUDE FARALDO
b. 1936 - France
Contact: French Film Office, 745 Fifth Avenue, New York,
    NY 10151, 212/832-8860

LA JEUNE MORTE   1970, French
BOF   1972, French
THEMROC   CIC, 1972, French
TABARNAC   M.D. Films, 1975, French
LES FLEURS DU MIEL   Contrechamp, 1976, French
DEUX LIONS AU SOLEIL   Gaumont, 1980, French
FLAGRANT DESIRE   Hemdale, 1986, French-U.S.

JAMES FARGO*
(Louis James Fargo)
August 4, 1938 - Republic, Washington
Agent: Scott Harris, Harris & Goldberg - Los Angeles,
    213/553-5200
Business Manager: Howard Bernstein, Kaufman & Bernstein,
    1900 Avenue of the Stars, Los Angeles, CA 90067,
    213/277-1900

THE ENFORCER   Warner Bros., 1976
EVERY WHICH WAY BUT LOOSE   Warner Bros., 1978
CARAVANS   Universal, 1979, U.S.-Iranian
GAME FOR VULTURES   New Line Cinema, 1980, British
FORCED VENGEANCE   MGM/United Artists, 1982
GUS BROWN AND MIDNIGHT BREWSTER (TF)
    Kaledonia Productions/ Scomi, 1985
THE LAST ELECTRIC KNIGHT (TF)   Walt Disney
    Productions, 1986
VOYAGE OF THE ROCK ALIENS   WHEN THE RAIN
    BEGINS TO FALL   KGA/Inter Planetary Pictures/Curb
    Communications, 1988, filmed in 1984
BORN TO RACE   MGM/UA, 1988
RIDING THE EDGE   Trans World Entertainment, 1989
MISSION MORAY   Integrity, 1990
THE ICE RUNNER   Four Seasons Entertainment, 1990

MIKE FARRELL*

b. February 6, 1939 - St. Paul, Minnesota
Address: P.O. Box 5961 - Suite 306, Sherman Oaks, CA
   91413, 818/986-4199
Agent: Audrey Caan, Triad Artists, Inc. - Los Angeles,
   213/556-2727

RUN TILL YOU FALL (TF)   CBS Entertainment, 1988

JOHN FASANO

Agent: Steve Rabineau, ICM - Los Angeles, 213/550-4000

ROCK 'N ROLL NIGHTMARE   Shapiro Glickenhaus
   Entertainment, 1987
BLACK ROSES   Shapiro Entertainment, 1988
THE JITTERS   Gaga Communications, 1989

WILLIAM C. FAURE

Contact: Department of Interior, Civitas Building, Struhen
   Street, Pretoria 0002, South Africa, 12/48-2551

SHAKA ZULU (MS)   Harmony Gold/Tele-Munchen, 1986,
   South African

LINDA FEFERMAN

Agent: The Gersh Agency - Beverly Hills, 213/274-6611

SEVEN MINUTES IN HEAVEN   Warner Bros., 1986

STEVE FEKE

Agent: David Wardlow, Camden Artists - Los Angeles,
   213/556-2022

KEYS TO FREEDOM   RPB Pictures/Queens Cross
   Productions, 1990, U.S.-Malaysian

DENNIS FELDMAN*

Agent: ICM - Los Angeles, 213/550-4000

REAL MEN   MGM/UA, 1987

FEDERICO FELLINI

b. January 20, 1920 - Rimini, Italy
Home: Via Margutta 110, Rome, Italy, 06/6780173

VARIETY LIGHTS   co-director with Alberto Lattuada,
   Pathe Contemporary, 1950, Italian
THE WHITE SHEIK   Pathe Contemporary, 1952, Italian
I VITELLONI   API Productions, 1953, Italian
LOVE IN THE CITY   co-director with Michelangelo
   Antonioni, Alberto Lattuada, Carlo Lizzani, Francesco
   Maselli & Dino Risi, Italian Films Export, 1953, Italian
LA STRADA   Trans-Lux, 1954, Italian
IL BIDONE   Astor, 1955, Italian
NIGHTS OF CABIRIA   Lopert, 1957, Italian
LA DOLCE VITA★   Astor, 1960, Italian
BOCCACCIO '70   co-director with Luchino Visconti &
   Vittorio De Sica, Embassy, 1962, Italian
8-1/2★   Embassy, 1963, Italian
JULIET OF THE SPIRITS   Rizzoli, 1965, Italian-French-
   West German
SPIRITS OF THE DEAD   *HISTOIRES EXTRAORDINAIRES*
   co-director with Roger Vadim & Louis Malle, American
   International, 1969, French- Italian
FELLINI SATYRICON★   United Artists, 1970, Italian-French
THE CLOWNS   Levitt-Pickman, 1971, Italian-French-West
   German, originally made for television
FELLINI'S ROMA   United Artists, 1972, Italian-French
AMARCORD★   New World, 1974, Italian

CASANOVA   *IL CASANOVA DI FEDERICO FELLINI*
   Universal, 1977, Italian
ORCHESTRA REHEARSAL   New Yorker, 1979, Italian-
   West German, originally made for television
CITY OF WOMEN   New Yorker, 1981, Italian-French
AND THE SHIP SAILS ON   Triumph/Columbia, 1983,
   Italian-French
GINGER AND FRED   MGM/UA, 1986, Italian-French-
   West German
INTERVISTA   Aljosha Productions/Cinecitta/RAI,
   1987, Italian
LA VOCE DELLA LUNA   Penta Distribuzione, 1990,
   Italian-French

KERRY FELTHAM*

b. March 20, 1939 - Edmonton, Alberta, Canada
Home: 16131 Sunset Blvd. - Apt. 7, Pacific Palisades, CA
   90272, 213/454-6806
Agent: Linne Radmin, ICM - Los Angeles, 213/550-4000

THE GREAT CHICAGO CONSPIRACY CIRCUS   New Line
   Cinema, 1970

GEORG J. FENADY*

b. July 2, 1930 - Toledo, Ohio
Home: 602 N. Cherokee, Los Angeles, CA 90004,
   213/466-5001
Agent: Mark Lichtman, Shapiro-Lichtman Agency -
   Los Angeles, 213/859-8877

ARNOLD   Cinerama Releasing Corporation, 1974
TERROR IN THE WAX MUSEUM   Cinerama Releasing
   Corporation, 1974
THE NIGHT THE BRIDGE FELL DOWN (TF)   Irwin Allen
   Productions/Warner Bros. TV, 1983
CAVE-IN! (TF)   Irwin Allen Productions/Warner Bros.
   TV, 1983

MICHAEL FERGUSON

b. 1937 - Surrey, England
Address: c/o Flickering Images, Ltd., 8 the Causeway,
   Teddington, Middlesex TW11 0HE, England, 71/943-2390
Agent: Roger Carey Management, 52 Old Brompton Road,
   London SW5 0BE, England, 71/373-4948

THE SANDBAGGERS (TF)   Yorkshire TV, 1978, British
AIRLINE (TF)   Yorkshire TV, 1980, British
EDMUND KEAN (TF)   Yorkshire TV, 1981, British
PRIDE OF OUR ALLEY (TF)   Yorkshire TV, 1982, British
KILLER WAITING (TF)   Yorkshire TV, 1983, British
THE GLORY BOYS (TF)   Yorkshire TV/Alan Landsburg
   Productions, 1984, British-U.S.
LYTTON'S DIARY (TF)   Thames TV, 1985, British
THE BILL (TF)   Thames TV, 1987, British

ABEL FERRARA*

Agent: William Morris Agency - Beverly Hills, 213/274-7451

DRILLER KILLER   Rochelle Films, 1979
MS. 45   Rochelle Films, 1981
FEAR CITY   Chevy Chase Distribution, 1985
THE GLADIATOR (TF)   Walker Brothers Productions/New
   World TV, 1986
CRIME STORY (TF)   Michael Mann Company/New
   World TV, 1986
CHINA GIRL   Vestron, 1987
CAT CHASER   Vestron, 1989
KING OF NEW YORK   Reteitalia/Scena Film, 1990,
   Italian-U.S.

BRAN FERREN
Business: Associates and Ferren, Wainscott Northwest
   Road, Wainscott, NY 11975

FUNNY (FD)   Original Cinema, 1989

JOSE FERRER*
(Jose Vincente Ferrer de Otero y Cintron)
b. January 8, 1912 - Santurce, Puerto Rico
Home: P.O. Box 616, Coconut Grove, FL 33133,
   305/442-2662
Agent: Don Buchwald and Associates - New York City,
   212/867-1070

THE SHRIKE   Universal, 1955
THE COCKLESHELL HEROES   Columbia, 1956, British
THE GREAT MAN   Universal, 1956
I ACCUSE!   MGM, 1958
THE HIGH COST OF LOVING   MGM, 1958
RETURN TO PEYTON PLACE   20th Century-Fox, 1961
STATE FAIR   20th Century-Fox, 1962

MEL FERRER
b. August 25, 1917 - Elberon, New Jersey
Agent: William Morris Agency - Beverly Hills, 213/274-7451

THE GIRL OF THE LIMBERLOST   Columbia, 1945
VENDETTA   RKO Radio, 1950
THE SECRET FURY   RKO Radio, 1950
GREEN MANSIONS   MGM, 1959
EVERY DAY IS A HOLIDAY *CABRIOLA*   Columbia,
   1966, Spanish

MARCO FERRERI
b. May 11, 1928 - Milan, Italy
Home: Piazza Mattei 10, Rome, Italy, 06/6569631

EL PISITO   1958, Spanish
LOS CHICOS   1959, Spanish
EL COCHECITO   1960, Spanish
LE ITALIANE E L'AMORE   co-director, Magic Film,
   1961, Italian
THE CONJUGAL BED   *UNA STORIA MODERNA:*
   L'APE REGINA   Embassy, 1963, Italian-French
THE APE WOMAN   Embassy, 1964, Italian
CONTROSESSO   co-director with Franco Rossi, Jacques
   Romain, Gianni Puccini & Mino Guerrini, Adelphia
   Cinematografica/France Cinema Production, 1964,
   Italian-French
KISS THE OTHER SHEIK   *OGGI, DOMANI E DO*
   PODOMANI   co-director with Eduardo de Filippo &
   Luciano Salce, MGM, 1965, Italian-French
MARCIA NUNZIALE   Sancro Film/Transinter Film, 1966,
   Italian-French
L'HAREM   Sancro Film, 1967, Italian
THE MAN WITH THE BALLOONS   Sigma III, 1968,
   French-Italian
DILLINGER E' MORTO   Pegaso Film, 1969, Italian
THE SEED OF MAN   SRL, 1970, Italian
L'UDIENZA   Vides, 1971, Italian
LIZA   Horizon, 1972, French-Italian
LA GRANDE BOUFFE   ABKCO, 1973, French-Italian
TOUCHEZ PAS LA FEMME BLANCHE   1974,
   French-Italian
THE LAST WOMAN   Columbia, 1976, Italian-French
BYE BYE MONKEY   Fida, 1978, Italian
CHIEDO ASILO   Gaumont, 1979, Italian-French-Tahitian

TALES OF ORDINARY MADNESS   Fred Baker Films,
   1983, Italian-French
THE STORY OF PIERA   UGC, 1983, Italian-French-
   West German
IL FUTURO E' DONNA   Faso Film, 1984, Italian
I LOVE YOU   UGC, 1986, French-Italian
COME SONO BUONI I BIANCHI   23 Giugno/Iberoamericana/
   Camera One-Michel Seydoux/JMS Films, 1987, Italian-
   Spanish-French
LE BANQUET DE PLATON   FIT Productions/FR3/La Sept/
   BEMA, 1989, French-Italian
LA CASA DEL SORRISO   Titanus, 1990, Italian

ROBERT A. FERRETTI
FEAR   CineTel Films, 1988

MICHAEL FIELDS
Agent: William Morris Agency - Beverly Hills, 213/274-7451

NOON WINE (TF)   Noon Wine Company, 1985
BRIGHT ANGEL   Hemdale, 1990

MIKE FIGGIS
Agent: William Morris Agency - Beverly Hills, 213/274-7451

STORMY MONDAY   Atlantic Releasing Corporation,
   1988, British
INTERNAL AFFAIRS   Paramount, 1990
LIEBESTRAUM   Pathe Entertainment, 1991

CHARLES FINCH
Contact: British Academy of Film & Television Arts,
   195 Piccadilly, London W1, England, 71/734-0022

PRICELESS BEAUTY   Gruppo BEMA/Reteitalia,
   1989, Italian

KEN FINKLEMAN*
Agent: CAA - Beverly Hills, 213/288-4545

AIRPLANE II: THE SEQUEL   Paramount, 1983
HEAD OFFICE   Tri-Star, 1986

ALBERT FINNEY
b. May 9, 1936 - Salford, England
Agent: ICM - Los Angeles, 213/550-4000

CHARLIE BUBBLES   Regional, 1968, British

SAM FIRSTENBERG*
b. 1950 - Israel
Address: 467 S. Almont Drive, Beverly Hills, CA 90211,
   213/275-4258
Agent: CAA - Beverly Hills, 213/288-4545

ONE MORE CHANCE   Cannon, 1981
REVENGE OF THE NINJA   MGM/UA/Cannon, 1983
NINJA III: THE DOMINATION   Cannon, 1984
BREAKIN' 2 ELECTRIC BOOGALOO   Tri-Star/
   Cannon, 1984
AMERICAN NINJA   Cannon, 1985
AVENGING FORCE   Cannon, 1986
AMERICAN NINJA 2: THE CONFRONTATION
   Cannon, 1987
RIVERBEND   Intercontinental Releasing Corporation, 1990
THE DAY WE MET   Roy Productions Ltd., 1990, Israeli

MICHAEL FIRTH
b. New Zealand
Business: P.O. Box 37-177, Parnell, Auckland, New
    Zealand, 09/399-699

OFF THE EDGE   Pentacle, 1977, New Zealand
HEART OF THE STAG   New World, 1984, New Zealand
SYLVIA   MGM/UA Classics, 1985, New Zealand
THE LEADING EDGE   Southern Light Pictures/Everard
    Films, 1987, New Zealand

MICHAEL FISCHA
MY MOM'S A WEREWOLF   Crown International, 1989
WITCH BITCH   Shapiro Glickenhaus Entertainment, 1989
CRACK HOUSE   Cannon, 1989

MAX FISCHER
b. 1929 - Alexandria, Egypt
Address: 4691 Bonavista Avenue, Montreal, Quebec
    H3W 2C6, Canada, 514/482-5827

MEWS EN MEIJN   1965, Dutch
DREAMS   1970, Dutch
THE LUCKY STAR   Pickman Films, 1981, Canadian
KILLING 'EM SOFTLY   Intermarket Pictures Corporation,
    1985, Canadian
LE PALANQUIN DES LARMES (MS)   1986,
    Canadian-French

BERND FISCHERAUER
Contact: German Film & TV Academy, Pommernallee 1,
    1 Berlin 19, West Germany, 0311/302-6096

BLOOD AND HONOR: YOUTH UNDER HITLER (MS)
    Daniel Wilson Productions/ SWF Baden/Taurus Film,
    1982, U.S.-West German

DAVID FISHELSON
CITY NEWS   co-director with Zoe Zinman, Cinecom, 1983

DAVID FISHER
b. April 21, 1948 - Nashville, Tennessee
Home: 14144 Dickens, Apt. 115, Sherman Oaks, CA
    91423, 818/907-1368

LIAR'S MOON   Crown International, 1982
TOY SOLDIERS   New World, 1984

JACK FISHER
TORN APART   Castle Hill Productions, 1990

MARY ANN FISHER
LORDS OF THE DEEP   Concorde, 1989

BILL FISHMAN
Agent: The Gersh Agency - Beverly Hills, 213/274-6611
Business: Fisher & Preachman, 1310 Main Street, Venice,
    CA 90291, 213/392-1896

TAPEHEADS   Avenue Pictures, 1988

JACK FISK*
b. December 19, 1945 - Ipava, Illinois
Agent: InterTalent - Los Angeles, 213/271-0600

RAGGEDY MAN   Universal, 1981
VIOLETS ARE BLUE   Columbia, 1986
DADDY'S DYIN'...WHO'S GOT THE WILL?
    MGM/UA, 1990

PAUL FLAHERTY*
Agent: Nancy Geller, ICM - Los Angeles, 213/550-4341

18 AGAIN   New World, 1988
WHO'S HARRY CRUMB?   Tri-Star, 1989
BILLY CRYSTAL: MIDNIGHT TRAIN TO MOSCOW (CTD) ☆
    Dalrymple Productions/Jennilind Productions, 1989

RICHARD FLEISCHER*
b. December 8, 1916 - Brooklyn, New York
Contact: Directors Guild of America - Los Angeles,
    213/289-2000

CHILD OF DIVORCE   RKO Radio, 1946
BANJO   RKO Radio, 1947
DESIGN FOR DEATH   RKO Radio, 1948
SO THIS IS NEW YORK   United Artists, 1948
BODYGUARD   Columbia, 1948
MAKE MINE LAUGHS   RKO Radio, 1949
THE CLAY PIGEON   RKO Radio, 1949
FOLLOW ME QUIETLY   RKO Radio, 1949
TRAPPED   Eagle Lion, 1949
ARMORED CAR ROBBERY   RKO Radio, 1950
THE NARROW MARGIN   RKO Radio, 1952
THE HAPPY TIME   Columbia, 1952
ARENA   MGM, 1953
20,000 LEAGUES UNDER THE SEA   Buena Vista, 1954
VIOLENT SATURDAY   20th Century-Fox, 1955
THE GIRL IN THE RED VELVET SWING   20th Century-
    Fox, 1955
BANDIDO   United Artists, 1956
BETWEEN HEAVEN AND HELL   20th Century-Fox, 1956
THE VIKINGS   United Artists, 1958
THESE THOUSAND HILLS   20th Century-Fox, 1959
COMPULSION   20th Century-Fox, 1959
CRACK IN THE MIRROR   20th Century-Fox, 1960
THE BIG GAMBLE   20th Century-Fox, 1961
BARABBAS   Columbia, 1962, Italian
FANTASTIC VOYAGE   20th Century-Fox, 1966
DR. DOLITTLE   20th Century-Fox, 1967
THE BOSTON STRANGLER   20th Century-Fox, 1968
CHE!   20th Century-Fox, 1969
TORA! TORA! TORA!   co-director with Kinji Fukasaku and
    Toshio Masuda, 20th Century-Fox, 1970, U.S.-Japanese
10 RILLINGTON PLACE   Columbia, 1971, British
SEE NO EVIL   Columbia, 1971, British
THE LAST RUN   MGM, 1971
THE NEW CENTURIONS   Columbia, 1972
SOYLENT GREEN   MGM, 1972
THE DON IS DEAD   Universal, 1973
THE SPIKES GANG   United Artists, 1974
MR. MAJESTYK   United Artists, 1974
MANDINGO   Paramount, 1975
THE INCREDIBLE SARAH   Reader's Digest, 1976, British
CROSSED SWORDS   THE PRINCE AND THE PAUPER
    Warner Bros., 1978, British
ASHANTI   Columbia, 1979, Swiss-U.S.
THE JAZZ SINGER   AFD, 1980
TOUGH ENOUGH   20th Century-Fox, 1983
AMITYVILLE 3-D   Orion, 1983
CONAN THE DESTROYER   Universal, 1984
RED SONJA   MGM/UA, 1985
MILLION DOLLAR MYSTERY   DEG, 1987

PETER FLEISCHMANN
Contact: German Film & TV Academy, Pommernallee 1,
    1 Berlin 19, West Germany, 0311/302-6096

HARD TO BE A GOD   Hallelujah Film/Sovinfilm/Dovzhenko
    Studio/Garance/Mediactuel, 1990, West German-Soviet-
    French-Swiss

FI

F
I
L
M

D
I
R
E
C
T
O
R
S

ANDREW FLEMING*
Contact: Directors Guild of America - Los Angeles,
213/289-2000

BAD DREAMS   20th Century Fox, 1988

GORDON FLEMYNG
b. March 7, 1934 - Glasgow, Scotland
Home: 1 Albert Road, Wilmslow, Cheshire SK9 5HT,
England, 0625/524198
Agent: Duncan Heath Associates, 162-170 Wardour Street,
London W1, England, 71/439-1471

SOLD FOR SPARROW   Schoenfield, 1962, British
FIVE TO ONE   Allied Artists, 1963, British
JUST FOR FUN   Columbia, 1963
DR. WHO AND THE DALEKS   Continental, 1966, British
DALEKS - INVASION EARTH 2150 A.D.   Continental,
1966, British
THE SPLIT   MGM, 1968
GREAT CATHERINE   Warner Bros., 1968, British
THE LAST GRENADE   Cinerama Releasing Corporation,
1970, British
A GOOD HUMAN STORY (TF)   Granada TV, 1977, British
MIRAGE (TF)   Granada TV, 1978, British
THE WEDDING (TF)   Tyne Tees, 1983, British
FLIGHT INTO HELL (MS)   Australian Broadcasting
Corporation/WWF/Andre Litik Film Productions, 1985,
Australian-West German
CLOUD WALTZER (TF)   Yorkshire TV/Atlantic Video
Ventures, 1987, British

THEODORE J. FLICKER*
b. June 6, 1930 - Freehold, New Jersey
Business Manager: Marvin Freedman, Freedman,
Kinzelberg & Broder, 1801 Avenue of the Stars,
Los Angeles, CA 90067, 213/277-0700

THE TROUBLEMAKER   Janus, 1964
THE PRESIDENT'S ANALYST   Paramount, 1967
UP IN THE CELLAR   American International, 1970
PLAYMATES (TF)   ABC Circle Films, 1972
GUESS WHO'S SLEEPING IN MY BED? (TF)   ABC Circle
Films, 1973
JUST A LITTLE INCONVENIENCE (TF)   Universal TV,
1977
JACOB TWO-TWO MEETS THE HOODED FANG
Cinema Shares International, 1978, Canadian
LAST OF THE GOOD GUYS (TF)   Columbia TV, 1978
WHERE THE LADIES GO (TF)   Universal TV, 1980
SOGGY BOTTOM, U.S.A.   Cinemax Marketing &
Distribution, 1981

JOHN FLOREA*
Contact: Directors Guild of America - Los Angeles,
213/289-2000

INVISIBLE STRANGLER   Seymour Borde & Associates,
1984
HOT CHILD IN THE CITY   Mediacom Filmworks, 1987

JOHN FLYNN*
Home: 574 Latimer Road, Santa Monica, CA 90402,
213/454-6850
Agent: Jeremy Zimmer, Bauer Benedek Agency -
Los Angeles, 213/275-2421

THE SERGEANT   Warner Bros., 1968
THE JERUSALEM FILE   MGM, 1972, U.S.-Israeli

THE OUTFIT   MGM, 1974
ROLLING THUNDER   American International, 1978
DEFIANCE   American International, 1980
MARILYN: THE UNTOLD STORY (TF)   co-director with
Jack Arnold & Lawrence Schiller, Lawrence Schiller
Productions, 1980
TOUCHED   Lorimar Productions/Wildwoods Partners, 1983
BEST SELLER   Orion, 1987
LOCK UP   Tri-Star, 1989

LAWRENCE D. FOLDES
b. November 4, 1959 - Los Angeles, California
Business: Star Cinema Production Group, Inc.,
6253 Hollywood Blvd. - Suite 927, Los Angeles, CA
90028, 213/463-2000
Attorney: Ronald G. Gabler, 9606 Santa Monica Blvd.,
Beverly Hills, CA 90210, 213/205-8908

MALIBU HIGH   Crown International, 1979
DON'T GO NEAR THE PARK   Cannon, 1981
THE GREAT SKYCOPTER RESCUE   Cannon, 1982
YOUNG WARRIORS   Cannon, 1983
NIGHTFORCE   Vestron, 1987

JAMES FOLEY*
Agent: CAA - Beverly Hills, 213/288-4545

RECKLESS   MGM/UA, 1984
AT CLOSE RANGE   Orion, 1986
WHO'S THAT GIRL   Warner Bros., 1987
AFTER DARK, MY SWEET   Avenue Pictures, 1990

PETER FONDA*
b. February 23, 1939 - New York, New York
Home: Indian Hill Ranch, 38 Box 2024, Livingston, MO
59047, 406/222-3686
Agent: Richard Shepherd/Mickey Freiberg, The Artists
Agency - Los Angeles, 213/277-7779
Business Manager: Nanas, Stern, Biers & Company, 9454
Wilshire Blv d. - Suite 405, Beverly Hills, CA 90212,
213/273-2501

THE HIRED HAND   Universal, 1971
IDAHO TRANSFER   Cinemation, 1975
WANDA NEVADA   United Artists, 1979

ALLEN FONG
(Fong Yu-Ping)
Contact: Hong Kong International Film Festival, 5th Floor,
High Block City Hall, Edinburgh Place, Hong Kong,
(3) 72-1193

FATHER AND SON   1983, Hong Kong
AH YING   Array Films, 1984, Hong Kong
JUST LIKE WEATHER   SIL-Metropole Organization,
1986, Hong Kong
DANCING BULL   Dancing Bull Production Company,
1990, Hong Kong

LLOYD FONVIELLE
Agent: ICM - Los Angeles, 213/550-4000

GOTHAM (CTF)   Showtime/Phoenix Entertainment Group/
Keith Addis & Associates, 1988

BRYAN FORBES*

b. July 22, 1926 - Stratford-Atte-Bow, England
Home: Seven Pines, Wentworth, Surrey GU25 4QP,
    England 9904-2349
Agent: APA - Los Angeles, 213/273-0744

WHISTLE DOWN THE WIND   Pathe-America,
    1962, British
THE L-SHAPED ROOM   Columbia, 1963, British
SEANCE ON A WET AFTERNOON   Artixo, 1964, British
KING RAT   Columbia, 1965, British
THE WRONG BOX   Columbia, 1966, British
THE WHISPERERS   United Artists, 1967, British
DEADFALL   20th Century-Fox, 1968, British
THE MADWOMAN OF CHAILLOT   Warner Bros.,
    1969, British
LONG AGO TOMORROW   *THE RAGING MOON*
    Cinema 5, 1971, British
THE STEPFORD WIVES   Columbia, 1975
THE SLIPPER AND THE ROSE: THE STORY OF
    CINDERELLA   Universal, 1976, British
INTERNATIONAL VELVET   MGM/United Artists,
    1978, British
SUNDAY LOVERS   co-director with Edouard Molinaro,
    Dino Risi & Gene Wilder, MGM/United Artists, 1981,
    U.S.-British-Italian-French
PHILIP MARLOWE - PRIVATE EYE   *CHANDLERTOWN*
    (CMS)   co-director with Peter Hunt, David Wickes &
    Sidney Hayers, HBO/David Wickes Television Ltd./
    London Weekend Television, 1983, British
BETTER LATE THAN NEVER   Warner Bros.,
    1983, British
THE NAKED FACE   Cannon, 1985
THE ENDLESS GAME (CTF)   TVS Films/Reteitalia/Pixit,
    1990, British-Italian

GREG FORD

Business: Warner Bros. Animation, 4000 Warner Blvd.,
    Burbank, CA 91522, 818/954-6000

DAFFY DUCK'S QUACKBUSTERS (AF)   co-director with
    Terry Lennon, Warner Bros., 1988

STEVE FORD

THE DUNGEONMASTER   co-director, Empire
    Pictures, 1985

STEPHEN H. FOREMAN*

Home: Spruceton Road, H.C. 181, Westkill, NY 12492,
    518/989-6692
Messages: 212/242-4772
Agent: Mickey Freiberg, The Artists Agency - Los Angeles,
    213/277-7779

COUGAR! (TF)   ABC Circle Films, 1984

MILOS FORMAN*

b. February 18, 1932 - Caslav, Czechoslovakia
Agent: Robert Lantz, The Lantz Office - New York City,
    212/586-0200

COMPETITION   Brandon, 1963, Czech
BLACK PETER   Billings, 1964, Czech
LOVES OF A BLONDE   Prominent, 1966, Czech
THE FIREMAN'S BALL   Cinema 5, 1968, Czech
TAKING OFF   Universal, 1971

VISIONS OF EIGHT (FD)   co-director with Yuri Ozerov, Mai
    Zetterling, Arthur Penn, Michael Pfleghar, Kon Ichikawa,
    Claude Lelouch & John Schlesinger, Cinema 5, 1973
ONE FLEW OVER THE CUCKOO'S NEST ★★   United
    Artists, 1976
HAIR   United Artists, 1979
RAGTIME   Paramount, 1981
AMADEUS★★   Orion, 1984
VALMONT   Orion, 1989, French-British

ROBERT FORSTER

b. July 13, 1941 - Rochester, New York
Agent: Charter Management - Los Angeles, 213/278-1690

HOLLYWOOD HARRY   Shapiro Entertainment, 1985

BILL FORSYTH*

(William David Forsyth)
b. Scotland
Agent: CAA - Beverly Hills, 213/288-4545

THAT SINKING FEELING   Samuel Goldwyn Company,
    1979, Scottish
GREGORY'S GIRL   Samuel Goldwyn Company,
    1982, Scottish
LOCAL HERO   Warner Bros., 1983, British-Scottish
COMFORT AND JOY   Universal, 1984, British-Scottish
HOUSEKEEPING   Columbia, 1987
BREAKING IN   Samuel Goldwyn Company, 1989

GILES FOSTER

Agent: Peters, Fraser & Dunlop, The Chambers, Chelsea
    Harbour, Lots Road, London SW10 0XF,
    England, 71/376-7676

LAST SUMMER'S CHILD (TF)   BBC, 1982, British
THE AERODROME (TF)   BBC, 1983, British
DUTCH GIRLS (TF)   London Weekend TV, 1984, British
SILAS MARNER (TF)   BBC, 1985, British
NORTHANGER ABBEY (TF)   BBC/Arts & Entertainment
    Network, 1986, British
HOTEL DULAC (TF)   Channel Four, 1986, British
CONSUMING PASSIONS   Samuel Goldwyn Company,
    1988, British
THE TREE OF HANDS   Greenpoint/Granada/British Screen,
    1989, British

JODIE FOSTER

Agent: ICM - Los Angeles, 213/550-4000

LITTLE MAN TATE   Orion, 1991

ROBERT FOWLER*

Home: 3561 Canada Street, Los Angeles, CA 90065
Agent: ICM - Los Angeles, 213/550-4000

BELOW THE BELT   Atlantic Releasing Corporation, 1980

WILLIAM A. FRAKER*

b. 1923 - Los Angeles, California
Home: 2572 Outpost Drive, Hollywood, CA 90068
Agent: Phil Gersh, The Gersh Agency - Beverly Hills,
    213/274-6611

MONTE WALSH   National General, 1970
A REFLECTION OF FEAR   Columbia, 1973, British
THE LEGEND OF THE LONE RANGER   Universal/
    AFD, 1981
B.L. STRYKER: THE DANCER'S TOUCH (TF)   Blue Period
    Productions/T.W.S. Productions/Universal TV, 1989

111

FREDDIE FRANCIS

b. 1917 - London, England
Home: 12 Ashley Drive, Jersey Road, Osterley, Middlesex
7W7 5QA, England
Agent: CCA Personal Management Ltd., 4 Court Lodge,
48 Sloane Square, London SW1W 8AT, England,
71/730-8857

TWO AND TWO MAKE SIX   Union, 1962, British
THE BRAIN *VENGEANCE*   Garrick, 1962,
British-West German
PARANOIAC   Universal, 1964, British
NIGHTMARE   Universal, 1964, British
THE EVIL OF FRANKENSTEIN   Universal, 1964, British
TRAITOR'S GATE   Columbia, 1964, British-West German
DR. TERROR'S HOUSE OF HORRORS   Paramount,
1965, British
HYSTERIA   MGM, 1965, British
THE SKULL   Paramount, 1965, British
THE PSYCHOPATH   Paramount, 1966, British
THE DEADLY BEES   Paramount, 1967, British
THEY CAME FROM BEYOND SPACE   Embassy,
1967, British
TORTURE GARDEN   Columbia, 1968, British
DRACULA HAS RISEN FROM THE GRAVE   Warner
Bros., 1969, British
MUMSY, NANNY, SONNY & GIRLY   *GIRLY*   Cinerama
Releasing Corporation, 1970, British
TROG   Warner Bros., 1970, British
THE HAPPENING OF THE VAMPIRE   1971, European
TALES FROM THE CRYPT   Cinerama Releasing
Corporation, 1972, British
TALES THAT WITNESS MADNESS   Paramount,
1973, British
THE CREEPING FLESH   Columbia, 1973, British
SON OF DRACULA   Cinemation, 1974, British
CRAZE   Warner Bros., 1974, British
THE GHOUL   Rank, 1974, British
LEGEND OF THE WEREWOLF   Tyburn, 1975, British
THE DOCTOR AND THE DEVILS   20th Century Fox,
1985, British
DARK TOWER   directed under pseudonym of Ken Barnett,
Spectrafilm, 1989, Canadian

KARL FRANCIS

Contact: British Academy of Film & Television Arts, 195
Piccadilly, London W1, England, 71/734-0022

THE MOUSE AND THE WOMAN   Facelift, 1981, British
AND NOTHING BUT THE TRUTH   *GIRO CITY*   Castle
Hill Productions, 1982, British
THE HAPPY ALCOHOLIC   1984, Welsh
BOY SOLDIER (TF)   Cine Cymru Productions/Channel
Four, 1986, Welsh
ANGRY EARTH   Bloom Street Productions, 1989, Welsh

CAROL FRANK

Agent: Shorr, Stille & Associates - Los Angeles,
213/859-6160

SORORITY HOUSE MASSACRE   Concorde, 1987

ROBERT FRANK

b. November 9, 1924 - Zurich, Switzerland
Agent: ICM - Los Angeles, 213/550-4000

PULL MY DAISY   co-director with Alfred Leslie, G-String
Productions, 1959
THE SIN OF JESUS   Off-Broadway Productions, 1961
O.K. END HERE   September 20 Productions, 1963

ME AND MY BROTHER   Two Faces Company, 1965-68
CONVERSATIONS IN VERMONT (FD)   Dilexi
Foundation, 1969
LIFE-RAFT EARTH (FD)   Portola Institute, 1969
ABOUT ME: A MUSICAL   1971
COCKSUCKER BLUES   *CS BLUES* (FD)   Rolling Stones
Productions, 1972
KEEP BUSY   1975
LIFE DANCES ON....   1980
ENERGY AND HOW TO GET IT   1981
THIS SONG FOR JACK   1983
CANDY MOUNTAIN   co-director with Rudy Wurlitzer,
International Film Exchange, 1987, Swiss-French-
Canadian

JOHN FRANKENHEIMER*

b. February 19, 1930 - Malba, New York
Agent: Jeff Berg, ICM - Los Angeles, 213/550-4205

THE YOUNG STRANGER   Universal, 1957
THE YOUNG SAVAGES   United Artists, 1961
ALL FALL DOWN   MGM, 1962
BIRDMAN OF ALCATRAZ   United Artists, 1962
THE MANCHURIAN CANDIDATE   United Artists, 1962
SEVEN DAYS IN MAY   Paramount, 1964
THE TRAIN   United Artists, 1965, U.S.-French-Italian
SECONDS   Paramount, 1966
GRAND PRIX   MGM, 1966
THE FIXER   MGM, 1968, British
THE EXTRAORDINARY SEAMAN   MGM, 1969
THE GYPSY MOTHS   MGM, 1969
I WALK THE LINE   Columbia, 1970
THE HORSEMEN   Columbia, 1971
THE ICEMAN COMETH   American Film Theatre, 1973
IMPOSSIBLE OBJECT   Valoria, 1973, French-Italian
99 AND 44/100 % DEAD   20th Century-Fox, 1974
FRENCH CONNECTION II   20th Century-Fox, 1975
BLACK SUNDAY   Paramount, 1976
PROPHECY   Paramount, 1979
THE CHALLENGE   Embassy, 1982
THE HOLCROFT COVENANT   Universal, 1985
52 PICK-UP   Cannon, 1986
DEAD-BANG   Warner Bros., 1989
THE FOURTH WAR   New Age Releasing, 1990

CARL FRANKLIN

Business: Concorde Pictures, 11600 San Vicente Blvd.,
Los Angeles, CA 90049, 213/826-0978

EYE OF THE EAGLE II: INSIDE THE ENEMY   Concorde,
1989, U.S.- Filipino
FULL FATHOM FIVE   Concorde, 1990

HOWARD FRANKLIN

Agent: CAA - Beverly Hills, 213/288-4545

QUICK CHANGE   co-director with Bill Murray, Warner
Bros., 1990

RICHARD FRANKLIN*

b. July 15, 1948 - Melbourne, Australia
Agent: Daniel Ostroff, The Daniel Ostroff Agency -
Los Angeles, 213/278-2020

BELINDA   Aquarius, 1972, Australian
LOVELAND   Illustrated, 1973, Australian
THE TRUE STORY OF ESKIMO NELL   *DICK DOWN
UNDER*   Quest Films/ Filmways Australasian
Distributors, 1975, Australian

FANTASM   Filmways Australasian, 1977, Australian
PATRICK   Cinema Shares International, 1979, Australian
ROAD GAMES   Avco Embassy, 1981, Australian
PSYCHO II   Universal, 1983
CLOAK & DAGGER   Universal, 1984
LINK   Thorn EMI/Cannon, 1986, U.S.-British
BEAUTY & THE BEAST (TF)   Wtt Thomas
    Productions, 1987
A FINE ROMANCE (TF)   Phoenix Entertainment
    Group, 1988
F/X 2   Orion, 1991

J A M E S   F R A W L E Y *
Business: Maya Films Ltd., 500 S. Sepulveda Blvd.,
    Los Angeles, CA 90049

THE CHRISTIAN LICORICE STORE   National
    General, 1971
KID BLUE   20th Century-Fox, 1973
DELANCEY STREET: THE CRISIS WITHIN (TF)
    Paramount TV, 1975
THE BIG BUS   Paramount, 1976
THE MUPPET MOVIE   AFD, 1979, British
THE GREAT AMERICAN TRAFFIC JAM (TF)   Ten-Four
    Productions, 1980
THE OUTLAWS (TF)   Limekiln and Templar Productions/
    Universal TV, 1984
FRATERNITY VACATION   New World, 1985
WARM HEARTS, COLD FEET (TF)   Lorimar-
    Telepictures, 1987
ASSAULT AND MATRIMONY (TF)   Michael Filerman
    Productions/NBC Productions, 1987
COLUMBO: MURDER - A SELF PORTRAIT (TF)
    Universal TV, 1989

S T E P H E N   F R E A R S
b. Leicester, England
Agent: William Morris Agency - Beverly Hills, 213/274-7451

GUMSHOE   Columbia, 1971, British
ABEL'S WILL (TF)   BBC, 1977, British
BLOODY KIDS (TF)   Black Lion Films, 1983, British
SAIGON - YEAR OF THE CAT (TF)   Thames TV,
    1983, British
THE HIT   Island Alive, 1984, British
MY BEAUTIFUL LAUNDRETTE (TF)   Orion Classics,
    1985, British
LOVING WALTER (TF)   Central TV Productions,
    1986, British
PRICK UP YOUR EARS   Samuel Goldwyn Company,
    1987, British
DECEMBER FLOWER (TF)   Granada TV, 1987, British
SAMMY AND ROSIE GET LAID   Cinecom, 1987, British
DANGEROUS LIAISONS   Warner Bros., 1988
THE GRIFTERS   Miramax Films, 1990

H E R B   F R E E D *
Agent: Norman G. Rudman, Slaff, Mosk & Rudman, 9200
    Sunset Blvd., Los Angeles, CA 90069, 213/275-5351

AWOL   BFB, 1972
HAUNTS   Intercontinental, 1977
BEYOND EVIL   IFI-Scope III, 1980
GRADUATION DAY   IFI-Scope III, 1981
TOMBOY   Crown International, 1985
SURVIVAL GAME   Trans World Entertainment, 1987

J E R R O L D   F R E E D M A N *
Agent: Robert Wunsch, Richland/Wunsch Agency -
    Los Angeles, 213/278-1955

KANSAS CITY BOMBER   MGM, 1972
A COLD NIGHT'S DEATH (TF)   ABC Circle Films, 1973
BLOOD SPORT (TF)   Danny Thomas Productions, 1973

THE LAST ANGRY MAN (TF)   Screen Gems/Columbia
    TV, 1974
SOME KIND OF MIRACLE (TF)   Lorimar Productions, 1979
THIS MAN STANDS ALONE (TF)   Roger Gimbel
    Productions/EMI TV/Abby Mann Productions, 1979
THE STREETS OF L.A. (TF)   George Englund
    Productions, 1979
THE BOY WHO DRANK TOO MUCH (TF)   MTM
    Enterprises, 1980
BORDERLINE   AFD, 1980
THE VICTIMS (TF)   Hajeno Productions/Warner
    Bros. TV, 1982
LEGS (TF)   The Catalina Production Group/Radio City Music
    Hall Productions/ Comworld Productions, 1983
THE SEDUCTION OF GINA (TF)   Bertinelli-Jaffee
    Productions, 1984
BEST KEPT SECRETS (TF)   ABC Circle Films, 1984
SEDUCED (TF)   Catalina Production Group/Comworld
    Productions, 1985
THOMPSON'S LAST RUN (TF)   Cypress Point
    Productions, 1986
NATIVE SON   Cinecom, 1986
UNHOLY MATRIMONY (TF)   Edgar J. Scherick Associates/
    Taft Entertainment TV, 1988
THE COMEBACK (TF)   CBS Entertainment, 1989
NIGHT WALK (TF)   Galatea Productions/CBS
    Entertainment, 1989

R O B E R T   F R E E D M A N *
Home: 213/276-9383

GOIN' ALL THE WAY   Saturn International, 1982

J O A N   F R E E M A N *
Agent: William Morris Agency - Beverly Hills, 213/274-7451

STREETWALKIN'   Concorde, 1985
SATISFACTION   20th Century Fox, 1988

R I C K   F R I E D B E R G *
Business Manager: M. Kenneth Suddleson, Irell & Manella,
    1800 Avenue of the Stars, Los Angeles, CA 90067,
    213/879-2600

PRAY TV K-GOD   Filmways, 1980
OFF THE WALL   Jensen Farley Pictures, 1983

R I C H A R D   F R I E D E N B E R G
Agent: The Daniel Ostroff Agency - Los Agency,
    213/278-2020

THE LIFE AND TIMES OF GRIZZLY ADAMS   Sunn
    Classic, 1976
FRONTIER FREMONT   Sunn Classic, 1976
THE DEERSLAYER (TF)   Sunn Classic Productions, 1978
THE BERMUDA TRIANGLE   Sunn Classic, 1979

W I L L I A M   F R I E D K I N *
b. August 29, 1935 - Chicago, Illinois
Agent: CAA - Beverly Hills, 213/278-4545

GOOD TIMES   Columbia, 1967
THE BIRTHDAY PARTY   Continental, 1968, British
THE NIGHT THEY RAIDED MINSKY'S   United Artists, 1968
THE BOYS IN THE BAND   National General, 1970
THE FRENCH CONNECTION ★★   20th Century-Fox, 1971
THE EXORCIST★   Warner Bros., 1973
SORCERER   Universal/Paramount, 1977
THE BRINK'S JOB   Universal, 1978
CRUISING   United Artists, 1980
DEAL OF THE CENTURY   Warner Bros., 1983

TO LIVE AND DIE IN L.A.   MGM/UA, 1985
PUTTING IT TOGETHER - THE MAKING OF 'THE
    BROADWAY ALBUM' (CTD)   Barwood Films/CBS
    Music Video Enterprises/HBO, 1986
C.A.T. SQUAD (TF)   NBC Productions, 1986
RAMPAGE   DEG, 1987
C.A.T. SQUAD: PYTHON WOLF (TF)   NBC
    Productions, 1988
THE GUARDIAN   Universal, 1990

JEFFREY FRIEDMAN
Agent: Curtis Brown, Ltd. - Los Angeles, 213/461-0148

FACES OF THE ENEMY (TD)   co-director, PBS, 1987
COMMON THREADS: STORIES FROM THE
    QUILT (CTD)   co-director with Robert Epstein, Telling
    Pictures/The Couturie Company, 1989

KEN FRIEDMAN
Contact: Writers Guild of America, East - New York City,
    212/245-6180

MADE IN USA   DEG, 1986

KIM FRIEDMAN*
Agent: David Gersh, The Gersh Agency - Beverly Hills,
    213/274-6611

BEFORE AND AFTER (TF)   The Konigsberg
    Company, 1979

RICHARD FRIEDMAN
PHANTOM OF THE MALL: ERIC'S REVENGE   Fries
    Distribution, 1989

BILL FROELICH
Agent: Ken Gross, Robinson, Weintraub, Gross &
    Associates - Los Angeles, 213/653-5802

RETURN TO HORROR HIGH   New World, 1987

WILLIAM FRUET
b. 1933 - Lethbridge, Alberta, Canada
Business: Jaguar Productions Ltd., 51 Olive Avenue,
    Toronto, Ontario M6G 1T7, Canada, 416/535-3569

WEDDING IN WHITE   Avco Embassy, 1973, Canadian
THE HOUSE BY THE LAKE   *DEATH WEEKEND*
    American International, 1977, Canadian
SEARCH AND DESTROY   *STRIKING BACK*   Film
    Ventures International, 1979
FUNERAL HOME   *CRIES IN THE NIGHT*   MPM,
    1981, Canadian
BAKER COUNTY USA   *TRAPPED*   Jensen Farley
    Pictures, 1982
SPASMS   Producers Distribution Company,
    1983, Canadian
FULL CIRCLE AGAIN (TF)   1984, Canadian
BEDROOM EYES   Film Gallery/Aquarius, 1984, Canadian
KILLER PARTY   MGM/UA, 1986, Canadian
CHASING RAINBOWS (MS)   co-director with Mark
    Blandford, Bruce Pittman & Susan Martin, CBC,
    1986, Canadian
BLUE MONKEY   Spectrafilm, 1987, Canadian

ROY FRUMKES
b. July 22, 1944 - New York, New York
Business: Bat Track Productions, 166 West 83rd Street,
    New York, NY 10024, 212/873-6626

DOCUMENT OF THE DEAD (FD)   Roy Frumkes
    Productions, 1980
BURT'S BIKERS (TD)   NBC, 1984

ROBERT FUEST
b. 1927 - London, England
Home: Sunnyside Radford, Tlmsbury, Avon, England,
    076/171043
Agent: Leading Players, 31 Kings Road, London SW3,
    England

JUST LIKE A WOMAN   Monarch, 1966, British
AND SOON THE DARKNESS   Levitt-Pickman,
    1970, British
WUTHERING HEIGHTS   American International,
    1971, British
THE ABOMINABLE DR. PHIBES   American International,
    1971, British
DR. PHIBES RISES AGAIN   American International,
    1972, British
THE LAST DAYS OF MAN ON EARTH   *THE FINAL
    PROGRAMME*   New World, 1974, British
THE DEVIL'S RAIN   Bryanston, 1975, U.S.-Mexican
REVENGE OF THE STEPFORD WIVES (TF)   Edgar J.
    Scherick Productions, 1980
APHRODITE   Atlantic Releasing Corporation, 1982, French

KINJI FUKASAKU
Contact: Directors Guild of Japan, Tsukada Building, 8-33
    Udagawa-cho, Shibuya-ku, Tokyo 150, Japan, 3/461-4411

(The following is an incomplete list of Mr. Fukasaku's credits)

THE GREEN SLIME   MGM, 1969, U.S.-Japanese
TORA! TORA! TORA!   co-director with Richard Fleischer &
    Toshio Masuda, 20th Century-Fox, 1970, U.S.-Japanese
OHKAMI-TO BUTA-TO NINGEN   1972, Japanese
THE YAKUZA PAPERS   1973, Japanese
MESSAGE FROM SPACE   United Artists, 1978, Japanese
THE SHOGUN'S SAMURAI   Toei, 1979, Japanese
VIRUS   Haruki Kadokawa Productions, 1980, Japanese
DEVIL RESUCITATION   Haruki Kadokawa Productions,
    1980, Japanese
KAMATA MARCH   Haruki Kadokawa Productions,
    1980, Japanese
THE FALL GUY   Shochiku, 1982, Japanese
UNDER THE FLAG OF THE RISING SUN   Toho,
    1982, Japanese
SHANGHAI VANCE KING   Cine Saison/Asahi TV/Shochiku,
    1984, Japanese
LEGEND OF THE DOGS OF SATOMI   Toei, 1984,
    Japanese
HOUSE ON FIRE   Takawa-Sato Productions, 1986,
    Japanese
SURE DEATH IV   Shochiku, 1987, Japanese

LUCIO FULCI
b. June 17, 1927 - Rome, Italy
Home: via Chiana 148, Rome, Italy, 06/845-8200

I LADRI   I.C.M. Fenix Film, 1959, Italian
I RAGAZZI DEL JUKE-BOX   Era Cinematografica,
    1959, Italian
URLATORI ALLA SBARRA   Era Cinematografica,
    1960, Italian
COLPO GOBBO ALL'ITALIANA   Mirafilm/Marcus
    Produzione Cinematografica, 1962, Italian
I DUE DELLA LEGIONE   Ultra Film, 1962, Italian
LE MASSAGGIATRICI   Panda/Gallus Film, 1962,
    Italian-French
UNO STRANO TIPO   Giovanni Addessi, 1963, Italian
GLI IMBROGLIONI   Produzione D.S./Tecisa Film, 1963,
    Italian-Spanish
I MANIACI   Hesperia Cinematografica, 1964, Italian

I DUE EVASI DI SING SING   Mega/Turris, 1964, Italian
002 AGENTI SEGRETISSIMI   Mega Film, 1964, Italian
I DUE PERICOLI PUBBLICI   Aster Film, 1965, Italian
COME INGUAIAMMO L'ESERCITO   Five Film,
   1965, Italian
002 OPERAZIONE LUNA   Ima/Agata, 1966,
   Italian-Spanish
I DUE PARA'   Ima/Agata, 1966, Italian-Spanish
COME SVALIGIAMMO LA BANCA D'ITALIA   Anteaos,
   1966, Italian
LE COLT CANTARONO LA MORTE E FU TEMPO DI
   MASSACRO   R.F. Mega, 1966, Italian
COME RUBAMMO LA BOMBA ATOMICA   Five Film,
   1967, Italian
IL LUNGO, IL CORTO, IL GATTO   Five Film/Fono Roma,
   1967, Italian
OPERAZIONE SAN PIETRO   Ultra Film, 1967, Italian
UNA SULL'ALTRA   Empire Film, 1969, Italian
BEATRICE CENCI   Filmena, 1969, Italian
UNA LUCERTOLA CON LA PELLE DI DONNA   Apollo
   Film, 1971, Italian
ALL'ONOREVOLE PIACCIONO LE DONNE   New Film
   Productions, 1972, Italian
NON SI SEVIZIA UN PAPERINO   Medusa, 1972, Italian
ZANNA BIANCA   Oceania Produzioni, 1973, Italian
IL RITORNO DI ZANNA BIANCA   Coralta Cinematografica,
   1974, Italian
IL CAVALIER COSTANTE NICOSIA DEMONIACO
   OVVERO DRACULA IN BRIANZA   Coralta
   Cinematografica, 1975, Italian
I QUATTRO DELL'APOCALISSE   Coralta Cinematografica,
   1976, Italian
LA PRETORA   Coralta Cinematografica, 1976, Italian
SETTE NOTE IN NERO   Cinecompany, 1977, Italian
SELLA D'ARGENTO   Rizzoli Film, 1978, Italian
ZOMBI 2   Variety Film, 1979, Italian
PAURA NELLA CITTA' DEI MORTI VIVENTI   Dania
   Film/Medusa Distribuzione/National Cinematografica,
   1980, Italian
BLACK CAT   Selenia Cinematografica, 1980, Italian
...E TU VIVRAI NEL TERRORE! L'ALDILA'   Fulvia Film,
   1980, Italian
LUCA IL CONTRABBANDIERE   Primex Italiana/C.M.R.
   Cinematografica, 1980, Italian
QUELLA VILLA ACCANTO AL CIMITERO   Fulvia Film,
   1981, Italian
LO SQUARTATORE DI NEW YORK   Fulvia Film,
   1981, Italian
MANHATTAN BABY   Fulvia Film, 1982, Italian
I GUERRIERI DELL'ANNO 2072   Regency Productions,
   1983, Italian
MURDEROCK, UCCIDE A PASSO DI DANZA   Scena
   Film, 1984, Italian
DANGEROUS OBSESSION   IL MIELE DEL DIAVOLO
   Celebrity Home Entertainment, 1986, Italian
AENIGMA   A.M. Trading International, 1987, Italian
HOUSE OF DOOM (MS)   co-director with Umberto Lenzi,
   1989, Reteitalia/Dania Film, 1989, Italian

SAMUEL FULLER*
b. August 12, 1911 - Worcester, Massachusetts
Home: 8 bis rue de la Baume, Paris 75008, France
Agent: Charles Silverberg - Los Angeles, 213/322-4500

I SHOT JESSE JAMES   Screen Guild, 1949
THE BARON OF ARIZONA   Lippert, 1950
THE STEEL HELMET   Lippert, 1951
FIXED BAYONETS!   20th Century-Fox, 1951
PARK ROW   United Artists, 1952
PICKUP ON SOUTH STREET   20th Century-Fox, 1953

HELL AND HIGH WATER   20th Century-Fox, 1954
HOUSE OF BAMBOO   20th Century-Fox, 1955
RUN OF THE ARROW   20th Century-Fox, 1957
FORTY GUNS   20th Century-Fox, 1957
CHINA GATE   20th Century-Fox, 1957
VERBOTEN!   Columbia, 1958
THE CRIMSON KIMONO   Columbia, 1959
UNDERWORLD U.S.A.   Columbia, 1961
MERRILL'S MARAUDERS   Warner Bros., 1962
SHOCK CORRIDOR   Allied Artists, 1963
THE NAKED KISS   Allied Artists, 1964
SHARK!   Heritage, 1970, U.S.-Mexican
DEAD PIGEON ON BEETHOVEN STREET   Emerson,
   1972, West German
THE BIG RED ONE   United Artists, 1980
WHITE DOG   Paramount, 1982
THIEVES AFTER DARK   Parafrance, 1983, French
STREET OF NO RETURN   Thunder Films International/
   Animatografo Producoes/FR3, 1989, French-Portuguese

TEX FULLER
STRANDED   New Line Cinema, 1987

ALLEN FUNT*
b. 1914 - New York, New York
Contact: Directors Guild of America - New York City,
   212/581-0370

WHAT DO YOU SAY TO A NAKED WOMAN?   United
   Artists, 1970
MONEY TALKS   United Artists, 1971

SIDNEY J. FURIE*
b. February 28, 1933 - Toronto, Canada
Business: Furie Productions, Inc., 9169 Sunset Blvd.,
   Los Angeles, CA 90069
Agent: Peter Rawley, ICM - Los Angeles, 213/550-4000

A DANGEROUS AGE   Ajay, 1959, Canadian
A COOL SOUND FROM HELL   1959, Canadian
DR. BLOOD'S COFFIN   United Artists, 1960, British
THE SNAKE WOMAN   United Artists, 1960, British
DURING ONE NIGHT   NIGHT OF PASSION   Astor,
   1961, British
THREE ON A SPREE   United Artists, 1961, British
WONDERFUL TO BE YOUNG!   THE YOUNG ONES
   Paramount, 1961, British
THE BOYS   Gala, 1962, British
THE LEATHER BOYS   Allied Artists, 1964, British
SWINGER'S PARADISE   Universal, 1965, British
THE IPCRESS FILE   Universal, 1965, British
THE APPALOOSA   Universal, 1966
THE NAKED RUNNER   Warner Bros., 1967, British
THE LAWYER   Paramount, 1970
LITTLE FAUSS AND BIG HALSY   Paramount, 1970
LADY SINGS THE BLUES   Paramount, 1972
HIT!   Paramount, 1973
SHEILA LEVINE IS DEAD AND LIVING IN NEW YORK
   Paramount, 1975
GABLE AND LOMBARD   Universal, 1976
THE BOYS IN COMPANY C   Columbia, 1978
THE ENTITY   20th Century-Fox, 1983
PURPLE HEARTS   The Ladd Company/Warner Bros., 1984
IRON EAGLE   Tri-Star, 1986
SUPERMAN IV: THE QUEST FOR PEACE   Warner
   Bros., 1987
IRON EAGLE II   Tri-Star, 1988, Canadian-Israeli
THE TAKING OF BEVERLY HILLS   Columbia, 1991

115

G

MITCHELL GABOURIE
BUYING TIME   MGM/UA, 1989

MICHAEL GABRIEL
Business: Walt Disney Production, 500 S. Buena Vista
Street, Burbank, CA 91521, 818/560-1000

THE RESCUERS DOWN UNDER (AF)   Buena
Vista, 1990

ALAN GADNEY
b. January 1, 1941 - Dayton, Ohio
Business: Festival Films, P.O. Box 10180, Glendale, CA
91209, 213/222-8626 HH

WEST TEXAS   American Media Productions/American
Films Ltd., 1973
MOONCHILD   Filmmakers Ltd./American
Films Ltd., 1974

GEORGE GAGE*
Home: 31316 Broad Beach Road, Malibu, CA 90265,
213/457-3395

SKATEBOARD   Universal, 1978
FLESHBURN   Crown International, 1984

CLAUDE GAGNON*
b. 1949 - St.-Hyacinthe, Quebec, Canada
Address: 824 Des Colibris, Longueuil, Quebec J4G 2C1,
Canada, 514/670-1061
Business: Aska Film International Inc., 1600 Avenue de
Lorimier - Suite 211, Montreal, Quebec H2K 3W5,
Canada, 514/521-7103

KEIKO   1987, Canadian
LA ROSE, PIERROT ET LA LUCE   Cinephile,
1982, Canadian
VISAGE PALE   Yoshimura-Gagnon, 1985, Canadian
THE KID BROTHER   Kinema Amerika/Yoshimura-
Gagnon/Toho, 1987, Canadian-Japanese-U.S.
THE PIANIST   Aska Film, 1991, Canadian

RENÉ GAINVILLE
Attorney: Marvin B. Meyer, Rosenfeld, Meyer and
Susman, 9601 Wilshire Blvd., Beverly Hills, CA
90210, 213/272-4536

THE MAN FROM MYKONOS   Comptoir Francais du Film,
1967, French
LE DEMONIAQUE   CCFC Distribution, 1968, French
THE YOUNG COUPLE   UGC/Transworld Attractions,
1969, French
ALISE AND CHLOÉ   Oceanic, 1970, French
LE COMPLOT   CIC, 1975, French
UN BON SAMARITAIN   FR3, 1976, French
L'ASSOCIÉ   Columbia, 1980, French

TIMOTHY GALFAS*
b. December 31, 1934 - Atlanta, Georgia
Agent: Scott Harris, Harris & Goldberg - Los Angeles,
213/553-5200

BOGARD   L-T Films, 1975
THE BLACK STREETFIGHTER   New Line Cinema, 1976
REVENGE FOR A RAPE (TF)   Albert S. Ruddy
Productions, 1976
BLACK FIST   Worldwide, 1977
MANEATERS ARE LOOSE! (TF)   Mona Productions/
Finnegan Associates, 1978
SUNNYSIDE   American International, 1979

JOHN A. GALLAGHER
b. March 1, 1955 - New York, New York
Home: 212/260-5917
Agent: Richard Parks, The Parks Agency, 138 East 16th St.,
#5B, New York, NY 10003, 212/254-9067
Attorney: Benton P. Levy, Epstein & Levy, 1780 Broadway,
New York, NY 10019, 212/765-5038

BEACH HOUSE   New Line Cinema, 1982
THIS IS BARBARA BARONDESS: ONE LIFE IS NOT
ENOUGH (FD)   Theatre Lab Productions, 1985
SECRETS OF PRO WRESTLING (HVD)   Diamond
Entertainment, 1988
SECRETS OF PRO WRESTLING, VOLUME TWO (HVD)
Diamond Entertainment, 1989
STREET HUNTER   21st Century Distribution, 1990

JOSE LUIS GARCI
b. 1944 - Madrid, Spain
Agent: Paul Kohner, Inc. - Los Angeles, 213/550-1060

ASSIGNATURA PENDIENTE   1976, Spanish
SOLOS EN LA MADRUGADA   Jose Luis Tafur Productions,
1977, Spanish
LAS VERDES PRADERAS   1979, Spanish
EL CRACK   Nickelodeon/Acuarius, 1981, Spanish
TO BEGIN AGAIN (A VOLVER EMPEAZAR)   20th Century-
Fox International Classics, 1982, Spanish
EL CRACK 2   Lola Films/Nickelodeon, 1983,
Spanish-Peruvian
SESION CONTINUA   Nickelodeon, 1984, Spanish
COURSE COMPLETED (ASIGNATURA APROBADA)
Nickelodeon, 1987, Spanish

HERB GARDNER*
Agent: Lantz-Harris - New York City, 212/586-0200

THE GOODBYE PEOPLE   Embassy, 1984

JACK GARFEIN*
b. July 2, 1930 - Mukacevo, Czechoslovakia
Business: Harold Clurman Theatre, 412 West 42nd Street,
New York, NY 10036, 212/695-5429
Attorney: Jerome Luie, Cohn, Glickstein, Lurie, 1370 Avenue
of the Americas, New York, NY 10019, 212/757-4000

THE STRANGE ONE   END AS A MAN   Columbia, 1957
SOMETHING WILD   United Artists, 1961

PATRICK GARLAND
b. 1936 - London, England
Agent: Spokesmen, Ltd., 1 Craven Hill, London W2,
England

THE SNOW GOOSE (TF)   NBC, 1971
A DOLL'S HOUSE   Paramount, 1973, Canadian-U.S.

TONY GARNETT
b. England
Agent: William Morris Agency - Beverly Hills,
213/274-7451

PROSTITUTE   Mainline Films, 1979, British
DEEP IN THE HEART *HANDGUN*   Warner Bros., 1981

LILA GARRETT*
b. November 21, 1925 - New York, New York
Address: 10390 Wilshire Blvd. - Suite 1509, Los Angeles,
CA 90024, 213/274-8041
Agent: CAA - Beverly Hills, 213/288-4545

TERRACES (TF)   Charles Fries Productions/
Worldvision, 1977
WHO GETS THE FRIENDS? (TF)   CBS
Entertainment, 1988
BRIDESMAIDS (TF)   Motown Productions/Qintex
Entertainment/ Deaune Productions, 1989

MICK GARRIS*
Agent: CAA - Beverly Hills, 213/288-4545

CRITTERS 2   New Line Cinema, 1988

JEROME GARY*
Business: Gary/Richardson, 127 Broadway - Suite 205,
Santa Monica, CA 90401, 213/393-5928

STRIPPER (FD)   20th Century Fox, 1985
TRAXX   DEG, 1988

ELEANOR GAVER
SLIPPING INTO DARKNESS   MCEG, 1990

COSTA - GAVRAS*
(Konstantinos Gavras)
Home: 244 Rue St. Jacques, Paris 75005, France
Agent: William Morris Agency - Beverly Hills,
213/274-7451

THE SLEEPING CAR MURDERS   7 Arts, 1966, French
SHOCK TROOPS *UN HOMME DE TROP*   United Artists,
1968, French- Italian
Z★   Cinema 5, 1969, French-Algerian
THE CONFESSION   Paramount, 1970, French
STATE OF SIEGE   Cinema 5, 1973, French
SPECIAL SECTION   Universal, 1975, French-Italian-
West German
CLAIR DE FEMME   Atlantic Releasing Corporation, 1979,
French-Italian-West German
MISSING   Universal, 1982
HANNA K.   Universal Classics, 1983, French
CONSEIL DE FAMILLE   European Classics,
1986, French
BETRAYED   MGM/UA, 1988
MUSIC BOX   Tri-Star, 1989

JOE GAYTON
Agent: InterTalent - Los Angeles, 213/271-0600

WARM SUMMER RAIN   Cinema Corporation of
America, 1989

GYULA GAZDAG
b. 1947 - Budapest, Hungary
Business: UCLA Film and TV Department, 405 Hilgard
Avenue, Los Angeles, CA 90024, 213/206-6851

THE WHISTLING COBBLESTONE   Mafilm Studio,
1971, Hungarian
THE RESOLUTION (FD)   co-director with Judit Ember,
Bela Balazs Studio, 1972, Hungarian
SINGING ON THE TREADMILL   Mafilm-Hunnia Studio,
1974, Hungarian
SWAP   Objektiv Studio, 1977, Hungarian
LOST ILLUSIONS   Objektiv Studio, 1982, Hungarian
THE BANQUET   Hungarian TV/Mafilm-Objektiv Studio,
1982, Hungarian
PACKAGE TOUR (FD)   New Yorker, 1984, Hungarian
A HUNGARIAN FAIRY TALE   Objektiv Studio,
1988, Hungarian
STAND OFF   Objektiv Studio/Mafilm, 1989, Hungarian

BEN GAZZARA*
b. August 28, 1930 - New York, New York
Contact: Directors Guild of America - Los Angeles,
213/289-2000

BEYOND THE OCEAN   Scena International/Reteitalia,
1990, Italian

VANYOSKA GEE
b. 1948
Business: Mountain Top Films, 48 East Broadway - Suite 3,
New York, NY 10002, 212/741-1814

KRIK? KRAK! TALES OF A NIGHTMARE   co-director
with Jac Avila, Mountain Top Films, 1988, Haitian-
U.S.-Canadian

DAVID GELFAND
DOTTIE (TF)   Dottie Films Inc., 1987

JAMES GEORGE
ROVER DANGERFIELD (AF)   co-director with Bob Seeley,
Warner Bros., 1991

THEODORE GERSHUNY
Contact: Writers Guild of America, East - New York City,
212/245-6180

LOVE, DEATH   1973
SILENT NIGHT, BLOODY NIGHT   Cannon, 1974
SUGAR COOKIES   Troma, 1977
DEATHHOUSE   Cannon, 1981

NICOLAS GESSNER
SOMEONE BEHIND THE DOOR   GSF, 1971, French
THE LITTLE GIRL WHO LIVES DOWN THE LANE
American International, 1977, U.S.-Canadian-French
IT RAINED ALL NIGHT THE DAY I LEFT   Caneuram/
Israfilm/COFCI, 1981, Canadian-Israeli-French
QUICKER THAN THE EYE   Condor Productions,
1989, Swiss
TENNESSEE NIGHTS   Condor Productions/Allianz Films/
Intermedia/WDR, 1989, U.S.-Swiss

JOE GIANNONE
MADMAN   Jensen Farley Pictures, 1982

DUNCAN GIBBINS*
Agent: The Brandt Company - Studio City, 818/506-7747

FIRE WITH FIRE   Paramount, 1986
EVE OF DESTRUCTION   Orion, 1990

BRIAN GIBSON*
b. September 22, 1944 - Reading, England
Address: 1299 Ocean Avenue - Suite 620, Santa Monica,
   CA 90401, 213/451-0744
Agent: Jim Wiatt, ICM - Los Angeles, 213/550-4000

BLUE REMEMBERED HILLS (TF)   1979, British
BREAKING GLASS   Paramount, 1980, British
POLTERGEIST II: THE OTHER SIDE   MGM/UA, 1986
THE MURDERERS AMONG US: THE SIMON
   WIESENTHAL STORY (CTF)   HBO Pictures/Robert
   Cooper Productions/TVS Films/Citadel Entertainment/
   Hungarian TV, 1989, U.S.-British-Hungarian
DRUG WARS: THE CAMARENA STORY (MS)   ZZY Inc.
   Productions/World International Network, 1990
THE JOSEPHINE BAKER STORY (CTF)   HBOPictures/
   Anglia TV/John Kemeny Productions, 1991,
   U.S.-British-Canadian

BRIAN GILBERT
Agent: CAA - Beverly Hills, 213/288-4545

SHARMA AND BEYOND   Cinecom, 1984, British,
   originally made for television
FRENCH LESSON   THE FROG PRINCE   Warner Bros.,
   1984, British
VICE VERSA   Columbia, 1988
NOT WITHOUT MY DAUGHTER   Pathe
   Entertainment, 1991

LEWIS GILBERT*
b. March 6, 1920 - London, England
Address: c/o Baker Rooke, Clement House, 99 Aldwych,
   London WC2 BJY, England
Attorney: Norman Tyre, Gang, Tyre & Brown - Los Angeles,
   213/463-4863

THE LITTLE BALLERINA   General Film Distributors,
   1947, British
ONCE A SINNER   Butcher, 1950, British
WALL OF DEATH   THERE IS ANOTHER SIDE   Realart,
   1951, British
THE SCARLET THREAD   Butcher, 1951, British
HUNDRED HOUR HUNT   EMERGENCY CALL   Greshler,
   1952, British
TIME GENTLEMEN PLEASE!   Eros, 1952, British
THE SLASHER   COSH BOY   Lippert, 1953, British
JOHNNY ON THE RUN   co-director with Vernon Harris,
   Associated British Film Distributors/Children's Film
   Foundation, 1953, British
BREAK TO FREEDOM   ALBERT R.N.   United Artists,
   1953, British
THE GOOD DIE YOUNG   United Artists, 1954, British
THE SEA SHALL NOT HAVE THEM   United Artists,
   1954, British
CAST A DARK SHADOW   DCA, 1955, British
REACH FOR THE SKY   Rank, 1956, British
PARADISE LAGOON   THE ADMIRABLE CRICHTON
   Columbia, 1957, British
CARVE HER NAME WITH PRIDE   Lopert, 1958, British

A CRY FROM THE STREETS   Tudor, 1959, British
FERRY TO HONG KONG   20th Century-Fox,
   1959, British
SINK THE BISMARCK!   20th Century-Fox, 1960, British
SKYWATCH   LIGHT UP THE SKY   Continental,
   1960, British
LOSS OF INNOCENCE   THE GREENGAGE SUMMER
   Columbia, 1961, British
DAMN THE DEFIANT!   H.M.S. DEFIANT   Columbia,
   1962, British
THE SEVENTH DAWN   United Artists, 1964, U.S.-British
ALFIE   Paramount, 1966, British
YOU ONLY LIVE TWICE   United Artists, 1967, British
THE ADVENTURERS   Paramount, 1970
FRIENDS   Paramount, 1971, British-French
PAUL AND MICHELLE   Paramount, 1974, British-French
OPERATION DAYBREAK   Warner Bros., 1975, British
SEVEN NIGHTS IN JAPAN   EMI, 1976, British-French
THE SPY WHO LOVED ME   United Artists, 1977,
   British-U.S.
MOONRAKER   United Artists, 1979, British-French
EDUCATING RITA   Columbia, 1983, British
NOT QUITE PARADISE   NOT QUITE JERUSALEM   New
   World, 1985, British
SHIRLEY VALENTINE   Paramount, 1989, British
STEPPING OUT   Paramount, 1991, U.S.-British

DAVID GILER*
Contact: Directors Guild of America - Los Angeles,
   213/289-2000

THE BLACK BIRD   Columbia, 1975

STUART GILLARD
b. 1946 - Coronation, Alberta, Canada
Business: Triton Productions, Inc., 11365 Ventura Blvd. -
   Suite 365, Studio City, CA 91604, 818/769-1053
Agent: Lynn Kinney, 1235 Bay Street - Suite 501, Toronto,
   Ontario M5R 3K4, Canada, 416/926-1507

PARADISE   Avco Embassy, 1982, Canadian
THE RETURN OF THE SHAGGY DOG (TF)   Walt
   Disney TV, 1987
A MAN CALLED SARGE   Cannon, 1990

TERRY GILLIAM
b. November 22, 1940 - Minneapolis, Minnesota
Address: 51 South Hill Park, London NW3, England
Agent: CAA - Beverly Hills, 213/288-4545

MONTY PYTHON AND THE HOLY GRAIL   co-director
   with Terry Jones, Cinema 5, 1974, British
JABBERWOCKY   Cinema 5, 1977, British
TIME BANDITS   Avco Embassy, 1981, British
BRAZIL   Universal, 1985, British
THE ADVENTURES OF BARON MUNCHAUSEN
   Columbia, 1989, British
THE FISHER KING   Columbia, 1991

FRANK D. GILROY*
b. October 13, 1925 - New York, New York
Agent: William Morris Agency - Beverly Hills,
   213/274-7451

DESPERATE CHARACTERS   ITC, 1971
JOHN O'HARA'S GIBBSVILLE (TF)   Columbia TV, 1975
THE TURNING POINT OF JIM MALLOY (TF)   David Gerber
   Company/Columbia TV, 1975
FROM NOON TILL THREE   United Artists, 1976

ONCE IN PARIS...   Atlantic Releasing Corporation, 1978
REX STOUT'S NERO WOLFE (TF)   Emmett Lavery, Jr.
    Productions/Paramount TV, 1979
THE GIG   Castle Hill Productions, 1985
THE LUCKIEST MAN IN THE WORLD   Co-Star
    Entertainment, 1989

MILTON MOSES GINSBERG
COMING APART   Kaleidoscope, 1969
THE WEREWOLF OF WASHINGTON   Diplomat, 1973

ROBERT GINTY
Agent: Steve Tellez, APA - Los Angeles, 213/237-0744

THE BOUNTY HUNTER   Action International, 1989
VIETNAM, TEXAS   Epic Pictures, 1990

BOB GIRALDI*
Business: Giraldi Suarez Productions, 581 Sixth Avenue,
    New York, NY 10011, 212/691-9200
Agent: CAA - Beverly Hills, 213/288-4545

NATIONAL LAMPOON'S MOVIE MADNESS   co-director
    with Henry Jaglom, United Artists, 1982
CLUB MED (TF)   Lorimar Productions, 1986
HIDING OUT   DEG, 1987

BERNARD GIRARD
b. 1930

THE GREEN-EYED BLONDE   Warner Bros., 1957
RIDE OUT FOR REVENGE   United Artists, 1958
AS YOUNG AS WE ARE   Paramount, 1958
THE PARTY CRASHERS   Paramount, 1958
A PUBLIC AFFAIR   Parade, 1962
DEAD HEAT ON A MERRY-GO-ROUND
    Paramount, 1966
MAD ROOM   Columbia, 1969
HUNTERS ARE FOR KILLING (TF)   Cinema Center, 1970
THE HAPPINESS CAGE   THE MIND SNATCHERS
    Cinerama Releasing Corporation, 1972
GONE WITH THE WEST   International Cinefilm, 1975

AMOS GITAI
Contact: Israel Film Centre, Ministry of Industry & Trade,
    30 Agron Street, P.O. Box 299, Jerusalem 94190,
    Israel, 02/210297

FIELD DIARY (FD)   1982, Israeli
PINEAPPLE (TD)   1983, French
BANGKOK BAHRAIN (TD)   Channel Four, 1984, British
ESTHER   1986, Israeli
BRAND NEW DAY (FD)   1987, Israeli
BERLIN JERUSALEM   Agav Films/Channel Four/La Sept/
    Nova Films/RAI-2/Orthel Films/NOS/Transfax/La Maison
    de Culture du Havre/Hubert Bals Fund/CNC, 1989,
    French- Israeli

DAVID GLADWELL
b. April 2, 1935 - Gloucester, England
Address: 8 Caldervale Road, London SW4 9LZ,
    England, 71/622-6843

REQUIEM FOR A VILLAGE   BFI Production Board,
    1977, British
MEMOIRS OF A SURVIVOR   EMI, 1982, British
O ALIEN! (TF)   1984, British
EARTHSTARS (TF)   1985, British

PAUL MICHAEL GLASER*
b. Cambridge, Massachusetts
Agent: Alan Greenspan, ICM - Los Angeles,
    213/550-4428

AMAZONS (TF)   ABC Circle Films, 1984
BAND OF THE HAND   Tri-Star, 1986
THE RUNNING MAN   Tri-Star, 1987

LESLI LINKA GLATTER*
Agent: CAA - Beverly Hills, 213/288-4545

INTO THE HOMELAND (CTF)   HBO Pictures/Capistrano
    Pictures, 1987

MICHIE GLEASON
BROKEN ENGLISH   Lorimar, 1981
SUMMER HEAT   Atlantic Releasing Corporation, 1987

JOHN GLEN
b. May 15, 1932 - Sunbury on Thames, England
Address: 9A Barkston Gardens, London SW5, England
Agent: Sanford-Beckett-Skouras & Associates - Los Angeles,
    213/208-2100

FOR YOUR EYES ONLY   United Artists, 1981, British
OCTOPUSSY   MGM/UA, 1983, British
A VIEW TO A KILL   MGM/UA, 1985, British
THE LIVING DAYLIGHTS   MGM/UA, 1987, British
LICENCE TO KILL   MGM/UA, 1989, British

PIERRE WILLIAM GLENN
Contact: French Film Office, 745 Fifth Avenue, New York,
    NY 10151, 212/832-8860

TERMINUS   END OF THE LINE   Hemdale, 1986,
    French-West German

PETER GLENVILLE*
b. October 28, 1913 - London, England
Business Manager: Elliot J. Lefkowitz, 641 Lexington
    Avenue, New York, NY 10022, 212/758-0860

THE PRISONER   Columbia, 1955, British
ME AND THE COLONEL   Columbia, 1958
SUMMER AND SMOKE   Paramount, 1961
TERM OF TRIAL   Warner Bros., 1963, British
BECKET★   Paramount, 1964, British
HOTEL PARADISO   MGM, 1966, British
THE COMEDIANS   MGM, 1967, British

JAMES GLICKENHAUS*
b. July 24, 1950 - New York, New York
Agent: William Morris Agency - Beverly Hills,
    213/274-7451
Business: Shapiro Glickenhaus Entertainment, 12001
    Ventura Place - 4th Floor, Studio City, CA 91604,
    818/766-8500 or: 1619 Broadway, New York, NY 10019,
    212/265-1150

THE ASTROLOGER   Interstar, 1977
THE EXTERMINATOR   Avco Embassy, 1980
THE SOLDIER   Embassy, 1982
THE PROTECTOR   Warner Bros., 1985,
    U.S.-Hong Kong
SHAKEDOWN   Universal, 1988

KURT GLOOR
b. November 8, 1942 - Zurich, Switzerland
Business: Filmproduktion AG, Spiegelgasse 27, CH-8001
   Zurich, Switzerland, 47-87-66

DIE PLOTZLICHE EINSAMKEIT DES KONRAD STEINER
   Kurt Gloor Filmproduktion, 1975, Swiss
LEHMANNS LETZTER (TF)   Swiss TV, 1977, Swiss
DER CHINESE (TF)   Bavaria Filmproduktion Munich,
   1978, West German
DER ERFINDER   Kurt Gloor Filmproduktion, 1980, Swiss
MANN OHNE GEDACHTNIS   Kurt Gloor Filmproduktion,
   1984, Swiss

VADIM GLOWNA
Contact: German Film & TV Academy, Pommernallee 1,
   1 Berlin 19, West Germany, 0311/302-6096

DESPERADO CITY   New Line Cinema, 1981,
   West German
DEVIL'S PARADISE   Atossa/ZDF, 1987, West German

JEAN-LUC GODARD
b. December 3, 1930 - Paris, France
Address: 99 Avenue du Roule, 92200 Neuilly, France,
   04/747-0910
Contact: French Film Office, 745 Fifth Avenue, New York,
   NY 10151, 212/832-8860

BREATHLESS   *A BOUT DE SOUFFLE*   Films Around
   the World, 1960, French
A WOMAN IS A WOMAN   Pathe Contemporary,
   1961, French
SEVEN CAPITAL SINS   co-director with Roger Vadim,
   Sylvaine Dhomme, Edouard Molinaro, Philippe
   De Broca, Claude Chabrol, Jacques Demy, Marie-Jose
   Nat, Dominique Paturel, Jean-Marc Tennberg &
   Perrette Pradier, Embassy, 1962, French-Italian
MY LIFE TO LIVE   Pathe Contemporary, 1962, French
ROGOPAG   co-director, 1962, French
LE PETIT SOLDAT   West End, 1963, French
LES CARABINIERS   West End, 1963, French
CONTEMPT   *LE MEPRIS*   Embassy, 1964, French-Italian
LES PLUS BELLES ESCROQUERIES DU MONDE
   co-director, 1964, French-Italian-Japanese
BAND OF OUTSIDERS   Royal Films International,
   1964, French
THE MARRIED WOMAN   Royal Films International,
   1964, French
SIX IN PARIS   New Yorker, co-director, French
ALPHAVILLE   Pathe Contemporary, 1965, French
PIERROT LE FOU   Pathe Contemporary, 1965, French
MASCULINE FEMININE   Royal Films International, 1966,
   French-Swedish
MADE IN U.S.A.   Pathe Contemporary, 1966, French
TWO OR THREE THINGS I KNOW ABOUT HER   New
   Line Cinema, 1967, French
THE OLDEST PROFESSION   *LES PLUS VIEUX METIER
   DU MONDE*   co-director with Franco Indovina,
   Mauro Bolognini, Philippe de Broca, Michael Pfleghar,
   Claude Autant-Lara, Goldstone, 1967, Italian-French-
   West German
FAR FROM VIETNAM (FD)   co-director with Alain Resnais,
   William Klein, Agnes Varda, Joris Ivens & Claude
   Lelouch, New Yorker, 1967, French
LA CHINOISE   Leacock-Pennebaker, 1967, French
WEEKEND   Grove Press, 1968, French-Italian
UN FILM COMME LES AUTRES   1968, French
AMORE E RABBIA   co-director, 1969, Italian-French
LE GAI SAVOIR   EYR, 1969, French

ONE A.M.   Leacock-Pennebaker, 1969, French
SYMPATHY FOR THE DEVIL   *1 + 1*   New Line Cinema,
   1969, British
BRITISH SOUNDS   *SEE YOU AT MAO* (TF)   Kestrel
   Productions, co-director with Jean-Pierre Gorin,
   1969, British
WIND FROM THE EAST   co-director with Jean-Pierre Gorin,
   New Line Cinema, 1969, French-Italian-West German
PRAVDA (FD)   co-director with Jean-Pierre Gorin, 1969,
   French-Czech
LOTTE IN ITALIA (FD)   co-director with Jean-Pierre Gorin,
   RAI, 1970, Italian
VLADIMIR ET ROSA   co-director with Jean-Pierre Gorin,
   1971, French
TOUT VA BIEN   co-director with Jean-Pierre Gorin, New
   Yorker, 1972, French-Italian
LETTER TO JANE: INVESTIGATION OF A STILL
   co-director with Jean-Pierre Gorin, New Yorker,
   1972, French
NUMERO DEUX   Zoetrope, 1975, French
COMMENT ÇA VA   1976, French
ICI ET AILLEURS   MK2 Diffusion, 1976, French
SUR ET SOUS LA COMMUNICATION (TD)   INA,
   1977, French
FRANCE/TOUR/DETOUR/DEUX/ENFANTS (TD)
   co-director with Anne-Marie Mieville, Zoetrope,
   1980, Swiss-French
EVERY MAN FOR HIMSELF   *SAUVE QUI PEUT LA VIE*
   New Yorker/Zoetrope, 1980, Swiss-French
PASSION   United Artists Classics, 1983, French-Swiss
FIRST NAME: CARMEN   Spectrafilm, 1983, French-Swiss
HAIL MARY   New Yorker, 1985, French-Swiss
DETECTIVE   Spectrafilm, 1985, French
GRANDEUR ET DECADENCE D'UN PETIT COMMERCE DE
   CINEMA (TF) Hamster Productions, 1986, French
SOIGNE TA DROITE (KEEP UP YOUR RIGHT!)   Galaxy,
   1987, French-Swiss
KING LEAR   Cannon, 1987, U.S.-Swiss
ARIA   co-director, Miramax Films, 1987, British
NOUVELLE VAGUE   Vega Film, 1990, Swiss

GARY GODDARD*
Agent: CAA - Beverly Hills, 213/288-4545

MASTERS OF THE UNIVERSE   Cannon, 1987

JIM GODDARD
b. February 2, 1936 - London, England
Agent: CAA - Beverly Hills, 213/288-4545

A TALE OF TWO CITIES (TF)   Norman Rosemont
   Productions/Marble Arch Productions, 1980, U.S.-British
REILLY - ACE OF SPIES (MS)   co-director with Martin
   Campbell, Euston Films Ltd., 1984
KENNEDY (MS)   Central Independent Television
   Productions/Alan Landsburg Productions, 1983,
   British-U.S.
HITLER'S S.S.: PORTRAIT IN EVIL (TF)   Colason Limited
   Productions/Edgar J. Scherick Associates, 1985,
   British-U.S.
PARKER   Virgin Films, 1985, British
SHANGHAI SURPRISE   MGM/UA, 1986, British-U.S.
THE IMPOSSIBLE SPY (CTF)   HBO Showcase/BBC/
   Quartet International/IMGC, 1987, British-Israeli
THE FOUR MINUTE MILE (TF)   Oscar-Sullivan Productions/
   Centre Films, 1988, Australian

JILL GODMILOW
FAR FROM POLAND (FD)   Film Forum, 1984
WAITING FOR THE MOON   Skouras Pictures, 1987,
   U.S.-French-British- West German

MENAHEM GOLAN*
b. May 31, 1929 - Tiberias, Israel
Business: 21st Century Film Corp., 8200 Wilshire Blvd.,
    Beverly Hills, CA 90211, 213/658-3000

EL DORADO   1963, Israeli
TRUNK TO CAIRO   American International, 1967,
    Israeli-West German
THE GIRL FROM THE DEAD SEA   1967, Israeli
TEVYE AND HIS SEVEN DAUGHTERS   Noah Films,
    1968, Israeli
FORTUNA   Trans-American, 1969, Israeli
WHAT'S GOOD FOR THE GOOSE   National
    Showmanship, 1969, British
MARGO   Cannon, 1970, Israeli
LUPO!   Cannon, 1970, Israeli
QUEEN OF THE ROAD   Noah Films, 1970, Israeli
KATZ AND KARASSO   Noah Films, 1971, Israeli
THE GREAT TELEPHONE ROBBERY   Noah Films,
    1972, Israeli
ESCAPE TO THE SUN   Cinevision, 1972, Israeli-West
    German-French
KAZABLAN   MGM, 1973, Israeli
LEPKE   Warner Bros., 1975
DIAMONDS   Avco Embassy, 1975, U.S.-Israeli-Swiss
THE AMBASSADOR   Noah Films, 1976, Israeli
OPERATION THUNDERBOLT   Cinema Shares
    International, 1978, Israeli
THE URANIUM CONSPIRACY   Noah Films, 1978,
    Israeli-West German
THE MAGICIAN OF LUBLIN   Cannon, 1979,
    Israeli-West German-U.S.
THE APPLE   Cannon, 1980, U.S.-West German
ENTER THE NINJA   Cannon, 1981
OVER THE BROOKLYN BRIDGE   MGM/UA/
    Cannon, 1984
THE DELTA FORCE   Canon, 1986
OVER THE TOP   Cannon, 1987
HANNA'S WAR   Cannon, 1988
MACK THE KNIFE   21st Century Distribution, 1989

GREGG GOLD
HOUSE OF THE RISING SUN   Mediacom
    Productions, 1987

JACK GOLD
b. June 28, 1930 - London, England
Home: 18 Avenue Road, London N6, England, 71/348-5482
Agent: InterTalent - Los Angeles, 213/271-0600

THE BOFORS GUN   Universal, 1968, British
THE RECKONING   Columbia, 1969, British
CATHOLICS (TF)   Sidney Glazier Productions,
    1973, British
WHO?   Allied Artists, 1975, British-West German
MAN FRIDAY   Avco Embassy, 1975, British
ACES HIGH   Cinema Shares International, 1977, British
THE MEDUSA TOUCH   Warner Bros., 1978, British
THE SAILOR'S RETURN   Euston Films Ltd., 1978
THE NAKED CIVIL SERVANT (TF)   Thames TV,
    1978, British
CHARLIE MUFFIN   Euston Films Ltd., 1980, British
LITTLE LORD FAUNTLEROY (TF)   Norman Rosemont
    Productions, 1980, U.S.- British
PRAYING MANTIS   Portman Productions/Channel Four,
    1982, British
RED MONARCH   Enigma Films/Goldcrest Films &
    Television Ltd., 1983, British
GOOD AND BAD AT GAMES (TF)   Portman Quintet
    Productions, 1983, British

SAKHAROV (CTF)   HBO Premiere Films/Titus Productions,
    1984, U.S.-British
THE CHAIN   Rank, 1985, British
NOEL COWARD'S 'ME AND THE GIRLS' (TF)   BBC/Quintet
    Films/Arts & Entertainment Network, 1985, British-U.S.
MURROW (CTF)   HBO Premiere Films/Titus Productions/
    TVS Ltd. Productions, 1986, U.S.-British
ESCAPE FROM SOBIBOR (TF)☆ Rule-Starger Productions/
    Zenith Productions, 1987, U.S.-British
STONES FOR IBARRA (TF)   Titus Productions, 1988
THE TENTH MAN (TF)   Rosemont Productions/William Self
    Productions, 1988, U.S.-British
THE ROSE AND THE JACKAL (CTF)   Steve White
    Productions/PWD Productions, 1990

DAN GOLDBERG
Agent: CAA - Beverly Hills, 213/288-4545

FEDS   Warner Bros., 1988

GARY DAVID GOLDBERG*
Agent: Jim Preminger Agency - Los Angeles, 213/475-9491

DAD   Universal, 1989

MARK GOLDBLATT*
Agent: The Gersh Agency - Beverly Hills, 213/274-6611

DEAD HEAT   New World, 1988
THE PUNISHER   New World, 1989

DAN GOLDEN
DARK OBSESSIONS   Concorde, 1990

JOHN GOLDEN
Contact: Writers Guild of America, West - Los Angeles,
    213/550-1000

FAT GUY GOES NUTZOID   Troma, 1986
THE BOILER ROOM   Eureka Productions, 1987
THE BIG GIVER   Coho Media/New Street Partners, 1988
MANHATTAN MOONSHINE   Coho Media, 1988

PAUL GOLDING
Contact: Writers Guild of America, West - Los Angeles,
    213/550-1000

PULSE   Columbia, 1988

ALLAN GOLDSTEIN*
Home: 2509 Green Valley Road, Los Angeles, CA 90046,
    213/656-9332
Agent: Devra Lieb, Triad Artists, Inc. - Los Angeles,
    213/556-2727

THE HOUSE OF DIES DREAR (TF)   Children's Television
    Workshop, 1984
THE RETURN OF HICKEY (TF)   Bar Harbour Film Inc.
    Productions/Siren Pictures Corporation/Global TV
    Network, 1988
THE OUTSIDE CHANCE OF MAXIMILIAN GLICK   South
    Gate Entertainment, 1988, Canadian
COLD FRONT   Cold Front Productions, 1989, Canadian
THE BEGINNING OF THE FIRM (TF)   Ronald J. Kahn
    Productions/ Scholastic Productions/Bar Harbour Film Inc.
    Productions/ Siren Pi ctures Corp./The Global TV Network,
    1989, U.S.- Canadian
THE PHONE CALL (TF)   3 Themes, 1989, Canadian
CHAINDANCE   Chaindance Productions, 1990, Canadian

SCOTT GOLDSTEIN
FLANAGAN *WALLS OF GLASS* United Film
  Distribution, 1985
MIND GAME Spirit Films, 1990

JAMES GOLDSTONE*
b. June 8, 1931 - Los Angeles, California
Agent: The Brandt Company - Studio City, 818/5067747

SCALPLOCK (TF) Columbia TV, 1966
CODE NAME: HERACLITUS (TF) Universal TV, 1967
IRONSIDE (TF) Universal TV, 1967
SHADOW OVER ELVERON (TF) Universal TV, 1968
JIGSAW Universal, 1968
A MAN CALLED GANNON Universal, 1969
WINNING Universal, 1969
A CLEAR AND PRESENT DANGER (TF)☆ Universal
  TV, 1970
BROTHER JOHN Columbia, 1971
RED SKY AT MORNING Universal, 1971
THE GANG THAT COULDN'T SHOOT STRAIGHT
  MGM, 1972
THEY ONLY KILL THEIR MASTERS 1973
CRY PANIC (TF) Spelling-Goldberg
  Productions, 1974
DR. MAX (TF) CBS, Inc., 1974
THINGS IN THEIR SEASON (TF) Tomorrow
  Entertainment, 1974
JOURNEY FROM DARKNESS (TF) Bob Banner
  Associates, 1975
ERIC (TF) Lorimar Productions, 1975
SWASHBUCKLER Universal, 1976
ROLLERCOASTER Universal, 1977
STUDS LONIGAN (MS) Lorimar Productions, 1979
WHEN TIME RAN OUT Warner Bros., 1980
KENT STATE (TF)☆☆ Inter Planetary Productions/
  Osmond Communications, 1981
CHARLES & DIANA: A ROYAL LOVE STORY (TF)
  St. Lorraine Productions, 1982
CALAMITY JANE (TF) CBS Entertainment, 1983
RITA HAYWORTH: THE LOVE GODDESS (TF) The
  Susskind Co, 1983
SENTIMENTAL JOURNEY (TF) Lucille Ball
  Productions/Smith-Richmond Productions/20th
  Century Fox TV, 1984
THE SUN ALSO RISES (TF) Furia-Oringer Productions/
  20th Century Fox TV, 1984
DREAMS OF GOLD: THE MEL FISHER STORY (TF)
  Inter Planetary Productions, 1986
EARTH*STAR VOYAGER (TF) Walt Disney TV/Marstar
  Productions, 1988

STEVE GOMER*
Contact: Directors Guild of America - Los Angeles,
  213/289-2000

SWEET LORRAINE Angelika Films, 1987
LOVE & OTHER SORROWS (TF) Learning in Focus/
  American Playhouse, 1989

SERVANDO GONZALEZ
b. May 15, 1925 - Mexico City, Mexico
Contact: Azteca Films, 555 N. La Brea Avenue, P.O.
  Box 36095, Hollywood, CA 90036, 213/938-2413

YANCO Azteca Films, 1960, Mexican
LOS MEDIOCRES Azteca Films, 1962, Mexican
THE FOOL KILLER Allied Artists, 1965
VIENTO NEGRO 1965, Mexican
EL ULTIMO TUNEL IMC/Conacine/F.F.C.C.,
  1987, Mexican

BERT I. GORDON*
b. September 24, 1922 - Kenosha, Wisconsin
Agent: Ronald Leif, Contemporary Artists - Beverly Hills,
  213/278-8250

KING DINOSAUR Lippert, 1955
BEGINNING OF THE END Republic, 1957
CYCLOPS American International, 1957
THE AMAZING COLOSSAL MAN American
  International, 1957
ATTACK OF THE PUPPET PEOPLE American
  International, 1958
WAR OF THE COLOSSAL BEAST American
  International, 1958
THE SPIDER American International, 1958
THE BOY AND THE PIRATES United Artists, 1960
TORMENTED Allied Artists, 1960
THE MAGIC SWORD United Artists, 1962
VILLAGE OF THE GIANTS Embassy, 1965
PICTURE MOMMY DEAD Embassy, 1966
HOW TO SUCCEED WITH SEX Medford, 1970
NECROMANCY American International, 1972
THE MAD BOMBER Cinemation, 1973
THE POLICE CONNECTION *DETECTIVE
  GERONIMO* 1973
THE FOOD OF THE GODS American International, 1976
EMPIRE OF THE ANTS American International, 1977
THE COMING 1981
DOING IT 1984
THE BIG BET Golden Communications, 1986
MALEDICTION Henry Plitt Productions, 1989

BETTE GORDON
Home: 393 Greenwich Street, New York, NY 10013,
  212/226-3408
Agent: Scott Yoselow, The Gersh Agency - New York City,
  212/997-1818

VARIETY Horizon Films, 1985
SEVEN WOMEN, SEVEN SINS co-director, ZDF, 1987,
  West German-French- U.S.-Austrian-Belgian

BRYAN GORDON*
Agent: Leading Artists - Beverly Hills, 213/858-1999

CAREER OPPORTUNITIES Universal, 1990

KEITH GORDON
b. 1961 - Bronx, New York
Contact: Screen Actors Guild - Los Angeles,
  213/465-4600

THE CHOCOLATE WAR MCEG, 1988

MICHAEL GORDON*
b. September 6, 1909 - Baltimore, Maryland
Home: 550 Veteran Avenue - Apt. 204, Los Angeles, CA
  90024, 213/208-3039
Business: UCLA Theatre Arts Department, 405 Hilgard
  Avenue, Los Angeles, CA 90024, 213/825-5761

BOSTON BLACKIE GOES HOLLYWOOD
  Columbia, 1942
UNDERGROUND AGENT Columbia, 1942
ONE DANGEROUS NIGHT Columbia, 1943
CRIME DOCTOR Columbia, 1943
THE WEB Universal, 1947
ANOTHER PART OF THE FOREST Universal, 1948
AN ACT OF MURDER Universal, 1948

THE LADY GAMBLES Universal, 1949
WOMAN IN HIDING Universal, 1950
CYRANO DE BERGERAC United Artists, 1950
I CAN GET IT FOR YOU WHOLESALE 20th Century-
    Fox, 1951
THE SECRET OF CONVICT LAKE 20th Century-
    Fox, 1951
WHEREVER SHE GOES Mayer-Kingsley, 1953,
    Australian
PILLOW TALK Universal, 1959
PORTRAIT IN BLACK Universal, 1960
BOYS' NIGHT OUT MGM, 1962
FOR LOVE OR MONEY Universal, 1963
MOVE OVER, DARLING 20th Century-Fox, 1963
A VERY SPECIAL FAVOR Universal, 1965
TEXAS ACROSS THE RIVER Universal, 1966
THE IMPOSSIBLE YEARS MGM, 1968
HOW DO I LOVE THEE? Cinerama Releasing
    Corporation, 1970

STUART GORDON

Agent: Jeremy Zimmer, Bauer Benedek Agency -
    Los Angeles, 213/275-2421

H.P. LOVECRAFT'S RE-ANIMATOR RE-ANIMATOR
    Empire Pictures, 1985
FROM BEYOND Empire Pictures, 1986
DOLLS Empire Pictures, 1987
DAUGHTER OF DARKNESS (TF) King Phoenix
    Entertainment, 1990
ROBOTJOX Triumph Releasing Corporation, 1990

BERRY GORDY*

b. November 28, 1929
Business: Motown Records Corporation, 6255 Sunset
    Blvd., Hollywood, CA 90028, 213/468-3500

MAHOGANY Paramount, 1975

CLAUDE GORETTA

b. June 23, 1929 - Geneva, Switzerland
Contact: Swiss Film Center, Munstergasse 18, 8001 Zurich,
    Switzerland, 01/472860

LE FOU 1970, Swiss
LE JOUR DES NOCES (TF) 1971, Swiss
L'INVITATION Janus, 1973, Swiss
THE WONDERFUL CROOK PAS SI MERCHANT
    QUE CA... New Yorker, 1975, Swiss-French
THE LACEMAKER New Yorker, 1977, Swiss-French
LES CHEMINS DE L'EXIT OU LES DERNIERES ANNEES
    DE JEAN JACQUES ROUSSEAU (MS) TFI/SSR/
    Telecip/BBC/RTB/SRC/TV60, 1978, French
BONHEUR TOI-MEME Phenix Films/FR3, 1980, French
THE GIRL FROM LORRAINE LA PROVINCIALE New
    Yorker, 1981, French
THE DEATH OF MARIO RICCI New Line Showcase,
    1983, Swiss-French
ORFEO Antenne-2/Radio France/Total Foundation for
    Music/SSR/Instituto Luce/ SRC, 1985, French-Swiss-
    Italian-Canadian
SI LE SOLEIL NE REVENAIT PAS JMH Productions/
    Television Suisse Romande/ Marion's Films/Sara Films/
    Canal Plus, 1987, Swiss-French
LE RAPPORT DU GENDARME (TF) Television Suisse
    Romande, 1987, Swiss

JEAN-PIERRE GORIN

Contact: French Film Office, 745 Fifth Avenue, New York,
    NY 10151, 212/832-8860

BRITISH SOUNDS SEE YOU AT MAO (TF) co-director
    with Jean-Luc Godard, Kestrel Films, 1969, British
WIND FROM THE EAST co-director with Jean-Luc Godard,
    New Line Cinema, 1969, French-Italian-West German
PRAVDA (FD) co-director with Jean-Luc Godard, 1969,
    French-Czech
LOTTE IN ITALIA (FD) co-director with Jean-Luc Godard,
    RAI, 1970, Italian
VLADIMIR ET ROSA co-director with Jean-Luc Godard,
    1971, French
TOUT VA BIEN co-director with Jean-Luc Godard, New
    Yorker, 1972, French-Italian
LETTER TO JANE: INVESTIGATION OF A STILL
    co-director with Jean-Luc Godard, New Yorker,
    1972, French
POTO AND CABENGO (FD) 1982, French
ORDINARY PLEASURES 1985, French

CHARLES GORMLEY

Contact: British Academy of Film & Television Arts,
    195 Piccadilly, London W1, England, 71/734-0022

LIVING APART TOGETHER (TF) Channel Four,
    1982, British
GOSPEL ACCORDING TO VIC JUST ANOTHER MIRACLE
    Skouras Pictures, 1986, British

MICHAEL GORNICK

CREEPSHOW II New World, 1987

HIDEO GOSHA

Contact: Directors Guild of Japan, Tsukada Building, 8-33
    Udagawa-cho, Shibuya-ku, Tokyo 150, Japan, 3/461-4411

GOYOKIN Toho, 1969, Japanese
HUNTER IN THE DARK 1970, Japanese
THE WOLVES Toho, 1972, Japanese
TENCHU Japanese Film Exchange, 1972, Japanese
ONIMASA East West Classics, 1982, Japanese
YOKIRO Filmtribe Distribution Company/Toei,
    1984, Japanese
CRACKED 1985, Japanese
THE PADDLE Toei, 1985, Japanese
FIREFLIES OF THE NORTH Toei, 1985, Japanese
USUGESHO Shochiku, 1986, Japanese
DEATH SHADOWS Shochiku, 1987, Japanese
TOKYO BORDELLO Toei, 1987, Japanese
A WOMAN WHO WOULDN'T MARRY Shochiku,
    1987, Japanese
FIRE OVER THE WOMEN'S CASTLE Toei,
    1987, Japanese
THE GATES OF FLESH Toei, 1988, Japanese
THE FOUR DAYS OF SNOW AND BLOOD Shochiku,
    1989, Japanese

PETER GOTHAR

b. 1947 - Pecs, Hungary
Contact: Hungarofilm, Bathory utca 10, H-1054 Budapest,
    Hungary, tel.: 116650

A PRICELESS DAY Budapest Studio, 1979, Hungarian
TIME STANDS STILL Budapest Studio, 1982, Hungarian
TIME Mafilm, 1986, Hungarian
JUST LIKE AMERICA Mafilm Hunnia Studio, 1987,
    Hungarian-U.S.

CARL GOTTLIEB*
b. March 18, 1938
Agent: Larry Grossman & Associates - Beverly Hills,
213/550-8127

CAVEMAN   United Artists, 1981
AMAZON WOMEN ON THE MOON   co-director with John
Landis, Joe Dante, Robert K. Weiss & Peter Horton,
Universal, 1987

LISA GOTTLIEB*
Agent: Tom Chasin, The Chasin Agency - Beverly Hills,
213/278-7505

JUST ONE OF THE BOYS   Columbia, 1985

MICHAEL GOTTLIEB*
Business: Harmony Pictures, 2921 W. Alameda Avenue,
Burbank, CA 91505, 818/846-6700
Agent: William Morris Agency - Beverly Hills, 213/274-7451

MANNEQUIN   20th Century Fox, 1987
THE SHRIMP ON THE BARBIE   directed under pseuonym
of Alan Smithee, Vestron, 1990

RICHARD GOVERNOR
GHOST TOWN   Trans World Entertainment, 1988

MARY GRACE
Business: Gracefilms, Inc., 279 So. Beverly Drive -
Suite 872, Beverly Hills, CA 90211, 213/273-9404

THE PRINCESS AND THE DWARF   Gracefilms, 1990

WILLIAM A. GRAHAM*
Agent: CAA - Beverly Hills, 213/288-4545

THE DOOMSDAY FLIGHT (TF)   Universal TV, 1966
THE OUTSIDER (TF)   Universal TV, 1967
WATERHOLE #3   Paramount, 1967
CHANGE OF HABIT   Universal, 1968
THE LEGEND OF CUSTER (TF)   20th Century-Fox, 1968
SUBMARINE X-1   United Artists, 1969, British
TRIAL RUN (TF)   Universal TV, 1969
THEN CAME BRONSON (TF)   Universal TV, 1969
THE INTRUDERS (TF)   Universal TV, 1970
CONGRATULATIONS, IT'S A BOY! (TF)   Aaron Spelling
Productions, 1971
THIEF (TF)   Metromedia Productions/Stonehenge
Productions, 1971
MARRIAGE: YEAR ONE (TF)   Universal TV, 1971
JIGSAW (TF)   Universal TV, 1972
MAGIC CARPET (TF)   Universal TV, 1972
HONKY   Jack H. Harris Enterprises, 1972
COUNT YOUR BULLETS   CRY FOR ME, BILLY   Brut
Productions, 1972
BIRDS OF PREY (TF)   Tomorrow Entertainment, 1973
MR. INSIDE/MR. OUTSIDE (TF)   D'Antoni
Productions, 1973
POLICE STORY (TF)   Screen Gems/Columbia TV, 1973
SHIRTS/SKINS (TF)   MGM TV, 1973
WHERE THE LILIES BLOOM   United Artists, 1974
TOGETHER BROTHERS   20th Century-Fox, 1974
GET CHRISTIE LOVE! (TF)   Wolper Productions, 1974
LARRY (TF)   Tomorrow Entertainment, 1974
TRAPPED BENEATH THE SEA (TF)   ABC Circle
Films, 1974
BEYOND THE BERMUDA TRIANGLE (TF)   Playboy
Productions, 1975
PERILOUS VOYAGE (TF)   Universal TV, 1976
SHARK KILL (TF)   D'Antoni-Weitz Productions, 1976

21 HOURS AT MUNICH (TF)   Filmways, 1976
PART 2 SOUNDER   Gamma III, 1976
MINSTREL MAN (TF)   Roger Gimbel Productions/
EMI TV, 1977
THE AMAZING HOWARD HUGHES (TF)   Roger Gimbel
Productions/EMI TV, 1977
CONTRACT ON CHERRY STREET (TF)   Columbia
TV, 1977
CINDY (TF)   John Charles Walters Productions, 1978
ONE IN A MILLION: THE RON LeFLORE STORY (TF)
Roger Gimbel Productions/EMI TV, 1978
AND I ALONE SURVIVED (TF)   Jerry Leider-OJL
Productions, 1978
TRANSPLANT (TF)   Time-Life Productions, 1979
ORPHAN TRAIN (TF)   Roger Gimbel Productions/
EMI TV, 1979
GUYANA TRAGEDY: THE STORY OF JIM JONES (TF)☆
The Konigsberg Company, 1980
RAGE (TF)   Diane Silver Productions/Charles Fries
Productions, 1980
DEADLY ENCOUNTER (TF)   Roger Gimbel Productions/
EMI TV, 1982
M.A.D.D.: MOTHERS AGAINST DRUNK DRIVERS (TF)
Universal TV, 1983
THE LAST NINJA (TF)   Paramount TV, 1983
HARRY TRACY   Quartet/Films Inc., 1983, Canadian
WOMEN OF SAN QUENTIN (TF)   David Gerber Company/
MGM-UA TV, 1983
THE CALENDAR GIRL MURDERS (TF)   Tisch-Avnet
Productions, 1984
SECRETS OF A MARRIED MAN (TF)   ITC
Productions, 1984
MUSSOLINI: THE UNTOLD STORY (MS)   Trian
Productions, 1985
THE LAST DAYS OF FRANK AND JESSE JAMES (TF)
Joseph Cates Productions, 1986
GEORGE WASHINGTON: THE FORGING OF A NATION
(TF)   David Gerber Company/MGM TV, 1986
POLICE STORY II: THE FREEWAY KILLINGS (TF)   David
Gerber Productions/MGM-UA TV/Columbia TV, 1987
PROUD MEN (TF)   Cowboy Productions/Agamemnon Films
Productions/ von Zerneck-Samuels Productions, 1987
SUPERCARRIER (TF)   Fries Entertainment/Richard
Hayward-Real Tinsel Productions, 1988
STREET OF DREAMS (TF)   Bill Stratton-Myrtos
Productions/Phoenix Entertainment Group, 1988
TRUCK ONE (TF)   Grosso-Jacobson Productions/NBC
Productions, 1989
GORE VIDAL'S BILLY THE KID   BILLY THE KID   (CTF)
von Zerneck-Sertner Productions, 1989
TRUE BLUE (TF)   Grosso-Jacobson Productions/NBC
Productions, 1989
MONTANA (CTF)   HBO Productions/Zoetrope Studios/
Roger Gimbel Productions, 1990
RETURN TO THE BLUE LAGOON   Columbia, 1991

LEE GRANT*
(Lyova Rosenthal)
b. October 31, 1927 - New York, New York
Agent: Joel Dean, Camden Artists - Los Angeles,
213/556-2022

TELL ME A RIDDLE   Filmways, 1980
THE WILLMAR 8 (FD)   California Newsreel, 1981
WHEN WOMEN KILL (CTD)   HBO/Joseph Feury
Productions, 1983
A MATTER OF SEX (CTD)   Willmar 8 Productions/
Orion TV, 1984
WHAT SEX AM I? (CTD)   Joseph Feury Productions, 1985
DOWN AND OUT IN AMERICA (CTD)   Joseph Feury
Productions, 1985

NOBODY'S CHILD (TF)   Joseph Feury Productions/
   Gaylord Production Company, 1986
STAYING TOGETHER   Hemdale, 1989
NO PLACE LIKE HOME (TF)   Feury-Grant Productions/
   Orion TV, 1989

MICHAEL GRANT
b. 1952 - Toronto, Ontario, Canada
Home: 463 Puerto Del Mar, Pacific Palisades, CA 90272,
   213/454-1356

THE BROTHERS KEEPER (TF)   1978, Canadian
FATAL ATTRACTION   *HEAD ON*   Greentree Productions,
   1980, Canadian

ALEX GRASSHOFF*
b. December 10, 1930 - Boston, Massachusetts
Home: 7845 Torreyson Drive, Los Angeles, CA 90046,
   213/874-5020
Agent: Lake & Douroux - Beverly Hills, 213/284-8182

THE JAILBREAKERS   American International, 1960
YOUNG AMERICANS (FD)   Columbia, 1967
JOURNEY TO THE OUTER LIMITS (FD)   1974
THE LAST DINOSAUR (TF)   co-director with Tom Kotani,
   1977, U.S.-Japanese
SMOKEY AND THE GOODTIME OUTLAWS   Howco
   International, 1978
J.D. & THE SALT FLAT KID   Samuel Goldwyn
   Company, 1978
WACKY TAXI   1982
A BILLION FOR BORIS   Comworld, 1985

WALTER GRAUMAN*
b. March 17, 1922 - Milwaukee, Wisconsin
Home: 244 Barlock Avenue, Los Angeles, CA 90049,
   213/472-3160
Agent: Bob Broder, Broder-Kurland-Webb-Uffner Agency -
   Los Angeles, 213/656-9262

THE DISEMBODIED   Allied Artists, 1957
LADY IN A CAGE   United Artists, 1964
633 SQUADRON   United Artists, 1964, British
A RAGE TO LIVE   United Artists, 1965
I DEAL IN DANGER   20th Century-Fox, 1966
DAUGHTER OF THE MIND (TF)   20th Century-Fox, 1969
THE LAST ESCAPE   United Artists, 1970
THE OLD MAN WHO CRIED WOLF (TF)   Aaron Spelling
   Productions, 1970
CROWHAVEN FARM (TF)   Aaron Spelling
   Productions, 1970
THE FORGOTTEN MAN (TF)   Walter Grauman
   Productions, 1971
PAPER MAN (TF)   20th Century-Fox TV, 1971
THEY CALL IT MURDER (TF)   20th Century-Fox TV, 1971
DEAD MEN TELL NO TALES (TF)   20th Century-
   Fox TV, 1971
THE STREETS OF SAN FRANCISCO (TF)   QM
   Productions, 1972
MANHUNTER (TF)   QM Productions, 1974
FORCE FIVE (TF)   Universal TV, 1975
MOST WANTED (TF)   QM Productions, 1976
ARE YOU IN THE HOUSE ALONE? (TF)   Charles Fries
   Productions, 1978
CRISIS IN MID-AIR (TF)   CBS Entertainment, 1979
THE GOLDEN GATE MURDERS (TF)   Universal TV, 1979
THE TOP OF THE HILL (TF)   Fellows-Keegan Company/
   Paramount TV, 1980
TO RACE THE WIND (TF)   Walter Grauman
   Productions, 1980

THE MEMORY OF EVA RYKER (TF)   Irwin Allen
   Productions, 1980
PLEASURE PALACE (TF)   Norman Rosemont Productions/
   Marble Arch Productions, 1980
JACQUELINE SUSANN'S VALLEY OF THE
   DOLLS 1981 (MS)   20th Century-Fox TV, 1981
BARE ESSENCE (MS)   Warner Bros. TV, 1982
ILLUSIONS (TF)   CBS Entertainment, 1983
COVENANT (TF)   Michael Filerman Productions/20th
   Century Fox TV, 1985
OUTRAGE! (TF)   Irwin Allen Productions/
   Columbia TV, 1986
WHO IS JULIA? (TF)   CBS Entertainment, 1986
SHAKEDOWN ON THE SUNSET STRIP (TF)   CBS
   Entertainment, 1988

GARY GRAVER
Agent: Skip Nicholson Agency - Sherman Oaks,
   818/906-2700

THE EMBRACERS   Joseph Brenner Associates, 1967
TEXAS LIGHTNING   Film Ventures International, 1981
TRICK OR TREAT   Lone Star, 1983
PARTY CAMP   Lightning Pictures, 1987
MOON IN SCORPIO   Trans World Entertainment, 1988
NERDS OF A FEATHER   International Investment
   Holdings Ltd., 1990
EVIL SPIRITS   Grand Am Ltd., 1990

JOHN GRAY
Agent: CAA - Beverly Hills, 213/288-4545

BILLY GALVIN   Vestron, 1986
WHEN HE'S NOT A STRANGER (TF)   Ohlmeyer
   Communications Co., 1989

MIKE GRAY*
Agent: William Morris Agency - Beverly Hills, 213/274-7451

WAVELENGTH   New World, 1983

KJELL GREDE
b. 1936 - Stockholm, Sweden
Contact: Swedish Film Institute, P.O. Box 27126, S-10252
   Stockholm, Sweden, 08/630510

HUGO AND JOSEPHINE   1967, Swedish
HARRY MUNTER   1969, Swedish
CLAIRE LUST   1972, Swedish
A SIMPLE MELODY   1979, Swedish
HIP, HIP, HURRAH!   Swedish Film Institute/Sandrews Film
   & Teater/Palle Fogtdal/Danish Film Institute/Norsk Film,
   1987, Swedish-Danish-Norwegian
GOOD EVENING MR. WALLENBERG   Sandrews/Swedish
   Film Institute/SVT-2, 1990, Swedish

JANET GREEK*
Agent: The Gersh Agency - Beverly Hills, 213/274-6611

THE LADIES CLUB   directed under pseudonym of A.K.
   Allen, New Line Cinema, 1986
SPELLBINDER   MGM/UA, 1988

BRUCE SETH GREEN*
Home: 1729 Bryn Mawr Avenue, Santa Monica, CA 90405,
   213/452-1463
Agent: Ronald Leif, Contemporary Artists - Beverly Hills,
   213/278-8250

RAGS TO RICHES (TF)   Leonard Hill Films/New
   World TV, 1987

IN SELF DEFENSE (TF)   Leonard Hill Films, 1987
PERFECT PEOPLE (TF)   Robert Greenwald
  Productions, 1988
MANHUNT: SEARCH FOR THE NIGHT STALKER (TF)
  Leonard Hill Films, 1989
THE LAKER GIRLS (TF)   Viacom Productions/Finnegan-
  Pinchuk Productions/Valente-Hamilton
  Productions, 1990

DAVID GREEN
b. London, England
Agent: Diane Cairns, ICM - Los Angeles, 213/550-4000

WHICKER'S WORLD, CALIFORNIA (MS)   Yorkshire TV,
  1980, British
WILFRED AND EILEEN - A LOVE STORY (TF)   BBC,
  1981, British
EAST LYNNE (TF)   BBC, 1983, British
THE GOLDEN LAND (TF)   BBC, 1984, British
CAR TROUBLE   CineTel Films, 1986, British
1914 - ALL OUT (TF)   Yorkshire TV, 1986, British
BUSTER   Hemdale, 1988, British
FIRE BIRDS   Buena Vista, 1990

GUY GREEN*
b. 1913 - Somerset, England
Agent: Phil Gersh, The Gersh Agency - Beverly Hills,
  213/274-6611

RIVER BEAT   Lippert, 1954, British
POSTMARK FOR DANGER   PORTRAIT OF ALISON
  RKO Radio, 1955, British
TEARS FOR SIMON   LOST   Republic, 1956, British
TRIPLE DECEPTION   HOUSE OF SECRETS   Rank,
  1956, British
THE SNORKEL   Columbia, 1958, British
DESERT PATROL   SEA OF SAND   Universal,
  1958, British
S.O.S. PACIFIC   Universal, 1960, British
THE ANGRY SILENCE   Valiant, 1960, British
THE MARK   Continental, 1961, British
LIGHT IN THE PIAZZA   MGM, 1962
DIAMOND HEAD   Columbia, 1963
A PATCH OF BLUE   MGM, 1965
A MATTER OF INNOCENCE   PRETTY POLLY
  Universal, 1968, British
THE MAGUS   20th Century-Fox, 1968, British
A WALK IN THE SPRING RAIN   Columbia, 1970
LUTHER   American Film Theatre, 1974
JACQUELINE SUSANN'S ONCE IS NOT ENOUGH
  ONCE IS NOT ENOUGH   Paramount, 1975
THE DEVIL'S ADVOCATE   Filmworld Distributors, 1978,
  West German
JENNIFER: A WOMAN'S STORY (TF)   Marble Arch
  Productions, 1979
THE INCREDIBLE JOURNEY OF DR. MEG LAUREL (TF)
  Columbia TV, 1979
JIMMY B. & ANDRE (TF)   Georgia Bay
  Productions, 1980
INMATES: A LOVE STORY (TF)   Henerson-Hirsch
  Productions/Finnegan Associates, 1981
ISABEL'S CHOICE (TF)   Stuart Miller-Pantheon
  TV, 1981
STRONG MEDICINE (TF)   Telepictures Productions/TVS
  Ltd. Productions, 1986, U.S.-British

TERRY GREEN
Contact: British Academy of Film & Television Arts,
  195 Piccadilly, London W1, England, 71/734-0022

FATHER JIM   East End Films Ltd., 1990, British

WALON GREEN*
b. December 15, 1936 - Baltimore, Maryland
Home: 3089 Seahorse, Ventura, CA 93001,
  805/642-2366
Agent: Judy Scott-Fox, William Morris Agency -
  Beverly Hills, 213/274-7451

SPREE (FD)   co-director with Mitchell Leisen, United
  Producers, 1967
THE HELLSTROM CHRONICLE (FD)   Cinema 5, 1971
THE SECRET LIFE OF PLANTS (FD)   Paramount, 1978

PETER GREENAWAY
b. 1942 - England
Contact: British Academy of Film & Television Arts,
  195 Piccadilly, London W1, England, 71/734-0022

THE FALLS   British Film Institute, 1980, British
ACT OF GOD   British Film Institute, 1981, British
THE DRAUGHTMAN'S CONTRACT   United Artists Classics,
  1983, British
MODERN AMERICAN COMPOSERS 1: CAGE AND
  MONK (TD)   Trans Atlantic Films/Channel Four,
  1984, British
MODERN AMERICAN COMPOSERS 2: GLASS AND
  ASHLEY (TD)   Trans Atlantic Films/Channel Four,
  1984, British
A ZED AND TWO NOUGHTS   Skouras Pictures, 1985,
  British-Dutch
DROWNING BY NUMBERS   Galaxy International,
  1988, British
THE COOK, THE THIEF, HIS WIFE AND HER LOVER
  Miramax Films, 1989, Dutch-French
PROSPERO'S BOOKS   Allarts, 1990, Dutch-British

BRUCE GREENBERG
DEAD GIRLS DON'T DANCE   Security Industries, 1990

RICHARD ALAN GREENBERG*
Business: Greenberg Associates, 350 West 39th Street,
  New York, NY, 10018, 212/239-6767
Agent: Triad Artists, Inc. - Los Angeles, 213/556-2727

LITTLE MONSTERS   MGM/UA, 1989

DANFORD B. GREENE
Home: 558 E. Channel Road, Santa Monica, CA 90402,
  213/459-2369
Agent: Phil Gersh, The Gersh Agency - Beverly Hills,
  213/274-6611

THE SECRET DIARY OF SIGMUND FREUD   TLC Films/
  20th Century Fox, 1984

DAVID GREENE*
b. February 22, 1921 - Manchester, England
Agent: CAA - Beverly Hills, 213/288-4545

THE SHUTTERED ROOM   Warner Bros.,
  1966, British
SEBASTIAN   Paramount, 1968, British
THE STRANGE AFFAIR   Paramount, 1968, British
I START COUNTING   United Artists, 1969, British
THE PEOPLE NEXT DOOR   Avco Embassy, 1970
MADAME SIN (TF)   ITC, 1971, British
GODSPELL   Columbia, 1973
THE COUNT OF MONTE CRISTO (TF)   Norman
  Rosemont Productions/ ITC, 1975, U.S.-British

ELLERY QUEEN (TF) Universal TV, 1975
RICH MAN, POOR MAN (MS) co-director with Boris
    Sagal, Universal TV, 1976
ROOTS (MS)☆☆ co-director with Marvin J. Chomsky,
    John Erman & Gilbert Moses, Wolper
    Productions, 1977
LUCAN (TF) MGM TV, 1977
THE TRIAL OF LEE HARVEY OSWALD (TF)   Charles
    Fries Productions, 1977
GRAY LADY DOWN Universal, 1978
FRIENDLY FIRE (TF)☆☆ Marble Arch Productions, 1979
A VACATION IN HELL (TF) David Greene Productions/
    Finnegan Associates, 1979
THE CHOICE (TF) David Greene Productions/Finnegan
    Associates, 1981
HARD COUNTRY Universal/AFD, 1981
WORLD WAR III (TF) Finnegan Associates/David
    Greene Productions, 1982
REHEARSAL FOR MURDER (TF) Levinson-Link
    Productions/Robert Papazian Productions, 1982
TAKE YOUR BEST SHOT (TF) Levinson-Link
    Productions/Robert Papazian Productions, 1982
GHOST DANCING (TF) Herbert Brodkin Productions/
    The Eugene O'Neill Memorial Theatre Center/Titus
    Productions, 1983
PROTOTYPE (TF) Levinson-Link Productions/Robert
    Papazian Productions, 1983
THE GUARDIAN (CTF) HBO Premiere Films/Robert
    Cooper Productions/Stanley Chase Productions,
    1984, U.S.-Canadian
SWEET REVENGE (TF) David Greene Productions/
    Robert Papazian Productions, 1984
FATAL VISION (TF)☆ NBC Productions, 1984
GUILTY CONSCIENCE (TF) Levinson-Link Productions/
    Robert Papazian Productions, 1985
MURDER AMONG FRIENDS (TF) Tisch-Avnet
    Productions/ABC Circle Films, 1985
THIS CHILD IS MINE (TF) Beth Polson Productions/
    Finnegan Associates/ Telepictures Productions, 1985
TRIPLECROSS (TF) TAP Productions/ABC Circle
    Films, 1986
VANISHING ACT (TF) Robert Cooper Productions,
    1986, U.S.-Canadian
MILES TO GO... (TF) Keating-Shostak Productions,
    1986, U.S.-Canadian
CIRCLE OF VIOLENCE: A FAMILY DRAMA (TF)
    Sheldon Pinchuk Productions/ Rafshoon
    Communications/Finnegan Associates/Telepictures
    Productions, 1986
THE BETTY FORD STORY (TF) David L. Wolper
    Productions/Warner Bros. TV, 1987
AFTER THE PROMISE (TF) Tamara Asseyev
    Productions/New World TV, 1987
INHERIT THE WIND (TF) Vincent Pictures Productions/
    David Greene- Robert Papazian Productions, 1988
LIBERACE: BEHIND THE MUSIC (TF) Canadian
    International Studios/ Kushner-Locke Productions,
    1988, U.S.-Canadian
RED EARTH, WHITE EARTH (TF) Robert Papazian
    Productions/Alan M. Levin Productions, 1989
THE PENTHOUSE (TF) Greene-White Productions/
    Spectator Films, 1989
SMALL SACRIFICES (TF) Louis Rudolph Films/Motown
    Productions/Allarcom Ltd./Fries Entertainment, 1989,
    U.S.-Canadian
IN THE BEST INTEREST OF THE CHILD (TF) Papazian-
    Hirsch Entertainment, 1990

SPARKY GREENE*
b. November 13, 1948 - Chicago, Illinois
Business: Titan Films, 73 Market Street, Venice, CA 90291,
    213/349-9319

A SAVAGE HUNGER THE OASIS Shapiro
    Entertainment, 1984

PAUL GREENGRASS
Contact: British Academy of Film & Television Arts,
    195 Piccadilly, London W1, England, 71/734-0022

RESURRECTED Film Four International/British Screen/St.
    Pancras, 1989, British

BUD GREENSPAN*
Home: 252 East 61st Street, New York, NY 10021
Business: Cappy Productions, 33 East 68th Street, New
    York, NY 10021, 212/249-1800

THE GLORY OF THEIR TIMES (TD) Cappy
    Productions, 1977
WILMA (TF) Cappy Productions, 1977
16 DAYS TO GLORY (FD) Paramount, 1985
SEOUL '88: 16 DAYS OF GLORY (CTD) Cappy
    Productions/The Disney Channel, 1989
TIME CAPSULE: THE 1936 BERLIN OLYMPIC GAMES (TD)
    Cappy Productions, 1989

MAGGIE GREENWALD
Agent: Lloyd Segan, Irvin Arthur Associates - Beverly Hills,
    213/276-7493

HOME REMEDY Kino International, 1988
THE KILL OFF Films Around the World, 1989

ROBERT GREENWALD*
b. August 28, 1945 - New York, New York
Agent: ICM - Los Angeles, 213/550-4000

SHARON: PORTRAIT OF A MISTRESS (TF) Moonlight
    Productions/ Paramount TV, 1977
KATIE: PORTRAIT OF A CENTERFOLD (TF) Moonlight
    Productions/Warner Bros. TV, 1978
FLATBED ANNIE & SWEETIE PIE: LADY TRUCKERS (TF)
    Moonlight Productions/Filmways, 1979
XANADU Universal, 1980
FORTY DAYS FOR DANNY (TF) Moonlight Productions/
    Filmways, 1982
IN THE CUSTODY OF STRANGERS (TF) Moonlight
    Productions/Filmways, 1982
THE BURNING BED (TF)☆ Tisch-Avnet Productions, 1984
SHATTERED SPIRITS (TF) Sheen-Greenblatt Productions/
    Robert Greenwald Productions, 1986
ON FIRE (TF) Robert Greenwald Productions, 1987
SWEET HEARTS DANCE Tri-Star, 1988

DAVID GREENWALT*
Agent: Bill Douglass, ICM - Los Angeles, 213/550-4178

SECRET ADMIRER Orion, 1985
HELP WANTED: KIDS (TF) Stan Rogow
    Productions, 1986
DOUBLE SWITCH (TF) Walt Disney TV, 1987
RUDE AWAKENING co-director with Aaron Russo,
    Orion, 1989
EXILE (TF) Walt Disney TV, 1990

COLIN GREGG
b. 1947 - Cheltenham, England
Office: Colin Gregg Productions, Floor 2, 1/6 Falconberg
   Court, London W1, England, 71/734-0632
Agent: Linda Seifert Associates, 8A Brunswick Gardens,
   London W8 4AJ, England, 71/229-5163

BEGGING THE RING (TF)   BBC/Colin Gregg Films,
   1978, British
THE TRESPASSER (TF)   LWT/Polytel, 1981
REMEMBRANCE (TF)   Channel Four/Film on Four,
   1982, British
TO THE LIGHTHOUSE (TF)   BBC/UMF/Colin Gregg Ltd.,
   1983, British
LAMB   Limehouse/Flickers/Channel Four, 1985, British
UNFINISHED BUSINESS (TF)   BBC, 1986, British
WE THINK THE WORLD OF YOU   Cinecom,
   1988, British

ANDREW GRIEVE
Contact: Lemon & Durbridge, 24 Pottery Lane, London
   W11 4ZZ, England, 71/727-1346

STORYBOOK INTERNATIONAL (MS)   HTV,
   1984, British
SUSPICION   Hemisphere, 1986, British
ON THE BLACK HILL   British Film Institute/Channel Four/
   British Screen, 1987, British

CHARLES B. GRIFFITH
Agent: Jim Preminger Agency - Los Angeles,
   213/475-9491

FORBIDDEN ISLAND   Columbia, 1959
HATSANKANIM   1961, Israeli
EAT MY DUST   New World, 1976
UP FROM THE DEPTHS   New World, 1979
DR. HECKLE AND MR. HYPE   Cannon, 1980
SMOKEY BITES THE DUST   New World, 1981
WIZARDS OF THE LOST KINGDOM II   Concorde, 1989

MARK GRIFFITHS
Agent: Leading Artists - Beverly Hills, 213/858-1999

RUNNING HOT   New Line Cinema, 1984
HARDBODIES   Columbia, 1984
HARDBODIES 2   CineTel Films, 1986
HEROES STAND ALONE   Concorde, 1989
A CRY IN THE WILD   Concorde, 1990

GARY GRILLO*
Agent: Barry Perelman Agency - Los Angeles,
   213/274-5999

AMERICAN JUSTICE   The Movie Store, 1986

ALAN GRINT
Agent: Alan Greenspan, ICM - Los Angeles,
   213/550-4428

SHERLOCK HOLMES (TF)   Granada TV, 1985, British
LOST EMPIRES (TF)   Granada TV, 1986, British
THE SECRET GARDEN (TF)   Rosemont Productions,
   1987, U.S.-British
AGATHA CHRISTIE'S 'THE MAN IN THE BROWN
   SUIT' (TF)   Alan Shayne Productions/Warner
   Bros. TV, 1989

ULU GROSBARD*
b. January 9, 1929 - Antwerp, Belgium
Home: 29 West 10th Street, New York, NY 10011
Agent: Sam Cohn, ICM - New York City, 212/556-5610

THE SUBJECT WAS ROSES   MGM, 1968
WHO IS HARRY KELLERMAN AND WHY IS HE SAYING
   THOSE TERRIBLE THINGS ABOUT ME?   National
   General, 1971
STRAIGHT TIME   Warner Bros., 1978
TRUE CONFESSIONS   United Artists, 1981
FALLING IN LOVE   Paramount, 1984

LARRY GROSS*
Agent: CAA - Beverly Hills, 213/288-4545

3:15   Dakota Entertainment, 1986

DAVID GROSSMAN*
Home: 6140 Glen Tower, Los Angeles, CA 90068,
   213/466-9134
Agent: Stephen E. Marks, ICM - Los Angeles, 213/550-4000

FROG (TF)   Platypus Productions, 1988

ROBERT GUENETTE*
b. January 12, 1935 - Holyoke, Massachusetts
Business: 1551 S. Robertson Blvd., Los Angeles, CA 90035,
   213/785-9312
Agent: Steve Waterman, ICM - Los Angeles, 213/550-4000

THE TREE   Guenette, 1969
THE MYSTERIOUS MONSTERS   Sunn Classic, 1976
THE AMAZING WORLD OF PSYCHIC PHENOMENA   Sunn
   Classic, 1976
THE MAN WHO SAW TOMORROW   Warner Bros., 1981

JAMES WILLIAM GUERCIO*
Home: Caribou Ranch, Nederland, Colorado 80466,
   303/258-3215
Agent: Jeff Berg, ICM - Los Angeles, 213/550-4205

ELECTRA GLIDE IN BLUE   United Artists, 1973

RUY GUERRA
b. August 23, 1931 - Lourenco Marques, Mozambique
Contact: Concine/National Cinema Council, Rua Mayrink
   Veiga 28, Rio de Janeiro, Brazil, 2/233-8329

OS CAFAJESTES   1962, Brazilian
OS FUZIS   1964, Brazilian
SWEET HUNTERS   1969, French
OS DEUSES E OS MORTOS   1970, Brazilian
A QUIEDA   co-director, 1978, Brazilian
MEUDA, MEMORIA E MASSACRE (FD)   1979,
   Mozambique
ERENDIRA   MGM/UA, 1983, French-Mexican
OPERA DO MALANDRO   Samuel Goldwyn Company,
   1986, Brazilian
FABULA DE LA BELA PALOMERA   Network Group/
   Television Espanola/ New Latin American Film
   Foundation, 1988, Spanish- Brazilian
KUARUP   Grapho Pictures/Guerra Films, 1989, Brazilian

CHRISTOPHER GUEST*
Agent: Alan Greenspan, ICM - Los Angeles, 213/550-4428

THE BIG PICTURE   Columbia, 1989

VAL GUEST

b. 1911 - London, England
Agent: Tim Stone, Stone-Manners Agency - Los Angeles, 213/275-9599 or: Denis Selinger, ICM - London, 71/629-8080

MISS LONDON LTD.   General Film Distributors, 1943, British
BEES IN PARADISE   General Film Distributors, 1944, British
GIVE US THE MOON   General Film Distributors, 1944, British
I'LL BE YOUR SWEETHEART   General Film Distributors, 1945, British
JUST WILLIAM'S LUCK   United Artists, 1947, British
WILLIAM COME TO TOWN   United Artists, 1948, British
MURDER AT THE WINDMILL   Grand National, 1949, British
MISS PILGRIM'S PROGRESS   Grand National, 1950, British
THE BODY SAID NO   Eros, 1950, British
MISTER DRAKE'S DUCK   United Artists, 1951, British
PENNY PRINCESS   Universal, 1952, British
LIFE WITH THE LYONS   Exclusive, 1954, British
THE RUNAWAY BUS   Eros, 1954, British
MEN OF SHERWOOD FOREST   Astor, 1954, British
DANCE LITTLE LADY   Renown, 1954, British
THEY CAN'T HANG ME   Independent Film Distributors, 1955, British
THE LYONS IN PARIS   Exclusive, 1955, British
BREAK IN THE CIRCLE   20th Century-Fox, 1955, British
THE CREEPING UNKNOWN   THE QUATERMASS EXPERIMENT   United Artists, 1955, British
IT'S A WONDERFUL WORLD   Renown, 1956, British
THE WEAPON   Republic, 1956, British
THE SHIP WAS LOADED   CARRY ON ADMIRAL   Renown, 1957, British
ENEMY FROM SPACE   QUATERMASS II   United Artists, 1957, British
THE ABOMINABLE SNOWMAN OF THE HIMALAYAS   20th Century-Fox, 1957, British
THE CAMP ON BLOOD ISLAND   Columbia, 1958, British
UP THE CREEK   Dominant, 1958, British
FURTHER UP THE CREEK   Warner Bros., 1958, British
EXPRESSO BONGO   Continental, 1959, British
YESTERDAY'S ENEMY   Columbia, 1959
LIFE IS A CIRCUS   1960, British
HELL IS A CITY   Columbia, 1960, British
STOP ME BEFORE I KILL   THE FULL TREATMENT   Columbia, 1961, British
THE DAY THE EARTH CAUGHT FIRE   Universal, 1962, British
JIGSAW   Beverly, 1962, British
80,000 SUSPECTS   Rank, 1963, British
CONTEST GIRL   THE BEAUTY JUNGLE   Continental, 1964, British
WHERE THE SPIES ARE   MGM, 1965, British
CASINO ROYALE   co-director with Ken Hughes, John Huston, Joseph McGrath & Robert Parrish, Columbia, 1967, British
ASSIGNMENT K   Columbia, 1968, British
WHEN DINOSAURS RULED THE EARTH   Warner Bros., 1969, British
TOOMORROW   FRD, 1970, British
THE PERSUADERS   1971, British
AU PAIR GIRLS   Cannon, 1972, British
CONFESSIONS OF A WINDOW CLEANER   Columbia, 1974, British
KILLER FORCE   American International, 1975, British-Swiss

THE SHILLINGBURY BLOWERS   ...AND THE BAND PLAYED ON   Inner Circle, 1980, British
DANGEROUS DAVIES - THE LAST DETECTIVE   ITC/Inner Circle/ Maidenhead Films, 1980, British
THE BOYS IN BLUE   MAM Ltd./Apollo Leisure Group, 1983, British
MARK OF THE DEVIL (TF)   1983, British
IN POSSESSION (TF)   1984, British
CHILD'S PLAY (TF)   1985, British

JOHN GUILLERMIN*

b. November 11, 1925 - London, England
Agent: CAA - Beverly Hills, 213/288-4545

TORMENT   Adelphi, 1949, British
SMART ALEC   Grand National, 1951, British
TWO ON THE TILES   Grand National, 1951, British
FOUR DAYS   Grand National, 1951, British
BACHELOR IN PARIS   SONG OF PARIS   Lippert, 1952, British
MISS ROBIN HOOD   Associated British Film Distributors, 1952, British
OPERATION DIPLOMAT   Butcher, 1953, British
ADVENTURE IN THE HOPFIELDS   British Lion/Children's Film Foundation, 1954, British
THE CROWDED DAY   Adelphi, 1954, British
DUST AND GOLD   1955, British
THUNDERSTORM   Allied Artists, 1955, British
TOWN ON TRIAL   Columbia, 1957, British
THE WHOLE TRUTH   Columbia, 1958, British
I WAS MONTY'S DOUBLE   NTA Pictures, 1958, British
TARZAN'S GREATEST ADVENTURE   Paramount, 1959, British-U.S.
THE DAY THEY ROBBED THE BANK OF ENGLAND   MGM, 1960, British
NEVER LET GO   Rank, 1960, British
WALTZ OF THE TOREADORS   Continental, 1962, British
TARZAN GOES TO INDIA   MGM, 1962, British-U.S.-Swiss
GUNS AT BATASI   20th Century-Fox, 1964, British-U.S.
RAPTURE   International Classics, 1965, British-French
THE BLUE MAX   20th Century-Fox, 1966, British, U.S.
P.J.   Universal, 1968
HOUSE OF CARDS   Universal, 1969
THE BRIDGE AT REMAGEN   United Artists, 1969
EL CONDOR   National General, 1970
SKYJACKED   MGM, 1972
SHAFT IN AFRICA   MGM, 1973
THE TOWERING INFERNO   20th Century-Fox, 1974
KING KONG   Paramount, 1976
DEATH ON THE NILE   Paramount, 1978, British
MR. PATMAN   Film Consortium, 1980, Canadian
SHEENA   Columbia, 1984
KING KONG LIVES   DEG, 1986
THE TRACKER (CTF)   HBO Pictures/Lance Hool Productions, 1988

PAUL GUNCZLER

b. December 9, 1957 - Augsburg, West Germany
Business: Bagel Film, Herzog-Johann-Str. 26, 8000 Munich 60, West Germany

GEWALT IM FILM (TD)   co-director with Benjamin Wilchfort, 1983, West German
DIE NACHT AM SEE   KS-Produktion, 1984, West German
SCHIZOPHRENE BEGEGNUNGEN   ZFI/Bagel Film, 1988, West German

Gu

FILM
DIRECTORS
GUIDE

F I L M   D I R E C T O R S

129

ERIK GUSTAVSON

Agent: The Chasin Agency - Beverly Hills, 213/278-7505

BLACKOUT   Norsk Film, 1985, Norwegian
HERMAN   Kummunenes Filmcentral, 1990, Norwegian

TOMAS GUTIERREZ ALEA

b. December 11, 1928 - Havana, Cuba
Contact: Instituto Cubano de Arte Y Ciencias
    Cinematograficas, Calle 23, No. 1155, Vedado,
    Havana, Cuba

EL MEGANO   co-director, 1955, Cuban
ESTA TIERRA NEUSTRA   1959, Cuban
ASEMBLEA GENERAL   1960, Cuban
MUERTE AL INVASOR   co-director, 1961, Cuban
HISTORIAS DE LA REVOLUCION   1961, Cuban
LAS DOCE SILLAS   1962, Cuban
CUMBITE   1964, Cuban
LA MUERTE DE AN BUROCRATA   1966, Cuban
MEMORIES OF UNDERDEVELOPMENT   Tricontinental,
    1968, Cuban
UNA PELEA CUBANA CONTRA LOS DEMONIOS
    1971, Cuban
EL ARTE DEL TOBACO   1974, Cuban
THE LAST SUPPER   Tricontinental, 1976, Cuban
LOS SOBREVIVIENTES   ICAIC, 1979, Cuban
UP TO A POINT   New Yorker, 1984, Cuban
CARTAS DEL PARQUE   ICAIC, 1988, Cuban

AMOS GUTMAN

Contact: Israel Film Centre, Ministry of Industry & Trade,
    30 Agron Street, P.O. Box 299, Jerusalem 94190,
    Israel, 02/210297

DRIFTING   1984, Israeli
BAR 51   Shapira Films, 1986, Israeli
HIMMO, KING OF JERUSALEM   Rearguard Productions,
    1987, Israeli

NATHANIEL GUTMAN

Contact: Israel Film Centre, Ministry of Industry & Trade,
    30 Agron Street, P.O. Box 299, Jerusalem 94190,
    Israeli, 02/210297

DEADLINE   Skouras Pictures, 1987, West German-Israeli
TWICE UPON A TIME   Creative, 1990, West German

ANDRE GUTTFREUND*

Contract: Directors Guild of America - Los Angeles,
    213/289-2000

BREACH OF CONTRACT   Atlantic Releasing
    Corporation, 1984

CLAUDIO GUZMAN*

Agent: David Shapira & Associates - Sherman Oaks,
    818/906-0322

ANTONIO   Guzman Productions, 1973
LINDA LOVELACE FOR PRESIDENT   General Film, 1975
WILLA (TF)   co-director with Joan Darling, GJL
    Productions/Dove, Inc., 1979
THE HOSTAGE TOWER (TF)   Jerry Leider
    Productions, 1980
FOR LOVERS ONLY (TF)   Henerson-Hirsch Productions/
    Caesar's Palace Productions, 1982

STEPHEN GYLLENHAAL*

b. October 4, 1949 - Cleveland, Ohio
Agent: CAA - Beverly Hills, 213/288-4545

CERTAIN FURY   New World, 1985, Canadian
THE ABDUCTION OF KARI SWENSON (TF)   NBC
    Productions, 1987
PROMISED A MIRACLE (TF)   Dick Clark Productions/
    Republic Pictures Roni Weisberg Productions, 1988
LEAP OF FAITH (TF)   Hart, Thomas & Berlin
    Productions, 1988
FAMILY OF SPIES (MS)   King Phoenix
    Entertainment, 1990
KILLING IN A SMALL TOWN (TF) ☆   The IndieProd Co./
    Hearst Entertainment Prods., 1990

H

TAYLOR HACKFORD*

b. 1945
Agent: CAA - Beverly Hills, 213/288-4545

THE IDOLMAKER   United Artists, 1980
AN OFFICER AND A GENTLEMAN   Paramount, 1982
AGAINST ALL ODDS   Columbia, 1984
WHITE NIGHTS   Columbia, 1985
CHUCK BERRY: HAIL! HAIL! ROCK 'N' ROLL! (FD)
    Universal, 1987
EVERYBODY'S ALL-AMERICAN   Warner Bros., 1988

ROSS HAGEN

Contact: Writers Guild of America, West - Los Angeles,
    213/550-1000

B.O.R.N.   The Movie utfit, 1989
CLICK: THE CALENDAR GIRL KILLER   co-director with
    John Stewart, Crown International, 1990

RUSSELL HAGG

Agent: Writers & Artists Agency - Los Angeles, 213/820-2240

CASH & CO. (MS)   co-director with George Miller,
    Homestead Films/Network Seven, 1975, Australian
TANDARRA (MS)   co-director, Homestead Films/Network
    Seven, 1976
RAW DEAL   Greater Union Film Distributors, 1977,
    Australian
TAXI (TF)   Network Seven, 1979, Australian

PIERS HAGGARD

b. 1939 - Scotland
Home: 35 Digby Mansions, London W6, England,
    71/741-0812
Agent: William Morris Agency - Beverly Hills, 213/274-7451

WEDDING NIGHT   *I CAN'T...I CAN'T*   American
    International, 1969, Irish
THE BLOOD ON SATAN'S CLAW   *SATAN'S SKIN*
    Cannon, 1971, British
THE QUATERMASS CONCLUSION   Euston Films Ltd.,
    1979, British
THE FIENDISH PLOT OF DR. FU MANCHU   Orion/Warner
    Bros., 1980, British

MRS. REINHARDT (TF)   BBC/WNET-13, 1981,
   British-U.S.
VENOM   Paramount, 1982, British
ROLLING HOME (TF)   BBC, 1982, British
MARKS (TF)   BBC, 1982, British
DESERT OF LIES (TF)   BBC, 1983, British
WATERS OF THE MOON (TF)   BBC, 1983, British
KNOCKBACK (TF)   BBC, 1984, British
DISNEY'S RETURN TO TREASURE ISLAND *RETURN
   TO TREASURE ISLAND* (CMS)   The Disney Channel/
   Harlech TV, 1986, U.S.-British
VISITORS (TF)   BBC, 1987, British
A SUMMER STORY (TF)   Atlantic Releasing Corporation,
   1988, British
THE FULFILLMENT OF MARY GRAY (TF)   Mary
   Gray Inc./Lee Caplin Productions/Indian Neck
   Entertainment, 1989
BACK HOME (CTF)   TVS Films/Veronmead Productions/
   Citadel Entertainment, 1990, British

LARRY HAGMAN*

b. September 21, 1931 - Fort Worth, Texas
Business: Majlar Productions, 23730 Malibu Colony,
   Malibu, CA 90265, 213/456-5210

BEWARE! THE BLOB *SON OF BLOB*   Jack H. Harris
   Enterprises, 1972

STUART HAGMANN*

b. September 2, 1942 - Sturgeon Bay, Wisconsin
Business Manager: Howard M. Borris, Howard Borris &
   Company, 8484 Wilshire Blvd. - Suite 500, Beverly Hills,
   CA 90211, 213/665-3991

THE STRAWBERRY STATEMENT   MGM, 1970
BELIEVE IN ME   MGM, 1971
SHE LIVES (TF)   ABC Circle Films, 1973
TARANTULAS: THE DEADLY CARGO (TF)   Alan
   Landsburg Productions, 1977

STEVEN HAHN

STARCHASER: THE LEGEND OF ORIN (AF)   Atlantic
   Releasing Corporation, 1985

ZAFAR HAI

THE PERFECT MURDER   Merchant Ivory Productions,
   1988, British-Indian

RANDA HAINES*

Contact: Directors Guild of America - Los Angeles,
   213/289-2000

UNDER THIS SKY (TF)   Red Cloud Productions/
   PBS, 1979
THE JILTING OF GRANNY WEATHERALL (TF)
   Learning in Focus/American Short Story, 1980
SOMETHING ABOUT AMELIA (TF)☆ Leonard Goldberg
   Productions, 1984
ALFRED HITCHCOCK PRESENTS (TF)   co-director
   with Steve DeJarnatt, Joel Oliansky & Fred Walton,
   Universal TV, 1985
CHILDREN OF A LESSER GOD   Paramount, 1986

WILLIAM (BILLY) HALE*

Agent: Alan Greenspan, ICM - Los Angeles, 213/550-4428

HOW I SPENT MY SUMMER VACATION (TF)
   Universal TV, 1967
GUNFIGHT IN ABILENE   Universal, 1967

JOURNEY TO SHILOH   Universal, 1968
NIGHTMARE (TF)   CBS, Inc., 1974
THE GREAT NIAGARA (TF)   Playboy Productions, 1974
CROSSFIRE (TF)   QM Productions, 1975
THE KILLER WHO WOULDN'T DIE (TF)   Paramount
   TV, 1976
STALK THE WILD CHILD (TF)   Charles Fries
   Productions, 1976
RED ALERT (TF)   The Jozak Company/Paramount
   TV, 1977
S.O.S. TITANIC (TF)   Roger Gimbel Productions/EMI TV/
   Argonaut Films Ltd., 1979, U.S.-British
MURDER IN TEXAS (TF)   Dick Clark Productions/Billy Hale
   Films, 1981
ONE SHOE MAKES IT MURDER (TF)   The Fellows-
   Keegan Company/Lorimar Productions, 1982
THE DEMON MURDER CASE (TF)   Dick Clark
   Productions/Len Steckler Productions, 1983
LACE (MS)   Lorimar Productions, 1984
LACE 2 (MS)   Lorimar Productions, 1985
HAREM (TF)   Highgate Pictures, 1986
THE MURDER OF MARY PHAGAN (TF)   George Stevens,
   Jr. Productions/ Century Tower Productions, 1988
LIBERACE (TF)   The Liberace Foundation for the
   Performing and Creative Arts/Dick Clark Productions/
   Republic Pictures, 1988
PEOPLE LIKE US (TF)   ITC, 1990

JACK HALEY, JR.*

b. October 25, 1933 - Los Angeles, California
Contact: Directors Guild of America - Los Angeles,
   213/289-2000

NORWOOD   Paramount, 1970
THE LOVE MACHINE   Columbia, 1971
THAT'S ENTERTAINMENT! (FD)   MGM/United
   Artists, 1974
THAT'S ENTERTAINMENT, PART 2 (FD)   co-director
   with Gene Kelly, MGM/ United Artists, 1976
THAT'S DANCING! (FD)   MGM/UA, 1985

ADRIAN HALL*

Home: 201 Washington Street, Providence RI 02903,
   401/521-1100

THE HOUSE OF MIRTH (TF)   Cinelit Productions/
   WNET-13, 1981

KENNETH J. HALL

GHOST WRITER   Rumar Films, 1989

PETER HALL

b. November 22, 1930 - Bury St. Edmunds, Suffolk, England
Address: The Wall House, Mongewall Park, Wallingford,
   Berkshire, England
Agent: Laurie Evans, ICM - London, 71/629-8080

WORK IS A FOUR LETTER WORD   Universal,
   1968, British
A MIDSUMMER NIGHT'S DREAM   Eagle, 1968, British
PERFECT FRIDAY   Chevron, 1970, British
THE HOMECOMING   American Film Theatre, 1973, British
AKENFIELD (FD)   Angle Films, 1975, British
SHE'S BEEN AWAY   BBC Films, 1989, British
ORPHEUS DESCENDING (CTF)   Nederlander TV & Film
   Productions/ Turnet Network TV, 1990

Ha

**FILM
DIRECTORS
GUIDE**

**F
I
L
M

D
I
R
E
C
T
O
R
S**

131

DANIEL HALLER*

b. 1926 - Los Angeles, California
Home: 5364 Jed Smith Road, Hidden Hills, CA 91302,
    818/888-7936
Agent: Irv Schechter, Irv Schechter Company - Beverly
    Hills, 213/278-8070

DIE, MONSTER, DIE! American International, 1965,
    U.S.-British
DEVIL'S ANGELS American International, 1967
THE WILD RACERS American International, 1968
PADDY Allied Artists, 1970, Irish
PIECES OF DREAMS United Artists, 1970
THE DUNWICH HORROR American
    International, 1970
THE DESPERATE MILES (TF) Universal TV, 1975
MY SWEET LADY (TF) Universal TV, 1976
BLACK BEAUTY (MS) Universal TV, 1978
LITTLE MO (TF) Mark VII Ltd./Worldvision, 1978
BUCK ROGERS IN THE 25TH CENTURY
    Universal, 1979
HIGH MIDNIGHT (TF) The Mirisch Corporation/
    Universal TV, 1979
GEORGIA PEACHES (TF) New World TV, 1980
FOLLOW THAT CAR New World, 1981
MICKEY SPILLANE'S MARGIN FOR MURDER (TF)
    Hamner Productions, 1981
KNIGHT RIDER (TF) Glen A. Larson Productions/
    Universal TV, 1982

TODD HALLOWELL*

Home: 5022 Willowcrest Avenue, North Hollywood, CA
    91601, 818/506-4319

LOVE OR MONEY Hemdale, 1990

LASSE HALLSTROM*

b. 1946 - Stockholm, Sweden
Agent: Spyros Skouras, Sanford-Beckett-Skouras &
    Associates - Los Angeles, 213/208-2100

A LOVER AND HIS LASS 1975, Swedish
ABBA - THE MOVIE Warner Bros., 1977, Swedish
FATHER TO BE 1979, Swedish
THE ROOSTER 1981, Swedish
HAPPY WE 1983, Swedish
MY LIFE AS A DOG★ Skouras Pictures, 1985, Swedish
THE CHILDREN OF BULLERBY VILLAGE Svensk
    Filmindustri, 1986, Swedish
MORE ABOUT THE CHILDREN OF BULLERBY VILLAGE
    Svensk Filmindustri, 1987, Swedish
ONCE AROUND Universal, 1990

DAVID HAMILTON

Contact: French Film Office, 745 Fifth Avenue, New
    York, NY 10151, 212/832-8860

BILITIS Topar, 1976, French
TENDRE COUSINES Crown International, 1980, French
LAURA, LES OMBRES DE L'ETE Les Films de L'Alma/
    CORA, 1979, French
PREMIERS DESIRS AMLF, 1983, French-West German
UN ETE A SAINT TROPEZ (FD) Fugio & Associates/JVC,
    1983, French- Japanese
TATIANA UGC, 1984, French

GUY HAMILTON*

b. September, 1922 - Paris, France
Home: 22 Mont Port, Puerto Andraitx , Mallorca, Palma de
    Mallorca, Spain, tel.: 67-15-32
Agent: Denis Selinger, ICM - London, 71/629-8080

THE RINGER British Lion, 1952, British
THE INTRUDER Associated Artists, 1953, British
AN INSPECTOR CALLS Associated Artists, 1954, British
THE COLDITZ STORY Republic, 1955, British
CHARLEY MOON British Lion, 1956, British
STOWAWAY GIRL *MANUELA* Paramount, 1957, British
THE DEVIL'S DISCIPLE United Artists, 1959, British
A TOUCH OF LARCENY Paramount, 1960, British
THE BEST OF ENEMIES *I DUE NEMICI* Columbia,
    1962, Italian-British
MAN IN THE MIDDLE 20th Century-Fox, 1964,
    British-U.S.
GOLDFINGER United Artists, 1964, British
THE PARTY'S OVER Allied Artists, 1966, British
FUNERAL IN BERLIN Paramount, 1966, British
BATTLE OF BRITAIN United Artists, 1969, British
DIAMONDS ARE FOREVER United Artists, 1971, British
LIVE AND LET DIE United Artists, 1973, British
THE MAN WITH THE GOLDEN GUN United Artists,
    1974, British
FORCE 10 FROM NAVARONE American
    International, 1978
THE MIRROR CRACK'D AFD, 1980, British
EVIL UNDER THE SUN Universal/AFD, 1982, British
REMO WILLIAMS: THE ADVENTURE BEGINS...
    Orion, 1985
TRY THIS ON FOR SIZE Film Number One, 1989, French

STRATHFORD HAMILTON*

Home: 8280 Grandview Drive, Los Angeles, CA 90046,
    213/656-0888
Agent: Tim Stone, Stone-Manners Agency, 213/275-9599

BLUEBERRY HILL MGM/UA, 1988
DIVING IN Skouras Pictures, 1990

JOHN HANCOCK*

b. February 9, 1939 - Kansas City, Missouri
Home: 21531 Deerpath Lane, Malibu, CA 90265,
    213/456-3627
Agent: Alan Greenspan, ICM - Los Angeles, 213/550-4428

LET'S SCARE JESSICA TO DEATH Paramount, 1971
BANG THE DRUM SLOWLY Paramount, 1973
BABY BLUE MARINE Columbia, 1976
CALIFORNIA DREAMING American International, 1979
WEEDS DEG, 1987
STEAL THE SKY (CTF) HBO Pictures/Yoram Ben Ami
    Productions/ Paramount TV, 1988
PRANCER Orion, 1989

IZHAK HANOOKA

RED NIGHTS Trans World Entertainment, 1988

BRIAN HANNANT

Contact: Australian Film Commission, 9229 Sunset Blvd.,
    Los Angeles, CA 90069, 213/275-7074

THREE TO GO co-director with Peter Weir & Oliver Howes,
    Commonwealth Film Unit, 1971, Australian
FLASHPOINT Film Australia, 1972, Australian
THE TIME GUARDIAN Hemdale, 1987, Australian

CURTIS HANSON*
Agent: Jim Berkus, Leading Artists - Beverly Hills, 213/858-1999

THE AROUSERS SWEET KILL New World, 1976
THE LITTLE DRAGONS Aurora, 1980
LOSIN' IT Embassy, 1983, Canadian-U.S.
THE CHILDREN OF TIMES SQUARE (TF) Gross-Weston Productions/Fries Entertainment, 1986
THE BEDROOM WINDOW DEG, 1987
BAD INFLUENCE Triumph Releasing Corporation, 1990

JOHN HANSON
b. March 7, 1942 - St. Paul, Minnesota
Business: New Front Films, 125 W. Richmond Avenue, Point Richmond, CA 94801, 415/231-0225
Agent: Scott Harris, Harris & Goldberg - Los Angeles, 213/553-5200

NORTHERN LIGHTS co-director with Rob Nilsson, Cine Manifest/New Front Films, 1978
WILDROSE Troma, 1984
SMART MONEY Skouras Pictures, 1988

JOSEPH C. HANWRIGHT*
Home: P.O. Box 478, Ketchum, ID 83340, 208/726-3594

UNCLE JOE SHANNON United Artists, 1979

JOSEPH HARDY*
b. March 8, 1929 - Carlsbad, New Mexico
Agent: CAA - Beverly Hills, 213/288-4545

GREAT EXPECTATIONS (TF) Transcontinental Film Productions, 1974, British
A TREE GROWS IN BROOKLYN (TF) 20th Century-Fox TV, 1974
LAST HOURS BEFORE MORNING (TF) Charles Fries Productions/MGM TV, 1975
THE SILENCE (TF) Palomar Pictures International, 1975
JAMES AT 15 (TF) 20th Century-Fox TV, 1977
THE USERS (TF) Aaron Spelling Productions, 1978
LOVE'S SAVAGE FURY (TF) Aaron Spelling Productions, 1979
THE SEDUCTION OF MISS LEONA (TF) Edgar J. Scherick Associates, 1980
DREAM HOUSE (TF) Hill-Mandelker Films/Time-Life Productions, 1981
THE DAY THE BUBBLE BURST (TF) Tamara Productions/20th Century-Fox TV/The Production Company, 1982
NOT IN FRONT OF THE CHILDREN (TF) Tamtco Productions/The Edward S. Feldman Company, 1982
TWO MARRIAGES (TF) Lorimar Productions/Raven's Claw Productions, 1983

ROBIN HARDY
b. February 10, 1929 - England
Address: c/o Robert Lasky, 1150 Fifth Avenue, New York, NY 10128

THE WICKER MAN Warner Bros., 1975, British
THE FANTASIST ITC, 1986, Irish

DAVID HARE
b. 1947 - Sussex, England
Agent: ICM - Los Angeles, 213/550-1000

DREAMS OF LEAVING (TF) 1980, British
LICKING HITLER (TF) 1983, British

WETHERBY MGM/UA Classics, 1985, British
PARIS BY NIGHT Cineplex Odeon, 1988, British
STRAPLESS Granada Film Productions/Film Four International, 1989, British
HEADING HOME BBC/Screen Two, 1991, British

DEAN HARGROVE*
b. July 27, 1938 - Iola, Kansas
Business: Dean Hargrove Productions, 100 Universal City Plaza - Bldg. 107, Rm. 3E, Universal City, CA 91608, 818/777-8305
Agent: Norman Kurland, Broder-Kurland-Webb-Uffner Agency - Los Angeles, 213/656-9262

THE MANCHU EAGLE CAPER MYSTERY United Artists, 1975
THE BIG RIP-OFF (TF) Universal TV, 1975
THE RETURN OF THE WORLD'S GREATEST DETECTIVE (TF) Universal TV, 1976
DEAR DETECTIVE (TF) CBS, 1979

TSUI HARK
(Xu Ke)
b. 1951 - Vietnam
Business: Film Workshop Company Ltd., 748A Nathan Road 11/F, Kowloon, Hong Kong

THE BUTTERFLY MURDERS 1979, Hong Kong
WE'RE GOING TO EAT YOU 1980, Hong Kong
DANGEROUS ENCOUNTER - FIRST KIND 1980, Hong Kong
ALL THE WRONG CLUES 1981, Hong Kong
ZU: WARRIORS FROM THE MAGIC MOUNTAIN 1983, Hong Kong
ACES GO PLACES III: OUR MAN FROM BOND STREET 1984, Hong Kong
SHANGHAI BLUES Film Workshop Company Ltd., 1984, Hong Kong
PEKING OPERA BLUES Gordon's Films, 1986, Hong Kong
A BETTER TOMORROW III: LOVE & DEATH IN SAIGON Golden Princess/Film Workshop, 1989, Hong Kong
SWORDSMAN co-director with King Hu, Ann Hui, Ching Siu Tung, Lee Wai Man & Kam Yeung Wah, Film Workshop Company, 1990, Hong Kong

RENNY HARLIN
(Lauri Harjula)
b. Finland
Agent: William Morris Agency - Beverly Hills, 213/274-7451
Business: Larmark Productions, c/o Kenoff, Labowitz & Machtinger - Los Angeles, 213/552-0808

BORN AMERICAN Concorde/Cinema Group, 1986
PRISON Empire Pictures, 1988
A NIGHTMARE ON ELM STREET PART 4: THE DREAM MASTER New Line Cinema, 1988
THE ADVENTURES OF FORD FAIRLANE 20th Century Fox, 1990
DIE HARD 2 20th Century Fox, 1990

ROBERT HARMON*
Agent: William Morris Agency - Beverly Hills, 213/274-7451

THE HITCHER Tri-Star, 1986
THE TENDER Triumph Releasing Corporation, 1990

CURTIS HARRINGTON *
b. September 17, 1928 - Los Angeles, California
Agent: Spyros Skouras, Sanford-Beckett-Skouras &
   Associates - Los Angeles, 213/208-2100

NIGHT TIDE   Universal, 1963
QUEEN OF BLOOD   American International, 1966
GAMES   Universal, 1967
HOW AWFUL ABOUT ALLAN (TF)   Aaron Spelling
   Productions, 1970
WHO SLEW AUNTIE ROO?   American International,
   1971, British
WHAT'S THE MATTER WITH HELEN?   United
   Artists, 1971
THE CAT CREATURE (TF)   Screen Gems/Columbia
   TV, 1973
KILLER BEES (TF)   RSO Films, 1974
THE KILLING KIND   Media Trend, 1974
THE DEAD DON'T DIE (TF)   Douglas S. Cramer
   Productions, 1975
RUBY   Dimension, 1977
DEVIL DOG: THE HOUND OF HELL (TF)   Zeitman-
   Landers-Roberts Productions, 1978
MATA HARI   Cannon, 1985

DAMIAN HARRIS
Agent: ICM - Los Angeles, 213/550-4000

THE RACHEL PAPERS   MGM/UA, 1989, British

DENNY HARRIS
Business: Denny Harris of California, Inc., 12166 W.
   Olympic Blvd., Los Angeles, CA 90064, 213/826-6565

SILENT SCREAM   American Cinema, 1980

FRANK HARRIS
KILLPOINT   Crown International, 1984
LOW BLOW   Crown International, 1986
THE PATRIOT   Crown International, 1986
AFTERSHOCK   Prism Entertainment, 1990

HARRY HARRIS *
b. September 8, 1922 - Kansas City, Missouri
Agent: Ronald Leif, Contemporary Artists, Beverly Hills,
   213/278-8250

THE RUNAWAYS (TF)   Lorimar Productions, 1975
THE SWISS FAMILY ROBINSON (TF)   Irwin Allen Produc-
   tions/20th Century- Fox TV, 1975
RIVKIN: BOUNTY HUNTER (TF)   Chiarascurio
   Productions/Ten-Four Productions, 1981
A DAY FOR THANKS ON WALTON'S MOUNTAIN (TF)
   Lorimar Productions/ Amanda Productions, 1982
ALICE IN WONDERLAND (TF)   Irwin Allen Productions/
   Procter & Gamble Productions/Columbia TV, 1985
EIGHT IS ENOUGH: A FAMILY REUNION (TF)   Lorimar
   TV, 1987

JAMES B. HARRIS *
b. August 3, 1928 - New York, New York
Business: James B. Harris Productions, 248-1/2 Lasky
   Drive, Beverly Hills, CA 90212, 213/273-4270
Attorney: Louis C. Blau, Loeb & Loeb, 10100 Santa
   Monica Blvd., Los Angeles, CA 90067, 213/552-7700

THE BEDFORD INCIDENT   Columbia, 1965
SOME CALL IT LOVING   Cine Globe, 1973

FAST-WALKING   Pickman Films, 1982
COP   Atlantic Releasing Corporation, 1988

RICHARD HARRIS
b. October 1, 1932 - Limerick, Ireland
Agent: William Morris Agency - Beverly Hills, 213/274-7451

THE HERO   *BLOOMFIELD*   Avco Embassy, 1972,
   Israeli-British

WENDELL B. HARRIS, JR.
CHAMELEON STREET   Prismatic One, Inc./Filmworld
   International Productions, 1990

JOHN HARRISON
Agent: Ken Stovitz, ICM - Los Angeles, 213/550-4218

BEAUTIFUL DREAMERS   Cinexus/Famous Players/C-FP
   Distribution/National Film Board of Canada,
   1990, Canadian
TALES FROM THE DARKSIDE: THE MOVIE
   Paramount, 1990

KEN HARRISON *
b. 1942 - Poetry, Texas
Contact: Directors Guild of America - Los Angeles,
   213/289-2000

1918   Cinecom, 1985
ON VALENTINE'S DAY   Angelika Films, 1986
KATHERINE ANNE PORTER: THE EYE OF MEMORY (TF)
   KERA-Dallas/Fort Worth/Lumiere Productions/American
   Masters, 1986
STORY OF A MARRIAGE (MS)   co-director with Howard
   Cummings, Indian Falls Corporation/American Playhouse/
   WGBH-Boston, 1987

BRUCE HART *
b. January 15, 1938 - New York, New York
Home: 200 West 86th Street, New York, NY 10024,
   212/724-1948

SOONER OR LATER (TF)   Laughing Willow Company/
   NBC, 1979

CHRISTOPHER HART
Agent: The Artists Agency - Los Angeles, 213/277-7779

EAT AND RUN   New World, 1986

DEREK HART
Contact: British Academy of Film & Television Arts,
   195 Piccadilly, London W1, England, 71/734-0022

BACKSTAGE AT THE KIROV (FD)   Armand Hammer
   Productions, 1983

HAL HARTLEY
THE UNBELIEVABLE TRUTH   Miramax Films, 1990
TRUST   Zenith Productions, 1991, U.S.-British

PHILIP HARTMAN
Agent: William Morris Agency - Beverly Hills, 213/274-7451

NO PICNIC   Gray City/Great Jones Film Group/Films
   Charas, 1988

ANTHONY HARVEY*

b. June 3, 1931 - London, England
Address: 101 Park Avenue - 43rd Floor, New York, NY
   10178, 212/661-8200
Agent: Paul Kohner, Inc. - Los Angeles, 213/550-1060 or:
   Derek Gibson/ David Booth, John Redway and
   Associates Ltd., 5 Denmark Street, London
   WC2H 8LP, England, 71/836-2001

DUTCHMAN   Continental, 1967, British
THE LION IN WINTER★   Avco Embassy, 1968, British
THEY MIGHT BE GIANTS   Universal, 1971
THE GLASS MENAGERIE (TF)   Talent Associates, 1973
THE ABDICATION   Warner Bros., 1974, British
THE DISAPPEARANCE OF AIMEE (TF)   Tomorrow
   Entertainment, 1976
PLAYERS   Paramount, 1979
EAGLE'S WING   International Picture Show, 1980, British
RICHARD'S THINGS   New World, 1981, British
THE PATRICIA NEAL STORY (TF)   co-director with
   Anthony Page, Lawrence Schiller Productions, 1981
SVENGALI (TF)   Robert Halmi Productions, 1983
THE ULTIMATE SOLUTION OF GRACE QUIGLEY
   GRACE QUIGLEY   Cannon, 1984

MASANORI HATA

Contact: Directors Guild of Japan, Tsukada Building,
   8-33 Udagawa-cho, Shibuya-ku, Tokyo 150, Japan,
   3/461-4411

THE ADVENTURES OF MILO AND OTIS   THE ADVEN-
   TURES OF CHATRAN   Columbia, 1986, Japanese

BOB HATHCOCK

Business: Walt Disney Productions, 500 S. Buena Vista ,
   Burbank, CA 91521, 818/560-1000

DUCK TALES, THE MOVIE: TREASURES OF THE LOST
   LAMP (AF)   Buena Vista, 1990

MAURICE HATTON

Business: Mithras Film, 3 Cambridge Gate, Regent's Park,
   London NW1, England, 71/486-1400

AMERICAN ROULETTE   Film Four International/British
   Screen/Mandemar Group, 1988, British

NICK HAVINGA*

Agent: The Cooper Agency - Los Angeles, 213/277-8422

SINGLE WOMEN, MARRIED MAN (TF)   Michele Lee
   Productions/CBS Entertainment, 1989

KAIZO HAYASHI

b. 1957 - Kyoto, Japan
Business: Eizo Tantei Sha Co., 201 Koyama - Bldg. 1,
   1-26-5, Umegaoka, Setagaya-ku, Toyko 154, Japan,
   03/439-2603

TO SLEEP SO AS TO DREAM   Cine Seson, 1985,
   Japanese
CIRCUS BOYS   CBS-Sont, 1989, Japanese
ZIPANG   Toho, 1989, Japanese

SIDNEY HAYERS*

b. Edinburgh, Scotland
Agent: Irv Schechter Company - Beverly Hills, 213/278-8070

VIOLENT MOMENT   Anglo-Amalgamated, 1959, British
THE WHITE TRAP   Anglo-Amalgamated, 1959, British
CIRCUS OF HORRORS   American International,
   1960, British

THE MALPAS MYSTERY   Anglo-Amalgamated,
   1960, British
ECHO OF BARBARA   Rank, 1961, British
BURN, WITCH, BURN   NIGHT OF THE EAGLE   American
   International, 1962, British
THIS IS MY STREET   Anglo-Amalgamated, 1963, British
THREE HATS FOR LISA   Anglo-Amalgamated,
   1963, British
THE TRAP   Rank, 1966, British
FINDERS KEEPERS   United Artists, 1967, British
THE SOUTHERN STAR   Columbia, 1969, French-British
MISTER JERICO (TF)   ITC, 1970, British
IN THE DEVIL'S GARDEN   ASSAULT   Hemisphere,
   1971, British
THE FIRECHASERS   Rank, 1971, British
INN OF THE FRIGHTENED PEOPLE   TERROR FROM
   UNDER THE HOUSE/ REVENGE   Hemisphere,
   1973, British
DEADLY STRANGERS   Fox-Rank, 1974, British
DIAGNOSIS: MURDER   CIC, 1975, British
WHAT CHANGED CHARLEY FARTHING?   Stirling Gold,
   1976, British
ONE WAY   Silhouette Film Productions, 1976
THE SEEKERS (TF)   Universal TV, 1978
THE LAST CONVERTIBLE (MS)   co-director with Jo
   Swerling, Jr. & Gus Trikonis, Roy Huggins Productions/
   Universal TV, 1979
CONDOMINIUM (TF)   Universal TV, 1980
PHILIP MARLOWE - PRIVATE EYE   CHANDLERTOWN
   (CMS)   co-director with Bryan Forbes, Peter Hunt &
   David Wickes, HBO/David Wickes Television Ltd./London
   Weekend Television, 1983, British

JACK HAZAN

Contact: British Academy of Film & Television Arts,
   195 Piccadilly, London W1, England, 71/734-0022

A BIGGER SPLASH   Lagoon Associates, 1975, British
RUDE BOY   co-director with David Mingay, Atlantic
   Releasing Corporation, 1980, British

SIMON HEATH

b. Australia
Address: c/o Denny Bond, Management 3, Lazy Creek
   Ranch, 4570 Encino Avenue, Encino, CA 91316,
   818/783-3713

BULLAMAKANKA   Bullamakanka Film Productions,
   1984, Australian
CHARLY'S WEB   Budei Holdings, 1986, Australian

AMY HECKERLING*

b. May 7, 1954 - Bronx, New York
Agent: David Gersh, The Gersh Agency - Beverly Hills,
   213/274-6611

FAST TIMES AT RIDGEMONT HIGH   Universal, 1982
JOHNNY DANGEROUSLY   20th Century Fox, 1984
NATIONAL LAMPOON'S EUROPEAN VACATION   Warner
   Bros., 1985
LOOK WHO'S TALKING   Tri-Star, 1989
LOOK WHO'S TALKING TOO   Tri-Star, 1991

ROB HEDDEN*

Home: 11235 Aqua Vista Street, Studio City, CA 91602,
   818/505-9501
Agent: Roberta Kent, STE Representation - Beverly Hils,
   213/550-3982

FRIDAY THE 13TH, PART VIII: JASON TAKES
   MANHATTAN Paramount, 1989

**F
I
L
M

D
I
R
E
C
T
O
R
S**

RICHARD T. HEFFRON*
b. October 6, 1930 - Chicago, Illinois
Agent: CAA - Beverly Hills, 213/288-4545

DO YOU TAKE THIS STRANGER? (TF)   Universal
    TV, 1971
FILLMORE (FD)   20th Century-Fox, 1972
TOMA (TF)   Universal TV, 1973
OUTRAGE! (TF)   ABC Circle Films, 1973
NEWMAN'S LAW   Universal, 1974
THE MORNING AFTER (TF)   Wolper Productions, 1974
THE ROCKFORD FILES (TF)   Universal TV, 1974
THE CALIFORNIA KID (TF)   Universal TV, 1974
LOCUSTS (TF)   Paramount TV, 1974
I WILL FIGHT NO MORE FOREVER (TF)   Wolper
    Productions, 1975
DEATH SCREAM (TF)   RSO Films, 1975
TRACKDOWN   United Artists, 1976
FUTUREWORLD   American International, 1976
YOUNG JOE, THE FORGOTTEN KENNEDY (TF)   ABC
    Circle Films, 1977
OUTLAW BLUES   Warner Bros., 1977
SEE HOW SHE RUNS (TF)   CLN Productions, 1978
TRUE GRIT: A FURTHER ADVENTURE (TF)   Paramount
    TV, 1978
FOOLIN' AROUND   Columbia, 1978
A RUMOR OF WAR (TF)   Charles Fries Productions, 1980
A WHALE FOR THE KILLING (TF)   Play Productions/
    Beowuif Productions, 1981
I, THE JURY   20th Century-Fox, 1982
A KILLER IN THE FAMILY (TF)   Stan Margulies
    Productions/Sunn Classic Pictures, 1983
THE MYSTIC WARRIOR (MS)   David L. Wolper-Stan
    Margulies Productions/ Warner Bros. TV, 1984
V: THE FINAL BATTLE (TF)   Blatt-Singer Productions/
    Warner Bros. TV, 1984
ANATOMY OF AN ILLNESS (TF)   Hamner Productions/
    CBS Entertainment, 1984
NORTH AND SOUTH (MS)   Wolper Productions/Warner
    Bros. TV, 1985
SAMARITAN (TF)   Levine-Robins Productions/Fries
    Entertainment, 1986
GUILTY OF INNOCENCE: THE LENELL GETER
    STORY (TF)   Embassy TV, 1986
CONVICTED: A MOTHER'S STORY (TF)   NBC
    Productions, 1987
NAPOLEON AND JOSEPHINE: A LOVE STORY (TF)
    David L. Wolper Productions/Warner Bros. TV, 1987
BROKEN ANGEL (TF)   The Stan Margulies Company/
    MGM-UA TV, 1988
PANCHO BARNES (TF)   Blue Andre Productions/
    Orion TV, 1988
LA REVOLUTION FRANCAISE: LES ANNEES TERRIBLES
    Ariane Films/ Films A2/Laura Films/Les Productions
    Alliance/Alcor Films, 1989, French-West German-
    Italian-Canadian

CHRIS HEGEDUS
Business: Pennebaker Associates, 21 West 86th Street,
    New York, NY 10024, 212/496-9199

TOWN BLOODY HALL (FD)   co-director with D.A.
    Pennebaker, Pennebaker Associates, 1980
ROCKABY (TD)   co-director with D.A. Pennebaker,
    Pennebaker Associates, 1983
DANCE BLACK AMERICA (FD)   co-director with D.A.
    Pennebaker, Pennebaker Associates, 1985
ROCKY X (FD)   co-director with D.A. Pennebaker,
    Pennebaker Associates, 1986
DEPECHE MODE 101 (FD)   co-director with D.A.
    Pennebaker & David Dawkins, Westwood One
    Radio, 1989

JEROME HELLMAN*
b. September 4, 1928 - New York, New York
Business: Jerome Hellman Productions, 68 Malibu Colony
    Drive, Malibu, CA 90265, 213/456-3361

PROMISES IN THE DARK   Orion/Warner Bros., 1979

MONTE HELLMAN*
b. July 12, 1932 - New York, New York
Address: 11075 Santa Monica Blvd. - Suite 275,
    Los Angeles, CA 90025, 213/479-5581
Agent: Andy Freedman/Mary Cross, Susan Smith &
    Associates - Beverly Hills, 213/852-4777

BEAST FROM HAUNTED CAVE   Allied Artists, 1959
BACK DOOR TO HELL   20th Century-Fox, 1964
FLIGHT TO FURY   Harold Goldman Associates, 1967,
    U.S.-Filipino
THE SHOOTING   American International, 1966
RIDE IN THE WHIRLWIND   American International, 1966
TWO-LANE BLACKTOP   Universal, 1971
COCKFIGHTER   BORN TO KILL   New World, 1974
CHINA 9 LIBERTY 37   Titanus, 1978, Italian
IGUANA   Enterprise Iguana Film Productions, 1988, Italian
SILENT NIGHT, DEADLY NIGHT III: BETTER WATCH OUT
    International Video Enterprises, 1989

GUNNAR HELLSTROM*
Business: Artist Film, Toro, 14992 Nynashamn, Sweden,
    46/752-31160

THE NAME OF THE GAME IS KILL (TF)   Universal
    TV, 1968
MARK, I LOVE YOU (TF)   The Aubrey Company, 1980
RASKENSTAM   Sandrews, 1983, Swedish

HENRI HELMAN
Contact: French Film Office, 745 Fifth Avenue, New York,
    NY 10151, 212/832-8860

LE COEUR FROID   Films Moliere, 1977, French
WHERE IS PARSIFAL?   Tri-Star, 1984, British

DAVID HELPERN, JR.
I'M A STRANGER HERE MYSELF (FD)   October
    Films, 1974
HOLLYWOOD ON TRIAL (FD)   Lumiere, 1976
SOMETHING SHORT OF PARADISE   American
    International, 1979

DAVID HEMMINGS*
b. November 18, 1941 - Guildfold, England
Agent: Tim Stone, Stone-Manners Agency - Los Angeles,
    213/275-9599 or Michael Whitehall, 125 Gloucester Road,
    London SW7, England, 71/244-8466

RUNNING SCARED   Paramount, 1972, British
THE 14   MGM-EMI, 1973, British
JUST A GIGOLO   United Artists Classics, 1978,
    West German
THE SURVIVOR   Hemdale, 1981, Australian
TREASURE OF THE YANKEE ZEPHYR   RACE TO THE
    YANKEE ZEPHYR   Artists Releasing Corporation/Film
    Ventures International, 1984, New Zealand-British
THE KEY TO REBECCA (TF)   Taft Entertainment TV/Castle
    Combe Productions, 1985, U.S.-British
WEREWOLF (TF)   Lycanthrope Productions/Tri-Star
    TV, 1987

IN THE HEAT OF THE NIGHT (TF)   The Fred Silverman
    Company/Jadda Productions/MGM-UA TV, 1988
DAVY CROCKETT: RAINBOW IN THE THUNDER (TF)
    Echo Cove Productions/Walt Disney TV, 1988
QUANTUM LEAP (TF)   Belisarius Productions/Universal
    TV, 1989
HARDBALL (TF)   Columbia TV/NBC Productions, 1989

CLARK HENDERSON

SAIGON COMMANDOS   Concorde, 1988
HIGHRIDERS   Concorde, 1990

FRANK HENENLOTTER

Business: Ievins/Henenlotter, 443 West 43rd Street #1,
    New York, NY 10036, 212/265-2166

BASKET CASE   Analysis, 1982
BRAIN DAMAGE   Palisades Entertainment, 1988
FRANKENHOOKER   Shapiro Glickenhaus
    Entertainment, 1990
BASKET CASE 2   Shapiro Glickenhaus
    Entertainment, 1990

BUCK HENRY*

b. 1930 - New York, New York
Agent: William Morris Agency - Beverly Hills, 213/274-7451

HEAVEN CAN WAITH   co-director with Warren Beatty,
    Paramount, 1978
FIRST FAMILY   Warner Bros., 1980

STEPHEN HEREK

b. November 10, 1958 - San Antonio, Texas
Agent: Bauer Benedek Agency - Los Angeles,
    213/275-2421

CRITTERS   New Line Cinema, 1985
BILL & TED'S EXCELLENT ADVENTURE   Orion, 1989
THE GIFTED ONE (TF)   Richard Rothstein Productions/
    NBC Productions, 1989
THE REAL WORLD   Warner Bros., 1991

JAIME HUMBERTO HERMOSILLO

b. 1942 - Aguascalientes, Mexico
Home: Ostia 2943-6, Providencia, Guadalajara, Jalisco,
    Mexico, C.P. 44620, 36/423226
Agent: Rene Fuentes-Chao, Cinevista, Inc., 353 West 39th
    Street, New York, NY 10018, 212/947-4373

LA VERDADERA VOCACION DE MAGDALENA   Azteca
    Films, 1971, Mexican
EL SENOR DE OSANTO   Azteca Films, 1972, Mexican
EL CUMPLEANOS DEL PERRO   Azteca Films,
    1974, Mexican
LA PASION SEGUN BERENICE   Azteca Films,
    1977, Mexican
NAUFRAGIO   Azteca Films, 1978, Mexican
MATINEE   Azteca Films, 1978, Mexican
EL AMOR LIBRE   Azteca Films, 1979, Mexican
LAS APARIENCIAS ENGANAN   Azteca Films,
    1982, Mexican
MARIA DE MI CORAZON   Azteca Films, 1983, Mexican
CONFIDENCIAS   Azteca Films, 1984, Mexican
DONA HERLINDA AND HER TWO SONS   Cinevista,
    1985, Mexican
EL ETERNO ESPLENDOR   Azteca Films, 1987, Mexican
CLANDESTINO DESTINO   Clasa Films Mundiales,
    1987, Mexican

EL VERANO DE LA SENORITA FORBES   Television
    Espanola/TVE/ ICAIC, 1988, Cuban-Mexican-Spanish
INTIMIDADES EN UN CUARTO DE BANO   Profesionales y
    Sociedad Cooperativa de Producciones/Cinematografica
    Jose Revueltas, 1990, Mexican

TIBOR HERNANDI

FELIX THE CAT (AF)   New World, 1990

ANTHONY HERRERA

THE WIDE NET (TF)   Wide Net Company/WGBH-
    Boston, 1987

ROWDY HERRINGTON*

Home: 4157 Sunswept Drive, Studio City, CA 91604
Agent: Arnold Rifkin, Triad Artists, Inc. - Los Angeles,
    213/556-2727

JACK'S BACK   Cinema Group, 1988
ROAD HOUSE   MGM/UA, 1989

MARSHALL HERSKOVITZ*

Agent: CAA - Beverly Hills, 213/288-4545

COMING OF AGE AT JEFFERSON HALL (CTF)
    Showtime, 1985

MICHAEL HERZ

b. May 9, 1949 - New York, New York
Business: Troma, Inc., 733 Ninth Avenue, New York, NY
    10019, 212/757-4555

SQUEEZE PLAY!   co-director with Samuel Weil,
    Troma, 1980
WAITRESS!   co-director with Samuel Weil, Troma, 1982
STUCK ON YOU!   co-director with Samuel Weil,
    Troma, 1983
THE FIRST TURN-ON!   co-director with Samuel Weil,
    Troma, 1984
THE TOXIC AVENGER   co-director with Samuel Weil,
    Troma, 1984
THE TOXIC AVENGER: PART II   co-director with Samuel
    Weil, Troma, 1988
TROMA'S WAR   co-director with Samuel Weil,
    Troma, 1988

JOHN HERZFELD*

Agent: William Morris Agency - Beverly Hills, 213/274-7451

TWO OF A KIND   20th Century-Fox, 1983
DADDY (TF)   Robert Greenwald Productions, 1987
A FATHER'S REVENGE (TF)   Shadowplay-Rosco
    Productions/ Phoenix Entertainment Group, 1988
THE RYAN WHITE STORY (TF)   The Landsburg
    Company, 1989
THE PREPPIE MURDER (TF)   Jack Grossbart Productions/
    Spectator Films, 1989

WERNER HERZOG

b. September 5, 1942 - Sachrang, Germany
Address: Neureutherstrasse 20, D-8000, Munich 13,
    West Germany
Contact: German Film & TV Academy, Pommernallee 1,
    1 Berlin 19, West Germany, 0311/302-6096

DIE FLIEGENDEN ARZTE VON OSTAFRIKA   1968,
    West German
SIGNS OF LIFE   Werner Herzog Filmproduktion, 1968,
    West German

BEHINDERTE ZUNKUFT   1970, West German
EVEN DWARFS STARTED SMALL   New Line Cinema,
   1971, West German
LAND OF SILENCE AND DARKNESS (FD)   New Yorker,
   1972, West German
AGUIRRE, THE WRATH OF GOD   New Yorker, 1973,
   West German- Mexican-Peruvian
THE MYSTERY OF KASPAR HAUSER   EVERY MAN FOR
   HIMSELF AND GOD AGAINST ALL   Cinema 5, 1974,
   West German
HEART OF GLASS   New Yorker, 1976, West German
STROSZEK   New Yorker, 1977, West German
FATA MORGANA   New Yorker, 1978, West German
WOYZECK   New Yorker, 1979, West German
NOSFERATU THE VAMPYRE   20th Century-Fox, 1979,
   West German-French- U.S.
GOD'S ANGRY MAN (FD)   1980, West German
FITZCARRALDO   New World, 1982, West German
WHERE THE GREEN ANTS DREAM   Orion Classics,
   1984, West German
COBRA VERDE   DEG, 1988, West German
A PATRIARCH IN WINTER (FD)   1990, West Germany

JON HESS
Agent: CAA - Beverly Hills, 213/288-4545

THE LAWLESS LAND   Concorde, 1988
WATCHERS   Universal, 1988, Canadian
ASSASSINATION WITH CAUSE   L.A. Film Group/
   Tamaulipas S.A., 1990, U.S.-Mexican
ALLIGATOR II: THE RETURN   Brandon Chase
   Productions, 1990
NOT OF THIS WORLD (TF)   Barry & Enright Productions,
   1990

GORDON HESSLER*
b. 1930 - Berlin, Germany
Home: 8910 Holly Place, Los Angeles, CA 90046,
   213/654-9890
Agent: Triad Artists, Inc. - Los Angeles, 213/556-2727

THE WOMAN WHO WOULDN'T DIE   CATACOMBS
   Warner Bros., 1965, British
THE OBLONG BOX   American International, 1969, British
THE LAST SHOT YOU HEAR   20th Century-Fox,
   1969, British
SCREAM AND SCREAM AGAIN   American International,
   1970, British
CRY OF THE BANSHEE   American International,
   1970, British
MURDERS IN THE RUE MORGUE   American
   International, 1971, British
EMBASSY   Hemdale, 1973, British
SCREAM, PRETTY PEGGY (TF)   Universal TV, 1973
SKYWAY TO DEATH (TF)   Universal TV, 1974
HITCHHIKE! (TF)   Universal TV, 1974
A CRY IN THE WILDERNESS (TF)   Universal TV, 1974
BETRAYAL (TF)   Metromedia Productions, 1974
THE GOLDEN VOYAGE OF SINBAD   Columbia,
   1974, British
TRACCO DI VELENO IN UNA COPPA DI CHAMPAGNE
   Arden, 1975, Italian
THE STRANGE POSSESSION OF MRS. OLIVER (TF)
   The Shpetner Company, 1977
PUZZLE (TF)   Australian Broadcasting Commission/
   Trans-Atlantic Enterprises, 1978, Australian
SECRETS OF THREE HUNGRY WIVES (TF)   Penthouse
   Productions, 1978
KISS MEETS THE PHANTOM OF THE PARK (TF)
   Hanna-Barbera Productions/ KISS Productions, 1978

BEGGERMAN, THIEF (TF)   Universal TV, 1980
THE SECRET WAR OF JACKIE'S GIRLS (TF)   Public Arts
   Productions/ Penthouse Productions/Universal TV, 1980
ESCAPE FROM EL DIABLO   Cinema Presentations
   International, 1983, U.S.- Spanish-British
PRAY FOR DEATH   American Distribution Group, 1985
RAGE OF HONOR   American Distribution Group, 1986
THE MISFIT BRIGADE   WHEELS OF TERROR   Trans
   World Entertainment, 1987, U.S.-British
THE GIRL IN A SWING   Millimeter Films, 1989,
   British-Danish
OUT ON BAIL   Trans World Entertainment, 1989,
   U.S.-South African
SHOGUN MAYEDA   Mayeda Productions, 1990

CHARLTON HESTON
b. October 4, 1923 - Evanston, Illinois
Agent: ICM - Los Angeles, 213/550-4000

ANTONY AND CLEOPATRA   Rank, 1973,
   British-Spanish-Swiss
MOTHER LODE   Agamemnon Films, 1982, Canadian
A MAN FOR ALL SEASONS (CTF)   Agamemnon Films/
   British Lion, 1988, U.S.-British

FRASER C. HESTON
Agent: Sanford-Beckett-Skouras & Associates - Los Angeles,
   213/208-2100
Contact: Writers Guild of America, West - Los Angeles,
   213/550-1000

TREASURE ISLAND (CTF)   Agamemnon Films/British Lion,
   1990, British-U.S.

ROD HEWITT
Business: Those Who Ride Productions - Los Angeles,
   213/874-3168

VERNE MILLER   Alive Films, 1987

DOUGLAS HEYES*
Business Manager: Clarke Lilly Associates, 333 Apolena
   Avenue, Balboa Island, CA 92662, 714/833-3347

KITTEN WITH A WHIP   Universal, 1964
BEAU GESTE   Universal, 1966
THE LONELY PROFESSION (TF)   Universal TV, 1969
POWDERKEG (TF)   Filmways/Rodphi, 1969
DRIVE HARD, DRIVE FAST (TF)   Universal TV, 1973
CAPTAINS AND THE KINGS (MS)   co-director with Allen
   Reisner, Universal TV, 1976
ASPEN (MS)   Universal TV, 1977
THE FRENCH ATLANTIC AFFAIR (TF)   Aaron Spelling
   Productions/MGM TV, 1979
THE HIGHWAYMAN (TF)   Glen A. Larson Productions/20th
   Century Fox TV, 1987

CHRISTOPHER HIBLER*
Agent: The Sheri Mann Agency - Los Angeles, 213/850-1777

FATAL CONFESSION: A FATHER DOWLING MYSTERY
   (TF)   The Fred Silverman Company/Strathmore
   Productions/Viacom, 1987
FATHER DOWLING MYSTERIES: THE MISSING BODY
   MYSTERY (TF) The Fred Silverman Company/Dean
   Hargrove Productions, 1989

BRUCE HICKEY
NECROPOLIS   Empire Pictures, 1986

ANTHONY HICKOX

Business: Hickox Films - Los Angeles, 213/876-8423

WAXWORK   Vestron, 1988
SUNDOWN: THE VAMPIRE IN RETREAT   Vestron, 1990
BLACK CREEK   Victory Pictures, 1990

GEORGE ROY HILL*

b. December 20, 1922 - Minneapolis, Minnesota
Business: 75 Rockefeller Plaza - Suite 1719, New York, NY
    10019, 212/484-7182
Business Manager: Edwins, Brown, McGladrey,
    Hendrickson & Pulle, 1133 Avenue of the Americas,
    New York, NY 10019, 212/382-0024

PERIOD OF ADJUSTMENT   MGM, 1962
TOYS IN THE ATTIC   United Artists, 1963
THE WORLD OF HENRY ORIENT   United Artists, 1964
HAWAII   United Artists, 1966
THOROUGHLY MODERN MILLIE   Universal, 1967
BUTCH CASSIDY AND THE SUNDANCE KID★   20th
    Century-Fox, 1969
SLAUGHTERHOUSE-FIVE   Universal, 1971
THE STING★★   Universal, 1973
THE GREAT WALDO PEPPER   Universal, 1975
SLAP SHOT   Universal, 1977
A LITTLE ROMANCE   Orion/Warner Bros., 1979,
    U.S.-French
THE WORLD ACCORDING TO GARP   Warner
    Bros., 1982
THE LITTLE DRUMMER GIRL   Warner Bros., 1984
FUNNY FARM   Warner Bros., 1988

JACK HILL*

b. January 28, 1933 - Los Angeles, California
Home: 16918 Schoolcraft Street, Van Nuys, CA 91406,
    818/342-6877
Agent: Mark Lichtman, Shapiro-Lichtman Agency -
    Los Angeles, 213/859-8877

BLOOD BATH   co-director with Stephanie Rothman,
    American International, 1966
SPIDER BABY   THE LIVER EATERS/CANNIBAL
    ORGY   1968
PIT STOP   Distributors International, 1969
THE BIG DOLL HOUSE   New World, 1971
THE BIG BIRD CAGE   New World, 1972
COFFY   American International, 1973
FOXY BROWN   American International, 1974
THE SWINGING CHEERLEADERS   Centaur, 1974
SWITCHBLADE SISTERS   Centaur, 1975

JAMES HILL*

b. 1919 - England
Home: 1 Abdale Road, London W12, England, 71/743-7208
Agent: The Lantz Office - Los Angeles, 213/858-1144 or:
    Jean Diamond, London Management, 235-241 Regent
    Street, London W1A 2J7, England, 71/493-1610

THE STOLEN PLANS   Associated British Film Distributors/
    Children's Film Foundation, 1952, British
THE CLUE OF THE MISSING APE   Associated British Film
    Distributors/Children's Film Foundation, 1953, British
PERIL FOR THE GUY   British Lion/Children's Film
    Foundation, 1956, British
MYSTERY IN THE MINE   Children's Film Foundation,
    1959, British
THE KITCHEN   British Lion, 1961, British
THE DOCK BRIEF   MGM, 1962, British
LUNCH HOUR   Bryanston, 1962, British

SEASIDE SWINGERS   EVERY DAY'S A HOLIDAY
    Embassy, 1964, British
A STUDY IN TERROR   Columbia, 1966, British
BORN FREE   Columbia, 1966, British
THE CORRUPT ONES   THE PEKING MEDALLION
    Warner Bros., 1967, West German-French-Italian
CAPTAIN NEMO AND THE UNDERWATER CITY   MGM,
    1970, British
AN ELEPHANT CALLED SLOWLY   American Continental,
    1971, British
BLACK BEAUTY   Paramount, 1971, British-
    West German-Spanish
THE BELSTONE FOX   FREE SPIRIT   Cine III,
    1973, British
CHRISTIAN THE LION   THE LION AT WORLD'S END
    co-director with Bill Travers, Scotia American,
    1974, British
WORZEL GUMMIDGE (TF)   1978, British
THE WILD AND THE FREE (TF)   BSR Productions/Marble
    Arch Productions, 1980
YOU KNOW WHAT I MEAN (TF)   1982, British
THE FETCHIT (TF)   1983, British
OWAIN GLYNDWR - PRINCE OF WALES (TF)   OPIX/S4C,
    1983, British
THE YOUNG VISITERS (TF)   Channel Four, 1984, British

WALTER HILL*

b. January 10, 1942 - Long Beach, California
Agent: Jeff Berg, ICM - Los Angeles, 213/550-4205

HARD TIMES   Columbia, 1975
THE DRIVER   20th Century-Fox, 1978
THE WARRIORS   Paramount, 1979
THE LONG RIDERS   United Artists, 1980
SOUTHERN COMFORT   20th Century-Fox, 1981
48 HRS.   Paramount, 1982
STREETS OF FIRE   Universal, 1984
BREWSTER'S MILLIONS   Universal, 1985
CROSSROADS   Columbia, 1986
EXTREME PREJUDICE   Tri-Star, 1987
RED HEAT   Tri-Star, 1988
JOHNNY HANDSOME   Tri-Star, 1989
ANOTHER 48 HRS.   Paramount, 1990

ARTHUR HILLER*

b. November 22, 1923 - Edmonton, Alberta, Canada
Agent: Phil Gersh, The Gersh Agency - Beverly Hills,
    213/274-6611

THE CARELESS YEARS   United Artists, 1957
THE MIRACLE OF THE WHITE STALLIONS
    Buena Vista, 1963
THE WHEELER DEALERS   MGM, 1963
THE AMERICANIZATION OF EMILY   MGM, 1964
PROMISE HER ANYTHING   Paramount, 1966
PENELOPE   MGM, 1966
TOBRUK   Universal, 1967
THE TIGER MAKES OUT   Columbia, 1967
POPI   United Artists, 1969
THE OUT-OF-TOWNERS   Paramount, 1970
LOVE STORYH   Paramount, 1970
PLAZA SUITE   Paramount, 1971
THE HOSPITAL   United Artists, 1971
MAN OF LA MANCHA   United Artists, 1972, Italian-U.S.
THE CRAZY WORLD OF JULIUS VROODER   20th
    Century-Fox, 1974
THE MAN IN THE GLASS BOOTH   American Film
    Theatre, 1975
W.C. FIELDS AND ME   Universal, 1976
SILVER STREAK   20th Century-Fox, 1975
THE IN-LAWS   Columbia, 1979

NIGHTWING   Columbia, 1979
MAKING LOVE   20th Century-Fox, 1981
AUTHOR! AUTHOR!   20th Century-Fox, 1982
ROMANTIC COMEDY   MGM/UA, 1983
THE LONELY GUY   Universal, 1984
TEACHERS   MGM/UA, 1984
OUTRAGEOUS FORTUNE   Buena Vista, 1987
SEE NO EVIL, HEAR NO EVIL   Tri-Star, 1989
TAKING CARE OF BUSINESS   Buena Vista, 1990
MARRIED TO IT   Orion, 1991

WILLIAM BYRON HILLMAN*
b. Evergreen, Illinois
Home: P.O. Box 321, Tarzana, CA 91356, 818/705-3456
Agent: Richard Brustein, The Brustein Company -
   Los Angeles, 213/286-0990

BETTA BETTA   Commonwealth United, 1971
THE TRAIL RIDE   Gulf States, 1973
THE PHOTOGRAPHER   Avco Embassy, 1974
THE MAN FROM CLOVER GROVE   American
   Cinema, 1977
THETUS   Rachel's Releasing Corporation, 1979
DOUBLE EXPOSURE   Crown International, 1982
THE MASTER   Front Line Releasing, 1984
LONER   International Film Completion Corporation, 1987
RAGIN' CAJUN   Double Helix Films, 1990

DAVID HINTON
THE MAKING OF A LEGEND: "GONE WITH THE WIND"
   (CTD) Turner Entertainment/Selznick Properties Ltd.,
   1988

BETTINA HIRSCH
Agent: The Gersh Agency - Beverly Hills, 213/274-6611

MUNCHIES   Concorde, 1987

RUPERT HITZIG*
Business: 73 Market Street, Venice, CA 90291,
   213/396-5937
Agent: Larry Becsey, The Agency - Los Angeles,
   213/551-3000

NIGHT VISITOR   MGM/UA, 1989
BACKSTREET STRAYS   Vidmark, 1990

JACK B. HIVELY*
Home: 8265 Mannix Drive, Los Angeles, CA 90046,
   213/654-2188
Agent: Lew Sherrell Agency - Los Angeles, 213/461-9955

(The following is an incomplete list of Mr. Hively's credits)

THE ADVENTURES OF HUCKLEBERRY FINN (TF)
   Sunn Classic Productions, 1981
CALIFORNIA GOLD RUSH (TF)   Sunn Classic
   Productions, 1981

YIM HO
(Yen Hao)
b. 1952 - Hong Kong
Contact: Hong Kong International Film Festival, 5th Floor,
   High Block City Hall, Edinburgh Place, Hong Kong,
   (3) 72-1193

THE EXTRAS   1978, Hong Kong
THE HAPPENINGS   1979, Hong Kong

WEDDING BELLS, WEDDING BELLES   1980, Hong Kong
HOMECOMING   Bluebird Movie Enterprises/Target Film
   Company, 1984, Hong Kong
BUDDHA'S LOCK   Shenzhen Film Enterprise/Highland Film
   Enterprise, 1987, Chinese-Hong Kong

LYNDALL HOBBS*
Agent: The Gersh Agency - Beverly Hills, 213/274-6611

BACK TO THE BEACH   Paramount, 1987

GREGORY HOBLIT*
Agent: Peter Benedek, Bauer Benedek Agency -
   Los Angeles, 213/275-2421

L.A. LAW (TF)   20th Century Fox TV, 1986
ROE VS. WADE (TF)☆   The Manheim Company/NBC
   Productions, 1989

VICTORIA HOCHBERG*
Home: 6825 Alta Loma Terrace, Hollywood, CA 90068,
   213/874-5064
Agent: Jim Kellem, APA - Los Angeles, 213/273-0744

JACOB HAVE I LOVED (TF)   KCET-LA/Victoria Hochberg
   Productions, 1989
SWEET 15 (TF)   Richard Soto Productions, 1990

MIKE HODGES*
b. July 29, 1932 - Bristol, England
Home: "Websley" Durweston, Blandford Farm, Dorset,
   England, 02/585-3188
Agent: Terence Baker, Hatton & Baker, 18 Jermyn Street,
   London W1, England, 71/439-2971

SUSPECT (TF)   Thames TV, 1968, British
RUMOUR (TF)   Thames TV, 1969, British
THE MANIPULATOR (TF)   London Weekend TV,
   1971, British
GET CARTER   MGM, 1971, British
PULP   United Artists, 1972, British
THE TERMINAL MAN   Warner Bros., 1974
FLASH GORDON   Universal, 1980, British
MISSING PIECES (TF)   Entheos Unlimited Productions/
   TTC, 1983
SQUARING THE CIRCLE (TF)   TVS Ltd./Metromedia
   Producers Corporation/ Brittanic Film and TV Ltd., 1984,
   British-U.S.
MORONS FROM OUTER SPACE   Universal, 1985, British
MIXED DOUBLES (TF)   Telepictures Productions, 1986
FLORIDA STRAITS (CTF)   HBO Premiere Films/Robert
   Cooper Productions, 1986
A PRAYER FOR THE DYING   Samuel Goldwyn Company,
   1987, British
BLACK RAINBOW   Goldcrest, 1989, British-U.S.

MICHAEL HOFFMAN
Agent: William Morris Agency - Los Angeles, 213/274-7451

PRIVILEGED   New Yorker, 1982, British
RESTLESS NATIVES   Orion Classics, 1985, British
PROMISED LAND   Vestron, 1988
SOME GIRLS   MGM/UA, 1988

PETER HOFFMAN
VALENTINO RETURNS   Vidmark International, 1989

TAMAR SIMON HOFFS*
Home: 27428 Pacific Coast Highway, Malibu, CA 90265,
213/393-7800
Agent: Phil Gersh, The Gersh Agency - Beverly Hills,
213/274-6611

THE ALLNIGHTER   Universal, 1987

GRAY HOFMEYR
SCHWEITZER   Concorde, 1990

JACK HOFSISS*
b. September 28, 1950 - Brooklyn, New York
Agent: William Morris Agency - Beverly Hills, 213/274-7451

I'M DANCING AS FAST AS I CAN   Paramount, 1982
FAMILY SECRETS (TF)   Katz-Gallin/Half-Pint
   Productions/Karoger Productions, 1984

ROD HOLCOMB*
Home: 1337 East Boston Street, Altadena, CA 91001,
818/794-0700
Agent: Elliot Webb, Broder-Kurland-Webb-Uffner Agency -
Los Angeles, 213/656-9262

CAPTAIN AMERICA (TF)   Universal TV, 1979
MIDNIGHT OFFERINGS (TF)   Stephen J. Cannell
   Productions, 1981
THE GREATEST AMERICAN HERO (TF)   Stephen J.
   Cannell Productions, 1981
THE QUEST (TF)   Stephen J. Cannell Productions, 1982
MOONLIGHT (TF)   co-director with Jackie Cooper,
   both directed under pseudonym of Alan Smithee,
   Universal TV, 1982
THE A TEAM (TF)   Stephen J. Cannell Productions, 1983
THE RED-LIGHT STING (TF)   J.E. Productions/Universal
   TV, 1984
NO MAN'S LAND (TF)   Jadda Productions/Warner
   Bros. TV, 1984
THE CARTIER AFFAIR (TF)   Hill-Mandelker
   Productions, 1984
TWO FATHERS' JUSTICE (TF)   A. Shane
   Company, 1985
STARK (TF)   CBS Entertainment, 1985
STITCHES   directed under pseudonym of Alan Smithee,
   International Film Marketing, 1985
CHASE (TF)   CBS Entertainment, 1985
BLIND JUSTICE (TF)   CBS Entertainment, 1986
STILLWATCH (TF)   Zev Braun Pictures/Interscope
   Communications/Potomac Productions, 1987
THE LONG JOURNEY HOME (TF)   Andrea Baynes
   Productions/Grail Productions/ Lorimar-
   Telepictures, 1987
WISEGUY (TF)   Stephen J. Cannell Productions, 1987
CHINA BEACH (TF)   Sacret Inc. Productions/Warner Bros.
   TV, 1988
WOLF (TF)   CBS Entertainment, 1989
CHAINS OF GOLD   New Line Cinema, 1990

AGNIESZKA HOLLAND
b. 1948 - Warsaw, Poland
Agent: Triad Artists, Inc. - Los Angeles, 213/556-2727

SUNDAY'S CHILDREN (TF)   1976, Polish
PROVINCIAL ACTORS   New Yorker, 1979, Polish
FEVER   Film Polski, 1980, Polish
WOMAN ON HER OWN   1981, Polish
ANGRY HARVEST   European Classics, 1985,
   West German

TO KILL A PRIEST   Columbia, 1988, U.S.-French
EUROPA, EUROPA   Films du Losange/CCC Filmkunst,
   1989, French-West German
THE LION'S DEN   CCR/BR, 1989, West German

SAVAGE STEVE HOLLAND*
Agent: CAA - Beverly Hills, 213/288-4545

BETTER OFF DEAD   Warner Bros., 1985
ONE CRAZY SUMMER   Warner Bros., 1986
HOW I GOT INTO COLLEGE   20th Century Fox, 1989

TODD HOLLAND*
Agent: CAA - Beverly Hills, 213/288-4545

THE WIZARD   Universal, 1989

TOM HOLLAND*
b. July 11 - Poughkeepsie, New York
Agent: CAA - Beverly Hills, 213/288-4545

FRIGHT NIGHT   Columbia, 1985
FATAL BEAUTY   MGM/UA, 1987
CHILD'S PLAY   MGM/UA, 1988

ALLEN HOLLEB
Agent: William Morris Agency - Beverly Hills, 213/274-7451

CANDY STRIPE NURSES   New World, 1974
SCHOOL SPIRIT   Concorde/Cinema Group, 1985

JAY HOLMAN
LIFE UNDER WATER (TF)   H.J. Holman Productions, 1989

FRED HOLMES
Contact: Texas Film Commission, P.O. Box 12728, 201 East
   5th Street - Suite B-6, Austin, TX 78711, 512/469-9111

DAKOTA   Miramax Films, 1988

ROGER HOLZBERG
Agent: APA - Los Angeles, 213/273-0744

MIDNIGHT CROSSING   Vestron, 1988

ALLAN HOLZMAN*
Contact: Directors Guild of America - Los Angeles,
   213/289-2000

FORBIDDEN WORLD   New World, 1982
OUT OF CONTROL   New World, 1985
GRUNT! THE WRESTLING MOVIE   New World, 1985
PROGRAMMED TO KILL   co-director with Robert Short,
   Trans World Entertainment, 1987

INOSHIRO (ISHIRO) HONDA
Contact: Directors Guild of Japan, Tsukada Building, 8-33
   Udagawa-cho, Shibuya-ku, Tokyo 150, Japan, 3/461-4411

GODZILLA, KING OF THE MONSTERS   GOJIRA
   co-director with Terry Morse, Embassy, 1954,
   Japanese-U.S.
HALF HUMAN   DCA, 1957, Japanese
RODAN   DCA, 1957, Japanese
VARAN THE UNBELIEVABLE   Crown International, 1958,
   Japanese-U.S.
THE MYSTERIANS   Columbia, 1959, Japanese

THE H-MAN   Columbia, 1959, Japanese
BATTLE IN OUTER SPACE   Columbia, 1960, Japanese
MOTHRA   Columbia, 1962, Japanese
GORATH   Brenco, 1962, Japanese
KING KONG VS. GODZILLA   Universal, 1963, Japanese
GODZILLA VS. THE THING   *GODZILLA VS. MOTHRA*
   American International, 1964, Japanese
FRANKENSTEIN CONQUERS THE WORLD   American
   International, 1964, Japanese
ATTACK OF THE MUSHROOM PEOPLE   *MATANGO*
   American International, 1964, Japanese
DAGORA, THE SPACE MONSTER   Toho, 1965,
   Japanese
ATRAGON   American International, 1965, Japanese
GHIDRAH, THE THREE-HEADED MONSTER
   Continental, 1966, Japanese
KING KONG ESCAPES   Universal, 1968, Japanese
DESTROY ALL MONSTERS   American International, 1969,
   Japanese
GODZILLA'S REVENGE   UPA, 1969, Japanese
LATITUDE ZERO   National General, 1970, Japanese
YOG - MONSTER FROM SPACE   American
   International, 1971, Japanese

ELLIOTT HONG
KILL THE GOLDEN GOOSE   Lone Star, 1979
THEY CALL ME BRUCE?   *A FISTFUL OF CHOPSTICKS*
   Artists Releasing Corporation/Film Ventures
   International, 1982
HOT AND DEADLY   Saturn International, 1983

JAMES HONG
Business: Universe II Productions, Inc., 11684 Ventura
   Blvd. - Suite 948, Studio City, CA 91604, 818/763-2028

THE VINEYARD   co-director with Bill Rice, Northstar
   Entertainment, Inc., 1988

HARRY HOOK
Agent: CAA - Beverly Hills, 213/288-4545

SINS OF THE FATHERS   NFS, 1982, British
THE KITCHEN TOTO   Cannon, 1987, British-Kenyan
LORD OF THE FLIES   Columbia, 1990

KEVIN HOOKS*
b. September 19, 1958 - Philadelphia, Pennsylvania
Business: Hooksfilm Ltd., 3518 Cahuenga Blvd. - Suite 106,
   Hollywood, CA 90068, 213/876-4040
Agent: Alan Greenspan, ICM - Los Angeles, 213/550-4428

VIETNAM WAR STORY (CTF)   co-director with
   Georg Stanford Brown & Ray Danton, Nexus
   Productions, 1987
ROOTS: THE GIFT (TF)   Wolper Productions/Warner
   Bros. TV, 1988
HEATWAVE (CTF)   The Avnet-Kerner Company/Turner
   Network TV, 1990

LANCE HOOL
b. May 11, 1948 - Mexico City, Mexico
Agent: William Morris Agency - Beverly Hills,
   213/274-7451

MISSING IN ACTION 2: THE BEGINNING   Cannon,
   1984
STEEL DAWN   Vestron, 1987

TOBE HOOPER*
b. 1943 - Austin, Texas
Agent: Triad Artists, Inc. - Los Angeles, 213/556-2727

THE TEXAS CHAINSAW MASSACRE   Bryanston, 1974
EATEN ALIVE   Virgo International, 1977
SALEM'S LOT (TF)   Warner Bros. TV, 1979
THE FUNHOUSE   Universal, 1981
POLTERGEIST   MGM/UA, 1982
LIFEFORCE   Tri-Star, 1985, British
INVADERS FROM MARS   Cannon, 1986
THE TEXAS CHAINSAW MASSACRE 2   Cannon, 1986
SPONTANEOUS COMBUSTION   Taurus
   Entertainment, 1990

JOHN HOPKINS
TORMENT   co-director with Samson Asianian,
   New World, 1986

STEPHEN HOPKINS
b. Jamaica
Agent: Lloyd Segan, Irvin Arthur Associates - Beverly Hills,
   213/276-7493

DANGEROUS GAME   Four Seasons Entertainment,
   1987, Australian
A NIGHTMARE ON ELM STREET 5: THE DREAM CHILD
   New Line Cinema, 1989
PREDATOR 2   20th Century Fox, 1990

DENNIS HOPPER*
b. May 17, 1936 - Dodge City, Kansas
Agent: CAA - Beverly Hills, 213/288-4545

EASY RIDER   Columbia, 1969
THE LAST MOVIE   Universal, 1971
OUT OF THE BLUE   Discovery Films, 1982, Canadian
COLORS   Orion, 1988
BACKTRACK   Vestron, 1990
HOT SPOT   Orion, 1990

PETER HORTON*
Agent: Bauer Benedek Agency - Los Angeles, 213/275-2421

AMAZON WOMEN ON THE MOON   co-director with Joe
   Dante, John Landis, Carl Gottlieb & Robert K. Weiss,
   Universal, 1987

BOB HOSKINS
b. December 26, 1942 - Bury St. Edmunds, Suffolk, England
Agent: MLR Representation, 200 Fulham Road, London
   SW10, England

THE RAGGEDY RAWNEY   Four Seasons Entertainment,
   1988, British

DAN HOSKINS
CHROME HEARTS   International Film Marketing, 1990

HSIAO-HSIEN HOU
(See Hou HSIAO-HSIEN)

JOHN HOUGH*
b. November 21, 1941 - London, England
Agent: Phil Gersh, The Gersh Agency - Beverly Hills,
   213/274-6611

WOLFHEAD   1970, British

SUDDEN TERROR *EYEWITNESS* National General, 1971, British
THE PRACTICE 1971, British
TWINS OF EVIL Universal, 1972, British
TREASURE ISLAND National General, 1972, British-French-West German- Spanish
THE LEGEND OF HELL HOUSE 20th Century-Fox, 1974, British
DIRTY MARY CRAZY LARRY 20th Century-Fox, 1974
ESCAPE TO WITCH MOUNTAIN Buena Vista, 1975
BRASS TARGET MGM/United Artists, 1978
THE WATCHER IN THE WOODS Buena Vista, 1980
THE INCUBUS Artists Releasing Corporation/Film Ventures International, 1982, Canadian
TRIUMPHS OF A MAN CALLED HORSE Jensen Farley Pictures, 1983, U.S.- Mexican
BLACK ARROW (CTF) Harry Alan Towers Productions/ Pan-Atlantic Pictures Productions, 1985, British
BIGGLES Compact Yellowbill/Tambarle, 1986, British
AMERICAN GOTHIC Vidmark, 1987, British
A HAZARD OF HEARTS (TF) The Grade Company/ Gainsborough Pictures, 1987, British
HOWLING IV...THE ORIGINAL NIGHTMARE Allied Entertainment, 1988, British
DANGEROUS LOVE (TF) The Grade Company/ Gainsborough Pictures, 1988, British
THE LADY AND THE HIGHWAYMAN (TF) The Grade Company/Gainsborough Pictures, 1989, British
A GHOST IN MONTE CARLO (CTF) The Grade Co./ Gainsborough Pictures, 1990, British

ROBERT (BOBBY) HOUSTON

Agent: Harris & Goldberg - Los Angeles, 213/553-5200

SHOGUN ASSASSIN director of U.S. version, New World, 1980, Japanese- U.S.
BAD MANNERS *GROWING PAINS* New World, 1984
TRUST ME Cinecom, 1989

ELLEN HOVDE*

Home: 43 Morton Street, New York, NY 10014, 212/242-5096

GREY GARDENS (FD) co-director with Albert Maysles, David Maysles & Muffie Meyer, 1975
ENORMOUS CHANGES AT THE LAST MINUTE co-director with Mirra Bank, TC Films International, 1985

CY HOWARD*

b. September 27, 1915 - Milwaukee, Wisconsin
Home: 10230 Sunset Blvd., Los Angeles, CA 90024, 213/276-2615

LOVERS AND OTHER STRANGERS Cinerama Releasing Corporation, 1970
EVERY LITTLE CROOK AND NANNY MGM, 1972
IT COULDN'T HAPPEN TO A NICER GUY (TF) The Jozak Company, 1974

RON HOWARD*

b. March 1, 1954 - Duncan, Oklahoma
Business: Imagine Films Entertainment, Inc., 1925 Century Park East, Los Angeles, CA 90067, 213/277-1665
Agent: CAA - Beverly Hills, 213/288-4545

GRAND THEFT AUTO New World, 1978
COTTON CANDY (TF) Major H Productions, 1978
SKYWARD (TF) Major H-Anson Productions, 1980

THROUGH THE MAGIC PYRAMID (TF) Major H Productions, 1981
NIGHT SHIFT The Ladd Company/Warner Bros., 1982
SPLASH Buena Vista, 1984
COCOON 20th Century Fox, 1985
GUNG HO Paramount, 1986
WILLOW MGM/UA, 1988
PARENTHOOD Universal, 1989
BACKDRAFT Universal, 1991

HOU HSIAO-HSIEN

b. 1947 - Mei County, Kwantung, China
Contact: Coordination Council for North American Affairs, Information & Communications Division, 900 N. Western Avenue, Los Angeles, CA 90029, 213/461-3665

GREEN, GREEN GRASS OF HOME 1982, Taiwanese
GROWING UP 1982, Taiwanese
THE SANDWICH MAN 1983, Taiwanese
THE BOYS FROM FENGKUEI 1983, Taiwanese
A SUMMER AT GRANDPA'S 1985, Taiwanese
A TIME TO LIVE AND A TIME TO DIE Central Motion Picture Corporation, 1985, Taiwanese
DUST IN THE WIND International Film Circuit, 1987, Taiwanese
DAUGHTER OF THE NILE PV Films, 1988, Taiwanese
A CITY OF SADNESS Era International Ltd./3-H Films, Ltd., 1989, Taiwanese

KING HU
(Hu Chin Ch'uan)

b. April 29, 1931 - Peking, China
Business: King Hu Film Productions, 10C Fa Po Street - Suite 2F, Yau Yat Chuen, Kowloon, Hong Kong, 3/818675

ETERNAL LOVE co-director, Shaw Brothers, 1963, Hong Kong
SONS OF THE GOOD EARTH Shaw Brothers, 1964, Hong Kong
COME DRINK WITH ME Union Film Company, 1966, Hong Kong
DRAGON GATE INN Union Film Company, 1967, Hong Kong
A TOUCH OF ZEN Union Film Company, 1968, Hong Kong
FOUR MOODS co-director, 1970, Hong Kong
THE FATE OF LEE KHAN King Hu Film Productions, 1973, Hong Kong
THE VALIANT ONES King Hu Film Productions, 1974, Hong Kong
RAINING ON THE MOUNTAIN King Hu Film Productions, 1977, Hong Kong
LEGEND OF THE MOUNTAIN King Hu Film Productions, 1978, Hong Kong
THE REJUVENATOR King Hu Film Productions, 1981, Taiwanese
ALL THE KING'S MEN Sunny Overseas Corporation/ CMPC, 1983, Hong Kong
THE WHEEL OF LIFE co-director with Li Hsing & Pai Ching-Jui, 1983, Taiwanese
THE WORLDS' BEST MEN 1984, Taiwanese
SWORDSMAN co-director with Tsui Hark, Ann Hui, Ching Siu Tung, Lee Wai Man & Kam Yeung Wah, Film Workshop Company, 1990, Hong Kong

JIANXIN HUANG
(See Huang JIANXIN)

JEAN-LOUP HUBERT
b. 1949 - France
Business: Camera Noire, 9 bis rue Labie, 75017 Paris,
    04/572-4717

L'ANNER PROCHAINE SI TOUT VA BIEN   1981, French
LA SMALA   1984, French
THE GRAND HIGHWAY   Miramax Films, 1987, French
APRES LA GUERRE   AMLF, 1989, French

TOM HUCKABEE
b. September 2, 1955 - Fort Worth, Texas
Home: 2488 Cheremoya Avenue, Hollywood, CA 90068,
    213/463-3831

TAKING TIGER MOUNTAIN   co-director with Kent Smith,
    Horizon, 1983

JOHN W. HUCKERT
b. June 26, 1954 - Washington, D.C.
Address: P.O. Box 2270, Hollywood, CA 90028,
    213/660-3549

ORANGE SUNSHINE: THE REINCARNATION OF
    LUDWIG VAN BEETHOVEN   Huckert
    Productions, 1972
ERNIE & ROSE   Huckert Productions, 1982
THE PASSING   Huckert Productions, 1983

REGINALD HUDLIN
Agent: Ronda Gomez-Quinones, Triad Artists, Inc. -
    Los Angeles, 213/556-2727

HOUSE PARTY   New Line Cinema, 1990

GARY HUDSON
THUNDER RUN   Cannon, 1986

HUGH HUDSON
Agent: CAA - Beverly Hills, 213/288-4545

CHARIOTS OF FIRE★   The Ladd Company/Warner
    Bros., 1981, British
GREYSTOKE: THE LEGEND OF TARZAN, LORD OF
    THE APES   Warner Bros., 1984, British-U.S.
REVOLUTION   Warner Bros., 1985, British-Norwegian
LOST ANGELS   Orion, 1989

ROY HUGGINS*
July 18, 1914 - Litelle, Washington
Business: Public Arts, Inc., 1928 Mandeville Canyon,
    Los Angeles, CA 90049, 213/476-7892

HANGMAN'S KNOT   Columbia, 1952
THE YOUNG COUNTRY (TF)   Universal TV, 1970

CAROL HUGHES
Contact: Writers Guild of America, West - Los Angeles,
    213/550-1000

MISSING LINK   co-director with David Hughes,
    Universal, 1988

DAVID HUGHES
Contact: Writers Guild of America, West - Los Angeles,
    213/550-1000

MISSING LINK   co-director with Carol Hughes,
    Universal, 1988

JOHN HUGHES*
b. February 18, 1950 - Lansing, Michigan
Agent: CAA - Beverly Hills, 213/288-4545

SIXTEEN CANDLES   Universal, 1984
THE BREAKFAST CLUB   Universal, 1985
WEIRD SCIENCE   Universal, 1985
FERRIS BUELLER'S DAY OFF   Paramount, 1986
PLANES, TRAINS AND AUTOMOBILES   Paramount, 1987
SHE'S HAVING A BABY   Paramount, 1988
UNCLE BUCK   Universal, 1989

KENNETH (KEN) HUGHES
b. January 19, 1922 - Liverpool, England
Home: 2218 Beachwood Drive - Apt. 301, Los Angeles, CA
    90068, 213/469-7716
Agent: Bob Eisenbach, Robert Eisenbach Agency -
    Los Angeles, 213/273-0801

WIDE BOY   Realart, 1952, British
HEAT WAVE   THE HOUSE ACROSS THE LAKE   Lippert,
    1954, British
BLACK 13   Archway, 1954, British
THE BRAIN MACHINE   RKO Radio, 1955, British
THE CASE OF THE RED MONKEY   LITTLE RED MONKEY
    Allied Artists, 1955, British
THE DEADLIEST SIN   CONFESSION   Allied Artists,
    1955, British
THE ATOMIC MAN   TIMESLIP   Allied Artists, 1955, British
JOE MACBETH   Columbia, 1956, British
WICKED AS THEY COME   Columbia, 1957, British
THE LONG HAUL   Columbia, 1957, British
JAZZ BOAT   Columbia, 1960, British
IN THE NICK   Columbia, 1960, British
THE TRIALS OF OSCAR WILDE   Kinglsey International,
    1960, British
PLAY IT COOLER   Columbia, 1961, British
THE SMALL WORLD OF SAMMY LEE   7 Arts,
    1963, British
OF HUMAN BONDAGE   MGM, 1964, British
ARRIVEDERCI, BABY!   DROP DEAD, DARLING
    Paramount, 1966, British
CASINO ROYALE   co-director with Val Guest, John
    Huston, Joseph McGrath & Robert Parrish, Columbia,
    1967, British
CHITTY CHITTY BANG BANG   United Artists, 1968, British
CROMWELL   Columbia, 1970, British
THE INTERNECINE PROJECT   Allied Artists, 1974, British
ALFIE DARLING   OH! ALFIE   1975, British
SEXTETTE   Crown International, 1978
NIGHT SCHOOL   TERROR EYES   Paramount, 1981

ROBERT C. HUGHES
HUNTER'S BLOOD   Concorde, 1987
MEMORIAL VALLEY MASSACRE   Concorde, 1988
ZADAR! COW FROM HELL   Stone Peach
    Productions, 1989
DOWN THE DRAIN   RCA-Columbia Home Video/Trans
    World Entertainment/Epic Pictures, 1990

TERRY HUGHES*
Home: 4633 Arcola Avenue, Toluca Lake, CA 91602,
    818/954-6470
Agent: William Morris Agency - Beverly Hills, 213/274-7451

MONTY PYTHON LIVE AT THE HOLLYWOOD BOWL
    Columbia, 1982, British
SUNSET LIMOUSINE (TF)   Witzend Productions/ITC, 1983
FOR LOVE OR MONEY (TF)   Robert Papazian Productions/
    Henerson-Hirsch Productions, 1984

ANN HUI
(Xu Anhua)
b. 1947 - Manchuria, China
Contact: Hong Kong International Film Festival, 5th Floor,
   High Block City Hall, Edinburgh Place, Hong Kong,
   (3)72-1193

THE SECRET   1979, Hong Kong
THE SPOOKY BUNCH   1980, Hong Kong
THE STORY OF WOO VIET   1981, Hong Kong
BOAT PEOPLE   Spectrafilm, 1983, Hong Kong
LOVE IN A FALLEN CITY   Shaw Brothers, 1984,
   Hong Kong
THE ROMANCE OF BOOK AND SWORD   Yeung Tse Ke
   Movie Enterprises/ SIL-Metropole Organisation, 1987,
   Hong Kong
STARRY IS THE NIGHT   Shaw Bros., 1988, Hong Kong
SONG OF THE EXILE   Cos Films Co. Ltd., 1990, Hong
   Kong-Taiwanese
SWORDSMAN   co-directed with King Hu, Tsui Hark, Ching
   Siu Tung, Lee Wai Man & Kam Yeung Wah, Film
   Workshop Company, 1990, Hong Kong

DANIELE HUILLET
Contact: French Film Office, 745 Fifth Avenue, New York,
   NY 10151, 212/832-8860

OTHON   co-director with Jean-Marie Straub,
   1969, French
GESCHICHTSUNTERRICHT   co-director with Jean-Marie
   Straub, 1972, West German
MOSES AND AARON   co-director with Jean-Marie Straub,
   New Yorker, 1975, West German
I CANI DEL SINAI   co-director with Jean-Marie Straub,
   1976, Italian
DELLA NUBE ALLA RESISTENZA   co-director with
   Jean-Marie Straub, 1979, Italian
CLASS RELATIONS   *KLASSENVERHALF-NISSE*
   co-director with Jean-Marie Straub, New Yorker,
   1984, West German-French
DER TOD DES EMPEDOKLES   co-director with
   Jean-Marie Straub, Janus/Les Films du Losange,
   1986, West German-French

DONALD HULETTE
b. November 29, 1937 - Los Angeles, California
Home: 8835 Crescent Drive, Los Angeles, CA 90046,
   213/654-9680

BREAKER BREAKER   American International, 1978
A GREAT RIDE   Manson International, 1978
TENNESSEE STALLION   Vestron, 1983
YOU'RE IT   Merlin Film Corporation, 1987

EDWARD HUME
Contact: Writers Guild of America, West - Los Angeles,
   213/550-1000

STRANGER ON MY LAND (TF)   Edgar J. Scherick
   Associates/Taft Entertainment TV, 1988

SAMO HUNG
b. January 7, 1952 - Hong Kong
Contact: Hong Kong International Film Festival, 5th Floor,
   High Block City Hall, Edinburgh Place, Hong Kong,
   (3) 72-1193

SPOOKY ENCOUNTERS   1980, Hong Kong
PRODIGAL SON   1983, Hong Kong
WINNERS AND SINNERS   1983, Hong Kong

WHEELS ON MEALS   1984, Hong Kong
TWINKLE, TWINKLE, LUCKY STARS   1985, Hong Kong
EASTERN CONDORS   1987, Hong Kong

JACKSON HUNSICKER
THE FROG PRINCE   Cannon, 1987, U.S.-Israeli
ODD BALL HALL   The Movie Group, 1989

PETER HUNT*
b. March 11, 1928 - London, England
Home: 2229 Roscomare Road, Los Angeles, CA 90077,
   213/472-1911
Agent: Martin Shapiro, Shapiro-Lichtman Agency -
   Los Angeles, 213/859-8877

ON HER MAJESTY'S SECRET SERVICE   United Artists,
   1969, British
GOLD   Allied Artists, 1974, British
SHOUT AT THE DEVIL   American International,
   1976, British
GULLIVER'S TRAVELS   EMI, 1977, British-Belgian
THE BEASTS ARE ON THE STREETS (TF)
   Hanna-Barbera Productions, 1978
DEATH HUNT   20th Century-Fox, 1981
PHILIP MARLOWE - PRIVATE EYE   *CHANDLERTOWN*
   (CMS)   co-director with Bryan Forbes, Sidney Hayers &
   David Wickes, HBO/David Wickes Television Ltd./London
   Weekend Television, 1983, British
THE LAST DAYS OF POMPEII (MS)   David Gerber
   Company/Columbia TV/ Centerpoint Films/RAI, 1984,
   U.S.-British-Italian
WILD GEESE II   Universal, 1985, British
HYPER SAPIEN   Taliafilm II, 1986
ASSASSINATION   Cannon, 1987

PETER H. HUNT*
b. December 19, 1938 - Pasadena, California
Home: 1799 Westridge Road, Los Angeles, CA 90049,
   213/472-1863
Agent: CAA - Beverly Hills, 213/288-4545

1776   Columbia, 1972
FLYING HIGH (TF)   Mark Carliner Productions, 1978
BULLY   Maturo Image, 1978
WHEN SHE WAS BAD... (TF)   Ladd Productions/Henry
   Jaffe Enterprises, 1979
RENDEZVOUS HOTEL (TF)   Mark Carliner
   Productions, 1979
LIFE ON THE MISSISSIPPI (TF)   The Great Amwell
   Company/Nebraska ETV Network/WNET-13/Taurus
   Films, 1980
THE PRIVATE HISTORY OF A CAMPAIGN THAT
   FAILED (TF)   The Great Amwell Company/Nebraska
   ETV Network/WNET-13, 1981
THE MYSTERIOUS STRANGER (TF)   The Great Amwell
   Company/Nebraska ETV Network/WNET-13/MR Film/
   Taurus Films, 1982
SKEEZER (TF)   Margie-Lee Enterprises/The Blue Marble
   Company/Marble Arch Productions, 1982
MASQUERADE (TF)   Renee Valente Productions/Glen A.
   Larson Productions/20th Century-Fox TV, 1983
THE PARADE (TF)   Hill-Mandelker Productions, 1984
SINS OF THE PAST (TF)   Sinpast Entertainment Company
   Productions, 1984
IT CAME UPON THE MIDNIGHT CLEAR (TF)
   Schenck-Cardea Productions/ Columbia TV/LBS
   Communications, 1984
THE ADVENTURES OF HUCKLEBERRY FINN (TF)
   The Great Amwell Company, 1986
CHARLEY HANNAH (TF)   A. Shane Company, 1986

Hu

FILM
DIRECTORS
GUIDE

F
I
L
M

D
I
R
E
C
T
O
R
S

TIM HUNTER*
Agent: Jeremy Zimmer, Bauer Benedek Agency -
   Los Angeles, 213/275-2421

TEX   Buena Vista, 1982
SYLVESTER   Columbia, 1985
RIVER'S EDGE   Hemdale, 1987
PAINT IT BLACK   Vestron, 1990

CAROLINE HUPPERT
Contact: French Film Office, 745 Fifth Avenue, New York,
   NY 10151, 212/832-8860

SINCERELY CHARLOTTE   New Line Cinema,
   1986, French

HARRY HURWITZ*
Agent: Mark Lichtman, Shapiro-Lichtman Agency -
   Los Angeles, 213/859-8877

THE PROJECTIONIST   Maron Films Limited, 1971
THE COMEBACK TRAIL   Dynamite Entertainment/
   Rearguard Productions, 1971
RICHARD   co-director with Lorees Yerby, Billings, 1972
CHAPLINESQUE, MY LIFE AND HARD TIMES
   Xanadu, 1972
FAIRY TALES   directed under pseudonym of Harry
   Tampa, 1978
NOCTURNA   directed under pseudonym of Harry Tampa,
   Compass International, 1979
SAFARI 3000   United Artists, 1982
THE ROSEBUD BEACH HOTEL   Almi Pictures, 1985
THAT'S ADEQUATE   South Gate Entertainment, 1989

SAMUEL HURWITZ
b. April 20, 1965 - Poughkeepsie, New York
Contact: 213/871-6907

ON THE MAKE   Taurus Entertainment, 1989

WARIS HUSSEIN*
b. 1938 - Lucknow, India
Address: 1422 N. Sweetzer Avenue - Suite 307,
   Los Angeles, CA 90069
Agent: Elliot Webb, Broder-Kurland-Webb-Uffner Agency -
   Los Angeles, 213/656-9262

THANK YOU ALL VERY MUCH   *A TOUCH OF LOVE*
   Columbia, 1969, British
QUACKSER FORTUNE HAS A COUSIN IN THE BRONX
   UMC, 1970, British
MELODY   *S.W.A.L.K.*   Levitt-Pickman, 1971, British
THE POSSESSION OF JOEL DELANEY
   Paramount, 1972
HENRY VIII AND HIS SIX WIVES   Levitt-Pickman,
   1973, British
DIVORCE HIS/DIVORCE HERS (TF)   World Film
   Services, 1973
AND BABY MAKES SIX (TF)   Alan Landsburg
   Productions, 1979
DEATH PENALTY (TF)   Brockway Productions/NBC
   Productions, 1980
THE HENDERSON MONSTER (TF)   Titus
   Productions, 1980
BABY COMES HOME (TF)   Alan Landsburg
   Productions, 1980
CALLIE & SON (TF)   Rosilyn Heller Productions/Hemdale
   Presentations/City Films/Motown Productions, 1981
COMING OUT OF THE ICE (TF)   The Konigsberg
   Company, 1982

LITTLE GLORIA...HAPPY AT LAST (TF)   Edgar J. Scherick
   Associates/Metromedia Producers Corporation, 1982
   U.S.-Canadian-British
PRINCESS DAISY (MS)   NBC Productions/Steve Krantz
   Productions, 1983
THE WINTER OF OUR DISCONTENT (TF)   Lorimar
   Productions, 1983
SURVIVING (TF)   Telepictures Productions, 1985
ARCH OF TRIUMPH (TF)   Newland-Raynor Productions/
   HTV, 1985, U.S.-British
COPACABANA (TF)☆☆   Dick Clark Cinema Productions/
   Stiletto Ltd., 1985
WHEN THE BOUGH BREAKS (TF)   Taft Entertainment TV/
   TDF Productions, 1986
INTIMATE CONTACT (MS)   Zenith Productions/Central TV,
   1987, British
DOWNPAYMENT ON MURDER (TF)   Adam Productions/
   20th Century Fox TV, 1987
THE RICHEST MAN IN THE WORLD: THE ARISTOTLE
   ONASSIS STORY (TF) The Kongsberg-Sanitsky
   Company, 1988
KILLER INSTINCT (TF)   Millar-Bromberg Productions/ITC,
   1988
THOSE SHE LEFT BEHIND (TF)   NBC Productions, 1989
THE SHELL SEEKERS (TF)   Marian Rees Associates/
   Central Films Ltd., 1989, U.S.-British
FORBIDDEN NIGHTS (TF)   Tristine Rainer Productions/
   Warner Bros. TV, 1990

DANNY HUSTON*
Agent: Leading Artists - Beverly Hills, 213/858-1999

BIGFOOT (TF)   Walt Disney TV, 1987
MR. NORTH   Samuel Goldwyn Company, 1988

JIMMY HUSTON
Agent: ICM - Los Angeles, 213/550-4000

DEATH RIVER   Omni, 1977
DARK SUNDAY   Intercontinental, 1978
BUCKSTONE COUNTY PRISON   Film Ventures
   International, 1978
SEABO   E.O. Corporation, 1978
FINAL EXAM   MPM, 1981
THE SLEUTH SLAYER   Private Eye Productions, 1984
MY BEST FRIEND IS A VAMPIRE   Kings Road, 1988

BRIAN G. HUTTON*
b. 1935 - New York, New York
Contact: Directors Guild of America - Los Angeles,
   213/289-2000

WILD SEED   Universal, 1965
THE PAD (...AND HOW TO USE IT)   Universal, 1966
SOL MADRID   MGM, 1968
WHERE EAGLES DARE   MGM, 1969, British
KELLY'S HEROES   MGM, 1970, U.S.-Yugoslavian
X Y & ZEE   *ZEE & CO.*   Columbia, 1972, British
NIGHT WATCH   Avco Embassy, 1973, British
THE FIRST DEADLY SIN   Filmways, 1980
HIGH ROAD TO CHINA   Warner Bros., 1983,
   U.S.-Yugoslavian
RYDER   Jolson-Jay Productions, 1990

WILLARD HUYCK*
Agent: CAA - Beverly Hills, 213/288-4545

MESSIAH OF EVIL   International Cinefilm, 1975
FRENCH POSTCARDS   Paramount, 1979

146

BEST DEFENSE   Paramount, 1984
HOWARD THE DUCK   Universal, 1986

NESSA HYAMS*
Contact: Directors Guild of America - New York City,
    212/581-0370

LEADER OF THE BAND   New Century/Vista, 1987

PETER HYAMS*
b. July 26, 1943 - New York, New York
Agent: ICM - Los Angeles, 213/550-4000

ROLLING MAN (TF)   ABC Circle Films, 1972
GOODNIGHT MY LOVE (TF)   ABC Circle Films, 1972
BUSTING   United Artists, 1974
OUR TIME   Warner Bros., 1974
PEEPER   20th Century-Fox, 1976
CAPRICORN ONE   20th Century-Fox, 1978
HANOVER STREET   Columbia, 1979
OUTLAND   The Ladd Company/Warner Bros., 1981
THE STAR CHAMBER   20th Century-Fox, 1983
2010   MGM/UA, 1984
RUNNING SCARED   MGM/UA, 1986
THE PRESIDIO   Paramount, 1988
NARROW MARGIN   Tri-Star, 1990

I

LEON ICHASO
Agent: CAA - Beverly Hills, 213/288-4545

EL SUPER   co-director with Orlando Jimenez-Leal,
    Columbia, 1979
CROSSOVER DREAMS   Miramax, 1985
TALES FROM THE HOLLYWOOD HILLS: A TABLE AT
    CIRO'S (TF)   WNET/ Zenith Productions/KCET, 1987
THE TAKE (CTF)   Cine-Nevada Inc./MCA-TV/USA
    Network, 1990

KON ICHIKAWA
b. November 20, 1915 - Ise, Mie Prefecture, Japan
Contact: Directors Guild of Japan, Tsukada Building,
    8-33 Udagawa-cho, Shibuya-ku, Tokyo 150, Japan,
    3/461-4411

A GIRL AT DOJO TEMPLE   Toho, 1946, Japanese
A FLOWER BLOOMS   Toho, 1948, Japanese
365 NIGHTS   Toho, 1948, Japanese
HUMAN PATTERNS   Toho, 1949, Japanese
ENDLESS PASSION   Toho, 1949, Japanese
SANSHIRO OF GINZA   Toho, 1950, Japanese
HEAT AND MUD   Toho, 1950, Japanese
PURSUIT AT DAWN   Toho, 1950, Japanese
NIGHTSHADE FLOWER   Toho, 1951, Japanese
THE LOVER   Toho, 1951, Japanese
THE MAN WITHOUT A NATIONALITY   Toho,
    1951, Japanese
STOLEN LOVE   Toho, 1951, Japanese
RIVER SOLO FLOWS   Toho, 1951, Japanese
WEDDING MARCH   Toho, 1951, Japanese
MR. LUCKY   Toho, 1952, Japanese

YOUNG PEOPLE   Toho, 1952, Japanese
THE WOMAN WHO TOUCHED LEGS   Toho,
    1952, Japanese
THIS WAY - THAT WAY   Daiei, 1952, Japanese
MR. PU   Toho, 1953, Japanese
THE BLUE REVOLUTION   Toho, 1953, Japanese
THE YOUTH OF HEIJI ZENIGATA   Toho, 1953, Japanese
ALL OF MYSELF   Toho, 1954, Japanese
A BILLIONAIRE   Toho, 1954, Japanese
TWELVE CHAPTERS ABOUT WOMEN   Toho,
    1954, Japanese
GHOST STORY OF YOUTH   Nikkatsu, 1955, Japanese
THE HEART   Nikkatsu, 1955, Japanese
THE BURMESE HARP   *HARP OF BURMA*   Brandon,
    1956, Japanese
PUNISHMENT ROOM   Daiei, 1956, Japanese
NIHOMBASHI   Daiei, 1956, Japanese
THE CROWDED STREETCAR   Daiei, 1957, Japanese
THE PIT   Daiei, 1957, Japanese
THE MEN OF TOHOKU   Toho, 1957, Japanese
CONFLAGRATION   Daiei, 1958, Japanese
MONEY AND THREE BAD MEN   1958, Japanese
GOODBYE - GOOD DAY   Daiei, 1959, Japanese
ODD OBSESSION   Harrison Pictures, 1959, Japanese
FIRES ON THE PLAIN   Daiei, 1959, Japanese
POLICE AND SMALL GANGSTERS   1959, Japanese
A WOMAN'S TESTAMENT   co-director with Kozaburo
    Yoshimura & Yasuzo Masamura, Daiei, 1959, Japanese
A GINZA VETERAN   1960, Japanese
BONCHI   Daiei, 1960, Japanese
HER BROTHER   Daiei, 1960, Japanese
TEN DARK WOMEN   Daiei, 1961, Japanese
THE BROKEN COMMANDMENT   Daiei, 1962, Japanese
BEING TWO ISN'T EASY   Daiei, 1962, Japanese
AN ACTOR'S REVENGE   *THE REVENGE OF UKENO-JO*
    Daiei, 1963, Japanese
ALONE ON THE PACIFIC   Nikkatsu, 1963, Japanese
MONEY TALKS   Daiei, 1964, Japanese
TOKYO OLYMPIAD (FD)   American International, 1965,
    Japanese
THE TALE OF GENJI (MS)   1966, Japanese
TOPO GIGIO E SEI LADRI   Kon Ichikawa Productions/
    Perego, 1967, Italian- Japanese
TO LOVE AGAIN   Toho, 1972, Japanese
THE WANDERERS   Kon Ichikawa Productions/ATG,
    1973, Japanese
VISIONS OF EIGHT (FD)   co-director with Yuri Ozerov, Mai
    Zetterling, Arthur Penn, Michael Pfleghar, Milos Forman,
    Claude Lelouch & John Schlesinger, Cinema 5, 1973
I AM A CAT   Toho, 1975, Japanese
BETWEEN WOMEN AND WIVES   co-director with Shiro
    Toyoda, Toho, 1976, Japanese
THE INUGAMI FAMILY   Toho, 1976, Japanese
THE DEVIL'S BOUNCING BALL SONG   Toho,
    1977, Japanese
ISLAND OF HORRORS   Toho, 1977, Japanese
QUEEN BEE   Toho, 1978, Japanese
FIREBIRD   Toho, 1978, Japanese
THE HOUSE OF THE HANGING ON HOSPITAL HILL
    Toho, 1979, Japanese
THE OLD CITY   *KOTO*   Toho, 1980, Japanese
HAPPINESS   Toho, 1982, Japanese
THE MAKIOKA SISTERS   RS/58, 1983, Japanese
FINE SNOW   Toho, 1983, Japanese
OHAN   Toho, 1984, Japanese
THE HARP OF BURMA   Toho, 1985, Japanese
ROKUMEIKAN   Marugen Production Company,
    1986, Japanese
FILM ACTRESS   Toho, 1987, Japanese
PRINCESS FROM THE MOON   Toho, 1987, Japanese

ERIC IDLE*
b. March 29, 1943 - England
Agent: ICM - Los Angeles, 213/550-4000

ALL YOU NEED IS CASH *THE RUTLES* (TF)
  co-director with Gary Weis, Rutles Corps Productions,
  1978, British

HASSAN ILDARI
FACE OF THE ENEMY Independent Network, 1989

KWON-TAEK IM
(See Im KWON-TAEK)

SHOHEI IMAMURA
b. 1926 - Tokyo, Japan
Contact: Directors Guild of Japan, Tsukada Building,
  8-33 Udagawa-cho, Shibuya-ku, Tokyo 150, Japan,
  3/461-4411

STOLEN DESIRE Nikkatsu, 1958, Japanese
NISHI GINZA STATION Nikkatsu, 1958, Japanese
ENDLESS DESIRE Nikkatsu, 1958, Japanese
MY SECOND BROTHER Nikkatsu, 1959, Japanese
PIGS AND BATTLESHIPS Nikkatsu, 1961, Japanese
THE INSECT WOMAN Nikkatsu, 1963, Japanese
INTENTIONS OF MURDER *UNHOLY DESIRE* Nikkatsu,
  1964, Japanese
THE PORNOGRAPHERS East West Classics,
  1966, Japanese
A MAN VANISHES Imamura Productions/Nihon Eiga
  Shinsha/ATG, 1967, Japanese
THE PROFOUND DESIRE OF THE GODS Nikkatsu,
  1968, Japanese
HISTORY OF POST-WAR JAPAN AS TOLD BY A BAR
  HOSTESS (FD) Toho, 1970, Japanese
KARAYUKI-SAN, THE MAKING OF A PROSTITUTE (TD)
  Shibata Organization, 1975, Japanese
VENGEANCE IS MINE Shochiku, 1979, Japanese
EIJANAIKA Shochiku, 1981, Japanese
THE BALLAD OF NARAYAMA Kino International/Janus,
  1983, Japanese
ZEGEN Toei, 1987, Japanese
BLACK RAIN Angelika Films, 1989, Japanese

SAMUEL (SHMUEL) IMBERMAN
Contact: Israel Film Centre, Ministry of Industry & Trade,
  30 Agron Street, P.O. Box 299, Jerusalem 94190, Israel,
  02/210297

I DON'T GIVE A DAMN Trans World Entertainment,
  1987, Israeli
TEL AVIV - LOS ANGELES Galia Communic Ltd./
  Five-Five Productions, 1988, Israeli

MARKUS IMHOOF
b. 1941 - Winterthur, Switzerland
Contact: Swiss Film Center, Muenstergasse 18, CH-8001
  Zurich, Switzerland, 01/472-860

FLUCHTGEFAHR 1974, Swiss
TAUWETTER 1978, Swiss
ISEWIXER 1979, Swiss
THE BOAT IS FULL Quartet, 1980, Swiss
DIE REISE Regina Ziegler Filmproduktion/Limbo
  Film/WDR/SRG, 1986, West German-Swiss
THE MOUNTAIN Bernard Lang Productions,
  1990, Swiss

KEVIN INCH*
Contact: Directors Guild of America - Los Angeles,
  213/289-2000

REMINGTON STEELE: THE STEELE THAT WOULDN'T
  DIE (TF) MTM Productions, 1987
CARLY'S WEB (TF) MTM Enterprises, 1987

OTAR IOSELLIANI
b. Georgia, Soviet Union
Contact: French Film Office, 745 Fifth Avenue, New York, NY
  1015l, 2l2-832-8860

THE FALL OF THE LEAVES Soviet
THERE WAS AT ONE TIME A MOCKINGBIRD Soviet
PASTORALE Soviet
LES FAVOURIS DE LA LUNE 1984, French
ET LA LUMIERE FUT Films du Triangle/La Sept/Direkt
  Film/RAI, 1989, French-West German-Italian

DANIEL IROM*
Address: P.O. Box 1868, Madison Square Station, NY
  10159, 212/288-0529

BUM RAP Millennium Productions, 1988

JOHN IRVIN*
b. May 7, 1940 - England
Home: 6 Lower Common South, London SW15, England,
  71/789-1514
Agent: ICM - Los Angeles, 213/550-4000

TINKER, TAILOR, SOLDIER, SPY (TF) BBC/Paramount
  TV, 1979, British
THE DOGS OF WAR United Artists, 1981, U.S.-British
GHOST STORY Universal, 1981
CHAMPIONS Embassy, 1983, British
TURTLE SUMMER Samuel Goldwyn Company,
  1985, British
RAW DEAL DEG, 1986
HAMBURGER HILL Paramount, 1987
NEXT OF KIN Warner Bros., 1989
EMINENT DOMAIN SVS Films, 1990,
  Canadian-French-Israeli

DAVID IRVING
Agent: Triad Artists, Inc. - Los Angeles, 213/556-2727

GOOD-BYE, CRUEL WORLD Sharp Features, 1982
RUMPELSTILTSKIN Cannon, 1987, U.S.-Israeli
SLEEPING BEAUTY Cannon, 1987, U.S.-Israeli
THE EMPEROR'S NEW CLOTHES Cannon, 1987,
  U.S.-Israeli
C.H.U.D. II Vestron, 1989
PERFUME OF THE CYCLONE The Movie Group, 1990

RICHARD IRVING*
b. February 13, 1917 - New York, New York
Home: 492 S. Spalding Drive, Beverly Hills, CA 90212,
  213/277-6083
Business Manager: Elaine Berke, Berke Management
  Company, 15910 Ventura Blvd. - Suite 1215, Encino,
  CA 91436

ISTANBUL EXPRESS (TF) Universal TV, 1968
PRESCRIPTION: MURDER (TF) Universal TV, 1968
BREAKOUT (TF) Universal TV, 1970
RANSOM FOR A DEAD MAN (TF) Universal TV, 1971
CUTTER (TF) Universal TV, 1972

THE SIX-MILLION DOLLAR MAN (TF)   Universal
    TV, 1973
THE ART OF CRIME (TF)   Universal TV, 1975
EXO-MAN (TF)   Universal TV, 1977
SEVENTH AVENUE (MS)   co-director with Russ
    Mayberry, Universal TV, 1977
CLASS OF '65 (TF)   Universal TV, 1978
THE JESSE OWENS STORY (TF)   Harve Bennett
    Productions/Paramount TV, 1984

ALBERTO ISAAC

b. Colima, Mexico
Contact: Azteca Films, 555 N. La Brea Avenue, P.O. Box
    36095, Hollywood, CA 90036, 213/938-2413

EN ESTE PUEBLO NO HAY LADRONES   Azteca Films,
    1965, Mexican
LA OLIMPIADA EN MEXICO (FD)   Azteca Films,
    1968, Mexican
LAS VISITACIONES DEL DIABLO   Azteca Films,
    1971, Mexican
LOS DIAS DE AMOR   Azteca Films, 1971, Mexican
EL RINCON DE LAS VIRGINES   Azteca Films,
    1972, Mexican
TIVOLI   Azteca Films, 1974, Mexican
CUARTELAZO   Azteca Films, 1976, Mexican
LAS NOCHES DE PALOMA   Azteca Films,
    1978, Mexican
TIEMPO DE LOBOS   Azteca Films, 1982, Mexican
UN HOGAR MUY DECENTE   Azteca Films,
    1987, Mexican
LAS BATALLAS EN EL DESIERTO   Conacine,
    1987, Mexican
MARIANA, MARIANA   Azteca Films, 1988, Mexican
NAVIDAD SANGRIENTE   Conacine, 1989, Mexican
MATAN A CHINTO   Conacine/Estudios Churubusco,
    1990, Mexican

JAMES ISAAC

Agent: Triad Artists, Inc. - Los Angeles, 213/556-2727

THE HORROR SHOW   MGM/UA, 1989

ROBERT ISCOVE*

b. Toronto, Ontario, Canada
Address: 16045 Royal Oak Road, Encino, CA 91436,
    818/981-7836
Agent: CAA - Beverly Hills, 213/288-4545

CHAUTAUQUA GIRL (TF)   CBC, 1983, Canadian
LOVE & LARCENY (TF)   CBC, 1985, Canadian
THE PRODIGIOUS HICKEY (TF)   Ronald J. Kahn
    Productions/American Playhouse, 1987
MURDER IN BLACK AND WHITE (TF)   Titus
    Productions, 1990

GERALD I. ISENBERG*

b. May 13, 1940 - Cambridge, Massachusetts
Agent: ICM - Los Angeles, 213/550-4000

SEIZURE: THE STORY OF KATHY MORRIS (TF)
    The Jozak Company, 1980

SOGO ISHII

b. 1957 - Hakata, Fukuoka, Japan
Contact: Directors Guild of Japan, Tsukada Building,
    8-33 Udagawa-cho, Shibuya-ku, Tokyo 150, Japan,
    3/461-4411

PANIC IN HIGH SCHOOL   1978, Japanese

CRAZY THUNDER ROAD   1980, Japanese
SHUFFLE   1981, Japanese
BURST CITY   1982, Japanese
REVENGE OF ASIA   1983, Japanese
THE CRAZY FAMILY   THE BACK-JET FAMILY   Art Theatre
    Guild, 1984, Japanese
HALF-MAN (FD)   1986, Japanese

NEIL ISRAEL*

Agent: Alan Greenspan, ICM - Los Angeles, 213/550-4428

TUNNELVISION   co-director with Brad Swirnoff,
    World Wide, 1976
AMERICATHON   United Artists, 1979
BACHELOR PARTY   20th Century Fox, 1984
MOVING VIOLATIONS   20th Century Fox, 1985
COMBAT HIGH (TF)   Frank von Zerneck Productions/
    Lynch-Biller Productions, 1986
THE COVER GIRL AND THE COP (TF)   Barry-Enright
    Productions/Alexander Productions, 1988
SKETCHES   New Line Cinema, 1990

PETER ISRAELSON*

Home: 114 East 87th Street, New York, NY 10128
Agent: Triad Artists, Inc. - Los Angeles, 213/556-2727
Attorney: Levinson, Israel & Bell, 12-1/2 East 82nd Street,
    New York, NY 10028, 212/472-8888

SIDE OUT   Tri-Star, 1990

JUZO ITAMI

b. 1933 - Kyoto, Japan
Attorney: Paul Sandberg, Denton, Hall, Burgin & Warrens -
    Los Angeles, 213/282-8888
Business: Itami Films Inc., 335 No. Maple Drive - Suite 352,
    Beverly Hills, CA 90210, 213/285-6244

THE FUNERAL   New Yorker, 1985
TAMPOPO   New Yorker, 1986, Japanese
A TAXING WOMAN   Original Cinema, 1987, Japanese
A TAXING WOMAN RETURNS   New Yorker,
    1988, Japanese

JAMES IVORY*

b. June 7, 1928 - Berkeley, California
Agent: CAA - Beverly Hills, 213/288-4545

THE HOUSEHOLDER   Royal Films International, 1963,
    Indian-U.S.
SHAKESPEARE WALLAH   Continental, 1966, Indian
THE GURU   20th Century-Fox, 1969, British-Indian
BOMBAY TALKIE   Dia Films, 1970, Indian
SAVAGES   Angelika, 1972
THE WILD PARTY   American International, 1975
AUTOBIOGRAPHY OF A PRINCESS (TF)   Merchant Ivory
    Productions, 1975
SWEET SOUNDS   Merchant Ivory Productions, 1976
ROSELAND   Cinema Shares International, 1977
THE 5:48 (TF)   PBS, 1979
HULLABALOO OVER GEORGIA & BONNIE'S PICTURES
    Corinth, 1979
THE EUROPEANS   Levitt-Pickman, 1979, British
JANE AUSTEN IN MANHATTAN   Contemporary, 1980
QUARTET   New World, 1981, British-French
HEAT AND DUST   Universal Classics, 1983, British
THE BOSTONIANS   Almi Pictures, 1984
A ROOM WITH A VIEW ★   Cinecom, 1986, British
MAURICE   Cinecom, 1987, British
SLAVES OF NEW YORK   Tri-Star, 1989
MR. & MRS. BRIDGE   Miramax Films, 1990

J

DONALD G. JACKSON

Home: 7007 Comanche Avenue, Canoga Park, CA
91306, 818/716-9539

I LIKE TO HUNT PEOPLE   New World, 1985
ROLLERBLADE   New World, 1985
HELL COMES TO FROGTOWN   co-director with
R.J. Kizer, New World, 1988
ROLLERBLADE WARRIORS   Golden Circle
Productions, 1988

LEWIS JACKSON

Contact: Writers Guild of America, East - New York City,
212/245-6180

YOU BETTER WATCH OUT   *CHRISTMAS EVIL*
Edward R. Pressman Productions, 1980

MICK JACKSON

Contact: British Academy of Film & Television Arts,
195 Piccadilly, London W1, England, 71/734-0022

THREADS (TF)   Western-World TV/BBC/Nine Network,
1984, British-American
YURI NOSENKO, KGB (CTF)   HBO Showcase/BBC/
Premiere TV, 1986, U.S.- British
DOUBLE HELIX   *LIFE STORY*   (TF)   BBC,
1987, British
A VERY BRITISH COUP (TF)   Skreba Films/Channel
Four, 1988, British
CHATTAHOOCHIE   Hemdale, 1989
L.A. STORY   Tri-Star, 1991

SIMCHA JACOBOVICI

Business: Matara Film Productions, Inc., 957 Broadview
Avenue - Unit D, Toronto, Ontario M4K 2R5, Canada,
416/422-1270 or 416/423-8122

FALASHA: EXILE OF THE BLACK JEWS (FD)   Matara
Film Productions, 1983, Canadian
DEADLY CURRENTS: INSIDE THE... (TF)   Reunion
Film, 1989, Canadian

LAWRENCE-HILTON JACOBS

Contact: Screen Actors Guild - Hollywood, 213-465-4600

ANGELS OF THE CITY   PM Entertainment Group, 1990

JOSEPH JACOBY

b. September 22, 1942 - Brooklyn, New York
Agent: CAA - Beverly Hills, 213/288-4545

SHAME, SHAME, EVERYBODY KNOWS HER NAME
JER, 1970
HURRY UP OR I'LL BE THIRTY   Avco Embassy, 1973
THE GREAT BANK HOAX   *SHENANIGANS*   Warner
Bros., 1979

JUST JAECKIN*

b. 1940
Address: 8 Villa Mequillet, 92200 Neuilly, France,
04/624-4627
Contact: Directors Guild of America - Los Angeles,
213/289-2000

EMMANUELLE   Columbia, 1974, French
THE STORY OF O   Allied Artists, 1975, French
THE FRENCH WOMAN   *MADAME CLAUDE*   Monarch,
1979, French
THE LAST ROMANTIC LOVER   New Line Cinema, 1980,
French
GIRLS   Caneuram Films, 1980, Canadian-French-Israeli
COLLECTIONS PRIVEES   co-director with Shuji Terayama
& Walerian Borowczyk, Jeudi Films/Toei/French Movies,
1979, French-Japanese
LADY CHATTERLEY'S LOVER   Cannon, 1982,
French-British
THE PERILS OF GWENDOLINE   *GWENDOLINE*   Samual
Goldwyn Company, 1984, French

RAY JAFELICE

Contact: Academy of Canadian Cinema & Television, 633
Yonge Street - 2nd Floor, Toronto, Ontario M4Y 1Z9,
Canada, 416/967-0315

THE CARE BEARS' ADVENTURE IN WONDERLAND (AF)
Cineplex Odeon, 1987, Canadian

STANLEY JAFFE*

b. July 31, 1940 - New Rochelle, New York
Business: 660 Madison Avenue, New York, NY 10021,
212/421-4410
Agent: CAA - Beverly Hills, 213/288-4545
Business Manager: Martin Eisman, Eisman & Company,
2001 Palmer Avenue, Larchmont, NY 10538

WITHOUT A TRACE   20th Century-Fox, 1983

STEVEN CHARLES JAFFE*

Address: c/o Pati Passu Productions, 5555 Melrose Avenue,
Hollywood, CA 90028, 213/468-5841
Agent: Camden Artists - Los Angeles, 213/556-2022

SCARAB   1982

HENRY JAGLOM*

b. January 26, 1941 - London, England
Business: International Rainbow Pictures, The Penthouse,
9165 Sunset Blvd., Los Angeles, CA 90069,
213/271-0202 or 888 Seventh Avenue - 34th Floor,
New York, NY 10106, 212/245-8300

A SAFE PLACE   Columbia, 1971
TRACKS   Castle Hill Productions, 1976
SITTING DUCKS   Speciality Films, 1980
NATIONAL LAMPOON'S MOVIE MADNESS   co-director
with Bob Giraldi, United Artists, 1981
CAN SHE BAKE A CHERRY PIE?   Castle Hill Productions/
Quartet Films, 1983
ALWAYS   Samuel Goldwyn Company, 1985
SOMEONE TO LOVE   Rainbow/Castle Hill Productions,
1987
NEW YEAR'S DAY   International Rainbow Pictures, 1988
EATING   International Rainbow Pictures, 1989
VENICE/VENICE   International Rainbow Pictures, 1990

PATRICK JAMAIN

Contact: Academy of Canadian Cinema and Television,
  633 Yonge Street - 2nd Floor, Toronto, Ontario
  M4Y 1Z9, Canada, 416/967-0315

HONEYMOON   International Film Marketing, 1985,
  Canadian-French

JERRY JAMESON*

b. Hollywood, California
Contact: Jeff Cooper, The Cooper Agency - Los Angeles,
  213/277-8422

BRUTE CORPS   General Films, 1971
THE DIRT GANG   American International, 1972
THE BAT PEOPLE   American International, 1974
HEATWAVE! (TF)   Universal TV, 1974
THE ELEVATOR (TF)   Universal TV, 1974
HURRICANE (TF)   Metromedia Productions, 1974
TERROR ON THE 4TH FLOOR (TF)   Metromedia
  Productions, 1974
THE SECRET NIGHT CALLER (TF)   Charles Fries
  Productions/Penthouse Productions, 1975
THE DEADLY TOWER (TF)   MGM TV, 1975
THE LIVES OF JENNY DOLAN (TF)   Ross Hunter
  Productions/Paramount TV, 1975
THE CALL OF THE WILD (TF)   Charles Fries
  Productions, 1976
THE INVASION OF JOHNSON COUNTY (TF)   Roy
  Huggins Productions/ Universal TV, 1976
AIRPORT '77   Universal, 1977
SUPERDOME (TF)   ABC Circle Films, 1978
A FIRE IN THE SKY (TF)   Bill Driskill Productions, 1978
RAISE THE TITANIC   AFD, 1980, British-U.S.
HIGH NOON - PART II: THE RETURN OF WILL
  KANE (TF)   Charles Fries Productions, 1980
STAND BY YOUR MAN (TF)   Robert Papazian
  Productions/Peter Guber-Jon Peters Productions, 1981
KILLING AT HELL'S GATE (TF)   CBS Entertainment, 1981
HOTLINE (TF)   Wrather Entertainment International/
  Ron Samuels Productions, 1982
STARFLIGHT: THE PLANE THAT COULDN'T LAND (TF)
  Orgolini-Nelson Productions, 1983
COWBOY (TF)   Bercovici-St. Johns Productions/
  MGM TV, 1983
THIS GIRL FOR HIRE (TF)   Barney Rosenzweig
  Productions/Orion TV, 1983
LAST OF THE GREAT SURVIVORS (TF)   CBS
  Entertainment, 1984
THE COWBOY AND THE BALLERINA (TF)   Cowboy
  Productions, 1984
STORMIN' HOME (TF)   CBS Entertainment, 1985
ONE POLICE PLAZA (TF)   CBS Entertainment, 1986
THE RED SPIDER (TF)   CBS Entertainment, 1988
TERROR ON HIGHWAY 91 (TF)   Katy Film
  Productions, 1989
FIRE AND RAIN (CTF)   Wilshire Court Productions, 1989

MIKLOS JANCSO

b. September 27, 1921 - Vac, Hungary
Contact: Hungarofilm, 1054 Bathory utca 10, Budapest,
  Hungary, tel.: 116650

THE BELLS HAVE GONE TO ROME   Mafilm,
  1958, Hungarian
THREE STARS   co-director, Mafilm, 1960, Hungarian
CANTATA   Studio Budapest, 1963, Hungarian
MY WAY HOME   Mafilm, 1964, Hungarian
THE ROUND-UP   Altura, 1965, Hungarian

THE RED AND THE WHITE   Brandon, 1967,
  Hungarian-Soviet
SILENCE AND CRY   Mafilm, 1967, Hungarian
THE CONFRONTATION   Mafilm, 1967, Hungarian
WINTER WIND   *SIROKKO*   Marquise Film/Mafilm, 1969,
  French-Hungarian
LA PACIFISTA   Cinematografia Lombarda, 1970,
  Italian-French-West German
AGNUS DEI   Mafilm, 1971, Hungarian
LA TECNICA E IL RITO   RAI, 1971, Italian
RED PSALM   Mafilm, 1972, Hungarian
ROMA RIVUOLE CESARE   RAI, 1973, Italian
SZERELEM, ELEKTRA   Studio Hunnia, 1974, Hungarian
PRIVATE VICES - PUBLIC VIRTUE   1976,
  Italian-Yugoslavian
MASTERWORK   1977, Hungarian
HUNGARIAN RHAPSODY   Studio Dialog/Hungarofilm,
  1978, Hungarian
ALLEGRO BARBARO   Mafilm, 1979, Hungarian
HEART OF A TYRANT   Sacis, 1981, Italian-Hungarian
HUZSIKA (TD)   Magyar TV, 1984, Hungarian
OMEGA, OMEGA... (TD)   Dialog Studios/Mafilm/Magyar TV,
  1985, Hungarian
BUDAPEST (FD)   1985, Italian
DAWN   Odessa Films, 1986, French
SEASON OF MONSTERS   Dialog Studio/Mafilm,
  1987, Hungarian
JESUS CHRIST'S HOROSCOPE   Mafilm, 1989, Hungarian

LEE JANG-HO

b. January 16, 1945 - Seoul, Korea

STARS' HOME   1974, South Korean
THE RAIN YESTERDAY   1974, South Korean
DEEP LOVE   1975, South Korean
FINE WINDY DAYS   1980, South Korean
THE SONS OF DARKNESS   1981, South Korean
COME UNTO DAWN   1981, South Korean
DANCE OF THE WIDOW   1983, South Korean
DECLARATION OF FOOLS   1983, South Korean
BETWEEN KNEE AND KNEE   1984, South Korean
THE ENTERTAINER ER WOO-DONG   1985, South Korean
ALIEN BASEBALL TEAM   1986, South Korean
A MAN WITH THREE COFFINS   1988, South Korean
MISS RHINOCEROS AND MR. KORANDO   1989,
  South Korean

ANNABEL JANKEL*

Agent: CAA - Beverly Hills, 213/288-4545

THE MAX HEADROOM STORY (TF)   co-director with
  Rocky Morton, 1985, British
D.O.A.   co-director with Rocky Morton, Buena Vista, 1988

DEREK JARMAN

Address: c/o Mundy Ellis, British Film Institute, 81 Dean
  Street, London W1, England

SEBASTIANE   co-director with Paul Humfress, Discopat,
  1977, British
JUBILEE   Libra, 1979, British
THE TEMPEST   World Northal, 1980, British
IN THE SHADOW OF THE SUN   ICA, 1981, British
ANGELIC CONVERSATIONS   British Film Institute,
  1985, British
CARAVAGGIO   British Film Institute, 1986, British
ARIA   co-director, RCA VP/Virgin Vision, 1987, British
THE LAST OF ENGLAND   International Film Circuit,
  1987, British
WAR REQUIEM   Movie Visions, 1988, British

JIM JARMUSCH

b. Akron, Ohio
Business: Black Snake Productions, Inc., 24 Prince Street -
    Suite 7, New York, NY 10012, 212/226-1341

PERMANENT VACATION   Gray City, 1982
STRANGER THAN PARADISE   Samuel Goldwyn
    Company, 1984
DOWN BY LAW   Island Pictures, 1986
MYSTERY TRAIN   Orion Classics, 1989, U.S.-Japanese

CHARLES JARROTT*

b. June 6, 1927 - London, England
Agent: Tom Chasin, The Chasin Agency - Beverly Hills,
    213/278-7505
Business Manager: Jess Morgan, Jess Morgan &
    Company, Inc., 5750 Wilshire Blvd., - Suite 590,
    Los Angeles, CA 90036, 213/937-1552

ANNE OF THE THOUSAND DAYS   Universal,
    1969, British
MARY, QUEEN OF SCOTS   Universal, 1971, British
LOST HORIZON   Columbia, 1972
THE DOVE   Paramount, 1974
THE LITTLEST HORSE THIEVES   ESCAPE FROM THE
    DARK   Buena Vista, 1977, U.S.-British
THE OTHER SIDE OF MIDNIGHT   20th Century-Fox, 1977
THE LAST FLIGHT OF NOAH'S ARK   Buena Vista, 1980
CONDORMAN   Buena Vista, 1981
THE AMATEUR   20th Century-Fox, 1981, Canadian
A MARRIED MAN (TF)   London Weekend TV Productions/
    Lionhead Productions, 1984, British
THE BOY IN BLUE   20th Century Fox, 1985, Canadian
POOR LITTLE RICH GIRL: THE BARBARA HUTTON
    STORY (MS)   Lester Persky Productions/ITC
    Productions, 1987
THE WOMAN HE LOVED (TF)   The Larry Thompson
    Organization/HTV/ New World TV, 1988, U.S.-British
JUDITH KRANTZ'S TILL WE MEET AGAIN   TILL WE
    MEET AGAIN (MS)   Steve Krantz Productions/
    Yorkshire TV, 1989, U.S.-British
NIGHT OF THE FOX (TF)   ITC Entertainment, 1990,
    U.S.-British

LAURENCE JARVIK

b. October 30, 1956 - New York, New York
Business: The Jarvik-Strickland Company, 944 Berkeley
    Street, Santa Monica, CA 90403, 213/828-7794

WHO SHALL LIVE AND WHO SHALL DIE? (FD)   Kino
    International, 1981

ROLAND JEFFERSON

Agent: Ben Kamssler, Swanson Agency - Los Angeles,
    213/652-5385

PERFUME   NTN Productions/FEC Entertainment
    Group, 1989

LIONEL JEFFRIES

b. 1926 - London, England
Agent: ICM - London, 01/629-8080

THE RAILWAY CHILDREN   Universal, 1971, British
THE AMAZING MR. BLUNDEN   Goldstone, 1972, British
BAXTER!   National General, 1973, British
THE WATER BABIES   Pethurst International/Film Polski,
    1978, British-Polish
WOMBLING FREE   Satori, 1979, British

MICHAEL JENKINS

Agent: Richard Shepherd, The Artists Agency - Los Angeles,
    213/277-7779

REBEL   Vestron, 1985, Australian
SHARK'S PARADISE (TF)   McElroy & McElroy,
    1986, Australian
THE DIRTWATER DYNASTY (MS)   co-director with John
    Power, Kennedy Miller Productions, 1988, Australian
EMERALD CITY   Limelight Productions, 1989, Australian
CONFIDENCE   New Century/Vista, 1989, Australian

NORMAN JEWISON*

b. July 21, 1926 - Toronto, Canada
Business: Yorktown Productions Ltd., 9336 West Washington
    Blvd., Culver City, CA 90232, 213/202-3434
Agent: William Morris Agency - Beverly Hills, 213/274-7451
Business Manager: Capell, Flekman, Coyne & Co. -
    Beverly Hills, 213/553-0310

40 POUNDS OF TROUBLE   Universal, 1962
THE THRILL OF IT ALL   Universal, 1963
SEND ME NO FLOWERS   Universal, 1964
THE ART OF LOVE   Universal, 1965
THE CINCINNATI KID   MGM, 1965
THE RUSSIANS ARE COMING THE RUSSIANS ARE
    COMING   United Artists, 1966
IN THE HEAT OF THE NIGHT ★   United Artists, 1967
THE THOMAS CROWN AFFAIR   United Artists, 1968
GAILY, GAILY   United Artists, 1969
FIDDLER ON THE ROOF ★   United Artists, 1971
JESUS CHRIST SUPERSTAR   Universal, 1973
ROLLERBALL   United Artists, 1975
F.I.S.T.   United Artists, 1978
...AND JUSTICE FOR ALL   Columbia, 1979
BEST FRIENDS   Warner Bros., 1982
A SOLDIER'S STORY   Columbia, 1984
AGNES OF GOD   Columbia, 1985
MOONSTRUCK ★   MGM/UA, 1987
IN COUNTRY   Warner Bros., 1989

HUANG JIANXIN

Contact: China Film Import & Export Office, 2500 Wilshire
    Blvd. - Suite 1028, Los Angeles, CA 90057, 213/380-7520

THE BLACK CANNON INCIDENT   China Film Import &
    Export, 1985, Chinese
THE STAND-IN   China Film Import & Export,
    1987, Chinese
SAMSARA   China Film Import & Export, 1989, Chinese

ORLANDO JIMENEZ-LEAL

EL SUPER   co-director with Leon Ichaso, Columbia, 1979
IMPROPER CONDUCT (FD)   co-director with Nestor
    Almendros, Cinevista/ Promovision International,
    1984, French
THE OTHER CUBA (FD)   Cinevista/Promovision
    International, 1985, French

XIE JIN

b. 1923 - Shaoxing, China
Contact: China Film Import & Export Office, 2500 Wilshire
    Blvd. - Suite 1028, Los Angeles, CA 90057, 213/380-7520

A CRISIS   China Film Import & Export, 1954, Chinese
A WAVE OF UNREST   China Film Import & Export,
    1954, Chinese
RENDEZVOUS AT ORCHARD BRIDGE   China Film Import
    & Export, 1954, Chinese

WOMAN BASKETBALL PLAYER NUMBER 5   China Film
     Import & Export, 1957, Chinese
THE RED DETACHMENT OF WOMEN   China Film
     Import & Export, 1960, Chinese
BIG LI, YOUNG LI, AND OLD LI   China Film Import &
     Export, 1962, Chinese
TWO STAGE SISTERS   China Film Import & Export,
     1964, Chinese
YOUTH   China Film Import & Export, 1977, Chinese
AH, CRADLE   China Film Import & Export, 1980, Chinese
THE LEGEND OF TIANYUAN MOUNTAIN   China Film
     Import & Export, 1981, Chinese
THE HERDSMAN   China Film Import & Export,
     1982, Chinese
QIU JIN   China Film Import & Export, 1983, Chinese
REEDS AT THE FOOT OF THE MOUNTAIN   China Film
     Import & Export, 1984, Chinese
HIBISCUS TOWN   China Film Import & Export,
     1986, Chinese
THE LAST ARISTOCRATS   China Film Import & Export,
     1989, Chinese

ROBERT JIRAS
Contact: Writers Guild of America, East - New York City,
     212/245-6180

I AM THE CHEESE   Libra Cinema 5, 1983

MIKE JITTLOV
THE WIZARD OF SPEED AND TIME   Shapiro
     Glickenhaus Entertainment, 1988

PHIL JOANOU*
b. November 20, 1961
Agent: CAA - Beverly Hills, 213/288-4545

THREE O'CLOCK HIGH   Universal, 1987
U2 RATTLE AND HUM (FD)   Paramount, 1988
STATE OF GRACE   Orion, 1990

ALEJANDRO JODOROWSKY
(Alexandro Jodorowsky)
b. Bolivia

FANDO AND LIS   Cannon, 1970, Mexican
EL TOPO   ABKCO, 1971, Mexican
THE HOLY MOUNTAIN   ABKCO, 1974, Mexican
TUSK   Yank Films-Films 21, 1980, French
SANTA SANGRE   Expanded Entertainment,
     1989, Italian
THE RAINBOW THIEF   Timothy Burrill Productions,
     1990, British

STEVE JODRELL
Contact: Australian Film Commission, 9229 Sunset Blvd.,
     Los Angeles, CA 90069, 213/275-7074

SHAME   Skouras Pictures, 1988, Australian

MICHAEL JOENS
MY LITTLE PONY - THE MOVIE (AF)   DEG, 1986

ARTHUR JOFFE
Contact: French Film Office, 745 Fifth Avenue, New York,
     NY 10151, 212/832-8860

HAREM   Sara Films, 1985, French
LA COMEDIE D'UN JOUR   UGC, 1990, French

MARK JOFFE
Agent: The Brandt Company - Studio City, 818/506-7747

GRIEVOUS BODY HARM   Fries Entertainment,
     1989, Australian
TOY SOLDIERS   Lea Films, 1990, Australian
SPOTSWOOD   Meridian Films, 1991, Australian

ROLAND JOFFE
b. November 1945 - London, England
Business: Lightmotive, 4000 Warner Blvd., Burbank, CA
     91522, 818/954-2976
Agent: The Artists Agency - Los Angeles, 213/277-7779

THE LEGION HALL BOMBING (TF)   BBC, 1978, British
THE SPONGERS (TF)   BBC, 1978, British
NO, MAMA, NO (TF)   Thames TV, 1979, British
UNITED KINGDOM (TF)   BBC, 1981, British
THE KILLING FIELDS ★   Warner Bros., 1984, British
THE MISSION ★   Warner Bros., 1986, British
FAT MAN AND LITTLE BOY   Paramount, 1989

ALAN JOHNSON*
Agent: Jim Lenny, 9701 Wilshire Blvd., Beverly Hills, CA
     90212, 213/271-2174

TO BE OR NOT TO BE   20th Century-Fox, 1983
SOLARBABIES   MGM/UA, 1986

JED JOHNSON
ANDY WARHOL'S BAD   New World, 1977

KENNETH JOHNSON*
b. October 26, 1942 - Pine Bluff, Arkansas
Address: 4528 Colbath Avenue, Sherman Oaks, CA 91423,
     818/905-5255
Agent: Bauer Benedek - Los Angeles, 213/275-2421

THE INCREDIBLE HULK (TF)   Universal TV, 1977
SENIOR TRIP (TF)   Kenneth Johnson Productions, 1981
V (TF)   Kenneth Johnson Productions/Warner
     Bros. TV, 1984
HOT PURSUIT (TF)   Kenneth Johnson Productions/NBC
     Productions, 1984
SHADOW CHASERS (TF)   Kenneth Johnson Productions/
     Brian Grazer Productions/Warner Bros. TV, 1985
THE LIBERATORS (TF)   Kenneth Johnson Productions/
     Walt Disney TV, 1987
SHORT CIRCUIT 2   Tri-Star, 1988
ALIEN NATION (TF)   20th Television Corp., 1989

LAMONT JOHNSON*
b. September 20, 1922 - Stockton, California
Agent: The Brandt Company - Studio City, 818/506-7747

THIN ICE   20th Century-Fox, 1961
A COVENANT WITH DEATH   Warner Bros., 1966
KONA COAST   Warner Bros., 1968
DEADLOCK (TF)   Universal TV, 1969
THE MACKENZIE BREAK   United Artists, 1970
MY SWEET CHARLIE (TF) ☆   Universal TV, 1970
A GUNFIGHT   Paramount, 1971
THE GROUNDSTAR CONSPIRACY   Universal, 1972,
     U.S.-Canadian
YOU'LL LIKE MY MOTHER   Universal, 1972
THAT CERTAIN SUMMER (TF) ☆   Universal TV, 1972
THE LAST AMERICAN HERO   20th Century-Fox, 1973
VISIT TO A CHIEF'S SON   United Artist, 1974
THE EXECUTIONS OF PRIVATE SLOVIK (TF) ☆
     Universal TV, 1974

FEAR ON TRIAL (TF) ☆   Alan Landsburg
    Productions, 1975
LIPSTICK   Paramount, 1976
ONE ON ONE   Warner Bros., 1977
SOMEBODY KILLED HER HUSBAND   Columbia, 1978
PAUL'S CASE (TF)   Learning in Focus, 1979
OFF THE MINNESOTA STRIP (TF)   Cherokee
    Productions/Universal TV, 1980
CATTLE ANNIE AND LITTLE BRITCHES   Universal, 1981
CRISIS AT CENTRAL HIGH (TF)   Time-Life
    Productions, 1981
ESCAPE FROM IRAN: THE CANADIAN CAPER (TF)
    Canamedia Productions, 1981, Canadian
DANGEROUS COMPANY (TF)   The Dangerous
    Company/Finnegan Associates, 1982
LIFE OF THE PARTY: THE STORY OF BEATRICE (TF)
    Welch-Welch Productions/Columbia TV, 1982
SPACEHUNTER: ADVENTURES IN THE FORBIDDEN
    ZONE   Columbia, 1983, Canadian-U.S.
ERNIE KOVACS: BETWEEN THE LAUGHTER (TF) ☆
    ABC Circle Films, 1984
WALLENBERG: A HERO'S STORY (TF) ☆☆   Dick
    Berg-Stonehenge Productions/Paramount TV, 1985
UNNATURAL CAUSES (TF) ☆   Blue Andre Productions/
    ITC Productions, 1986
GORE VIDAL'S LINCOLN (TF) ☆☆   Chris-Rose
    Productions/Finnegan-Pinchuk Company, 1988
THE KENNEDYS OF MASSACHUSETTS (MS) ☆
    Edgar J. Scherick Associates/ Orion TV, 1990
VOICES WITHIN: THE LIVES OF TRUDDI CHASE (TF)
    Itzbinzo Long Productions/P.A. Productions/New
    World TV, 1990

PATRICK READ JOHNSON
Agent: CAA - Beverly Hills, 213/288-4545

SPACED INVADERS   Buena Vista, 1990

JIM JOHNSTON*
Address: 6254 Afton Avenue, Los Angeles, CA 90028,
    213/469-1999
Business: Johnston Films, Inc., 140 East 39th Street,
    New York, NY 10016, 212/683-7500

BLUE DeVILLE (TF)   B & E Enterprises Ltd./NBC
    Productions, 1986

JOE JOHNSTON*
Home: 38 Convent Court, San Rafael, CA 94901,
    415/459-2580
Agent: Favored Artists Agency - Los Angeles,
    213/653-3816

HONEY, I'VE SHRUNK THE KIDS   Buena Vista, 1989

AMY JONES
Agent: ICM - Los Angeles, 213/550-4000

SLUMBER PARTY MASSACRE   Santa Fe, 1982
LOVE LETTERS   New World, 1983
MAID TO ORDER   New Century/Vista, 1987

DAVID JONES*
b. February 19, 1934 - Poole, Dorset, England
Home: 227 Clinton Street, Brooklyn, NY 11201,
    718/834-0810
Agent: Triad Artists, Inc. - Los Angeles, 213/556-2727

BETRAYAL   20th Century-Fox International Classics,
    1983, British
84 CHARING CROSS ROAD   Columbia, 1987, British

THE CHRISTMAS WIFE (CTF)   HBO Showcase, 1988
JACKNIFE   Cineplex Odeon, 1989

EUGENE S. JONES*
Home: 461 Bellagio Terrace, Los Angeles, CA 90049,
    213/476-6375

A FACE OF WAR (FD)   Commonwealth, 1968
TWO MEN OF KARAMOJA   THE WILD AND THE
    BRAVE (FD)   Tomorrow Entertainment, 1974
HIGH ICE (TF)   ESJ Productions, 1980

JAMES CELLAN JONES
(See James CELLAN-JONES)

L.Q. JONES*
Business: 2144 N. Cahuenga Blvd., Hollywood, CA 90068,
    213/463-4426

A BOY AND HIS DOG   Pacific Film Enterprises, 1975

ROBERT JONES
b. November 2, 1942 - Boston, Massachusetts
Business: Still River Films, 1834 Harvard Blvd., Hollywood,
    CA 90027, 213/469-2846
Agent: Fred Amsel & Associates - Beverly Hills,
    213/855-1200

CARRY IT ON (FD)   United Productions of America, 1970
MISSION HILL   Atlantic Releasing Corporation, 1983

TERRY JONES
b. 1942 - Colwyn Bay, Wales
Address: 6 Cambridge Gate, London NW1 4JR, England,
    71/487-4485
Agent: Anne James, Monty Python Office - London,
    71/487-4485

MONTY PYTHON AND THE HOLY GRAIL   co-director with
    Terry Gilliam, Cinema 5, 1974, British
MONTY PYTHON'S LIFE OF BRIAN   Orion/Warner Bros.,
    1979, British
MONTY PYTHON'S THE MEANING OF LIFE   Universal,
    1983, British
PERSONAL SERVICES   Vestron, 1987, British
ERIK THE VIKING   Orion, 1989, British

GLENN JORDAN*
April 5, 1936 - San Antonio, Texas
Agent: CAA - Beverly Hills, 213/288-4545

FRANKENSTEIN (TF)   Dan Curtis Productions, 1973
THE PICTURE OF DORIAN GRAY (TF)   Dan Curtis
    Productions, 1973
SHELL GAME (TF)   Thoroughbred Productions, 1975
ONE OF MY WIVES IS MISSING (TF)   Spelling-Goldberg
    Productions, 1975
DELTA COUNTY, U.S.A. (TF)   Leonard Goldberg
    Productions/Paramount TV, 1977
SUNSHINE CHRISTMAS (TF)   Universal TV, 1977
IN THE MATTER OF KAREN ANN QUINLAN (TF)   Warren
    V. Bush Productions, 1977
THE DISPLACED PERSON (TF)   Learning in Focus, 1977
LES MISERABLES (TF) ☆   Norman Rosemont Productions/
    ITV Entertainment, 1978
SON RISE: A MIRACLE OF LOVE (TF)   Rothman-Wohl
    Productions/Filmways, 1979
THE FAMILY MAN (TF)   Time-Life Productions, 1979
THE WOMEN'S ROOM (TF)   Philip Mandelker Productions/
    Warner Bros. TV, 1980

NEIL SIMON'S ONLY WHEN I LAUGH   Columbia, 1981
THE PRINCESS AND THE CABBIE (TF)   Freyda Rothstein
   Productions/Time-Life Productions, 1981
LOIS GIBBS AND THE LOVE CANAL (TF)   Moonlight
   Productions/Filmways, 1982
THE BUDDY SYSTEM   20th Century Fox, 1984
HEARTSOUNDS (TF)   Embassy TV, 1984
MASS APPEAL   Universal, 1984
TOUGHLOVE (TF)   Fries Entertainment, 1985
DRESS GRAY (TF)   Frank von Zerneck Productions/
   Warner Bros. TV, 1986
PROMISE (TF) ☆☆   Garner-Duchow Productions/Warner
   Bros. TV, 1986
SOMETHING IN COMMON   New World TV/Freyda
   Rothstein Productions/Littke- Grossbart
   Productions, 1986
JOSEPH WAMBAUGH'S ECHOES IN THE DARKNESS
   ECHOES IN THE DARKNESS (MS) ☆   Litke-
   Grossbart Productions/New World TV, 1987
JESSE (TF)   Turman-Foster Company/Jordan Productions/
   Republic Pictures, 1988
HOME FIRES BURNING (TF)   Marian Rees
   Associates, 1989
CHALLENGER (TF)   The IndieProd Company/King
   Phoenix Entertainment/George Englund, Jr.
   Productions, 1990

NEIL JORDAN
b. Sligo, Ireland
Contact: British Academy of Film & TV Arts, 195 Piccadilly,
   London W1, England, 71/734-0022

DANNY BOY   *ANGEL*   Triumph/Columbia, 1983, Irish
THE COMPANY OF WOLVES   Cannon, 1984, British
MONA LISA   Island Pictures, 1986, British
HIGH SPIRITS   Tri-Star, 1988, British
WE'RE NO ANGELS   Paramount, 1989
THE MIRACLE   Miramax Films, 1990, British-U.S.

JON JOST
Address: c/o Hansen, 115 East 92nd Street, New York,
   NY 10128

SPEAKING DIRECTLY: SOME AMERICAN NOTES   Jon
   Jost Films, 1974
ANGEL CITY   Jon Jost Films, 1977
LAST CHANTS FOR A SLOW DANCE   Jon Jost
   Films, 1977
CHAMELEON   Jon Jost Films, 1978
STAGE FRIGHT   Jon Jost Films, 1981
SLOW MOVES   Jon Jost Films, 1983
BELL DIAMOND   Jon Jost Films, 1986
UNCOMMON SENSES   Jon Jost Films, 1987
LAUGHING REMBRANDT   Jon Jost Films, 1988

NATHAN JURAN*
b. September 1, 1907 - Austria
Home: 623 Via Horquilla, Palos Verdes Estates, CA 90274

THE BLACK CASTLE   Universal, 1952
GUNSMOKE   Universal, 1953
LAW AND ORDER   Universal, 1953
THE GOLDEN BLADE   Universal, 1953
TUMBLEWEED   Universal, 1953
HIGHWAY DRAGNET   Allied Artists, 1954
DRUMS ACROSS THE RIVER   Universal, 1954
THE CROOKED WEB   Columbia, 1955
THE DEADLY MANTIS   Universal, 1957
HELLCATS OF THE NAVY   Columbia, 1957
TWENTY MILLION MILES TO EARTH   Columbia, 1957

ATTACK OF THE 50 FOOT WOMAN   Allied Artists, 1958
BRAIN FROM PLANET AROUS   Howco International, 1958
THE 7TH VOYAGE OF SINBAD   Columbia, 1958
GOOD DAY FOR A HANGING   Columbia, 1959
FLIGHT OF THE LOST BALLOON   Woolner Brothers, 1961
JACK THE GIANT KILLER   United Artists, 1962
SIEGE OF THE SAXONS   Columbia, 1963, British
FIRST MEN IN THE MOON   Columbia, 1964, British
EAST OF SUDAN   Columbia, 1964, British
LAND RAIDERS   Columbia, 1970
THE BOY WHO CRIED WEREWOLF   Universal, 1973

PAUL JUSTMAN
GIMME AN F   20th Century Fox, 1984

K

GASTON KABORÉ
b. 1951 - Upper Volta

WEND KUUNI   1982, Burkina Faso
ZAN BOKO   1988, Burkina Faso

GEORGE KACZENDER*
b. April 19, 1933 - Budapest, Hungary
Agent: Tom Chasin, The Chasin Agency - Beverly Hills,
   213/278-7505

DON'T LET THE ANGELS FALL   National Film Board of
   Canada, 1968, Canadian
THE GIRL IN BLUE   *U-TURN*   Cinerama Releasing
   Corporation, 1973, Canadian
IN PRAISE OF OLDER WOMEN   Avco Embassy,
   1978, Canadian
AGENCY   Taft International, 1980, Canadian
YOUR TICKET IS NO LONGER VALID   RSL Productions/
   Ambassador, 1981, Canadian
CHANEL SOLITAIRE   United Film Distribution, 1981,
   French-British
PRETTYKILL   Spectrafilm, 1987, Canadian

HARUKI KADOKAWA
Business: Haruki Kadokawa Films, Inc., 5-24-5, Bunkyo-ku,
   Tokyo, Japan, 03/817-8552 or Kadokawa Productions,
   U.S. Inc., 8981 Sunset Blvd., Los Angeles, CA 90069,
   213/273-5825

THE LAST HERO   Haruki Kadokawa Films,
   1982, Japanese
THE CURTAIN CALL   Haruki Kadokawa Films, 1984,
   Japanese
CABARET   Haruki Kadokawa Films, 1986, Japanese
HEAVEN AND EARTH   Triton Pictures, 1990, Japanese

JEREMY PAUL KAGAN*
b. December 14, 1945 - Mt. Vernon, New York
Agent: Lou Pitt, ICM - Los Angeles, 213/550-4321

UNWED FATHER (TF)   Wolper Productions, 1974
JUDGE DEE AND THE MONASTERY MURDERS (TF)
   ABC Circle Films, 1974
KATHERINE (TF)   The Jozak Company, 1975

HEROES   Universal, 1977
SCOTT JOPLIN   Universal, 1977
THE BIG FIX   Universal, 1978
THE CHOSEN   20th Century-Fox International
     Classics, 1982
THE STING II   Universal, 1983
THE JOURNEY OF NATTY GANN   Buena Vista, 1985
COURAGE (TF)   Highgate Pictures/New
     World TV, 1986
CONSPIRACY: TRIAL OF THE CHICAGO 8 (CTF)
     Jeremy Kagan Productions/Inter Planetary
     Productions, 1987
BIG MAN ON CAMPUS   Vestron, 1989
DESCENDING ANGEL (CTF)   HBO Pictures, 1990

CHEN KAIGE
b. 1952 - Beijing, China
Contact: China Film Import & Export Office, 2500 Wilshire
     Blvd. - Suite 1028, Los Angeles, CA 90057,
     213/380-7520

YELLOW EARTH   China Film Import & Export,
     1984, Chinese
FORCED TAKE-OFF (TF)   1985, Chinese
THE BIG PARADE   China Film Import & Export,
     1986, Chinese
KING OF THE CHILDREN   Orion Classics,
     1988, Chinese
LIFE ON THE STRING   China Film Import & Export,
     1990, Chinese

CONSTANCE KAISERMAN
MY LITTLE GIRL   Hemdale, 1986

JAY KAMEN
b. July 21, 1953 - New York, New York
Home: 3233 DeWitt Drive, Hollywood, CA 90068,
     213/876-4173

TRANSFORMATIONS   Empire Pictures, 1988

STEVEN KAMPMANN
Agent: InterTalent - Los Angeles, 213/271-0600

STEALING HOME   co-director with Will Aldis, Warner
     Bros., 1988
CLIFFORD   Orion, 1991

JEFF KANEW*
Agent: ICM - Los Angeles, 213/550-4000

BLACK RODEO (FD)   Cinerama Releasing
     Corporation, 1972
NATURAL ENEMIES   Cinema 5, 1979
EDDIE MACON'S RUN   Universal, 1983
REVENGE OF THE NERDS   20th Century Fox, 1984
GOTCHA!   Universal, 1985
TOUGH GUYS   Buena Vista, 1986
TROOP BEVERLY HILLS   Columbia/WEG, 1989

MAREK KANIEVSKA *
b. London, England
Agent: Duncan Heath & Associates, 162 Wardour Street,
     London W1, England, 71/439-1471
Business: RSA/USA, 192 Lexington Avenue - 16th Floor,
     New York, NY 10016, 212/725-1900

ANOTHER COUNTRY   Orion Classics, 1984, British
LESS THAN ZERO   20th Century Fox, 1987

GARSON KANIN*
b. November 24, 1912 - Rochester, New York
Business: TFT Corporation, 200 West 57th Street -
     Suite 1203, New York, NY 10019, 212/586-7850

A MAN TO REMEMBER   RKO Radio, 1938
NEXT TIME I MARRY   RKO Radio, 1938
THE GREAT MAN VOTES   RKO Radio, 1939
BACHELOR MOTHER   RKO Radio, 1939
MY FAVORITE WIFE   RKO Radio, 1940
THEY KNEW WHAT THEY WANTED   Columbia, 1940
TOM, DICK AND HARRY   RKO Radio, 1941
THE TRUE GLORY   co-director with Carol Reed,
     Columbia, 1945
WHERE IT'S AT   United Artists, 1969
SOME KIND OF NUT   United Artists, 1969

ALEXIS KANNER
b. May 2, 1952 - Luchon, France
Contact: Screen Actors Guild - Hollywood, 213/465-4600

HELLO THE UNIVERSAL   1982, British
KINGS AND DESPERATE MEN, a hostage incident
     1985, Canadian
DOWNTOWN FARMER   1988

HAL KANTER*
b. December 18, 1918 - Savannah, Georgia
Business Manager: James Harper & Associates, 13063
     Ventura Blvd., Studio City, CA 91604, 818/788-8683

LOVING YOU   Paramount, 1957
I MARRIED A WOMAN   Universal, 1958
ONCE UPON A HORSE   Universal, 1958
FOR THE LOVE OF IT (TF)   Charles Fries Productions/
     Neila Productions, 1980

ED KAPLAN*
Agent: Bill Douglass, ICM - Los Angeles, 213/550-4178

WALKING ON AIR (TF)   WonderWorks, 1987
CHIPS, THE WAR DOG (CTF)   W.G. Productions, 1990

JONATHAN KAPLAN*
b. November 25, 1947 - Paris, France
Agent: CAA - Beverly Hills, 213/288-4545

THE STUDENT TEACHERS   New World, 1973
THE SLAMS   MGM, 1973
TRUCK TURNER   American International, 1974
NIGHT CALL NURSES   New World, 1974
WHITE LINE FEVER   Columbia, 1975
MR. BILLION   20th Century-Fox, 1976
OVER THE EDGE   Orion/Warner Bros., 1979
THE 11TH VICTIM (TF)   Marty Katz Productions/
     Paramount TV, 1979
THE HUSTLER OF MUSCLE BEACH (TF)   Furia-Oringer
     Productions, 1980
THE GENTLEMAN BANDIT (TF)   Highgate
     Pictures, 1981
HEART LIKE A WHEEL   20th Century-Fox, 1983
GIRLS OF THE WHITE ORCHID (TF)   Hill-Mandelker
     Films, 1983
PROJECT X   20th Century Fox, 1987
THE ACCUSED   Paramount, 1988
IMMEDIATE FAMILY   Columbia, 1989
LOVE FIELD   Orion, 1990

NELLY KAPLAN

b. 1936 - Buenos Aires, Argentina
Business: Cythere Films, 34 Avenue Champs Elysees,
    Paris 75008, France, 04/289-0767

GUSTAVE MOREAU (FD) Cythere Films, 1961, French
ABEL GANCE HIER ET DEMAIN (FD) Cythere Films,
    1963, French
LE REGARD PICASSO (FD) Cythere Films, 1966, French
A VERY CURIOUS GIRL LE FIANCEE DU PIRATE
    Regional, 1970, French
PAPA LES PETITS BATEAUX Cythere Films,
    1971, French
NEA NEA - A YOUNG EMMANUELLE Libra,
    1976, French
CHARLES ET LUCIE Nu-Image, 1980, French
ABEL GANCE ET SON NAPOLEON (FD) Cythere Films,
    1983, French
PATTES DE VELOURS (TF) Antenne-2, 1986, French

JANICE KARMAN

THE CHIPMUNK ADVENTURE (AF) Samuel Goldwyn
    Company, 1986

ERIC KARSON*

Business: Karsonfilms, Inc., 11818 Riverside Drive,
    North Hollywood, CA 91607, 818/508-7680
Agent: Mark Lichtman, Shapiro-Lichtman Agency -
    Los Angeles, 213/859-8877

DIRT co-director with Cal Naylor, American
    Cinema, 1979
THE OCTAGON American Cinema, 1980
OPPOSING FORCE HELL CAMP Orion, 1986
BLACK EAGLE Taurus Entertainment, 1988
ANGEL TOWN Taurus Entertainment, 1990

LAWRENCE KASDAN*

b. January 14, 1949 - Miami Beach, Florida
Agent: Bauer Benedek Agency - Beverly Hills,
    213/275-2421

BODY HEAT The Ladd Company/Warner Bros., 1981
THE BIG CHILL Columbia, 1983
SILVERADO Columbia, 1985
THE ACCIDENTAL TOURIST Warner Bros., 1988
I LOVE YOU TO DEATH Tri-Star, 1990

ELLIOTT KASTNER*

b. January 7, 1933 - New York, New York
Business: Pinewood Studios, Iver Heath, Bucks, England,
    075/36-56437

LIKEWISE co-director with Arthur Sherman, Cinema
    Group, 1988

MILTON KATSELAS*

b. December 22, 1933 - Pittsburgh, Pennsylvania
Personal Manager: Ronald Muchnick Personal
    Management - Los Angeles, 213/934-3183
Business: Beverly Hills Playhouse, 254 S. Robertson
    Blvd., Beverly Hills, CA 90211, 213/855-1556

BUTTERFLIES ARE FREE Columbia, 1972
40 CARATS Columbia, 1973
REPORT TO THE COMMISSIONER United Artists, 1975
WHEN YOU COMIN' BACK, RED RYDER?
    Columbia, 1979

STRANGERS: THE STORY OF A MOTHER AND A
    DAUGHTER (TF) Chris-Rose Productions, 1979
THE RULES OF MARRIAGE (TF) Entheos Unlimited
    Productions/Brownstone Productions/20th Century-Fox
    TV, 1982

LEE H. KATZIN*

b. April 12, 1935 - Detroit, Michigan
Home: 13425 Java Drive, Beverly Hills, CA 90210,
    213/278-7726
Agent: Martin Shapiro, Shapiro-Lichtman Agency -
    Los Angeles, 213/859-8877

HONDO AND THE APACHES MGM, 1967
HEAVEN WITH A GUN MGM, 1969
WHAT EVER HAPPENED TO AUNT ALICE? Cinerama
    Releasing Corporation, 1969
THE PHYNX Warner Bros., 1970
LE MANS National General, 1970
ALONG CAME A SPIDER (TF) 20th Century-
    Fox TV, 1970
THE SALZBURG CONNECTION 20th Century-Fox, 1972
VISIONS... (TF) CBS, Inc., 1972
THE VOYAGE OF THE YES (TF) Bing Crosby
    Productions, 1973
THE STRANGER (TF) Bing Crosby Productions, 1973
ORDEAL (TF) 20th Century-Fox TV, 1973
SAVAGES (TF) Spelling-Goldberg Productions, 1974
STRANGE HOMECOMING (TF) Alpine Productions/
    Worldvision, 1974
THE LAST SURVIVORS (TF) Bob Banner
    Associates, 1975
SKY HEI$T (TF) Warner Bros. TV, 1975
QUEST (TF) David Gerber Company/
    Columbia TV, 1976
THE MAN FROM ATLANTIS (TF) Solow Production
    Company, 1977
RELENTLESS (TF) CBS, Inc., 1977
THE BASTARD (TF) Universal TV, 1978
ZUMA BEACH (TF) Edgar J. Scherick Associates/Warner
    Bros. TV, 1978
TERROR OUT OF THE SKY (TF) Alan Landsburg
    Productions, 1978
REVENGE OF THE SAVAGE BEES (TF) 1979
SAMURAI (TF) Danny Thomas Productions/
    Universal TV, 1979
DEATH RAY 2000 (TF) Woodruff Productions/QM
    Productions, 1981
THE NEIGHBORHOOD (TF) David Gerber Company/
    Columbia TV, 1982
AUTOMAN (TF) Kushner-Locke Company/Glen A. Larson
    Productions/20th Century-Fox TV, 1983
SPENSER: FOR HIRE (TF) John Wilder Productions/
    Warner Bros. TV, 1985
THE DIRTY DOZEN: THE DEADLY MISSION (TF)
    MGM-UA TV/Jadran Film, 1987, U.S.-Yugoslavian
WORLD GONE WILD Lorimar, 1988
THE DIRTY DOZEN: THE FATAL MISSION (TF)
    MGM-UA TV, 1988
JAKE SPANNER, PRIVATE EYE (CTF) Andrew J. Fenady
    Productions/ Scotti-Vinnedge TV/USA Network, 1989

JONATHAN KAUFER*

b. March 14, 1955 - Los Angeles, California
Agent: ICM - Los Angeles, 213/550-4000

SOUP FOR ONE Warner Bros., 1982

Ka

FILM
DIRECTORS
GUIDE

**F
I
L
M
D
I
R
E
C
T
O
R
S**

CHARLES KAUFMAN
Agent: Triad Artists, Ltd. - Los Angeles, 213/556-2727

THE SECRET DREAMS OF MONA Q   Troma, 1977
MOTHER'S DAY   United Film Distribution, 1980
WHEN NATURE CALLS   Troma, 1985
JAKARTA   MCEG, 1989, Indonesian- U.S.,
    filmed in 1986

JIM KAUFMAN
b. 1949 - Montreal, Quebec, Canada
Address: 241 Clarke Avenue, Montreal, Quebec H3Z 2E3,
    Canada, 514/931-7463

MAKE MINE CHARTREUSE   1986, U.S.-Canadian
SHADES OF LOVE   1987, Canadian-U.S.
FORGIVING HARRY (TF)   1987, Canadian
THE THRILLER (TF)   3 Themes, 1989, Canadian
BACK STAB   Allegro Films/Westwind, 1990, Canadian
A STAR FOR TWO   Stick Films International/Line
    Productions/Cine-Video Plus, 1991, French-Canadian

LLOYD KAUFMAN
b. November 30, 1945 - New York, New York
Business: Troma, Inc., 733 Ninth Avenue, New York, NY
    10019, 212/757-4555

SQUEEZE PLAY!   co-director with Michael Herz under
    pseudonym of Samuel Weil, Troma, 1980
WAITRESS!   co-director with Michael Herz under
    pseudonym of Samuel Weil, Troma, 1982
STUCK ON YOU!   co-director with Michael Herz under
    pseudonym of Samuel Weil, Troma, 1983
THE FIRST TURN-ON!   co-director with Michael Herz
    under pseudonym of Samuel Weil, Troma, 1984
THE TOXIC AVENGER   co-director with Michael Herz
    under pseudonym of Samuel Weil, Troma, 1984
NUKE 'EM HIGH   CLASS OF NUKE 'EM HIGH
    co-director with Michael Herz under pseudonym
    of Samuel Weil, Troma, 1985
THE TOXIC AVENGER: PART II   co-director with
    Michael Herz under pseudonym of Samuel Weil,
    Troma, 1988
TROMA'S WAR   co-director with Michael Herz under
    pseudonym of Samuel Weil, Troma, 1988
THE TOXIC AVENGER, PART III: THE LAST
    TEMPTATION OF TOXIE co-director with Michael
    Herz, Troma, 1989

PHILIP KAUFMAN*
b. October 23, 1936 - Chicago, Illinois
Agent: CAA - Beverly Hills, 213/288-4545

GOLDSTEIN   co-director with Benjamin Manaster,
    Altura, 1965
FEARLESS FRANK   American International, 1969
THE GREAT NORTHFIELD, MINNESOTA RAID
    Universal, 1972
THE WHITE DAWN   Paramount, 1974
INVASION OF THE BODY SNATCHERS   United
    Artists, 1978
THE WANDERERS   Orion/Warner Bros., 1979
THE RIGHT STUFF   The Ladd Company/Warner
    Bros., 1983
THE UNBEARABLE LIGHTNESS OF BEING
    Orion, 1988
HENRY AND JUNE   Universal, 1990

AKI KAURISMÄKI
b. 1957 - Finland
Business: Villealfa Film Productions, Minna
    Canthinkatu 20, SF-00250, Helsinki, Finland,
    0/41-37-88

CRIME AND PUNISHMENT   Villealfa Film Productions,
    1983, Finnish
CALAMARI UNION   Villealfa Film Productions,
    1985, Finnish
SHADOWS IN PARADISE   Villealfa Film Productions,
    1986, Finnish
HAMLET GOES BUSINESS   Villealfa Film Productions,
    1987, Finnish
ARIEL   Kino International, 1989, Finnish
LENINGRAD COWBOYS GO FINNISH   Villealfa Film
    Productions/ Swedish Film Institute, 1989,
    Finnish-Swedish
I HIRED A CONTRACT KILLER   Villealfa Film Productions/
    Swedish Film Institute, 1990, Finnish-Swedish
THE MATCH FACTORY GIRL   Villealfa Film Productions/
    Swedish Film Institute, 1990, Finnish-Swedish

MIKA KAURISMÄKI
b. 1955 - Finland
Business: Villealfa Film Productions, Minna
    Canthinkatu 20, SF-00250, Helsinki, Finland,
    0/41-37-88

THE WORTHLESS   Villealfa Film Productions,
    1982, Finnish
THE CLAN   Villealfa Film Productions, 1984, Finnish
ROSSO   Villealfa Film Productions, 1985, Finnish
HELSINKI-NAPOLI: ALL NIGHT LONG   Villealfa Film
    Productions, 1987, Finnish
CHA CHA CHA   Villealfa Film Productions/Swedish Film
    Institute, 1989, Finnish-Swedish
PAPER STAR   Villealfa Film Productions/Swedish Film
    Institute, 1990, Finnish-Swedish
AMAZON   Diane Silver Productions/Villealfa Film
    Productions, 1990, U.S.-Finnish-Swiss-French

ANWAR KAWADRI
b. January 17, 1953 - Damascus, Syria
Address: 115 Wendell Road, London W12 9SD, England,
    71/740-1341

SEX WITH THE STARS   ITC, 1980, British
NUTCRACKER   Rank, 1983, British
CLAUDIA'S STORY (TF)   ITC, 1986, British
OUT OF TIME   Alexander's Treasure Projects/Tamido Film
    Productions, 1989, British-Egyptian

GILBERT LEE KAY
b. June 28 - Chicago, Illinois
Home: 105 Barbara Street, Louisville, CO 80027

THREE BAD SISTERS   United Artists, 1956
NOW IT CAN BE TOLD   Toronto-Lisboa
    Productions, 1961
THE SECRET DOOR   Allied Artists, 1961, British
THE TOWER   1965, Spanish
A HARVEST OF EVIL   1966, Spanish
RAGAN   1967, Spanish
WHITE COMANCHE   RKO, 1968, Spanish
DEVIL MAY CARE   1969, Spanish
MAYBE SEPTEMBER   1970, Spanish

JONATHON KAY
Contact: 213/829-5070

WALKING AFTER MIDNIGHT (FD)   Kay's Film
   Productions, 1988, Canadian

ROBERT KAYLOR*
Agent: Michele Wallerstein, Wallerstein Company, Inc. -
   Beverly Hills, 213/859-4804

DERBY (FD)   Cinerama Releasing Corporation, 1971
CARNY   United Artists, 1980
NOBODY'S PERFECT   Moviestore Entertainment, 1990

ELIA KAZAN*
(Elia Kazanjoglou)
b. September 7, 1909 - Constantinople, Turkey
Home: 174 East 95th Street, New York, NY 10128

A TREE GROWS IN BROOKLYN   20th
   Century-Fox, 1945
SEA OF GRASS   20th Century-Fox, 1947
BOOMERANG!   20th Century-Fox, 1947
GENTLEMAN'S AGREEMENT ★★   20th Century-
   Fox, 1947
PINKY   20th Century-Fox, 1949
PANIC IN THE STREETS   20th Century-Fox, 1950
A STREETCAR NAMED DESIRE ★   Warner Bros., 1951
VIVA ZAPATA!   20th Century-Fox, 1952
MAN ON A TIGHTROPE   20th Century-Fox, 1953
ON THE WATERFRONT ★★   Columbia, 1954
EAST OF EDEN ★   Warner Bros., 1955
BABY DOLL   Warner Bros., 1956
A FACE IN THE CROWD   Warner Bros., 1957
WILD RIVER   20th Century-Fox, 1960
SPLENDOR IN THE GRASS   Warner Bros., 1961
AMERICA AMERICA ★   Warner Bros., 1963
THE ARRANGEMENT   Warner Bros., 1969
THE VISITORS   United Artists, 1972
THE LAST TYCOON   Paramount, 1975

JAMES KEACH
Agent: The Gersh Agency - Beverly Hills, 213/274-6611

THE FORGOTTEN (CTF)   Keach-Railsback Productions/
   Wilshire Court Productions, 1989
FALSE IDENTITY   RKO Pavilion/Prism
   Entertainment, 1990

DIANE KEATON
(Diane Hall)
b. January 5, 1949 - Santa Ana, California
Agent: William Morris Agency - Beverly Hills, 213/274-7451

HEAVEN (FD)   Island Pictures, 1987

DON KEESLAR
BOG   Marshall Films, 1978
THE CAPTURE OF GRIZZLY ADAMS (TF)   Sunn Classic
   Productions, 1982

DAVID KEITH*
b. 1954 - Knoxville, Tennessee
Agent: Jim Wiatt, ICM - Los Angeles, 213/550-4000

THE CURSE   Trans World Entertainment, 1987

SACRIFICE   Trans World Entertainment, 1988
THE FURTHER ADVENTURES OF TENNESSEE BUCK
   Trans World Entertainment, 1988

HARVEY KEITH*
Address: 1541 N. Laurel - Suite 202, Los Angeles, CA
   90046, 213/859-5519
Agent: Lauri Apelian, The Chasin Agency - Beverly Hills,
   213/278-7505

MONDO NEW YORK   Fourth and Broadway Films/Island
   Pictures, 1988
JEZEBEL'S KISS   Shapiro Glickenhaus Entertainment,
   1990

ASAAD KELADA*
Agent: Bob Broder, Broder-Kurland-Webb-Uffner Agency -
   Los Angeles, 213/656-9262

THE FACTS OF LIFE GOES TO PARIS (TF)   Embassy
   TV, 1982

FREDERICK KING KELLER
TUCK EVERLASTING   1981
VAMPING   Atlantic Releasing Corporation, 1984
MY DARK LADY   Film Gallery/Artist Entertainment
   Group, 1987

BARNET KELLMAN*
b. November 9, 1947 - New York, New York
Home: 718 Broadway - Apt. 88, New York, NY 10003,
   212/477-2615
Agent: InterTalent - Los Angeles, 213/271-0600

KEY EXCHANGE   TLC Films/20th Century Fox, 1985

GENE KELLY*
(Eugene Curran Kelly)
b. August 23, 1912 - Pittsburgh, Pennsylvania
Contact: Directors Guild of America - Los Angeles,
   213/289-2000

ON THE TOWN   co-director with Stanley Donen,
   MGM, 1949
SINGIN' IN THE RAIN   co-director with Stanley Donen,
   MGM, 1952
IT'S ALWAYS FAIR WEATHER   co-director with Stanley
   Donen, MGM, 1955
INVITATION TO THE DANCE   MGM, 1956
THE HAPPY ROAD   co-director with Noel Howard,
   MGM, 1957
THE TUNNEL OF LOVE   MGM, 1958
GIGOT   20th Century-Fox, 1962
A GUIDE FOR THE MARRIED MAN   20th Century-
   Fox, 1967
HELLO, DOLLY!   20th Century-Fox, 1969
THE CHEYENNE SOCIAL CLUB   National General, 1970
THAT'S ENTERTAINMENT, PART 2   co-director with Jack
   Haley, Jr., MGM/United Artists, 1976

NANCY KELLY
b. March 1953 - North Adams, Massachusetts
Business: Mother Lode Productions, 397 Miller Avenue -
   Suite 1, Mill Valley, CA 94941, 415/381-3573
Attorney: Peter S. Buchanan, 170 Columbus Avenue -
   5th Floor, San Francisco, CA 94133

THOUSAND PIECES OF GOLD   American Playhouse
   Theatrical Films/Maverick Films International/Film Four
   International, 1990

Ke

**F
I
L
M**

**D
I
R
E
C
T
O
R
S**

PATRICK KELLY*
Agent: William Morris Agency - New York, 212/586-5100
Business: Kelly Pictures, Inc., 31 West 21st Street,
New York, NY 10010, 212/929-6176

BEER   Orion, 1985

BURT KENNEDY*
b. September 3, 1922 - Muskegon, Michigan
Home: 13138 Magnolia Blvd., Sherman Oaks, CA 91403,
818/986-8759
Agent: Sanford-Beckett-Skouras & Associates -
Los Angeles, 213/208-2100

THE CANADIANS   20th Century-Fox, 1961
MAIL ORDER BRIDE   MGM, 1963
THE ROUNDERS   MGM, 1965
THE MONEY TRAP   MGM, 1966
RETURN OF THE SEVEN   United Artists, 1966
WELCOME TO HARD TIMES   MGM, 1967
THE WAR WAGON   Universal, 1967
SUPPORT YOUR LOCAL SHERIFF   United Artists, 1969
YOUNG BILLY YOUNG   United Artists, 1969
THE GOOD GUYS AND THE BAD GUYS   Warner
Bros., 1969
DIRTY DINGUS MAGEE   MGM, 1970
SUPPORT YOUR LOCAL GUNFIGHTER   United
Artists, 1971
HANNIE CAULDER   Paramount, 1971, British
THE DESERTER   Paramount, 1971, Italian-Yugoslavian
THE TRAIN ROBBERS   Warner Bros., 1973
SHOOTOUT IN A ONE-DOG TOWN (TF)   Hanna-Barbera
Productions, 1974
SIDEKICKS (TF)   Warner Bros. TV, 1974
ALL THE KIND STRANGERS (TF)   Cinemation TV, 1974
THE KILLER INSIDE ME   Warner Bros., 1976
HOW THE WEST WAS WON (MS)   co-director with Daniel
Mann, MGM TV, 1977
THE RHINEMANN EXCHANGE (MS)   Universal TV, 1977
KATE BLISS & THE TICKER TAPE KID (TF)   Aaron
Spelling Productions, 1978
THE WILD WILD WEST REVISITED (TF)   CBS
Entertainment, 1979
THE CONCRETE COWBOYS (TF)   Frankel Films, 1979
MORE WILD WILD WEST   CBS Entertainment, 1980
WOLF LAKE   *THE HONOR GUARD*   Filmcorp
Distribution, 1981, Canadian
THE ALAMO: 13 DAYS TO GLORY (TF)   Briggle,
Hennessy, Carrothers Productions/The Finnegan
Company/Fries Entertainment, 1987
DOWN THE LONG HILLS (TF)   The Finnegan Company/
Walt Disney TV, 1987
THE TROUBLE WITH SPIES   DEG, 1987
ONCE UPON A TEXAS TRAIN (TF)   CBS
Entertainment, 1988
WHERE THE HELL'S THAT GOLD?!! (TF)   Willie Nelson
Productions/ Brigade Productions/Konigsberg-Sanitsky
Company, 1988

MICHAEL KENNEDY
b. 1954 - Prince Edward Island, Canada

CARIBE   Miramax Films, 1988, Canadian
ERIK   Miramax Films, 1989, Canadian

TOM KENNEDY*
Agent: Mitch Kaplan, Kaplan-Stahler Agency -
Beverly Hills, 213/653-4483

TIME WALKER   New World, 1983

GARY KENT
RAINY DAY FRIENDS   Powerdance Films, 1985

IRVIN KERSHNER*
b. April 29, 1923 - Philadelphia, Pennsylvania
Agent: CAA - Beverly Hills, 213/288-4545

STAKEOUT ON DOPE STREET   Warner Bros., 1958
THE YOUNG CAPTIVES   Paramount, 1959
THE HOODLUM PRIEST   United Artists, 1961
A FACE IN THE RAIN   Embassy, 1963
THE LUCK OF GINGER COFFEY   Continental,
1964, Canadian
A FINE MADNESS   Warner Bros., 1966
THE FLIM-FLAM MAN   20th Century-Fox, 1967
LOVING   Columbia, 1970
UP THE SANDBOX   National General, 1972
S*P*Y*S   20th Century-Fox, 1974, British-U.S.
THE RETURN OF A MAN CALLED HORSE   United
Artists, 1976
RAIN ON ENTEBBE (TF) ☆   Edgar J. Scherick Associates/
20th Century-Fox TV, 1977
EYES OF LAURA MARS   Columbia, 1978
THE EMPIRE STRIKES BACK   20th Century-Fox, 1980
NEVER SAY NEVER AGAIN   Warner Bros., 1983
TRAVELING MAN (CTF) ☆   HBO Pictures, 1989
ROBOCOP 2   Orion, 1990

BRUCE KESSLER*
b. March 23, 1936 - California
Home: 4335 Marina City Drive - Apt. 740, Marina del Rey,
CA 90292, 213/823-2394
Agent: The Cooper Agency - Los Angeles, 213/277-8422

ANGELS FROM HELL   American International, 1968
KILLERS THREE   American International, 1968
THE GAY DECEIVERS   Fanfare, 1969
SIMON, KING OF WITCHES   Fanfare, 1971
MURDER IN PEYTON PLACE (TF)   20th Century-
Fox TV, 1977
THE TWO-FIVE (TF)   Universal TV, 1978
DEATH MOON (TF)   Roger Gimbel Productions/
EMI TV, 1978
CRUISE INTO TERROR (TF)   Aaron Spelling
Productions, 1978

MUSTAPHA KHAN
IMAGINING AMERICA (TF)   co-director with Ralph Bakshi,
Matt Mahurin & Ed Lachman, Vanguard Films, 1989

MICHEL KHLEIFI
b. Palestine
Contact: National Tourist Office, 61 Rue de Marche Aux
Herbes, B1000 Brussels, Belgium, 02/513-8940

LA MEMOIRE FERTILE (FD)   1980, Belgian
WEDDING IN GALILEE   Kino International, 1987,
Belgian-French- West German
ANTHEM OF THE STONES   1990, Belgian

MICHAEL KIDD*
b. August 12, 1919 - Brooklyn, New York
Agent: William Morris Agency - Beverly Hills,
213/274-7451

MERRY ANDREW   MGM, 1958

FRITZ KIERSCH
b. July, 1951 - Alpine, Texas
Agent: Larry Becsey, The Agency - Los Angeles,
   213/551-3000

CHILDREN OF THE CORN   New World, 1984
TUFF TURF   New World, 1985
WINNERS TAKE ALL   Apollo Pictures, 1987
UNDER THE BOARDWALK   New World, 1989
FATAL CHARM   New Line Cinema, 1990

KRZYSZTOF KIESLOWSKI
Contact: Ministry of Culture and Arts, Cinematography
   Authority, Krakowskie Przedmiecie 21/23, 00071
   Warsaw, Poland, tel.: 268072

DEKALOG (MS)   Polish TV/Sender Freies Berlin, 1990,
   Polish-West German
CITY LIFE (FD)   co-director, Nederlands Film Museum/
   International Art Film, 1990, Dutch

GERARD KIKOINE
DRAGONARD   Cannon, 1987, British
MASTER OF DRAGONARD HILL   Cannon, 1988, British
EDGE OF SANITY   Millimeter Films, 1989,
   British-Hungarian
BURIED ALIVE   The Movie Group, 1989, British

BRUCE KIMMEL*
b. December 8, 1947 - Los Angeles, California
Home: 3680 Fredonia Drive, Los Angeles, CA 90068,
   213/874-1571
Agent: Tim Stone, Stone-Manners Agency - Los Angeles,
   213/275-9599

THE FIRST NUDIE MUSICAL   co-director with Mark
   Haggard, Paramount, 1976
SPACESHIP *THE CREATURE WASN'T NICE*   Almi
   Cinema 5, 1982

JOHN KINCADE
TERMINAL ENTRY   United Film Distribution, 1987
BACK TO BACK   Concorde, 1990

TIM KINCAID
ESCAPE FROM BAD GIRLS DORMITORY   Films Around
   the World, 1985
BREEDERS   Empire Pictures, 1986
MUTANT HUNT   Tycin Entertainment, 1986
ROBOT HOLOCAUST   Tycin Entertainment, 1987
THE OCCULTIST   Urban Classics, 1989
SHE'S BACK   Vestron, 1989

ALLAN KING
b. 1930 - Vancouver, British Columbia, Canada
Business: Allan King Associates Ltd., 965 Bay Street -
   Suite 2209, Toronto, Ontario M5S 2A3, Canada,
   416/962-0181
Agent: Triad Artists, Inc. - Los Angeles, 213/556-2727 or:
   Great North Artists Management Inc., 345 Adelaide
   Street West - Suite 500, Toronto, Ontario M5V 1R5,
   416/593-2587

PEMBERTON VALLEY (FD)   CBC, 1957, Canadian
A MATTER OF PRIDE (FD)   CBC, 1961, Canadian
COMING OF AGE IN IBIZA *RUNNING AWAY BACK-
   WARDS* (FD)   CBC, 1964, Canadian
WARRENDALE (FD)   Grove Press, 1968, Canadian

A MARRIED COUPLE (FD)   Aquarius, 1970, Canadian
COME ON CHILDREN (FD)   Allan King Associates,
   1972, Canadian
WHO HAS SEEN THE WIND   Astral Bellevue,
   1977, Canadian
MARIA (TF)   CBC, 1977, Canadian
ONE-NIGHT STAND   Janus, 1978, Canadian
SILENCE OF THE NORTH   Universal, 1981, Canadian
READY FOR SLAUGHTER (TF)   CBC, 1983, Canadian
THE LAST SEASON (TF)   1986, Canadian
TERMINI STATION   Astral Bellevue Pathe,
   1989, Canadian

RICK KING*
Home: 143 Ocean Park Blvd., Santa Monica, CA 90405,
   213/399-9219
Agent: Toby Jaffe, Leading Artists - Beverly Hills,
   213/858-1999

HARD CHOICES   Lorimar, 1986
HOTSHOT   International Film Marketing, 1987
THE KILLING TIME   New World, 1987
FORCED MARCH   A-Pix, 1989
PRAYER OF THE ROLLERBOYS   Gaga America/Fox-
   Lorber Associates/Academy Entertainment,
   1990, U.S.-Japanese

STEPHEN KING
b. 1947 - Maine
Agent: CAA - Beverly Hills, 213/288-4545

MAXIMUM OVERDRIVE   DEG, 1986

ZALMAN KING*
Agent: Triad Artists, Inc. - Los Angeles, 213/556-2727

WILDFIRE   Zupnick Enterprises/Jody Ann
   Productions, 1987
TWO MOON JUNCTION   Lorimar, 1988
WILD ORCHID   Triumph Releasing Corporation, 1990

ALAN KINGSBERG
Agent: Scott Yoselow, The Gersh Agency - New York City,
   212/997-1818

ALMOST PARTNERS (TF)   South Carolina Educational TV
   Network, 1987

RICHARD KINON*
Agent: Alan Greenspan, ICM - Los Angeles, 213/550-4000

THE LOVE BOAT (TF)   co-director with Alan Myerson,
   Douglas S. Cramer Productions, 1976
THE NEW LOVE BOAT (TF)   Douglas S. Cramer
   Productions, 1977
ALOHA PARADISE (TF)   Aaron Spelling Productions, 1981

KLAUS KINSKI
PAGANINI   Medusa, 1989, Italian

ROBERT KIRK*
Address: 11693 San Vicente Blvd. - Suite 234, Los Angeles,
   CA 90049, 213/653-9060
Agent: Spyros Skouras, Sanford-Beckett-Skouras &
   Associates - Los Angeles, 213/208-2100

DESTROYER   Moviestore Entertainment, 1988

Ki

FILM
DIRECTORS
GUIDE

F
I
L
M

D
I
R
E
C
T
O
R
S

161

EPHRAIM KISHON

Contact: Israel Film Centre, Ministry of Industry & Trade,
30 Agron Street, P.O. Box 299, Jerusalem 94190,
Israel, 02/210297

SALLAH   Palisades International, 1963, Israeli
THE BIG DIG   Canal, 1969, Israeli
THE POLICEMAN   Cinema 5, 1972, Israeli
ERVINKA   1974, Israeli
FOX IN THE CHICKEN COOP   Hashu'alim Ltd.,
1978, Israeli
THE MARRIAGE CONTRACT (TF)   1983, West German

R. J. KIZER

b. September 27, 1952 - Long Island City, New York
Home: 3267 Deronda Drive, Los Angeles, CA 90068,
213/469-3321

GODZILLA 1985   co-director with Kohji Yamamoto,
New World, 1985, Japanese-U.S.
HELL COMES TO FROGTOWN   co-director with
Donald G. Jackson, New World, 1987

ROBERT KLANE*

Agent: ICM - Los Angeles, 213/550-4000

THANK GOD IT'S FRIDAY   Columbia, 1978

DENNIS KLEIN

Agent: Leading Artists - Beverly Hills, 213/858-1999

ONE MORE SATURDAY NIGHT   Columbia, 1986

WILLIAM KLEIN

b. 1926 - New York, New York
Address: 9 Rue Falguiere, 75015 Paris, France,
04/326-9376
Contact: French Film Office, 745 Fifth Avenue, New York,
NY 10151, 212/832-8860

QUI ETES-VOUS POLLY MAGGOO?   1966, French
FAR FROM VIETNAM (FD)   co-director with Jean-Luc
Godard, Joris Ivens, Alain Resnais & Agnes Varda,
New Yorker, 1967, French
MISTER FREEDOM   1969, French
FLOAT LIKE A BUTTERFLY - STING LIKE A BEE (FD)
Delpire Advico/Films Paris-New York, 1969, French
FESTIVAL PANAFRICAIN (FD)   1969, French
ELDRIDGE CLEAVER (FD)   1970, French
LE COUPLE TEMOIN   Planfilm, 1977, French
THE FRENCH (FD)   AAA, 1981, French
MODE IN FRANCE (FD)   KVIV Productions, 1985, French

RANDAL KLEISER*

b. July 20, 1946
Agent: Jim Wiatt, ICM - Los Angeles, 213/550-4000
Business: Randal Kleiser Productions, 3050 Runyan
Canyon Road, Los Angeles, CA 90046, 213/850-5511

ALL TOGETHER NOW (TF)   RSO Films, 1975
DAWN: PORTRAIT OF A TEENAGE RUNAWAY (TF)
Douglas S. Cramer Productions, 1976
THE BOY IN THE PLASTIC BUBBLE (TF)   Spelling-
Goldberg Productions, 1976
THE GATHERING (TF) ☆   Hanna-Barbera
Productions, 1977
GREASE   Paramount, 1978
THE BLUE LAGOON   Columbia, 1980
SUMMER LOVERS   Filmways, 1982

GRANDVIEW, U.S.A.   Warner Bros., 1984
FLIGHT OF THE NAVIGATOR   Buena Vista, 1986
BIG TOP PEE-WEE   Paramount, 1988
GETTING IT RIGHT   MCEG, 1989, U.S.-British
WHITE FANG   Buena Vista, 1990

MAX J. KLEVEN*

Home: 2.2 Ranch, 33150 Barber Road, Agua Dulce, CA
91350, 805/268-1681

RUCKUS   International Vision Productions, 1982
THE NIGHT STALKER   PSO, 1987
BORDER HEAT   MCEG, 1988
W.B., BLUE AND THE BEAN   The Movie Group, 1988

ELEM KLIMOV

b. 1933 - Volgograd, U.S.S.R.
Contact: Union of Soviet Filmmakers, Vassilievskaya 13,
Moscow, U.S.S.R., tel.: 250-4114

WELCOME, OR NO ENTRY FOR UNAUTHORIZED
PERSONS   1964, Soviet
ADVENTURES OF A DENTIST   1965, Soviet
SPORT, SPORT, SPORT   1971, Soviet
AND NONETHELESS I BELIEVE   co-director, 1974, Soviet
LARISSA (FD)   1980, Soviet
RASPUTIN   *AGONIYA*   International Film Exchange,
1982, Soviet
FAREWELL TO MATYORA   International Film Exchange,
1982, Soviet
COME AND SEE   International Film Exchange,
1985, Soviet

HERBERT KLINE*

b. March 13, 1909 - Chicago, Illinois
Home: 1280 N. Laurel Avenue, Los Angeles, CA 90046,
213/650-1437 or: 42 Beak Street, London, England,
01/439-3654
Business: Eagle Films, 236 West 27th Street, New York, NY
10001, 212/675-1339

CRISIS (FD)   1938
LIGHTS OUT IN EUROPE (FD)   1939
THE FORGOTTEN VILLAGE (FD)   1941
MY FATHER'S HOUSE (FD)   Mayer-Burstyn, 1946
THE KID FROM CLEVELAND   Republic, 1949
THE FIGHTER   United Artists, 1951
JACK LONDON'S TALES OF ADVENTURE (TF)   1952
WALLS OF FIRE (FD)   Mentor Productions, 1974
THE CHALLENGE: A TRIBUTE TO MODERN ART (FD)
New Line Cinema, 1975
ACTING: LEE STRASBERG AND THE ACTORS STUDIO
(FD)   Davada Enterprises, 1981
GREAT THEATRES OF THE WORLD (FD)   1987

STEVE KLOVES

Agent: Bauer Benedek Agency - Beverly Hills, 213/275-2421

THE FABULOUS BAKER BOYS   20th Century Fox, 1989

ROBERT KNIGHTS

b. 1942
Address: The Top Flat, 41 Lancaster Lane, Hampstead
NW3 4HB, England
Agent: Duncan Heath & Associates, 162/170 Wardour Street,
London W1V 3AT, England, 71/439-1471

A BIT OF SINGING AND DANCING (TF)   Granada TV/
WGBH-Boston, 1981, British-U.S.
THE EBONY TOWER (TF)   Granada TV, 1984, British

TENDER IS THE NIGHT (CMS)   Showtime/BBC/Seven
Network, 1985, U.S.- British-Australian
PORTERHOUSE BLUE (MS)   Picture Partnership
Productions/Channel Four, 1987, British
THE OLD JEST (TF)   Lawson Productions/Television
South, 1988, British
THE DAWNING (TF)   TVS Entertainment/Vista
Organization, 1988, British
AND A NIGHTINGALE SANG (TF)   Portman Productions/
Tyne Tees TV, 1988, British

MASAKI KOBAYASHI
b. February 14, 1916 - Otaru City, Hokkaido, Japan
Contact: Directors Guild of Japan, Tsukada Building,
8-33 Ugagawa-cho, Shibuya-ku, Tokyo 150, Japan,
3/461-4411

MY SONS' YOUTH   Shochiku, 1952, Japanese
SINCERITY   Shochiku, 1953, Japanese
THE THICK-WALLED ROOM   Shochiku,
1953, Japanese
THREE LOVES   Shochiku, 1954, Japanese
SOMEWHERE BENEATH THE WIDE SKY   Shochiku,
1954, Japanese
BEAUTIFUL DAYS   Shochiku, 1955, Japanese
THE SPRING   Shochiku, 1956, Japanese
I'LL BUY YOU   Shochiku, 1956, Japanese
BLACK RIVER   Shochiku, 1957, Japanese
THE HUMAN CONDITION, PART I (NO GREATER LOVE)
Shochiku, 1959, Japanese
THE HUMAN CONDITION, PART II (ROAD TO ETERNITY)
Shochiku, 1959, Japanese
THE HUMAN CONDITION, PART III (A SOLDIER'S
PRAYER)   Shochiku, 1961, Japanese
THE INHERITANCE   Shochiku, 1962, Japanese
HARAKIRI *SEPPUKU*   Shochiku, 1962, Japanese
KWAIDAN   Continental, 1964, Japanese
REBELLION *SAMURAI REBELLION*   Toho,
1967, Japanese
HYMN TO A TIRED MAN   Toho, 1968, Japanese
INN OF EVIL   Toho, 1971, Japanese
FOSSILS (MS)   Fuji TV, 1975, Japanese
FIERY AUTUMN   Toho, 1978, Japanese
THE TOKYO TRIAL (FD)   Kodansha Ltd.,
1984, Japanese
THE EMPTY TABLE   Marugen/Herald Ace, 1985,
Japanese

HOWARD W. KOCH*
b. April 11, 1916 - New York, New York
Business: 5555 Melrose Avenue, Hollywood, CA 90038,
213/468-5996

SHIELD FOR MURDER   co-director with Edmond O'Brien,
United Artists, 1954
BIG HOUSE, U.S.A.   United Artists, 1955
UNTAMED YOUTH   Warner Bros., 1957
BOP GIRL   United Artists, 1957
JUNGLE HEAT   United Artists, 1957
THE GIRL IN BLACK STOCKINGS   United Artists, 1957
FORT BOWIE   United Artists, 1958
VIOLENT ROAD   Warner Bros., 1958
FRANKENSTEIN - 1970   Allied Artists, 1958
ANDY HARDY COMES HOME   MGM, 1958
THE LAST MILE   United Artists, 1959
BORN RECKLESS   Warner Bros., 1959
BADGE 373   Paramount, 1973

OJA KODAR
Contact: Bill Krohn - Los Angeles, 213/969-9074

JADED   Olpal Productions, 1989

PANCHO KOHNER
b. January 7, 1939 - Los Angeles, California
Contact: Writers Guild of America, West - Los Angeles,
213/550-1000

THE BRIDGE IN THE JUNGLE   United Artists,
1971, Mexican
MR. SYCAMORE   Film Ventures International, 1975

AMOS KOLLEK
b. Israel
Contact: Israel Film Centre, Ministry of Industry & Trade,
30 Agron Street, P.O. Box 299, Jerusalem, Israel,
02/210297

WORLDS APART   1980, Israeli
GOODBYE NEW YORK   Castle Hill Productions,
1985, U.S.-Israeli
FOREVER, LULU   Tri-Star, 1987
HIGH STAKES   Vidmark Entertainment, 1989

JAMES KOMACK*
b. August 3, 1930 - New York, New York
Agent: ICM - Los Angeles, 213/550-4000
Business Manager: Marvin "Dusty" Snyder, Oppenheim,
Appel, Dixon & Co., 2029 Century Park East - Suite 1300,
Los Angeles, CA 90067, 213/277-0400

PORKY'S REVENGE   20th Century Fox, 1985,
U.S.-Canadian

ANDREI KONCHALOVSKY*
(Andrei Mikhalkov-Konchalovsky)
b. August 20, 1937 - U.S.S.R.
Agent: CAA - Beverly Hills, 213/288-4545

A BOY AND A PIGEON   Mosfilm, 1960, Soviet
THE FIRST TEACHER   Mosfilm/Kirghizfilm, 1965, Soviet
ASYA'S HAPPINESS   Mosfilm, 1967, Soviet
A NEST OF GENTRY   Corinth, 1969, Soviet
UNCLE VANYA   Mosfilm, 1971, Soviet
A LOVER'S ROMANCE   Mosfilm, 1974, Soviet
SIBERIADE   IFEX Film, 1979, Soviet
MARIA'S LOVERS   Cannon, 1984
RUNAWAY TRAIN   Cannon, 1985
DUET FOR ONE   Cannon, 1986
SHY PEOPLE   Cannon, 1987
HOMER AND EDDIE   Skouras Pictures, 1989
TANGO & CASH   Warner Bros., 1989

JACKIE KONG
Contact: Bob Brenner, Esq. - Los Angeles, 213/553-2525

THE BEING   BFV Films, 1983
NIGHT PATROL   New World, 1984
THE UNDERACHIEVERS   Lightning Pictures, 1987
BLOOD DINER   Vestron, 1987

BARBARA KOPPLE*
Business: Cabin Creek Films, 58 East 11th Street, New York,
NY 10003, 212/533-7157

HARLAN COUNTY, U.S.A. (FD)   Cabin Creek Films, 1976
KEEPING ON (TF)   Many Mansions Institute, 1983

JOHN KORTY*

b. July 22, 1936 - Lafayette, Indiana
Agent: Bob Wunsch, Richland /Wunsch Agency -
    Los Angeles, 213/278-1955
Business: Korty Films, Inc., 200 Miller Avenue, Mill Valley,
    CA 94941, 415/383-6900

CRAZY QUILT   Farallon, 1965
FUNNYMAN   New Yorker, 1967
RIVERRUN   Columbia, 1970
THE PEOPLE (TF)   Metromedia Productions/American
    Zoetrope, 1972
GO ASK ALICE (TF)   Metromedia Productions, 1973
CLASS OF '63 (TF)   Metromedia Productions/Stonehenge
    Productions, 1973
SILENCE   Cinema Financial of America, 1974
THE AUTOBIOGRAPHY OF MISS JANE
    PITTMAN (TF) ☆☆   Tomorrow Entertainment, 1974
THE MUSIC SCHOOL (TF)   Learning in Focus, 1975
ALEX & THE GYPSY   20th Century-Fox, 1976
FAREWELL TO MANZANAR (TF)   Korty Films/
    Universal TV, 1976
WHO ARE THE DE BOLTS? ...AND WHERE DID
    THEY GET 19 KIDS? (FD)   Pyramid Films, 1977
FOREVER (TF)   Roger Gimbel Productions/EMI TV, 1978
OLIVER'S STORY   Paramount, 1979
A CHRISTMAS WITHOUT SNOW (TF)   Korty Films/The
    Konigsberg Company, 1980
TWICE UPON A TIME (AF)   co-director with Charles
    Swenson, The Ladd Company/Warner Bros., 1983
THE HAUNTING PASSION (TF)   BSR Productions/
    ITC, 1983
SECOND SIGHT: A LOVE STORY (TF)   Entheos
    Unlimited Productions/T.T.C. Enterprises, 1984
THE EWOK ADVENTURE (TF)   Lucasfilm Ltd./Korty
    Films, 1984
A DEADLY BUSINESS (TF)   Thebaut-Frey Productions/
    Taft Entertainment TV, 1986
RESTING PLACE (TF) ☆   Marian Rees Associates, 1986
BABY GIRL SCOTT (TF)   Polson Company Productions/
    The Finnegan-Pinchuk Company, 1987
EYE ON THE SPARROW (TF)   Sarabande Productions/
    Republic Pictures, 1987
WINNIE (TF)   All Girls Productions/NBC
    Productions, 1988
CAST THE FIRST STONE (TF)   Mench Productions/
    Columbia TV, 1989
A SON'S PROMISE (TF)   Marian Rees Associates, 1990

WALDEMAR KORZENIOWSKY

THE CHAIR   Angelika Films, 1987

TOM KOTANI

THE LAST DINOSAUR (TF)   co-director with
    Alex Grasshoff, Rankin-Bass Productions, 1977,
    U.S.-Japanese
THE BERMUDA DEPTHS (TF)   Rankin-Bass
    Productions, 1978
THE IVORY APE (TF)   Rankin-Bass Productions, 1980,
    U.S.-Japanese
THE BUSHIDO BLADE   Aquarius, 1982, U.S.-Japanese

TED KOTCHEFF*

b. April 7, 1931 - Toronto, Canada
Agent: CAA - Beverly Hills, 213/288-4545

TIARA TAHITI   Zenith International, 1962, British
LIFE AT THE TOP   Columbia, 1965, British
TWO GENTLEMEN SHARING   American International,
    1969, British

OUTBACK   *WAKE IN FRIGHT*   United Artists,
    1971, Australian
BILLY TWO HATS   United Artists, 1972, British
THE APPRENTICESHIP OF DUDDY KRAVITZ   Paramount,
    1974, Canadian
FUN WITH DICK & JANE   Columbia, 1977
WHO IS KILLING THE GREAT CHEFS OF EUROPE?
    Warner Bros., 1978
NORTH DALLAS FORTY   Paramount, 1979
SPLIT IMAGE   Orion, 1982
FIRST BLOOD   Orion, 1982, Canadian
UNCOMMON VALOR   Paramount, 1983
JOSHUA THEN AND NOW   20th Century Fox,
    1985, Canadian
SWITCHING CHANNELS   Columbia, 1988
WINTER PEOPLE   Columbia, 1989
WEEKEND AT BERNIE'S   20th Century Fox, 1989

YAPHET KOTTO

b. November 15, 1937 - New York, New York
Agent: The Artists Group - Los Angeles, 213/552-1100

THE LIMIT   *TIME LIMIT/SPEED LIMIT 65*   Cannon, 1972
NIGHTMARES OF THE DEVIL   Edgewood
    Productions, 1988

JIM KOUF

Agent: Jim Wyatt, ICM - Los Angeles,
    213/550-4000

MIRACLES   Orion, 1986
DISORGANIZED CRIME   Buena Vista, 1989

STEVEN KOVACS

'68   New World, 1988

BERNARD L. KOWALSKI*

August 2, 1929 - Brownsville, Texas
Home: 17524 Community Street, Northridge, CA 91324,
    818/987-2433
Agent: Irv Schechter, Irv Schechter Company - Beverly Hills,
    213/278-8070

HOT CAR GIRL   Allied Artists, 1958
NIGHT OF THE BLOOD BEAST   American
    International, 1958
THE GIANT LEECHES   American International, 1959
BLOOD AND STEEL   20th Century-Fox, 1959
KRAKATOA, EAST OF JAVA   Cinerama Releasing
    Corporation, 1969
STILETTO   Avco Embassy, 1969
MACHO CALLAHAN   Avco Embassy, 1970
HUNTERS ARE FOR KILLING (TF)   1970
TERROR IN THE SKY (TF)   Paramount TV, 1971
BLACK NOON (TF)   Fenady Associates/Screen
    Gems, 1971
WOMEN IN CHAINS (TF)   Paramount TV, 1972
TWO FOR THE MONEY (TF)   Aaron Spelling
    Productions, 1972
THE WOMAN HUNTER (TF)   Bing Crosby
    Productions, 1972
SHE CRIED MURDER (TF)   1973
Sssssss   Universal, 1973
IN TANDEM (TF)   D'Antoni Productions, 1974
FLIGHT TO HOLOCAUST (TF)   Aycee Productions/First
    Artists, 1977
THE NATIVITY (TF)   D'Angelo-Bullock-Allen Productions/
    20th Century-Fox TV, 1978
MARCIANO (TF)   ABC Circle Films, 1979
B.A.D. CATS (TF)   Aaron Spelling Productions, 1980

TURNOVER SMITH (TF)   Wellington Productions, 1980
NIGHTSIDE (TF)   Stephen J. Cannell Productions/Glen A.
   Larson Productions/ Universal TV, 1980
MIRACLE AT BEEKMAN'S PLACE (TF)   Em/BE
   Productions, 1988
NASHVILLE BEAT (CTF)   Buck Productions/RDK
   Productions/NAC Productions, 1989

JERRY KRAMER*
Contact: Directors Guild of America - Los Angeles,
   213/289-2000

MODERN GIRLS   Atlantic Releasing Corporation, 1986
MOONWALKER   co-director with Colin Chilvers, Warner
   Bros., 1988

ROBERT KRAMER
b. June, 1939 - New York, New York
Contact: French Film Office, 745 Fifth Avenue, New York,
   NY 10151, 212/832-8860

FALN (FD)   1965
IN THE COUNTRY   Newsreel, 1968
THE EDGE   Film-Makers, 1968
PEOPLE'S WAR (FD)   co-director, Newsreel, 1969
ICE   New Yorker, 1970
MILESTONES   co-director with John Douglas,
   Stone, 1975
SCENES FROM THE PORTUGUESE CLASS
   STRUGGLE (FD)   1977
GUNS   S.N.D., 1980, French
BIRTH   1982, French
A TOUT ALLURE   INA, 1982, French
UNSER NAZI   Cannon International, 1984,
   West German-French
DIESEL   Distributeurs Associes, 1985, French
ACROSS THE HEART   Films du Passage/Garance,
   1987, French
DOC'S KINGDOM   Garance/Filmargem, 1988, French

STANLEY KRAMER*
b. September 29, 1913 - New York, New York
Home: 12386 Ridge Circle, Los Angeles, CA 90049,
   213/472-0065
Agent: Paul Kohner, Inc. - Los Angeles, 213/550-1060

NOT AS A STRANGER   United Artists, 1955
THE PRIDE AND THE PASSION   United Artists, 1957
THE DEFIANT ONES ★   United Artists, 1958
ON THE BEACH   United Artists, 1959
INHERIT THE WIND   United Artists, 1960
JUDGMENT AT NUREMBERG ★   United Artists, 1961
IT'S A MAD, MAD, MAD, MAD WORLD   United
   Artists, 1963
SHIP OF FOOLS   Columbia, 1965
GUESS WHO'S COMING TO DINNER ★   Columbia, 1967
THE SECRET OF SANTA VITTORIA   United Artists, 1969
R.P.M.*   Columbia, 1970
BLESS THE BEASTS & CHILDREN   Columbia, 1971
OKLAHOMA CRUDE   Columbia, 1973
THE DOMINO PRINCIPLE   Avco Embassy, 1977
THE RUNNER STUMBLES   20th Century-Fox, 1979

ALEXIS KRASILOVSKY
b. July 5, 1950 - Juneau, Alaska
Business: Rafael Film, P.O. Bos 3091, Los Angeles, CA
   90051, 213/662-5746

END OF THE ART WORLD   Rafael Film, 1971
BLOOD   Rafael Film, 1975

CREATED AND CONSUMED BY LIGHT   Rafael Film, 1976
CHILDBIRTH DREAM   Rafael Film, 1978
BEALE STREET (TF)   co-director, Real to Reel
   Productions, 1978
EXILE   Rafael Film, 1984

PAUL KRASNY*
b. August 8, 1935 - Cleveland, Ohio
Agent: Barry Perelman Agency - Los Angeles, 213/274-5999
Business: Pako Films Ltd., 3620 Goodland Drive, Studio City,
   CA 91604, 818/506-4200

THE D.A.: CONSPIRACY TO KILL (TF)   Universal TV/Mark
   VII Ltd., 1971
THE ADVENTURES OF NICK CARTER (TF)   Universal
   TV, 1972
THE LETTERS (TF)   co-director with Gene Nelson, ABC
   Circle Films, 1973
CHRISTINA   International Amusements, 1974
BIG ROSE (TF)   20th Century-Fox TV, 1974
JOE PANTHER   Artists Creation & Associates, 1976
CENTENNIAL (MS)   co-director with Harry Falk, Bernard
   McEveety & Virgil Vogel, Universal TV, 1978
THE ISLANDER (TF)   Universal TV, 1978
WHEN HELL WAS IN SESSION (TF)   Aubrey-Hamner
   Productions, 1979
240-ROBERT (TF)   Rosner TV/Filmways TV
   Productions, 1979
ALCATRAZ: THE WHOLE SHOCKING STORY (TF)   Pierre
   Cossette Productions, 1980
FUGITIVE FAMILY (TF)   Aubrey-Hamner Productions, 1980
TERROR AMONG US (TF)   David Gerber Company, 1981
FLY AWAY HOME (TF)   An Lac Productions/Warner
   Bros. TV, 1981
TIME BOMB (TF)   Barry Weitz Films/Universal TV, 1984
STILL CRAZY LIKE A FOX (TF)   Schenck-Cardea
   Productions/Columbia TV, 1987
KOJAK (TF)   Universal TV, 1989

GERARD KRAWCZYK
b. May 17, 1953 - Paris, France
Business: International Paranoiac Productions, 9-11 Rue
   Clisson, 75013 Paris, France, 04/570-8538
Contact: French Film Office, 745 Fifth Avenue, New York, NY
   10151, 212/832-8860

MEME LES MOULES ONT DU VAGUE A L'AME
   1982, French
I HATE ACTORS   Galaxy International, 1986, French
L'ETE EN PENTE DOUCE   AAA, 1987, French

JOHN KRISH
Business: Sierra Productions Ltd., 8-8 Old Bond Street,
   London W1

THE SALVAGE GANG   Children's Film Foundation,
   1958, British
THE WILD AFFAIR   Goldstone, 1963, British
THE UNEARTHLY STRANGER   American International,
   1964, British
DECLINE AND FALL OF A BIRD WATCHER   20th Century-
   Fox, 1969, British
THE MAN WHO HAD POWER OVER WOMEN   Avco
   Embassy, 1971, British
JESUS   co-director with Peter Sykes, Warner Bros.,
   1979, British
OUT OF THE DARKNESS   Children's Film & TV
   Foundation/Rank, 1985, British

Kr

ALLEN KROEKER

b. 1951 - St. Boniface, Manitoba, Canada
Home: 633 Bay Street - Apt. 2701, Toronto, Ontario M5G
2G4, Canada, 416/593-5138
Agent: Jerry Adler, Sy Fischer Company - Los Angeles,
213/969-2949

HOW MUCH LAND DOES A MAN NEED (TF)   1979,
Canadian
TRAMP AT THE DOOR (TF)   Can West, 1985, Canadian
FRONTIER (MS)   Primedia, 1986, Canadian
HEAVEN ON EARTH (TF)   Primedia-Opix/CBC/BBC
Wales/Allied Entertainment/Telefilm Canada/Ontario
Film Development Corporation, 1987, Canadian-Welsh
AGE-OLD FRIENDS (CTF)   Granger Productions/HBO
Showcase, 1989, U.S.-Canadian
KOOTENAI BROWN   Festival Films, 1990, Canadian

WILLIAM KRONICK*

Business: 8489 West Third Street, Los Angeles, CA 90048,
213/656-8150
Agent: Ben Conway & Associates - Los Angeles,
213/271-8133

THE 500-POUND JERK (TF)   Wolper Productions, 1973
TO THE ENDS OF THE EARTH (TD)   Armand Hammer
Productions, 1984

JEREMY JOE KRONSBERG*

Agent: Naomi Gurian, The Gurian Agency - Los Angeles,
213/550-0400

GOING APE!   Paramount, 1981

STANLEY KUBRICK*

b. July 26, 1928 - Bronx, New York
Business: Pinewood Studios, Iver Heath, Bucks, England,
0753/651-700
Attorney: Louis C. Blau, Loeb & Loeb, 10100 Santa
Monica Blvd., Los Angeles, CA 90067, 213/552-7774

FEAR AND DESIRE   Joseph Burstyn, Inc., 1954
KILLER'S KISS   United Artists, 1955
THE KILLING   United Artists, 1956
PATHS OF GLORY   United Artists, 1957
SPARTACUS   Universal, 1960
LOLITA   MGM, 1962, British
DR. STRANGELOVE OR: HOW I LEARNED TO STOP
WORRYING AND LOVE THE BOMB ★   Columbia,
1964, British
2001: A SPACE ODYSSEY ★   MGM, 1968, British
A CLOCKWORK ORANGE ★   Warner Bros.,
1971, British
BARRY LYNDON ★   Warner Bros., 1975, British
THE SHINING   Warner Bros., 1980, British
FULL METAL JACKET   Warner Bros., 1987, British

ANDREW J. KUEHN*

Business: Kaleidoscope Films Ltd., 844 N. Seward Street,
Hollywood, CA 90038, 213/465-1151

TERROR IN THE AISLES (FD)   Universal, 1984
ROLLING IN THE AISLES (FD)   Tri-Star, 1987

BUZZ KULIK*

b. 1923 - New York, New York
Agent: William Morris Agency - Beverly Hills, 213/274-7451

THE EXPLOSIVE GENERATION   United Artists, 1961
THE YELLOW CANARY   20th Century-Fox, 1963

READY FOR THE PEOPLE   Warner Bros., 1964
WARNING SHOT   Paramount, 1968
SERGEANT RYKER   *THE CASE AGAINST PAUL RYKER*
Universal, 1968, originally filmed for television in 1963
VILLA RIDES!   Paramount, 1968
RIOT   Paramount, 1969
VANISHED (TF)   Universal TV, 1971
OWEN MARSHALL, COUNSELOR AT LAW (TF)   Universal
TV, 1971
BRIAN'S SONG (TF) ☆   Screen Gems/Columbia TV, 1971
TO FIND A MAN   *THE BOY NEXT DOOR/SEX AND THE
TEENAGER*   Columbia, 1972
INCIDENT ON A DARK STREET (TF)   20th Century-Fox
TV, 1973
PIONEER WOMAN (TF)   Filmway, 1973
SHAMUS   Columbia, 1973
BAD RONALD (TF)   Lorimar Productions, 1974
REMEMBER WHEN (TF)   Danny Thomas Productions/
The Raisin Company, 1974
CAGE WITHOUT A KEY (TF)   Columbia TV, 1975
MATT HELM (TF)   Columbia TV, 1975
BABE (TF) ☆   MGM TV, 1975
THE LINDBERGH KIDNAPPING CASE (TF)   Columbia
TV, 1976
COREY: FOR THE PEOPLE (TF)   Columbia TV, 1977
KILL ME IF YOU CAN (TF)   Columbia TV, 1977
ZIEGFELD: THE MAN AND HIS WOMEN (TF)   Frankovich
Productions/Columbia TV, 1978
FROM HERE TO ETERNITY (MS)   Bennett-Katleman
Productions/Columbia TV, 1979
THE HUNTER   Paramount, 1980
SIDNEY SHELDON'S RAGE OF ANGELS   *RAGE OF
ANGELS* (TF)   Furia-Oringer Productions/NBC
Productions, 1983
GEORGE WASHINGTON (MS)   David Gerber Company/
MGM-UA TV, 1984
KANE & ABEL (MS)   Schrekinger Communications/Embassy
TV, 1985
WOMEN OF VALOR (TF)   Inter Planetary Productions/Jeni
Productions, 1986
HER SECRET LIFE (TF)   Phoenix Entertainment
Group, 1987
TOO YOUNG THE HERO (TF)   Rick-Dawn Productions/
Pierre Cossette Productions/The Landsburg
Company, 1988
AROUND THE WORLD IN 80 DAYS (MS)   Harmony Gold/
ReteEuropa/Valente-Baerwald Productions, 1989

AKIRA KUROSAWA

b. March 23, 1910 - Tokyo, Japan
Business: Kurosawa Production Inc., 3-2-1, Kirigaoka,
Midori-ku, Yokohama, Japan 227, 045/922-0850

SANSHIRO SUGATA   Toho, 1943, Japanese
THE MOST BEAUTIFUL   Toho, 1944, Japanese
THOSE WHO TREAD ON THE TIGER'S TAIL   Toho,
1945, Japanese
SANSHIRO SUGATA - PART TWO   Toho, 1945, Japanese
NO REGRETS FOR OUR YOUTH   Toho, 1946, Japanese
THOSE WHO MAKE TOMORROW   Toho, 1946, Japanese
ONE WONDERFUL SUNDAY   Toho, 1947, Japanese
DRUNKEN ANGEL   Toho, 1948, Japanese
THE QUIET DUEL   Daiei, 1949, Japanese
STRAY DOG   Toho, 1949, Japanese
SCANDAL   Shochiku, 1959, Japanese
RASHOMON   RKO Radio, 1950, Japanese
THE IDIOT   Shochiku, 1951, Japanese
IKIRU   Brandon, 1952, Japanese
SEVEN SAMURAI   Landmark Releasing, 1954, Japanese
I LIVE IN FEAR   Brandon, 1955, Japanese
THE LOWER DEPTHS   Brandon, 1957, Japanese

THRONE OF BLOOD *THE CASTLE OF THE SPIDER'S WEB* Brandon, 1957, Japanese
THE HIDDEN FORTRESS *THREE BAD MEN IN A HIDDEN FORTRESS* Toho, 1958, Japanese
THE BAD SLEEP WELL Toho, 1960, Japanese
YOJIMBO Seneca International, 1961, Japanese
SANJURO Toho, 1962, Japanese
HIGH AND LOW East West Classics, 1963, Japanese
RED BEARD Toho, 1965, Japanese
DODES'KA'DEN Janus, 1970, Japanese
DERSU UZALA New World, 1975, Soviet-Japanese
KAGEMUSHA: THE SHADOW WARRIOR 20th Century-Fox, 1980, Japanese
RAN ★ Orion Classics, 1985, French-Japanese
AKIRA KUROSAWA'S DREAMS *DREAMS* Warner Bros., 1990, Japanese-U.S.

DIANE KURYS
b. 1949 - France
Agent: Triad Artists, Inc. - Los Angeles, 213/556-2727

PEPPERMINT SODA *DIABOLO MENTHE* New Yorker, 1977, French
COCKTAIL MOLOTOV Putnam Square, 1980, French
ENTRE NOUS *COUP DE FOUDRE* United Artists Classics, 1983, French
A MAN IN LOVE Cinecom, 1987, French
C'EST LA VIE *LE BAULE-LES PINS* Samuel Goldwyn Company, 1990, French

EMIR KUSTURICA
b. Sarajevo, Yugoslavia
Contact: Incovent Ltd., 1900 Avenue of the Stars - Suite 1500, Los Angeles, CA 90067, 213/277-7881

DO YOU REMEMBER DOLLY BELL? International Home Cinema, 1981, Yugoslavian
WHEN FATHER WAS AWAY ON BUSINESS Cannon, 1985, Yugoslavian
TIME OF THE GYPSIES Columbia, 1989, Yugoslavian

FRAN RUBEL KUZUI
Agent: CAA - Beverly Hills, 213/288-4545

TOKYO POP Spectrafilm, 1988

STANLEY KWAN
Contact: Hong Kong International Film Festival, 5th Floor, High Block City Hall, Edinburgh Place, Hong Kong, (3) 72-1193

ROUGE 1988, Hong Kong
FULL MOON IN NEW YORK Shiobu Film Co., 1990, Hong Kong

KEN KWAPIS*
Agent: CAA - Beverly Hills, 213/288-4545

SESAME STREET PRESENTS: FOLLOW THAT BIRD Warner Bros., 1985
VIBES Columbia, 1988
HE SAID, SHE SAID co-director with Marisa Silver, Paramount, 1991

JEFF KWITNY
Agent: Irvin Arthur Associates - Beverly Hills, 213/276-7493

ICED Mikon Releasing Corporation, 1988
THE TRAIN International Movie Service, 1989, Italian

IM KWON-TAEK
b. May 2, 1936 - Kwangju, Jonlanamdo, Korea

(The following is an incomplete list of Mr. Im's credits)

GOOD-BYE! DUMAN RIVER 1961, South Korean
THE GREAT LONG FOR HUSBAND 1963, South Korean
WAR AND WOMAN TEACHER 1966, South Korean
WEEDS 1973, South Korean
TESTIMONY 1973, South Korean
WANGSIBRI STREET 1976, South Korean
WAR! NAKDONG RIVER! 1976, South Korean
THE FAMILY TREE BOOK 1978, South Korean
THE HIDDEN HERO 1979, South Korean
MANDALA 1981, South Korean
VILLAGE IN THE MIST 1982, South Korean
GILSODOM Hwa Chun Trading Company, 1985, South Korean
TICKET 1986, South Korean
SURROGATE WOMAN 1986, South Korean
COME, COME, COME UPWARD Motion Picture Promotion Corporation, 1989, South Korean

L

ED LACHMAN
IMAGINING AMERICA (TF) co-director with Ralph Bakshi, Matt Mahurin & Mustapha Khan, Vanguard Films, 1989

MORT LACHMAN*
b. March 20, 1918 - Seattle, Washington
Agent: Bernie Weintraub, Robinson, Weintraub, Gross & Associates - Los Angeles, 213/653-5802

THE GIRL WHO COULDN'T LOSE (TF)☆☆ Filmways, 1975

JOHN LAFIA
Agent: William Morris Agency - Beverly Hills, 213/274-7451

THE BLUE IGUANA Paramount, 1988
CHILD'S PLAY II Universal, 1990

RON LAGOMARSINO*
Agent: William Morris Agency - New York City, 212/903-1328

DINNER AT EIGHT (CTF) Think Entertainment/Turner Network TV, 1989

HARVEY LAIDMAN*
b. February 22, 1942 - Cleveland, Ohio
Agent: Louis Bershad, Century Artists Ltd. - Beverly Hills, 213/273-4366

STEEL COWBOY (TF) Roger Gimbel Productions/ EMI TV, 1978
FLATBUSH (TF) Lorimar Productions, 1979
THE BOY WHO LOVED TROLLS (TF) Q Productions, 1984

JOHN LAING

Contact: New Zealand Film Commission, P.O. Box 11546, Wellington, New Zealand, 4/859-754

BEYOND REASONABLE DOUBT   Endeavour Productions/New Zealand Film Commission, 1980, New Zealand
THE LOST TRIBE   Meridian Films/Film Investment Corporation of New Zealand/ New Zealand Film Commission, 1983, New Zealand
OTHER HALVES   Finlayson Hill Productions, 1985, New Zealand
DANGEROUS ORPHANS   Cinepro/New Zealand Film Commission, 1986, New Zealand

MARLENA LAIRD*

b. March 21, 1949 - London, England
Home: 6208 Mulholland Highway, Hollywood, CA 90068, 213/465-6400
Agent: Ronald Leif, Contemporary Artists - Beverly Hills, 213/278-8250

FRIENDSHIP, SECRETS AND LIES   co-director with Ann Zane Shanks, Wittman-Riche Productions/Warner Bros. TV, 1979

FRANK LaLOGGIA

Business: LaLoggia Productions - Los Angeles, 213/462-3055

FEAR NO EVIL   Avco Embassy, 1981
LADY IN WHITE   New Century/Vista, 1987

MARY LAMBERT

Agent: William Morris Agency - Beverly Hills, 213/274-7451

SIESTA   Lorimar, 1987, British
PET SEMATARY   Paramount, 1989

MARY LAMPSON

UNDERGROUND (FD)   co-director with Emile de Antonio & Haskell Wexler, New Yorker, 1976
UNTIL SHE TALKS (TF)   Alaska Street Productions, 1983

BURT LANCASTER*

b. November 2, 1913 - New York, New York
Agent: ICM - Los Angeles, 213/550-4000

THE MIDNIGHT MAN   co-director with Roland Kibbee, Universal, 1974

JOHN LANDIS*

b. 1951 - Chicago, Illinois
Agent: CAA - Beverly Hills, 213/288-4545

SCHLOCK   Jack H. Harris Enterprises, 1973
THE KENTUCKY FRIED MOVIE   United Film Distribution, 1977
NATIONAL LAMPOON'S ANIMAL HOUSE Universal, 1978
THE BLUES BROTHERS   Universal, 1980
AN AMERICAN WEREWOLF IN LONDON Universal, 1981
TWILIGHT ZONE - THE MOVIE   co-director with Steven Spielberg, Joe Dante & George Miller, Warner Bros., 1983
TRADING PLACES   Paramount, 1983
COMING SOON (CTD)   Universal Pay TV, 1983
INTO THE NIGHT   Universal, 1985
SPIES LIKE US   Warner Bros., 1985

THREE AMIGOS   Orion, 1986
AMAZON WOMEN ON THE MOON   co-director with Joe Dante, Carl Gottlieb, Robert K. Weiss & Peter Horton, Universal, 1987
COMING TO AMERICA   Paramount, 1988

MICHAEL LANDON*
(Eugene Orowitz)

b. October 31, 1937 - Forest Hills, New York
Contact: Directors Guild of America - Los Angeles, 213/289-2000

IT'S GOOD TO BE ALIVE (TF)   Metromedia Productions, 1974
LITTLE HOUSE ON THE PRAIRIE (TF)   NBC Productions, 1974
THE LONELIEST RUNNER (TF)   NBC Productions, 1976
KILLING STONE (TF)   Universal TV, 1978
FATHER MURPHY (TF)   NBC Productions, 1981
LITTLE HOUSE: THE LAST FAREWELL (TF)   NBC Productions/Ed Friendly Productions, 1984
SAM'S SON   Invictus Entertainment Corporation, 1984
HIGHWAY TO HEAVEN (TF)   Michael Landon Productions, 1984
WHERE PIGEONS GO TO DIE (TF)   Michael Landon Productions/World International Network, 1990

ALAN LANDSBURG*

b. May 10, 1933 - New York, New York
Business: Alan Landsburg Productions, Inc., 1554 S. Sepulveda Blvd., Los Angeles, CA 90025, 213/473-9641

BLACK WATER GOLD (TF)   Metromedia Productions, 1970

ANDREW LANE

Business: Crawford/Lane Productions, 14101 Valleyheart Drive - Suite 205, Sherman Oaks, CA 91423, 818/501-2076
Agent: Richland-Wunsch Agency - Los Angeles, 213/278-1955

JAKE SPEED   New World, 1986
MORTAL PASSIONS   MGM/UA, 1990

CHARLES LANE

Agent: William Morris Agency - Beverly Hills, 213/274-7451

SIDEWALK STORIES   Island Pictures, 1989

ERIC LANEUVILLE*

Home: 5138 W. Slauson Avenue, Los Angeles, CA 90056, 213/293-1277
Agent: Kaplan-Stahler Agency - Los Angeles, 213/653-4483

THE GEORGE McKENNA STORY (TF)   Alan Landsburg Productions, 1986
MIGHTY PAWNS (TF)   WonderWorks/PBS, 1987
SECRET WITNESS (TF)   Just Greene Productions/CBS Entertainment, 1988
A BRAND NEW LIFE (TF)   NBC Productions, 1989

RICHARD LANG*

Agent: Sanford-Beckett-Skouras & Associates - Los Angeles, 213/208-2100

FANTASY ISLAND (TF)   Spelling-Goldberg Productions, 1977
THE HUNTED LADY (TF)   QM Productions, 1977
NOWHERE TO RUN (TF)   MTM Enterprises, 1978
NIGHT CRIES (TF)   Charles Fries Productions, 1978

DR. SCORPION (TF) Universal TV, 1978
VEGA$ (TF) Aaron Spelling Productions, 1978
THE WORD (MS) Charles Fries Productions/Stonehenge
   Productions, 1978
THE MOUNTAIN MEN Columbia, 1980
A CHANGE OF SEASONS 20th Century-Fox, 1980
MATT HOUSTON (TF) Largo Productions/Aaron Spelling
   Productions, 1982
DON'T GO TO SLEEP (TF) Aaron Spelling
   Productions, 1982
SHOOTING STARS (TF) Aaron Spelling
   Productions, 1983
DARK MIRROR (TF) Aaron Spelling
   Productions, 1984
VELVET (TF) Aaron Spelling Productions, 1984
OBSESSED WITH A MARRIED WOMAN (TF)
   Sidaris-Camhe Productions/The Feldman-Meeker
   Company, 1985
IN LIKE FLYNN (TF) Glen A. Larson Productions/
   20th Century Fox TV/Astral Film Productions, 1985,
   U.S.-Canadian
KUNG FU: THE MOVIE (TF) Lou-Step Productions/
   Warner Bros. TV, 1985
HOUSTON KNIGHTS (TF) co-director with Gary Nelson,
   Jay Bernstein Productions/Columbia TV, 1987
PERRY MASON: THE CASE OF THE SINISTER
   SPIRIT (TF) The Fred Silverman Company/
   Strathmore Productions/Viacom Productions, 1987
CHRISTMAS COMES TO WILLOW CREEK (TF) Blue
   Andre Productions/ITC Productions, 1987
THE ROAD RAIDERS (TF) New East Entertainment/
   Universal TV, 1989

ROCKY LANG*
Agent: William Morris Agency - Beverly Hills,
   213/274-7451

ALL'S FAIR Moviestore Entertainment, 1989
RACE FOR GLORY New Century/Vista, 1989

MICHAEL LANGE*
Agent: Mark Lichtman, Shapiro-Lichtman Agency -
   Los Angeles, 213/859-8877

PARADISE (TF) co-director with Clifford Bole, CBS, 1989

TED LANGE*
Agent: Arnold Soloway, The Artists Group - Los Angeles,
   213/552-1100

OTHELLO Uptown Films, 1989

MURRAY LANGSTON
Contact: Screen Actors Guild - Hollywood,
   213/465-4600

WISHFUL THINKING Broadstar Entertainment, 1989

SIMON LANGTON*
b. November 5, 1941 - Amersham, England
Agent: CAA - Beverly Hills, 213/288-4545

SMILEY'S PEOPLE (MS)☆ BBC/Paramount TV,
   1982, British
THE LOST HONOR OF KATHRYN BECK (TF) Open
   Road Productions, 1984
ANNA KARENINA (TF) Rastar Productions/Colgems
   Productions, 1985

THE WHISTLE BLOWER Hemdale, 1987
CASANOVA (TF) Konigsberg-Sanitsky Company/
   Reteitalia, 1987, U.S.-Italian
LAGUNA HEAT (CTF) HBO Pictures/Jay Weston
   Productions, 1987

CLAUDE LANZMANN
Business: Aleph Films, 18 rue Marbeuf, 75008 Paris,
   France, 04/723-5547
Contact: French Film Office, 745 Fifth Avenue, New York,
   NY 10151, 212/832-8860

PORQUOI ISRAEL? (FD) New Yorker, 1973, French
SHOAH (FD) New Yorker, 1985, French

JAMES LAPINE
Contact: Writers Guild of America, East - New York City,
   212/245-6180

IMPROMPTU Hemdale, 1990, U.S.-French

SHELDON LARRY*
b. October 3, 1949 - Toronto, Ontario, Canada
Address: 3010 Paulcrest Avenue, Los Angeles, CA 90046,
   213/650-1004 or: 143 West 21st Street, New York, NY
   10011, 212/243-7174
Agent: Alan Greenspan, ICM - Los Angeles,
   213/550-4428

TERMINAL CHOICE Almi, 1985, Canadian
FIRST STEPS (TF) CBS Entertainment, 1985
BEHIND ENEMY LINES (TF) TVS Productions/MTM
   Enterprises, 1985, British- U.S.
HOME (TF) Leonard Goldberg Productions, 1986
HOT PAINT (TF) Catalina Production Group/MGM-UA
   TV, 1988
BURNING BRIDGES (TF) Andrea Baynes Productions/
   Lorimar TV, 1990

GLEN A. LARSON*
Contact: Directors Guild of America - Los Angeles,
   213/289-2000

CHAMELEONS (TF) Glen A. Larson Productions/NBC
   Productions, 1989

STAN LATHAN*
b. July 8, 1945 - Philadelphia, Pennsylvania
Contact: Directors Guild of America - Los Angeles,
   213/289-2000

SAVE THE CHILDREN (FD) Paramount, 1973
AMAZING GRACE United Artists, 1974
THE SKY IS GRAY (TF) Learning in Focus, 1980
DENMARK VESEY'S REBELLION (TF) WPBT-
   Miami, 1982
BEAT STREET Orion, 1984
BOOKER (TF) KQED-Frisco, 1984
GO TELL IT ON THE MOUNTAIN (TF) Learning in
   Focus, 1984
UNCLE TOM'S CABIN (CTF) Edgar J. Scherick
   Productions/Taft Entertainment TV, 1987
THE CHILD SAVER (TF) Michael Filerman Productions/
   NBC Productions, 1988
AN EIGHT IS ENOUGH WEDDING (TF) Lorimar
   TV, 1989

ALBERTO LATTUADA
b. November 13, 1914 - Milan, Italy
Address: Via N. Paganini, 7 Rome, Italy, 06/862035

GIACOMO L'IDEALISTA   1942, Italian
LA FRECCIA NEL FIANCO   1943, Italian
LA NOSTRA GUERRA   1943, Italian
IL BANDITO   Lux Film, 1946, Italian
IL DELITTO DI GIOVANNI EPISCOPO   Lux Film,
    1947, Italian
SENZA PIETA '   Lux Film, 1948, Italian
LUCI DEL PO   1949, Italian
VARIETY LIGHTS   co-director with Federico Fellini,
    Pathe Contemporary, 1950, Italian
ANNA   Italian Films Export, 1951, Italian
IL CAPPOTTO   Faro Film, 1952, Italian
LA LUPA   Republic, 1953, Italian
LOVE IN THE CITY   co-director, Italian Films Export,
    1953, Italian
LA SPIAGGIA   Titanus, 1954, Italian
SCUOLA ELEMENTARE   Titanus/Societe General de
    Cinematographie, 1954, Italian-French
GUENDALINA   Carlo Ponti/Les Films Marceau, 1957,
    Italian-French
TEMPEST   Paramount, 1958, Italian-
    French-Yugoslavian
I DOLCI INGANNI   Carlo Ponti/Titanus, 1960, Italian
LETTERA DI UNA NOVIZIA   Champion/Euro International,
    1960, Italian
L'IMPREVISTO   Documento Film/Orsay Film, 1961,
    Italian-French
MAFIOSO   Zenith International, 1962, Italian
LA STEPPA   Zebra Film/Aera Film, 1962, Italian
LA MANDRAGOLA   Arco Film/Lux Compagnie
    Cinematographie, 1965, Italian- French
MATCHLESS   United Artists, 1966, Italian
DON GIOVANNI IN SICILIA   Adelphia, 1967, Italian
FRAULEIN DOKTOR   Paramount, 1969,
    Italian-Yugoslavian
L'AMICA   Fair Film, 1969, Italian
VENGA A PRENDERE IL CAFFE' DA NOI   Mass Film,
    1970, Italian
WHITE SISTER   BIANCO, ROSSOE...   Columbia,
    1971, Italian-French- Spanish
SONO STATO IO   Dear Film, 1973, Italian
LE FARO DA PADRE   Clesi Cinematografica,
    1974, Italian
LA BAMBINA   1974, Italian
CUORE DI CANE   Italnoleggio, 1975, Italian
OH, SERAFINA   Cineriz, 1976, Italian
COSI' COME SEI   CEIAD, 1978, Italian-Spanish
LA CICALA   PIC, 1979, Italian
CHRISTOPHER COLUMBUS (MS)   RAI/Clesi
    Cinematografica/Antenne-2/ Bavaria Atelier/
    Lorimar Productions, 1985, Italian-West German-
    U.S.- French
UNA SPINA DEL CUORE   Titanus, 1985, Italian
FRATELLI (MS)   Solaris Cinematografica/Reteitalia/Beta
    Film, 1988, Italian-West German
AMORI (TF)   co-director, Reteitalia, 1989, Italian

FRANK LAUGHLIN
Home: 415/931-8024
Business Manager: Ronald Dorfman, 15910
    Ventura Blvd. - Suite 1501, Encino, CA 91436,
    818/906-8555

THE TRIAL OF BILLY JACK   Taylor-Laughlin, 1974
THE MASTER GUNFIGHTER   Taylor-Laughlin, 1975

MICHAEL LAUGHLIN
STRANGE BEHAVIOR   DEAD KIDS   World Northal,
    1981, New Zealand- Australian
STRANGE INVADERS   Orion, 1983, Canadian
MESMERIZED   RKO/Challenge Corporation Services,
    1984, New Zealand- Australian-British

TOM LAUGHLIN*
b. 1938 - Minneapolis, Minnesota
Contact: Directors Guild of America - Los Angeles,
    213/289-2000

THE PROPER TIME   Lopert, 1960
THE YOUNG SINNER   United Screen Arts, 1965
BORN LOSERS   directed under pseudonym of T.C. Frank,
    American International, 1967
BILLY JACK   directed under pseudonym of T.C. Frank,
    Warner Bros., 1973
BILLY JACK GOES TO WASHINGTON   Taylor-
    Laughlin, 1978
THE RETURN OF BILLY JACK   Billy Jack Productions,
    1986, unfinished

GERARD LAUZIER
Contact: French Film Office, 745 Fifth Avenue, New York, NY
    10151, 212/832-8860

TU EMPECHES TOUT LE MONDE DE DORMIR
    1982, French
PETIT CON   Samuel Goldwyn Company, 1984, French
LA TETE DANS LE SAC   Parafrance, 1984, French

JEAN-CLAUDE LAUZON
b. 1953 - Montreal, Quebec, Canada
Contact: Academy of Canadian Cinema and Television,
    633 Yonge Street - 2nd Floor, Toronto, Ontario M4Y 1Z9,
    Canada, 416/967-0315

NIGHT ZOO   UN ZOO LA NUIT   FilmDallas, 1987,
    Canadian

ARNOLD LAVEN*
b. February 23, 1922 - Chicago, Illinois
Home: 15954 Valley Vista, Encino, CA 91436,
    818/981-4551
Agent: Jerry Adler, Sy Fischer Company - Los Angeles,
    213/208-0455

WITHOUT WARNING   United Artists, 1952
VICE SQUAD   United Artists, 1953
DOWN THREE DARK STREETS   United Artists, 1954
THE RACK   MGM, 1956
THE MONSTER THAT CHALLENGED THE WORLD
    United Artists, 1957
SLAUGHTER ON TENTH AVENUE   Universal, 1957
ANNA LUCASTA   United Artists, 1958
GERONIMO   United Artists, 1962
THE GLORY GUYS   United Artists, 1965
ROUGH NIGHT IN JERICHO   Universal, 1967
SAM WHISKEY   United Artists, 1969

MARTIN LAVUT
b. 1939 - Montreal, Quebec, Canada
Home: 367 Sackville Street, Toronto, Ontario M5A 3G5,
    Canada, 416/929-9677
Agent: Ralph Zimmerman, Great North Artists Management,
    350 Dupont Street, Toronto, Ontario M5R 1V9, Canada,
    416/925-2051

MARSHALL McLUHAN (TD)   1965, Canadian

LENI RIEFENSTAHL, HITLER'S CAMERA (TD)
   1965, Canadian
AT HOME   1968, Canadian
THE LIFE GAME (TF)   1970, Canadian
WITHOUT A HOBBY, IT'S NO LIFE (TF)
   1973, Canadian
ORILLIA: OUR TOWN (TF)   1974, Canadian
MIDDLE GAME (TF)   1974, Canadian
MELONY (TF)   1974, Canadian
TOGETHERNESS (TF)   1975, Canadian
SAM, GRACE, DOUG AND THE DOG (TF)
   1976, Canadian
THIS WILL DO FOR TODAY (TF)   1977, Canadian
NORTHERN LIGHTS (TF)   1980, Canadian
WAR BRIDES (TF)   1980, Canadian
RUMOURS OF GLORY (TF)   Rumours of Glory
   Productions/Extra Modern Productions Ltd.,
   1981, Canadian
MAGGIE AND PIERRE (TF)   1983, Canadian
CHARLIE GRANT'S WAR (TF)   1984, Canadian
RED RIVER (TF)   1985, Canadian
THE MARRIAGE BED (TF)   1986, Canadian
PALAIS ROYALE   Spectrafilm, 1988, Canadian

TOM LAW
TAX SEASON   Prism Entertainment, 1990

RAY LAWRENCE
Contact: Australian Film Commission, 9229 Sunset Blvd.,
   Los Angeles, CA 90069, 213/275-7074

BLISS   New World, 1985, Australian

DAVID LAYTON
DEMON HUNTERS   Golden Harvest, 1989,
   Hong Kong

JOE LAYTON*
b. May 3, 1931 - New York, New York
Personal Manager: Roy Gerber Associates, 9200 Sunset
   Blvd. - Suite 620, Los Angeles, CA 90069,
   213/550-0100

RICHARD PRYOR LIVE ON THE SUNSET STRIP (FD)
   Columbia, 1982

ASHLEY LAZARUS
Contact: British Academy of Film & Television Arts,
   195 Piccadilly, London W1, England, 71/734-0022

FOREVER YOUNG, FOREVER FREE   E'LOLLIPOP
   Universal, 1976, British
GOLDEN RENDEZVOUS   Rank, 1977, British

PAUL LEAF*
b. May 2, 1929 - New York, New York
Home: 2800 Neilson Way, Santa Monica, CA 90405,
   213/392-5276
Business Manager: Alan U. Schwartz, Shea & Gould,
   1800 Avenue of the Stars, Los Angeles, CA 90067,
   213/277-1000

TOP SECRET (TF)   Jemmin, Inc./Sheldon Leonard
   Productions, 1978
SERGEANT MATLOVICH VS. THE U.S. AIR FORCE (TF)
   Tomorrow Entertainment, 1978

LARRY LEAHY
13 O'CLOCK   co-director with Frank Mazzola, Third Coast
   Entertainment, 1988

DAVID LEAN*
b. March 25, 1908 - Croydon, England
Contact: Kent Jones & Done, Churchill House, 47 Regent
   Road, Stoke-on-Trent, England

IN WHICH WE SERVE   co-director with Noel Coward,
   Universal, 1942, British
THIS HAPPY BREED   Universal, 1944, British
BLITHE SPIRIT   United Artists, 1945, British
BRIEF ENCOUNTER   Universal, 1946, British
GREAT EXPECTATIONS★   Universal, 1947, British
OLIVER TWIST   United Artists, 1948, British
ONE WOMAN'S STORY   THE PASSIONATE FRIENDS
   Universal, 1949, British
MADELEINE   Universal, 1950, British
BREAKING THE SOUND BARRIER   THE SOUND BARRIER
   United Artists, 1952, British
HOBSON'S CHOICE   United Artists, 1954, British
SUMMERTIME   SUMMER MADNESS★   United Artists,
   1955, British
THE BRIDGE ON THE RIVER KWAI★★   Columbia,
   1957, British
LAWRENCE OF ARABIA★★   Columbia, 1962, British
DOCTOR ZHIVAGO★   MGM, 1965, British
RYAN'S DAUGHTER   MGM, 1970, British
A PASSAGE TO INDIA★   Columbia, 1984, British

NORMAN LEAR*
b. July 27, 1922 - New Haven, Connecticut
Business: Act III Communications, 1800 Century Park East -
   Suite 200, Los Angeles, CA 90067, 213/553-3636

COLD TURKEY   United Artists, 1971

PATRICE LECONTE
Contact: French Film Office, 745 Fifth Avenue, New York,
   NY 10151, 212/832-8860

MONSIEUR HIRE   Orion Classics, 1989, French
LE MARI DE LA COIFFEUSE   AMLF, 1990, French

MIMI LEDER*
Agent: InterTalent - Los Angeles, 213/271-0600

NIGHTINGALES (TF)   Aaron Spelling Productions, 1988

PAUL LEDUC
b. March 1942 - Mexico City, Mexico
Contact: Azteca Films, 555 N. La Brea Avenue, P.O. Box
   36095, Hollywood, CA 90036, 213/938-2413

REED: INSURGENT MEXICO   New Yorker,
   1970, Mexican
ETNOCIDIA, NOTAS SOBRE MEZQUITAL (TD)   Azteca
   Films, 1976, Mexican- Canadian
ESTUDIOS PARA UN RETRATO (FD)   Azteca Films,
   1978, Mexican
FRANCIS BACON (FD)   Azteca Films, 1978, Mexican
MONJAS CORONADAS (FD)   Azteca Films,
   1978, Mexican
HISTORIAS PROHIBIDAS DE PULGARCITO   Azteca
   Films, 1980, Mexican

LA CABEZA DE LA HIDRA (TF)   Azteca Films,
   1981, Mexican
FRIDA: NATURALEZA VIVA   Azteca Films,
   1985, Mexican
HAMBRE COMO VES?   Azteca Films, 1986, Mexican
BARROCO   Television Espanola/Opulo Films/ICAIC/
   Quinto Centenario, 1989, Spanish-Cuban

DOO-YONG LEE
(See Lee DOO-YONG)

JANG-HO LEE
(See Lee JANG-HO)

JOANNA LEE*
Business: 11250 Ventura Blvd. - Suite 200, Studio City,
   CA 91604, 818/509-0371
Agent: Mickey Freiberg, The Artists Agency - Los Angeles,
   213/277-7779
Business Manager: Betty Beall, CPA, 9696 Culver Blvd. -
   Suite 203, Culver City, CA 90232, 213/558-8110

MIRROR, MIRROR (TF)   Christiana Productions, 1979
CHILDREN OF DIVORCE (TF)   Christiana Productions/
   Marble Arch Productions, 1980

JOE LEE
THE COURIER   co-director with Frank Deasy, Vestron,
   1988, Irish-British

SPIKE LEE
(Shelton Jackson Lee)
b. Atlanta, Georgia
Business: Forty Acres & A Mule Productions, 124 DeKalb
   Avenue, Brooklyn, NY 11217, 718/624-3703

JOE'S BED-STUY BARBERSHOP: WE CUT HEADS
   First Run Features, 1983
SHE'S GOTTA HAVE IT   Island Pictures, 1986
SCHOOL DAZE   Columbia, 1988
DO THE RIGHT THING   Universal, 1989
MO' BETTER BLUES   Universal, 1990
JUNGLE FEVER   Universal, 1991

ROBERT LEEDS*
Agent: Brandon & Rodgers - Los Angeles, 213/273-6173

RETURN OF THE BEVERLY HILLBILLIES (TF)
   CBS, 1981

MICHEL LEGRAND
Contact: French Film Office, 745 Fifth Avenue, New York,
   NY 10151, 212/832-8860

CINQ JOURS EN JUIN   Compagnie Francaise
   Cinematographique/ Productions Michel Legrand/
   Films A2, 1989, French

ERNEST LEHMAN
b. 1920 - New York, New York
Agent: The Gersh Agency - Beverly Hills, 213/274-6611
Business Manager: Henry J. Bamberger, 2049
   Century Park East, Los Angeles, CA 90067,
   213/553-0581

PORTNOY'S COMPLAINT   Warner Bros., 1972

MICHAEL LEHMANN
Agent: CAA - Beverly Hills, 213/288-4545

HEATHERS   New World, 1989
MEET THE APPLEGATES   Triton Pictures, 1990
HUDSON HAWK   Tri-Star, 1991

PETER LEHNER
MEGAVILLE   Heritage Entertainment/White Noise
   Productions, 1990

ARNOLD LEIBOVIT
THE FANTASY FILM WORLDS OF GEORGE PAL (FD)
   Leibovit Productions, 1986
THE PUPPETOON MOVIE (FD)   Expanded
   Entertainment, 1987

NEIL LEIFER
Agent: William Morris Agency - Beverly Hills,
   213/274-7451

TRADING HEARTS   Cineworld, 1988

MIKE LEIGH
Agent: Peters, Fraser & Dunlop, The Chambers, Chelsea
   Harbour, Lots Road, London SW10 OXF,
   England, 71/376-7676

BLEAK MOMENTS   1971, British
MEANTIME (TF)   Channel Four/Mostpoint/Central
   Film, 1983
HIGH HOPES   Skouras Pictures, 1988, British
UNTITLED   Film Four International, 1990, British

CHRISTOPHER LEITCH*
Agent: William Morris Agency - Beverly Hills,
   213/274-7451

TEEN WOLF TOO   Atlantic Releasing Corporation, 1987
COURAGE MOUNTAIN   Triumph Releasing Corporation,
   1989, U.S.-French

DAVID LEIVICK
GOSPEL (FD)   co-director with Frederick Ritzenberg,
   20th Century-Fox, 1983

DAVID LELAND
Agent: CAA - Beverly Hills, 213/388-4545

WISH YOU WERE HERE   Atlantic Releasing
   Corporation, 1987, British
CHECKING OUT   Warner Bros., 1989, U.S.-British
THE BIG MAN   Miramax Films, 1990, British

CLAUDE LELOUCH
b. October 30, 1937 - Paris, France
Address: 15 Avenue Hoche, 75008 Paris, France,
   04/227-0089
Contact: French Film Office, 745 Fifth Avenue, New York,
   NY 10151, 212/832-8860

LE PROPRE DE L'HOMME   1960, French
L'AMOUR AVEC DES SI   1963, French
LA FEMME SPECTACLE   1964, French
TO BE A CROOK   *UNE FILLE ET DES FUSILS*   Comet,
   1965, French
LES GRAND MOMENTS   1965, French

A MAN AND A WOMAN★ Allied Artists, 1966, French
LIVE FOR LIFE United Artists, 1967, French
FAR FROM VIETNAM (FD) co-director with Jean-Luc
Godard, Joris Ivens, William Klein, Alain Resnais &
Agnes Varda, New Yorker, 1967, French
GRENOBLE (FD) co-director with Francois Reichenbach,
United Producers of America, 1968, French
LIFE LOVE DEATH Lopert, 1969, French
LOVE IS A FUNNY THING UN HOMME QUI ME PLAIT
United Artists, 1970, French-Italian
THE CROOK United Artists, 1971, French
SMIC, SMAC, SMOC GSF, 1971, French
MONEY MONEY MONEY L'AVENTURE C'EST
L'AVENTURE GSF, 1972, French
HAPPY NEW YEAR LA BONNE ANNEE Avco
Embassy, 1973, French- Italian
VISIONS OF EIGHT (FD) co-director with Yuri Ozerov,
Mai Zetterling, Michael Pfleghar, Kon Ichikawa, Milos
Forman & John Schlesinger, Cinema 5, 1973
AND NOW MY LOVE TOUTE UNE VIE Avco Embassy,
1975, French-Italian
MARIAGE 1975, French
CAT AND MOUSE Quartet, 1975, French
THE GOOD AND THE BAD Paramount, 1976, French
SECOND CHANCE SI C'ETAIT A REFAIRE United
Artists Classics, 1976, French
ANOTHER MAN, ANOTHER CHANCE United Artists,
1977, U.S.-French
ROBERT ET ROBERT Quartet, 1978, French
A NOUS DEUX AMLF, 1979, French-Canadian
BOLERO LES UNS ET LES AUTRES/WITHIN MEMORY
Double 13/Sharp Features, 1982, French
EDITH AND MARCEL Miramax, 1983, French
VIVA LA VIE UGC, 1984, French
PARTIR REVENIR UGC, 1985, French
A MAN AND A WOMAN: 20 YEARS LATER Warner
Bros., 1986, French
BANDITS ATTENTION BANDITS Grange
Communications/Jerry Winters, 1987, French
L'ITINERAIRE D'UN ENFANT GATE Films 13/Cerito
Films, 1988, French-West German
IL Y A DES JOURS...ET DES LUNES AFMD,
1990, French

JAMES LEMMO
HEART New World, 1987
TRIPWIRE New Line Cinema, 1990

JACK LEMMON*
b. February 8, 1925 - Boston, Massachusetts
Agent: CAA - Beverly Hills, 213/288-4545
Business: Jalem Productions, Inc., 141 El Camino -
Suite 201, Beverly Hills, CA 90212, 213/278-7750
Business Manager: Marvin Freedman, Freedman,
Kinzelberg & Broder, 1801 Avenue of the Stars - Suite
911, Los Angeles, CA 90067, 213/277-0700

KOTCH Cinerama Releasing Corporation, 1971

RUSTY LEMORANDE*
Home: 1699 Woods Drive, Los Angeles, CA 90069,
213/656-3528
Business Manager: Craig Jacobson, Hansen, Jacobson &
Teller, 335 N. Maple - Suite 270, Beverly Hills, CA 90210,
213/271-8777

JOURNEY TO THE CENTER OF THE EARTH
Cannon, 1989

TERRY LENNON
Business: Warner Bros. Animation, 4000 Warner Blvd.,
Burbank, CA 91522, 818/954-6000

DAFFY DUCK'S QUACKBUSTERS (AF) co-director with
Greg Ford, Warner Bros., 1988

MALCOLM LEO*
b. October 9, 1944 - New York, New York
Agent: Michael Peretzian, William Morris Agency -
Beverly Hills, 213/274-7451
Business: Malcolm Leo Productions, 6536 Sunset Blvd.,
Los Angeles, CA 90028, 213/464-4448

HEROES OF ROCK AND ROLL (TD) co-director with
Andrew Solt, ABC, 1979
THIS IS ELVIS (FD) co-director with Andrew Solt, Warner
Bros., 1981
IT CAME FROM HOLLYWOOD (FD) co-director with
Andrew Solt, Paramount, 1982
SUPER NIGHT OF ROCK AND ROLL (TD) Malcolm Leo
Productions, 1984
THE BEACH BOYS: AN AMERICAN BAND (FD)
Vestron, 1985
WILL ROGERS - LOOK BACK IN LAUGHTER (CTD)
Malcolm Leo Productions, 1987
ROLLING STONE - TWENTY YEARS OF ROCK 'N ROLL
(TD) Malcolm Leo Productions, 1987

HERBERT B. LEONARD*
b. October 8, 1922 - New York, New York
Address: 5300 Fulton Avenue, Van Nuys, CA 91401,
818/783-0457
Agent: Irwin Moss, Preferred Artists - Encino, 818/990-0305

THE PERILS OF PAULINE Universal, 1967
GOING HOME MGM, 1971

TERRY LEONARD*
Home: 11244 Darling Road, Agua Dulce, CA 91350,
805/268-1577
Agent: Jan Leonard, Artists Creative Management, 12001
Ventura Place - Suite 328, Studio City, CA 91604,
818/769-0469

DEATH BEFORE DISHONOR New World, 1987

JOHN LEONE*
Agent: Camden Artists - Los Angeles, 213/278-6885

THE GREAT SMOKEY ROADBLOCK THE LAST OF
THE COWBOYS Dimension, 1978

PO-CHIH LEONG
(Liang Puzhi)
b. 1939 - London, England
Contact: Hong Kong International Film Festival, 5th Floor,
High Block City Hall, Edinburgh Place, Hong Kong,
(3) 72-1193

JUMPING ASH 1976, Hong Kong
FOXBAT 1977, Hong Kong
ITCHY FINGERS 1977, Hong Kong
NO BIG DEAL 1979, Hong Kong
SUPER FOOL 1981, Hong Kong
HE LIVES BY NIGHT 1982, Hong Kong
BANANA COP 1984, Hong Kong

HONG KONG 1941   D&B/Bo Ho, 1985, Hong Kong
TIME TRAVELLER   1985, Hong Kong
THE ISLAND   1985, Hong Kong
PING PONG   Samuel Goldwyn Company, 1985, British
CARRY ON DANCING   co-director with Kam Kwok-Leung,
  D&B Films, 1989, Hong Kong

SERGE LePERON
Contact: French Film Office, 745 Fifth Avenue, New York,
  NY 10151, 212/832-8860

LAISSE BETON   Luna Films, 1984, French

MARK L. LESTER*
b. November 26, 1948 - Cleveland, Ohio
Agent: The Chasin Agency - Beverly Hills,
  213/278-7805

TRICIA'S WEDDING   Lester Pictures, 1971
TWILIGHT OF THE MAYAS   Lester Pictures, 1972
STEEL ARENA   L-T, 1973
TRUCK STOP WOMEN   L-T, 1974
WHITE HOUSE MADNESS   Lester Pictures, 1975
BOBBI JO AND THE OUTLAW   American
  International, 1976
STUNTS   New Line Cinema, 1977
GOLD OF THE AMAZON WOMEN (TF)   Mi-Ka
  Productions, 1979
ROLLER BOOGIE   United Artists, 1979
CLASS OF 1984   United Film Distribution,
  1982, Canadian
FIRESTARTER   Universal, 1984
COMMANDO   20th Century Fox, 1985
ARMED AND DANGEROUS   Columbia, 1986
CLASS OF 1999   Taurus Entertainment, 1990

RICHARD LESTER*
b. January 19, 1932 - Philadelphia, Pennsylvania
Agent: CAA - Beverly Hills, 213/288-4545

RING-A-DING RHYTHM   *IT'S TRAD, DAD*   Columbia,
  1962, British
THE MOUSE ON THE MOON   United Artists,
  1963, British
A HARD DAY'S NIGHT   United Artists, 1964, British
THE KNACK...AND HOW TO GET IT   Lopert,
  1965, British
HELP!   United Artists, 1965, British
A FUNNY THING HAPPENED ON THE WAY TO THE
  FORUM   United Artists, 1966, British
TEENAGE REBELLION   *MONDO TEENO*
  co-director with Norman Herbert, Trans-American,
  1967, British-U.S.
HOW I WON THE WAR   United Artists, 1967, British
PETULIA   Warner Bros., 1968, U.S.-British
THE BED SITTING ROOM   United Artists,
  1969, British
THE THREE MUSKETEERS (THE QUEEN'S DIAMONDS)
  20th Century-Fox, 1974, British
JUGGERNAUT   United Artists, 1974, British
THE FOUR MUSKETEERS (MILADY'S REVENGE)   20th
  Century-Fox, 1975, British
ROYAL FLASH   20th Century-Fox, 1976, British
ROBIN AND MARIAN   Columbia, 1976, British
THE RITZ   Warner Bros., 1976
BUTCH AND SUNDANCE: THE EARLY DAYS   20th
  Century-Fox, 1979

CUBA   United Artists, 1979
SUPERMAN II   Warner Bros., 1981, U.S.-British
SUPERMAN III   Warner Bros., 1983, U.S.-British
FINDERS KEEPERS   Warner Bros., 1984
RETURN OF THE MUSKETEERS   Universal, 1989,
  British-Spanish-French
GET BACK (FD)   Buena Vista, 1990, British

SHELDON LETTICH
Agent: Linne Radmin, ICM - Los Angeles, 213/550-4000

WRONG BET   Imperial Entertainment, 1990

DON LETTS
THE PUNK ROCK MOVIE (FD)   Cinematic, 1978

JAY LEVEY
Agent: William Morris Agency - Beverly Hills,
  213/274-7451

U.H.F.   Orion, 1989

WILLIAM A. LEVEY*
b. March 31, 1943 - Stamford, Connecticut
Agent: John LaRocca, LaRocca Talent Group - Burbank,
  818/849-7731

BLACKENSTEIN   LFG, 1973
TO BE A ROSE   Cinemation, 1974
WAM BAM THANK YOU SPACEMAN   Box Office
  International, 1975
SLUMBER PARTY '57   Cannon, 1977
THE HAPPY HOOKER GOES TO WASHINGTON
  Cannon, 1977
SKATETOWN, U.S.A.   Columbia, 1979
LIGHTNING: THE WHITE STALLION   Cannon, 1986
COMMITTED   Trans World Entertainment, 1988
HELLGATE   Ghost Town Film Management/
  Distant Horizon/Anant Singh Productions, 1989,
  Australian-British

ALAN J. LEVI*
b. St. Louis, Missouri
Home: 3951 Longridge Avenue, Sherman Oaks, CA
  91423, 818/981-3417

GEMINI MAN (TF)   Universal TV, 1976
THE RETURN OF THE INCREDIBLE HULK (TF)
  Universal TV, 1977
GO WEST, YOUNG GIRL (TF)   Bennett-Katleman
  Productions/Columbia TV, 1978
THE IMMIGRANTS (TF)   Universal TV, 1978
THE LEGEND OF THE GOLDEN GUN (TF)   Bennett-
  Katleman Productions/ Columbia TV, 1979
SCRUPLES (TF)   Lou-Step Productions/Warner Bros.
  TV, 1980
THE LAST SONG (TF)   Ron Samuels Productions/
  Motown Pictures, 1980
THE STEPFORD CHILDREN (TF)   Edgar J. Scherick
  Productions/Taft Entertainment TV, 1987
ISLAND SONS (TF)   Universal TV, 1987
THE RETURN OF SAM McCLOUD (TF)   Michael Sloan
  Productions/Universal TV, 1989
THE BIONIC SHOWDOWN: THE SIX-MILLION DOLLAR
  MAN AND THE BIONIC WOMAN (TF)   Universal
  TV, 1989

PETER LEVIN*
b. Trenton, New Jersey
Agent: Ken Gross, Robinson, Weintraub, Gross &
Associates - Los Angeles, 213/653-5802

HEART IN HIDING (TF)   Filmways, 1973
PALMERSTOWN, U.S.A. (TF)   Haley-TAT
Productions, 1980
THE COMEBACK KID (TF)   ABC Circle Films, 1980
RAPE AND MARRIAGE: THE RIDEOUT CASE (TF)
Stonehenge Productions/ Blue Greene Productions/
Lorimar Productions, 1980
THE MARVA COLLINS STORY (TF)   NRW
Features, 1981
WASHINGTON MISTRESS (TF)   Lorimar
Productions, 1982
THE ROYAL ROMANCE OF CHARLES AND DIANA (TF)
Chrysalis-Yellen Productions, 1982
A DOCTOR'S STORY (TF)   Embassy TV, 1984
A REASON TO LIVE (TF)   Rastar Productions/Robert
Papazian Productions, 1985
CALL TO GLORY: JFK (TF)   Tisch-Avnet Productions/
Paramount TV, 1985
BETWEEN THE DARKNESS AND THE DAWN (TF)
Doris Quinlan Productions/Warner Bros. TV, 1985
NORTHSTAR (TF)   Daniel Grodnik Productions/Clyde
Phillips Productions/Warner Bros. TV, 1986
"POPEYE" DOYLE (TF)   December 3rd Productions/
Robert Singer Productions/20th Century
Fox TV, 1986
HOUSTON: THE LEGEND OF TEXAS (TF)   Taft
Entertainment TV/J.D. Feigelson Productions, 1987
SWORN TO SILENCE (TF)   Daniel H. Blatt-Robert
Singer Productions, 1987
HOSTAGE (TF)   CBS Entertainment, 1988
IN THE HEAT OF THE NIGHT (TF)   NBC, 1988
THE LITTLEST VICTIMS (TF)   CBS
Entertainment, 1989
LADY IN A CORNER   Sagaponack Films/Pantheon
Pictures/Allen Leicht Productions/Fries
Entertainment, 1989

SIDNEY LEVIN*
Contact: Directors Guild of America - Los Angeles,
213/289-2000

LET THE GOOD TIMES ROLL (FD)   co-director with
Robert J. Abel, Columbia, 1973
THE GREAT BRAIN   Osmond Distribution
Company, 1978

BARRY LEVINSON*
Agent: CAA - Beverly Hills, 213/288-4545

DINER   MGM/United Artists, 1982
THE NATURAL   Tri-Star, 1984
YOUNG SHERLOCK HOLMES   Paramount, 1985
TIN MEN   Buena Vista, 1987
GOOD MORNING, VIETNAM   Buena Vista, 1987
RAIN MAN★★   MGM/UA, 1988
AVALON   Tri-Star, 1990

GENE LEVITT*
b. May 28, 1920 - New York, New York
Agent: Triad Artists, Inc. - Los Angeles, 213/556-2727
Business Manager: Henry J. Bamberger, 2049 Century Park
East, Los Angeles, CA 90067, 213/553-0581

ANY SECOND NOW (TF)   Universal TV, 1969
RUN A CROOKED MILE (TF)   Universal TV, 1969

ALIAS SMITH AND JONES (TF)   Universal TV, 1971
COOL MILLION (TF)   Universal TV, 1972
THE PHANTOM OF HOLLYWOOD   MGM TV, 1974
SHE'LL BE SWEET (MS)   Australian Broadcasting
Commission/Trans-Atlantic Enterprises,
1979, Australian

EDMOND LEVY*
b. September 26, 1929 - Toronto, Ontario, Canada
Home: 135 Central Park West, New York, NY 10023,
212/595-7666
Agent: Sandy Landau - New York City, 212/539-7546

TROUBLE IN THE FAMILY (TF)   Harold Mayer Productions,
1972, Canadian
MOM, THE WOLFMAN AND ME (TF)   Time-Life
Productions, 1981
STRESS (TD)   Time-Life Productions, 1982

RALPH LEVY*
Home: 206 McKenzie Street, Santa Fe, NM 87501,
505/983-7545

BEDTIME STORY   Universal, 1964
DO NOT DISTURB   20th Century-Fox, 1965

DAVID LEWIS
DANGEROUS CURVES   Lightning Pictures, 1988

HERSCHELL GORDON LEWIS
LIVING VENUS   Creative Services, 1960
THE ADVENTURES OF LUCKY PIERRE   directed under
the pseudonym of Lewis H. Gordon, 1961
DAUGHTER OF THE SUN   directed under the pseudonym
of Lewis H. Gordon, 1962
NATURE'S PLAYMATES   directed under the pseudonym of
Lewis H. Gordon, Dore Productions, 1962
BOIN-N-G   directed under the pseudonym of Lewis H.
Gordon, Box Office Spectaculars, 1963
BLOOD FEAST   Box Office Spectaculars, 1963
GOLDILOCKS AND THE THREE BEARS *GOLDILOCKS'
THREE CHICKS* directed under the pseudonym of Lewis
H. Gordon, Dore Productions, 1963
BELL, BARE AND BEAUTIFUL   directed under the
pseudonym of Lewis H. Gordon, Griffith
Productions, 1963
SCUM OF THE EARTH *DEVIL'S CAMERA* directed
under the pseudonym of Lewis H. Gordon, Box Office
Spectaculars, 1963
2000 MANIACS   Box Office Spectaculars, 1964
MOONSHINE MOUNTAIN   Herschell Gordon Lewis
Productions, 1964
COLOR ME BLOOD RED   Jacqueline Kay, Inc., 1965
MONSTER A GO-GO *TERROR AT HALFDAY* directed
under the pseudonym of Sheldon Seymour, 1965
SIN, SUFFER AND REPENT   director of additional scenes,
1965, British-U.S.
JIMMY, THE BOY WONDER   Mayflower Pictures, 1966
ALLEY TRAMP   directed under the pseudonym of Armand
Parys, United Picture Organization, 1966
AN EYE FOR AN EYE   Creative Film Enterprises, 1966
SANTA CLAUS VISITS THE LAND OF MOTHER
GOOSE   1967
SUBURBAN ROULETTE   Argent Film Productions, 1967
SOMETHING WEIRD   Mayflower Pictures, 1967
A TASTE OF BLOOD   Creative Film Enterprises, 1967
THE GRUESOME TWOSOME   Mayflower Pictures, 1967

175

THE GIRL, THE BODY, AND THE PILL   Creative Film
Enterprises, 1967
BLAST-OFF GIRLS   Creative Film Enterprises, 1967
THE ECSTASIES OF WOMEN   directed under the
pseudonym of Mark Hansen, United Pictures
Organization, 1969
LINDA AND ABILENE   directed under the pseudonym of
Mark Hansen, United Pictures Organization, 1969
MISS NYMPHET'S ZAP-IN   directed under the pseudonym
of Sheldon Seymour, Mayflower Pictures, 1970
THE WIZARD OF GORE   Mayflower Pictures, 1970
THIS STUFF'LL KILL YA!   Ultima Productions, 1971
YEAR OF THE YAHOO!   International Arts
Corporation, 1972
BLACK LOVE   directed under the pseudonym of R.L.
Smith, Lewis Motion Picture Enterprises, 1972
THE GORE-GORE GIRLS   Lewis Motion Picture
Enterprises, 1972

JERRY LEWIS*
(Joseph Levitch)
b. March 16, 1926 - Newark, New Jersey
Address: 3305 West Spring Mountain Road, Las Vegas,
NV 89102, 702/362-9730
Agent: William Morris Agency - Beverly Hills,
213/274-7451

THE BELLBOY   Paramount, 1960
THE LADIES' MAN   Paramount, 1961
THE ERRAND BOY   Paramount, 1962
THE NUTTY PROFESSOR   Paramount, 1963
THE PATSY   Paramount, 1964
THE FAMILY JEWELS   Paramount, 1965
THREE ON A COUCH   Columbia, 1966
THE BIG MOUTH   Columbia, 1967
ONE MORE TIME   United Artists, 1970, British
WHICH WAY TO THE FRONT?   Warner Bros., 1970
HARDLY WORKING   20th Century-Fox, 1981
SMORGASBORD   Warner Bros., 1983

JOSEPH H. LEWIS*
b. April 6, 1900 - New York, New York
Home: 14069 Marquesas Way, Marina del Rey, CA
90292, 213/823-3372

NAVY SPY   co-director with Crane Wilbur, 1937
COURAGE OF THE WEST   1937
SINGING OUTLAW   1937
THE SPY RING   INTERNATIONAL SPY   1938
BORDER WOLVES   1938
THE LAST STAND   1938
TWO-FISTED RANGERS   1940
BLAZING SIX-SHOOTERS   1940
TEXAS STAGECOACH   1940
THE MAN FROM TUMBLEWEEDS   1940
BOYS OF THE CITY   1940
THE RETURN OF WILD BILL   1940
THAT GANG OF MINE   Monogram, 1940
THE INVISIBLE GHOST   Monogram, 1941
PRIDE OF THE BOWERY   Monogram, 1941
CRIMINALS WITHIN   1941
ARIZONA CYCLONE   1941
BOMBS OVER BURMA   Producers Releasing
Corporation, 1942
THE SILVER BULLET   1942
SECRETS OF A CO-ED   SILENT WITNESS   1942
THE BOSS OF HANGTOWN MESA   1942
THE MAD DOCTOR OF MARKET STREET
Universal, 1942
MINSTREL MAN   1944

THE FALCON IN SAN FRANCISCO   RKO Radio, 1945
MY NAME IS JULIA ROSS   Columbia, 1945
SO DARK THE NIGHT   Columbia, 1946
THE SWORDSMAN   Columbia, 1947
THE RETURN OF OCTOBER   Columbia, 1948
THE UNDERCOVER MAN   Columbia, 1949
GUN CRAZY   DEADLY IS THE FEMALE   United
Artists, 1949
A LADY WITHOUT PASSPORT   MGM, 1950
RETREAT, HELL!   Warner Bros., 1952
DESPERATE SEARCH   MGM, 1953
CRY OF THE HUNTED   MGM, 1953
THE BIG COMBO   Allied Artists, 1955
A LAWLESS STREET   Columbia, 1955
THE 7TH CAVALRY   Columbia, 1956
THE HALLIDAY BRAND   United Artists, 1957
TERROR IN A TEXAS TOWN   United Artists, 1958

ROBERT M. LEWIS*
b. November 9, 1934 - New York, New York
Agent: Alan Greenspan, ICM - Los Angeles,
213/550-4428
Attorney: Franklin Rohner, 11111 Santa Monica Blvd. -
Suite 1615, Los Angeles, CA 90025, 213/477-5001

THE ASTRONAUT (TF)   Universal TV, 1972
THE ALPHA CAPER (TF)   Universal TV, 1973
MONEY TO BURN (TF)   Universal TV, 1973
MESSAGE TO MY DAUGHTER (TF)   Metromedia
Productions, 1973
PRAY FOR THE WILDCATS (TF)   ABC Circle
Films, 1974
THE DAY THE EARTH MOVED (TF)   ABC Circle
Films, 1975
THE INVISIBLE MAN (TF)   Universal TV, 1975
GUILTY OR INNOCENT: THE SAM SHEPPARD MURDER
CASE (TF)   Universal TV, 1975
NO ROOM TO RUN (TF)   Australian Broadcasting
Commission/Trans-Atlantic Enterprises,
1977, Australian
THE NIGHT THEY TOOK MISS BEAUTIFUL (TF)   Don
Kirshner Productions, 1977
RING OF PASSION (TF)   20th Century-Fox TV, 1980
S*H*E (TF)   Martin Bregman Productions, 1980
IF THINGS WERE DIFFERENT (TF)   Bob Banner
Associates, 1980
ESCAPE (TF)   Henry Jaffe Enterprises, 1980
A PRIVATE BATTLE (TF)   Procter & Gamble Productions/
Robert Halmi, Inc., 1980
FALLEN ANGEL (TF)   Green-Epstein Productions/
Columbia TV, 1981
THE MIRACLE OF KATHY MILLER (TF)   Rothman-Wohl
Productions/Universal TV, 1981
CHILD BRIDE OF SHORT CREEK (TF)   Lawrence
Schiller-Paul Monash Productions, 1981
DESPERATE LIVES (TF)   Fellows-Keegan Company/
Lorimar Productions, 1982
BETWEEN TWO BROTHERS (TF)   Turman-Foster
Company/Finnegan Associates, 1982
COMPUTERCIDE (TF)   Anthony Wilson
Productions, 1982
SUMMER GIRL (TF)   Bruce Lansbury Productions/Roberta
Haynes Productions/ Finnegan Associates, 1983
AGATHA CHRISTIE'S 'A CARIBBEAN MYSTERY' (TF)
Stan Margulies Productions/Warner Bros. TV, 1983
AGATHA CHRISTIE'S 'SPARKLING CYANIDE' (TF)   Stan
Margulies Productions/Warner Bros. TV, 1983
FLIGHT 90: DISASTER ON THE POTOMAC (TF)   Sheldon
Pinchuk Productions/Finnegan Associates, 1984
CITY KILLER (TF)   Stan Shpetner Productions, 1984

A SUMMER TO REMEMBER (TF)   Inter Planetary
    Productions, 1985
EMBASSY (TF)   Stan Margulies Company/ABC Circle
    Films, 1985
LOST IN LONDON (TF)   Emmanuel Lewis Entertainment
    Enterprises/D'Angelo Productions/Group W.
    Productions, 1985
FIREFIGHTER (TF)   Forest Hills Productions/Embassy
    TV, 1986
A STRANGER WAITS (TF)   Bruce Lansbury Productions/
    Edgar Lansbury Productions/Lewisfilm Ltd./New Century
    TV Productions, 1987
DEEP DARK SECRETS (TF)   Gross-Weston Productions/
    Fries Entertainment, 1987
THE SECRET LIFE OF KATHY McCORMICK (TF)
    Tamara Asseyev Productions/New World TV, 1988
LADYKILLERS (TF)   Barry Weitz Films/ABC Circle
    Films, 1988
DEAD RECKONING (CTF)   Houston Lady Productions,
    1990

ROBERT LIDDLE
Agent: Tom Chasin, The Chasin Agency - Beverly Hills,
    213/278-7505

ATTLA   1981

JEFF LIEBERMAN*
Home: 217 S. Crescent Drive, Beverly Hills, CA 90212,
    213/278-4150
Agent: The Agency - Los Angeles, 213/551-3000

SQUIRM   American International, 1976
BLUE SUNSHINE   Cinema Shares International, 1979
DOCTOR FRANKEN (TF)   co-director with Marvin J.
    Chomsky, Titus Productions/Janus Productions, 1980
JUST BEFORE DAWN   Picturmedia Limited, 1981
REMOTE CONTROL   Vista Organization, 1988

ROBERT LIEBERMAN*
Agent: Alan Greenspan, ICM - Los Angeles, 213/550-4428

FIGHTING BACK (TF)   MTM Enterprises, 1980
WILL: G. GORDON LIDDY (TF)   A. Shane
    Company, 1982
TABLE FOR FIVE   Warner Bros., 1983

ROBERT H. LIEBERMAN
b. February 4, 1941
Business: Ithaca Filmworks, 400 Nelson Road, Ithaca,
    NY 14850, 607/273-8801
Agent: Maureen Walters, Curtis-Brown Ltd., 10 Astor
    Place, New York, NY 10003, 212/473-5400
Attorney/Personal Manager: Jay Kramer, 135 East 55th
    Street, New York, NY 10022, 212/753-5420

HONG KONG AND ONWARD (FD)   Gamma Films, 1967
FACES IN A FAMINE (FD)   Ithaca Filmworks, 1986

PETER LILIENTHAL
Contact: German Film & TV Academy, Pommernallee 1,
    1 Berlin 19, West Germany, 0311/302-6096

LA VICTORIA (FD)   1973, West German
ER HERRSCHT RUHE IM LAND   Filmverlag Der
    Autoren, 1976, West German
DAVID   Kino International, 1979, West German
THE UPRISING   Kino International, 1981, El Salvador

DEAR MR. WONDERFUL   Joachim von Vietinghoff
    Produktion/Westdeutscher Rundfunk/Sender Freis Berlin,
    1982, West German
THE AUTOGRAPH   Cine-International, 1984, West
    German-French
DAS SCHWEIGEN DES DICHTERS   Edgar Reitz
    Filmproduktion, 1986, West German

VIVECA LINDFORS
b. December 29, 1920 - Uppsala, Sweden
Contact: Screen Actors Guild - Hollywood, 213/465-4600

UNFINISHED BUSINESS...   American Film Institute, 1987

MICHAEL LINDSAY-HOGG*
b. May 5, 1940 - New York, New York
Agent: William Morris Agency - Beverly Hills, 213/274-7451

LET IT BE (FD)   United Artists, 1970, British
NASTY HABITS   Brut Productions, 1977, British
BRIDESHEAD REVISITED (MS)☆   co-director with Charles
    Sturridge, Granada TV/WNET-13/NDR Hamburg, 1982,
    British-U.S.-West German
DOCTOR FISCHER OF GENEVA (TF)   Consolidated
    Productions/BBC, 1985, British
NAZI HUNTER: THE BEATE KLARSFELD STORY (TF)
    William Kayden Productions/Orion TV/Silver Chalice/
    Revcom/George Walker TV/TF1/ SFP, 1986,
    U.S.-British-French
THE LITTLE MATCH GIRL (TF)   NBC Productions, 1987
MURDER BY MOONLIGHT (TF)   Tamara Asseyev
    Productions/London Weekend TV/Viacom, 1989,
    U.S.-British
THE STRANGE CASE OF DR. JEKYLL AND MR. HYDE
    (CTF)   Think Entertainment, 1989
THE OBJECT OF BEAUTY   Avenue Pictures, 1990, British

RON LINK
Agent: William Morris Agency - Beverly Hills, 213/274-7451

ZOMBIE HIGH   Cinema Group, 1987

ART LINSON*
b. Chicago, Illinois
Agent: William Morris Agency - Beverly Hills, 213/274-7451

WHERE THE BUFFALO ROAM   Universal, 1980
THE WILD LIFE   Universal, 1984

AARON LIPSTADT*
b. November 12, 1952 - Southington, Connecticut
Agent: Alan Greenspan, ICM - Los Angeles, 213/550-4428

ANDROID   Island Alive/New Realm, 1982
CITY LIMITS   Atlantic Releasing Corporation, 1985
POLICE STORY: MONSTER MANOR (TF)   Columbia
    TV, 1988
PAIR OF ACES (TF)   Pedernales Films/Once Upon A
    Time Films, 1990

STEVEN LISBERGER*
b. April 24, 1951 - Rye, New York
Agent: Jeff Berg, ICM - Los Angeles, 213/550-4205

ANIMALYMPICS (AF)   Lisberger Studios, 1980
TRON   Buena Vista, 1982
HOT PURSUIT   Paramount, 1987
SLIPSTREAM   Entertainment Film Productions,
    1989, British

DAVID LISTER

b. June 4, 1947 - Barberton, South Africa
Home: 87 Athol Street, Waverley, Johannesburg 2090,
South Africa, 011/786-4096

RIDING HIGH (MS)   SABC-TV, 1983, South African
RIVER HORSE LAKE (MS)   SABC-TV, 1984,
South African
MY FRIEND ANGELO (TF)   IFC, 1985, South African
JOHN ROSS, AN AFRICAN ADVENTURE (MS)
SABC-TV, 1986, South African
THE SEA TIGER (MS)   IFC/Toron, 1987, South African
BARNEY BARNATO (MS)   IFC/Toron/Tele-Saar, 1988,
South African-West German
THE RUTANGA TAPES   The Movie Group, 1989,
Namibian

MIGUEL LITTIN

b. August 9, 1942 - Palmilla, Colchagua, Chile
Contact: Azteca Films, 555 N. La Brea Avenue, P.O. Box
36095, Hollywood, CA 90036, 213/938-2413

EL CHACAL DE NAHUELTORO   1970, Chilean
COMPANERO PRESIDENTE (FD)   1971, Chilean
LA TIERRA PROMETIDA   1972, Chilean
LETTERS FROM MARUSIA   Azteca Films,
1975, Mexican
EL RECURSO DEL METODO   Azteca Films, 1978,
Mexican-French-Cuban
LA VIUDA DE MONTIEL   Azteca Films, 1980, Mexican
ALSINO AND THE CONDOR   1982, Cuban-Nicaraguan
ACTA GENERAL DE CHILE (FD)   Alfil Uno
Cinematografica/TVE, 1986, Cuban
SANDINO   Incine/Television Espanola/Reteitalia, 1990,
Nicaraguan-Spanish-Italian

DWIGHT H. LITTLE*

Agent: William Morris Agency - Beverly Hills, 213/274-7451

KGB - THE SECRET WAR   LETHAL   Cinema
Group, 1986
GETTING EVEN   American Distribution Group, 1986
HALLOWEEN 4   Galaxy International, 1988
BLOODSTONE   Omega Pictures, 1989
THE PHANTOM OF THE OPERA   21st Century
Distribution, 1989
SCREWFACE   20th Century Fox, 1990

LYNNE LITTMAN*

Home: 6620 Cahuenga Terrace, Los Angeles, CA 90068,
213/467-6802

NUMBER OUR DAYS (FD)   1977
TESTAMENT   Paramount, 1983
IN HER OWN TIME (FD)   Direct Cinema Limited, 1985

CARLO LIZZANI

b. April 3, 1917 - Rome, Italy
Home: Via F. Corridoni 7, Rome, Italy, 06/350185

ACHTUNG! BANDITI!   Cooperative Spettori Produtti
Cinematografici, 1951, Italian
AL MARGINI DELLA METROPOLI   Elios Film,
1953, Italian
LOVE IN THE CITY   co-director, Italian Films
Export, 1953
CRONACHE DI POVERI AMANTI   Cooperative Spettori
Produtti Cinematografici, 1954, Italian
LO SVITATO   Galatea/ENIC, 1956, Italian

BEHIND THE GREAT WALL   LA MURAGLIA CINESE   (FD)
Continental, 1958, Italian
ESTERINA   Italia Prod. Film, 1959, Italian
IL GOBBO   Dino De Laurentiis Cinematografica,
1960, Italian
IL CARABINIERE A CAVALLO   Maxima Film, 1961, Italian
IL PROCESSO DI VERONA   Duilio Cinematografica/Dino
De Laurentiis Cinematografica, 1963, Italian
LA VITA AGRA   Film Napoleon, 1964, Italian
AMORI PERICLOSI   co-director with Giulio Questi &
Alfredo Giannetti, Zebra Film/Fulco Film/Aera Film,
1964, Italian-French
LA CELESTINA P... R...   Aston Film, 1965, Italian
THE DIRTY GAME   GUERRE SECRETE   co-director
with Terence Young, Christian-Jacque & Werner
Klinger, American International, 1966, French-Italian-
West German
THRILLING   co-director with Ettore Scola & Gian Luigi
Polidori, Dino De Laurentiis Cinematografica,
1965, Italian
SVEGLIATI E UCCIDI   Sanson Film/Castoro Film,
1966, Italian
THE HILLS RUN RED   UN FIUME DI DOLLARI   directed
under pseudonym of Lee W. Beaver, United Artists,
1966, Italian
REQUIESCANT   Castoro Film, 1967, Italian
THE VIOLENT FOUR   BANDITI A MILANO   Paramount,
1968, Italian
L'AMANTE DI GRAMIGNA   Dino De Laurentiis
Cinematografica, 1969, Italian
AMORE E RABBIA   co-director with Bernardo Bertolucci,
Pier Paolo Pasolini, Jean-Luc Godard & Marco Bellocchio,
Castoro Film, 1969, Italian
BARBAGIA   Dino De Laurentiis Cinematografica,
1969, Italian
ROMA BENE   Castoro Film, 1971, Italian
TORINO NERA   Dino De Laurentiis Cinematografica,
1972, Italian
CRAZY JOE   Columbia, 1974, Italian-U.S.
THE LAST FOUR DAYS   MUSSOLINI - ULTIMO ATTO
Group 1, 1974, Italian
SAN BABILA ORE 20: UN DELITTO INUTILE   Agora,
1976, Italian
KLEINHOFF HOTEL   Capitol, 1977, Italian
FONTAMARA   Sacis, 1980, Italian
LA CASA DEL TAPPETO GIALLO   Gaumont, 1983, Italian
ROME: THE IMAGE OF A CITY (FD)   Transworld Film,
1983, Italian
NUCLEO ZERO   Diamant Film/RAI, 1984, Italian
MAMMA EBE   Clemi Cinematografica, 1985, Italian
UN' ISOLA (TF)   RAI, 1986, Italian
UNA MOGLIE (TF)   Regency Film/RAI, 1987, Italian
CARO GORBACIOV   UIP, 1988, Italian
THE MISSING FORMULA (MS)   Reteitalia/Titanus/Dean
Film, 1989, Italian

LUIS LLOSA

b. Peru
Agent: CAA - Beverly Hills, 213-288-4545

HOUR OF THE ASSASSIN   Concorde, 1987,
U.S.-Peruvian
CRIME ZONE   Concorde, 1989, U.S.-Peruvian

KENNETH LOACH

b. June 17, 1936 - Nuneaton, Warwickshire, England
Address: 46 Charlotte Street, London W1, England
Agent: Judy Daish Agency, 83 Eastbourne Mews, London
W2, 71/262-1101

DIARY OF A YOUNG MAN (TF)   1964, British

THREE CLEAR SUNDAYS (TF) 1965, British
THE END OF ARTHUR'S MARRIAGE (TF) 1965, British
UP THE JUNCTION (TF) 1965, British
COMING OUT PARTY (TF) 1965, British
CATHY COME HOME (TF) 1966, British
IN TWO MINDS (TF) 1966, British
THE GOLDEN VISION (TF) 1968, British
THE BIG FLAME (TF) 1968, British
POOR COW National General, 1968, British
IN BLACK AND WHITE (TF) 1969, British
KES United Artists, 1970, British
THE RANK AND FILE (TF) 1971, British
WEDNESDAY'S CHILD FAMILY LIFE Cinema 5,
   1972, British
BLACK JACK Boyd's Company, 1979, British
THE GAMEKEEPER ATV, 1980, British
AUDITIONS (TF) ATV, 1980, British
LOOKS AND SMILES Black Lion Films/Kestrel Films/
   MK2, 1981, British- French
THE RED AND THE BLUE (TF) 1983, British
WHICH SIDE ARE YOU ON? (TD) London Weekend
   TV, 1984
SINGING THE BLUES IN RED FATHERLAND Angelika
   Films, 1986, British-West German-French
HIDDEN AGENDA Hemdale, 1990, British

TONY LO BIANCO*
b. New York, New York
Home: 141 S. Roxbury Drive, Beverly Hills, CA 90212,
   213/274-1827
Business Manager: Unicorn Entertainment Inc., 365 West
   End Avenue, New York, NY 10024, 212/362-0368

TOO SCARED TO SCREAM The Movie Store, 1984

VICTOR LOBL*
Agent: Steve Glick, William Morris Agency - Beverly Hills,
   213/274-7451

BRAKER (TF) Blatt-Singer Productions/Centerpoint
   Productions/ MGM-UA TV, 1985
THE REVOLT OF MOTHER (TF) Learning in
   Focus, 1988
BEAUTY AND THE BEAST (TF) Witt-Thomas
   Productions/Ron Koslow Films/Republic Pictures
   Corporation, 1989

SONDRA LOCKE*
b. May 28, 1947 - Shelbyville, Tennessee
Agent: Jeremy Zimmer, Bauer Benedek Agency -
   Los Angeles, 213/275-2421

RATBOY Warner Bros., 1986
IMPULSE Warner Bros., 1990

DOUG LODATO
Address: c/o Wilson, Sonsini, Goodrich & Rosati -
   San Francisco, 415/493-9300

BEST SHOT Triax, 1990

BRUCE LOGAN*
Contact: Directors Guild of America - Los Angeles,
   213/289-2000

VENDETTA Concorde, 1986

ROBERT LOGAN
UP YOUR ALLEY Seymour Borde & Associates, 1989
REPOSSESSED Morgan Creek Productions, 1990

DIMITRI LOGOTHETIS
Agent: The Chasin Agency - Beverly Hills, 213/278-7505

PRETTY SMART New World, 1987
SLAUGHTERHOUSE ROCK Artists Entertainment
   Group, 1988
CHAMPIONS FOREVER (FD) Ion Pictures, 1989
THE CLOSER Ion Pictures, 1990

LOUIS LOMBARDO*
Home: 5455 Longridge Avenue, Van Nuys, CA 91401,
   818/902-0422
Agent: Jay Gilbert Talent Agency - Los Angeles,
   213/656-8090

RUSSIAN ROULETTE Avco Embassy, 1975,
   U.S.-Canadian
P.K. AND THE KID Castle Hill Productions, 1987,
   filmed in 1982

ULLI LOMMEL
b. West Germany
Business: Horizons Productions, 1134 N. Ogden Drive,
   West Hollywood, CA 90046, 213/654-6911

TENDERNESS OF THE WOLVES Monument, 1973,
   West German
DER MANN VON OBERZALZBERG - ADOLF UND
   MARLENE Albatros Produktion/Trio Film, 1976,
   West German
BLANK GENERATION International Harmony, 1979,
   West German
COCAINE COWBOYS International Harmony, 1979,
   West German
THE BOOGEY MAN Jerry Gross Organization, 1980
A TASTE OF SIN Ambassador, 1983
BRAINWAVES MPM, 1983
THE DEVONSVILLE TERROR MPM, 1983
STRANGERS IN PARADISE New West, 1984
REVENGE OF THE STOLEN STARS New West, 1985
DEFENSE PLAY Kodiak Films, 1986
IFO Kodiak Films, 1986
OVERKILL United Independent Films, 1987
A YEAR AT LINCOLN PLAINS Horizons Productions, 1987
WAR BIRDS Vidmark Entertainment/Hess Kallberg
   Associates/ Skyhawk Enterprises, 1989
COLD HEAT Skyhawk Enterprises, 1989
THE BIG SWEAT Falcon Arts and Entertainment, 1990
DESTINATION UNKNOWN Hess Kallberg
   Associates, 1990

RICHARD LONCRAINE
b. October 20, 1946 - Cheltenham, England
Agent: Lee Rosenberg, Triad Artists, Inc. - Los Angeles,
   213/556-2727

RADIO WONDERFUL 1972, British
FLAME Goodtime Enterprises, 1975, British
THE HAUNTING OF JULIA FULL CIRCLE Discovery
   Films, 1977, British-Canadian
OY VAY MARIA (TF) 1977, British
THE VANISHING ARMY (TF) BBC, 1978, British
SECRET ORCHARDS (TF) Granada TV, 1979, British
BLADE ON THE FEATHER (TF) London Weekend TV,
   1980, British

BRIMSTONE AND TREACLE   United Artists Classics,
   1982, British
THE MISSIONARY   Columbia, 1982, British
BELLMAN AND TRUE   Island Pictures, 1987, British

JERRY LONDON*
b. September 21, 1937 - Los Angeles, California
Agent: CAA - Beverly Hills, 213/288-4545

KILLDOZER (TF)   Universal TV, 1974
McNAUGHTON'S DAUGHTER (TF)   Universal TV, 1976
COVER GIRLS (TF)   Columbia TV, 1977
ARTHUR HAILEY'S WHEELS (MS)   Universal TV, 1978
EVENING IN BYZANTIUM (TF)   Universal TV, 1978
WOMEN IN WHITE (MS)   NBC, 1979
SWAN SONG (TF)   Renee Valente Productions/Topanga
   Services Ltd./20th Century-Fox, 1980
SHOGUN (MS)☆   Paramount TV/NBC Entertainment,
   1980, U.S.-Japanese
FATHER FIGURE (TF)   Finnegan Associates/Time-Life
   Productions, 1980
THE CHICAGO STORY (TF)   Eric Bercovici Productions/
   MGM TV, 1981
THE ORDEAL OF BILL CARNEY (TF)   Belle Company/
   Comworld Productions, 1981
THE GIFT OF LIFE (TF)   CBS Entertainment, 1982
THE SCARLET AND THE BLACK (TF)   Bill McCutchen
   Productions/ITC/RAI, 1983, U.S.-Italian
ARTHUR HAILEY'S HOTEL   HOTEL   (TF)   Aaron
   Spelling Productions, 1983
CHIEFS (MS)   Highgate Pictures, 1983
ELLIS ISLAND (MS)   Pantheon Pictures/Telepictures
   Productions, 1984, U.S.-British
MacGRUDER AND LOUD (TF)   Aaron Spelling
   Productions, 1985
HOLLYWOOD BEAT (TF)   Aaron Spelling
   Productions, 1985
DARK MANSIONS (TF)   Aaron Spelling Productions, 1986
IF TOMORROW COMES (MS)   CBS Entertainment, 1986
MANHUNT FOR CLAUDE DALLAS (TF)   London
   Films, Inc., 1986
HARRY'S HONG KONG (TF)   Aaron Spelling
   Productions, 1987
RENT-A-COP   Kings Road Productions, 1988
DADAH IS DEATH (TF)   Steve Krantz Productions/
   Roadshow, Coote & Carroll Productions/Samuel
   Goldwyn TV, 1988, U.S.-Australian
KISS SHOT (TF)   Lonson Productions/Whoop Inc., 1989
THE HAUNTING OF SARAH HARDY (TF)   USA
   Network, 1989
MICHELANGELO: A SEASON OF GIANTS (CMS)   Tiber
   Cinematografica/RAI/Turner Network TV, 1990,
   Italian-U.S.

JACK LORD
(John Joseph Ryan)
b. December 30, 1928 - New York, New York
Business: Lord & Lady Enterprises, Inc., 4999 Kahala
   Avenue, Honolulu, HI 96816, 808/735-5070
Business Manager: J. William Hayes, Executive Business
   Management, Inc., 132 S. Rodeo Drive, Beverly Hills,
   CA 90212, 213/858-2013

M STATION: HAWAII (TF)   Lord & Lady
   Enterprises, 1980

JEAN-CLAUDE LORD
b. 1943 - Montreal, Quebec, Canada
Address: 311 rue Notre-Dame, Saint-Lambert, Quebec
   J4P 2K2, Canada, 514/466-2602

DELIVREZ-NOUS DU MAL   Cooperativo, 1965, Canadian
LES COLOMBES   Les Films Jean-Claude Lord,
   1972, Canadian
BINGO   Les Films Mutuels, 1974, Canadian
PARLEZ-NOUS D'AMOUR   Les Films Mutuels,
   1977, Canadian
ECLAIR AU CHOCOLAT   Les Films Mutuels,
   1978, Canadian
VISITING HOURS   20th Century-Fox, 1982, Canadian
COVERGIRL   New World, 1984, Canadian
THE VINDICATOR   FRANKENSTEIN '88   20th Century
   Fox, 1985, Canadian
TOBY McTEAGUE   Filmline International Productions/
   Telefilm/Societe Generale du Cinema/CBS/Radio-Canada
   TV Network, 1985, Canadian
HE SHOOTS, HE SCORES (MS)   Communications Claude
   Heroux/CBC/Societe Radio-Canada/O'Keefe Breweries/
   TF-1/Telefilm Canada, 1986, Canadian- French
TADPOLE AND THE WHALE   New World Mutual,
   1988, Canadian
EDDIE AND THE CRUISERS II: EDDIE LIVES   Scotti Bros.,
   1989, U.S.-Canadian
MINDFIELD   Cinegem, 1990, Canadian

EMIL LOTEANU
b. November 6, 1936 - Bukovina, U.S.S.R.
Contact: Union of Soviet Filmmakers, Vassilievskaya 13,
   Moscow, U.S.S.R., tel.: 250-4114

WAIT FOR US AT DAWN   Moldovafilm, 1963, Soviet
RED MEADOWS   Moldovafilm, 1966, Soviet
FRESCOS ON THE WHITE   Moldovafilm, 1968, Soviet
THIS INSTANT   Moldovafilm, 1969, Soviet
LAUTARY   Moldovafilm, 1972, Soviet
MY WHITE CITY   Moldovafilm, 1973, Soviet
INTO THE SUNSET   Mosfilm, 1976, Soviet
THE SHOOTING PARTY   Mosfilm, 1978, Soviet
ANNA PAVLOVA: A WOMAN FOR ALL TIME   Cinema
   Development Corporation, 1985, Soviet-British-French

CHARLIE LOVENTHAL
Contact: Writers Guild of America, East - New York City,
   212/245-6180

THE FIRST TIME   New Line Cinema, 1983
MY DEMON LOVER   New Line Cinema, 1987

BERT LOVITT
PRINCE JACK   Castle Hill Productions, 1984

STEVE LOVY
CIRCUITRY MAN   IRS World Media, 1990

RICHARD LOWENSTEIN
Agent: Triad Artists, Inc. - Los Angeles, 213/556-2727

STRIKEBOUND   TRM Productions, 1985, Australian
DOGS IN SPACE   Skouras Pictures, 1987, Australian
AUSTRALIAN MADE (FD)   Hoyts Distribution,
   1987, Australian

DICK LOWRY*

b. Bartlesville, Oklahoma
Agent: John Gaines, APA - Los Angeles, 213/273-0744

OHMS (TF)   Grant-Case-McGrath Enterprises, 1980
KENNY ROGERS AS THE GAMBLER (TF)   Kragen &
   Co., 1980
THE JAYNE MANSFIELD STORY (TF)   Alan Landsburg
   Productions, 1980
ANGEL DUSTED (TF)   NRW Features, 1981
COWARD OF THE COUNTY (TF)   Kraco
   Productions, 1981
A FEW DAYS IN WEASEL CREEK (TF)   Hummingbird
   Productions/Warner Bros., 1981
RASCALS AND ROBBERS: THE SECRET ADVENTURES
   OF TOM SAWYER AND HUCKLEBERRY FINN (TF)
   CBS Entertainment, 1982
MISSING CHILDREN: A MOTHER'S STORY (TF)
   Kayden-Gleason Productions, 1982
LIVING PROOF: THE HANK WILLIAMS, JR. STORY (TF)
   Procter & Gamble Productions/Telecom Entertainment/
   Melpomene Productions, 1983
SMOKEY AND THE BANDIT PART 3   Universal, 1983
KENNY ROGERS AS THE GAMBLER - THE ADVENTURE
   CONTINUES (TF)   Lion Share Productions, 1983
OFF SIDES (TF)   Ten-Four Productions, 1984,
   filmed in 1980
WET GOLD (TF)   Telepictures Productions, 1984
THE TOUGHEST MAN IN THE WORLD (TF)   Guber-
   Peters Productions/ Centerpoint Productions, 1984
AGATHA CHRISTIE'S 'MURDER WITH MIRRORS' (TF)
   Hajeno Productions/Warner Bros. TV, 1985
WILD HORSES (TF)   Wild Horses Productions/
   Telepictures Productions, 1985
DREAM WEST (MS)   Sunn Classic Pictures, 1986
AMERICAN HARVEST (TF)   Ruth-Stratton Productions/
   The Finnegan Company, 1987
KENNY ROGERS AS THE GAMBLER III: THE LEGEND
   CONTINUES (TF)   Lion Share Productions, 1987
CASE CLOSED (TF)   Houston Motion Picture
   Entertainment Inc./CBS Entertainment, 1988
IN THE LINE OF DUTY: THE FBI MURDERS (TF)
   Telecom Entertainment/World International
   Network, 1988
UNCONQUERED (TF)   Alexandra Film Productions/
   Double Helix Films/Dick Lowry Productions, 1989
HOWARD BEACH: MAKING THE CASE FOR MURDER
   (TF)   Patchett- Kaufman Entertainment Productions/
   WIN, 1989
MIRACLE LANDING (TF)   CBS Entertainment, 1990
ARCHIE: TO RIVERDALE AND BACK AGAIN (TF)
   Patchett Kaufman Entertainment/DIC Enterprises, 1990

NANNI LOY

b. October 23, 1925 - Cagliari, Sardinia, Italy
Home: Piazza Rondanini 33, Rome, Italy, 06/654-0721

PAROLA DI LADRO   co-director with Gianni Puccini,
   Panal Film, 1957, Italian
IL MARITO   co-director with Gianni Puccini, Fortuna
   Film/Chamartin, 1957, Italian-Spanish
AUDACE COLPO DEI SOLITI IGNOTI   Titanus/Vides/
   SGC, 1959, Italian
UN GIORNO DA LEONI   Lux Film/Vides/Galatea,
   1961, Italian
THE FOUR DAYS OF NAPLES   MGM, 1962, Italian
MADE IN ITALY   Royal Films International, 1965,
   Italian-French
IL PADRE DI FAMIGLIA   Ultra/CFC/Marianne Productions,
   1967, Italian- French

ROSOLINO PATERNO' SOLDATO   Dino De Laurentiis
   Cinematografica, 1970, Italian
WHY   *DETENUTO IN ATTESA DI GIUDIZIO*   Documento
   Film, 1971, Italian
SISTEMO L'AMERICA E TORNO   Documento Film,
   1973, Italian
SIGNORE E SIGNORI BUONANOTTE   co-director, Titanus,
   1976, Italian
CAFE EXPRESS   Summit Features, 1980, Italian
TESTA O CROCE   Filmauro, 1982, Italian
WHERE'S PICONE?   *MI MANDA PICONE*   Italtoons,
   1984, Italian
AMICI MIEI III   Filmauro, 1985, Italian
AMORI (TF)   co-director, Reteitalia, 1989, Italian
SCUGNIZZI   Titanus, 1989, Italian

ARTHUR LUBIN

b. July 25, 1901 - Los Angeles, California
Home: 2881 Seattle Drive, Los Angeles, CA 90046,
   213/876-6024

A SUCCESSFUL FAILURE   Monogram, 1934
GREAT GOD GOLD   Monogram, 1935
HONEYMOON LIMITED   1935
TWO SINNERS   Republic, 1935
FRISCO WATERFRONT   Republic, 1935
THE HOUSE OF A THOUSAND CANDLES   Republic, 1936
YELLOWSTONE   Universal, 1936
MYSTERIOUS CROSSING   Universal, 1937
CALIFORNIA STRAIGHT AHEAD   Universal, 1937
I COVER THE WAR   Universal, 1937
IDOL OF THE CROWDS   Universal, 1937
ADVENTURE'S END   Universal, 1937
MIDNIGHT INTRUDER   Universal, 1938
THE BELOVED BRAT   Warner Bros., 1938
PRISON BREAK   Universal, 1938
SECRETS OF A NURSE   Universal, 1938
RISKY BUSINESS   Universal, 1939
BIG TOWN CZAR   Universal, 1939
MICKEY THE KID   Republic, 1939
CALL A MESSENGER   Universal, 1939
THE BIG GUY   Universal, 1940
BLACK FRIDAY   Universal, 1940
GANGS OF CHICAGO   Republic, 1940
I'M NOBODY'S SWEETHEART NOW   Universal, 1940
MEET THE WILDCAT   Universal, 1940
WHO KILLED AUNT MAGGIE?   Universal, 1940
SAN FRANCISCO DOCKS   Universal, 1941
WHERE DID YOU GET THAT GIRL?   Universal, 1941
BUCK PRIVATES   Universal, 1941
IN THE NAVY   Universal, 1941
HOLD THAT GHOST   Universal, 1941
KEEP 'EM FLYING   Universal, 1941
RIDE 'EM COWBOY   Universal, 1942
EAGLE SQUADRON   Universal, 1942
WHITE SAVAGE   Universal, 1943
THE PHANTOM OF THE OPERA   Universal, 1943
ALI BABA AND THE 40 THIEVES   Universal, 1944
DELIGHTFULLY DANGEROUS   United Artists, 1945
THE SPIDER WOMAN STRIKES BACK   Universal, 1946
NIGHT IN PARADISE   Universal, 1946
NEW ORLEANS   United Artists, 1947
IMPACT   United Artists, 1949
FRANCIS   Universal, 1950
QUEEN FOR A DAY   United Artists, 1951
FRANCIS GOES TO THE RACES   Universal, 1951
RHUBARB   Paramount, 1951
FRANCIS GOES TO WEST POINT   Universal, 1952
IT GROWS ON TREES   Universal, 1952
SOUTH SEA WOMAN   Warner Bros., 1953
FRANCIS COVERS THE BIG TOWN   Universal, 1953

FRANCIS JOINS THE WACS   Universal, 1954
FRANCIS IN THE NAVY   Universal, 1955
FOOTSTEPS IN THE FOG   Columbia, 1955
LADY GODIVA   Universal, 1955
STAR OF INDIA   United Artists, 1953, British-Italian
THE FIRST TRAVELING SALESLADY   RKO Radio, 1956
ESCAPADE IN JAPAN   Universal, 1957
THE THIEF OF BAGHDAD   MGM, 1961, Italian-French
THE INCREDIBLE MR. LIMPET   Universal, 1964
HOLD ON!   MGM, 1966
RAIN FOR A DUSTY SUMMER   Do'Bar, 1971,
    Spanish-U.S.

GEORGE LUCAS
b. January 14, 1944 - Modesto, California
Business: Lucasfilm Ltd., P.O. Box 668, San Anselmo,
    CA 94960

THX 1138   Warner Bros., 1971
AMERICAN GRAFFITI★   Universal, 1973
STAR WARS★   20th Century-Fox, 1977

FRANCESCO LUCENTE
Contact: Academy of Canadian Cinema & Television, 653
    Yonge Street - 2nd Floor, Toronto, Ontario M4Y 1Z9,
    Canada, 416/967-0315

THE VIRGIN QUEEN OF ST. FRANCIS HIGH   Crown
    International, 1987, Canadian

DANIELE LUCHETTI
b. July 25, 1960 - Rome, Italy
Home: viale Oceano Atlantico 31, Rome, Italy,
    06/501-4889

JUKE BOX   co-director, Gaumont, 1983, Italian
DOMANI ACCADRA'   Sacher Film/RAI-1/So.Fin.A.,
    1987, Italian

SIDNEY LUMET*
b. June 25, 1924 - Philadelphia, Pennsylvania
Agent: CAA - Beverly Hills, 213/288-4545

TWELVE ANGRY MEN★   United Artists, 1957
STAGE STRUCK   RKO Radio, 1958
THAT KIND OF WOMAN   Paramount, 1959
THE FUGITIVE KIND   United Artists, 1960
A VIEW FROM THE BRIDGE   Allied Artists, 1961,
    French-Italian
LONG DAY'S JOURNEY INTO NIGHT   Embassy, 1962
FAIL SAFE   Columbia, 1964
THE PAWNBROKER   Landau/Allied Artists, 1965
THE HILL   MGM, 1965, British
THE GROUP   United Artists, 1965
THE DEADLY AFFAIR   Columbia, 1967, British
BYE BYE BRAVERMAN   Warner Bros., 1968
THE SEA GULL   Warner Bros., 1968, British
THE APPOINTMENT   MGM, 1969
LAST OF THE MOBILE HOT-SHOTS   Warner Bros., 1970
KING: A FILMED RECORD...MONTGOMERY TO
    MEMPHIS (FD)   co-director with Joseph L.
    Mankiewicz, Maron Films Limited, 1970
THE ANDERSON TAPES   Columbia, 1971
CHILD'S PLAY   Paramount, 1972
THE OFFENSE   United Artists, 1973, British
SERPICO   Paramount, 1973
LOVIN' MOLLY   Columbia, 1974
MURDER ON THE ORIENT EXPRESS   Paramount,
    1974, British
DOG DAY AFTERNOON★   Warner Bros., 1975

NETWORK★   MGM/United Artists, 1976
EQUUS   United Artists, 1977, British
THE WIZ   Universal, 1978
JUST TELL ME WHAT YOU WANT   Columbia, 1980
PRINCE OF THE CITY   Orion/Warner Bros., 1981
DEATHTRAP   Warner Bros., 1982
THE VERDICT★   20th Century-Fox, 1982
DANIEL   Paramount, 1983
GARBO TALKS   MGM/UA, 1984
POWER   20th Century Fox, 1986
THE MORNING AFTER   20th Century Fox, 1986
RUNNING ON EMPTY   Warner Bros., 1988
FAMILY BUSINESS   Tri-Star, 1989
Q&A   Tri-Star, 1990

BIGAS LUNA
(Jose Juan Bigas Luna)
Contact: Ministry of Culture, Motion Picture Division, Avenida
    de Burgos, 5, 28036 Madrid, Spain, 91/202-5351

TATUAJE   1976, Spanish
BILBAO, UNA HISTORIA DEL AMOR   Figaro Films/Ona/
    Pepon Coromina, 1978, Spanish
CANICHE   Figaro Films, 1979, Spanish
REBORN   Diseno y Produccion de Films/Diamant/Laurel,
    1982, Spanish- Italian-U.S.
ANGUISH   Spectrafilm, 1987, Spanish
LOS AMORES DE LULU   Iberoamericana, 1990, Spanish

IDA LUPINO*
b. February 4, 1918 - London, England
Contact: Directors Guild of America - Los Angeles,
    213/289-2000

OUTRAGE   RKO Radio, 1950
HARD, FAST AND BEAUTIFUL   RKO Radio, 1951
THE HITCH-HIKER   RKO Radio, 1953
THE BIGAMIST   Filmmakers, 1953
THE TROUBLE WITH ANGELS   Columbia, 1966

TONY LURASCHI
THE OUTSIDER   Paramount, 1980, U.S.-Irish

STEVEN LUSTGARDEN
b. August 1, 1951

AMERICAN TABOO   Motion Pictures International, 1983
AMERICAN HERO   Appaloosa Films, 1986

WILLIAM LUSTIG
b. February 1, 1955 - Bronx, New York
Home: 2427 Liberty Lane, Topanga, CA 90290,
    213/455-0030

THE VIOLATION OF CLAUDIA   Lustig Productions, 1977
MANIAC   Analysis, 1981
VIGILANTE   Artists Releasing Corporation/Film Ventures
    International, 1983
MANIAC COP   Shapiro Entertainment, 1987
HIT LIST   New Line Cinema, 1989
RELENTLESS   New Line Cinema, 1989
MANIAC COP II   Cordell Productions, 1990

DAVID LYNCH*
b. January 20, 1946 - Missoula, Montana
Agent: CAA - Beverly Hills, 213/288-4545

ERASERHEAD   Libra, 1978
THE ELEPHANT MAN★   Paramount, 1980, British-U.S.

DUNE   Universal, 1984
BLUE VELVET★   DEG, 1986
TWIN PEAKS (TF) ☆   Lynch-Frost Productions/Propaganda
    Films/World Vision Enterprises, 1990
WILD AT HEART   Samuel Goldwyn Company, 1990

PAUL LYNCH*
b. November 6, 1946
Agent: Barry Perelman Agency - Los Angeles,
    213/274-5999
Business Manager: Stan Nugit, 1750 Ocean Park Avenue -
    Suite 204, Los Angeles, CA, 213/450-7020

THE HARD PART BEGINS   Cinepix, 1974, Canadian
BLOOD AND GUTS   Ambassador, 1978, Canadian
PROM NIGHT   Avco Embassy, 1980, Canadian
HUMONGOUS   Avco Embassy, 1982, Canadian
CROSS-COUNTRY   New World, 1983, Canadian
FLYING   Golden Harvest, 1985
BULLIES   Universal, 1986, Canadian
MANIA   co-director with John Sheppard & D.M.
    Robertson, Simcom Productions, 1986, Canadian
BLINDSIDE   Norstar Entertainment, 1987, Canadian
REALLY WEIRD TALES (CTF)   co-director, HBO/Atlantis
    Films, 1987, U.S.- Canadian
GOING TO THE CHAPEL (TF)   The Furia Organization/
    Finnegan- Pinchuk Productions, 1988
SHE KNOWS TOO MUCH (TF)   The Fred Silverman
    Company/Finnegan- Pinchuk Productions/
    MGM TV, 1989
MURDER BY NIGHT (CTF)   USA Network, 1989
DOUBLE YOUR PLEASURE (TF)   Steve White
    Productions/Spectator Films, 1989

ADRIAN LYNE*
Agent: ICM - Los Angeles, 213/550-4000

FOXES   United Artists, 1980
FLASHDANCE   Paramount, 1983
9-1/2 WEEKS   MGM/UA, 1986
FATAL ATTRACTION★   Paramount, 1987
JACOB'S LADDER   Tri-Star, 1990

JONATHAN LYNN*
b. 1943 - Bath, England
Agent: CAA - Beverly Hills, 213/288-4545

CLUE   Paramount, 1985
NUNS ON THE RUN   20th Century Fox, 1990, British

M

DICK MAAS
Agent: Triad Artists, Inc. - Los Angeles, 213/556-2727

RIGOR MORTIS   1981, Dutch
THE LIFT   Island Alive/Media Home Entertainment,
    1983, Dutch
FLODDER   Concorde Films, 1986, Dutch
AMSTERDAMNED   Vestron, 1987, Dutch

PETER MACDONALD*
Home: 23 Wensleydale Road, Hampton, Middlesex,
    England TW122LP, 01/979-5142
Agent: Jeremy Zimmer, Bauer Benedek Agency -
    Los Angeles, 213/274-2521

RAMBO III   Tri-Star, 1988

ALEXANDER MACKENDRICK
b. 1912 - Boston, Lincolnshire, England

TIGHT LITTLE ISLAND   WHISKEY GALORE!   Rank,
    1949, British
THE MAN IN THE WHITE SUIT   Rank, 1951, British
CRASH OF SILENCE   MANDY   Universal, 1952, British
HIGH AND DRY   THE MAGGIE   Universal, 1954, British
THE LADYKILLERS   Continental, 1956, British
SWEET SMELL OF SUCCESS   United Artists, 1957
A BOY TEN FEET TALL   SAMMY GOING SOUTH
    Paramount, 1963, British
A HIGH WIND IN JAMAICA   20th Century-Fox,
    1965, British
DON'T MAKE WAVES   MGM, 1967

JOHN MACKENZIE*
b. Edinburgh, Scotland
Home: 7 Clifton Hill, London NW8, England, 71/624-4233
Agent: Bauer Benedek Agency - Los Angeles, 213/275-2421

ONE BRIEF SUMMER   Cinevision, 1970, British
UNMAN, WITTERING & ZIGO   Paramount, 1971, British
THE CHEVIOT (TF)   1973, British
THE STAG AND THE BLACK (TF)   1973, British
BLACK OIL (TF)   1973, British
SHUTDOWN (TF)   1974, British
JUST ANOTHER SATURDAY (TF)   1975, British
MADE   International Co-productions, 1975, British
DOUBLE DARE (TF)   1976, British
PASSAGE TO ENGLAND (TF)   1976, British
RED SHIFT (TF)   1977, British
JUST A BOY'S GAME (TF)   BBC, 1979, British
A SENSE OF FREEDOM (TF)   J. Isaacs Productions/STV,
    1979, British
THE LONG GOOD FRIDAY   Embassy, 1982, British
BEYOND THE LIMIT   THE HONORARY CONSUL
    Paramount, 1983, British
THE INNOCENT   TVS Ltd./Tempest Films, 1985, British
ACT OF VENGEANCE (CTF)   HBO Premiere Films/Telepix
    Canada Corporation, 1986, U.S.-Canadian
THE FOURTH PROTOCOL   Lorimar, 1987, British
THE LAST OF THE FINEST   Orion, 1990

WILL MACKENZIE*
Agent: Elliot Webb, Broder-Kurland-Webb-Uffner Agency -
    Los Angeles, 213/656-9262

FAMILY TIES VACATION (TF)   Paramount TV/Ubu
    Productions/NBC Entertainment, 1985
A HOBO'S CHRISTMAS (TF)   Joe Byrnne-Falrose
    Productions/Phoenix Entertainment, 1987
WORTH WINNING   20th Century Fox, 1989

STEPHEN MACLEAN
Agent: William Morris Agency - Beverly Hills, 213/274-7451

AROUND THE WORLD IN 80 WAYS   Alive Films,
    1987, Australian

W. H. MACY
LIP SERVICE (CTF)   HBO Showcase/Cinehaus, 1988

JOHN MADDEN
Agent: William Morris Agency - Beverly Hills, 213/274-7451

AFTER THE WAR (MS)   Granada TV, 1989, British

LEE MADDEN*
Home: 16918 Marquez Avenue, Pacific Palisades, CA
    90272, 213/454-6255

HELL'S ANGELS '69   American International, 1969
ANGEL UNCHAINED   American International, 1970
THE MANHANDLERS   Premiere, 1975
THE NIGHT GOD SCREAMED   Cinemation, 1973
OUT OF THE DARKNESS   NIGHT CREATURES
    Dimension, 1978
GHOST FEVER   directed under pseudonym of Alan
    Smithee, Miramax, 1987

PAUL M. MADDEN
b. April 26, 1950 - Boston
Business: Madden Movies, Inc., 415 United Street, Key
    West, FL 33040, 305/296-7434
Attorney: Keith Fleer, Sinclair, Tennenbaum, 335 North
    Maple Drive, Beverly Hills, CA 90210, 213/285-6222

SUMMER JOB   SVS Films, 1989
MEDIUM RARE   Limelight Films, 1989

KENNETH MADSEN
b. Denmark
Address: Guldbergsgade 29F, 2200 Copenhagen,
    Denmark, 45/35360036
Attorney: 1990 Kenmad Inc., c/o Weisbarth, Alman &
    Michaelson, 156 West 56th Street, New York,
    NY 10019

A DAY IN OCTOBER   Panorama Film International,
    1991, U.S.-Danish

GUY MAGAR*
Home: 7185 Woodrow Wilson Drive, Los Angeles, CA
    90068, 213/461-9009
Business: Renegade Films, 8033 Sunset Blvd. -
    Suite 1102, Los Angeles, CA 90046, 213/466-0786

RETRIBUTION   United Film Distribution, 1987

ALBERT MAGNOLI*
Agent: Jim Wiatt, ICM - Los Angeles, 213/550-4000

PURPLE RAIN   Warner Bros., 1984
AMERICAN ANTHEM   Columbia, 1986

DEZSO MAGYAR*
Home: 1247 22nd Street - Apt. 3, Santa Monica, CA
    90404, 213/453-66217
Agent: Paul Kohner, Inc. - Los Angeles, 213/550-1060

THE AGITATORS   Hungarofilm, 1969, Hungarian
THREE GIRLS   Hungarian
PUNITIVE EXPEDITION   Hungarian
RAPPACINI'S DAUGHTER (TF)   Learning in Focus, 1980
SUMMER (TF)   Cinelit Productions/WNET-13, 1981
KING OF AMERICA (TF)   Center for Television in the
    Humanities, 1982
NO SECRETS   Curb/Esquire Films, 1990

BARRY MAHON
(Jackson B. Mahon)
Contact: Sinetron Corporation - North Hollywood,
    818/762-5674

WHITE SLAVE RACKET   Independent, 1953
CUBAN REBEL GIRLS   Joseph Brenner Associates, 1957
GIRLS INC.   Independent, 1960
HOUSEWIVES INC.   Independent, 1960
SMORGASBROAD   Independent, 1960
PROSTITUTES PROTECTIVE SOCIETY
    Independent, 1961
THE BEAST THAT KILLED WOMEN   Independent, 1962
FANNY HILL MEETS LADY CHATTERLEY
    Independent, 1967
FANNY HILL MEETS THE RED BARON
    Independent, 1967
FANNY HILL MEETS DR. EROTICO   Independent, 1967
THE WONDERFUL LAND OF OZ   Childhood
    Productions, 1968
SANTA'S CHRISTMAS ELF   Cineworld, 1969

MATT MAHURIN
IMAGINING AMERICA (TF)   co-director with Ralph Bakshi,
    Mustapha Khan & Ed Lachman, Vanguard Films, 1989

NORMAN MAILER*
b. January 31, 1923 - Long Beach, New Jersey
Contact: Directors Guild of America - Los Angeles,
    213/289-2000

WILD 90   Supreme Mix, 1968
BEYOND THE LAW   Grove Press, 1968
MAIDSTONE   Supreme Mix, 1971
TOUGH GUYS DON'T DANCE   Cannon, 1987

LECH MAJEWSKI*
Business: AGF Associates - New York, 212/864-7097

THE FLIGHT OF THE SPRUCE GOOSE   Michael
    Hausman/Filmhaus, 1986
PRISONER OF RIO   Multi Media AG/Samba Corporation,
    1988, Swiss

JOHNNY MAK
(Mai Dangxiong)
b. 1949 - Hong Kong
Business: Johnny Mak Productions Ltd., Room 608 - Tower
    1, 30 Canton Road, Silvercord, Kowloon, Hong Kong,
    (3) 693966

LONG ARM OF THE LAW   Johnny Mak Productions/Bo Ho
    Films, 1984, Hong Kong
RED GUARDS IN HONG KONG   Golden Communications,
    1987, Hong Kong

DUSAN MAKAVEJEV
b. October 13, 1932 - Belgrade, Yugoslavia
Agent: Toby Jaffe, Leading Artists - Beverly Hills,
    213/858-1999

MAN IS NOT A BIRD   Grove Press, 1965, Yugoslavian
LOVE AFFAIR; OR THE CASE OF THE MISSING
    SWITCHBOARD OPERATOR   Brandon,
    1966, Yugoslavian
INNOCENCE UNPROTECTED   Grove Press,
    1968, Yugoslavian
WR - MYSTERIES OF THE ORGANISM   Cinema 5,
    1971, Yugoslavian

SWEET MOVIE   Biograph, 1975, French-Canadian-
   West German
MONTENEGRO   *MONTENEGRO, OR PIGS AND PEARLS*
   Atlantic Releasing Corporation, 1981, Swedish
THE COCA COLA KID   Cinecom/Film Gallery,
   1985, Australian
MANIFESTO   Cannon, 1988, U.S.-Yugoslavian

KAROLY MAKK

b. 1925 - Hungary
Contact: Hungarofilm, Bathory utca 10, H-1054, Budapest,
   Hungary, tel.: 116650

LILOMFI   1954, Hungarian
WARD NO. 8   1955, Hungarian
THE HOUSE UNDER THE ROCKS   1958, Hungarian
THE FANATICS   1961, Hungarian
THE LOST PARADISE   1962, Hungarian
THE LAST BUT ONE   1963, Hungarian
A CLOUDLESS VACATION   1967, Hungarian
BEFORE GOD AND MAN   1967, Hungarian
LOVE   Ajay, 1971, Hungarian
CAT'S PLAY   1974, Hungarian
A VERY MORAL NIGHT   1978, Hungarian
BEHIND THE BRICK WALL   1980, Hungarian
ANOTHER WAY   1983, Hungarian
LILY IN LOVE   New Line Cinema, 1985, Hungarian-U.S.
THE LAST MANUSCRIPT   Mafilm/Studio Dialog,
   1987, Hungarian

TERRENCE MALICK*

b. November 30, 1943 - Ottawa, Illinois
Agent: Writers Guild of America - Los Angeles,
   213550-1000

BADLANDS   Warner Bros., 1974
DAYS OF HEAVEN   Paramount, 1978

LOUIS MALLE*

b. October 30, 1932 - Thumeries, France
Agent: Sam Cohn, ICM - New York City, 212/556-5600

FONTAINE DE VAUCLUSE   1953, French
STATION 307   1955, French
THE SILENT WORLD (FD)   co-director with
   Jacques-Yves Cousteau, Columbia, 1956, French
FRANTIC   *ASCENSEUR POUR L'ECHAFAUD*   Times,
   1957, French
THE LOVERS   Zenith International, 1958, French
ZAZIE   *ZAZIE DANS LE METRO*   Astor, 1960, French
A VERY PRIVATE AFFAIR   MGM, 1962, French-Italian
THE FIRE WITHIN   Governor, 1963, French
VIVA MARIA!   United Artists, 1965, French-Italian
THE THIEF OF PARIS   *LE VOLEUR*   Lopert, 1967,
   French-Italian
SPIRITS OF THE DEAD   *HISTOIRES
   EXTRAORDINAIRES*   co-director with Federico
   Fellini & Roger Vadim, American International, 1969,
   French-Italian
CALCUTTA (FD)   1969, French
PHANTOM INDIA (TD)   Olympic, 1969, French
MURMUR OF THE HEART   *LE SOUFFLE AU COEUR*
   Palomar, 1971, French
HUMAIN, TROP HUMAIN (FD)   New Yorker,
   1972, French
PLACE DE LA REPUBLIQUE (FD)   NEF Diffusion,
   1974, French

LACOMBE LUCIEN   20th Century-Fox, 1974,
   French-Italian-West German
BLACK MOON   20th Century-Fox, 1975, French
PRETTY BABY   Paramount, 1978
ATLANTIC CITY★   Paramount, 1981, Canadian-French
MY DINNER WITH ANDRE   New Yorker, 1981
CRACKERS   Universal, 1984
ALAMO BAY   Tri-Star, 1985
AND THE PURSUIT OF HAPPINESS   *GOD'S COUNTRY*
   (FD)   Pretty Mouse Films, 1985
AU REVOIR LES ENFANTS (GOODBYE CHILDREN)
   Orion Classics, 1987, French-West German
MAY FOOLS   *MILOU EN MAI*   Orion Classics,
   1990, French

BRUCE MALMUTH*

b. February 4, 1934 - Brooklyn, New York
Business: Soularview Productions, Inc., 9981 Robbins Drive,
   Beverly Hills, CA 90212, 213/277-4555
Agent: Irv Schechter Company - Beverly Hills, 213/278-8070

FORE PLAY   co-director with John G. Avildsen & Robert
   McCarty, Cinema National, 1975
NIGHTHAWKS   Universal, 1981
THE MAN WHO WASN'T THERE   Paramount, 1983
WHERE ARE THE CHILDREN?   Columbia, 1986
HARD TO KILL   Warner Bros., 1990

NANCY MALONE*

Business: Lilac Productions, 4507 Auckland Avenue,
   North Hollywood, CA 91602, 818/506-5130

THERE WERE TIMES, DEAR (TF)   Lilac Productions, 1987

WILLIAM MALONE

Agent: CAA - Beverly Hills, 213/288-4545

SCARED TO DEATH   Lone Star, 1982
CREATURE   Cardinal Releasing, 1985

DAVID MAMET*

b. November 30, 1947 - Chicago, Illinois
Agent: Rosenstone/Wender - New York City,
   212/832-8330

HOUSE OF GAMES   Orion, 1987
THINGS CHANGE   Columbia, 1988

ROBERT MANDEL*

Contact: Directors Guild of America - Los Angeles,
   213/289-2000

INDEPENDENCE DAY   Warner Bros., 1983
TOUCH & GO   Tri-Star, 1986
F/X   Orion, 1986
BIG SHOTS   20th Century Fox, 1987
PERFECT WITNESS (CTF)   HBO Pictures/Granger
   Productions, 1989

LUIS MANDOKI

Agent: Alan Greenspan, ICM - Los Angeles, 213/550-4428

MOTEL   1983, Mexican
GABY - A TRUE STORY   Tri-Star, 1987, U.S.-Mexican
WHITE PALACE   Universal, 1990

JOSEPH MANDUKE*

Agent: Ronald Leif, Contemporary Artists - Beverly Hills,
213/278-8250

JUMP   Cannon, 1971
CORNBREAD, EARL AND ME   American
International, 1975
KID VENGEANCE   Irwin Yablans, 1977, U.S.-Israeli
BEATLEMANIA   American Cinema, 1981
OMEGA SYNDROME   New World, 1987
THE GUMSHOE KID   Skouras Pictures, 1989

FRANCIS MANKIEWICZ

b. 1944 - Shanghai, China
Address: 711 Stuart, Montreal, Quebec H2V 3H4,
Canada, 514/495-8055
Agent: Great Northern Artists Management, 350 Dupont
Street, Toronto, Ontario M5R 1V9, Canada,
416/925-2051

VALENTIN (TF)   1973, Canadian
LE TEMPS D'UNE CHASSE   Cinepix, 1973, Canadian
LES BONS DEBARRAS—GOOD RIDDANCE
International Film Exchange, 1981, Canadian
LES BEAUX SOUVENIRS   National Film Board of
Canada, 1982, Canadian
AND THEN YOU DIE (TF)   CBC, 1987, Canadian
LES PORTES TOURNANTES   Malofilm Group/UGC/
Canal Plus/ACPAV, 1988, Canadian-French
LOVE AND HATE: THE STORY OF COLIN AND JOANNE
THATCHER (MS)   CBC, 1989, Canadian

JOSEPH L. MANKIEWICZ*

b. February 11, 1909 - Wilkes-Barre, Pennsylvania
Home: 491 Guard Hill Road, Bedford, NY 10506
Agent: Ben Benjamin, William Morris Agency - New York
City, 212/556-5652

DRAGONWYCK   20th Century-Fox, 1946
SOMEWHERE IN THE NIGHT   20th Century-Fox, 1946
THE LATE GEORGE APLEY   20th Century-Fox, 1947
THE GHOST AND MRS. MUIR   20th Century-Fox, 1947
ESCAPE   20th Century-Fox, 1948
A LETTER TO THREE WIVES★★   20th Century-
Fox, 1949
HOUSE OF STRANGERS   20th Century-Fox, 1949
NO WAY OUT   20th Century-Fox, 1950
ALL ABOUT EVE★★   20th Century-Fox, 1950
PEOPLE WILL TALK   20th Century-Fox, 1951
FIVE FINGERS★   20th Century-Fox, 1952
JULIUS CAESAR   MGM, 1953
THE BAREFOOT CONTESSA   United Artists, 1954,
U.S.-Italian
GUYS AND DOLLS   MGM, 1955
THE QUIET AMERICAN   United Artists, 1958
SUDDENLY LAST SUMMER   Columbia, 1960
CLEOPATRA   20th Century-Fox, 1963
THE HONEY POT   United Artists, 1967,
British-U.S.-Italian
THERE WAS A CROOKED MAN   Warner Bros., 1970
KING: A FILMED RECORD...MONTGOMERY TO
MEMPHIS (FD)   co-director with Sidney Lumet,
Maron Films Limited, 1970
SLEUTH★   20th Century-Fox, 1972, British

TOM MANKIEWICZ*

b. June 1, 1942 - Los Angeles, California
Agent: ICM - Los Angeles, 213/550-4000

HART TO HART (TF)   Spelling-Goldberg Productions, 1979

DRAGNET   Universal, 1987
DELIRIOUS   MGM/UA, 1990

ABBY MANN*

(Abraham Goodman)
b. 1927 - Philadelphia, Pennsylvania
Agent: ICM - Los Angeles, 213/550-4000

KING (MS) ☆   Abby Mann Productions/Filmways, 1978

DANIEL MANN*

b. August 8, 1912 - New York, New York
Home: 6328 Frondosa Drive, Malibu, CA 90265,
213/457-9889
Business Manager: Berke Management Company, 15910
Ventura Blvd. - Suite 1215, Encino, CA 91436,
818/990-2631

COME BACK, LITTLE SHEBA   Paramount, 1952
ABOUT MRS. LESLIE   Paramount, 1954
THE ROSE TATTOO   Paramount, 1955
I'LL CRY TOMORROW   MGM, 1955
TEAHOUSE OF THE AUGUST MOON   MGM, 1956
HOT SPELL   Paramount, 1958
THE LAST ANGRY MAN   Columbia, 1959
THE MOUNTAIN ROAD   Columbia, 1960
BUTTERFIELD 8   MGM, 1960
ADA   MGM, 1961
FIVE FINGER EXERCISE   Columbia, 1962
WHO'S GOT THE ACTION?   Paramount, 1962
WHO'S BEEN SLEEPING IN MY BED?   Paramount, 1963
JUDITH   Paramount, 1965, U.S.-British-Israeli
OUR MAN FLINT   20th Century-Fox, 1966
FOR LOVE OF IVY   Cinerama Releasing Corporation, 1968
A DREAM OF KINGS   National General, 1969
WILLARD   Cinerama Releasing Corporation, 1971
THE REVENGERS   National General, 1972, U.S.-Mexican
INTERVAL   Avco Embassy, 1973, U.S.-Mexican
MAURIE   *BIG MO*   National General, 1973
LOST IN THE STARS   American Film Theatre, 1974
JOURNEY INTO FEAR   Stirling Gold, 1976, Canadian
HOW THE WEST WAS WON (MS)   co-director with Burt
Kennedy, MGM TV, 1977
MATILDA   American International, 1978
PLAYING FOR TIME (TF)   Syzygy Productions, 1980
THE DAY THE LOVING STOPPED (TF)   Monash-Zeitman
Productions, 1981
THE MAN WHO BROKE 1,000 CHAINS (CTF)   HBO
Pictures/Journey Entertainment, 1987

DELBERT MANN*

b. January 30, 1920 - Lawrence, Kansas
Agent: William Morris Agency - Beverly Hills, 213/274-7451

MARTY★★   United Artists, 1955
THE BACHELOR PARTY   United Artists, 1957
DESIRE UNDER THE ELMS   Paramount, 1958
SEPARATE TABLES   United Artists, 1959
MIDDLE OF THE NIGHT   Columbia, 1959
THE DARK AT THE TOP OF THE STAIRS   Warner
Bros., 1960
THE OUTSIDER   Universal, 1961
LOVER, COME BACK   Universal, 1962
THAT TOUCH OF MINK   Universal, 1962
A GATHERING OF EAGLES   Universal, 1963
DEAR HEART   Warner Bros., 1964
QUICK BEFORE IT MELTS   MGM, 1965
MISTER BUDDWING   MGM, 1966
FITZWILLY   United Artists, 1967

HEIDI (TF)   Omnibus Productions, 1968
THE PINK JUNGLE   Universal, 1968
DAVID COPPERFIELD (TF)   Omnibus Productions/
 Sagittarius Productions, 1970, British-U.S.
KIDNAPPED   American International, 1971, British
JANE EYRE (TF)   Omnibus Productions/Sagittarius
 Productions, 1971, British-U.S.
SHE WAITS (TF)   Metromedia Productions, 1972
NO PLACE TO RUN (TF)   ABC Circle Films, 1972
THE MAN WITHOUT A COUNTRY (TF)   Norman
 Rosemont Productions, 1973
A GIRL NAMED SOONER (TF)   Frederick Brogger
 Associates/20th Century-Fox TV, 1975
BIRCH INTERVAL   Gamma III, 1976
FRANCIS GARY POWERS: THE TRUE STORY OF
 THE U-2 SPY INCIDENT (TF)   Charles Fries
 Productions, 1976
TELL ME MY NAME (TF)   Talent Associates, 1977
BREAKING UP (TF) ☆   Time-Life Productions, 1978
LOVE'S DARK RIDE (TF)   Mark VII Ltd./
 Worldvision, 1978
HOME TO STAY (TF)   Time-Life Productions, 1978
THOU SHALT NOT COMMIT ADULTERY (TF)   Edgar J.
 Scherick Associates, 1978
TORN BETWEEN TWO LOVERS (TF)   Alan Landsburg
 Productions, 1979
ALL QUIET ON THE WESTERN FRONT (TF) ☆   Norman
 Rosemont Productions/ Marble Arch Productions, 1979
TO FIND MY SON (TF)   Green-Epstein Productions/
 Columbia TV, 1980
NIGHT CROSSING   Buena Vista, 1982
BRONTE   Charlotte Ltd. Partnership/Radio Telefis
 Eireann, 1983, U.S-Irish
THE GIFT OF LOVE: A CHRISTMAS STORY (TF)
 Telecom Entertainment/Amanda Productions, 1983
LOVE LEADS THE WAY (CTF)   Hawkins-Permut
 Productions, 1984
A DEATH IN CALIFORNIA (TF)   Mace Neufeld
 Productions/Lorimar Productions, 1985
THE LAST DAYS OF PATTON (TF)   Entertainment
 Partners, 1986
THE TED KENNEDY, JR. STORY (TF)   Entertainment
 Partners, 1986
APRIL MORNING (TF)   Robert Halmi, Inc./Samuel
 Goldwyn TV, 1988

FARHAD MANN*
Home: 1125 Chantilly Road, Bel Air, CA 90077,
 213/850-7404
Agent: Alan Greenspan, ICM - Los Angeles,
 213/550-4428

NICK KNIGHT (TF)   Barry Weitz Films/Robirdle Pictures/
 New World TV, 1989
FACE OF FEAR (TF)   Lee Rich Productions/Warner Bros.
 TV, 1990

MICHAEL MANN*
Agent: Jeff Berg, ICM - Los Angeles, 213/550-4205

THE JERICHO MILE (TF)   ABC Circle Films, 1979
THIEF   United Artists, 1981
THE KEEP   Paramount, 1983
MANHUNTER   DEG, 1986
L.A. TAKEDOWN (TF)   AJAR Inc./Movies Film
 Productions/Cia Ibero de T.V. S.A./World International
 Network, 1989

RON MANN
b. 1958 - Toronto, Ontario, Canada
Agent: The Colbert Agency, 303 Davenport Road, Toronto,
 Ontario M5R 1K5, 416/964-3302
Business: Sphinx Productions Ltd., 41 Riderwood Drive,
 Willowdale, Ontario M2L 2E7, Canada, 416/445-7492

IMAGINE THE SOUND   Harmony Films, 1981, Canadian
POETRY IN MOTION (FD)   Sphinx, 1983, Canadian
LISTEN TO THE CITY   Spectrafilm, 1984, Canadian
COMIC BOOK CONFIDENTIAL (FD)   Cinecom,
 1988, Canadian
TWIST (FD)   Cineplex Odeon, 1990, Canadian

KIM MANNERS*
Agent: Sanford-Beckett-Skouras & Associates - Los Angeles,
 213/208-2100

21 JUMP STREET (TF)   Stephen J. Cannell
 Productions, 1987
K-9000 (TF)   Fries Entertainment, 1989

MICHELLE MANNING*
Business Manager: Zeiderman, Oberman & Associates,
 500 S. Sepulveda Blvd. - Suite 500, Los Angeles, CA
 90049, 213/476-5333

BLUE CITY   Paramount, 1986

PETER MANOOGIAN
THE DUNGEONMASTER   co-director, Empire
 Pictures, 1985
ELIMINATORS   Empire Pictures, 1986
ENEMY TERRITORY   Empire Pictures, 1987
ARENA   Triumph Releasing Corporation, 1990

RON MARCARELLI
ORIGINAL INTENT   Mission of Hope Productions, 1990

TERRY MARCEL*
(Terence G. Marcel)
b. 1942 - Oxford, England
Address: 4 Gaston Bell Close, Richmond, Surrey, England,
 71/940-3310
Agent: Maureen Moore, London Management, 235 Regent
 Street, London W1A 2JT, England, 71/493-1610

THERE GOES THE BRIDGE   Vanguard, 1980, British
HAWK THE SLAYER   ITC, 1980, British
PRISONERS OF THE LOST UNIVERSE (CTF)
 Marcel-Robertson Productions/ Showtime, 1983, British
JANE AND THE LOST CITY   Marcel-Robertson
 Productions/Glen Films Productions, 1987, British

ANTONIO MARGHERITI
(See Anthony B. DAWSON)

STUART MARGOLIN*
b. January 31 - Davenport, Iowa
Home: Box 478, Ganges, Salt Spring Island, British Columbia
 V0S 1E0, Canada, 604/537-4224
Agent: Alan Greenspan, ICM - Los Angeles, 213/550-4428

SUDDENLY, LOVE (TF)   Ross Hunter Productions, 1978
A SHINING SEASON (TF)   Green-Epstein Productions/T-M
 Productions/ Columbia TV, 1979
BRET MAVERICK (TF)   Comanche Productions/Warner
 Bros. TV, 1981

Ma

FILM DIRECTORS GUIDE

FILM DIRECTORS

THE LONG SUMMER OF GEORGE ADAMS (TF)
Warner Bros. TV, 1982
THE GLITTER DOME (CTF)   HBO Premiere Films/
Telepictures Productions/ Trincomali Productions,
1984, U.S.-Canadian
THE ROOM UPSTAIRS (TF)   Marian Rees Associates/
The Alexander Group, 1987
THE FACTS OF LIFE DOWN UNDER (TF)   Embassy TV/
Crawford Productions, 1987, U.S.-Australian
PARAMEDICS   Vestron, 1988
DONNA D'ONORE   Lux TV/Reteitalia, 1990, Italian

JEFF MARGOLIS*

Agent: Dan Schrier, ICM - Los Angeles, 213/550-4000

RICHARD PRYOR LIVE IN CONCERT (FD)   Special
Event Entertainment, 1979

CHEECH MARIN
(Richard Marin)
b. July 13, 1946 - Los Angeles, California
Agent: CAA - Beverly Hills, 213/288-4545

BORN IN EAST L.A.   Universal, 1987

PETER MARIS
TERROR SQUAD   1987
VIPER   Fries Distribution, 1988
MINISTRY OF VENGEANCE   Concorde, 1989

MONTE MARKHAM*
b. June 21, 1938 - Manatee, Florida
Home: P.O. Box 4200, Malibu, CA 90265

DEFENSE PLAY   Trans World Entertainment, 1988

PETER MARKLE*

Agent: CAA - Beverly Hills, 213/288-4545

THE PERSONALS   New World, 1982
HOT DOG...THE MOVIE   MGM/UA, 1984
YOUNGBLOOD   MGM/UA, 1986
DESPERATE (TF)   Toots Productions/Warner
Bros. TV, 1987
BAT-21   Tri-Star, 1988
BREAKING POINT (CTF)   Avnet-Kerner Company, 1989
EL DIABLO (CTF)   HBO Pictures/Wizan-Black Films, 1990

ROBERT MARKOWITZ*
Business: Moon River Productions Ltd., 11521 Amanda
Drive, Studio City, CA 91604
Agent: William Morris Agency - Beverly Hills, 213/274-7451

THE STORYTELLER (TF)   Universal TV, 1977
THE DEADLIEST SEASON (TF)   Titus Productions, 1977
VOICES   MGM/United Artists, 1979
THE WALL (TF)   Cinetex International/Time-Life
Productions, 1982, U.S-Polish
A LONG WAY HOME (TF)   Alan Landsburg
Productions, 1981
PRAY TV (TF)   ABC Circle Films, 1982
PHANTOM OF THE OPERA (TF)   Robert Halmi Inc., 1983
MY MOTHER'S SECRET LIFE (TF)   Furia-Oringer
Productions/ABC Circle Films, 1984
KOJAK: THE BELARUS FILE (TF)   Universal TV, 1985
CHILDREN OF THE NIGHT (TF)   Robert Guenette
Productions, 1985
ALEX: THE LIFE OF A CHILD (TF)   Mandy
Productions, 1986

ADAM: HIS SONG CONTINUES (TF)   Alan Landsburg
Productions, 1986
A DANGEROUS LIFE (CTF)   HBO/McElroy & McElroy/
FilmAccord Corporation/Australian Broadcasting
Corporation/Zenith Productions, 1988, U.S.-Australian
A CRY FOR HELP: THE TRACEY THURMAN STORY (TF)
Dick Clark Productions, 1989
TOO YOUNG TO DIE? (TF)   von Zerneck-Sertner
Films, 1990

ARTHUR MARKS*
b. August 2, 1927 - Los Angeles, California
Business Manager: Robert Brenner, Gibson, Hoffman &
Pancione, 1888 Century Park East - Suite 1777,
Los Angeles, CA 90067, 213/556-4660

CLASS OF '74   co-director with Mack Bing, Crest, 1972
BONNIE'S KIDS   General Film Corporation, 1973
THE ROOM MATES   General Film Corporation, 1973
DETROIT 9000   General Film Corporation, 1973
A WOMAN FOR ALL MEN   General Film Corporation, 1975
BUCKTOWN   American International, 1975
FRIDAY FOSTER   American International, 1975
J.D.'S REVENGE   American International, 1976
THE MONKEY HUSTLE   American International, 1976

MALCOLM MARMORSTEIN
Agent: Preferred Artists - Encino, 818/990-0305

DEAD MEN DON'T DIE   Waymar Productions, 1990

EUGENE MARNER*
Home: 141 Bergen Street, Brooklyn, NY 11217,
718/875-8205

CIVILIZATION AND THE JEWS (TD)   PBS, 1984
BEAUTY AND THE BEAST   Cannon, 1987, U.S.-Israeli
PUSS IN BOOTS   Cannon, 1987, U.S.-Israeli

LEON MARR
b. 1948 - Toronto, Ontario, Canada
Address: 19 Beech Avenue, Toronto, Ontario M4E 3H3,
Canada, 416/691-1215
Agent: William Morris Agency - Beverly Hills, 213/274-7451

CLARE'S WISH (TF)   1979, Canadian
FLOWERS IN THE SAND (TF)   1980, Canadian
DANCING IN THE DARK   New World, 1986, Canadian

FRANK MARSHALL*
Business: Amblin Entertainment, 100 Universal City
Plaza - Bungalow 477, Universal City, CA 91608,
818/777-4600

ARACHNOPHOBIA   Buena Vista, 1990

GARRY MARSHALL*
b. November 13, 1934 - New York, New York
Business Manager: Diane Frazen, Henderson Productions,
10067 Riverside Drive, North Hollywood, CA 91602,
818/985-6417

YOUNG DOCTORS IN LOVE   20th Century-Fox, 1982
THE FLAMINGO KID   20th Century Fox, 1984
NOTHING IN COMMON   Tri-Star, 1986
OVERBOARD   MGM/UA, 1987
BEACHES   Buena Vista, 1988
PRETTY WOMAN   Buena Vista, 1990

PENNY MARSHALL*
b. October 15, 1942 - New York, New York
Agent: CAA - Beverly Hills, 213/288-4545

JUMPIN' JACK FLASH   20th Century Fox, 1986
BIG   20th Century Fox, 1988
AWAKENINGS   Columbia, 1990

FRANK MARTIN
Business: Point Blank, 6936 Pacific View Drive,
    Los Angeles, CA 90068

JOHN HUSTON: THE MAN, THE MOVIES,
    THE MAVERICK (CTD)   Point Blank, 1988

CHUCK MARTINEZ
Agent: Lloyd Segan, Irvin Arthur Associates - Beverly Hills,
    213/278-5934

SNACKS   New World, 1985
NICE GIRLS DON'T EXPLODE   New World, 1987

RICHARD MARTINI
Personal Manager: MCEG Management, 11355
    W. Olympic Blvd. - Suite 500, Los Angeles, CA 90064,
    213/208-3262
Agent: The Agency - Los Angeles, 213/551-3000

YOU CAN'T HURRY LOVE   MCEG, 1989
LIMIT UP   New Line Cinema, 1989

LESLIE H. MARTINSON*
b. Boston, Massachusetts
Home: 2288 Coldwater Canyon Blvd., Beverly Hills, CA
    90210, 213/271-4127
Agent: Mitch Kaplan, Kaplan-Stahler Agency -
    Beverly Hills, 213/271-4127

THE ATOMIC KID   Republic, 1954
HOT ROD GIRL   American International, 1956
HOT ROD RUMBLE   Allied Artists, 1957
LAD: A DOG   co-director with Aram Avakian, Warner
    Bros., 1961
PT 109   Warner Bros., 1963
BLACK GOLD   Warner Bros., 1963
F.B.I. CODE 98   Warner Bros., 1964
FOR THOSE WHO THINK YOUNG   United Artists, 1964
BATMAN   20th Century-Fox, 1966
FATHOM   20th Century-Fox, 1967
THE CHALLENGERS (TF)   Universal TV, 1970
MRS. POLLIFAX - SPY   United Artists, 1971
HOW TO STEAL AN AIRPLANE (TF)   Universal
    TV, 1971
ESCAPE FROM ANGOLA   Doty-Dayton, 1976
CRUISE MISSILE   Eichberg Film/Cinelux-Romano Film/
    Mundial Film/Cine-Luce/ Noble Productions/FPDC,
    1978, West German-Spanish-U.S.-Iranian
RESCUE FROM GILLIGAN'S ISLAND (TF)   Sherwood
    Schwartz Productions, 1978
THE KID WITH THE BROKEN HALO (TF)   Satellite
    Productions, 1982
THE KID WITH THE 200 I.Q. (TF)   Guillaume-Margo
    Productions/Zephyr Productions, 1983
THE FANTASTIC WORLD OF D.C. COLLINS (TF)
    Guillaume-Margo Productions/Zephyr
    Productions, 1984

ANDREW MARTON*
(Endre Marton)
b. January 26, 1904 - Budapest, Hungary
Home: 8856 Appian Way, Los Angeles, CA 90046,
    213/654-1297

GYPSY COLT   MGM, 1954
PRISONER OF WAR   MGM, 1954
MEN OF THE FIGHTING LADY   MGM, 1954
GREEN FIRE   MGM, 1955
SEVEN WONDERS OF THE WORLD   co-director, Stanley
    Warner Cinema Corporation, 1956
UNDERWATER WARRIOR   MGM, 1958
THE LONGEST DAY   co-director with Ken Annakin &
    Bernhard Wicki, 20th Century-Fox, 1962
IT HAPPENED IN ATHENS   20th Century-Fox, 1962
THE THIN RED LINE   Allied Artists, 1964
CRACK IN THE WORLD   Paramount, 1965, British
CLARENCE, THE CROSS-EYED LION   MGM, 1965
AROUND THE WORLD UNDER THE SEA   MGM, 1966
BIRDS DO IT   Columbia, 1966
AFRICA - TEXAS STYLE!   Paramount, 1967, British-U.S.

MIKE MARVIN
Agent: Irv Schechter Company - Beverly Hills,
    213/278-8070

HAMBURGER...THE MOTION PICTURE   FM
    Entertainment, 1986
THE WRAITH   New Century/Vista, 1986

PAUL MASLANSKY*
b. November 23, 1933 - New York, New York
Business Manager: Robert Morgan, Morgan & Martindale,
    10780 Santa Monica Blvd. - Suite 250, Los Angeles, CA
    90025, 213/474-0810

SUGAR HILL   American International, 1974

QUENTIN MASTERS*
b. July 12, 1946 - Australia
Address: SW1 One Limited, 21 Cabul Road, London SW11,
    England, 01/228-5228

THUMB TRIPPING   Avco Embassy, 1973
THE STUD   Trans-American, 1978, British
THE PSI FACTOR   1981, British
A DANGEROUS SUMMER   Filmco Ltd.,
    1982, Australian
MIDNITE SPARES   Filmco Australia, 1983, Australian

PETER MASTERSON*
b. June 1, 1934 - Houston, Texas
Agent: Writers and Artists Agency - Los Angeles,
    213/820-2240
Business: Tejas Productions, 1165 Fifth Avenue - Apt. 15A,
    New York, NY 10029, 212/427-4055

THE TRIP TO BOUNTIFUL   Island Pictures/Film
    Dallas, 1985
FULL MOON IN BLUE WATER   Trans World
    Entertainment, 1988
NIGHT GAME   Trans World Entertainment, 1989
BLOOD RED   Hemdale, 1990
CONVICTS   New Line Cinema, 1990

NICO MASTORAKIS

b. April 28, 1941 - Athens, Greece
Agent: The Artists Group - Los Angeles, 213/552-1100
Business: Omega Pictures, 8760 Shoreham Drive - Suite 501, Los Angeles, CA 90069, 213/855-0516

DEATH HAS BLUE EYES   Omega Pictures, 1974, British
ISLAND OF DEATH   Omega Pictures, 1975, British
THE NEXT ONE *THE TIME TRAVELLER*   Allstar Productions, 1982, British-Greek
BLIND DATE   New Line Cinema, 1984, British-Greek
SKYHIGH   Omega Pictures, 1985
THE ZERO BOYS   Omega Pictures, 1986
DOUBLE EXPOSURE   United Film Distribution, 1987
THE WIND   Omega Pictures, 1987
GLITCH!   Omega Pictures, 1988
NIGHTMARE AT NOON   Omega Pictures, 1990, filmed in 1987
HIRED TO KILL   co-director with Peter Rader, Omega Pictures, 1990
IN THE COLD OF THE NIGHT   Omega Pictures, 1990
NINJA ACADEMY   Omega Pictures, 1990

ARMAND MASTROIANNI

b. Brooklyn, New York
Home: 248 Ridgecrest Avenue, Staten Island, NY 10312, 718/948-1051
Agent: William Morris Agency - Beverly Hills, 213/274-7451

HE KNOWS YOU'RE ALONE   MGM/United Artists, 1980
THE CLAIRVOYANT *THE KILLING HOUR*   20th Century-Fox, 1983
THE SUPERNATURALS   Republic Entertainment/ Sandy Howard Productions, 1985
DISTORTIONS   Cori Films, 1987
CAMERON'S CLOSET   SVS Films, 1989
DOUBLE REVENGE   Smart Egg Releasing, 1989

VIVIAN MATALON*

b. October 11, 1929 - Manchester, England
Home: P.O. Box 632, Sharon, CT 06069, 203/364-5190
Agent: Clifford Stevens, STE Representation Ltd. - New York City, 212/246-1030

PRIVATE CONTENTMENT (TF)   WNET-13/South Carolina Educational TV, 1982

CHARLES MATTHAU*

b. December 10, 1964 - New York, New York
Agent: William Morris Agency - Beverly Hills, 213/274-7451
Business: The Matthau Company, 10100 Santa Monica Blvd. - Suite 2200, Los Angeles, CA 90067, 213/454-3336

DOIN' TIME ON PLANET EARTH   Cannon, 1988

WALTER MATTHAU
(Walter Matuschanskavasky)

b. October 1, 1920 - New York, New York
Agent: William Morris Agency - Beverly Hills, 213/274-7451

GANGSTER STORY   RCIP-States Rights, 1960

BURNY MATTINSON

THE GREAT MOUSE DETECTIVE (AF)   co-director with Ron Clements, Dave Michener & John Musker, Buena Vista, 1986

SALLY MATTISON

Business: Concorde Pictures, 11600 San Vicente Blvd., Los Angeles, CA 90049, 213/826-0978

NIGHT LIGHT   Concorde, 1990

RONALD F. MAXWELL*

b. January 5, 1947
Agent: Harris-Goldberg Agency - Los Angeles, 213/553-5200
Business Manager: Sean Corrigan, DeLoitte-Touche - Los Angeles, 213/277-3000
Attorney: Eric Weissman, 9665 Wilshire Blvd., Beverly Hills, CA 90212, 213/858-7888

SEA MARKS (TF)   PBS, 1976
VERNA: USO GIRL (TF) ☆   WNET-13, 1978
LITTLE DARLINGS   Paramount, 1980
THE NIGHT THE LIGHTS WENT OUT IN GEORGIA   Avco Embassy, 1981
KIDCO   20th Century-Fox, 1983
PARENT TRAP II (TF)   The Landsburg Company/Walt Disney TV, 1987

BRADFORD MAY*

Home: 2949 Deep Canyon Drive, Beverly Hills, CA 90210, 213/273-0125
Agent: Audrey Caan, Triad Artists, Inc. - Los Angeles, 213/556-2727

THE LADY FORGETS (TF)   Leonard Hill Films, 1989

ELAINE MAY*
(Elaine Berlin)

b. April 21, 1932 - Philadelphia, Pennsylvania
Business Manager: Julian Schlossberg, Castle Hill Productions, 1414 Avenue of the Americas, New York, NY 10019, 212/888-0080

A NEW LEAF   Paramount, 1971
THE HEARTBREAK KID   20th Century-Fox, 1972
MIKEY AND NICKY   Paramount, 1977
ISHTAR   Columbia, 1987

RUSS MAYBERRY*

Agent: Sanford-Beckett-Skouras & Associates - Los Angeles, 213/208-2100

THE JESUS TRIP   EMCO, 1971
PROBE (TF)   Warner Bros. TV, 1972
A VERY MISSING PERSON (TF)   Universal TV, 1972
FER-DE-LANCE (TF)   Leslie Stevens Productions, 1974
SEVENTH AVENUE (MS)   co-director with Richard Irving, Universal TV, 1977
STONESTREET: WHO KILLED THE CENTERFOLD MODEL? (TF)   Universal TV, 1977
THE 3,000 MILE CHASE (TF)   Universal TV, 1977
THE YOUNG RUNAWAYS (TF)   NBC, 1978
THE MILLION DOLLAR DIXIE DELIVERY (TF)   NBC, 1978
THE REBELS (MS)   Universal TV, 1979
UNIDENTIFIED FLYING ODDBALL   Buena Vista, 1979
THE $5.20 AN HOUR DREAM (TF)   Thompson-Sagal Productions/Big Deal Inc./Finnegan Associates, 1980
MARRIAGE IS ALIVE AND WELL (TF)   Lorimar Productions, 1980
REUNION (TF)   Barry Weitz Films, 1980
A MATTER OF LIFE AND DEATH (TF)   Big Deal Inc./ Raven's Claw Productions/Lorimar Productions, 1981
SIDNEY SHORR (TF)   Hajeno Productions/Warner Bros. TV, 1981

THE FALL GUY (TF)   Glen A. Larson Productions/20th
    Century-Fox TV, 1981
SIDE BY SIDE: THE TRUE STORY OF THE OSMOND
    FAMILY (TF) Osmond Productions/Comworld
    Productions, 1982
ROOSTER (TF)   Glen A. Larson Productions/Tugboat
    Productions/20th Century- Fox TV, 1982
MANIMAL (TF)   Glen A. Larson Productions/20th
    Century-Fox TV, 1983
CHALLENGE OF A LIFETIME (TF)   Moonlight
    Productions, 1985
A PLACE TO CALL HOME (TF)   Big Deal Productions/
    Crawford Productions/ Embassy TV, 1987,
    U.S.-Australian
DANGER DOWN UNDER (TF)   Weintraub Entertainment
    Goup/Hoyts Productions Ltd., 1988, U.S.-Australian

PAUL MAYERSBERG
b. 1941
Agent: William Morris Agency - Beverly Hills, 213/274-7451

CAPTIVE *HEROINE*   CineTel Films, 1986,
    British-French
NIGHTFALL   Concorde, 1988
THE LAST SAMURAI   Goldenberg Films, 1990

TONY MAYLAM*
b. May 26, 1943 - London, England
Business: Worldwide Productions, 303-315 Cricklewood
    Broadway, London NW2, England, 452/809-0214

WHITE ROCK (FD)   EMI, 1977, British
THE RIDDLE OF THE SANDS   Satori, 1979, British
THE BURNING   Orion, 1982
THE SINS OF DORIAN GRAY (TF)   Rankin-Bass
    Productions, 1983

ALBERT MAYSLES
b. November 26, 1926 - Brookline, Massachusetts
Business: Maysles Films, Inc., 250 West 54th Street,
    New York, NY 10019

PSYCHIATRY IN RUSSIA (FD)   1955
YOUTH IN POLAND (FD)   co-director with David
    Maysles, 1962
SHOWMAN (FD)   co-director with David Maysles, 1962
WHAT'S HAPPENING: THE BEATLES IN THE USA (FD)
    co-director with David Maysles, 1964
MEET MARLON BRANDO (FD)   co-director with David
    Maysles, 1965
WITH LOVE FROM TRUMAN (FD)   co-director with David
    Maysles, 1966
SALESMAN (FD)   co-director with David Maysles &
    Charlotte Zwerin, Maysles Film, 1969
GIMME SHELTER (FD)   co-director with David Maysles &
    Charlotte Zwerin, Cinema 5, 1971
CHRISTO'S VALLEY CURTAIN (FD)   co-director with
    David Maysles & Ellen Giffard, 1972
GREY GARDENS (FD)   co-director with David Maysles,
    Ellen Hovde & Muffie Meyer, 1975
RUNNING FENCE (FD)   co-director with David Maysles &
    Charlotte Zwerin, 1977
VLADIMIR HOROWITZ: THE LAST ROMANTIC (TD) ☆
    co-director with David Maysles, Cami Video, 1985
ISLANDS (FD)   co-director with David Maysles & Charlotte
    Zwerin, Maysles Films, 1986
OZAWA (TD)   co-director with David Maysles, Deborah
    Dickson & Susan Froemke, Columbia Artists, 1986

HOROWITZ PLAYS MOZART (FD)   co-director with
    Susan Froemke & Charlotte Zwerin, 1987
JESSYE NORMAN SINGS CARMEN (HVD)   co-director
    with Susan Froemke & Charlotte Zwerin, Cami
    Video, 1989

PAUL MAZURSKY*
b. April 25, 1930 - Brooklyn, New York
Agent: Jeff Berg, ICM - Los Angeles, 213/550-4000

BOB & CAROL & TED & ALICE   Columbia, 1969
ALEX IN WONDERLAND   MGM, 1970
BLUME IN LOVE   Warner Bros., 1973
HARRY AND TONTO   20th Century-Fox, 1974
NEXT STOP, GREENWICH VILLAGE   20th
    Century-Fox, 1976
AN UNMARRIED WOMAN   20th Century-Fox, 1978
WILLIE AND PHIL   20th Century-Fox, 1980
TEMPEST   Columbia, 1982
MOSCOW ON THE HUDSON   Columbia, 1984
DOWN AND OUT IN BEVERLY HILLS   Buena
    Vista, 1986
MOON OVER PARADOR   Universal, 1988, U.S.-Brazilian
ENEMIES, A LOVE STORY   20th Century Fox, 1989
SCENES FROM A MALL   Buena Vista, 1991

FRANK MAZZOLA
13 O'CLOCK   co-director with Frank Leahy, Third Coast
    Entertainment, 1988

CARLO MAZZACURATI
b. March 2, 1956 - Padua, Italy
Contact: SACIS, via Tomacelli 139, 00186 Rome, Italy,
    06/396841

NOTTE ITALIANA   Sacher Film/RAI/So.Fin.A.,
    1987, Italian
IL PRETE BELLO   Nickelodeon/Partner's Production/RAI-3,
    1989, Italian

JIM McBRIDE*
Home: 1059 S. Alfred Street, Los Angeles, CA 90035,
    213/935-9578
Agent: Daniel Ostroff, The Daniel Ostroff Agency - Los
    Angeles, 213/278-2020

DAVID HOLZMAN'S DIARY   Grove Press, 1967
MY GIRLFRIEND'S WEDDING   1968
GLEN AND RANDA   UMC, 1971
A HARD DAY FOR ARCHIE *HOT TIMES* 1973,
    re-released under title MY EROTIC FANTASIES in 1974
    with additional footage by another director
BREATHLESS   Orion, 1983
THE BIG EASY   Columbia, 1987
GREAT BALLS OF FIRE   Orion, 1989

ROBERT McCARTY
Home: 222 West 83rd Street - Apt. 11-C, New York, NY
    10024, 212/580-1034
Attorney: Franklin Weinrib, Ruddel & Vassallo, 950 Third
    Avenue, New York, NY 10022

LIGHT FANTASTIC   Embassy, 1965
I COULD NEVER HAVE SEX WITH A MAN WHO HAS
    SO LITTLE REGARD FOR MY HUSBAND
    Cinema 5, 1973
FORE PLAY   co-director with John G. Avildsen & Bruce
    Malmuth, Cinema National, 1975

GEORGE McCOWAN*

Agent: Martin Shapiro, Shapiro-Lichtman Agency -
Los Angeles, 213/859-8877

THE MONK (TF)   Thomas-Spelling Productions, 1969
THE BALLAD OF ANDY CROCKER (TF)   Thomas-
Spelling Productions, 1969
CARTER'S ARMY (TF)   Thomas-Spelling
Productions, 1970
THE LOVE WAR (TF)   Thomas-Spelling
Productions, 1970
THE OVER-THE-HILL GANG RIDES AGAIN (TF)
Thomas-Spelling Productions, 1970
RUN, SIMON, RUN (TF)   Aaron Spelling
Productions, 1970
LOVE, HATE, LOVE (TF)   Aaron Spelling
Productions, 1971
CANNON (TF)   QM Productions, 1971
THE FACE OF FEAR (TF)   QM Productions, 1971
IF TOMORROW COMES (TF)   Aaron Spelling
Productions, 1971
WELCOME HOME, JOHNNY BRISTOL (TF)   Cinema
Center, 1972
THE MAGNIFICENT SEVEN RIDE!   United Artists, 1972
FROGS   American International, 1972
MURDER ON FLIGHT 502 (TF)   Spelling-Goldberg
Productions, 1975
SHADOW OF THE HAWK   Columbia, 1976, Canadian
SEPARATION (TF)   CFTO-TV, 1978, Canadian
RETURN TO FANTASY ISLAND (TF)   Spelling-Goldberg
Productions, 1978
THE RETURN OF THE MOD SQUAD (TF)   Thomas-
Spelling Productions, 1979
THE SHAPE OF THINGS TO COME   Film Ventures
International, 1979, Canadian
SANITY CLAUSE (TF)   co-director with David Barlow,
Canadian Broadcasting Corporation, 1990, Canadian

JIM McCULLOUGH, SR.

MOUNTAINTOP MOTEL MASSACRE   New World, 1985
THE AURORA ENCOUNTER   New World, 1986

DON McDOUGALL*

Home: 1269 Shadybrook Drive, Beverly Hills, CA 90210,
213/265-4578

ESCAPE TO MINDANAO (TF)   Universal TV, 1968
WILD WOMEN (TF)   Aaron Spelling Productions, 1970
THE AQUARIANS (TF)   Ivan Tors Productions, 1975
THE HEIST (TF)   Paramount TV, 1972
THE MARK OF ZORRO (TF)   20th Century-Fox, 1974
THE MISSING ARE DEADLY (TF)   Lawrence Gordon
Productions, 1975

RODDY McDOWALL

b. September 17, 1928 - London, England
Contact: Screen Actors Guild - Hollywood, 213/465-4600

TAM LIN   *THE DEVIL'S WIDOW*   American
International, 1971

BERNARD McEVEETY*

Contact: Directors Guild of America - Los Angeles,
213/289-2000

RIDE BEYOND VENGEANCE   Columbia, 1966
A STEP OUT OF LINE (TF)   Cinema Center, 1971
THE BROTHERHOOD OF SATAN   Columbia, 1971
KILLER BY NIGHT (TF)   Cinema Center, 1972

NAPOLEON AND SAMANTHA   Buena Vista, 1972
ONE LITTLE INDIAN   Buena Vista, 1973
THE BEARS AND I   Buena Vista, 1974
THE MACAHANS (TF)   Albert S. Ruddy Productions/
MGM TV, 1976
THE HOSTAGE HEART (TF)   Andrew J. Fenady
Associates/MGM TV, 1977
DONOVAN'S KID (TF)   NBC, 1979
CENTENNIAL (MS)   co-director with Harry Falk, Paul Krasny
& Virgil Vogel, Universal TV, 1979
ROUGHNECKS (TF)   Douglas Netter Productions/
Metromedia Producers Corporations, 1980

VINCENT McEVEETY*

Home: 14561 Mulholland Drive, Los Angeles, CA 90077,
213/783-4674
Agent: Shapiro-Lichtman Agency - Los Angeles,
213/859-8877

THIS SAVAGE LAND (TF)   1968
FIRECREEK   Warner Bros., 1968
CUTTER'S TRAIL (TF)   CBS Studio Center, 1970
THE MILLION DOLLAR DUCK   Buena Vista, 1971
THE BISCUIT EATER   Buena Vista, 1972
CHARLEY AND THE ANGEL   Buena Vista, 1972
WONDER WOMAN (TF)   Warner Bros. TV, 1974
SUPERDAD   Buena Vista, 1972
THE CASTAWAY COWBOY   Buena Vista, 1974
THE STRONGEST MAN IN THE WORLD   Buena
Vista, 1975
THE LAST DAY (TF)   Paramount TV, 1975
THE TREASURE OF MATECUMBE   Buena Vista, 1976
GUS   Buena Vista, 1976
HERBIE GOES TO MONTE CARLO   Buena Vista, 1976
THE APPLE DUMPLING GANG RIDES AGAIN   Buena
Vista, 1979
HERBIE GOES BANANAS   Buena Vista, 1980
AMY   Buena Vista, 1981
MCCLAIN'S LAW (TF)   Eric Bercovici Productions/
Epipsychidion Inc., 1982
BLOOD SPORT (TF)   Spelling-Goldberg Productions/
Columbia TV, 1986
GUNSMOKE: RETURN TO DODGE (TF)   CBS
Entertainment, 1987

DARREN McGAVIN*

b. May 7, 1922 - Spokane, Washington
Home: 8643 Holloway Plaza, Los Angeles, CA 90069,
213/855-0271
Agent: Jack Gilardi, ICM - Los Angeles, 213/550-4000

HAPPY MOTHER'S DAY - LOVE, GEORGE
Cinema 5, 1973

DON McGLYNN

Home: 314 S. Alexandria Avenue - Apt. 405, Los Angeles,
CA 90020, 213/389-0173

ART PEPPER: NOTES FROM A JAZZ SURVIVOR (FD)
Winter Moon Productions, 1982
JAZZ PROFILES: JOE WILLIAMS (FD)   Productions in
Tempo, 1985
THE SOUNDIES (FD)   Euphoria Productions, 1986
THE MILLS BROTHERS STORY (FD)   Storyville Films/
Winter Moon Productions, 1986
TV'S FIRST MUSIC VIDEOS (FD)   Storyville Films/Winter
Moon Productions, 1988
THE SPIKE JONES STORY (FD)   Storyville Films/Winter
Moon Productions, 1988
HOLLYWOOD MAVERICKS (TD)   American Film Institute/
NHK Enterprises, 1990, U.S.-Japanese

PATRICK McGOOHAN*
b. May 19, 1928 - New York, New York
Contact: Directors Guild of America - Los Angeles,
213/289-2000

CATCH MY SOUL   Cinerama Releasing
    Corporation, 1974
COLUMBO: AGENDA FOR MURDER (TF)   Universal
    TV, 1990

JOSEPH McGRATH
Business: McGrath and Mack, 10 Lower John Street,
    London W1, England, 71/437-4983
Agent: Denis Selinger, ICM - London, 71/629-8080

CASINO ROYALE   co-director with Val Guest,
    Ken Hughes, John Huston & Robert Parrish,
    Columbia, 1967, British
30 IS A DANGEROUS AGE, CYNTHIA   Columbia,
    1968, British
THE BLISS OF MRS. BLOSSOM   Paramount,
    1969, British
NER IST WER?   1970, West German
THE MAGIC CHRISTIAN   Commonwealth United,
    1970, British
DIGBY, THE BIGGEST DOG IN THE WORLD
    Cinerama Releasing Corporation,
    1974, British
THE GREAT McGONAGALL   Scotia American,
    1975, British
I'M NOT FEELING MYSELF TONIGHT   New Realm,
    1976, British
THE STRANGE CASE OF THE END OF CIVILISATION
    AS WE KNOW IT (TF)   Shearwater Films/London
    Weekend TV, 1978, British
RISING DAMP   ITC, 1980, British
NIGHT TRAIN TO MURDER (TF)   Thames TV,
    1983, British
WHAT THE DICKENS? (TF)   HTV, 1984, British
JUST DESSERTS (TF)   1986, British
STARLETS   1987, British

THOMAS McGUANE
Home: Hoffman Route, Livingston, Montana 59047
Agent: Jeff Berg, ICM - Los Angeles, 213/550-4000

92 IN THE SHADE   United Artists, 1975

GEORGE McINDOE
b. May 17, 1949 - Montrose, Scotland
Home: P.O. Box 66, Santa Monica, CA 90406,
    213/276-7554
Agent: Marc Sullivan, DOC Management,
    14 St. Georges Drive, London WC1, England,
    71/834-9226

STAGE SCHOOL (TF)   Speake Films, 1971, British
THE ROLLER SKATING GROUPIE   Rainbow Film
    Productions, 1971, British
THE STUDIO KIDS (TF)   BMPC Ltd., 1973, British
LAZY DAYS (TF)   Sean Barry Productions,
    1973, British
HYDE PARK POP (FD)   co-director, Unit Two Film
    Productions, 1973, British

ANDREW V. McLAGLEN*
b. July 28, 1920 - London, England
Home: 3110 San Juan Valley Road, P.O. Box 1056,
    Friday Harbor, WA 98250, 206/378-4990
Agent: Tom Chasin, The Chasin Agency - Beverly Hills,
    213/278-7505
Business: Stanmore Productions, Inc., 1900 Avenue of
    the Stars - Suite 2270, Los Angeles, CA 90067,
    213/277-1900

GUN THE MAN DOWN   United Artists, 1956
MAN IN THE VAULT   Universal, 1956
THE ABDUCTORS   20th Century-Fox, 1957
FRECKLES   20th Century-Fox, 1960
THE LITTLE SHEPHERD OF KINGDOM COME   20th
    Century-Fox, 1961
McLINTOCK!   United Artists, 1963
SHENANDOAH   Universal, 1965
THE RARE BREED   Universal, 1966
MONKEYS, GO HOME!   Buena Vista, 1967
THE WAY WEST   United Artists, 1967
THE BALLAD OF JOSIE   Universal, 1968
THE DEVIL'S BRIGADE   United Artists, 1968
BANDOLERO!   20th Century-Fox, 1968
HELLFIGHTERS   Universal, 1969
THE UNDEFEATED   20th Century-Fox, 1969
CHISUM   Warner Bros., 1970
ONE MORE TRAIN TO ROB   Universal, 1971
FOOLS' PARADE   Columbia, 1971
SOMETHING BIG   National General, 1971
CAHILL, U.S. MARSHAL   Warner Bros., 1973
MITCHELL   Allied Artists, 1975
THE LOG OF THE BLACK PEARL (TF)   Universal TV/
    Mark VII Ltd., 1975
STOWAWAY TO THE MOON (TF)   20th Century-
    Fox TV, 1975
BANJO HACKETT: ROAMIN' FREE (TF)   Bruce Lansbury
    Productions/Columbia TV, 1976
THE LAST HARD MEN   20th Century-Fox, 1976
MURDER AT THE WORLD SERIES (TF)   ABC Circle
    Films, 1977
THE FANTASTIC JOURNEY (TF)   Bruce Lansbury
    Productions/Columbia TV, 1977
BREAKTHROUGH   *SERGEANT STEINER*   Maverick
    Pictures International, 1978, West German
THE WILD GEESE   Allied Artists, 1979, British
ffolkes   *NORTH SEA HIJACK*   Universal, 1980, British
THE SEA WOLVES   Paramount, 1981, British
THE SHADOW RIDERS (TF)   The Pegasus Group Ltd./
    Columbia TV, 1982
THE BLUE AND THE GRAY (MS)   Larry White-Lou Reda
    Productions/Columbia TV, 1982
TRAVIS McGEE (TF)   Hajeno Productions/Warner
    Bros. TV, 1983
SAHARA   MGM/UA/Cannon, 1984
THE DIRTY DOZEN: THE NEXT MISSION (TF)   MGM-UA
    TV, 1985
ON WINGS OF EAGLES (MS)   Edgar J. Scherick
    Productions/Taft Entertainment TV, 1986
RETURN FROM THE RIVER KWAI   Screenlife
    Establishment/Leisure Time Productions, 1989, British
EYE OF THE WIDOW   Adlar Productions/Bureau
    Productions, 1990, French

TOM McLOUGHLIN*
Agent: William Morris Agency - Beverly Hills, 213/274-7451

ONE DARK NIGHT   Comworld, 1983
FRIDAY THE 13TH, PART VI: JASON LIVES
    Paramount, 1986

DATE WITH AN ANGEL   DEG, 1987
FRIDAY THE 13TH - THE PROPHECIES (TF)
   Triumphant Entertainment Corporation of Canada/
   Hometown Films, 1989, Canadian-U.S.

MARY McMURRAY
b. March 31, 1949 - Manchester, England
Agent: Jeremy Conway Ltd., 109 Jermyn Street,
   London W1, England, 71/839-2121

THE ASSAM GARDEN   The Moving Picture Company,
   1985, British
TO HAVE AND TO HOLD (TF)   London Weekend TV,
   1986, British
BORN IN THE R.S.A. (TF)   Channel Four, 1986, British

JOHN McNAUGHTON
Agent: Scott Yoselow, The Gersh Agency - New York City,
   212/997-1818 or: Ron Bernstein, The Gersh Agency -
   Beverly Hills, 213/274-6611

HENRY...PORTRAIT OF A SERIAL KILLER
   Greycat, 1989
THE BORROWER   Film Finances, 1990

JOHN McTIERNAN*
b. January 8, 1951 - Albany, New York
Agent: William Morris Agency - Beverly Hills, 213/274-7451

NOMADS   Atlantic Releasing Corporation, 1985
PREDATOR   20th Century Fox, 1987
DIE HARD   20th Century Fox, 1988
THE HUNT FOR RED OCTOBER   Paramount, 1990

PETER MEDAK*
b. Budapest, Hungary
Home: 1712 N. Stanley, Los Angeles, CA 90046,
   213/969-8849
Business Manager: Fred Altman & Company, 9255 Sunset
   Blvd. - Suite 901, Los Angeles, CA 90069, 213/278-4201

NEGATIVES   Continental, 1968, British
A DAY IN THE DEATH OF JOE EGG   Columbia,
   1972, British
THE RULING CLASS   Avco Embassy, 1972, British
THE THIRD GIRL FROM THE LEFT (TF)   Playboy
   Productions, 1973
GHOST IN THE NOONDAY SUN   Columbia, 1974, British
THE ODD JOB   Columbia, 1978, British
THE CHANGELING   AFD, 1980, Canadian
THE BABYSITTER (TF)   Moonlight Productions/
   Filmways, 1980
ZORRO, THE GAY BLADE   20th Century-Fox, 1981
MISTRESS OF PARADISE (TF)   Lorimar
   Productions, 1981
CRY FOR THE STRANGERS (TF)   David Gerber
   Company/MGM TV, 1982
THE MEN'S CLUB   Atlantic Releasing Corporation, 1986
THE KRAYS   Miramax Films, 1990, British

DON MEDFORD*
Home: 13900 Panay Way - Apt. R-216, Marina Del Rey,
   CA 90292, 213/827-3519
Agent: Jerry Zeitman, The Agency - Los Angeles,
   213/551-3000

TO TRAP A SPY   MGM, 1966
THE HUNTING PARTY   United Artists, 1970
INCIDENT IN SAN FRANCISCO (TF)   QM
   Productions, 1971

THE ORGANIZATION   United Artists, 1971
THE NOVEMBER PLAN   1976
THE CLONE MASTER (TF)   Mel Ferber Productions/
   Paramount TV, 1978
COACH OF THE YEAR (TF)   A. Shane Company, 1980
SIZZLE (TF)   Aaron Spelling Productions, 1981
HELL TOWN (TF)   Breezy Productions, 1985

CARY MEDOWAY*
b. May 16, 1949 - Philadelphia, Pennsylvania
Agent: Martin Shapiro, Shapiro-Lichtman Agency -
   Los Angeles, 213/859-8877

PARADISE MOTEL   Saturn International, 1985
THE HEAVENLY KID   Orion, 1985

FRANCIS MEGAHY
Business: Bedford Productions, Canalot Studios,
   222 Kensal Road, London W10, England

FREELANCE   1970, British
ONLY TAKES TWO   1978, British
SEWERS OF GOLD   1981, British
MINDER ON THE ORIENT EXPRESS (TF)   1986, British
TAFFIN   MGM/UA, 1988, U.S.-Irish
MINDER VI (MS)   co-director with Roy Ward Baker, Terry
   Green & Bill Brayne, Euston Films, 1988, British

KETAN MEHTA
Contact: Films Division, Ministry of Information & Broadcasting, 24 Dr G Beshmukh Marg, Bombay 40026, India,
   36-l46l

BHAVNI DHAVAI   1981, Indian
SPICES   Upfront Films/Cinema Four, 1986, Indian

ANDRE MELANCON
b. 1942 - Rouyn, Quebec, Canada
Home: Ruisseau-Nord, St-Ours sur le Richelieu, Quebec
   JOG 1PO, Canada, 514/785-5586

DES ARMES ET LES HOMMES (TF)   1972, Canadian
LES OREILLES MENE L'ENQUETTE (TF)   1973, Canadian
LES TACOTS (TF)   1973, Canadian
LE VIOLON DE GASTON (TF)   1974, Canadian
LES VRAIS PERDANTS (TF)   1977, Canadian
COMME LES SIX DOIGTS DE LA MAIN (TF)
   1978, Canadian
LA PAROLE AUX ENFANTS (TF)   1979, Canadian
L'ESPACE D'UN ETE (TF)   1980, Canadian
ZIG ZAGS (TF)   1982, Canadian
THE DOG WHO STOPPED THE WAR   New World,
   1984, Canadian
CECI EST MON CORPS (TF)   1986, Canadian
BACH ET BOTTINE   Cinema Plus, 1987, Canadian
SUMMER OF THE COLT   Productions La Fete/GEA
   Cinematografia, 1989, Canadian-Argentine
RAFALES   Aska Films, 1990, Canadian

IB MELCHIOR*
b. September 17, 1917 - Copenhagen, Denmark
Home: 8228 Marmont Lane, Los Angeles, CA 90069,
   213/654-6679
Agent: Tanya Chasman, Jack Rose Agency - Los Angeles,
   213/463-7300

THE ANGRY RED PLANET   American International, 1960
THE TIME TRAVELERS   American International, 1964

BILL MELENDEZ

Business: Bill Melendez Productions, 439 N. Larchmont
Blvd., Los Angeles, CA 90004, 213/463-4101

A BOY NAMED CHARLIE BROWN (AF)   National
General, 1968
SNOOPY, COME HOME (AF)   National General, 1972
DICK DEADEYE, OR DUTY DONE (AF)   Intercontinental,
1976, British
RACE FOR YOUR LIFE, CHARLIE BROWN (AF)
Paramount, 1978
BON VOYAGE, CHARLIE BROWN (AND DON'T COME
BACK!) (AF)   Paramount, 1980
HAPPILY EVER AFTER (ATF)   JZM Productions, 1985
THIS IS AMERICA, CHARLIE BROWN (AMS)   co-director
with Everett Brown & Sam Jaimes, Lee Mendelson-
Bill Melendez Productions/Charles Schulz Creative
Associates/United Media, 1988-89
TWO DADDIES? (ATF)   co-director with Dick Horn &
Eddie Raddage, JZM Productions/Bill Melendez
Productions/WonderWorks, 1989

JEFFREY MELMAN*

Home: 142 S. Windsor Blvd., Los Angeles, CA 90004,
213/939-8584
Agent: InterTalent - Los Angeles, 213/271-0600

A FAMILY FOR JOE (TF)   Grosso-Jacobson Productions/
NBC Productions, 1990

GEORGE MENDELUK*

b. March 20, 1948 - Augsburg, West Germany
Business: World Classic Pictures, 6263 Tapia Drive,
Malibu, CA 90265, 213/457-9911
Agent: Michael Margules, Irv Schechter Company -
Beverly Hills, 213/278-8070

STONE COLD DEAD   Dimension, 1979, Canadian
THE KIDNAPPING OF THE PRESIDENT   Crown
International, 1980, Canadian
DOIN' TIME   The Ladd Company/Warner Bros., 1984
MEATBALLS III *SUMMER JOB*   TMS Pictures,
1986, Canadian
BY THE RIVERS OF BABYLON (TF)   Universal TV, 1989

RAMON MENENDEZ

Contact: Writers Guild of America, West - Los Angeles,
213/550-1000

STAND AND DELIVER   Warner Bros., 1988

CHRIS MENGES

Agent: Leading Artists - Beverly Hills, 213/858-1999

A WORLD APART   Atlantic Releasing Corporation,
1988, British
CRISSCROSS   Pathe Entertainment, 1991

JIRI MENZEL

b. February 23, 1938 - Prague, Czechoslovakia
Contact: Czechoslovak Filmexport, Department of
Coproductions & Service Facilities, Vaclavske Namesti
28, 111-45 Prague 1, Czechoslovakia, tel.: 268412

CRIME AT A GIRL'S SCHOOL   1965, Czech
THE DEATH OF MR. BALTISBERGER   1965, Czech
CLOSELY WATCHED TRAINS   Sigma III, 1966, Czech
CAPRICIOUS SUMMER   Sigma III, 1968, Czech
CRIME IN A NIGHT CLUB   1968, Czech
WHOEVER LOOKS FOR GOLD   1975, Czech

SECLUSION NEAR A FOREST   1977, Czech
MAGICIANS OF THE SILVER SCREEN   1979, Czech
CUTTING IT SHORT   1980, Czech
SNOWDROP FEAST   1983, Czech
MY SWEET LITTLE VILLAGE   Circle Releasing,
1986, Czech
THE END OF THE GOOD OLD DAYS   Barrandov Film
Studios/Czechoslovak Film, 1989, Czech

KIETH MERRILL*

b. May 22, 1940 - Utah
Home: 10696 Mora Drive, Los Altos Hills, CA 94022,
415/941-8720

THE GREAT AMERICAN COWBOY (FD)   Sun
International, 1974
THREE WARRIORS   United Artists, 1978
TAKE DOWN   Buena Vista, 1979
WINDWALKER   Pacific International, 1980
MR. KRUEGER'S CHRISTMAS (TF)   Bonneville
Productions, 1980
HARRY'S WAR   Taft International, 1981
THE CHEROKEE TRAIL (TF)   Walt Disney
Productions, 1981

MATTHEW MESHEKOFF*

Address: 170 Fifth Avenue, New York, NY 10010,
212/243-4369
Agent: Alan Greenspan, ICM - Los Angeles, 213/550-4428

THE RULES OF THE GAME   Outlaw Productions/Once
Upon A Time Films, 1990

PHILIP F. MESSINA

Contact: Writers Guild of America, West - Los Angeles,
213/550-1000

SPY (CTF)   Deadly Productions/Wilshire Court
Productions, 1989

MARTA MESZAROS

b. September 19, 1931 - Budapest, Hungary
Contact: Hungarofilm, Bathory utca 10, H-1054 Budapest,
Hungary, tel.: 116650

THE GIRL   Mafilm Studio, 1968, Hungarian
BINDING SENTIMENTS   Mafilm Studio, 1969, Hungarian
DON'T CRY, PRETTY GIRLS   Mafilm Studio,
1970, Hungarian
RIDDANCE   Studio Hunnia, 1973, Hungarian
ADOPTION   Studio Hunnia, 1975, Hungarian
NINE MONTHS   Studio Hunnia, 1976, Hungarian
THE TWO OF THEM   Studio Dialog, 1977, Hungarian
JUST LIKE AT HOME   Studio Hunnia, 1978, Hungarian
EN COURS DE ROUTE   1979, French
THE HEIRESSES   1980, Hungarian
MOTHER AND DAUGHTER   1981, Hungarian-French
DIARY FOR MY CHILDREN   Budapest Studio,
1982, Hungarian
THE LAND OF MIRAGES   1983, Hungarian
DIARY FOR MY LOVE   Budapest Studio/Mafilm,
1987, Hungarian
BYE BYE RED RIDING HOOD   Productions La Fete/
Budapest Studio, 1989, Canadian-Hungarian

ALAN METTER*

Agent: Bauer Benedek Agency - Los Angeles, 213/275-2421

GIRLS JUST WANT TO HAVE FUN   New World, 1985
BACK TO SCHOOL   Orion, 1986

MOVING   Warner Bros., 1988
COLD DOG SOUP   HandMade Films, 1990

ALAN METZGER*
Home: 145 West 86th Street, New York, NY 10024,
   212/586-8418
Agent: Triad Artists, Inc. - Los Angeles, 213/556-2727

KOJAK: THE PRICE OF JUSTICE (TF)   MCA/Universal
   TV, 1987
TOP OF THE HILL (TF)   Stephen J. Cannell
   Productions, 1989
THE CHINA LAKE MURDERS (CTF)   Papazian-Hirsch
   Entertainment, 1990

RADLEY METZGER
b. 1930

DARK ODYSSEY   co-director with William Kyriaskys,
   ERA, 1961
DICTIONARY OF SEX   1964
THE DIRTY GIRLS   1965
THE ALLEY CATS   1966
CARMEN, BABY   Audubon, 1967, U.S.-Yugoslavian-
   West German
THERESE AND ISABELLE   Audubon, 1968,
   West German-U.S.
CAMILLE 2000   Audubon, 1969, Italian
THE LICKERISH QUARTET   Audubon, 1970,
   U.S.-Italian-West German
LITTLE MOTHER   Audubon, 1972
SCORE   Audubon, 1973
NAKED CAME THE STRANGER   directed under
   pseudonym of Henry Paris, Catalyst, 1975
THE PRIVATE AFTERNOONS OF PAMELA MANN
   directed under pseudonym of Henry Paris, Hudson
   Valley, 1975
ESOTIKA, EROTIKA, PSICOTIKA FAB   1975,
   Italian-Monocan
THE PUNISHMENT OF ANNE   1975
THE IMAGE   Audubon, 1976
THE OPENING OF MISTY BEETHOVEN   directed under
   pseudonym of Henry Paris, Catalyst, 1976
BARBARA BROADCAST   directed under pseudonym of
   Henry Paris, Crescent, 1977
MARASCHINO CHERRY   directed under pseudonym of
   Henry Paris, 1978
THE CAT AND THE CANARY   Quartet, 1978, British
THE TALE OF TIFFANY LUST   directed under pseudonym
   of Henry Paris, Entertainment Ventures, 1981
THE PRINCESS AND THE CALL GIRL   Highbridge Film
   Productions, 1984

NICHOLAS MEYER*
b. New York, New York
Agent: William Morris Agency - Beverly Hills, 213/274-7451

TIME AFTER TIME   Orion/Warner Bros., 1979
STAR TREK II: THE WRATH OF KHAN   Paramount, 1982
THE DAY AFTER (TF) ☆   ABC Circle Films, 1983
VOLUNTEERS   Tri-Star, 1985
THE DECEIVERS   Cinecom, 1988
PATRIOTS   Pathe Entertainment, 1991

RUSS MEYER*
b. March 21, 1922 - Oakland, California
Business RM Films International Inc., P.O. Box 3748,
   Hollywood, CA 90028, 213/466-7791

THE IMMORAL MR. TEAS   Pedram, 1959
EVE AND THE HANDYMAN   Eve, 1961
EROTICA   Eve, 1961
THE IMMORAL WEST AND HOW IT WAS LOST
   Eve, 1961
EUROPE IN THE RAW   Eve, 1963
HEAVENLY BODIES   Eve, 1963
KISS ME QUICK!   Eve, 1964
LORNA   Eve, 1965
ROPE OF FLESH   Eve, 1965
FANNY HILL: MEMOIRS OF A WOMAN OF PLEASURE
   Pan World, 1965, U.S.-West German
MOTOR PSYCHO   Eve, 1965
FASTER PUSSYCAT, KILL! KILL!   Eve, 1965
MONDO TOPLESS   Eve, 1966
HOW MUCH LOVING DOES A NORMAL COUPLE NEED?
   Eve, 1967
GOOD MORNING...AND GOODBYE   Eve, 1967
COMMON LAW CABIN   Eve, 1967
FINDERS KEEPERS, LOVERS WEEPERS   Eve, 1968
RUSS MEYER'S VIXEN   Eve, 1968
CHERRY, HARRY AND RAQUEL   Eve, 1969
BEYOND THE VALLEY OF THE DOLLS   20th
   Century-Fox, 1970
THE SEVEN MINUTES   20th Century-Fox, 1971
SWEET SUZY! *BLACKSNAKE*   Signal 166, 1975
SUPERVIXENS   RM Films, 1975
RUSS MEYER'S UP!   RM Films, 1976
BENEATH THE VALLEY OF THE ULTRAVIXENS   RM
   Films, 1979
THE BREAST OF RUSS MEYER   RM Films, 1987

MIKE MICHAELS
b. December 15, 1946 - Ohio
Business: Studio M Productions, 8715 Waikiki Station,
   Honolulu, HI 96815, 808/734-3345

THE WORLD OF TRAVEL: SRI LANKA (TD)   Studio M
   Productions, 1981
THE WORLD OF TRAVEL: BANGKOK (FD)   Studio M
   Productions, 1982
THE WORLD OF TRAVEL: LAS VEGAS (FD)   Studio M
   Productions, 1984
THE WORLD OF TRAVEL: KOREA (TD)   Studio M
   Productions, 1984
THE WORLD OF TRAVEL: NEW ZEALAND (TD)   Studio M
   Productions, 1985
THE WORLD OF TRAVEL: ROME (TD)   Studio M
   Productions, 1985
THE WORLD OF TRAVEL: MALAYSIA (TD)   Studio M
   Productions, 1986
THE WORLD OF TRAVEL: SINGAPORE (TD)   Studio M
   Productions, 1986
THE WORLD OF TRAVEL: OSAKA (FD)   Studio M
   Productions, 1987

RICHARD MICHAELS*
b. February 15, 1936
Agent: David Gersh, The Gersh Agency - Beverly Hills,
   213/274-6611
Business Manager: David G. Licht, 9171 Wilshire Blvd.,
   Beverly Hills, CA 90210, 213/278-1920

HOW COME NOBODY'S ON OUR SIDE?   American Films
   Ltd., 1975
DEATH IS NOT THE END   Libert Films International, 1976
ONCE AN EAGLE (MS)   co-director with E.W. Swackhamer,
   Universal TV, 1976
CHARLIE COBB: NICE NIGHT FOR HANGING (TF)
   Universal TV, 1977
HAVING BABIES II (TF)   The Jozak Company, 1977

LEAVE YESTERDAY BEHIND (TF)   ABC Circle
   Films, 1978
MY HUSBAND IS MISSING (TF)   Bob Banner
   Associates, 1978
...AND YOUR NAME IS JONAH (TF)   Charles Fries
   Productions, 1979
HOMEWARD BOUND (TF)   Tisch-Avnet
   Productions, 1980
ONCE UPON A FAMILY (TF)   Universal TV, 1980
THE PLUTONIUM INCIDENT (TF)   Time-Life
   Productions, 1980
SCARED STRAIGHT! ANOTHER STORY (TF)   Golden
   West TV, 1980
BERLIN TUNNEL 21 (TF)   Cypress Point Productions/
   Filmways, 1981
THE CHILDREN NOBODY WANTED (TF)   Blatt-Singer
   Productions, 1981
BLUE SKIES AGAIN   Warner Bros., 1983
ONE COOKS, THE OTHER DOESN'T (TF)   Kaleidoscope
   Films Ltd./Lorimar Productions, 1983
SADAT (TF)   Blatt-Singer Productions/Columbia TV, 1983
JESSIE (TF)   Lindsay Wagner Productions/
   MGM-UA TV, 1984
SILENCE OF THE HEART (TF)   David A. Simons
   Productions/Tisch-Avnet Productions, 1984
HEART OF A CHAMPION: THE RAY MANCINI
   STORY (TF)   Rare Titles Productions/Robert
   Papazian Productions, 1985
ROCKABYE (TF)   Roger Gimbel Productions/Peregrine
   Entertainment/Bertinelli Productions, 1986
I'LL TAKE MANHATTAN (MS)   co-director with Douglas
   Hickox, Steve Krantz Productions, 1987
RED RIVER (TF)   Catalina Production Group/
   MGM-UA TV, 1988
INDISCREET (TF)   Karen Mack Productions/HTV/Republic
   Pictures, 1988, U.S.-British
LOVE AND BETRAYAL (TF)   Gross-Weston Productions/
   ITC Entertainment Group, 1989

DAVE MICHENER
THE GREAT MOUSE DETECTIVE (AF)   co-director with
   Dave Clements, Burny Mattinson & John Musker,
   Buena Vista, 1986

GEORGE MIHALKA
b. 1952 - Budapest, Hungary
Home: 2030 Lambert Closse - Suite 4, Montreal, Quebec
   H3H 1Z8, Canada, 514/937-4740

MY BLOODY VALENTINE   Paramount, 1981, Canadian
PICK-UP SUMMER   PINBALL SUMMER   Film Ventures
   International, 1981, Canadian
SCANDALE   Vivafilm/Cine 360, 1982, Canadian
ETERNAL EVIL   Seymour Borde & Associates, 1987,
   Canadian-U.S.
OFFICE PARTY   Miramax Films, 1988, Canadian
LE CHEMIN DE DAMES (TF)   Cinema Plus/Les
   Producteurs TV-Films Associes/National Film Board
   for Radio-Quebec, 1988, Canadian
STRAIGHT LINE (TF)   1988, Canadian-U.S.

TED V. MIKELS
STRIKE ME DEADLY   1963
THE DOCTORS   1963
ONE SHOCKING MOMENT   SUBURBAN AFFAIR   1964
THE BLACK KLANSMAN   I CROSSED THE COLOR
   LINE   SGS Productions, 1965
THE UNDERTAKER AND HIS PALS   1966
THE ASTRO-ZOMBIES   Gemini Films, 1967

UP YOUR TEDDY BEAR   1968
THE GIRL IN GOLD BOOTS   1968
THE CORPSE GRINDERS   1972
BLOOD ORGY OF THE SHE-DEVILS   Gemini Films, 1973
THE DOLL SQUAD   SEDUCE AND DESTROY   1974
THE WORM EATERS   New American, 1975
ALEX JOSEPH AND HIS WIVES   THE REBEL
   BREED   1978
DEVIL'S GAMBIT   1982
OPERATION OVERKILL   1982
TEN VIOLENT WOMEN   1982
SPACE ANGELS   1985
ANGEL OF VENGEANCE   Majestic, 1987

NIKITA MIKHALKOV
b. October 21, 1945 - Moscow, U.S.S.R.
Contact: Union of Soviet Filmmakers, Vassilievskaya 13,
   Moscow, U.S.S.R., tel.: 250-4114

AT HOME AMONG STRANGERS   1974, Soviet
A SLAVE OF LOVE   Cinema 5, 1976, Soviet
AN UNFINISHED PIECE FOR PLAYER PIANO   Corinth,
   1977, Soviet
FIVE EVENINGS   IFEX Film, 1979, Soviet
OBLOMOV   IFEX Film, 1981, Soviet
FAMILY RELATIONS   Mosfilm, 1983, Soviet
WITHOUT WITNESS   IFEX Film, 1984, Soviet
DARK EYES   Island Pictures, 1987, Italian-French

ANDREI MIKHALKOV-
KONCHALOVSKY
(See Andrei KONCHALOVSKY)

RENTARO MIKUNI
Contact: Directors Guild of Japan, Tsukada Building, 8-33
   Udagawa-cho, Shibuya-ku, Tokyo 150, Japan, 3/461-4411

SHINRAN - THE PATH TO PURITY   Shochiku,
   1987, Japanese

KATHY MILANI
b. November 25, 1963 - New Haven, Connecticut
Business: Generic Films, Inc., P.O. Box 2715, Waterbury,
   CT 06723, 203/756-3017

B-MOVIE   Generic Films, 1988

CHRISTOPHER MILES
b. April 19, 1939 - London, England
Agent: Michael Whitehall, 125 Gloucester Road, London
   SW7 4TE, England, 71/244-8466
Business: Milesian Film Productions Ltd., 10 Selwood Place,
   London SW7 3QQ, England, 71/373-8858

UP JUMPED A SWAGMAN   Anglo-Amalgamated/
   Warner-Pathe, 1966, British
THE VIRGIN AND THE GYPSY   Chevron, 1970, British
TIME FOR LOVING   Hemdale, 1972, British
ZINOTCHKA (TF)   BBC, 1973, British
THE MAIDS   American Film Theatre, 1975,
   British-Canadian
THAT LUCKY TOUCH   Allied Artists, 1975, British
ALTERNATIVE 3 (TF)   1976, British
NECK (TF)   ITV/Anglia, 1978, British
PRIEST OF LOVE   Filmways, 1981, British
DALEY'S DECATHLON (TF)   BBC/Milesian Films,
   1982, British
THE MARATHON (TF)   Channel Four, 1983, British

APHRODISIAC (TF)   1984, British
LORD ELGIN AND SOME STONES OF NO VALUE (TF)
    Milesian Films/ Channel Four/ERT-TV, 1985,
    British-Greek

JOHN MILIUS*
b. April 11, 1944 - St. Louis, Missouri
Agent: ICM - Los Angeles, 213/550-4000

DILLINGER   American International, 1973
THE WIND AND THE LION   MGM/United
    Artists, 1975
BIG WEDNESDAY   Warner Bros., 1978
CONAN THE BARBARIAN   Universal, 1982
RED DAWN   MGM/UA, 1984
FAREWELL TO THE KING   Orion, 1989
FLIGHT OF THE INTRUDER   Paramount, 1990

GAVIN MILLAR
b. January 11, 1938 - Clydebank, Scotland
Home: 16 Compton Terrace, London N1 2UN, England,
    07/226-0210
Agent: Judy Daish, 83 Eastbourne Mews, London
    W2 6LQ, England, 71/262-1101

THE GOLDWYN TOUCH (TD)   BBC, 1973, British
AN IMAGINATIVE WOMAN (TF)   BBC, 1973, British
BUSBY BERKELEY - THE YEARS AT WARNERS (TD)
    BBC, 1974, British
GOODBYE (TF)   BBC, 1975, British
TRAVELS WITH A DONKEY (TF)   BBC, 1978, British
CREAM IN MY COFFEE (TF)   London Weekend TV,
    1980, British
INTENSIVE CARE (TF)   BBC, 1982, British
STAN'S LAST GAME (TF)   BBC, 1983, British
SECRETS   Samuel Goldwyn Company,
    1983, British
THE WEATHER IN THE STREETS (TF)   Rediffusion
    Films/BBC/Britannia TV, 1983, British
UNFAIR EXCHANGES (TF)   BBC, 1984, British
THE RUSSIAN SOLDIER (TF)   BBC, 1985, British
DREAMCHILD   Universal, 1985, British
STOOP (TF)   London Weekend TV, 1987, British
TIDY ENDINGS (CTF)   HBO Showcase/Sandollar
    Productions, 1988
THE MOST DANGEROUS MAN IN THE WORLD (TF)
    BBC/ Iberoamericana/Celtic Films, 1988, British
DANNY, THE CHAMPION OF THE WORLD   Portobello
    Productions/British Screen/Thames TV/The Disney
    Channel/WonderWorks/Children's Film & Television
    Foundation, 1989, British-U.S.

STUART MILLAR*
b. 1929 - New York, New York
Home: 300 Central Park East - Suite 15G, New York,
    NY 10024, 212/873-5515

WHEN THE LEGENDS DIE   20th Century-Fox, 1972
ROOSTER COGBURN   Universal, 1975
VITAL SIGNS (TF)   CBS Entertainment, 1986
THE O'CONNORS (TF)   CBS Entertainment, 1989

CATHERINE MILLER
DARLINGS OF THE GODS (MS)   Thames TV/Australian
    Broadcasting Corporation/Film Victoria, 1989,
    British-Australian

CLAUDE MILLER
Contact: French Film Office, 745 Fifth Avenue, New York,
    NY 10151, 212/832-8860

THE BEST WAY   *LA MEILLEURE FACON DE MARCHER*
    1976, French
DITES LUI QUE JE L'AIME   1977, French
GARDE A VUE   1981, French
MARTELLE RANEE   1983, French
CHARLOTTE AND LULU   *L'EFFRONTEE*   New Yorker,
    1985, French
THE LITTLE THIEF   Miramax Films, 1989, French

DAVID MILLER*
b. November 28, 1909 - Paterson, New Jersey
Home: 1843 Thayer Avenue, Los Angeles, CA 90025,
    213/474-8542

BILLY THE KID   MGM, 1941
SUNDAY PUNCH   MGM, 1942
FLYING TIGERS   Republic, 1942
TOP O' THE MORNING   Paramount, 1948
LOVE HAPPY   United Artists, 1949
OUR VERY OWN   RKO Radio, 1950
SATURDAY'S HERO   Columbia, 1951
SUDDEN FEAR   RKO Radio, 1952
TWIST OF FATE   *THE BEAUTIFUL STRANGER*   United
    Artists, 1954, British
DIANE   MGM, 1956
THE OPPOSITE SEX   MGM, 1956
THE STORY OF ESTHER COSTELLO   Columbia, 1957
HAPPY ANNIVERSARY   United Artists, 1959
MIDNIGHT LACE   Universal, 1961
BACK STREET   Universal, 1961
LONELY ARE THE BRAVE   Universal, 1962
CAPTAIN NEWMAN, M.D.   Universal, 1964
HAMMERHEAD   Columbia, 1968, British
HAIL, HERO!   National General, 1969
EXECUTIVE ACTION   National General, 1973
BITTERSWEET LOVE   Avco Embassy, 1976
LOVE FOR RENT (TF)   Warren V. Bush Productions, 1979
THE BEST PLACE TO BE (TF)   Ross Hunter
    Productions, 1979
GOLDIE AND THE BOXER (TF)   Orenthal Productions/
    Columbia TV, 1979
GOLDIE AND THE BOXER GO TO HOLLYWOOD (TF)
    Orenthal Productions/Columbia TV, 1981

GEORGE MILLER*
b. March 3, 1945 - Cinchilla, Queensland, Australia
Business: Kennedy Miller Productions, 30 Orwell Street,
    Kings Cross, Sydney, Australia
Business Manager: Arnold Burk, Gang, Tyre & Brown, Inc.,
    6400 Sunset Blvd., Los Angeles, CA 90028,
    213/463-4863

MAD MAX   American International, 1979, Australian
THE ROAD WARRIOR   *MAD MAX II*   Warner Bros.,
    1982, Australian
THE DISMISSAL (MS)   co-director with Phillip Noyce,
    George Ogilvie, Carl Schultz & John Power, 1983,
    Australian
TWILIGHT ZONE - THE MOVIE   co-director with John
    Landis, Steven Spielberg & Joe Dante, Warner
    Bros., 1983
MAD MAX BEYOND THUNDERDOME   co-director with
    George Ogilvie, Warner Bros., 1985, Australian
THE WITCHES OF EASTWICK   Warner Bros., 1987

GEORGE MILLER*
(George Trumbull Miller)
Address: 3 Reed Street, Albert Park, Victoria, 3206, Australia, 03/690-5663
Agent: Don Klein, Irv Schechter Company - Beverly Hills, 213/278-8070

CASH & CO. (MS)   co-director with Russell Hagg, Homestead Films/Network Seven, 1975, Australian
AGAINST THE WIND (MS)   co-director with Simon Wincer, Pegasus Productions, 1978, Australian
THE LAST OUTLAW (MS)   co-director with Kevin Dobson, Network Seven/ Pegasus Productions, 1980, Australian
THE MAN FROM SNOWY RIVER   20th Century-Fox, 1982, Australian
ALL THE RIVERS RUN (CMS)   co-director with Pino Amenta, Crawford Productions/Nine Network, 1984, Australian
THE AVIATOR   MGM/UA, 1985
ANZACS: THE WAR DOWN UNDER   ANZACS (MS) co-director with Pino Amenta & John Dixon, Burrowes Dixon Productions, 1985, Australian
COOL CHANGE   Hoyts, 1986, Australian
LES PATTERSON SAVES THE WORLD   Hoyts Distribution, 1987, Australian
THE FAR COUNTRY (MS)   Crawford Productions, 1987, Australian
THE CHRISTMAS VISITOR   BUSHFIRE MOON (CTF) Entertainment Media/ The Disney Channel/Wonder Works, 1987, Australian-U.S.
THE NEVERENDING STORY II   Warner Bros., 1990, West German

HARVEY MILLER*
b. June 15, 1935 - New York, New York
Home: 5538 Calhoun Avenue, Van Nuys, CA 91401, 818/997-6760
Agent: ICM - Los Angeles, 213/550-4000

BAD MEDICINE   20th Century Fox, 1985

JASON MILLER*
b. April 22, 1939 - New York, New York
Agent: Mickey Freiberg, The Artists Agency - Los Angeles, 213/277-7779

THAT CHAMPIONSHIP SEASON   Cannon, 1982

JONATHAN MILLER
b. July 21, 1934 - London, England
Business: BBC Television Center, Wood Lane, London W12, England

TAKE A GIRL LIKE YOU   Columbia, 1970, British

MICHAEL MILLER*
Agent: Alan Greenspan, ICM - Los Angeles, 213/550-4000
Business Manager: Henry Levine, Henry Levine & Associates, 9100 Wilshire Blvd. - Suite 517, Beverly Hills, CA 91210, 213/274-8691

STREET GIRLS   New World, 1975
JACKSON COUNTY JAIL   New World, 1976
OUTSIDE CHANCE (TF)   New World Productions /Miller-Begun Productions, 1978
SILENT RAGE   Columbia, 1982
NATIONAL LAMPOON'S CLASS REUNION   20th Century-Fox, 1983

SILENT WITNESS (TF)   Robert Greenwald Productions, 1985
CRIME OF INNOCENCE (TF)   Ohlmeyer Communications Company, 1985
A CASE OF DEADLY FORCE (TF)   Telecom Entertainment, 1986
CAN YOU FEEL ME DANCING? (TF)   Robert Greenwald Productions, 1986
ROSES ARE FOR THE RICH (TF)   Phoenix Entertainment Group, 1987
NECESSITY (TF)   Barry-Enright Productions/Alexander Productions, 1988
DANGEROUS PASSION (TF)   Stormy Weathers/Davis Entertainment TV, 1990

MOLLIE MILLER*
Home: 2190 Moreno Drive, Los Angeles, CA 90039, 213/664-0807
Agent: CAA - Beverly Hills, 213/288-4545

THE B.R.A.T. PATROL (TF)   Mark H. Ovitz Productions/ Walt Disney Productions, 1986
STUDENT EXCHANGE (TF)   Walt Disney TV, 1987
TALES FROM THE HOLLYWOOD HILLS: THE CLOSED SET (TF)   WNET-NY/Zenith Productions, 1988
PARENT TRAP: HAWAIIAN HONEYMOON (TF)   Walt Disney TV, 1989

NEAL MILLER
b. Chicago, Illinois
Business: Rubicon Film Productions, 505 Chicago Avenue, Evanston, IL 60202

UNDER THE BILTMORE CLOCK (TF)   Rubicon Film Productions/KTCA/ American Playhouse, 1985

ROBERT ELLIS MILLER*
b. July 18, 1932 - New York, New York
Agent: Phil Gersh, The Gersh Agency - Beverly Hills, 213/274-6611
Business Manager: McGuire Management, 1901 Avenue of the Stars, Los Angeles, CA 90067, 213/277-5902

ANY WEDNESDAY   Warner Bros., 1966
SWEET NOVEMBER   Warner Bros., 1967
THE HEART IS A LONELY HUNTER   Warner Bros., 1968
THE BUTTERCUP CHAIN   Warner Bros., 1970, British
BIG TRUCK AND POOR CLARE   Kastner-Ladd-Winkler/ Pashanel-Topol- Gottesman, 1972, U.S-Israel
THE GIRL FROM PETROVKA   Universal, 1974
JUST AN OLD SWEET SONG (TF)   MTM Enterprises, 1976
ISHI: THE LAST OF HIS TRIBE (TF)   Edward & Mildred Lewis Productions, 1978
THE BALTIMORE BULLET   Avco Embassy, 1980
MADAME X (TF)   Levenback-Riche Productions/Universal TV, 1981
REUBEN, REUBEN   20th Century-Fox International Classics, 1983
HER LIFE AS A MAN (TF)   LS Entertainment, 1984
THE OTHER LOVER (TF)   Larry Thompson Productions/ Columbia TV, 1985
INTIMATE STRANGERS (TF)   Nederlander TV & Film Productions/Telepictures Productions, 1986
BRENDA STARR   New World, 1989, filmed in 1987
HAWKS   Skouras Pictures, 1989, British
BED AND BREAKFAST   Schwartzman Pictures, 1990

SHARRON MILLER*
b. Enid, Oklahoma
Agent: CAA - Beverly Hills, 213/288-4545

PLEASURES (TF)   Catalina Production Group/Columbia
   TV, 1986
PIGEON FEATHERS (TF)   Learning in Focus, 1988
LITTLE GIRL LOST (TF)   Marian Rees Associates, 1988
THE OUTSIDERS (TF)   co-director with Alan Shapiro,
   Zoetrope Studios/ Papazian-Hirsch Productions, 1990

WALTER C. MILLER*
Home: 2401 Crest View Drive, Los Angeles, CA 90046,
   213/656-2819

THE BORROWERS (TF)   Walt DeFaria Productions/20th
   Century-Fox TV, 1973
CAN I SAVE MY CHILDREN? (TF) ☆   Stanley L. Colbert
   Co-Production Associates/20th Century-Fox TV, 1974

BILL MILLING
CAGED FURY   21st Century Film Corp., 1989

REGINALD MILLS
PETER RABBIT & TALES OF BEATRIX POTTER   MGM,
   1971, British

MICHAEL MINER
Agent: Bauer Benedek Agency - Los Angeles, 213/275-2421

DEADLY WEAPON   Empire Pictures, 1989

STEPHEN C. (STEVE) MINER*
b. June 18, 1951 - Chicago, Illinois
Agent: David Gersh, The Gersh Agency - Beverly Hills,
   213/274-6611
Business: 1137 Second Street - Suite 103, Santa Monica,
   CA 90403, 213/393-0291

FRIDAY THE 13TH PART 2   Paramount, 1981
FRIDAY THE 13TH PART 3   Paramount, 1982
HOUSE   New World, 1986
SOUL MAN   New World, 1986
WARLOCK   New World, 1989

DAVID MINGAY
Contact: British Academy of Film & Television Arts,
   195 Piccadilly, London W1, England, 71/734-0022

RUDE BOY   co-director with Jack Hazan, Atlantic
   Releasing Corporation, 1980, British
SOPHISTICATED LADY (FD)   co-director with David
   Robinson, 1990, British

JOSEPH MINION
Agent: William Morris Agency - Beverly Hills, 213/274-7451

DADDY'S BOYS   Concorde, 1988

MERATA MITA
Contact: New Zealand Film Commission, P.O. Box 11546,
   Wellington, New Zealand, 4/859-754

PATU! (FD)   Awatea Films, 1983, New Zealand
MAURI   Awatea Films, 1988, New Zealand
MANA WAKA (FD)   Te Puea Estate/Turangawaewae Marae
   Productions, 1990, New Zealand

SOLLACE MITCHELL
Agent: CAA - Beverly Hills, 213/288-4545

CALL ME   Vestron, 1988

MOSHE MIZRAHI
b. 1931 - Egypt
Agent: The Gersh Agency - Beverly Hills, 213/274-6611
Business: Rosa Productions, 5 rue D'Artois, 75008 Paris,
   France, 04/359-4704

LES STANCES A SOPHIE   Prodis, 1971, French
I LOVE YOU ROSA   Leisure Media, 1973, Israeli
THE HOUSE ON CHELOUCHE STREET   Productions
   Unlimited, 1974, Israeli
DAUGHTERS! DAUGHTERS!   Steinmann-Baxter,
   1975, Israeli
RACHEL'S MAN   Allied Artists, 1976, Israeli
MADAME ROSA   *LA VIE DEVANT SOI*   Atlantic Releasing
   Corporation, 1978, French
I SENT A LETTER TO MY LOVE   *CHERE INCONNUE*
   Atlantic Releasing Corporation, 1980, French
LA VIE CONTINUE   Triumph/Columbia, 1982, French
UNE JEUNESSE   1983, French
WAR AND LOVE   Cannon, 1985
EVERY TIME WE SAY GOODBYE   Tri-Star,
   1987, Israeli
MANGECLOUS   AAA, 1988, French
A MAN OF INFLUENCE (MS)   Mod Film/TF1/Reteitalia,
   1990, French-Italian-Canadian

DAVID MOESSINGER*
Home: 3861 Kingswood Road, Sherman Oaks, CA 91403
Agent: Dan Richland, Richland/Wunsch Agency -
   Los Angeles, 213/278-1955

MOBILE TWO (TF)   Universal TV/Mark VII Ltd., 1975

JOHN MOFFITT*
Agent: ICM - Los Angeles, 213/550-4000
Personal Manager: Bernie Brillstein, The Brillstein
   Company, 9200 Sunset Blvd., Los Angeles, CA 90069,
   213/275-6135

LOVE AT STAKE   *BURNIN' LOVE*   Tri-Star, 1988

EDOUARD MOLINARO
b. May 13, 1928 - Bordeaux, France
Agent: Artmedia, 10 Avenue Georges V, 75008 Paris,
   France, 04/723-7860
Contact: French Film Office, 745 Fifth Avenue, New York,
   NY 10151, 212/832-8860

BACK TO THE WALL   Ellis, 1958, French
DES FEMMES DISPARAISSENT   1959, French
UNE FILLE POUR L'ETE   1960, French
THE PASSION OF SLOW FIRE   *LA MORT DE BELLE*
   Trans-Lux, 1961, French
SEVEN CAPITAL SINS   co-director with Jean-Luc Godard,
   Roger Vadim, Sylvaine Dhomme, Philippe De Broca,
   Claude Chabrol, Jacques Demy, Marie-Jose Nat,
   Dominique Paturel, Jean-Marc Tennberg & Perrette
   Pradier, Embassy, 1962, French-Italian
LES ENNEMIS   1962, French
ARSENE LUPIN CONTRE ARSENE LUPIN
   1962, French
UNE RAVISSANTE IDIOTE   1964, French
MALE HUNT   Pathe Contemporary, 1965, French-Italian
QUAND PASSENT LES FAISANS   1965, French

TO COMMIT A MURDER *PEAU D'ESPION*
   Cinerama Releasing Corporation, 1967,
   French-Italian-West German
OSCAR 1968, French
HIBERNATUS 1969, French
MON ONCLE BENJAMIN 1969, French
LA LIBERTEEN CROUPE 1970, French
LES AVEUX LES PLUS DOUX MGM, 1971, French
LA MANDARINE Prodis, 1972, French-Italian
A PAIN IN THE A— *L'EMMERDEUR* Corwin-Mahler,
   1973, French
LE GANG DES OTAGES Gaumont, 1973, French
L'IRONIE DU SORT CFDC, 1974, French
THE PINK TELEPHONE SJ International, 1975, French
DRACULA PERE ET FILS Gaumont, 1976, French
L'HOMME PRESSE AMLF, 1977, French
LA CAGE AUX FOLLES ★ United Artists, 1979,
   French-Italian
LA PITIE DANGEREUSE (TF) Christine Gouze-Renal
   Progefi/Antenne-2, 1979, French
CAUSE TOUJOURS...TU M'INTERESSES Albina
   Productions, 1979, French
SUNDAY LOVERS co-director with Bryan Forbes,
   Dino Risi & Gene Wilder, MGM/United Artists, 1981,
   U.S.-British-Italian-French
LA CAGE AUX FOLLES II United Artists, 1981,
   French-Italian
POUR 100 BRIQUES, T'AS PLUS RIENI UGC,
   1982, French
JUST THE WAY YOU ARE MGM/UA, 1984
L'AMOUR EN DOUCE European Classics, 1985, French
PALACE Parafrance, 1985, French-West German
ENCHANTE Renn Productions, 1988, French
A GAUCHE EN SORTANT DE L'ACENSEUR AMLF,
   1988, French

RAUNI MOLLBERG
b. 1929 - Hameenlinna, Finland
Contact: Federation of Finnish Film Directors, Mariankatu
   15B, SF-00250 Helsinki, Finland, 0/654426

THE EARTH IS A SINFUL SONG Seaberg,
   1973, Finnish
PRETTY GOOD FOR A HUMAN BEING 1977, Finnish
MILKA 1980, Finnish
THE UNKNOWN SOLDIER 1985, Finnish
FRIENDS, COMRADES Filmi-Molle Oy/Swedish Film
   Institute/Norsk Film, 1990, Finnish-Swedish-Norwegian

PAUL MONES
Agent: Leading Artists - Beverly Hills, 213/858-1999

THE BEAT Vestron, 1987

MARIO MONICELLI
b. May 16, 1915 - Viareggio, Italy
Address: Via del Babuino, 135 Rome, Italy, 06/6566126

I RAGAZZI DELLA VIA PAAL co-director with Alberto
   Mondadori, 1935, Italian
PIOGGIA D'ESTATE Zacconi, 1937, Italian
AL DIAVOLO LA CELEBRITA co-director with Steno,
   Produttori Associati, 1949, Italian
TOTO' CERCA CASA co-director with Steno, ATA,
   1949, Italian
VITA DA CANI co-director with Steno, ATA, 1950, Italian
E ARRIVATO IL CAVALIERE co-director with Steno,
   ATA/Excelsa Film, 1950, Italian

GUARDIE E LADRI co-director with Steno, Carlo Ponti/
   Dino De Laurentiis Cinematografica/Golden Film,
   1951, Italian
TOTO' E I RE DI ROMA co-director with Steno, Golden
   Film/Humanitas Film, 1952, Italian
THE UNFAITHFULS co-director with Steno, Allied Artists,
   1953, Italian
PROIBITO Documento Film/UGC/Cormoran Film,
   1954, Italian
TOTO' E CAROLINA Rosa, 1955, Italian
UN EROE DEI NOSTRI TEMPI Titanus/Vides,
   1955, Italian
DONATELLA Sud Film, 1956, Italian
THE TAILOR'S MAID *PADRI E FIGLI* Trans-Lux,
   1957, Italian
IL MEDICO E LO STREGONE Royal Film/Francinex,
   1957, Italian-French
BIG DEAL ON MADONNA STREET *I SOLITI IGNOTTI*
   United Motion Picture Organization, 1958, Italian
THE GREAT WAR United Artists, 1959, Italian
THE PASSIONATE THIEF Embassy, 1960, Italian
BOCCACCIO '70 co-director with Federico Fellini, Vittorio
   De Sica & Luchino Visconti, Embassy, 1962, Italian
THE ORGANIZER *I COMPAGNI* Continental, 1963,
   Italian-French-Yugoslavian
HIGH INFIDELITY co-director with Franco Rossi, Elio Petri
   & Luciano Salce, Magna, 1964, Italian-French
CASANOVA '70 Embassy, 1965, Italian-French
L'ARMATA BRANCALEONE Fair Film, 1966, Italian
THE QUEENS *LE FATE* co-director with Luciano Salce,
   Mauro Bolognini & Antonio Pietrangeli, Royal Films
   International, 1966, Italian-French
RAGAZZA CON LA PISTOLA Documento Film,
   1968, Italian
CAPRICCIO ALL'ITALIANA co-director with Steno, Mauro
   Bolognini & Pier Paolo Pasolini, Dino De Laurentiis
   Cinematografica, 1968, Italian
TO'E MORTA LA NONNA Vides, 1969, Italian
LE COPPIE co-director with Alberto Sordi & Vittorio De
   Sica, Documento Film, 1970, Italian
BRANCALEONE ALLE CROCIATE Fair Film, 1970, Italian
LADY LIBERTY *MORTADELLA* United Artists,
   1971, Italian
VOGLIAMO I COLONNELLI Dean Film, 1973, Italian
ROMANZO POPOLARE Capitolina, 1975, Italian
MY FRIENDS Allied Artists, 1975, Italian
CARO MICHELE Cineriz, 1976, Italian
SIGNORE E SIGNORI BUONANOTTE co-director, Titanus,
   1976, Italian
UN BORGHESE PICCOLO PICCOLO Cineriz, 1977, Italian
VIVA ITALIA! *I NUOVI MOSTRI* co-director with Dino Risi
   & Ettore Scola, Cinema 5, 1978, Italian
LOVERS AND LIARS *TRAVELS WITH ANITA*
   Levitt-Pickman, 1979, Italian-French
HURRICANE ROSY United Artists, 1979, Italian-French-
   West German
CAMERA D'ALBERGO Filmauro/Nouvelle Cinevog, 1980,
   Italian-French
LE COPPIE co-director with Alberto Sordi, Documento
   Film, 1980, Italian
IL MARCHESE DEL GRILLO Opera/RAI, 1981,
   Italian-French
AMICI MIEI II Sacis, 1982, Italian
BERTOLDO BERTOLDINO E...CACASENNO Gaumont,
   1984, Italian
LE DUE VITE DI MATTIA PASCAL Sacis, 1985,
   Italian-French-West German
SPERIAMO CHE SIA FEMMINA Clemi Cinematografica/
   Producteurs Associes, 1986, Italian-French
I PICARI Clemi Cinematografica, 1987, Italian
IL MALE OSCURO Clemi Cinematografica, 1989, Italian

Mo

FILM
DIRECTORS
GUIDE

CHRISTOPHER MONGER
b. November 9, 1950 - Wales
Home: 115 S. Catalina, Los Angeles, CA 90004,
213/388-4788
Agent: Brenda Beckett, Sanford-Beckett-Skouras &
Associates - Los Angeles, 213/208-2100

ENOUGH CUTS FOR A MURDER 1979, British
REPEATER WAC Films, 1980, British
VOICE OVER WAC Films, 1981, British
THE MABINOGI (TD) S4C/Channel Four, 1984,
Welsh-British
CRIME PAYS *MAE'N TALU WITHE* Thread Cross Films/
Channel Four, 1986, British
WAITING FOR THE LIGHT Triumph Releasing
Corporation, 1990

MEREDITH MONK
BOOK OF DAYS Tatge-Lasseur Productions/Foundation
for the Arts/La Sept/Alive From Off Center, 1988

PHILIPPE MONNIER
Contact: French Film Office, 745 Fifth Avenue, New York,
NY 10151, 212/832-8860

A TALE OF TWO CITIES (TF) Granada TV/Dune of
France/Antenne-2, 1989, British-French

GIULIANO MONTALDO
b. February 22, 1930 - Genua, Italy
Home: Via Paolo Emilio 32, Rome, Italy, 06/351842
Agent: Carol Levi, via G. Carducci 10, Rome, Italy 00187,
06/486961

TIRO AL PICCIONE Ajace Cinematografica, 1961, Italian
EXTRACONIUGALE co-director, D.S. Produzione,
1965, Italian
UNA BELLA GRINTA Ager Film/Clodio Cinematografica,
1965, Italian
GRAND SLAM *AD OGNI COSTO* Paramount, 1968,
Italian-Spanish-West German
GOTT MIT UNS Clesi Cinematografica/Jadran, 1969,
Italian-Yugoslavian
MACHINE GUN McCAIN *GLI INTOCCABILI* 1969,
Italian-Yugoslavian
SACCO AND VANZETTI UMC, 1971, Italian
GIORDANO BRUNO Champion/Les Films Concordia,
1973, Italian-French
L'AGNESE VA A MORIRE Indipendenti Regionali,
1976, Italian
CIRCUITO CHIUSO Filmalpha/RAI, 1978, Italian
IL GIOCATTOLO Titanus, 1978, Italian
MARCO POLO (MS) RAI/Franco Cristaldi Productions/
Vincenzo Labella Productions, 1982, Italian
CONTROL (CTF) HBO Showcase/Alliance Entertainment
Corporation/ Cristaldifilm/Les Films Ariane, 1987,
Italian-Canadian-French
THE GOLD-RIMMED GLASSES European Classics,
1987, Italian- French-Yugoslavian
TEMPO DI UCCIDERE Titanus, 1989, Italian-French

MONTY MONTGOMERY
THE LOVELESS co-director with Kathryn Bigelow,
Atlantic Releasing Corporation, 1981

PATRICK MONTGOMERY
THE COMPLEAT BEATLES (FD) TeleCulture, 1984,
originally released by MGM/UA Home Video in 1982

ROCK & ROLL: THE EARLY DAYS (HVD) co-director with
Pamela Page, RCA/Columbia Home Video/Fox-Lorber/
Archive Film Productions, 1984
BRITISH ROCK: THE FIRST WAVE (HVD) co-director with
Pamela Page, RCA/Columbia Home Video/Archive Film
Productions, 1985

IRVING J. MOORE*
Agent: Ronald Leif, Contemporary Artists - Beverly Hills,
213/278-8250

THE MAKING OF A MALE MODEL (TF) Aaron Spelling
Productions, 1983
DALLAS: PHANTOM OF THE OIL RIG (TF) co-director with
Michael Preece, Lorimar TV, 1989

MICHAEL MOORE
b. Flint, Michigan
Business: Center for Alternative Media, 2025 Pennsylvania
Avenue - Suite 918, Washington, D.C. 20006,
202/287-4974

ROGER & ME (FD) Warner Bros., 1989

RICHARD MOORE*
b. October 4, 1925 - Jacksonville, Illinois
Home: 1219 Sunset Plaza Drive, Los Angeles, CA 90069,
213/855-1144

CIRCLE OF IRON Avco Embassy, 1979

RONALD W. MOORE
FUTURE-KILL International Film Marketing, 1985

TOM MOORE*
Agent: CAA - Beverly Hills, 213/288-4545

'NIGHT, MOTHER Universal, 1986
MAYBE BABY (TF) Perry Lafferty Productions/von Zerneck-
Samuels Productions, 1988
DANIELLE STEEL'S FINE THINGS *FINE THINGS* The
Cramer Co./NBC Productions, 1990

PHILIPPE MORA*
Agent: TomMarion Rosenberg Office - Los Angeles,
212/653-7383

TROUBLE IN MOLOPOLIS Mora Productions,
1969, British
SWASTIKA (FD) Cinema 5, 1974, British
BROTHER, CAN YOU SPARE A DIME? (FD) Dimension,
1975, Canadian
MAD DOG *MAD DOG MORGAN* Cinema Shares
International, 1976, Australian
THE BEAST WITHIN United Artists, 1982
THE RETURN OF CAPTAIN INVINCIBLE *LEGEND IN
LEOTARDS* New World, 1983, Australian
A BREED APART Orion, 1983
HOWLING II...YOUR SISTER IS A WEREWOLF
Thorn-EMI, 1985, British
DEATH OF A SOLDIER Scotti Brothers,
1986, Australian
HOWLING III *THE MARSUPIALS: THE HOWLING III*
Square Pictures, 1987, Australian
COMMUNION New Line Cinema, 1989

202

CHRISTOPHER MORAHAN
b. July 9, 1929 - London, England
Business: Greenpoint Films, 5A Noel Street, London W1,
    England, 71/437-6492
Agent: William Morris Agency - Beverly Hills,
    213/274-7451

TALKING TO A STRANGER (TF)   BBC, 1966, British
THE GORGE (TF)   BBC, 1968, British
DIAMONDS FOR BREAKFAST   Paramount,
    1968, British
ALL NEAT IN BLACK STOCKINGS   National General,
    1969, British
THE JEWEL IN THE CROWN (MS) ☆ co-director with
    Jim O'Brien, Granada TV, 1984, British
IN THE SECRET STATE   Greenpoint Films,
    1985, British
CLOCKWISE   Universal, 1986, British
AFTER PILKINGTON (TF)   BBC, 1987, British
TROUBLES (TF)   Little Bird Productions/London
    Weekend TV, 1988, British
THE HEAT OF THE DAY (TF)   Granada TV,
    1989, British
PAPER MASK   FFI/British Screen, 1990, British

JACOBO MORALES
b. Puerto Rico
Contact: Puerto Rico Film Institute, P.O. Box 2350,
    San Juan, Puerto Rico, 00936

DIOS LOS CRIAS   1980, Puerto Rican
NICOLAS Y LOS DEMAS   Puerto Rican
LO QUE LE PASO A SANTIAGO   Dios los Crias
    Producciones/ Pedro Muniz Producciones, 1989,
    Puerto Rican

RICK MORANIS
Agent: APA - Los Angeles, 213/273-0744

STRANGE BREW   co-director with Dave Thomas,
    MGM/UA, 1983, Canadian

JEANNE MOREAU
b. January 23, 1928 - Paris, France
Contact: French Film Office, 745 Fifth Avenue, New York,
    NY 10151, 212/832-8860

LUMIERE   New World, 1976, French
L'ADOLESCENTE   Landmark Releasing, 1979,
    French-West German

NANNI MORETTI
b. August 19, 1953 - Brunico, Bolzano, Italy
Home: via Pindemonte 22, Rome, Italy, 06/582593

IO SONO UN AUTARCHICO   Nanni Moretti, 1976, Italian
ECCE BOMBO   Filmalpha/Alphabeta, 1978, Italian
SOGNI D'ORO   Operafilm/RAI, 1981, Italian
BIANCA   Faso Film/Reteitalia, 1984, Italian
LA MESSA E' FINITA   Faso Film, 1985, Italian
PALOMBELLA ROSSA   Titanus, 1989, Italian-French

W. T. MORGAN
Home: 733 Levering Avenue, Los Angeles, CA 90024,
    213/208-4198

THE UNHEARD MUSIC (FD)   Skouras Pictures, 1985
A MATTER OF DEGREES   Backbeat Productions/New
    Front Films, Linus Associates/George Gund/Fujisankei
    Communications, 1990

YOSHIMITSU MORITA
Contact: Directors Guild of Japan, Tsukada Building, 8-33
    Udagawa-cho, Shibuya-ku, Tokyo 150, Japan, 3/461-4411

THE FAMILY GAME   New Yorker, 1985, Japanese
SOREKARA (AND THEN)   New Yorker, 1986, Japanese
THE MERCENARIES   Fuji Television Network Film Division,
    1987, Japanese
ALL FOR BUSINESS' SAKE   Toho, 1987, Japanese
BAKAYARD! I'M PLENTY MAD   Shochiku, 1989, Japanese

DAVID BURTON MORRIS*
b. Kansas City, Missouri
Home: 3640 Dixie Canyon Place, Sherman Oaks, CA
    91423, 818/906-0239
Agent: William Morris Agency - Beverly Hills, 213/274-7451

LOOSE ENDS   Twyman Films, 1975
PURPLE HAZE   Triumph/Columbia, 1983
PATTI ROCKS   FilmDallas, 1987
HOME TOWN BOY MAKES GOOD (CTF)   HBO, 1989
VIETNAM WAR STORY: THE LAST DAYS (CTF)
    co-director with Luis Soto & Sandy Smolan, HBO, 1989

ERROL MORRIS
Agent: CAA - Beverly Hills, 213/288-4545

GATES OF HEAVEN (FD)   1978
VERNON, FLORIDA (FD)   1981
THE THIN BLUE LINE   Miramax Films, 1988
A BRIEF HISTORY OF TIME   Amblin
    Entertainment, 1990

HOWARD MORRIS*
b. September 4, 1919 - New York, New York
Business Manager: Perry & Neidorf, 315 S. Beverly Drive,
    Beverly Hills, CA 90212, 213/553-0171

WHO'S MINDING THE MINT?   Columbia, 1967
WITH SIX YOU GET EGGROLL   National General, 1968
DON'T DRINK THE WATER   Avco Embassy, 1969
OH! BABY, BABY, BABY... (TF)   Alan Landsburg
    Productions, 1974
GOIN' COCONUTS   Osmond Distribution, 1978

JUDY MORRIS
Contact: Australian Film Commission, 9229 Sunset Blvd.,
    Los Angeles, CA 90069, 213/275-7074

LUIGI'S LADIES   Hoyts Distribution, 1989, Australian

BRUCE MORRISON
b. New Zealand
Address: P.O. Box 46-090, Herne Bay, Auckland,
    New Zealand

CONSTANCE   Mirage Films/New Zealand Film
    Commission, 1984, New Zealand
SHAKER RUN   Challenge Film Corporation, 1985,
    New Zealand
TEARAWAY   *QUEEN CITY ROCKER*   Spectrafilm,
    1987, New Zealand

PAUL MORRISSEY
b. 1939 - New York, New York

FLESH   Warhol, 1968
TRASH   Warhol, 1970
ANDY WARHOL'S WOMEN   Warhol, 1971

FILM
DIRECTORS
GUIDE

F
I
L
M

D
I
R
E
C
T
O
R
S

HEAT   Warhol, 1972
L'AMOUR   co-director with Andy Warhol, Altura, 1973
ANDY WARHOL'S FRANKENSTEIN   *FLESH FOR FRANKENSTEIN*   Bryanston, 1974, Italian-French
ANDY WARHOL'S DRACULA   *BLOOD FOR DRACULA*   Bryanston, 1974, Italian-French
THE HOUND OF THE BASKERVILLES   Atlantic Releasing Corporation, 1979, British
MADAME WANG'S   1981
FORTY-DEUCE   Island Alive, 1982
MIXED BLOOD   Sara Films, 1984, U.S.-French
BEETHOVEN'S NEPHEW   FilmDallas, 1985, French-West German-Austrian
SPIKE OF BENSONHURST   FilmDallas, 1988

ROCKY MORTON
Agent: CAA - Beverly Hills, 213/288-4545

THE MAX HEADROOM STORY (TF)   co-director with Annabel Jankel, 1985, British
D.O.A.   co-director with Annabel Jankel, Buena Vista, 1988

GILBERT MOSES*
b. August 20, 1942 - Cleveland, Ohio
Agent: Stuart Kaplan, Irv Schechter Company - Beverly Hills, 213/278-8070

WILLIE DYNAMITE   Universal, 1974
ROOTS (MS) ☆   co-director with Marvin J. Chomsky, John Erman & David Greene, Wolper Productions, 1977
THE GREATEST THING THAT ALMOST HAPPENED (TF)   Charles Fries Productions, 1977
THE FISH THAT SAVED PITTSBURGH   United Artists, 1979
A FIGHT FOR JENNY (FT)   Robert Greenwald Productions, 1986
RUNAWAY (TF)   WonderWorks Inc., 1989

HARRY MOSES*
Business: 1560 Broadway - Suite 600, New York, NY 10036, 212/840-8400
Agent: David Guc, The Gersh Agency - New York City, 212/997-1818

THORNWELL (TF)   MTM Enterprises, 1981
THE TRIAL OF BERNHARD GOETZ (TF)   Litchfield Films, 1988

JON MOSTOW
Business: McGuffin Productions, Television Center, 6311 Romaine Street, Hollywood, CA 90038, 213/461-8880
Agent: Hess-Kallberg Associates - Hollywood, 213/850-5714

BLACK ANGEL   Hess-Kallberg Productions, 1991

CAROLINE AHLFORS MOURIS
BEGINNER'S LUCK   co-director with Frank Mouris, New World, 1986

FRANK MOURIS
BEGINNER'S LUCK   co-director with Caroline Ahlfors Mouris, New World, 1986

LOUIS MOURNEAU
TO DIE STANDING   Concorde, 1990, U.S.-Peruvian

MALCOLM MOWBRAY*
Agent: CAA - Beverly Hills, 213/288-4545

A PRIVATE FUNCTION   Island Alive, 1984, British
OUT COLD   Hemdale, 1989
THE BOYFRIEND SCHOOL   Hemdale, 1990

JOHN LLEWELLYN MOXEY*
b. 1920 - Burlingham, England
Agent: Jeff Cooper, The Cooper Agency - Los Angeles, 213/277-8422

HORROR HOTEL   *CITY OF THE DEAD*   Trans-World, 1960, British
FOXHOLE IN CAIRO   Paramount, 1961, British
DEATH TRAP   Anglo-Amalgamated, 1962, British
THE 20,000 POUND KISS   Anglo-Amalgamated, 1963, British
RICOCHET   Warner-Pathe, 1963, British
DOWNFALL   Embassy, 1964, British
FACE OF A STRANGER   Warner-Pathe, 1964, British
STRANGLER'S WEB   Embassy, 1965, British
PSYCHO-CIRCUS   *CIRCUS OF FEAR*   American International, 1967, British
THE TORMENTOR   ITC, 1967, British
SAN FRANCISCO INTERNATIONAL AIRPORT (TF)   Universal TV, 1970
THE HOUSE THAT WOULD NOT DIE (TF)   Aaron Spelling Productions, 1970
ESCAPE (TF)   Paramount TV, 1971
THE LAST CHILD (TF)   Aaron Spelling Productions, 1971
A TASTE OF EVIL (TF)   Aaron Spelling Productions, 1971
THE DEATH OF ME YET! (TF)   Aaron Spelling Productions, 1971
THE NIGHT STALKER (TF)   ABC, Inc., 1972
HARDCASE (TF)   Hanna-Barbera Productions, 1972
THE BOUNTY MAN (TF)   ABC Circle Films, 1972
HOME FOR THE HOLIDAYS (TF)   ABC Circle Films, 1972
GENESIS II (TF)   Warner Bros. TV, 1973
THE STRANGE AND DEADLY OCCURENCE (TF)   Metromedia Productions, 1974
WHERE HAVE ALL THE PEOPLE GONE? (TF)   Metromedia Productions, 1974
FOSTER AND LAURIE (TF)   Charles Fries Productions, 1975
CHARLIE'S ANGELS (TF)   Spelling-Goldberg Productions, 1976
CONSPIRACY OF TERROR (TF)   Lorimar Productions, 1976
NIGHTMARE IN BADHAM COUNTY (TF)   ABC Circle Films, 1976
SMASH-UP ON INTERSTATE 5 (TF)   Filmways, 1976
PANIC IN ECHO PARK (TF)   Edgar J. Scherick Associates, 1977
INTIMATE STRANGERS (TF)   Charles Fries Productions, 1977
THE PRESIDENT'S MISTRESS (TF)   Stephen Friedman/Kings Road Productions, 1978
THE COURAGE AND THE PASSION (TF)   David Gerber Company/Columbia TV, 1978
SANCTUARY OF FEAR (TF)   Marble Arch Productions, 1979
THE POWER WITHIN (TF)   Aaron Spelling Productions, 1979
THE SOLITARY MAN (TF)   Universal TV, 1979
EBONY, IVORY AND JADE (TF)   Frankel Films, 1979
THE CHILDREN OF AN LAC (TF)   Charles Fries Productions, 1980
THE MATING SEASON (TF)   Highgate Pictures, 1980
NO PLACE TO HIDE (TF)   Metromedia Producers Corporation, 1981

THE VIOLATION OF SARAH McDAVID (TF)   CBS
Entertainment, 1981
KILLJOY (TF)   Lorimar Productions, 1981
I, DESIRE (TF)   Green-Epstein Productions/Columbia
TV, 1982
THE CRADLE WILL FALL (TF)   Cates Films Inc./Procter &
Gamble Productions, 1983
THROUGH NAKED EYES (TF)   Charles Fries
Productions, 1983
WHEN DREAMS COME TRUE (TF)   I & C
Productions, 1985
BLACKE'S MAGIC (TF)   Universal TV, 1986
SADIE AND SON (TF)   Norton Wright Productions/Kenny
Rogers Organization/ ITC Productions, 1987
LADY MOBSTER (TF)   Danjul Films/Frank von Zerneck
Productions, 1988
OUTBACK BOUND (TF)   Andrew Gottlieb Productions/
CBS Entertainment, 1988

ALLAN MOYLE*

Home: 454 West 49th Street, New York, NY 10019,
212/247-7952
Agent: Jan McCormack, 11342 Dona Lisa Drive, Studio
City, CA 97604, 213/650-3801

MONTREAL MAIN   co-director with Frank Vitale &
Maxine McGillivray, President Films/Canadian Film
Development Corporation, 1978, Canadian
THE RUBBER GUN   Schuman-Katzka, 1978, Canadian
TIMES SQUARE   AFD, 1980
PUMP UP THE VOLUME   New Line Cinema, 1990,
U.S.-Canadian

RUSSELL MULCAHY*

b. 1953 - Melbourne, Australia
Contact: Directors Guild of America - Los Angeles,
213/289-2000

DEREK AND CLIVE GET THE HORN (FD)   Peter Cook
Productions, 1981, British
RAZORBACK   Warner Bros., 1984, Australian
HIGHLANDER   20th Century Fox, 1986, British-U.S.
HIGHLANDER 2 - THE QUICKENING   Davis-Panzer
Productions, 1990, British-U.S.

ROBERT MULLIGAN*

b. August 23, 1925 - Bronx, New York
Agent: Robert Stein, Leading Artists - Beverly Hills,
213/858-1999

FEAR STRIKES OUT   Paramount, 1957
THE RAT RACE   Paramount, 1960
THE GREAT IMPOSTER   Universal, 1961
COME SEPTEMBER   Universal, 1961
THE SPIRAL ROAD   Universal, 1962
TO KILL A MOCKINGBIRD ★★   Universal, 1962
LOVE WITH THE PROPER STRANGER   Paramount, 1964
BABY, THE RAIN MUST FALL   Columbia, 1965
INSIDE DAISY CLOVER   Warner Bros., 1966
UP THE DOWN STAIRCASE   Warner Bros., 1967
THE STALKING MOON   National General, 1969
THE PURSUIT OF HAPPINESS   Columbia, 1971
SUMMER OF '42   Warner Bros., 1971
THE OTHER   20th Century-Fox, 1972
THE NICKEL RIDE   20th Century-Fox, 1975
BLOODBROTHERS   Warner Bros., 1979
SAME TIME, NEXT YEAR   Universal, 1979
KISS ME GOODBYE   20th Century-Fox, 1982
CLARA'S HEART   Warner Bros., 1988
MAN IN THE MOON   Pathe Entertainment, 1991

MARK MULLIN
COOL BLUE   Cinema Corporation of America, 1990

JAG MOHAN MUNDHRA
b. October 29, 1948 - India
Agent: Marshak-Wykoff Agency - Beverly Hills, 213/278-7222
Business: Scorpion Entertainment Group, 8756 Holloway
Drive, Los Angeles, CA 90069, 213/652-6824

SURAAG   1982, Indian
KAMLA   1985, Indian
OPEN HOUSE   I.R.C./Prism Entertainment, 1987
DEATH MASK   Filmtrust, 1987
HACK-O-LANTERN   Legacy Entertainment/Spencer
Films, 1989
NIGHT EYES   Amritraj-Baldwin Entertainment, 1990
LAST CALL   Prism Entertainment, 1990
DOWN AND DIRTY   Prism Entertainment, 1990

IAN MUNE
Business: Mirage Entertainment Ltd., P.O. Box 1113,
Auckland, New Zealand, 09/790-097

CAME A HOT FRIDAY   Mirage Films, 1984, New Zealand
BRIDGE TO NOWHERE   Mirage Films, 1985,
New Zealand

JIMMY T. MURAKAMI
Business: Murakami/Wolf/Swenson, Inc., 1463 Tamarind
Avenue, Hollywood, CA 90028, 213/462-6473

BATTLE BEYOND THE STARS   New World, 1979
WHEN THE WIND BLOWS (AF)   Kings Road, 1988, British

WALTER MURCH*
Contact: Directors Guild of America - Los Angeles, 213/289-
2000

RETURN TO OZ   Buena Vista, 1985

FREDI M. MURER
Contact: Swiss Film Center, Munstergasse 18, 8001 Zurich,
Switzerland, 01/472-860

ALPINE FIRE   Vestron, 1986, Swiss

JIM MURO
Business: Chaos Productions, 166 West 83rd Street,
New York, NY 10024

STREET TRASH   Lightning Pictures, 1987

EDDIE MURPHY
b. April 3, 1961 - Brooklyn, New York
Agent: ICM - Los Angeles, 213/550-4000

HARLEM NIGHTS   Paramount, 1989

EDWARD MURPHY
RAW FORCE   American Panorama, 1982
HEATED VENGEANCE   Media Home Entertainment/
Jungle Production Corporation, 1985

GEOFF MURPHY
Agent: InterTalent - Los Angeles, 213/271-0600

WILDMAN   1976, New Zealand
GOODBYE PORK PIE   Samuel Goldwyn Company,
1980, New Zealand

UTU   Pickman Films, 1983, New Zealand
THE QUIET EARTH   Skouras Pictures,
    1985, New Zealand
NEVER SAY DIE   Everard Films, 1988, New Zealand
RED KING, WHITE KNIGHT (CTF)   HBO Pictures/
    Zenith Productions/ John Kemeny Productions/
    Citadel Entertainment, 1989, U.S.-British-Canadian
YOUNG GUNS II   20th Century Fox, 1990

BILL MURRAY*
b. September 21, 1950 - Chicago, Illinois
Contact: Directors Guild of America - Los Angeles,
    213/289-2000

QUICK CHANGE   co-director with Howard Franklin,
    Warner Bros., 1990

DON MURRAY
b. July 29, 1929 - Hollywood, California
Agent: F.A.M.E. - Los Angeles, 213/656-7590

THE CROSS AND THE SWITCHBLADE   Dick
    Ross, 1970

JOHN MUSKER
Business: Walt Disney Studios, 500 S. Buena Vista Street,
    Burbank, CA 91521, 818/560-1000

THE GREAT MOUSE DETECTIVE (AF)   co-director with
    Ron Clements, Burny Mattinson & Dave Michener,
    Buena Vista, 1986
THE LITTLE MERMAID (AF)   co-director with Ron
    Clements, Buena Vista, 1989

FLOYD MUTRUX*
(Charles Floyd Mutrux)
Agent: William Morris Agency - Beverly Hills,
    213/274-7451

DUSTY AND SWEETS McGEE   Warner Bros., 1971
ALOHA, BOBBY AND ROSE   Columbia, 1975
AMERICAN HOT WAX   Paramount, 1978
THE HOLLYWOOD KNIGHTS   Columbia, 1980

ALAN MYERSON*
Agent: Scott Harris, Harris & Goldberg - Los Angeles,
    213/553-5200
Personal Manager: George Shapiro, Shapiro-West,
    141 El Camino Drive, Beverly Hills, CA 90212,
    213/278-8896

STEELYARD BLUES   Warner Bros., 1973
THE LOVE BOAT (TF)   co-director with Richard Kinon,
    Douglas S. Cramer Productions, 1976
PRIVATE LESSONS   Jensen Farley Pictures, 1981
POLICE ACADEMY 5: ASSIGNMENT MIAMI BEACH
    Warner Bros., 1988

N

MARVA NABILI
NIGHTSONGS (TF)   FN Films/American Playhouse, 1984

IVAN NAGY*
b. January 23, 1938 - Budapest, Hungary
Home: 10128 Empyrean Way, Los Angeles, CA 90067,
    213/552-4724
Agent: Mark Lichtman, Shapiro-Lichtman Agency - Beverly
    Hills, 213/859-8877

BAD CHARLESTON CHARLIE   International Cinema, 1973
MONEY, MARBLES AND CHALK   American
    International, 1973
FIVE MINUTES OF FREEDOM   Cannon, 1973
DEADLY HERO   Avco Embassy, 1976
MIND OVER MURDER (TF)   Paramount TV, 1979
ONCE UPON A SPY (TF)   David Gerber Company/
    Columbia TV, 1980
MIDNIGHT LACE (TF)   Four R Productions/Universal
    TV, 1981
A GUN IN THE HOUSE (TF)   Channing-Debin-Locke
    Company, 1981
JANE DOE (TF)   ITC, 1983
A TOUCH OF SCANDAL (TF)   Doris M. Keating
    Productions/Columbia TV, 1984
PLAYING WITH FIRE (TF)   Zephyr Productions, 1985
ENCOUNTERS (TF)   Larry A. Thompson Productions/
    Donna Mills Productions/Columbia TV, 1986

MIRA NAIR
b. 1957 - Orissa, India
Business: Mirabai Films, 6 Rivington Street, New York, NY
    10002, 212/254-7826

SO FAR FROM INDIA (FD)   Mirabai Films, 1982
INDIA CABARET (FD)   Mirabai Films, 1985
SALAAM BOMBAY!   Cinecom, 1988, Indian-British-French
MISSISSIPPI MASALA   Cinecom, 1991, U.S.-British

MICHAEL NANKIN
b. December 26, 1955 - Los Angeles, California
Agent: ICM - Los Angeles, 213/550-4000

MIDNIGHT MADNESS   co-director with David Wechter,
    Buena Vista, 1981

LEON NARBEY
Contact: New Zealand Film Commission, P.O. Box 11546,
    Wellington, New Zealand, 4/859-754

ILLUSTRIOUS ENERGY   Challenge Film Corporation/
    Cinepro Productions/ New Zealand Film Commission,
    1987, New Zealand

SILVIO NARIZZANO*
b. February 8, 1928 - Montreal, Quebec, Canada
Home: 20155 Observation Drive, Topanga, CA 90290,
    213/455-3558
Agent: The Agency - Los Angeles, 213/551-3000

DIE! DIE! MY DARLING! *FANATIC* Columbia,
    1965, British

GEORGY GIRL   Columbia, 1967, British
BLUE   Paramount, 1968, British
LOOT   Cinevision, 1972, British
REDNECK   International Amusements, 1975,
   British-Italian
THE SKY IS FALLING   1976, Canadian
WHY SHOOT THE TEACHER   Quartet, 1977, Canadian
COME BACK, LITTLE SHEBA (TF)   Granada TV,
   1977, British
THE CLASS OF MISS MacMICHAEL   Brut Productions,
   1979, British
STAYING ON (TF)   Granada TV, 1980, British
CHOICES   1981, Canadian

GREGORY NAVA
b. April 10, 1949 - San Diego, California
Agent: Jeff Berg, ICM - Los Angeles, 213/550-4000

THE CONFESSIONS OF AMANS   Independent
   Productions, 1976
EL NORTE   Cinecom/Island Alive, 1984
A TIME OF DESTINY   Columbia, 1988

CAL NAYLOR*
Home: 17606 Posetano Road, Pacific Palisades, CA
   90272, 213/454-7229

DIRT   co-director with Eric Karson, American
   Cinema, 1979

RONALD NEAME*
b. April 23, 1911 - London, England
Agent: Ben Benjamin, ICM - Los Angeles, 213/550-4000
Business: Kimridge Corporation, 2317 Kimridge Road,
   Beverly Hills, CA 90210, 213/271-2970

TAKE MY LIFE   Eagle Lion, 1947, British
THE GOLDEN SALAMANDER   Eagle Lion, 1950, British
THE PROMOTER   *THE CARD*   Universal, 1952, British
MAN WITH A MILLION   *THE MILLION POUND NOTE*
   United Artists, 1954, British
THE MAN WHO NEVER WAS   20th Century-Fox,
   1956, British
THE SEVENTH SIN   MGM, 1957
WINDOM'S WAY   Rank, 1958, British
THE HORSE'S MOUTH   United Artists, 1959, British
TUNES OF GLORY   Lopert, 1960, British
ESCAPE FROM ZAHRAIN   Paramount, 1962
I COULD GO ON SINGING   United Artists, 1963, British
THE CHALK GARDEN   Universal, 1964, British
MISTER MOSES   United Artists, 1965, British
A MAN COULD GET KILLED   co-directed with Cliff Owen,
   Universal, 1966
GAMBIT   Universal, 1966
THE PRIME OF MISS JEAN BRODIE   20th Century-Fox,
   1969, British
SCROOGE   National General, 1970, British
THE POSEIDON ADVENTURE   20th Century-Fox, 1972
THE ODESSA FILE   Columbia, 1974,
   British-West German
METEOR   American International, 1979
HOPSCOTCH   Avco Embassy, 1980
FIRST MONDAY IN OCTOBER   Paramount, 1981
FOREIGN BODY   Orion, 1986, British

HAL NEEDHAM*
b. March 6, 1931 - Memphis, Tennessee
Agent: Camden Artists - Los Angeles, 213/556-2022
Business: Bandit Productions, 3518 Cahuenga Blvd.
   West - Suite 110, Los Angeles, CA 90068, 213/876-8052

SMOKEY AND THE BANDIT   Universal, 1977

HOOPER   Warner Bros., 1978
THE VILLAIN   Columbia, 1979
DEATH CAR ON THE FREEWAY (TF)   Shpetner
   Productions, 1979
STUNTS UNLIMITED (TF)   Lawrence Gordon Productions/
   Paramount TV, 1980
SMOKEY AND THE BANDIT, PART II   Universal, 1980
THE CANNONBALL RUN   20th Century-Fox, 1981
MEGAFORCE   20th Century-Fox, 1982
STROKER ACE   Universal, 1983
CANNONBALL RUN II   Warner Bros., 1984
RAD   Tri-Star, 1986
BODY SLAM   DEG, 1987
B.L. STRYKER (TF)   Blue Period Productions/TWS
   Productions/ Universal TV, 1989

ALBERTO NEGRIN
Home: via Compagno 56, Rome, Italy, 06/302-9917

MUSSOLINI: THE DECLINE AND FALL OF IL DUCE (CTF)
   HBO Premiere Films/ RAI/Antenne-2/Beta Film/TVE/RTSI,
   1985, U.S.-Italian-French-West German
IL SECRETO DEL SAHARA (MS)   RAI/TF1/TVE/Beta
   Film/Racing Pictures, 1987, Italian-French-
   West German-Spanish
VOYAGE OF TERROR: THE ACHILLE LAURO AFFAIR (TF)
   RAI/Tribune Entertainment/TF1/Taurusfilm/ORF/HR/
   Filmalpha, 1990, Italian-U.S.-French-West German

JEAN NEGULESCO*
b. February 29, 1900 - Craiova, Romania
Home: Marabella Club, Malaga, Costa Del Sol, Spain,
   011/345-2776-524
Business Manager: Harold Weiser, 20508 Mandel Street,
   Canoga Park, CA 91306, 818/998-2536

SINGAPORE WOMAN   Warner Bros., 1941
THE MASK OF DIMITRIOS   Warner Bros., 1944
THE CONSPIRATORS   Warner Bros., 1944
THREE STRANGERS   Warner Bros., 1946
NOBODY LIVES FOREVER   Warner Bros., 1946
HUMORESQUE   Warner Bros., 1947
DEEP VALLEY   Warner Bros., 1947
JOHNNY BELINDA★   Warner Bros., 1948
ROAD HOUSE   20th Century Fox, 1948
THE FORBIDDEN STREET   *BRITANNIA MEWS*   20th
   Century-Fox, 1949
UNDER MY SKIN   20th Century-Fox, 1950
THREE CAME HOME   20th Century-Fox, 1950
THE MUDLARK   20th Century-Fox, 1950
TAKE CARE OF MY LITTLE GIRL   20th Century-Fox, 1951
PHONE CALL FROM A STRANGER   20th Century-
   Fox, 1952
LYDIA BAILEY   20th Century-Fox, 1952
LURE OF THE WILDERNESS   20th Century-Fox, 1952
O. HENRY'S FULL HOUSE   co-director with Howard Hawks,
   Henry King & Henry Koster, 20th Century-Fox, 1952
TITANIC   20th Century-Fox, 1953
HOW TO MARRY A MILLIONAIRE   20th Century-Fox, 1953
SCANDAL AT SCOURIE   MGM, 1953
THREE COINS IN THE FOUNTAIN   20th Century-
   Fox, 1954
A WOMAN'S WORLD   20th Century-Fox, 1954
DADDY LONG LEGS   20th Century-Fox, 1955
THE RAINS OF RANCHIPUR   20th Century-Fox, 1955
BOY ON A DOLPHIN   20th Century-Fox, 1957
THE GIFT OF LOVE   20th Century-Fox, 1958
A CERTAIN SMILE   20th Century-Fox, 1958
COUNT YOUR BLESSINGS   MGM, 1959
THE BEST OF EVERYTHING   20th Century-Fox, 1959
JESSICA   United Artists, 1962, U.S.-Italian-French

THE PLEASURE SEEKERS 20th Century-Fox, 1964
HELLO - GOODBYE 20th Century-Fox, 1970
THE INVINCIBLE SIX Continental, 1970, U.S.-Iranian

DAVID NELSON*

b. October 24, 1936 - New York, New York
Contact: Directors Guild of America - Los Angeles,
213/289-2000

DEATH SCREAMS ABA Productions, 1981
LAST PLANE OUT New World, 1983
A RARE BREED New World, 1984

GARY NELSON*

Agent: CAA - Beverly Hills, 213/288-4545

MOLLY AND LAWLESS JOHN Producers Distribution
Corporation, 1972,
SANTEE Crown International, 1973
THE GIRL ON THE LATE, LATE SHOW (TF) Screen
Gems/Columbia TV, 1974
MEDICAL STORY (TF) David Gerber Company/
Columbia TV, 1975
PANACHE (TF) Warner Bros. TV, 1976
WASHINGTON: BEHIND CLOSED DOORS (MS) ☆
Paramount TV, 1977
FREAKY FRIDAY Buena Vista, 1977
TO KILL A COP (TF) David Gerber Company/
Columbia TV, 1978
THE BLACK HOLE Buena Vista, 1979
THE PRIDE OF JESSE HALLAM (TF) The Konigsberg
Company
SEVEN BRIDES FOR SEVEN BROTHERS (TF) David
Gerber Company/ MGM-UA TV, 1982
JIMMY THE KID New World, 1983
MURDER IN COWETA COUNTY (TF) Telecom
Entertaiment/The International Picture Show Co., 1983
MICKEY SPILLANE'S 'MURDER ME, MURDER YOU' (TF)
Jay Bernstein Productions/Columbia TV, 1983
FOR LOVE AND HONOR (TF) David Gerber Company/
MGM-UA TV, 1983
THE BARON AND THE KID (TF) Telecom
Entertainment, 1984
LADY BLUE (TF) David Gerber Productions/
MGM-UA TV, 1985
AGATHA CHRISTIE'S 'MURDER IN THREE ACTS' (TF)
Warner Bros. TV, 1986
ALLAN QUATERMAIN AND THE LOST CITY OF GOLD
Cannon, 1987
HOUSTON KNIGHTS (TF) co-director with Richard Lang,
Jay Bernstein Productions/Columbia TV, 1987
JAMES CLAVELL'S NOBLE HOUSE NOBLE HOUSE (MS)
Noble House Productions Ltd./De Laurentiis
Entertainment Group, 1988
SHOOTER (TF) UBU Productions/Paramount TV, 1988
GET SMART, AGAIN! (TF) Phoenix Entertainment Group/
IndieProd Co., 1989

GENE NELSON*

(Gene Berg)
b. March 24, 1920 - Seattle, Washington
Business: Tangene Productions, 3431 Vinton Avenue,
Los Angeles, CA 90034, 213/837-0484

HAND OF DEATH 20th Century-Fox, 1962
HOOTENANNY HOOT MGM, 1962
KISSIN' COUSINS MGM, 1964
YOUR CHEATIN' HEART MGM, 1964
HARUM SCARUM MGM, 1965
THE COOL ONES Warner Bros., 1967

WAKE ME WHEN THE WAR IS OVER (TF) Thomas-
Spelling Productions, 1969
THE LETTERS (TF) co-director with Paul Krasny,
ABC Circle Films, 1973
THE BARON AND THE KID (TF) Telecom
Entertainment, 1984

AVI NESHER

Agent: InterTalent - Los Angeles, 213/271-0600

THE TROUPE *HALAHAKA* Eastways Productions,
1978, Israeli
DIZENGOFF 99 Shapira Films, 1970, Israeli
SHE American National Enterprises, 1983, Italian
RAGE AND GLORY Interpictures, 1985, Israeli
BREAKING Zygmunt P. Barwaz Productions, 1985, Israeli
NAMELESS Dino De Laurentiis Communications, 1990

MIKE NEWELL*

b. 1942
Agent: Alan Greenspan, ICM - Los Angeles, 213/550-4428

THE MAN IN THE IRON MASK (TF) Norman Rosemont
Productions/ITC, 1977, U.S.-British
THE AWAKENING Orion/Warner Bros., 1980
BLOOD FEUD (TF) 20th Century-Fox TV/Glickman-
Selznick Productions, 1983
BAD BLOOD Southern Pictures/New Zealand Film
Commission, 1983, New Zealand
DANCE WITH A STRANGER Samuel Goldwyn Company,
1985, British
THE GOOD FATHER Skouras Pictures, 1986, British
AMAZING GRACE AND CHUCK Tri-Star, 1987
SOURSWEET First Film Company/Zenith, 1988, British
COMMON GROUND (TF) Daniel H. Blatt Productions/
Lorimar TV, 1990

JOHN NEWLAND*

b. November 23, 1917 - Cincinnati, Ohio
Agent: Sanford-Beckett-Skouras & Associates - Los Angeles,
213/208-2100

THAT NIGHT Universal, 1957
THE VIOLATORS Universal, 1957
THE SPY WITH MY FACE MGM, 1966
MY LOVER, MY SON MGM, 1970, British
THE DEADLY HUNT (TF) Four Star International, 1971
CRAWLSPACE (TF) Titus Productions, 1972
DON'T BE AFRAID OF THE DARK (TF) Lorimar
Productions, 1972
WHO FEARS THE DEVIL *THE LEGEND OF HILLBILLY
JOHN* Jack H. Harris Enterprises, 1974
A SENSITIVE, PASSIONATE MAN (TF) Factor-Newland
Production Corporation, 1977
OVERBOARD (TF) Factor-Newland Production
Corporation, 1978
THE SUICIDE'S WIFE (TF) Factor-Newland Production
Corporation, 1979

ANTHONY NEWLEY

b. September 24, 1931 - London, England
Agent: ICM - Los Angeles, 213/550-4000

CAN HIERONYMOUS MERKIN EVER FORGET MERCY
HUMPPE AND FIND TRUE HAPPINESS? Regional,
1969, British
SUMMERTREE Columbia, 1971

PAUL NEWMAN*
b. January 26, 1925 - Cleveland, Ohio
Agent: CAA - Beverly Hills, 213/288-4545

RACHEL, RACHEL   Warner Bros., 1968
SOMETIMES A GREAT NOTION   *NEVER GIVE AN INCH*
   Universal, 1971
THE EFFECT OF GAMMA RAYS ON MAN-IN-THE-MOON
   MARIGOLDS   20th Century-Fox, 1973
THE SHADOW BOX (TF) ☆   The Shadow Box Film
   Company, 1980
HARRY & SON   Orion, 1984
THE GLASS MENAGERIE   Cineplex Odeon, 1987

PAUL NICHOLAS*
(Lutz Schaarwaechter)
Contact: Directors Guild of America - Los Angeles,
   213/289-2000

BAD BLOOD   *JULIE DARLING*   Twin Continental, 1982,
   Canadian-West German
CHAINED HEAT   Jensen Farley Pictures, 1983
THE NAKED CAGE   Cannon, 1986

ALLAN NICHOLLS*
b. April 8, 1945 - Montreal, Quebec, Canada
Home: P.O. Box 466, Montgomery Center, VT 05471,
   802/326-4566

DEAD RINGER   Feature Films, 1982

MIKE NICHOLS*
(Michael Igor Peschkowsky)
b. November 6, 1931 - Berlin, Germany
Agent: Sam Cohn, ICM - New York City, 212/556-6810
Attorney: Marvin B. Meyer, Rosenfeld, Meyer & Susman -
   Beverly Hills, 213/858-7700

WHO'S AFRAID OF VIRGINIA WOOLF?★   Warner
   Bros., 1966
THE GRADUATE★★   Avco Embassy, 1967
CATCH-22   Paramount, 1970
CARNAL KNOWLEDGE   Avco Embassy, 1971
THE DAY OF THE DOLPHIN   Avco Embassy, 1973
THE FORTUNE   Columbia, 1975
GILDA LIVE (FD)   Warner Bros., 1980
SILKWOOD★   20th Century-Fox, 1983
HEARTBURN   Paramount, 1986
BILOXI BLUES   Universal, 1988
WORKING GIRL★   20th Century Fox, 1988
POSTCARDS FROM THE EDGE   Columbia, 1990

JACK NICHOLSON*
b. April 22, 1927 - Neptune, New Jersey
Agent: Sandy Bresler, Bresler, Kelly & Associates -
   Encino, 818/905-1155
Business Manager: Guild Management Corporation -
   Los Angeles, 213/277-9711

DRIVE, HE SAID   Columbia, 1971
GOIN' SOUTH   Paramount, 1979
THE TWO JAKES   Paramount, 1990

TED NICOLAOU
THE DUNGEONMASTER   co-director, Empire
   Pictures, 1985
TERRORVISION   Empire Pictures, 1986

JOHN NICOLELLA*
Agent: InterTalent - Los Angeles, 213/271-0600

FINISH LINE (CTF)   Guber-Peters Entertainment
   Productions/Phoenix Entertainment Group, 1989
MICKEY SPILLANE'S MIKE HAMMER: MURDER TAKES
   ALL (TF) Jay Bernstein Productions/Columbia TV, 1989
ROCK HUDSON (TF)   The Konigsberg-Sanitsky
   Company, 1990

GEORGE T. NIERENBERG
b. Roslyn Heights, New York

THE HOLLOW   GTN Productions, 1975
NO MAPS ON MY TAPS (FD)   GTN Productions, 1980
SAY AMEN, SOMEBODY (FD)   United Artists
   Classics, 1983
THAT RHYTHM, THOSE BLUES (FD)   1989

ROB NILSSON
Agent: Sanford-Beckett-Skouras & Assoc. - Los Angeles,
   213/277-6211

NORTHERN LIGHTS   co-director with John Hanson,
   Cine-Manifest, 1979
ON THE EDGE   Skouras Pictures, 1986
SIGNAL 7   Myron-Taylor Productions, 1986
HEAT AND SUNLIGHT   New Front Alliance/Snowball
   Productions, 1987

LEONARD NIMOY*
b. March 26, 1931 - Boston, Massachusetts
Agent: The Gersh Agency - Beverly Hills, 213/274-6611

STAR TREK III: THE SEARCH FOR SPOCK
   Paramount, 1984
STAR TREK IV: THE VOYAGE HOME   Paramount, 1986
THREE MEN AND A BABY   Buena Vista, 1987
THE GOOD MOTHER   Buena Vista, 1988
UNTITLED   Paramount, 1990

NIGEL NOBLE
VOICES OF 'SARAFINA!' (FD)   New Yorker, 1988

RON NORMAN
b. November 2, 1953 - New York, New York
Business: Horizons Productions, 1134 N. Ogden Drive,
   Los Angeles, CA 90046, 213/654-6911

A DEATH   Venice Pictures, 1979
VT   Marshfield Productions, 1980
RENNIE   Horizons Productions, 1982
HORIZONS   Horizons Productions, 1983

ZACK NORMAN
Contact: Screen Actors Guild - Hollywood, 213/465-4600

RICH BOYS   *CHIEF ZABU*   co-director with Neil Cohen
   under pseudonym of Howard Zuker, International Film
   Marketing, 1988

AARON NORRIS
Personal Manager: Jim Rogers and Associates, 8285
   Sunset Blvd. - Suite 1, Los Angeles, CA 90046

BRADDOCK: MISSING IN ACTION III   Cannon, 1988
PLATOON LEADER   Cannon, 1988
DELTA FORCE 2: THE COLOMBIAN CONNECTION
   Cannon, 1990

F
I
L
M

D
I
R
E
C
T
O
R
S

BILL L. NORTON
(William Lloyd Norton)
b. August 13, 1943 - California
Agent: William Morris Agency - Beverly Hills, 213/274-7451

CISCO PIKE   Columbia, 1971
GARGOYLES (TF)   Tomorrow Entertainment, 1972
MORE AMERICAN GRAFFITI   Universal, 1979
BABY - SECRET OF THE LOST LEGEND   Buena
    Vista, 1985
THREE FOR THE ROAD   New Century/Vista, 1987
TOUR OF DUTY (TF)   Zev Braun Productions/New
    World TV, 1987
GRAND SLAM (TF)   Bill L. Norton Productions/New
    World TV, 1990

NOEL NOSSECK*
Agent: Jeff Benson, Barrett, Benson, McCartt & Weston -
    Los Angeles, 213/277-4998

BEST FRIENDS   Crown International, 1973
LAS VEGAS LADY   Crown International, 1976
YOUNGBLOOD   American International, 1978
DREAMER   20th Century-Fox, 1979
KING OF THE MOUNTAIN   Universal, 1981
RETURN OF THE REBELS (TF)   Moonlight Productions/
    Filmways, 1981
THE FIRST TIME (TF)   Moonlight Productions, 1982
NIGHT PARTNERS (TF)   Moonlight Productions II, 1983
SUMMER FANTASIES (TF)   Moonlight
    Productions II, 1984
STARK: MIRROR IMAGE (TF)   CBS Entertainment, 1986
A DIFFERENT AFFAIR (TF)   Rogers-Samuels
    Productions, 1987
ROMAN HOLIDAY (TF)   Jerry Ludwig Enterprises/
    Paramount TV, 1987
AARON'S WAY: THE HARVEST (TF)   Blinn-Thorpe
    Productions/ Lorimar Telepictures, 1988
FULL EXPOSURE: THE SEX TAPES SCANDAL (TF)
    Von Zerneck- Sertner Films, 1989
FOLLOW YOUR HEART (TF)   Force Ten Productions/
    Danson-Fauci Productions/NBC Productions, 1990

GEOFFREY NOTTAGE
Agent: Alan Greenspan, ICM - Los Angeles, 213/550-4428

WOMEN OF THE SUN (TF)   co-director, 1981, Australian
WHITE MAN'S LEGEND (TF)   1983, Australian
JOE WILSON (MS)   1986, Australian
THE LIZARD KING (TF)   1987, Australian

THIERRY NOTZ
b. Switzerland
Business: Concorde Pictures, 11600 San Vicente Blvd.,
    Los Angeles, CA 90049, 213/826-0978

THE TERROR WITHIN   Concorde, 1989
WATCHERS II   Concorde, 1990

BLAINE NOVAK
Agent: Lauri Apelian, The Chasin Agency - Beverly Hills,
    213/278-7505

GOOD TO GO   Island Pictures, 1986

AMRAM NOWAK
THE CAFETERIA (TF)   Amram Nowak Associates, 1984
ISAAC IN AMERICA: A JOURNEY WITH ISAAC
    BASHEVIS SINGER (FD)   Amram Nowak
    Associates, 1986

NEIL SIMON: NOT JUST FOR LAUGHS (TD)   American
    Masters/WNET-TV/ Amram Nowak Association for the
    Arts, 1989

CYRUS NOWRASTEH
b. 1956 - U.S.A.
Agent: Patty Detroit, ICM - Los Angeles, 213/550-4000

THREAT   Daystar Productions, 1989

PHILLIP NOYCE
b. Griffith, New South Wales, Australia
Agent: Joan Scott, Writers & Artists Agency - Los Angeles,
    213/820-2240

BACKROADS   Cinema Ventures, 1978, Australian
NEWSFRONT   New Yorker, 1979, Australian
THE DISMISSAL (MS)   co-director with George Miller,
    George Ogilvie, Carl Schultz & John Power, 1983,
    Australian
HEATWAVE   New Line Cinema, 1982, Australian
THE COWRA BREAKOUT (MS)   co-director with Chris
    Noonan, Kennedy-Miller Productions, 1985, Australian
ECHOES OF PARADISE   *SHADOWS OF THE PEACOCK*
    Castle Hill Productions/Quartet Films, 1987, Australian
DEAD CALM   Warner Bros., 1989, Australian
BLIND FURY   Tri-Star, 1989

SIMON NUCHTERN
b. Belgium
Agent: Jack Tantleff, The Tantleff Office, 360 West 20th
    Street - Suite 4F, New York, NY 10011, 212/627-2105
Business: August Films, 321 West 44th Street, New York,
    NY 10036, 212/582-7025

GIRL GRABBERS   RAF Distribution, 1968
TO HEX WITH SEX   RAF Industries, 1969
THE COWARDS   Jaylo, 1970
WHAT DO I TELL THE BOYS AT THE STATION?
    August, 1972
THE BROAD COALITION   August, 1972
THE BODYGUARD   Aquarius, 1976
SILENT MADNESS   Almi Pictures, 1984
NEW YORK NIGHTS   International Talent Marketing, 1984
SAVAGE DAWN   MAG Enterprises/Gregory Earls
    Productions, 1985

VICTOR NUÑEZ
Home: 227 Westminster Drive, Tallahassee, FL 32304,
    904/575-2696 or 904/618-3662
Agent: Paul Kohner, Inc. - Los Angeles, 213/550-5060

GAL YOUNG UN   Nuñez Films, 1979
A FLASH OF GREEN   Spectrafilm, 1984

TREVOR NUNN
b. January 14, 1940 - Ipswich, Suffolk, England
Business: Homevale Ltd., 28/29 Southampton Street,
    London WC2E 7JA, England, 71/240-5435
Attorney: Bill Fournier, Campbell Hooper, 35 Old Queen
    Street, London SW1H 9JD, England, 71/222-9070

HEDDA   Brut Productions, 1975, British
LADY JANE   Paramount, 1986, British

RAPHAEL NUSSBAUM
W.A.R.: WOMEN AGAINST RAPE   The Clark Film
    Company, 1987
PRIVATE ROAD (NO TRESPASSING)   Trans World
    Entertainment, 1987

FRANCESCO NUTI
b. May 17, 1955 - Prato, Italy
Home: via G. Nicotera 29, Rome, Italy, 06/353155

CASABLANCA CASABLANCA   Union P.N./C.G. Silver
    Film, 1985, Italian
STREGATI   Union P.N./C.G. Silver Film, 1986, Italian
CARUSO PASCOSKI DI PADRE POLACCO   Union
    P.N./Cecchi Gori Group/ Tiger Cinematografica,
    1988, Italian
WILLY SIGNORI E VENGO DA LONTANO   Warner
    Bros. Italia, 1990, Italian

DAVID NUTTER*
Agent: Jody Levine, Harris & Goldberg - Los Angeles,
    213/553-5200

CEASE FIRE   Cineworld, 1985

BRUNO NUYTTEN
b. 1945 - Paris, France
Contact: French Film Office, 745 Fifth Avenue, New York,
    NY 10151, 212/832-8860

CAMILLE CLAUDEL   Orion Classics, 1988, French

CHRISTIAN I. NYBY II*
b. June 1, 1941 - Glendale, California
Agent: Irv Schechter, Irv Schechter Company -
    Beverly Hills, 213/278-8070

THE RANGERS (TF)   Universal TV/Mark VII Ltd., 1974
PINE CANYON IS BURNING (TF)   Universal TV, 1977
RIPTIDE (TF)   Stephen J. Cannell Productions, 1984
WACO & RINEHART (TF)   Touchstone Films TV, 1987
PERRY MASON: THE CASE OF THE SCANDALOUS
    SCOUNDREL (TF)   The Fred Silverman Company/
    Strathmore Productions/Viacom, 1987
PERRY MASON: THE CASE OF THE AVENGING
    ACE (TF)   The Fred Silverman Company/Strathmore
    Productions/Viacom, 1988
A WHISPER KILLS (TF)   Sandy Hook Productions/Steve
    Tisch Company/Phoenix Entertainment Group, 1988
TOO GOOD TO BE TRUE (TF)   Newland-Raynor
    Productions, 1988
PERRY MASON: THE CASE OF THE LETHAL LESSON
    (TF)   The Fred Silverman Company/Dean Hargrove
    Productions/Viacom, 1989
PERRY MASON: THE CASE OF THE MUSICAL MURDER
    (TF)   The Fred Silverman Company/Dean Hargrove
    Productions/Viacom, 1989
PERRY MASON: THE CASE OF THE ALL-STAR
    ASSASSIN (TF)   The Fred Silverman Company/Dean
    Hargrove Productions/Viacom, 1989
PERRY MASON: THE CASE OF THE PARISIAN
    PARADOX (TF)   The Fred Silverman Company/Dean
    Hargrove Productions/Viacom, 1990
PERRY MASON: THE CASE OF THE POISONED
    PEN (TF)   The Fred Silverman Company/Dean
    Hargrove Productions/Viacom, 1990
PERRY MASON: THE CASE OF THE DESPERATE
    DECEPTION (TF)   The Fred Silverman Company/
    Dean Hargrove Productions/Viacom, 1990

PETER NYDRLE
b. November 16, 1954 - Prague, Czechoslovakia
Business: Peter Nydrle Productions, P.O. Box 582,
    Beverly Hills, CA 90213, 213/659-6967

EUGENE AMONG US   F.A.M.U., 1981, Czech

RON NYSWANER
Contact: Writers Guild of America, West - Los Angeles,
    213/550-1000

THE PRINCE OF PENNSYLVANIA   New Line
    Cinema, 1988

DAN O'BANNON
b. 1946 - St. Louis, Missouri
Agent: Morton Agency - Los Angeles, 213/824-4089

THE RETURN OF THE LIVING DEAD   Orion, 1985

JIM O'BRIEN
b. February 15, 1947 - Dundee, Scotland
Agent: Judy Daish Agency, 83 Eastbourne Mews,
    London W2, England, 71/262-1101

SHADOWS ON OUR SKIN (TF)   BBC, 1980, British
JAKE'S END (TF)   BBC, 1981, British
THE JEWEL IN THE CROWN (MS) ☆   co-director with
    Christopher Morahan, Granada TV, 1984, British
THE MONOCLED MUTINEER (TF)   BBC, 1986, British
THE DRESSMAKER   Euro-American, 1988, British

JOHN O'BRIEN
THE BIG DIS   co-director with Gordon Eriksen, Pyramid
    Films, 1989

JEFFREY OBROW
THE DORM THAT DRIPPED BLOOD *PRANKS* co-director
    with Stephen Carpenter, New Image Releasing, 1982
THE POWER   co-director with Stephen Carpenter, Artists
    Releasing Corporation/ Film Ventures International, 1984
THE KINDRED   co-director with Stephen Carpenter, FM
    Entertainment, 1987

MIKE OCKRENT
Agent: Saraband Associates, 265 Liverpool Road, London
    N1 1LX, England, 71/609-5313

DANCIN' THRU THE DARK   Palace Pictures/British Screen/
    BBC Films/Formost Films, 1990, British

JACK O'CONNELL
GREENWICH VILLAGE STORY   Lion International, 1963
REVOLUTION (FD)   Lopert, 1968
SWEDISH FLY GIRLS *CHRISTA* American International,
    1971, U.S.-Danish

JAMES O'CONNOLLY
Address: 61 Edith Grove, London SW10, England,
    71/352-1242

THE HI-JACKERS   Butcher, 1964, British
SMOKESCREEN   Butcher, 1964, British
THE LITTLE ONES   Columbia, 1965, British
BERSERK!   Columbia, 1968, British
THE VALLEY OF GWANG!   Warner Bros., 1969, British

SOPHIE'S PLACE *CROOKS AND CORONETS* Warner
Bros., 1969, British
HORROR ON SNAPE ISLAND *BEYOND THE FOG*
Fanfare, 1972, British
MISTRESS PAMELA Fanfare, 1974, British

PAT O'CONNOR*
b. Ireland
Agent: CAA - Beverly Hills, 213/288-4545

CAL Warner Bros., 1984, Irish
A MONTH IN THE COUNTRY Orion Classics,
1987, British
STARS AND BARS Columbia, 1988
THE JANUARY MAN MGM/UA, 1989
FOOLS OF FORTUNE New Line Cinema, 1990, British

DAVID ODELL

Agent: ICM - Los Angeles, 213/550-4000

MARTIANS GO HOME Taurus Entertainment, 1990

MICHAEL O'DONOGHUE*
Agent: William Morris Agency - Beverly Hills, 213/274-7451

MR. MIKE'S MONDO VIDEO New Line Cinema, 1979

GEORGE OGILVIE
Contact: Australian Film Commission, 9229 Sunset Blvd.,
Los Angeles, CA 90069, 213/275-7074

THE DISMISSAL (MS) co-director with George Miller,
Phillip Noyce, Carl Schultz & John Power,
1983, Australian
BODYLINE (MS) co-director with Carl Schultz, Denny
Lawrence & Lex Marinos, 1984, Australian
MAD MAX BEYOND THUNDERDOME co-director with
George Miller, Warner Bros., 1985, Australian
SHORT CHANGED Greater Union, 1985, Australian
THE PLACE AT THE COAST Daedalus Films,
1986, Australian
THE SHIRALEE (MS) SAFC Productions,
1988, Australian
PRINCESS KATE (TF) Australian Children's TV
Foundation/Australian Broadcasting Corporation/
Revcom, 1990, Australian
THE CROSSING Beyond International, 1990, Australian

KOHEI OGURI
b. 1945 - Japan
Contact: Directors Guild of Japan, Tsukada Building, 8-33
Udagawa-cho, Shibuya-ku, Tokyo 150, Japan, 3/461-4411

MUDDY RIVER Japan Film Center, 1981, Japanese
FOR KAYAKO Theatre Group Himawari, 1986, Japanese
THE STING OF DEATH Shochiku, 1990, Japanese

GERRY O'HARA
b. 1924 - Boston, Lincolnshire, England
Address: Flat K, 51 Elm Park Gardens, London SW10,
England, 71/352-6153

MODELS, INC. *THAT KIND OF GIRL* Mutual,
1963, British
A GAME FOR THREE LOSERS Embassy, 1963, British
THE PLEASURE GIRLS Times, 1965, British
MAROC 7 Paramount, 1966, British
AMSTERDAM AFFAIR Lippert, 1968, British
FIDELIA 1970, British
ALL THE RIGHT NOISES 20th Century-Fox,
1971, British

THE BRUTE Rank, 1976, British
LEOPARD IN THE SNOW New World, 1978,
Canadian-British
THE BITCH Brent Walker Productions, 1979, British
FANNY HILL Playboy Enterprises, 1983, British
STRICTLY FOR CASH Harry Alan Towers Productions,
1984, British

MICHAEL O'HERLIHY*
b. April 1, 1928 - Dublin, Ireland
Agent: Contemporary Artists - Beverly Hills, 213/278-8250
Business Manager: Turner Accountancy Corporation, 9200
Sunset Blvd. - Suite 604, Los Angeles, CA 90069,
213/273-4260

THE FIGHTING PRINCE OF DONEGAL Buena Vista,
1966, British-U.S.
THE ONE AND ONLY GENUINE, ORIGINAL FAMILY BAND
Buena Vista, 1967
SMITH! Buena Vista, 1969
DEADLY HARVEST (TF) CBS, Inc., 1972
YOUNG PIONEERS (TF) ABC Circle Films, 1976
KISS ME, KILL ME (TF) Columbia TV, 1976
YOUNG PIONEERS' CHRISTMAS (TF) ABC Circle
Films, 1976
PETER LUNDY AND THE MEDICINE HAT STALLION (TF)
Ed Friendly Productions, 1977
BACKSTAIRS AT THE WHITE HOUSE (MS) Ed Friendly
Productions, 1979
THE FLAME IS LOVE (TF) Ed Friendly Productions/
Friendly-O'Herlihy Ltd., 1979
DALLAS COWBOYS CHEERLEADERS II (TF) Aubrey-
Hamner Productions, 1980
DETOUR TO TERROR (TF) Orenthal Productions/Playboy
Productions/Columbia TV, 1980
THE GREAT CASH GIVEAWAY GETAWAY (TF)
Penthouse Productions/Cine Guarantors, Inc., 1980
CRY OF THE INNOCENT (TF) Tara Productions, 1980
DESPERATE VOYAGE (TF) Barry Weitz Films/Joe Wizan
TV Productions, 1980
A TIME FOR MIRACLES (TF) ABC Circle Films, 1980
THE MILLION DOLLAR FACE (TF) Nephi-Hamner
Productions, 1981
I MARRIED WYATT EARP (TF) Osmond TV
Productions, 1983
TWO BY FORSYTH (TF) Tara Productions/Mobil
Corporation, 1984, U.S.-Irish
HOOVER VS. THE KENNEDYS: THE SECOND CIVIL
WAR (TF) Sunrise Films/Selznick-Glickman
Productions, 1987, Canadian

TOM O'HORGAN*
Contact: Directors Guild of America - New York City,
212/581-0370

FUTZ Commonwealth United, 1969
RHINOCEROS American Film Theatre, 1974

KIHACHI OKAMOTO
Contact: Directors Guild of Japan, Tsukada Building, 8-33
Udagawa-cho, Shibuya-ku, Tokyo 150, Japan, 3/461-4411

(The following is an incomplete list of Mr. Okamoto's credits)

SAMURAI ASSASSIN Toho, 1964, Japanese
THE EMPEROR AND THE GENERAL *THE LONGEST DAY
IN JAPAN* Toho, 1967, Japanese
THE SWORD OF DOOM Toho, 1967, Japanese
THE HUMAN BULLET 1968, Japanese
KILL! 1968, Japanese
RED LION 1969, Japanese

ZATOICHI MEETS YOJIMBO   1970, Japanese
TOKKAN   1975, Japanese
DIXIELAND DAIMYO   Daiei, 1987, Japanese

STEVEN OKAZAKI
b. March 12, 1952 - Los Angeles, California
Agent: Paul J. Yamamoto, Writers and Artists Agency -
   Los Angeles, 213/820-2240

SURVIVORS (TD)   1982
UNFINISHED BUSINESS (FD)   Mouchette Films, 1985
LIVING ON TOKYO TIME   Skouras Pictures, 1987

JOEL OLIANSKY*
b. October 11, 1935 - New York, New York
Agent: Tanya Lopez, ICM - Los Angeles, 213/550-4264

THE COMPETITION Columbia, 1980
ALFRED HITCHCOCK PRESENTS (TF)   co-director with
   Steve DeJarnatt, Randa Haines & Fred Walton,
   Universal TV, 1985
THE SILENCE AT BETHANY   Keener Productions/
   American Playhouse Theatrical Films, 1988

DAVID OLIVER
CAVEGIRL   Crown International, 1985

HECTOR OLIVERA
b. 1931 - Olivos, Argentina
Contact: Aries International, S.A., Lavalle 1860,
   1051 Buenos Aires, Argentina, tel.: 46-9249

PSEXOANALISIS   Aries Films, 1967, Argentine
LAS VENGANZAS DE BETO SANCHEZ   Aries Films,
   1972, Argentine
LA PATAGONIA REBELDE   Aries Films, 1974, Argentine
EL MUERTO   Aries Films, 1975, Argentine
LA NONA   Aries Films, 1978, Argentine
LOS VIERNES DE LA ETERNIDAD   Aries Films,
   1981, Argentine
BUENOS AIRES ROCK 82 (FD)   Aries Films,
   1983, Argentine
A FUNNY DIRTY LITTLE WAR   NO HABRA MAS
   PENAS NI OLVIDO   Cinevista, 1984, Argentine
WIZARDS OF THE LOST KINGDOM   Concorde/Cinema
   Group, 1985, U.S.-Argentine
BARBARIAN QUEEN   Concorde/Cinema Group, 1985,
   U.S.-Argentine
COCAINE WARS   Concorde, 1986, U.S.-Argentine
NIGHT OF THE PENCILS   Marquis Pictures,
   1986, Argentine
TWO TO TANGO   Concorde, 1989, U.S.-Argentine
MIDNIGHT BLACK   Concorde, 1990, U.S.-Argentine
THE GOSPEL ACCORDING TO MARCUS   Ibero-
   Americana Films/Aries Cinematografica, 1990,
   Spanish-Argentine

MARTY OLLSTEIN
Agent: Chris Nassif, CNA & Associates - Los Angeles,
   213/556-4343

DANGEROUS LOVE   Concorde, 1988

ERMANNO OLMI
b. July 24, 1931 - Bergamo, Italy
Home: via Rigoni di Sotto 36, Asiago, Italy, 0424/63220

IL TEMPO SI E FERMATO   Sezione Cinema Edison
   Volta, 1959, Italian
THE SOUND OF TRUMPETS   Janus, 1961, Italian

THE FIANCES   Janus, 1963, Italian
AND THERE CAME A MAN   Brandon, 1965, Italian
UN CERTO GIORNO   Cinema Spa/Italnoleggio,
   1968, Italian
I RECUPERANTI (TF)   RAI/Produzione Palumbo,
   1969, Italian
DURANTE L'ESTATE (TF)   RAI, 1971, Italian
LA CIRCOSTANZA (TF)   RAI/Italnoleggio, 1974, Italian
THE TREE OF WOODEN CLOGS   New Yorker, 1979,
   Italian, originally made for televison
CAMMINACAMMINA   Grange Communications,
   1983, Italian
MILANO '83 (FD)   1983, Italian
LONG LIVE THE LADY   International Film Exchange,
   1987, Italian
LA LEGGENDA DEL SANTO BEVITORE   Columbia Italia,
   1988, Italian

WILLIAM OLSEN
b. December 17, 1950 - North Carolina
Agent: Arthur Bicknell, Abrams Artists & Associates, 420
   Madison Avenue - Suite 1400, New York, NY 10017,
   212/935-8980

THE HAUNTED PALACE (TF)   Poe Society, 1978
GETTING IT ON   Comworld, 1983
ROCKIN' ROAD TRIP   Troma, 1985
AFTER SCHOOL   Moviestore Entertainment, 1989
RETURN TO EDEN   Quest Entertainment, 1989

DAVID O'MALLEY
b. June 14, 1944 - Woodsoncket, Rhode Island
Agent: The Daniel Ostroff Agency - Los Angeles,
   213/278-2020

MOUNTAIN MAN   Taft Entertainment, 1978
THE CHAMPION (TF)   Ammi Productions, 1982
AWESOME LOTUS   Double "O" Associates, 1983
KID COLTER   TMS Pictures, 1985
EASY WHEELS   Fries Distribution, 1989

RON O'NEAL
b. September 1, 1937 - Utica, New York
Agent: 213/857-1234

SUPERFLY T.N.T.   Paramount, 1973

ROBERT VINCENT O'NEIL*
Agent: Lew Weitzman, The Sy Fischer Company -
   Los Angeles, 213/969-2900

THE LOVING TOUCH   Medford, 1970
BLOOD MANIA   Crown International, 1971
WONDER WOMEN   1973
PACO   Cinema National, 1975
ANGEL   New World, 1984
AVENGING ANGEL   New World, 1985

MARCEL OPHULS
b. November 1, 1927 - Frankfurt-am-Main, Germany
Contact: French Film Office, 745 Fifth Avenue, New York,
   NY 10151, 212/832-8860

MATISSE   1960, French
LOVE AT TWENTY   co-director with Francois Truffaut,
   Andrzej Wajda, Renzo Rossellini & Shintaro Ishihara,
   Embassy, 1962, French-Italian- Japanese-Polish-
   West German
BANANA PEEL   Pathe Contemporary, 1965, French-Italian
FEU A VOLONTE   1965, French-Italian

MUNICH, OU LA PRIX POUR CENT ANS (TD)
1967, French
CLAVIGO (TF)   1970, French
THE HARVEST OF MY LAI (TD)   1970, French
AMERICA REVISITED (TD)   1971, French
ZWEI GANZE TAGE (TF)   1971, West German
THE SORROW AND THE PITY (FD)   Cinema 5, 1972,
French-Swiss-West German
A SENSE OF LOSS (FD)   Cinema 5, 1972, U.S.-Swiss
THE MEMORY OF JUSTICE (FD)   Paramount, 1976,
British-West German
KORTNER GESCHICHTE (TD)   1980, West German
YORKTOWN, LE SANS D'UNE BETAILLE (TD)
1982, French
HOTEL TERMINUS: THE LIFE AND TIMES OF KLAUS
BARBIE (FD)   Samuel Goldwyn Company,
1988, French

PEER J. OPPENHEIMER
Contact: Writers Guild of America, West - Los Angeles,
213/550-1000

TERROR IN PARADISE   Concorde, 1990, U.S.-Filipino

DOMINIC ORLANDO
KNIGHTS OF THE CITY   New World, 1986

STUART ORME
Agent: Alan Greenspan, ICM - Los Angeles, 213/550-4428

THE FEAR (MS)   Euston Films, 1987, British
THE HEIST (CTF)   HBO Pictures/Chris-Rose Productions/
Paramount TV, 1989
THE WOLVES OF WILLOUGHBY CHASE   Zenith
Productions, 1990, British
HANDS OF A MURDERER (TF)   Storke-Fuisz Productions/
Yorkshire TV, 1990, British-U.S.

PETER ORMROD
EAT THE PEACH   Skouras Pictures, 1986, Irish

EMMERICH OROSS
b. September 20, 1940 - Hungary
Home: P.O. Box 46163, Denver, CO 80201, 303/825-5612
or 303/830-4092
Business Manager: Jonathan L. Handler, Talent
Management, 5655 Radford Avenue, North Hollywood,
CA 91607, 818/713-5977

FORM OF LIFE (TD)   1966, Hungarian
DESIGN FOR AUTOMOBILES (TD)   1966, Hungarian
TESTAMENTUM HUNGARORUM (TD)   1967, Hungarian
SOUTH AMERICAN PHOTOGRAPHS (TF)
1969, Hungarian
THE WITCH DOCTORS OF THE ORINOCO (TD)
1969, Hungarian
AGAIN   1969, Hungarian
THE PIAROA INDIANS (TD)   1970, Hungarian
KODALY'S METHODS (FD)   1970, Hungarian
THE PRINCESS (TF)   1970, Hungarian
PHOTOMEDITATION (TF)   1971, Hungarian
MADAMA BUTTERFLY (TF)   Racana Company, 1984
LAST CALL   Vu Jade Productions, 1985

JAMES ORR*
Agent: William Morris Agency - Beverly Hills, 213/274-7451

BREAKING ALL THE RULES   New World,
1985, Canadian
THEY STILL CALL ME BRUCE   co-director with Johnny
Yune, Shapiro Entertainment, 1987

YOUNG HARRY HOUDINI (TF)   Walt Disney TV, 1987
MR. DESTINY   Buena Vista, 1990

NAGISA OSHIMA
b. March 31, 1932 - Kyoto, Japan
Contact: Directors Guild of Japan, Tsukada Building, 8-33
Udagawa-cho, Shibuya-ku, Tokyo 150, Japan, 3/461-4411

A TOWN OF LOVE AND HOPE   Shochiku, 1959,
Japanese
CRUEL STORY OF YOUTH   Shochiku, 1960, Japanese
THE SUN'S BURIAL   Shochiku, 1960, Japanese
NIGHT AND FOG IN JAPAN   Shochiku, 1960, Japanese
THE CATCH   Palace Productions/Taiho, 1961, Japanese
SHIRO TOKISADA FROM AMAKUSA   *THE*
REVOLUTIONARY   Toei, 1962, Japanese
A SMALL CHILD'S FIRST ADVENTURE   Nissei Insurance
Company, 1964, Japanese
IT'S ME HERE, BELLETT   Society of Japanese Film
Directors, 1964, Japanese
THE PLEASURES OF THE FLESH   Sozosha/Shochiku,
1965, Japanese
THE DIARY OF YUNBAGI (FD)   Sozosha/Shibata
Organization, 1965, Japanese
VIOLENCE AT NOON   Sozosha/Shochiku, 1966,
Japanese
BAND OF NINJA   Sozosha/Art Theatre Guild,
1967, Japanese
A TREATISE IN JAPANESE BAWDY SONGS   Sozosha/
Shochiku, 1967, Japanese
JAPANESE SUMMER: DOUBLE SUICIDE   Sozosha/
Shochiku, 1967, Japanese
DEATH BY HANGING   Grove Press, 1968, Japanese
THREE RESURRECTED DRUNKARDS   Sozosha/
Shochiku, 1968, Japanese
DIARY OF A SHINJUKU BURGLAR   Grove Press,
1968, Japanese
BOY   Grove Press, 1969, Japanese
THE MAN WHO LEFT HIS WILL ON FILM   Sozosha/ATG,
1970, Japanese
DEAR SUMMER SISTER   New Yorker, 1973, Japanese
THE CEREMONY   New Yorker, 1974, Japanese
IN THE REALM OF THE SENSES   Surrogate Releasing,
1976, Japanese
EMPIRE OF PASSION   *CORRIDA OF LOVE*   Barbary
Coast, 1980, Japanese
MERRY CHRISTMAS, MR. LAWRENCE   Universal, 1983,
British-Japanese
MAX MON AMOUR   Greenwich Films/Films A2,
1986, French

CLIFF OSMOND
b. February 26, 1937
Agent: Shapiro-Lichtman Agency - Los Angeles,
213/859-8877

THE PENITENT   Cineworld, 1988

SAM O'STEEN*
b. November 6, 1923
Business Manager: Robert Morgan, Tucker, Morgan &
Martindale - Los Angeles, 213/274-0891

A BRAND NEW LIFE (TF)   Tomorrow Entertainment, 1973
I LOVE YOU, GOODBYE (TF)   Tomorrow
Entertainment, 1974
QUEEN OF THE STARDUST BALLROOM (TF) ☆
Tomorrow Entertainment, 1975
HIGH RISK (TF)   Danny Thomas Productions/
MGM TV, 1976
SPARKLE   Warner Bros., 1976

LOOK WHAT'S HAPPENED TO ROSEMARY'S BABY (TF)
    Paramount TV, 1976
THE BEST LITTLE GIRL IN THE WORLD (TF)   Aaron
    Spelling Productions, 1981
KIDS DON'T TELL (TF)   Chris-Rose Productions/Viacom
    Productions, 1985

THADDEUS O'SULLIVAN
Contact: British Academy of Film & Television Arts,
    195 Piccadilly, London W1, England, 71/732-0022

DECEMBER BRIDE   British Screen/Film Four
    International, 1990, Irish-British

DOMINIQUE OTHENIN-GIRARD
HALLOWEEN 5   Galaxy, 1989
NIGHT ANGEL   Fries Entertainment, 1990

LINDA OTTO*
Contact: Directors Guild of America - Los Angeles,
    213/289-2000

UNSPEAKABLE ACTS (TF)   The Landsburg
    Company, 1990

FILIPPO OTTONI
Home: via E. Gianturco 11, Rome, Italy, 06/360-5087

QUESTO SI' CHE E'AMORE   Creative Films Century,
    1977, Italian
DETECTIVE SCHOOL DROPOUTS   Cannon, 1986,
    U.S.-Italian
STRAY DAYS   Cannon, 1987, Italian

IDRISSA OUEDRAOGO
b. 1954 - Bandora, Upper Volta (Burkina Faso)

YAM DAABO   1987, Burkina Faso-French
YAABA   New Yorker, 1989, Burkina Faso-French-Swiss
TILAI   Les Films de l'Avenir/Waka Film/Rhea Film,
    1990, Burkina Faso-French-Swiss

GERARD OURY
(Max-Gerard Houry Tannenbaum)
b. April 29, 1919 - Paris, France
Address: c/o Horstig, 76 Avenue Champs Elysees, 75008
    Paris, France, 04/359-9310
Contact: French Film Office, 745 Fifth Avenue, New York,
    NY 10151, 212/832-8860

LA MAIN CHAUDE   Films de France, 1960, French
THE MENACE   Warner Bros., 1961, French
CRIME DOES NOT PAY   Embassy, 1962, French-Italian
THE SUCKER   Royal Films International, 1966,
    French-Italian
DON'T LOOK NOW...WE'RE BEING SHOT AT LA
    GRANDE VADROVILLE   Cinepix, 1966, French-British
THE BRAIN   Paramount, 1969, French-Italian
DELUSIONS OF GRANDEUR   Joseph Green Pictures,
    1971, French
THE MAD ADVENTURES OF 'RABBI' JACOB   20th
    Century-Fox, 1974, French-Italian
LA CARAPATE   Gaumont, 1978, French
LE COUP DU PARAPLUIE   Gaumont, 1980, French
L'AS DES AS   Gaumont/Cerito Rene Chateau, 1982,
    French-West German
LA VENGEANCE DU SERPENT A PLUMES   AMLF,
    1984, French

LEVY AND GOLIATH LEVI ET GOLIATH Kino
    International, 1986, French
VANILLE FRAISE   Ariane Films/Cristaldi Film, 1989,
    French-Italian

HORACE OVE
Business: Anancy Films, 3 Kelly Street, London NW1 8PG,
    England, 71/482-3332

PRESSURE   British Film Institute, 1974, British
A HOLE IN BABYLON (TF)   BBC, 1979, British
THE PROFESSIONALS (MS)   London Weekend TV,
    1980, British
THE GARLAND (TF)   BBC, 1981, British
WHO SHALL WE TELL? (TF)   Channel Four, 1985, British
DABBAWALLAHS (TF)   Channel Four, 1985, British
PLAYING AWAY (TF)   Channel Four, 1986, British

CLIFF OWEN
b. April 22, 1919 - London, England
Address: 20 Marlborough Place, London NW8, England

OFFBEAT   1961, British
A PRIZE OF ARMS   British Lion, 1961, British
THE WRONG ARM OF THE LAW   Continental,
    1963, British
A MAN COULD GET KILLED   co-director with Ronald
    Neame, Universal, 1966
THAT RIVIERA TOUCH   Continental, 1966, British
WHAT HAPPENED AT CAMPO GRANDE? THE
    MAGNIFICENT TWO   Alan Enterprises, 1967, British
THE VENGEANCE OF SHE   20th Century-Fox,
    1968, British
STEPTOE AND SON   MGM-EMI, 1972, British
OOH...YOU ARE AWFUL   Lion International, 1973, British
NO SEX PLEASE - WE'RE BRITISH   Columbia-Warner,
    1973, British
THE BAWDY ADVENTURES OF TOM JONES   Universal,
    1975, British
GET CHARLIE TULLY   TBS Distributing Corporation,
    1976, British

DON OWEN
b. 1935 - Toronto, Ontario, Canada
Home: Glenstreams, RR#1, Locust Hill, Ontario LOH 1JO,
    Canada, 416/294-5163
Business: Zebra Films, 55 Charles Street East - Suite 303,
    Toronto, Ontario M4Y 1S9, Canada, 416/926-8086

NOBODY WAVED GOODBYE   Cinema 5, 1964, Canadian
THE ERNIE GAME   CBC/National Film Board of Canada,
    1967, Canadian
PARTNERS   Astral Films, 1976, Canadian
UNFINISHED BUSINESS   Zebra Films/National Film Board
    of Canada/CBC, 1984, Canadian
TURNABOUT   Zebra Films, 1988, Canadian

FRANK OZ*
(Frank Oznowicz)
b. May 25, 1944 - Hereford, England
Agent: CAA - Beverly Hills, 213/288-4545

THE DARK CRYSTAL   co-director with Jim Henson,
    Universal/AFD, 1982, British
THE MUPPETS TAKE MANHATTAN   Tri-Star, 1984
LITTLE SHOP OF HORRORS   The Geffen Company/
    Warner Bros., 1986
DIRTY ROTTEN SCOUNDRELS   Orion, 1988

P

ANTHONY PAGE*
b. September 21, 1935 - Bangalore, India
Agent: Audrey Caan, Triad Artists, Inc. - Los Angeles,
213/556-2727

INADMISSABLE EVIDENCE   Paramount, 1968, British
ALPHA BETA   Cine III, 1976, British
F. SCOTT FITZGERALD IN HOLLYWOOD (TF)   Titus
   Productions, 1976
I NEVER PROMISED YOU A ROSE GARDEN   New
   World, 1977
ABSOLUTION   Trans World Entertainment, 1979, British
THE LADY VANISHES   Rank, 1979, British
THE PATRICIA NEAL STORY (TF)   co-director with
   Anthony Harvey, Lawrence Schiller Productions, 1981
BILL (TF)   Alan Landsburg Productions, 1981
JOHNNY BELINDA (TF)   Dick Berg-Stonehenge
   Productions/Lorimar Productions, 1982
GRACE KELLY (TF)   The Kota Company/
   Embassy TV, 1983
BILL: ON HIS OWN (TF)   Alan Landsburg
   Productions, 1983
FORBIDDEN (CTF)   HBO Premiere Films/Mark Forstater
   Productions/Clasart/ Anthea Productions, 1985,
   U.S.-British-West German
MURDER: BY REASON OF INSANITY (TF)   LS
   Entertainment, 1985
SECOND SERVE (TF)   Linda Yellen Productions/
   Lorimar-Telepictures, 1986
MONTE CARLO (TF)   New World TV/Phoenix
   Entertainment Group/Collins-Holm Productions/
   Highgate Pictures, 1986
PACK OF LIES (TF)   Robert Halmi, Inc., 1987
SCANDAL IN A SMALL TOWN (TF)   Carliner-Rappoport
   Productions, 1988
THE NIGHTMARE YEARS (CMS)   Consolidated
   Productions, 1989
FINAL WARNING (CTF)   Carolco TV Productions, 1990

PAMELA PAGE
ROCK & ROLL: THE EARLY DAYS (HVD)   co-director
   with Patrick Montgomery, RCA/Columbia Home Video/
   Fox-Lorber/Archive Film Productions, 1984
BRITISH ROCK: THE FIRST WAVE (HVD)   co-director
   with Patrick Montgomery, RCA/Columbia Home Video/
   Archive Film Productions, 1985

ALAN J. PAKULA*
b. April 7, 1928 - New York, New York
Agent: William Morris Agency - Beverly Hills, 213/274-7451
Business: The Pakula Company, 330 West 58th Street -
   Suite 5H, New York, NY 10019, 212/664-0640

THE STERILE CUCKOO   Paramount, 1969
KLUTE   Warner Bros., 1971
LOVE AND PAIN AND THE WHOLE DAMNED THING
   Columbia, 1973, British-U.S.
THE PARALLAX VIEW   Paramount, 1974
ALL THE PRESIDENT'S MEN ★   Warner Bros., 1976
COMES A HORSEMAN   United Artists, 1978
STARTING OVER   Paramount, 1979

ROLLOVER   Orion/Warner Bros., 1981
SOPHIE'S CHOICE   Universal/AFD, 1982
DREAM LOVER   MGM/UA, 1986
ORPHANS   Lorimar, 1987
SEE YOU IN THE MORNING   Warner Bros., 1989
PRESUMED INNOCENT   Warner Bros., 1990

EUZHAN PALCY
Agent: William Morris Agency - Beverly Hills, 213/274-7451

SUGAR CANE ALLEY   Orion, 1983, French
A DRY WHITE SEASON   MGM/UA, 1989

ROSPO PALLENBERG*
Home: 9021 Burroughs Road, Los Angeles, CA 90046,
   213/654-0380
Agent: ICM - Los Angeles, 213/550-4000

CUTTING CLASS   Republic Pictures, 1989

TONY PALMER
Address: 4 Kensington Park Gardens, London W11,
   England, 71/727-3541
Business: Isolde Film Productions - London, 71/323-4050

(The following is an incomplete list of Mr. Palmer's credits)

FAREWELL CREAM (FD)   1968, British
200 MOTELS   co-director with Frank Zappa, United Artists,
   1971, British
BIRD ON A WIRE (FD)   EMI, 1974, British
A TIME THERE WAS   A PROFILE OF BENJAMIN
   BRITTEN (TD)   London Weekend TV, 1980, British
THE SPACE MOVIE (FD)   International Harmony,
   1980, British
WAGNER (MS)   London Trust Productions/Richard Wagner
   Productions/Ladbroke Productions/Hungarofilm, 1983,
   British-Hungarian-Austrian
GEORGE FREDERIC HANDEL (1685-1759)   Arts
   International, 1985, British
TESTIMONY (TF)   European Classics, 1987, British
MARIA CALLAS: AN OPERATIC BIOGRAPHY (TD)   Isolde
   Films/London Trust Productions, 1988, British
RICHARD BURTON: IN FROM THE COLD (TD)   Isolde
   Films/Thames TV, 1989
THE CHILDREN   Isolde Films/Film Four International/Arbo
   Films & Maram GmbH/Bayerlische Landesantalt, 1990,
   British-West German

CONRAD E. PALMISANO*
Contact: Directors Guild of America - Los Angeles,
   213/289-2000

SPACE RAGE   Vestron, 1985
BUSTED UP   Shapiro Entertainment, 1987, Canadian

BRUCE PALTROW*
b. November 26, 1943 - New York, New York
Agent: ICM - Los Angeles, 213/550-4000

A LITTLE SEX   Universal, 1982

NORMAN PANAMA*
b. April 21, 1914 - Chicago, Illinois
Agent: Mitchell Kaplan, Kaplan-Stahler Agency -
   Los Angeles, 213/653-4483

THE REFORMER AND THE REDHEAD   co-director with
   Melvin Frank, MGM, 1950

STRICTLY DISHONORABLE   co-director with Melvin
    Frank, MGM, 1951
CALLAWAY WENT THATAWAY   co-director with Melvin
    Frank, MGM, 1951
ABOVE AND BEYOND   co-director with Melvin Frank,
    MGM, 1952
KNOCK ON WOOD   co-director with Melvin Frank,
    Paramount, 1954
THE COURT JESTER   co-director with Melvin Frank,
    Paramount, 1956
THAT CERTAIN FEELING   co-director with Melvin Frank,
    Paramount, 1956
THE TRAP   Paramount, 1959
THE ROAD TO HONG KONG   United States, 1962
NOT WITH MY WIFE, YOU DON'T!   Warner Bros., 1966
HOW TO COMMIT MARRIAGE   Cinerama Releasing
    Corporation, 1969
THE MALTESE BIPPY   MGM, 1969
COFFEE, TEA OR ME? (TF)   CBS, Inc., 1973
I WILL, I WILL...FOR NOW   20th Century-Fox, 1976
BARNABY AND ME   Trans-Atlantic Enterprises, 1978

GLEB PANFILOV
b. May 21, 1937 - Magnitogorsk, U.S.S.R.
Contact: Union of Soviet Filmmakers, Vassilievskaya 13,
    Moscow, U.S.S.R., tel.: 250-4114

ACROSS THE STREAM AND FIRE   Lenfilm,
    1968, Soviet
THE DEBUT   Lenfilm, 1970, Soviet
MAY I HAVE THE FLOOR?   Lenfilm, 1975, Soviet
VALENTINA, VALENTINA   1981, Soviet
VASSA   1983, Soviet
THEME   International Film Exchange, 1984, Soviet
MOTHER   Cinefin/Mosfilm/RAI, 1990, Italian-Soviet

PEKKA PARIKKA
b. May 2, 1939 - Helsinki, Finland
Contact: Federation of Finnish Film Directors, Mariankatu
    15B, SF-00250, Helsinki, Finland, 0/654426

POHJANMAA   Finnkino, 1988, Finnish
THE WINTER WAR   *TALVISOTA*   Finnkino,
    1989, Finnish

DOMONIC PARIS
b. September 28, 1950

DRACULA'S LAST RITES   Cannon, 1980
SPLITZ   Film Ventures International, 1984
AMAZING MASTERS   Vestron, 1986
FILMHOUSE FEVER   Lightning Video, 1986

HENRY PARIS
(See Radley METZGER)

CHOI-SU PARK
(See Park CHOI-SU)

ALAN PARKER*
b. February 14, 1944 - London, England
Agent: CAA - Beverly Hills, 213/288-4545

THE EVACUEES (TF)   BBC, 1975, British
BUGSY MALONE   Paramount, 1976, British
MIDNIGHT EXPRESS ★   Columbia, 1978, British
FAME   MGM/United Artists, 1980
SHOOT THE MOON   MGM/United Artists, 1982

PINK FLOYD - THE WALL   MGM/UA, 1982, British
BIRDY   Tri-Star, 1984
A TURNIP HEAD'S GUIDE TO THE BRITISH CINEMA (TD)
    Thames TV, 1985, British
ANGEL HEART   Tri-Star, 1987
MISSISSIPPI BURNING ★   Orion, 1988
COME SEE THE PARADISE   20th Century Fox, 1990

CARY PARKER
b. Atlanta, Georgia
Agent: Leading Artists - Beverly Hills, 213/858-1999

THE GIRL IN THE PICTURE   Samuel Goldwyn Company,
    1986, British

FRANCINE PARKER*
Agent: Martin Shapiro, Shapiro-Lichtman Agency -
    Los Angeles, 213/859-8877

F.T.A. (FD)   American International, 1972

WALTER F. PARKES
Agent: InterTalent - Los Angeles, 213271-0600

THE CALIFORNIA REICH (FD)   co-director with Keith F.
    Critchlow, Paramount Home Video, 1977

GORDON PARKS*
b. November 30, 1912 - Fort Scott, Kansas
Home: 860 U.N. Plaza, New York, NY 10017
Agent: ICM - Los Angeles, 213/550-4000

THE LEARNING TREE   Warner Bros., 1969
SHAFT   MGM, 1971
SHAFT'S BIG SCORE!   MGM, 1972
THE SUPER COPS   MGM, 1974
LEADBELLY   Paramount, 1976
SUPER COPS (TF)   MGM TV, 1976
SOLOMON NORTHUP'S ODYSSEY (TF)   Past
    America, Inc., 1985

MICHAEL PARKS
b. 1938 - Corona, California
Contact: Screen Actors Guild - Hollywood, 213/465-4600

THE RETURN OF JOSEY WALES   Reel Movies
    International, 1986

EDWARD PARONE*
Agent: Mitch Kaplan, Kaplan-Stahler Agency - Beverly Hills,
    213/653-4483

PROMISE HIM ANYTHING... (TF)   ABC Circle Films, 1975
LETTERS FROM FRANK (TF)   The Jozak Company/
    Cypress Point Productions, 1979

LARRY PARR
Contact: New Zealand Film Commission, P.O. Box 11546,
    Wellington, New Zealand, 4/859-754

A SOLDIER'S TALE   Atlantic Releasing Corporation,
    1988, New Zealand-U.S.

JAMES D. PARRIOTT*
Agent: Leading Artists - Beverly Hills, 213/858-1999

MISFITS OF SCIENCE (TF)   James D. Parriott
    Productions/Universal TV, 1985
HEART CONDITION   New Line Cinema, 1990

ROBERT PARRISH*
b. January 4, 1916 - Columbus, Georgia
Business Manager: Jess S. Morgan & Co., 6420 Wilshire
    Blvd., Los Angeles, CA 90048, 213/651-1601

CRY DANGER   RKO Radio, 1951
THE MOB   Columbia, 1951
THE SAN FRANCISCO STORY   Warner Bros., 1952
ASSIGNMENT - PARIS   Columbia, 1952
MY PAL GUS   20th Century-Fox, 1952
SHOOT FIRST   ROUGH SHOOT   United Artists,
    1953, British
THE PURPLE PLAIN   United Artists, 1954, British
LUCY GALLANT   Paramount, 1955
FIRE DOWN BELOW   Columbia, 1957
SADDLE THE WIND   MGM, 1957
THE WONDERFUL COUNTRY   United Artists, 1959
IN THE FRENCH STYLE   Columbia, 1963, French-U.S.
UP FROM THE BEACH   20th Century-Fox, 1965
CASINO ROYALE   co-director with Val Guest,
    Ken Hughes, John Huston & Joseph McGrath,
    Columbia, 1967, Columbia
THE BOBO   Warner Bros., 1967, British
DUFFY   Columbia, 1968, British
JOURNEY TO THE FAR SIDE OF THE SUN
    DOPPELGANGER   Universal, 1969, British
A TOWN CALLED BASTARD   A TOWN CALLED HELL
    Scotia International, 1971, British-Spanish
THE DESTRUCTORS   THE MARSEILLES CONTRACT
    American International, 1974, British-French
MISSISSIPPI BLUES (FD)   co-director with Bertrand
    Tavernier, Little Bear Productions/Odessa Films,
    1984, French

MICHAEL PART
b. March 29, 1949 - Sheboygan, Wisconsin
Home: Wicked Scherzo Productions, 14248 Dickens
    Street - Apt. 115, Sherman Oaks, CA 91423,
    818/906-8566
Agent: Robert Hohman, Triad Artists - Los Angeles,
    213/556-2727

STARBIRDS (ATF)   3B Productions Ltd., 1982, Japanese
REVENGE OF THE DEFENDERS (ATF)   3B Productions
    Ltd., 1982, Japanese
SHADOW WORLD (ATF)   3B Productions Ltd., 1983,
    Japanese
THE RAFT ADVENTURES OF HUCK AND JIM (ATF)
    3B Productions Ltd., 1984, Japanese

GORAN PASKALJEVIC
Contact: Incovent Ltd., 1900 Avenue of the Stars - Suite
    1500, Los Angeles, CA 90067, 213/277-7881

THE BEACH GUARD IN WINTER   Center FRZ,
    1976, Yugoslavian
THE DOG THAT LIKED TRAINS   Yugoslav Film Releasing,
    1978, Yugoslavian
THE DAYS ARE PASSING   Yugoslav Film Releasing,
    1980, Yugoslavian
SPECIAL TREATMENT   International Home Cinema,
    1982, Yugoslavian
TWILIGHT TIME   MGM/UA, 1983, U.S.-Yugoslavian
THE ILLUSORY SUMMER OF '68   1984, Yugoslavian
GUARDIAN ANGEL   Jugoart-Singidinum/Morava Film,
    1987, Yugoslavian
TIME OF MIRACLES   Metropolitan Films,
    1990, Yugoslavian

JOHN PASQUIN*
Agent: CAA - Beverly Hills, 213/288-4545

OUT ON THE EDGE (TF)   Rick Dawn Enterprises/The Steve
    Tisch Company/King Phoenix Entertainment, 1989

IVAN PASSER*
b. July 10, 1933 - Prague, Czechoslovakia
Agent: Larry Becsey, The Agency - Los Angeles,
    213/551-3000

A BORING AFTERNOON   1965, Czech
INTIMATE LIGHTING   Altura, 1965, Czech
BORN TO WIN   United Artists, 1971
LAW AND DISORDER   Columbia, 1974
CRIME AND PASSION   American International, 1976
SILVER BEARS   Columbia, 1978
CUTTER'S WAY   CUTTER AND BONE   United Artists
    Classics, 1981
CREATOR   Universal, 1985
HAUNTED SUMMER   Cannon, 1988
FOURTH STORY (CTF)   Konigsberg-Sanitsky Productions/
    Viacom, 1990

MICHAEL PATE
b. 1920 - Sydney, Australia
Business: Pisces Productions, 21 Bundarra Road, Bellevue
    Hill, NSW, 2023, Australia, 02/30-4208

TIM   Satori, 1979, Australian

RAJU PATEL
IN THE SHADOW OF KILIMANJARO   Scotti Brothers, 1986

SHARAD PATEL
b. India
Agent: Soren Fischer Associates, 14 Glebe House, Fitzroy
    Mews, London W1P 5DP, England, 71/437-6862

AMIN: THE RISE AND FALL   THE RISE AND FALL OF
    IDI AMIN   Twin Continental, 1983, British-Kenyan

MATTHEW PATRICK
Agent: William Morris Agency - Beverly Hills, 213/274-7451

HIDER IN THE HOUSE   Vestron, 1989

JOHN PATTERSON*
Agent: William Morris Agency - Beverly Hills, 213/274-7451

INDEPENDENCE (TF)   Sunn Classic Pictures, 1987
GIDEON OLIVER: SLEEP WELL, PROFESSOR OLIVER
    (TF) Wolf Films/Crescendo Productions/Logo Productions/
    Universal TV, 1989
A DEADLY SILENCE (TF)   Robert Greenwald
    Productions, 1989
TAKEN AWAY (TF)   Hart, Thomas & Berlin
    Productions, 1989
A MOTHER'S COURAGE: THE MARY THOMAS STORY
    (TF)   Interscope Communications/Chet Walker
    Enterprises/ Walt Disney TV, 1989

RAY PATTERSON
GOBOTS: BATTLE OF THE ROCK LORDS (AF)
    Clubhouse/Atlantic Releasing Corporation, 1986

WILLI PATTERSON*
Agent: Linda Seifert, 8A Brunswick Gardens, London W8
4AJ, England, 71/229-5163

TIMESLIP (TF)   Yorkshire TV, 1984, British
DREAMS LOST, DREAMS FOUND (CTF)   Atlantic Video
Ventures Productions/ Yorkshire TV, 1987, British
OUT OF THE SHADOWS (CTF)   Showtime/Yorkshire
TV/Atlantic Videoventures Productions, 1988, British

MICHAEL PATTINSON
Agent: Triad Artists, Inc. - Los Angeles, 213/556-2727

MOVING OUT   Pattinson Ballantine Pictures,
1982, Australian
GROUND ZERO   Avenue Pictures, 1987, Australian
WENDY CRACKED A WALNUT   Australian Broadcasting
Corporation/ Australian Classic Films, 1990, Australian

STEVEN PAUL
b. May 16, 1958 - New York, New York
Business: Paul Entertainment, Inc., 8776 Sunset Blvd.,
Los Angeles, CA 90069, 213/652-9320

FALLING IN LOVE AGAIN   International Picture Show
Company, 1980
SLAPSTICK OF ANOTHER KIND   *SLAPSTICK*
Entertainment Releasing Corporation/International Film
Marketing, 1983
ETERNITY   Preferred Films, 1990

STUART PAUL
Business: Paul Entertainment, Inc., 8776 Sunset Blvd.,
Los Angeles, CA 90069, 213/652-9320

EMANON   Paul Releasing, 1987

DAVID PAULSEN*
Agent: The Richland/Wunsch Agency - Los Angeles,
213/278-1955
Attorney: Donald Walerstein, Rohner-Walerstein, 9225
Sunset Blvd., Los Angeles, CA 90069, 213/274-6182

SAVAGE WEEKEND   *THE UPSTATE MURDERS*
Cannon, 1976
SCHIZOID   Cannon, 1980

GEORGE PAVLOU
b. November 5, 1953
Agent: CCA, 5 Court Lodge, 48 Sloane Square, London
SW1, England, 71/730-8857

UNDERWORLD   Empire Pictures, 1985, British
RAWHEAD REX   Empire Pictures, 1987, British

MICHAEL PEARCE
JAMES JOYCE'S WOMEN   Universal, 1985
INITIATION   International Film Management/Goldfarb
Distributors, 1987, Australian

RICHARD PEARCE*
Agent: Bauer Benedek Agency - Beverly Hills, 213/275-2421

THE GARDENER'S SON (TF)   RIP/Filmhaus, 1977
SIEGE (TF)   Titus Productions, 1978
NO OTHER LOVE (TF)   Tisch-Avnet Productions, 1979
HEARTLAND   Levitt-Pickman, 1979
THRESHOLD   20th Century-Fox International Classics,
1983, Canadian

SESSIONS (TF)   Roger Gimbel Productions/EMI TV/
Sarabande Productions, 1983
COUNTRY   Buena Vista, 1984
NO MERCY   Tri-Star, 1987
DEAD MAN OUT (CTF)   HBO Showcase/Citadel
Entertainment Productions/ Granada TV, 1989,
U.S.-Canadian-British
THE FINAL DAYS (TF) ☆   The Samuels Film Company,
1989
THE LONG WALK HOME   New Century/Vista, 1990

RON PECK
Contact: British Academy of Film & Television Arts,
195 Piccadilly, London W1, England, 71/734-0022

EMPIRE STATE   Virgin/Miracle, 1987, British

LARRY PEERCE*
b. Bronx, New York
Address: 225 West 34th Street - Suite 1012, New York, NY
10125, 212/564-6656
Agent: The Brandt Company - Studio City, 818/506-7747

ONE POTATO, TWO POTATO   Cinema 5, 1964
THE BIG T.N.T. SHOW (FD)   American International, 1966
THE INCIDENT   20th Century-Fox, 1967
GOODBYE, COLUMBUS   Paramount, 1969
THE SPORTING CLUB   Avco Embassy, 1971
A SEPARATE PEACE   Paramount, 1972
ASH WEDNESDAY   Paramount, 1973
THE STRANGER WHO LOOKS LIKE ME (TF)
Filmways, 1974
THE OTHER SIDE OF THE MOUNTAIN   Universal, 1975
TWO-MINUTE WARNING   Universal, 1976
THE OTHER SIDE OF THE MOUNTAIN - PART 2
Universal, 1978
THE BELL JAR   Avco Embassy, 1979
WHY WOULD I LIE?   MGM/United Artists, 1980
LOVE CHILD   The Ladd Company/Warner Bros., 1982
I TAKE THESE MEN (TF)   Lillian Gallo Productions/United
Artists TV, 1983
HARD TO HOLD   Universal, 1984
LOVE LIVES ON (TF)   Script-Song Productions/ABC Circle
Films, 1985
THE FIFTH MISSILE (TF)   Bercovici-St. Johns Productions/
MGM-UA TV, 1986
PRISON FOR CHILDREN (TF)   Knopf-Simons Productions/
Viacom Productions, 1987
QUEENIE (MS)   von Zerneck-Samuels Productions/
Highgate Pictures, 1987
ELVIS AND ME (TF)   Navarone Productions/New
World TV, 1988
WIRED   Taurus Entertainment, 1989
THE NEON EMPIRE (CMS)   Richard Maynard Productions/
Fries Entertainment, 1989

ARTHUR PENN*
b. September 27, 1922 - Philadelphia, Pennsylvania
Agent: Sam Cohn, ICM - New York City, 212/556-6810

THE LEFT-HANDED GUN   Warner Bros., 1958
THE MIRACLE WORKER ★   United Artists, 1962
MICKEY ONE   Columbia, 1965
THE CHASE   Columbia, 1966
BONNIE AND CLYDE ★   Warner Bros., 1967
ALICE'S RESTAURANT ★   United Artists, 1969
LITTLE BIG MAN   National General, 1970
NIGHT MOVES   Warner Bros., 1975
THE MISSOURI BREAKS   United Artists, 1976
FOUR FRIENDS   Filmways, 1981

TARGET   Warner Bros., 1985
DEAD OF WINTER   MGM/UA, 1987
PENN & TELLER GET KILLED   Warner Bros., 1989

LEO PENN*
Agent: Sanford-Beckett-Skouras & Assciates -
    Los Angeles, 213/208-2100

A MAN CALLED ADAM   Embassy, 1966
QUARANTINED (TF)   Paramount TV, 1970
TESTIMONY OF TWO MEN (MS)   co-director with Larry
    Yust, Universal TV, 1977
THE DARK SECRET OF HARVEST HOME (TF)
    Universal TV, 1978
MURDER IN MUSIC CITY (TF)   Frankel Films, 1979
HELLINGER'S LAW (TF)   Universal TV, 1981
JUDGMENT IN BERLIN   New Line Cinema, 1988
COLUMBO GOES TO THE GUILLOTINE (TF)
    Universal TV, 1989

D. A. PENNEBAKER
(Don Alan Pennebaker)
b. 1930 - Evanston, Illinois
Business: Pennebaker Associates, 21 West 86th Street,
    New York, NY 10024, 212/496-9199

DON'T LOOK BACK (FD)   Leacock-Pennebaker, 1967
MONTEREY POP (FD)   Leacock-Pennebaker, 1967
COMPANY (FD)   Pennebaker Associates, 1970
SWEET TORONTO   *KEEP ON ROCKIN'* (FD)
    Pennebaker Associates, 1972
THE ENERGY WAR (TD)   Pennebaker Associates/
    Corporation for Public Broadcasting, 1979
ELLIOTT CARTER (FD)   Pennebaker Associates, 1980
TOWN BLOODY HALL (FD)   co-director with Chris
    Hegedus, Pennebaker Associates, 1980
DeLOREAN (TD)   Pennebaker Associates, 1981
ROCKABY (TD)   co-director with Chris Hegedus,
    Pennebaker Associates, 1983
ZIGGY STARDUST AND THE SPIDERS FROM MARS
    20th Century-Fox International Classics/Miramax Films,
    1983, filmed in 1973
DANCE BLACK AMERICA (FD)   co-director with Chris
    Hegedus, Pennebaker Associates, 1985
ROCKY X (FD)   co-director with Chris Hegedus,
    Pennebaker Associates, 1986
JIMI (FD)   Pennebaker Associates, 1986
DEPECHE MODE 101 (FD)   co-director with Chris
    Hegedus & David Dawkins, Westwood One Radio, 1989

EAGLE PENNELL
b. Texas
Contact: Tom Garvin, Ervin, Cohen & Jessup, 9401
    Wilshire Blvd., Beverly Hills, CA 90212, 213/273-6333

THE WHOLE SHOOTIN' MATCH   First Run
    Features, 1979
LAST NIGHT AT THE ALAMO   Cinecom, 1983
CITY LIFE   City Life Foundation, 1988
ICE HOUSE   Upfront Films, 1989
CITY LIFE (FD)   co-director, Nederlands Film Museum/
    International Art Film, 1990, Dutch

DAVID WEBB PEOPLES
Contact: Shapiro-Lichtman Agency - Los Angeles,
    213/859-8877

THE BLOOD OF HEROES   *THE SALUTE OF THE
    JUGGER*   New Line Cinema, 1989, U.S.-Australian

CLARE PEPLOE
Contact: British Academy of Film & Television Arts,
    195 Piccadilly, London W1, England, 71/734-0022

HIGH SEASON   Hemdale, 1987, British

GEORGE PEPPARD*
b. October 1, 1928 - Detroit, Michigan
Business: Lime Tree Productions - Beverly Hills,
    213/275-4748
Agent: Barbara Carswell Management, 321 S. Beverly Blvd. -
    Suite M, Beverly Hills, CA 90212, 213/556-6632

FIVE DAYS FROM HOME   Universal, 1977

ETIENNE PERIER
Business: Films de la Tour, 4 rue Arsene Houssaye, 75008
    Paris, 04/225-0117
Contact: French Film Office, 745 Fifth Avenue, New York,
    NY 10151, 212/832-8860

BOBOSSE   1959, Belgian
MEURTRE EN 45 TOURS   1960, Belgian
BRIDGE TO THE SUN   MGM, 1961, U.S.-French
SWORDSMAN OF SIENA   MGM, 1962, Italian-French
DIS-MOI QUI TUER   1965, Belgian
DES GARCONS ET DES FILLES   1968, French
RUBLO DE LOS CARAS   1969, Spanish
WHEN EIGHT BELLS TOLL   Cinerama Releasing
    Corporation, 1971, British
ZEPPELIN   Warner Bros., 1971, British
A MURDER IS A MURDER...IS A MURDER   Levitt-Pickman,
    1972, French
LA MAIN A COUPER   Planfilm, 1974, French-Italian
THE INVESTIGATION   *UN SI JOLI VILLAGE*   Quartet/
    Films Inc., 1978, French
LA PART DU FEU   Planfilm, 1978, French
LA CONFUSION DES SENTIMENTS (TF)   Christine
    Gouze-Renel Progefi/FR3, 1979, French
VENEZIA ROSSO SANGUE   Scena/Reteitalia/Clea
    Productions/ President Film, 1989, Italian-French

ZORAN PERISIC
b. March 16, 1940 - Yugoslavia
Agent: Eric L'Epine Smith, 10 Wyndham Place, London W1H
    1AS, England, 71/724-0739
Business: Courier Films Ltd., Unit 1, North Weyland Estate,
    Walton on Thames, England, 0932/246551

SKY BANDITS   Galaxy International, 1986, British

ANTHONY PERKINS*
b. April 14, 1932 - New York, New York
Agent: The Gersh Agency - Beverly Hills, 213/274-6611

PSYCHO III   Universal, 1986
LUCKY STIFF   New Line Cinema, 1989

FRANK PERRY*
b. 1930 - New York, New York
Home: 104 East 68th Street, New York, NY 10021,
    212/535-2910
Business: Corsair Pictures, 1740 Broadway - 23rd Floor,
    New York, NY 10019, 212/603-0652
Agent: Michael Black, ICM - Los Angeles/New York,
    213/550-4000 or 212/556-5600

DAVID AND LISA ★   Continental, 1962
LADYBUG, LADYBUG   United Artists, 1963
THE SWIMMER   Columbia, 1968

LAST SUMMER   Allied Artists, 1969
TRILOGY   Allied Artists, 1969
DIARY OF A MAD HOUSEWIFE   Universal, 1970
DOC   United Artists, 1971
PLAY IT AS IT LAYS   Universal, 1972
MAN ON A SWING   Paramount, 1974
RANCHO DeLUXE   United Artists, 1975
DUMMY (TF)   The Konigsberg Company/Warner Bros.
   TV, 1979
SKAG (TF) ☆   NBC, 1980
MOMMIE DEAREST   Paramount, 1981
MONSIGNOR   20th Century-Fox, 1982
COMPROMISING POSITIONS   Paramount, 1985
HELLO AGAIN   Buena Vista, 1987

BILL PERSKY*
b. 1931 - New Haven Connecticut
Agent: CAA - Beverly Hills, 213/288-4545

ROLL, FREDDY, ROLL! (TF)   ABC Circle Films, 1974
HOW TO PICK UP GIRLS! (TF)   King-Hitzig
   Productions, 1978
SERIAL   Paramount, 1980
WAIT TILL YOUR MOTHER GETS HOME (TF)
   Blue-Greene Productions/NBC Productions, 1983
TRACKDOWN: FINDING THE GOODBAR KILLER (TF)
   Grosso-Jacobson Productions, 1983
FOUND MONEY (TF)   Cypress Point Productions/Warner
   Bros. TV, 1983

BARBARA PETERS*
(Barbara Peeters)
Business: The Big Movie Company, 4243 Bakman Avenue,
   Studio City, CA 91602, 818/762-5883
Agent: Ronald Leif, Contemporary Artists - Beverly Hills,
   213/278-8250

THE DARK SIDE OF TOMORROW   co-director with
   Jacque Beerson, Able, 1970
BURY ME AN ANGEL   New World, 1972
SUMMER SCHOOL TEACHERS   New World, 1975
JUST THE TWO OF US   Boxoffice International, 1975
STARHOPS   First American, 1978
HUMANOIDS FROM THE DEEP   New World, 1980

WOLFGANG PETERSEN
b. West Germany
Agent: Tom Chasin, The Chasin Agency - Beverly Hills,
   213/278-7505

THE CONSEQUENCE   Libra, 1977, West German
BLACK AND WHITE LIKE DAY AND NIGHT   New Yorker,
   1978, West German
DAS BOOT (THE BOAT) ★   Triumph/Columbia, 1981,
   West German
THE NEVERENDING STORY   Warner Bros., 1984,
   West German
ENEMY MINE   20th Century Fox, 1985
SHATTERED   Pathe Entertainment, 1991,
   U.S.-West German

KRISTINE PETERSON
Business: Concorde Pictures, 11600 Concorde Pictures,
   Los Angeles, CA 90049, 213/826-0978

DEADLY DREAMS   Concorde, 1988
BODY CHEMISTRY   Concorde, 1990

CHRIS PETIT
b. 1949 - England
Contact: British Academy of Film & Television Arts,
   195 Piccadilly, London W1, England, 71/732-0022

RADIO ON   British Film Institute/Road Movies, 1979,
   British-West German
AN UNSUITABLE JOB FOR A WOMAN   Boyd's Co.,
   1982, British
FLYING FISH OVER HOLLYWOOD (FD)   1983, British
FLIGHT TO BERLIN   Road Movies/British Film Institute/
   Channel Four, 1984, West German-British
CHINESE BOXES   Chris Sievernich Productions/Palace
   Productions, 1984, West German-British

ANN PETRIE*
Home: 225 West 106th Street - Penthouse K, New York, NY
   10025, 212/866-8676

MOTHER TERESA (FD)   co-director with Jeanette Petrie,
   Petrie Productions, 1986

DANIEL PETRIE*
b. November 26, 1920 - Glace Bay, Nova Scotia, Canada
Address: 13201 Haney Place, Los Angeles, CA 90049,
   213/451-9157
Agent: The Richland/Wunsch Agency - Los Angeles,
   213/278-1955

THE BRAMBLE BUSH   Warner Bros., 1960
A RAISIN IN THE SUN   Columbia, 1961
THE MAIN ATTRACTION   MGM, 1962
STOLEN HOURS   United Artists, 1963
THE IDOL   Embassy, 1966, British
THE SPY WITH A COLD NOSE   Embassy, 1966, British
SILENT NIGHT, LONELY NIGHT (TF)   Universal TV, 1969
THE CITY (TF)   Universal TV, 1971
A HOWLING IN THE WOODS (TF)   Universal TV, 1971
MOON OF THE WOLF (TF)   Filmways, 1972
HEC RAMSEY (TF)   Universal TV/Mark VII Ltd., 1972
TROUBLE COMES TO TOWN (TF)   ABC Circle
   Films, 1973
THE NEPTUNE FACTOR   20th Century-Fox,
   1973, Canadian
MOUSEY (TF)   Universal TV/Associated British Films,
   1974, U.S.-British
THE GUN AND THE PULPIT (TF)   Danny Thomas
   Productions, 1974
BUSTER AND BILLIE   Columbia, 1974
RETURNING HOME (TF)   Lorimar Productions/Samuel
   Goldwyn Productions, 1975
ELEANOR AND FRANKLIN (TF) ☆☆   Talent
   Associates, 1976
SYBIL (TF)   Lorimar Productions, 1976
LIFEGUARD   Paramount, 1976
ELEANOR AND FRANKLIN: THE WHITE HOUSE
   YEARS (TF) ☆☆   Talent Associates, 1977
THE QUINNS (TF)   Daniel Wilson Productions, 1977
THE BETSY   Allied Artists, 1978
RESURRECTION   Universal, 1980
FORT APACHE, THE BRONX   20th Century-Fox, 1981
SIX PACK   20th Century-Fox, 1982
THE DOLLMAKER (TF)   Finnegan Associates/IPC Films,
   Inc./Dollmaker Productions, 1984
THE BAY BOY   Orion, 1984, Canadian-French
HALF A LIFETIME (CTF)   HBO Showcase/Astral Film
   Enterprises/Martin Bregman Productions, 1986,
   U.S.-Canadian

SQUARE DANCE   Island Pictures, 1986
ROCKET GIBRALTAR   Columbia, 1988
COCOON: THE RETURN   20th Century Fox, 1988
MY NAME IS BILL W. (TF) ☆   Garner-Duchow
   Productions, 1989

DONALD PETRIE*
Agent: Bob Wunsch, Richland/Wunsch Agency -
   Los Angeles, 213/278-1955

MYSTIC PIZZA   Samuel Goldwyn Company, 1988
OPPORTUNITY KNOCKS   Universal, 1990

JEANETTE PETRIE
MOTHER TERESA (FD)   co-director with Ann Petrie,
   Petrie Productions, 1986

JOSEPH PEVNEY*
b. 1920 - New York, New York
Business Manager: T.J. Smith, 17826 Chatsworth Street,
   Granada Hills, CA 91344, 818/366-1144

SHAKEDOWN   Universal, 1950
UNDERCOVER GIRL   Universal, 1950
AIR CADET   Universal, 1951
IRON MAN   Universal, 1951
THE LADY FROM TEXAS   Universal, 1951
THE STRANGE DOOR   Universal, 1951
MEET DANNY WILSON   Universal, 1952
FLESH AND FURY   Universal, 1952
JUST ACROSS THE STREET   Universal, 1952
BECAUSE OF YOU   Universal, 1952
DESERT LEGION   Universal, 1953
IT HAPPENS EVERY THURSDAY   Universal, 1953
BACK TO GOD'S COUNTRY   Universal, 1953
YANKEE PASHA   Universal, 1954
PLAYGIRL   Universal, 1954
THREE RING CIRCUS   Paramount, 1954
SIX BRIDGES TO CROSS   Universal, 1955
FOXFIRE   Universal, 1955
FEMALE ON THE BEACH   Universal, 1955
AWAY ALL BOATS   Universal, 1956
CONGO CROSSING   Universal, 1956
ISTANBUL   Universal, 1956
TAMMY AND THE BACHELOR   Universal, 1957
THE MIDNIGHT STORY   Universal, 1957
MAN OF A THOUSAND FACES   Universal, 1957
TWILIGHT FOR THE GODS   Universal, 1958
TORPEDO RUN   MGM, 1958
CASH McCALL   Warner Bros., 1960
THE PLUNDERERS   Allied Artists, 1960
THE CROWDED SKY   Warner Bros., 1960
PORTRAIT OF A MOBSTER   Warner Bros., 1961
THE NIGHT OF THE GRIZZLY   Paramount, 1966
MY DARLING DAUGHTERS' ANNIVERSARY (TF)
   Universal TV, 1973
WHO IS THE BLACK DAHLIA? (TF)   Douglas S. Cramer
   Productions, 1975
MYSTERIOUS ISLAND OF BEAUTIFUL WOMEN (TF)
   Alan Landsburg Productions, 1977
PRISONERS OF THE SEA   McLane Enterprises, 1985

JOHN PEYSER*
b. August 10, 1916 - New York, New York
Home: 19721 Redwing Street, Woodland Hills, CA 91364,
   818/884-7730
Agent: Martin Shapiro, Shapiro-Lichtman Agency -
   Los Angeles, 213/859-8877

UNDERSEA GIRL   Allied Artists, 1958
THE MURDER MEN   MGM, 1964

THE YOUNG WARRIORS   Universal, 1967
HONEYMOON WITH A STRANGER (TF)   20th Century-
   Fox TV, 1969
MASSACRE HARBOR   United Artists, 1970
CENTER FOLD GIRLS   Dimension, 1974
STUNT SEVEN (TF)   Martin Poll Productions, 1979

WILLIAM PHELPS*
Home: 9019 Elevado Street, Los Angeles, CA 90069,
   213/271-9466
Agent: Warden/White/Van Duren - Santa Monica,
   213/315-4725

THE NORTH SHORE   Universal, 1987

LEE PHILIPS*
b. Brooklyn, New York
Home: 11939 Gorham Avenue - Suite 104, Los Angeles,
   CA 90049, 213/820-7464
Agent: William Morris Agency - Beverly Hills, 213/274-7451

GETTING AWAY FROM IT ALL (TF)   Palomar Pictures
   International, 1972
THE GIRL MOST LIKELY TO... (TF)   ABC Circle
   Films, 1973
THE STRANGER WITHIN (TF)   Lorimar Productions, 1974
THE RED BADGE OF COURAGE (TF)   20th Century-
   Fox TV, 1974
SWEET HOSTAGE (TF)   Brut Productions, 1975
LOUIS ARMSTRONG - CHICAGO STYLE (TF)   Charles
   Fries Productions, 1975
JAMES A. MICHENER'S DYNASTY (TF)   David Paradine
   TV, 1976
WANTED: THE SUNDANCE WOMAN (TF)   20th Century-
   Fox TV, 1976
THE SPELL (TF)   Charles Fries Productions, 1977
THE WAR BETWEEN THE TATES (TF)   Talent
   Associates, 1977
SPECIAL OLYMPICS (TF)   Roger Gimbel Productions/
   EMI TV, 1978
THE COMEDY COMPANY (TF)   Merrit Malloy-Jerry Adler
   Productions, 1978
SALVAGE (TF)   Bennett-Katleman Productions/
   Columbia TV, 1979
VALENTINE (TF)   Malloy-Philips Productions/Edward S.
   Feldman Company, 1979
HARDHAT AND LEGS (TF)   Syzygy Productions, 1980
CRAZY TIMES (TF)   Kayden-Gleason Productions/George
   Reeves Productions/Warner Bros. TV, 1981
ON THE RIGHT TRACK   20th Century-Fox, 1981
A WEDDING ON WALTON'S MOUNTAIN (TF)   Lorimar
   Productions/Amanda Productions, 1982
MAE WEST (TF) ☆   Hill-Mandelker Films, 1982
GAMES MOTHER NEVER TAUGHT YOU (TF)   CBS
   Entertainment, 1982
LOTTERY! (TF)   Rosner TV Productions/Orion TV, 1983
HAPPY (TF)   Bacchus Films Inc., 1983
SAMSON AND DELILAH (TF)   Catalina Production Group/
   Comworld Productions, 1984
SPACE (MS)   co-director with Joseph Sargent, Stonehenge
   Productions/Paramount TV, 1985
AMERICAN GEISHA (TF)   Interscope Communications/
   Stonehenge Productions, 1986
THE BLUE LIGHTNING (TF)   Alan Sloan Productions/
   The Seven Network/Coote-Carroll Australia/Roadshow,
   1986, U.S.-Australian
BARNUM (TF)   Robert Halmi, Inc./Filmline International,
   1986, U.S.- Canadian
SIDNEY SHELDON'S WINDMILLS OF THE GODS
   WINDMILLS OF THE GODS (TF)   Dove Productions/
   ITC Productions, 1988

KING OF THE OLYMPICS (TF)   Harmony Gold/Rete
Europa/SFP Productions, 1988, U.S.-Italian
MONEY, POWER, MURDER (TF)   Skids Productions/
CBS Entertainment, 1989

MAURICE PHILLIPS
Agent: The Brandt Company - Studio City, 818/506-7747

RIDERS OF THE STORM   *THE AMERICAN WAY*
Miramax Films, 1986, British
ENID IS SLEEPING   Vestron, 1990

MAURICE PIALAT
b. August 21, 1925 - Puy-de-Dome, France
Contact: French Film Office, 745 Fifth Avenue, New York,
NY 10151, 212/832-8860

ME   *L'ENFANCE NUE*   Altura Films Limited,
1968, French
NOUS NE VIEILLIRONS PAS ENSEMBLE   Corona,
1972, French
LA GUEULE OUVERTE   Lido Films La Boetie,
1974, French
GRADUATE FIRST   *PASSE TON BAC D'ABORD*
1979, French
LOULOU   Gaumont, 1979, French
A NOS AMOURS   Les Films du Livradois/Gaumont/FR3,
1983, French
POLICE   Island Pictures, 1985, French
UNDER THE SUN OF SATAN   Alive Films, 1987, French
VAN GOGH   Erato Films, 1991, French

VASILY PICHUL
Contact: Union of Soviet Filmmakers, Vassilievskaya 13,
Moscow, U.S.S.R., tel.: 250-4114

LITTLE VERA   International Film Exchange, 1988, Soviet
DARK IS THE NIGHT ON THE BLACK SEA   Podaro/
Sacis/Silvia D'Amico/RAI, 1990, Soviet-Italian

REX PICKETT
Agent: Robert Hohman/Ronda Gomez-Quinones, Triad
Artists, Inc. - Los Angeles, 213/556-2727

FROM HOLLYWOOD TO DEADWOOD   Island
Pictures, 1988

CHARLES B. PIERCE
THE LEGEND OF BOGGY CREEK   Howco
International, 1973
BOOTLEGGERS   Howco International, 1974
WINTERHAWK   Howco International, 1975
THE WINDS OF AUTUMN   Howco International, 1976
THE TOWN THAT DREADED SUNDOWN   American
International, 1977
GREYEAGLE   American International, 1977
THE NORSEMEN   American International, 1978
THE EVICTORS   American International, 1979
SACRED GROUND   Pacific International, 1983
BOGGY CREEK II   Howco International, 1985
HAWKEN'S BREED   Vidmark, 1989
LEGEND OF THE JERSEY DEVIL   Paragon Pictures, 1990

FRANK PIERSON*
b. May 12, 1925 - New York, New York
Agent: Bauer Benedek Agency - Los Angeles, 213/275-2421

THE LOOKING GLASS WAR   Columbia, 1970, British
THE NEON CEILING (TF)   Universal TV, 1971
A STAR IS BORN   Warner Bros., 1976
KING OF THE GYPSIES   Paramount, 1978

SAM PILLSBURY
Agent: Alan Greenspan, ICM - Los Angeles, 213/550-4428

THE SCARECROW   Rob Whitehouse Productions, 1982,
New Zealand
HEART OF THE HIGH COUNTRY (MS)   Phillips/
Whitehouse, 1985, New Zealand-British
STARLIGHT HOTEL   Republic Pictures, 1987,
New Zealand
ZANDALEE   Electric Pictures, 1990

HAROLD PINTER
b. October 10, 1930 - London, England
Home: 52 Campden Hill Square, London W8, England
Business: c/o ACTAC Ltd., 16 Cadogan Lane, London SW1,
England, 71/235-2797
Agent: Judy Daish, 83 Eastbourne Mews, London W2 6LQ,
England, 71/262-1101

BUTLEY   American Film Theatre, 1974, British

ERNEST PINTOFF*
b. December 15, 1931 - Watertown, Connecticut
Agent: Ronald Leif, Contemporary Artists - Beverly Hills,
213/278-8250

HARVEY MIDDLEMAN, FIREMAN   Columbia, 1965
WHO KILLED MARY WHAT'S'ERNAME   Cannon, 1971
DYNAMITE CHICKEN   EYR, 1972
HUMAN FEELINGS (TF)   Crestview Productions/
Worldvision, 1978
JAGUAR LIVES   American International, 1979
LUNCH WAGON   *LUNCH WAGON GIRLS*   Seymour Borde
Associates, 1981
ST. HELENS   Davis-Panzer Productions, 1981

GLEN PITRE
b. 1955 - Louisiana
Agent: William Morris Agency - Beverly Hills, 213/274-7451

BELIZAIRE THE CAJUN   Skouras Pictures, 1986

BRUCE PITTMAN
b. 1950 - Toronto, Ontario, Canada
Business: Chrysalis Productions, 191 Logan Avenue,
Toronto, Ontario M4M 2N2, Canada, 416/469-0459

THE MARK OF CAIN   Brightstar Films, 1985, Canadian
CONFIDENTIAL   Cineplex Odeon, 1986, Canadian
HELLO MARY LOU: PROM NIGHT II   *THE HAUNTING OF
HAMILTON HIGH*   Samuel Goldwyn Company, 1987,
Canadian
CHASING RAINBOWS (MS)   co-director with William Fruet,
Mark Blandford & Susan Martin, CBC, 1988, Canadian
WHERE THE SPIRIT LIVES (TF)   Amazing Spirit
Productions/CBC/ Mid-Canada TV/TV Ontario,
1989, Canadian

LEONG PO-CHIH
(See Po-Chih LEONG)

AMOS POE
Agent: William Morris Agency - Beverly Hills, 213/274-7451

THE FOREIGNER   Amos Poe Visions, 1978
SUBWAY RIDERS   Hep Pictures, 1981
ALPHABET CITY   Atlantic Releasing Corporation, 1984

S. LEE POGOSTIN*

Contact: Directors Guild of America - Los Angeles,
213/289-2000

HARD CONTRACT   20th Century-Fox, 1969

SIDNEY POITIER*

b. February 20, 1924 - Miami, Florida
Agent: CAA - Beverly Hills, 213/288-4545
Business: Verdon-Cedric Productions, Ltd., 9350 Wilshire
   Blvd., Beverly Hills, CA 90212, 213/274-7253

BUCK AND THE PREACHER   Columbia, 1972
A WARM DECEMBER   National General, 1973
UPTOWN SATURDAY NIGHT   Warner Bros., 1974
LET'S DO IT AGAIN   Warner Bros., 1975
A PIECE OF THE ACTION   Warner Bros., 1977
STIR CRAZY   Columbia, 1980
HANKY PANKY   Columbia, 1982
FAST FORWARD   Columbia, 1985
GHOST DAD   Universal, 1990

ROMAN POLANSKI

b. August 18, 1933 - Paris, France
Address: 43 Avenue Montaigne, 75008 Paris, France
Agent: ICM - Los Angeles, 213/500-4000

KNIFE IN THE WATER   Kanawha, 1963, Polish
THE BEAUTIFUL SWINDLERS   LES PLUS BELLES
   ESCROQUERIES DU MONDE   co-director with Ugo
   Grigoretti, Claude Chabrol & Hiromichi Horikawa, Jack
   Ellis Films, 1964, French-Italian-Japanese-Dutch
REPULSION   Royal Films International, 1965, British
CUL-DE-SAC   Sigma III, 1966, British
THE FEARLESS VAMPIRE KILLERS, OR PARDON ME
   BUT YOUR TEETH ARE IN MY NECK   DANCE OF
   THE VAMPIRES   MGM, 1967, British
ROSEMARY'S BABY   Paramount, 1968
MACBETH   Columbia, 1971, British
WHAT?   Avco Embassy, 1973, Italian-French-
   West German
CHINATOWN ★   Paramount, 1974
THE TENANT   Paramount, 1976, French-U.S.
TESS ★   Columbia, 1980, French-British
PIRATES   Cannon, 1986, French-Tunisian
FRANTIC   Warner Bros., 1988

STEPHEN POLIAKOFF

Contact: British Academy of Film & Televison Arts,
   195 Piccadilly, London W1, England, 71/734-0022

HIDDEN CITY   Hidden City Films/Channel Four,
   1987, British
UNTITLED   BBC, 1989, British

BARRY POLLACK

COOL BREEZE   MGM, 1972
THIS IS A HIJACK   Fanfare, 1973

SYDNEY POLLACK*

b. July 1, 1934 - South Bend, Indiana
Agent: CAA - Beverly Hills, 213/288-4545

THE SLENDER THREAD   Paramount, 1965
THIS PROPERTY IS CONDEMNED   Paramount, 1966
THE SCALPHUNTERS   United Artists, 1968
CASTLE KEEP   Columbia, 1969
THEY SHOOT HORSES, DON'T THEY? ★   Cinerama
   Releasing Corporation, 1969
JEREMIAH JOHNSON   Warner Bros., 1972

THE WAY WE WERE   Columbia, 1973
THE YAKUZA   Warner Bros., 1975
3 DAYS OF THE CONDOR   Paramount, 1975
BOBBY DEERFIELD   Columbia, 1977
THE ELECTRIC HORSEMAN   Columbia, 1979
ABSENCE OF MALICE   Columbia, 1981
TOOTSIE ★   Columbia, 1982
OUT OF AFRICA ★★   Universal, 1985
HAVANA   Universal, 1990

ABRAHAM POLONSKY*

b. December 5, 1910 - New York, New York
Agent: The Gersh Agency - Beverly Hills, 213/274-6611
Attorney: Shanks, Davis & Remer - New York City,
   212/986-0440

FORCE OF EVIL   MGM, 1948
TELL THEM WILLIE BOY IS HERE   Universal, 1969
ROMANCE OF A HORSETHIEF   Allied Artists, 1971

GILLO PONTECORVO

b. November 19, 1919 - Pisa, Italy
Home: via Paolo Frisi 18, Rome, Italy, 06/877672

DIE WINDROSE   co-director, 1956, East German
LA GRANDE STRADA AZZURRA   Ge-Si Malenotti/Play Art/
   Eichberg/Triglav Film, 1957, Italian-Yugoslavian
KAPO'   Vides/Zebra Film/Cineriz, 1960, Italian
BATTLE OF ALGIERS ★   Rizzoli, 1967, Italian-Algerian
BURN!   QUEIMADA!   United Artists, 1970, Italian-French
OPERATION OGRO   CIDIF, 1979, Italian-Spanish-French

MAURIZIO PONZI

b. May 8, 1939 - Rome
Home: Vicolo del Bologna 51, Rome, Italy, 06/589-2877

I VISIONARI   21 Marzo Cinematografica, 1969, Italian
EQUINOZIO   San Diego, 1971, Italian
IL CASO RAOUL   Iskra Cinematografica, 1975, Italian
MADONNA CHE SILENZIO C'E' STASERA   Hera
   International Film/Mirage Film, 1982, Italian
SON CONTENTO   Hera International Film, 1983
THE POOL HUSTLERS   IO CHIARA E LO SCURO   Orion
   Classics, 1983, Italian
AURORA (TF)   Roger Gimbel Productions/The Peregrine
   Producers Group/Sacis, 1984, U.S.-Italian
IL TENENTE DEI CARABINIERI   Columbia, 1986, Italian
NOI UOMINI DURI   CDI, 1987, Italian
IL VOLPONE   Maura Film/Cecchi Gori/Tiger
   Cinematografica, 1988, Italian
VOLEVO I PANTOLINI   Penta Distribuzione, 1990, Italian

PETRU POPESCU

b. Romania
Agent: APA - Los Angeles, 213/273-0744

DEATH OF AN ANGEL   20th Century Fox, 1985

TED POST*

b. March 31, 1918 - Brooklyn, New York
Business Manager: Norman Blumenthal, 12233 W.
   Olympic Blvd., Los Angeles, CA 90064, 213/207-4464

THE PEACEMAKER   United Artists, 1956
THE LEGEND OF TOM DOOLEY   Columbia, 1959
HANG 'EM HIGH   United Artists, 1968
BENEATH THE PLANET OF THE APES   20th
   Century-Fox, 1970
NIGHT SLAVES (TF)   Bing Crosby Productions, 1970
DR. COOK'S GARDEN (TF)   Paramount TV, 1970
YUMA (TF)   Aaron Spelling Productions, 1971

FIVE DESPERATE WOMEN (TF)   Aaron Spelling
   Productions, 1971
DO NOT FOLD, SPINDLE OR MUTILATE (TF)   Lee Rich
   Productions, 1971
THE BRAVOS (TF)   Universal TV, 1972
SANDCASTLES (TF)   Metromedia Productions, 1972
THE BABY   Scotia International, 1973, British
THE HARRAD EXPERIMENT   Cinerama Releasing
   Corporation, 1973
MAGNUM FORCE   Warner Bros., 1973
WHIFFS   20th Century-Fox, 1975
GOOD GUYS WEAR BLACK   American Cinema, 1978
GO TELL THE SPARTANS   Avco Embassy, 1978
DIARY OF A TEENAGE HITCHHIKER (TF)   The
   Shpetner Company, 1979
THE GIRLS IN THE OFFICE (TF)   ABC Circle Films, 1979
NIGHTKILL (TF)   Cine Artists, 1980
CAGNEY & LACEY (TF)   Mace Neufeld Productions/
   Filmways, 1981
STAGECOACH (TF)   Raymond Katz Productions/
   Heritage Entertainment, 1986

DENNIS POTTER
b. May 17, 1935 - Forest of Dean, Gloucester, England
Contact: Writers Guild of America, West - Los Angeles,
   213/550-1000

BLACKEYES   BBC/Paravision/Blackeyes Ltd.,
   1990, British

SALLY POTTER
b. England
Address: 20 Kellet House, Tankerton Street, London
   WC1H 8HW, England, 71/837-4631

THE GOLD DIGGERS   British Film Institute/Channel
   Four, 1984, British
TEARS, LAUGHTER, FEARS AND RAGE (TD)
   1987, British

GERALD POTTERTON
b. 1931 - London, England
Home: R.R. #3, Brome Lake, Cowansville, Quebec
   J2K 3G8, Canada, 514/263-3282
Business: The Potterton Studio, 1568 Summerhill Avenue,
   Montreal, Quebec H3H 1B9, Canada, 514/931-5753

HEAVY METAL (AF)   Columbia, 1981, Canadian

TRISTRAM POWELL
b. April 1940 - Oxford, England
Agent: Douglas Rae Management, 28 Charing Cross
   Road, London WC2, England, 71/836-3903

THE GHOST WRITER (TF)   WGBH-Boston/Malone-Gill
   Productions/BBC, 1984, U.S.-British
NUMBER 27 (TF)   BBC, 1988, British
AMERICAN FRIENDS   Prominent Features, 1991, British

MICHAEL PREECE*
b. September 15, 1936 - Los Angeles, California
Home: 15278 Friends Street, Pacific Palisades, CA 90272,
   213/459-4475
Agent: Spyros Skouras, Sanford-Beckett-Skouras &
   Associates - Los Angeles, 213/208-2100

THE PRIZE FIGHTER   New World, 1979
PARADISE CONNECTION (TF)   Woodruff Productions/
   QM Productions, 1979
DALLAS: PHANTOM OF THE OIL RIG (TF)   co-director with
   Irving J. Moore, Lorimar TV, 1989

MICHAEL PRESSMAN*
b. July 1, 1950 - New York, New York
Home: 451 Linnie Canal, Venice, CA 90291, 213/301-1834
Agent: Elliot Webb, Broder-Kurland-Webb-Uffner Agency -
   Los Angeles, 213/656-9262

THE GREAT TEXAS DYNAMITE CHASE   New World, 1976
THE BAD NEWS BEARS IN BREAKING TRAINING
   Paramount, 1977
LIKE MOM, LIKE ME (TF)   CBS Entertainment, 1978
BOULEVARD NIGHTS   Warner Bros., 1979
THOSE LIPS, THOSE EYES   United Artists, 1980
SOME KIND OF HERO   Paramount, 1982
DOCTOR DETROIT   Universal, 1983
THE IMPOSTER (TF)   Gloria Monty Productions/Comworld
   Productions, 1984
AND THE CHILDREN SHALL LEAD (TF)   Rainbow TV
   Workshop, 1985
PRIVATE SESSIONS (TF)   The Belle Company/Seltzer-
   Gimbel Productions/ Raven's Claw Productions/Comworld
   Productions, 1985
FINAL JEOPARDY (TF)   Frank von Zerneck
   Productions, 1985
THE CHRISTMAS GIFT (TF)   Rosemont Productions/Sunn
   Classic Pictures, 1986
HAUNTED BY HER PAST (TF)   Norton Wright Productions/
   ITC Productions, 1987
TO HEAL A NATION (TF)   Lionel Chetwynd Productions/
   Orion TV/ von Zerneck-Samuels Productions, 1988
SHOOTDOWN (TF)   Leonard Hill Films, 1988
INCIDENT AT DARK RIVER (CTF)   Farrell-Minoff
   Productions/Turner Network TV, 1989
MAN AGAINST THE MOB: THE CHINATOWN MURDERS
   (TF)   von Zerneck-Sertner Productions, 1989

GAYLENE PRESTON
Contact: New Zealand Film Commission, P.O. Box 11546,
   Wellington, New Zealand, 4/859-754

DARK OF THE NIGHT   *MR. WRONG*   Quartet, 1985,
   New Zealand
RUBY AND RATA   Preston Laing Productions, 1990,
   New Zealand

RUBEN PREUSS*
Home: 11926 Hartsook Street, North Hollywood, CA 91607,
   818/508-7514

IN DANGEROUS COMPANY   Manson International, 1988
DECEPTIONS   Alpha Entertainment, 1989

PRINCE
(Rogers Nelson)
b. Minneapolis, Minnesota
Agent: CAA - Beverly Hills, 213/288-4545

UNDER THE CHERRY MOON   Warner Bros., 1986
SIGN 'O' THE TIMES   Cineplex Odeon, 1987
GRAFFITI BRIDGE   Warner Bros., 1990

HAROLD PRINCE
b. January 30, 1928
Business: 1270 Avenue of the Americas, New York, NY,
   212/399-0960

SOMETHING FOR EVERYONE   National General,
   1970, British
A LITTLE NIGHT MUSIC   New World, 1978, Austrian-U.S.

DAVID A. PRIOR

Business: Action International Pictures, 1022 N. Palm
    Avenue, Los Angeles, CA 90069, 213/659-4399

CHASE   Action International, 1987
DEADLY PREY   Action International, 1987
MANKILLERS   Action International, 1987
NIGHTWARS   Action International, 1987
BATTLEGROUND   Action International, 1989
C.O.P.S.   Action International, 1989
JUNGLE ASSAULT   Action International, 1989
FUTURE FORCE   Action International, 1989
THE LOST PLATOON   Action International, 1989
FINAL SANCTION   American-Independent, 1990
BACK TO THE PAST   American-Independent, 1990
RAPID FIRE   Action International, 1990

RICHARD PRYOR*

b. December 1, 1940 - Peoria, Illinois
Agent: ICM - Los Angeles, 213/550-4000
Attorney: Bloom & Dekom Hergott - Los Angeles,
    213/278-8622

RICHARD PRYOR HERE AND NOW (FD)
    Columbia, 1983
JO JO DANCER, YOUR LIFE IS CALLING
    Columbia, 1986

LUIS PUENZO*

Agent: Triad Artists, Inc. - Los Angeles, 213/556-2727

THE OFFICIAL STORY   Historias Cinematograficas,
    1985, Argentine
OLD GRINGO   Columbia, 1989

ABRAHAM PULIDO

b. March 18, 1953 - Caracas, Venezuela
Business: E. Films, 107 West 89th Street - Apt. 2B,
    New York, NY 10024, 212/721-1945

LILY   Creacolor, 1983, Venezuelan

EVELYN PURCELL*

Agent: William Morris Agency - Beverly Hills, 213/274-7451
Personal Manager: Barbara Carswell Management, 321
    S. Beverly Drive - Suite M, Beverly Hills, CA 90212,
    213/556-0563

NOBODY'S FOOL   Island Pictures, 1986
THE LAND OF LITTLE RAIN   Denver Center for the
    Performing Arts/Mayport Productions/Brockman
    Seawell, 1988

JOSEPH PURCELL*

Home: 13627 Morrison Street, Sherman Oaks, CA
    91423, 818/789-9294

THE DELOS ADVENTURE   American Cine
    Marketing, 1987

DOROTHY ANN PUZO*

Home: 12050 Valleyheart Drive - Apt. 303, Studio City, CA
Agent: Harold Greene, 8455 Beverly Blvd. - Suite 309,
    Los Angeles, CA 90048, 213/852-4959

COLD STEEL   CineTel, 1987

JOE PYTKA*

Business: 408 Boulevard of the Allies, Pittsburgh, PA
    25229, 412/391-7919
Agent: Alan Greenspan, ICM - Los Angeles, 213/550-4428

LET IT RIDE   Paramount, 1989

ALBERT PYUN*

Agent: Leading Artists - Beverly Hills, 213/858-1999

THE SWORD AND THE SORCERER   Group 1, 1982
RADIOACTIVE DREAMS   DEG, 1986
DANGEROUSLY CLOSE   Cannon, 1986
VICIOUS LIPS   Empire Pictures, 1987
DOWN TWISTED   Cannon, 1987
ALIEN FROM L.A.   Cannon, 1988
CYBORG   Cannon, 1989
DECEIT   21st Century Distribution, 1989
CAPTAIN AMERICA   21st Century Distribution, 1990

JOHN QUESTED

Business: Goldcrest Films and Television, 36-44 Brewer
    Street, London W1, England, 71/436-8696

PHILADELPHIA, HERE I COME   Irish
HERE ARE LADIES   Arthur Cantor Films, 1971, Irish
LOOPHOLE   MGM/United Artists, 1981, British

FOLCO QUILICI

DANGER ADRIFT (TF)   RAI/CBS Entertainment, 1989,
    Italian-U.S.

ANTHONY QUINN

b. April 21, 1915 - Chihuahua, Mexico
Agent: Barrett, Benson, McCartt & Weston - Los Angeles,
    213/553-2600

THE BUCCANEER   Paramount, 1959

GENE QUINTANO

Agent: Steve Rabineau, ICM - Los Angeles, 213/550-4315

HONEYMOON ACADEMY   Triumph Releasing
    Corporation, 1990
WHY ME?   Triumph Releasing Corporation, 1990

JOSE QUINTERO*

b. October 15, 1924 - Panama City, Panama
Home: 4300 Parva Avenue, Los Angeles, CA 90027,
    213/662-3264
Business Manager: Jim Harty & Associates, 1741 N. Ivar
    Avenue - Suite 209, Los Angeles, CA 90028,
    213/464-6188

THE ROMAN SPRING OF MRS. STONE   Warner
    Bros., 1961

R

FONS RADEMAKERS
b. September 5, 1920 - Rosendaal, Brabant, Netherlands
Business: Fons Rademakers Productie B.V., Prinsengracht
685, 1017 JT Amsterdam, Netherlands, 20/221298
Agent: Paul Kohner, Inc. - Los Angeles, 213/550-1060

*(The following is an incomplete list of Mr. Rademakers'
credits)*

VILLAGE ON THE RIVER   1958, Dutch
THAT JOYOUS EVE   1960, Dutch
THE KNIFE   1961, Dutch
THE SPITTING IMAGE   1963, Dutch
THE DANCE OF THE HERON   1966, Dutch
MIRA   1971, Dutch
BECAUSE OF THE CATS   1973, Dutch
MAX HAVELAAR   1976, Dutch
MY FRIEND   1979, Dutch
THE ASSAULT   Cannon, 1987, Dutch
THE ROSE GARDEN   Cannon, 1989, West German

PETER RADER
Contact: 213/454-2223

GRANDMOTHER'S HOUSE   Omega Pictures, 1989
HIRED TO KILL   co-director with Nico Mastorakis, Omega
Pictures, 1990

MICHAEL RADFORD
Agent: Triad Artists, Inc. - Los Angeles, 213/556-2727
Address: 3B Pickering Mews, London W2 5AD, England

VAN MORRISON IN IRELAND (FD)   Caledonia-Angle Films,
1981, British
THE WHITE BIRD PASSES (TF)   BBC, 1981, British
ANOTHER TIME, ANOTHER PLACE   Samuel Goldwyn
Company, 1983, British
1984   Atlantic Releasing Corporation, 1984, British
WHITE MISCHIEF   Columbia, 1987, British

BOB RADLER
BEST OF THE BEST   Taurus Entertainment/SVS
Films, 1989

MICHAEL RAE
LASERBLAST   Irwin Yablans, 1978

MICHAEL RAEBURN
b. January 22, 1943 - Cairo, Egypt
Business: Signfour Films Ltd., 10 Spencer Park, London
SW18, England, 71/874-0205
Agent: Tim Corrie, Peters, Fraser & Dunlop, The Chambers,
Chelsea Harbour, Lots Road, London SW10 OXF,
England, 71/376-7676

KILLING HEAT   *THE GRASS IS SINGING*   Satori, 1983,
British-Swedish-Zambian
SOWETO   General Entertainment/S&S Productions/
Nigerian TV, 1987, British-Finnish-Nigerian

BOB RAFELSON*
b. 1935 - New York, New York
Agent: Peter Rawley, ICM - Los Angeles, 213/550-4000

HEAD   Columbia, 1968
FIVE EASY PIECES   Columbia, 1970
THE KING OF MARVIN GARDENS   Columbia, 1972
STAY HUNGRY   United Artists, 1976
THE POSTMAN ALWAYS RINGS TWICE
Paramount, 1981
BLACK WIDOW   20th Century Fox, 1987
MOUNTAINS OF THE MOON   Tri-Star, 1990

STEWART RAFFILL*
Home: P.O. Box 117, Tarzana, CA 91356, 818/991-8987
Agent: Jerry Adler, The Sy Fischer Company - Studio City,
818/769-5003

THE TENDER WARRIOR   Safari, 1971
THE ADVENTURES OF THE WILDERNESS FAMILY
Pacific International, 1975
ACROSS THE GREAT DIVIDE   Pacific International, 1976
THE SEA GYPSIES   Warner Bros., 1978
HIGH RISK   American Cinema, 1981
THE ICE PIRATES   MGM/UA, 1983
THE PHILADELPHIA EXPERIMENT   New World, 1984
MAC AND ME   Orion, 1988
MANNEQUIN ON THE MOVE   Winstar Productions/
Gladden Entertainment, 1990

"I do believe that a director's function is interpretive, that a director
has to be able to project himself into Shakespearean England, or
outer space. Those things are what distinguishes a director in terms
of his ability to recognize the commonality of experience, or the
humanity in everyone, and to project himself firmly into that."

EDWARD ZWICK

ALAN RAFKIN*

b. July 23, 1938 - New York, New York
Home: 1008 St. Bimini Circle, Palm Springs, CA
    619/323-4058
Personal Manager: The Brillstein Company, 9200 Sunset
    Blvd., Los Angeles, CA 90069, 213/275-6135

SKI PARTY   American International, 1965
THE GHOST AND MR. CHICKEN   Universal, 1966
THE RIDE TO HANGMAN'S TREE   Universal, 1967
NOBODY'S PERFECT   Universal, 1968
THE SHAKIEST GUN IN THE WEST   Universal, 1968
ANGEL IN MY POCKET   Universal, 1969
HOW TO FRAME A FIGG   Universal, 1971
LET'S SWITCH (TF)   Universal TV, 1975

SAM RAIMI

Agent: InterTalent - Los Angeles, 213/271-0600

THE EVIL DEAD   New Line Cinema, 1983
CRIMEWAVE   *BROKEN HEARTS AND NOSES*
    Columbia, 1985
EVIL DEAD 2   Rosebud Releasing Corporation, 1987
DARKMAN   Universal, 1990

ALVIN RAKOFF

b. 1937 - Toronto, Canada
Home: Alvin Rakoff Productions Ltd., 1 The Orchard,
    Chiswick, London W4 1JZ, England, 71/994-1269
Agent: Paul Kohner, Inc. - Los Angeles, 213/550-1060

HOT MONEY GIRL   *THE TREASURE OF SAN TERESA*
    United Producers Releasing Organization, 1959, British
ROOM 43   *PASSPORT TO SHAME*   British Lion,
    1959, British
ON FRIDAY AT ELEVEN   British Lion, 1961,
    West German-British
WORLD IN MY POCKET   MGM, 1962, West German-
    French-Italian
THE COMEDY MAN   Continental, 1964, British
CROSSPLOT   United Artists, 1969, British
HOFFMAN   Levitt-Pickman, 1971, British
SAY HELLO TO YESTERDAY   Cinerama Releasing
    Corporation, 1971, British
THE ADVENTURES OF DON QUIXOTE (TF)   Universal
    TV/BBC, 1973, U.S.-British
KING SOLOMON'S TREASURE   Filmco Limited,
    1978, Canadian
CITY ON FIRE!   Avco Embassy, 1979, Canadian
DEATH SHIP   Avco Embassy, 1980, Canadian
DIRTY TRICKS   Avco Embassy, 1981, Canadian
A VOYAGE ROUND MY FATHER (TF)   Thames TV/D.L.
    Taffner Ltd., 1983, British
THE FIRST OLYMPICS—ATHENS 1896 (MS)   Larry
    White-Gary Allison Productions/Columbia TV, 1984
PARADISE POSTPONED (MS)   Euston Films,
    1985, British

ALEXANDER RAMATI

Contact: Writers Guild of America - Los Angeles,
    213/550-1000

SANDS OF BEERSHEBA   *REBELS AGAINST THE LIGHT*
    Landau-Unger, 1964, U.S.-Israeli
THE ASSISI UNDERGROUND   Cannon, 1985,
    Italian-British
AND THE VIOLINS STOPPED PLAYING   David Films/
    Film Polski, 1989, Polish-U.S.

HAROLD RAMIS*

b. November 21, 1944 - Chicago, Illinois
Agent: CAA - Beverly Hills, 213/288-4545

CADDYSHACK   Orion/Warner Bros., 1980
NATIONAL LAMPOON'S VACATION   Warner Bros., 1983
CLUB PARADISE   Warner Bros., 1986

PATRICK RAND

Agent: William Morris Agency - Beverly Hills, 213/274-7451

MOM   Triumph Releasing Corporation, 1990

JOHN RANDALL

b. January 22, 1929 - Oakland, California
Business: Cinetex, P.O. Box 3584, Chula Vista, CA 92011,
    619/420-2053

DEADLY REEF   Cinetex, 1978
J. J. GARCIA   Filmrand, 1984

TONY RANDEL

Agent: Todd Moyer, Vanguard - Los Angles, 213/829-5000

HELLBOUND: HELLRAISER II   New World, 1988,
    British-U.S.
CHILDREN OF THE NIGHT   Fangoria Films, 1990

ARTHUR RANKIN, JR.

Business: Rankin-Bass Productions, Inc., 1 East 53rd
    Street, New York, NY 10022, 212/759-7721

WILLY McBEAN AND HIS MAGIC MACHINE (AF)   1967
THE HOBBIT (ATF)   co-director with Jules Bass,
    Rankin-Bass Productions, 1979
THE RETURN OF THE KING (ATF)   co-director with
    Jules Bass, Rankin-Bass Productions, 1979
THE LAST UNICORN (AF)   co-director with Jules Bass,
    Jensen Farley Pictures, 1982
THE FLIGHT OF DRAGONS (ATF)   co-director with
    Jules Bass, Rankin-Bass Productions, 1986
THE WIND IN THE WILLOWS (ATF)   co-director with Jules
    Bass, Rankin-Bass Productions, 1987, filmed in 1985

FREDERIC RAPHAEL

b. 1931 - Chicago, Illinois
Agent: William Morris Agency - Los Angeles, 213/550-4000

SOMETHING'S WRONG (TF)   BBC, 1978, British
WOMEN AND MEN (CTF)   co-director with Tony Richardson
    & Ken Russell, HBO Showcase, 1990

I. C. RAPOPORT*

Home: 559 Muskingum Avenue, Pacific Palisades, CA
    90272, 213/454-3120
Agent: Elliot Webb, Broder-Kurland-Webb-Uffner Agency -
    Los Angeles, 213/656-9262

THOU SHALT NOT KILL (TF)   Edgar J. Scherick
    Associates/Warner Bros. TV, 1982

JEAN-PAUL RAPPANEAU

Contact: French Film Office, 745 Fifth Avenue, New York,
    NY 10151, 212/832-8860

LA VIE DE CHATEAU   1965, French
LES MARIES DE L'AN   1970, French
LE SAUVAGE   1975, French
TOUT FEU TOUT FLAMME   1982, French
CYRANO DE BERGERAC   Orion Classics, 1990, French

IRVING RAPPER

b. 1898 - London, England
Home: 1033 Hilgard Avenue, Los Angeles, CA 90024,
213/208-8717

SHINING VICTORY   Warner Bros., 1941
ONE FOOT IN HEAVEN   Warner Bros., 1941
THE GAY SISTERS   Warner Bros., 1942
NOW, VOYAGER   Warner Bros., 1942
THE ADVENTURES OF MARK TWAIN   Warner
    Bros., 1944
THE CORN IS GREEN   Warner Bros., 1945
RHAPSODY IN BLUE   Warner Bros., 1945
DECEPTION   Warner Bros., 1946
THE VOICE OF THE TURTLE   Warner Bros., 1947
ANNA LUCASTA   Columbia, 1949
THE GLASS MENAGERIE   Warner Bros., 1950
ANOTHER MAN'S POISON   United Artists, 1952, British
BAD FOR EACH OTHER   Columbia, 1954
FOREVER FEMALE   Paramount, 1954
STRANGE INTRUDER   Allied Artists, 1956
THE BRAVE ONE   Universal, 1956
MARJORIE MORNINGSTAR   Warner Bros., 1958
THE MIRACLE   Warner Bros., 1959
THE STORY OF JOSEPH AND HIS BRETHREN
    GIUSEPPE VENDUTO DAI FRATELLI   co-director
    with Luciano Ricci, Colorama, 1960, Italian
PONTIUS PILATE   US Films, 1962, Italian-French
THE CHRISTINE JORGENSEN STORY   United
    Artists, 1970
BORN AGAIN   Avco Embassy, 1978

STEVE RASH*

Home: P.O. Box 455, Forest Grove, PA 18922

THE BUDDY HOLLY STORY   Columbia, 1978
UNDER THE RAINBOW   Orion/Warner Bros., 1981
VANISHING AMERICA (CTF)   Showtime, 1985
CAN'T BUY ME LOVE   Buena Vista, 1987
QUEENS LOGIC   New Century/Vista, 1990

DANIEL RASKOV

WEDDING BAND   I.R.S. World Media, 1990
MASTERS OF MENACE   New Line Cinema, 1990

HARRY RASKY*

b. 1928 - Toronto, Ontario, Canada
Business: CBC, Box 500, Terminal A, Toronto, Ontario
    M5W 1E6, Canada 416/975-6888
Business Manager: Bill Barnes, 900 Third Avenue,
    New York, NY 10022, 212/838-4788

PANAMA: DANGER ZONE (TD)   1960
THE LION AND THE CROSS (TD)   1961
MAHATMA: THE GREAT SOUL (TD)   1962
ELEANOR ROOSEVELT: FIRST LADY OF THE
    WORLD (TD)   1963
THE NOBEL PRIZE (TD)   1964
CUBA AND CASTRO TODAY (TD)   1965
HALL OF KINGS (TD)   1967
ZOOS OF THE WORLD (TD)   1968
THE LEGEND OF SILENT NIGHT (TD)   1969
UPON THIS ROCK (FD)   Levitt-Pickman, 1971
THE WIT AND WORLD OF G. BERNARD SHAW (TD)
    1972, Canadian-British
AN INVITATION TO THE ROYAL WEDDING (TD)   1973,
    Canadian-U.S.
TENNESSEE WILLIAMS' SOUTH (TD)   1973, Canadian
NEXT YEAR IN JERUSALEM (TD)   1973, Canadian

HOMAGE TO CHAGALL: THE COLORS OF LOVE (FD)
    CBC/Maragall Productions, 1975
TRAVELS THROUGH LIFE WITH LEACOCK (TD)
    1976, Canadian
ARTHUR MILLER ON HOME GROUND (FD)
    1979, Canadian
THE SONG OF LEONARD COHEN (TD)   1979, Canadian
THE MAN WHO HID ANNE FRANK (TD)   1980, Canadian
THE SPIES WHO NEVER WERE (TD)   1981, Canadian
BEING DIFFERENT (TD)   Astral Films, 1981, Canadian
STRATASPHERE (TD)   1982, Canadian
RAYMOND MASSEY: ACTOR OF THE CENTURY (TD)
    1982, Canadian
THE MYSTERY OF HENRY MOORE (TD)   1984, Canadian
KARSH, THE SEARCHING EYE (TD)   1986, Canadian
TO MEND THE WORLD (TD)   CBC, 1987, Canadian
DEGAS (TD)   1988, Canadian
NORTHROP FRYE (TD)   1989, Canadian

TINA RATHBORNE

Home: 397 Washington Street, New York, NY 10013,
    212/925-5986
Agent: ICM - Los Angeles, 213/550-4000

THE JOY THAT KILLS (TF)   Cypress Point
    Productions, 1985
ZELLY & ME   Columbia, 1988

DAVID RATHOD

b. July 15, 1952 - Chicago, Illinois
Business: P.O. Box 536, Fairfax, CA 94930, 415/457-3500

WEST IS WEST   Rathod Productions, 1989

OUSAMA RAWI*

b. May 3, 1939 - Baghdad, Iraq
Business: Rawi Sherman, 41 Peter Street, Toronto,
    Ontario M5V 2G2, Canada, 416/593-5969

THE HOUSEKEEPER   *A JUDGEMENT IN STONE*   Castle
    Hill Productions, 1986, Canadian

FRED OLEN RAY

Business: American-Independent Productions, Inc.,
    6515 Sunset Blvd. - Suite 402, Hollywood, CA 90028,
    213/856-9369

SCALPS   21st Century Distribution, 1984
THE TOMB   Trans World Entertainment, 1985
COMMANDO SQUAD   Trans World Entertainment, 1986
ARMED RESPONSE   CineTel, 1986
CYCLONE   CineTel, 1987
PRISON SHIP: THE ADVENTURES OF TAURA, PART I
    STAR SLAMMER   Worldwide Entertainment, 1987
DEMENTED DEATH FARM MASSACRE   co-director with
    Donn Davison, Troma, 1987
DEEP SPACE   Trans World Entertainment, 1987
HOLLYWOOD CHAINSAW HOOKERS   Camp Motion
    Pictures/ American-Independent , 1988
DEMON SWORD   American-Independent, 1989
THE PHANTOM EMPIRE   American-Independent, 1989,
    filmed in 1986
BEVERLY HILLS VAMP   American-Independent, 1989
WARLORDS   American-Independent, 1989
ALIENATOR   American-Independent, 1989
HAUNTING FEAR   American-Independent, 1990
BAD GIRLS FROM MARS   Vidmark, 1990
MOB BOSS   Vidmark, 1990
SPIRITS   Cinema Group Productions, 1990

SATYAJIT RAY

b. May 2, 1921 - Calcutta, India
Address: Flat 8, 1/1 Bishop Lefroy Road,
   Calcutta 20, India
Contact: Films Division, Ministry of Information &
   Broadcasting, 24 Dr G Beshmukh Marg, Bombay
   40026, India, 36-1461

PATHER PANCHALI   Harrison, 1955, Indian
APARAJITO   Harrison, 1956, Indian
PARAS PATHAR   1957, Indian
THE MUSIC ROOM   Harrison, 1958, Indian
THE WORLD OF APU   Harrison, 1959, Indian
DEVI   Harrison, 1960, Indian
RABINDRANATH TAGORE   1961, Indian
TWO DAUGHTERS   Janus, 1961, Indian
KANCHENJUNGHA   Harrison, 1962, Indian
ABHIJAN   1962, Indian
MAHANAGAR   1963, Indian
CHARULATA *THE LONELY WIFE*   Trans-World,
   1964, Indian
KAPURUSH-O-MAHAPURUSH   1966, Indian
NAYAK   1966, Indian
CHIRIAKHANA   1967, Indian
GOOPY GYNE BAGHA BYNE   Purnima Pictures,
   1968, Indian
DAYS AND NIGHTS IN THE FOREST   Pathe
   Contemporary, 1970, Indian
THE ADVERSARY   Audio Brandon, 1971, Indian
SIKKIM   1971, Indian
THE INNER EYE   1972, Indian
SIMABADDHA   1972, Indian
DISTANT THUNDER   Cinema 5, 1973, Indian
SONAR KELLA   1974, Indian
BALA   1976, Indian
THE MIDDLEMAN   Bauer International,
   1976, Indian
THE CHESS PLAYERS   Creative, 1977, Indian
JOI BABA FELUNATH   1978, Indian
HEERAK RAJAR DESHE   1979, Indian
THE ELEPHANT GOD   R.D. Bansal & Company,
   1979, Indian
THE KINGDOM OF DIAMONDS (TF)   GOVWB,
   1980, Indian
SADGATI   1982, Indian
THE HOME AND THE WORLD   European Classics,
   1984, Indian
GANASHATRU   National Film Development Corporation
   of India, 1989, Indian
THE BRANCHES OF THE TREE   Erato Film/DD
   Productions/AAA/Satyajit Ray Productions, 1990,
   French-Indian

ERIC RED

Agent: Bauer Benedek Agency - Los Angeles,
   213/275-2421

COHEN & TATE   Hemdale, 1988

ROBERT REDFORD*

b. August 18, 1937 - Santa Monica, California
Business: Wildwood Productions, 100 University City
   Plaza, Universal City, CA 91608, 818/777-5505
Agent: CAA - Beverly Hills, 213/288-4545

ORDINARY PEOPLE★★   Paramount, 1980
THE MILAGRO BEANFIELD WAR   Universal, 1988

JERRY REED*

b. March 20, 1937
Address: 116 Wilson Peak - Suite 210, Brentwood, TN
   37027, 615/377-3038

WHAT COMES AROUND   W.O. Associates, 1986

CLIVE REES

Address: 11 Portland Mews, London W1V 3FJ, England,
   71/439-1555

WHEN THE WHALES CAME   20th Century Fox,
   1989, British

JERRY REES

Agent: Bauer Benedek Agency - Los Angeles, 213/275-2421

THE BRAVE LITTLE TOASTER (AF)   Hyperion-Kushner-
   Locke Productions, 1987
THE MARRYING MAN   Buena Vista, 1991

GEOFFREY REEVE

b. October 28, 1932 - Tring, Hertfordshire, England
Home: Oldgarth, South Newington, Near Banbury,
   Oxfordshire 0X15 4JW, England, 0295/721337
Business: Geoff Reeve Pictures Ltd., Cannon Elstree
   Studios, Borehamwood, Herts WD6 1JG, England,
   71/953-1600

PUPPET ON A CHAIN   co-director with Don Sharp,
   Cinerama Releasing Corporation, 1972, British
CARAVAN TO VACCARES   Bryanston, 1976,
   British-French
SOUVENIR (CTF)   Fancyfree Productions Ltd.,
   1988, British

PATRICK REGAN*

b. January 23, 1939 - Los Angeles, California
Home: 3680 Will Rogers Station, Santa Monica, CA 90403,
   213/393-2734
Business: Silver-Regan Productions, The Culver Studios,
   9336 W. Washington Blvd., Culver City, CA 90230,
   213/559-0346

KISS DADDY GOODBYE   Pendragon Film Ltd./Wrightwood
   Entertainment, 1981

GODFREY REGGIO

KOYAANISQATSI   Island Alive/New Cinema, 1983
POWAQQATSI   Cannon, 1988

FRANÇOIS REICHENBACH

b. July 3, 1922 - Paris, France
Home: 20 rue Bayen, 75017 Paris, France, 04/572-0153
Business: Films du Prisme, 72 bis Rue de la Tour, 75016
   Paris, France, 04/504-4229
Contact: French Film Office, 745 Fifth Avenue, New York,
   NY 10151, 212/832-8860

L'AMERIQUE INSOLITE (FD)   1960, French
UN COEUR GROS COMME CA (FD)   1961, French
LES AMOUREAUX DU "FRANCE" (FD)   co-director with
   Pierre Grimblat, 1963, French
GRENOBLE (FD)   co-director with Claude Lelouch, United
   Producers of America, 1968, French
MEXICO MEXICO (FD)   1969, French
ARTHUR RUBINSTEIN: LOVE OF LIFE (FD)   co-director
   with Gerard Patris, New Yorker, 1970, French

L'INDISCRETE (FD) 1970, French
MEDICINE BALL CARAVAN (FD) Warner Bros., 1971, French-U.S.
YEHUDI MENUHIN - CHEMIN DE LUMIERE (FD) co-director with Bernard Gavoty, 1971, French
LA RAISON DU PLUS FOU Gaumont, 1973, French
JOHNNY HALLYDAY (FD) Prodis, 1972, French
LE HOLD-UP AU CRAYON (FD) Films du Prisme, 1973, French
DON'T YOU HEAR THE DOGS BARK? co-director with Noel Howard, 1975, Mexican-French
SEX O'CLOCK USA (FD) 1976
ANOTHER WAY TO LIVE (FD) 1976
PELE (FD) Televisa, 1977, French-Mexican
HOUSTON, TEXAS (FD) Camera One/TFI/Prisme Films, 1980, French
FRANÇOIS REICHENBACH'S JAPAN (FD) CIDIF, 1983, French

MARK REICHERT
UNION CITY Kinesis, 1980

ALASTAIR REID*
b. July 21, 1939 - Edinburgh, Scotland
Address: The Old Stores, Curload, St. Gregory, Taunton, Somerset, England, 08/236-9645
Agent: Louisa Stevenson, PTA, Bugle House, 21a Noel Street, London W1V 3PD, England, 71/434-9513

BABY LOVE Avco Embassy, 1969, British
THE NIGHT DIGGER MGM, 1971, British
SOMETHING TO HIDE 1971, British
SIX FACES (TF) 1972, British
A BURNT-OUT CASE (TF) 1973, British
THE FILE ON JILL HATCH (TF) WNET-13/BBC, 1983, U.S.-British
MAN ON THE SCREEN (TF) 1983, British
THE SECRET SERVANT (TF) BBC/Channel 7, 1984, British-Australian
THE DEAD OF JERICHO (TF) Zenith Productions, 1986, British
THE STORY OF A RECLUSE (TF) BBC, 1987, British
THE WOLVERCOTE TONGUE (TF) Zenith Productions, 1987, British
TRAFFIK (MS) Picture Partnership Productions/Channel Four, 1989, British

JOHN REID
Business: Plumb Productions Ltd., P.O. Box 2070, Wellington, New Zealand, 4/851-283

MIDDLE AGE SPREAD Endeavour Productions/New Zealand Film Commission, 1979, New Zealand
CARRY ME BACK Kiwi Films/New Zealand Film Commission, 1982, New Zealand
LEAVE ALL FAIR Pacific Films, 1985, New Zealand

MAX REID*
b. November 19, 1944 - Berkeley, California
Home: 15243 Earlham Street, Pacific Palisades, CA 90272, 213/459-5196
Agent: Jeff Thal, The Lantz Office - Los Angeles, 213/858-1144

WILD THING Atlantic Releasing Corporation, 1987, U.S.-Canadian
TEEN ANGEL (CTF) The Disney Channel, 1989
MATCH POINT (CTF) The Disney Channel, 1989
SNAKE EYES Jacques Sandoz Productions, 1990, French

WILLIAM REILLY
MEN OF RESPECT Central City Films, 1990

CARL REINER*
b. March 20, 1922 - Bronx, New York
Home: 714 N. Rodeo Drive, Beverly Hills, CA
Agent: William Morris Agency - Beverly Hills, 213274-7451
Business Manager: George Shapiro, Shapiro-West, 141 El Camino Drive, Beverly Hills, CA 90212, 213/278-8896

ENTER LAUGHING Columbia, 1967
THE COMIC Columbia, 1969
WHERE'S POPPA? United Artists, 1970
THE ONE AND ONLY Paramount, 1978
OH, GOD! Warner Bros., 1978
THE JERK Universal, 1979
DEAD MEN DON'T WEAR PLAID Universal, 1979
THE MAN WITH TWO BRAINS Warner Bros., 1983
ALL OF ME Universal, 1984
SUMMER RENTAL Paramount, 1985
SUMMER SCHOOL Paramount, 1987
BERT RIGBY, YOU'RE A FOOL Warner Bros., 1989
SIBLING RIVALRY Columbia, 1991

JEFFREY REINER
BLOOD AND CONCRETE IRS World Media, 1990

LUCAS REINER
THE SPIRIT OF '76 Black Diamond Productions, 1990

ROB REINER*
b. March 6, 1945 - Beverly Hills, California
Agent: CAA - Beverly Hills, 213/288-4545
Business: Castle Rock Entertainment, 335 N. Maple Drive - Suite 135, Beverly Hills, CA 90210, 213/285-2300

THIS IS SPINAL TAP Embassy, 1984
THE SURE THING Embassy, 1985
STAND BY ME Columbia, 1986
THE PRINCESS BRIDE 20th Century Fox, 1987
WHEN HARRY MET SALLY... Columbia, 1989
MISERY Columbia, 1990

AL REINERT
Business: Apollo Associates, 1815 Norfolk Street, Houston, TX 77098

FOR ALL MANKIND (FD) Apollo Associates, 1989

DEBORAH REINISCH
Agent: Bauer Benedek Agency - Los Angeles, 213/275-2421

ASK ME AGAIN (TF) DBR Films Ltd./American Playhouse, 1989
ANDRE'S MOTHER (TF) DBR Films, 1990

ALLEN REISNER*
b. New York, New York
Home: 9165 Cordell Drive, Los Angeles, CA 90069, 213/274-2844
Agent: Arnold Soloway, The Artists Group - Los Angeles, 213/552-1100

ST. LOUIS BLUES Paramount, 1958
ALL MINE TO GIVE THE DAY THEY GAVE BABIES AWAY Universal, 1958
TO DIE IN PARIS (TF) co-director with Charles Dubin, Universal TV, 1968

YOUR MONEY OR YOUR WIFE (TF)   Brentwood
   Productions, 1972
CAPTAINS AND THE KINGS (MS)   co-director with
   Douglas Heyes, Universal TV, 1976
MARY JANE HARPER CRIED LAST NIGHT (TF)
   Paramount TV, 1977
COPS AND ROBIN (TF)   Paramount TV, 1978
THE LOVE TAPES (TF)   Christiana Productions/
   MGM TV, 1980

KAREL REISZ*
b. July 21, 1926 - Ostrava, Czechoslovakia
Address: 2 Lower St. James Street, London W1, England,
   01/437-7015
Agent: Sam Cohn, ICM - New York City, 213/556-5600

WE ARE THE LAMBETH BOYS   Rank, 1958, British
SATURDAY NIGHT AND SUNDAY MORNING
   Continental, 1961, British
NIGHT MUST FALL   Embassy, 1964, British
MORGAN! *MORGAN: A SUITABLE CASE FOR
   TREATMENT* Cinema 5, 1966, British
ISADORA *THE LOVES OF ISADORA* Universal,
   1969, British
THE GAMBLER   Paramount, 1974
WHO'LL STOP THE RAIN   United Artists, 1978
THE FRENCH LIEUTENANT'S WOMAN   United Artists,
   1981, British
SWEET DREAMS   Tri-Star, 1985
EVERYBODY WINS   Orion, 1990, British-U.S.

IVAN REITMAN*
b. October 26, 1946 - Czechoslovakia
Agent: CAA - Beverly Hills, 213/288-4545

FOXY LADY   Ivan Reitman Productions, 1971, Canadian
CANNIBAL GIRLS   American International, 1973,
   Canadian
MEATBALLS   Paramount, 1979, Canadian
STRIPES   Columbia, 1981
GHOSTBUSTERS   Columbia, 1984
LEGAL EAGLES   Universal, 1986
TWINS   Universal, 1988
GHOSTBUSTERS II   Columbia, 1989
KINDERGARTEN COP   Universal, 1991

NORMAN RENE
LONGTIME COMPANION   Samuel Goldwyn
   Company, 1990

BARBARA RENNIE
Agent: CAA - Beverly Hills, 213/288-4545

SACRED HEARTS (TF)   Channel Four, 1985, British
ECHOES   Working Title Productions/Channel Four, 1
   988, British

ALAIN RESNAIS
b. June 3, 1922 - Vannes, France
Address: 70 rue des Plantes, 75014 Paris, France
Contact: French Film Office, 745 Fifth Avenue, New York,
   NY 10151, 212/832-8860

HIROSHIMA, MON AMOUR   Zenith, 1959, French
LAST YEAR AT MARIENBAD   Astor, 1961, French-Italian
MURIEL   Lopert, 1963, French-Italian
LA GUERRE EST FINIE   Brandon, 1966, French-Swedish
FAR FROM VIETNAM (FD)   co-director with Jean-Luc
   Godard, William Klein, Claude Lelouch, Agnes Varda &
   Joris Ivens, New Yorker, 1967, French

JE T'AIME, JE T'AIME   New Yorker, 1968, French-Spanish
STAVISKY   Cinemation, 1974, French
PROVIDENCE   Cinema 5, 1977, French-Swiss
MON ONCLE D'AMERIQUE   New World, 1980, French
LIFE IS A BED OF ROSES   *LA VIE EST UN ROMAN*
   Spectrafilm, 1983, French
L'AMOUR A MORT   Roissy Film, 1984, French
MELO   European Classics, 1986, French
I WANT TO GO HOME   MK2/Films A2/La Sept,
   1989, French

ROBERT RESNIKOFF
Agent: Bauer Benedek Agency - Los Angeles, 213/275-2421

THE FIRST POWER   Orion, 1990

BURT REYNOLDS*
b. February 11, 1936 - Waycross, Georgia
Agent: William Morris Agency - Beverly Hills, 213/274-7451
Business Manager: Global Business Management -
   Beverly Hills, 213/278-4141

GATOR   United Artists, 1976
THE END   United Artists, 1978
SHARKY'S MACHINE   Orion/Warner Bros., 1982
STICK   Universal, 1985

GENE REYNOLDS*
b. April 4, 1925 - Cleveland, Ohio
Agent: CAA - Beverly Hills, 213/288-4545

IN DEFENSE OF KIDS (TF)   MTM Enterprises, 1983
DOING LIFE (TF)   Castilian Productions/Phoenix
   Entertainment Group, 1986
TALES FROM THE HOLLYWOOD HILLS: GOLDEN
   LAND (TF)   WNET-NY/ Zenith Productions, 1988

KEVIN REYNOLDS*
b. January 17, 1952 - San Antonio, Texas
Agent: William Morris Agency - Beverly Hills, 213/274-7451
Business: Windmill Films, Inc., 5201 Lake Jackson, Waco,
   TX 76710, 213/506-1690

FANDANGO   Warner Bros., 1985
THE BEAST   Columbia, 1988

MARK REZYKA
b. 1949 - Breslau, Poland

SOUTH OF RENO   Open Road Productions/Pendulum
   Productions, 1987

DAVID LOWELL RICH*
b. August 31, 1920 - New York, New York
Home: 12216 Linda Flora Drive, Ojai, CA 93023,
   805/649-1042
Agent: Christine Foster, The Agency - Los Angeles,
   213/551-3000

NO TIME TO BE YOUNG   Columbia, 1957
SENIOR PROM   Columbia, 1958
HEY BOY! HEY GIRL!   Columbia, 1959
HAVE ROCKET, WILL TRAVEL   Columbia, 1959
SEE HOW THEY RUN (TF)   Universal TV, 1964
MADAME X   Universal, 1966
THE PLAINSMAN   Universal, 1966
ROSIE!   Universal, 1967
WINGS OF FIRE (TF)   Universal TV, 1967
THE BORGIA STICK (TF)   Universal TV, 1967

A LOVELY WAY TO DIE   Universal, 1968
THREE GUNS FOR TEXAS   co-director with Paul
    Stanley & Earl Bellamy, Universal, 1968
MARCUS WELBY, M.D. (TF)   Universal TV, 1969
EYE OF THE CAT   Universal, 1969
THE MASK OF SHEBA (TF)   MGM TV, 1970
BERLIN AFFAIR (TF)   Universal TV, 1970
THE SHERIFF (TF)   Screen Gems/Columbia TV, 1971
ASSIGNMENT: MUNICH (TF)   MGM TV, 1972
LIEUTENANT SCHUSTER'S WIFE (TF)   Universal
    TV, 1972
ALL MY DARLING DAUGHTERS (TF)   Universal TV, 1972
THAT MAN BOLT   co-director with Henry Levin,
    Universal, 1972
THE JUDGE AND JAKE WYLER (TF)   Universal TV, 1972
SET THIS TOWN ON FIRE (TF)   Universal TV, 1973
THE HORROR AT 37,000 FEET (TF)   CBS, Inc., 1973
BROCK'S LAST CASE (TF)   Talent Associates/Universal
    TV, 1973
CRIME CLUB (TF)   CBS, Inc., 1973
BEG, BORROW...OR STEAL (TF)   Universal TV, 1973
SATAN'S SCHOOL FOR GIRLS (TF)   Spelling-Goldberg
    Productions, 1973
RUNAWAY! (TF)   Universal TV, 1973
DEATH RACE (TF)   Universal TV, 1973
THE CHADWICK FAMILY (TF)   Universal TV, 1974
THE SEX SYMBOL (TF)   Screen Gems/Columbia, 1974
ALOHA MEANS GOODBYE (TF)   Universal TV, 1974
THE DAUGHTERS OF JOSHUA CABE RETURN (TF)
    Spelling-Goldberg Productions, 1975
ADVENTURES OF THE QUEEN (TF)   20th Century-
    Fox TV, 1975
YOU LIE SO DEEP, MY LOVE (TF)   Universal TV, 1975
BRIDGER (TF)   Universal TV, 1976
THE SECRET LIFE OF JOHN CHAPMAN (TF)   The
    Jozak Company, 1976
THE STORY OF DAVID (TF)   co-director with Alex Segal,
    Mildred Freed Alberg Productions/Columbia TV, 1976
SST - DEATH FLIGHT (TF)   ABC Circle Films, 1977
RANSOM FOR ALICE! (TF)   Universal TV, 1977
TELETHON (TF)   ABC Circle Films, 1977
THE DEFECTION OF SIMAS KUDIRKA (TF) ☆☆   The
    Jozak Company/ Paramount TV, 1978
A FAMILY UPSIDE DOWN (TF)   Ross Hunter-Jacques
    Mapes Film/Paramount TV, 1978
LITTLE WOMEN (TF)   Universal TV, 1978
THE CONCORDE - AIRPORT '79   Universal, 1979
NURSE (TF)   Robert Halmi, Inc., 1980
ENOLA GAY (TF)   The Production Company/
    Viacom, 1980
CHU CHU AND THE PHILLY FLASH   20th Century-
    Fox, 1981
THURSDAY'S CHILD (TF)   The Catalina Production
    Group/Viacom, 1983
THE FIGHTER (TF)   Martin Manulis Productions/The
    Catalina Production Group, 1983
I WANT TO LIVE (TF)   United Artists Corporation, 1983
THE SKY'S THE LIMIT (TF)   Palance-Levy
    Productions, 1984
HIS MISTRESS (TF)   David L. Wolper Productions/
    Warner Bros. TV, 1984
THE HEARST AND DAVIES AFFAIR (TF)   ABC Circle
    Films, 1985
SCANDAL SHEET (TF)   Fair Dinkum Productions, 1985
THE DEFIANT ONES (TF)   MGM-UA TV, 1986
CHOICES (TF)   Robert Halmi, Inc., 1986
CONVICTED (TF)   Larry A. Thompson Productions, 1986
INFIDELITY (TF)   Mark-Jett Productions/ABC Circle
    Films, 1987

JOHN RICH*
b. July 6, 1925 - Rockaway Beach, New York
Agent: CAA - Beverly Hills, 213/288-4545

WIVES AND LOVERS   Paramount, 1963
THE NEW INTERNS   Columbia, 1964
ROUSTABOUT   Paramount, 1964
BOEING BOEING   Paramount, 1965
EASY COME, EASY GO   Paramount, 1967

RICHARD RICH
THE FOX AND THE HOUND (AF)   co-director with Art
    Stevens & Ted Berman, Buena Vista, 1981
THE BLACK CAULDRON (AF)   co-director with Ted
    Berman, Buena Vista, 1985

DICK RICHARDS*
b. 1936
Agent: The Gersh Agency - Beverly Hills, 213/274-6611

THE CULPEPPER CATTLE CO.   20th Century-Fox, 1972
RAFFERTY AND THE GOLD DUST TWINS   Warner
    Bros., 1975
FAREWELL, MY LOVELY   Avco Embassy, 1975
MARCH OR DIE   Columbia, 1977, British
DEATH VALLEY   Universal, 1981
MAN, WOMAN AND CHILD   Paramount, 1983
HEAT   New Century/Vista, 1987

H. CLIVE RICHARDS
b. Jamaica
Contact: Lee Collver, Oakwood Station, 265 S. Western
    Avenue - #74343, Los Angeles, CA 90004, 213/664-6622

JAMMIN'   1989

LLOYD RICHARDS*
Address: 90 York Square, New Haven, CT 06511,
    203/436-1586

ROOTS: THE NEXT GENERATIONS (MS)   co-director with
    John Erman, Charles S. Dubin & Georg Stanford Brown,
    Wolper Productions, 1979

MARK RICHARDSON
Agent: The Gersh Agency - New York City, 212/997-1818

GOLDDIGGER   Long Island Expressway Productions, 1990

PETER RICHARDSON
Contact: British Academy of Film & Televison Arts,
    195 Piccadilly, London W1, England, 71/734-0022

THE SUPERGRASS   Hemdale, 1985, British
EAT THE RICH   New Line Cinema, 1987, British
THE COMIC STRIP PRESENTS...THE STRIKE (TF)
    co-director with Pete Richens, Channel Four,
    1988, British

TONY RICHARDSON*
(Cecil Antonio Richardson)
b. June 5, 1928 - Shipley, England
Business: 1478 N. Kings Road, Los Angeles, CA 90069,
    213/656-5314
Agent: William Morris Agency - Beverly Hills, 213/274-7451

LOOK BACK IN ANGER   Warner Bros., 1958, British
THE ENTERTAINER   Continental, 1960, British

SANCTUARY   20th Century-Fox, 1961
A TASTE OF HONEY   Continental, 1962, British
THE LONELINESS OF THE LONG DISTANCE RUNNER
   Continental, 1962, British
TOM JONES★★   Lopert, 1963, British, re-released
   by The Samuel Goldwyn Company in 1989
THE LOVED ONE   MGM, 1965
MADEMOISELLE   Lopert, 1966, French-British
THE SAILOR FROM GIBRALTER   Lopert, 1967, British
THE CHARGE OF THE LIGHT BRIGADE   United Artists,
   1968, British
LAUGHTER IN THE DARK   Lopert, 1969, British-French
HAMLET   Columbia, 1969, British
NED KELLY   United Artists, 1970, British
A DELICATE BALANCE   American Film Theatre, 1973
DEAD CERT   United Artists, 1973, British
JOSEPH ANDREWS   Paramount, 1977, British
A DEATH IN CANAAN (TF)   Chris-Rose Productions/
   Warner Bros. TV, 1978
THE BORDER   Universal, 1982
THE HOTEL NEW HAMPSHIRE   Orion, 1984
PENALTY PHASE (TF)   Tamara Asseyev Productions/
   New World TV, 1986
BERYL MARKHAM: A SHADOW ON THE SUN (TF)
   Tamara Asseyev Productions/New World TV, 1988
THE PHANTOM OF THE OPERA (TF)   Saban-Scherick
   Productions, 1990
WOMEN AND MEN (CTF)   co-director with Ken Russell &
   Frederic Raphael, HBO Showcase, 1990
BLUE SKY   Orion, 1991

WILLIAM RICHERT*
Contact: Directors Guild of America - Los Angeles,
   213/289-2000

FIRST POSITION (FD)   Roninfilm, 1973
WINTER KILLS   Avco Embassy, 1979
THE AMERICAN SUCCESS CO. *SUCCESS* Columbia,
   1979, West German-U.S.
A NIGHT IN THE LIFE OF JIMMY REARDON   20th
   Century Fox, 1988

ANTHONY RICHMOND*
b. July 7, 1942 - London, England
Business Manager: Harry Schaffer, Guild Management,
   9911 W. Pico Blvd., Los Angeles, CA 90035,
   213/277-9711

DEJA VU   Cannon, 1985, British

W. D. RICHTER*
Agent: Shapiro-Lichtman Agency - Los Angeles,
   213/859-8877

THE ADVENTURES OF BUCKAROO BANZAI: ACROSS
   THE 8TH DIMENSION   20th Century Fox, 1984
LATE FOR DINNER   Columbia, 1991

TOM RICKMAN*
(James Thomas Rickman)
Agent: CAA - Beverly Hills, 213/288-4545

THE RIVER RAT   Paramount, 1984

PHILIP RIDLEY
Contact: British Academy of Film & Television Arts,
   195 Piccadilly, London W1, England, 71/734-0022

THE REFLECTING SKIN   Zenith/BBC/British Screen,
   1990, British-Canadian

WILLIAM RIEAD
SCORPION   Crown International, 1986

LENI RIEFENSTAHL
(Helene Bertha Amalie Riefenstahl)
b. August 22, 1902 - Berlin, Germany
Contact: German Film & TV Academy, Pommernallee 1,
   1 Berlin 19, West Germany, 0311/302-6096

THE BLUE LIGHT   Du World, 1932, German
SIEG DES GLAUBENS   1933, German
TRIUMPH OF THE WILL (FD)   Contemporary,
   1935, German
TAG DER FREIHEIT - UNSERE WEHRMACHT (FD)
   1935, German
OLYMPIAD, PART I: FESTIVAL OF THE NATIONS (FD)
   Contemporary, 1938, German
OLYMPIAD, PART II: FESTIVAL OF BEAUTY (FD)
   Contemporary, 1938, German
TIEFLAND   1954, West German

ADAM RIFKIN
Agent: William Morris Agency - Beverly Hills, 213/274-7451

NEVER ON TUESDAY   Cinema Group, 1988
TALE OF TWO SISTERS   Vista Street Entertainment, 1989

WOLF RILLA
Home: Moulin de la Camandoule, Chemin N-D des Cypre,
   83440 France

VILLAGE OF THE DAMNED   MGM, 1960, British
THE WORLD TEN TIMES OVER   1962, British
PAX?   1968, British
THE GREATER GOOD (TF)   BBC, 1972, British
ROSIE   1975, British
TRAINING SALESMEN (FD)   1980, British

ARTURO RIPSTEIN
b. 1943 - Mexico City, Mexico
Contact: Azteca Films, 555 N. La Brea Avenue, P.O. Box
   36095, Hollywood, CA 90036, 213/938-2413

TIEMPO DE MORIR   Azteca Films, 1965, Mexican
H.O.   Azteca Films, 1966, Mexican
LOS RECUERDOS DEL PORVENIR   Azteca Films,
   1968, Mexican
LA HORA DE LOS NINOS   Azteca Films, 1969, Mexican
EL CASTILLO DE LA PUREZA   Azteca Films,
   1972, Mexican
EL SANTO OFICIO   Azteca Films, 1974, Mexican
FOXTROT   New World, 1975, Mexican-Swiss
LECUMBERRI   Azteca Films, 1976, Mexican
EL LUGAR SIN LIMITES   Azteca Films, 1977, Mexican
CADENA PERPETUA   Azteca Films, 1978, Mexican
LA TIA ALEXANDRA   Azteca Films, 1980, Mexican
LA SEDUCCION   Azteca Films, 1983, Mexican
RASTRO DE LA MUERTE   Azteca Films, 1983, Mexican
EL OTRO   Azteca Films, 1984, Mexican
EL IMPERIO DE LA FORTUNA   Conacine, 1986, Mexican
MENTIRASPIADOSOS   Filmicas Internacionales/Fondo de
   Apoyo, 1989, Mexican

DINO RISI
b. December 23, 1917 - Milan, Italy
Home: Residence Aldrovandi, via Aldrovandi, Rome,
   Italy, 06/804556

VACANZE COL GANGSTER   Mambretti Film, 1952, Italian

VIALE DELLA SPERANZA   Mambretti Film/ENIC,
    1953, Italian
LOVE IN THE CITY   co-director with Michelangelo
    Antonioni, Federico Fellini, Alberto Lattuada, Carlo
    Lizzani & Francesco Maselli, Italian Films Export,
    1953, Italian
IL SEGNO DI VENERE   Titanus, 1955, Italian
SCANDAL IN SORRENTO   *PANE, AMORE E...*   DCA,
    1955, Italian
POOR BUT BEAUTIFUL   Trans-Lux, 1956, Italian-French
LA NONNA SABELLA   Titanus/Franco-London Films,
    1957, Italian-French
BELLE MA POVERE   Titanus, 1957, Italian
VENEZIA, LA LUNA E TU   Titanus/Societe Generale de
    Cinematographie, 1958, Italian-French
POVERI MILIONARI   Titanus, 1958, Italian
IL VEDOVO   Paneuropa/Cino Del Duca, 1959, Italian
LOVE AND LARCENY   *IL MATTATORE*   Major Film,
    1960, Italian-French
UN AMORE A ROMA   CEI Incom/Fair Film/Laetitia Film/
    Les Films Cocinor/ Alpha Film, 1960, Italian-French-
    West German
A PORTE CHIUSE   Fair Film/Cinematografica Rire/
    Societe Generale de Cinematographie/Ultra Film/Lyre
    Film/Roxy Film, 1960, Italian- French-West German
UNA VITA DIFFICILE   Dino De Laurentiis
    Cinematographica, 1961, Italian
LA MARCIA SU ROMA   Fair Film/Orsay Films, 1962,
    Italian-French
THE EASY LIFE   *IL SORPASSO*   Embassy, 1962, Italian
IL GIOVEDI   Dino De Laurentiis Cinematografica/Center
    Film, 1963, Italian
15 FROM ROME   *I MOSTRI*   McAbee, 1963,
    Italian-French
IL GAUCHO   Fair Film/Clemente Lococo, 1964,
    Italian-Argentinian
BAMBOLE!   co-director with Luigi Comencini, Franco
    Rossi & Mauro Bolognini, Royal Films International,
    1965, Italian
I COMPLESSI   co-director with Franco Rossi & Luigi Filippo
    D'Amico, Documento Film/SPCE, 1965, Italian-French
WEEKEND, ITALIAN STYLE   *L'OMBRELLONE*   Marvin
    Films, 1965, Italian- French-Spanish
I NOSTRI MARITI   co-director with Luigi Filippo D'Amico &
    Luigi Zampa, Documento Film, 1966, Italian
TREASURE OF SAN GENNARO   *OPERAZIONE SAN
    GENNARO*   Paramount, 1966, Italian-French-
    West German
THE TIGER AND THE PUSSYCAT   *IL TIGRE*
    Embassy, 1967, Italian-U.S.
THE PROPHET   Joseph Green Pictures, 1967, Italian
STRAZIAMI DA MI BACI SAZIAMI   FIDA Cinematografica/
    Productions Jacques Roitfeld, 1968, Italian-French
VEDO NUDO   Dean Film/Jupiter Generale
    Cinematografica, 1969, Italian
IL GIOVANE NORMALE   Dean Film/Italnoleggio,
    1969, Italian
THE PRIEST'S WIFE   Warner Bros., 1970, Italian-French
NOI DONNE SIAMO FATTE COSI'   Apollo International
    Film, 1971, Italian
IN NOME DEL POPOLO ITALIANO   Apollo International
    Film, 1972, Italian
MORDI E FUGGI   C.C. Champion/Les Films Concordia,
    1973, Italian-French
HOW FUNNY CAN SEX BE?   *SESSOMATTO*   In-Frame,
    1973, Italian
TELEFONI BIANCHI   Dean Film, 1975, Italian
SCENT OF A WOMAN   20th Century-Fox, 1976, Italian
ANIMA PERSA   Dean Film/Les Productions Fox Europe,
    1977, Italian-French

LA STANZA DEL VESCOVO   Merope Film/Carlton Film
    Export/Societe Nouvelle Prodis, 1977, Italian-French
VIVA ITALIA!   *I NUOVI MOSTRI*   co-director with Mario
    Monicelli & Ettore Scola, Cinema 6, 1978, Italian
PRIMO AMORE   Dean Film, 1978, Italian
CARO PAPA'   Dean Film/AMLF/Prospect Film, 1979,
    Italian-French-Canadian
SUNDAY LOVERS   co-director with Bryan Forbes, Edouard
    Molinaro & Gene Wilder, MGM/United Artists, 1980,
    U.S.-British-Italian-French
SONO FOTOGENICO   Dean Film/Marceau Cocinor, 1980,
    Italian-French
GHOST OF LOVE   Dean Film/AMLF/Roxy Film, 1981,
    Italian-French-West German
SESSO E VOLENTIERI   Dean Film, 1982, Italian
LA VITA CONTINUA (MS)   RAI, 1984, Italian
LE BON ROI DAGOBERT   Gaumount, 1984, French-Italian
SCEMO DI GUERRA   Titanus, 1985, Italian-French
IL COMMISSARIO LO GATTO   Dean Film/Reteitalia,
    1987, Italian
TERESA   Dean Film/Reteitalia, 1987, Italian
TWO WOMEN (TF)   Reteitalia, 1989, Italian
AMORI (TF)   co-director, Reteitalia, 1989, Italian
TOLGO IL DISTURBO   International Dean Film/Starlet
    International/ Flore, 1990, Italian-French

MARCO RISI

b. June 4, 1951 - Milan, Italy
Home: via Misurina 78, Rome, Italy, 06/327-9692

APPUNTI SU HOLLYWOOD (TD)   Rail, 1978, Italian
VADO A VIVERE DA SOLO   Numero Uno Cinematografica,
    1981, Italian
UN RAGAZZO, UNA RAGAZZA   Numero Uno
    Cinematografica, 1983, Italian
COLPO DI FULMINE   Numero Uno Cinematografica,
    1984, Italian
SOLDATI. 365 ALL' ALBA   Numero Uno Cinematografica/
    Reteitalia, 1987, Italian
MERY PER SEMPRE   Numero Uno Cinematografica,
    1989, Italian
RAGAZZI FUORI   Numero Uno Cinematografica,
    1990, Italian

MICHAEL RITCHIE*

b. 1938 - Waukesha, Wisconsin
Address: 22 Miller Avenue, Mill Valley, CA 94941,
    415/383-2564
Agent: Sam Cohn, ICM - New York City, 212/556-5600
Business Manager: Marvin Freedman, Freedman,
    Kinzelberg & Broder, 1801 Avenue of the Stars -
    Suite 911, Los Angeles, CA 90067, 213/277-0700

THE OUTSIDER (TF)   Universal TV, 1967
THE SOUND OF ANGER (TF)   Universal TV, 1968
DOWNHILL RACER   Paramount, 1969
PRIME CUT   National General, 1972
THE CANDIDATE   Warner Bros., 1972
SMILE   United Artists, 1975
THE BAD NEWS BEARS   Paramount, 1976
SEMI-TOUGH   United Artists, 1978
AN ALMOST PERFECT AFFAIR   Paramount, 1979
THE ISLAND   Universal, 1980
DIVINE MADNESS (FD)   The Ladd Company/Warner
    Bros., 1980
THE SURVIVORS   Columbia, 1983
FLETCH   Universal, 1985
WILDCATS   Warner Bros., 1986
THE GOLDEN CHILD   Paramount, 1986
THE COUCH TRIP   Orion, 1988
FLETCH LIVES   Universal, 1989

MARTIN RITT*
b. March 2, 1920 - New York, New York
Agent: ICM - Los Angeles, 213/550-4000
Business Manager: Larry Martindale, Tucker, Morgan,
    Martindale, 9200 Sunset Blvd., Los Angeles, CA
    90069, 213/274-0891

EDGE OF THE CITY   MGM, 1957
NO DOWN PAYMENT   20th Century-Fox, 1957
THE LONG HOT SUMMER   MGM, 1958
THE BLACK ORCHID   Paramount, 1959
THE SOUND AND THE FURY   20th Century-Fox, 1959
FIVE BRANDED WOMEN   Paramount, 1960,
    Italian-Yugoslavian-U.S.
PARIS BLUES   United Artists, 1961
HEMINGWAY'S ADVENTURES OF A YOUNG MAN
    20th Century-Fox, 1962
HUD★   Paramount, 1963
THE OUTRAGE   MGM, 1964
THE SPY WHO CAME IN FROM THE COLD   Paramount,
    1965, British
HOMBRE   20th Century-Fox, 1967
THE BROTHERHOOD   Paramount, 1968
THE MOLLY MAGUIRES   Paramount, 1970
THE GREAT WHITE HOPE   20th Century-Fox, 1970
SOUNDER   20th Century-Fox, 1972
PETE N' TILLIE   Universal, 1972
CONRACK   20th Century-Fox, 1974
THE FRONT   Columbia, 1976
CASEY'S SHADOW   Columbia, 1978
NORMA RAE   20th Century-Fox, 1979
BACK ROADS   Warner Bros., 1981
CROSS CREEK   Universal/AFD, 1983
MURPHY'S ROMANCE   Columbia, 1985
NUTS   Universal, 1987
STANLEY & IRIS   MGM/UA, 1990

JOE RITTER
BEACH BALLS   Concorde, 1988
THE NEW GLADIATORS   Concorde, 1989

FREDERICK RITZENBERG
GOSPEL (FD)   co-director with David Leivick, 20th
    Century-Fox, 1983

JOAN RIVERS*
b. June 8, 1933 - New York, New York
Contact: Dorothy Melvin - Los Angeles,
    213/933-3764

RABBIT TEST   Avco Embassy, 1978

JACQUES RIVETTE
b. March 1, 1978 - Rouen, France
Address: 20 Boulevard de la Bastille, 75012 Paris, France

AUX QUATRE COINS   1950, French
LE QUADRILLE   1950, French
LE DIVERTISSEMENT   1952, French
LE COUP DE BERGER   1956, French
PARIS BELONGS TO US   1961, French
THE NUN   Altura, 1966, French
JEAN RENOIR, LE PATRON (FD)   1966, French
L'AMOUR FOU   1968, French
OUT 1: SPECTRE   Sunchild Productions, 1974, French
CELINE AND JULIE GO BOATING   1974, French
DUELLE   Valoria, 1976, French
NOROIT   Sunchild Productions, 1976, French
MERRY-GO-ROUND   1979, French

LE PONT DU NORD   Gerik Distribution, 1981, French
PARIS S'EN VA   1981, French
LOVE ON THE GROUND   Spectrafilm, 1984, French
HURLEVENT   *WUTHERING HEIGHTS*   AMLF,
    1985, French
LA BANDE DES QUARTRE   1989, French-Swiss

ADAM ROARKE
TRESPASSES   co-director with Loren Bivens, Shapiro
    Entertainment, 1987

ALAIN ROBBE-GRILLET
b. August 18, 1922 - Brest, France
Home: 18 Boulevard Maillot, 92200 Neuilly, France,
    1/722-3122

L'IMMORTELLE   Grove Press, 1963, French
TRANS-EUROP-EXPRESS   Trans-American,
    1967, French
THE MAN WHO LIES   Grove Press, 1968, French-Czech
L'EDEN ET APRES   Como Films, 1971,
    French-Czech-Tunisian
GLISSMENTS PROGRESSIFS DU PLAISIR   SNETC,
    1974, French
LE JEU AVEC LE FEU   Arcadie Productions, 1975,
    Italian-French
LA BELLE CAPTIVE   Argos Films, 1983, French

SEYMOUR ROBBIE*
Home: 9980 Liebe Drive, Beverly Hills, CA 90210,
    213/274-6713
Agent: Alan Greenspan, ICM - Beverly Hills,
    213/550-4428

C.C. AND COMPANY   Avco Embassy, 1970
MARCO   Cinerama Releasing Corporation, 1974

JEROME ROBBINS*
(Jerome Rabinowitz)
b. October 11, 1918 - Weehawken, New Jersey
Contact: Directors Guild of America - New York City,
    212/581-0370

WEST SIDE STORY★★   co-director with Robert Wise,
    United Artists, 1961

MATTHEW ROBBINS*
b. New York
Agent: ICM - Los Angeles, 213/550-4000

CORVETTE SUMMER   MGM/United Artists, 1978
DRAGONSLAYER   Paramount, 1981, U.S.-British
THE LEGEND OF BILLIE JEAN   Tri-Star, 1985
*batteries not included   Universal, 1987
MOTHERS, DAUGHTERS & LOVERS (TF)   Katz-Huyck
    Film Productions/NBC Productions, 1989

MIKE ROBE*
Agent: CAA - Beverly Hills, 213/288-4545

WITH INTENT TO KILL (TF)   London Productions, 1984
NEWS AT ELEVEN (TF)   Turman-Foster Productions/
    Finnegan Associates, 1986
MURDER ORDAINED (TF)   Zev Braun Productions/
    Interscope Communications, 1987
GO TOWARD THE LIGHT (TF)   Corapeak Productions/The
    Polson Company, 1988

GUTS & GLORY: THE RISE AND FALL OF OLIVER
NORTH (TF)   Mike Robe Productions/Papazian-Hirsch
Entertainment, 1989
CHILD IN THE NIGHT (TF)   Mike Robe Productions, 1990
SON OF THE MORNING STAR (TF)   Republic Pictures/
The Mount Company, 1990

GENEVIEVE ROBERT
Agent: CAA - Beverly Hills, 213/288-4545

CASUAL SEX?   Universal, 1988

YVES ROBERT
b. June 19, 1920 - Saumur, France
Contact: French Film Office, 745 Fifth Avenue, New York,
NY 10151, 212/832-8860

LES HOMMES NE PENSENT QU'A ÇA   1954, French
SIGNE ARSENE LUPIN   1959, French
LA FAMILLE FENOUILLARD   1961, French
LA GUERRE DES BOUTONS   LGE, 1962, French
BEBERT ET L'OMNIBUS   1963, French
LES COPAINS   1964, French
MONNAIRE DE SINGE   1965, French
VERY HAPPY ALEXANDER *ALEXANDER*   Cinema 5,
1968, French
CLERAMBARD   1969, French
THE TALL BLOND MAN WITH ONE BLACK SHOE
Cinema 5, 1972, French
SALUT L'ARTISTE   Exxel, 1973, French
RETURN OF THE TALL BLOND MAN WITH ONE
BLACK SHOE   Lanir Releasing, 1974, French
PARDON MON AFFAIRE *AN ELEPHANT CA TROMPE
ENORMEMENT*   First Artists, 1976, French
PARDON MON AFFAIRE, TOO! *NOUS IRONS TOUS
AU PARADIS*   First Artists, 1977, French
COURAGE FUYONS   Gaumont, 1979, French
LE JUMEAU   AAA, 1984, French
LE GLOIRE DE MON PERE   Gaumont, 1990, French

ALAN ROBERTS
Contact: Writers Guild of America, West - Los Angeles,
213/550-1000

THE ZODIAC COUPLES   co-director with Bob Stein,
SAE, 1970
PANORAMA BLUE   Ellman Film Enterprises, 1974
YOUNG LADY CHATTERLEY   PRO International, 1977
THE HAPPY HOOKER GOES HOLLYWOOD
Cannon, 1980
FLASHDANCE FEVER   Shapiro Entertainment, 1983
PRIVATE PROPERTY   Park Lane Productions, 1985

DEBORAH ROBERTS
Contact: Writers Guild of America, West - Los Angeles,
213/550-1000

FRANKENSTEIN GENERAL HOSPITAL   New Star
Entertainment, 1988

CLIFF ROBERTSON*
b. September 9, 1925 - La Jolla, California
Agent: Michael Black, ICM - Los Angeles,
213/550-4000
Business: P.O. Box 55049, Sherman Oaks, CA 91403,
818/988-1130

J.W. COOP   Columbia, 1972
THE PILOT   Summit Features, 1981

TOM G. ROBERTSON
GOOD OLD BOY (TF)   Multimedia Entertainment/The
Disney Channel/ WonderWorks, 1989

JOHN ROBINS
Home: 6637 Zumirez Drive, Malibu, CA 90265,
213/457-9966
Business Manager: Stanley Margolis, Financial Management
Inc., 6404 Wilshire Blvd. - Suite 1230, Los Angeles, CA
90048, 213/651-4141

HOT RESORT   Cannon, 1985

BRUCE ROBINSON
b. May 2, 1946 - London, England
Agent: CAA - Beverly Hills, 213/288-4545

WITHNAIL AND I   Cineplex Odeon, 1987, British
HOW TO GET AHEAD IN ADVERTISING   Warner Bros.,
1989, British

MARK ROBINSON
(John Mark Robinson)
b. 1949 - Toronto, Ontario, Canada
Business: Modern Productions, 1424 W. Washington Blvd.,
Venice, CA 90291, 213/306-1400
Agent: William Morris Agency - Beverly Hills, 213/274-7451

ROADHOUSE 66   Atlantic Releasing Corporation, 1984
KID   Tapestry Films, 1990

PHIL ALDEN ROBINSON*
Agent: William Morris Agency - Beverly Hills, 213/274-7451

IN THE MOOD *THE WOO WOO KID*   Lorimar, 1987
FIELD OF DREAMS   Universal, 1989

MARC ROCCO
Agent: Triad Artists, Inc. - Los Angeles, 213/556-2727

SCENES FROM THE GOLDMINE   Hemdale, 1988
DREAM A LITTLE DREAM   Vestron, 1989

FRANC RODDAM*
(Francis George Roddam)
b. April 29 - Stockton, England
Agent: ICM - Los Angeles, 213/550-4000

MINI (TF)   BBC, 1975, British
DUMMY (TF)   ATV Network, 1977, British
QUADROPHENIA   World Northal, 1979, British
THE LORDS OF DISCIPLINE   Paramount, 1983
THE BRIDE   Columbia, 1985, British
ARIA   co-director, Miramax Films, 1987, British
WAR PARTY   Hemdale, 1988

NICOLAS ROEG*
b. December 15, 1928 - London, England
Home: 2E Oxford-Cambridge Mansions, Old Marylebone
Road, London NW1, England, 71/262-8612
Agent: Hatton & Baker, 18 Jermyn Street, London SW1Y
6HN, England, 71/439-2971

PERFORMANCE   co-director with Donald Cammell,
Warner Bros., 1970, British
WALKABOUT   20th Century-Fox, 1971, British-Australian
DON'T LOOK NOW   Paramount, 1974, British-Italian
THE MAN WHO FELL TO EARTH   Cinema 5,
1976, British

BAD TIMING/A SENSUAL OBSESSION   World Northal,
   1980, British
EUREKA   MGM/UA Classics, 1984, British
INSIGNIFICANCE   Island Alive, 1985, British
CASTAWAY   Cannon, 1986, British
ARIA   co-director, Miramax Films, 1987, British
TRACK 29   Island Pictures, 1988
TENNESSEE WILLIAMS' SWEET BIRD OF YOUTH
   SWEET BIRD OF YOUTH (TF)   Atlantic/Kushner-
   Locke Productions, 1989
THE WITCHES   Warner Bros., 1990, British
COLD HEAVEN   New Line Cinema, 1990

MICHAEL ROEMER
b. January 1, 1928 - Berlin, Germany
Contact: Yale School of Art, Box 1605A, Yale Station,
   New Haven, CT 06520, 203/432-2600

A TOUCH OF THE TIMES   1949
THE INFERNO   *CORTILE CASCINO, ITALY* (FD)
   co-director with Robert M. Young, Robert M. Young
   Productions, 1962
NOTHING BUT A MAN   co-director with Robert M. Young,
   Cinema 5, 1965
FACES OF ISRAEL (FD)   1967
THE PLOT AGAINST HARRY   New Yorker, 1969-1989
DYING (TD)   WGBH-Boston, 1976
PILGRIM, FAREWELL   Post Mills Productions, 1980
HAUNTED (TF)   Post Mills Productions/WGBH-
   Boston, 1984

DOUG ROGERS*
Address: 846 S. Robertson, Los Angeles, CA 90035,
   213/659-9511

DENNIS THE MENACE (TF)   DIC Enterprises
   Productions, 1987

LIONEL ROGOSIN
b. 1924 - New York, New York

ON THE BOWERY (FD)   Film Representations, 1957
COME BACK, AFRICA (FD)   Rogosin, 1959
GOOD TIMES, WONDERFUL TIMES (FD)   Rogosin, 1966
BLACK ROOTS (FD)   Rogosin, 1970
BLACK FANTASY (FD)   Impact, 1972
WOODCUTTERS OF THE DEEP SOUTH (FD)
   Rogosin, 1973

ERIC ROHMER
(Jean-Marie Maurice Scherer)
b. April 4, 1920 - Nancy, France
Business: 26 Avenue Pierre-ler-de-Serbie, 75008,
   Paris, France
Contact: French Film Office, 745 Fifth Avenue, New York,
   NY 10151, 212/832-8860

LE SIGNE DU LION   1959, French
LA CARRIERE DE SUZANNE   Films du Losange,
   1963, French
PARIS VU PAR...   co-director, New Yorker, 1965, French
LA COLLECTIONNEUSE   Pathe Contemporary,
   1967, French
MY NIGHT AT MAUD'S   Pathe Contemporary,
   1970, French
CLAIRE'S KNEE   *L'AMOUR, L'APRES-MIDI*   Columbia,
   1971, French
CHLOE IN THE AFTERNOON   Columbia, 1972, French

THE MARQUISE OF O...   New Line Cinema, 1976,
   French-West German
PERCEVAL   *PERCEVAL LE GALLOIS*   New Yorker,
   1978, French
THE AVIATOR'S WIFE   New Yorker, 1981, French
LE BEAU MARIAGE   United Artists Classics, 1982, French
PAULINE AT THE BEACH   Orion Classics, 1983, French
FULL MOON IN PARIS   *LES NUITS DE LA PLEINE LUNE*
   Orion Classics, 1984, French
SUMMER   *LE RAYON VERT*   Orion Classics,
   1985, French
FOUR ADVENTURES OF REINETTE AND MIRABELLE
   New Yorker, 1987, French
BOYFRIENDS AND GIRLFRIENDS   *L'AMI DE MON AMIE*
   Orion Classics, 1987, French
CONTE DE PRINTEMPS   Orion Classics, 1990, French

SUSAN ROHRER
MOTHER'S DAY (CTF)   CBN Producers Group, 1989

SUTTON ROLEY*
b. Belle Vernon, Pennsylvania
Home: 777 Arden Road, Pasadena, CA 91106,
   818/449-2491

HOW TO STEAL THE WORLD   MGM, 1966
SWEET, SWEET RACHEL (TF)   ABC, Inc., 1971
THE LONERS   Fanfare, 1972
SNATCHED (TF)   ABC Circle Films, 1973
SATAN'S TRIANGLE (TF)   Danny Thomas
   Productions, 1975
CHOSEN SURVIVORS   Columbia, 1974

TONY ROMAN
Business: Outpost Entertainment Group, 270 N. Canon
   Drive, Beverly Hills, CA 90210, 213/281-7575

BREAKING NEW YORK STYLE   Rene Malo Film,
   1986, Canadian

MARK ROMANEK
b. Chicago, Illinois

STATIC   Cinecom, 1985

EDDIE ROMERO
b. July 7, 1924 - Negros Oriental, Philippines
Contact: Philippine Motion Picture Producers Association,
   514 Burke Building, Escolta Manila, Philippines, 2/48-7731

THE DAY OF THE TRUMPET   1957, U.S.-Filipino
LOST BATALLION   American International,
   1962, Filipino-U.S.
THE RAIDERS OF LEYTE GULF   Hemisphere, 1963,
   Filipino-U.S.
MORO WITCH DOCTOR   20th Century-Fox, 1964,
   Filipino-U.S.
THE KIDNAPPERS   *MAN ON THE RUN*   1964
THE WALLS OF HELL   co-director with Gerardo De Leon,
   Hemisphere, 1964, U.S.-Filipino
THE RAVAGERS   Hemisphere, 1965, U.S.-Filipino
MANILA OPEN CITY   1967, Filipino
BEAST OF THE YELLOW NIGHT   New World,
   1970, Filipino
TWILIGHT PEOPLE   Dimension, 1972, U.S.-Filipino
BEAST OF BLOOD   Marvin Films, 1971, U.S.-Filipino
BLACK MAMA, WHITE MAMA   American International,
   1973, U.S.-Filipino
BEYOND ATLANTIS   Dimension, 1973, U.S.-Filipino

SAVAGE SISTERS   American International,
   1974, U.S.-Filipino
THE WOMAN HUNT   New World, 1975, U.S.-Filipino
GANITO KAMI NOON, PAANO KAYO NGAYON?
   1976, Filipino
SUDDEN DEATH   Topar, 1977, U.S.-Filipino
SINO'NG KAPILING, SINO'NG KASIPING?
   1977, Filipino
AGUILA   Bancom Audiovision Corporation,
   1980, Filipino
DESIRE   Hemisphere, 1983, Filipino
HARI SA HARI, LAHI SA LAHI   co-director with Hsiao
   Lang & Chao Lili, Cultural Center of the Philippines/
   Beijing Film Studios, 1987, Filipino-Chinese
WHITEFORCE   Eastern Film Management/FGH
   Corporation, 1989, Australian-Filipino

GEORGE A. ROMERO
b. 1939
Agent: David Gersh, The Gersh Agency - Beverly Hills,
   213/274-6611

NIGHT OF THE LIVING DEAD   Continental, 1968
THERE'S ALWAYS VANILLA   Cambist, 1972
THE CRAZIES   *CODE NAME: TRIXIE*   Cambist, 1972
HUNGRY WIVES   Jack H. Harris Enterprises, 1973
MARTIN   Libra, 1978
DAWN OF THE DEAD   United Film Distribution, 1979
KNIGHTRIDERS   United Film Distribution, 1981
CREEPSHOW   Warner Bros., 1982
DAY OF THE DEAD   United Film Distribution, 1985
MONKEY SHINES   Orion, 1988
TWO EVIL EYES   co-director with Dario Argento, Taurus
   Entertainment, 1990, Italian

DARRELL ROODT
Contact: Department of Interior, Civitas Building, Struben
   Street, Pretoria 0002, South Africa, 12/48-2551

PLACE OF WEEPING   New World, 1986, South African
CITY OF BLOOD   Distant Horizon International, 1987,
   South African
TENTH OF A SECOND   Distant Horizon International,
   1987, South African
THE STICK   New World, 1987, South African
JOBMAN   Gibraltar Releasing, 1990, South African

CONRAD ROOKS
CHAPPAQUA   Regional, 1968
SIDDHARTHA   Columbia, 1973

TOM ROPELEWSKI*
Agent: ICM - Los Angeles, 213/550-4000

MADHOUSE   Orion, 1990

BERNARD ROSE
Agent: CAA - Beverly Hills, 213/288-4545

PAPERHOUSE   Vestron, 1988, British
CHICAGO JOE & THE SHOWGIRL   New Line Cinema,
   1990, British

LES ROSE
Agent: Jeanine Edwards/Fifi Oscard - New York City,
   212/764-1100

THREE CARD MONTE   Arista, 1977, Canadian
TITLE SHOT   Arista, 1979, Canadian

HOG WILD   Avco Embassy, 1980, Canadian
GAS   Paramount, 1981, Canadian
GORDON PINSENT AND THE LIFE AND TIMES OF
   EDWIN ALONZO BOYD (TF)   Poundmaker Productions,
   1982, Canadian
ISAAC LITTLEFEATHERS   Lauron Productions,
   1985, Canadian
COVERT ACTION   Spooks Productions/CBC,
   1987, Canadian

MICKEY ROSE
Agent: Larry Grossman & Associates - Beverly Hills,
   213/5508127

STUDENT BODIES   Paramount, 1981

MARTIN ROSEN
Address: 305 San Anselmo Avenue, San Anselmo, CA
   94960, 415/456-1414

WATERSHIP DOWN (AF)   Avco Embassy, 1978, British
THE PLAGUE DOGS (AF)   Nepenthe Productions,
   1982, British
STACKING   Spectrafilm, 1987

ROBERT L. ROSEN*
b. January 7, 1937 - Palm Springs, California
Attorney: Marty Weiss, 12301 Wilshire Blvd. - Suite 203,
   Los Angeles, CA 90025, 213/820-8872

COURAGE   New World, 1984

ANITA ROSENBERG
Agent: Paul Kohner, Inc. - Los Angeles, 213/550-1060

ASSAULT OF THE KILLER BIMBOS   Empire
   Pictures, 1988

STUART ROSENBERG*
b. 1928 - New York, New York
Agent: William Morris Agency - Beverly Hills,
   213/274-7451

MURDER, INC.   co-director with Burt Balaban, 20th
   Century-Fox, 1960
QUESTION 7   De Rochemont, 1961, U.S.-West German
FAME IS THE NAME OF THE GAME (TF)   Universal
   TV, 1966
ASYLUM FOR A SPY (TF)   Universal TV, 1967
COOL HAND LUKE   Warner Bros., 1967
THE APRIL FOOLS   National General, 1969
MOVE   20th Century-Fox, 1970
WUSA   Paramount, 1970
POCKET MONEY   National General, 1972
THE LAUGHING POLICEMAN   20th Century-Fox, 1973
THE DROWNING POOL   Warner Bros., 1975
VOYAGE OF THE DAMNED   Avco Embassy,
   1977, British
LOVE AND BULLETS   AFD, 1979
THE AMITYVILLE HORROR   American
   International, 1979
BRUBAKER   20th Century-Fox, 1980
THE POPE OF GREENWICH VILLAGE   MGM/UA, 1984
LET'S GET HARRY   directed under pseudonym of Alan
   Smithee, Tri-Star, 1986
HOME GROWN   E.K. Gaylord II/Martin Poll
   Productions, 1990

RALPH ROSENBLUM*
b. October 13, 1925 - New York, New York
Home: 155 West 91st Street, New York, NY 10024,
    212/595-7975
Agent: The Gersh Agency - Beverly Hills, 213/274-6611

THE GREATEST MAN IN THE WORLD (TF)   Learning in
    Focus, 1979
ANY FRIEND OF NICHOLAS NICKLEBY IS A FRIEND
    OF MINE (TF)   Rubicon Productions, 1982
STIFFS   Serious Productions, 1986

MARK ROSENTHAL
Agent: InterTalent - Los Angeles, 213/271-0600

THE IN CROWD   Orion, 1988

RICK ROSENTHAL*
b. 1950 - New York, New York
Agent: William Morris Agency - Beverly Hills, 213/274-7451

HALLOWEEN II   Universal, 1981
BAD BOYS   Universal/AFD, 1983
AMERICAN DREAMER   Warner Bros., 1984
CODE OF VENGEANCE (TF)   Universal TV, 1985
HARD COPY (TF)   Universal TV, 1987
RUSSKIES   New Century/Vista, 1987
DISTANT THUNDER   Paramount, 1988
NASTY BOYS (TF)   Wolf Films/Universal TV, 1989

ROBERT J. ROSENTHAL
Contact: Writers Guild of America, West - Los Angeles,
    213/550-1000

MALIBU BEACH   Crown International, 1978
ZAPPED!   Embassy, 1982

FRANCESCO ROSI
b. November 15, 1922 - Naples, Italy
Home: via Gregoriana 36, Rome, Italy, 06/6791742

LA SFIDA   Lux/Vices/Suevia Film, 1958, Italian-Spanish
I MAGLIARI   Vides/Titanus, 1959, Italian
SALVATORE GIULIANO   CCM Films, 1962,
    Italian-French
LE MANI SULLA CITTA'   Galatea Film, 1963, Italian
THE MOMENT OF TRUTH   Rizzoli, 1965,
    Italian-Spanish
MORE THAN A MIRACLE   C'ERA UNA VOLTA   MGM,
    1967, Italian-French
UOMINI CONTRO   Prima Cinematografica/Jadran Film,
    1970, Italian-Yugoslavian
THE MATTEI AFFAIR   Paramount, 1973, Italian
LUCKY LUCIANO   Avco Embassy, 1974, Italian
CADAVERI ECCELENTI   United Artists, 1976,
    Italian-French
EBOLI   CHRIST STOPPED AT EBOLI   Franklin Media,
    1980, Italian-French
THREE BROTHERS   New World, 1981, Italian
BIZET'S CARMEN   CARMEN   Triumph/Columbia, 1984,
    Italian-French
CHRONICLE OF A DEATH FORETOLD   Mediactuel/
    Italmedia/Soprofilms/ Focine, 1986, Italian-French-
    Colombian
DIMENTICARE PALERMO   Mario & Vittorio Cecchi Gori/
    Pentafilm/Reteitalia, 1990, Italian

MARK ROSMAN
Agent: CAA - Beverly Hills, 213/288-4545

THE HOUSE ON SORORITY ROW   Artists Releasing
    Corporation/Film Ventures International, 1983
TIME FLYER (TF)   Three Blind Mice Productions, 1986
SPOT MARKS THE X (CTF)   Catalina Production
    Group, 1986

MARK ROSNER*
Home: 2655 Creston Drive, Los Angeles, CA 90068,
    213/469-7510
Agent: CAA - Beverly Hills, 213/288-4545

DREAM STREET (TF)   The Bedford Falls Company/
    Finnegan- Pinchuk Productions/MGM-UA TV, 1989

COURTNEY SALE ROSS
IN SEARCH OF ROTHKO (FD)   Atlantic Richfield
    Company, 1979

HERBERT ROSS*
b. May 13, 1927 - New York, New York
Agent: CAA - Beverly Hills, 213/288-4545

GOODBYE, MR. CHIPS   MGM, 1969, British
THE OWL AND THE PUSSYCAT   Columbia, 1970
T.R. BASKIN   Paramount, 1971
PLAY IT AGAIN, SAM   Paramount, 1972
THE LAST OF SHEILA   Warner Bros., 1973
FUNNY LADY   Columbia, 1975
THE SUNSHINE BOYS   MGM/United Artists, 1975
THE SEVEN-PER-CENT SOLUTION   Universal,
    1976, British
THE TURNING POINT★   20th Century-Fox, 1977
THE GOODBYE GIRL   Warner Bros., 1977
CALIFORNIA SUITE   Columbia, 1978
NIJINSKY   Paramount, 1980
PENNIES FROM HEAVEN   MGM/United Artists, 1981
I OUGHT TO BE IN PICTURES   20th Century-Fox, 1982
MAX DUGAN RETURNS   20th Century-Fox, 1983
FOOTLOOSE   Paramount, 1984
PROTOCOL   Warner Bros., 1984
THE SECRET OF MY SUCCESS   Universal, 1987
DANCERS   Cannon, 1987
STEEL MAGNOLIAS   Tri-Star, 1989
MY BLUE HEAVEN   Warner Bros., 1990
TRUE COLORS   Paramount, 1991

BOBBY ROTH*
(Robert J. Roth)
Address: 7469 Melrose Avenue - Suite 35, Los Angeles,
    CA 90046, 213/651-0288
Agent: William Morris Agency - Beverly Hills, 213/274-7451

INDEPENDENCE DAY   Unifilm, 1977
THE BOSS' SON   Circle Associates, 1980
CIRCLE OF POWER   MYSTIQUE/BRAINWASH/THE
    NAKED WEEKEND   Televicine, 1983
HEARTBREAKERS   Orion, 1984
TONIGHT'S THE NIGHT (TF)   Indieprod Productions/
    Phoenix Entertainment Group, 1987
THE MAN WHO FELL TO EARTH (TF)   David Gerber
    Productions/ MGM TV, 1987
BAJA OKLAHOMA (CTF)   HBO Pictures/Rastar
    Productions, 1988
DEAD SOLID PERFECT (CTF)   HBO Pictures/David
    Merrick Productions, 1988

THE MAN INSIDE   New Line Cinema, 1990, French-U.S.
RAINBOW DRIVE (CTF)   Dove Inc./ITC Entertainment/
   Viacom Pictures, 1990

JOE ROTH*
b. June 13, 1948 - New York, New York
Business: Twentieth Century Fox Film Corporation, P.O.
   Box 900, Beverly Hills, CA 90213, 213/277-2211
Agent: CAA - Beverly Hills, 213/288-4545

STREETS OF GOLD   20th Century Fox, 1986
REVENGE OF THE NERDS II: NERDS IN PARADISE
   20th Century Fox, 1987
COUPE DE VILLE   Universal, 1990

STEPHANIE ROTHMAN
Contact: Writers Guild of America, West - Los Angeles,
   213/550-1000

BLOOD BATH   co-director with Jack Hill, American
   International, 1966
IT'S A BIKINI WORLD   American International, 1967
THE STUDENT NURSES   New World, 1970
THE VELVET VAMPIRE   New World, 1971
GROUP MARRIAGE   Dimension, 1972
TERMINAL ISLAND   Dimension, 1973
THE WORKING GIRLS   Dimension, 1974

RICHARD ROTHSTEIN*
Agent: ICM - Los Angeles, 213/550-4000

BATES MOTEL (TF)   Universal TV, 1987

PETER ROWE
b. July 23, 1947 - Winnipeg, Manitoba, Canada
Business: Rosebud Films Ltd., 14013 Captains Row -
   Suite 315, Marina del Rey, CA 90292, 213/827-8029

THE NEON PALACE   Acme Idea & Sale, 1971, Canadian
FINAL EDITION (TF)   CBC, 1980, Canadian
TAKEOVER (TF)   CBC, 1981, Canadian
LOST!   Rosebud Films, 1985, Canadian
ARCHITECTS OF FEAR   Palette Productions,
   1986, Canadian
TAKE TWO   TBJ Films, 1988

PATRICIA ROZEMA
b. 1958 - Ontario, Canada
Address: 212 Robert Street, Toronto, Ontario
   M5S 2K7, Canada,

I'VE HEARD THE MERMAIDS SINGING   Miramax Films,
   1987, Canadian
WHITE ROOM   Vos Productions, 1990, Canadian

MICHAEL RUBBO
b. 1938 - Melbourne, Australia
Home: 719 de l'Epee, Montreal, Quebec H2V 3V1,
   Canada, 514/274-3148

SOLZHENITSYN'S CHILDREN...ARE MAKING A LOT
   OF NOISE IN PARIS (FD)   Le Cinema Parallele,
   1979, Canadian
THE PEANUT BUTTER SOLUTION   New World,
   1985, Canadian
TOMMY TRICKER AND THE STAMP TRAVELER
   Productions La Fete, 1988, Canadian
VINCENT AND ME   Productions La Fete, 1990, Canadian

JOSEPH RUBEN*
Address: 1026A 14th Street - Suite A, Santa Monica, CA
   90403, 213/341-1257
Agent: Bauer Benedek Agency - Los Angeles, 213/275-2421

THE SISTER-IN-LAW   Crown International, 1975
THE POM-POM GIRLS   Crown International, 1976
JOYRIDE   American International, 1977
OUR WINNING SEASON   American International, 1978
GORP   American International, 1980
DREAMSCAPE   20th Century Fox, 1984
THE STEPFATHER   New Century/Vista, 1987
TRUE BELIEVER   Columbia, 1989
SLEEPING WITH THE ENEMY   20th Century Fox, 1991

KATT SHEA RUBEN
Business: Concorde Pictures, 11600 San Vicente Blvd.,
   Los Angeles, CA 90049, 213/826-0978

STRIPPED TO KILL   Concorde, 1987
DANCE OF THE DAMNED   Concorde, 1989
STRIPPED TO KILL II   Concorde, 1989
STREETS   Concorde, 1990

PERCIVAL RUBENS
THE FOSTER GANG   1964, South African-British
THREE DAYS OF FIRE   1967, Italian
STRANGERS AT SUNRISE   1969
MISTER KINGSTREETS WAR   1970
SABOTEURS   1974, South African-West German- British
THE MIDNIGHT CALLER   1980
SURVIVAL ZONE   1981
RAW TERROR   1985
WILD COUNTRY   1988
OKAVANGO   Transworld Entertainment, 1989
SWEET MURDER   Transatlantic Pictures, 1990

RICK RUBIN
TOUGHER THAN LEATHER   New Line Cinema, 1988

ALAN RUDOLPH*
b. December 18, 1943 - Los Angeles, California
Agent: CAA - Beverly Hills, 213/288-4545

PREMONITION   TransVue, 1972
TERROR CIRCUS   BARN OF THE NAKED DEAD   1973
WELCOME TO L.A.   United Artists/Lions Gate, 1977
REMEMBER MY NAME   Columbia/Lagoon
   Associates, 1979
ROADIE   United Artists, 1980
ENDANGERED SPECIES   MGM/UA, 1982
RETURN ENGAGEMENT (FD)   Island Alive, 1983
CHOOSE ME   Island Alive/New Cinema, 1984
SONGWRITER   Tri-Star, 1984
TROUBLE IN MIND   Alive Films, 1985
MADE IN HEAVEN   Lorimar, 1987
THE MODERNS   Alive Films, 1988
LOVE AT LARGE   Orion, 1990
MORTAL THOUGHTS   Columbia, 1991

LOUIS RUDOLPH*
Contact: Directors Guild of America - Los Angeles,
   213/289-2000

DOUBLE STANDARD (TF)   Louis Rudolph Productions/
   Fenton Entertainment Group/Fries Entertainment, 1988

RAUL RUIZ
b. July 25, 1941 - Puerto Montt, Chile
Contact: French Film Office, 745 Fifth Avenue, New York, NY 10151, 212/832-8860

TRES TRISTES TIGRES   1968, Chilean
QUE HACER?   1970, Chilean
LA COLONIA PENAL   1971, Chilean
NADIE DIJO NADA   1971, Chilean
LA EXPROPRIACION   1972, Chilean
EL REALISMO SOCIALISTA   1973, Chilean
PALOMILLA BRAVA (FD)   1973, Chilean
PALOMITO BLANCA   1973, Chilean
DIALOGO DE EXILADOS   1974, French
MENSCH VERSTREUT UND WELT VERKEHRT   1975, West German
LA VOCATION SUSPENDUE   1977, French
THE HYPOTHESIS OF THE STOLEN PAINTING   Coralie Films International, 1979, French
DE GRAND EVENEMENT ET DES GENS ORDINAIRES   1979, French
IMAGES DU DEBAT   1979, French
JEUX   1979, French
LA VILLE NOUVELLE   1980, French
L'OR GRIS   1980, French
PAGES D'UN CATALOGUE   1980, French
FAHSTROM   1980, West German
LE BORGNE   1981, French
THE TERRITORY   1981, Portuguese
HET DAK VAN DE WALVIS   1982, Dutch
LES TROIS COURONNES DU MATELOT   1982, French
BERENICE   1983, French
LA PRESENCE REELLE   1983, French
LA VILLE DES PIRATES   Les Films du Passage/Metro Films, 1983, French- Portuguese
POINT DE FUITE   1983, French-Portuguese
VOYAGE AUTOUR D'UNE MAIN   1983, French
ADVENTURES A L'ILE DE MADERE   1984, French
L'EVEILLE DU PONT DE L'ALMA   Les Films du Passage, 1983, French
LES DESTINS DE MANOEL   1985, French
TREASURE ISLAND   Cannon, 1986, French
REGIME SANS PAIN   Lasa Films, 1986, French
MAMMAME   Maison de la Culture du Havre, 1986, French
LA CHOUETTE AVEUGLE   La Sept/Night Productions/ Radio Television Suisse Romande, 1987, French-Swiss
MEMOIRE DES APPARENCES: LA VIE EST UN SONGE   INA/Maison de la Culture du Havre/La Sept/Ministere des Affaires Etrangeres/CNC/ Ministere de PPT, 1987, French
THE GOLDEN BOAT   Symbolic Exchange/Duende Pictures, 1990

RICHARD RUSH*
b. 1930 - New York, New York
Agent: CAA - Beverly Hills, 213/288-4545

TOO SOON TO LOVE   Universal, 1960
OF LOVE AND DESIRE   20th Century-Fox, 1963
FICKLE FINGER OF FATE   Pro International, 1967
THUNDER ALLEY   American International, 1967
HELL'S ANGELS ON WHEELS   American International, 1967
A MAN CALLED DAGGER   MGM, 1968
PSYCH-OUT   American International, 1968
THE SAVAGE SEVEN   American International, 1968
GETTING STRAIGHT   Columbia, 1970
FREEBIE AND THE BEAN   Warner Bros., 1974
THE STUNT MAN★   20th Century-Fox, 1980

CHUCK RUSSELL*
Agent: Robert Stein, Leading Artists - Beverly Hills, 213/858-1999

A NIGHTMARE ON ELM STREET, PART 3: DREAM WARRIORS   New Line Cinema, 1987
THE BLOB   Tri-Star, 1988

JAY RUSSELL
Business Manager: Michael Adler, Mitchell, Silberberg, Knupp, 11377 W. Olympic Blvd., Los Angeles, CA 90064

END OF THE LINE   Orion Classics, 1988

KEN RUSSELL*
b. July 3, 1927 - Southampton, England
Agent: Peter Rawley, ICM - Los Angeles, 213/550-4000

FRENCH DRESSING   Warner-Pathe, 1963, British
THE DEBUSSY FILM (TF)   BBC, 1965, British
ISADORA DUNCAN, THE BIGGEST DANCER IN THE WORLD (TF)   BBC, 1966, British
BILLION DOLLAR BRAIN   United Artists, 1967, British
DANTE'S INFERNO (TF)   BBC, 1967, British
SONG OF SUMMER (TF)   BBC, 1968, British
THE DANCE OF THE SEVEN VEILS (TF)   BBC, 1970, British
WOMEN IN LOVE★   United Artists, 1970, British
THE MUSIC LOVERS   United Artists, 1971, British
THE DEVILS   Warner Bros., 1971, British
THE BOY FRIEND   MGM, 1971, British
SAVAGE MESSIAH   MGM, 1972, British
MAHLER   Mayfair, 1974, British
TOMMY   Columbia, 1975, British
LISZTOMANIA   Warner Bros., 1975, British
VALENTINO   United Artists, 1977, British
CLOUDS OF GLORY: WILLIAM AND DOROTHY (TF)   Granada TV, 1978, British
CLOUDS OF GLORY: THE RIME OF THE ANCIENT MARINER (TF)   Granda TV, 1978, British
ALTERED STATES   Warner Bros., 1980
CRIMES OF PASSION   New World, 1984
GOTHIC   Vestron, 1987, British
SALOME'S FIRST NIGHT   Vestron, 1988, British
THE LAIR OF THE WHITE WORM   Vestron, 1988, British
THE RAINBOW   Vestron, 1989, British
WOMEN AND MEN (CTF)   co-director with Frederic Raphael & Tony Richardson, HBO Showcase, 1990

AARON RUSSO
RUDE AWAKENING   co-director with David Greenwalt, Orion, 1989

MARK RUTLAND
PRIME SUSPECT   Premiere Pictures, 1988

MARK RYDELL*
b. March 23, 1934
Agent: Jeff Berg, ICM - Los Angeles, 213/550-4000

THE FOX   Claridge, 1968
THE REIVERS   National General, 1969
THE COWBOYS   Warner Bros., 1972
CINDERELLA LIBERTY   20th Century-Fox, 1974
HARRY AND WALTER GO TO NEW YORK   Columbia, 1976
THE ROSE   20th Century-Fox, 1979
ON GOLDEN POND ★   Universal/AFD, 1981
THE RIVER   Universal, 1984

S

WILLIAM SACHS*

Agent: Barry Salomon, The Artists Group - Los Angeles,
213/552-1100

SECRETS OF THE GODS   Film Ventures
International, 1976
THERE IS NO THIRTEEN   Film Ventures
International, 1977
THE INCREDIBLE MELTING MAN   American
International, 1977
VAN NUYS BLVD.   Crown International, 1979
GALAXINA   Crown International, 1980
HOT CHILI   Cannon, 1985
JUDGMENT   Juvie Productions, 1990
CONCRETE WAR   Cobra Entertainment
Group, 1990

ALAN SACKS

Contact: Writers Guild of America, West - Los Angeles,
213/550-1000

DU BEAT-E-O   H-Z-H Presentation, 1984

JAMES STEVEN SADWITH*

b. October 20, 1952 - Plainfield, New Jersey
Agent: InterTalent - Los Angeles, 213/271-0600

BLUFFING IT (TF)   Ohlmeyer Communications, 1987
BABY M (TF)   ABC Circle Films, 1988

HENRI SAFRAN

b. October 7, 1932 - Paris, France
Contact: Mitch Consultancy, 98 Bay Road, Waverton,
NSW, 2060, Australia, 02/922-6566

TROUBLE SHOOTER (MS)   1975, Australian
SOFTLY SOFTLY (MS)   1975, Australian
ELEPHANT BOY   1975, Australian
LOVE STORY (MS)   1976, Australian
STORM BOY   South Australian Film Corporation,
1976, Australian
NORMAN LOVES ROSE   Atlantic Releasing Corporation,
1981, Australian
THE WILD DUCK   RKR Releasing, 1983, Australian
PRINCE AND THE GREAT RACE   BUSH CHRISTMAS
Quartet/Films Inc., 1983, Australian
A FORTUNATE LIFE (MS)   co-director with Marcus Cole,
PBL Productions, 1986, Australian
THE LANCASTER MILLER AFFAIR (MS)   Lancaster
Miller Productions, 1986, Australian
THE RED CRESCENT   Somerset Films,
1987, Australian
JACK SIMPSON (TF)   Transmedia Productions/
Roadshow/Coote & Carroll/Film Australia,
1988, Australian
BONY (TF)   Reg Grundy Organization/Seven Network/
Beta/Taurus, 1990, Australian-West German

GENE SAKS*

b. November 8, 1921 - New York, New York
Business Manager: Wallin, Simon, Black & Co.,1350 Avenue
of the Americas, New York, NY 10019

BAREFOOT IN THE PARK   Paramount, 1966
THE ODD COUPLE   Paramount, 1968
CACTUS FLOWER   Columbia, 1969
LAST OF THE RED HOT LOVERS   Paramount, 1972
MAME   Warner Bros., 1974
BRIGHTON BEACH MEMOIRS   Universal, 1986
TCHIN-TCHIN   CEP, 1990, Italian

JAMES SALTER

Agent: Joan Brandt, Sterling Lord Literistic, 1 Madison
Avenue, New York, NY 10010

THREE   United Artists, 1969, British

PAUL SALTZMAN

b. 1943 - Toronto, Ontario, Canada
Business: Sunrise Films Ltd., 160 Perth Avenue, Toronto,
Ontario M6P 3X5, Canada, 416/535-2900

INDIA (FD)   1973
WHEN WE FIRST MET (CTF)   Learning Corporation of
America, 1984
VALENTINE'S REVENGE (TF)   Learning Corporation
of America/Family Communications/Sunrise
Films, Ltd., 1986

GLEN SALZMAN

b. 1951 - Montreal, Quebec, Canada
Business: Cineflics Ltd., 215 Albany Avenue - Suite 302,
Toronto, Ontario M5R 3C7, Canada, 416/531-2612

HOME FREE (TF)   co-director with Rebecca Yates,
1976, Canadian
ANOTHER KIND OF MUSIC (TF)   co-director with Rebecca
Yates, 1977, Canadian
NIKKOLINA (TF)   co-director with Rebecca Yates,
1978, Canadian
CORLETTO & SON (TF)   co-director with Rebecca Yates,
1980, Canadian
REACHING OUT (TF)   co-director with Rebecca Yates,
1980, Canadian
INTRODUCING...JANET (TF)   co-director with Rebecca
Yates, 1981, Canadian
JEN'S PLACE (TF)   co-director with Rebecca Yates,
1982, Canadian
MILK AND HONEY   co-director with Rebecca Yates,
Castle Hill Productions, 1987, Canadian-British

JAY SANDRICH*

b. February 24, 1932 - Los Angeles, California
Agent: CAA - Beverly Hills, 213/288-4545

THE CROOKED HEARTS (TF)   Lorimar
Productions, 1972
WHAT ARE BEST FRIENDS FOR? (TF)   ABC Circle
Films, 1973
NEIL SIMON'S SEEMS LIKE OLD TIMES   SEEMS LIKE
OLD TIMES   Columbia, 1980
THE LONELY HEARTS (TF)   Lorimar Productions, 1984

JONATHAN SANGER*
Address: 6525 Sunset Blvd. - 6th Floor, Hollywood, CA
    90028, 213/ 462-4705
Agent: The Gersh Agency - Beverly Hills, 213/274-6611
Business Manager: Freedman, Kinzelberg & Broder, 2121
    Avenue of the Stars - Suite 9000, Los Angeles, CA
    90067, 213/277-0700

CODE NAME: EMERALD   MGM/UA, 1985

JIMMY SANGSTER*
b. December 2, 1927 - England
Agent: Shapiro-Lichtman Agency - Los Angeles,
    213/859-8877

THE HORROR OF FRANKENSTEIN   Levitt-Pickman,
    1970, British
LUST FOR A VAMPIRE   American Continental,
    1971, British
FEAR IN THE NIGHT   International Co-Productions,
    1972, British

CIRIO H. SANTIAGO
Contact: Manila Film Center, CCP Complex, Rexas Blvd.,
    Manila, Philippines, tel.: 832-1125

WOMEN IN CAGES   New World, 1972, U.S.-Filipino
BAMBOO GODS AND IRON MEN   American
    International, 1974, U.S.-Filipino
TNT JACKSON   New World, 1975, U.S.-Filipino
COVER GIRL MODELS   New World, 1975,
    U.S.-Filipino
THE MUTHERS   Dimension, 1976, U.S.-Filipino
VAMPIRE HOOKERS   Capricorn Three,
    1978, U.S.-Filipino
DEATH FORCE   Capricorn Three, 1978, U.S.-Filipino
FIRECRACKER   New World, 1981, U.S.-Filipino
CAGED FURY   Saturn International, 1984,
    U.S.-Filipino
DESERT WARRIOR   Concorde, 1985, U.S.-Filipino
THE DESTROYERS   Concorde/Cinema Group,
    1985, U.S.-Filipino
NAKED VENGEANCE   Concorde/Cinema Group, 1986
SILK   Concorde/Cinema Group, 1986, U.S.-Filipino
EYE OF THE EAGLE   Premiere International,
    1986, Filipino
FINAL MISSION   Westbrook-M.P. Films/D.S. Pictures,
    1986, Filipino-U.S.
THE DEVASTATOR   Concorde, 1986
DEMON OF PARADISE   Concorde, 1987
KILLER INSTINCT   Eastern Film Management
    Corporation, 1987, Filipino
EQUALIZER 2000   Concorde, 1987, U.S.-Filipino
FAST GUN   Juno Media/Premiere International,
    1987, Filipino
THE SISTERHOOD   Concorde, 1988, U.S.-Filipino
THE EXPENDABLES   Concorde, 1988, U.S.-Filipino
FUTURE HUNTERS   Lightning Pictures, 1989,
    U.S.-Filipino
SILK 2   Concorde, 1989, U.S.-Filipino
NAM ANGELS   Concorde, 1989, U.S.-Filipino
LAST STAND AT LANG VEI   Concorde, 1990,
    U.S.-Filipino
FULL BATTLE GEAR   Concorde, 1990, U.S.-Filipino
DUNE WARRIORS   Concorde, 1990, U.S.-Filipino
BEHIND ENEMY LINES   Concorde, 1990,
    U.S.-Filipino

DAVID SAPERSTEIN*
Agent: Susan Schulman Agency - New York City,
    212/713-1633

A KILLING AFFAIR   Hemdale, 1988
BEYOND THE STARS   PERSONAL CHOICE   Moviestore
    Entertainment, 1989

DERAN SARAFIAN
Agent: Triad Artists, Inc. - Los Angeles, 213/556-2727

ALIEN PREDATOR   Trans World Entertainment, 1987
INTERZONE   Trans World Entertainment, 1987
TO DIE FOR   Skouras Pictures, 1989
DUSTED   Dusted Productions, 1990

RICHARD C. SARAFIAN*
b. April 28, 1932 - New York, New York
Agent: Jerry Kalajian, Sanford-Beckett-Skouras -
    Los Angeles, 213/208-2100
Business Manager: John Mitchell, 1341 Ocean Avenue -
    Suite 108, Santa Monica, CA 90401, 213/479-0311

TERROR AT BLACK FALLS   Beckman, 1962
ANDY   Universal, 1965
SHADOW ON THE LAND (TF)   Screen Gems/
    Columbia TV, 1968
RUN WILD, RUN FREE   Columbia, 1969, British
FRAGMENT OF FEAR   Columbia, 1971, British
MAN IN THE WILDERNESS   Warner Bros., 1971
VANISHING POINT   20th Century-Fox, 1971
LOLLY-MADONNA XXX   MGM, 1973
THE MAN WHO LOVED CAT DANCING   MGM, 1973
ONE OF OUR OWN (TF)   Universal TV, 1975
THE NEXT MAN   Allied Artists, 1976
A KILLING AFFAIR (TF)   Columbia TV, 1977
SUNBURN   Paramount, 1979, U.S.-British
DISASTER ON THE COASTLINER (TF)   Moonlight
    Productions/ Filmways, 1979
THE GOLDEN MOMENT: AN OLYMPIC LOVE
    STORY (TF)   Don Ohlmeyer Productions/Telepictures
    Corporation, 1980
THE GANGSTER CHRONICLES (TF)   Universal TV, 1981
SPLENDOR IN THE GRASS (TF)   Katz-Gallin Productions/
    Half-Pint Productions/Warner Bros. TV, 1981
THE BEAR   Embassy, 1984
LIBERTY (TF)   Robert Greenwald Productions, 1986
EYE OF THE TIGER   Scotti Bros., 1986
STREET JUSTICE   Lorimar/Sandy Howard
    Productions, 1989
SOLAR CRISIS   Japan America Picture Co., 1990,
    Japanese-U.S.

JOSEPH SARGENT*
(Giuseppe Danielle Sorgente)
b. July 25, 1925 - Jersey City, New Jersey
Agent: Martin Shapiro, Shapiro-Lichtman Agency -
    Los Angeles, 213/859-8877

ONE SPY TOO MANY   MGM, 1966
THE HELL WITH HEROES   Universal, 1968
THE SUNSHINE PATRIOT (TF)   Universal TV, 1968
THE IMMORTAL (TF)   Paramount TV, 1969
COLOSSUS: THE FORBIN PROJECT   Universal, 1970
TRIBES (TF)☆   20th Century-Fox, 1970
MAYBE I'LL COME HOME IN THE SPRING (TF)
    Metromedia Productions, 1971

LONGSTREET (TF)   Paramount TV, 1971
MAN ON A STRING (TF)   Screen Gems/
     Columbia TV, 1972
THE MAN   Paramount, 1972
THE MARCUS-NELSON MURDERS (TF) ☆☆   Universal
     TV, 1973
THE MAN WHO DIED TWICE (TF)   Cinema Center, 1973
SUNSHINE (TF)   Universal TV, 1973
WHITE LIGHTNING   United Artists, 1973
THE TAKING OF PELHAM 1-2-3   United Artists, 1974
HUSTLING (TF)   Filmways, 1975
FRIENDLY PERSUASION (TF)   International TV
     Productions/ Allied Artists, 1975
THE NIGHT THAT PANICKED AMERICA (TF)
     Paramount TV, 1975
MacARTHUR   Universal, 1977
GOLDENGIRL   Avco Embassy, 1979
AMBER WAVES (TF) ☆   Time-Life Productions, 1980
COAST TO COAST   Paramount, 1980
FREEDOM (TF)   Hill-Mandelker Films, 1981
THE MANIONS OF AMERICA (MS)   co-director with
     Charles S. Dubin, Roger Gimbel Productions/
     EMI TV/Argonaut Films Ltd., 1981
TOMORROW'S CHILD (TF)   20th Century-Fox TV, 1982
NIGHTMARES   Universal, 1983
CHOICES OF THE HEART (TF)   Katz-Gallin/Half-Pint
     Productions, 1983
MEMORIAL DAY (TF)   Charles Fries Productions, 1983
TERRIBLE JOE MORAN (TF)   Robert Halmi, Inc., 1984
SPACE (MS)   co-director with Lee Philips, Stonehenge
     Productions/Paramount TV, 1985
LOVE IS NEVER SILENT (TF)☆☆   Marian Rees
     Associates, 1985
PASSION FLOWER (TF)   Doris Keating Productions/
     Columbia TV, 1986
THERE MUST BE A PONY (TF)   R.J. Productions/
     Columbia TV, 1986
OF PURE BLOOD (TF)   K-M Productions/Joseph Sargent
     Productions/Warner Bros. TV, 1986
JAWS THE REVENGE   Universal, 1987
DAY ONE (TF)   Aaron Spelling Productions/Paragon
     Motion Pictures, David W. Rintels Productions, 1989
THE KAREN CARPENTER STORY (TF)   Weintraub
     Entertainment Group, 1989
CAROLINE? (TF) ☆   Barry & Enright Productions, 1990
THE INCIDENT (TF)   Qintex Entertainment, 1990
THE LAST ELEPHANT (CTF)   The National Audubon
     Society/Turner Network TV, 1990
A GREEN JOURNEY (TF)   Orion TV, 1990

MARINA SARGENTI
MIRROR, MIRROR   Shapiro Glickenhaus
     Entertainment, 1990

MICHAEL SARNE
b. August 6, 1939 - London, England
Home: 61 Campden Hill Towers, London W11 3QP,
     England, 71/727-8047
Agent: Eric L'Epine Smith, 10 Wyndham Place,
     London W11, England, 71/724-0739

LA ROUTE DE ST. TROPEZ   1966, French
JOANNA   20th Century-Fox, 1968, British
MYRA BRECKINRIDGE   20th Century-Fox, 1970
INTIMIDADE   VERA VERAO   Relevo Productions,
     1972, Brazilian
TROUBLE WITH A BATTERY   Luna Films,
     1986, Spanish

PETER SASDY*
b. Budapest, Hungary
Address: 3236 Bennett Drive, Los Angeles, CA 90068,
     213/850-6719
Agent: Martin Shapiro, Shapiro-Lichtman Agency -
     Los Angeles, 213/859-8877

TASTE THE BLOOD OF DRACULA   Warner Bros.,
     1970, British
COUNTESS DRACULA   20th Century-Fox, 1972, British
HANDS OF THE RIPPER   Universal, 1972, British
DOOMWATCH   Avco Embassy, 1972, British
THE STONE TAPE (TF)   1973, British
NOTHING BUT THE NIGHT   Cinema Systems,
     1975, British
THE DEVIL WITHIN HER   I DON'T WANT TO BE BORN
     20th Century-Fox, 1976, British
WELCOME TO BLOOD CITY   EMI, 1977, British
IF WINTER COMES (TF)   1981, British
THE LONELY LADY   Universal, 1983
THE SECRET DIARY OF ADRIAN MOLE (MS)   Thames TV,
     1985, British
THE GROWING PAINS OF ADRIAN MOLE (TF)   Thames
     TV, 1987, British
IMAGINARY FRIENDS (TF)   Thames TV, 1987, British
ENDING UP (TF)   Thames TV, 1989, British

RON SATLOF*
Agent: David Shapira, David Shapira & Associates -
     Sherman Oaks, 818/906-0322

BENNY & BARNEY: LAS VEGAS UNDERCOVER (TF)
     Universal TV, 1977
WAIKIKI (TF)   Aaron Spelling Productions, 1980
THE MURDER THAT WOULDN'T DIE (TF)
     Universal TV, 1980
HUNTER (TF)   Stephen J. Cannell Productions, 1984
J.O.E. AND THE COLONEL (TF)   Mad Dog Productions/
     Universal TV, 1985
PERRY MASON RETURNS (TF)   Intermedia Productions/
     Strathmore Productions/Viacom Productions, 1985
PERRY MASON: THE CASE OF THE NOTORIOUS
     NUN (TF)   Intermedia Productions/Strathmore
     Productions/Viacom Productions, 1986
PERRY MASON: THE CASE OF THE SHOOTING
     STAR (TF)   Intermedia Entertainment Company/
     Strathmore Productions/Viacom
PERRY MASON: THE CASE OF THE LOST LOVE (TF)
     The Fred Silverman Company/Strathmore Productions/
     Viacom Productions, 1987
PERRY MASON: THE CASE OF THE MURDERED
     MADAM (TF)   The Fred Silverman Company/Strathmore
     Productions/Viacom, 1987
JAKE AND THE FATMAN (TF)   The Fred Silverman
     Company/Strathmore Productions/Viacom, 1987
PERRY MASON: THE CASE OF THE LADY IN THE
     LAKE (TF)   The Fred Silverman Company/Strathmore
     Productions/Viacom, 1988
ORIGINAL SIN (TF)   Larry A. Thompson Organization/New
     World TV, 1989
THE LOVE BOAT: A VALENTINE VOYAGE (TF)   Aaron
     Spelling Productions/ Douglas C. Cramer Company, 1990

JUNYA SATO
Contact: Directors Guild of Japan, Tsukada Building, 8-33
     Udagawa-cho, Shibuya-ku, Tokyo 150, Japan, 3/461-4411

(The following is an incomplete list of Mr. Sato's credits)

THE GO MASTERS   Daiei, 1983, Japanese-Chinese

THE SHAPE OF THE LAND   Dentsu-Mainiche
  Broadcasting System, 1986, Japanese
THE SILK ROAD   *DUN-HUANG*   New World/Trans
  Atlantic Pictures, 1988, Japanese-Chinese
UNDER THE AURORA   Toei, 1990, Japanese-Soviet

CARLOS SAURA
b. January 4, 1932 - Huesca, Spain
Contact: Ministry of Culture, Motion Picture Division,
  Avenida de Burgos 5, 28036 Madrid, Spain,
  341/202-5351

CUENCA   1959, Spanish
LOS GOLFOS   1962, Spanish
LLANTO POR UN BANDITO   1964, Spanish
THE HUNT   Trans-Lux, 1966, Spanish
PEPPERMINT FRAPPE   Elias Querejeta Productions,
  1967, Spanish
STRESS ES TRES TRES   Elias Querejeta Productions,
  1968, Spanish
HONEYCOMB   *LA MADRIGUERA*   CineGlobe,
  1969, Spanish
THE GARDEN OF DELIGHTS   Perry/Fleetwood,
  1970, Spanish
ANA Y LOS LOBOS   1973, Spanish
COUSIN ANGELICA   New Yorker, 1974, Spanish
CRIA!   *CRIA CUERVOS*   Jason Allen, 1976, Spanish
ELISA, VIDA MIA   Elias Querejeta Productions,
  1977, Spanish
LOS OJOS VENDADOS   Elias Querejeta Productions,
  1978, Spanish
MAMA CUMPLE CIEN ANOS   Elias Querejeta
  Productions/Films Moliere/Pierson Productions,
  1979, Spanish-French
DEPRISA, DEPRISA   Films Moliere, 1981,
  Spanish-French
BLOOD WEDDING   New Yorker, 1981, Spanish
SWEET HOURS   New Yorker, 1982, Spanish
ANTONIETA   Gaumont/Conacine/Nuevo Cine, 1982,
  French-Mexican
CARMEN   Orion Classics, 1983, Spanish
LOS ZANCOS   Emiliano Piedra Productions,
  1984, Spanish
EL AMOR BRUJO (LOVE, THE MAGICIAN)   Orion
  Classics, 1986, Spanish
EL DORADO   Iberoamericana/Chrysalide Film/Canal Plus/
  FR3/TVE/RAI/Sacis, 1988, Spanish-French-Italian
LA NOCHE OSCURA   Iberoamericana/La Generale
  D'Images/TVE, 1989, Spanish-French
AY, CARMELA!   Miramax Films, 1990, Spanish-Italian

CLAUDE SAUTET
b. February 23, 1924 - Montrouge, France
Contact: French Film Office, 745 Fifth Avenue, New York,
  NY 10151, 212/832-8860

BONJOUR SOURIRE   Vox, 1955, French
THE BIG RISK   United Artists, 1960, French-Italian
L'ARME A GAUCHE   1965, French
THE THINGS OF LIFE   Columbia, 1970, French
MAX ET LES FERRAILLEURS   CFDC, 1971, French
CESAR AND ROSALIE   Cinema 5, 1972,
  French-Italian-West German
VINCENT, FRANÇOIS, PAUL AND THE OTHERS
  Joseph Green Pictures, 1974, French-Italian
MADO   Joseph Green Pictures, 1976, French
A SIMPLE STORY   Quartet, 1979, French
UN MAUVAIS FIL   Sara Films/Antenne-2, 1980, French

GARCON   Sara Film/Renn Productions, 1983, French
A FEW DAYS WITH ME   Galaxy International,
  1988, French

PIERRE SAUVAGE
b. Le Cambon-Sur-Ligny, France
Address: Friends of Le Chambon, 8033 Sunset Blvd. -
  Suite 784, Los Angeles, CA 90046, 213/650-1774

WEAPONS OF THE SPIRIT (FD)   First Run Features, 1989

TELLY SAVALAS*
b. 1926 - Garden City, New Jersey
Business Manager: Tucker, Morgan, Martindale,
  9200 Sunset Blvd. - Suite 418, Los Angeles, CA 90069,
  213/274-0981

BEYOND REASON   Allwyn Pictures/Arthur
  M. Sarkissian, 1977

PHILIP SAVILLE
b. London, England
Agent: Merrily Kane, The Artists Agency - Los Angeles,
  213/277-7779

STOP THE WORLD - I WANT TO GET OFF   Warner Bros.,
  1966, British
OEDIPUS THE KING   Regional, 1968, British
THE BEST HOUSE IN LONDON   MGM, 1969, British
THE RAINBIRDS (TF)   BBC, 1970, British
SECRETS   Lone Star, 1971, British
GANGSTERS (TF)   BBC, 1975, British
COUNT DRACULA (TF)   1977, British
THE JOURNAL OF BRIDGET HITLER (TF)   1980, British
BOYS FROM THE BLACKSTUFF (TF)   1982, British
THOSE GLORY, GLORY DAYS   Cinecom, 1983, British,
  originally made for television
SHADEY   Skouras Pictures, 1986, British
MANDELA (CTF)   Titus Productions/Polymuse Inc./
  TVS Ltd., 1987, U.S.-British
WONDERLAND   *THE FRUIT MACHINE*   Vestron,
  1988, British
FIRST BORN (TF)   BBC/Australian Broadcasting
  Corporation/TV New Zealand, 1989,
  British-Australian-New Zealand
MAX AND HELEN (CTF)   Citadel Entertainment, 1990
FELLOW TRAVELLER (CTF)   British Film Institute/BBC
  Films/HBO Showcase, 1990, British-U.S.

TOM SAVINI
NIGHT OF THE LIVING DEAD   Columbia, 1990

NANCY SAVOCA
Business: Forward Films, 2445 Hering Avenue, Bronx,
  NY 10469
Agent: William Morris Agency - Beverly Hills, 213/274-7451

TRUE LOVE   MGM/UA, 1989
DOGFIGHT   Warner Bros., 1991

JOHN SAXON
(Carmine Orrico)
b. August 5, 1936 - New York, New York
Contact: Screen Actors Guild - Hollywood, 213/465-4600

DEATH HOUSE   Nick Marino Presents, 1988

JOHN SAYLES
b. September 28, 1950 - Schenectady, New York
Contact: Writers Guild of America, East -
   New York City, 212/245-6180

RETURN OF THE SECAUCUS SEVEN   Libra/Specialty
   Films, 1980
LIANNA   United Artists Classics, 1983
BABY IT'S YOU   Paramount, 1983
THE BROTHER FROM ANOTHER PLANET
   Cinecom, 1984
MATEWAN   Cinecom, 1987
EIGHT MEN OUT   Orion, 1988

JOSEPH L. SCANLAN*
Agent: Mitchell Kaplan, Kaplan-Stahler Agency -
   Beverly Hills, 213/653-4483

OUR MAN FLINT: DEAD ON TARGET (TF)   20th
   Century-Fox TV, 1976
STARTING OVER (TF)   1979, Australian
SPRING FEVER   Comworld, 1983, Canadian
NIGHTSTICK   Production Distribution Company,
   1987, Canadian
THE RETURN OF BEN CASEY (TF)   Cooper Canadian
   Films, Inc., 1988, Canadian

ALLEN SCHAAF
b. December 6, 1942 - San Francisco, California
Business: Tenth Street Production Group, Inc., 147 10th
   Street, San Francisco, CA 94103, 415/621-3395

DRACULA'S DISCIPLE   Tenth Street Production
   Group, 1984

GEORGE SCHAEFER*
b. December 16, 1920 - Wallingford, Connecticut
Agent: CAA - Beverly Hills, 213/288-4545

MACBETH   British Lion, 1961, British
PENDULUM   Columbia, 1969
GENERATION   Avco Embassy, 1969
DOCTOR'S WIVES   Columbia, 1971
A WAR OF CHILDREN (TF)☆   Tomorrow Entertainment,
   1972
F. SCOTT FITZGERALD AND "THE LAST OF THE
   BELLES" (TF)   Titus Productions, 1974
ONCE UPON A SCOUNDREL   Image International,
   1974, U.S.-Mexican
IN THIS HOUSE OF BREDE (TF)   Tomorrow
   Entertainment, 1975
AMELIA EARHART (TF)   Universal TV, 1976
THE GIRL CALLED HATTER FOX (TF)   Roger Gimbel
   Productions/EMI TV, 1978
FIRST YOU CRY (TF)   MTM Enterprises, 1978
AN ENEMY OF THE PEOPLE   Warner Bros., 1978
WHO'LL SAVE OUR CHILDREN? (TF)   Time-Life
   Productions, 1978
BLIND AMBITION (TF)   Time-Life Productions, 1979
MAYFLOWER: THE PILGRIMS' ADVENTURE (TF)
   Syzygy Productions, 1979
THE BUNKER (TF)   Time-Life Productions/SFP France/
   Antenne-2, 1981, U.S.-French
A PIANO FOR MRS. CIMINO (TF)   Roger Gimbel
   Productions/EMI TV, 1982
RIGHT OF WAY (CTF)   HBO Premiere Films, Schaefer-
   Karpf Productions/Post- Newsweek Video, 1983
CHILDREN IN THE CROSSFIRE (TF)   Schaefer-Karpf
   Productions/Prendergast- Brittcadia Productions/
   Gaylord Production Company, 1984

STONE PILLOW (TF)   Schaefer-Karpf Productions/Gaylord
   Productions, 1985
MRS. DELAFIELD WANTS TO MARRY (TF)   Schaefer-
   Karpf Productions/ Gaylord Production Company, 1986
LAURA LANSING SLEPT HERE (TF)   Schaefer-Karpf-
   Eckstein Productions/Gaylord Production Company, 1988

FRANKY (FRANCIS) SCHAEFFER
Business: (508) 462-8055

WIRED TO KILL   American Distribution Group, 1986
RISING STORM   Gibraltar Releasing, 1989
HEAD HUNTER   Academy Entertainment/Gibraltar
   Releasing, 1990

JERRY SCHAFER*
Home: 3661 S. Maryland Parkway - Apt. 35-47, Las Vegas,
   NV 89109, 702/796-1934
Agent: Sanford International Entertainment, P.O. Box 25202,
   Las Vegas, NV 89114, 702/737-1100

FISTS OF STEEL   FoS Productions, 1989

DON SCHAIN*
Home: 1865 N. Fuller Avenue - Apt. 203, Los Angeles,
   CA 90046, 818/851-8455

GINGER   Joseph Brenner Associates, 1971
THE ABDUCTORS   Joseph Brenner Associates, 1972
A PLACE CALLED TODAY   Avco Embassy, 1972
GIRLS ARE FOR LOVING   Continental, 1973
TOO HOT TO HANDLE   Derio Productions, 1978

JERRY SCHATZBERG*
b. New York, New York
Agent: Alan Greenspan, ICM - Los Angeles, 213/550-4428
Business Manager: Herb Bard, Bard & Kass, 551 Fifth
   Avenue, New York, NY 10176, 212/599-2880

PUZZLE OF A DOWNFALL CHILD   Universal, 1970
PANIC IN NEEDLE PARK   20th Century-Fox, 1971
SCARECROW   Warner Bros., 1973
SWEET REVENGE   DANDY, THE ALL-AMERICAN GIRL
   MGM/United Artists, 1976
THE SEDUCTION OF JOE TYNAN   Universal, 1979
HONEYSUCKLE ROSE   Warner Bros., 1980
MISUNDERSTOOD   MGM/UA, 1984
NO SMALL AFFAIR   Columbia, 1984
STREET SMART   Cannon, 1987
CLINTON AND NADINE (CTF)   HBO Pictures/ITC, 1988
REUNION   Les Films Ariane/FR3/NEF Film Produktion und
   Vertriebs/C26 Films/Tac Ltd./Arbo-Film Maran, 1989,
   French-British-West German

HANS SCHEEPMAKER
Contact: Ministry of Cultural Affairs, Steenvoordelaan 370,
   Rijswijk (Z.H.), Netherlands, 070/949233

FIELD OF HONOR   Cannon, 1986, U.S.-Dutch

ROBERT SCHEERER*
b. Santa Barbara, California
Agent: The Cooper Agency - Los Angeles, 213/277-8422

HANS BRINKER (TF)   NBC, 1969
ADAM AT SIX A.M.   National General, 1970
THE WORLD'S GREATEST ATHLETE   Buena Vista, 1973
POOR DEVIL (TF)   Paramount TV, 1973

TARGET RISK (TF)   Universal TV, 1975
IT HAPPENED AT LAKEWOOD MANOR (TF)   Alan
    Landsburg Productions, 1977
HAPPILY EVER AFTER (TF)   Tri-Media II, Inc./
    Hamel-Somers Entertainment, 1978
HOW TO BEAT THE HIGH COST OF LIVING   American
    International, 1980
MATLOCK: THE HUNTING PARTY (TF)   The Fred
    Silverman Company/Dean Hargrove Productions/
    Viacom, 1989

MAXIMILIAN SCHELL

b. December 8, 1930 - Vienna, Austria
Agent: ICM - Los Angeles, 213/550-4000

FIRST LOVE   UMC, 1970, Swiss-West German
THE PEDESTRIAN   Cinerama Releasing Corporation,
    1974, West German-Swiss- Israeli
END OF THE GAME   20th Century-Fox, 1976, West
    German-Italian
TALES FROM THE VIENNA WOODS   Cinema 5, 1979,
    Austrian-West German
MARLENE (FD)   Alive Films, 1984, West German
AN AMERICAN PLACE   OKO/B.A., 1989,
    West German-U.S.

HENNING SCHELLERUP*

Home: 1710 Camino Palmero - Apt. 12, Los Angeles, CA
    90046, 213/876-1752

THE BLACK BUNCH   Entertainment Pyramid, 1973
SWEET JESUS, PREACHER MAN   MGM, 1973
THE BLACK ALLEYCATS   Entertainment Pyramid, 1974
THE TIME MACHINE (TF)   Sunn Classic
    Productions, 1978
IN SEARCH OF HISTORIC JESUS   Sunn Classic, 1979
BEYOND DEATH'S DOOR   Sunn Classic, 1979
THE LEGEND OF SLEEPY HOLLOW   Sunn
    Classic, 1979
THE ADVENTURES OF NELLIE BLY (TF)   Sunn
    Classic, 1981
CAMP-FIRE GIRLS   Rainbow Spectrum Film Co., 1984
BERSERKER   Shapiro Entertainment, 1987

CARL SCHENKEL

b. Switzerland

OUT OF ORDER   Sandstar Releasing Corporation,
    1984, West German
BAY COVEN (TF)   Guber-Peters Company/Phoenix
    Entertainment Group, 1987
THE MIGHTY QUINN   MGM/UA, 1989
SILENCE LIKE GLASS   Moviestore Entertainment,
    1989, West German

FRED SCHEPISI*

b. December 26, 1939 - Melbourne, Australia
Agent: Sam Cohn, ICM - New York City, 212/556-6810

LIBIDO   co-director with John B. Murray, Tim Burstall &
    David Baker, Producers & Directors Guild of Australia,
    1973, Australian
THE DEVIL'S PLAYGROUND   Entertainment Marketing,
    1976, Australian
THE CHANT OF JIMMIE BLACKSMITH   New Yorker,
    1978, Australian
BARBAROSA   Universal/AFD, 1982, West German
ICEMAN   Universal, 1984
PLENTY   20th Century-Fox, 1985, British

ROXANNE   Columbia, 1987
A CRY IN THE DARK   *EVIL ANGELS*   Warner Bros.,
    1988, Australian
THE RUSSIA HOUSE   Pathe Entertainment, 1990

JEFFREY NOYES SCHER

Business: Northwinds Entertainment, 3 Sheridan Square -
    Apt. 8A, New York, NY 10014

PRISONERS OF INERTIA   Northwinds Entertainment, 1989

PAUL SCHIBLI

Contact: Academy of Canadian Cinema and Television, 653
    Yonge Street - 2nd Floor, Toronto, Ontario M4Y 1Z9,
    Canada, 416/967-0315

THE NUTCRACKER PRINCE (AF)   Warner Bros., 1990,
    Canadian

RICHARD SCHICKEL*

Home: 9051 Dicks Street, Los Angeles, CA 90069

THE MEN WHO MADE THE MOVIES (TD)   PBS, 1972
INTO THE MORNING: WILLA CATHER'S AMERICA (TD)
    PBS, 1978
FUNNY BUSINESS (TD)   CBS, 1978
THE HORROR SHOW (TD)   CBS, 1979
JAMES CAGNEY, THAT YANKEE DOODLE DANDY (TD)
    PBS, 1981
MINNELLI ON MINNELLI: LIZA REMEMBERS
    VINCENTE (TD)   PBS, 1987
MYRNA LOY: SO NICE TO COME HOME TO (CTD)
    LORAC Productions, 1990

SUZANNE SCHIFFMAN

Contact: French Film Office, 745 Fifth Avenue, New York,
    NY 10151, 212/832-8860

SORCERESS   *LA MOINE ET LA SORCIERE*   European
    Classics, 1987, French-U.S.
FEMME DE PAPIER   Pierre Grise Productions/La Sept/La
    Cine/ Canal Plus, 1989, French

LAWRENCE J. SCHILLER*

b. December 28, 1936 - New York, New York
Business: The New Ingot Company, 4827 N. Sepulveda
    Blvd. - Suite 400, Sherman Oaks, CA 91403,
    818/906-0926
Agent: David Wardlow, Camden Artists - Beverly Hills,
    213/278-6885

THE LEXINGTON EXPERIENCE (FD)   Corda, 1971
THE AMERICAN DREAMER (FD)   co-director with L.M. Kit
    Carson, EYR, 1971
HEY, I'M ALIVE! (TF)   Charles Fries Productions/
    Worldvision, 1975
MARILYN: THE UNTOLD STORY (TF)   co-director
    with Jack Arnold & John Flynn, Lawrence Schiller
    Productions, 1980
THE EXECUTIONER'S SONG (TF)   Film
    Communications Inc., 1982
PETER THE GREAT (MS)   co-director with Marvin J.
    Chomsky, PTG Productions/NBC Productions, 1986
MARGARET BOURKE-WHITE (CTF)   Turner Network TV/
    Project VII/ Central TV Enterprises, 1989
THE PLOT TO KILL HITLER (TF)   Wolper Productions/
    Bernard Sofronski Productions/Warner Bros. TV, 1990

TOM SCHILLER

Agent: Mike Hamilburg, Mike Hamilburg Agency, 292
S. La Cienega Blvd. - Suite 212, Beverly Hills, CA
90211, 213/657-1501

NOTHING LASTS FOREVER   MGM/UA Classics, 1984

THOMAS SCHLAMME*

Address: 1619 Broadway - 9th Floor, New York, NY
10019, 212/603-0609
Agent: William Morris Agency - Beverly Hills, 213/274-7451

MISS FIRECRACKER   Corsair Pictures, 1989

GEORGE SCHLATTER*

b. December 31, 1932
Business: George Schlatter Productions, 8321 Beverly
Blvd., Los Angeles, CA 90048, 213/655-1400
Agent: William Morris Agency - Beverly Hills, 213/274-7451

NORMAN...IS THAT YOU?   MGM/United Artists, 1976

JOHN SCHLESINGER*

b. February 16, 1926 - London, England
Home: 10 Victoria Road, London W8 5RD, England,
01/937-3983
Agent: Jeff Berg, ICM - Los Angeles, 213/550-4000

A KIND OF LOVING   Continental, 1962, British
BILLY LIAR   Continental, 1963, British
DARLING★   Embassy, 1965, British
FAR FROM THE MADDING CROWD   MGM,
1967, British
MIDNIGHT COWBOY★★   United Artists, 1969
SUNDAY BLOODY SUNDAY★   United Artists,
1970, British
VISIONS OF EIGHT (FD)   co-director with Yuri Ozerov,
Mai Zetterling, Arthur Penn, Michael Pfleghar, Kon
Ichikawa, Milos Forman & Claude Lelouch,
Cinema 5, 1973
THE DAY OF THE LOCUST   Paramount, 1975
MARATHON MAN   Paramount, 1976
YANKS   Universal, 1979, British
HONKY TONK FREEWAY   Universal/AFD, 1981
AN ENGLISHMAN ABROAD (TF)   BBC, 1983, British
THE FALCON AND THE SNOWMAN   Orion, 1985
THE BELIEVERS   Orion, 1987
MADAME SOUSATZKA   Universal, 1988, British
PACIFIC HEIGHTS   20th Century Fox, 1990

VOLKER SCHLONDORFF*

b. 1939 - Wiesbaden, Germany
Business: c/o Bioskop Film, Turkenstrasse 91, 8000
Munich 40, West Germany
Agent: Sam Cohn, ICM - New York City, 212/556-5600

YOUNG TORLESS   Kanawha, 1966,
West German-French
A DEGREE OF MURDER   Universal, 1967,
West German
MICHAEL KOHLHAAS   Columbia, 1969, West German
THE SUDDEN WEALTH OF THE POOR PEOPLE OF
KOMBACK   New Yorker, 1970, West German
BAAL (TF)   Hessischer Rundfunk/Bayerischer Rundfunk/
Hallelujah Film, 1970, West German
DIE MORAL DER RUTH HALBFASS   Hallelujah Film/
Hessischer Rundfunk, 1971, West German
A FREE WOMAN   STROHFEUER   New Yorker, 1971,
West German

UBERNACHTUNG IN TIROL (TF)   Hessischer Rundfunk,
1974, West German
GEORGINAS GRUNDE (TF)   West Deutscher Rundfunk/
ORTF, 1975, West German-Austrian
THE LOST HONOR OF KATHARINA BLUM   co-director with
Margaretha Von Trotta, New World, 1975, West German
COUP DE GRACE   Cinema 5, 1976, West German
NUR ZUM SPASS - NUR ZUM SPIEL (TD)   Kaleidoskop
Valeska Gert/ Bioskop Film, 1977
DEUTSCHLAND IM HERBST (FD)   co-director, Filmverlag
der Autoren/Hallelujah Film/Kairos Film, 1978,
West German
THE TIN DRUM   New World, 1980, West German
CIRCLE OF DECEIT   DIE FALSCHUNG   United Artists
Classics, 1982, West German-French
KRIEG UND FRIEDEN (FD)   co-director with Heinrich Boll,
Alexander Kluge, Stefan Aust & Axel Engstfeld,
TeleCulture, 1983, West German
SWANN IN LOVE   Orion Classics, 1984,
French-West German
DEATH OF A SALESMAN (TF)☆   Roxbury and Punch
Productions, 1985
A GATHERING OF OLD MEN (TF)   Consolidated
Productions/Jennie & Company/ Zenith Productions, 1987
THE HANDMAID'S TAIL   Cinecom, 1990
PASSAGIER FABER   Bioskop/Argos Film/Hellas,
1990, West German

JULIAN SCHLOSSBERG

Business: Castle Hill Productions, 1414 Avenue of the
Americas, New York, NY 10019, 212/888-0080

NO NUKES (FD)   co-director with Danny Goldberg &
Anthony Potenza, Warner Bros., 1980
GOING HOLLYWOOD - THE 30'S (FD)   Castle Hill
Productions, 1984
GOING HOLLYWOOD - THE WAR YEARS (FD)   Castle Hill
Productions, 1988

OLIVER SCHMITZ

Contact: Department of the Interior, Civitas Building,
Struben Street, Pretoria 0002, South Africa, 12/48-2551

MAPANTSULA   Ray Wave Productions, 1988,
South African-Australian-British

DAVID SCHMOELLER

Business: The Schmoeller Corporation, 2244 Stanley Hills
Drive, Los Angeles, CA 90046, 213/654-0748
Agent: Martin Shapiro, Shapiro-Lichtman Agency -
Los Angeles, 213/859-8877

TOURIST TRAP   Compass International, 1979
THE SEDUCTION   Avco Embassy, 1981
CRAWLSPACE   Empire Pictures, 1986
CATACOMBS   Empire Pictures, 1988
PUPPET MASTER   Full Moon Entertainment, 1989
THE ARRIVAL   Del Mar Entertainment, 1990

PAUL SCHNEIDER*

Agent: Alan Greenspan, ICM - Los Angeles, 213/550-4428

SOMETHING SPECIAL   WILLY MILLY / I WAS A
TEENAGE BOY   Cinema Group, 1986
THE LEFTOVERS (TF)   Walt Disney TV, 1986
DANIEL AND THE TOWERS (TF)   Mark Taper
Forum, 1987
14 GOING ON 30 (TF)   Walt Disney TV, 1988
DANCE 'TIL DAWN (TF)   Konigsberg-Sanitsky
Productions, 1989

BABYCAKES (TF)   Konigsberg-Sanitsky
    Productions, 1989
MY BOYFRIEND'S BACK (TF)   Interscope
    Communications, 1989
HOW TO MURDER A MILLIONAIRE (TF)   Robert
    Greenwald Productions, 1990

ROBERT A. SCHNITZER
Business: Robert Schnitzer Productions, Inc., 7135
    Hollywood Blvd. - Suite 410, Los Angeles, CA 90046,
    213/850-1122

NO PLACE TO HIDE   American Films Ltd., 1975
THE PREMONITION   Avco Embassy, 1976
KANDYLAND   New World, 1988

RENEN SCHORR
Contact: Israel Film Centre, Ministry of Industry & Trade,
    30 Agron Street, P.O. Box 299, Jerusalem, Israel,
    02/210297

LATE SUMMER BLUES   Kino International, 1988, Israeli

DALE SCHOTT
Contact: Academy of Canadian Cinema and Television,
    633 Yonge Street - Second Floor, Toronto, Ontario
    M4Y 1Z9, Canada, 416/967-0315

CARE BEARS MOVIE II: A NEW GENERATION (AF)
    Columbia, 1986, Canadian

LEONARD SCHRADER
Contact: Henry Holmes - Los Angeles, 213/278-1111

NAKED TANGO   Sugarloaf/Gotan Productions/Towa
    Productions, 1990

PAUL SCHRADER*
b. July 22, 1946 - Grand Rapids, Michigan
Agent: ICM - Los Angeles, 213/550-4000

BLUE COLLAR   Universal, 1978
HARDCORE   Columbia, 1979
AMERICAN GIGOLO   Paramount, 1980
CAT PEOPLE   Universal, 1982
MISHIMA: A LIFE IN FOUR CHAPTERS   Warner Bros.,
    1985, Japanese-U.S.
LIGHT OF DAY   Tri-Star, 1987
PATTY HEARST   Atlantic Releasing Corporation, 1988
THE COMFORT OF STRANGERS   Erre Produzioni/
    Sovereign Pictures/Reteitalia, 1990, Italian-U.S.

MYRL SCHREIBMAN*
Home: 15913 Enadia Way, Van Nuys, CA 91406,
    818/989-3637
Agent: Christine Foster, The Agency - Los Angeles,
    213/551-3000

THE ITALIAN   Caracosta Films, 1979
ANGEL OF H.E.A.T.   Summa Vista, 1982
SO COOL   Chariot VII Productions, 1990

WILLIAM SCHREINER
Contact: Writers Guild of America, West - Los Angeles,
    213/550-1000

A SINFUL LIFE   New Line Cinema, 1989

BARBET SCHROEDER*
b. August 26, 1941 - Teheran, Iran
Business: Les Films du Losange, 26 Avenue Pierre de
    Serbie, Paris 75116, France, 04/472-5412

MORE   Cinema 5, 1969, Luxembourg
THE VALLEY obscured by clouds   Lagoon Associates,
    1972, French
IDI AMIN DADA   *GENERAL IDI AMIN DADA* (FD)   Tinc,
    1974, French
MAITRESSE   Tinc, 1976, French
KOKO, A TALKING GORILLA (FD)   New Yorker,
    1978, French
TRICHEURS   Gaumont, 1983, French-West German
BARFLY   Cannon, 1987
REVERSAL OF FORTUNE   Warner Bros., 1990

MICHAEL SCHROEDER*
b. November 12, 1952 - Klamath Falls, Oregon
Agent: David Gersh, The Gersh Agency - Beverly Hills,
    213/274-6611

MORTUARY ACADEMY   Landmark Releasing, 1987
OUT OF THE DARK   New Line Cinema, 1989
DAMNED RIVER   MGM/UA, 1989

CARL SCHULTZ*
b. September 19, 1939 - Budapest, Hungary
Agent: Martha Luttrell, ICM - Los Angeles, 213/550-4491

THE TICHBORNE AFFAIR (TF)   Australian Broadcasting
    Commission, 1977, Australian
BLUE FIN   Roadshow Distributors, 1978, Australian
RIDE ON STRANGER (TF)   Australian Broadcasting
    Commission, 1979, Australian
GOODBYE PARADISE   New South Wales Film
    Corporation, 1982, Australian
CAREFUL HE MIGHT HEAR YOU   TLC Films/20th
    Century Fox, 1983, Australian
THE DISMISSAL (MS)   co-director with George Miller, Phillip
    Noyce, George Ogilvie & John Power, 1983, Australian
BODYLINE (MS)   co-director with George Ogilvie, Denny
    Lawrence & Lex Marinos, 1984, Australian
TOP KID (TF)   Australian Children's Television Foundation/
    Australian Film Commission/ Film Victoria/New South
    Wales Film Corporation, 1985, Australian
BULLSEYE   Cinema Group, 1986, Australian
TRAVELLING NORTH   Cineplex Odeon, 1987, Australian
THE SEVENTH SIGN   Tri-Star, 1988
CASSIDY (MS)   Five Arrow Films/Australian Broadcasting
    Corporation/Archive Film, 1989, Australian
WHICH WAY HOME (CMS)   McElroy and McElroy/Network
    Ten Australia/Turner Network TV, 1990, Australian-U.S.

MICHAEL SCHULTZ*
b. November 10, 1938 - Milwaukee, Wisconsin
Agent: Alan Greenspan, ICM - Los Angeles, 213/550-4428

TOGETHER FOR DAYS   Olas, 1973
HONEYBABY, HONEYBABY   Kelly-Jordan, 1974
COOLEY HIGH   American International, 1975
CAR WASH   Universal, 1976
GREASED LIGHTNING   Warner Bros., 1977
WHICH WAY IS UP?   Universal, 1978
SGT. PEPPER'S LONELY HEARTS CLUB BAND
    Universal, 1978
SCAVENGER HUNT   20th Century-Fox, 1979
CARBON COPY   Avco Embassy, 1981

BENNY'S PLACE (TF)   Titus Productions, 1982
FOR US, THE LIVING (TF)   Charles Fries
   Productions, 1983
THE JERK, TOO (TF)   40 Share Productions/
   Universal TV, 1984
BERRY GORDY'S THE LAST DRAGON   *THE LAST
   DRAGON*   Tri-Star, 1985
KRUSH GROOVE   Warner Bros., 1985
TIMESTALKERS (TF)   Fries Entertainment/Newland-
   Raynor Productions, 1987
DISORDERLIES   Warner Bros., 1987
THE SPIRIT (TF)   von Zerneck-Samuels Productions/
   Warner Bros. TV, 1987
ROCK 'N' ROLL MOM (TF)   Walt Disney TV, 1988
TARZAN IN MANHATTAN (TF)   American First Run
   Studios, 1989
JURY DUTY: THE COMEDY (TF)   Steve White
   Productions/Spectator Films, 1990

JOEL SCHUMACHER*
b. 1942 - New York, New York
Agent: CAA - Beverly Hills, 213/288-4545

THE VIRGINIA HILL STORY (TF)   RSO Films, 1974
AMATEUR NIGHT AT THE DIXIE BAR & GRILL (TF)
   Motown/Universal TV, 1979
THE INCREDIBLE SHRINKING WOMAN   Universal, 1981
D.C. CAB   Universal, 1983
ST. ELMO'S FIRE   Columbia, 1985
THE LOST BOYS   Warner Bros., 1987
COUSINS   Paramount, 1989
FLATLINERS   Columbia, 1990

ARNOLD SCHWARTZMAN
GENOCIDE (FD)   Simon Wiesenthal Center, 1982

ETTORE SCOLA
b. May 10, 1931 - Trevico, Italy
Home: via Bertoloni 1/E, Rome, Italy, 06/875-174

LET'S TALK ABOUT WOMEN   *SE PERMETTETE,
   PARLIAMO DI DONNE*   Embassy, 1964,
   Italian-French
LA CONGIUNTURA   Fair Film/Les Films Concordia,
   1965, Italian-French
THRILLING   co-director, 1966, Italian
THE DEVIL IN LOVE   *L'ARCIDIAVOLO*   Warner Bros.,
   1966, Italian
RIUSCIRANNO I NOSTRI EROI A TROVARE L'AMICO
   MISTERIOSAMENTE SCOMPARSO IN AFRICA?
   Documento Film, 1968, Italian
IL COMMISSARIO PEPE   Dean Film, 1969, Italian
THE PIZZA TRIANGLE   *DRAMMA DELLA GELOSIA -
   TUTTI I PARTICOLARI IN CRONACA*   Warner Bros.,
   1970, Italian-Spanish
MY NAME IS ROCCO PAPALEO   Rumson, 1971, Italian
LA PIU BELLA SERATA DELLA MIA VITA   Dino De
   Laurentiis Cinematografica, 1972, Italian
TREVICO-TORINO...VIAGGIO NEL FIAT NAM
   1973, Italian
WE ALL LOVED EACH OTHER SO MUCH   Cinema 5,
   1975, Italian
DOWN AND DIRTY   *BRUTTI, SPORCHI E CATTIVI*
   New Line Cinema, 1976, Italian
SIGNORE E SIGNORI BUONANOTTE   co-director,
   Titanus, 1976, Italian
A SPECIAL DAY   Cinema 5, 1977, Italian
VIVA ITALIA!   *I NUOVI MOSTRI*   co-director with Mario
   Monicelli & Dino Risi, Cinema 5, 1978, Italian

LA TERRAZZA   United Artists, 1980, Italian-French
PASSIONE D'AMORE   Putnam Square, 1982,
   Italian-French
LA NUIT DE VARENNES   Triumph/Columbia, 1982,
   French-Italian
LE BAL   Almi Classics, 1983, French-Italian-Algerian
MACARONI   Paramount, 1985, Italian
THE FAMILY   Vestron, 1987, Italian
SPLENDOR   RAI/Studio EL, 1988, Italian
CHE ORA E'?   RAI/Studio EL, 1989, Italian
IL VIAGGIO DI CAPITAN FRACASSA   Tiger
   Cinematografica/Gaumont, 1990, Italian-French

MARTIN SCORSESE*
b. November 17, 1942 - Flushing, New York
Agent: CAA - Beverly Hills, 213/288-4545

WHO'S THAT KNOCKING AT MY DOOR?   Joseph Brenner
   Associates, 1968
BOXCAR BERTHA   American International, 1972
MEAN STREETS   Warner Bros., 1973
ALICE DOESN'T LIVE HERE ANYMORE   Warner
   Bros., 1974
ITALIANAMERICAN (FD)   1974
TAXI DRIVER   Columbia, 1976
NEW YORK, NEW YORK   United Artists, 1977
AMERICAN BOY (FD)   Scorsese Productions, 1978
THE LAST WALTZ   United Artists, 1978
RAGING BULL★   United Artists, 1978
THE KING OF COMEDY   20th Century-Fox, 1983
AFTER HOURS   The Geffen Company/Warner
   Bros., 1985
THE COLOR OF MONEY   Buena Vista, 1986
THE LAST TEMPTATION OF CHRIST★   Universal, 1988
NEW YORK STORIES   co-director with Woody Allen &
   Francis Ford Coppola, Buena Vista, 1989
GOODFELLAS   Warner Bros., 1990

GEORGE C. SCOTT*
b. October 18, 1927 - Wise, Virginia
Agent: Jane Deacy Agency - New York City,
   212/752-4865
Business Manager: Becker & London - New York City,
   212/541-7070

RAGE   Warner Bros., 1972
THE SAVAGE IS LOOSE   Campbell Devon, 1974

JAMES SCOTT
b. July 9, 1941 - Wells, England
Business: Flamingo Pictures, 47 Lonsdale Square, London
   N1 1EW, England
Agent: Triad Artists, Inc. - Los Angeles, 213/556-2727

EVERY PICTURE TELLS A STORY   Channel Four,
   1984, British
STRIKE IT RICH   Millimeter Films, 1990, British-U.S.

OZ SCOTT*
Agent: The Brandt Company - Studio City, 818/506-7747

BUSTIN' LOOSE   Universal, 1981
DREAMLAND   co-director with Nancy Baker & Joel
   Schulman, First Run Features, 1983
BRIDE OF BOOGEDY (TF)   Walt Disney TV, 1987
CRASH COURSE (TF)   Fries Entertainment, 1988
CLASS CRUISE (TF)   Portoangelo Productions, 1989

RIDLEY SCOTT*
b. England
Agent: Jeff Berg, ICM - Los Angeles, 213/550-4000

THE DUELLISTS Paramount, 1978, British
ALIEN 20th Century-Fox, 1979, U.S.-British
BLADE RUNNER The Ladd Company/Warner Bros., 1982
LEGEND Universal, 1986, British
SOMEONE TO WATCH OVER ME Columbia, 1987
BLACK RAIN Paramount, 1989
THELMA AND LOUISE Pathe Entertainment, 1991

TONY SCOTT*
b. England
Agent: CAA - Beverly Hills, 213/288-4545

THE HUNGER MGM/UA, 1983, British
TOP GUN Paramount, 1986
BEVERLY HILLS COP II Paramount, 1987
REVENGE Columbia, 1990
DAYS OF THUNDER Paramount, 1990

GEORGE SCRIBNER
Business: Walt Disney Productions, 500 S. Buena Vista
Street, Burbank, CA 91521, 213/845-3141

OLIVER AND COMPANY (AF) Buena Vista, 1988

SANDRA SEACAT
IN THE SPIRIT Castle Hill Productions, 1990

JOHN SEALE
Agent: William Morris Agency - Beverly Hills, 213/274-7451

TILL THERE WAS YOU McElroy & McElroy,
1990, Australian

PAUL SEED
b. September 18, 1947 - Devon, England
Home: 132 Kyverdale Road, London N16 6PU, England
Agent: Tim Corrie, Peters, Fraser & Dunlop, The
Chambers, Chelsea Harbour, Lots Road, London
SW10 0XF,71/376-7676

ACROSS THE WATER (TF) BBC, 1982, British
WYNNE & PENKOVSKY MAN FROM MOSCOW (TF)
BBC, 1984, British
INAPPROPRIATE BEHAVIOUR (TF) BBC, 1986, British
EVERY BREATH YOU TAKE (TF) Granada TV,
1987, British
THE PICNIC (TF) BBC, 1987, British
CAPITAL CITY (MS) co-director with Sarah Hellings &
Mike Vardy, Euston Films/Thames TV, 1989, British

ROBERT SEELEY
ROVER DANGERFIELD (AF) co-director with James
George, Warner Bros., 1991

ARTHUR ALLAN SEIDELMAN*
b. New York, New York
Agent: William Morris Agency - Beverly Hills, 213/274-7451
Business: Entertainment Professionals, Inc., 11300 W.
Olympic Blvd. - Suite 870, Los Angeles, CA 90064,
213/473-4747

HERCULES IN NEW YORK HERCULES GOES
BANANAS/HERCULES Filmpartners, 1970
CHILDREN OF RAGE LSF, 1975, U.S.-Israeli

ECHOES Entertainment Professionals, 1983
SIN OF INNOCENCE (TF) Renee Valente Productions/
Jeremac Productions/ 20th Century Fox TV, 1986
KATE'S SECRET (TF) Andrea Baynes Productions/
Columbia TV, 1986
GLORY DAYS (CTF) HBO, 1986
THE CALLER Empire Pictures, 1987
POKER ALICE (TF) New World TV, 1987
LITTLE GIRL LOST (TF) The Landsburg Company, 1987
THE BEST KEPT SECRET (TF) The Landsburg
Company, 1987
AN ENEMY AMONG US (TF) Helios Productions, 1987
STRANGE VOICES (TF) Forrest Hills Productions/Dacks-
Geller Productions/ TLC, 1987
ADDICTED TO HIS LOVE (TF) Green-Epstein Productions/
Columbia TV, 1988
A FRIENDSHIP IN VIENNA (CTF) Finnegan-Pinchuk
Productions, 1988
THE PEOPLE ACROSS THE LAKE (TF) Bill McCutchen
Productions/ Columbia TV, 1988
FALSE WITNESS (TF) Valente-Kritzer-EPI Productions/
New World TV, 1989

SUSAN SEIDELMAN*
Agent: Sam Cohn, ICM - New York City, 212/556-6810

SMITHEREENS New Line Cinema, 1982
DESPERATELY SEEKING SUSAN Orion, 1985
MAKING MR. RIGHT Orion, 1987
COOKIE Warner Bros., 1989
SHE-DEVIL Orion, 1990

ARNAUD SELIGNAC
Contact: French Film Office, 745 Fifth Avenue, New York,
NY 10151, 212/832-8860

DREAM ONE Columbia, 1984, British-French
SUEURS FROIDES (MS) co-director, 1988, French

JACK M. SELL*
b. September 15, 1954 - Albany, Georgia
Business: Sell Pictures, Inc., 9454 Wilshire Blvd. - Suite 600,
Beverly Hills, CA 90212, 213/874-5402
Business Manager: Adrienne Richmond, Richmond
Communications Inc., 2000 N. Highland Avenue - Suite 3,
Los Angeles, CA 90068, 213/851-8740

THE PSYCHOTRONIC MAN International Harmony, 1980
OUTTAKES Marketechnics, 1987
DEADLY SPYGAMES Sell Entertainment/Double
Helix, 1989

CHARLES E. SELLIER, JR.
Agent: The Schallert Agency - Beverly Hills,
213/276-2044

THE CAPTURE OF GRIZZLY ADAMS (TF) NBC
Entertainment, 1981
IN SEARCH OF A GOLDEN SKY Comworld, 1983
SMOOTH MOVES SNOW BALLING Comworld, 1984
SILENT NIGHT, DEADLY NIGHT Tri-Star, 1984
THE ANNIHILATORS New World, 1986

DAVID SELTZER*
Agent: CAA - Beverly Hills, 213/288-4545

LUCAS 20th Century Fox, 1986
PUNCHLINE Columbia, 1988

ARNA SELZNICK
b. 1948 - Toronto, Ontario, Canada
Address: 79 Blantyre Avenue, Scarborough, Ontario
M1N 2R6, Canada, 416/698-9888

THE CARE BEARS MOVIE (AF)   Samuel Goldwyn
Company, 1985, Canadian

OUSMANE SEMBENE
b. January 1, 1923 - Ziguinchor, Senegal
Contact: SIDEC, 12 rue Beranger Ferraud, B P 335,
Dakar, Senegal

BLACK GIRL   LA NOIRE DE...   New Yorker,
1966, Senegalese
MANDABI   Grove Press, 1968, Senegalese
EMITAI   New Yorker, 1974, Senegalese
XALA   New Yorker, 1974, Senegalese
CEDDO   New Yorker, 1977, Senegalese
CAMP DE THIAROYE   co-director with Thierno
Faty Sow, New Yorker, 1988,
Senegalese-Algerian-Tunisian-Italian

MRINAL SEN
b. May 4, 1923 - East Bengal, India
Contact: Films Division, Ministry of Information &
Broadcasting, 24 Dr G Beshmukh Marg, Bombay
40026, India, 36-1461

THE DAWN   1956, Indian
UNDER THE BLUE SKY   1959, Indian
THE WEDDING DAY   1960, Indian
OVER AGAIN   1961, Indian
AND AT LAST   1962, Indian
THE REPRESENTATIVE   1964, Indian
UP IN THE CLOUDS   1965, Indian
TWO BROTHERS   1967, Indian
MOVING PERSPECTIVES (FD)   1967, Indian
MR. SHOME   1969, Indian
THE WISH-FULFILLMENT   1970, Indian
INTERVIEW   1971, Indian
CALCUTTA 71   1972, Indian
AN UNFINISHED STORY   1972, Indian
THE GUERILLA FIGHTER   1973, Indian
CHORUS   1974, Indian
THE ROYAL HUNT   1976, Indian
THE OUTSIDERS   1977, Indian
THE MAN WITH THE AXE   1978, Indian
AND QUIET ROLLS THE DAWN   1979, Indian
IN SEARCH OF FAMINE   1980, Indian
THE KALEIDOSCOPE   1981, Indian
THE CASE IS CLOSED   1981, Indian
PORTRAIT OF A NEW MAN   1984, Indian
THE RUINS   Jagadish/Pushpa Chowkhani, 1984, Indian
GENESIS   Scarabee/French Ministry of Culture/Films
de la Dreve/Cactus Film/ Mrinal Sen Productions,
1986, French-Belgian-Swiss-Indian
SUDDENLY, ONE DAY   National Film Development
Corporation of India/ Doordarshan, 1989, Indian
CITY LIFE (FD)   co-director, Nederlands Film Museum/
International Art Film, 1990, Dutch

RALPH SENENSKY*
b. May 1, 1923 - Mason City, Iowa
Agent: Shapiro-Lichtman Agency - Los Angeles,
213/859-8877

A DREAM FOR CHRISTMAS (TF)   Lorimar
Productions, 1973
THE FAMILY KOVACK (TF)   Playboy Productions, 1974

DEATH CRUISE (TF)   Spelling-Goldberg Productions, 1974
THE FAMILY NOBODY WANTED (TF)   Universal TV, 1975
THE NEW ADVENTURES OF HEIDI (TF)   Pierre Cossette
Enterprises, 1978
DYNASTY (TF)   Aaron Spelling Productions/Fox-Cat
Productions, 1981

MICHAEL SERESIN*
Contact: Directors Guild of America - Los Angeles,
213/289-2000

HOMEBOY   Redbury Ltd./Elliott Kastner Productions, 1988

YAHOO SERIOUS
(Greg Pead)
Contact: Australian Film Commission, 9229 Sunset Blvd.,
Los Angeles, CA 90069, 213/275-7074

YOUNG EINSTEIN   Warner Bros., 1988, Australian

COLINE SERREAU
Agent: Triad Artists, Inc. - Los Angeles, 213/556-2727

PORQUOI PAS?   1979, French
3 MEN AND A CRADLE   Samuel Goldwyn Company,
1985, French
MAMA, THERE'S A MAN IN YOUR BED   ROMAULD ET
JULIETTE   Miramax Films, 1988, French

ALEX SESSA
Business: Aries International, S.A., Lavalle 1860, 1051
Buenos Aires, Argentina, tel.: 46-9249

AMAZONS   Concorde, 1987, U.S.-Argentine
STORMQUEST   Aries Film/Benlux Investment,
1988, Argentine
THE EYE OF THE HURRICANE   Aries Film/Bouchard
Productions, 1988, Argentine

PHILIPPE SETBON
Contact: French Film Office, 745 Fifth Avenue, New York,
NY 10151, 212/832-8860

MISTER FROST   SVS Films, 1990, French-British

JOHN SEXTON
Contact: Australian Film Commission, 9229 Sunset Blvd.,
Los Angeles, CA 90069, 213/275-7074

OUTBACK   International Film Management/Burrowes Film
Group/John Sexton Productions, 1990, Australian

NICHOLAS SGARRO*
Agent: Louis Bershad, Century Artists - Beverly Hills,
213/273-4366

THE HAPPY HOOKER   Cannon, 1975
THE MAN WITH THE POWER (TF)   Universal TV, 1977
BERRENGER'S (TF)   co-director with Larry Elikann,
Roundelay Productions/Lorimar Productions, 1985
FORTUNE DANE (TF)   Stormy Weathers Productions/
The Movie Company Enterprises/The Rosenzweig
Company, 1986

MICHAEL SHACKLETON
Address: 5 Queen Street, London W1, England, 71/499-6452

SURVIVOR (HVF)   Vestron Video/Omega Entertainment/
Matrix Motion Pictures, 1988

SUSAN SHADBURNE
Business: Millenium Pictures, Inc., 2580 N.W. Upshur,
    Portland, OR 97210, 503/227-7041

SHADOW PLAY   New World, 1986
GRANDPA'S MUSICAL TOYS (HVF)   Price Stern Sloan/
    Wee Sing Productions, 1988

KRISHNA SHAH*
b. May 10, 1938 - India
Business: 7135 Hollywood Blvd. - Suite 104, Los Angeles,
    CA 90046, 213/876-9236
Agent: David Shapira & Associates - Sherman Oaks,
    818/906-0322

RIVALS   *SINGLE PARENT*   Avco Embassy, 1972
THE RIVER NIGER   Cine Artists, 1976
SHALIMAR   *THE DEADLY THIEF*   Judson Productions/
    Laxmi Productions, 1978, U.S.-Indian
CINEMA-CINEMA (FD)   Shahab Ahmed Productions,
    1980, Indian
HARD ROCK ZOMBIES   Cannon, 1985
AMERICAN DRIVE-IN   Cinevest, 1985

LINA SHANKLIN
Business: Films That Make A Difference, Inc., 408 Linnie
    Canal Court, Venice, CA 90291, 213/827-4472

SUMMERSPELL   Summerspell Productions, 1983

ANN SHANKS*
b. New York, New York
Home: 160 East 65th Street, New York, NY 10021,
    212/861-8282
Agent: William Morris Agency - New York City,
    212/586-5100

FRIENDSHIPS, SECRETS AND LIES (TF)   co-director
    with Marlena Laird, Wittman-Riche Productions/
    Warner Bros. TV, 1979

JOHN PATRICK SHANLEY*
b. October 13, 1950 - New York, New York
Agent: William Morris Agency - Beverly Hills,
    213/274-7451

JOE VERSUS THE VOLCANO   Warner Bros., 1990

ALAN SHAPIRO
Agent: William Morris Agency - Beverly Hills,
    213/274-7451

TIGER TOWN (CTF)   Thompson Street Pictures, 1983
THE CHRISTMAS STAR (TF)   Lake Walloon
    Productions/Catalina Production Group/Walt
    Disney TV, 1986
THE OUTSIDERS (TF)   co-director with Sharron Miller,
    Zoetrope Studios/ Papazian-Hirsch Productions, 1990

KEN SHAPIRO*
b. 1943 - New Jersey
Contact: 20115 Observation Drive, Topanga, CA 90290,
    213/455-1222

THE GROOVE TUBE   Levitt-Pickman, 1974
MODERN PROBLEMS   20th Century-Fox, 1981

MELVIN SHAPIRO*
Contact: Directors Guild of America - Los Angeles,
    213/289-2000

SAMMY STOPS THE WORLD (FD)   Elkins, 1979

PAUL SHAPIRO
b. 1955 - Regina, Saskatchewan, Canada
Address: 41 Shanly Street - Suite 10, Toronto, Ontario
    M6H 1S2, Canada, 416/537-0031
Business: Martin-Paul Productions Ltd., 12 McMurrich Street,
    Toronto, Ontario M5R 2A2, Canada, 416/968-9375

THE UNDERSTUDY (TF)   1975, Canadian
CLOWN WHITE (TF)   Martin-Paul Productions,
    1980, Canadian
R.W. (TF)   Atlantis Films, 1982, Canadian
HOCKEY NIGHT (TF)   Martin-Paul Productions/CBS,
    1984, Canadian
MIRACLE AT MOREAUX (TF)   Atlantis Films,
    1985, Canadian
THE TRUTH ABOUT ALEX (CTF)   Scholastic Productions/
    Insight Productions, 1987, Canadian
ROAD TO AVONLEA (CMS)   Sullivan Films/The Disney
    Channel/CBC, 1990, Canadian-U.S.

JIM SHARMAN
Contact: M & L Casting Consultants, 49 Darlinghurst Road,
    Kings Cross, NSW, 2100, Australia, 02/358-3111

SHIRLEY THOMPSON VERSUS THE ALIENS   Kolossal
    Piktures, 1972, Australian
SUMMER OF SECRETS   Greater Union Film Distribution,
    1976, Australian
THE ROCKY HORROR PICTURE SHOW   20th Century-
    Fox, 1976, British
THE NIGHT THE PROWLER   International Harmony,
    1978, Australian
SHOCK TREATMENT   20th Century-Fox, 1981, British

ALAN SHARP*
Agent: Paul Kohner, Inc. - Los Angeles, 213/550-1060

LITTLE TREASURE   Tri-Star, 1985

DON SHARP
b. April, 1922 - Hobart, Tasmania
Home: 80 Castelnau, Barnes, London SW13 9EX, England,
    71/748-4333
Agent: Denis Selinger, ICM - London, 71/629-8080

THE GOLDEN AIRLINER   British Lion/Children's Film
    Foundation, 1955, British
THE ADVENTURES OF HAL 5   Children's Film Foundation,
    1958, British
THE IN-BETWEEN AGE   *THE GOLDEN DISC*   Allied
    Artists, 1958, British
THE PROFESSIONALS   American International,
    1960, British
LINDA   British Lion, 1961, British
IT'S ALL HAPPENING   *THE DREAM MAKER*   Universal,
    1963, British
KISS OF THE VAMPIRE   Universal, 1963, British
THE DEVIL-SHIP PIRATES   Columbia, 1964, British
WITCHCRAFT   20th Century-Fox, 1964, British
THE FACE OF FU MANCHU   7 Arts, 1965, British
CURSE OF THE FLY   20th Century-Fox, 1965, British

RASPUTIN - THE MAD MONK *I KILLED RASPUTIN*
20th Century-Fox, 1966, British-French-Italian
BANG, BANG, YOU'RE DEAD! *OUR MAN IN
MARRAKESH* American International,
1966, British
THE BRIDES OF FU MANCHU 7 Arts, 1966, British
THOSE FANTASTIC FLYING FOOLS *BLAST
OFF/JULES VERNE'S ROCKET TO THE MOON*
American International, 1967, British
TASTE OF EXCITEMENT Crispin, 1968, British
THE VIOLENT ENEMY 1969, British
PUPPET ON A CHAIN co-director with Geoffrey Reeve,
Cinerama Releasing Corporation, 1972, British
THE DEATH WHEELERS *PSYCHOMANIA* Scotia
International, 1973, British
DARK PLACES Cinerama Releasing Corporation,
1974, British
HENNESSY American International, 1975, British
CALLAN Cinema National, 1975, British
THE FOUR FEATHERS (TF) Norman Rosemont
Productions/Trident Films Ltd., 1978, U.S.-British
THE 39 STEPS International Picture Show Company,
1978, British
BEAR ISLAND Taft International, 1980,
Canadian-British
Q.E.D. (TF) 1982, British
WHAT WAITS BELOW Blossom Pictures, 1984
A WOMAN OF SUBSTANCE (MS) Artemis Portman
Productions, 1984, British
TUSITALA (MS) Australian Broadcasting Corporation/
Portman Productions/ Channel Four, 1986,
Australian-British
HOLD THE DREAM (TF) Robert Bradford Productions/
Taft Entertainment TV, 1986, U.S.-British
TEARS IN THE RAIN (CTF) British Lion/Yorkshire TV/
Atlantic Videoventures, 1988, British

IAN SHARP
b. November 13, 1946 - Clitheroe, Lancashire, England
Agent: Alan Greenspan, ICM - Los Angeles,
213/550-4000

THE MUSIC MACHINE Norfolk International Pictures/
Target International Pictures, 1979, British
THE FINAL OPTION *WHO DARES WINS* MGM/UA,
1983, British
ROBIN OF SHERWOOD (TF) HTV/Goldcrest Films &
Television, 1983, British
THE CORSICAN BROTHERS (TF) Rosemont
Productions, 1985, British-U.S.
C.A.T.S. EYES (TF) TVS, 1985, British
YESTERDAY'S DREAMS (MS) Central TV,
1987, British
CODENAME: KYRIL (TF) HTV/Incito Productions,
1988, British
TWIST OF FATE (TF) Henry Plitt-Larry White
Productions/ HTV/Columbia TV, 1989, British-U.S.
PRIDE AND EXTREME PREJUDICE (CTF) F.F.S.
Productions/Taurusfilm/ Blair Communications, 1990,
British-West German-U.S.
SECRET WEAPON (CTF) Griffin-Elysian Productions/
TVS/ABC-Australia, 1990, U.S.-British-Australian

PETER SHATALOW
b. Brussels, Belgium
Address: 1438 Queen Street East, Toronto, Ontario
M4L 1E1, Canada, 416/461-3614

BLUE CITY SLAMMERS Cineplex Odeon,
1988, Canadian

WILLIAM SHATNER*
b. March 22, 1931 - Montreal, Quebec, Canada
Agent: Triad Artists, Inc. - Los Angeles, 213/556-2727

STAR TREK V: THE FINAL FRONTIER
Paramount, 1989

MELVILLE SHAVELSON*
b. April 1, 1917 - Brooklyn, New York
Agent: William Morris Agency - Beverly Hills,
213/274-7451

THE SEVEN LITTLE FOYS Paramount, 1955
BEAU JAMES Paramount, 1957
HOUSEBOAT Paramount, 1958
THE FIVE PENNIES Paramount, 1959
IT STARTED IN NAPLES Paramount, 1960
ON THE DOUBLE Paramount, 1961
THE PIDGEON THAT TOOK ROME Paramount, 1962
A NEW KIND OF LOVE Paramount, 1963
CAST A GIANT SHADOW United Artists, 1966
YOURS, MINE AND OURS United Artists, 1968
THE WAR BETWEEN MEN AND WOMEN National
General, 1972
MIXED COMPANY United Artists, 1974
THE LEGEND OF VALENTINO (TF) Spelling-Goldberg
Productions, 1975
THE GREAT HOUDINIS (TF) ABC Circle Films, 1976
IKE (MS) co-director with Boris Sagal, ABC
Circle Films, 1979
THE OTHER WOMAN (TF) CBS Entertainment, 1983
DECEPTIONS (TF) co-director with Robert Chenault,
Louis Rudolph Productions/ Consolidated Productions/
Columbia TV, 1985, U.S.-British

LARRY SHAW*
Address: 2121 Kress Street, Los Angeles, CA 90046,
213/650-8440
Agent: Alan Greenspan, ICM - Los Angeles,
213/550-4000

POLICE STORY: COP KILLER (TF) Columbia TV, 1988
FEAR STALK (TF) Donald March Productions/ITC
Entertainment Group/CBS Entertainment, 1989

ROBERT SHAYE
Business: New Line Cinema, 116 N. Robertson Blvd. -
Suite 200, Los Angeles, CA 90048, 213/854-5811

BOOK OF LOVE New Line Cinema, 1990

LINDA SHAYNE
Agent: Shapiro-Lichtman Agency - Los Angeles,
213/859-8877

PURPLE PEOPLE EATER Concorde, 1988

JACK SHEA*
b. August 1, 1928 - New York, New York
Address: 8439 Sunset Blvd., Los Angeles, CA 90069,
213/656-9263
Business Manager: Freedman, Kinzelberg & Broder,
2121 Avenue of the Stars, Los Angeles, CA 90067,
213/277-0700

DAYTON'S DEVILS Commonwealth United, 1968
THE MONITORS Commonwealth United, 1969

DONALD SHEBIB

b. 1938 - Toronto, Canada
Agent: Jerry Adler, The Adler Agency - Los Angeles,
   213/278-3456
Business: Evdon Films Ltd., 312 Wright Avenue, Toronto,
   Ontario M6R 1L9, Canada, 416/536-8969

GOIN' DOWN THE ROAD   Chevron, 1970, Canadian
RIP-OFF   Alliance, 1971, Canadian
BETWEEN FRIENDS   Eudon Productions,
   1973, Canadian
SECOND WIND   Health and Entertainment Corporation
   of America, 1976, Canadian
FISH HAWK   Avco Embassy, 1981, Canadian
HEARTACHES   MPM, 1982, Canadian
RUNNING BRAVE   directed under pseudonym of D.S.
   Everett, Buena Vista, 1983, Canadian
THE CLIMB   CineTel Films, 1987, Canadian
THE LITTLE KIDNAPPERS (CTF)   Jones Maple Leaf/The
   Disney Channel/CBC/Resnick-Margellos Productions,
   1990, Canadian

MARTIN SHEEN*

(Ramon Estevez)
b. August 3, 1940 - Dayton, Ohio
Agent: Glennis Liberty, The Liberty Agency - Los Angeles,
   213/824-7937

CADENCE   The Movie Group, 1990

STANLEY SHEFF

LOBSTER MAN FROM MARS   Electric Pictures, 1989

RIKI SHELACH

Public Relations: Chen Sedan Public Relations, 11 Rabina
   Street, Tel Aviv 69395, Israel, 3/412669
Contact: Israel Film Centre, Ministry of Industry & Trade,
   30 Agron Street, P.O. Box 299, Jerusalem 94190,
   Israel, 02/210297

THE LAST WINTER   Triumph/Columbia,
   1983, Israeli
MERCENARY FIGHTERS   Cannon, 1988

JAMES SHELDON*

(James Schleifer)
b. November 12 - New York, New York
Home: 9428 Lloydcrest Drive, Beverly Hills, CA 90210,
   213/275-2210
Agent: Irv Schechter Company - Beverly Hills,
   213/278-8070

GIDGET GROWS UP (TF)   Screen Gems/Columbia
   TV, 1969
WITH THIS RING (TF)   The Jozak Company/
   Paramount TV, 1978
THE GOSSIP COLUMNIST (TF)   Universal TV, 1980

SIDNEY SHELDON*

b. February 11, 1917 - Chicago, Illinois
Agent: CAA - Beverly Hills, 213/288-4545
Business Manager: Gerald Breslauer, Breslauer,
   Jacobson & Rutman - Los Angeles, 213/282-0477

DREAM WIFE   MGM, 1953
THE BUSTER KEATON STORY   Paramount, 1957

RON SHELTON*

b. September 15, 1945 - Santa Barbara, California
Business: Raleigh Studios, 650 N. Bronson, Los Angeles,
   CA 90004, 213/462-5095
Agent: Geoffrey Sanford, Sanford-Beckett-Tobias-Skouras
   Agency - Los Angeles, 213/208-2100

BULL DURHAM   Orion, 1988
BLAZE   Buena Vista, 1989

SAM SHEPARD

(Samuel Shepard Rogers)
b. November 5, 1943 - Fort Sheridan, Illinois
Agent: ICM - Los Angeles, 213/550-4000

FAR NORTH   Alive Films, 1988

JOHN SHEPPARD

b. 1956 - Toronto, Ontario, Canada
Home: 62 Kilkenny Drive, Agincourt, Ontario M1W 1K1,
   Canada, 416/499-1580
Agent: Barry Perelman Agency - Los Angeles,
   213/274-5999

MANIA   co-director with Paul Lynch & D.M. Robertson,
   Simcom Productions, 1986, Canadian
HIGHER EDUCATION   Norstar Releasing,
   1987, Canadian

ADRIAN SHERGOLD

Agent: Duncan Heath 162/170 Wardour Street, London
   W1V 3AT, England, 71/439-1471

CHRISTABEL (MS)   BBC, 1988, British

JIM SHERIDAN

b. Dublin, Ireland
Agent: CAA - Beverly Hills, 213/288-4545

MY LEFT FOOT ★   Miramax Films, 1989, Irish-British
THE FIELD   Granada International, 1990, Irish-British

EDWIN (ED) SHERIN*

b. January 15, 1930 - Harrisburg, Pennsylvania
Business: 2920 Neilson Way - Suite 404, Santa Monica,
   CA 90405, 213/396-5726
Agent: William Morris Agency - Beverly Hills, 213/274-7451

VALDEZ IS COMING   United Artists, 1971
MY OLD MAN'S PLACE *GLORY BOY*   Cinerama
   Releasing Corporation, 1972
THE FATHER CLEMENTS STORY (TF)   Zev Braun
   Productions/Interscope Communications, 1987
LENA: MY 100 CHILDREN (TF)   Robert Greenwald
   Productions, 1987
SETTLE THE SCORE (TF)   Steve Sohmer Inc. Productions/
   ITC Entertainment Group, 1989
DAUGHTER OF THE STREETS (TF)   Adam Productions/
   20th Century Fox TV, 1990

ARTHUR SHERMAN*

Contact: Directors Guild of America - Los Angeles,
   213/289-2000

LIKEWISE   co-director with Elliott Kastner, Cinema
   Group, 1989

GARY A. SHERMAN*

Agent: David Wardlow, Camden Artists - Los Angeles,
   213/556-2022

RAW MEAT *DEATH LINE* American International, 1973
DEAD AND BURIED Avco Embassy, 1981
VICE SQUAD Avco Embassy, 1982
MYSTERIOUS TWO (TF) Alan Landsburg
   Productions, 1982
WANTED DEAD OR ALIVE New World, 1986
POLTERGEIST III MGM/UA, 1988
LISA MGM/UA, 1990

GEORGE SHERMAN*

b. July 14, 1908 - New York, New York
Business Manager: Cleo Ronson, Ron Sher Productions,
   317 N. Palm Drive, Beverly Hills, CA 90210,
   213/858-7720

WILD HORSE RODEO Republic, 1938
THE PURPLE VIGILANTES Republic, 1938
OUTLAWS OF SONORA Republic, 1938
RIDERS OF THE BLACK HILLS Republic, 1938
PALS OF THE SADDLE Republic, 1938
OVERLAND STAGE RAIDERS Republic, 1938
RHYTHM OF THE SADDLE Republic, 1938
SANTA FE STAMPEDE Republic, 1938
RED RIVER RANGE Republic, 1938
MEXICALI ROSE Republic, 1939
THE NIGHT RIDERS Republic, 1939
THREE TEXAS STEERS Republic, 1939
WYOMING OUTLAW Republic, 1939
COLORADO SUNSET Republic, 1939
NEW FRONTIER Republic, 1939
COWBOYS FROM TEXAS Republic, 1939
THE KANSAS TERRORS Republic, 1939
ROVIN' TUMBLEWEEDS Republic, 1939
SOUTH OF THE BORDER Republic, 1939
GHOST VALLEY RAIDERS Republic, 1940
ONE MAN'S LAW Republic, 1940
THE TULSA KID Republic, 1940
TEXAS TERRORS Republic, 1940
COVERED WAGON DAYS Republic, 1940
ROCKY MOUNTAIN RANGERS Republic, 1940
UNDER TEXAS SKIES Republic, 1940
THE TRAIL BLAZERS Republic, 1940
LONE STAR RAIDERS Republic, 1940
FRONTIER VENGEANCE Republic, 1940
WYOMING WILDCAT Republic, 1941
THE PHANTOM COWBOY Republic, 1941
TWO GUN SHERIFF Republic, 1941
DESERT BANDIT Republic, 1941
KANSAS CYCLONE Republic, 1941
DEATH VALLEY OUTLAWS Republic, 1941
A MISSOURI OUTLAW Republic, 1941
CITADEL OF CRIME Republic, 1941
THE APACHE KID Republic, 1941
ARIZONA TERRORS Republic, 1942
STAGECOACH EXPRESS Republic, 1942
JESSE JAMES JR. Republic, 1942
THE CYCLONE KID Republic, 1942
THE SOMBRERO KID Republic, 1942
X MARKS THE SPOT Republic, 1942
LONDON BLACKOUT MURDERS Republic, 1942
THE PURPLE V Republic, 1943
THE MANTRAP Republic, 1943
THE WEST SIDE KID Republic, 1943
MYSTERY BROADCAST Republic, 1943
THE LADY AND THE MONSTER Republic, 1944
STORM OVER LISBON Republic, 1944

THE CRIME DOCTOR'S COURAGE Columbia, 1945
THE GENTLEMAN MISBEHAVES Columbia, 1946
RENEGADES Columbia, 1946
TALK ABOUT A LADY Columbia, 1946
THE BANDIT OF SHERWOOD FOREST co-director with
   Henry Levin, Columbia, 1946
PERSONALITY KID Columbia, 1947
SECRETS OF THE WHISTLER Columbia, 1947
LAST OF THE REDMEN Columbia, 1947
RELENTLESS Columbia, 1948
BLACK BART Universal, 1948
RIVER LADY Universal, 1948
LARCENY Universal, 1948
RED CANYON Universal, 1949
CALAMITY JANE AND SAM BASS Universal, 1949
YES SIR, THAT'S MY BABY Universal, 1949
SWORD IN THE DESERT Universal, 1949
SPY HUNT Universal, 1950
THE SLEEPING CITY Universal, 1950
FEUDIN', FUSSIN' AND A-FIGHTIN' Universal, 1950
COMANCHE TERRITORY Universal, 1950
TOMAHAWK Universal, 1951
TARGET UNKNOWN Universal, 1951
THE RAGING TIDE Universal, 1951
THE GOLDEN HORDE Universal, 1951
STEEL TOWN Universal, 1952
AGAINST ALL FLAGS Universal, 1952
THE BATTLE AT APACHE PASS Universal, 1952
BACK AT THE FRONT Universal, 1952
THE LONE HAND Universal, 1953
WAR ARROW Universal, 1953
VEILS OF BAGDAD Universal, 1953
BORDER RIVER Universal, 1954
DAWN AT SOCORRO Universal, 1954
CHIEF CRAZY HORSE Universal, 1955
COUNT THREE AND PRAY Universal, 1955
THE TREASURE OF PANCHO VILLA Universal, 1955
COMANCHE Universal, 1956
REPRISAL! Columbia, 1956
THE HARD MAN Columbia, 1957
THE LAST OF THE FAST GUNS Universal, 1958
TEN DAYS TO TULARA United Artists, 1958
THE SON OF ROBIN HOOD 20th Century-Fox, 1959
THE FLYING FONTAINES Columbia, 1959
HELL BENT FOR LEATHER Universal, 1960
FOR THE LOVE OF MIKE 20th Century-Fox, 1960
THE ENEMY GENERAL Columbia, 1960
THE WIZARD OF BAGHDAD 20th Century-Fox, 1960
THE FIERCEST HEART 20th Century-Fox, 1961
PANIC BUTTON Gorton, 1964
MURIETA Warner Bros., 1965, Spanish
SMOKY 20th Century-Fox, 1966
BIG JAKE National General, 1971

VINCENT SHERMAN*

b. July 16, 1906 - Vienna, Georgia
Home: 6355 Sycamore Meadows Drive, Malibu, CA 90265,
   213/457-2229

THE RETURN OF DOCTOR X Warner Bros., 1939
SATURDAY'S CHILDREN Warner Bros., 1940
THE MAN WHO TALKED TOO MUCH Warner Bros., 1940
FLIGHT FROM DESTINY Warner Bros., 1942
UNDERGROUND Warner Bros., 1941
ALL THROUGH THE NIGHT Warner Bros., 1942
THE HARD WAY Warner Bros., 1942
OLD ACQUAINTANCE Warner Bros., 1942
IN OUR TIME Warner Bros., 1944
MR. SKEFFINGTON Warner Bros., 1945
PILLOW TO POST Warner Bros., 1945
NORA PRENTISS Warner Bros., 1947

Sh

FILM
DIRECTORS
GUIDE

F I L M   D I R E C T O R S

THE UNFAITHFUL   Warner Bros., 1947
THE ADVENTURES OF DON JUAN   Warner Bros., 1949
THE HASTY HEART   Warner Bros., 1949
BACKFIRE   Warner Bros., 1950
THE DAMNED DON'T CRY   Warner Bros., 1950
HARRIET CRAIG   Columbia, 1950
GOODBYE, MY FANCY   Warner Bros., 1951
LONE STAR   MGM, 1952
AFFAIR IN TRINIDAD   Columbia, 1952
DIFENDO IL MIO AMORE   1956, Italian
THE GARMENT JUNGLE   Columbia, 1957
THE NAKED EARTH   20th Century-Fox, 1959
THE YOUNG PHILADELPHIANS   Warner Bros., 1959
ICE PALACE   Warner Bros., 1960
A FEVER IN THE BLOOD   Warner Bros., 1961
THE SECOND TIME AROUND   20th Century-Fox, 1961
THE YOUNG REBEL   CERVANTES   American
   International, 1968, Italian- Spanish-French
THE LAST HURRAH (TF)   O'Connor-Becker Productions/
   Columbia TV, 1977
LADY OF THE HOUSE (TF)   co-director with Ralph
   Nelson, Metromedia Productions, 1978
WOMEN AT WEST POINT (TF)   Green-Epstein
   Productions/Alan Sacks Productions, 1979
BOGIE: THE LAST HERO (TF)   Charles Fries
   Productions, 1980
THE DREAM MERCHANTS (TF)   Columbia TV, 1980
TROUBLE IN HIGH TIMBER COUNTRY (TF)
   Witt-Thomas Productions/Warner Bros. TV, 1980

FRANK SHIELDS
NO CAUSE FOR ALARM   International Film
   Management/Jadran Film, 1990, U.S.-Yugoslavian

PETER SHILLINGFORD
b. London, England
Home: Shillingford & Company, 231 S. Orange Drive,
   Los Angeles, CA 90036, 213/939-2881

TODAY MEXICO - TOMORROW THE WORLD
   Shillingford & Company/ Rank, 1970, British
THE MAKING OF 'STAR WARS' (TD)   co-director,
   Lucasfilm/20th Century-Fox TV, 1977
THE ENGLISH GIRL ABROAD   Border Films,
   1979, British

GILBERT SHILTON*
b. 1945
Address: 315 S. Beverly Drive - Suite 412, Beverly Hills,
   CA 90212, 213/553-0171
Agent: Ken Gross, Robinson, Weintraub, Gross &
   Associates - Los Angeles, 213/643-5802

SPEARFIELD'S DAUGHTER (MS)   Robert Halmi, Inc./
   Channel Seven, 1986, U.S.-Australian

NELSON SHIN
THE TRANSFORMERS - THE MOVIE (AF)   DEG, 1986

KANETO SHINDO
b. April 22, 1922 - Hiroshima Prefecture, Japan
Contact: Directors Guild of Japan, Tsukada Building,
   8-33 Udagawa-cho, Shibuya-ku, Tokyo 150, Japan,
   3/461-4411

STORY OF MY LOVING WIFE   1951, Japanese
AVALANCHE   1952, Japanese
CHILDREN OF THE ATOM BOMB   1952, Japanese
EPITOME   1953, Japanese

A LIFE OF A WOMAN   1953, Japanese
GUTTER   1954, Japanese
WOLVES   1955, Japanese
SILVER DOUBLE SUICIDE   1956, Japanese
BANK OF DEPARTURE   1956, Japanese
AN ACTRESS   1956, Japanese
GUYS OF THE SEA   1957, Japanese
SORROW IS ONLY FOR WOMEN   1957, Japanese
DAI GO FUKURYU-MARU   1959, Japanese
THE WORLD'S BEST BRIDE   1959, Japanese
GRAFFITI BLACKBOARD   1959, Japanese
THE ISLAND   Zenith International, 1960, Japanese
HUMAN BEING   1962, Japanese
MOTHER   1962, Japanese
ONIBABA   Toho, 1964, Japanese
A SCOUNDREL   1965, Japanese
INSTINCT   1966, Japanese
MONUMENT OF TOTSUSEKI   1966, Japanese
FOUR SEASONS OF TATESHINA   1966, Japanese
ORIGIN OF SEX   1967, Japanese
A BLACK CAT IN THE BUSH   1968, Japanese
STRONG WOMAN AND WEAK MAN   1968, Japanese
HEAT HAZE   1969, Japanese
TENTACLES   1970, Japanese
NAKED 19-YEAR-OLD   1970, Japanese
IRON RING   1972, Japanese
A PAEAN   1972, Japanese
HEART   1973, Japanese
MY WAY   1974, Japanese
LIFE OF A FILM DIRECTOR: RECORD OF KENJI
   MIZOGUCHI (FD)   1975, Japanese
LIFE OF CHIKUZAN   1977, Japanese
HOKUSAI, UKIYOE MASTER   1982, Japanese
THE HORIZON   Toho, 1984, Japanese
A DECIDUOUS TREE   Kindai Eikyo, 1987, Japanese
SAKUR TAI 8-6 (FD)   Kindai Eiga Kyokai, 1988, Japanese

MASAHIRO SHINODA
b. March 9, 1931 - Gifu Prefecture, Japan
Address: 1-11-16 Kita-Senzoku, Ota-ku, Tokyo 145, Japan,
   03/723-4060
Business Manager: Herald Ace Inc., No. 1 Ekimae Building,
   2-20-15, Shimbashi, Minato-ku, Tokyo 105, Japan,
   03/573-1150

ONE WAY TICKET FOR LOVE   Shochiku, 1960, Japanese
DRY LAKE   Shochiku, 1960, Japanese
MY FACE RED IN THE SUNSET   Shochiku,
   1961, Japanese
EPITAPH TO MY LOVE   Shochiku, 1961, Japanese
SHAMISEN AND MOTORCYCLE   Shochiku,
   1961, Japanese
OUR MARRIAGE   Shochiku, 1962, Japanese
GLORY ON THE SUMMIT: BURNING YOUTH   Shochiku,
   1962, Japanese
TEARS ON THE LION'S MANE   Shochiku, 1962,
   Japanese
PALE FLOWER   Shochiku, 1963, Japanese
ASSASSINATION   Toho, 1964, Japanese
WITH BEAUTY AND SORROW   Shochiku,
   1965, Japanese
SAMURAI SPY   Films Inc., 1965, Japanese
PUNISHMENT ISLAND   Films Inc., 1966, Japanese
CLOUDS AT SUNSET   Hyogensha/Shochiku,
   1967, Japanese
DOUBLE SUICIDE   Toho, 1969, Japanese
THE SCANDALOUS ADVENTURES OF BURAIKAN   Toho,
   1970, Japanese
SILENCE   Toho, 1971, Japanese
SAPPORO WINTER OLYMPIC GAMES (FD)   Toho,
   1972, Japanese

THE PETRIFIED FOREST   Hyogensha/Toho,
   1973, Japanese
HIMIKO   Hyogensha/ATG, 1974, Japanese
UNDER THE CHERRY BLOSSOMS   Geiensha/Toho,
   1975, Japanese
NIHON-MARU SHIP (FD)   1976, Japanese
SADO'S ONDEKO-ZA (FD)   1976, Japanese
THE BALLAD OF ORIN   Kino International, 1977,
   Japanese
DEMON POND   Kino International, 1979, Japanese
ISLAND OF EVIL SPIRITS   Kadokawa/Toei,
   1981, Japanese
MacARTHUR'S CHILDREN   Orion Classics,
   1984, Japanese
GONZA THE SPEARMAN   Shochiku/Hyogensha,
   1986, Japanese
DIE TANZERIN   Manfred Durniok Productions/Herald
   Ace, 1990, West German-Japanese

JACK SHOLDER*

Agent: Alan Greenspan, ICM - Los Angeles, 213/550-4428
Attorney: Henry E. Schays, Goldstein, Schrank, Selegstein,
   99 Park Avenue, New York, NY 10016, 212/986-3036

ALONE IN THE DARK   New Line Cinema, 1982
A NIGHTMARE ON ELM STREET, PART 2: FREDDY'S
   REVENGE   New Line Cinema, 1985
THE HIDDEN   New Line Cinema, 1987
RENEGADES   Universal, 1989
GRAND TOUR (CTF)   HBO Pictures, 1989
BY DAWN'S EARLY LIGHT (CTF)   HBO Pictures/
   Paravision International, 1990

SIG SHORE

Contact: Writers Guild of America, East - New York City,
   212/245-6180

THAT'S THE WAY OF THE WORLD   *SHINING STAR*
   United Artists, 1975
THE ACT   Artists Releasing Corporation/Film Ventures
   International, 1984
SUDDEN DEATH   Marvin Films, 1985
THE SURVIVALIST   Skouras Pictures, 1987
THE RETURN OF SUPERFLY   Triton Pictures, 1990

ROBERT SHORT*

b. December 22, 1950 - Santa Monica, California
Business: Robert Short Productions, 4228 Glencoe
   Avenue, Marina del Rey, CA 90292, 213/306-6842

PROGRAMMED TO KILL   co-director with Allan Holzman,
   Trans World Entertainment, 1987

CHARLES SHYER*

b. October 11, 1941 - Los Angeles, California
Agent: Jeff Berg, ICM - Los Angeles, 213/550-4000

IRRECONCILABLE DIFFERENCES   Warner Bros., 1984
BABY BOOM   MGM/UA, 1987

ANDY SIDARIS*

b. February 20, 1933 - Chicago, Illinois
Business: The Sidaris Company, 9229 Sunset Blvd. -
   Suite 208, Los Angeles, CA 90069, 213/278-5056

THE RACING SCENE (FD)   Filmways, 1970
STACEY   New World, 1973
SEVEN   American International, 1979

MALIBU EXPRESS   Malibu Bay Films, 1984
HARD TICKET TO HAWAII   Malibu Bay Films, 1987
PICASSO TRIGGER   Malibu Bay Films, 1988
SAVAGE BEACH   Malibu Bay Films, 1989
GUNS   Malibu Bay Films, 1990

GEORGE SIDNEY*

b. October 4, 1916 - Long Island City, New York
Home: 910 N. Rexford Drive, Beverly Hills, CA 90210

FREE AND EASY   MGM, 1941
PACIFIC RENDEZVOUS   MGM, 1942
PILOT NO. 5   MGM, 1943
THOUSANDS CHEER   MGM, 1943
BATHING BEAUTY   MGM, 1944
ANCHORS AWEIGH   MGM, 1945
THE HARVEY GIRLS   MGM, 1946
HOLIDAY IN MEXICO   MGM, 1946
CASS TIMBERLANE   MGM, 1947
THE THREE MUSKETEERS   MGM, 1948
THE RED DANUBE   MGM, 1949
KEY TO THE CITY   MGM, 1950
ANNIE GET YOUR GUN   MGM, 1950
SHOW BOAT   MGM, 1951
SCARAMOUCHE   MGM, 1952
YOUNG BESS   MGM, 1953
KISS ME KATE   MGM, 1953
JUPITER'S DARLING   MGM, 1955
THE EDDY DUCHIN STORY   Columbia, 1956
JEANNE EAGELS   Columbia, 1957
PAL JOEY   Columbia, 1957
WHO WAS THAT LADY?   Columbia, 1960
PEPE   Columbia, 1960
BYE BYE BIRDIE   Columbia, 1963
A TICKLISH AFFAIR   MGM, 1963
VIVA LAS VEGAS   MGM, 1964
THE SWINGER   Paramount, 1966
HALF A SIXPENCE   Paramount, 1968, British

DON SIEGEL*

b. October 26, 1912 - Chicago, Illinois
Home: 645 Barberry Way, Nipomo, CA 93444,
   805/343-5566
Business Manager: Dick deBlois, Mejia & Company, 9171
   Wilshire Blvd. - Suite 541, Beverly Hills, CA 90210,
   213/273-7769

THE VERDICT   Warner Bros., 1946
NIGHT UNTO NIGHT   Warner Bros., 1949
THE BIG STEAL   RKO Radio, 1949
DUEL AT SILVER CREEK   Universal, 1952
NO TIME FOR FLOWERS   RKO Radio, 1952
COUNT THE HOURS   RKO Radio, 1953
CHINA VENTURE   Columbia, 1953
RIOT IN CELL BLOCK 11   Allied Artists, 1954
PRIVATE HELL 36   Filmmakers, 1954
AN ANNAPOLIS STORY   Allied Artists, 1955
INVASION OF THE BODY SNATCHERS   Allied
   Artists, 1956
CRIME IN THE STREETS   Allied Artists, 1956
BABY FACE NELSON   Allied Artists, 1957
SPANISH AFFAIR   Paramount, 1958, Spanish
THE LINEUP   Columbia, 1958
THE GUN RUNNERS   United Artists, 1958
HOUND DOG MAN   20th Century-Fox, 1959
EDGE OF ETERNITY   Columbia, 1959
FLAMING STAR   20th Century-Fox, 1960
HELL IS FOR HEROES   Paramount, 1962
THE KILLERS   Universal, 1964
THE HANGED MAN (TF)   Universal TV, 1964

STRANGER ON THE RUN (TF)   Universal TV, 1967
MADIGAN   Universal, 1968
COOGAN'S BLUFF   Universal, 1968
DEATH OF A GUNFIGHTER   co-director with Robert
    Totten, both directed under pseudonym of Allen
    Smithee, Universal, 1969
TWO MULES FOR SISTER SARA   Universal, 1970,
    U.S.-Mexican
THE BEGUILED   Universal, 1971
DIRTY HARRY   Warner Bros., 1972
CHARLEY VARRICK   Universal, 1973
THE BLACK WINDMILL   Universal, 1974, British
THE SHOOTIST   Paramount, 1976
TELEFON   MGM/United Artists, 1977
ESCAPE FROM ALCATRAZ   Paramount, 1979
ROUGH CUT   Paramount, 1980
JINXED   MGM/UA, 1982

ROBERT J. SIEGEL*
Contact: Directors Guild of America - New York City,
    212/581-0370

PARADES   Cinerama Releasing Corporation, 1972

JAMES SIGNORELLI*
Contact: Directors Guild of Ameica - Los Angeles,
    213/289-2000

EASY MONEY   Orion, 1983
ELVIRA, MISTRESS OF THE DARK   New World, 1988

SLOBODAN SIJAN
Contact: Yugoslavia Film, Knez Mihailova 19, 11000
    Belgrade, Yugoslavia, 011/625-860

WHO'S SINGING OVER THERE?   Centar Film,
    1982, Yugoslavian
THE MARATHON FAMILY   Centar Film,
    1984, Yugoslavian
HOW I WAS SYSTEMATICALLY DESTROYED BY
    AN IDIOT   Paris-Union Film, 1984, Yugoslavian
STRANGLER VS. STRANGLER   Centar Film, 1986,
    Yugoslavian
SECRET INGREDIENT   Hemdale, 1988,
    U.S.-Yugoslavian

JOEL SILBERG*
(Yoel Zilberg)
Address: 12 Mishmar-Hagwul Street, Afeka, Israel 69697,
    03/415-640
Agent: The Gersh Agency - Beverly Hills, 213/274-6611

(The following is an incomplete list of Mr. Silberg's credits)

GET ZORKIN   1968, Israeli
GAMLIEL   1972, Israeli
THE RABBI AND THE SHIKSE   Roll Films,
    1976, Israeli
MILLIONAIRE IN TROUBLE   Shapira Films,
    1978, Israeli
MARRIAGE, TEL AVIV STYLE   Noah Films,
    1979, Israeli
MY MOTHER THE GENERAL   Noah Films,
    1981, Israeli
BREAKDANCIN'   MGM/UA/Cannon, 1984
RAPPIN'   Cannon, 1985
BAD GUYS   Interpictures, 1986
CATCH THE HEAT   *FEEL THE HEAT*   Trans World
    Entertainment, 1987
LAMBADA   Warner Bros., 1990

ANDREW SILVER
Business: Silver Productions, 260 Beacon Street, Boston,
    MA 02116, 617/ 266-6482 or: 24 Central Park South,
    New York, NY 10019, 212/355-5291

RETURN   Silver Productions, 1985

JOAN MICKLIN SILVER*
b. May 24, 1935 - Omaha, Nebraska
Agent: Broder-Kurland-Webb-Uffner Agency - Los Angeles,
    213/656-9262
Business: Midwest Film Productions, 600 Madison Avenue,
    New York, NY 10022, 212/355-0282

HESTER STREET   Midwest Film Productions, 1975
BETWEEN THE LINES   Midwest Film Productions, 1977
HEAD OVER HEELS   *CHILLY SCENES OF WINTER*
    United Artists, 1979
HOW TO BE A PERFECT PERSON IN JUST THREE
    DAYS (TF)   PBS, 1984
FINNEGAN BEGIN AGAIN (CTF)   HBO Premiere Films/
    Zenith Productions/ Jennie & Co. Film Productions,
    1985, U.S.-British
CROSSING DELANCEY   Warner Bros., 1988
LOVERBOY   Tri-Star, 1989

MARISA SILVER
b. April 23, 1960 - Cleveland, Ohio
Agent: Alan Greenspan, ICM - Los Angeles, 213/550-4428

OLD ENOUGH   Orion Classics, 1984
PERMANENT RECORD   Paramount, 1988
VITAL SIGNS   20th Century Fox, 1990
HE SAID, SHE SAID   co-director with Ken Kwapis,
    Paramount, 1991

RAPHAEL D. SILVER*
Business: Midwest Film Productions, 600 Madison Avenue,
    New York, NY 10022, 212/355-0282

ON THE YARD   Midwest Film Productions, 1979
A WALK ON THE MOON   Skouras Pictures, 1987

MARC SILVERMAN
Business: 62 West Productions, 62 West 70th Street,
    New York, NY 10023, 212/595-5464

LE FILM NOIR   Worthwhile Pictures, 1983
RUMSEY STATUES (FD)   Dubin/Rumsey Foundation, 1986

ELLIOT SILVERSTEIN*
b. 1927 - Boston, Massachusetts
Agent: Phil Gersh, The Gersh Agency - Beverly Hills,
    213/274-6611

BELLE SOMMARS   Columbia, 1962
CAT BALLOU   Columbia, 1965
THE HAPPENING   Columbia, 1967
A MAN CALLED HORSE   National General, 1970
DEADLY HONEYMOON   *NIGHTMARE HONEYMOON*
    MGM, 1974
THE CAR   Universal, 1977
BETRAYED BY INNOCENCE (TF)   Inter Planetary Pictures/
    CBS Entertainment, 1986
NIGHT OF COURAGE (TF)   Titus Productions/The Eugene
    O'Neill Memorial Theater Center, 1987
FIGHT FOR LIFE (TF)   Fries Entertainment, 1987
RICH MEN, SINGLE WOMEN (TF)   Aaron Spelling
    Productions, 1990

ANTHONY SIMMONS

Agent: Hatton and Baker, 18 Jermyn Street, London
  SW1Y 6HN, England, 71/439-2971
Business: West One Film Producers Ltd., c/o Robert
  Rosner, Palladium House, 1-4 Argyll Street,
  London W1, England

YOUR MONEY OR YOUR WIFE   Rank, 1960, British
FOUR IN THE MORNING   West One, 1965, British
THE OPTIMISTS   *THE OPTIMISTS OF NINE ELMS*
  Paramount, 1973, British
BLACK JOY   Hemdale, 1977, British
ON GIANT'S SHOULDERS (TF)   BBC, 1979, British
SUPERGRAN (TF)   Newcastle, 1984, British
DAY AFTER THE FAIR (TF)   BBC/Bill Kenwright Films
  Ltd./Arts & Entertainment Network, 1987, British
LITTLE SWEETHEART   Columbia, 1988, U.S.-British

ADAM SIMON

BRAIN DEAD   Concorde, 1990

FRANCIS SIMON

THE CHICKEN CHRONICLES   Avco Embassy, 1977

ROGER L. SIMON*

Agent: Bauer Benedek Agency - Los Angeles,
  213/275-2421

MY MAN ADAM   Tri-Star, 1985

YVES SIMONEAU

Address: 5046 rue Clark, Montreal, Quebec H2T 2T8,
  Canada, 514/271-7593
Agent: InterTalent - Los Angeles, 213/551-3000

LES CELEBRATIONS   Le Loup Blanc, 1979, Canadian
LES YEUX ROUGES OU LES VERITES ACCIDENTELLES
  Les Films du Crepuscule, 1982, Canadian
POURQUOI L'ETRANGE MONSIEUR ZOLOCK
  S'INTERESSAIT-IL TANT A LA BANDE DESSINEE?
  Salon International du Livre du Quebec,
  1983, Canadian
POUVOIR INTIME   Cinema Group, 1986, Canadian
LES FOUS DE BASSAN   1987, Canadian
DAN LE VENTRE DU DRAGON   Quebec-Amerique/Lenox
  Productions, 1989, Canadian
PERFECTLY NORMAL   Bialystock & Bloom Ltd.,
  1989, Canadian

MICHAEL A. SIMPSON

Business: Double Helix Films, Inc., 303 West 76th Street -
  Suite B, New York, NY 10023

IMPURE THOUGHTS   ASA Communications, 1986
FUNLAND   Vestron, 1987
SLEEPAWAY CAMP II: UNHAPPY CAMPERS   Double
  Helix, 1988
SLEEPAWAY CAMP III: TEENAGE WASTELAND
  Double Helix, 1988
FAST FOOD   Fries Distribution, 1989

FRANK SINATRA*

b. December 12, 1915 - Hoboken, New Jersey
Business Manager: Nathan Golden, 8501 Wilshire Blvd. -
  Suite 250, Beverly Hills, CA 90211, 213/855-0850

NONE BUT THE BRAVE   Warner Bros., 1964,
  U.S.-Japanese

ANDREW SINCLAIR

Contact: British Academy of Film & Television Arts, 195
  Piccadilly, London W1, England, 71/732-0022

THE BREAKING OF BUMBO   Timon/ABPC, 1971, British
UNDER MILD WOOD   Altura, 1973, British
BLUE BLOOD   Mallard Productions, 1975, British

GERALD SETH SINDELL

b. April 15, 1944 - Cleveland, Ohio
Home: 9655 Yoakum Drive, Beverly Hills, CA 90210,
  213/275-3353
Agent: Jim Preminger Agency - Los Angeles, 213/475-9491

DOUBLE-STOP   World Entertainment, 1967
HARPY (TF)   Cinema Center 100, 1970
TEENAGER   National Cinema, 1974
H.O.T.S.   Derio Productions, 1979

ALEXANDER SINGER*

b. 1932 - New York, New York
Agent: Sheri Mann Agency - Los Angeles, 213/850-1777

A COLD WIND IN AUGUST   Lopert, 1961
PSYCHE 59   Royal Films International, 1964, British
LOVE HAS MANY FACES   Columbia, 1965
CAPTAIN APACHE   Scotia International, 1971, British
GLASS HOUSES   Columbia, 1972
THE FIRST 36 HOURS OF DR. DURANT (TF)
  Columbia TV, 1975
TIME TRAVELERS (TF)   Irwin Allen Productions/20th
  Century-Fox TV, 1976
THE MILLION DOLLAR RIP-OFF (TF)   Charles Fries
  Productions, 1976
HUNTERS OF THE REEF (TF)   Writers Company
  Productions/Paramount TV, 1978
THE RETURN OF MARCUS WELBY, M.D. (TF)   Marstar
  Productions/ Universal TV, 1984

RALPH S. SINGLETON*

Business: R. S. Singleton Productions, c/o Perry & Neidorf,
  315 S. Beverly Dr., #412, Beverly Hills, CA 90212,
  213/553-0171
Agent: Harold Cohen, Associated Management -
  Los Angeles, 213/550-0570

GRAVEYARD SHIFT   Paramount, 1990

GARY SINISE*

Agent: Bill Douglass, ICM - Los Angeles, 213/550-4178

MILES FROM HOME   Cinecom, 1988

BERNHARD SINKEL

Contact: German Film & TV Academy, Pommernallee 1,
  1 Berlin 19, West Germany, 0311/302-6096

SINS OF THE FATHERS   *FATHERS AND SONS* (MS)
  Bavaria Atelier/ WDR/Taurus Film/FR3/ORF/RAI,
  1987, West German-French-Italian
HEMINGWAY (MS)   Alcor Films/Daniel Wilson Productions/
  DWP/Cine Alliance/Channel Four/RAI/TFI/ZDF, 1988,
  West German-U.S.- French-British-Italian

HAL SITOWITZ*

Agent: Triad Artists, Inc. - Los Angeles, 213/556-2727

A LAST CRY FOR HELP (TF)   Myrt-Hal Productions/
  Viacom, 1979

VILGOT SJOMAN
(David Harald Vilgot Sjoman)
b. December 2, 1924 - Stockholm, Sweden
Contact: Swedish Film Institute, P.O. Box 27126,
    102 52 Stockholm, Sweden, 08/63-0510

THE SWEDISH MISTRESS   1962, Swedish
491   Peppercorn-Wormser, 1964, Swedish
THE DRESS   1964, Swedish
STIMULANTIA   co-director, 1965, Swedish
MY SISTER, MY LOVE   *SYSKONBADD 1782*   Sigma III,
    1966, Swedish
I AM CURIOUS (YELLOW)   Grove Press, 1967, Swedish
I AM CURIOUS (BLUE)   Grove Press, 1968, Swedish
YOU'RE LYING   Grove Press, 1969, Swedish
BLUSHING CHARLIE   1970, Swedish
TILL SEX DO US PART   TROLL   Astro, 1971, Swedish
THE KARLSSON BROTHERS   1972, Swedish
A HANDFUL OF LOVE   1974, Swedish
THE GARAGE   1975, Swedish
TABU   Svensk Filminstitut, 1977, Swedish
LINUS AND THE MYSTERIOUS RED BRICK HOUSE
    Svensk Filmindustri, 1979, Swedish
I AM BLUSHING   1982, Swedish
MALACCA   Filmstallet/TV-2/Swedish Film Institute/Vilgot
    Sjoman Film, 1986, Swedish
THE PITFALL   Facta & Fiction/Swedish TV/Swedish Film
    Institute/Sandrews, 1989, Swedish

CALVIN SKAGGS
THE FIG TREE (TF)   KERA/Lumiere Productions/
    WonderWorks, 1987

JERZY SKOLIMOWSKI*
b. May 5, 1938 - Warsaw, Poland
Home: 514 Alta Avenue, Santa Monica, CA, 213/451-1010
Agent: ICM - Los Angeles, 213/550-4000

IDENTIFICATION MARKS: NONE   New Yorker,
    1964, Polish
WALKOVER   New Yorker, 1965, Polish
BARRIER   Film Polski, 1966, Polish
LE DEPART   Pathé Contemporary, 1967, Belgian
HANDS UP!   1967, Polish
DIALOGUE   co-director, 1968, Czech
THE ADVENTURES OF GIRARD   United Artists, 1969,
    British-Swiss
DEEP END   Paramount, 1971, British-West German
KING, QUEEN, KNAVE   Avco Embassy, 1972, West
    German-British
THE SHOUT   Films Inc., 1979, British
MOONLIGHTING   Universal Classics, 1982, British
SUCCESS IS THE BEST REVENGE   Triumph/Columbia,
    1984, British
THE LIGHTSHIP   Castle Hill Productions, 1985,
    U.S.-West German
TORRENTS OF SPRING   Millimeter Films, 1989,
    Italian-French

BOB SKOTAK
Agent: The Chasin Agency - Beverly Hills, 213/278-7505

INVASION EARTH: THE ALIENS ARE HERE   New
    World, 1987

LANE SLATE*
Agent: CAA - Beverly Hills, 213/288-4545

CLAY PIGEON   co-director with Tom Stern, MGM, 1971
DEADLY GAME (TF)   MGM TV, 1977

AVIVA SLESIN*
b. February 5, 1946 - Shaulen, Lithuania
Address: 155 East 77th Street - Apt. 5A, New York, NY
    10021, 212/734-1940

DIRECTED BY WILLIAM WYLER (FD)   Topgallant
    Productions/Tatge Productions, 1986
THE TEN YEAR LUNCH: THE WIT AND LEGEND OF THE
    ALGONQUIN ROUND TABLE (FD)   Aviva Films, 1987

JON SMALL
THE TEDDY BEAR HABIT   Advocate Productions, 1990

JOHN SMALLCOMBE
Contact: British Academy of Film & Television Arts,
    195 Piccadilly, London W1, England, 71/734-0022

AN AFRICAN DREAM   Hemdale, 1988, British

ROBERT J. SMAWLEY*
Home: 11838 Sheldon - Apt. 5, Sun Valley, CA 91352,
    818/896-1711

MURPHY'S FAULT   Triax Entertainment Group,
    1989, British
AMERICAN EAGLE   Triax Entertainment Group, 1990
RIVER OF DIAMONDS   Karat Film/IMV, 1990,
    West German

JACK SMIGHT*
b. March 9, 1926 - Minneapolis, Minnesota
Agent: Tom Chasin, The Chasin Agency - Beverly Hills,
    213/278-7505

I'D RATHER BE RICH   Universal, 1964
THE THIRD DAY   Warner Bros., 1965
HARPER   Warner Bros., 1966
KALEIDOSCOPE   Warner Bros., 1966, British
THE SECRET WAR OF HARRY FRIGG   Universal, 1968
NO WAY TO TREAT A LADY   Paramount, 1968
STRATEGY OF TERROR   *IN DARKNESS WAITING*
    Universal, 1969, originally made for television
THE ILLUSTRATED MAN   Warner Bros., 1969
RABBIT, RUN   Warner Bros., 1970
THE TRAVELING EXECUTIONER   MGM, 1970
THE SCREAMING WOMAN (TF)   Universal TV, 1972
BANACEK: DETOUR TO NOWHERE (TF)   Universal
    TV, 1972
THE LONGEST NIGHT (TF)   Universal TV, 1972
PARTNERS IN CRIME (TF)   Universal TV, 1973
DOUBLE INDEMNITY (TF)   Universal TV, 1973
LINDA (TF)   Universal TV, 1973
FRANKENSTEIN: THE TRUE STORY (TF)   Universal
    TV, 1973
AIRPORT 1975   Universal, 1974
MIDWAY   Universal, 1976
DAMNATION ALLEY   20th Century-Fox, 1977
ROLL OF THUNDER, HEAR MY CRY (TF)   Tomorrow
    Entertainment, 1978
FAST BREAK   Columbia, 1979
LOVING COUPLES   20th Century-Fox, 1980
REMEMBRANCE OF LOVE (TF)   Doris Quinlan
    Productions/Comworld Productions, 1982
NUMBER ONE WITH A BULLET   Cannon, 1987
THE FAVORITE   Ascona Films, 1989, Swiss

BUD SMITH*
Agent: Bauer Benedek Agency - Los Angeles, 213/275-2421

JOHNNY BE GOOD   Orion, 1988

CHARLES MARTIN SMITH
b. October 30, 1953 - Van Nuys, California
Agent: Leading Artists - Beverly Hills, 213/858-1999

TRICK OR TREAT   DEG, 1986
BORIS AND NATASHA   New Line Cinema, 1990

CLIVE A. SMITH
b. England
Business: Nelvana Productions, 32 Atlantic Avenue,
   Toronto, Ontario M6K 1X8, Canada, 416/588-5571

ROCK & RULE (AF)   MGM/UA, 1983, Canadian
RING OF POWER (AF)   1984, Canadian

HOWARD SMITH
Business: The Village Voice, 842 Broadway, New York,
   NY 10003, 212/475-3300

MARJOE (FD)   co-director with Sarah Kernochan,
   Cinema 5, 1972
GIZMO! (FD)   New Line Cinema, 1977

KENT SMITH
TAKING TIGER MOUNTAIN   co-director with Tom
   Huckabee, Horizon, 1983

MEL SMITH
b. 1952 - London, England
Contact: British Academy of Film & Television Arts,
   195 Piccadilly, London W1, England, 71/734-0022

THE TALL GUY   Miramax Films, 1989, British

ALAN SMITHEE*
(Allen Smithee)
b. 1967 - Los Angeles, California
Contact: Directors Guild of America - Los Angeles,
   213/289-2000

DEATH OF A GUNFIGHTER   (Don Siegel/Robert Totten)
   Universal, 1967
FADE IN   (Jud Taylor)   Paramount, 1968
THE CHALLENGE (TF)   20th Century-Fox TV, 1970
CITY IN FEAR   (Jud Taylor) (TF)   Trans World
   International, 1980
FUN AND GAMES   (Paul Bogart) (TF)   Kanin-Gallo
   Productions/Warner Bros. TV, 1980
MOONLIGHT   (Jackie Cooper/Rod Holcomb) (TF)
   Universal TV, 1982
STITCHES   (Rod Holcomb)   International Film
   Marketing, 1985
LET'S GET HARRY   (Stuart Rosenberg)   Tri-Star, 1986
MORGAN STEWART'S COMING HOME   (Terry Winsor/
   Paul Aaron)   New Century/Vista, 1987
RIVIERA (TF)   MTM Productions, 1987
GHOST FEVER   (Lee Madden)   Miramax, 1987
I LOVE N.Y.   (Gianni Bozzacchi)   Manhattan Films, 1988
THE SHRIMP ON THE BARBIE   (Michael Gottlieb)
   Vestron, 1990, U.S.-New Zealand

Note: Alan Smithee is the pseudonym designated by the
Directors Guild of America for those members who wish
to remove their names from the n-screen and advertising
credits of a particular film. This is usually he result of
studio and/or network interference with their intended cut
of a film, and therefore a loss of creative control - M.S.

SANDY SMOLAN
RACHEL RIVER   Taurus Entertainment, 1987
VIETNAM WAR STORY: THE LAST DAYS (CTF)
   co-director with David Burton Morris & Luis Soto,
   HBO, 1989

SHERRY SNELLER
ROBINSON CRUSOE   PSM Entertainment, 1987

MARK S. SOBEL*
b. June 10, 1956 - Toronto, Ontario, Canada
Agent: Stone-MannersAgency - Los Angeles, 213/275-9599
Business Manager: Ken Stein Management - Los Angeles,
   213/969-8417

ACCESS CODE   Intercontinental Releasing, 1984
SWEET REVENGE   Concorde, 1987

STEVEN SODERBERGH
b. January 14, 1963 - Atlanta, Georgia
Agent: Pat Dollard, Leading Artists - Beverly Hills,
   213/858-1999

sex, lies, and videotape   Miramax Films, 1989

RAINER SOEHNLEIN
b. May 6, 1941 - Coburg, Germany
Agent: Peter Rawley, ICM - Los Angeles, 213/550-4000

MARIANNE AND SOFIE   Jugendfilm, 1984, West German

FERNANDO E. SOLANAS
b. Argentina
Contact: French Film Office, 745 Fifth Avenue, New York,
   NY 10151, 212/832-8860

HOUR OF THE FURNACES (FD)   1966, Argentine
TANGOS: THE EXILE OF GARDEL   New Yorker,
   1986, French
SUR   Pacific Productions/Cinesur/Instituto de
   Cinematografica, 1988, Argentine-French

TODD SOLONDZ
FEAR, ANXIETY AND DEPRESSION   Samuel Goldwyn
   Company, 1989

ALFRED SOLE*
b. July 2, 1943 - Paterson, New Jersey
Home: 9032 Vista Grande, West Hollywood, CA 90069,
   213/859-7531
Agent: ICM - Los Angeles, 213/550-4000

ALICE, SWEET ALICE   *COMMUNION/HOLY TERROR*
   Allied Artists, 1977
TANYA'S ISLAND   International Film Exchange/Fred
   Baker Films, 1981, Canadian
PANDEMONIUM   MGM/UA, 1982

ANDREW SOLT*
b. December 13, 1947 - London, England
Agent: William Morris Agency - Beverly Hills, 213/274-7451
Business: Andrew Solt Productions, 9121 Sunset Blvd.,
   Los Angeles, CA 90069, 213/276-9522

HEROES OF ROCK AND ROLL (TD)   co-director with
   Malcolm Leo, ABC, 1979
THIS IS ELVIS (FD)   co-director with Malcolm Leo,
   Warner Bros., 1981

IT CAME FROM HOLLYWOOD (FD)   co-director with
    Malcolm Leo, Paramount, 1982
IMAGINE: JOHN LENNON (FD)   Warner Bros., 1988

OLA SOLUM
b. 1943 - Norway
Contact: Norwegian Cinema and Film Foundation,
    Stortingsgt. 16, N-0161 Oslo 1, Norway, 2/412702

ORION'S BELT   New World, 1985, Norwegian
DEADLY ILLUSION   Cinema Group, 1987,
    British-Norwegian
WANDERERS   Norsk Film, 1989, Norwegian

STEPHEN SOMMERS
Agent: Bauer Benedek Agency - Los Angeles, 213/275-2421

CATCH ME IF YOU CAN   MCEG, 1989

SUSAN SONTAG
DUET FOR CANNIBALS   Grove Press, 1969, Swedish
BROTHER CARL   New Yorker, 1972, Swedish
PROMISED LANDS (FD)   New Yorker, 1974, French

ALBERTO SORDI
b. June 15, 1920 - Rome, Italy
Home: via Druso 45, Rome, Italy, 06/513-7778

FUMO DI LONDRA   Fono Roma, 1966, Italian
SCUSI, LEI E' FAVOREVOLE O CONTRARIO?   Fono
    Roma, 1966, Italian
UN ITALIANO IN AMERICA   Euro International Film,
    1967, Italian
AMORE MIO AIUTAMI   Documento Film, 1969, Italian
LE COPPIE   co-director, Documento Film, 1970, Italian
POLVERE DI STELLE   Capitolina Produzioni
    Cinematografiche, 1973, Italian
FINCHE' C'E' GUERRA C'E' SPERANZA   Rizzoli Film,
    1974, Italian
IL COMUNE SENSO DEL PUDORE   Rizzoli Film,
    1976, Italian
DOVE VAI IN VACANZA?   co-director, Rizzoli Film,
    1978, Italian
IO E CATERINA   Italian International Films/Cathago
    Film, 1980, Italian- French
IO SO CHE TU SAI CHE IO SO   Scena Film,
    1982, Italian
IN VIAGGIO CON PAPA'   Scena Film, 1982, Italian
STORIA DI UN ITALIANO (MS)   RAI, 1982, Italian
IL TASSINARO   Italian International Films, 1982, Italian
TUTTI DENTRO   Scena Film, 1984, Italian
UN TASSINARO A NEW YORK   Italian International
    Films, 1987, Italian

CARLOS SORIN
Agent: Triad Artists, Inc. - Los Angeles, 213/556-2727

LA PELICULA DEL REY   1987, Argentine
EVERSMILE, NEW JERSEY   J&M Entertainment, 1989,
    Argentine- British

DIMITRI SOTIRAKIS*
(Jim Sotos)
b. September 17, 1935 - New York, New York
Home: 3805 Goodland Avenue, Studio City, CA 91604,
    818/769-6553

THE LAST VICTIM   Howard Mahler Films, 1975
FORCED ENTRY   Century International, 1980
SWEET SIXTEEN   Century International, 1981

HOT MOVES   Cardinal Releasing, 1984
BEVERLY HILLS BRATS   Taurus Entertainment, 1989

LUIS SOTO*
Business: Cool Moss, Inc., 165 N. Orange Drive,
    Los Angeles, CA 90036, 213/939-8417
Agent: Lawrence A. Mirisch, Triad Artists, Inc. -
    Los Angeles, 213/556-2727

THE HOUSE OF RAMON IGLESIA (TF)   LFS
    Productions, 1986
VIETNAM WAR STORY: THE LAST DAYS (CTF)
    co-director with David Burton Morris & Sandy Smolan,
    HBO, 1989

JIM SOTOS
(See Dimitri SOTIRAKIS)

LARRY G. SPANGLER
THE SOUL OF NIGGER CHARLEY   Paramount, 1973
A KNIFE FOR THE LADIES   Bryanston, 1974
THE LIFE AND TIMES OF XAVIERA HOLLANDER
    Mature, 1974
JOSHUA   Lone Star, 1976
SILENT SENTENCE   Intercontinental, 1983

TERESA SPARKS
b. June 27, 1952 - Kentucky
Agent: Joel Millner, J. Michael Bloom, Ltd. - Los Angeles,
    213/275-6800

OVER THE SUMMER   Shine Productions, 1984

PENELOPE SPHEERIS
b. New Orleans, Louisiana
Agent: William Morris Agency - Beverly Hills, 213/274-7451

THE DECLINE OF WESTERN CIVILIZATION (FD)
    Spheeris Films Inc., 1981
SUBURBIA *THE WILD SIDE*   New World, 1984
THE BOYS NEXT DOOR   New World, 1985
HOLLYWOOD VICE SQUAD   Concorde/Cinema
    Group, 1986
DUDES   Cineworld, 1987
THE DECLINE OF WESTERN CIVILIZATION II: THE
    METAL YEARS (FD)   New Line Cinema, 1988

SCOTT SPIEGEL
Agent: Leading Artists - Beverly Hills, 213/858-1999
INTRUDER   Phantom Productions, 1989

STEVEN SPIELBERG*
b. December 18, 1947 - Cincinnati, Ohio
Business: Amblin Entertainment, 100 Universal City Plaza -
    Bungalow 477, Universal City, CA 91608, 818/777-1000
Agent: CAA - Beverly Hills, 213/288-4545

NIGHT GALLERY (TF)   co-director with Boris Sagal & Barry
    Shear, Universal TV, 1969
DUEL (TF)   Universal TV, 1971
SOMETHING EVIL (TF)   Belford Productions/CBS
    International, 1972
SAVAGE (TF)   Universal TV, 1973
THE SUGARLAND EXPRESS   Universal, 1974
JAWS   Universal, 1975
CLOSE ENCOUNTERS OF THE THIRD KIND★
    Columbia, 1977
1941   Universal/Columbia, 1979
RAIDERS OF THE LOST ARK★   Paramount, 1981
E.T. THE EXTRA-TERRESTRIAL★   Universal, 1982

TWILIGHT ZONE - THE MOVIE   co-director with John
    Landis, Joe Dante & George Miller, Warner Bros., 1983
INDIANA JONES AND THE TEMPLE OF DOOM
    Paramount, 1984
THE COLOR PURPLE   Warner Bros., 1985
EMPIRE OF THE SUN   Warner Bros., 1987
INDIANA JONES AND THE LAST CRUSADE
    Paramount, 1989
ALWAYS   Universal, 1989

ROGER SPOTTISWOODE*
b. England
Agent: InterTalent - Los Angeles, 213/271-0600

TERROR TRAIN   20th Century-Fox, 1980, Canadian
THE PURSUIT OF D.B. COOPER   Universal, 1982
THE RENEGADES (TF)   Lawrence Gordon Productions/
    Paramount TV, 1982
UNDER FIRE   Orion, 1983
THE BEST OF TIMES   Universal, 1986
THE LAST INNOCENT MAN (CTF)   HBO Pictures/
    Maurice Singer Productions, 1987
SHOOT TO KILL   Buena Vista, 1988
THIRD DEGREE BURN (CTF)   HBO Pictures/MTM
    Entertainment/Paramount TV, 1989
TIME FLIES WHEN YOU'RE ALIVE (CTF)   HBO
    Showcase/Kings Road Entertainment, 1989
TURNER & HOOCH   Buena Vista, 1989
AIR AMERICA   Tri-Star, 1990

G. D. SPRADLIN
Agent: The Mishkin Agency - Los Angeles, 213/274-5261

THE ONLY WAY HOME   Regional, 1972

ROBIN SPRY*
b. October 25, 1939 - Toronto, Canada
Home: 5330 Durocher, Montreal, Quebec H2V 3Y1,
    Canada, 514/277-1503
Business: Telescene Productions, 444 St. Paul Street East,
    Montreal, Quebec M2Y 3V1, Canada, 514/288-1638
Agent: Laurie Rotenberg, The Talent Group, 387 Bloor
    Street East, Toronto, Ontario, Canada, 416/961-3304

FLOWERS ON A ONE WAY STREET (FD)
    1968, Canadian
PROLOGUE   Vaudeo, 1969, Canadian
ACTION: THE OCTOBER CRISIS OF 1970 (FD)
    National Film Board of Canada, 1974
ONE MAN   National Film Board of Canada, 1977,
    Canadian
DRYING UP THE STREETS   CBC, 1978, Canadian
DON'T FORGET - JE ME SOUVIENS (TF)   CBC,
    1979, Canadian
HIT AND RUN   Agora Productions, 1981, Canadian
SUZANNE   20th Century-Fox, 1982, Canadian
KEEPING TRACK   Shapiro Entertainment,
    1987, Canadian
OBSESSED   HITTING HOME   New Star Entertainment,
    1988, Canadian

RAYMOND ST. JACQUES
(James Arthur Johnson)
b. 1930 - Hartford, Connecticut
Agent: Contemporary Artists - Beverly Hills, 213/278-8250

BOOK OF NUMBERS   Avco Embassy, 1973

CHRISTOPHER ST. JOHN
TOP OF THE HEAP   Fanfare, 1972

SYLVESTER STALLONE*
b. July 6, 1946 - New York, New York
Agent: CAA - Beverly Hills, 213/288-4545

PARADISE ALLEY   Universal, 1978
ROCKY II   United Artists, 1979
ROCKY III   MGM/UA, 1982
STAYING ALIVE   Paramount, 1983
ROCKY IV   MGM/UA, 1985

TERENCE STAMP
b. July 23, 1939 - London, England
Contact: Screen Actors Guild - Hollywood, 213/465-4600

STRANGER IN THE HOUSE   Multifilm Productions, 1990

PAUL STANLEY*
Agent: Irv Schechter Company - Beverly Hills, 213/278-8070

CRY TOUGH   United Artists, 1959
THREE GUNS FOR TEXAS   co-director with David Lowell
    Rich & Earl Bellamy, Universal, 1968
SOLE SURVIVOR (TF)   Cinema Center, 1969
RIVER OF MYSTERY (TF)   Universal TV, 1971
NICKY'S WORLD (TF)   Tomorrow Entertainment, 1974
CRISIS IN SUN VALLEY (TF)   Columbia TV, 1978
THE ULTIMATE IMPOSTER (TF)   Universal TV, 1979

RICHARD STANLEY
Contact: Writers Guild of America, West - Los Angeles,
    213/550-1000

HARDWARE   Miramax Films, 1990, British-U.S.

RINGO STARR
(Richard Starkey)
b. July 7, 1940 - Liverpool, England

BORN TO BOOGIE (FD)   MGM-EMI, 1972, British

RAY DENNIS STECKLER
DRIVERS IN HELL   WILD ONES ON WHEELS   1961
WILD GUITAR   Fairway International, 1962
THE INCREDIBLY STRANGE CREATURES WHO
    STOPPED LIVING AND BECAME MIXED-UP ZOMBIES
    Fairway International, 1962
THE THRILL KILLERS   1964
RAT PFINK A-BOO-BOO   1964
SCREAM OF THE BUTTERFLY   1965
LEMON GROVE KIDS MEET THE MONSTERS   1966
SINTHIA, THE DEVIL'S DOLL   1968
SUPER COOL   BODY FEVER/THE LAST ORIGINAL
    B-MOVIE   1969
THE CHOOPER   BLOOD SHACK   1971
BLOODY JACK THE RIPPER   1972, unreleased
THE HOLLYWOOD STRANGLER MEETS THE SKID ROW
    SLASHER   1979

JEFF STEIN
Agent: Alan Greenspan, ICM - Los Angeles, 213/550-4000

THE KIDS ARE ALRIGHT (FD)   New World, 1979, British

KEN STEIN
Business: Concorde Pictures, 11600 San Vicente Blvd.,
    Los Angeles, CA 90049, 213/826-0978

PRIMARY TARGET   Concorde, 1990
RAIN OF DEATH   Concorde, 1990

DAVID STEINBERG*

b. August 9, 1942 - Winnipeg, Canada
Business: MTM, 4024 Radford Avenue - Administration
    Bldg. Rm. 377, Studio City, CA 91604, 818/760-6068
Agent: William Morris Agency - Beverly Hills,
    213/274-7451

PATERNITY   Paramount, 1981
GOING BERSERK   Universal, 1983, Canadian

ZIGGY STEINBERG

Attorney: Ted Steinberg, Esq. - Los Angeles,
    213/553-4070

THE BOSS'S WIFE   Tri-Star, 1987

DANIEL STEINMANN

SAVAGE STREETS   Entermark Corporation, 1985
FRIDAY THE 13TH PART V - A NEW BEGINNING
    Paramount, 1985
SUBTERRANEANS   Empire Pictures, 1988

MARTIN STELLMAN

Contact: British Academy of Film & Television Arts, 195
    Piccadilly, London W1, England, 71/734-0022

FOR QUEEN AND COUNTRY   Zenith Productions,
    1988, British

LEONARD B. STERN*

b. December 23, 1923 - New York, New York
Business: 410 N. La Cienega Blvd., Los Angeles, CA
    90048, 213/657-6100
Agent: The Sy Fischer Agency - Los Angeles,
    213/470-0917

ONCE UPON A DEAD MAN (TF)   Universal TV, 1971
THE SNOOP SISTERS (TF)   Universal TV, 1972
JUST YOU AND ME, KID   Columbia, 1979

SANDOR STERN*

b. July 13, 1936 - Timmins, Ontario, Canada
Agent: Elliot Webb, Broder-Kurland-Webb-Uffner
    Agency - Los Angeles, 213/656-9262

THE SEEDING OF SARAH BURNS (TF)   Michael Klein
    Productions, 1979
MUGGABLE MARY: STREET COP (TF)   CBS
    Entertainment, 1982
MEMORIES NEVER DIE (TF)   Groverton Productions/
    Scholastic Productions/ Universal TV, 1982
PASSIONS (TF)   Carson Production Group/Wizan TV
    Enterprises, 1984
JOHN & YOKO - A LOVE STORY (TF)   Carson
    Production Group, 1985
ASSASSIN (TF)   Sankan Productions, 1986
EASY PREY (TF)   New World TV/Rene Malo
    Productions, 1987, U.S.-Canadian
PROBE (TF)   MCA Television Ltd., 1988
SHATTERED INNOCENCE (TF)   Green-Epstein
    Productions/Lorimar TV, 1988
GLITZ (TF)   Robert Cooper Films, 1988
PIN   New World, 1989, Canadian
WITHOUT HER CONSENT (TF)   Raymond Katz
    Enterprises/Half Pint Productions/Carla Singer
    Productions, 1990
AMITYVILLE: THE EVIL ESCAPES (TF)   Steve White
    Productions/ Spectator Films, 1990

STEVEN HILLIARD STERN*

b. November 1, 1937 - Timmins, Ontario, Canada
Home: 4321 Clear Valley Drive, Encino, CA 91436,
    818/788-3607
Agent: Elliot Webb, Broder-Kurland-Webb-Uffner Agency -
    Los Angeles, 213/656-9262

B.S. I LOVE YOU   20th Century-Fox, 1971
NEITHER BY DAY NOR BY NIGHT   Motion Pictures
    International, 1972, U.S.-Israeli
THE HARRAD SUMMER   Cinerama Releasing
    Corporation, 1974
ESCAPE FROM BOGEN COUNTY (TF)   Paramount
    TV, 1977
THE GHOST OF FLIGHT 401 (TF)   Paramount TV, 1978
DOCTORS' PRIVATE LIVES (TF)   David Gerber
    Company/Columbia TV, 1978
GETTING MARRIED (TF)   Paramount TV, 1978
FAST FRIENDS (TF)   Columbia TV, 1979
ANATOMY OF A SEDUCTION (TF)   Moonlight
    Productions/Filmways, 1979
YOUNG LOVE, FIRST LOVE (TF)   Lorimar
    Productions, 1979
RUNNING   Columbia, 1979, Canadian-U.S.
PORTRAIT OF AN ESCORT (TF)   Moonlight
    Productions/Filmways, 1980
THE DEVIL AND MAX DEVLIN   Buena Vista, 1981
MIRACLE ON ICE (TF)   Moonlight Productions/
    Filmways, 1981
A SMALL KILLING (TF)   Orgolini-Nelson Productions/
    Motown Productions, 1982
THE AMBUSH MURDERS (TF)   David Goldsmith
    Productions/Charles Fries Productions, 1982
PORTRAIT OF A SHOWGIRL (TF)   Hamner
    Productions, 1982
NOT JUST ANOTHER AFFAIR (TF)   Ten-Four
    Productions, 1982
FORBIDDEN LOVE (TF)   Gross-Weston Productions, 1982
RONA JAFFE'S MAZES AND MONSTERS   McDermott
    Productions/Procter & Gamble Productions, 1982
BABY SISTER (TF)   Moonlight Productions II, 1983
STILL THE BEAVER (TF)   Bud Austin Productions/
    Universal TV, 1983
AN UNCOMMON LOVE (TF)   Beechwood Productions/
    Lorimar Productions, 1983
GETTING PHYSICAL (TF)   CBS Entertainment, 1984
DRAW! (CTF)   HBO Premiere Films/Astral Film Productions/
    Bryna Company, 1984, U.S.-Canadian
OBSESSIVE LOVE (TF)   Onza Inc./Moonlight
    Productions, 1984
THE PARK IS MINE (CTF)   HBO Premiere Films/Astral Film
    Productions/ICC, 1985, U.S.-Canadian
MURDER IN SPACE (CTF)   Robert Cooper Productions/
    Zenith Productions/CTV Network, 1985, Canadian-British
THE UNDERGRADS (CTF)   Sharmhill Productions/The
    Disney Channel, 1985, U.S.-Canadian
HOSTAGE FLIGHT (TF)   Frank von Zerneck Films, 1985
YOUNG AGAIN (TF)   Sharmhill Productions/Walt Disney
    Productions, 1986, U.S.-Canadian
MANY HAPPY RETURNS (TF)   Alan M. Levin & Steven H.
    Stern Films, 1986, U.S.-Canadian
ROLLING VENGEANCE   Apollo Pictures, 1987,
    U.S.-Canadian
NOT QUITE HUMAN (TF)   Sharmhill Productions/Walt
    Disney TV, 1987
WEEKEND WAR (TF)   Pompian-Atamvan Productions/
    Columbia TV, 1988
CROSSING THE MOB (TF)   Bateman Company
    Productions/Interscope Communications, 1988
LOVE & MURDER   Norstar Entertainment, 1990, Canadian
PERSONALS (CTF)   Sharmhill Productions/Wilshire Court
    Productions, 1990, Canadian-U.S.
MONEY   Andre Djaoui Productions, 1990, French-
    Italian-Canadian

JEAN-FRANÇOIS STEVENIN
b. 1944 - France
Contact: French Film Office, 745 Fifth Avenue, New York,
    NY 10151, 212/832-8860

PASSE MONTAGNE   1979, French
DOUBLE MESSIEURS   Sagamore Cinema/Mallia Films/
    FR3, 1986, French

ART STEVENS
THE FOX AND THE HOUND (AF)   co-director with Ted
    Berman & Richard Rich, Buena Vista, 1981

DAVID STEVENS*
Agent: Irv Schwartz, The Agency - Los Angeles,
    213/551-3000

NUMBER 96 (MS)   1974, Australian
THE SULLIVANS (MS)   co-director with Simon Wincer,
    1976, Australian
THE JOHN SULLIVAN STORY (TF)   Crawford
    Productions/Nine Network/Australian Film
    Commission, 1979, Australian
A TOWN LIKE ALICE (MS)   Seven Network/Victorian Film
    Corporation, 1981, Australian
THE CLINIC   Film House/Generation Films,
    1982, Australian
UNDERCOVER   Filmco, 1983, Australian
WOMEN OF THE SUN (MS)   co-director with Stephen
    Wallace, James Ricketson & Geoffrey Nottage,
    Generation Films, 1983, Australian
A THOUSAND SKIES (MS)   Dimsey Ginn Ltd.,
    1985, Australian
ALWAYS AFTERNOON (MS)   The Special Broadcasting
    Service/Norddeutsche Rundfunk/Multimedia/Primetime
    TV, 1987, Australian-West German- British
KANSAS   Trans World Entertainment, 1988

GEORGE STEVENS, JR.
b. April 3, 1932 - Los Angeles, California
Business: New Liberty Productions, American Film
    Institute, John F. Kennedy Center, Washington D.C.
    20566, 202/828-4020

AMERICA AT THE MOVIES (FD)   American Film
    Institute, 1976
GEORGE STEVENS: A FILMMAKER'S JOURNEY (FD)
    Castle Hill Productions, 1984

LESLIE STEVENS
b. February 3, 1924 - Washington, D.C.
Contact: Writers Guild of America, West - Los Angeles,
    213/550-1000

PRIVATE PROPERTY   Citation, 1960
INCUBUS   1961
HERO'S ISLAND   United Artists, 1962
DELLA   Four Star, 1964
FANFARE FOR A DEATH SCENE   Four Star, 1967
I LOVE A MYSTERY (TF)   Universal TV, 1973
THREE KINDS OF HEAT   Cannon, 1987

STELLA STEVENS
b. October 1, 1938 - Hot Coffee, MS
Contact: Screen Actors Guild - Los Angeles, 213/465-4600

THE RANCH   Sky Nest Productions, 1989, Canadian

ALAN STEWART
GHETTO BLASTERS   CHVP Inc., 1989

DOUGLAS DAY STEWART*
Agent: Martin Bauer, Bauer Benedek Agency -
    Beverly Hills, 213/275-2421

THIEF OF HEARTS   Paramount, 1984
LISTEN TO ME   WEG/Columbia, 1989

JOHN STEWART
CLICK: THE CALENDAR GIRL KILLER   co-director with
    Ross Hagen, Crown International, 1989
CARTEL   Cobra Entertainment Group, 1989
THUNDER AND LIGHTNING   Red Rock
    Productions, 1990

LARRY STEWART*
Contact: Directors Guild of America - Los Angeles,
    213/289-2000

THE INITIATION   New World, 1984

JOHN STIX
b. November 14, 1920 - St. Louis, Missouri

THE GREAT ST. LOUIS BANK ROBBERY   co-director with
    Charles Guggenheim, United Artists, 1959
FAMILY BUSINESS (TF)   Screenscope Inc./South Carolina
    Educational TV Network, 1983

JOHN STOCKWELL*
Agent: Tracey Jacobs, ICM - Los Angeles, 213/550-4000

UNDER COVER   Cannon, 1987

ANDREW L. STONE*
b. July 16, 1902 - Oakland, California
Home: 10478 Wyton Drive, Los Angeles, CA 90024,
    213/279-2427
Agent: Phil Gersh, The Gersh Agency - Beverly Hills,
    213/274-6611

SOMBRAS DE GLORIA   Sono Arts, 1930
HELL'S HEADQUARTERS   Capitol, 1932
THE GIRL SAID NO   Grand National, 1937
STOLEN HEAVEN   Paramount, 1938
SAY IT IN FRENCH   Paramount, 1938
THE GREAT VICTOR HERBERT   Paramount, 1939
THERE'S MAGIC IN MUSIC   Paramount, 1941
STORMY WEATHER   20th Century-Fox, 1943
HI DIDDLE DIDDLE   RKO Radio, 1943
SENSATIONS OF 1945   United Artists, 1944
BEDSIDE MANNER   United Artists, 1945
THE BACHELOR'S DAUGHTER   United Artists, 1946
FUN ON A WEEKEND   United Artists, 1947
HIGHWAY 301   Warner Bros., 1950
CONFIDENCE GIRL   United Artists, 1951
THE STEEL TRAP   20th Century-Fox, 1952
A BLUEPRINT FOR MURDER   20th Century-Fox, 1953
THE NIGHT HOLDS TERROR   Columbia, 1955
JULIE   MGM, 1956
CRY TERROR!   MGM, 1958
THE DECKS RAN RED   MGM, 1958
THE LAST VOYAGE   MGM, 1960
RING OF FIRE   MGM, 1961
THE PASSWORD IS COURAGE   MGM, 1963, British
NEVER PUT IT IN WRITING   Allied Artists, 1964, British
THE SECRET OF MY SUCCESS   MGM, 1965, British
SONG OF NORWAY   Cinerama Releasing
    Corporation, 1970
THE GREAT WALTZ   MGM, 1972

NORMAN STONE
Contact: British Academy of Film & Television Arts,
195 Piccadilly, London W1, England, 71/734-0022

CROSSING TO FREEDOM (TF)   Procter & Gamble
Productions/Stan Margulies Productions/Granada TV,
1990, U.S.-British

OLIVER STONE*
b. November 15, 1946 - New York, New York
Agent: CAA - Beverly Hills, 213/288-4545

SEIZURE   Cinerama Releasing Corporation,
1974, Canadian
THE HAND   Orion/Warner Bros., 1981
SALVADOR   Hemdale, 1986
PLATOON★★   Orion, 1986
WALL STREET   20th Century Fox, 1987
TALK RADIO   Universal, 1988
BORN ON THE FOURTH OF JULY★★   Universal, 1989
THE DOORS   Tri-Star, 1991

TOM STOPPARD
b. July 3, 1937 - Czechoslovakia
Agent: Fraser & Dunlop - London, 71/734-7311

ROSENKRANTZ AND GUILDENSTERN ARE DEAD
Cinecom, 1990

HOWARD STORM*
b. New York, New York
Agent: Robinson, Weintraub, Gross & Associates -
Los Angeles, 213/653-5802

ONCE BITTEN   Samuel Goldwyn Company, 1985

MARK STORY*
Business: Story Piccolo Guliner, Inc., 35 East 21st Street,
New York, NY 10010, 212/529-9090

ODD JOBS   Tri-Star, 1986

MARK STOUFFER*
Address: P.O. Box 2638, Santa Barbara, CA 93120,
805/965-4140

MAN OUTSIDE   Stouffer Enterprise Film Partners, 1987

JEAN-MARIE STRAUB
b. January 8, 1933 - Metz, Germany
Contact: French Film Office, 745 Fifth Avenue, New York,
NY 10151, 212/832-8860

NICHT VERSOHNT ODER, ES HILFT NUR GEWALT,
WO GEWALT HERRSCHT   1965, West German
THE CHRONICLE OF ANNA MAGDALENA BACH
New Yorker, 1968, West German
OTHON   co-director with Daniele Huillet, 1969, French
GESCHICHTSUNTERRICHT   co-director with Daniele
Huillet, 1972, West German
MOSES AND AARON   co-director with Daniele Huillet,
New Yorker, 1975, West German
I CANI DEL SINAI   co-director with Daniele Huillet,
1976, Italian
DELLA NUBE ALLA RESISTENZA   co-director with
Daniele Huillet, 1979, Italian
CLASS RELATIONS   *KLASSENVERHALF-NISSE*
co-director with Daniele Huillet, New Yorker, 1984,
West German-French
DER TOD DES EMPEDOKLES   co-director with Daniele
Huillet, Janus Film/Les Films du Losange, 1987,
West German-French

BARBRA STREISAND*
b. April 24, 1942 - New York, New York
Agent: CAA - Beverly Hills, 213/288-4545

YENTL   MGM/UA, 1983
THE PRINCE OF TIDES   Columbia, 1991

JOSEPH STRICK*
b. July 6, 1923 - Braddock, Pennsylvania
Home: 266 River Road, Grandview, NY 10960,
914/359-9527
Agent: David Dworski & Associates - Los Angeles,
213/273-6173

THE SAVAGE EYE   co-director with Ben Maddow &
Sidney Meyers, Trans-Lux, 1959
THE BALCONY   Continental, 1963
THE HECKLERS (TF)   1966, British
ULYSSES   Continental, 1967
TROPIC OF CANCER   Paramount, 1970
ROAD MOVIE   Grove Press, 1974
A PORTRAIT OF THE ARTIST AS A YOUNG MAN   Howard
Mahler Films, 1979
UNDERWORLD   Angelika Films, 1990

BRIAN STUART
SORCERESS   New World, 1982

MEL STUART*
b. September 2, 1928
Address: 1551 S. Robertson Blvd., Los Angeles, CA
90035, 213/785-9080
Agent: Christine Foster, The Agency - Los Angeles,
213/551-3000

THE MAKING OF THE PRESIDENT (TD)   David Wolper
Productions, 1960
THE MAKING OF THE PRESIDENT (TD)   David Wolper
Productions, 1964
FOUR DAYS IN NOVEMBER (FD)   United Artists, 1965
CHINA: ROOTS OF MADNESS (TD)   David Wolper
Productions, 1967
RISE AND FALL OF THE THIRD REICH (TD)   David Wolper
Productions, 1968
THE MAKING OF THE PRESIDENT (TD)   David Wolper
Productions, 1968
IF IT'S TUESDAY, THIS MUST BE BELGIUM   United
Artists, 1969
I LOVE MY WIFE   Universal, 1970
WILLY WONKA AND THE CHOCOLATE FACTORY
Paramount, 1971, British
ONE IS A LONELY NUMBER   MGM, 1972
WATTSTAX (FD)   Columbia, 1973
BRENDA STARR (TF)   Wolper Productions, 1976
LIFE GOES TO THE MOVIES (TD)   David Wolper
Productions, 1976
OSCAR GOES TO WAR (TD)   David Wolper
Productions, 1977
MEAN DOG BLUES   American International, 1978
RUBY AND OSWALD (TF)   Alan Landsburg
Productions, 1978
THE TRIANGLE FACTORY FIRE SCANDAL (TF)   Alan
Landsburg Productions/Don Kirshner Productions, 1979
THE CHISHOLMS (MS)   Alan Landsburg Productions, 1979
THE WHITE LIONS   Alan Landsburg Productions, 1979
SOPHIA LOREN: HER OWN STORY (TF)   Roger Gimbel
Productions/EMI TV, 1980
WITH PETER BEARD IN AFRICA (TD)   co-director with
Robert H. Nixon, NDEFU Productions, 1988

JOHN STURGES*
b. January 3, 1911 - Oak Park, Illinois
Contact: Roberta Soules, 726 Upham, San Luis Obispo, CA
    93401, 805/544-0464

THUNDERBOLT   co-director with William Wyler,
    Monogram, 1945
THE MAN WHO DARED   Columbia, 1946
SHADOWED   Columbia, 1946
ALIAS MR. TWILIGHT   Columbia, 1946
FOR THE LOVE OF RUSTY   Columbia, 1947
KEEPER OF THE BEES   Columbia, 1947
BEST MAN WINS   Columbia, 1948
THE SIGN OF THE RAM   Columbia, 1948
THE WALKING HILLS   Columbia, 1949
THE CAPTURE   RKO Radio, 1950
MYSTERY STREET   MGM, 1950
RIGHT CROSS   MGM, 1950
THE MAGNIFICENT YANKEE   MGM, 1950
KIND LADY   MGM, 1951
THE PEOPLE AGAINST O'HARA   MGM, 1951
IT'S A BIG COUNTRY   co-director with Charles Vidor,
    Richard Thorpe, Don Hartman, Don Weis, Clarence
    Brown & William Wellman, MGM, 1952
THE GIRL IN WHITE   MGM, 1952
JEOPARDY   MGM, 1953
FAST COMPANY   MGM, 1953
ESCAPE FROM FORT BRAVO   MGM, 1953
BAD DAY AT BLACK ROCK★   MGM, 1955
UNDERWATER!   RKO Radio, 1955
THE SCARLET COAT   MGM, 1955
BACKLASH   MGM, 1956
GUNFIGHT AT THE O.K. CORRAL   Paramount, 1957
THE LAW AND JAKE WADE   MGM, 1958
THE OLD MAN AND THE SEA   Warner Bros., 1958
LAST TRAIN FROM GUN HILL   Paramount, 1959
NEVER SO FEW   MGM, 1959
THE MAGNIFICENT SEVEN   United Artists, 1960
BY LOVE POSSESSED   United Artists, 1961
SERGEANTS 3   United Artists, 1962
A GIRL NAMED TAMIKO   Paramount, 1963
THE GREAT ESCAPE   United Artists, 1963
THE SATAN BUG   United Artists, 1965
THE HALLELUJAH TRAIL   United Artists, 1965
HOUR OF THE GUN   United Artists, 1967
ICE STATION ZEBRA   MGM, 1968
MAROONED   Columbia, 1969
JOE KIDD   Universal, 1972
CHINO   THE VALDEZ HORSES   Intercontinental,
    1973, Italian-Spanish-French
McQ   Warner Bros., 1974
THE EAGLE HAS LANDED   Columbia, 1977, British

CHARLES STURRIDGE
b. June 24, 1951 - London, England
Agent: Peters, Fraser & Dunlop, The Chambers, Chelsea
    Harbour, Lots Road, London SW10 0XF, England,
    71/376-7676

BRIDESHEAD REVISITED (MS) ☆   co-director with
    Michael Lindsay-Hogg, Granada TV/WNET-13/NDR
    Hamburg, 1982, British-U.S.-West German
SOFT TARGETS (TF)   BBC, 1982, British
RUNNERS   Goldcrest Films & TV, 1983, British
ARIA   co-director, Miramax Films, 1987, British
A HANDFUL OF DUST   New Line Cinema, 1988, British

ELISEO SUBIELA
b. Buenos Aires, Argentina
Contact: Instituto Nacional de Cinematografica, Lima 319,
    1073 Buenos Aires, Argentina, tel.: 370-028

LA CONQUISTA DEL PARAISO   1981, Argentine

MAN FACING SOUTHEAST   FilmDallas, 1987, Argentine
ULTIMAS IMAGENES DEL NAUFRAGIO   Films
    Cinequanon/Enrique Marti/ Virrey Olaguer 7 Feliu,
    1989, Argentine-Spanish

ANDREW SUGARMAN
BASIC TRAINING   The Movie Store, 1985

FRED G. SULLIVAN
COLD RIVER   1978
THE BEER DRINKER'S GUIDE TO FITNESS AND
    FILMMAKING   SULLIVAN'S PAVILLION   Adirondack
Alliance Film Corporation, 1987

KEVIN SULLIVAN*
b. May 28, 1955 - Toronto, Ontario, Canada
Agent: Alan Greenspan, ICM - Los Angeles, 213/550-4428

KRIEGHOFF (TF)   Sullivan Films, Inc., 1981, Canadian
THE WILD PONY (TF)   Sullivan Films, Inc., 1982,
    Canadian
ANNE OF GREEN GABLES (MS)   Anne of Green Gables
    Productions/PBS WonderWorks/CBS/60 Film Productions/
    ZDF/City TV/Telefilm Canada, 1985, Canadian-U.S.-
    West German
ANNE OF AVONLEA: THE CONTINUING STORY OF ANNE
    OF GREEN GABLES (MS)   Sullivan Films/CBC/The
    Disney Channel/PBS WonderWorks/ Telefilm Canada,
    1987, Canadian-U.S.
LOOKING FOR MIRACLES (CTF)   Sullivan Films/CBC/The
    Disney Channel/ Telefilm Canada, 1989, Canadian-U.S.
LANTERN HILL (CTF)   Sullivan Films/The Disney
    Channel, 1990

JEREMY SUMMERS
Agent: Eric L'Epine Smith, 10 Wyndham Place, London
    W1H 1AS, England, 71/724-0739

DEPTH CHARGE   British Lion, 1960, British
CROOKS IN CLOISTERS   Warner-Pathe, 1964, British
FERRY CROSS THE MERSEY   United Artists,
    1965, British
SAN FERRY ANN   British Lion, 1966, British
DATELINE DIAMONDS   Rank, 1966, British
HOUSE OF 1,000 DOLLS   American International,
    1967, British
FIVE GOLDEN DRAGONS   Warner-Pathe, 1968, British
THE VENGEANCE OF FU MANCHU   Warner Bros.,
    1968, British
FALLEN HERO (TF)   Granada TV, 1979, British
TOURIST (TF)   Castle Combe Productions/Paramount
    TV, 1980
A KIND OF LOVING (TF)   Granada TV, 1981, British

SHIRLEY SUN
Business: Sun Productions, 110 Greene Street - Suite 12G,
    New York, NY 10012

IRON AND SILK   Shirley Sun Productions, 1990,
    U.S.-Chinese

CEDRIC SUNDSTRÖM
Agent: Jerry Davidson, 20th Century Artists Inc. -
    Los Angeles, 213/850-5516
Address: 5 Stanton Road, Barnes, SW 13, London, England

THE MOUNTAIN (TF)   CMS Film Productions, 1984, British
CAPTIVE RAGE   Moviestore Entertainment, 1988, British
FAIR TRADE   The Movie Group, 1988

THE SHADOWED MIND   Have Beam X, 1988,
   British-Austrian
AMERICAN NINJA 3: BLOOD HUNT   Cannon, 1989
EDGAR ALLAN POE'S HOUSE OF HORROR
   Cannon, 1989
THE REVENGER   American-Independent, 1990

HAL SUTHERLAND
PINOCCHIO AND THE EMPEROR OF THE NIGHT (AF)
   New World, 1987

E. W. SWACKHAMER*
Agent: Shapiro-Lichtman Agency - Los Angeles,
   213/859-8877
Business Manager: Murray Neidorf, Perry & Neidorf,
   315 S. Beverly Drive, Beverly Hills, CA 90213,
   213/553-0171

IN NAME ONLY (TF)   Screen Gems/Columbia
   TV, 1969
MAN AND BOY   Levitt-Pickman, 1972
GIDGET GETS MARRIED (TF)   Screen Gems/
   Columbia TV, 1972
DEATH SENTENCE (TF)   Spelling-Goldberg
   Productions, 1974
DEATH AT LOVE HOUSE (TF)   Spelling-Goldberg
   Productions, 1976
ONCE AN EAGLE (MS)   co-director with Richard
   Michaels, Universal TV, 1976
QUINCY, M.E. (TF)   Glen A. Larson Productions/
   Universal TV, 1976
NIGHT TERROR (TF)   Charles Fries Productions, 1977
SPIDER-MAN (TF)   Charles Fries Productions, 1977
THE DAIN CURSE (MS☆   Martin Poll
   Productions, 1978
THE WINDS OF KITTY HAWK (TF)   Charles Fries
   Productions, 1978
VAMPIRE (TF)   MTM Enterprises, 1979
THE DEATH OF OCEAN VIEW PARK (TF)   Furia-Oringer
   Productions/Playboy Productions, 1979
REWARD (TF)   Jerry Adler Productions/Espirit
   Enterprises/Lorimar Productions, 1980
TENSPEED AND BROWNSHOE (TF)   Stephen J. Cannell
   Productions, 1980
THE OKLAHOMA CITY DOLLS (TF)   IKE Productions/
   Columbia TV, 1981
LONGSHOT   GG Productions, 1981
COCAINE AND BLUE EYES (TF)   Orenthal Productions/
   Columbia TV, 1983
MALIBU (TF)   Hamner Productions/Columbia TV, 1983
CARPOOL (TF)   Charles Fries Productions/Cherryhill
   Productions, 1983
THE ROUSTERS (TF)   Stephen J. Cannell
   Productions, 1983
BROTHERS-IN-LAW (TF)   Stephen J. Cannell
   Productions, 1985
COMMAND 5 (TF)   Paramount TV, 1985
BRIDGE ACROSS TIME (TF)   Fries
   Entertainment, 1985
THE RETURN OF DESPERADO (TF)   Walter Mirisch
   Productions/Charles E. Sellier, Jr. Productions/
   Universal TV, 1988
DESPERADO: THE OUTLAW WARS (TF)   Walter Mirisch
   Productions/Charles E. Sellier, Jr. Productions/
   Universal TV, 1989
CHRISTINE CROMWELL: THINGS THAT GO BUMP
   IN THE NIGHT (TF)   Wolf Film Productions/
   Universal TV, 1989

BOB SWAIM
b. November 2, 1943 - Evanston, Illinois
Agent: Jeff Berg, ICM - Los Angeles, 213/550-4000 or
   Sam Cohn, ICM - New York City, 212/556-5600

LA NUIT DE SAINT-GERMAIN-DES-PRES   Filmologies,
   1977, French
LA BALANCE   Spectrafilm, 1982, French
HALF MOON STREET   20th Century Fox, 1986, British
MASQUERADE   MGM/UA, 1988

BOB SWEENEY*
Agent: Frank Cooper, The Cooper Agency - Los Angeles,
   213/277-8422

RETURN TO MAYBERRY (TF)   Strathmore Productions/
   Viacom Productions, 1986
IF IT'S TUESDAY, IT STILL MUST BE BELGIUM (TF)
   Eisenstock & Mintz Productions, 1987

CHARLES SWENSON
Business: Murakami/Wolf/Swenson, Inc., 1463 Tamarind
   Avenue, Hollywood, CA 90028, 213/462-6473

DIRTY DUCK (AF)   New World, 1977
THE MOUSE AND HIS CHILD (AF)   co-director with
   Fred Wolf, Sanrio, 1977
TWICE UPON A TIME (AF)   co-director with John Korty,
   The Ladd Company/ Warner Bros., 1983

JO SWERLING, JR.*
b. June 18, 1931 - Los Angeles, California
Home: 4415 Saugus Avenue - Apt. 303, Sherman Oaks,
   CA 91403
Agent: Sam Adams, Triad Artists, Inc. - Los Angeles,
   213/556-2727

THE LAST CONVERTIBLE (MS)   co-director with Sidney
   Hayers & Gus Trikonis, Roy Huggins Productions/
   Universal TV, 1979

DAVID SWIFT*
b. 1919 - Minneapolis, Minnesota
Business Manager: Peter Dekom, Bloom & Dekom, 9255
   Sunset Blvd., Los Angeles, CA 90069, 213/278-8622

POLLYANNA   Buena Vista, 1960
THE PARENT TRAP   Buena Vista, 1961
THE INTERNS   Columbia, 1962
LOVE IS A BALL   United Artists, 1962
UNDER THE YUM YUM TREE   Columbia, 1963
GOOD NEIGHBOR SAM   Columbia, 1964
HOW TO SUCCEED IN BUSINESS WITHOUT REALLY
   TRYING   United Artists, 1967

SAUL SWIMMER
FORCE OF IMPULSE   Sutton, 1961
MRS. BROWN, YOU'VE GOT A LOVELY DAUGHTER
   MGM, 1968, British
COMETOGETHER   Allied Artists, 1971, U.S.-Italian
THE CONCERT FOR BANGLADESH (FD)   20th Century-
   Fox, 1972
THE BLACK PEARL   Diamond, 1977
WE WILL ROCK YOU (FD)   Mobilevision/Yellowbill,
   1983, Canadian

BRAD SWIRNOFF
Agent: The Artists Agency - Los Angeles, 213/277-7779

TUNNELVISION   co-director with Neil Israel, World
    Wide, 1976
AMERICAN RASPBERRY   Cannon, 1980

MICHAEL SWITZER*
Agent: Alan Greenspan, ICM - Los Angeles, 213/550-4428

RAGS TO RICHES (TF)   Leonard Hill Films, 1987
FRANK NITTI: THE ENFORCER (TF)   Leonard Hill
    Films, 1988
POLICE STORY: THE FAR TURN (TF)   Columbia
    TV, 1989
HEROES AND VILLAINS (TF)   Leonard Hill Films, 1990
THE STORY OF THE BEACH BOYS: SUMMER
    DREAMS (TF)   Leonard Hill Films, 1990
REVEALING EVIDENCE (TF)   T.W.S. Productions/
    Universal TV, 1990

HANS-JURGEN SYBERBERG
b. December 8, 1935 - Germany
Contact: German Film & TV Academy, Pommernallee 1,
    1 Berlin 19, West Germany, 0311/302-6096

FUNFTER AKT, SIEBTE SZENE. FRITZ KORTNER
    PROBT KABALE UND LIEBE (FD)   1965,
    West German
ROMY. ANATOMIE EINES GESICHT (FD)   1965,
    West German
FRITZ KORTNER SPRICHT MONOLOGE FUR EINE
    SCHALLPLATTE (FD)   1966
DIE GRAFFEN POCCI - EINIGE KAPITEL ZUR
    GESCHICHTE EINER FAMILIE (FD)   1967,
    West German
SCARABEA - WIENVIEL ERDE BRAUCHT DER MENSCH?
    1968, West German
SEX-BUSINESS - MADE IN PASSING (FD)   1969,
    West German
SAN DOMINGO   co-director with Christian Blackwood,
    1970, West German
NACH MEINEM LETZEN UMZUG   1970, West German
THEODOR HIERNEIS ODER: WIE MAN EHEM.
    HOFKOCH WIRD   1972, West German
LUDWIG: REQUIEM FOR A VIRGIN KING   Zoetrope,
    1972, West German
KARL MAY   7MS Film Gesellschaft, 1974, West German
WINIFRED WAGNER (FD)   WINIFRED WAGNER UND
    DIE GESCHICHTE DES HAUSES WAHNFRIED VON
    1914-1975   Bauer International, 1978, West German
HITLER: A FILM FROM GERMANY   Zoetrope, 1980,
    West German
PARSIFAL   Triumph/Columbia, 1981,
    French-West German
DIE NACHT   TMS Film, 1985, West German

PETER SYKES
b. June 17, 1939 - Melbourne, Australia
Address: 66 Highgate Hill - No. 6, London NW19, England,
    71/272-1664
Agent: Jonathan Clowes, 22 Prince Albert Street, London
    NW1, England

THE COMMITTEE   Planet, 1968, British
DEMONS OF THE MIND   MGM-EMI, 1972, British
THE HOUSE IN NIGHTMARE PARK   MGM-EMI,
    1973, British
STEPTOE AND SON RIDE AGAIN   MGM-EMi,
    1973, British

LEGEND OF SPIDER FOREST   *VENOM*   New Line
    Cinema, 1974, British
TO THE DEVIL A DAUGHTER   EMI, 1976, British
CRAZY HOUSE   Constellation, 1977, British
JESUS   co-director with John Krish, Warner Bros.,
    1979, British
THE SEARCH FOR ALEXANDER THE GREAT (MS)
    Time-Life Productions/ Video Arts TV Productions,
    1981, U.S.-British

PAUL SYLBERT*
Home: 52 East 64th Street - Suite 3, New York, NY
    10021, 212/308-9078

THE STEAGLE   Avco Embassy, 1971

ISTVAN SZABO
b. February 18, 1938 - Budapest, Hungary
Agent: Paul Kohner, Inc. - Los Angeles, 213/550-1060

AGE OF ILLUSIONS   Brandon, 1964, Hungarian
FATHER   Continental, 1966, Hungarian
LOVE FILM   Mafilm, 1970, Hungarian
25, FIREMAN'S STREET   Unifilm, 1970, Hungarian
PREMIERE (TF)   Hungarian TV, 1974, Hungarian
BUDAPEST TALES   Hunnia Studios, 1976, Hungarian
CONFIDENCE   Mafilm, 1979, Hungarian
THE GREEN BIRD   Teleculture, 1979, West German
MEPHISTO   Analysis, 1980, Hungarian-West German
COLONEL REDL   Orion Classics, 1985, West German-
    Austrian-Hungarian
HANUSSEN   Studio Objektiv/CCC Filmkunst/Hungarofilm/
    MOKEP, 1988, Hungarian-West German
MEETING VENUS   Warner Bros., 1991, British-U.S.

JEANNOT SZWARC*
b. November 21, 1937 - Paris, France
Business: Terpsichore Productions, P.O. Box 8639,
    Calabasas, CA 91302, 818/888-5301
Agent: David Gersh, The Gersh Agency - Beverly Hills,
    213/274-6611

NIGHT OF TERROR (TF)   Paramount TV, 1972
THE WEEKEND SUN (TF)   Paramount TV, 1972
THE DEVIL'S DAUGHTER (TF)   Paramount TV, 1973
YOU'LL NEVER SEE ME AGAIN (TF)   Universal TV, 1973
LISA, BRIGHT AND DARK (TF)   Bob Banner
    Associates, 1973
A SUMMER WITHOUT BOYS (TF)   Playboy
    Productions, 1973
THE SMALL MIRACLE (TF)   FCB Productions/Alan
    Landsburg Productions, 1973
EXTREME CLOSE-UP   National General, 1973
CRIME CLUB (TF)   Universal TV, 1975
BUG   Paramount, 1975
CODE NAME: DIAMOND HEAD (TF)   QM
    Productions, 1977
JAWS 2   Universal, 1978
SOMEWHERE IN TIME   Universal, 1980
ENIGMA   Embassy, 1982, British-French
SUPERGIRL   Warner Bros., 1984, British
SANTA CLAUS: THE MOVIE   Tri-Star, 1985, U.S.-British
THE MURDERS IN THE RUE MORGUE (TF)   Robert Halmi,
    Inc./International Film Productions, 1986
GRAND LARCENY (TF)   Robert Halmi, Inc., 1988
HONOR BOUND   MGM/UA, 1990, U.S.-French

T

JEAN-CHARLES TACCHELLA
b. September 23, 1925 - Cherbourg, France
Home: 8 bis Boulevard de Lesseps, Versailles 78000,
    France, 3/950-4764
Agent: Jean-Paul Faure, Agence IPF, 2 Rue Jules
    Chaplain, Paris, France, 325-5163

VOYAGE TO GRAND TARTARIE   New Line Cinema,
    1973, French
COUSIN COUSINE   Libra, 1975, French
THE BLUE COUNTRY   Quartet, 1977, French
IT'S A LONG TIME THAT I'VE LOVED YOU   SOUPCON
    Durham/Pike, 1979, French
CROQUE LA VIE   Prodis, 1981, French
ESCALIER C   AMLF, 1985, French
L'HEURE SIMENON (TF)   TF1, 1986, French
TRAVELLING AVANT   Erato Film/La Sept,
    1987, French
LES DAMES GALANTES   Gaumont, 1990,
    French-Canadian-Italian

ROBERT TAICHER
INSIDE OUT   Hemdale, 1986

RENEE TAJIMA
WHO KILLED VINCENT CHIN? (FD)   co-director with
    Christine Choy, 1988
BEST HOTEL ON SKID ROW (FD)   co-director with
    Christine Choy, 1990

TIBOR TAKACS*
b. 1954 - Budapest, Hungary
Business: New Frontier Films, 618 Adelaide Street West,
    Toronto, Ontario M6J 1A9, Canada, 416/366-3966
Agent: Donald Kopaloff, The Kopaloff Company -
    Los Angeles, 213/203-8430

METAL MESSIAH   Mega Media Communications
    Corporation, 1977, Canadian
THE TOMORROW MAN   PRISONER 984   (TF)
    Mega Media Communications Corporation,
    1979, Canadian
THE GREAT AMERICAN TRAGEDY   Gilmark Picture
    Corporation, 1984, Canadian
THE GATE   New Century/Vista, 1987, Canadian
I, MADMAN   Trans World Entertainment, 1989
THE GATE II: TRESPASSERS   Alliance Entertainment,
    1990, Canadian

YOJIRO TAKITA
Contact: Directors Guild of Japan, Tsukada Building,
    8-33 Udagawa-cho, Shibuya-ku, Tokyo 150, Japan,
    3/461-4411

COMIC MAGAZINE   M&R Films/Cinecom,
    1986, Japanese
YEN FAMILY   Herald Ace/Nippon Herald Films,
    1988, Japanese

LEN TALAN
HANSEL AND GRETEL   Cannon, 1987, U.S.-Israeli

BILL TANNEBRING*
b. March 9, 1937 - Bermuda
Business: Tannebring Rose Associates, 10300 N. Central
    Expressway, Dallas, TX 75231, 214/363-3464

VOYEUR   Crystal Productions, 1984

TERREL TANNEN
Agent: William Morris Agency - Beverly Hills, 213/274-7451

SHADOWS IN THE STORM   Vidmark, 1990

WILLIAM TANNEN*
Agent: Tom Chasen - Los Angeles, 213/278-7505

FLASHPOINT   Tri-Star, 1984
DEADLY ILLUSION   co-director with Larry Cohen, CineTel
    Films, 1987
HERO AND THE TERROR   Cannon, 1988

HARRY TAMPA
(See Harry HURWITZ)

ALAIN TANNER
b. December 6, 1929 - Geneva, Switzerland
Contact: Swiss Film Center, Munstergasse 18, 8001 Zurich,
    Switzerland, 01/472860

LES APPRENTIS (FD)   1964, Swiss
UNE VILLE A CHANDIGARH   1966, Swiss
CHARLES, DEAD OR ALIVE   New Yorker, 1969,
    Swiss-French
LA SALAMANDRE   New Yorker, 1971, Swiss
LA RETOUR D'AFRIQUE   Alain Tanner/Groupe 5,
    1973, Swiss
THE MIDDLE OF THE WORLD   New Yorker, 1974, Swiss
JONAH WHO WILL BE 25 IN THE YEAR 2000   New Yorker,
    1976, Swiss
MESSIDOR   New Yorker, 1979, Swiss-French
LIGHT YEARS AWAY   New Yorker, 1981, Swiss-French
IN THE WHITE CITY   Gray City, 1983, Swiss
NO MAN'S LAND   New Yorker, 1985, French-Swiss
LA VALLEE FANTOME   MK2, 1987, French-Swiss
A FLAME IN MY HEART   Roxie Releasing, 1987, Swiss
LA FEMME DE ROSE HILL   Filmograph, 1989,
    Swiss-French- West German

DANIEL TAPLITZ
Agent: Linne Radmin, ICM - Los Angeles, 213/550-4474

NIGHTLIFE (CTF)   Cine Enterprises Mexico/MTE,
    1989, U.S.-Mexican

DANIEL TARADASH*
b. January 29, 1913 - Louisville, Kentucky
Agent: Ben Benjamin, ICM - Los Angeles, 213/550-4000

STORM CENTER   Columbia, 1956

MAX TASH*
Agent: CAA - Beverly Hills, 213/288-4545

THE RUNNIN' KIND   MGM/UA, 1989

NADIA TASS

Agent: CAA - Beverly Hills, 213/288-4545

MALCOLM   Vestron, 1986, Australian
RIKKY AND PETE   MGM/UA, 1988, Australian
THE BIG STEAL   Hoyts Distribution, 1990, Australian
OVER THE HILL   Glasshouse Pictures/Village Roadshow, 1990, Australian

BERTRAND TAVERNIER

b. April 25, 1941 - Lyon, France
Agent: ICM - Los Angeles, 213/550-4000

LES BAISERS   co-director, 1963, French
LA CHANCE ET L'AMOUR   co-director, 1964, French
THE CLOCKMAKER OF ST. PAUL   Joseph Green Pictures, 1974, French
LET JOY REIGN SUPREME *QUE LA FETE COMMENCE...* SJ International, 1975, French
THE JUDGE AND THE ASSASSIN   Libra, 1976, French
SPOILED CHILDREN   Corinth, 1977, French
FEMMES FATALES   1979, French
DEATH WATCH   Quartet, 1980, French-West German
A WEEK'S VACATION *UNE SEMAINE DE VACANCES* Biograph, 1982, French
COUP DE TORCHON *CLEAN SLATE* Biograph/Quartet/ Films Inc./The Frank Moreno Company, 1982, French
MISSISSIPPI BLUES   co-director with Robert Parrish, Little Bear Productions/ Odessa Films, 1984, French
A SUNDAY IN THE COUNTRY   MGM/UA Classics, 1984, French
ROUND MIDNIGHT   Warner Bros., 1986, U.S.-French
BEATRICE *LA PASSION BEATRICE* Samuel Goldwyn Company, 1987, French
LIFE AND NOTHING BUT...   Orion Classics, 1989, French-Italian
DADDY NOSTALGIE   Avenue Pictures, 1990, French

PAOLO TAVIANI

b. November 8, 1931 - San Miniato, Italy
Home: via dell'Ongaro 41, Rome, Italy, 06/5817231

UN UOMO DA BRUCIARE   co-director with Vittorio Taviani & Valentino Orsini, Moira Film/Ager Film/ Sancro Film, 1963, Italian
I FUORILEGGE DEL METRIMONIO   co-director with Vittorio Taviani & Valentino Orsini, Ager Film/Filmcoop/ D'errico Film, 1963, Italian
SOVVERSIVI   co-director with Vittorio Taviani, Ager Film, 1967, Italian
SOTTO IL SEGNO DELLO SCORPIONE   co-director with Vittorio Taviani, Ager Film, 1969, Italian
SAN MICHELE AVEVA UN GALLO (TF)   co-director with Vittorio Taviani, Igor Film/RAI, 1971, Italian
ALLONSANFAN   co-director with Vittorio Taviani, Italtoons/Wonder Movies, 1974, Italian
PADRE PADRONE   co-director with Vittorio Taviani, New Yorker, 1977, Italian originally made for television
THE MEADOW   co-director with Vittorio Taviani, New Yorker, 1979, Italian- French
THE NIGHT OF THE SHOOTING STARS *LA NOTTE DI SAN LORENZO*   co-director with Vittorio Taviani, United Artists Classics, 1981, Italian
KAOS   co-director with Vittorio Taviani, MGM/UA Classics, 1985, Italian
GOOD MORNING, BABYLON   co-director with Vittorio Taviani, Vestron, 1987, Italian-French-U.S.
IL SOLE ANCHE DI NOTTE   co-director with Vittorio Taviani, Film 3, 1989, Italian

VITTORIO TAVIANI

b. September 20, 1929 - San Miniato, Italy
Home: via Orti D'Alibert 4, Rome, Italy, 06/6541834

UN UOMO DA BRUCIARE   co-director with Paolo Taviani & Valentino Orsini, Moira Film/Ager Film/ Sancro Film, 1963, Italian
I FUORILEGGE DEL METRIMONIO   co-director with Paolo Taviani & Valentino Orsini, Ager Film/Filmcoop/ D'errico Film, 1963, Italian
SOVVERSIVI   co-director with Paolo Taviani, Ager Film, 1967, Italian
SOTTO IL SEGNO DELLO SCORPIONE   co-director with Paolo Taviani, Ager Film, 1969, Italian
SAN MICHELE AVEVA UN GALLO (TF)   co-director with Paolo Taviani, Igor Film/RAI, 1971, Italian
ALLONSANFAN   co-director with Paolo Taviani, Italtoons/Wonder Movies, 1974, Italian
PADRE PADRONE   co-director with Paolo Taviani, New Yorker, 1977, Italian, originally made for television
THE MEADOW   co-director with Paolo Taviani, New Yorker, 1979, Italian-French
THE NIGHT OF THE SHOOTING STARS *LA NOTTE DI SAN LORENZO*   co-director with Paolo Taviani, United Artists Classics, 1981, Italian
KAOS   co-director with Paolo Taviani, MGM/UA Classics, 1985, Italian
GOOD MORNING, BABYLON   co-director with Paolo Taviani, Vestron, 1987, Italian-French-U.S.
IL SOLE ANCHE DI NOTTE   co-director with Paolo Taviani, Film 3, 1989, Italian

BAZ TAYLOR

Address: 17 Alexander Street, London W2, England, 01/727-1191
Agent: Duncan Heath, 162/170 Wardour Street, London W1V 3AT, England, 71/439-1471

LOVEJOY (TF)   BBC, 1985, British
DEMPSEY & MAKEPEACE - THE MOVIE   1986, British
WHERE THERE'S A WILL (TF)   1987, British
THE YOUNG CHARLIE CHAPLIN (TF)   Thames TV, 1989, British
LAST TANGLE IN PARIS   The Movie Group, 1991, U.S.-Fernch

DON TAYLOR*

b. December 13, 1920 - Freeport, Pennsylvania
Agent: Phil Gersh, The Gersh Agency - Beverly Hills, 213/274-6611

EVERTHING'S DUCKY   Columbia, 1961
RIDE THE WILD SURF   Columbia, 1964
JACK OF DIAMONDS   MGM, 1967, U.S.-West German
SOMETHING FOR A LONELY MAN (TF)   Universal TV, 1968
THE FIVE MAN ARMY   MGM, 1970, Italian
WILD WOMEN (TF)   Aaron Spelling Productions, 1970
ESCAPE FROM THE PLANET OF THE APES   20th Century-Fox, 1971
HEAT OF ANGER (TF)   Metromedia Productions, 1972
TOM SAWYER   United Artists, 1973
NIGHT GAMES (TF)   Paramount TV, 1974
HONKY TONK (TF)   MGM TV, 1974
ECHOES OF A SUMMER   Cine Artists, 1976, U.S.-Canadian
THE MAN-HUNTER (TF)   Universal TV, 1976
THE GREAT SCOUT AND CATHOUSE THURSDAY   American International, 1976

A CIRCLE OF CHILDREN (TF)   Edgar J. Scherick
    Associates/ 20th Century-Fox TV, 1977
THE ISLAND OF DR. MOREAU   American
    International, 1977
DAMIEN - OMEN II   20th Century-Fox, 1978
THE GIFT (TF)   The Jozak Company/Cypress Point
    Productions/ Paramount TV, 1979
THE FINAL COUNTDOWN   United Artists, 1980
THE PROMISE OF LOVE (TF)   Pierre Cossette
    Productions, 1980
BROKEN PROMISE (TF)   1981
RED FLAG: THE ULTIMATE GAME (TF)   Marble Arch
    Productions, 1981
DROP-OUT FATHER (TF)   CBS Entertainment, 1982
LISTEN TO YOUR HEART (TF)   CBS Entertainment, 1983
SEPTEMBER GUN (TF)   QM Productions/Taft
    Entertainment/Brademan-Self Productions, 1983
HE'S NOT YOUR SON (TF)   CBS Entertainment, 1984
MY WICKED, WICKED WAYS: THE LEGEND OF ERROL
    FLYNN (TF)   CBS Entertainment, 1985
SECRET WEAPONS (TF)   Goodman-Rosen
    Productions/ITC Productions, 1985
GOING FOR THE GOLD: THE BILL JOHNSON
    STORY (TF)   ITC Productions/ Sullivan-Carter
    Interests/Goodman-Rosen Productions, 1985
CLASSIFIED LOVE (TF)   CBS Entertainment, 1986
GHOST OF A CHANCE (TF)   Stuart-Phoenix Productions/
    Thunder Bird Road Productions/Lorimar-Telepictures
    Productions, 1987
THE DIAMOND TRAP (TF)   Jay Bernstein Productions/
    Columbia TV, 1988

JUD TAYLOR*
b. February 25, 1940
Agent: Alan Berger, ICM - Los Angeles, 213/550-4311

FADE-IN   directed under pseudonym of Allen Smithee,
    Paramount, 1968
WEEKEND OF TERROR (TF)   Paramount TV, 1970
SUDDENLY SINGLE (TF)   Chris-Rose Productions, 1971
REVENGE (TF)   Mark Carliner Productions, 1972
THE ROOKIES (TF)   Aaron Spelling Productions, 1972
SAY GOODBYE, MAGGIE COLE (TF)   Spelling-Goldberg
    Productions, 1972
HAWKINS ON MURDER (TF)   Arena-Leda Productions/
    MGM TV, 1973
WINTER KILL (TF)   Andy Griffith Enterprises/
    MGM TV, 1974
THE DISAPPEARANCE OF FLIGHT 412 (TF)   Cinemobile
    Productions, 1975
SEARCH FOR THE GODS (TF)   Warner Bros. TV, 1975
FUTURE COP (TF)   Paramount TV, 1976
RETURN TO EARTH (TF)   King-Hitzig Productions, 1976
WOMAN OF THE YEAR (TF)   MGM TV, 1976
TAIL GUNNER JOE (TF) ☆   Universal TV, 1977
MARY WHITE (TF)   Radnitz/Mattel Productions, 1977
CHRISTMAS MIRACLE IN CAUFIELD, U.S.A. (TF)   20th
    Century-Fox TV, 1977
THE LAST TENANT (TF)   Titus Productions, 1978
LOVEY: A CIRCLE OF CHILDREN, PART II (TF)
    Time-Life Productions, 1978
FLESH AND BLOOD (TF)   The Jozak Company/Cypress
    Point Productions/ Paramount TV, 1979
CITY IN FEAR (TF)   directed under pseudonym of Alan
    Smithee, Trans World International, 1980
ACT OF LOVE (TF)   Cypress Point Productions/
    Paramount TV, 1980
MURDER AT CRESTRIDGE (TF)   Jaffe-Taylor
    Productions, 1981
A QUESTION OF HONOR (TF)   Roger Gimbel
    Productions/EMI TV/Sonny Grosso Productions, 1982

PACKIN' IT IN (TF)   Roger Gimbel Productions/Thorn
    EMI TV/Jones-Reiker Ink Corporation, 1983
LICENSE TO KILL (TF)   Marian Rees Associates/
    D. Petrie Productions, 1984
OUT OF THE DARKNESS (TF)   Grosso-Jacobson
    Productions/Centerpoint Productions, 1985
DOUBLETAKE (TF)   Titus Productions, 1985
BROKEN VOWS (TF)   Brademan-Self Productions/
    Robert Halmi, Inc., 1987
FOXFIRE (TF)   Marian Rees Associates, 1987
THE GREAT ESCAPE II: THE UNTOLD STORY (TF)
    co-director with Paul Wendkos, Spectator Films/
    Michael Jaffe Films, 1988
THE OLD MAN AND THE SEA (TF)   Storke Enterprises/
    Green Pond Productions/Yorkshire TV, 1990
END RUN (TF)   Titus Productions, 1990

RENEE TAYLOR*
b. March 19, 1945
Address: 613 N. Arden Drive, Beverly Hills, CA 90210,
    213/274-8965

IT HAD TO BE YOU   co-director with Joseph Bologna,
    Limelite Studios, 1989

ROBERT TAYLOR
THE NINE LIVES OF FRITZ THE CAT (AF)   American
    International, 1974
HEIDI'S SONG (AF)   Paramount, 1982

RODERICK TAYLOR*
Agent: ICM - Los Angeles, 213/550-4000

INSTANT KARMA   Rosenbloom Entertainment, 1990

LEWIS TEAGUE*
b. 1941
Agent: David Gersh, The Gersh Agency - Beverly Hills,
    213/274-6611

DIRTY O'NEIL   co-director with Howard Freen, American
    International, 1974
THE LADY IN RED   New World, 1979
ALLIGATOR   Group 1, 1980
FIGHTING BACK   Paramount, 1982
CUJO   Warner Bros., 1983
STEPHEN KING'S CAT'S EYE   CAT'S EYE
    MGM/UA, 1985
THE JEWEL OF THE NILE   20th Century-Fox, 1985
SHANNON'S DEAL (TF)   Stan Rogow Productions/NBC
    Productions, 1989
COLLISION COURSE   DEG, 1990, filmed in 1988
NAVY SEALS   Orion, 1990

JULIEN TEMPLE
b. November 26, 1953 - London, England
Agent: William Morris Agency - Beverly Hills, 213/274-7451
Business: Nitrate Films Ltd., 47 Dean Street, London W1,
    England, 01/734-0386

THE GREAT ROCK 'N' ROLL SWINDLE   Kendon Films/
    Matrix Best/Virgin Records, 1980, British
THE SECRET POLICEMAN'S OTHER BALL (FD)   Miramax,
    1981, British
IT'S ALL TRUE (TF)   Island Pictures/BBC, 1983, British
RUNNING OUT OF LUCK   Nitrate Film Ltd./Julien Temple
    Production Company, 1985, British
ABSOLUTE BEGINNERS   Orion, 1986, British
EARTH GIRLS ARE EASY   Vestron, 1989

CONNY TEMPLEMAN
Contact: British Academy of Film & Television Arts,
195 Piccadilly, London W1, England, 71/734-0022

NANOU   Umbrella-Caulfield Films Ltd./National Film Finance
Corporation/Curzon Film Distributors Ltd./French Ministry
of Culture, 1986, British-French

KEVIN S. TENNEY
WITCHBOARD   Cinema Group, 1986
NIGHT OF THE DEMONS   International Film
Marketing, 1988
WITCHTRAP   Cinema Plus/GCO Pictures/Mentone
Pictures, 1989
PEACEMAKER   Fries Entertainment, 1990

HIROSHI TESHIGAHARA
b. 1927 - Tokyo, Japan
Contact: Directors Guild of Japan, Tsukada Building,
8-33 Udagawa-cho, Shibuya-ku, Tokyo 150, Japan,
3/461-4411

THE PITFALL   1961, Japanese
THAT TENDER AGE   co-director, 1964,
Canadian-French-Italian-Japanese
WOMAN IN THE DUNES   1964, Japanese
THE FACE OF ANOTHER   1966, Japanese
MAN WITHOUT A MAP   1968, Japanese
SUMMER SOLDIERS   1972, Japanese
OUT OF WORK FOR YEARS   1975, Japanese
RIKYU   Shochiku, 1989, Japanese

JOAN TEWKESBURY*
b. 1937 - Redlands, California
Agent: CAA - Beverly Hills, 213/288-4545

OLD BOYFRIENDS   Avco Embassy, 1979
THE TENTH MONTH (TF)   Joe Hamilton
Productions, 1979
THE ACORN PEOPLE (TF)   Rollins-Joffe-Morra-Brezner
Productions, 1980
COLD SASSY TREE (CTF)   Faye Dunaway Productions/
Ohlmeyer Communications/Turner Network TV, 1989

PETER TEWKSBURY
b. 1924

SUNDAY IN NEW YORK   MGM, 1964
EMIL AND THE DETECTIVES   Buena Vista, 1964
DOCTOR, YOU'VE GOT TO BE KIDDING   MGM, 1967
STAY AWAY, JOE   MGM, 1968
THE TROUBLE WITH GIRLS   MGM, 1969
SECOND CHANCE (TF)   Metromedia Productions, 1972

ANNA THOMAS
b. July 12, 1948 - Stuttgart, West Germany
Agent: Jeff Berg, ICM - Los Angeles, 213/550-4000

THE HAUNTING OF M   Independent Productions, 1981

ANTONY THOMAS
Contact: Writers Guild of America, West - Los Angeles,
213/550-1000

S.P.O.O.K.S.   Vestron, 1990

DAVE THOMAS*
Business: DWT Productions Inc., 336 Keewatin Avenue,
Toronto, Ontario, Canada, 416/487-8296
Agent: ICM - Los Angeles, 213/550-4000

STRANGE BREW   co-director with Rick Moranis,
MGM/UA, 1983, Canadian
THE EXPERTS   Paramount, 1989

GERALD THOMAS
b. December 10, 1920 - Hull, England
Business: Pinewood Studios, Iver Heath, Buckinghamshire
SLO 0NH, England, 0753/656634
Contact: British Academy of Film & Television Arts,
195 Piccadilly, London W1, England, 71/734-0022

CIRCUS FRIENDS   British Lion/Children's Film
Foundation, 1956, British
TIMELOCK   DCA, 1957, British
THE CIRCLE   THE VICIOUS CIRCLE   Kassler,
1957, British
THE DUKE WORE JEANS   Anglo-Amalgamated,
1958, British
CHAIN OF EVENTS   British Lion, 1958, British
CARRY ON SERGEANT   Governor, 1958, British
CARRY ON NURSE   Governor, 1959, British
PLEASE TURN OVER   Columbia, 1959, British
WATCH YOUR STERN   Magna, 1960, British
BEWARE OF CHILDREN   NO KIDDING   American
International, 1960, British
CARRY ON CONSTABLE   Governor, 1960, British
ROOMMATES   RAISING THE WIND   Herts-Lion
International, 1961, British
CARRY ON REGARDLESS   Anglo-Amalgamated,
1961, British
A SOLITARY CHILD   British Lion, 1961, British
TWICE ROUND THE DAFFODILS   Anglo-Amalgamated,
1962, British
CARRY ON CRUISING   Governor, 1962, British
THE SWINGIN' MAIDEN   THE IRON MAIDEN   Columbia,
1962, British
NURSE ON WHEELS   Janus, 1963, British
CARRY ON CABBY   Anglo-Amalgamated/Warner-Pathé,
1963, British
CARRY ON JACK   Anglo-Amalgamated/Warner-Pathé,
1964, British
CARRY ON SPYING   Governor, 1964, British
CARRY ON CLEO   Governor, 1964, British
THE BIG JOB   Anglo-Amalgamated/Warner-Pathé,
1966, British
CARRY ON COWBOY   Anglo-Amalgamated/Warner-Pathé,
1966, British
CARRY ON SCREAMING   Anglo-Amalgamated/Warner-
Pathé, 1966, British
FOLLOW THAT CAMEL   Schoenfeld Film Distributing,
1967, British
CARRY ON DOCTOR   Rank, 1968, British
CARRY ON...UP THE KHYBER   Rank, 1969, British
CARRY ON CAMPING   Rank, 1969, British
CARRY ON UP THE JUNGLE   Rank, 1970, British
CARRY ON AGAIN, DOCTOR   Rank, 1970, British
CARRY ON AT YOUR CONVENIENCE   Rank,
1971, British
CARRY ON HENRY   Rank, 1971, British
CARRY ON LOVING   Rank, 1971, British
CARRY ON ABROAD   Rank, 1972, British
CARRY ON MATRON   Rank, 1972, British
BLESS THIS HOUSE   Rank, 1973, British
CARRY ON BEHIND   Rank, 1976, British

CARRY ON ENGLAND   Rank, 1976, British
CARRY ON EMMANUELLE   Rank, 1978, British
THAT'S CARRY ON   Rank, 1978, British
CARRY ON COMEDY CLASSICS (TF)   Thames TV,
   1983, British
THE SECOND VICTORY   Filmworld Distributors, 1987,
   Australian-British

JOHN G. THOMAS
BANZAI RUNNER   Montage Films, 1987
ARIZONA HEAT   Spectrum Entertainment, 1988

RALPH THOMAS
b. August 10, 1915 - Hull, England
Home: 20 Hyde Park Gardens Mews, London W2, England,
   71/262-6402
Agent: Denis Selinger, ICM - London, 71/629-8080

HELTER SKELTER   General Film Distributors,
   1949, British
ONCE UPON A DREAM   General Film Distributors,
   1949, British
TRAVELLER'S JOY   General Film Distributors,
   1949, British
THE CLOUDED YELLOW   General Film Distributors,
   1950, British
ISLAND RESCUE   *APPOINTMENT WITH VENUS*
   Universal, 1951, British
THE ASSASSIN   *THE VENETIAN BIRD*   United Artists,
   1952, British
THE DOG AND THE DIAMONDS   Associated British Film
   Distributors/Children's Film Foundation, 1953, British
A DAY TO REMEMBER   Republic, 1953, British
DOCTOR IN THE HOUSE   Republic, 1954, British
MAD ABOUT MEN   General Film Distributors,
   1954, British
DOCTOR AT SEA   Republic, 1955, British
ABOVE US THE WAVES   Republic, 1955, British
THE IRON PETTICOAT   MGM, 1956, British
CHECKPOINT   Rank, 1956, British
DOCTOR AT LARGE   Universal, 1957, British
CAMPBELL'S KINGDOM   Rank, 1957, British
A TALE OF TWO CITIES   Rank, 1958, British
THE WIND CANNOT READ   20th Century-Fox,
   1959, British
THE 39 STEPS   20th Century-Fox, 1959, British
UPSTAIRS AND DOWNSTAIRS   20th Century-Fox,
   1959, British
CONSPIRACY OF HEARTS   Paramount, 1960, British
DOCTOR IN LOVE   Governor, 1960, British
NO LOVE FOR JOHNNIE   Embassy, 1961, British
NO, MY DARLING DAUGHTER   Zenith, 1961, British
A PAIR OF BRIEFS   Rank, 1962, British
YOUNG AND WILLING   *THE WILD AND THE WILLING*
   Universal, 1962, British
DOCTOR IN DISTRESS   Governor, 1963, British
AGENT 8 3/4   *HOT ENOUGH FOR JUNE*   Continental,
   1963, British
McGUIRE, GO HOME!   *THE HIGH BRIGHT SUN*
   Continental, 1964, British
CARNABY, M.D.   *DOCTOR IN CLOVER*   Continental,
   1965, British
DEADLIER THAN THE MALE   Universal, 1966, British
SOME GIRLS DO   United Artists, 1968, British
THE HIGH COMMISSIONER   *NOBODY RUNS FOREVER*
   Cinerama Releasing Corporation, 1968, British
DOCTOR IN TROUBLE   Rank, 1970, British
PERCY   MGM, 1971, British
QUEST FOR LOVE   Rank, 1971, British

IT'S A 2'6" ABOVE THE GROUND WORLD   British Lion,
   1972, British
THE LOVE BAN   1973, British
IT'S NOT THE SIZE THAT COUNTS   *PERCY'S
   PROGRESS*   Joseph Brenner Associates,
   1974, British
A NIGHTINGALE SANG IN BERKELEY SQUARE   S.
   Benjamin Fisz Productions/Nightingale Productions,
   1980, British

RALPH L. THOMAS*
b. Sao Luiz, Maranhao, Brazil
Address: 8480 Harold Way, Los Angeles, CA 90069,
   213/858-6006
Business: Thomlee Productions Inc., 365 Markham Street,
   Toronto, Ontario M6G 2K8, Canada, 416/922-8700
Agent: David Wardlow, Camden Artists - Beverly Hills,
   213/278-6885

TYLER (TF)   CBC, 1977, Canadian
CEMENTHEAD (TF)   CBC, 1978, Canadian
A PAID VACATION (TF)   CBC, 1979, Canadian
AMBUSH AT IROQUOIS POINT (TF)   CBC,
   1979, Canadian
TICKET TO HEAVEN   United Artists Classics,
   1981, Canadian
THE TERRY FOX STORY (CTF)   HBO Premiere Films/
   Robert Cooper Films II, 1983, Canadian
APPRENTICE TO MURDER   New World, 1987, Canadian
THE FIRST SEASON   Orange Productions,
   1989, Canadian

ERNEST THOMPSON
b. 1950
Agent: InterTalent - Los Angeles, 213/271-0600

1969   Atlantic Releasing Corporation, 1988

HARRY THOMPSON
THE PASSAGE   Spectrum Films, 1988

J. LEE THOMPSON*
b. 1914 - Bristol, England
Home: 9595 Lime Orchard Road, Beverly Hills, CA 90210,
   213/858-3958
Business Manager: Dick deBlois, 9171 Wilshire Blvd.,
   Beverly Hills, CA 90210, 213/273-7769

MURDER WITHOUT CRIME   Associated British Picture
   Corporation, 1950, British
THE YELLOW BALLOON   Allied Artists, 1952, British
THE WEAK AND THE WICKED   Allied Artists, 1954, British
COCKTAILS IN THE KITCHEN   *FOR BETTER OR WORSE*
   Associated British Picture Corporation, 1954, British
AS LONG AS THEY'RE HAPPY   Rank, 1955, British
AN ALLIGATOR NAMED DAISY   Rank, 1955, British
BLONDE SINNER   *YIELD TO THE NIGHT*   Allied Artists,
   1956, British
THE GOOD COMPANIONS   Rank, 1957, British
WOMAN IN A DRESSING GOWN   Warner Bros.,
   1957, British
DESERT ATTACK   *ICE COLD IN ALEX*   20th Century-Fox,
   1958, British
NO TREES IN THE STREET   Associated British Picture
   Corporation, 1959, British
TIGER BAY   Continental, 1959, British
FLAME OVER INDIA   *NORTH WEST FRONTIER*   20th
   Century-Fox, 1959, British

I AIM AT THE STARS   Columbia, 1960,
    U.S.-West German
THE GUNS OF NAVARONE ★   Columbia, 1961,
    U.S.-British
CAPE FEAR   Universal, 1962
TARAS BULBA   United Artists, 1962
KINGS OF THE SUN   United Artists, 1963
WHAT A WAY TO GO!   20th Century-Fox, 1964
JOHN GOLDFARB, PLEASE COME HOME   20th
    Century-Fox, 1965
RETURN FROM THE ASHES   United Artists,
    1965, British-U.S.
EYE OF THE DEVIL   MGM, 1967, British
BEFORE WINTER COMES   Columbia, 1969, British
THE CHAIRMAN   20th Century-Fox, 1969, British
MACKENNA'S GOLD   Columbia, 1969
BROTHERLY LOVE   COUNTRY DANCE   MGM,
    1970, British
CONQUEST OF THE PLANET OF THE APES   20th
    Century-Fox, 1972
A GREAT AMERICAN TRAGEDY (TF)   Metromedia
    Productions, 1972
BATTLE FOR THE PLANET OF THE APES   20th
    Century-Fox, 1973
HUCKLEBERRY FINN   United Artists, 1974
THE BLUE KNIGHT (TF)   Lorimar Productions, 1975
THE REINCARNATION OF PETER PROUD   American
    International, 1975
ST. IVES   Warner Bros., 1976
WIDOW (TF)   Lorimar Productions, 1976
THE WHITE BUFFALO   United Artists, 1977
THE GREEK TYCOON   Universal, 1978
THE PASSAGE   United Artists, 1979, British
CABOBLANCO   Avco Embassy, 1981
HAPPY BIRTHDAY TO ME   Columbia,
    1981, Canadian
CODE RED (TF)   Irwin Allen Productions/
    Columbia TV, 1981
10 TO MIDNIGHT   Cannon, 1983
THE EVIL THAT MEN DO   Tri-Star, 1984
THE AMBASSADOR   MGM/UA/Cannon, 1984
KING SOLOMON'S MINES   Cannon, 1985
MURPHY'S LAW   Cannon, 1986
FIREWALKER   Cannon, 1986
DEATH WISH 4: THE CRACKDOWN   Cannon, 1988
MESSENGER OF DEATH   Cannon, 1988
KINJITE (FORBIDDEN SUBJECTS)   Cannon, 1989

ROB THOMPSON*

Home: 1302 N. Sweetzer Avenue - Apt. 401, Los Angeles,
    CA 90069, 213/650-2070
Agent: Ronda Gomez-Quinones, Triad Artists, Inc. -
    Los Angeles, 213/556-2727

TALES FROM THE HOLLYWOOD HILLS: PAT HOBBY
    TEAMED WITH GENIUS (TF)   WNET/Zenith
    Productions, 1987

ROBERT C. THOMPSON*

b. May 31, 1937 - Palmyra, New York
Home: 4536 Mary Ellen Avenue, Sherman Oaks, CA
    91423, 818/995-0273
Business Manager: Group Three Management, 13914
    Addison Street, Sherman Oaks, CA 92423,
    818/501-3714

BUD AND LOU (TF)   Bob Banner Associates, 1978

CHRIS THOMSON*

Contact: Directors Guild of America - Los Angeles,
    213/289-2000

(The following is an incomplete list of Mr. Thomson's credits)

MOVING TARGET (TF)   Lewis B. Chesler Productions/
    Bateman Company Productions/Finnegan-Pinchuk
    Company/ MGM-UA TV, 1988
STRINGER (TF)   co-director with Ken Cameron & Kathy
    Mueller, Australian Broadcasting Corporation/
    Televenture Film Productions, 1988, Australian-British
THE RAINBOW WARRIOR CONSPIRACY (TF)   Golden
    Dolphin Productions/ATNT/Television New Zealand,
    1989, Australian-New Zealand
SHE WAS MARKED FOR MURDER (TF)   Jack Grossbart
    Productions, 1989
SWIMSUIT (TF)   Musifilm Productions/American First
    Run Studios, 1989
THE DELINQUENTS   Warner Bros. International,
    1989, Australian

JERRY THORPE*

b. 1930
Home: 865 S. Bundy Drive, Los Angeles, CA 90049
Agent: Barrett, Benson, McCartt & Weston - Los Angeles,
    213/277-4998

THE VENETIAN AFFAIR   MGM, 1968
DAY OF THE EVIL GUN   MGM, 1968
DIAL HOT LINE (TF)   Universal TV, 1970
LOCK, STOCK AND BARREL (TF)   Universal TV, 1971
THE CABLE CAR MURDER (TF)   Warner Bros.
    TV, 1971
KUNG FU (TF)   Warner Bros. TV, 1972
COMPANY OF KILLERS   THE PROTECTORS
    Universal, 1972
SMILE JENNY, YOU'RE DEAD (TF)   Warner Bros.
    TV, 1974
THE DARK SIDE OF INNOCENCE (TF)   Warner Bros.
    TV, 1976
I WANT TO KEEP MY BABY (TF)   CBS, Inc., 1976
THE POSSESSED (TF)   Warner Bros. TV, 1977
STICKIN' TOGETHER (TF)   Blinn-Thorpe Productions/
    Viacom, 1978
A QUESTION OF LOVE (TF)   Viacom, 1978
THE LAZARUS SYNDROME (TF)   Blinn-Thorpe
    Productions/Viacom, 1979
ALL GOD'S CHILDREN (TF)   Blinn-Thorpe Productions/
    Viacom, 1980
HAPPY ENDINGS (TF)   Blinn-Thorpe Productions, 1983
BLOOD AND ORCHIDS (TF)   Lorimar Productions, 1986

RICHARD THORPE*
(Rollo Smolt Thorpe)

b. February 24, 1896 - Hutchinson, Kansas
Home: 1550 S. Camino Real - Apt. 222, Palm Springs, CA
    92264, 619/323-5347

BRINGING HOME THE BACON   Artclass, 1924
ROUGH RIDIN'   Artclass, 1924
FAST AND FEARLESS   Action, 1924
HARD HITTIN' HAMILTON   Action, 1924
RARIN' TO GO   Action, 1924
RIP ROARIN' ROBERTS   Artclass, 1924
THUNDERING ROMANCE   Artclass, 1924
WALLOPING WALLACE   Artclass, 1924
THE DESERT DEMON   Artclass, 1925
SADDLE CYCLONE   Artclass, 1925
FULL SPEED   Artclass, 1925
DOUBLE ACTION DANIELS   Artclass, 1925

FAST FIGHTIN' Artclass, 1925
GALLOPING ON Artclass, 1925
GOLD AND GRIT Artclass, 1925
ON THE GO Artclass, 1925
QUICKER 'N LIGHTNIN' Artclass, 1925
A STREAK OF LUCK Artclass, 1925
TEARIN' LOOSE Artclass, 1925
THE BANDIT BUSTER Associated Exhibitors, 1926
COLLEGE DAYS Tiffany, 1926
DOUBLE DEALING Artclass, 1926
THE FIGHTING CHEAT Artclass, 1926
RAWHIDE Associated Exhibitors, 1926
TWIN TRIGGERS Artclass, 1926
THE BONANZA BUCKAROO Associated Exhibitors, 1926
COMING AN' GOING Artclass, 1926
THE DANGEROUS DUB Associated Exhibitors, 1926
DEUCE HIGH Artclass, 1926
EASY GOING Artclass, 1926
RIDING RIVALS Artclass, 1926
ROARING RIDER Artclass, 1926
SPEEDY SPURS Artclass, 1926
TRUMPIN' TROUBLE Artclass, 1926
TWISTED TRIGGERS Associated Exhibitors, 1926
BETWEEN DANGERS Pathé, 1927
THE CYCLONE COWBOY Pathé, 1927
THE FIRST NIGHT Tiffany, 1927
THE GALLOPING GOBS Pathé, 1927
THE INTERFERIN' GENT Pathé, 1927
THE MEDDLIN' STRANGER Pathé, 1927
PALS IN PERIL Pathé, 1927
RIDE 'EM HIGH Pathé, 1927
THE RIDIN' ROWDY Pathé, 1927
ROARIN' BRONCS Pathé, 1927
SKEDADDLE GOLD Pathé, 1927
THE OBLIGIN' BUCKAROO Pathé, 1927
TEARIN' INTO TROUBLE Pathé, 1927
THE DESERT OF THE LOST Pathé, 1927
SODA WATER COWBOY Pathé, 1927
WHITE PEBBLES Pathé, 1927
THE VANISHING WEST Mascot, 1928, serial
VULTURES OF THE SEA Mascot, 1928, serial
THE COWBOY CAVALIER Pathé, 1928
DESPERATE COURAGE Pathé, 1928
THE VALLEY OF HUNTED MEN Pathé, 1928
BALLYHOO BUSTER Pathé, 1928
THE FLYING BUCKAROO Pathé, 1928
SADDLE MATES Pathé, 1928
THE FATAL WARNING Mascot, 1929, serial
KING OF THE KONGO Mascot, 1929, serial
THE BACHELOR GIRL Columbia, 1929, serial
THE LONE DEFENDER Mascot, 1930, serial
BORDER ROMANCE Tiffany, 1930
THE DUDE WRANGLER Sono-Art World Wide, 1930
WINGS OF ADVENTURE Tiffany, 1930
UNDER MONTANA SKIES TIffany, 1930
THE UTAH KID Tiffany, 1930
THE THOROUGHBRED Tiffany, 1930
KING OF THE WILD Mascot, 1931, serial
THE LAWLESS WOMAN Chesterfield, 1931
THE LADY FROM NOWHERE Chesterfield, 1931
WILD HORSES co-director with Sidney Algier,
    M.H. Hoffman, 1931
SKY SPIDER Action, 1931
GRIEF STREET Chesterfield, 1931
NECK AND NECK Sono-Art World Wide, 1931
THE DEVIL PLAYS Chesterfield, 1931
CROSS EXAMINATION Artclass, 1932
MURDER AT DAWN Big Four, 1932
FORGOTTEN WOMEN Monogram, 1932
PROBATION Chesterfield, 1932
MIDNIGHT LADY Chesterfield, 1932
ESCAPADE Invincible, 1932

FORBIDDEN COMPANY Invincible, 1932
BEAUTY PARLOR Chesterfield, 1932
THE KING MURDER Chesterfield, 1932
THE THRILL OF YOUTH Invincible, 1932
SLIGHTLY MARRIED Chesterfield, 1932
WOMEN WON'T TELL Chesterfield, 1933
THE SECRETS OF WU SIN Chesterfield, 1933
LOVE IS DANGEROUS Chesterfield, 1933
FORGOTTEN Invincible, 1933
STRANGE PEOPLE Chesterfield, 1933
I HAVE LIVED Chesterfield, 1933
NOTORIOUS BUT NICE Chesterfield, 1933
MAN OF SENTIMENT Chesterfield, 1933
RAINBOW OVER BROADWAY Chesterfield, 1933
MURDER ON THE CAMPUS Chesterfield, 1934
THE QUITTER Chesterfield, 1934
CITY PARK Chesterfield, 1934
STOLEN SWEETS Chesterfield, 1934
GREEN EYES Chesterfield, 1934
CHEATING CHEATERS Universal, 1934
SECRET OF THE CHATEAU Universal, 1935
STRANGE WIVES Universal, 1935
LAST OF THE PAGANS MGM, 1935
THE VOICE OF BUGLE ANN MGM, 1936
TARZAN ESCAPES MGM, 1936
DANGEROUS NUMBER MGM, 1937
NIGHT MUST FALL MGM, 1937
DOUBLE WEDDING MGM, 1937
MAN-PROOF MGM, 1938
LOVE IS A HEADACHE MGM, 1938
THE FIRST 100 YEARS MGM, 1938
THE TOY WIFE MGM, 1938
THE CROWD ROARS MGM, 1938
THREE LOVES HAS NANCY MGM, 1938
THE ADVENTURES OF HUCKLEBERRY FINN
    MGM, 1939
TARZAN FINDS A SON MGM, 1939
THE EARL OF CHICAGO MGM, 1940
TWENTY-MULE TEAM MGM, 1940
WYOMING MGM, 1940
THE BAD MAN MGM, 1941
BARNACLE BILL MGM, 1941
TARZAN'S SECRET TREASURE MGM, 1941
JOE SMITH, AMERICAN MGM, 1942
TARZAN'S NEW YORK ADVENTURE MGM, 1942
APACHE TRAIL MGM, 1942
WHITE CARGO MGM, 1942
THREE HEARTS FOR JULIA MGM, 1943
ABOVE SUSPICION MGM, 1943
CRY HAVOC MGM, 1943
TWO GIRLS AND A SAILOR MGM, 1944
THE THIN MAN GOES HOME MGM, 1945
THRILL OF A ROMANCE MGM, 1945
HER HIGHNESS AND THE BELLBOY MGM, 1945
WHAT NEXT, CORPORAL HARGROVE? MGM, 1945
FIESTA MGM, 1947
THIS TIME FOR KEEPS MGM, 1947
ON AN ISLAND WITH YOU MGM, 1948
A DATE WITH JUDY MGM, 1948
THE SUN COMES UP MGM, 1949
BIG JACK MGM, 1949
CHALLENGE TO LASSIE MGM, 1949
MALAYA MGM, 1950
THE BLACK HAND MGM, 1950
THREE LITTLE WORDS MGM, 1950
VENGEANCE VALLEY MGM, 1951
THE GREAT CARUSO MGM, 1951
THE UNKNOWN MAN MGM, 1951
IT'S A BIG COUNTRY co-director with Charles Vidor,
    John Sturges, Don Hartman, Clarence Brown,
    William Wellman & Don Weis, MGM, 1952

CARBINE WILLIAMS   MGM, 1952
IVANHOE   MGM, 1952
THE PRISONER OF ZENDA   MGM, 1952
THE GIRL WHO HAD EVERYTHING   MGM, 1953
ALL THE BROTHERS WERE VALIANT   MGM, 1953
KNIGHTS OF THE ROUND TABLE   MGM, 1954
THE FLAME AND THE FLESH   MGM, 1954
THE STUDENT PRINCE   MGM, 1954
ATHENA   MGM, 1954
THE PRODIGAL   MGM, 1955
QUENTIN DURWARD   MGM, 1955
TEN THOUSAND BEDROOMS   MGM, 1957
TIP ON A DEAD JOCKEY   MGM, 1957
JAILHOUSE ROCK   MGM, 1957
THE HOUSE OF THE SEVEN HAWKS   MGM,
   1959, British
KILLERS OF KILIMANJARO   Columbia, 1959, British
THE TARTARS   MGM, 1961, Italian-Yugoslavian
THE HONEYMOON MACHINE   MGM, 1961
THE HORIZONTAL LIEUTENANT   MGM, 1962
FOLLOW THE BOYS   MGM, 1963
FUN IN ACAPULCO   Paramount, 1963
THE GOLDEN HEAD   Cinerama, 1965, Hungarian-U.S.
THE TRUTH ABOUT SPRING   Universal, 1965,
   British-U.S.
THAT FUNNY FEELING   Universal, 1965
THE SCORPIO LETTERS (TF)   MGM TV, 1967
THE LAST CHALLENGE   MGM, 1967

KAREN THORSEN
Contact: Writers Guild of America, East - New York City,
   212/245-6180

JAMES BALDWIN: THE PRICE OF THE TICKET (TD)
   Nobody Knows Productions/Maysles Films/WNET-TV/
   American Masters, 1989

ERIC TILL*
b. 1929- London, England
Home: 62 Chaplin Crescent, Toronto, Ontario M5P 1A3,
   Canada, 416/488-4068

A GREAT BIG THING   Argofilms, 1967, British
HOT MILLIONS   MGM, 1968, British
THE WALKING STICK   MGM, 1970, British
TALKING TO A STRANGER (TF)   1971, Canadian
FOLLOW THE NORTH STAR (TF)   1972, Canadian
A FAN'S NOTES   Warner Bros., 1972, Canadian
ALL THINGS BRIGHT AND BEAUTIFUL   *IT SHOULDN'T
   HAPPEN TO A VET*   World Northal, 1978, British
WILD HORSE HANK   Film Consortium of Canada,
   1979, Canadian
AN AMERICAN CHRISTMAS CAROL (TF)   ABC, 1979
MARY AND JOSEPH: A STORY OF FAITH (TF)
   Lorimar Productions/CIP- Europaische Treuhand AG,
   1979, U.S.-West German
MAD SHADOWS (TF)   1979, Canadian
EYE OF THE BEHOLDER (TF)   1980, Canadian
IMPROPER CHANNELS   Crown International,
   1981, Canadian
IF YOU COULD SEE WHAT I HEAR   Jensen Farley
   Pictures, 1982, Canadian
SHOCKTRAUMA (TF)   1983, Canadian
GENTLE SINNERS (TF)   CBC, 1983, Canadian
BRIDGE TO TERABITHIA (TF)   Twenty Minute
   Productions/Kicking Horse Productions,
   1985, Canadian

THE CUCKOO BIRD (TF)   CBC, 1985, Canadian
TURNING TO STONE (TF)   CBC, 1985, Canadian
GLENN GOULD: A PORTRAIT (TD)   co-director,
   1985, Canadian
THE CHALLENGE (TF)   CBC/Lauron Productions,
   1989, Canadian

MARK TINKER*
Agent: Alan Greenspan, ICM - Los Angeles,
   213/550-4428

PRIVATE EYE (TF)   Yerkovich Productions/
   Universal TV, 1987
CAPITAL NEWS (TF)   MTM Enterprises, 1990

JAMES TOBACK*
Home: 11 East 87th Street, New York, NY 10028,
   212/427-5606
Agent: Jeff Berg, ICM - Los Angeles, 213/550-4000
Business Manager: David Kaufman, Kaufman & Nachbar,
   100 Merrick Road, Rockville Centre, NY, 516/536-5760

FINGERS   Brut Productions, 1978
LOVE AND MONEY   Paramount, 1982
EXPOSED   MGM/UA, 1983
THE PICK-UP ARTIST   20th Century-Fox, 1987
THE BIG BANG (FD)   Triton Pictures, 1989

STEPHEN TOBOLOWSKY
Agent: Triad Artists, Inc. - Los Angeles,
   213/556-2727

TWO IDIOTS IN HOLLYWOOD   FilmDallas, 1989

AUGUSTO TOMAYO
WELCOME TO OBLIVION   Concorde, 1990,
   U.S.-Peruvian

RALPH TOPOROFF*
Contact: Directors Guild of America - Los Angeles,
   213/289-2000

AMERICAN BLUE NOTE   Vested Interests
   Productions, 1989

BURT TOPPER*
b. July 31, 1928 - New York, New York
Address: 8447 Wilshire Blvd. - Suite102, Beverly Hills, CA
   90211, 213/823-6434

HELL SQUAD   American International, 1958
TANK COMMANDOS   American International, 1959
THE DIARY OF A HIGH SCHOOL BRIDE   American
   International, 1959
WAR IS HELL   Allied Artists, 1964
THE STRANGLER   Allied Artists, 1964
THE DEVIL'S 8   American International, 1968
THE HARD RIDE   American International, 1971
THE DAY THE LORD GOT BUSTED   American, 1976

RIP TORN*
b. February 6, 1931 - Temple, Texas
Agent: J. Michael Bloom - Los Angeles, 213/275-6800

THE TELEPHONE   New World, 1988

GIUSEPPE TORNATORE
b. May 27, 1956 - Bagheria, Palermo, Italy
Home: via Santamaura 7, Rome, Italy, 06/356-2106

IL CAMORRISTA   Aria Cinematografica/Titanus/Reteitalia,
   1986, Italian
CINEMA PARADISO   *NUOVO CINEMA PARADISO*
   Miramax Films, 1989, Italian-French
EVERYBODY'S FINE   Miramax Films, 1990, Italian
ESPECIALLY ON SUNDAY   co-director with Giuseppe
   Bertolucci, Ricky Tognazzi & Francesco Barilli, Pacific
   Pictures, 1990, Italian

JOE TORNATORE
GROTESQUE   Concorde, 1988

CINZIA TH TORRINI
b. 1954 - Florence, Italy
Home: via della Giuliana 85, Rome, Italy, 06/356-8976

GIOCARE D'AZZARDO   Cassiopea/Grokenberger,
   1982, Italian
HOTEL COLONIAL   Hemdale, 1987, U.S.-Italian
PLAGIO   co-director with Silvia Napolitano, RAI/WDR/
   Tangram/The Senate of West Berlin, 1990,
   Italian-West German

ROBERT TOTTEN*
b. February 5, 1937 - Los Angeles, California
Address: 13819 Riverside Drive, Sherman Oaks, CA
   91403, 818/986-3970
Agent: Jerry Kalajian, Sanford-Beckett-Skouras &
   Associates - Los Angeles, 213/208-2100

THE QUICK AND THE DEAD   Beckman, 1963
DEATH OF A GUNFIGHTER   co-director with Don Siegel,
   both directed under pseudonym of Allen Smithee,
   Universal, 1967
THE WILD COUNTRY   Buena Vista, 1971
THE RED PONY (TF)   Universal TV/Omnibus
   Productions, 1973
HUCKLEBERRY FINN (TF)   ABC Circle Films, 1975
PONY EXPRESS RIDER   Doty-Dayton, 1976
THE SACKETTS (TF)   Douglas Netter Enterprises/M.B.
   Scott Productions/ Shalako Enterprises, 1979
DARK BEFORE DAWN   PSM Entertainment, 1988

ROBERT TOWNE*
Agent: Jeff Berg, ICM - Los Angeles, 213/550-4000

PERSONAL BEST   The Geffen Company/Warner
   Bros., 1982
TEQUILA SUNRISE   Warner Bros., 1988

BUD TOWNSEND
Home: 5917 Blairstone Drive, Culver City, CA 90230,
   213/870-1559
Agent: The Gersh Agency - Beverly Hills, 213/274-6611

NIGHTMARE IN WAX   Crown International, 1969
THE FOLKS AT RED WOLF INN   *TERROR HOUSE*
   Scope III, 1972
ALICE IN WONDERLAND   General National
   Enterprises, 1976
COACH   Crown International, 1978
LOVE SCENES   Playboy Enterprises, 1984

PAT TOWNSEND
Business: Crown International Pictures, 292 S. La
   Cienega Blvd., Beverly Hills, CA 90211, 213/657-6700

THE BEACH GIRLS   Crown International, 1982

ROBERT TOWNSEND*
Agent: Leading Artists - Beverly Hills, 213/858-1999

HOLLYWOOD SHUFFLE   Samuel Goldwyn
   Company, 1987
EDDIE MURPHY RAW   Paramount, 1987
THE FIVE HEARTBEATS   20th Century Fox, 1990

IAN TOYNTON
Address: 1 Prospect Cottages, Lee Common, Great
   Missenden, Bucks HP16 9JP, England, 024020
Agent: Peters, Fraser & Dunlop, The Chambers, Chelsea
   Harbour, Lots Road, London SW10 OXF, England,
   71/376-7676

THE SAINT: THE BRAZILIAN CONNECTION (TF)   Saint
   Productions/ London Weekend TV/CD & MG/Toro
   GMBH/Taffner Ramsay Productions, 1989, British
PIECE OF CAKE (MS)   Holmes Associates Productions/
   London Weekend TV, 1990, British

JEAN-CLAUDE TRAMONT*
b. May 5, 1934 - Brussels, Belgium
Agent: Peter Rawley, ICM - Los Angeles, 213/550-4000

LE POINT DE MIRE   Warner-Columbia, 1977, French
ALL NIGHT LONG   Universal, 1981
AS SUMMERS DIE (CTF)   HBO Premiere Films/
   Chris-Rose Productions/Baldwin/Aldrich Productions/
   Lorimar-Telepictures Productions, 1986

MARK W. TRAVIS*
Home: 357 So. Orange Grove Avenue, Los Angeles, CA
   90036, 213/930-1400
Personal Manager: Alan Lasoff, MCEG Management,
   11355 W. Olympic Blvd., Los Angeles, CA 90064,
   213/208-8899
Agent: InterTalent - Los Angeles, 213/271-0600

DIVE   Warner Bros., 1990

TOM TRBOVICH*
Home: 20140 Pacific Coast Highway, Malibu, CA 90265,
   213/456-9417
Agent: Larry Grossman & Associates - Beverly Hills,
   213/550-8127

FREE RIDE   Galaxy International, 1986

BRIAN TRENCHARD-SMITH
b. 1946
Business: Trenchard Productions, 26 Maranta Street,
   Hornsby, Sydney, Australia, 477-6913

THE WORLD OF KUNG FU (TF)   1974, Australian
THE KUNG FU KILLERS (TF)   1974, Australian
THE LOVE EPIDEMIC   Hexagon Production,
   1975, Australian
THE MAN FROM HONG KONG   The Movie Company/
   Golden Harvest, 1975, Australian-Hong Kong
DEATHCHEATERS   Trenchard Productions/D.L. Taffner,
   1976, Australian

STUNT ROCK   1978, British
THE DAY OF THE ASSASSIN   1981, Mexican
TURKEY SHOOT   Second FGH Film Consortium,
    1982, Australian
BMX BANDITS   Nilsen Premiere, 1985, Australian
JENNY KISSED ME   Nilsen Premiere, 1985, Australian
THE QUEST   Miramax, 1986, Australian
DEAD END DRIVE-IN   New World, 1986, Australian
THE DAY OF THE PANTHER   International Film Marketing,
    1987, Australian
OUT OF THE BODY   David Hannay Productions,
    1988, Australian
STRIKE OF THE PANTHER   Virgo Productions/TVM
    Studios/Mandemar Group, 1988, Australian
THE SIEGE OF FIREBASE GLORIA   Fries Entertainment,
    1989, U.S.-Filipino-Australian
DELTA FORCE - THE KILLING GAME   Global Pictures,
    1990

BARBARA TRENT
Business: Empowerment Project, 1653 18th Street - Suite 3,
    Santa Monica, CA 90404, 213/828-8807

COVERUP: BEHIND THE IRAN-CONTRA AFFAIR (FD)
    Empowerment Project, 1988

DALE TREVILLION
Agent: ICM - Los Angeles, 213/550-4000

ONE MAN FORCE   Shapiro Glickenhaus
    Entertainment, 1989

JESUS SALVADOR TREVINO*
Home: 6042 Springvale Drive, Los Angeles, CA 90042,
    213/258-0802
Agent: Alan Greenspan, ICM - Los Angeles,
    213/550-4428

RAICES DE SANGRE   Conacine, 1977, Mexican
MARIPOSA (TF)   Rainbow Productions, 1979
SEGUIN (TF)   KCET, 1982
YO SOY (TD)   co-director with Jose Luis Ruiz, WNET/
    KCET/KAET, 1985

GUS TRIKONIS*
b. New York, New York
Agent: William Morris Agency - Beverly Hills,
    213/274-7451

FIVE THE HARD WAY   Fantascope, 1969
THE SWINGING BARMAIDS   Premiere, 1975
SUPERCOCK   Hagen-Wayne, 1975
NASHVILLE GIRL   New World, 1976
MOONSHINE COUNTY EXPRESS   New World, 1977
NEW GIRL IN TOWN   New World, 1977
THE EVIL   New World, 1978
THE DARKER SIDE OF TERROR (TF)   Shaner-Ramrus
    Productions/Bob Banner Associates, 1979
SHE'S DRESSED TO KILL (TF)   Grant-Case-McGrath
    Enterprises/Barry Weitz Films, 1979
THE LAST CONVERTIBLE (MS)   co-director with Sidney
    Hayers & Jo Swerling, Jr., Roy Huggins Productions/
    Universal TV, 1979
FLAMINGO ROAD (TF)   MF Productions/Lorimar
    Productions, 1980
TOUCHED BY LOVE   Columbia, 1980
ELVIS AND THE BEAUTY QUEEN (TF)   David Gerber
    Company/Columbia TV, 1981
TAKE THIS JOB AND SHOVE IT   Avco Embassy, 1981

TWIRL (TF)   Charles Fries Productions, 1981
MISS ALL-AMERICAN BEAUTY (TF)   Marian Rees
    Associates, 1982
DEMPSEY (TF)   Charles Fries Productions, 1983
DANCE OF THE DWARFS   Dove, Inc., 1983
FIRST AFFAIR (TF)   CBS Entertainment, 1983
MALICE IN WONDERLAND (TF)   ITC Productions, 1985
MIDAS VALLEY (TF)   Edward S. Feldman Company/
    Warner Bros. TV, 1985
LOVE ON THE RUN (TF)   NBC Productions, 1985
OPEN ADMISSIONS (TF)   The Mount Company/Viacom
    Productions, 1988

JAN TROELL
b. July 23, 1931 - Limhamn, Skane, Sweden
Contact: Swedish Film Institute, P.O. Box 27126,
    102 52 Stockholm, Sweden, 08/63-0510

4 X 4   co-director, 1965, Swedish-Finnish-
    Norwegian-Danish
HERE'S YOUR LIFE   Brandon, 1966, Swedish
EENY, MEENY, MINY, MO WHO SAW HIM DIE?
    Svensk Filmindustri, 1968, Swedish
THE EMIGRANTS UTVANDRARNA ★   Warner Bros.,
    1972, Swedish
THE NEW LAND NYBYGGARNA   Warner Bros.,
    1973, Swedish
ZANDY'S BRIDE   Warner Bros., 1974
BANG!   Svensk Filminstitut, 1977, Swedish
HURRICANE   Paramount, 1979
THE FLIGHT OF THE EAGLE   Summit Features, 1982,
    Swedish-West German- Norwegian
SAGOLANDET (FD)   Swedish Film Institute,
    1988, Swedish

MASSIMO TROISI
b. February 19, 1953 - San Giorgio a Cremano, Italy
Home: via Lima 22, Rome, Italy, 06/844-9081

RICOMINCIO DA TRE   Italian International Films,
    1981, Italian
SCUSATE IL RITARDO   Yarno Cinematografica,
    1983, Italian
NON CI RESTA CHE PIANGERE   co-director with
    Roberto Benigni, Yarno Cinematografica/Best
    International Films, 1984, Italian
LA VIE DEL SIGNORE SONO FINITE   Esterno
    Mediterraneo Film/Cecchi Gori Group/Tiger
    Cinematografica/RAI, 1987, Italian

MARC C. TROPIA
Business: Vantage Point Entertainment, P.O. Box 60171,
    San Diego, CA 92106, 619/225-9206
Agent: Harry S. Hamlin, Motion Picture Production Institute,
    5410 SW 127 Place, Miami, FL 33175, 305/553-8256

MIAMI BEACH BUG POLICE   co-director with Tano Tropia,
    Cinemaworld Pictures, 1986
FRIARS ROAD   Vantage Point Entertainment, 1986

TANO TROPIA
Business: Vantage Point Entertainment, P.O. Box 60171,
    San Diego, CA 92106, 619/225-9206
Agent: Harry S. Hamlin, Motion Picture Production Institute,
    5410 SW 127 Place, Miami, FL 33175, 305/553-8256

MIAMI BEACH BUG POLICE   co-director with Marc C.
    Tropia, Cinemaworld Pictures, 1986

FERNANDO TRUEBA
b. January 18, 1955 - Madrid, Spain
Contact: Ministry of Culture, Motion Picture Division, Avenida
    de Burgos, 5, 28036 Madrid, Spain, 91/202-5351

OPERA PRIMA   La Salamandra, 1980, Spanish
CHICHO, O MIENTRAS EL CUERPO AGUANTE   Opera
    Films, 1982, Spanish
SAL GORDA   1983, Spanish
TWISTED OBSESSION   *THE MAD MONKEY*   IVE,
    1989, Spanish-French

DOUGLAS TRUMBULL*
Agent: Scott Yoselow, The Gersh Agency - New York City,
    212/997-1818
Business Manager: Larry Goldberg, Nagler & Schneider,
    9460 Wilshire Blvd. - Suite 410, Beverly Hills, CA 90212,
    213/274-8201

SILENT RUNNING   Universal, 1972
BRAINSTORM   MGM/UA, 1983

HARK TSUI
(See Tsui HARK)

SLAVA TSUKERMAN
b. Moscow, U.S.S.R.
Telephone: (212) 620-0110

LIQUID SKY   Cinevista, 1983

MICHAEL TUCHNER*
b. June 24, 1934 - Berlin, Germany
Home: 1329 Olive Drive - Apt. C, Los Angeles, CA 90069,
    213/654-2073

VILLAIN   MGM, 1971, British
FEAR IS THE KEY   Paramount, 1973, British
MR. QUILP   Avco Embassy, 1975, British
BAR MITZVAH BOY (TF)   BBC, 1976, British
THE LIKELY LADS   EMI, 1976, British
THE ONE AND ONLY PHYLLIS DIXEY (TF)   Thames TV,
    1979, British
SUMMER OF MY GERMAN SOLDIER (TF)   Highgate
    Productions, 1978
HAYWIRE (TF)   Pando Productions/Warner Bros. TV, 1980
THE HUNCHBACK OF NOTRE DAME (TF)   Norman
    Rosemont Productions/ Columbia TV, 1982, U.S.-British
PAROLE (TF)   RSO Films, 1982
TRENCHCOAT   Buena Vista, 1983
ADAM (TF)   Alan Landsburg Productions, 1983
NOT MY KID (TF)   Beth Polson Productions/Finnegan
    Associates, 1985
GENERATION (TF)   Embassy TV, 1985
AMOS (TF)   The Bryna Company/Vincent Pictures, 1985
TRAPPED IN SILENCE (TF)   Reader's Digest
    Productions, 1986
AT MOTHER'S REQUEST (TF)   Vista Organization
    Ltd., 1987
MISTRESS (TF)   Jaffe-Lansing Productions/Republic
    Pictures, 1987
INTERNAL AFFAIRS (TF)   Titus Productions, 1988
DESPERATE FOR LOVE (TF)   Vishudda Productions/
    Andrew Adelson Productions/Lorimar
    Telepictures, 1989
THE MISADVENTURES OF MR. WILT   *WILT*   Samuel
    Goldwyn Company, 1990, British

RICHARD TUGGLE*
b. August 8, 1948 - Coral Gables, Florida
Agent: Martin Bauer, Bauer Benedek Agency -
    Beverly Hills, 213/275-2321

TIGHTROPE   Warner Bros., 1984
OUT OF BOUNDS   Columbia, 1986

SANDY TUNG*
Home: 8377 Gregory Way, Beverly Hills, CA 90211,
    213/852-4941
Agent: Martin Shapiro, Shapiro-Lichtman Agency -
    Los Angeles, 213/859-8877

BROKEN PROMISE   *A MARRIAGE*   Cinecom, 1983
ACROSS THE TRACKS   Rosenbloom
    Entertainment, 1990

SOPHIA TURKIEWICZ
b. Poland
Contact: Australian Film Commission, 9229 Sunset Blvd.,
    Los Angeles, CA 90069, 213/275-7074

SILVER CITY   Samuel Goldwyn Company,
    1984, Australian

ROSE MARIE TURKO
b. April 14, 1951 - Orleans, France
Personal Manager: Greg Moscoe, Literary Management,
    P.O. Box 5430, Playa del Rey, CA 90293

SCARRED   *STREET LOVE*   Seymour Borde &
    Associates, 1983
THE DUNGEONMASTER   co-director, Empire
    Pictures, 1985

LAWRENCE TURMAN*
b. 1926 - Los Angeles, California
Address: 340 S. Roxbury Drive, Beverly Hills, CA 90212

MARRIAGE OF A YOUNG STOCKBROKER   20th
    Century-Fox, 1971
SECOND THOUGHTS   Universal, 1983

CLIVE TURNER
Contact: British Academy of Film & Television Arts,
    195 Piccadilly, London W1, England, 71/734-0022

HOWLING V   Allied Vision, 1989, British

JON TURTELTAUB
THINK BIG   Motion Picture Corporation of
    America, 1990
AUTOBAHN   Motion Picture Corporation of
    America, 1991

TRACY TYNAN
b. London, England
Attorney: Frank Gruber, 9601 Wilshire Blvd., Beverly Hills,
    CA 90210, 213/274-5638

A GREAT BUNCH OF GIRLS (FD)   co-director with Mary
    Ann Braubach, Cowgirl Productions, 1978

U

V

LIV ULLMANN
b. December 16, 1939 - Tokyo, Japan
Agent: Paul Kohner, Inc. - Los Angeles, 213/550-1060

LOVE   co-director with Annette Cohen, Nancy Dowd &
   Mai Zetterling, Velvet Films, 1982, Canadian

RON UNDERWOOD
TREMORS   Universal, 1990
CITY SLICKERS   Columbia, 1991

MICHAEL TOSHIYUKI UNO*
Agent: Alan Greenspan, ICM - Los Angeles, 213/550-4428

HOME FIRES (CMS)   Edgar J. Scherick Productions, 1987
THE WASH   Skouras Pictures, 1988

PETER USTINOV*
b. April 16, 1921 - London, England
Home: Rue de Silly, 91200 Boulogne, France, 1/603-8753
Agent: William Morris Agency - London, 01/734-9361

SCHOOL FOR SECRETS   General Film Distributors,
   1946, British
VICE VERSA   General Film Distributors, 1948, British
PRIVATE ANGELO   co-director with Michael Anderson,
   Associated British Picture Corporation, 1949, British
ROMANOFF AND JULIET   Universal, 1961
BILLY BUDD   Allied Artists, 1962, British
LADY L   MGM, 1966, U.S.-Italian-French
HAMMERSMITH IS OUT   Cinerama Releasing
   Corporation, 1972
MEMED, MY HAWK   Filmworld Distributors, 1984,
   British-Yugoslavian

JAMIE UYS
Contact: Department of Interior, Civitas Building, Struben
   Street, Pretoria 0002, South Africa, 12/48-2551

(The following is an incomplete list of Mr. Uys' credits)

DINGAKA   Embassy, 1965, South African
AFTER YOU, COMRADE   Continental, 1967, South African
LOST IN THE DESERT   Columbia-Warner, 1971,
   South African
ANIMALS ARE BEAUTIFUL PEOPLE (FD)   *BEAUTIFUL
   PEOPLE*   Warner Bros., 1974, South African
THE GODS MUST BE CRAZY   TLC Films/20th
   Century-Fox, 1979, Botswana
BEAUTIFUL PEOPLE II (FD)   1983, South African
THE GODS MUST BE CRAZY 2   WEG/Columbia,
   1989, Botswana

ROGER VADIM*
(Roger Vadim Plemiannikov)
b. January 26, 1928 - Paris, France
Agent: The Robert Littman Company - Beverly Hills,
   213/278-1572

AND GOD CREATED WOMAN   Kingsley
   International, 1956, French
NO SUN IN VENICE   *SAIT-ON JAMAIS?*   Kingsley
   International, 1957, French-Italian
THE NIGHT HEAVEN FELL   *LES BIJOUTIERS DU
   CLAIR DE LUNES*   Kingsley International,
   1957, French-Italian
LES LIAISONS DANGEREUSES   *DANGEROUS
   LIAISONS 1960*   Astor, 1959, French-Italian,
   re-released in 1989 by Interama
BLOOD AND ROSES   *ET MOURIR DE PLAISIR*
   Paramount, 1960, Italian
PLEASE, NOT NOW!   *LA BRIDE SUR LE COU*   20th
   Century-Fox, 1961, French
SEVEN CAPITAL SINS   co-director with Jean-Luc
   Godard, Sylvaine Dhomme, Edouard Molinaro,
   Philippe De Broca, Claude Chabrol, Jacques Demy,
   Marie-Jose Nat, Dominique Paturel, Jean-Marc
   Tennberg & Perrette Pradier, Embassy, 1962,
   French-Italian
LOVE ON A PILLOW   *LE REPOS DU GUERRIER*
   Royal Films International, 1962, French-Italian
OF FLESH AND BLOOD   *LES GRANDS CHEMINS*
   Times, 1963, French- Italian
VICE AND VIRTUE   MGM, 1963, French
NUTTY, NAUGHTY CHATEAU   *CHATEAU EN SUEDE*
   Lopert, 1963, French- Italian
CIRCLE OF LOVE   *LA RONDE*   Continental,
   1964, French
THE GAME IS OVER   *LA CUREE*   Royal Films
   International, 1966, French- Italian
SPIRITS OF THE DEAD   *HISTOIRES
   EXTRAORDINAIRES*   co-director with Federico
   Fellini & Louis Malle, American International, 1968,
   Italian- French
BARBARELLA   Paramount, 1968, Italian-French
PRETTY MAIDS ALL IN A ROW   MGM, 1971
HELLE   Cocinor, 1972, French
MS. DON JUAN   *DON JUAN ETAIT UNE FEMME*
   Scotia American, 1973, French
CHARLOTTE   *LA JEUNE FILLE ASSASSINEE*
   Gamma III, 1974, French
UNE FEMME FIDELE   FFCM, 1976, French
NIGHT GAMES   Avco Embassy, 1980, French
THE HOT TOUCH   Astral Bellevue, 1981, Canadian
SURPRISE PARTY   Uranium Films, 1982, French
COME BACK   Comeci, 1983, French
AND GOD CREATED WOMAN   Vestron, 1988

LUIS VALDEZ*
b. June 26, 1940 - Delano, California
Agent: Joan Scott, Writers and Artists Agency -
   Los Angeles, 213/820-2240

ZOOT SUIT   Universal, 1981
LA BAMBA   Columbia, 1987

283

BRUCE VAN DUSEN
COLD FEET   Cinecom, 1984

BUDDY VAN HORN*
Messages: 213/462-2301
Home: 4409 Ponca Avenue, Toluca Lake, CA 91602,
   213/462-2301
Agent: Phil Gersh, The Gersh Agency - Beverly Hills,
   213/274-6611

ANY WHICH WAY YOU CAN   Warner Bros., 1980
THE DEAD POOL   Warner Bros., 1988
PINK CADILLAC   Warner Bros., 1989

KEES VAN OOSTRUM*
b. July 5, 1954 - Amsterdam, Netherlands
Attorney: Peter Nichols, Weissmann, Wolff, Bergman,
   Coleman & Schulman, 9665 Wilshire Blvd., Suite 900,
   Beverly Hills, CA 90212, 213/858-7888

MISSING PERSONS: FOUR TRUE STORIES (CTD)
   Dave Bell Associates, 1984
HET BITTERE KRUID   Verenigde Nederlandsche
   Filmcompagnie, 1985, Dutch

MARIO VAN PEEBLES*
Agent: William Morris Agency - Beverly Hills, 213/274-7451

NEW JACK CITY   Warner Bros., 1991

MELVIN VAN PEEBLES
b. 1932 - Chicago, Illinois
Home: 353 West 56th Street - Apt. 10F, New York, NY
   10019, 212/489-6570
Agent: William Morris Agency - Beverly Hills, 213/274-7451

THE STORY OF A THREE-DAY PASS   Sigma III,
   1968, French
WATERMELON MAN   Columbia, 1970
SWEET SWEETBACK'S BAADASSSSSS SONG
   Cinemation, 1971
DON'T PLAY US CHEAP   Movin On Distribution, 1972
IDENTITY CRISIS   Block & Chip Productions, 1989

WILLIAM VANDERKLOOT
Business: Double Helix Films, Inc., 303 West 76th
   Street - Suite B, New York, NY 10023

MACE   Film Ventures International, 1987

NORMAN THADDEUS VANE
Agent: Stan Goldberg, Artists Directions - Los Angeles,
   213/273-0600
Business: Screen Writers Productions, 1411 N. Harper
   Avenue, Los Angeles, CA 90046, 213/656-9260

FRIGHTMARE   Saturn International, 1983
THE BLACK ROOM   co-director with Elly Kenner,
   CI Films, 1984
KING OF THE CITY   CLUB LIFE   Troma, 1986
NIGHTLIFE   SVS Films, 1989

GUS VAN SANT
Agent: William Morris Agency - Beverly Hills, 213/274-7451

MALA NOCHE   Northern Film Company, 1985
DRUGSTORE COWBOY   Avenue Pictures, 1989

CARLO VANZINA
b. 1952 - Florence, Italy
Home: via Pezzana 9, Rome, Italy, 06/877319

LUNA DI MIELE IN TRE   Irrigazione Cinematografica,
   1976, Italian
FIGLIO DELLE STELLE   San Francisco, 1979, Italian
ARRIVANO I GATTI   Adap/Mondial/Laser, 1979, Italian
I FICHISSIMI   Dean International, 1981, Italian
ECCEZZIUNALE VERAMENTE   Cinemedia, 1982, Italian
VIUUULENTEMENTE...MIA   Horizont Produzioni,
   1982, Italian
SAPORE DI MARE   Dean International, 1982, Italian
IL RAS DEL QUARTIERE   Ypsilon Cinematografica/
   Italian International Films, 1983, Italian
MYSTERE   Tris Film, 1983, Italian
VACANZE DI NATALE   Filmauro, 1983, Italian
AMARSI UN PO'   C.G. Silver Film, 1984, Italian
VACANZE IN AMERICA   C.G. Silver Film, 1984, Italian
SOTTO IL VESTITO NIENTE   Faso Film, 1985, Italian
YUPPIES, I GIOVANI DI SUCCESSO   Filmauro,
   1986, Italian
VIA MONTENAPOLEONE   Reteitalia/C.G. Silver Film/
   Video 80, 1987, Italian
I MIEI PRIMI QUARANT' ANNI   Columbia, 1987, Italian
MONTECARLO GRAN CASINO'   Filmauro, 1988, Italian
THE MATCH   Mario & Vittorio Cecchi Gori/C.G. Silver,
   1989, Italian
LA FINTE BIONDE   Reteitalia, 1989, Italian
TRE COLONNE IN CRONACA   Pixit/Pentafilm,
   1990, Italian

AGNES VARDA
b. May 30, 1928 - Brussels, Belgium
Contact: French Film Office, 745 Fifth Avenue, New
   York, NY 10151, 212/832-8860

LA POINTE COURTE   1954, French
CLEO FROM 5 TO 7   Zenith, 1962, French
LE BONHEUR   Clover, 1965, French
LES CREATURES   New Yorker, 1966, French-Swedish
FAR FROM VIETNAM (FD)   co-director with Jean-Luc
   Godard, Claude Lelouch, Alain Resnais, William Klein &
   Joris Ivens, New Yorker, 1967, French
LIONS LOVE   Raab, 1969
NAUSICAA (TF)   1970, French
DAGUERREOTYPES (FD)   1975, French
ONE SINGS, THE OTHER DOESN'T   Cinema 5,
   1977, French
MUR MURS (FD)   Cine-Tamaris, 1981, French
DOCUMENTEUR: AN EMOTION PICTURE   Cine-
   Tamaris, 1981, French
VAGABOND   SANS TOIT NI LOI   Grange
   Communications/IFEX Film, 1985, French
JANE B. PAR AGNES V.   Cine-Tamaris/La Sept,
   1987, French
KUNG FU MASTER   Heritage Entertainment,
   1988, French

FRANCIS VEBER*
b. July 28, 1937 - Neuilly Sur Seine, France
Agent: CAA - Beverly Hills, 213/288-4545

THE TOY   Show Biz Company, 1976, French
LE CHEVRE   European International, 1981, French
LES COMPERES   European International, 1983, French
LES FUGITIFS   Gaumont, 1986, French
THREE FUGITIVES   Buena Vista, 1989

ISELA VEGA

b. Sonora, Mexico
Contact: Isela Vega Video, 1076 El Centro Avenue, Hollywood, CA 90038, 213/465-5438

LAS AMANTES DEL SENOR DE LA NOCHE   Fenix Cinematografica S.A./Avpasa, S.A., 1983, Mexican

MIKE VEJAR*

(Lawrence Mike Vejar)
Home: 2239 Penmar Avenue, Venice, CA 90271, 213/398-8704
Agent: Carole Bennett, The Bennett Agency - Los Angeles, 213/471-2251

HAWAIIAN HEAT (TF)   James D. Parriott Productions/ Universal TV, 1984
DOUBLE AGENT (TF)   Walt Disney TV, 1987

MICHAEL VENTURA

Agent: Sanford-Beckett-Tobias-Skouras Agency - Los Angeles, 213/277-6211

"I'M ALMOST NOT CRAZY..." JOHN CASSAVETES: THE MAN AND HIS WORK (FD)   Cannon, 1984

CARLO VERDONE

b. 1950 - Rome, Italy
Home: via dei Banchi Vecchi, 61, Rome, Italy, 06/656-8902

UN SACCO BELLO   Medusa Distribuzione, 1980, Italian
BIANCO, ROSSO E VERDONE   Medusa Distribuzione, 1981, Italian
BOROTALCO   Intercapital, 1981, Italian
ACQUA E SAPONE   Intercapital, 1983, Italian
I DUE CARABINIERI   C.G. Silver Film, 1984, Italian
TROPPO FORTE   Scena Film Produzioni, 1985, Italian
IO E MIA SORELLA   C.G. Silver, 1988, Italian
COMPAGNI DI SCUOLA   Mario & Vittorio Cecchi Gori, 1989, Italian
IL BAMBINO E IL POLIZIOTTO   Pentafilm, 1990, Italian

PAUL VERHOEVEN

b. 1938 - Holland
Business: Riverside Pictures B.V., Koningslaan 17, 1075 AA Amsterdam, Netherlands, 20/640-401
Agent: The Marion Rosenberg Office - Los Angeles, 213/653-7383

WAT ZIEN IK   Rob Houwer Film, 1971, Dutch
TURKISH DELIGHT   Cinemation, 1973, Dutch
KEETJE TIPPEL   Cinema National, 1975, Dutch
SOLDIER OF ORANGE   Samuel Goldwyn Company, 1977, Dutch
SPETTERS   Samuel Goldwyn Company, 1980, Dutch
THE 4TH MAN   Spectrafilm, 1983, Dutch
FLESH + BLOOD   Orion, 1985, U.S.-Dutch
ROBOCOP   Orion, 1987
TOTAL RECALL   Tri-Star, 1990

HENRI VERNEUIL

(Achod Malakian)
b. October 15, 1920 - Rodosto, Turkey
Business: V. Films, 12 Bis Rue Keppler, 75016 Paris, France, 723-5068

LA TABLE AUX CREVES   1951, French
BRELAN D'AS   1952, French

FORBIDDEN FRUIT   Films Around the World, 1952, French
LE BOULANGER DE VALORGUE   1953, French
CARNAVAL   1953, French
THE MOST WANTED MAN IN THE WORLD   *ENNEMI PUBLIC NO. 1*   Astor, 1953, French-Italian
THE SHEEP HAS FIVE LEGS   United Motion Picture Organization, 1954, French
LES AMANTS DU TAGE   1955, French
DES GENS SANS IMPORTANCE   1955, French
PARIS-PALACE-HOTEL   1956, French
WHAT PRICE MURDER   *UNE MANCHE ET LA BELLE*   United Motion Picture Organization, 1957, French
MAXIME   Interworld, 1958, French
THE BIG CHIEF   Continental, 1959, French-Italian
THE COW AND I   *LA VACHE ET LE PRISONNIER*   Zenith, 1959, French-West German
L'AFFAIRE D'UNE NUIT   1960, French
LA FRANCAISE ET L'AMOUR   co-director, Auerbach Film Enterprises/Kingsley International, 1960, French
LE PRESIDENT   1961, French-Italian
THE LIONS ARE LOOSE   Franco-London, 1961, French-Italian
A MONKEY IN WINTER   MGM, 1962, French
ANY NUMBER CAN WIN   *MELODIE EN SOUS-SOL*   MGM, 1963, French
GREED IN THE SUN   MGM, 1964, French
WEEKEND AT DUNKIRK   *WEEKEND A ZUYDCOOTE*   20th Century-Fox, 1965, French-Italian
THE 25TH HOUR   MGM, 1967, French-Italian-Yugoslavian
GUNS FOR SAN SEBASTIAN   *LA BATAILLE DE SAN SEBASTIAN*   MGM, 1968, French-Italian-Mexican
THE SICILIAN CLAN   20th Century-Fox, 1970, French
THE BURGLARS   Columbia, 1972, French-Italian
THE SERPENT   *NIGHT FLIGHT TO MOSCOW*   Avco Embassy, 1973, French- Italian-West German
THE NIGHT CALLER   *PEUR SUR LA VILLE*   Columbia, 1975, French-Italian
LE CORPS DE MON ENNEMI   AMLF, 1976, French
I...COMME ICARE   V Films/SFP/Antenne-2, 1979, French
MILLE MILLIARDS DE DOLLARS   V Films/Films A2, 1982, French
LES MORFALOUS   AAA, 1984, French

STEPHEN F. VERONA*

b. September 11, 1940 - Illinois
Home: 1251 Stone Canyon Road, Bel Air, CA 90024, 213/476-7387
Agent: Mark Harris, David Shapira & Associates - Sherman Oaks, 818/906-0322

THE LORDS OF FLATBUSH   co-director with Martin Davidson, Columbia, 1974
PIPE DREAMS   Avco Embassy, 1976
BOARDWALK   Atlantic Releasing Corporation, 1979
TALKING WALLS   Drummond Productions, 1987

DANIEL VIGNE

Agent: CAA - Beverly Hills, 213/288-4545

LES HOMMES   Cocinor, 1973, French-Italian
THE RETURN OF MARTIN GUERRE   European International, 1983, French
ONE WOMAN OR TWO   Orion Classics, 1985, French
COMEDIE D'ETE   Partners Productions, 1989, French

CAMILO VILA

b. December 14, 1947 - Havana, Cuba
Agent: Stuart M. Miller, APA - Los Angeles, 213/273-0744

A LITTLE RAIN   Three C Productions, 1976
LOS GUSANOS   South American Shorts, 1977
THE UNHOLY   Vestron, 1988
OPTIONS   Vestron, 1989

CHUCK VINCENT

b. Garden City, Michigan
Business: Platinum Pictures, 11-12 44th Avenue, Long Island
   City, NY 11101, 718/786-3701

BLUE SUMMER   Monarch, 1971
WHILE THE CAT'S AWAY   Monarch, 1971
THE APPOINTMENT   New Line Cinema, 1971
MRS. BARRINGTON   Monarch, 1972
LETCHER   Command, 1974
HEAVY LOAD   Command, 1975
AMERICAN TICKLER   Platinum Pictures, 1976
BANG BANG   *PORN FLAKES*   Platinum Pictures, 1976
FAREWELL SCARLET   Command, 1976
VISIONS   Platinum Pictures, 1977
DIRTY LILLY   Bunnco, 1978
HOT T-SHIRTS   Cannon, 1979
BAD PENNY   Platinum Pictures, 1979
JACK AND JILL   Platinum Pictures, 1980
SUMMER CAMP   Seymour Borde & Associates, 1981
BON APPETIT   Distribpix, 1981
MISBEHAVIN'   Distribpix, 1981
THAT LUCKY STIFF   Distribpix, 1981
IN LOVE   Platinum Pictures, 1982
C.O.D.   Lone Star, 1982
GAMES WOMEN PLAY   Platinum Pictures, 1982
ROOMMATES   Platinum Pictures, 1982
THIS LADY IS A TRAMP   Bunnco, 1982
DIRTY LOOKS   Platinum Pictures, 1983
PUSS 'N BOOTS   Platinum Pictures, 1983
JACK AND JILL II   Platinum Pictures, 1984
PREPPIES   Platinum Pictures, 1984
HOLLYWOOD HOT TUBS   Seymour Borde &
   Associates, 1984
HOUSE OF THE RISING SUN   Platinum Pictures, 1985
SEX APPEAL   Seymour Borde & Associates, 1986
IF LOOKS COULD KILL   Platinum Pictures, 1986
WIMPS   Platinum Pictures, 1987
POMPEII   *WARRIOR QUEEN*   Seymour Borde &
   Associates, British- Italian, 1987
SLAMMER GIRLS   Lightning Pictures, 1987
YOUNG NURSES IN LOVE   Platinum Pictures, 1987
DERANGED   Platinum Pictures, 1987
NEW YORK'S FINEST   Platinum Pictures, 1988
SATISFACTION   Platinum Pictures, 1988
SENSATIONS   Platinum Pictures, 1988
SEXPOT   Platinum Pictures, 1988
THRILLED TO DEATH   Platinum Pictures, 1989
BAD BLOOD   Platinum Pictures, 1989
PARTY INCORPORATED   Platinum Pictures, 1989
CLEO/LEO   Platinum Pictures, 1989
BEDROOM EYES II   Distant Horizon, 1989
WILDEST DREAMS   Platinum Pictures, 1990
ENRAPTURE   Platinum Pictures, 1990

JESSE VINT

Contact: Screen Actors Guild - Los Angeles, 213/465-4600

ANOTHER CHANCE   Moviestore Entertainment, 1988

WILL VINTON

Business: Will Vinton Productions, Inc., 1400 NW 22nd
   Street, Portland, OR 97210, 503/225-1130

THE ADVENTURES OF MARK TWAIN (AF)   Atlantic
   Releasing Corporation, 1985

MARCELA FERNANDEZ VIOLANTE

b. June 9, 1941 - Mexico City, Mexico
Contact: Azteca Films, 555 N. La Brea Avenue, P.O. Box
   36095, Hollywood, CA 90036, 213/938-2413

DE TODOS MODOS JUAN TE LLAMAS   Azteca Films,
   1976, Mexican
CANANEA   Azteca Films, 1979, Mexican
MISTERIO   Azteca Films, 1981, Mexican
EN EL PAIS DE LOS PIES LIGEROS   Azteca Films,
   1983, Mexican
NOCTURNO AMOR QUE TE VAS   UNAM/D.A.C.,
   1987, Mexican

VIRGIL W. VOGEL*

b. Peoria, Illinois
Address: 10350 Santa Monica Blvd. - Suite 350,
   Los Angeles, CA 90025, 213/553-9709
Agent: Irv Schechter Company - Beverly Hills,
   213/278-8070

THE MOLE PEOPLE   Universal, 1956
THE KETTLES ON OLD McDONALD'S FARM
   Universal, 1957
THE LAND UNKNOWN   Universal, 1957
INVASION OF THE ANIMAL PEOPLE   co-director with
   Jerry Warren, ADP, 1962
THE SWORD OF ALI BABA   Universal, 1965
THE RETURN OF JOE FORRESTER (TF)   Columbia
   TV, 1975
THE DEPUTIES (TF)   1976
LAW OF THE LAND (TF)   QM Productions, 1976
CENTENNIAL (MS)   co-director with Paul Krasny, Harry
   Falk & Bernard McEveety, Universal TV, 1978
POWER (TF)   co-director with Barry Shear, David Gerber
   Company/Columbia TV, 1980
PORTRAIT OF A REBEL: MARGARET SANGER (TF)
   Marvin Minoff Productions/David Paradine TV, 1980
BEULAH LAND (MS)   co-director with Harry Falk, David
   Gerber Company/Columbia TV, 1980
TODAY'S FBI (TF)   David Gerber Company, 1981
STREET HAWK (TF)   Limekiln and Templar Productions/
   Universal TV, 1985
CONDOR (TF)   Jaygee Productions/Orion TV, 1986
DESPERADO (TF)   Walter Mirisch Productions/Charles E.
   Sellier Productions/Universal TV, 1987
LONGARM (TF)   Universal TV, 1988

MAX VON SYDOW

b. April 10, 1929 - Lund, Sweden
Agent: InterTalent - Los Angeles, 213/271-0600

KATINKA   Nordiskfilm/Svensk Filmindustri/Danish Film
   Institute/British Film Institute/Film Four International,
   1988, Danish-Swedish-British

MARGARETHE von TROTTA
b. February 21, 1942 - Berlin, Germany
Contact: German Film & TV Academy, Pommernallee 1,
    1 Berlin 19, West Germany, 0311/302-6096

THE LOST HONOR OF KATHARINA BLUM   co-director
    with Volker Schlondorff, New World, 1975,
    West German
THE SECOND AWAKENING OF CHRISTA KLAGES
    Bioskop Film/WDR/First City Films/Cinema of Women,
    1977, West German
SCHWESTERN ODER DIE BALANCE DES GLUCKS
    Bioskop Film/First City Films/Blue Dolphin Films, 1979,
    West German
MARIANNE AND JULIANNE DIE BLEIRNE ZEIT 1981,
    West German
SHEER MADNESS RS/58, 1983, West German
ROSA LUXEMBOURG New Yorker, 1986, West German
PAURA E AMORE Erre Productions/Reteitalia/Bioskop
    Film/Cinemax Generale D'Images, 1988, Italian-French-
    West German
IL RITORNO Scena Film, 1990, Italian

ORIN WACHSBERG
STARLIGHT Starlight Ltd. Partnership, 1986

DANIEL WACHSMANN
Contact: Israel Film Centre, Ministry of Industry & Trade,
    30 Agron Street, P.O. Box 299, Jerusalem 94190, Israel,
    02/210297

TRANSIT Jacob Goldwasser Productions, 1979, Israeli
HOT WIND *HAMSIN* Hemdale, 1982, Israeli
THE APPOINTED 21st Century Distribution,
    1990, Israeli

JONATHAN WACKS
b. 1948
Agent: Jeremy Zimmer, Bauer Benedek Agency - Los
    Angeles, 213/275-2421

POWWOW HIGHWAY Warner Bros., 1989, U.S.-British

MICHAEL WADLEIGH*
Attorney: Robert C. Boffa, Rosenfeld, Meyer & Susman,
    9601 Wilshire Blvd., Beverly Hills, CA 90210

WOODSTOCK (FD) Warner Bros., 1970
WOLFEN Orion/Warner Bros., 1981

JANE WAGNER*
b. February 2, 1935 - Morristown, Tennessee
Home: 213/275-5161
Agent: ICM - Los Angeles, 213/550-4000

MOMENT BY MOMENT Universal, 1978

RALPH WAITE*
b. June 22, 1928 - White Plains, New York
Business Manager: Global Business Management,
    9000 Sunset Blvd. - Suite 1115, Los Angeles, CA
    90069, 213/278-4141

ON THE NICKEL Rose's Park, 1980

ANDRZEJ WAJDA
b. March 6, 1926 - Suwalki, Poland
Agent: Georges Beaume, 3 Quai Malaquais, 75006 Paris,
    France, 04/325-2831
Contact: Ministry of Culture and Arts, Cinematography
    Authority, Krakowskie Przedmiecie 21/23, 00071
    Warsaw, Poland, tel.: 268072

A GENERATION WFF Wroclaw, 1954, Polish
JE VAIS VERS LE SOLEIL WFD Warsaw, 1955,
    French-Polish
KANAL Frankel, 1957, Polish
ASHES AND DIAMONDS Janus, 1958, Polish
LOTNA KADR Unit, 1959, Polish
INNOCENT SORCERERS KADR Unit, 1960, Polish
SAMSON Droga-KADR Unit, 1961, Polish
SIBERIAN LADY MACBETH Avala Film, 1961, Polish
LOVE AT TWENTY co-director with Francois Truffaut,
    Renzo Rossellini, Shintaro Ishihara & Marcel Ophuls,
    Embassy, 1962, French-Italian-Japanese-Polish-
    West German
ASHES 1965, Polish
GATES TO PARADISE 1967, British
EVERYTHING FOR SALE New Yorker, 1968, Polish
HUNTING FLIES 1969, Polish
LANDSCAPE AFTER BATTLE New Yorker, 1970, Polish
THE BIRCH-WOOD 1971, Polish
PILATUS UND ANDERE (TF) 1972, West German
THE WEDDING Film Polski, 1972, Polish
THE PROMISED LAND Film Polski, 1974, Polish
SHADOW LINE 1976, Polish
MAN OF MARBLE New Yorker, 1977, Polish
WITHOUT ANESTHETIC New Yorker, 1979, Polish
THE GIRLS FROM WILKO 1979, Polish-French
THE CONDUCTOR Film Polski, 1980, Polish
ROUGH TREATMENT Film Polski, 1980, Polish
MAN OF IRON United Artists Classics, 1981, Polish
DANTON Triumph/Columbia, 1983, French-Polish
A LOVE IN GERMANY Triumph/Columbia, 1983,
    West German-French
CHRONICLE OF LOVE AFFAIRS Film Polski/Film Group
    Perspektyva, 1985, Polish
LES POSSEDES Gaumont, 1988, French
KORCZAK Erato Films/Les Films du Losange/MK2,
    1990, West German-French-Polish

CHRIS WALAS*
(Christophe James Walas)
Agent: William Morris Agency - Beverly Hills, 213/274-7451
Business: 415/479-5040

THE FLY II 20th Century Fox, 1989, U.S.-Canadian

DORIAN WALKER
Agent: The Artists Agency - Los Angeles, 213/277-7779

MAKING THE GRADE MGM/UA/Cannon, 1984
TEEN WITCH Trans World Entertainment, 1989

GILES WALKER
b. 1946 - Dundee, Scotland
Address: 4039 Grand Avenue, Montreal, Quebec H4B 2X4,
Canada, 514/483-3270

DESCENT   1975, Canadian
TWICE UPON A TIME   1979, Canadian
THE MASCULINE MYSTIQUE (FD)   co-director with John
Smith, 1985, Canadian
90 DAYS   Cinecom, 1985, Canadian
THE LAST STRAW   National Film Board of Canada,
1987, Canadian
CADDIE WOODLAWN (CTF)   Churchill Entertainment/
WonderWorks/ The Disney Channel, 1989,
Canadian-U.S.
PRINCE IN EXILE   Cinepix/National Film Board of Canada,
1989, Canadian

NANCY WALKER*
b. May 10, 1922 - Philadelphia, Pennsylvania
Agent: Lionel Larner Ltd., 850 Seventh Avenue, New York,
NY 10019, 212/246-3105

CAN'T STOP THE MUSIC   AFD, 1980

PETER WALKER
Address: 23 Bentick Street, London W1, England

I LIKE BIRDS   1966, British
GIRLS FOR MEN ONLY   1967, British
SCHOOL FOR SEX   1968, British
STRIP POKER   Miracle, 1969, British
COOL IT CAROL!   Miracle, 1970, British
MAN OF VIOLENCE   Miracle, 1971, British
DIE SCREAMING, MARIANNE   1971, British
THE FLESH AND BLOOD SHOW   Tigon, 1972, British
THE FOUR DIMENSIONS OF GRETA   Hemdale,
1972, British
TIFFANY JONES   Hemdale, 1973, British
HOUSE OF WHIPCORD   Miracle, 1974, British
FRIGHTMARE   Miracle, 1975, British
HOUSE OF MORTAL SIN   Miracle, 1976, British
SCHIZO   Warner Bros., 1976, British
THE COMEBACK   Enterprise, 1978, British
HOME BEFORE MIDNIGHT   Heritage/EMI, 1979, British
HOUSE OF THE LONG SHADOWS   MGM/UA/Cannon,
1983, British
BLIND SHOT   Agincourt Ventures Ltd., 1988, British

GARY WALKOW
Agent: Tom Chasin, The Chasin Agency - Beverly Hills,
213/278-7505

THE TROUBLE WITH DICK   Fever Dream Production
Company, 1987

RICK WALLACE*
Home: 4960 Ambrose Avenue, Los Angeles, CA 90027,
213/664-8614
Agent: Alan Berger, ICM - Los Angeles, 213/550-4000

CALIFORNIA GIRLS (TF)   ABC Circle Films, 1985
A TIME TO LIVE (TF)   Blue Andre Productions/ITC
Productions, 1985
ACCEPTABLE RISKS (TF)   ABC Circle Films, 1986
A FATHER'S HOMECOMING (TF)   NBC
Productions, 1988

TOMMY LEE WALLACE*
Agent: Harris & Goldberg - Los Angeles, 213/553-5200

HALLOWEEN III: SEASON OF THE WITCH
Universal, 1982
ALOHA SUMMER   HANAUMA BAY   Spectrafilm, 1988
FRIGHT NIGHT PART 2   New Century/Vista, 1989
IT (TF)   Konigsberg-Sanitsky Productions/Green-Epstein
Productions/Lorimar TV, 1990

FRED WALTON*
(Frederick R. Walton)
Agent: The Brandt Company - Studio City, 818/506-7747

WHEN A STRANGER CALLS   Columbia, 1979
HADLEY'S REBELLION   American Film Distributors, 1984
ALFRED HITCHCOCK PRESENTS (TF)   co-director with
Steve DeJarnatt, Randa Haines & Joel Oliansky,
Universal TV, 1985
APRIL FOOL'S DAY   Paramount, 1986
THE ROSARY MURDERS   New Line Cinema, 1987
I SAW WHAT YOU DID (TF)   Universal TV, 1988
TRAPPED (CTF)   Cine Enterprises, 1989
MURDER IN PARADISE (TF)   Bill McCutchen
Productions/Columbia TV, 1990

SAM WANAMAKER*
b. June 14, 1919 - Chicago, Illinois
Home: 352 N. Croft Avenue, Los Angeles, CA 90048,
213/653-9759

THE FILE ON THE GOLDEN GOOSE   United Artists,
1969, British
THE EXECUTIONER   Columbia, 1970, British
CATLOW   MGM, 1971, U.S.-Spanish
SINBAD AND THE EYE OF THE TIGER   Columbia,
1977, British
MY KIDNAPPER, MY LOVE (TF)   Roger Gimbel
Productions/EMI TV, 1980
THE KILLING OF RANDY WEBSTER (TF)   Roger Gimbel
Productions/EMI TV, 1981

PETER WANG
(Wang Zhengfang)
b. Beijing, China
Business: Peter Wang Films, Inc., 594 Broadway -
Suite 906, New York, NY 10012

A GREAT WALL   Orion Classics, 1986, U.S.-Chinese
THE LASER MAN   Original Cinema, 1988
FIRST DATE   Peter Wang Films, 1989, Taiwanese

WAYNE WANG
b. January 12, 1949 - Hong Kong
Agent: William Morris Agency - Beverly Hills, 213/274-7451
Business: C.I.M. Productions, 665 Bush Street, San
Francisco, CA 94108, 415/433-2342

A MAN, A WOMAN, AND A KILLER   co-director with
Rick Schmidt, 1975
CHAN IS MISSING   New Yorker, 1982
DIM SUM: A LITTLE BIT OF HEART   Orion
Classics, 1985
SLAMDANCE   Island Pictures, 1987
EAT A BOWL OF TEA   Columbia, 1989
LIFE IS CHEAP...BUT TOILET PAPER IS EXPENSIVE
LIFE IS CHEAP   Silverlight Entertainment, 1989,
U.S.-Hong Kong

DAVID S. WARD*
b. October 25, 1945
Agent: CAA - Beverly Hills, 213/288-4545

CANNERY ROW   MGM/United Artists, 1981
MAJOR LEAGUE   Paramount, 1989
KING RALPH I   Universal, 1991

VINCENT WARD
b. 1956 - New Zealand
Agent: William Morris Agency - Beverly Hills, 213/274-7451

A STATE OF SIEGE   1978, New Zealand
IN SPRING ONE PLANTS ALONE   1981, New Zealand
VIGIL   John Maynard Productions/Film Investment
   Corporation of New Zealand/New Zealand Film
   Commission, 1984, New Zealand
THE NAVIGATOR: AN ODYSSEY ACROSS TIME   *THE
   NAVIGATOR - A MEDIEVAL ODYSSEY*   Circle
   Releasing, 1988, Australian-New Zealand

CLYDE WARE*
b. December 22, 1936 - West Virginia
Home: 1252 N. Laurel Avenue, Los Angeles, CA 90046,
   213/650-8205
Agent: Barry Perelman Agency - Los Angeles,
   213/274-5999
Business Manager: Gerald Chapnick, Zeiderman, Oberman
   & Associates, 500 S. Sepulveda Blvd., Los Angeles, CA
   90049, 213/476-5333

NO DRUMS, NO BUGLES   Cinerama Releasing
   Corporation, 1971
THE STORY OF PRETTY BOY FLOYD (TF)   Universal
   TV, 1974
THE HATFIELDS AND THE McCOYS (TF)   Charles
   Fries Productions, 1975
THREE HUNDRED MILES FOR STEPHANIE (TF)   Edward
   S. Feldman Company/Yellow Ribbon Productions/
   PKO, 1981
WHEN THE LINE GETS THROUGH   Lorimar, 1985
HUMAN ERROR   Wouk-Ware Productions, 1989
ANOTHER TIME, ANOTHER PLACE   Wouk-Ware
   Productions, 1989
BAD JIM   21st Century Distribution, 1990

CHARLES MARQUIS WARREN*
b. December 16, 1917 - Baltimore, Maryland
Home: 3250 Cornell Road, Agoura Hills, CA 91301,
   818/706-0692

LITTLE BIG HORN   Lippert, 1951
HELLGATE   Lippert, 1952
ARROWHEAD   Paramount, 1953
FLIGHT TO TANGIER   Paramount, 1953
SEVEN ANGRY MEN   Allied Artists, 1955
TENSION AT TABLE ROCK   Universal, 1956
THE BLACK WHIP   20th Century-Fox, 1956
TROOPER HOOK   United Artists, 1957
BACK FROM THE DEAD   20th Century-Fox, 1957
THE UNKNOWN TERROR   20th Century-Fox, 1957
COPPER SKY   20th Century-Fox, 1957
RIDE A VIOLENT MILE   20th Century-Fox, 1957
DESERT HELL   20th Century-Fox, 1958
CATTLE EMPIRE   20th Century-Fox, 1958
BLOOD ARROW   20th Century-Fox, 1958
CHARRO!   National General, 1969

MARK WARREN*
b. September 24, 1938
Agent: Gil Barnett, Sue Goldin Talent - Los Angeles,
   213/852-1441
Business: Mew Productions, 3528 10th Avenue,
   Los Angeles, CA 90018, 213/732-0554

COME BACK CHARLESTON BLUE   Warner Bros., 1972
TULIPS   co-director with Rex Bromfield & Al Waxman,
   all directed under pseudonym of Stan Ferris,
   Avco Embassy, 1981, Canadian
THE KINKY COACHES AND THE POM-POM
   PUSSYCATS   *CRUNCH*   Summa Vista,
   1981, Canadian

JOHN WATERS
b. April 22, 1946 - Baltimore, Maryland
Agent: InterTalent - Los Angeles, 213/271-0600

MONDO TRASHO   Film-Makers, 1970
PINK FLAMINGOS   Saliva Films, 1974
FEMALE TROUBLE   New Line Cinema, 1975
DESPERATE LIVING   New Line Cinema, 1977
POLYESTER   New Line Cinema, 1981
HAIRSPRAY   New Line Cinema, 1988
CRY-BABY   Universal, 1990

PETER WATKINS
b. October 29, 1935 - Norbiton, England
Contact: Swedish Film Institute, Film House, Box 27126,
   102 52 Stockholm, Sweden

CULLODEN (TF)   BBC, 1964, British
THE WAR GAME   Pathe Contemporary, 1966, British
PRIVILEGE   Universal, 1967, British
GLADIATORS   1969, Swedish
PUNISHMENT PARK   Sherpix, 1971, British
EDVARD MUNCH   New Yorker, 1974,
   Swedish-Norwegian
70-TALETS   Manniskor, 1975, Swedish
FALLEN   1975, Swedish
EVENING LAND   Panorama-ASA, 1977, Danish
THE JOURNEY (FD)   Swedish Peace and Arbitration
   Society/Peter Watkins Productions/Cinergy Films/
   Sky Works Charitable Foundation, 1987,
   Swedish-Canadian

JOHN WATSON*
b. 1947 - England
Home: 619 18th Street, Manhattan Beach, CA 90266,
   213/545-4148
Agent: William Morris Agency - Beverly Hills, 213/274-7451

THE ZOO GANG   co-director with Pen Densham,
   New World, 1985

JOHN WATSON
DEATHSTALKER   New World, 1983, U.S.-Argentine

PAUL WATSON
b. February 17, 1942 - London, England
Address: 103 Grandison Road, London SW11, England
Agent: Duncan Heath & Associates, 162 Wardour Street,
   London W1, England, 71/439-1471

THE ROTHKO CONSPIRACY (TF)   BBC/Lionheart TV,
   1983, British
REVELATIONS (TD)   BBC, 1988, British

FILM
DIRECTORS
GUIDE

F
I
L
M

D
I
R
E
C
T
O
R
S

289

ROY WATTS
HAMBONE AND HILLIE   New World, 1984

KEENEN IVORY WAYANS
b. June 8, 1958 - New York, New York
Agent: InterTalent - Los Angeles, 213/271-0600

I'M GONNA GIT YOU SUCKA   MGM/UA, 1989

AL WAXMAN*
b. 1935 - Toronto, Ontario, Canada
Personal Manager: Sandy Wernick, The Brillstein Company,
   9200 Sunset Blvd. - Suite 428, Los Angeles, CA 90069,
   213/275-6135
Agent: Barrett, Benson, McCartt & Weston - Los Angeles,
   213/277-4998

THE CROWD INSIDE   National General, 1971, Canadian
MY PLEASURE IS MY BUSINESS   Brian Distributing
   Corporation, 1975, Canadian-West German
TULIPS   co-director with Rex Bromfield & Mark Warren,
   all directed under pseudonym of Stan Ferris, Avco
   Embassy, 1981, Canadian

PETER WEBB
Address: 1 Park Village East, London NW1, England,
   71/387-8077
Agent: William Morris Agency - London, 71/434-2191

GIVE MY REGARDS TO BROAD STREET   20th Century
   Fox, 1984, British

WILLIAM WEBB*
Contact: Directors Guild of America - Los Angeles,
   213/289-2000

DIRTY LAUNDRY   Seymour Borde & Associates, 1987
DISCOVERY BAY   Big Guy Productions, 1987
PARTY LINE   SVS Films, 1988
THE BANKER   Westwind Productions, 1989

BRUCE WEBER*
Contact: Directors Guild of America - Los Angeles,
   213/289-2000

BROKEN NOSES (FD)   Little Bear Films, 1987
LET'S GET LOST (FD)   Zeitgeist Films, 1988

NICHOLAS WEBSTER*
b. July 24, 1922 - Spokane, Washington
Home: 4135 Fulton Avenue, Sherman Oaks, CA 91423,
   818/906-9793

DEAD TO THE WORLD   United Artists, 1961
GONE ARE THE DAYS!   *PURLIE VICTORIOUS*
   Trans-Lux, 1963
SANTA CLAUS CONQUERS THE MARTIANS
   Embassy, 1964
MISSION MARS   Allied Artists, 1968
NO LONGER ALONE   World Wide, 1978, British
MANBEAST (TF)   Alan Landsburg Productions, 1981

DAVID WECHTER*
b. June 27, 1956 - Los Angeles, California
Agent: William Morris Agency - Beverly Hills, 213/274-7451

MIDNIGHT MADNESS   co-director with Michael Nankin,
   Buena Vista, 1980
THE BIKINI SHOP   *THE MALIBU BIKINI SHOP*
   International Film Marketing, 1986

STEPHEN WEEKS
b. 1948
Address: Penhow Castle, Nr. Newport, Gwent.,
   Penhow WP6 3AD, England, 0633/400800

GAWAIN AND THE GREEN KNIGHT   United Artists,
   1972, British
I, MONSTER   Cannon, 1974, British
CLASH OF THE SWORDS   Cannon, 1984, British

SAMUEL WEIL
(*see Lloyd KAUFMAN*)

PAUL WEILAND*
Address: 14 Newburgh Street, London W1V 1LF, England,
   11/434-9231

LEONARD PART 6   Columbia, 1987

CLAUDIA WEILL*
b. 1947 - New York, New York
Home: 2800 Seattle Drive, Los Angeles, CA 90046,
   213/850-1772
Agent: William Morris Agency - Beverly Hills, 213/274-7451

THE OTHER HALF OF THE SKY: A CHINA MEMOIR (FD)
   co-director with Shirley MacLaine, 1975
GIRLFRIENDS   Warner Bros., 1978
IT'S MY TURN   Columbia, 1980
JOHNNY BULL (TF)   Titus Productions/Eugene O'Neill
   Memorial Theatre Center, 1986

HAL WEINER
THE IMAGEMAKER   Castle Hill Productions, 1986

BOB WEINSTEIN
Business: Miramax Films, 18 East 48th Street, New York,
   NY 10017, 212/888-2662

PLAYING FOR KEEPS   co-director with Harvey Weinstein,
   Universal, 1986

HARVEY WEINSTEIN*
Business: Miramax Films, 18 East 48th Street, New York,
   NY 10017, 212/888-2662

PLAYING FOR KEEPS   co-director with Bob Weinstein,
   Universal, 1986

SANDRA WEINTRAUB
THE WOMEN'S CLUB   Weintraub-Cloverleaf/Scorsese
   Productions, 1987

PETER WEIR*
b. August 8, 1944 - Sydney, Australia
Agent: William Morris Agency - Beverly Hills, 213/274-7451

THREE TO GO   co-director with Brian Hannant &
   Oliver Howes, Commonwealth Film Unit Production,
   1971, Australian
THE CARS THAT EAT PEOPLE   *THE CARS THAT ATE
   PARIS*   New Line Cinema, 1974, Australian
PICNIC AT HANGING ROCK   Atlantic Releasing
   Corporation, 1975, Australian
THE PLUMBER   Barbary Coast, 1978, Australian,
   originally made for television

THE LAST WAVE   World Northal, 1978, Australian
GALLIPOLI   Paramount, 1981, Australian
THE YEAR OF LIVING DANGEROUSLY   MGM/UA,
    1983, Australian
WITNESS★   Paramount, 1985
THE MOSQUITO COAST   Warner Bros., 1986
DEAD POETS SOCIETY★   Buena Vista, 1989
GREEN CARD   Buena Vista, 1991, Australian-French

D O N   W E I S *

b. May 13, 1922 - Milwaukee, Wisconsin
Agent: Shapiro-Lichtman Agency - Los Angeles,
    213/859-8877

BANNERLINE   MGM, 1951
IT'S A BIG COUNTRY   co-director with Charles Vidor,
    Richard Thorpe, John Sturges, Don Hartman, Clarence
    Brown & William Wellman, MGM, 1951
JUST THIS ONCE   MGM, 1952
YOU FOR ME   MGM, 1952
I LOVE MELVIN   MGM, 1953
REMAINS TO BE SEEN   MGM, 1953
A SLIGHT CASE OF LARCENY   MGM, 1953
THE AFFAIRS OF DOBIE GILLIS   MGM, 1953
HALF A HERO   MGM, 1953
THE ADVENTURES OF HAJJI BABA   20th Century-
    Fox, 1954
RIDE THE HIGH IRON   Columbia, 1957
MR. PHAROAH AND HIS CLEOPATRA   1959
THE GENE KRUPA STORY   Columbia, 1960
CRITIC'S CHOICE   Warner Bros., 1963
LOOKING FOR LOVE   MGM, 1964
PAJAMA PARTY   American International, 1964
BILLIE   United Artists, 1965
THE GHOST IN THE INVISIBLE BIKINI   American
    International, 1966
THE KING'S PIRATE   Universal, 1967
THE LONGEST 100 MILES (TF)   Universal TV, 1967
NOW YOU SEE IT, NOW YOU DON'T (TF)   Universal
    TV, 1968
DID YOU HEAR THE ONE ABOUT THE TRAVELING
    SALESLADY? Universal, 1968
DEADLOCK (TF)   Universal TV, 1969
THE MILLIONAIRE (TF)   Don Fedderson Productions, 1978
ZERO TO SIXTY   First Artists, 1978
THE MUNSTERS' REVENGE (TF)   Universal TV, 1981

G A R Y   W E I S *

Contact: Directors Guild of America - Los Angeles,
    213/289-2000

JIMI HENDRIX (FD)   co-director with Joe Boyd & John
    Head, Warner Bros., 1973
ALL YOU NEED IS CASH (TF)   THE RUTLES   co-director
    with Eric Idle, Rutles Corps Productions, 1978, British
80 BLOCKS FROM TIFFANY'S (FD)   Above Average
    Productions, 1980
WHOLLY MOSES   Columbia, 1980
YOUNG LUST   RSO Films, 1982
MARLEY (FD)   Island Alive, 1985

S A M   W E I S M A N *

Agent: Jeremy Zimmer, Bauer Benedek Agency -
    Los Angeles, 213/275-2421

SUNSET BEAT (TF)   Patrick Hasburgh Productions, 1990

R O B E R T   K .   W E I S S *

Business: Universal Studios - Building 157, Room 209,
    100 Universal City Plaza, Universal City, CA 91608,
    818/777-1981

THE COMPLEAT AL (CTF)   Showtime/CBS-Fox, 1985
AMAZON WOMEN ON THE MOON   co-director with Joe
    Dante, Carl Gottlieb, Peter Horton & John Landis,
    Universal, 1987

E L L E N   W E I S S B R O D

LISTEN UP: THE LIVES OF QUINCY JONES (FD)   Warner
    Bros., 1990

W I M   W E N D E R S

b. August 14, 1945 - Dusseldorf, West Germany
Business: Gray City Inc., 853 Broadway, New York, NY
    10007, 212/473-3600

SUMMER IN THE CITY (DEDICATED TO THE KINKS)
    1970, West German
THE GOALIE'S ANXIETY AT THE PENALTY KICK
    Bauer International, 1972, West German
THE SCARLET LETTER   Bauer International, 1973,
    West German-Spanish
ALICE IN THE CITIES   New Yorker, 1974, West German
THE WRONG MOVE   New Yorker, 1975, West German
KINGS OF THE ROAD   Bauer International, 1976,
    West German
THE AMERICAN FRIEND   New Yorker, 1977, West
    German-French
LIGHTNING OVER WATER   NICK'S MOVIE   co-director
    with Nicholas Ray, Pari Films, 1980,
    West German-Swiss-U.S.
THE STATE OF THINGS   Gray City, 1982,
    U.S.-West German-Portuguese
HAMMETT   Orion/Warner Bros., 1982
PARIS, TEXAS   TLC Films/20th Century Fox, 1984,
    West German-French
TOKYO-GA (FD)   Wim Wenders Produktion/Gray
    City/Chris Sievernich Produktion, 1985,
    West German-U.S.
WINGS OF DESIRE   DER HIMMEL UBER BERLIN
    Orion Classics, 1987, West German-French
AUFZEICHNUNGEN ZU KLEIDERN UND STADTEN (FD)
    Road Movies, 1989, West German
UNTIL THE END OF THE WORLD   Road Movies/Argos
    Films, 1991, West German-French
FAR AWAY, SO CLOSE (FD)   Road Movies,
    1991, West German

P A U L   W E N D K O S *

b. September 20, 1922 - Philadelphia, Pennsylvania
Agent: CAA - Beverly Hills, 213/288-4545

THE BURGLAR   Columbia, 1957
THE CASE AGAINST BROOKLYN   Columbia, 1958
TARAWA BEACHHEAD   Columbia, 1958
GIDGET   Columbia, 1959
FACE OF A FUGITIVE   Columbia, 1959
BATTLE OF THE CORAL SEA   Columbia, 1959
BECAUSE THEY'RE YOUNG   Columbia, 1960
GIDGET GOES HAWAIIAN   Columbia, 1961
ANGEL BABY   Allied Artists, 1961
TEMPLE OF THE SWINGING DOLL   20th Century-
    Fox, 1961
GIDGET GOES TO ROME   Columbia, 1963
RECOIL   Lion, 1963
JOHNNY TIGER   Universal, 1966

ATTACK ON THE IRON COAST   United Artists,
    1968, U.S.-British
HAWAII FIVE-O (TF)   Leonard Freeman Productions, 1968
GUNS OF THE MAGNIFICENT SEVEN   United
    Artists, 1969
FEAR NO EVIL (TF)   Universal TV, 1969
CANNON FOR CORDOBA   United Artists, 1970
THE BROTHERHOOD OF THE BELL (TF)   Cinema
    Center, 1970
THE MEPHISTO WALTZ   20th Century-Fox, 1971
TRAVIS LOGAN, D.A. (TF)   QM Productions, 1971
A TATTERED WEB (TF)   Metromedia Productions, 1971
A LITTLE GAME (TF)   Universal TV, 1971
A DEATH OF INNOCENCE (TF)   Mark Carliner
    Productions, 1971
THE DELPHI BUREAU (TF)   Warner Bros. TV, 1972
THE FAMILY RICO (TF)   CBS, Inc., 1972
HAUNTS OF THE VERY RICH (TF)   ABC Circle
    Films, 1972
FOOTSTEPS (TF)   Metromedia Productions, 1972
THE STRANGERS IN 7A (TF)   Palomar Pictures
    International, 1972
HONOR THY FATHER (TF)   Metromedia Productions, 1973
TERROR ON THE BEACH (TF)   20th Century-Fox
    TV, 1973
THE UNDERGROUND MAN (TF)   Paramount TV, 1974
THE LEGEND OF LIZZIE BORDEN (TF)   Paramount
    TV, 1975
DEATH AMONG FRIENDS (TF)   Douglas S. Cramer
    Productions/Warner Bros. TV, 1975
SPECIAL DELIVERY   American International, 1976
THE DEATH OF RICHIE (TF)   Henry Jaffe
    Enterprises, 1977
SECRETS (TF)   The Jozak Company, 1977
GOOD AGAINST EVIL (TF)   Frankel-Bolen Productions/
    20th Century-Fox TV, 1977
HAROLD ROBBINS' 79 PARK AVENUE   *79 PARK
    AVENUE* (MS)   Universal TV, 1978
BETRAYAL (TF)   Roger Gimbel Productions/EMI TV, 1978
A WOMAN CALLED MOSES (TF)   Henry Jaffe
    Enterprises, 1978
THE ORDEAL OF PATTY HEARST (TF)   Finnegan
    Associates/David Paradine TV, 1979
ACT OF VIOLENCE (TF)   Emmett G. Lavery, Jr.
    Productions/Paramount TV, 1979
THE ORDEAL OF DR. MUDD (TF)   BSR Productions/
    Marble Arch Productions, 1980
A CRY FOR LOVE (TF)   Charles Fries Productions/Alan
    Sacks Productions, 1980
THE FIVE OF ME (TF)   Jack Farren Productions/
    Factor-Newland Production Corporation, 1981
GOLDEN GATE (TF)   Lin Bolen Productions/Warner
    Bros. TV, 1981
FARRELL FOR THE PEOPLE (TF)   InterMedia
    Entertainment/TAL Productions/ MGM-UA TV, 1982
COCAINE: ONE MAN'S SEDUCTION (TF)   Charles Fries
    Productions/David Goldsmith Productions, 1983
INTIMATE AGONY (TF)   Henerson-Hirsch Productions/
    Robert Papazian Productions, 1983
BOONE (TF)   Lorimar Productions, 1983
CELEBRITY (MS)   NBC Productions, 1984
SCORNED AND SWINDLED (TF)   Cypress Point
    Productions, 1984
THE EXECUTION (TF)   Newland-Raynor Productions/
    Comworld Productions, 1985
THE BAD SEED (TF)   Hajeno Productions/Warner Bros.
    TV, 1985
PICKING UP THE PIECES (TF)   CBS Entertainment, 1985
SISTER MARGARET AND THE SATURDAY NIGHT
    LADIES (TF)   Poolhouse Productions, 1986

RAGE OF ANGELS: THE STORY CONTINUES (MS)   NBC
    Productions, 1986
BLOOD VOWS: THE STORY OF A MAFIA WIFE (TF)
    Louis Rudolph Films/ Fries Entertainment, 1987
SIX AGAINST THE ROCK (TF)   Schaefer-Karpf-Epstein
    Productions/Gaylord Production Company, 1987
RIGHT TO DIE (TF)   Ohlmeyer Communications, 1987
THE TAKING OF FLIGHT 847: THE ULI DERICKSON
    STORY (TF) ☆   Columbia TV, 1988
THE GREAT ESCAPE II: THE UNTOLD STORY (TF)
    co-director with Jud Taylor, Spectator Films/Michael
    Jaffe Films, 1988
FROM THE DEAD OF NIGHT (TF)   Shadowplay Films/
    Phoenix Entertainment Group, 1989
CROSS OF FIRE (TF)   Leonard Hill Films, 1989
BLIND FAITH (TF)   NBC Productions, 1990

RICHARD WENK

Contact: Writers Guild of America, West - Los Angeles,
    213/550-1000

VAMP   New World, 1986

JEFF WERNER*

Home: 4211 Kester Avenue, Studio City, CA 91403,
    818/981-8651
Agent: Jerry Adler, The Sy Fischer Company -
    Los Angeles, 213/969-2900

CHEERLEADERS' WILD WEEKEND   Dimension, 1979
DIE LAUGHING   Orion/Warner Bros., 1980

PETER WERNER*

b. January 17, 1947 - New York, New York
Home: 415 Mesa Road, Santa Monica, CA 90402,
    213/459-0374
Agent: David Gersh, The Gersh Agency - Beverly Hills,
    213/274-6611

FINDHORD (FD)   Moving Pictures, 1976
BATTERED (TF)   Henry Jaffe Enterprises, 1978
AUNT MARY (TF)   Henry Jaffe Enterprises, 1979
DON'T CRY, IT'S ONLY THUNDER   Sanrio, 1981,
    U.S.-Japanese
HARD KNOX (TF)   A. Shane Company, 1984
I MARRIED A CENTERFOLD (TF)   Moonlight II
    Productions, 1984
PRISONERS   20th Century Fox, 1984, New Zealand
WOMEN IN SONG (TD)   KCET/Marc Robertson
    Productions, 1985
SINS OF THE FATHER (TF)   Fries Entertainment, 1985
OUTLAWS (TF)   Mad Dog Productions/Universal TV, 1986
LBJ: THE EARLY YEARS (TF)   Louis Rudolph Films/
    Fries Entertainment, 1987
NO MAN'S LAND   Orion, 1987
THE IMAGE (CTF)   HBO Pictures/Citadel
    Entertainment, 1990
HIROSHIMA: OUT OF THE ASHES (TF)   Robert
    Greenwald Productions, 1990

LINA WERTMULLER
*(Arcangela Felice Assunta Wertmuller von Elgg
Spanol von Braueich)*
b. August 14, 1928 - Rome, Italy
Home: Piazza Coltilde 5, Rome, Italy, 06/360-7501

I BALISCHI   22 Dicembre/Galatea, 1963, Italian
LET'S TALK ABOUT MEN   *QUESTA VOLTA
    PARLIAMO DI UOMINI*   Allied Artists, 1965, Italian

RITA LA ZANZARA   Mondial, 1966, Italian
NON STUZZICATE LA ZANZARA   Mondial, 1967, Italian
THE SEDUCTION OF MIMI   *MIMI METALLURGICO FERITO
    NELL'ONORE*   New Line Cinema, 1972, Italian
LOVE AND ANARCHY   *FILM D'AMORE E D'ANARCHIA*
    Peppercorn- Wormser, 1973, Italian
ALL SCREWED UP   *TUTTO A POSTE E NIENTE IN
    ORDINE*   New Line Cinema, 1974, Italian
SWEPT AWAY BY AN UNUSUAL DESTINY IN THE BLUE
    SEA OF AUGUST   Cinema 5, 1974, Italian
SEVEN BEAUTIES   *PASQUALINO SETTEBELLEZZE* ★
    Cinema 5, 1976, Italian
THE END OF THE WORLD IN OUR USUAL BED IN A
    NIGHT FULL OF RAIN   Warner Bros., 1978, Italian-U.S.
BLOOD FEUD   *FATTO DI SANGUE FRA DUE UOMINI PER
    CAUSA DI UNA VEDOVA (SI SOSPETTANO MOVENTI
    POLITICI)*   AFD, 1980, Italian
A JOKE OF DESTINY lying in wait around the corner like a
    street bandit,   Samuel Goldwyn Company, 1983, Italian
SOTTO, SOTTO   Triumph/Columbia, 1984, Italian
CAMORRA   *UN COMPLICATO INTRIGO DI DONNE,
    VICOLI E DELITTI*   Cannon, 1986, Italian
SUMMER NIGHT WITH GREEK PROFILE, ALMOND EYES
    AND SCENT OF BASIL   New Line Cinema,
    1986, Italian
IL DECIMO CLANDESTINO (TF)   Reteitalia, 1989, Italian
IN UNA NOTTE DI CHIARO DI LUNA   Italian International
    Films/RAI/ Istituto Luce/Carthago, 1989, Italian
SABATO DOMENICA LUNEDI   Nuova Champion/
    Filminvest, 1990, Italian

ERIC WESTON*
Agent: Ken Stovitz, ICM - Los Angeles, 213/550-4000

THEY WENT THAT-A-WAY AND THAT-A-WAY
    International Picture Show Company, 1979
EVILSPEAK   The Frank Moreno Company, 1982
MARVIN AND TIGE   *LIKE FATHER AND SON*   20th
    Century-Fox International Classics, 1983
THE IRON TRIANGLE   Scotti Bros., 1989

HASKELL WEXLER*
b. February 6, 1926 - Chicago, Illinois
Agent: Sanford-Beckett-Tobias-Skouras & Associates -
    Los Angeles, 213/208-2100
Business: Perigo Productions, Inc., 3659 Las Flores Canyon
    Road, Malibu, CA 90265, 213/456-3438

MEDIUM COOL   Paramount, 1969
BRAZIL: A REPORT ON TORTURE (FD)   co-director with
    Saul Landau, 1971
INTRODUCTION TO THE ENEMY (FD)   co-director, 1974
UNDERGROUND (FD)   co-director with Emile De Antonio &
    Mary Lampson, New Yorker, 1976
BUS II (FD)   co-director with Bonnie Bass Parker & Tom
    Tyson, 1983
LATINO   Cinecom, 1985

TONY WHARMBY*
Agent: Barrett, Benson, McCartt & Weston - Los Angeles,
    213/553-2600

DEMPSEY AND MAKEPEACE (TF)   London Weekend TV,
    1985, British
SORRY, WRONG NUMBER (CTF)   USA Network, 1989
VOICE OF THE HEART (TF)   Robert Bradford Productions,
    1990, British-U.S.
THE KISSING PLACE (TF)   Cynthia Cherbak Productions/
    Wilshire Court Productions, 1990

CLAUDE WHATHAM
Address: Camp House, Camp, Miserden, Stroud,
    Gloucestershire, England

CIDER WITH ROSIE (TF)   1972, British
THAT'LL BE THE DAY   EMI, 1974, British
ALL CREATURES GREAT AND SMALL (TF)   Talent
    Associates/EMI TV, 1975, British
SWALLOWS AND AMAZONS   LDS, 1977, British
SWEET WILLIAM   Kendon Films, 1980, British
HOODWINK   CB Films, 1982, Australian
MURDER IS EASY (TF)   David L. Wolper-Stan Margulies
    Productions/Warner Bros. TV, 1982
MURDER ELITE (TF)   Tyburn Productions, 1985, British
JUMPING THE QUEUE (TF)   BBC, 1987, British
BUDDY'S SONG   Curbishley-Baird Productions,
    1990, British

JIM WHEAT
Agent: The Gersh Agency - Beverly Hills, 213/274-6611

LIES   co-director with Ken Wheat, International Film
    Marketing, 1983
EWOKS: THE BATTLE FOR ENDOR (TF)   co-director
    with Ken Wheat, Lucasfilm Ltd., 1985
AFTER MIDNIGHT   co-director with Ken Wheat,
    MGM/UA, 1989

KEN WHEAT
Agent: The Gersh Agency - Beverly Hills, 213/274-6611

LIES   co-director with Jim Wheat, International Film
    Marketing, 1983
EWOKS: THE BATTLE FOR ENDOR (TF)   co-director
    with Jim Wheat, Lucasfilm Ltd., 1985
AFTER MIDNIGHT   co-director with Jim Wheat,
    MGM/UA, 1989

DAVID WHEATLEY
Contact: British Academy of Film & Television Arts,
    195 Piccadilly, London W1, England, 71/734-0022

THE MAGIC TOYSHOP   Roxie Releasing, 1986, British

ANNE WHEELER
b. 1946 - Edmonton, Alberta, Canada
Home: 10904 - 126th Street, Edmonton, Alberta T5M OP3,
    Canada, 403/451-0219

A WAR STORY   National Film Board of Canada,
    1981, Canadian
LOYALTIES   Norstar Releasing, 1986, Canadian-British
COWBOYS DON'T CRY   Cineplex Odeon,
    1988, Canadian
BYE BYE BLUES   Circle Releasing, 1989, Canadian
ANGEL SQUARE   Festival Films, 1990, Canadian

DAVID WICKES
Agent: Derek Webster/David Booth, John Redway and
    Associates Ltd., 5 Denmark Street, London WC2H 8LP,
    England, 71/836-2001

SWEENEY   EMI, 1977, British
SILVER DREAM RACER   Almi Cinema 5, 1980, British
PHILIP MARLOWE - PRIVATE EYE   *CHANDLERTOWN*
    co-director with Sidney Hayers, Bryan Forbes & Peter
    Hunt, HBO/David Wickes Television Ltd./London
    Weekend Television, 1983, British

JACK THE RIPPER (TF)   Euston Films/Thames TV/Hill-
O'Connor Entertainment/Lorimar TV, 1988, British-U.S.
JEKYLL & HYDE (TF)   King-Phoenix Entertainment/
London Weekend TV, 1990, U.S.-British

BERNHARD WICKI*
b. October 28, 1919 - St. Polten, Austria
Home: Restelbergstrasse 60, 8 Zurich, Switzerland,
00411-361-37-45
Agent: A.M. Cordes, Alexander Agency, William Morris
Organization, Lamontstrasse 9, 8 Munich 80, West
Germany, 089-47-60-81

WARUM SIND SIE GEGEN UNS?   1958, West German
THE BRIDGE   Allied Artists, 1959, West German
DAS WUNDER DES MALACHIAS   1961, West German
THE LONGEST DAY   co-director with Ken Annakin &
Andrew Marton, 20th Century-Fox, 1962
THE VISIT   20th Century-Fox, 1964, West German-
Italian-French-U.S.
MORITURI   *THE SABOTEUR, CODE NAME "MORITURI"*
20th Century-Fox, 1965
TRANSIT   1966, West German
QUADRIGA   co-director, 1967, West German
DAS FALSCHE GEWICHT   1971, West German
DIE EROBERUNG DER ZITADELLE   Scorpion Film,
1977, West German
DIE GRUNSTEIN-VARIANTE   Futura Film, 1985,
West German
DAS SPINNENNETZ   Beta/Kirch Group/Provobis/
ZDF/ORF/RAI/TVE, 1989, West German

BO WIDERBERG
b. June 8, 1930 - Malmo, Sweden
Contact: Swedish Film Institute, P.O. Box 27126, 102 52
Stockholm, Sweden, 08/63-0510

THE BABY CARRIAGE   Europa Film, 1962, Swedish
RAVEN'S END   New Yorker, 1963, Swedish
LOVE 65   Europa Film, 1965, Swedish
THIRTY TIMES YOUR MONEY   Europa Film,
1965, Swedish
ELVIRA MADIGAN   Cinema 5, 1967, Swedish
THE WHITE GAME   co-director, 1968, Swedish
ADALEN '31   Paramount, 1971, Swedish-U.S.
JOE HILL   Paramount, 1971, Swedish-U.S.
FIMPEN   1974, Swedish
MAN ON THE ROOF   Cinema 5, 1977, Swedish
VICTORIA   1979, Swedish-West German
GRISFESTEN   Nordiskfilm/Svensk Filmindustri/TV2/
Drakfilm/Svenska Filminstitut, 1983, Swedish-Danish
THE MAN FROM MAJORCA   Swedish Film Institute/
Drakfilm/Svensk Filmindustri/SVT2/Filmhuset KB/Crone
Film Sales, 1985, Swedish-Danish
THE SERPENT'S WAY UP THE NAKED ROCK
European Classics, 1987, Swedish

KEN WIEDERHORN*
Agent: David Gersh, The Gersh Agency - Beverly Hills,
213/274-6611

SHOCK WAVES   Joseph Brenner Associates, 1977
KING FRAT   Mad Makers, 1979
EYES OF A STRANGER   Warner Bros., 1981
MEATBALLS PART II   Tri-Star, 1984
RETURN OF THE LIVING DEAD PART II
Lorimar, 1988

ROBERT WIEMER
b. January 30, 1938 - Detroit, Michigan
Business: Tigerfilm, Inc., 3960 Laurel Canyon Blvd. -
Suite 381, Studio City, CA 91604, 213/461-8668

MY SEVENTEENTH SUMMER (TF)   BMC, Inc., 1980
WITCH'S SISTER (TF)   BMC, Inc., 1981
DO ME A FAVOR (TF)   BMC, Inc., 1982
ANNA TO THE INFINITE POWER (TF)   Tigerfilm, 1983
SOMEWHERE, TOMORROW   Comworld, 1984
THE NIGHT TRAIN TO KATHMANDU (TF)   Golden Tiger
Pictures, 1988

BILLY WILDER*
(Samuel Wilder)
b. June 22, 1906 - Vienna, Austria
Agent: Paul Kohner, Inc. - Los Angeles, 213/550-1060

MAUVAISE GRAINE   co-director with Alexander Esway,
1933, German
THE MAJOR AND THE MINOR   Paramount, 1942
FIVE GRAVES TO CAIRO   Paramount, 1943
DOUBLE INDEMNITY★   Paramount, 1944
THE LOST WEEKEND★★   Paramount, 1945
THE EMPEROR WALTZ   Paramount, 1948
A FOREIGN AFFAIR   Paramount, 1948
SUNSET BOULEVARD★★   Paramount, 1950
THE BIG CARNIVAL   *ACE IN THE HOLE*
Paramount, 1951
STALAG 17★   Paramount, 1953
SABRINA★   Paramount, 1954
THE SEVEN YEAR ITCH   20th Century-Fox, 1955
THE SPIRIT OF ST. LOUIS   Warner Bros., 1957
LOVE IN THE AFTERNOON   Allied Artists, 1957
WITNESS FOR THE PROSECUTION★   United
Artists, 1958
SOME LIKE IT HOT★   United Artists, 1959
THE APARTMENT★★   United Artists, 1960
ONE, TWO, THREE   United Artists, 1961
IRMA LA DOUCE   United Artists, 1963
KISS ME, STUPID   Lopert, 1964
THE FORTUNE COOKIE   United Artists, 1966
THE PRIVATE LIFE OF SHERLOCK HOLMES   United
Artists, 1970, U.S.-British
AVANTI!   United Artists, 1972, U.S.-Italian
THE FRONT PAGE   Universal, 1974
FEDORA   United Artists, 1979, West German-French
BUDDY BUDDY   MGM/United Artists, 1981

GENE WILDER*
(Jerry Silberman)
Agent: CAA - Beverly Hills, 213/288-4545

THE ADVENTURE OF SHERLOCK HOLMES' SMARTER
BROTHER   20th Century-Fox, 1975
THE WORLD'S GREATEST LOVER   20th Century-
Fox, 1977
SUNDAY LOVERS   co-director with Bryan Forbes,
Edouard Molinaro & Dino Risi, MGM/United Artists,
1981, U.S.-British-French-Italian
THE WOMAN IN RED   Orion, 1984
HAUNTED HONEYMOON   Orion, 1986

JOHN WILDER*
Agent: CAA - Beverly Hills, 213/288-4545

NORMAN ROCKWELL'S 'BREAKING HOME TIES'
BREAKING HOME TIES (TF)   ABC, 1987

GORDON WILES*

Home: 24 Delphinus, Irvine, CA 92715, 714/854-4484

GINGER IN THE MORNING   National Film, 1974

ETHAN WILEY

Agent: Jim Crabbe, William Morris Agency - Beverly Hills,
    213/274-7451

HOUSE II: THE SECOND STORY   New World, 1987

ANTHONY WILKINSON*

Address: 3726 Barham Blvd. - Suite B210, Los Angeles,
    CA 90068, 213/851-5416
Agent: Dan Redler, APA - Los Angeles, 213/273-0744

THE KING OF LOVE (TF)   Sarabande Productions/
    MGM-UA TV, 1987

ANSON WILLIAMS*

b. Los Angeles, California
Agent: APA - Los Angeles, 213/273-0744

THE LONE STAR KID (TF)   Major H/Anson
    Productions, 1986
YOUR MOTHER WEARS COMBAT BOOTS (TF)
    Kushner-Locke Productions, 1989
DREAM DATE (TF)   Frederic Golchan-Robert Kosberg
    Productions/ Gary Hoffman-Neal Israel Productions/
    Saban International, 1989
LITTLE WHITE LIES (TF)   Larry A. Thompson
    Organization/New World TV, 1989

OSCAR WILLIAMS*

b. May 20, 1944 - St. Croix, Virgin Islands
Home: 856 S. St. Andrews Place, Los Angeles, CA
    90005, 213/387-6487
Agent: David Dworski & Associates - Los Angeles,
    213/273-6173

THE FINAL COUNTDOWN   New World, 1972
FIVE ON THE BLACK HAND SIDE   United
    Artists, 1973
HOT POTATO   Warner Bros., 1976

PAUL WILLIAMS*

b. November 12, 1943 - New York, New York
Home: 990 Hanley Avenue, Los Angeles, CA 90049,
    213/471-0669

OUT OF IT   United Artists, 1969
THE REVOLUTIONARY   United Artists, 1970
DEALING: OR THE BERKELEY-TO-BOSTON FORTY-
    BRICK LOST-BAG BLUES   Warner Bros., 1972
NUNZIO   Universal, 1978
MISS RIGHT   IAP, 1981, Italian
A LIGHT IN THE AFTERNOON   Starfighter
    Productions, 1986
MIRROR, MIRROR II   Orphane Eyes
    Productions, 1990

RICHARD WILLIAMS

b. March 19, 1933 - Toronto, Canada
Business: Richard Williams Animation, 13 Soho Square,
    London W1V 5FB, England, 01/437-4455

RAGGEDY ANN AND ANDY (AF)   20th Century-
    Fox, 1977

FRED WILLIAMSON

b. March 5, 1938 - Gary, Indiana
Business: Po' Boy Productions, 5907 W. Pico Blvd., West
    Los Angeles, CA 90035, 213/855-1285

ADIOS AMIGO   Atlas, 1976
MEAN JOHNNY BARROWS   Atlas, 1976
DEATH JOURNEY   Atlas, 1976
NO WAY BACK   Atlas, 1976
MR. MEAN   Lone Star/Po' Boy, 1977, Italian-U.S.
ONE DOWN TWO TO GO   Almi Films, 1982
THE LAST FIGHT   Marvin Films, 1983
THE BIG SCORE   Almi Distribution, 1983
FOXTRAP   Snizzlefritz Distribution, 1986, Italian-U.S.
THE MESSENGER   Snizzlefritz Distribution, 1987,
    U.S.-Italian
JUSTICE DONE   Arista, 1990
CRITICAL ACTION   21st Century Distribution, 1990
THE KILL REFLEX   RCA-Columbia Home Video/Epic, 1990

GORDON WILLIS*

Business Manager: Ron Taft - New York City,
    212/586-8844

WINDOWS   United Artists, 1979

BRUCE WILSON

b. February 3, 1942 - Burlington, Wisconsin
Home: 305 W. Garfield, Seattle, WA 98119, 206/282-9581

DOUBLES   Shaprio Entertainment, 1978
BOMBS AWAY   TMS Pictures, 1985

HUGH WILSON*

b. August 21, 1943 - Miami, Florida
Agent: William Morris Agency - Beverly Hills,
    213/274-7451
Personal Manager: The Brillstein Company -
    Los Angeles, 213/275-6135
Business Manager: John Mucci & Associates -
    Los Angeles, 213/273-1301

POLICE ACADEMY   The Ladd Company/Warner
    Bros., 1984
RUSTLERS' RHAPSODY   Paramount, 1985
BURGLAR   Warner Bros., 1987

JIM WILSON

HOLLYWOOD DREAMING   American Twist/Boulevard
    Productions, 1986

RICHARD WILSON*

b. December 25, 1915 - McKeesport, Pennsylvania
Home: 501 Ocean Front, Santa Monica, CA 90402,
    213/395-0012
Attorney: Gunther Schiff, Finley, Kumble, Wagner, 9100
    Wilshire Blvd., Beverly Hills, CA 90212,
    213/550-6100

MAN WITH THE GUN   United Artists, 1955
THE BIG BOODLE   United Artists, 1957
RAW WIND IN EDEN   Universal, 1958
AL CAPONE   Allied Artists, 1959
PAY OR DIE   Allied Artists, 1960
WALL OF NOISE   Warner Bros., 1963
INVITATION TO A GUNFIGHTER   United Artists, 1964
THREE IN THE ATTIC   American International, 1968

SANDRA (SANDY) WILSON
b. 1947 - Penticton, British Columbia, Canada
Address: 2576 West 6th Avenue, Vancouver, British
Columbia V6K 1W5, Canada, 604/734-4688
Agent: Joan Scott, Writers and Artists Agency - Los Angeles,
213/829-2240

MY AMERICAN COUSIN   Spectrafilm, 1985, Canadian
MAMA'S GOING TO BUY YOU A MOCKINGBIRD (TF)
CBC, 1988, Canadian
AMERICAN BOYFRIENDS   Alliance Entertainment,
1989, Canadian

SIMON WINCER*
Home: 17 Bickleigh Yale Road, Mooroolbark,
Victoria 3128, Australia
Agent: CAA - Beverly Hills, 213/288-4545

TANDARRA (MS)   1976, Australian
THE SULLIVANS (MS)   co-director with David Stevens,
1976, Australian
AGAINST THE WIND (MS)   co-director with George Miller,
Pegasus Productions, 1978, Australian
THE DAY AFTER HALLOWEEN   SNAPSHOT   Group 1,
1979, Australian
HARLEQUIN   New Image, 1980, Australian
PHAR LAP   20th Century-Fox, 1983, Australian
D.A.R.Y.L.   Paramount, 1985
THE GIRL WHO SPELLED FREEDOM (TF)   Knopf-
Simons Productions/ITC Productions/Walt Disney
Productions, 1986
THE LAST FRONTIER (TF)   McElroy & McElroy
Productions, 1986, Australian
THE LIGHTHORSEMEN   Cinecom, 1987, Australian
BLUEGRASS (TF)   The Landsburg Company, 1988
LONESOME DOVE (MS)☆☆   Motown Productions/
Pangaea/Qintex Entertainment Inc., 1989
QUIGLEY DOWN UNDER   Pathe Entertainment, 1990,
U.S.-Australian

HARRY WINER*
b. May 4, 1947 - Detroit, Michigan
Agent: CAA - Beverly Hills, 213/288-4545

ONE OF A KIND (TF)   ABC, 1982
PAPER DOLLS (TF)   Mandy Productions/
MGM-UA TV, 1984
SINGLE BARS, SINGLE WOMEN (TF)   Carsey-Werner
Productions/Sunn Classic Pictures, 1984
MIRRORS (TF)   Leonard Hill Films, 1985
SPACECAMP   20th Century Fox, 1986
HEARTBEAT (TF)   Aaron Spelling Productions, 1988
I LOVE YOU PERFECT (TF)   Gross-Weston Productions/
Susan Dey Productions/Stephen J. Cannell
Productions, 1989

CHARLES WINKLER*
Agent: The Gersh Agency - Beverly Hills, 213/274-6611

YOU TALKIN' TO ME   MGM/UA, 1987

HENRY WINKLER*
b. October 30, 1946 - New York, New York
Address: P.O. Box 1764, Studio City, CA 91604,
213/468-5700
Agent: ICM - Los Angeles, 213/550-4000

A SMOKEY MOUNTAIN CHRISTMAS   Sandollar
Productions, 1986
MEMORIES OF ME   MGM/UA, 1988

IRWIN WINKLER*
b. May 28, 1931 - New York, New York
Contact: Directors Guild of America - Los Angeles,
213/289-2000

GUILTY BY SUSPICION   Warner Bros., 1990

TERENCE H. WINKLESS
Agent: William Morris Agency - Beverly Hills, 213/274-7451

THE NEST   Concorde, 1988
BLOODFIST   Concorde, 1989
PRIVATE OFFERINGS   Concorde, 1990

MICHAEL WINNER*
b. 1935 - London, England
Business: Scimitar Films, Ltd., 6-8 Sackville Street,
London W1X 1DD, England, 71/734-8385

CLIMB UP THE WALL   New Realm, 1960, British
SHOOT TO KILL   New Realm, 1960, British
OLD MAC   Carlyle, 1961, British
SOME LIKE IT COOL   Carlyle, 1961, British
MURDER ON THE CAMPUS   OUT OF THE SHADOW
New Realm, 1961, British
PLAY IT COOL   Allied Artists, 1962, British
THE COOL MIKADO   United Artists, 1962, British
WEST 11   Warner-Pathe, 1963, British
THE GIRL GETTERS   THE SYSTEM   American
International, 1964, British
YOU MUST BE JOKING!   Columbia, 1965, British
THE JOKERS   Universal, 1967, British
I'LL NEVER FORGET WHAT'S 'IS NAME   Regional,
1968, British
HANNIBAL BROOKS   United Artists, 1969, British
THE GAMES   20th Century-Fox, 1970, British
LAWMAN   United Artists, 1971
CHATO'S LAND   United Artists, 1972
THE NIGHTCOMERS   Avco Embassy, 1972, British
THE MECHANIC   United Artists, 1972
SCORPIO   United Artists, 1973
THE STONE KILLER   Columbia, 1973
DEATH WISH   Paramount, 1974
WON TON TON, THE DOG WHO SAVED HOLLYWOOD
Paramount, 1976
THE SENTINEL   Universal, 1977
THE BIG SLEEP   United Artists, 1978, British
FIREPOWER   AFD, 1979, British
DEATH WISH II   Filmways, 1982
THE WICKED LADY   MGM/UA/Cannon, 1983, British
SCREAM FOR HELP   Lorimar Distribution
International, 1984
DEATH WISH 3   Cannon, 1985
APPOINTMENT WITH DEATH   Cannon, 1988,
U.S.-British
A CHORUS OF DISAPPROVAL   South Gate
Entertainment, 1989, British
BULLSEYE!   21st Century Distribution, 1990, British

DAVID WINNING
b. 1961 - Calgary, Alberta, Canada
Business: Groundstar Entertainment Corporation,
918 16th Avenue NW - Suite 4001, Calgary, Alberta
T2M 0K3, Canada, 403/284-2889

STORM   Groundstar Entertainment, 1985, Canadian

TERRY WINSOR
PARTY PARTY   A&M Pictures, 1983, British
MORGAN STEWART'S COMING HOME   co-director with
Paul Aaron, both directed under pseudonym of Alan
Smithee, New Century/Vista, 1987

STAN WINSTON*
Agent: The Gersh Agency - Beverly Hills, 213/274-6611

PUMPKINHEAD   MGM/UA, 1988
UPWORLD   Vestron, 1990

DONOVAN WINTER
Business: Donwin Productions Ltd., 19 Bolton Street,
    London W1Y 8AD, England

THE TRUNK   Columbia, 1960, British
COME BACK, PETER   Donwin Productions, 1969, British
ESCORT GIRLS   Donwin Productions, 1973, British
THE DEADLY FEMALES   Donwin Productions,
    1976, British
GIVE US TOMORROW   Donwin Productions, 1978, British

DAVID WINTERS*
(David Weizer)
b. April 5, 1939 - London, England
Agent: Barry Perelman Agency - Los Angeles, 213/274-5999

DR. JEKYLL AND MR. HYDE   1973
WELCOME TO MY NIGHTMARE (FD)   Warner Bros., 1976
RACQUET   Cal-Am Artists, 1979
JAYNE MANSFIELD - AN AMERICAN TRAGEDY   1981
THE LAST HORROR FILM *FANATIC*   Twin
    Continental, 1982
MISSION KILL   Media Home Entertainment, 1985
THRASHIN'   Fries Entertainment, 1986
RAGE TO KILL   Action International, 1989
SPACE MUTINY   Action International, 1989
CODE NAME VENGEANCE   Action International, 1989

FRANZ PETER WIRTH
Contact: Filmforderungsantalt des Offentlichenrechts,
    Budapester Strasse 41, P.O. Box 301/87, 1000
    Berlin 31, West Germany, 49 30/261-6006

ARMS AND THE MAN *HELDEN*   Casino, 1958,
    West German
INSEL DER ROSEN (TF)   Suddeutscher Rundfunk, 1976,
    West German
BUDDENBROOKS (MS)   Taurus Film/Hessisher Rundfunk/
    TF-1/Film Polski, 1984, West German-French-Polish
A SQUARE OF SKY (MS)   1986, West German

HERBERT WISE*
(Herbert Weisz)
b. August 31, 1924 - Vienna, Austria
Home: 13 Despard Road, London N19 5NP, England,
    01/272-5047
Agent: Tim Corrie, Peters, Fraser & Dunlop, The
    Chambers, Chelsea Harbour, Lots Road, London
    SW10 OXF, England, 71/376-7676

ALONE AGAINST ROME   co-director with Riccardo
    Freda, Medallion, 1962, Italian
TO HAVE AND TO HOLD   Warner-Pathe, 1963, British
THE LOVERS!   British Lion, 1973, British
THE GATHERING STORM (TF)   BBC/Clarion
    Productions/Levien Productions, 1974, British
SKOKIE (TF)☆   Titus Productions, 1981
DEATH OF AN EXPERT WITNESS (MS)   Anglia TV,
    1982, British
LYTTON'S DIARY (TF)   1984, British
POPE JOHN PAUL II (TF)   Alvin Cooperman-Judith De
    Paul Productions/Taft Entertainment Company, 1984

REUNION AT FAIRBOROUGH (CTF)   HBO Premiere
    Films/Alan Wagner Productions/Alan King Productions/
    Columbia TV, 1985
THE CHRISTMAS TREE (TF)   1986, British
WELCOME HOME, BOBBY (TF)   Titus Productions, 1986
STRANGE INTERLUDE (TF)   Fries Entertainment, 1987
INSPECTOR MORSE III: THE GHOST IN THE
    MACHINE (TF)   Zenith Productions, 1988, British

ROBERT WISE*
b. September 10, 1914 - Winchester, Indiana
Business: Robert Wise Productions, 315 S. Beverly Drive -
    Suite 214, Beverly Hills, CA 90212, 213/284-7932
Agent: Phil Gersh, The Gersh Agency - Beverly Hills,
    213/274-6611

THE CURSE OF THE CAT PEOPLE   co-director with
    Gunther von Fritsch, RKO Radio, 1944
MADEMOISELLE FIFI   RKO Radio, 1944
THE BODY SNATCHER   RKO Radio, 1945
A GAME OF DEATH   RKO Radio, 1945
CRIMINAL COURT   RKO Radio, 1946
BORN TO KILL   RKO Radio, 1947
MYSTERY IN MEXICO   RKO Radio, 1948
BLOOD ON THE MOON   RKO Radio, 1948
THE SET-UP   RKO Radio, 1949
TWO FLAGS WEST   20th Century-Fox, 1950
THREE SECRETS   Warner Bros., 1950
THE HOUSE ON TELEGRAPH HILL   20th
    Century-Fox, 1951
THE DAY THE EARTH STOOD STILL   20th
    Century-Fox, 1951
THE CAPTIVE CITY   United Artists, 1952
SOMETHING FOR THE BIRDS   MGM, 1952
THE DESERT RATS   20th Century-Fox, 1953
DESTINATION GOBI   20th Century-Fox, 1953
SO BIG   Warner Bros., 1953
EXECUTIVE SUITE   MGM, 1954
HELEN OF TROY   Warner Bros., 1955, Italian-French
TRIBUTE TO A BAD MAN   MGM, 1956
SOMEBODY UP THERE LIKES ME   MGM, 1957
THIS COULD BE THE NIGHT   MGM, 1957
UNTIL THEY SAIL   MGM, 1957
RUN SILENT, RUN DEEP   United Artists, 1958
I WANT TO LIVE!★   United Artists, 1958
ODDS AGAINST TOMORROW   United Artists, 1959
WEST SIDE STORY★★   co-director with Jerome Robbins,
    United Artists, 1961
TWO FOR THE SEESAW   United Artists, 1962
THE HAUNTING   MGM, 1963, British-U.S.
THE SOUND OF MUSIC★★   20th Century-Fox, 1965
THE SAND PEBBLES   20th Century-Fox, 1966
STAR! *THOSE WERE THE HAPPY TIMES*   20th
    Century-Fox, 1968
THE ANDROMEDA STRAIN   Universal, 1971
TWO PEOPLE   Universal, 1973
THE HINDENBURG   Universal, 1975
AUDREY ROSE   United Artists, 1977
STAR TREK - THE MOTION PICTURE   Paramount, 1979
ROOFTOPS   New Century/Vista, 1989

CAROL WISEMAN
Address: 6 Westbourne Park Road, London W2 5PH,
    England, 71/229-3253
Agent: ICM - Los Angeles, 213/550-4428

BIG DEAL (MS)   BBC, 1985, British
A LITTLE PRINCESS (TF)   London Weekend TV,
    1987, British
CITY TAILS (TF)   Thames TV, 1988, British
MAY WINE   The Movie Group, 1990, French
THE FINDING (TF)   Thames TV, 1990, British

Wi

FILM
DIRECTORS
GUIDE

F I L M   D I R E C T O R S

297

FREDERICK WISEMAN
b. January 1, 1930 - Boston, Massachusetts
Agent: William Morris Agency - Beverly Hills, 213/274-7451
Home/Business: Zipporah Films, Inc., 1 Richdale Avenue - Suite 4, Cambridge, MASS 02140, 617/576-3603

TITICUT FOLLIES (FD)   Zipporah Films, 1967
HIGH SCHOOL (FD)   Zipporah Films, 1968
LAW AND ORDER (FD)   Zipporah Films, 1969
HOSPITAL (FD)☆☆   Zipporah Films, 1970
BASIC TRAINING (FD)   Zipporah Films, 1971
ESSENE (FD)   Zipporah Films, 1972
JUVENILE COURT (FD)   Zipporah Films, 1973
PRIMATE (FD)   Zipporah Films, 1974
WELFARE (FD)   Zipporah Films, 1975
MEAT (FD)   Zipporah Films, 1976
CANAL ZONE (FD)   Zipporah Films, 1977
SINAI FIELD MISSION (FD)   Zipporah Films, 1978
MANOEUVRE (FD)   Zipporah Films, 1979
MODEL (FD)   Zipporah Films, 1980
SERAPHITA'S DIARY   Zipporah Films, 1982
THE STORE (FD)   Zipporah Films, 1983
RACETRACK (FD)   Zipporah Films, 1985
DEAF (FD)   Zipporah Films, 1986
BLIND (FD)   Zipporah Films, 1986
MULTI-HANDICAPPED (FD)   Zipporah Films, 1986
ADJUSTMENT AND WORK (FD)   Zipporah Films, 1986
MISSLE (FD)   Zipporah Films, 1988
NEAR DEATH (FD)   Zipporah Films, 1989
CENTRAL PARK (TD)   Zipporah Films, 1990

STEPHEN WITHROW
FRIENDS, LOVERS AND LUNATICS *CRAZY HORSE/SHE DRIVES ME CRAZY*   Fries Entertainment, 1989, Canadian

WILLIAM WITNEY*
b. May 15, 1910 - Lawton, Oklahoma
Contact: Directors Guild of America - Los Angeles, 213/289-2000

THE TRIGGER TRIO   Republic, 1937
HI-YO SILVER   co-director with John English, Republic, 1940
HEROES OF THE SADDLE   Republic, 1940
OUTLAWS OF PINE RIDGE   Republic, 1942
THE YUKON PATROL   co-director with John English, Republic, 1942
HELLDORADO   Republic, 1946
APACHE ROSE   Republic, 1947
BELLS OF SAN ANGELO   Republic, 1947
SPRINGTIME IN THE SIERRAS   Republic, 1947
ON THE SPANISH TRAIL   Republic, 1947
THE GAY RANCHERO   Republic, 1948
UNDER CALIFORNIA SKIES   Republic, 1948
EYES OF TEXAS   Republic, 1948
THE FAR FRONTIER   Republic, 1949
THE LAST MUSKETEER   Republic, 1952
THE OUTCAST   Republic, 1954
HEADLINE HUNTERS   Republic, 1955
CITY OF SHADOWS   Republic, 1955
A STRANGE ADVENTURE   Republic, 1956
PANAMA SAL   Republic, 1957
YOUNG AND WILD   Republic, 1958
JUVENILE JUNGLE   Republic, 1958

THE COOL AND THE CRAZY   American International, 1958
THE BONNIE PARKER STORY   American International, 1958
PARATROOP COMMAND   American International, 1959
SECRET OF THE PURPLE REEF   20th Century-Fox, 1960
MASTER OF THE WORLD   American International, 1961
THE LONG ROPE   20th Century-Fox, 1961
APACHE RIFLES   20th Century-Fox, 1964
THE GIRLS ON THE BEACH   Paramount, 1965
ARIZONA RAIDERS   Columbia, 1965
FORTY GUNS TO APACHE PASS   Columbia, 1967
I ESCAPED FROM DEVIL'S ISLAND   United Artists, 1973
DARKTOWN STRUTTERS *GET DOWN AND BOOGIE* New World, 1975

WILLIAM D. (BILL) WITTLIFF*
Business: 510 Baylor, Austin, TX 78703, 512/476-6821
Agent: ICM - Los Angeles, 213/550-4000

RED HEADED STRANGER   Alive Films, 1987

PETER WITTMAN
PLAY DEAD   Troma, 1981
ELLIE   Shapiro Entertainment, 1984

IRA WOHL
BEST BOY (FD)   International Film Exchange, 1980

ANNETT WOLF
Address: L'Ermitage, 9291 Burton Way, Beverly Hills, CA 90210, 213/278-3344
Agent: Ed Millis, La Rocca Talent Group - Burbank, 818/841-8000
Attorney: Robert Myman, Shagin & Myman, 11777 San Vicente Blvd. - Suite 600, Los Angeles, CA 90049, 213/820-7717

CHARLES CHAPLIN: "THE MAN, THE DIRECTOR AND THE CLOWN" (TD)   1965, Danish
A TWIST OF LEMON (TD)   Danish TV, 1976, Danish
ELVIS IN CONCERT (TD)   Smith-Hemion Productions, 1977
THE WORLD OF INGMAR BERGMAN (TD)   1983

DAN WOLMAN
b. October 28, 1941 - Jerusalem, Israel
Contact: Israel Film Centre, Ministry of Industry & Trade, 30 Agron Street, P.O. Box 299, Jerusalem 94190, Israel, 02/210297

THE MORNING BEFORE SLEEP   Toda Films, 1969, Israeli
THE DREAMER   Cannon, 1979, Israeli
FLOCH   Aldan Films/Floch Ltd., 1972, Israeli
MY MICHAEL   Alfred Plaine, 1976, Israeli
HIDE AND SEEK   1980, Israeli
NANA   MGM/UA/Cannon, 1983, Italian-U.S.
BABY LOVE (LEMON POPSICLE V)   Noah Films, 1983, Israeli
SOLDIER OF THE NIGHT   Cannon, 1983, Israeli
ANCHORS AWEIGH (LEMON POPSICLE VI)   Noah Films, 1985, Israeli
CONTRACT FOR LOVE   Dan Wolman Productions, 1986, Israeli
THE GREAT DAYS, SMALL STORIES (FD)   1989, Israeli

LENNY WONG*
Contact: Directors Guild of America - Los Angeles,
213/289-2000

COMEDY'S DIRTIEST DOZEN (FD)   Fourth & Broadway
Films/Island Pictures, 1989

JOANNE WOODWARD*
b. February 27, 1930 - Thomasville, Georgia
Agent: William Morris Agency - Beverly Hills,
213/274-7451

COME ALONG WITH ME (TF)   Rubicon
Productions, 1982

CHUCK WORKMAN*
(Carl Workman)
Address: 195 S. Beverly Drive, Beverly Hills, CA 90212,
213/271-0964
Agent: APA - Los Angeles, 213/273-0744

THE MONEY   Coliseum, 1977
STOOGEMANIA   Atlantic Releasing Corporation, 1985
SUPERSTAR (FD)   Marilyn Lewis Entertainment
Enterprises, 1990

DAVID WORTH
WARRIOR OF THE LOST WORLD   Visto International,
1985, Italian
KICKBOXER   co-director with Mark DiSalle,
Cannon, 1989

CASPER WREDE
Contact: British Academy of Film & Television Arts, 195
Piccadilly, London W1, England, 71/734-0022

PRIVATE POTTER   MGM, 1964, British
ONE DAY IN THE LIFE OF IVAN DENISOVICH
Cinerama Releasing Corporation, 1971,
British-Norwegian
THE TERRORISTS   *RANSOM*   20th Century-Fox,
1975, British

PATRICK WRIGHT
b. November 28, 1939 - San Francisco, California
Business: The People People, Inc., 8776 Sunset Blvd.,
Los Angeles, CA 90069, 213/652-9320 or
213/256-5552

HOLLYWOOD HIGH   Lone Star, 1976

THOMAS J. WRIGHT*
Agent: CAA - Beverly Hills, 213/288-4545

TORCHLIGHT   International Film Marketing, 1984,
U.S.-Mexican
NO HOLDS BARRED   New Line Cinema, 1989
THE OPERATION (TF)   Moress, Nanas, Golden
Entertainment/Viacom, 1990
OVER THE EDGE (CTF)   USA Network, 1990
SNOW KILL (CTF)   Wilshire Court Productions, 1990

DONALD WRYE*
Agent: ICM - Los Angeles, 213/550-4000

THE MAN WHO COULD TALK TO KIDS (TF)   Tomorrow
Entertainment, 1973
BORN INNOCENT (TF)   Tomorrow Entertainment, 1974

DEATH BE NOT PROUD (TF)   Good Housekeeping
Productions/Westfall Productions, 1975
THE ENTERTAINER (TF)   RSO Films, 1976
IT HAPPENED ONE CHRISTMAS (TF)   Universal TV, 1977
ICE CASTLES   Columbia, 1979
THE HOUSE OF GOD   H.O.G.   United Artists, 1981
FIRE ON THE MOUNTAIN (TF)   Bonnard
Productions, 1982
DIVORCE WARS: A LOVE STORY (TF)   Wrye-
Konigsberg Films/Warner Bros. TV, 1982
THE FACE OF RAGE (TF)   Hal Sitowitz Productions/
Viacom, 1983
HEART OF STEEL (TF)   Beowulf Productions, 1983
AMERIKA (MS)   ABC Circle Films, 1987
83 HOURS 'TIL DAWN (TF)   Consolidated
Productions, 1990

RUDOLPH (RUDY) WURLITZER
Contact: Writers Guild of America , West - Los Angeles,
213/550-1000

CANDY MOUNTAIN   co-director with Robert Frank,
Metropolis Film, 1987, Swiss-French-Canadian

TRACY KEENAN WYNN*
b. February 28, 1945 - Los Angeles, California
Agent: CAA - Beverly Hills, 213/288-4545

HIT LADY (TF)   Spelling-Goldberg Productions, 1974

JIM WYNORSKI
b. August 14, 1950 - Long Island, New York
Personal Manager: L. Miller Management - Los Angeles,
213/392-5802

THE LOST EMPIRE   JGM Enterprises, 1984
CHOPPING MALL   Concorde/Cinema Group, 1986
DEATHSTALKER II   Concorde, 1986, U.S.-Argentine
BIG BAD MAMA II   Concorde, 1987
NOT OF THIS EARTH   Concorde, 1988
THE RETURN OF SWAMP THING   Lightyear
Entertainment, 1989
TRANSYLVANIA TWIST   Concorde, 1989
THE HAUNTING OF MORELLA   Concorde, 1990

JIN XIE
(See Xie JIN)

YOJI YAMADA

b. 1931 - Japan
Contact: Shochiku Co., Ltd., 13-5, Tsukiji 1-Chome,
Chuo-ku, Tokyo 104, Japan, 03/542-5551

THE STRANGERS UPSTAIRS   Shochiku, 1961, Japanese
THE SUNSHINE GIRL   Shochiku, 1963, Japanese
HONEST FOOL   Shochiku, 1964, Japanese
HONEST FOOL - SEQUEL   Shochiku, 1964, Japanese
THE DONKEY COMES ON A TANK   Shochiku,
    1964, Japanese
THE TRAP   Shochiku, 1965, Japanese
GAMBLER'S LUCK   Shochiku, 1966, Japanese
THE LOVABLE TRAMP   Shochiku, 1966, Japanese
LET'S HAVE A DREAM   Shochiku, 1967, Japanese
SONG OF LOVE   Shochiku, 1967, Japanese
THE GREATEST CHALLENGE OF ALL   Shochiku,
    1967, Japanese
THE MILLION DOLLAR PURSUIT   Shochiku,
    1968, Japanese
THE SHY DECEIVER   Shochiku, 1968, Japanese
VAGABOND SCHEMER   Shochiku, 1969, Japanese
TORA-SAN, OUR LOVABLE TRAMP   Shochiku,
    1969, Japanese
TORA-SAN'S CHERISHED MOTHER   Shochiku,
    1969, Japanese
TORA-SAN'S RUNAWAY   Shochiku, 1970, Japanese
WHERE SPRING COMES LATE   Shochiku,
    1970, Japanese
TORA-SAN'S SHATTERED ROMANCE   Shochiku,
    1971, Japanese
TORA-SAN: THE GOOD SAMARITAN   Shochiku,
    1971, Japanese
TORA-SAN'S LOVE CALL   Shochiku, 1971, Japanese
TORA-SAN'S DEAR OLD HOME   Shochiku,
    1972, Japanese
HOME FROM THE SEA   Shochiku, 1972, Japanese
TORA-SAN'S DREAM COME TRUE   Shochiku,
    1972, Japanese
TORA-SAN'S FORGET-ME-NOT   Shochiku,
    1973, Japanese
TORA-SAN LOVES AN ARTIST   Shochiku,
    1973, Japanese
TORA-SAN'S LOVESICK   Shochiku, 1974, Japanese
TORA-SAN'S LULLABY   Shochiku, 1974, Japanese
TORA-SAN MEETS THE SONGSTRESS AGAIN   Shochiku,
    1975, Japanese
THE VILLAGE   Shochiku, 1975, Japanese
TORA-SAN, THE INTELLECTUAL   Shochiku,
    1975, Japanese
TORA-SAN'S SUNRISE, SUNSET   Shochiku,
    1976, Japanese
TORA-SAN'S HEART OF GOLD   Shochiku,
    1976, Japanese
TORA-SAN MEETS HIS LORDSHIP   Shochiku,
    1977, Japanese
THE YELLOW HANDKERCHIEF   Shochiku,
    1977, Japanese
TORA-SAN PLAYS CUPID   Shochiku, 1977, Japanese
STAGE-STRUCK TORA-SAN   Shochiku, 1978, Japanese
TALK-OF-THE-TOWN TORA-SAN   Shochiku,
    1978, Japanese

TORA-SAN, THE MATCHMAKER   Shochiku,
    1979, Japanese
TORA-SAN'S DREAM OF SPRING   Shochku,
    1979, Japanese
A DISTANT CRY FROM SPRING   Shochiku,
    1980, Japanese
TORA-SAN'S TROPICAL FEVER   Shochiku,
    1980, Japanese
FOSTER DADDY TORA-SAN   Shochiku, 1981, Japanese
TORA-SAN'S MANY-SPLINTERED LOVE   Shochiku,
    1981, Japanese
TORA-SAN'S PROMISE   Shochiku, 1981, Japanese
HEARTS AND FLOWERS FOR TORA-SAN   Shochiku,
    1982, Japanese
TORA-SAN, THE EXPERT   Shochiku, 1982, Japanese
TORA-SAN'S SONG OF LOVE   Shochiku, 1983, Japanese
TORA-SAN GOES RELIGIOUS?   Shochiku,
    1983, Japanese
MARRIAGE COUNSELOR TORA-SAN   Shochiku,
    1984, Japanese
TORA-SAN'S FORBIDDEN LOVE   Shochiku,
    1984, Japanese
TORA-SAN, THE GO-BETWEEN   Shochiku,
    1985, Japanese
TORA-SAN'S ISLAND ENCOUNTER   Shochiku,
    1985, Japanese
FINAL TAKE   Shochiku, 1986, Japanese
TORA-SAN'S BLUEBIRD FANTASY   Shochiku,
    1986, Japanese
TORA-SAN GOES NORTH   Shochiku, 1987, Japanese
TORA-SAN PLAYS DADDY   Shochiku, 1987, Japanese
HOPE AND PAIN   Shochiku, 1988, Japanese
TORA-SAN'S SALAD DATE MEMORIAL   Shochiku,
    1989, Japanese
TORA-SAN GOES TO VIENNA   Kino International/
    Shochiku, 1989, Japanese
TORA-SAN, MY UNCLE   Shochiku, 1990, Japanese

MITSUO YANAGIMACHI

b. 1944 - Ibaraki, Japan
Contact: Directors Guild of Japan, Tsukada Building,
    8-33 Udagawa-cho, Shibuya-ku, Tokyo 150, Japan,
    3/461-4411

GOD SPEED YOU, BLACK EMPEROR (FD)
    1976, Japanese
A 19-YEAR-OLD'S PLAN   1979, Japanese
FAREWELL TO THE LAND   1982, Japanese
HIMATSURI (FIRE FESTIVAL)   Kino International,
    1985, Japanese
SHADOW OF CHINA   Nippon Herald Films/Fuji TV/
    Marubeni/Nissho Iway, 1990, Japanese-U.S.

EDWARD YANG
(Yang Dechang)

b. 1947 - Shanghai, China
Contact: Coordination Council for North American Affairs,
    Information & Communications Division, 900 N. Western
    Avenue, Los Angeles, CA 90029, 213/461-3665

IN OUR TIME   co-director, 1982, Taiwanese
THAT DAY ON THE BEACH   Central Motion Picture
    Corporation, 1983, Taiwanese
TAIPEI STORY   Evergreen Film Production Company,
    1985, Taiwanese
THE TERRORIZERS   Central Motion Picture Corporation,
    1986, Taiwanese

BOB YARI
MIND GAMES   MGM/UA, 1989

PETER YATES*

b. July 24, 1929 - Aldershot, England
Agent: CAA - Beverly Hills, 213/288-4545

SUMMER HOLIDAY   American International,
   1963, British
ONE WAY PENDULUM   Lopert, 1964, British
ROBBERY   Avco Embassy, 1967, British
BULLITT   Warner Bros., 1968
JOHN AND MARY   20th Century-Fox, 1969
MURPHY'S WAR   Paramount, 1971, British
THE HOT ROCK   20th Century-Fox, 1972
THE FRIENDS OF EDDIE COYLE   Paramount, 1973
FOR PETE'S SAKE   Columbia, 1974
MOTHER, JUGS AND SPEED   20th Century-Fox, 1976
THE DEEP   Columbia, 1977
BREAKING AWAY★   20th Century-Fox, 1979
EYEWITNESS   20th Century-Fox, 1981
KRULL   Columbia, 1983, U.S.-British
THE DRESSER★   Columbia, 1983, British
ELENI   Warner Bros., 1985
SUSPECT   Tri-Star, 1987
THE HOUSE ON CARROLL STREET   Orion, 1988
AN INNOCENT MAN   Buena Vista, 1989

REBECCA YATES

b. 1950 - London, England
Business: Cineflics Ltd., 215 Albany Avenue, Toronto,
   Ontario M5R 3C7, Canada, 416/531-2612

HOME FREE (TF)   co-director with Glen Salzman,
   1976, Canadian
ANOTHER KIND OF MUSIC (TF)   co-director with Glen
   Salzman, 1977, Canadian
NIKKOLINA (TF)   co-director with Glen Salzman,
   1978, Canadian
CORLETTO & SON (TF)   co-director with Glen Salzman,
   1980, Canadian
REACHING OUT (TF)   co-director with Glen Salzman,
   1980, Canadian
INTRODUCING...JANET (TF)   co-director with Glen
   Salzman, 1981, Canadian
JEN'S PLACE (TF)   co-director with Glen Salzman,
   1982, Canadian
MILK AND HONEY   co-director with Glen Salzman, Castle
   Hill Productions, 1987, Canadian

LINDA YELLEN*

b. Queens, New York
Agent: Wliam Morris Agency - Beverly Hills,
   213/274-7451

COME OUT, COME OUT   Beacon Productions, 1969
LOOKING UP   Levitt-Pickman, 1977
JACOBO TIMERMAN: PRISONER WITHOUT A NAME,
   CELL WITHOUT A NUMBER (TF)   Chrysalis-Yellen
   Productions, 1983

YEVGENY YEVTUSHENKO

Contact: Union of Soviet Filmmakers, Vassilievskaya 13,
   Moscow, U.S.S.R., tel.: 250-4114

THE KINDERGARTEN   IFEX Film, 1984, Soviet

HO YIM
(See Yim HO)

ZHANG YIMOU

Contact: China Film Import & Export Office, 2500 Wilshire
   Blvd. - Suite 1028, Los Angeles, CA 90057, 213/380-7520

RED SORGHUM   New Yorker, 1988, Chinese
MOANS IN THE DARK   China Film Co-Production Corpora-
   tion/ Tokuma Communications Company Ltd., 1989,
   Chinese-Japanese
JU DOU   co-director with Yang Fengliang, China Film
   Import and Export Company, 1990, Chinese-Japanese

BUD YORKIN*
(Alan David Yorkin)

b. February 22, 1926 - Washington, Pennsylvania
Address: 132 S. Rodeo Drive - Suite 300, Beverly Hills, CA
   90212, 213/274-8111
Agent: William Morris Agency - Beverly Hills, 213/274-7451

COME BLOW YOUR HORN   Paramount, 1963
NEVER TOO LATE   Warner Bros., 1965
DIVORCE AMERICAN STYLE   Columbia, 1967
INSPECTOR CLOUSEAU   United Artists, 1968, British
START THE REVOLUTION WITHOUT ME   Warner Bros.,
   1970, British
THE THIEF WHO CAME TO DINNER   Warner Bros., 1972
TWICE IN A LIFETIME   The Yorkin Company, 1985
ARTHUR 2 ON THE ROCKS   Warner Bros., 1988
LOVE HURTS   Vestron, 1990

YAKY YOSHA

Business: Yaky Yosha Ltd., 29 Lilienblum Street, Tel Aviv
   65133, Israel, 03/659108

SHALOM   Yaky Yosha Ltd., 1973, Israeli
ROCKINGHORSE   Sus-Etz, 1978, Israeli
THE VULTURE   New Yorker, 1981, Israeli
DEAD END STREET   Lelo Motza Ltd., 1982, Israeli
SUNSTROKE   Shapira Films, 1984, Israeli

FREDDIE YOUNG

b. 1902 - England
Address: 3 Roehampton Close, London SW15, England
Agent: London Management, 235/241 Regent Street,
   London W1, England, 71/493-1610

ARTHUR'S HALLOWED GROUND   Cinecom, 1983,
   British, originally made for television

JEFFREY YOUNG*

Contact: Directors Guild of America - New York City,
   212/581-0370

BEEN DOWN SO LONG IT LOOKS LIKE UP TO ME
   Paramount, 1971

ROBERT M. YOUNG*

b. November 22, 1924 - New York, New York
Agent: ICM - Los Angeles, 213/550-4000

THE INFERNO *CORTILE CASCINO, ITALY* (FD)
   co-director with Michael Roemer, Robert M. Young
   Film Productions, 1962
NOTHING BUT A MAN   co-director with Michael Roemer,
   Cinema 5, 1965
ALAMBRISTA!   Bobwin/Films Haus, 1977
SHORT EYES   The Film League, 1978
RICH KIDS   United Artists, 1979
ONE-TRICK PONY   Warner Bros., 1980

**F
I
L
M

D
I
R
E
C
T
O
R
S**

THE BALLAD OF GREGORIO CORTEZ Embassy, 1983
SAVING GRACE Columbia, 1986
EXTREMITIES Atlantic Releasing Corporation, 1986
WE ARE THE CHILDREN (TF) Paulist Pictures/Dan Fauci-Ted Danson Productions/The Furia Organization, 1987
DOMINICK AND EUGENE Orion, 1988
TRIUMPH OF THE SPIRIT Triumph Releasing Corporation, 1989, U.S.-Israeli
TALENT FOR THE GAME Paramount, 1990

ROBERT WILLIAM YOUNG
Home: 28 Kew Green, Kew, Surrey TW9 3BH, England, 01/948-2310
Business: Bainbridge, Robert, Young, 95 Dean Street, London W1V 5RB, England, 71/439-1144
Agent: Douglas Rae Management, 28 Charing Cross Road, London WC2H 0DB, England, 71/836-3903

VAMPIRE CIRCUS Rank, 1972, British
THE WORLD IS FULL OF MARRIED MEN New Realm, 1979, British
THE MAD DEATH (TF) BBC Scotland, 1981, Scottish
WORST WITCH (TF) Central TV, 1986, British
HARRY'S KINGDOM (TF) BBC, 1987, British
BLUE BLOOD (TF) Tele-Munchen, 1987, West German
THREE WISHES FOR JAMIE (TF) Hill-St. Johns Films/HTV Ltd./Columbia TV, 1987, British-U.S.

ROGER YOUNG*
b. May 13, 1942 - Champaign, Illinois
Agent: CAA - Beverly Hills, 213/288-4545

BITTER HARVEST (TF)☆ Charles Fries Productions, 1981
AN INNOCENT LOVE (TF) Steve Binder Productions, 1982
DREAMS DON'T DIE (TF) Hill-Mandelker Films, 1982
TWO OF A KIND (TF) Lorimar Productions, 1982
HARDCASTLE AND McCORMICK (TF) Stephen J. Cannell Productions, 1983
LASSITER Warner Bros., 1984
GULAG (CTF) Lorimar Productions/HBO Premiere Films, 1985
INTO THIN AIR (TF) Tony Ganz Productions/Major H Productions, 1985
UNDER SIEGE (TF) Ohlmeyer Communications Company/Telepictures Productions, 1986
LOVE AMONG THIEVES (TF) Robert A. Papazian Productions, 1987
THE SQUEEZE Tri-Star, 1987
THE BOURNE IDENTITY (TF) Alan Shayne Productions/Warner Bros. TV, 1988
MURDER IN MISSISSIPPI (TF) Wolper Productions/Bernard Sofronski Productions/Warner Bros. TV, 1990
LOVE AND LIES (TF) Freyda Rothstein Productions/ITC Entertainment Group, 1990

TERENCE YOUNG*
b. June 20, 1915 - Shanghai, China
Address: 23717 Long Valley Road, Calabasas, CA 91302, 818/340-7375
Agent: Kurt Frings Agency - Beverly Hills, 213/277-1103

MEN OF ARNHEM (FD) co-director with Brian Desmond Hurst, Army Film Unit, 1944, British
CORRIDOR OF MIRRORS Universal, 1948, British
ONE NIGHT WITH YOU Universal, 1948, British
WOMAN HATER Universal, 1948, British
THEY WERE NOT DIVIDED General Film Distributors, 1950, British
VALLEY OF THE EAGLES Lippert, 1951, British

THE FRIGHTENED BRIDE *THE TALL HEADLINES* Beverly, 1952, British
PARATROOPER *THE RED BERET* Columbia, 1953, British
THAT LADY 20th Century-Fox, 1954, British
STORM OVER THE NILE co-director with Zoltan Korda, Columbia, 1955, British
SAFARI Columbia, 1956, British
ZARAK Columbia, 1956, British
ACTION OF THE TIGER MGM, 1957, British
TANK FORCE *NO TIME TO DIE* Columbia, 1958, British
SERIOUS CHARGE Eros, 1959, British
BLACK TIGHTS Magna, 1960, French
PLAYGIRL AFTER DARK *TOO HOT TO HANDLE* Topaz, 1960, British
DUEL OF CHAMPIONS co-director with Ferdinando Baldi, Medallion, 1961, Italian-Spanish
DR. NO United Artists, 1962, British
FROM RUSSIA WITH LOVE United Artists, 1963, British
THE AMOROUS ADVENTURES OF MOLL FLANDERS Paramount, 1965, British
THUNDERBALL United Artists, 1965, British
THE DIRTY GAME *GUERRE SECRETE* co-director with Christian-Jaque, Carlo Lizzani & Werner Klinger, American International, 1966, French-Italian-West German
TRIPLE CROSS Warner Bros., 1966, British-French
THE POPPY IS ALSO A FLOWER Comet, 1966, European
WAIT UNTIL DARK Warner Bros., 1967
THE ROVER *L'AVVENTURIERO* Cinerama Releasing Corporation, 1967, I talian
MAYERLING MGM, 1969, British-French
THE CHRISTMAS TREE Continental, 1969, French-Italian
COLD SWEAT *DE LA PART DES COPAINS* Emerson, 1970, French
RED SUN National General, 1972, French-Italian-Spanish
THE VALACHI PAPERS *JOE VALACHI: I SEGRETI DI COSA NOSTRA* Columbia, 1972, Italian-French
WAR GODDESS *LE GUERRIERE DEL SNO NUDA* American International, 1973, Italian
THE KLANSMAN Paramount, 1974
SIDNEY SHELDON'S BLOODLINE Paramount, 1979
INCHON! MGM/UA, 1982, South Korean
THE JIGSAW MAN United Film Distribution, 1984, British

COREY YUEN
NO RETREAT NO SURRENDER New World, 1986, Hong Kong
NO RETREAT, NO SURRENDER II Shapiro Glickenhaus Entertainment, 1989, Hong Kong

JOHNNY YUNE
THEY STILL CALL ME BRUCE co-director with James Orr, Shapiro Entertainment, 1987

LARRY YUST*
Address: 500 S. Rossmore Avenue, Los Angeles, CA 90020, 213/934-4706
Agent: Ben Benjamin, ICM - Los Angeles, 213/550-4000

TRICK BABY Universal, 1973
HOMEBODIES Avco Embassy, 1974
TESTIMONY OF TWO MEN (TF) co-director with Leo Penn, Universal TV, 1977
"SAY YES" Cinetel, 1986

PETER YUVAL

Business: Action International Pictures, 10726 McCune
Avenue, Los Angeles, CA 90034, 213/559-8805

DEAD END CITY   Action International, 1989
TIME BURST - THE FINAL ALLIANCE   Action
International, 1989
FIREHEAD   Action International, 1990
THE SHOOTERS   Action International, 1990

BRIAN YUZNA

SOCIETY   Wild Street Pictures, 1989
THE BRIDE OF RE-ANIMATOR   Taurus Entertainment,
1990

Z

KRZYSZTOF ZANUSSI

b. July 17, 1939 - Warsaw, Poland
Agent: William Morris Agency - Beverly Hills, 213/274-7451

THE STRUCTURE OF CRYSTALS   1969, Polish
MOUNTAINS AT DUSK (TF)   1970, Polish
DIE ROLLE (TF)   1971, West German
FAMILY LIFE   1971, Polish
BEHIND THE WALL   1971, Polish
HYPOTHESIS (TF)   1972, Polish
ILLUMINATION   1973, Polish
THE CATAMOUNT KILLING   1974
NIGHT DUTY (TF)   1975, Polish
A WOMAN'S DECISION   Tinc, 1975, Polish
CAMOUFLAGE   Libra, 1977, Polish
THE SPIRAL   1978, Polish
WAYS IN THE NIGHT   TeleCulture, 1980, West German
THE CONSTANT FACTOR   New Yorker, 1980, Polish
CONTRACT   New Yorker, 1981, Polish
FROM A FAR COUNTRY (POPE JOHN PAUL II) (TF)
Trans World Film/ ITC/RAI/Film Polski, 1981,
British-Italian-Polish
IMPERATIV (TF)   TeleCulture, 1982, West German
THE UNAPPROACHABLE   TeleCulture, 1982,
West German
BLAUBART (TF)   Westdeutscher Rundfunk/DRS, 1984,
West German-Swiss
A YEAR OF THE QUIET SUN   Sandstar Releasing
Company, 1984, Polish- West German-U.S.
LE POUVOIR DU MAL   Films Moliere, 1985, French-Italian
WHEREVER YOU ARE   Mark Forstater Productions/
Gerhard Schmidt Filmproduktion/Film Polski, 1988,
British-West German- Polish
INVENTORY   Polish Film Unit TOR/Polish TV/Regina
Ziegler Filmproduktion, 1989, Polish-West German

FRANK ZAPPA

b. December 21, 1940 - Baltimore, Maryland
Address: P.O. Box 5265, North Hollywood, CA 91616
Agent: Triad Artists, Inc. - Los Angeles, 213/556-2727

200 MOTELS   co-director with Tony Palmer, United Artists,
1971, British
BABY SNAKES   Intercontinental Absurdities, 1979

JOHN ZARITSKY

b. 1943 - St-Catherines, Ontario, Canada
Business: K.A. Productions, 49 Cavell Avenue, Toronto,
Ontario M4J 1H5, Canada, 416/466-8202

JUST ANOTHER MISSING KID (TD)   1981, Canadian
TEARS ARE NOT ENOUGH (FD)   Pan-Canadian Film
Distributors, 1985, Canadian
THE REAL STUFF (TD)   K.A. Productions/Jack of Hearts
Productions/CBC, 1987, Canadian
BROKEN PROMISES (TD)   1988, Canadian
MY HUSBAND IS GOING TO KILL ME (TD)   PBS, 1988
THALIDOMIDE (TD)   1988, Canadian

FRANCO ZEFFIRELLI*

b. February 12, 1923 - Florence, Italy
Home: via Lucio Volumnio 37, Rome, Italy, 06/799441

CAMPING   1957, Italian
LA BOHEME   Warner Bros., 1965, Swiss
FLORENCE - DAYS OF DESTRUCTION (FD)
1966, Italian
THE TAMING OF THE SHREW   Columbia, 1967,
Italian-British
ROMEO AND JULIET★   Paramount, 1968, Italian-British
BROTHER SUN SISTER MOON   Paramount, 1973,
Italian-British
JESUS OF NAZARETH (MS)   Sir Lew Grade Productions/
ITC, 1978, British-Italian
THE CHAMP   MGM/United Artists, 1979
ENDLESS LOVE   Universal, 1981
I PAGLIACCI (TF)   1981, Italian
LA TRAVIATA   Universal Classics, 1982, Italian
CAVALLERIA RUSTICANA (TF)☆   1986, Italian
OTELLO   Cannon, 1986, Italian
YOUNG TOSCANINI   Carthago Films/Canal Plus/FR3/
La Sept/Italian International Pictures/RAI, 1988,
Italian-French
HAMLET   Nelson Entertainment, 1991, British

ROBERT ZEMECKIS*

b. 1952 - Chicago, Illinois
Agent: CAA - Beverly Hills, 213/288-4545

I WANNA HOLD YOUR HAND   Universal, 1977
USED CARS   Columbia, 1980
ROMANCING THE STONE   20th Century Fox, 1984
BACK TO THE FUTURE   Universal, 1985
WHO FRAMED ROGER RABBIT   Buena Vista, 1988
BACK TO THE FUTURE PART II   Universal, 1989
BACK TO THE FUTURE PART III   Universal, 1990

MAI ZETTERLING

b. May 24, 1925 - Vasteras, Sweden
Agent: Douglas Rae Management - London, 71/836-3903

LOVING COUPLES   Prominent, 1964, Swedish
NIGHT GAMES   Mondial, 1966, Swedish
DOCTOR GLAS   20th Century-Fox, 1968, Danish
THE GIRLS   New Line Cinema, 1969, Swedish
VINCENT THE DUTCHMAN   1972, Swedish
VISIONS OF EIGHT (FD)   co-director with Yuri Ozerov,
Arthur Penn, Michael Pfleghar, Kon Ichikawa, Milos
Forman, Claude Lelouch & John Schlesinger,
Cinema 5, 1973
WE HAVE MANY NAMES   1976, Swedish
STOCKHOLM (TD)   1977, Canadian

LOVE   co-director with Annette Cohen, Nancy Dowd &
   Liv Ullmann, Velvet Films, 1982, Canadian
SCRUBBERS   Orion Classics, 1983, British
AMAROSA   Sandrews/Swedish Film Institute,
   1986, Swedish

YIMOU ZHANG
(See Zhang YIMOU)

HOWARD ZIEFF*
b. 1943 - Los Angeles, California
Agent: CAA - Beverly Hills, 213/288-4545

SLITHER   MGM, 1973
HEARTS OF THE WEST   MGM/United Artists, 1975
HOUSE CALLS   Universal, 1978
THE MAIN EVENT   Warner Bros., 1979
PRIVATE BENJAMIN   Warner Bros., 1980
UNFAITHFULLY YOURS   20th Century Fox, 1984
THE DREAM TEAM   Universal, 1989

RAFAL ZIELINSKI
b. 1954 - Warsaw, Poland
Agent: Larry Becsey, The Agency - Los Angeles,
   213/551-3000

HEY BABE!   Rafal Productions/Canadian Film Development
   Corporation/L'Institut Quebecois du Cinema/Famous
   Players Ltd., 1980, Canadian
SCREWBALLS   New World, 1983, Canadian
LOOSE SCREWS   Concorde, 1985, Canadian
RECRUITS   Concorde, 1986, Canadian
VALET GIRLS   Empire Pictures, 1986
SPELLCASTER   Empire Pictures, 1987
STATE PARK   ITC, 1987, Canadian
SCREWBALL HOTEL   Universal, 1989, U.S.-British
GINGERALE AFTERNOON   Skouras Pictures, 1989
NIGHT WARRIOR   Kodiak Films, 1990

VERNON ZIMMERMAN*
Business Manager: Eric Weissmann, Weissmann, Wolff,
   Bergman, Coleman & Schulman, 9665 Wilshire Blvd. -
   Suite 900, Beverly Hills, CA 90212, 213/858-7888

DEADHEAD MILES   Paramount, 1971
UNHOLY ROLLERS   American International, 1972
FADE TO BLACK   American Cinema, 1980

MICHAEL A. ZINBERG*
Agent: Bob Broder, Broder-Kurland-Webb-Uffner -
   Los Angeles, 213/656-9262

TILL I KISSED YA (TF)   American Flyer Productions/
   Lorimar TV, 1990

ZOE ZINMAN
CITY NEWS   co-director with David Fishelson,
   Cinecom, 1983

FRED ZINNEMANN*
b. April 29, 1907 - Vienna, Austria
Office: 128 Mount Street, London W1, England, 71/499-8810
Agent: William Morris Agency - Beverly Hills, 213/274-7451

THE WAVE (FD)   co-director with Emilio Gomez Muriel,
   Strand, 1935, Mexican
KID GLOVE KILLER   MGM, 1942
EYES IN THE NIGHT   MGM, 1942
THE SEVENTH CROSS   MGM, 1944

LITTLE MR. JIM   MGM, 1946
MY BROTHER TALKS TO HORSES   MGM, 1947
THE SEARCH★   MGM, 1948, U.S.-Swiss
ACT OF VIOLENCE   MGM, 1949
THE MEN   Columbia, 1950
TERESA   MGM, 1951
HIGH NOON★   United Artists, 1952
THE MEMBER OF THE WEDDING   Columbia, 1953
FROM HERE TO ETERNITY★★   Columbia, 1953
OKLAHOMA!   Magna, 1955
A HATFUL OF RAIN   20th Century-Fox, 1957
THE NUN'S STORY★   Warner Bros., 1959
THE SUNDOWNERS★   Warner Bros., 1960
BEHOLD A PALE HORSE   Columbia, 1964
A MAN FOR ALL SEASONS★★   Columbia, 1966, British
THE DAY OF THE JACKAL   Universal, 1973,
   British-French
JULIA★   20th Century-Fox, 1977
FIVE DAYS ONE SUMMER   The Ladd Company/Warner
   Bros., 1982, British

PETER ZINNER
b. July 24, 1919 - Vienna, Austria

THE SALAMANDER   ITC, 1981, British-Italian-U.S.

JOSEPH ZITO*
b. May 14, 1946 - New York, New York
Home: 11637 Spy Glass Drive, Porter Ranch, CA 91326,
   818/366-3536
Agent: Larry Becsey, The Agency - Los Angeles,
   213/551-3000

ABDUCTION   United Film Distribution, 1981
THE PROWLER   Sandhurst Corporation, 1982
FRIDAY THE 13TH - THE FINAL CHAPTER
   Paramount, 1984
MISSING IN ACTION   Cannon, 1984
INVASION U.S.A.   Cannon, 1985
RED SCORPION   Shapiro Glickenhaus
   Entertainment, 1989

MILAN ZIUKOVIC
THE ART OF MURDER   Concorde, 1990

DAVID ZUCKER*
b. October 16, 1947 - Milwaukee, Wisconsin
Agent: CAA - Beverly Hills, 213/288-4545

AIRPLANE!   co-director with Jim Abrahams & Jerry
   Zucker, Paramount, 1980
TOP SECRET!   co-director with Jim Abrahams & Jerry
   Zucker, Paramount, 1984
RUTHLESS PEOPLE   co-director with Jim Abrahams &
   Jerry Zucker, Buena Vista, 1986
THE NAKED GUN: FROM THE FILES OF POLICE
   SQUAD!   Paramount, 1988

JERRY ZUCKER*
b. March 11, 1950 - Milwaukee, Wisconsin
Agent: CAA - Beverly Hills, 213/288-4545

AIRPLANE!   co-director with Jim Abrahams & David
   Zucker, Paramount, 1980
TOP SECRET!   co-director with Jim Abrahams & David
   Zucker, Paramount, 1984
RUTHLESS PEOPLE   co-director with Jim Abrahams &
   David Zucker, Buena Vista, 1986
GHOST   Paramount, 1990

ALBERT ZUGSMITH*
b. April 24, 1910 - Atlantic City, New Jersey
Business: Famous Players International, 1210 N. Wetherly
    Drive, Los Angeles, CA 90069, 213/275-8221

COLLEGE CONFIDENTIAL   Universal, 1960
SEX KITTENS GO TO COLLEGE   Allied Artists, 1960
THE PRIVATE LIVES OF ADAM AND EVE
    Universal, 1960
DONDI   Allied Artists, 1961
CONFESSIONS OF AN OPIUM EATER   *EVILS OF
    CHINATOWN*   Allied Artists, 1962
THE INCREDIBLE SEX REVOLUTION   1965
MOVIE STAR AMERICAN STYLE OR LSD -
    I HATE YOU   1966
ON HER BED OF ROSES   Famous Players
    International, 1966
THE VERY FRIENDLY NEIGHBORS   1969
TWO ROSES AND A GOLDEN ROD   1969

HOWARD ZUKER
(See Zack NORMAN)

FRANK ZUNIGA
(Francisco Zuniga)
b. March 20, 1936 - Gallup, New Mexico
Business: Pisces Productions, 948 N. Cahuenga Blvd. -
    Suite 212, Los Angeles, CA 90038, 213/461-6800

FURTHER ADVENTURES OF THE WILDERNESS FAMILY -
    PART 2   Pacific International, 1978
HEARTBREAKER   Monarex/Emerson Film
    Enterprises, 1983
THE GOLDEN SEAL   Samuel Goldwyn Company, 1983
WHAT COLOR IS THE WIND   Pisces Productions, 1984
STRANGE COMPANIONS (TF)   Walt Disney TV, 1987
FISTFIGHTER   Taurus Entertainment, 1989

MARCOS ZURINAGA
Contact: Puerto Rico Film Institute, P.O. Box 2350, San
    Juan, Puerto Rico, 00936

STEP AWAY   1979, Puerto Rican
LA GRAN FIESTA   Jack R. Crosby/The Frank Moreno
    Company, 1986, Puerto Rican
TANGO BAR   Beco Films/Zaga Films, 1988,
    Puerto Rican- Argentine

CHARLOTTE ZWERIN*
Home: 43 Morton Street, New York, NY 10014,
    212/645-1284

SALESMAN (FD)   co-director with Albert Maysles & David
    Maysles, Maysles Films, 1969
GIMME SHELTER (FD)   co-director with Albert Maysles &
    David Maysles, Cinema 5, 1971
RUNNING FENCE (FD)   co-director with Albert Maysles &
    David Maysles, 1977
ARSHILE GORKY (FD)   1982
DEKOONING ON DEKOONING (FD)   1983
ISLANDS (FD)   co-director with Albert Maysles & David
    Maysles, Maysles Films, 1986
HOROWITZ PLAYS MOZART (FD)   co-director with Albert
    Maysles & Susan Froemke, 1987
THELONIOUS MONK: STRAIGHT, NO CHASER (FD)
    Warner Bros., 1989
JESSYE NORMAN SINGS CARMEN (HVD)   co-director with
    Albert Maysles & Susan Froemke, Cami Video, 1989
THE FLANAGAN TOUCH (FD)   Charlotte Zwerin
    Productions, 1990

EDWARD ZWICK*
b. October 8, 1952 - Winnetka, Illinois
Agent: Jeff Berg, ICM - Los Angeles, 213/550-4000

PAPER DOLLS (TF)   Leonard Goldberg Productions, 1982
HAVING IT ALL (TF)   Hill-Mandelker Films, 1982
ABOUT LAST NIGHT...   Tri-Star, 1986
GLORY   Tri-Star, 1989

JOEL ZWICK*
Home: 18588 Linnet Street, Tarzana, CA 91356,
    818/881-8392
Agent: Irv Schechter Company - Beverly Hills, 213/278-8070

SECOND SIGHT   Warner Bros., 1989

"Movies are for me a piece of life. It isn't a job, it's everything. You can't make
them unless you're obsessed. They tend to take you over, like a spell. Even when
you're on holiday you're not really on holiday, because the characters and story
you're dealing with chase and catch you. Even when you're asleep, the tensions that
are running through the film you're naking are the tensions that enter your mind
like spirits and trap you. They guide your dreams as much as they guide your
waking. There's no escaping movies..."

PHILLIP NOYCE

HIS JOB, HIS HOME, HIS FAMILY. SOME PEOPLE WILL PAY ANYTHING FOR COCAINE.

Cocaine really is expensive. Look what it almost cost this man.

He's getting help at a Drug Rehabilitation Center. They got help from the United Way. All because the United Way got help from you.

Your single contribution helps provide therapy for a child with a learning disability, a program that sends a volunteer to do the shopping for a 79 year-old woman, and a place for a 12 year-old to toss a basketball around after school.

Or, in this case, rehabilitation for a cocaine abuser. A man who, without your help, could very well have ended up paying the ultimate price.

Ad Council

United Way

It brings out the best in all of us.

NOTABLE DIRECTORS
OF THE PAST

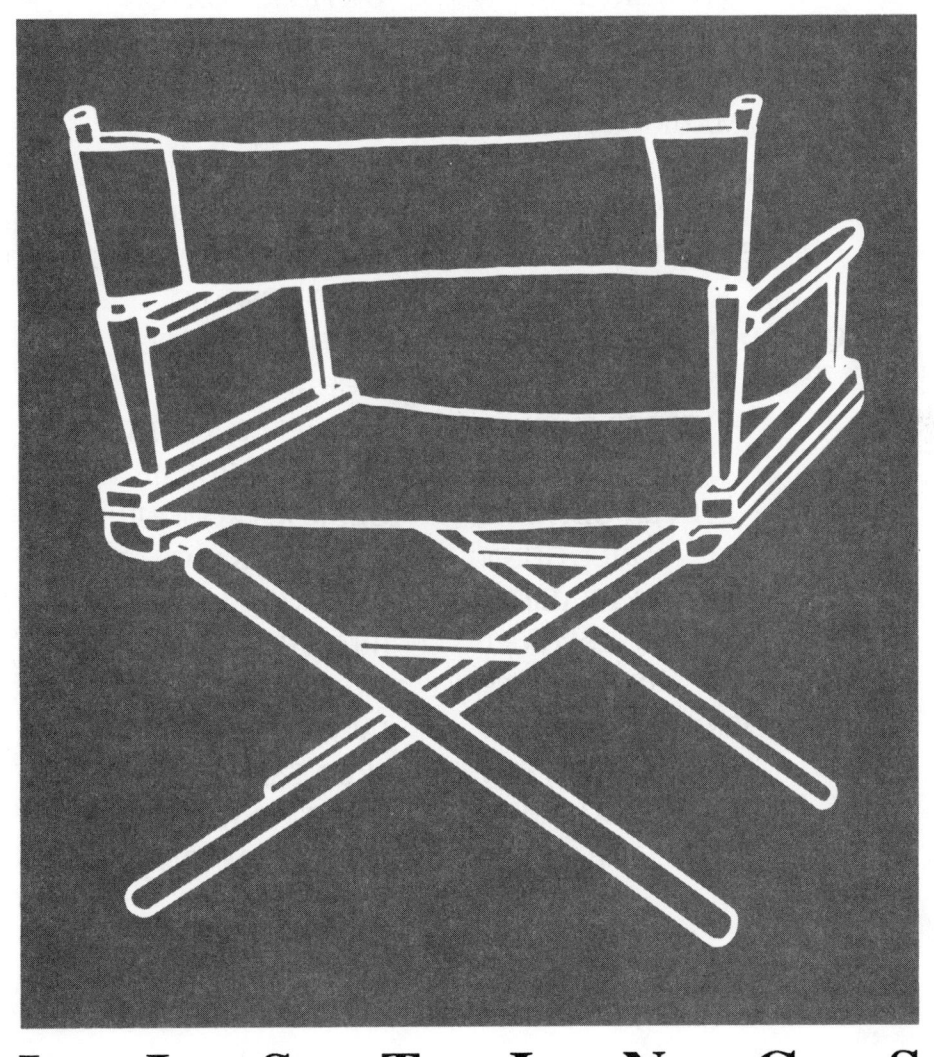

LISTINGS

IN MEMORIAM

LEM AMERO	REGINALD LE BORG
HOWARD BROOKNER	SERGIO LEONE
KARL BROWN	DAVID R. LOXTON
VITTORIO CAPRIOLI	MICHELE LUPO
ALAN CLARKE	ALEX MARCH
MAURICE CLOCHE	ULF MIEHE
BRUNO CORTINI	ARTHUR H. NADEL
MARC DANIELS	LAURENCE OLIVIER
EMILE DE ANTONIO	AMERICO ORTIZ DE ZARATE
JOHN DEXTER	GERD OSWALD
JACQUES DONIOL-VALCROZE	MICHAEL POWELL
ED EMSHWILLER	RICHARD QUINE
VICTOR FRENCH	BRUNELLO RONDI
MARC J. GASS	FREDERIC ROSSIF
STEVEN GETHERS	GEORGES ROUQUIER
BILL GUNN	LUCIANO SALCE
H. B. (TOBY) HALICKI	FRANKLIN J. SCHAFFNER
HARVEY HART	BILL SHERWOOD
JIM HENSON	R.G. SPRINGSTEEN
HERMAN HOFFMAN	JACK STARRETT
JORIS IVENS	FRED TAN
GEORGES LACOMBE	LUIS TRENKER
PHILIP LEACOCK	CHARLES MARQUIS WAREEN
CORNEL WILDE	

NOTABLE DIRECTORS
OF THE PAST

INTRODUCTION

The purpose of this section of the book is to honor the men and women of the past who left their imprints on motion picture history, from geniuses like Sergei Eisenstein and D.W. Griffith to B-movie specialists like William Beaudine and Edgar G. Ulmer. As with the main section, *Notable Directors of the Past* is selective by necessity, listing only a fraction of international filmmakers no longer living. If you feel we have excluded someone, please let us know.

Accurate information on early silent films—and even the first talkies—is sometimes extremely difficult to obtain. Different references provide different facts. There are often disagreements on year of distribution, distributors, even who directed what and with whom and, occasionally, the actual titles or alternate titles. Obviously, we would appreciate any and all corrections.

Also, running time criteria have been ignored for this section. Early films include one- and two-reelers and we could not afford to exclude these early examples of history however brief they may be.

A

ROBERT ALDRICH
b. August 9, 1918 - Cranston, Rhode Island
d. 1983

THE BIG LEAGUER   MGM, 1953
WORLD FOR RANSOM   Allied Artists, 1954
APACHE   United Artists, 1954
VERA CRUZ   United Artists, 1954
KISS ME DEADLY   United Artists, 1955
THE BIG KNIFE   United Artists, 1955
AUTUMN LEAVES   Columbia, 1956
ATTACK!   United Artists, 1956
THE ANGRY HILLS   MGM, 1959
TEN SECONDS TO HELL   United Artists, 1959, British
THE LAST SUNSET   Universal, 1961
SODOM AND GOMORRAH   20th Century-Fox, 1961,
    Italian-French-U.S.
WHAT EVER HAPPENED TO BABY JANE?   Warner
    Bros., 1962
HUSH...HUSH, SWEET CHARLOTTE   20th Century-Fox,
    1964
THE FLIGHT OF THE PHOENIX   20th Century-Fox, 1965
THE DIRTY DOZEN   MGM, 1967
THE LEGEND OF LYLAH CLARE   MGM, 1968
THE KILLING OF SISTER GEORGE   Cinerama
    Releasing Corporation, 1968
WHAT EVER HAPPENED TO AUNT ALICE?   Cinerama
    Releasing Corporation, 1968
TOO LATE THE HERO   Cinerama Releasing Corporation,
    1970
THE GRISSOM GANG   Cinerama Releasing Corporation,
    1971
ULZANA'S RAID   Universal, 1972
EMPEROR OF THE NORTH POLE   *EMPEROR OF THE
    NORTH*   20th Century-Fox, 1973
THE LONGEST YARD   Paramount, 1974
HUSTLE   Paramount, 1975
TWILIGHT'S LAST GLEAMING   Allied Artists, 1977,
    U.S.-West German
THE CHOIRBOYS   Universal, 1977
THE FRISCO KID   Warner Bros., 1979
...ALL THE MARBLES   MGM/United Artists, 1981

LEWIS ALLEN
b. December 25, 1905 - Shropshire, England
d. 1986

THE UNINVITED   Paramount, 1944
OUR HEARTS WERE YOUNG AND GAY   Paramount,
    1944
THE UNSEEN   Paramount, 1945
THOSE ENDEARING YOUNG CHARMS   RKO Radio,
    1945
THE PERFECT MARRIAGE   Paramount, 1947
THE IMPERFECT LADY   Paramount, 1947
DESERT FURY   Paramount, 1947
SO EVIL MY LOVE   Paramount, 1948
SEALED VERDICT   Paramount, 1948

CHICAGO DEADLINE   Paramount, 1949
APPOINTMENT WITH DANGER   Paramount, 1951
VALENTINO   Columbia, 1951
AT SWORD'S POINT   RKO Radio, 1952
SUDDENLY   United Artists, 1954
A BULLET FOR JOEY   United Artists, 1955
ILLEGAL   Warner Bros., 1955
ANOTHER TIME, ANOTHER PLACE   Paramount,
    1958
WHIRLPOOL   Continental, 1959, British

DOROTHY ARZNER
b. January 3, 1900 - San Francisco, California
d. 1979

FASHIONS FOR WOMEN   Paramount, 1927
TEN MODERN COMMANDMENTS   Paramount,
    1927
GET YOUR MAN   Paramount, 1927
MANHATTAN COCKTAIL   Paramount, 1928
THE WILD PARTY   Paramount, 1928
SARAH AND SON   Paramount, 1930
PARAMOUNT ON PARADE   co-director,
    Paramount, 1930
ANYBODY'S WOMAN   Paramount, 1930
HONOR AMONG LOVERS   Paramount, 1931
WORKING GIRLS   Paramount, 1931
MERRILY WE GO TO HELL   Paramount, 1932
CHRISTOPHER STRONG   RKO Radio, 1933
NANA   United Artists, 1934
CRAIG'S WIFE   Columbia, 1936
THE BRIDE WORE RED   MGM, 1937
DANCE, GIRL, DANCE   RKO Radio, 1940
FIRST COMES COURAGE   Columbia, 1943

HAL ASHBY
b. 1936 - Ogden, Utah
d. 1988

THE LANDLORD   United Artists, 1970
HAROLD AND MAUDE   Paramount, 1971
THE LAST DETAIL   Columbia, 1973
SHAMPOO   Columbia, 1975
BOUND FOR GLORY   United Artists, 1976
COMING HOME ★   United Artists, 1978
BEING THERE   United Artists, 1979
SECOND HAND HEARTS   Paramount, 1981
LOOKIN' TO GET OUT   Paramount, 1982
LET'S SPEND THE NIGHT TOGETHER (FD)
    Embassy, 1983
THE SLUGGER'S WIFE   Columbia, 1985
8 MILLION WAYS TO DIE   Tri-Star, 1986

ANTHONY ASQUITH
b. November 9, 1902 - London, England
d. 1968

SHOOTING STARS   New Era, 1928
UNDERGROUND   Pro Patria, 1928, British
THE RUNAWAY PRINCESS   VMG, 1929, German
A COTTAGE ON DARTMOOR   *ESCAPED FROM
    DARTMOOR*   Pro Patria, 1930, British
TELL ENGLAND   *THE BATTLE OF GALLIPOLI*
    co-director with Geoffrey Barkas,   Wardour, 1931,
    British
DANCE PRETTY LADY   Wardour, 1932, British
LUCKY NUMBER   Ideal, 1933, British

THE UNFINISHED SYMPHONY   co-director with
    Will Forst, Gaumont, 1934, British-German
I STAND CONDEMNED   *MOSCOW NIGHTS*
    United Artists, 1935, British
PYGMALION   co-director with Leslie Howard, MGM,
    1938, British
FRENCH WITHOUT TEARS   Paramount, 1940, British
A VOICE IN THE NIGHT   *FREEDOM RADIO*   Columbia,
    1941, British
QUIET WEDDING   Universal, 1941, British
COTTAGE TO LET   *BOMBSIGHT STOLEN*   Rank,
    1941, British
UNCENSORED   General Film Distributors, 1942, British
THE DEMI-PARADISE   *ADVENTURE FOR TWO*
    General Film Distributors, 1943, British
WE DIVE AT DAWN   General Film Distributors, 1943,
    British
WELCOME TO BRITAIN (FD)   co-director with
    Burgess Meredith, 1943, British
MAN OF EVIL   *FANNY BY GASLIGHT*   United Artists,
    1944, British
THE WAY TO THE STARS   *JOHNNY IN THE CLOUDS*
    United Artists, 1945, British
WHILE THE SUN SHINES   Pathé, 1947, British
THE WINSLOW BOY   British Lion Film Corporation,
    1948, British
THE WOMAN IN QUESTION   *FIVE ANGLES ON
    MURDER*   Columbia, 1950, British
THE BROWNING VERSION   Universal, 1951, British
THE IMPORTANCE OF BEING EARNEST   Universal,
    1952, British
PROJECT M-7   *THE NET*   Universal, 1953, British
CHANCE MEETING   *THE YOUNG LOVERS*
    Pacemaker Pictures, 1954, British
COURT MARTIAL   *CARRINGTON, V.C.*   Kingsley
    International, 1955, British
ORDERS TO KILL   United Motion Picture Organization,
    1958, British
THE DOCTOR'S DILEMMA   MGM, 1958, British
LIBEL   MGM, 1959, British
THE MILLIONAIRESS   20th Century-Fox, 1960,
    British
TWO LIVING, ONE DEAD   Emerson Films, 1961,
    British-Swedish
GUNS OF DARKNESS   Warner Bros., 1962, British
THE V.I.P.'S   MGM, 1963, British-U.S.
AN EVENING WITH THE ROYAL BALLET (FD)
    co-director with Anthony Havelock-Allan, Sigma III,
    1964, British
THE YELLOW ROLLS-ROYCE   MGM, 1965, British

ARAM AVAKIAN

b. New York, New York
d. 1987

LAD: A DOG   co-director with Leslie H. Martinson,
    Warner Bros., 1961
END OF THE ROAD   Allied Artists, 1970
COPS AND ROBBERS   United Artists, 1973
11 HARROWHOUSE   20th Century-Fox, 1974, British

B

LLOYD BACON

b. January 16, 1890 - San Jose, California
d. 1955

BROKEN HEARTS OF HOLLYWOOD   Warner Bros.,
    1926
PRIVATE IZZY MURPHY   Warner Bros., 1926
FINGER PRINTS   Warner Bros., 1927
WHITE FLANNELS   Warner Bros., 1927
THE HEART OF MARYLAND   Warner Bros., 1927
A SAILOR'S SWEETHEART   Warner Bros., 1927
BRASS KNUCKLES   Warner Bros., 1927
PAY AS YOU ENTER   Warner Bros., 1928
THE LION AND THE MOUSE   Warner Bros., 1928
WOMEN THEY TALK ABOUT   Warner Bros., 1928
THE SINGING FOOL   Warner Bros., 1928
STARK MAD   Warner Bros., 1929
NO DEFENSE   Warner Bros., 1929
HONKY TONK   Warner Bros., 1929
SAY IT WITH SONGS   Warner Bros., 1929
SO LONG LETTY   Warner Bros., 1929
THE OTHER TOMORROW   First National, 1930
SHE COULDN'T SAY NO   Warner Bros., 1930
A NOTORIOUS AFFAIR   First National, 1930
MOBY DICK   Warner Bros., 1930
THE OFFICE WIFE   Warner Bros., 1930
SIT TIGHT   Warner Bros., 1931
KEPT HUSBANDS   RKO, 1931
FIFTY MILLION FRENCHMEN   Warner Bros., 1931
GOLD DUST GERTIE   Warner Bros., 1931
HONOR OF THE FAMILY   First National, 1931
MANHATTAN PARADE   Warner Bros., 1932
FIREMAN SAVE MY CHILD   First National, 1932
THE FAMOUS FERGUSON CASE   First National,
    1932
ALIAS THE DOCTOR   co-director with Michael Curtiz,
    Warner Bros., 1932
MISS PINKERTON   First National, 1932
CROONER   First National, 1932
YOU SAID A MOUTHFUL   First National, 1932
42ND STREET   Warner Bros., 1933
PICTURE SNATCHER   Warner Bros., 1933
MARY STEVENS, M.D.   Warner Bros., 1933
FOOTLIGHT PARADE   Warner Bros., 1933
SON OF A SAILOR   First National, 1933
WONDER BAR   First National, 1934
A VERY HONORABLE GUY   First National, 1934
HE WAS HER MAN   Warner Bros., 1934
HERE COMES THE NAVY   Warner Bros., 1934
SIX-DAY BIKE RIDER   Warner Bros., 1934
DEVIL DOGS OF THE AIR   Warner Bros., 1935
IN CALIENTE   First National, 1935
BROADWAY GONDOLIER   Warner Bros., 1935
THE IRISH IN US   Warner Bros., 1935
FRISCO KID   Warner Bros., 1935
SONS O'GUNS   Warner Bros., 1936
CAIN AND MABEL   Warner Bros., 1936
GOLD DIGGERS OF 1937   Warner Bros., 1936
MARKED WOMAN   Warner Bros., 1937
EVER SINCE EVE   Warner Bros., 1937

SAN QUENTIN   Warner Bros., 1937
SUBMARINE D-1   First National, 1937
A SLIGHT CASE OF MURDER   Warner Bros., 1938
COWBOY FROM BROOKLYN   Warner Bros., 1938
RACKET BUSTERS   Warner Bros., 1938
BOY MEETS GIRL   Warner Bros., 1938
WINGS OF THE NAVY   Warner Bros., 1939
THE OKLAHOMA KID   Warner Bros., 1939
INDIANAPOLIS SPEEDWAY   Warner Bros., 1939
ESPIONAGE AGENT   Warner Bros., 1939
A CHILD IS BORN   Warner Bros., 1940
INVISIBLE STRIPES   Warner Bros., 1940
THREE CHEERS FOR THE IRISH   Warner Bros., 1940
BROTHER ORCHID   Warner Bros., 1940
KNUTE ROCKNE - ALL AMERICAN   Warner Bros.,
   1940
HONEYMOON FOR THREE   Warner Bros., 1941
FOOTSTEPS IN THE DARK   Warner Bros., 1941
AFFECTIONATELY YOURS   Warner Bros., 1941
NAVY BLUES   Warner Bros., 1941
LARCENY INC.   Warner Bros., 1941
WINGS FOR THE EAGLE   Warner Bros., 1941
SILVER QUEEN   Warner Bros., 1942
ACTION IN THE NORTH ATLANTIC   Warner Bros.,
   1943
THE SULLIVANS   20th Century-Fox, 1944
SUNDAY DINNER FOR A SOLDIER   20th Century-Fox,
   1944
CAPTAIN EDDIE   20th Century-Fox, 1945
HOME SWEET HOMICIDE   20th Century-Fox, 1946
WAKE UP AND DREAM   20th Century-Fox, 1946
I WONDER WHO'S KISSING HER NOW   20th Century-
   Fox, 1947
YOU WERE MEANT FOR ME   20th Century-Fox, 1948
GIVE MY REGARDS TO BROADWAY   20th Century-Fox,
   1948
DON'T TRUST YOUR HUSBAND   AN INNOCENT
   AFFAIR   United Artists, 1948
MOTHER IS A FRESHMAN   20th Century-Fox, 1949
IT HAPPENS EVERY SPRING   20th Century-Fox, 1949
MISS GRANT TAKES RICHMOND   Columbia, 1949
KILL THE UMPIRE   Columbia, 1950
THE GOOD HUMOR MAN   Columbia, 1950
THE FULLER BRUSH GIRL   Columbia, 1950
CALL ME MISTER   20th Century-Fox, 1951
THE FROGMEN   20th Century-Fox, 1951
GOLDEN GIRL   20th Century-Fox, 1951
THE I DON'T CARE GIRL   20th Century-Fox, 1953
THE GREAT SIOUX UPRISING   Universal, 1953
WALKING MY BABY BACK HOME   Universal, 1953
THE FRENCH LINE   RKO Radio, 1953
SHE COULDN'T SAY NO   RKO Radio, 1953

LIONEL BARRYMORE
(Lionel Blythe)
b. April 29, 1878 - Philadelphia, Pennsylvania
d. 1954

LIFE'S WHIRLPOOL   1917
MADAME X ★   MGM, 1929
HIS GLORIOUS NIGHT   MGM, 1929
THE UNHOLY NIGHT   MGM, 1929
THE ROGUE SONG   MGM, 1930
TEN CENTS A DANCE   MGM, 1931

MARIO BAVA
b. July 31, 1914 - San Remo, Italy
d. 1980

BLACK SUNDAY   *LA MASCHERA DEL DEMONIO*
   American International, 1960, Italian
ERIK THE CONQUEROR   *GLI INVASORI/FURY
   OF THE VIKINGS*   American International, 1961,
   Italian-French
HERCULES IN THE HAUNTED WORLD   *ERCOLE
   AL CENTRO DELLA TERRA*   Woolner Brothers, 1961,
   Italian
EVIL EYE   *LA RAGAZZA CHE SAPEVE TROPPO*
   American International, 1963, Italian
WHAT!   *LA FRUSTA E IL CORPO*   Futuramic Releasing
   Organization, 1963, Italian-French-British
BLACK SABBATH   *I TRE VOLTI DELLA PAURA*
   American International, 1963, U.S.-French-Italian
BLOOD AND BLACK LACE   *SEI DONNE PER
   L'ASSASSINO*   Allied Artists, 1964, Italian-French-
   Monocan
LA STRADA PER FORT ALAMO   1965, Italian
RAFFICA DI COLTELLI   1965, Italian
PLANET OF THE VAMPIRES   *PLANET OF BLOOD/
   TERRORE NELLO SPAZIO*   American International,
   1965, Italian-Spanish-U.S.
KILL BABY KILL   *OPERAZIONE PAURA*
   Europix-Consolidated, 1966, Italian
DR. GOLDFOOT AND THE GIRL BOMBS   *LE SPIE
   VENGONO DAL SEMIFREDDO*   American
   International, 1966, U.S.-Italian
KNIVES OF THE AVENGER   1967, Italian
DANGER: DIABOLIK   Paramount, 1967, Italian-French
CINQUE BAMBOLE PER LA LUNA DI AGOSTO
   1967, Italian
ROY COLT E WINCHESTER JACK   1970, Italian
HATCHET FOR THE HONEYMOON   *IL ROSSO
   SEGNO DELLA FOLLIA/UN'ACCETTA
   PER LA LUNA DI MIELE*   GGP, 1970, Italian-Spanish
ECOLOGIA DEL DELITTO   1970, Italian
ANTEFATTO   1971, Italian
BARON BLOOD   *GLI ORRORI DEL CASTELLO
   DE NORIMBERGA*   American International, 1972,
   Italian-West German
REAZIONE A CATENA   1973, Italian
QUANTE VOLTE...QUELLA NOTTE   1973, Italian
IL DIAVOLO E IL MORTO   1974, Italian
SHOCK   1977, Italian
BABY KONG   1977, Italian
LA VENERE DELL'ILLE   1979, Italian

WILLIAM BEAUDINE
b. January 15, 1892 - New York, New York
d. 1970

ALMOST A KING   1915
A BAD LITTLE GOOD MAN   1917
WATCH YOUR STEP   Goldwyn, 1922
CATCH MY SMOKE   1922
HEROES OF THE STREET   Warner Bros., 1922
HER FATAL MILLIONS   Metro, 1923
PENROD AND SAM   First National, 1923
THE PRINTER'S DEVIL   1923
THE COUNTRY KID   Warner Bros., 1923
BOY OF MINE   First National, 1923
DARING YOUTH   Principal, 1924
DAUGHTERS OF PLEASURE   Principal, 1924
WANDERING HUSBANDS   Producers Distributing
   Corporation, 1924

A SELF-MADE FAILURE First National, 1924
CORNERED Warner Bros., 1924
LOVER'S LANE Warner Bros., 1924
THE NARROW STREET Warner Bros., 1924
A BROADWAY BUTTERFLY Warner Bros., 1925
LITTLE ANNIE ROONEY United Artists, 1925
THAT'S MY BABY Paramount, 1926
THE SOCIAL HIGHWAYMAN Pearless-World, 1926
SPARROWS United Artists, 1926
THE CANADIAN Paramount, 1926
FRISCO SALLY LEVY MGM, 1927
THE LIFE OF RILEY First National, 1927
THE IRRESISTABLE LOVER Universal, 1927
THE COHENS AND THE KELLYS IN PARIS Universal, 1928
HEART TO HEART First National, 1928
HOME JAMES Universal, 1928
DO YOUR DUTY First National, 1928
GIVE AND TAKE Universal, 1928
FUGITIVES Fox, 1929
TWO WEEKS OFF First National, 1929
THE GIRL FROM WOOLWORTH'S First National, 1929
WEDDING RINGS First National, 1929
THOSE WHO DANCE Warner Bros., 1930
THE ROAD TO PARADISE Warner Bros., 1930
FATHER'S SON Warner Bros., 1931
THE LADY WHO DARED Warner Bros., 1931
THE MAD PARADE Paramount, 1931
PENROD AND SAM Warner Bros., 1931
MISBEHAVING LADIES Warner Bros., 1931
THE MEN IN HER LIFE Columbia, 1931
THREE WISE GIRLS Columbia, 1932
MAKE ME A STAR Paramount, 1932
CRIME OF THE CENTURY Paramount, 1933
HER BODYGUARD Paramount, 1933
THE OLD FASHIONED WAY Paramount, 1934
DANDY DICK BIP, 1934, British
TWO HEARTS IN HARMONY Wardour, 1935, British
BOYS WILL BE BOYS First National, 1935, British
MR. COHEN TAKES A WIFE Warner Bros., 1935, British
IT'S IN THE BAG Warner Bros., 1936, British
WHERE THERE'S A WILL First National, 1936, British
WINDBAG THE SAILOR Gaumont-British, 1936, British
EDUCATED EVANS First National, 1936
SAID O'REILLY TO McNAB SEZ O'REILLY TO McNAB Gaumont-British, 1937, British
TAKE IT FROM ME First National, 1937, British
FEATHER YOUR NEST Associated British Film Distributors, 1937, British
TORCHY GETS HER MAN Warner Bros., 1938
TORCHY BLANE IN CHINATOWN Warner Bros., 1939
MISBEHAVING HUSBANDS PRC, 1940
FEDERAL FUGITIVES PRC, 1941
EMERGENCY LANDING PRC, 1941
DESPERATE CARGO PRC, 1941
DUKE OF THE NAVY PRC, 1942
THE BROADWAY BIG SHOT Monogram, 1942
THE PANTHER'S CLAW PRC, 1942
THE MIRACLE KID PRC, 1942
MEN OF SAN QUENTIN PRC, 1942
GALLANT LADY PRC, 1942
ONE THRILLING NIGHT Monogram, 1942
THE PHANTOM KILLER Monogram, 1942
FOREIGN AGENT Monogram, 1942
THE LIVING GHOST Monogram, 1942
CLANCY STREET BOYS Monogram, 1943
THE APE MAN Monogram, 1943
SPOTLIGHT SCANDALS Monogram, 1943
HERE COMES KELLY Monogram, 1943
THE MYSTERY OF THE 13TH GUEST Monogram, 1943

WHAT A MAN! Monogram, 1944
VOODOO MAN Monogram, 1944
HOT RHYTHM Monogram, 1944
DETECTIVE KITTY O'DAY Monogram, 1944
FOLLOW THE LEADER Monogram, 1944
LEAVE IT TO THE IRISH Monogram, 1944
OH, WHAT A NIGHT! Monogram, 1944
SHADOW OF SUSPICION Monogram, 1944
BOWERY CHAMPS Monogram, 1944
CRAZY KNIGHTS Monogram, 1944
FASHION MODEL Monogram, 1945
COME OUT FIGHTING Monogram, 1945
BLONDE RANSOM Universal, 1945
SWINGIN' ON A RAINBOW Republic, 1945
BLACK MARKET BABIES Monogram, 1945
THE SHADOW RETURNS 1946
THE FACE OF MARBLE Monogram, 1946
DON'T GAMBLE WITH STRANGERS Monogram, 1946
SPOOK BUSTERS Monogram, 1946
BELOW THE DEADLINE Monogram, 1946
MR. HEX Monogram, 1946
PHILO VANCE RETURNS Producers Releasing Corporation, 1947
HARD-BOILED MAHONEY Monogram, 1947
TOO MANY WINNERS PRC, 1947
KILLER AT LARGE PRC, 1947
NEWS HOUNDS Monogram, 1947
GAS HOUSE KIDS GO WEST PRC, 1947
BOWERY BUCKAROOS Monogram, 1947
THE CHINESE RING THE RED HORNET Monogram, 1947
ANGEL'S ALLEY Monogram, 1948
JINX MONEY Monogram, 1948
JIGGS AND MAGGIE IN COURT co-director with Edward F. Cline, Monogram, 1948
THE SHANGHAI CHEST Monogram, 1948
THE GOLDEN EYE Monogram, 1948
KIDNAPPED Monogram, 1948
SMUGGLERS' COVE Monogram, 1948
THE FEATHERED SERPENT Monogram, 1948
INCIDENT Monogram, 1948
TUNA CLIPPER Monogram, 1949
FORGOTTEN WOMEN Monogram, 1949
TRAIL OF THE YUKON 1949
TOUGH ASSIGNMENT Lippert, 1949
BLUE GRASS OF KENTUCKY Monogram, 1950
JUGGS AND MAGGIE OUT WEST Monogram, 1950
COUNTY FAIR Monogram, 1950
THE PRINCE OF PEACE THE LAWTON STORY co-director with Harold Daniels, Hallmark Productions, 1951
BOWERY BATALLION Monogram, 1951
CUBAN FIREBALL Republic, 1951
GHOST CHASERS Monogram, 1951
LET'S GO NAVY! Monogram, 1951
HAVANA ROSE Republic, 1951
RODEO Monogram, 1952
JET JOB Monogram, 1952
HERE COME THE MARINES! Monogram, 1952
THE ROSE BOWL STORY Monogram, 1952
YUKON GOLD Allied Artists, 1953
JALOPY Allied Artists, 1952
ROAR OF THE CROWD Allied Artists, 1953
MURDER WITHOUT TEARS Allied Artists, 1953
YUKON VENGEANCE Allied Artists, 1954
PARIS PLAYBOYS Allied Artists, 1954
PRIDE OF THE BLUE GRASS Allied Artists, 1954
HIGH SOCIETY Allied Artists, 1955
JAIL BUSTERS Allied Artists, 1955
MOM AND DAD Hygienic Productions, 1957, filmed in 1944

IN THE MONEY   Allied Artists, 1957
WESTWARD HO THE WAGONS!   Buena Vista, 1957
TEN WHO DARED   Buena Vista, 1960
LASSIE'S GREATEST ADVENTURE   20th Century-Fox,
   1963, originally filmed for television
BILLY THE KID VS. DRACULA   Embassy, 1966
JESSE JAMES MEETS FRANKENSTEIN'S DAUGHTER
   Embassy, 1966

HARRY BEAUMONT

b. February 10, 1888 - Abilene, Kansas
d. 1966

THE CALL OF THE CITY   Essanay, 1915
TRUANT SOULS   Essanay, 1917
SKINNER'S DRESS SUIT   Essanay, 1917
SKINNER'S BUBBLE   Essanay, 1917
SKINNER'S BABY   Essanay, 1917
BURNING THE CANDLE   Essanay, 1917
FILLING HIS OWN SHOES   Essanay, 1917
BROWN OF HARVARD   Essanay, 1918
THIRTY A WEEK   Goldwyn, 1918
LITLE ROWDY   Triangle, 1919
WILD GOOSE CHASE   Triangle, 1919
A MAN AND HIS MONEY   Goldwyn, 1919
GO WEST YOUNG MAN   Goldwyn, 1919
ONE OF THE FINEST   Goldwyn, 1919
THE CITY OF COMRADES   Goldwyn, 1919
HEARTSEASE   Goldwyn, 1919
LORD AND LADY ALGY   Goldwyn, 1919
TOBY'S BOW   Goldwyn, 1919
THE GAY LORD QUEX   Goldwyn, 1919
THE GREAT ACCIDENT   Goldwyn, 1920
DOLLARS AND SENSE   Goldwyn, 1920
GOING SOME   Goldwyn, 1920
STOP THIEF!   Goldwyn, 1920
OFFICER 666   Goldwyn, 1920
THE FOURTEENTH LOVER   Metro, 1922
GLASS HOUSES   Metro, 1922
THE RAGGED HEIRESS   Fox, 1922
VERY TRULY YOURS   Fox, 1922
SEEING'S BELIEVING   Metro, 1922
THE FIVE DOLLAR BABY,   Metro, 1922
LIGHTS OF THE DESERT   Fox, 1922
THEY LIKE 'EM ROUGH   Metro, 1922
JUNE MADNESS   Metro, 1922
LOVE IN THE DARK   Metro, 1922
CRINOLINE AND ROMANCE   Metro, 1923
A NOISE IN NEWBORO   Metro, 1923
MAIN STREET   Warner Bros., 1923
THE GOLD DIGGERS   Warner Bros., 1923
BEAU BRUMMEL   Warner Bros., 1924
DON'T DOUBT YOUR HUSBAND   MGM, 1924
BABBITT   Warner Bros., 1924
THE LOVER OF CAMILLE   Warner Bros., 1924
A LOST LADY   Warner Bros., 1924
RECOMPENSE   Warner Bros., 1925
HIS MAJESTY BUNKER BEAN   Warner Bros., 1925
ROSE OF THE WORLD   Warner Bros., 1925
SANDY   Fox, 1926
WOMANPOWER   Fox, 1926
ONE INCREASING PURPOSE   Fox, 1927
FORBIDDEN HOURS   MGM, 1928
OUR DANCING DAUGHTERS   MGM, 1928
A SINGLE MAN   MGM, 1929
THE BROADWAY MELODY ★   MGM, 1929
SPEEDWAY   MGM, 1929
LORD BYRON OF BROADWAY   co-director with
   William Nigh, MGM, 1930
CHILDREN OF PLEASURE   MGM, 1930

THE FLORADORA GIRL   MGM, 1930
OUR BLUSHING BRIDES   MGM, 1930
THOSE THREE FRENCH GIRLS   MGM, 1930
DANCE FOOLS DANCE   MGM, 1931
LAUGHING SINNERS   MGM, 1931
THE GREAT LOVER   MGM, 1931
WEST OF BROADWAY   MGM, 1931
ARE YOU LISTENING?   MGM, 1932
UNASHAMED   MGM, 1932
FAITHLESS   MGM, 1932
MADE ON BROADWAY   MGM, 1933
WHEN LADIES MEET   MGM, 1933
SHOULD LADIES BEHAVE?   MGM, 1933
MURDER IN THE PRIVATE CAR   MGM, 1934
ENCHANTED APRIL   RKO, 1935
THE GIRL ON THE FRONT PAGE   Universal, 1936
WHEN'S YOUR BIRTHDAY?   RKO, 1937
MAISIE GOES TO RENO   MGM, 1944
TWICE BLESSED   MGM, 1945
UP GOES MAISIE   MGM, 1946
THE SHOW-OFF   MGM, 1946
UNDERCOVER MAISIE   MGM, 1947
ALIAS A GENTLEMAN   MGM, 1948

COMPTON BENNETT
(Robert Compton-Bennett)

b. January 15, 1900 - Tunbridge Wells, England
d. 1974

FIND, FIX AND STRIKE (FD)   1942, British
MEN OF ROCHDALE (FD)   1944, British
THE SEVENTH VEIL   Universal, 1945, British
THE YEARS BETWEEN   Universal, 1946, British
DAYBREAK   Rank, 1947, British
MY OWN TRUE LOVE   Paramount, 1949
THAT FORSYTE WOMAN   MGM, 1949
KING SOLOMON'S MINES   MGM, 1950
IT STARTED IN PARADISE   Astor, 1952, British
SO LITTLE TIME   MacDonald, 1952, British
DESPERATE MOMENT   Universal, 1953, British
GLORY AT SEA   *THE GIFT HORSE*   M&A Alexander,
   1952, British
AFTER THE BALL   Romulus Films, 1957, British
CITY AFTER MIDNIGHT   *THAT WOMAN OPPOSITE*
   RKO Radio, 1957, British
MAILBAG ROBBERY   *THE FLYING SCOT*
   Tudor Pictures, 1957, British
BEYOND THE CURTAIN   Rank, 1960, British
HOW TO UNDRESS IN PUBLIC WITHOUT UNDUE
   EMBARRASSMENT   1965, British

BUSBY BERKELEY
(William Berkeley Enos)

b. November 29, 1895 - Los Angeles, California
d. 1976

SHE HAD TO SAY YES   co-director with George
   Amy, First National, 1933
GOLD DIGGERS OF 1935   First National, 1935
BRIGHT LIGHTS   First National, 1935
I LIVE FOR LOVE   First National, 1935
STAGE STRUCK   First National, 1936
THE GO-GETTER   Warner Bros., 1937
HOLLYWOOD HOTEL   Warner Bros., 1937
MEN ARE SUCH FOOLS   Warner Bros., 1938
GARDEN OF THE MOON   Warner Bros., 1938
COMET OVER BROADWAY   Warner Bros., 1938
THEY MADE ME A CRIMINAL   Warner Bros., 1939

BABES IN ARMS   MGM, 1939
FAST AND FURIOUS   MGM, 1939
STRIKE UP THE BAND   MGM, 1940
FORTY LITTLE MOTHERS   MGM, 1940
BLONDE INSPIRATION   MGM, 1941
BABES ON BROADWAY   MGM, 1941
FOR ME AND MY GAL   MGM, 1942
THE GANG'S ALL HERE   20th Century-Fox, 1943
CINDERELLA JONES   Warner Bros., 1946
TAKE ME OUT TO THE BALL GAME   MGM, 1949

CURTIS BERNHARDT
(Kurt Bernhardt)
b. April 15, 1899 - Worms, Germany
d. 1981

QUALEN DER NACHT   1926, German
DIE WAISE VON LOWOOD   1926, German
KINDERSEELEN KLAGEN AN   1927, German
DAS MADCHEN MIT DEN FUNF NULLEN   1927,
   German
SCHINDERHANNES   THE PRINCE OF ROGUES
   1927, German
DAS LETZTE FORT   1928, German
DIE FRAU NACH DER MANN SICH SEHNT   THREE
   LOVES   1929, German
DIE LEZTE KOMPANIE   13 MEN AND A GIRL
   1930, German
DER MANN DER DEN MORD BEGING   1931,
   German
DER REBELL   co-director with Luis Trenker,
   1932, German
DER GROSSE RAUSCH   1932, German
DER TUNNEL   1933, German
L'OR DANS LA RUE   1934, French
THE BELOVED VAGABOND   1934, British
CARREFOUR   1938, French
NUIT DE DECEMBRE   1939, French
MY LOVE CAME BACK   Warner Bros., 1940
LADY WITH RED HAIR   Warner Bros., 1940
MILLION DOLLAR BABY   Warner Bros., 1941
JUKE GIRL   Warner Bros., 1942
HAPPY GO LUCKY   Paramount, 1943
CONFLICT   Warner Bros., 1945
MY REPUTATION   Warner Bros., 1946
DEVOTION   Warner Bros., 1946
A STOLEN LIFE   Warner Bros., 1946
POSSESSED   Warner Bros., 1947
HIGH WALL   MGM, 1948
THE DOCTOR AND THE GIRL   MGM, 1949
PAYMENT ON DEMAND   RKO Radio, 1951
SIROCCO   Columbia, 1951
THE BLUE VEIL   RKO Radio, 1951
THE MERRY WIDOW   MGM, 1952
MISS SADIE THOMPSON   Columbia, 1954
BEAU BRUMMEL   MGM, 1954
INTERRUPTED MELODY   MGM, 1955
GABY   MGM, 1956
STEPHANIE IN RIO   Casino, 1960, West German
DAMON AND PYTHIAS   IL TIRANO DI SIRACUSA
   MGM, 1962, Italian-U.S.
KISSES FOR MY PRESIDENT   Warner Bros., 1964

HERBERT J. BIBERMAN
d. March 4, 1900 - Philadelphia, Pennsylvania
d. 1971

ONE-WAY TICKET   Columbia, 1935

MEET NERO WOLFE   Columbia, 1936
KING OF CHINATOWN   Paramount, 1939
THE MASTER RACE   RKO Radio, 1944
SALT OF THE EARTH   Independent Productions, 1954
SLAVES   Continental, 1969

RICHARD BOLESLAWSKI
(Ryszard Srzednicki Boleslawsky)
b. February 4, 1889 - Warsaw, Poland
d. 1937

TRI VSTRECHI   1915, Russian
BREAD   co-director with Boris Suskevich, 1918, Soviet
THE MIRACLE OF THE VISTULA   1921, Polish
THE LAST OF THE LONE WOLF   Columbia, 1930
THE GAY DIPLOMAT   RKO, 1931
WOMAN PURSUED   RKO, 1931
RASPUTIN AND THE EMPRESS   MGM, 1933
STORM AT DAYBREAK   MGM, 1933
BEAUTY FOR SALE   MGM, 1933
FUGITIVE LOVERS   MGM, 1934
MEN IN WHITE   MGM, 1934
OPERATOR 13   MGM, 1934
THE PAINTED VEIL   MGM, 1934
CLIVE OF INDIA   20th Century-Fox, 1935
LES MISERABLES   20th Century-Fox, 1935
O'SHAUGHNESSY'S BOY   MGM, 1935
METROPOLITAN   20th Century-Fox, 1935
THREE GODFATHERS   MGM, 1936
THEODORA GOES WILD   Columbia, 1936
THE GARDEN OF ALLAH   United Artists, 1936
THE LAST OF MRS. CHEYNEY   co-director with
   George Fitzmaurice, MGM, 1937

FRANK BORZAGE
b. April 23, 1893 - Salt Lake City, Utah
d. 1962

THAT GAL OF BURKE'S   1916
MAMMY'S ROSE   co-director with James Douglass, 1916
LIFE'S HARMONY   co-director with Lorimer Johnson, 1916
THE SILKEN SPIDER   1916
THE CODE OF HONOR   1916
NELL DALE'S MEN FOLKS   1916
THE FORGOTTEN PRAYER   1916
THE COURTIN' OF CALLIOPE CLEW   1916
NUGGET JIM'S PARDNER   1916
THE DEMON OF FEAR   1916
LAND O' LIZARDS   SILENT SHELBY   Mutual, 1916
IMMEDIATE LEE   HAIR TRIGGER CASEY   Mutual, 1916
ENCHANTMENT   1916
THE PRIDE AND THE MAN   1916
DOLLARS OF DROSS   1916
WEE LADY BETTY   co-director with Charles Miller, 1917
FLYING COLORS   Triangle, 1917
UNTIL THEY GET ME   Triangle, 1917
THE ATOM   1918
THE GUN WOMAN   Triangle, 1918
THE SHOES THAT DANCED   Triangle, 1918
INNOCENT'S PROGRESS   Triangle, 1918
AN HONEST MAN   Triangle, 1918
SOCIETY FOR SALE   Triangle, 1918
WHO IS TO BLAME?   Triangle, 1918
THE GHOST FLOWER   Triangle, 1918
THE CURSE OF IKU   Essanay, 1918
TOTON   Triangle, 1919
PRUDENCE OF BROADWAY   Triangle, 1919
WHOM THE GODS DESTROY   First National, 1919

ASHES OF DESIRE   1919
HUMORESQUE   Paramount, 1920
THE DUKE OF CHIMNEY BUTTE   Federated, 1921
GET-RICH-QUICK WALLINGFORD   Paramount, 1921
BACK PAY   Paramount, 1922
BILLY JIM   Film Booking Offices, 1922
THE GOOD PROVIDER   Paramount, 1922
THE VALLEY OF SILENT MEN   Paramount, 1922
THE PRIDE OF PALOMAR   Paramount, 1922
THE NTH COMMANDMENT   Paramount, 1923
CHILDREN OF THE DUST   Associated First National, 1923
AGE OF DESIRE   Associated First National, 1923
SECRETS   First National, 1924
THE LADY   First National, 1925
DADDY'S GONE A-HUNTING   Metro-Goldwyn, 1925
LAZYBONES   Fox, 1925
WAGES FOR WIVES   Fox, 1925
THE CIRCLE   Metro-Goldwyn, 1925
THE FIRST YEAR   Fox, 1926
THE DIXIE MERCHANT   Fox, 1926
EARLY TO WED   Fox, 1926
MARRIAGE LICENSE?   Fox, 1926
SEVENTH HEAVEN ★★   Fox, 1927
STREET ANGEL   Fox, 1928
THE RIVER   Fox, 1929
LUCKY STAR   Fox, 1929
THEY HAD TO SEE PARIS   Fox, 1929
SONG O' MY HEART   Fox, 1930
LILIOM   Fox, 1930
DOCTORS' WIVES   Fox, 1930
YOUNG AS YOU FEEL   Fox, 1931
BAD GIRL ★★   Fox, 1931
AFTER TOMORROW   Fox, 1932
YOUNG AMERICA   Fox, 1932
A FAREWELL TO ARMS   Paramount, 1932
SECRETS   United Artists, 1933
A MAN'S CASTLE   Columbia, 1933
NO GREATER GLORY   Columbia, 1934
LITTLE MAN, WHAT NOW?   Universal, 1934
FLIRTATION WALK   First National, 1934
LIVING ON VELVET   First National, 1935
STRANDED   Warner Bros., 1935
SHIPMATES FOREVER   First National, 1935
DESIRE   Paramount, 1936
HEARTS DIVIDED   First National, 1936
GREEN LIGHT   Warner Bros., 1937
HISTORY IS MADE AT NIGHT   United Artists, 1937
BIG CITY   MGM, 1937
MANNEQUIN   MGM, 1937
THREE COMRADES   MGM, 1938
THE SHINING HOUR   MGM, 1938
DISPUTED PASSAGE   Paramount, 1939
STRANGE CARGO   MGM, 1940
THE MORTAL STORM   MGM, 1940
FLIGHT COMMAND   MGM, 1940
SMILIN' THROUGH   MGM, 1941
THE VANISHING VIRGINIAN   MGM, 1942
SEVEN SWEETHEARTS   MGM, 1942
STAGE DOOR CANTEEN   United Artists, 1943
HIS BUTLER'S SISTER   Universal, 1943
TILL WE MEET AGAIN   Paramount, 1944
THE SPANISH MAIN   RKO Radio, 1945
I'VE ALWAYS LOVED YOU   Republic, 1946
THE MAGNIFICENT DOLL   Universal, 1946
THAT'S MY MAN   Republic, 1947
MOONRISE   Republic, 1948
CHINA DOLL   United Artists, 1958
THE BIG FISHERMAN   Buena Vista, 1959

JOHN BOULTING

b. November 21, 1913 - Bray, Buckinghamshire, England
d. 1985

JOURNEY TOGETHER   RKO Radio, 1945, British
YOUNG SCARFACE   *BRIGHTON ROCK*   Mayer-Kingsley, 1947, British
SEVEN DAYS TO NOON   Mayer-Kingsley, 1950, British
THE MAGIC BOX   Rank, 1952, British
CREST OF THE WAVE   *SEAGULLS OVER SORRENTO* co-director with Roy Boulting, MGM, 1954, British
PRIVATE'S PROGRESS   DCA, 1956, British
LUCKY JIM   Kingsley International, 1957, British
I'M ALL RIGHT, JACK   Columbia, 1960, British
THE RISK   *SUSPECT*   co-director with Roy Boulting, Kingsley International, 1961, British
HEAVENS ABOVE!   Janus, 1963, British
ROTTEN TO THE CORE   Cinema 5, 1965, British

CHARLES J. BRABIN

b. April 17, 1883 - Liverpool, England
d. 1957

THE AWAKENING OF JOHN BOND   1911
THE MAN WHO DISAPPEARED   Edison, 1914
THE MIDNIGHT RIDE OF PAUL REVERE   1914
HOUSE OF THE LOST COURT   Edison, 1915
THE RAVEN   Essanay, 1915
THE PRICE OF FAME   Vitagraph, 1916
MARY JANE'S PA   Vitagraph, 1917
THE SIXTEENTH WIFE   Vitagraph, 1917
THE SECRET KINGDOM   co-director with Theodore Marston, Vitagraph, 1917
BABETTE   Vitagraph, 1917
PERSUASIVE PEGGY   Mayfair Shallenberger & Priest, 1917
THE ADOPTED SON   Metro, 1917
RED, WHITE AND BLUE BLOOD   Metro, 1917
BREAKERS AHEAD   Metro, 1918
SOCIAL QUICKSANDS   Metro, 1918
A PAIR OF CUPIDS   Metro, 1918
THE POOR RICH MAN   Metro, 1918
BUCHANAN'S WIFE   Fox, 1918
HIS BONDED WIFE   Metro, 1918
THOU SHALT NOT   Fox, 1919
KATHLEEN MAVOURNEEN   Fox, 1919
LA BELLE RUSSE   Fox, 1919
WHILE NEW YOUK SLEEPS   Fox, 1920
BLIND WIFES   Fox, 1920
FOOTFALLS   Fox, 1921
THE BROADWAY PEACOCK   Fox, 1922
THE LIGHTS OF NEW YORK   Fox, 1922
DRIVEN   Universal, 1923
SIX DAYS   Goldwyn, 1923
SO BIG   First National, 1925
STELLA MARIS   Universal, 1925
MISMATES   First National, 1926
TWINKLETOES   First National, 1926
FRAMED   First National, 1927
HARD-BOILED HAGGERTY   First National, 1927
THE VALLEY OF THE GIANTS   First National, 1927
BURNING DAYLIGHT   First National, 1928
THE WHIP   First National, 1928
THE BRIDGE OF SAN LUIS REY   MGM, 1929
THE SHIP FROM SHANGHAI   MGM, 1930
CALL OF THE FLESH   MGM, 1930

THE GREAT MEADOW   MGM, 1931
SPORTING BLOOD   MGM, 1931
THE BEAST OF THE CITY   MGM, 1932
NEW MORALS FOR OLD   MGM, 1932
THE WASHINGTON MASQUERADE   MGM, 1932
THE MASK OF FU MANCHU   MGM, 1932
THE SECRET OF MADAME BLANCHE   MGM, 1932
STAGE MOTHER   MGM, 1933
DAY OF RECKONING   MGM, 1932
A WICKED WOMAN   MGM, 1932

JOHN BRAHM
(Hans Brahm)
b. August 17, 1893 - Hamburg, Germany
d. 1982

BROKEN BLOSSOMS   Twickenham, 1936, British
COUNSEL FOR CRIME   Columbia, 1937
PENITENTIARY   Columbia, 1938
GIRL'S SCHOOL   Columbia, 1938
LET US LIVE   Columbia, 1939
RIO   Universal, 1939
ESCAPE TO GLORY   *SUBMARINE ZONE*   Columbia,
   1940
WILD GEESE CALLING   20th Century-Fox, 1941
THE UNDYING MONSTER   20th Century-Fox, 1942
TONIGHT WE RAID CALAIS   20th Century-Fox, 1943
WINTERTIME   20th Century-Fox, 1943
THE LODGER   20th Century-Fox, 1944
GUEST IN THE HOUSE   United Artist, 1944
HANGOVER SQUARE   20th Century-Fox, 1945
THE LOCKET   RKO RADIO, 1946
THE BRASHER DOUBLOON   20th Century-Fox, 1947
SINGAPORE   Universal, 1947
THE THIEF OF VENICE   1950, Italian
THE MIRACLE OF OUR LADY OF FATIMA   Warner Bros.,
   1952
FACE TO FACE   co-director with Bretaigne Windust,
   RKO Radio, 1952
THE DIAMOND QUEEN   Warner Bros., 1953
THE MAD MAGICIAN   Columbia, 1952
DIE GOLDENE PEST   1952, West German
SPECIAL DELIVERY   *VON HIMMEL GEFALLEN*
   Columbia, 1955, West German-U.S.
BENGAZI   RKO Radio, 1955
HOT RODS TO HELL   MGM, 1967

HERBERT BRENON
b. January 13, 1880 - Dublin, Ireland
d. 1958

ALL FOR HER   1912
THE CLOWN'S TRIUMPH   1912
LEAH THE FORSAKEN   1912
KATHLEEN MAVOURNEEN   1913
THE ANGEL OF DEATH   1913
IVANHOE   1913, British
THE ANARCHIST   1913
ABSINTHE   1914, French
ACROSS THE ATLANTIC   1914, British
NEPTUNE'S DAUGHTER   co-director with Otis Turner,
   1914
THE KREUTZER SONATA   1915
THE CLMENCEAU CASE   1915
THE TWO ORPHANS   1915
SIN   1915
THE SOUL OF BROADWAY   1915
WHOM THE GODS DESTROY   1916

A DAUGHTER OF THE GODS   1916
WAR BRIDES   1916
MARBLE HEART   1916
THE RULING PASSION   1916
THE ETERNAL SIN   1917
THE LONE WOLF   1917
THE FALL OF THE ROMANOFFS   1917
EMPTY POCKETS   1917
VICTORY AND PEACE   1918, British
THE PASSING OF THE THIRD FLOOR BACK   1918
PRINCIPESSA MISTERIOSA   1919, Italian
TWELVE: TEN   1919, British
A SINLESS SINNER   1919, British
CHAINS OF EVIDENCE   1920
THE PASSION FLOWER   1921
THE SIGN ON THE DOOR   1921
THE WONDERFUL THING   1921
ANY WIFE   1922
A STAGE ROMANCE   1922
SHACKLES OF GOLD   1922
MOONSHINE VALLEY   1922
THE CUSTARD CUP   1923
THE RUSTLE OF SILK   1923
SISTER AGAINST SISTER   1923
THE WOMAN WITH FOUR FACES   1923
THE SPANISH DANCER   1923
SHADOWS OF PARIS   1924
THE BREAKING POINT   1924
THE SIDE SHOW OF LIFE   1924
THE ALASKAN   1924
PETER PAN   1924
THE LITTLE FRENCH GIRL   1925
THE STREET OF FORGOTTEN MEN   1925
THE SONG AND DANCE MAN   1926
DANCING MOTHERS   1926
BEAU GESTE   Paramount, 1926
THE GREAT GATSBY   Paramount, 1926
GOD GAVE ME TWENTY CENTS   1926
A KISS FOR CINDERELLA   1926
THE TELEPHONE GIRL   1927
SORRELL AND SON ★   United Artists, 1927
LAUGH CLOWN LAUGH   1928
THE RESCUE   1929
LUMMOX   1930
THE CASE OF SERGEANT GRISHA   1930
BEAU IDEAL   1931
TRANSGRESSION   1931
GIRL OF THE RIO   1932
WINE, WOMEN AND SONG   1933
ROYAL CAVALCADE (FD)   1935, British
HONORS EASY   1935, British
LIVING DANGEROUSLY   1936, British
SOMEONE AT THE DOOR   1936, British
THE DOMINANT SEX   1937, British
SPRING HANDICAP   1937, British
THE LIVE WIRE   1937, British
HOUSEMASTER   1938, British
YELLOW SANDS   1938, Briitsh
BLACK EYES   1939, British
THE FLYING SQUAD   1940, British

CLARENCE BROWN
b. May 10, 1890 - Clinton, Massachusetts
d. 1987

THE GREAT REDEEMER   co-director with Maurice
   Tourneur, Metro, 1920
THE LAST OF THE MOHICANS   co-director with
   Maurice Tourneur, 1920

THE FOOLISH MATRONS   co-director with
    Maurice Tourneur, 1921
THE LIGHT IN THE DARK   Associated First National, 1922
DON'T MARRY FOR MONEY   Webster, 1923
THE ACQUITTAL   Universal, 1923
THE SIGNAL TOWER   Universal, 1924
BUTTERFLY   Universal, 1924
SMOULDERING FIRES   Universal, 1925
THE EAGLE   Universal, 1925
THE GOOSE WOMAN   Universal, 1925
KIKI   MGM, 1926
FLESH AND THE DEVIL   MGM, 1927
THE TRAIL OF '98   MGM, 1928
A WOMAN OF AFFAIRS   MGM, 1928
THE WONDER OF WOMEN   MGM, 1929
NAVY BLUES   MGM, 1929
ANNA CHRISTIE ★   MGM, 1930
ROMANCE ★   MGM, 1930
INSPIRATION   MGM, 1931
A FREE SOUL ★   MGM, 1931
POSSESSED   MGM, 1931
EMMA   MGM, 1932
LETTY LYNTON   MGM, 1932
THE SON-DAUGHTER   MGM, 1932
LOOKING FORWARD   MGM, 1933
NIGHT FLIGHT   MGM, 1933
SADIE MCKEE   MGM, 1934
CHAINED   MGM, 1934
ANNA KARENINA   MGM, 1935
AH WILDERNESS!   MGM, 1935
WIFE VERSUS SECRETARY   MGM, 1936
THE GORGEOUS HUSSY   MGM, 1936
CONQUEST   *MARIA WALEWSKA*   MGM, 1937
OF HUMAN HEARTS   MGM, 1938
IDIOT'S DELIGHT   MGM, 1939
THE RAINS CAME   MGM, 1939
EDISON THE MAN   MGM, 1940
COME LIVE WITH ME   MGM, 1941
THEY MET IN BOMBAY   MGM, 1941
THE HUMAN COMEDY ★   MGM, 1943
THE WHITE CLIFFS OF DOVER   MGM, 1944
NATIONAL VELVET ★   MGM, 1945
THE YEARLING ★   MGM, 1947
SONG OF LOVE   MGM, 1947
INTRUDER IN THE DUST   MGM, 1950
TO PLEASE A LADY   MGM, 1950
ANGELS IN THE OUTFIELD   MGM, 1951
IT'S A BIG COUNTRY   co-director with Charles
    Vidor, Richard Thorpe, John Sturges, Don Hartman,
    Don Weis & William Wellman, MGM, 1952
WHEN IN ROME   MGM, 1952
PLYMOUTH ADVENTURE   MGM, 1952

TOD BROWNING
b. July 12, 1882 - Louisville, Kentucky
d. 1962

JIM BLUDSO   co-director with Wilfred Lucas, Fine Arts-
    Triangle, 1917
A LOVE SUBLIME   co-director with Wilfred Lucas,
    Fine Arts-Triangle, 1917
HANDS UP   co-director with Wilfred Lucas, Fine Arts-
    Triangle, 1917
PEGGY THE WILL-0'-THE-WISP   Metro, 1917
THE JURY OF FATE   Metro, 1917
THE EYES OF MYSTERY   Metro, 1918
WHICH WOMAN   Bluebird-Universal, 1918
THE DECIDING KISS   Bluebird-Universal, 1918

REVENGE   Metro, 1918
THE LEGION OF DEATH   Metro, 1918
THE BRAZEN BEAUTY   Universal, 1918
SET FREE   Bluebird-Universal, 1918
THE UNPAINTED WOMAN   Universal, 1919
THE WICKED DARLING   Universal, 1919
THE EXQUISITE THIEF   Universal, 1919
A PETAL ON THE CURRENT   Universal, 1919
BONNIE BONNIE LASSIE   Universal, 1919
THE VIRGIN OF STAMBOUL   Universal, 1920
OUTSIDE THE LAW   Universal, 1921
NO WOMAN KNOWS   Universal, 1921
THE WISE KID   Universal, 1922
MAN UNDER COVER   Universal, 1922
UNDER TWO FLAGS   Universal, 1922
DRIFTING   Universal, 1923
WHITE TIGER   Universal, 1923
THE DAY OF FAITH   Goldwyn, 1923
THE DANGEROUS FLIRT   Film Booking Office, 1924
SILK STOCKING SAL   Film Booking Office, 1924
THE UNHOLY THREE   MGM, 1925
THE MYSTIC   MGM, 1925
DOLLAR DOWN   Truart, 1925
THE BLACK BIRD   MGM, 1926
THE ROAD TO MANDALAY   MGM, 1926
THE SHOW   MGM, 1927
THE UNKNOWN   MGM, 1927
LONDON AFTER MIDNIGHT   MGM, 1927
THE BIG CITY   MGM, 1928
WEST OF ZANZIBAR   MGM, 1928
WHERE EAST IS EAST   MGM, 1929
THE THIRTEENTH CHAIR   MGM, 1929
OUTSIDE THE LAW   Universal, 1930
DRACULA   Universal, 1931
THE IRON MAN   Universal, 1931
FREAKS   MGM, 1932
FAST WORKERS   MGM, 1933
MARK OF THE VAMPIRE   MGM, 1935
THE DEVIL DOLL   MGM, 1936
MIRACLES FOR SALE   MGM, 1939

LUIS BUÑUEL
b. February 22, 1900 - Calanda, Spain
d. 1983

UN CHIEN ANDALOU   co-director with Salvador Dali,
    1928, French
L'AGE D'OR   1930, French
LAS HURDES   1932, Spanish
GRAN CASINO   Azteca Films, 1947, Mexican
EL GRAN CALAVERA   Azteca Films, 1949,
    Mexican
LOS OLVIDADOS   *THE YOUNG AND THE
    DAMNED*   Mayer-Kingsley, 1950,
    Mexican
SUSANA   *DEMONIO Y CARNE*   Azteca Films,
    1951, Mexican
LA HIJA DEL ENGANO   Azteca Films, 1951,
    Mexican
UNA MUJER SIN AMOR   Azteca Films, 1951,
    Mexican
SUBIDA AL CIELO   *MEXICAN BUS RIDE*
    Azteca Films, 1951, Mexican
EL BRUTO   Azteca Films, 1952, Mexican
THE ADVENTURES OF ROBINSON CRUSOE
    United Artists, 1952, Mexican
EL   *THIS STRANGE PASSION*   Azteca Films,
    1952, Mexican

ABISMOS DE PASION *CUMBRES BORRASCOSAS/ WUTHERING HEIGHTS* Azteca Films, 1953, Mexican
LA ILUSION VIAJA EN TRANVIA Azteca Films, 1953, Mexican
EL RIO Y LA MUERTE Azteca Films, 1954, Mexican

THE CRIMINAL LIFE OF ARCHIBALDO DE LA CRUZ Azteca Films, 1955, Mexican
CELA S'APPELLE L'AURORE 1956, French-Italian
DEATH IN THE GARDEN Bauer International, 1956, French-Mexican
NAZARIN Altura Films Limited, 1959, Mexican
LA FIEVRE MONTE A EL PAO *REPUBLIC OF SIN* 1960, French-Mexican
THE YOUNG ONE Vitalite, 1961, Mexican
VIRIDIANA Kingsley International, 1961, Spanish-Mexican
THE EXTERMINATING ANGEL Altura Films Limited, 1962, Mexican
DIARY OF A CHAMBERMAID International Classics, 1964, French-Italian
SIMON OF THE DESERT Altura Films Limited, 1965, Mexican
BELLE DE JOUR Allied Artists, 1967, French-Italian
THE MILKY WAY United Artists, 1967, French-Italian
TRISTANA Maron Films Limited, 1970, Spanish-French-Italian
THE DISCREET CHARM OF THE BOURGEOISIE 20th Century-Fox, 1972, French
THE PHANTOM OF LIBERTE 20th Century-Fox, 1974, French
THAT OBSCURE OBJECT OF DESIRE First Artists, 1977, French

DAVID BUTLER
b. December 17, 1894 - San Francisco, California
d. 1979

HIGH SCHOOL HERO Fox, 1927
THE NEWS PARADE Fox, 1928
WIN THAT GIRL Fox, 1928
PREP AND PEP Fox, 1928
MASKED EMOTIONS co-director with Kenneth Hawks, 1929, Fox
FOX MOVIETONE FOLLIES OF 1929 Fox, 1929
CHASING THROUGH EUROPE co-director with Alfred Werker, Fox, 1929
SUNNY SIDE UP Fox, 1929
HIGH SOCIETY BLUES Fox, 1930
JUST IMAGINE Fox, 1930
A CONNECTICUT YANKEE Fox, 1931
DELICIOUS Fox, 1931
BUSINESS AND PLEASURE Fox, 1932
DOWN TO EARTH Fox, 1932
HANDLE WITH CARE Fox, 1932
HOLD ME TIGHT Fox, 1933
MY WEAKNESS Fox, 1933
BOTTOMS UP Fox, 1934
HANDY ANDY Fox, 1934
HAVE A HEART Fox, 1934
BRIGHT EYES Fox, 1934
THE LITTLE COLONEL 20th Century-Fox, 1935
DOUBTING THOMAS 20th Century-Fox, 1935
THE LITTLEST REBEL 20th Century-Fox, 1935
CAPTAIN JANUARY 20th Century-Fox, 1936
WHITE FANG 20th Century-Fox, 1936
PIGSKIN PARADE 20th Century-Fox, 1936

ALI BABA GOES TO TOWN 20th Century-Fox, 1937
YOU'RE A SWEETHEART Universal, 1937
KENTUCKY MOONSHINE 20th Century-Fox, 1938
STRAIGHT PLACE AND SHOW 20th Century-Fox, 1938
KENTUCKY 20th Century-Fox, 1938
EAST SIDE OF HEAVEN Universal, 1939
THAT'S RIGHT, YOU'RE WRONG RKO Radio, 1939
IF I HAD MY WAY Universal, 1940
YOU'LL FIND OUT RKO Radio, 1940
CAUGHT IN THE DRAFT Paramount, 1941
PLAYMATES RKO Radio, 1941
THE ROAD TO MOROCCO Paramount, 1942
THEY GOT ME COVERED RKO Radio, 1943
THANK YOUR LUCKY STARS Warner Bros., 1943
SHINE ON HARVEST MOON Warner Bros., 1944
THE PRINCESS AND THE PIRATE RKO Radio, 1944
SAN ANTONIO Warner Bros., 1945
TWO GUYS FROM MILWAUKEE Warner Bros., 1946
THE TIME, THE PLACE AND THE GIRL Warner Bros., 1946
MY WILD IRISH ROSE Warner Bros., 1947
TWO GUYS FROM TEXAS Warner Bros., 1948
JOHN LOVES MARY Warner Bros., 1949
LOOK FOR THE SILVER LINING Warner Bros., 1949
IT'S A GREAT FEELING Warner Bros., 1949
THE STORY OF SEABISCUIT Warner Bros., 1949
THE DAUGHTER OF ROSIE O'GRADY Warner Bros., 1950
TEA FOR TWO Warner Bros., 1950
THE LULLABY OF BROADWAY Warner Bros., 1951
PAINTING THE CLOUDS WITH SUNSHINE Warner Bros., 1951
WHERE'S CHARLEY? Warner Bros., 1952
APRIL IN PARIS Warner Bros., 1952
BY THE LIGHT OF THE SILVERY MOON Warner Bros., 1953
CALAMITY JANE Warner Bros., 1953
THE COMMAND Warner Bros., 1954
KING RICHARD AND THE CRUSADERS Warner Bros., 1954
JUMP INTO HELL Warner Bros., 1955
GLORY RKO Radio, 1956
THE GIRL HE LEFT BEHIND Warner Bros., 1956
THE RIGHT APPROACH 20th Century-Fox, 1961
C'MON, LET'S LIVE A LITTLE Paramount, 1967

EDWARD (EDDIE) BUZZELL
b. November 13, 1897 - Brooklyn, New York
d. 1985

THE BIG TIMER Columbia, 1932
HOLLYWOOD SPEAKS Columbia, 1932
VIRTUE Columbia, 1932
CHILD OF MANHATTAN Columbia, 1933
ANN CARVER'S PROFESSION Columbia, 1933
LOVE, HONOR AND OH BABY! Universal, 1933
CROSS COUNTRY CRUISE Universal, 1934
THE HUMAN SIDE Universal, 1934
TRANSIENT LADY Universal, 1935
THE GIRL FRIEND Columbia, 1935
THREE MARRIED MEN Paramount, 1936
THE LUCKIEST GIRL IN THE WORLD Universal, 1936
AS GOOD AS MARRIED Universal, 1937
PARADISE FOR THREE MGM, 1938
FAST COMPANY MGM, 1938
HONOLULU MGM, 1939
AT THE CIRCUS MGM, 1939
GO WEST MGM, 1940

THE GET-AWAY   MGM, 1941
MARRIED BACHELOR   MGM, 1941
SHIP AHOY   MGM, 1942
THE OMAHA TRAIL   MGM, 1942
THE YOUNGEST PROFESSION   MGM, 1943
BEST FOOT FORWARD   MGM, 1943
KEEP YOUR POWDER DRY   MGM, 1945
EASY TO WED   MGM, 1946
THREE WISE FOOLS   MGM, 1946
SONG OF THE THIN MAN   MGM, 1947
NEPTUNE'S DAUGHTER   MGM, 1949
A WOMAN OF DISTINCTION   Columbia, 1950
EMERGENCY WEDDING   Columbia, 1950
CONFIDENTIALLY CONNIE   MGM, 1953
AIN'T MISBEHAVIN'   Universal, 1955
MARY HAD A LITTLE...   1961, British

C

PASQUALE FESTA CAMPANILE
b. July 28, 1927 - Melfi, Italy
d. 1986

UN TENTATIVE SENTIMENTALE   co-director with
   Massimo Franciosa, 1963, Italian
WHITE VOICES   co-director with Massimo Franciosa,
   Rizzoli, 1964, Italian-French
LA COSTANZA DELLA REGIONE   1964, Italian
A MAIDEN FOR A PRINCE   Royal Films International,
   1965, Italian-French
ADULTERIO ALL' ITALIANA   1966, Italian
THE GIRL AND THE GENERAL   MGM, 1967, Italian-
   French
ON MY WAY TO THE CRUSADES, I MET A GIRL WHO...
   THE CHASTITY BELT   Warner Bros., 1969,
   Italian-U.S.
IL MARITO E MIO E L'AMAZZO QUANDO MI PARE
   1968, Italian
THE LIBERTINE   Audubon, 1968, Italian
DOVE VAI TUTTA NUDA?   1969, Italian
SCACCO ALLA REGINA   1970, Italian
CON QUALE AMORE CON QUANTO AMORE   1970,
   Italian
WHEN WOMEN HAD TAILS   Film Ventures International,
   1970, Italian
IL MERLO MASCHIO   1971, Italian
JUS PRIMA NOCTIS   1972, Italian
LA CALANDRIA   1972, Italian
WHEN WOMEN LOST THEIR TAILS   Film Ventures
   International, 1972, Italian-West German
L'EMIGRANTE   1973, Italian
RUGANTINO   1973, Italian
LA SCULACCIATA   1974, Italian
SOLDIER OF FORTUNE   1975, Italian
HUMUNQUS HECTOR   1976, Italian
CARA SPOSA   1977, Italian
AUTOSTOP   1977, Italian
PARLAMI D'AMORE MARIA   1977, Italian
IL RITORNO DI CASANOVA (TF)   1978, Italian
CORNE PERDERE UNA MOGLIE E TROVARE UN'
AMANTE   1978, Italian

BELLOW MA DANNATO   1979, Italian
GEGE BELLAVITA   1979, Italian

JOHN CASSAVETES
b. December 9, 1929 - New York, New York
d. 1989

SHADOWS   Lion International, 1961
TOO LATE BLUES   Paramount, 1962
A CHILD IS WAITING   United Artists, 1963
FACES   Continental, 1968
HUSBANDS   Columbia, 1970
MINNIE AND MOSKOWITZ   Universal, 1971
A WOMAN UNDER THE INFLUENCE ★   Faces
   International, 1974
THE KILLING OF A CHINESE BOOKIE   Faces
   International, 1976
OPENING NIGHT   Faces International, 1979
GLORIA   Columbia, 1980
LOVE STREAMS   Cannon, 1984
BIG TROUBLE   Columbia, 1986

WILLIAM CASTLE
b. April 24, 1914 - New York, New York
d. 1977

THE CHANCE OF A LIFETIME   Columbia, 1943
KLONDIKE KATE   Columbia, 1943
THE WHISTLER   Columbia, 1944
SHE'S A SOLDIER TOO   Columbia, 1944
THE MARK OF THE WHISTLER   Columbia, 1944
WHEN STRANGERS MARRY   Columbia, 1944
VOICE OF THE WHISTLE   Columbia, 1944
THE CRIME DOCTOR'S WARNING   Columbia, 1945
JUST BEFORE DAWN   Columbia, 1946
THE MYSTERIOUS INTRUDER   Columbia, 1946
THE RETURN OF RUSTY   Columbia, 1946
THE CRIME DOCTOR'S MAN HUNT   Columbia, 1946
THE CRIME DOCTOR'S GAMBLE   Columbia, 1947
TEXAS, BROOKLYN AND HEAVEN   United Artists, 1948
THE GENTLEMAN FROM NOWHERE   1948
JOHNNY STOOL PIGEON   Universal, 1949
UNDERTOW   Universal, 1949
IT'S A SMALL WORLD   Universal, 1950
THE FAT MAN   Universal, 1951
HOLLYWOOD STORY   Universal, 1951
CAVE OF OUTLAWS   Universal, 1951
SERPENT OF THE NILE   Columbia, 1953
FORT TI   Columbia, 1953
CONQUEST OF COCHISE   Columbia, 1953
SLAVES OF BABYLON   Columbia, 1953
DRUMS OF TAHITI   Columbia, 1954
CHARGE OF THE LANCERS   Columbia, 1954
BATTLE OF ROGUE RIVER   Columbia, 1954
JESSE JAMES VS. THE DALTONS   Columbia, 1954
THE IRON GLOVE   Columbia, 1954
THE LAW VS. BILLY THE KID   Columbia, 1954
MASTERSON OF KANSAS   Columbia, 1954
THE AMERICANO   Columbia, 1954
NEW ORLEANS UNCENSORED   Columbia, 1954
THE GUN THAT WON THE WEST   Columbia, 1955
DUEL ON THE MISSISSIPPI   Columbia, 1955
THE HOUSTON STORY   Columbia, 1956
URANIUM BOOM   Columbia, 1956
MACABRE   Allied Artists, 1958
HOUSE ON HAUNTED HILL   Allied Artists, 1959
THE TINGLER   Columbia, 1959
13 GHOSTS   Columbia, 1960

HOMICIDAL   Columbia, 1961
MR. SARDONICUS   Columbia, 1961
ZOTZ!   Columbia, 1962
13 FRIGHTENED GIRLS   Columbia, 1963
THE OLD DARK HOUSE   Columbia, 1963, British-U.S.
STRAIT-JACKET   Columbia, 1964
THE NIGHT WALKER   Universal, 1965
I SAW WHAT YOU DID   Universal, 1965
LET'S KILL UNCLE   Universal, 1966
THE BUSY BODY   Paramount, 1967
THE SPIRIT IS WILLING   Paramount, 1967
PROJECT X   Paramount, 1968
SHANKS   Paramount, 1974

CHARLES (CHARLIE) CHAPLIN

b. April 16, 1889 - London, England
d. 1977

CAUGHT IN A CABARET   co-director with Mabel Normand,
   Keystone, 1914
CAUGHT IN THE RAIN   Keystone, 1914
A BUSY DAY   Keystone, 1914
THE FATAL MALLET   Keystone, 1914
HER FRIEND THE BANDIT   co-director with Mabel
   Normand, Keystone, 1914
MABEL'S BUSY DAY   co-director with Mabel Normand,
   Keystone, 1914
MABEL'S MARRIED LIFE   co-director with Mabel
   Normand, Keystone, 1914
LAUGHING GAS   Keystone, 1914
THE PROPERTY MAN   Keystone, 1914
THE FACE ON THE BARROOM FLOOR   Keystone, 1914
RECREATION   Keystone, 1914
THE MASQUERADER   Keystone, 1914
HIS NEW PROFESSION   Keystone, 1914
THE ROUNDERS   Keystone, 1914
THE NEW JANITOR   Keystone, 1914
THOSE LOVE PANGS   Keystone, 1914
DOUGH AND DYNAMITE   Keystone, 1914
GENTLEMEN OF NERVE   Keystone, 1914
HIS MUSICAL CAREER   Keystone, 1914
HIS TRYSTING PLACE   Keystone, 1914
GETTING ACQUAINTED   Keystone, 1914
HIS PREHISTORIC PAST   Keystone, 1914
HIS NEW JOB   Essanay, 1915
A NIGHT OUT   Essanay, 1915
THE CHAMPION   Essanay, 1915
IN THE PARK   Essanay, 1915
A JITNEY ELOPEMENT   Essanay, 1915
THE TRAMP   Essanay, 1915
BY THE SEA   Essanay, 1915
WORK   Essanay, 1915
A WOMAN   Essanay, 1915
THE BANK   Essanay, 1915
SHANGHAIED   Essanay, 1915
A NIGHT IN THE SHOW   Essanay, 1915
CARMEN   Essanay, 1916
POLICE   Essanay, 1916
THE FLOORWALKER   Mutual, 1916
THE FIREMAN   Mutual, 1916
THE VAGABOND   Mutual, 1916
ONE A.M.   Mutual, 1916
THE COUNT   Mutual, 1916
THE PAWNSHOP   Mutual, 1916
BEHIND THE SCREEN   Mutual, 1916
THE RINK   Mutual, 1916
EASY STREET   Mutual, 1917
THE CURE   Mutual, 1917

THE IMMIGRANT   Mutual, 1917
THE ADVENTURER   Mutual, 1917
A DOG'S LIFE   First National, 1918
TRIPLE TROUBLE   Essanay, 1918
THE BOND   First National, 1918
SHOULDER ARMS   First National, 1918
SUNNYSIDE   First National, 1919
A DAY'S PLEASURE   First National, 1919
THE NUT   First National, 1921
THE KID   First National, 1921
THE IDLE CLASS   First National, 1921
PAY DAY   First National, 1922
THE PILGRIM   First National, 1923
A WOMAN OF PARIS   United Artists, 1923
THE GOLD RUSH   United Artists, 1925
THE CIRCUS ★   United Artists, 1928
CITY LIGHTS   United Artists, 1931
MODERN TIMES   United Artists, 1936
THE GREAT DICTATOR   United Artists, 1940
MONSIEUR VERDOUX   United Artists, 1947
LIMELIGHT   United Artists, 1952
A KING IN NEW YORK   Archway, 1957, British
A COUNTESS FROM HONG KONG   Universal, 1967,
   British

CHARLEY CHASE
(Charles Parrott)

b. October 20, 1893 - Baltimore, Maryland
d. 1940

THE ANGLERS   1914
DO-RE-MI-PA   1915
A DASH OF COURAGE   1916
CHASED INTO LOVE   1917
HELLO TROUBLE   1918
SHIP AHOY!   1919
KIDS IS KIDS   1920
SHERMAN SAID IT   1933
MIDSUMMER MUSH   1933
LUNCHEON AT TWELVE   1933
THE CRACKED ICEMAN   co-director with Eddie Dunn,
   1934
FOUR PARTS   co-director with Eddie Dunn, 1934
I'LL TAKE VANILLA   co-director with Eddie Dunn, 1934
ANOTHER WILD IDEA   co-director with Eddie Dunn, 1934
IT HAPPENED ONE DAY   co-director with Eddie Dunn,
   1934
SOMETHING SIMPLE   co-director with Walter Weems,
   1934
YOU SAID A HATEFUL!   1934
FATE'S FATHEAD   1934
THE CHASES OF PIMPLE STREET   1934
OKAY TOOTS!   co-director with William Terhune, 1936
POKER AT EIGHT   1936
SOUTHERN EXPOSURE   1936
THE FOUR-STAR BOARDER   1936
NURSE TO YOU   co-director with Jefferson Moffitt, 1936
MANHATTAN MONKEY BUSINESS   co-director with
   Harold Law, 1936
PUBLIC GHOST NO. 1   co-director with Harold Law, 1936
LIFE HESITATES AT 40   co-director with Harold Law,
   1936
THE COUNT TAKES THE COUNT   co-director with
   Harold Law, 1936
VAMP TILL READY   co-director with Harold Law, 1936
ON THE WRONG TREK   co-director with Harold Law,
   1936
NEIGHBORHOOD HOUSE   co-director with Harold Law,
   1936

ALBERT CHRISTIE

b. November 24, 1886 - London, Ontario, Canada
d. 1951

WHEN THE MUMMY CRIED FOR HELP   1915
ALL ABOARD   1915
ALMOST A KING   1915
LITTLE EGYPT MALONE   1915
MRS. PLUM'S PUDDING   co-director with Edmund Fraze, 1915
EDDIE'S LITTLE LOVE AFFAIR   1915
WANTED: A LEADING LADY   1915
LOVE AND A SAVAGE   1915
WANTED: A HUSBAND   1916
SEMINARY SCANDAL   1916
NEVER LIE TO YOUR WIFE   1916
FIVE LITTLE WIDOWS   1917
WHO'S LOONEY NOW?   1917
OUT OF THE NIGHT   1920
WEDDING BLUES   1920
THE RESTLESS SEX   1920
KISS AND MAKE UP   1921]
SEE MY LAWYER   1921
ONE STORMY KNIGHT   1922
THAT SON OF SHEIK   1922
THE CHASED BRIDE   1923
RECKLESS ROMANCE   1924
SAVAGE LOVE   1924
BRIGHT LIGHTS   1924
HOT DOGGIE   1925
MEET THE FOLKS   1927
DIVORCE MADE EASY   1929
CHARLEY'S AUNT   1930

EDWARD F. (EDDIE) CLINE

b. November 7, 1892 - Kenosha, Wisconsin
d. 1961

THE WINNING PUNCH   Keystone, 1916
HIS BUSTED TRUST   Keystone, 1916
SUNSHINE   Keystone, 1916
THE DOG CATCHER'S LOVE   Keystone, 1917
THE PAWNBROKER'S HEART   Keystone, 1917
A BEDROOM BLUNDER   Keystone, 1917
THAT NIGHT   Keystone, 1917
THE KITCHEN LADY   Keystone, 1918
THOSE ATHLETIC GIRLS   Keystone, 1918
HIS SMOTHERED LOVE   Keystone, 1918
THE SUMMER GIRLS   Keystone, 1918
WHOSE LITTLE WIFE ARE YOU?   Keystone, 1918
HIDE AND SEEK DETECTIVES   Keystone, 1918
CUPID'S DAY OFF   1919
EAST LYNNE WITH VARIATIONS   1919
WHEN LOVE IS BLIND   1919
HEARTS AND FLOWERS   1919
ONE WEEK   co-director with Buster Keaton, 1920
CONVICT 13   co-director with Buster Keaton, 1920
THE SCARECROW   co-director with Buster Keaton, 1920
NEIGHBORS   co-director with Buster Keaton, 1920
THE HAUNTED HOUSE   co-director with Buster Keaton, 1921
HARD LUCK   co-director with Buster Keaton, 1921
THE HIGH SIGN   co-director with Buster Keaton, 1921
THE PLAYHOUSE   co-director with Buster Keaton, 1921
THE BOAT   co-director with Buster Keaton, 1921
THE PALEFACE   co-director with Buster Keaton, 1922
COPS   co-director with Buster Keaton, 1922
MY WIFE'S RELATIONS   co-director with Buster Keaton, 1922

THE FROZEN NORTH   co-director with Buster Keaton, 1922
THE ELECTRIC HOUSE   co-director with Buster Keaton, 1922
DAY DREAMS   co-director with Buster Keaton, 1922
THE BALLOONATIC   co-director with Buster Keaton, 1923
THE LOVE NEST   co-director with Buster Keaton, 1923
THE THREE AGES   co-director with Buster Keaton, 1923
CIRCUS DAYS   First National, 1923
THE MEANEST MAN IN THE WORLD   First National, 1923
WHEN A MAN'S A MAN   First National, 1924
THE PLUMBER   1924
LITTLE ROBINSON CRUSOE   MGM, 1924
GOOD BAD BOY   Principal, 1924
CAPTAIN JANUARY   Principal, 1924
ALONG CAME RUTH   MGM, 1924
BASHFUL JIM   1925
TEE FOR TWO   1925
COLD TURKEY   1925
LOVE AND KISSES   1925
DANGEROUS CURVES BEHIND   1925
THE RAG MAN   MGM, 1925
OLD CLOTHES   MGM, 1925
THE GOSH-DARN MORTGAGE   1926
SPANKING BREEZES   1926
A LOVE SUNDAE   1926
THE GHOST OF FOLLY   1926
PUPPY LOVETIME   1926
SMITH'S BABY   1926
WHEN A MAN'S A PRINCE   1926
FLIRTY FOUR-FLUSHERS   1926
GOOSELAND   1926
A HAREM KNIGHT   1926
A BLONDE'S REVENGE   1926
THE JOLLY JILTER   1927
LET IT RAIN   Paramount, 1927
SOFT CUSHIONS   1927
THE GIRL FROM EVERYWHERE   1927
THE BULLFIGHTERS   1927
HOLD THAT POSE   1928
LOVE AT FIRST SIGHT   1928
LADIES' NIGHT IN A TURKISH BATH   1928
VAMPING VENUS   First National, 1928
MAN CRAZY   1928
THE HEAD MAN   First National, 1928
THE CRASH   First National, 1928
BROADWAY FEVER   Tiffany Star, 1929
HIS LUCKY DAY   Universal, 1929
THE FORWARD PASS   First National, 1929
IN THE NEXT ROOM   First National, 1930
SWEET MAMA   First National, 1930
LEATHERNECKING   RKO, 1930
THE WIDOW FROM CHICAGO   First National, 1930
HOOK, LINE AND SINKER   1930
CRACKED NUTS   1931
THE NAUGHTY FLIRT   First National, 1931
THE GIRL HABIT   Paramount, 1931
MILLION DOLLAR LEGS   Paramount, 1932
SO THIS IS AFRICA   Columbia 1933
PAROLE GIRL   1933
THE DUDE RANGER   Fox, 1934
PECK'S BAD BOY   Fox, 1934
WHEN A MAN'S A MAN   British Lion, 1935
THE COWBOY MILLIONAIRE   Fox, 1935
IT'S A GREAT LIFE   Paramount, 1936
F-MAN   Paramount, 1936
ON AGAIN, OFF AGAIN   RKO, 1937
FORTY NAUGHTY GIRLS   RKO, 1937
HIGH FLYERS   RKO, 1937
HAWAII CALLS   RKO, 1938

GO CHASE YOURSELF   RKO, 1938
BREAKING THE ICE   RKO, 1938
PECK'S BAD BOY WITH THE CIRCUS   FOX, 1938
MY LITTLE CHICKADEE   Universal, 1940
THE VILLAIN STILL PURSUED HER   RKO Radio, 1940
THE BANK DICK   Universal, 1940
MEET THE CHUMP   Universal, 1941
HELLO SUCKER   Universal, 1941
NEVER GIVE A SUCKER AN EVEN BREAK   Universal,
   1941
SNUFFY SMITH THE YARD BIRD   Monogram, 1942
WHAT'S COOKIN'?   Universal, 1942
PRIVATE BUCKAROO   Universal, 1942
GIVE OUT SISTERS   Universal, 1942
BEHIND THE EIGHT BALL   Universal, 1942
HE'S MY GUY   Universal, 1943
CRAZY HOUSE   Universal, 1943
SWINGTIME JOHNNY   Universal, 1944
GHOST CATCHERS   Universal, 1944
MOONLIGHT AND CACTUS   Universal, 1944
NIGHT CLUB GIRL   Universal, 1944
SLIGHTLY TERRIFIC   Universal, 1944
SEE MY LAWYER   Universal, 1945
PENTHOUSE RHYTHM   Universal, 1945
BRINGING UP FATHER   Monogram, 1946
JIGGS AND MAGGIE IN SOCIETY   Monogram, 1948
JIGGS AND MAGGIE IN COURT   co-director with
   William Beaudine, Monogram, 1948

HENRI-GEORGES CLOUZOT
b. November 20, 1907 - Niort, France
d. 1977

L'ASSASSIN HABITE AU 21   1941, French
LE CORBEAU   1934, French
QUAI DES ORFEVRES   1947, French
MANON   1949, French
RETOUR A LA VIE   co-director, 1949, French
MIQUETTE ET SA MERE   1950, French
THE WAGES OF FEAR   DCA, 1953, French
DIABOLIQUE   United Motion Picture Organization, 1955,
   French
THE MYSTERY OF PICASSO (FD)   Samuel Goldwyn
   Company, 1956, French
LES ESPIONS   1957, French
THE TRUTH   Kingsley International, 1960, French-Italian
LA PRISONNIERE   Avco Embassy, 1968, French-Italian
MESSA DA REQUIEM   1969, Swiss-West German

JEAN COCTEAU
b. July 5, 1889 - Maisons-Lafitte, France
d. 1963

THE BLOOD OF A POET   Brandon, 1930, French
BEAUTY AND THE BEAST   Lopert, 1946, French
L'AIGLE A DEUX TETES   1948, French
LES PARENTS TERRIBLES   1948, French
ORPHEUS   Discina International, 1950, French
LE TESTAMENT D'ORPHEE   1960, French

JACK CONWAY
b. July 17, 1887 - Graceville, Minnesota
d. 1952

THE OLD ARMCHAIR   1913
CAPTAIN McLEAN   1914
THE PENITENTS   Triangle, 1915

THE BECKONING TRAIL   Red Films, 1916
SOCIAL BUCCANEERS   Bluebird, 1916
THE MEASURE OF A MAN   Bluebird, 1916
THE MAINSPRING   Red Films, 1916
THE SILENT BATTLE   Bluebird, 1916
POLLY'S REDHEAD   POLLY REDHEAD   Bluebird,
   1917
JEWEL IN PAWN   A JEWEL IN THE PAWN   Bluebird,
   1917
THE LITTLE ORPHAN   Pathé, 1917
HER SOUL'S INSPIRATION   Bluebird, 1917
COME THROUGH   Universal, 1917
THE CHARMER   Bluebird, 1917
THE BOND OF FEAR   Triangle, 1917
BECAUSE OF A WOMAN   Triangle, 1917
LITTLE RED DECIDES   Triangle, 1918
HER DECISION   Triangle, 1918
YOU CAN'T BELIEVE EVERYTHING   Triangle, 1918
DOING THEIR BIT   1918
DIPLOMATIC MISSION   Vitagraph, 1918
DESERT LAW   Triangle, 1918
RESTLESS SOULS   Triangle, 1919
LOMBARDI LTD.   Metro, 1919
RIDERS OF THE DAWN   DESERT OF WHEAT
   W.W. Hodkinson, 1920
THE SERVANT IN THE HOUSE   FBO, 1920
THE DWELLING PLACE OF LIGHT   W.W. Hodkinson,
   1920
THE MONEY CHANGERS   Pathé, 1920
THE U.P. TRAIL   W.W. Hodkinson, 1920
THE SPENDERS   W. W. Hodkinson, 1921
THE KISS   Universal, 1921
A DAUGHTER OF THE LAW   Universal, 1921
THE KILLER   1921
THE LURE OF THE ORIENT   1921
THE RAGE OF PARIS   Universal, 1921
THE MILLIONAIRE   Universal, 1921
STEP ON IT!   Universal, 1922
ACROSS THE DEADLINE   Universal, 1922
ANOTHER MAN'S SHOES   Universal, 1922
DON'T SHOOT   Universal, 1922
THE LONG CHANCE   Universal, 1922
THE PRISONER   Universal, 1923
SAWDUST   Universal, 1923
WHAT WIVES WANT   Universal, 1923
QUICKSANDS   Selznick, 1923
TRIMMED IN SCARLET   Universal, 1923
LUCRETIA LOMBARD   Warner Bros., 1923
THE TROUBLE SHOOTER   Fox, 1924
THE HEART BUSTER   Fox, 1924
THE ROUGHNECK   Fox, 1924
THE HUNTED WOMAN   Fox, 1925
THE ONLY THING   MGM, 1925
SOUL MATES   MGM, 1926
BROWN OF HARVARD   MGM, 1926
THE UNDERSTANDING HEART   MGM, 1927
TWELVE MILES OUT   MGM, 1927
THE SMART SET   MGM, 1928
WHILE THE CITY SLEEPS   MGM, 1928
BRINGING UP FATHER   MGM, 1928
ALIAS JIMMY VALENTINE   MGM, 1928
OUR MODERN MAIDENS   MGM, 1929
UNTAMED   MGM, 1929
THEY LEARNED ABOUT WOMEN   co-director with
   Sam Wood, MGM, 1930
THE UNHOLY THREE   MGM, 1930
NEW MOON   MGM, 1931
THE EASIEST WAY   MGM, 1931
JUST A GIGOLO   MGM, 1931
ARSENE LUPIN   MGM, 1932
BUT THE FLESH IS WEAK   MGM, 1932

RED-HEADED WOMAN   MGM, 1932
HELL BELOW   MGM, 1933
THE NUISANCE   MGM, 1933
THE SOLITAIRE MAN   MGM, 1933
VIVA VILLA!   MGM, 1934
THE GIRL FROM MISSOURI   MGM, 1934
THE GAY BRIDE   MGM, 1934
ONE NEW YORK NIGHT   MGM, 1935
A TALE OF TWO CITIES   MGM, 1935
LIBELED LADY   MGM, 1936
SARATOGA   MGM, 1937
A YANK AT OXFORD   MGM, 1938
TOO YOUNG TO HANDLE   MGM, 1938
LET FREEDOM RING   MGM, 1939
LADY OF THE TROPICS   MGM, 1939
BOOM TOWN   MGM, 1940
LOVE CRAZY   MGM, 1941
HONKY-TONK   MGM, 1941
CROSSROADS   MGM, 1942
ASSIGNMENT IN BRITTANY   MGM, 1943
DRAGON SEED   co-director with Harold S. Bucquet,
   MGM, 1944
HIGH BARBAREE   MGM, 1947
THE HUCKSTERS   MGM, 1947
JULIA MISBEHAVES   MGM, 1948

MERIAN C. COOPER

b. October 24, 1893 - Jacksonville, Florida
d. 1973

GRASS   *GRASS: A NATION'S BATTLE FOR LIFE/*
   GRASS: THE EPIC OF A LOST TRIBE (FD)
   co-director with Ernest B. Schoedsack, Paramount, 1925
CHANG (FD)   co-director with Ernest B. Schoedsack,
   Paramount, 1927
THE FOUR FEATHERS   co-director with Ernest B.
   Schoedsack & Lothar Mendes, United Artists, 1933
KING KONG   co-director with Ernest B. Schoedsack,
   RKO Radio, 1933

JOHN CROMWELL

b. December 23, 1888 - Toledo, Ohio
d. 1979

CLOSE HARMONY   co-director with Edward Sutherland,
   Paramount, 1929
THE DANCE OF LIFE   co-director with Edward Sutherland,
   Paramount, 1929
THE MIGHTY   Paramount, 1929
STREET OF CHANCE   Paramount, 1930
THE TEXAN   Paramount, 1930
FOR THE DEFENSE   Paramount, 1930
TOM SAWYER   Paramount, 1930
SCANDAL SHEET   Paramount, 1931
UNFAITHFUL   Paramount, 1931
THE VICE SQUAD   Paramount, 1931
RICH MAN'S FOLLY   Paramount, 1931
THE WORLD AND THE FLESH   Paramount, 1932
SWEEPINGS   RKO, 1933
THE SILVER CORD   RKO, 1933
DOUBLE HARNESS   RKO, 1933
ANN VICKERS   RKO, 1933
SPITFIRE   RKO Radio, 1934
THIS MAN IS MINE   RKO Radio, 1934
OF HUMAN BONDAGE   RKO Radio, 1934
THE FOUNTAIN   RKO Radio, 1934
VILLAGE TALE   RKO Radio, 1935
JALNA   RKO Radio, 1935

I DREAM TOO MUCH   RKO Radio, 1935
LITTLE LORD FAUNTLEROY   United Artists, 1936
TO MARY - WITH LOVE   20th Century-Fox, 1936
BANJO ON MY KNEE   20th Century-Fox, 1936
THE PRISONER OF ZENDA   United Artists, 1937
ALGIERS   United Artists, 1938
MADE FOR EACH OTHER   United Artists, 1939
IN NAME ONLY   RKO Radio, 1939
ABE LINCOLN IN ILLINOIS   RKO Radio, 1940
VICTORY   Paramount, 1940
SO ENDS OUR NIGHT   United Artists, 1941
SON OF FURY   20th Century-Fox, 1942
SINCE YOU WENT AWAY   United Artists, 1944
THE ENCHANTED COTTAGE   RKO Radio, 1945
ANNA AND THE KING OF SIAM   20th Century-Fox, 1946
DEAD RECKONING   Columbia, 1947
NIGHT SONG   RKO Radio, 1947
CAGED   Warner Bros., 1950
THE COMPANY SHE KEEPS   RKO Radio, 1951
THE RACKET   RKO Radio, 1951
THE GODDESS   Columbia, 1958
THE SCAVENGERS   Paramount, 1959
A MATTER OF MORALS   United Artists, 1960,
   U.S.-Swedish

ALAN CROSLAND

b. August 10, 1894 - New York, New York
d. 1936

THE LIGHT IN DARKNESS   Edison, 1917
KIDNAPPED   Forum, 1917
THE APPLE TREE GIRL   Edison Perfection, 1917
THE WHIRLPOOL   Select, 1918
THE UNBELIEVER   Edison-Kleine, 1918
THE COUNTRY COUSIN   Select, 1919
THE FLAPPER   Select, 1920
YOUTHFUL FOLLY   Select, 1920
BROADWAY AND HOME   Select, 1920
GREATER THAN FLAME   Select, 1920
POINT OF VIEW   Select, 1920
WORLDS APART   Select, 1921
IS LIFE WORTH LIVING?   Select, 1921
ROOM AND BOARD   Paramount, 1921
SLIM SHOULDERS   W.W. Hodkinson, 1922
WHY ANNOUNCE YOUR MARRIAGE?   Select, 1922
THE PROPHET'S PARADISE   Select, 1922
SHADOWS OF THE SEA   Select, 1922
THE SNITCHING HOUR   Clark-Cornelius Corp., 1922
THE FACE IN THE FOG   Paramount, 1922
THE ENEMIES OF WOMEN   Goldwyn, 1923
UNDER THE RED ROBE   Goldwyn, 1923
THREE WEEKS   Goldwyn, 1924
MIAMI   W.W. Hodkinson, 1924
UNGUARDED WOMEN   Paramount, 1924
SINNERS IN HEAVEN   Paramount, 1924
CONTRABAND   Paramount, 1925
COMPROMISE   Warner Bros., 1925
BOBBED HAIR   Warner Bros., 1925
DON JUAN   Warner Bros., 1926
WHEN A MAN LOVES   Warner Bros., 1927
THE BELOVED ROGUE   United Artists, 1927
OLD SAN FRANCISCO   Warner Bros., 1927
THE JAZZ SINGER   Warner Bros., 1927
GLORIOUS BETSY   Warner Bros., 1928
THE SCARLET LADY   Columbia, 1928
ON WITH THE SHOW   Warner Bros., 1929
GENERAL CRACK   Warner Bros., 1929
THE FURIES   First National, 1930
SONG OF THE FLAME   First National, 1930
BIG BOY   Warner Bros., 1930

VIENNESE NIGHTS   Warner Bros., 1930
CAPTAIN THUNDER   Warner Bros., 1930
CHILDREN OF DREAMS   Warner Bros., 1931
THE SILVER LINING   United Artists, 1932
WEEK-ENDS ONLY   Fox, 1932
HELLO, SISTER   Fox, 19333
MASSACRE   First National, 1934
MIDNIGHT ALIBI   First National, 1934
THE PERSONALITY KID   Warner Bros., 1934
THE CASE OF THE HOWLING DOG   Warner Bros., 1934
THE WHITE COCKATOO   Warner Bros., 1935
IT HAPPENED IN NEW YORK   Universal, 1935
MR. DYNAMITE   Universal, 1935
LADY TUBBS   Universal, 1935
KING SOLOMON OF BROADWAY   Universal, 1935
THE GREAT IMPERSONATION   United Artists, 1935

JAMES CRUZE

(Jens Cruz Bosen)
b. March 27, 1884 - Ogden, Utah
d. 1942

TOO MANY MILLIONS   Paramount, 1918
THE DUB   Paramount, 1919
ALIAS MIKE MORAN   Paramount, 1919
THE ROARING ROADS   Paramount, 1919
YOU'RE FIRED   Paramount, 1919
THE LOVE BURGLAR   Paramount, 1919
VALLEY OF THE GIANTS   1919
AN ADVENTURE IN HEARTS   Paramount, 1919
HAWTHORNE OF THE U.S.A.   Paramount, 1919
THE LOTTERY MAN   Paramount, 1919
MRS. TEMPLE'S TELEGRAM   Paramount, 1920
TERROR ISLAND   Paramount, 1920
A FULL HOUSE   Paramount, 1920
THE SINS OF ST. ANTHONY   Paramount, 1920
WHAT HAPPENED TO JONES?   Paramount, 1920
ALWAYS AUDACIOUS   Paramount, 1920
THE CHARM SCHOOL   Paramount, 1921
THE DOLLAR-A-YEAR MAN   Paramount, 1921
FOOD FOR SCANDAL   Realart, 1921
LEAP YEAR   SKIRT SHY   Paramount, 1921
THE FAST FREIGHT   Paramount, 1921
GASOLINE GUS   Paramount, 1921
CRAZY TO MARRY   Paramount, 1921
ONE GLORIOUS DAY   Paramount, 1922
IS MATRIMONY A FAILURE?   Paramount, 1922
THE DICTATOR   Paramount, 1922
THE OLD HOMESTEAD   Paramount, 1922
THIRTY DAYS   Paramount, 1922
THE COVERED WAGON   Paramount, 1923
HOLLYWOOD   Paramount, 1923
RUGGLES OF RED GAP   Paramount, 1923
TO THE LADIES   Paramount, 1923
MERTON OF THE MOVIES   Paramount, 1924
THE FIGHTING COWARD   Paramount, 1924
THE GARDEN OF WEEDS   Paramount, 1924
THE CITY THAT NEVER SLEEPS   Paramount, 1924
THE ENEMY SEX   Paramount, 1924
THE PONY EXPRESS   Paramount, 1925
BEGGAR ON HORSEBACK   Paramount, 1925
THE GOOSE HANGS HIGH   Paramount, 1925
MARRY ME   Paramount, 1925
WELCOME HOME   Paramount, 1925
WAKING UP THE TOWN   United Artists, 1925
MANNEQUIN   Paramount, 1926
THE WAITER FROM THE RITZ   1926
OLD IRONSIDES   Paramount, 1926
WE'RE ALL GAMBLERS   Paramount, 1927

THE CITY GONE WILD   Paramount, 1927
ON TO RENO   Pathé, 1928
THE RED MARK   Pathé, 1928
EXCESS BAGGAGE   MGM, 1928
THE MATING CALL   Paramount, 1928
THE DUKE STEPS OUT   MGM, 1929
A MAN'S MAN   MGM, 1929
THE GREAT GABBO   Sono Art-World Wide, 1929
ONCE A GENTLEMAN   Sono Art-World Wide, 1930
SHE GOT WHAT SHE WANTED   Tiffany, 1930
SALVATION NELL   Tiffany, 1931
IF I HAD A MILLION   co-director, Paramount, 1932
WASHINGTON MERRY-GO-ROUND   1932
RACETRACK   World Wide, 1933
SAILOR BE GOOD   RKO, 1933
I COVER THE WATERFRONT   United Artists, 1933
MR. SKITCH   Fox, 1933
DAVID HARUM   Fox, 1934
THEIR BIG MOMENT   RKO, 1934
HELLDORADO   Fox, 1935
TWO-FISTED   Paramount, 1935
SUTTER'S GOLD   Universal, 1936
THE WRONG ROAD   Republic, 1937
PRISON NURSE   Republic, 1938
THE GANGS OF NEW YORK   Republic, 1938
COME ON LEATHERNECKS!   Republic, 1938

GEORGE CUKOR

b. July 7, 1899 - New York, New York
d. 1983

GRUMPY   co-director with Cyril Gardner, Paramount, 1930
THE VIRTUOUS SIN   co-director with Louis Gasnier, Paramount, 1930
THE ROYAL FAMILY OF BROADWAY   co-director with Cyril Gardner, Paramount, 1930
TARNISHED LADY   Paramount, 1931
GIRLS ABOUT TOWN   Paramount, 1931
WHAT PRICE HOLLYWOOD?   RKO Radio, 1932
A BILL OF DIVORCEMENT   RKO Radio, 1932
ROCKABYE   RKO Radio, 1932
OUR BETTERS   RKO Radio, 1933
DINNER AT EIGHT   MGM, 1933
LITTLE WOMEN ★   RKO Radio, 1933
DAVID COPPERFIELD   MGM, 1935
SYLVIA SCARLETT   RKO Radio, 1935
ROMEO AND JULIET   MGM, 1936
CAMILLE   MGM, 1937
HOLIDAY   Columbia, 1938
ZAZA   Paramount, 1939
THE WOMEN   MGM, 1939
THE PHILADELPHIA STORY   MGM, 1940
SUSAN AND GOD   MGM, 1940
A WOMAN'S FACE   MGM, 1941
TWO-FACED WOMAN   MGM, 1941
HER CARDBOARD LOVER   MGM, 1942
KEEPER OF THE FLAME   MGM, 1943
RESISTANCE AND OHM'S LAW (FD)   Army Signal Corps, 1944
GASLIGHT   MGM, 1944
WINGED VICTORY   20th Century-Fox, 1944
A DOUBLE LIFE   Universal, 1947
EDWARD, MY SON   MGM, 1949
ADAM'S RIB   MGM, 1949
A LIFE OF HER OWN   MGM, 1950
BORN YESTERDAY   Columbia, 1950
THE MODEL AND THE MARRIAGE BROKER   20th Century-Fox, 1951
THE MARRYING KIND   Columbia, 1952

PAT AND MIKE   MGM, 1952
THE ACTRESS   MGM, 1953
A STAR IS BORN   Warner Bros., 1954
IT SHOULD HAPPEN TO YOU   Columbia, 1954
BHOWANI JUNCTION   MGM, 1956
LES GIRLS   MGM, 1957
WILD IS THE WIND   Paramount, 1957
HELLER IN PINK TIGHTS   Paramount, 1960
SONG WITHOUT END   co-director with Charles
   Vidor, Columbia, 1960
LET'S MAKE LOVE   20th Century-Fox, 1960
THE CHAPMAN REPORT   Warner Bros., 1962
SOMETHING'S GOT TO GIVE   20th Century-Fox, 1962,
   incomplete
MY FAIR LADY ★★   Warner Bros., 1964
JUSTINE   20th Century-Fox, 1969
TRAVELS WITH MY AUNT   MGM, 1972, British
LOVE AMONG THE RUINS ☆☆ (TF)   ABC Circle Films,
   1975
THE BLUE BIRD   20th Century-Fox, 1976, U.S.-Soviet
THE CORN IS GREEN (TF)   Warner Bros. TV, 1979
RICH AND FAMOUS   MGM/United Artists, 1981

IRVING   CUMMINGS
b. Ocotober 9, 1888 - New York, New York
d. 1959

THE MAN FROM HELL'S RIVER   Western, 1922
FLESH AND BLOOD   Western, 1922
PAID BACK   Universal, 1922
BROAD DAYLIGHT   Universal, 1922
THE JILT   Universal, 1922
ENVIRONMENT   Principal, 1922
THE DRUG TRAFFICE   Western, 1923
EAST SIDE - WEST SIDE   Principal, 1923
BROKEN HEARTS OF BROADWAY   Western, 1923
STOLEN SECRETS   Universal, 1924
FOOLS' HIGHWAY   Universal, 1924
THE DANCING CHEAT   Universal, 1924
RIDERS UP   Universal, 1924
IN EVERY WOMAN'S LIFE   First National, 1924
THE ROSE OF PARIS   Universal, 1924
AS MAN DESIRES   First National, 1925
ONE YEAR TO LIVE   First National, 1925
THE DESERT FLOWER   First National, 1925
JUST A WOMAN   First National, 1925
INFATUATION   First National 1925
THE JOHNSTOWN FLOOD   Fox, 1926
RUSTLING FOR CUPID   Fox, 1926
THE MIDNIGHT KISS   Fox, 1926
THE COUNTRY BEYOND   Fox, 1926
BERTHA THE SEWING MACHINE GIRL   Fox, 1926
THE BRUTE   Warner Bros., 1927
THE PORT OF MISSING GIRLS   Brenda, 1928
DRESSED TO KILL   Fox, 1928
ROMANCE OF THE UNDERWORLD   *ROMANCE
   AND BRIGHT LIGHTS*   Fox, 1928
IN OLD ARIZONA ★   co-director with Raoul Walsh, Fox,
   1929
NOT QUITE DECENT   Fox, 1929
BEHIND THAT CURTAIN   Fox, 1929
CAMEO KIRBY   Fox, 1930
ON THE LEVEL   Fox, 1930
A DEVIL WITH WOMEN   Fox, 1930
A HOLY TERROR   Fox, 1932
THE CISCO KID   Fox, 1932
ATTORNEY FOR THE DEFENSE   Columbia, 1932
THE NIGHT CLUB LADY   Columbia, 1932
MAN AGAINST WOMAN   Columbia, 1932
MAN HUNT   RKO, 1933

THE WOMAN I STOLE   Columbia, 1933
THE MAD GAME   Fox, 1933
I BELIEVED IN YOU   Fox, 1934
GRAND CANARY   Fox, 1934
THE WHITE PARADE   Fox, 1934
IT'S A SMALL WORLD   Fox, 1935
CURLY TOP   Fox, 1935
NOBODY'S FOOL   Universal, 1936
THE POOR LITTLE RICH GIRL   20th Century-Fox, 1936
GIRLS' DORMITORY   20th Century-Fox, 1936
WHITE HUNTER   20th Century-Fox, 1936
VOGUES OF 1938   United Artists, 1937
MERRY-GO-ROUND OF 1938   Universal, 1937
LITTLE MISS BROADWAY   20th Century-Fox, 1938
JUST AROUND THE CORNER   20th Century-Fox, 1938
THE STORY OF ALEXANDER GRAHAM BELL
   20th Century-Fox, 1939
HOLLYWOOD CAVALCADE   20th Century-Fox, 1939
EVERYTHING HAPPENS AT NIGHT   20th Century-Fox,
   1939
LILILIAN RUSSELL   20th Century-Fox, 1940
DOWN ARGENTINE WAY   20th Century -Fox, 1940
THAT NIGHT IN RIO   20th Century-Fox, 1941
BELLE STARR   20th Century-Fox, 1941
LOUISIANA PURCHASE   Paramount, 1941
MY GAL SAL   20th Century-Fox, 1942
SPRINGTIME IN THE ROCKIES   20th Century-Fox, 1942
SWEET ROSIE O'GRADY   20th Century-Fox, 1943
WHAT A WOMAN!   Columbia, 1943
THE IMPATIENT YEARS   Columbia, 1944
THE DOLLY SISTERS   20th Century-Fox, 1945
DOUBLE DYNAMITE   RKO, 1951

MICHAEL   CURTIZ
(Mihaly Kertesz)
b. December 24, 1888 - Budapest, Hungary
d. 1962

AZ UTOLSO BOHÉM   1912, Hungarian
MA ES HOLNAP   1912, Hungarian
RABELEK   1913, Hungarian
HAZASOKIK AZ URAM   1913, Hungarian
AS EJSZAKA RABJA   1914, Hungarian
A TOLONE   1914, Hungarian
A KOLESONKERT CSECSEMOK   1914, Hungarian
A HERCEGNO PONGYOLABAN   1914, Hungarian
BANK BAN   1914, Hungarian
AKIT KETTEN SZERETNEK   1915, Hungarian
A MEDIKUS   1916, Hungarian
A KARTHAUZI   1916, Hungarian
A FEKETE SZIVARVANY   1916, Hungarian
DOKTOR UR   1916, Hungarian
A FARKAS   1916, Hungarian
MAKKHETES   1916, Hungarian
A MAGYAR FOLD EREJE   1916, Hungarian
AZ EZREDES   1917, Hungarian
ZOARD MESTER   1917, Hungarian
A VOROS SAMSON   1917, Hungarian
A FOLD EMBERE   1917, Hungarian
TATARJARAS   1917, Hungarian
LILIOM   1918, Hungarian
JUDAS   1918, Hungarian
LULU   1918, Hungarian
ALRAUNE   1918, Hungarian
DIE DAME MIT DEM SCHWARZEN HANDSCHUH
   1919, German
DIE GOTTESGEISSEL   1919, German
DER STERN VON DAMASKUS   1920, German
DIE DAME MIT DEN SONNENBLUMEN   1920, German

HERZOGIN SATANELLA   1920, German
BOCCACCIO   1920, German
CHERCHEZ LA FEMME   1921, German
FRAU DOROTHY'S BEKENNTNIS   1921, German
WEGE DES SCHRECKENS   *LABYRINTH DES GRAUENS*   1921, German
SODOM UND GOMORRAH   *LEGENDE VON SUNDE UND STAFE/THE QUEEN OF SIN AND THE SPECTACLE OF SODOM AND GOMORRAH*   1922-23, German
DIE LAWINE   *AVALANCHE*   1923, German
DER JUNGE MEDARDUS   1923, German
NAMENLOS   1923, German
EIN SPIEL UNS LEBEN   1924, German
HARUN AL RASCHID   1924, German
DIE SKLAVENKONIGIN   *MOON OF ISRAEL*   1924, German
CELIMENE - LA POUPEE DE MONTMARTRE   1925, French-Austrian-German
DER GOLDENE SCHMETTERLING   *THE ROAD TO HAPPINESS*   1926, Austrian-German-Danish
FLAKER NR. 13   1926, German
THE THIRD DEGREE   Warner Bros., 1927
A MILLION BID   Warner Bros., 1927
THE DESIRED WOMAN   Warner Bros., 1927
GOOD TIME CHARLEY   Warner Bros., 1927
TENDERLOIN   Warner Bros., 1928
NOAH'S ARK   Warner Bros., 1929
THE GLAD RAG DOLL   Warner Bros., 1929
THE MADONNA OF AVENUE A   Warner Bros., 1929
THE GAMBLERS   Warner Bros., 1929
HEARTS IN EXILE   Warner Bros., 1929
MAMMY   Warner Bros., 1930
UNDER A TEXAS MOON   Warner Bros., 1930
THE MATRIMONIAL BED   Warner Bros., 1930
BRIGHT LIGHTS   Warner Bros., 1930
A SOLDIER'S PLAYTHING   Warner Bros., 1930
RIVER'S END   Warner Bros., 1930
GOD'S GIFT TO WOMEN   Warner Bros., 1931
THE MAD GENIUS   Warner Bros., 1931
THE WOMAN FROM MONTE CARLO   Warner Bros., 1932
ALIAS THE DOCTOR   co-director with Lloyd Bacon, Warner Bros., 1932
THE STRANGE LOVE OF MOLLY LOUVAIN   Warner Bros., 1932
DOCTOR X   Warner Bros., 1932
CABIN IN THE COTTON   Warner Bros., 1932
20,000 YEARS IN SING SING   Warner Bros., 1933
THE MYSTERY OF THE WAX MUSEUM   Warner Bros., 1933
THE KEYHOLE   Warner Bros., 1933
PRIVATE DETECTIVE 62   Warner Bros., 1933
GOODBYE AGAIN   Warner Bros., 1933
THE KENNEL MURDER CASE   Warner Bros., 1933
FEMALE   Warner Bros., 1933
MANDALAY   Warner Bros., 1934
JIMMY THE GENT   Warner Bros., 1934
THE KEY   *HIGH PERIL*   Warner Bros., 1934
BRITISH AGENT   Warner Bros., 1934
BLACK FURY   Warner Bros., 1935
THE CASE OF THE CURIOUS BRIDE   Warner Bros., 1935
FRONT PAGE WOMAN   Warner Bros., 1935
LITTLE BIG SHOT   Warner Bros., 1935
CAPTAIN BLOOD   Warner Bros., 1935
THE WALKING DEAD   Warner Bros., 1936
THE CHARGE OF THE LIGHT BRIGADE   Warner Bros., 1936
STOLEN HOLIDAY   Warner Bros., 1937
MOUNTAIN JUSTICE   Warner Bros., 1937

KID GALAHAD   *THE BATTLING BELLHOP*   Warner Bros., 1937
THE PERFECT SPECIMEN   Warner Bros., 1937
GOLD IS WHERE YOU FIND IT   Warner Bros., 1938
THE ADVENTURES OF ROBIN HOOD   co-director with William Keighley, Warner Bros., 1938
FOUR'S A CROWD   Warner Bros., 1938
FOUR DAUGHTERS ★   Warner Bros., 1938
ANGELS WITH DIRTY FACES ★   Warner Bros., 1938
DODGE CITY   Warner Bros., 1939
DAUGHTERS COURAGEOUS   Warner Bros., 1939
THE PRIVATE LIVES OF ELIZABETH AND ESSEX   *ELIZABETH THE QUEEN*   Warner Bros., 1939
FOUR WIVES   Warner Bros., 1939
VIRGINIA CITY   Warner Bros., 1940
THE SEA HAWK   Warner Bros., 1940
SANTA FE TRAIL   Warner Bros., 1940
THE SEA WOLF   Warner Bros., 1941
DIVE BOMBER   Warner Bros., 1941
CAPTAINS OF THE CLOUDS   Warner Bros., 1942
YANKEE DOODLE DANDY ★   Warner Bros., 1942
CASABLANCA ★★   Warner Bros., 1943
MISSION TO MOSCOW   Warner Bros., 1943
THIS IS THE ARMY   Warner Bros., 1943
PASSAGE TO MARSEILLE   Warner Bros., 1944
JANIE   Warner Bros., 1944
ROUGHLY SPEAKING   Warner Bros., 1945
MILDRED PIERCE   Warner Bros., 1945
NIGHT AND DAY   Warner Bros., 1946
LIFE WITH FATHER   Warner Bros., 1947
THE UNSUSPECTED   Warner Bros., 1947
ROMANCE ON THE HIGH SEAS   Warner Bros., 1948
MY DREAM IS YOURS   Warner Bros., 1949
FLAMINGO ROAD   Warner Bros., 1949
THE LADY TAKES A SAILOR   Warner Bros., 1949
BRIGHT LEAF   Warner Bros., 1950
YOUNG MAN WITH A HORN   Warner Bros., 1950
THE BREAKING POINT   Warner Bros., 1950
FORCE OF ARMS   Warner Bros., 1951
JIM THORPE - ALL AMERICAN   Warner Bros., 1951
I'LL SEE YOU IN MY DREAMS   Warner Bros., 1951
THE STORY OF WILL ROGERS   Warner Bros., 1952
THE JAZZ SINGER   Warner Bros., 1953
TROUBLE ALONG THE WAY   Warner Bros., 1953
THE BOY FROM OKLAHOMA   Warner Bros., 1954
THE EGYPTIAN   20th Century-Fox, 1954
WHITE CHRISTMAS   Paramount, 1954
WE'RE NO ANGELS   Paramount, 1955
THE VAGABOND KING   Paramount, 1956
THE SCARLET HOUR   Paramount, 1956
THE BEST THINGS IN LIFE ARE FREE   20th Century-Fox, 1956
THE HELEN MORGAN STORY   Warner Bros., 1957
KING CREOLE   Paramount, 1958
THE PROUD REBEL   Buena Vista, 1958
THE HANGMAN   Paramount, 1959
THE MAN IN THE NET   United Artists, 1959
THE ADVENTURES OF HUCKLEBERRY FINN   MGM, 1960
A BREATH OF SCANDAL   Paramount, 1960
FRANCIS OF ASSISI   20th Century-Fox, 1961
THE COMANCHEROS   20th Century-Fox, 1961

PAUL CZINNER

b. 1890 - Budapest, Hungary
d. 1972

HOMO IMMANIS   *DER UNMENSCH*   1919, Austrian
INFERNO   1923, Austrian
NJU   1924, German

DER GEIGER VON FLORENZ   1926, German
LIEBE   1926, German
DONA JUANA   1927, German
FRAULEIN ELSE   1929, German
THE WOMAN HE SCORNED   *THE WAY OF LOST SOULS*
    Warner Bros.,   1930, British
ARIANE   *THE LOVES OF ARIANE*   1931, German
DER TRAUMENDE MUND   1932, German
CATHERINE THE GREAT   United Artist, 1934, British
ESCAPE ME NEVER   United Artists, 1935, British
AS YOU LIKE IT   co-director with Dallas Bower, 20th
    Century-Fox, 1936, British
DREAMING LIPS   co-director with Lee Garmes, United
    Artists, 1937, British
MELO   1938, French
STOLEN LIFE   Paramount, 1939, British
DON GIOVANNI   co-director with Maxwell Travers, 1955,
    British
THE BOLSHOI BALLET   RFD, 1960, British
DER ROSENKAVALIER   RFD, 1962, British
ROMEO AND JULIET   RFD, 1966, British

D

MORTON DA COSTA
(Morton Tecosky)
b. March 7, 1914 - Philadelphia, Pennsylvania
d.1989

AUNTIE MAME   Warner Bros., 1958
THE MUSIC MAN   Warner Bros., 1962
ISLAND OF LOVE   Warner Bros., 1963

MARC DANIELS
d. 1989

SQUEEZE A FLOWER   MGM-EMI, 1971, Australian
PLANET EARTH (TF)   Warner Bros. TV, 1974
SPECIAL PEOPLE: BASED ON A TRUE STORY (TF)   Joe
    Cates Productions/CTV Broadcasting Corporation, 1984,
    U.S. - Canadian
HE'S FIRED, SHE'S HIRED (TF)   CBS, 1984
VENGEANCE: THE STORY OF TONY CIMO (TF)   Neder-
    lander TV and Film Productions/Robirdie Pictures, 1986

DELMER DAVES
b. July 24, 1904 - San Francisco, California
d. 1977

DESTINATION TOKYO   Warner Bros., 1943
THE VERY THOUGHT OF YOU   Warner Bros., 1944
HOLLYWOOD CANTEEN   Warner Bros., 1944
PRIDE OF THE MARINES   Warner Bros., 1945
THE RED HOUSE   Warner Bros., 1947
DARK PASSAGE   Warner Bros., 1947
TO THE VICTOR   Warner Bros., 1948
A KISS IN THE DARK   Warner Bros., 1949
TASK FORCE   Warner Bros., 1949
BROKEN ARROW   20th Century-Fox, 1950

BIRD OF PARADISE   20th Century-Fox, 1951
RETURN OF THE TEXAN   20th Century-Fox, 1952
TREASURE OF THE GOLDEN CONDOR   20th
    Century-Fox, 1953
NEVER LET ME GO   MGM, 1953, British-U.S.
DEMETRIUS AND THE GLADIATORS   20th Century-Fox,
    1954
DRUM BEAT   Warner Bros., 1954
JUBAL   Columbia, 1956
THE LAST WAGON   20th Century-Fox, 1956
3:10 TO YUMA   Columbia, 1957
COWBOY   Columbia, 1958
KINGS GO FORTH   United Artists, 1958
THE BADLANDERS   MGM, 1958
THE HANGING TREE   Warner Bros., 1959
A SUMMER PLACE   Warner Bros., 1959
PARRISH   Warner Bros., 1961
SUSAN SLADE   Warner Bros., 1961
ROME ADVENTURE   Warner Bros., 1962
SPENCER'S MOUNTAIN   Warner Bros., 1963
YOUNGBLOOD HAWKE   Warner Bros., 1964
THE BATTLE OF THE VILLA FIORITA   Warner Bros.,
    1965, British-U.S.

J. SEARLE DAWLEY
d. 1950

RESCUED FROM AN EAGLE'S NEST   co-director with
    Edwin S. Porter, Edison, 1907
THE PRINCE AND THE PAUPER   Edison, 1909
HANSEL AND GRETEL   Edison, 1909
FAUST   Edison, 1909
BLUEBEARD   Edison, 1909
MICHAEL STROGOFF   Edison, 1910
FRANKENSTEIN   Edison, 1910
A CHRISTMAS CAROL   Edison, 1910
AIDA   co-director with Oscar Apfel, 1911
THE DOCTOR   1911
VAN BIBBER'S EXPERIMENT   1911
THE BATTLE OF BUNKER HILL   1911
UNDER THE TROPICAL SUN   1911
THE BATTLE OF TRAFALGAR   1911
TREASURE ISLAND   1912
THE CHARGE OF THE LIGHT BRIGADE   1912
PARTNERS FOR LIFE   1912
ALLADDIN UP-TO-DATE   1912
TESS OF THE D'URBERVILLES   co-director with
    Edwin S. Porter, Paramount, 1913
IN THE BISHOP'S CARRIAGE   co-director with
    Edwin S. Porter, Famous Players, 1913
CAPRICE   1913
AN HOUR BEFORE DAWN   1913
MARY STUART   1913
THE DIAMOND CROWN   1913
A GOOD LITTLE DEVIL   co-director with Edwin S. Porter,
    Famous Players, 1913
A DAUGHTER OF THE HILLS   1913
THE PORT OF DOOM   1913
AN AMERICAN CITIZEN   1914
THE OATH OF A VIKING   1914
MARTA OF THE LOWLANDS   1914
ONE OF MILLIONS   1914
IN THE NAME OF THE PRINCE OF PEACE   1914
ALWAYS IN THE WAY   1915
A DAUGHTER OF THE PEOPLE   1915
FOUR FEATHERS   1915
MICE AND MEN   1916
SNOW WHITE   1916
THE VALENTINE GIRL   1917

THE MYSTERIOUS MISS TERRY   1917
BAB'S MATINEE IDOL   1917
UNCLE TOM'S CABIN   1918
THE SEVEN SWANS   1918
THE LIE   1918
RICH MAN POOR MAN   1918
THE DEATH DANCE   1918
THE PHANTOM HONEY MOON   1919
EVERYBODY'S BUSINESS   1919
TWILIGHT   1919
HARVEST MOON   1920
A VIRGIN PARADISE   1921
BEYOND PRICE   1921
WHO ARE MY PARENTS?   1922
AS A MAN LIVES   1923
HAS THE WORLD GONE MAD?   1923
BROADWAY BROKE   1923

EMILE DE ANTONIO

b. 1920 - Scranton, Pennsylvania
d. 1989

POINT OF ORDER (FD)   Point, 1963
RUSH TO JUDGMENT (FD)   Impact, 1967
AMERICA IS HARD TO SEE (FD)   1968
IN THE YEAR OF THE PIG (FD)   Pathe Contemporary,
   1969
MILLHOUSE: A WHITE COMEDY   New Yorker, 1971
PAINTERS PAINTING (FD)   New Yorker, 1973
UNDERGROUND (FD)   co-director with Mary Lampson &
   Haskell Wexler, New Yorker, 1976
IN THE KING OF PRUSSIA   Turin Film Corporation, 1983
MR. HOOVER AND I (FD)   Turin Film Corporation, 1990

BASIL DEARDEN

b. January 1, 1911 - Westcliffe, England
d. 1971

THE BLACK SHEEP OF WHITEHALL   co-director
   with Will Hay, United Artists, 1941
THE GOOSE STEPS OUT   co-director with Will Hay,
   United Artists, 1942, British
MY LEARNED FRIEND   co-director with Will Hay,
   Ealing, 1943, British
THE BELLS GO DOWN   United Artists, 1943, British
HALFWAY HOUSE   Ealing, 1944, British
THEY CAME TO A CITY   Ealing, 1944, British
DEAD OF NIGHT   co-director with Alberto Cavalcanti,
   Robert Hamer & Charles Crichton, Universal, 1946,
   British
THE CAPTIVE HEART   Universal, 1946, British
FRIEDA   Universal, 1947, British
SARABAND   SARABAND FOR DEAD LOVERS
   Eagle Lion, 1948, British
TRAIN OF EVENTS   co-director with Sidney Cole
   & Charles Crichton, Rank, 1949, British
THE BLUE LAMP   Eagle Lion, 1950, British
CAGE OF GOLD   Ellis Films, 1950, British
POOL OF LONDON   Universal, 1951, British
I BELIEVE IN YOU   co-director with Michael Relph,
   Universal, 1952, British
THE GENTLE GUNMAN   Universal, 1952
THE SQUARE RING   co-director with Michael Relph,
   Republic, 1953, British
THE RAINBOW JACKET   Rank, 1954, British
OUT OF THE CLOUDS   co-director with Michael
   Relph, Rank, 1954, British

THE SHIP THAT DIED OF SHAME   Continental, 1955,
   British
WHO DONE IT?   RFD, 1956, British
THE SMALLEST SHOW ON EARTH   Times Film
   Corporation, 1957, British
VIOLENT PLAYGROUND   Lopert, 1958, British
SAPPHIRE   Universal, 1959, British
THE LEAGUE OF GENTLEMEN   Kingsley International,
   1960, British
MAN IN THE MOON   Trans-Lux, 1960, British
THE SECRET PARTNER   MGM, 1961, British
VICTIM   Pathé-America, 1961, British
ALL NIGHT LONG   Continental, 1961, British
WALK IN THE SHADOW   LIFE FOR RUTH   Continental,
   1962, British
THE MIND BENDERS   American International, 1963,
   British
A PLACE TO GO   Continental, 1964, British
WOMAN OF STRAW   United Artists, 1964, British
MASQUERADE   United Artists, 1965, British
KHARTOUM   United Artists, 1966, British
ONLY WHEN I LARF   Paramount, 1968, British
THE ASSASSINATION BUREAU   Paramount, 1969,
   British
THE MAN WHO HAUNTED HIMSELF   Levitt-Pickman,
   1970, British

FERNANDO DE FUENTES

b. December 13, 1895 - Vera Cruz, Mexico
d. 1952

EL ANONIMO   Azteca Films, 1932, Mexican
EL PRISONERO 13   Azteca Films, 1933, Mexican
LA CALANDRIA   Azteca Films, 1933, Mexican
EL COMPADRE MENDOZA   Azteca Films, 1934, Mexican
CRUZ DIABLO   Azteca Films, 1934, Mexican
VAMONOS CON PANCHO VILLA   Azteca Films, 1935,
   Mexican
LA FAMILIA DRESSEL   Azteca Films, 1935, Mexican
ALLA EN EL RANCHO GRANDE   Azteca Films, 1936,
   Mexican
BAJO EL CIELO DE MEXICAO   Azteca Films, 1937,
   Mexican
LA ZANDUNGA   Azteca Films, 1937, Mexican
LA CASA DEL OGRO   Azteca Films, 1937, Mexican
SU GRAN AVENTURA   Azteca Films, 1938, Mexican
PAPACITO LINDO   Azteca Films, 1938, Mexican
ALLA EN EL TROPICO   Azteca Films, 1940, Mexican
CREO EN DIOS   Azteca Films, 1941, Mexican
ASI SE QUIERE EN JALISCO   Azteca Films, 1942,
   Mexican
DONA BARBARA   Azteca Films, 1942, Mexican
LA SELVA DEL FUEGO   Azteca Films, 1945, Mexican
LA DEVORADOR   Azteca Films, 1946, Mexican
CANCION DE CUNA   Azteca Film, 1952, Mexican

ROY DEL RUTH

b. October 18, 1895 - Philadelphia, Pennsylvania
d. 1961

EVE'S LOVER   Warner Bros., 1925
HOGAN'S ALLEY   Warner Bros., 1925
THREE WEEKS IN PARIS   Warner Bros., 1926
THE MAN UPSTAIRS   Warner Bros., 1926
THE LITTLE IRISH GIRL   Warner Bros., 1926
FOOTLOOSE WIDOWS   Warner Bros., 1926
ACROSS THE PACIFIC   Warner Bros., 1926

WOLF'S CLOTHING   Warner Bros., 1927
THE FIRST AUTO   Warner Bros., 1927
HAM AND EGGS AT THE FRONT   Warner Bros., 1927
IF I WERE SINGLE   Warner Bros., 1928
FIVE AND TEN CENT ANNIE   Warner Bros., 1928
POWDER MY BACK   Warner Bros., 1928
THE TERROR   Warner Bros., 1928
BEWARE OF BACHELORS   Warner Bros., 1928
CONQUEST   Warner Bros., 1929
THE DESERT SONG   Warner Bros., 1929
THE HOTTENTOT   Warner Bros., 1929
THE GOLD DIGGERS OF BROADWAY   Warner Bros., 1929
THE AVIATOR   Warner Bros., 1930
HOLD EVERYTHING   Warner Bros., 1930
THE SECOND FLOOR MYSTERY   Warner Bros., 1930
THREE FACES EAST   Warner Bros., 1930
THE LIFE OF THE PARTY   Warner Bros., 1930
DIVORCE AMONG FRIENDS   Warner Bros., 1930
MY PAST   Warner Bros., 1931
THE MALTESE FALCON   Warner Bros., 1931
SIDE SHOW   Warner Bros., 1931
BLONDE CRAZY   *LARCENY LANE*   Warner Bros., 1931
TAXI   Warner Bros., 1932
BEAUTY AND THE BOSS   Warner Bros., 1932
WINNER TAKE ALL   Warner Bros., 1932
BLESSED EVENT   Warner Bros., 1932
EMPLOYEES' ENTRANCE   Warner Bros., 1933
THE MIND READER   Warner Bros., 1933
THE LITTLE GIANT   Warner Bros., 1933
BUREAU OF MISSING PERSONS   Warner Bros., 1933
CAPTURED   Warner Bros., 1933
LADY KILLER   Warner Bros., 1933
BULLDOG DRUMMOND STRIKES BACK   United Artists, 1934
UPPER WORLD   Warner Bros., 1934
KID MILLIONS   United Artists, 1934
BROADWAY MELODY OF 1936   MGM, 1935
FOLIES-BERGERE   United Artists, 1935
THANKS A MILLION   20th Century-Fox, 1935
IT HAD TO HAPPEN   20th Century-Fox, 1936
PRIVATE NUMBER   20th Century-Fox, 1936
BORN TO DANCE   MGM, 1936
ON THE AVENUE   20th Century-Fox, 1937
BROADWAY MELODY OF 1938   MGM, 1937
HAPPY LANDING   20th Century-Fox, 1938
MY LUCKY STAR   20th Century-Fox, 1938
TAIL SPIN   20th Century-Fox, 1939
THE STAR MAKER   Paramount, 1939
HERE I AM A STRANGER   20th Century-Fox, 1939
HE MARRIED HIS WIFE   20th Century-Fox, 1940
TOPPER RETURNS   United Artists, 1941
THE CHOCOLATE SOLDIER   MGM, 1941
MAISIE GETS HER MAN   MGM, 1942
DU BARRY WAS A LADY   MGM, 1943
BROADWAY RHYTHM   MGM, 1944
BARBARY COAST GENT   MGM, 1944
IT HAPPENED ON FIFTH AVENUE   Allied Artists, 1947
THE BABE RUTH STORY   Allied Artists, 1948
RED LIGHT   United Artists, 1949
ALWAYS LEAVE THEM LAUGHING   Warner Bros., 1949
THE WEST POINT STORY   Warner Bros., 1948
ON MOONLIGHT BAY   Warner Bros., 1951
STARLIFT   Warner Bros., 1951
ABOUT FACE   Warner Bros., 1952
STOP, YOU'RE KILLING ME   Warner Bros., 1953
THREE SAILORS AND A GIRL   Warner Bros., 1953
PHANTOM OF THE RUE MORGUE   Warner Bros., 1954
THE ALLIGATOR PEOPLE   20th Century-Fox, 1959
WHY MUST I DIE?   American International, 1960

CECIL B. DE MILLE
b. August 12, 1881 - Ashfield, Massachusetts
d. 1959

THE SQUAW MAN   co-director with Oscar Apfel, Jesse L. Lasky Feature Play Co., 1914
BREWSTER'S MILLIONS   co-director with Oscar Apfel, Jesse L. Lasky Feature Play Co., 1914
THE CALL OF THE NORTH   Jesse L. Lasky Feature Play Co., 1914
THE MAN ON THE BOX   co-director with Oscar Apfel & Wilfred Buckland, Jesse L. Lasky Feature Play Co., 1914
THE VIRGINIAN   Jesse L. Lasky Feature Play Co., 1914
WHAT'S HIS NAME   Jesse L. Lasky Feature Play Co., 1914
THE MAN FROM HOME   Jesse L. Lasky Feature Play Co., 1914
ROSE OF THE RANCHO   Jesse L. Lasky Feature Play Co., 1914
THE GIRL OF THE GOLDEN WEST   Paramount, 1915
THE WARRENS OF VIRGINIA   Paramount, 1915
THE UNAFRAID   Paramount, 1915
THE CAPTIVE   Paramount, 1915
THE WILD GOOSE CHASE   Paramount, 1915
THE ARAB   Paramount, 1915
CHIMMIE FADDEN   Paramount, 1915
KINDLING   Paramount, 1915
CARMEN   Paramount, 1915
CHIMMIE FADDEN OUT WEST   Paramount, 1915
THE CHEAT   Paramount, 1915
THE GOLDEN CHANCE   Paramount, 1915
TEMPTATION   Paramount, 1916
THE TRAIL OF THE LONESOME PINE   Paramount, 1916
THE HEART OF NORA FLYNN   Paramount, 1916
MARIA ROSA   Paramount, 1916
THE DREAM GIRL   Paramount, 1916
JOAN THE WOMAN   Paramount, 1917
ROMANCE OF THE REDWOODS   Paramount, 1971
THE LITTLE AMERICAN   Paramount, 1917
THE WOMAN GOD FORGOT   Paramount, 1917
THE DEVIL STONE   Paramount, 1917
THE WHISPERING CHORUS   Paramount, 1918
OLD WIVES FOR NEW   Paramount, 1918
YOU CAN'T HAVE EVERYTHING   Paramount, 1918
TILL I COME BACK TO YOU   Paramount, 1918
THE SQUAW MAN   Paramount, 1918
DON'T CHANGE YOUR HUSBAND   Paramount, 1919
FOR BETTER OR WORSE   Paramount, 1919
MALE AND FEMALE   Paramount, 1919
WHY CHANGE YOUR WIFE?   Paramount, 1920
SOMETHING TO THINK ABOUT   Paramount, 1920
FORBIDDEN FRUIT   Paramount, 1921
THE AFFAIRS OF ANATOL   Paramount, 1921
FOOL'S PARADISE   Paramount, 1921
SATURDAY NIGHT   Paramount, 1922
MANSLAUGHTER   Paramount, 1922
ADAM'S RIB   Paramount, 1923
THE TEN COMMANDMENTS   Paramount, 1923
TRIUMPH   Paramount, 1924
FEET OF CLAY   Paramount, 1924
THE GOLDEN BED   Paramount, 1925
THE ROAD TO YESTERDAY   Producers Distributing Corp., 1925
THE VOLGA BOATMAN   Producers Distributing Corp., 1926
THE KING OF KINGS   Pathé, 1927
THE GODLESS GIRL   Pathé, 1929
DYNAMITE   MGM, 1929
MADAME SATAN   MGM, 1930
THE SQUAW MAN   Paramount, 1931

THE SIGN OF THE CROSS   Paramount, 1932
THIS DAY AND AGE   Paramount, 1933
FOUR FRIGHTENED PEOPLE   Paramount, 1934
CLEOPATRA   Paramount, 1934
THE CRUSADES   Paramount, 1935
THE PLAINSMAN   Paramount, 1937
THE BUCCANEER   Paramount, 1938
UNION PACIFIC   Paramount, 1939
NORTH WEST MOUNTED POLICE   Paramount, 1940
REAP THE WILD WIND   Paramount, 1942
THE STORY OF DR. WASSELL   Paramount, 1944
UNCONQUERED   Paramount, 1947
SAMSON AND DELILAH   Paramount, 1949
THE GREATEST SHOW ON EARTH ★   Paramount, 1952
THE TEN COMMANDMENTS   Paramount, 1956

VITTORIO DE SICA
b. July 7, 1902 - Sora, Italy
d. 1974

ROSE SCARLATTE   1940, Italian
MADDALENA ZERO IN CONDOTTA   1941, Italian
TERESA VENERDI   1941, Italian
UN GARIBALDINO AL CONVENTO   1941, Italian
I BAMBINI CI GUARDANO   *THE CHILDREN ARE
    WATCHING US*   1943, Italian
LA PORTA DEL CIELO   1946, Italian
SHOESHINE   Lopert, 1946, Italian
THE BICYCLE THIEF   Mayer-Burstyn, 1949, Italian
MIRACLE IN MILAN   Joseph Burstyn, 1951, Italian
UMBERTO D   Harrison Pictures, 1952, Italian
INDISCRETION OF AN AMERICAN WIFE
    STAZIONE TERMINI   Columbia, 1953, U.S.-Italian
GOLD OF NAPLES   DCA, 1955, Italian
THE ROOF   Trans-Lux, 1956, Italian
TWO WOMEN   *LA CIOCIARA*   Embassy, 1960,
    Italian-French
IL GIUDIZIO UNIVERSALE   1961, Italian
BOCCACCIO '70   co-director with Federico Fellini
    & Luchino Visconti, Embassy, 1962, Italian-French
THE CONDEMNED OF ALTONA   20th Century-Fox, 1963,
    Italian-French
IL BOOM   Italian, 1963

YESTERDAY, TODAY AND TOMORROW   Embassy,
    1963, Italian-French
MARRIAGE ITALIAN STYLE   Embassy, 1964,
    Italian-French
UN MONDE NOUVEAU   1966, French-Italian
AFTER THE FOX   United Artists, 1966, Italian-U.S.-British
THE WITCHES   co-director, Lopert, 1967, Italian-French
WOMAN TIMES SEVEN   Avco Embassy, 1967,
    French-Italian-U.S.
A PLACE FOR LOVERS   *AMANTI*   MGM, 1968,
    Italian-French
SUNFLOWER   Avco Embassy, 1969, Italian-French
THE GARDEN OF THE FINZI-CONTINIS   Cinema 5, 1971,
    Italian-West German
LE COPPIE   co-director, 1971, Italian
LO CHIAMEREMO ANDREA   1972, Italian
A BRIEF VACATION   Allied Artists, 1973, Italian
THE VOYAGE   United Artists, 1974, Italian

JOHN DEXTER
b. 1935 - England
d. 1990

THE VIRGIN SOLDIERS   Columbia, 1970, British

PIGEONS   *THE SIDELONG GLANCES OF A PIGEON
    KICKER*   MGM, 1970
I WANT WHAT I WANT   Cinerama Releasing Corporation,
    1972, British

WILLIAM DIETERLE
(Wilhelm Dieterle)
b. July 15, 1893 - Ludwigshafen, Germany
d. 1972

DER MENSCH AM WEGE   1923, German
DER MANN DER NICHT LIEBEN DARK   *DAS
    GEHEIMNIS DES ABBE X*   1927, German
GESCHLECHT IN FESSELN   1928, German
DER HEILIGE UND IHR NARR   1928, German
FRUHLINGSRAUSCHEN   1929, German
ICH LEBE FUR DICH   1929, German
LUDWIG DER ZWEITE - KONIG VON BAYERN
    1929, German
DAS SCHWEIGEN IM WALDE   1929, German
EINE STUNDE GLUCK   1929, German
DEI TANZ GEHT WEITER   First National, 1930
DIE MASKE FALLT   First National, 1930
KISMET   First National, 1931, German
THE LAST FLIGHT   Warner Bros., 1931
HER MAJESTY LOVE   Warner Bros., 1932
MAN WANTED   Warner Bros., 1932
JEWEL ROBBERY   Warner Bros., 1932
THE CRASH   Warner Bros., 1932
SIX HOURS TO LIVE   Warner Bros., 1932
SCARLET DAWN   Warner Bros., 1932
LAWYER MAN   Warner Bros., 1932
GRAND SLAM   Warner Bros., 1933
ADORABLE   Warner Bros., 1933
THE DEVIL'S IN LOVE   Warner Bros., 1933
FEMALE   Warner Bros., 1933
FROM HEADQUARTERS   Warner Bros., 1933
FASHIONS OF 1934   Warner Bros., 1934
FOG OVER FRISCO   Warner Bros., 1934
MADAME DU BARRY   Warner Bros., 1934
THE FIREBIRD   Warner Bros., 1934
THE SECRET BRIDE   Warner Bros., 1935
A MIDSUMMER NIGHT'S DREAM   co-director with
    Max Reinhardt, Warner Bros., 1935
DR. SOCRATES   Warner Bros., 1935
THE STORY OF LOUIS PASTUER   Warner Bros., 1936
THE WHITE ANGEL   Warner Bros., 1936
SATAN MET A LADY   Warner Bros., 1936
THE GREAT O'MALLEY   Warner Bros., 1937
ANOTHER DAWN   Warner Bros., 1937
THE LIFE OF EMILE ZOLA ★   Warner Bros.,   1937
BLOCKADE   Warner Bros., 1938
JUAREZ   Warner Bros., 1939
THE HUNCHBACK OF NOTRE DAME   RKO Radio,
    1939
DR. EHRLICH'S MAGIC BULLET   Warner Bros.,
    1940
A DISPATCH FROM REUTERS   Warner Bros.,
    1940
THE DEVIL AND DANIEL WEBSTER   *ALL THAT
    MONEY CAN BUY*   RKO Radio, 1941
SYNCOPATION   RKO Radio, 1942
TENNESSEE JOHNSON   MGM, 1942
KISMET   MGM, 1944
I'LL BE SEEING YOU   United Artists, 1944
LOVE LETTERS   Paramount, 1945
THIS LOVE OF OURS   Universal, 1945
THE SEARCHING WIND   Paramount, 1946
THE ACCUSED   Paramount, 1948

PORTRAIT OF JENNIE   Selznick, 1948
ROPE OF SAND   Paramount, 1949
VOLCANO   United Artists, 1950, Italian-U.S.
PAID IN FULL   Paramount, 1950
DARK CITY   Paramount, 1950
SEPTEMBER AFFAIR   Paramount, 1951
PEKING EXPRESS   Paramount, 1951
RED MOUNTAIN   Paramount, 1951
THE TURNING POINT   Paramount, 1952
BOOTS MALONE   Columbia, 1952
SALOME   Columbia, 1953
ELEPHANT WALK   Paramount, 1954
MAGIC FIRE   Republic, 1956
OMAR KHAYYAM   Paramount, 1957
IL VENDICATORE   1959, Italian-Yugoslavian
DIE FASTNACHTSBEICHTE   1960, West German
HERRIN DER WELT   1960, West German
THE CONFESSION   Golden Eagle, 1965

JACK DONOHUE
(John Francis Donohue)
b. November 3, 1908 - New York, New York
d. 1984

CLOSE-UP   Eagle Lion, 1948
THE YELLOW CAB MAN   MGM, 1950
WATCH THE BRIDE   MGM, 1951
LICKY ME   Warner Bros., 1954
BABES IN TOYLAND   Buena Vista, 1961
MARRIAGE ON THE ROCKS   Warner Bros., 1965
ASSAULT ON A QUEEN   Paramount, 1965

ALEXANDER PETROVICH DOVZHENKO
b. September 12, 1894 - Sosnitsa, Ukraine, Russia
d. 1956

VASYA THE REFORMER   co-director with F. Lokatinsi &
    Yosef Rona, 1926, Soviet
THE DIPLOMATIC POUCH   1927, Soviet
ZVENIGORA   1928, Soviet
ARSENAL   1929, Soviet
EARTH   Vufku, 1930, Soviet
IVAN   1932, Soviet
AEROGARD   1935, Soviet
SHCHORS   1939, Soveit
VICTORY IN THE UKRAINE AND THE EXPULSION OF
    THE GERMANS FROM THE BOUNDARIES OF THE
    UKRAINIAN SOVIET EARTH   *VICTORY IN
    THE UKRAINE* (FD)   co-director, 1945, Soviet
LIFE IN BLOOM   1949, Soviet

CARL THEODOR DREYER
b. February 3, 1889 - Copenhagen, Denmark
d. 1968

THE PRESIDENT   1919, Danish
LEAVES FROM SATAN'S BOOK   1920, Danish
THE PARSON'S WIDOW   *THE WITCH WOMAN/
    THE FOURTH MARRIAGE OF DAME MARGARET*
    1920, Danish
LOVE ONE ANOTHER   1922, Danish
ONCE UPON A TIME   1922, Danish
MIKAEL   1924, German
MASTER OF THE HOUSE   1925, Danish
THE BRIDE OF GLOMDAL   1925, Danish

THE PASSION OF JOAN OF ARC   M.J. Gourland,
    1928, French
VAMPYR   *VAMPYR OU L'ETRANGE AVENTURE
    DE DAVID GRAY*   1932, French-German
DAY OF WRATH   George Schaefer, 1943, Danish
TWO PEOPLE   1945, Swedish
ORDET   Kingsley International, 1955, Danish
GERTRUD   Pathé Contemporary, 1964, Danish

E.A. DUPONT
(Ewald Andre Dupont)
b. December 25, 1891 - Leitz, Germany
d. 1956

DIE JANANERIN   1917, German
DAS GEHEIMNIS DES AMERIKA-DOCKA   1918, German
EUROPA POSTLAGERND   1918, German
DER LEBENDE SCHATTEN   1918, German
ES WERDE LICHT   co-director with Richard Oswald, 1918
DER AMM AUS NEAPEL   1918, German
DIE SCHWARZE SCHACHDAME   1918, German
DER TEUFEL   1918, German
DIE APACHEN   1919, German
DAS GRAND HOTEL BABYLON   1919, German
MORD OHNE TATER   1920, German
DER WEISSE PFAU   1920, German
DIE GEIERWALLY   1921, German
WHITECHAPEL   1921, German
KINDER DER FINSTERNIS   1922, German
SIE UND DIE DREI   1922, German
DAS ALTE GESETZ   1923, German
DIE GRUNE MANUELA   1923, German
DER DEMUTIGE UND DIE SANGERIN   1925, German
LVARIETY   Paramount, 1925, German
LOVE ME AND THE WORLD IS MINE   1928, British
MOULIN ROUGE   BIP, 1928, British
PICCADILLY   BIP, 1929, British
ATLANTIC   BIP, 1929, British
TWO WORLDS   BIP, 1930, British
CAPE FORLORN   *LOVE STORM*   BIP, 1931, British
SALTO MORTALE   *TRAPEZE*   1931, German
PETER VOSS DER MILLIONENDIEB   1932, German
DER LAUFER VON MARATHON   1933, German
LADIES MUST LOVE   Universal, 1933
THE BISHOP MISBEHAVES   MGM, 1935
A SON COMES HOME   Paramount, 1936
FORGOTTEN FACES   Paramount, 1936
A NIGHT OF MYSTERY   Paramount, 1937
ON SUCH A NIGHT   Paramount, 1937
LOVE ON TOAST   Paramount, 1937
HELL'S KITCHEN   co-director with Lewis Seiler, Warner
    Bros., 1939
THE SCARF   United Artists, 1951
PROBLEM GIRLS   Columbia, 1953
THE NEANDERTHAL MAN   United Artists, 1953
THE STEEL LADY   United Artists, 1953
RETURN TO TREASURE ISLAND   United Artists, 1954

JULIEN DUVIVIER
b. October 8, 1896 - Lille, France
d. 1967

HACELDMA   *LE PRIX DU SANG*   1919, French
LA REINCARNATION DE SERGE RENAUDIER
    1920, French
L'AGONIE DES AIGLES   1921, French
LES ROQUEVILLARD   1922, French
L'OURAGAN SUR LA MONTAGNE   1922, French

DER UNHEIMLICHE GAST 1922, German
LE REFLET DE CLAUDE MERCOEUR 1923, French
CREDO OU LA TRAGEDIE DE LOURDES 1924, French
COEURS FAROUCHES 1924, French
LA MACHINE A REFAIRE LA VIE (FD) co-director, 1924, French
L'OEUVRE IMMORTELLE 1924, Belgian
L'ABBE CONSTANTIN 1925, French
POIL DE CAROTTE 1925, French
L'AGONIE DE JERUSALEM 1926, French
L'HOMME A L'HISPANO 1926, French
LE MARIAGE DE MADEMOISELLE BEULEMANS 1927, French
LE MYSTERE DE LA TOUR EIFFEL 1927, French
LE TOURBILLON DE PARIS 1928, French
LA VIE MIRACULEUSE DE THERESE MARTIN 1929, French
LA DIVINE CROISIERE 1929, French
MAMAN COLIBRI 1929, French
AU BONHEUR DES DAMES 1930, French
DAVID GOLDER 1930, French
LES CINQ GENTLEMEN MAUDITS SOUS LA LUNE DU MAROC 1932, French
ALLO BERLIN? ICI PARIS! 1932, French
POIL DE CAROTTE 1932, French
LA VENUS DU COLLEGE 1932, French
LA TETE D'UN HOMME 1933, French
LA MACHINE A REFAIRE LA VIE 1933, French
LE PETIT ROI 1933, French
LA PAQUEBOT "TENACITY" 1934, French
MARIA CHAPDELAINE 1934, French
GOLGOTHA 1935, French
LA BANDERA 1935, French
THE GOLEM THE LEGEND OF PRAGUE United Artists, 1936, French-Czechoslovakian
L'HOMME DU JOUR 1936, French
LA BELLE EQUIPE 1936, French
PEPE LE MOKO Paris Film, 1936, French
UN CARNET DE BAL CHRISTINE 1937, French
THE GREAT WALTZ MGM, 1938
LA FIN DU JOUR 1939, French
LA CHARRETTE FANTOME 1939, French
UNTEL, PERE ET FILS HEART OF A NATION 1940, French
LYDIA United Artists, 1941
TALES OF MANHATTAN RKO, 1942
FLESH AND FANTASY Universal, 1943
THE IMPOSTOR Universal, 1944
PANIC Tricolore, 1946, French
ANNA KARENINA 20th Century-Fox, 1947, British
AU ROYAUME DES CIEUX WOMAN HUNT 1949, French
CAPTAIN BLACK JACK United Artists, 1950, French-British-Spanish
UNDER THE PARIS SKY Discina International, 1951, French
THE LITTLE WORLD OF DON CAMILLO Italian Films Export, 1951, French
ON TRIAL L'AFFAIRE MAURIZIUS New Realm, 1953, French-Italian
THE RETURN OF DON CAMILLO 1953, French-Italian
LA FETE A HENRIETTE HOLIDAY FOR HENRIETTE 1953, French
MARIANNE OF MY YOUTH United Motion Picture Organization, 1955, French
DEADLIER THAN THE MALE VOICI LE TEMPS DES ASSASSINS Continental, 1955, French
THE MAN IN THE RAINCOAT Kingsley International, 1956, French-Italian

POT BOUILLE THE HOUSE OF LOVERS Continental, 1957, French
A WOMAN LIKE SATAN THE FEMALE/LA FEMME ET LA PANTIN Lopert, 1958, French-Italian
MARIE OCTOBRE 1958, French
LA GRANDE VIE 1960, French-West German
BOULEVARD 1960, French
LA CHAMBRE ARDENTE THE CURSE AND THE COFFIN 1962, French-Italian-West German
THE DEVIL AND THE TEN COMMANDMENTS Union Films, 1962, French-Italian
CHAIR DE POULE HIGHWAY PICKUP 1963, French-Italian
DIABOLIQUEMENT VOTRE 1967, French-Italian-West German

A L L A N   D W A N
(Joseph Aloysius Dwan)
b. April 3, 1885 - Toronto, Ontario, Canada
d. 1981

BRANDISHING A BAD MAN 1911
RATTLESNAKES AND GUNPOWDER 1911
THE ANGEL OF PARADISE RANCH 1911
THE YIDDISHER COWBOY 1911
THE POISONED FLUME 1911
THREE MILLION DOLLARS 1911
THE GUNMAN 1911
THE GOLD LUST 1911
THE LOCKET 1912
THE MORMON 1912
FIDELITY 1912
THE COWARD 1912
THE HATERS 1912
THE GREEN EYED MONSTER 1912
THE MARAUDERS 1912
THE ANIMAL WITHIN 1912
THE BATTLEGROUND 1912
THE FEAR 1912
CALAMITY ANNE'S WARD 1912
THE POWER OF LOVE 1912
THE FUGITIVE 1913
CALAMITY ANN, DETECTIVE 1913
ANGEL OF THE CANYONS 1913
THE ANIMAL 1913
ANOTHER MAN'S LIFE 1913
ASHES OF THREE 1913
WHEN LUCK CHANGES 1913
CUPID THROWS A BRICK 1913
THE SPIRIT OF THE FLAG 1913
THE CALL TO ARMS 1913
CRIMINALS 1913
BACK TO LIFE 1913
THE MENACE 1913
THE LIE 1914
DISCORD AND HARMONY 1914
THE EMBEZZLER 1914
TRAGEDY OF WHISPERING CREEK 1914
THE FORBIDDEN ROOM 1914
RICHILIEU Universal, 1914
WILDFLOWER Paramount, 1914
THE COUNTY CHAIRMAN Paramount, 1914
THE STRAIGHT ROAD Paramount, 1914
THE UNWELCOME MRS. HATCH Paramount, 1914
HONOR OF THE MOUNTED 1914
THE HOPES OF BLIND ALLEY 1914
THE CONSPIRACY Paramount, 1914
THE DANCING GIRL Paramount, 1915
DAVID HARUM Paramount, 1915

Dw

**FILM
DIRECTORS
GUIDE**

**N
O
T
A
B
L
E

D
I
R
E
C
T
O
R
S

O
F

T
H
E

P
A
S
T**

THE LOVE ROUTE   Paramount, 1915
THE COMMANDING OFFICER   Paramount, 1915
MAY BLOSSOM   Pathé, 1915
THE PRETTY SISTER OF JOSE   Paramount, 1915
A GIRL OF YESTERDAY   Paramount, 1915
THE FOUNDLING   Paramount, 1915
JORDAN IS A HARD ROAD   Fine Arts-Triangle, 1915
BETTY OF GREYSTONE   Fine Arts-Triangle, 1916
THE HABIT OF HAPPINESS   Fine Arts-Triangle, 1916
THE GOOD BAD MAN   Fine Arts-Triangle, 1916
AN INNOCENT MAGDALENE   Fine Arts-Triangle, 1916
THE HALF-BREED   Fine Arts-Triangle, 1916
MANHATTAN MADNESS   Fine Arts-Triangle, 1916
FIFTY-FIFTY   Fine Arts-Triangle, 1916
PANTHEA   Selznick, 1917
THE FIGHTING ODDS   Goldwyn, 1917
A MODERN MUSKETEER   Artcraft, 1917
MR. FIX-IT   Artcraft, 1918
BOUND IN MOROCCO   Artcraft, 1918
HE COMES UP SMILING   1918, Artcraft
CHEATING CHEATERS   Select, 1919
GETTING MARY MARRIED   Select, 1919
THE DARK STAR   Artcraft, 1919
SOLDIERS OF FORTUNE   Realart, 1919
THE LUCK OF THE IRISH   Realart, 1920
THE FORBIDDEN THING   Associated Producers, 1920
A PERFECT CRIME   Associated Producers, 1921
A BROKEN DOLL   Associated Producers, 1921
THE SCOFFER   Realart, 1921
THE SINS OF MARTHA QUEED   Associated Exibitors,
   1921
IN THE HEART OF A FOOL   Associated First National,
   1921
THE HIDDEN WOMAN   Nanuet Amusement/American
   Releasing, 1922
SUPERSTITION   Artlee, 1922
ROBIN HOOD   United Artists, 1922
THE GLIMPSES OF THE MOON   Paramount, 1923
LAWFUL LARCENY   Paramount, 1923
ZAZA   Paramount, 1923
BIG BROTHER   Paramount, 1923
A SOCIETY SCANDAL   Paramount, 1924
MANHANDLED   Paramount, 1924
HER LOVE STORY   Paramount, 1924
WAGES OF VIRTUE   Paramount, 1924
ARGENTINE LOVE   Paramount, 1924
NIGHT LIFE OF NEW YORK   Paramount, 1925
COAST OF FOLLY   Paramount, 1925
STAGE STRUCK   Paramount, 1925
SEA HORSES   Paramount, 1926
PADLOCKED   Paramount, 1926
TIN GODS   Paramount, 1926
SUMMER BACHELORS   Fox, 1926
THE MUSIC MASTER   Fox, 1927
WEST POINT (FD)   1927
THE JOY GIRL   Fox, 1927
EAST SIDE, WEST SIDE   Fox, 1927
FRENCH DRESSING   First National, 1927
THE BIG NOISE   First National, 1928
THE IRON MASK   United Artists, 1929
TIDE OF EMPIRE   MGM, 1929
THE FAR CALL   Fox, 1929
FROZEN JUSTICE   Fox, 1929
SOUTH SEA ROSE   Fox, 1929
WHAT A WIDOW!   United Artists, 1930
MAN TO MAN   First National, 1930
CHANCES   First National, 1931
WICKED   Fox, 1931
WHILE PARIS SLEEPS   Fox, 1932
HER FIRST AFFAIR   Associated British, 1933, British

COUNSEL'S OPINION   London Films-Paramount,
   1933, British
I SPY *THE MORNING AFTER*   Wardour-Majestic, 1934
BLACK SHEEP   Fox, 1935
NAVY WIFE   20th Century-Fox, 1935
THE SONG AND DANCE MAN   20th Century-Fox, 1936
HUMAN CARGO   20th Century-Fox, 1936
HIGH TENSION   20th Century-Fox, 1936
15 MAIDEN LANE   20th Century-Fox, 1936
WOMAN-WISE   20th Century-Fox, 1937
THAT I MAY LIVE   20th Century-Fox, 1937
ONE MILE FROM HEAVEN   20th Century-Fox, 1937
HEIDI   20th Century-Fox, 1937
REBECCA OF SUNNYBROOK FARM   20th Century-Fox,
   1938
JOSETTE   20th Century-Fox, 1938
SUEZ   20th Century-Fox, 1938
THE THREE MUSKETEERS   20th Century-Fox, 1939
THE GORILLA   20th Century-Fox, 1939
FRONTIER MARSHAL   20th Century-Fox, 1939
SAILOR'S LADY   20th Century-Fox, 1940
YOUNG PEOPLE   20th Century-Fox, 1940
TRAIL OF THE VIGILANTES   Universal, 1940
LOOK WHO'S LAUGHING   RKO Radio, 1941
RISE AND SHINE   20th Century-Fox, 1941
FRIENDLY ENEMIES   United Artists, 1942
HERE WE GO AGAIN   RKO Radio, 1942
AROUND THE WORLD   RKO Radio, 1943
UP IN MABEL'S ROOM   United Artists, 1944
ABROAD WITH TWO YANKS   United Artists, 1944
BREWSTER'S MILLIONS   United Artists, 1945
GETTING GERTIE'S GARTER   United Artists, 1945
RENDEZVOUS WITH ANNIE   Republic, 1946
CALENDAR GIRL   Republic, 1947
NORTHWEST OUTPOST   Republic, 1947
DRIFTWOOD   Republic, 1947
THE INSIDE STORY   Republic, 1948
ANGEL IN EXILE   co-director with Philip Ford, Republic,
   1948
SANDS OF IWO JIMA   Republic, 1949
SURRENDER   Republic, 1950
BELLE LE GRANDE   Republic, 1951
THE WILD BLUE YONDER   Republic, 1951
I DREAM OF JEANIE   Republic, 1952
MONTANA BELLE   RKO Radio, 1952
THE WOMAN THEY ALMOST LYNCHED   Republic, 1953
SWEETHEARTS ON PARADE   Republic, 1953
FLIGHT NURSE   Republic, 1954
SILVER LODE   RKO Radio, 1954
PASSION   RKO Radio, 1954
CATTLE QUEEN OF MONTANA   RKO Radio, 1954
ESCAPE TO BURMA   RKO Radio, 1955
PEARL OF THE SOUTH PACIFIC   RKO Radio, 1955
TENNESSEE'S PARTNER   RKO Radio, 1955
SLIGHTLY SCARLET   RKO Radio, 1956
HOLD BACK THE NIGHT   Allied Artists, 1956
THE RIVER'S EDGE   20th Century-Fox, 1957
THE RESTLESS BREED   20th Century-Fox, 1957
ENCHANTED ISLAND   Warner Bros., 1958
MOST DANGEROUS MAN ALIVE   Columbia, 1961

E

SERGEI EISENSTEIN
b. January 23, 1898 - Riga, Latvia, Russia
d. 1948

STRIKE   Brandon, 1925, Soviet
THE BATTLESHIP POTEMKIN   *POTEMKIN*   Amkino, 1925, Soviet
OCTOBER   *TEN DAYS THAT SHOOK THE WORLD*   co-director with Grigori Alexandrov, Amkino, 1928, Soviet
THE GENERAL LINE   *OLD AND NEW*   co-director with Grigori Alexandrov, 1929, Soviet
STURM UBER LA SARRAZ   co-director with Hans Richter & Ivor Montagu, 1929, Swiss
ROMANCE SENTIMENTALE   co-director with Grigori Alexandrov, 1930, French
QUE VIVA MEXICO!   1931-32, Soviet, unfinished
BEZHIN MEADOW   1935-37, Soviet, unfinished
ALEXANDER NEVSKY   Amkino, 1938, Soviet
THE FERGANA CANAL   1939, Soviet, unfinished
IVAN THE TERRIBLE, PART I   Artkino, 1945, Soviet
IVAN THE TERRIBLE, PART II   Artkino, 1946, Soviet
IVAN THE TERRIBLE, PART III   1947, Soviet, unfinished

RAY ENRIGHT
(Raymond E. Enright)
b. March 25, 1896 - Anderson, Indiana
d. 1965

TRACKER BY THE POLICE   Warner Bros., 1927
JAWS OF STEEL   Warner Bros., 1927
THE GIRL FROM CHICAGO   Warner Bros., 1927
DOMESTIC TROUBLES   Warner Bros., 1928
LAND OF THE SILVER FOX   Warner Bros., 1928
THE LITTLE WILDCAT   Warner Bros., 1929
STOLEN KISSES   Warner Bros., 1929
KID GLOVES   Warner Bros., 1929
SKIN DEEP   Warner Bros., 1929
SONG OF THE WEST   Warner Bros., 1930
GOLDEN DAWN   Warner Bros., 1930
DANCING SWEETIES   Warner Bros., 1930
SCARLET PAGES   Warner Bros., 1930
PLAY GIRL   Warner Bros., 1932
THE TENDERFOOT   First National, 1932
BLONDIE JOHNSON   First National, 1933
THE SILK EXPRESS   Warner Bros., 1933
TOMORROW AT SEVEN   RKO, 1933
HAVANA WIDOWS   First National, 1933
I'VE GOT YOUR NUMBER   Warner Bros., 1934
20 MILLION SWEETHEARTS   First National, 1934
THE CIRCUS CLOWN   First National, 1934
DAMES   Warner Bros., 1934
THE ST. LOUIS KID   Warner Bros., 1934
WHILE THE PATIENT SLEPT   First National, 1935
TRAVELING SALESLADY   First National, 1935
ALIBI IKE   First National, 1935
WE'RE IN THE MONEY   Warner Bros., 1935
MISS PACIFIC FLEET   Warner Bros., 1935
SNOWED UNDER   First National, 1936
EARTHWORM TRACTORS   First National, 1936
CHINA CLIPPER   First National, 1936
SING ME A LOVE SONG   First National, 1937
READY, WILLING AND ABLE   Warner Bros., 1937
SLIM   Warner Bros., 1937
THE SINGING MARINE   Warner Bros., 1937
BACK IN CIRCULATION   Warner Bros., 1937
SWING YOUR LADY   Warner Bros., 1938
GOLD DIGGERS IN PARIS   Warner Bros., 1938
HARD TO GET   Warner Bros., 1938
GOING PLACES   Warner Bros., 1938
NAUGHTY BUT NICE   Warner Bros., 1939
ANGELS WASH THEIR FACES   Warner Bros., 1939
ON YOUR TOES   Warner Bros., 1939
BROTHER RAT AND A BABY   Warner Bros., 1940
AN ANGEL FROM TEXAS   Warner Bros., 1940
RIVER'S END   Warner Bros., 1940
THE WAGONS ROLL AT NIGHT   Warner Bros., 1941
THIEVES FALL OUT   Warner Bros., 1941
BAD MEN OF MISSOURI   Warner Bros., 1941
LAW OF THE TROPICS   Warner Bros., 1941
WILD BILL HICKOK RIDES   Warner Bros., 1942
THE SPOILERS   Universal, 1942
MEN OF TEXAS   Universal, 1942
SIN TOWN   Universal, 1942
GOOD LUCK, MR. YATES   Columbia, 1943
THE IRON MAJOR   RKO Radio, 1943
GUNG HO!   UNIVERSAL, 1943
CHINA SKY   RKO Radio, 1945
MAN ALIVE   RKO Radio, 1945
ONE WAY TO LOVE   Columbia, 1946
TRAIL STREE   RKO Radio, 1947
ALBUQUERQUE   Paramount, 1948
RETURN OF THE BAD MEN   RKO Radio, 1948
CORONER CREEK   Columbia, 1948
SOUTH OF ST. LOUIS   Warner Bros., 1949
MONTANA   Warner Bros., 1950
THE KANSAS RAIDERS   Universal, 1950
FLAMING FEATHER   Paramount, 1952
THE MAN FROM CAIRO   Lippert, 1953

CHESTER ERSKINE
b. November 29, 1905 - Vienna, Austria
d. 1986

MIDNIGHT   Universal, 1934
FRANKIE AND JOHNNY   Republic, 1935
THE EGG AND I   Universal, 1947
TAKE ONE FALSE STEP   Universal, 1949
A GIRL IN EVERY PORT   RKO Radio, 1952
ANDROCLES AND THE LION   RKO Radio, 1953

JEAN EUSTACHE
b. 1938 - Pessac, France
d. 1981

LES MAUVAISES FREQUENTATIONS   1963, French
LE PERE NOEL A LES YEUX BLEUS   Anouchka Films, 1966, French
LA ROSIERE DE PESSAC (I)   Jean Eustache Film, 1968, French
LE COCHON   Luc Moullet/Francoise Lebrun, 1970, French
NUMERO ZERO   Jean Eustache Film, 1971, French
THE MOTHER AND THE WHORE   New Yorker, 1973, French
MES PETITES AMOUREUSES   Elite Films, 1974, French
UNE SALE HISTOIRE   Les Films du Losange, 1977, French

LA ROSIERE DE PESSAC (II)   INA/ZDF/Mediane Films, 1979, French-West German
LE JARDIN DES DELICES DE JEROME BOSCH
   INA, 1979, French
LES PHOTOS D'ALIX   Mediane Films, 1980, French
OFFRE D'EMPLOI   INA, 1980, French

F

JOHN FARROW
b. February 10, 1904 - Sydney, Australia
d. 1963

WARLORD   Warner Bros., 1937
MEN IN EXILE   Warner Bros., 1937
WEST OF SHANGHAI   Warner Bros., 1937
SHE LOVED A FIREMAN   Warner Bros., 1938
THE INVISIBLE MENACE   Warner Bros., 1938
LITTLE MISS THOROUGHBRED   Warner Bros., 1938
MY BILL   Warner Bros., 1938
BROADWAY MUSKETEERS   Warner Bros., 1938
WOMEN IN THE WIND   Warner Bros., 1939
THE SAINT STRIKES BACK   RKO Radio, 1939
SORORITY HOUSE   RKO Radio, 1939
FIVE CAME BACK   RKO Radio, 1939
FULL CONFESSION   RKO Radio, 1939
RENO   RKO Radio, 1939
MARRIED AND IN LOVE   1940
A BILL OF DIVORCEMENT   RKO Radio, 1940
WAKE ISLAND   Paramount, 1942
THE COMMANDOS STRIKE AT DAWN
   Columbia, 1943
CHINA   Paramount, 1943
THE HITLER GANG   Paramount, 1944
YOU CAME ALONG   Paramount, 1945
TWO YEARS BEFORE THE MAST
   Paramount, 1946
CALIFORNIA   Paramount, 1947
EASY COME, EASY GO   Paramount, 1947
BLAZE OF NOON   Paramount, 1947
CALCUTTA   Paramount, 1947
THE BIG CLOCK   Paramount, 1948
BEYOND GLORY   Paramount, 1948
THE NIGHT HAS A THOUSAND EYES
   Paramount, 1948
ALIAS NICK BEAL   Paramount, 1949
RED, HOT AND BLUE   Paramount, 1949
WHERE DANGER LIVES   RKO Radio, 1950
COPPER CANYON   Paramount, 1950
HIS KIND OF WOMAN   RKO Radio, 1951
SUBMARINE COMMAND   Paramount, 1951
RIDE, VAQUERO   MGM, 1953
PLUNDER OF THE SUN   Warner Bros., 1953
BOTANY BAY   Paramount, 1953
HONDO   Warner Bros., 1953
A BULLET IS WAITING   Columbia, 1954
THE SEA CHASE   Warner Bros., 1955
BACK FROM ETERNITY   RKO Radio, 1956
THE UNHOLY WIFE   Universal, 1957
JOHN PAUL JONES   Warner Bros., 1959

RAINER WERNER FASSBINDER
b. May 31, 1946 - Bad Worishofen, Bavaria, West Germany
d. 1982

LIEBE IST KALTER ALS DER TOD   1969, West German
KATZELMACHER   1969, West German
GOTTER DER PEST   1970, West German
WHY DOES HERR R. RUN AMOK?   co-director with
   Michael Fengler, New Yorker, 1970, West German
THE AMERICAN SOLDIER   New Yorker, 1970,
   West German
DIE NIKLASHAUSER FAHRT   co-director with Michael
   Fengler, 1970, West German
RIO DAS MORTE   1971, West German
PIONIERE IN INGOLSTADT   1971, West German
WHITY   1971, West German
BEWARE THE HOLY WHORE   New Yorker, 1971,
   West German
THE MERCHANT OF FOUR SEASONS   New Yorker,
   1972, West German
THE BITTER TEARS OF PETRA VON KANT   New
   Yorker, 1972, West German
ACHT STUNDEN SIND KEIN TAG (MS)   1972,
   West German
WILDWECHSEL (TF)   1973, West German
WELT AM DRAHT (TF)   1973, West German
ALI: FEAR EATS THE SOUL   New Yorker, 1974,
   West German
MARTHA   1974, West German
EFFI BRIEST   New Yorker, 1974, West German
FOX AND HIS FRIENDS   *FAUSTRECHT DER FREIHEIT*
   New Yorker, 1975, West German
MOTHER KUSTERS GOES TO HEAVEN   New Yorker,
   1975, West German
FEAR OF FEAR   1976, West German
CHINESE ROULETTE   New Yorker, 1976, West German
SATAN'S BREW   New Yorker, 1976, West German
DEUTSCHLAND IM HERBST (FD)   co-director,
   Filmverlag der Autoren/Hallelujah Film/Kairos Film, 1978,
   West German
IN A YEAR OF 13 MONTHS   New Yorker, 1978,
   West German
DESPAIR   New Line Cinema, 1978, West German
BERLIN ALEXANDERPLATZ (MS)   1979, West German
THE MARRIAGE OF MARIA BRAUN   New Yorker,
   1979, West German
DIE DRITTE GENERATION   1979, West German
QUERELLE   Triumph/Columbia, 1983, West German

EMILIO (EL INDIO) FERNANDEZ
b. March 26, 1904 - El Hondo, Mexico
d. 1986

LA ISLA DE LA PASION   Azteca Films, 1941, Mexican
SOY PURO MEXICANO   Azteca Films, 1942, Mexican
FLOR SILVESTRE   Azteca Films, 1943, Mexican
MARIA CANDELARIA   Azteca Films, 1943, Mexican
LAS ABANDONADAS   Azteca Films, 1944, Mexican
BUGAMBILLIA   Azteca Films, 1945, Mexican
PEPITA JIMENEZ   Azteca Films, 1945, Mexican
THE PEARL   Azteca Films, 1946, Mexican
ENAMORADA   Azteca Films, 1947, Mexican
RIO ESCONDIDO   Azteca Films, 1947, Mexican
MACLOVIA   Azteca Films, 1948, Mexican
SALON MEXICO   Azteca Films, 1948, Mexican
PUEBLERINA   Azteca Films, 1949, Mexican
LA MALQUERIDA   Azteca Films, 1949, Mexican

DUELO EN LAS MONTANAS   Azteca Films, 1949,
    Mexican
THE TORCH   Eagle Lion, 1950, U.S.-Mexican
UN DIA DE VIDA   Azteca Films, 1950, Mexican
VICTIMAS DEL PECADO   Azteca Films, 1951, Mexican
LA BIENAMADA   Azteca Films, 1951, Mexican
ACAPULCO   Azteca Films, 1951, Mexican
ISLAS MARIAS   Azteca Films, 1951, Mexican
SUAVE PATRIA   Azteca Films, 1951, Mexican
SIEMPRE TUYA   Azteca Films, 1951, Mexican
TU Y EL MAR   Azteca Films, 1952, Mexican
CUANDO LEVANTA LA NIEBLA   Azteca Films, 1952,
    Mexican
LA RED   Azteca Films, 1953, Mexican
EL REPORTAJE   Azteca Films, 1953, Mexican
EL RAPTO   Azteca Films, 1953, Mexican
LA ROSA BLANCA   Azteca Films, 1954, Mexican
LA REBELION DE LOS COLGADOS   Azteca Films, 1954,
    Mexican
NOSOTROS DOS   1954, Spanish
LA TIERRA DEL FUEGO SE APAGA   1955, Argentine
UNA CITA DE AMOR   Azteca Films, 1956, Mexican
EL IMPOSTOR   Azteca Films, 1957, Mexican
PUEBLITO, O EL AMOR   Azteca Films, 1962, Mexican
UN DORADO DE PANCHO VILLA   Azteca Films, 1966,
    Mexican
AQUEL MEXICO LINDO   Azteca Films, 1968, Mexican
LA CHOCA   Azteca Films, 1973, Mexican
MEXICO NORTE   Azteca Films, 1974, Mexican
ZONA ROJA   Azteca Films, 1976, Mexican
EROTICA   Azteca Films, 1978, Mexican

JACQUES FEYDER
(Jacques Frederix)
b. July 21, 1885 - Ixelles, Belgium
d. 1948

M. PINSON - POLICIER   co-director with Gaston Ravel,
    1916, French
TETES DE FEMMES - FEMMES DE TETE   1916, French
LE PIED QUI ETREINT   1916, French
LE BLUFF   1916, French
UN CONSEIL D'AMI   1916, French
L'HOMME DE CONPAGNIE   1916, French
TIENS VOUS ETES A POITIERS?   1916, French
LA FRERE DE LAIT   1916, French
L'INSTINCT EST MAITRE   1917, French
LE BILLARD CASSE   1917, French
ABREGEONS LES FORMALITES!   1917, French
LA TROUVAILLE DE BUCHU   1917, French
LE PARDESSUS DE DEMI-SAISON   1917, French
LES VIEILLES FEMMES DE L'HOSPICE   1917, French
LE RAVIN SANS FOND   co-director with Raymond
    Bernard, 1917, French
LA FAUTE D'ORTHOGRAPHE   1919, French
L'ATLANTIDE   MISSING HUSBANDS   1921, French
CRAINQUEBILLE   1922, French
VISAGES D'ENFANTS   1925, Swiss
L'IMAGE   1925, French
GRIBICHE   1925, French
CARMEN   co-director with Francoise.Rosay, 1926, French
AU PAYS DU ROI LEPREUX   1927, French
THERESE RAQUIN   SHADOWS OF FEAR   1928, French
LES NOUVEAUX MESSIEURS   1928, French
THE KISS   MGM, 1929
DAYBREAK   MGM, 1931
SON OF INDIA   MGM, 1931
LE GRAND JEU   1934, French
PENSION MIMOSAS   1935, French

CARNIVAL IN FLANDERS   LA KERMESSE HEROIQUE
    American Tobis, 1935, French
LES GENS DU VOYAGE   1937, French
KNIGHT WITHOUT ARMOR   United Artists, 1937, British
FAHRENDES VOLK   1938, German
LA LOI DU NORD   1942, French-Norwegian
UNE FEMME DISPARAIT   1942, Swiss
MACADAM   1946, French

TERENCE FISHER
b. 1904 - London, England
d. 1980

COLONEL BOGEY   GFD, 1948, British
TO THE PUBLIC DANGER   GFD, 1948, British
PORTRAIT FROM LIFE   THE GIRL IN THE PAINTING
    Universal, 1948, British
SONG OF TOMORROW   GFD, 1948, British
MARRY ME!   GFD, 1949, British
THE ASTONISHED HEART   co-director with Anthony
    Darnborough, GFD, 1950, British
SO LONG AT THE FAIR   co-director with Anthony
    Darnborough, GFD, 1950, British
HOME TO DANGER   Eros, 1951, British
A DISTANT TRUMPET   Apex, 1952, British
MAN BAIT   THE LAST PAGE   Exclusive Films, 1952,
    British
STOLEN FACE   Exclusive Films, 1952, U.S.-British
WINGS OF DANGER   DEAD ON COURSE   Exclusive
    Films, 1952, British
FOUR-SIDED TRIANGLE   Exclusive Films, 1953,
    British
WOMAN IN HIDING   MANTRAP   United Artists, 1953,
    British
SPACEWAYS   Exclusive Films, 1953, British
BLOOD ORANGE   Exclusive Films, 1953, British
FINAL APPOINTMENT   Monarch, 1954, British
MASK OF DUST   RACE FOR LIFE   Exclusive Films,
    1954, British
THE BLACK GLOVE   FACE THE MUSIC   Exclusive Films,
    1954, British
CHILDREN GALORE   GFD, 1954, British
THE UNHOLY FOUR   THE STRANGER CAME HOME
    Exclusive Films, 1954, British
BLACKOUT   MURDER BY PROXY   Exclusive Films,
    1954, British
STOLEN ASSIGNMENT   1955, British
THE FLAW   Renown, 1955, British
THE LAST MAN TO HANG?   Columbia, 1956, British
THE CURSE OF FRANKENSTEIN   Warner Bros., 1957,
    British
KILL ME TOMORROW   Tudor Pictures, 1957, British
HORROR OF DRACULA   DRACULA   Universal, 1958,
    British
THE REVENGE OF FRANKENSTEIN   Columbia, 1958,
    British
THE HOUND OF THE BASKERVILLES   United Artists,
    1959, British
THE MUMMY   Universal, 1959, British
THE MAN WHO COULD CHEAT DEATH   Paramount,
    1959, British
THE STRANGLERS OF BOMBAY   Columbia, 1959,
    British
THE BRIDES OF DRACULA   Universal, 1960, British
THE SWORD OF SHERWOOD FOREST   Columbia, 1960,
    British
HOUSE OF FRIGHT   THE TWO FACES OF DR.
    JEKYLL   American International, 1960, British
THE CURSE OF THE WEREWOLF   Universal,
    1961, British

THE PHANTOM OF THE OPERA   Universal, 1962,
   British
SHERLOCK HOLMES AND THE DEADLY NECKLACE
   Screen Gems, 1962, West German-British
SHERLOCK HOLMES   1963, British
THE HORROR OF IT ALL   20th Century-Fox, 1964, British
THE EARTH DIES SCREAMING   20th Century-Fox, 1965,
   British
THE GORGON   Columbia, 1964, British
DRACULA - PRINCE OF DARKNESS   20th Century-Fox,
   1965, British
ISLAND OF TERROR   Universal, 1966, British
FRANKENSTEIN CREATED WOMAN   20th Century-Fox,
   1967, British
NIGHT OF THE BIG HEAT   Planet, 1967, British
THE DEVIL'S BRIDE   *THE DEVIL RIDES OUT*
   20th Century-Fox, 1968, British
FRANKENSTEIN MUST BE DESTROYED!   Warner Bros.,
   1970, British
FRANKENSTEIN AND THE MONSTER FROM HELL
   Paramount, 1974, British

GEORGE FITZMAURICE

b. February 13, 1985 - Paris, France
d. 1940

THE QUEST OF THE SACRED GEM   Pathé, 1914
THE BOMB BOY   1914
STOP THIEF!   Kleine, 1915
WHO'S WHO IN SOCIETY   Kleine, 1915
THE COMMUTERS   Kleine, 1915
THE MONEY MASTER   Kleine, 1915
VIA WIRELESS   Pathé, 1915
AT BAY   Pathé, 1915
NEW YORK   Pathé, 1916
BIG JIM GARRITY   Pathé, 1916
ARMS AND THE WOMAN   Pathé, 1916
THE TEST   Astra, 1916
THE ROMANTIC JOURNEY   Pathé, 1916
THE HUNTING OF THE HAWK   Pathé, 1917
BLIND MAN'S LUCK   Pathé, 1917
THE RECOIL   Pathé, 1917
THE IRON HEART   Pathé, 1917
THE MARK OF CAIN   Pathé, 1917
SYLVIA OF THE SECRET SERVICE   Pathé, 1917
INNOCENCE   Pathé, 1918
THE NAULAHKA   Pathé, 1918
THE HILLCREST MYSTERY   Pathé, 1918
THE NARROW PATH   Pathé, 1918
THE JAPANESE NIGHTINGALE   Pathé, 1918
COMMON CLAY   Pathé, 1919
THE WITNESS FOR THE DEFENSE   Paramount, 1919
THE CRY OF THE WEAK   Pathé, 1919
OUR BETTER SELVES   Pathé, 1919
PROFITEER   Pathé, 1919
THE AVALANCHE   Artclass-Paramount, 1919
A SOCIETY EXILE   Paramount, 1919
COUNTERFEIT   Paramount, 1919
ON WITH THE DANCE   Paramount, 1920
THE RIGHT TO LOVE   Paramount, 1920
IDOLS OF CLAY   Paramount, 1920
PAYING THE PIPER   Paramount, 1921
EXPERIENCE   Paramount, 1921
PETER IBBETSON   1921
FOREVER   Paramount, 1921
THREE LIVE GHOSTS   Paramount, 1922
THE MAN FROM HOME   Paramount, 1922
TO HAVE AND TO HOLD   Paramount, 1922
KICK IN   Paramount, 1922

BELLA DONNA   Paramount, 1923
THE CHEAT   Paramount, 1923
THE ETERNAL CITY   Associated First National, 1923
CYTHEREA   Associated First National, 1924
TARNISH   Associated First National, 1924
A THIEF IN PARADISE   First National, 1925
HIS SUPREME MOMENT   First National, 1925
THE DARK ANGEL   First National, 1925
THE SON OF THE SHEIK   United Artists, 1926
THE NIGHT OF LOVE   United Artists, 1927
THE TENDER HOUR   First National, 1927
ROSE OF THE GOLDEN WEST   First National, 1927
THE LOVE MART   First National, 1927
LILAC TIME   First National, 1928
THE BARKER   First National, 1928
HIS CAPTIVE WOMAN   First National, 1929
THE MAN AND THE MOMENT   First National, 1929
THE LOCKED DOOR   United Artists, 1929
TIGER ROSE   Warner Bros., 1929
THE BAD ONE   United Artists, 1930
RAFFLES   co-director with Harry D'Abbadie D'Arrast,
   United Artists, 1930
THE DEVIL TO PAY   United Artists, 1931
ONE HEAVENLY NIGHT   United Artists, 1931
STRANGERS MAY KISS   MGM, 1931
THE UNHOLY GARDEN   United Artists, 1931
MATA HARI   MGM, 1932
AS YOU DESIRE ME   MGM, 1932
ALL MEN ARE ENEMIES   MGM, 1934
PETTICOAT FEVER   MGM, 1936
SUZY   MGM, 1936
THE EMPEROR'S CANDLESTICKS   MGM, 1937
LIVE, LOVE AND LEARN   MGM, 1937
ARSENE LUPIN RETURNS   MGM, 1938
VACATION FROM LOVE   MGM, 1938
ADVENTURE IN LOVE   *ADVENTURE IN DIAMONDS*
   Paramount, 1940

ROBERT J. FLAHERTY

b. February 16, 1884 - Iron Mountain, Michigan
d. 1951

NANOOK OF THE NORTH (FD)   Pathé, 1922
THE POTTERY-MAKER (FD)   1925
MOANA (FD)   Paramount, 1926
THE TWENTY-FOUR DOLLAR ISLAND (FD)   1927
WHITE SHADOWS OF THE SOUTH SEAS
   co-director with W. S. Van Dyke, MGM, 1928
ACOMA, THE SKY CITY   Fox, 1928, unreleased
TABU   co-director with F.W. Murnau, Paramount, 1931
INDUSTRIAL BRITAIN (FD)   1933, British
MAN OF ARAN (FD)   Gaumont-British, 1934, British
ELEPHANT BOY   co-director with Zoltan Korda,
   United Artists, 1937, British
THE LAND (FD)   Department of Agriculture, 1942
LOUISIANA STORY (FD)   Lopert, 1948

VICTOR FLEMING

b. February 23, 1883 - Pasadena, California
d. 1949

WHEN THE CLOUDS ROLL BY   co-director with
   Ted Reed, United Artists, 1919
THE MOLLYCODDLE   United Artists, 1920
WOMAN'S PLACE   First National, 1921
MAMMA'S AFFAIR   Associated First National, 1921

THE LANE THAT HAD NO TURNING   Paramount, 1922
RED HOT ROMANCE   First National, 1922
ANNA ASCENDS   Paramount, 1922
DARK SECRETS   Paramount, 1923
LAW OF THE LAWLESS   Paramount, 1923
TO THE LAST MAN   Paramount, 1923
THE CALL OF THE CANYON   Paramount, 1923
EMPTY HANDS   Paramount, 1924
CODE OF THE SEA   Paramount, 1924
THE DEVIL'S CARGO   Paramount, 1925
ADVENTURE   Paramount, 1925
A SON OF HIS FATHER   Paramount, 1925
LORD JIM   Paramount, 1925
BLIND GODDESS   Paramount, 1926
MANTRAP   Paramount, 1926
THE ROUGH RIDERS   Paramount, 1927
THE WAY OF ALL FLESH   Paramount, 1927
HULA   Paramount, 1927
ABIE'S IRISH ROSE   Paramount, 1928
THE AWAKENING   Paramount, 1928
WOLF SONG   Paramount, 1929
THE VIRGINIAN   Paramount, 1929
COMMON CLAY   Fox, 1930
RENEGADES   Fox, 1930
AROUND THE WORLD IN 80 MINUTES   co-director with
    Douglas Fairbanks, United Artists, 1931
THE WET PARADE   MGM, 1932
RED DUST   MGM, 1932
THE WHITE SISTER   MGM, 1933
BOMBSHELL   MGM, 1933
TREASURE ISLAND   MGM, 1934
RECKLESS   MGM, 1935
THE FARMER TAKES A WIFE   Fox, 1935
CAPTAINS COURAGEOUS   MGM, 1937
TEST PILOT   MGM, 1938
THE WIZARD OF OZ   MGM, 1939
GONE WITH THE WIND ★★   MGM, 1939
DR. JEKYLL AND MR. HYDE   MGM, 1941
TORTILLA FLAT   MGM, 1942
A GUY NAMED JOE   MGM, 1943
ADVENTURE   MGM, 1946
JOAN OF ARC   RKO Radio, 1948

ROBERT FLOREY
b. September 14, 1900
d. 1979

ONE HOUR OF LOVE   Tiffany, 1927
THE ROMANTIC AGE   Columbia, 1927
FACE VALUE   Sterling, 1927
FIGHT CLUB   Paramount, 1928
THE HOLE IN THE WALL   Paramount, 1929
THE COCOANUTS   co-director with Joseph Santley,
    Paramount, 1929
THE BATTLE OF PARIS   Paramount, 1929
LA ROUTE EST BELLE   Paramount, 1930, Grench
L'AMOUR CHATTE   1930, French
LE BLANC ET LE NOIR   co-director with Marc Allegret,
    1930, French
MURDERS IN THE RUE MORGUE   Universal, 1932
THE MAN CALLED BACK   World Wide, 1932
THOSE WE LOVE   World Wide, 1932
GIRL MISSING   Warner Bros., 1933
EX-LADY   Warner Bros., 1933
THE HOUSE ON 56TH STREET   Warner Bros., 1933
BEDSIDE   First National, 1934
SMARTY   Warner Bros., 1934
REGISTERED NURSE   First National, 1934
I SELL ANYTHING   First National, 1934
I AM A THIEF   Warner Bros., 1935

THE WOMAN IN RED   First National, 1935
THE FLORENTINE DAGGER   Warner Bros., 1935
DON'T BET ON BLONDES   Warner Bros., 1935
GOING HIGHBROW   Warner Bros., 1935
THE PAY-OFF   Warner Bros., 1935
SHIP CAFE   Paramount, 1935
THE PREVIEW MURDER MYSTERY   Paramount, 1936
TILL WE MEET AGAIN   Paramount, 1936
HOLLYWOOD BOULEVARD   Paramount, 1936
OUTCAST   Paramount, 1937
KING OF GAMBLERS   Paramount, 1936
MOUNTAIN MUSIC   Paramount, 1937
THIS WAY PLEASE   Paramount, 1937
DAUGHTER OF SHANGHAI   Paramount, 1937
DANGEROUS TO KNOW   Paramount, 1938
KING OF ALCATRAZ   Paramount, 1938
DISBARRED   Paramount, 1939
HOTEL IMPERIAL   Paramount, 1939
THE MAGNIFICENT FRAUD   Paramount, 1939
DEATH OF A CHAMPION   Paramount, 1939
PAROLE FIXER   Paramount, 1940
WOMEN WITHOUT NAMES   Paramount, 1940
THE FACE BEHIND THE MASK   Columbia, 1941
MEET BOSTON BLACKIE   Columbia, 1941
TWO IN A TAXI   Columbia, 1941
DANGEROUSLY THEY LIVE   Warner Bros., 1942
LADY GANGSTER   directed under pseudonym of Florian
    Roberts, Warner Bros., 1942
THE DESERT SONG   Warner Bros., 1944
MAN FROM FRISCO   Republic, 1944
ROGER TOUHY - GANGSTER   20th Century-Fox, 1944
GOD IS MY CO-PILOT   Warner Bros., 1945
DANGER SIGNAL   Warner Bros., 1945
THE BEAST WITH FIVE FINGERS   Warner Bros., 1946
TARZAN AND THE MERMAIDS   RKO Rado, 1948
ROGUES' REGIMENT   Universal, 1948
OUTPOST IN MOROCCO   United Artists, 1949
THE CROOKED WAY   United Artists, 1949
THE VICIOUS YEARS   Film Classics, 1950
JOHNNY ONE-EYE   United Artists, 1950

JOHN FORD
(Sean Aloysius O'Feeney/Jack Ford)
b. February 1, 1895 - Cape Elizabeth, Maine
d. 1973

THE TORNADO   Universal, 1917
THE TRAIL OF HATE   Universal, 1917
THE SCRAPPER   Universal, 1917
THE SOUL HERDER   Universal, 1917
CHEYENNE'S PAL   Universal, 1917
STRAIGHT SHOOTING   Universal, 1917
THE SECRET MAN   Universal, 1917
A MARKED MAN   Universal, 1917
BUCKING BROADWAY   Universal, 1917
THE PHANTOM RIDERS   Universal, 1918
WILD WOMEN   Universal, 1918
THIEVES' GOLD   Universal, 1918
THE SCARLET DROP   Universal, 1918
HELL BENT   Universal, 1918
A WOMAN'S FOOL   Universal, 1918
THREE MOUNTED MEN   Universal, 1918
THE CRAVING   co-director with Francis Ford, Universal,
    1919
ROPED   Universal, 1919
THE FIGHTING BROTHERS   Universal, 1919
A FIGHT FOR LOVE   Universal, 1919
BY INDIAN POST   Universal, 1919
THE RUSTLERS   Universal, 1919

BARE FISTS   Universal, 1919
GUN LAW   Universal, 1919
THE GUN PACKER   Universal, 1919
RIDERS OF VENGEANCE   Universal, 1919
THE LAST OUTLAW   Universal, 1919
THE OUTCASTS OF POKER FLAT   Universal, 1919
THE AGE OF THE SADDLE   Universal, 1919
THE RIDER OF THE LAW   Universal, 1919
A GUN FIGHTIN' GENTLEMAN   Universal, 1919
MARKED MEN   Universal, 1919
THE PRINCE OF AVENUE A   Universal, 1920
THE GIRL IN NO. 29   Universal, 1920
HITCHIN' POSTS   Universal, 1920
JUST PALS   20th Century Brand, 1920
THE BIG PUNCH   20th Century Brand, 1921
THE FREEZE OUT   Universal, 1921
THE WALLOP   Universal, 1921
DESPERATE TRAILS   Universal, 1921
ACTION   Universal, 1921
SURE FIRE   Universal, 1921
JACKIE   William Fox, 1921
LITTLE MISS SMILES   William Fox, 1922
SILVER WINGS   co-director with Edwin Carewe,
    William Fox, 1922
THE VILLAGE BLACKSMITH   William Fox, 1922
THE FACE ON THE BARROOM FLOOR   William Fox,
    1923
THREE JUMPS AHEAD   William Fox, 1923
CAMEO KIRBY   William Fox, 1923
NORTH OF HUDSON BAY   William Fox, 1923
HOODMAN BLIND   William Fox, 1923
THE IRON HORSE   William Fox, 1924
HEARTS OF OAK   William Fox, 1924
LIGHTNIN'   William Fox, 1925
KENTUCKY PRIDE   William Fox, 1925
THE FIGHTING HEART   William Fox, 1925
THANK YOU   William Fox, 1925
3 BAD MEN   William Fox, 1926
THE BLUE EAGLE   William Fox, 1926
UPSTREAM   William Fox, 1927
MOTHER MACHREE   William Fox, 1928
FOUR SONS   William Fox, 1928
HANGMAN'S HOUSE   William Fox, 1928
RILEY THE COP   William Fox, 1928
STRONG BOY   William Fox, 1929
THE BLACK WATCH   William Fox, 1929
SALUTE   William Fox, 1929
MEN WITHOUT WOMEN   William Fox, 1930
BORN RECKLESS   William Fox, 1930
UP THE RIVER   William Fox, 1930
SEAS BENEATH   William Fox, 1931
THE BRAT   Fox Film Corporation, 1931
ARROWSMITH   United Artists, 1931
AIR MAIL   Universal, 1932
FLESH   MGM, 1932
PILGRIMAGE   Fox Film Corporation, 1933
DOCTOR BULL   Fox Film Corporation, 1933
THE LOST PATROL   RKO Radio, 1934
THE WORLD MOVES ON   Fox Film Corporation, 1934
JUDGE PRIEST   Fox Film Corporation, 1934
THE WHOLE TOWN'S TALKING   Columbia, 1935
THE INFORMER ★★   RKO Radio, 1935
STEAMBOAT ROUND THE BEND   20th Century-Fox,
    1935
THE PRISONER OF SHARK ISLAND   20th Century-Fox,
    1936
MARY OF SCOTLAND   RKO Radio, 1936
THE PLOUGH AND THE STARS   RKO Radio, 1936
WEE WILLIE WINKIE   20th Century-Fox, 1937
THE HURRICANE   United Artists, 1937
FOUR MEN AND A PRAYER   20th Century-Fox, 1938

SUBMARINE PATROL   20th Century-Fox, 1938
STAGECOACH ★   United Artists, 1939
YOUNG MR. LINCOLN   20th Century-Fox, 1939
DRUMS ALONG THE MOHAWK   20th Century-Fox, 1939
THE GRAPES OF WRATH ★★   20th Century-Fox, 1940
THE LONG VOYAGE HOME   United Artists, 1940
TOBACCO ROAD   20th Century-Fox, 1941
HOW GREEN WAS MY VALLEY ★★   20th Century-Fox,
    1941
THEY WERE EXPENDABLE   MGM, 1945
MY DARLING CLEMENTINE   20th Century-Fox, 1946
THE FUGITIVE   RKO Radio, 1947
FORT APACHE   RKO Radio, 1948
THREE GODFATHERS   MGM, 1948
SHE WORE A YELLOW RIBBON   RKO Ribbon, 1949
WHEN WILLIE COMES MARCHING HOME   20th
    Century-Fox, 1950
WAGON MASTER   RKO Radio, 1950
RIO GRANDE   Republic, 1950
THE QUIET MAN ★★   Republic, 1952
WHAT PRICE GLORY   20th Century-Fox, 1952
THE SUN SHINES BRIGHT   Republic, 1953
MOGAMBO   MGM, 1953
THE LONG GRAY LINE   Columbia, 1955
MISTER ROBERTS   co-director with Mervyn LeRoy,
    Warner Bros., 1955
THE SEARCHERS   Warner Bros., 1956
THE RISING OF THE MOON   Warner Bros., 1957
THE WINGS OF EAGLES   MGM, 1957
GIDEON OF SCOTLAND YARD   *GIDEON'S DAY*
    Columbia, 1958, British
THE LAST HURRAH   Columbia, 1958
THE HORSE SOLDIERS   United Artists, 1959
SERGEANT RUTLEDGE   Warner Bros., 1960
TWO RODE TOGETHER   Columbia, 1961
THE MAN WHO SHOT LIBERTY VALANCE
    Paramount, 1962
HOW THE WEST WAS WON   co-director with George
    Marshall & Henry Hathaway, MGM/Cinerama, 1963
DONOVAN'S REEF   Paramount, 1963
CHEYENNE AUTUMN   Warner Bros., 1964
7 WOMEN   MGM, 1965

CARL FOREMAN
b. July 23, 1914 - Chicago, Illinois
d. 1984

THE VICTORS   Columbia, 1963

BOB FOSSE
b. June 23, 1927 - Chicago, Illinois
d. 1987

SWEET CHARITY   Universal, 1969
CABARET ★★   Allied Artists, 1972
LENNY ★   United Artists, 1974
ALL THAT JAZZ ★   20th Century-Fox, 1979
STAR 80   The Ladd Company/Warner Bros., 1983

NORMAN FOSTER
(Norman Hoeffer)
b. December 13, 1900 - Richmond, Indiana
d. 1976

I COVER CHINATOWN   20th Century-Fox, 1936
FAIR WARNING   20th Century-Fox, 1937
THINK FAST, MR. MOTO   20th Century-Fox, 1937

THANK YOU, MR. MOTO 20th Century-Fox, 1937
WALKING DOWN BROADWAY 20th Century-Fox, 1938
MR. MOTO TAKES A CHANCE 20th Century-Fox, 1938
MYSTERIOUS MR. MOTO 20th Century-Fox, 1938
MR. MOTO'S LAST WARNING 20th Century-Fox, 1939
CHARLIE CHAN IN RENO 20th Century-Fox, 1939
MR. MOTO TAKES A VACATION 20th Century- Fox,
    1939
CHARLIE CHAN AT TREASURE ISLAND 20th
    Century-Fox, 1939
CHARLIE CHAN IN PANAMA 20th Century-Fox, 1940
VIVA CISCO KID 20th Century-Fox, 1940
RIDE, KELLY, RIDE 20th Century-Fox, 1941
SCOTLAND YARD 20th Century-Fox, 1941
JOURNEY INTO FEAR RKO Radio, 1942
IT'S ALL TRUE co-director with Orson Welles, RKO
    Radio, 1942, unfinished
SANTA 1943, Mexican
HORA DE LA VERDAD 1945, Mexican
RACHEL AND THE STRANGER RKO Radio, 1948
KISS THE BLOOD OFF MY HANDS Universal, 1948
TELL IT TO THE JUDGE Columbia, 1949
FATHER IS A BACHELOR co-director with Abby Berlin,
    Columbia, 1950
WOMAN ON THE RUN Universal, 1950
NAVAJO Lippert, 1952
SKY FULL OF MOON MGM, 1952
SOMBRERO MGM, 1953
DAVY CROCKETT, KING OF THE WILD FRONTIER
    Buena Vista, 1955
DAVY CROCKETT AND THE RIVER PIRATES
    Buena Vista, 1956
THE NINE LIVES OF ELFEGO BACA (TF) 1959
THE SIGN OF ZORRO co-director with Lewis R. Foster,
    Buena Vista, 1960
HANS BRINKER *THE SILVER SKATES* Buena Vista,
    1962
VON DRAKE IN SPAIN Buena Vista, 1962
INDIAN PAINT Crown International, 1966
BRIGHTY OF GRAND CANYON Feature Film
    Corporation, 1967
DEATHBED Wargay, 1973

GEORGES FRANJU
b. April 12, 1912 - Fougeres, France
d. 1987

LA TETE CONTRE LES MURS 1959, French
THE HORROR CHAMBER OF DR. FAUSTUS
    LES YEUX SANS VISAGE Lopert, 1960,
    French-Italian
PLEINS FEUX SUR L'ASSASSIN 1961, French
THERESE DESQUEYROUX 1962, French
JUDEX 1964, French
THOMAS L'IMPOSTEUR 1965, French
LA FAUTE DE L'ABBE MOURET 1970, French
L'HOMME SANS VISAGE 1974, French

MELVIN FRANK
b. August 13, 1913 - Chicago, Illinois
d. 1988

THE REFORMER AND THE REDHEAD co-director
    with Norman Panama, MGM, 1950
CALLAWAY WENT THATAWAY co-director with
    Norman Panama, MGM, 1951
STRICTLY DISHONORABLE co-director with Norman
    Panama, MGM, 1951

ABOVE AND BEYOND co-director with Norman Panama,
    MGM, 1952
KNOCK ON WOOD co-director with Norman Panama,
    Paramount, 1954
THE COURT JESTER co-director with Norman Panama,
    Paramount, 1956
THAT CERTAIN FEELING co-director with Norman
    Panama, Paramount, 1956
THE JAYHAWKERS Paramount, 1959
LI'L ABNER Paramount, 1959
THE FACTS OF LIFE United Artists, 1960
STRANGE BEDFELLOWS Universal, 1965
BUONA SERA, MRS. CAMPBELL United Artists, 1968
A TOUCH OF CLASS Avco Embassy, 1973, British
THE PRISONER OF SECOND AVENUE Warner Bros.,
    1975
THE DUCHESS AND THE DIRTWATER FOX 20th
    Century-Fox, 1976
LOST AND FOUND Columbia, 1979
WALK LIKE A MAN MGM/UA, 1987

SIDNEY FRANKLIN
b. March 21, 1893 - San Francisco, California
d. 1972

LET KATY DO IT co-director with Chester Franklin,
    Triangle, 1915
MARTHA'S VINDICATION co-director with Chester
    Franklin, Triangle, 1915
THE CHILDREN IN THE HOUSE co-director with Chester
    Franklin, Fine Arts-Triangle, 1916
GOING STRAIGHT co-director with Chester Franklin,
    Fine Arts-Triangle, 1916
THE LITTLE SCHOOLMA'AM co-director with Chester
    Franklin, Fine Arts-Triangle, 1916
GRETCHEN THE GREENHORN co-director with Chester
    Franklin, Fine Arts-Triangle, 1916
SISTER OF SIX co-director with Chester Franklin,
    Fine Arts-Triangle, 1916
JACK AND THE BEANSTALK co-director with Chester
    Franklin, Fox, 1917
ALADDIN AND THE WONDERFUL LAMP co-director with
    Chester Franklin, Fox, 1917
BABES IN THE WOODS co-director with Chester
    Franklin, Fox, 1917
FAN FAN co-director with Chester Franklin, Fox, 1918
TREASURE ISLAND co-director with Chester Franklin,
    Fox, 1918
ALI BABA AND THE FORTY THIEVES co-director
    with Chester Franklin, Fox, 1918
SIX SHOOTER ANDY Fox, 1918
CONFESSION Fox, 1918
THE BRIDE OF FEAR Fox, 1918
THE SAFETY CURTAIN Select, 1918
THE FORBIDDEN CITY Select, 1918
HER ONLY WAY Select, 1918
THE HEART OF WETONA Select, 1918
PROBATION WIFE Select, 1919
THE HOODLUM First National, 1919
HEART O' THE HILLS First National, 1919
TWO WEEKS First National, 1920
UNSEEN FORCES First National, 1920
NOT GUILTY Associated First National, 1921
COURAGE Associated First National, 1921
SMILIN' THROUGH Associated First National, 1922
THE PRIMITIVE LOVER Associated First National, 1922
EAST IS WEST Associated First National, 1922
BRASS Warner Bros., 1923
DULCY Associated First National, 1923

TIGER ROSE   Warner Bros., 1923
HER NIGHT OF ROMANCE   First National, 1924
LEARNING TO LOVE   First National, 1924
HER SISTER FROM PARIS   First National, 1925
BEVERLY OF GRAUSTARK   MGM, 1926
THE DUCHESS OF BUFFALO   MGM, 1926
QUALITY STREET   MGM, 1927
THE ACTRESS   MGM, 1928
WILD ORCHIDS   MGM, 1928
THE LAST OF MRS. CHEYNEY   MGM, 1929
DEVIL MAY CARE   MGM, 1930
THE LADY OF SCANDAL   MGM, 1930
A LADY'S MORALS   MGM, 1930
THE GUARDSMAN   MGM, 1931
PRIVATE LIVES   MGM, 1931
SMILIN' THROUGH   MGM, 1932
REUNION IN VIENNA   MGM, 1933
THE BARRETTS OF WIMPOLE STREET   MGM, 1934
THE DARK ANGEL   MGM, 1935
THE GOOD EARTH ★   MGM, 1937
THE BARRETTS OF WIMPOLE STREET   MGM, 1957

HUGO FREGONESE
b. April 18, 1908 - Buenos Aires, Argentina
d. 1987

PAMPA BARBARA   co-director with Lucas Demare, 1943,
   Argentine
DONDE MUEREN LAS PALABRAS   1946, Argentine
APENAS UN DELINCUENTE   1947, Argentine
DE HOMBRE A HOMBRE   1949, Argentine
ONE WAY STREET   Universal, 1950
SADDLE TRAMP   Universal, 1950
APACHE DRUMS   Universal, 1951
MARK OF THE RENEGADE   Universal, 1951
MY SIX CONVICTS   Universal, 1952
UNTAMED FRONTIER   Universal, 1952
BLOWING WILD   Warner Bros., 1953
DECAMERON NIGHTS   RKO Radio, 1953, British-U.S.
MAN IN THE ATTIC   20th Century-Fox, 1953
THE RAID   20th Century-Fox, 1954
BLACK TUESDAY   United Artists, 1955
I GIROVAGHI   1956, Italian
BEAST OF MARSEILLES   *THE SEVEN THUNDERS*
   Lopert, 1957, British
HARRY BLACK AND THE TIGER   20th Century-Fox, 1958,
   British
MARCO POLO   co-director with Piero Pierotti, American
   International, 1961, Italian-French
OLD SHATTERHAND   *SHATTERHAND*   Constantin,
   1964, West German-French-Italian-Yugoslavian
THE TESTAMENT OF DR. MABUSE   Thunder, 1964,
   West German-Italian-French
SAVAGE PAMPAS   Comet, 1966, Spanish-Argentine-U.S.
OPERAZIONE BALLABREK   co-director with Giuliano
   Cannimro, 1965, Italian
LA MALA VIDA   1973, Argentine
MAS ALLA DEL SOL   1975, Argentine

VICTOR FRENCH
b. December 4, 1934 - Santa Barbara, California
d. 1989

LITTLE HOUSE: LOOK BACK TO YESTERDAY (TF)   NBC
   Productions/Ed Friendly Productions, 1983
LITTLE HOUSE: BLESS ALL THE DEAR CHILDREN (TF)
   NBC Productions/ Ed Friendly Productions, 1984

KARL FREUND
b. January 16, 1890 - Koniginhof, Bohemia
d. 1969

THE MUMMY   Universal, 1932
MOONLIGHT AND PRETZELS   Universal, 1933
MADAME SPY   Universal, 1934
THE COUNTESS OF MONTE CRISTO   Universal, 1934
UNCERTAIN LADY   Universal, 1934
I GIVE MY LOVE   Universal, 1934
GIFT OF GAB   Universal, 1934
MAD LOVE   MGM, 1935

G

PAL GABOR
b. 1932 - Budapest, Hungary
d. 1987

FORBIDDEN GROUND   1968, Hungarian
JOURNEY WITH JACOB   1973, Hungarian
EPIDEMIC   1978, Hungarian
ANGI VERA   New Yorker, 1979, Hungarian
WASTED LIVES   Budapest Studio, 1982, Hungarian
BRADY'S ESCAPE   *THE LONG RUN*   Satori, 1984,
   U.S.-Hungarian
LA SPOSA ERA BELLISSIMA   Titanus, 1986, Italian-
   Hungarian

ABEL GANCE
b. October 25, 1889 - Paris, France
d. 1981

LA DIGUE   1911, French
LE NEGRE BLANC   co-director with Jean Joulout, 1912,
   French
IL Y A DES PIEDS AU PLAFOND   1912, French
LE MASQUE D'HORREUR   1912, French
UN DRAME AU CHATEAU D'ACRE   1915, French
LA FOLIE DU DOCTEUR TUBE   1915, French
L'ENIGME DE DIX HEURES   1915, French
LA FLEUR DES RUINES   1915, French
L'HEROISME DE PADDY   1915, French
STRASS ET COMPAGNIE   1915, French
FIORITURES   1916, French
LE FOU DE LA FALAISE   1916, French
CE QUE LES FLOTS RACONTENT   1916, French
LE PERISCOPE   1916, French
LES GAZ MORTELS   1916, French
LE DROIT A LA VIE   1916, French
BARBEROUSSE   1917, French
LA ZONE DE LA MORT   1917, French
MATER DOLOROSA   1917, French
LA DIXIEME SYMPHONIE   1918, French
J'ACCUSE   1919, French
LA ROUE   1923, French
AU SECOURS!   1923, French
NAPOLEON   Zoetrope, 1927, French
MARINES   1928, French
CRISTAUX   1928, French
LA FIN DU MONDE   1931, French
MATER DOLOROSA   1932, French
LE MAITRE DE FORGES   1933, French
POLICHE   1934, French

LA DAME AUX CAMELIAS   co-director with Fernand
    Rivers, 1934, French
LE ROMAN D'UN JEUNE HOMME PAUVRE
    1935, French
LUCRECE BORGIA   1935, French
JEROME PERREAU   *JEROME PERREAU, HEROS
    DES BARRICADES*   1936, French
UN GRAND AMOUR DE BEETHOVEN   1936,
    French
LE VOLEUR DE FEMMES   1936, French
J'ACCUSE   1938, French
LOUISE   1939, French
LE PARADIS PERDU   1939, French
LA VENUS AVEUGLE   1941, French
LE CAPITAINE FRACASSE   1943, French
QUATORZE JULIET   1953, French
LA TOUR DE NESLES   *THE TOWER OF LUST*
    1955, French
MAGIRAMA   1956, French
THE BATTLE OF AUSTERLITZ   *AUSTERLITZ*
    20th Century-Fox, 1960, French
CYRANO ET D'ARTAGNAN   1963, French-Italian-
    Spanish

TAY GARNETT
(William Taylor Garnett)
b. June 13, 1894 - Los Angeles, California
d. 1977

CELEBRITY   Pathé, 1928
THE SPIELER   Pathé, 1928
THE FLYING FOOL   Pathé, 1929
OH YEAH!   Pathé, 1929
OFFICER O'BRIEN   Pathé, 1930
HER MAN   Pathé, 1930
BAD COMPANY   Pathé, 1931
PRESTIGE   RKO, 1932
OKAY AMERICA   Universal, 1932
ONE WAY PASSAGE   Warner Bros., 1932
DESTINATION UNKNOWN   Universal, 1933
S.O.S. ICEBERG   co-director with Arnold Fanck,
    Universal, 1933, U.S.-German
CHINA SEAS   MGM, 1935
SHE COULDN'T TAKE IT   Columbia, 1935
PROFESSIONAL SOLDIER   20th Century-Fox, 1936
LOVE IS NEWS   20th Century-Fox, 1937
SLAVE SHIP   20th Century-Fox, 1937
STAND-IN   Warner Bros., 1937
JOY OF LIVING   RKO Radio, 1938
TRADE WINDS   United Artists, 1939
ETERNALLY YOURS   United Artists, 1939
SLIGHTLY HONORABLE   United Artists, 1940
SEVEN SINNERS   Universal, 1940
CHEERS FOR MISS BISHOP   United Artists, 1941
MY FAVORITE SPY   RKO Radio, 1942
BATAAN   MGM, 1943
THE CROSS OF LORRAINE   MGM, 1943
MRS. PARKINGTON   MGM, 1944
THE VALLEY OF DECISION   MGM, 1945
THE POSTMAN ALWAYS RINGS TWICE   MGM, 1946
WILD HARVEST   Paramount, 1947
A CONNECTICUT YANKEE IN KING ARTHUR'S
    COURT   Paramount, 1949
THE FIREBALL   20th Century-Fox, 1950
CAUSE FOR ALARM   MGM, 1951
SOLDIERS THREE   MGM, 1951
ONE MINUTE TO ZERO   RKO Radio, 1952
MAIN STREET TO BROADWAY   MGM, 1953
THE BLACK KNIGHT   Columbia, 1954, British

SEVEN WONDERS OF THE WORLD (FD)   co-director,
    Stanley Warner Cinema Corporation, 1956
THE NIGHT FIGHTERS   *A TERRIBLE BEAUTY*
    United Artists, 1960, British
CATTLE KING   MGM, 1963
THE DELTA FACTOR   American International,
    1971
THE MAD TRAPPER   Alaska Pictures, 1972
TIMBER TRAMP   Alaska Pictures, 1973

PIETRO GERMI
b. September 14, 1914 - Colombo, Liguaria, Italy
d. 1974

IL TESTIMONE   1945, Italian
GIOVENTU PERDUTA   *LOST YOUTH*   1947, Italian
IL NOME DELLA LEGGE   1949, Italian
IL CAMINO DELLA SPERANZA   1950, Italian
LA CITTA SI DIFENDE   *FOUR WAYS OUT*   1951, Italian
LA PRESIDENTESSA   1952, Italian
IL BRIGANTE DI TACCA DEL LUPO   1952, Italian
GELOSIA   1953, Italian
AMORI DI MEZZO SECOLO   co-director, 1954, Italian
THE RAILROAD MAN   *IL FERROVIERE*   Continental,
    1956, Italian
L'UOMO DI PAGLIA   1957, Italian
THE FACTS OF MURDER   *UN MALADETTO
    IMBROGLIO*   Seven Arts, 1959, Italian
DIVORCE ITALIAN STYLE ★   Embassy, 1961, Italian
SEDUCED AND ABANDONED   Continental, 1964,
    Italian-French
THE BIRDS, THE BEES AND THE ITALIANS
    SIGNORE E SIGNORI   Claridge, 1966, Italian
THE CLIMAX   *L'IMMORALE*   Lopert, 1967, Italian-French
SERAFINO   Royal Films International, 1968, Italian-
    French
TILL DIVORCE DO YOU PART   *LE CASTAGNE SONO
    BUONE*   1971, Italian
ALFREDO, ALFREDO   Paramount, 1973, Italian

STEVEN GETHERS*
b. June 8, 1922
d. 1989

BILLY: PORTRAIT OF A STREET KID (TF)   Mark Carliner
    Productions, 1977
DAMIEN...THE LEPER PRIEST (TF)   Tomorrow Entertain-
    ment, 1980
JACQUELINE BOUVIER KENNEDY (TF)   ABC Circle Films,
    1981
CONFESSIONS OF A MARRIED MAN (TF)   Gloria Monty
    Productions/ Comworld Productions, 1983
JENNY'S WAR (TF)   Louis Rudolph Productions/HTV/
    Columbia TV, 1985, U.S.-British
MERCY OR MURDER? (TF)   John J. McMahon Produc-
    tions/MGM-UA TV, 1987
MARCUS WELBY, M.D.: A HOLIDAY AFFAIR (TF)   Marstar
    Ltd./Condor Productions, 1988
TWO OF A KIND: THE CASE OF THE HILLSIDE STRAN-
    GLER (TF) ABC, 1989

ALAN GIBSON
b. April 28, 1938 - Canada
d. 1987

GOODBYE GEMINI   Cinerama Releasing Corporation,
    1970, British
CRESCENDO   Warner Bros., 1972, British

DRACULA TODAY   *DRACULA A.D. 1972*   Warner Bros.,
   1972, British
THE PLAYBOY OF THE WESTERN WORLD (TF)
   BBC, 1975, British
COUNT DRACULA AND HIS VAMPIRE BRIDE
   SATANIC RITES OF DRACULA   Dynamite
   Entertainment, 1978, British
CHECKERED FLAG OR CRASH   Universal, 1978
CHURCHILL AND THE GENERALS (TF)   BBC/Le Vien
   International, 1979, British
A WOMAN CALLED GOLDA (TF)   Harve Bennett
   Productions/Paramount TV, 1982
WITNESS FOR THE PROSECUTION (TF)   Norman
   Rosemont Productions/United Artists Productions, 1982,
   U.S.-British
HELEN KELLER - THE MIRACLE CONTINUES (TF)
   Castle Combe Productions/20th Century-Fox TV, 1984,
   U.S.-British
MARTIN'S DAY   MGM/UA, 1985, British

E D M U N D   G O U L D I N G
b. March 20, 1891 - London, England
d. 1959

SUN-UP   MGM, 1925
SALLY, IRENE AND MARY   MGM, 1925
PARIS   MGM, 1926
WOMEN LOVE DIAMONDS   MGM, 1927
LOVE   MGM, 1927
THE TRESPASSER   United Artists, 1929
PARAMOUNT ON PARADE   co-director, Paramount,
   1930
THE DEVIL'S HOLIDAY   Paramount, 1930
REACHING FOR THE MOON   United Artists, 1931
THE NIGHT ANGEL   Paramount, 1931
GRAND HOTEL   MGM, 1932
BLONDIE OF THE FOLLIES   MGM, 1932
RIPTIDE   MGM, 1934
THE FLAME WITHIN   MGM, 1935
THAT CERTAIN WOMAN   Warner Bros., 1937
WHITE BANNERS   Warner Bros., 1938
THE DAWN PATROL   Warner Bros., 1938
DARK VICTORY   Warner Bros., 1939
THE OLD MAID   Warner Bros., 1939
WE ARE NOT ALONE   Warner Bros., 1939
'TIL WE MEET AGAIN   Warner Bros., 1940
THE GREAT LIE   Warner Bros., 1941
FOREVER AND A DAY   co-director, RKO Radio, 1943
THE CONSTANT NYMPH   Warner Bros., 1943
CLAUDIA   20th Century-Fox, 1943
OF HUMAN BONDAGE   Warner Bros., 1946
THE RAZOR'S EDGE   20th Century-Fox, 1946
NIGHTMARE ALLEY   20th Century-Fox, 1947
EVERYBODY DOES IT   20th Century-Fox, 1949
MISTER 880   20th Century-Fox, 1950
WE'RE NOT MARRIED!   20th Century-Fox, 1952
DOWN AMONG THE SHELTERING PALMS   20th
   Century-Fox, 1953
TEENAGE REBEL   20th Century-Fox, 1956
MARDI GRAS   20th Century-Fox, 1958

A L F R E D   E .   G R E E N
b. 1889 - Ferris, California
d. 1960

LOST AND FOUND   Selig, 1917
THE PRINCESS OF PATCHES   Selig, 1917
LITTLE LOST SISTER   Selig, 1917
THE LAD AND THE LION   Selig, 1917

THE WEB OF CHANCE   Fox, 1919
THE DOUBLE-DYED DECEIVER   Goldwyn, 1920
SILK HUSBANDS AND CALICO WIVES   Equity, 1920
JUST OUT OF COLLEGE   Goldwyn, 1921
THE MAN WHO HAD EVERYTHING   Goldwyn, 1921
THROUGH THE BACK DOOR   co-director with
   Jack Pickford, United Artists, 1921
LITTLE LORD FAUNTLEROY   co-director with Jack
   Pickford, United Artists, 1921
COME ON OVER   Goldwyn, 1922
OUR LEADING CITIZEN   Paramount, 1922
THE BACHELOR DADDY   Paramount, 1922
THE GHOST BREAKER   Paramount, 1922
THE MAN WHO SAW TOMORROW   Paramount, 1922
BACK HOME AND BROKE   Paramount, 1922
THE NE'ER-DO-WELL   Paramount, 1923
WOMAN PROOF   Paramount, 1923
PIED PIPER MALONE   Paramount, 1924
IN HOLLYWOOD WITH POTASH AND PERLMUTTER
   First National, 1924
INEZ FROM HOLLYWOOD   First National, 1924
SALLY   First National, 1925
THE TALKER   1925
THE MAN WHO FOUND HIMSELF   Paramount, 1925
IRENE   First National, 1926
ELLA CINDERS   First National, 1926
IT MUST BE LOVE   First National, 1926
LADIES AT PLAY   First National, 1926
THE GIRL FROM MONTMARTRE   First National, 1926
IS ZAT SO?   Fox, 1927
THE AUCTIONEER   Fox, 1927
TWO GIRLS WANTED   Fox, 1927
COME TO MY HOUSE   Fox, 1927
HONOR BOUND   Fox, 1928
MAKING THE GRADE   Fox, 1929
DISRAELI   Warner Bros., 1929
THE GREEN GODDESS   Warner Bros., 1930
THE MAN FROM BLANKLEY'S   Warner Bros., 1930
OLD ENGLISH   Warner Bros., 1930
SWEET KITTY BELLAIRS   Warner Bros., 1930
SMART MONEY   Warner Bros., 1931
MEN OF THE SKY   Warner Bros., 1931
THE ROAD TO SINGAPORE   Warner Bros., 1931
UNION DEPOT   Warner Bros., 1932
IT'S TOUGH TO BE FAMOUS   Warner Bros., 1932
THE RICH ARE ALWAYS WITH US   Warner Bros., 1932
THE DARK HORSE   Warner Bros., 1932
SILVER DOLLAR   Warner Bros., 1932
PARACHUTE JUMPER   Warner Bros., 1933
BABY FACE   Warner Bros., 1933
THE NARROW CORNER   Warner Bros., 1933
I LOVED A WOMAN   Warner Bros., 1933
DARK HAZARD   Warner Bros., 1934
AS THE EARTH TURNS   Warner Bros., 1934
THE MERRY FRINKS   Warner Bros., 1934
HOUSEWIFE   Warner Bros., 1934
SIDE STREETS   Warner Bros., 1934
A LOST LADY   Warner Bros., 1934
GENTLEMAN ARE BORN   Warner Bros., 1934
SWEET MUSIC   Warner Bros., 1935
THE GIRL FROM 10TH AVENUE   Warner Bros., 1935
THE GOOSE AND THE GANDER   Warner Bros., 1935
HERE'S TO ROMANCE   Warner Bros., 1935
DANGEROUS   Warner Bros., 1935
COLLEEN   Warner Bros., 1936
THE GOLDEN ARROW   First National, 1936
THEY MET IN A TAXI   Columbia, 1936
TWO IN A CROWD   Universal, 1936
MORE THAN A SECRETARY   Columbia, 1936
LET'S GET MARRIED   Columbia, 1937
THE LEAGUE OF FRIGHTENED MEN   Columbia, 1937
MR. DODD TAKES THE AIR   Warner Bros., 1937

THOROUGHBREDS DON'T CRY   MGM, 1937
THE DUKE OF WEST POINT   United Artists, 1938
RIDE A CROOKED MILE   Paramount, 1938
KING OF THE TURF   United Artists, 1939
THE GRACIE ALLEN MURDER CASE   Paramount, 1939
20,000 MEN A YEAR   1939
SHOOTING HIGH   20th Century-Fox, 1940
SOUTH OF PAGO-PAGO   United Artists, 1940
FLOWING GOLD   Warner Bros., 1940
EAST OF THE RIVER   Warner Bros., 1940
ADVENTURE IN WASHINGTON   Columbia, 1941
BADLANDS OF DAKOTA   Universal, 1941
THE MAYOR OF 44TH STREET   RKO Radio, 1942
MEET THE STEWARTS   Columbia, 1942
APPOINTMENT IN BERLIN   Columbia, 1943
THERE'S SOMETHING ABOUT A SOLDIER   Columbia, 1943
MR. WINKLE GOES TO WAR   Columbia, 1944
STRANGE AFFAIR   Columbia, 1944
A THOUSAND AND ONE NIGHTS   Columbia, 1945
TARS AND SPARS   Columbia, 1946
THE JOLSON STORY   Columbia, 1946
THE FABULOUS DORSEYS   United Artists, 1947
COPACABANA   United Artists, 1947
FOUR FACES WEST   United Artists, 1948
THE GIRL FROM MANHATTAN   United Artists, 1948
COVER-UP   United Artists, 1949
THE JACKIE ROBINSON STORY   Eagle Lion, 1950
SIERRA   Universal, 1950
TWO GALS AND A GUY   United Artists, 1951
INVASION, U.S.A.   Columbia, 1953
PARIS MODEL   Columbia, 1953
THE EDDIE CANTOR STORY   Warner Bros., 1954
TOP BANANA   United Artists, 1954

TOM GRIES
b. December 20, 1922 - Chicago, Illinois
d. 1977

WILL PENNY   Paramount, 1968
100 RIFLES   20th Century-Fox, 1969
NUMBER ONE   United Artists, 1969
THE HAWAIIANS   United Artists, 1970
FOOLS   Cinerama Releasing Corporation, 1970
EARTH II (TF)   MGM TV, 1971
JOURNEY THROUGH ROSEBUD   GSF, 1972
TRUMAN CAPOTE'S THE GLASS HOUSE *THE GLASS HOUSE* (TF) ☆☆   Tomorrow Entertainment, 1972
LADY ICE   National General, 1973
A CALL TO DANGER (TF)   Paramount TV, 1973
THE CONNECTION (TF)   D'Antoni Productions, 1973
THE MIGRANTS (TF) ☆   CBS, Inc., 1974
QB VII (MS) ☆   Screen Gems/Columbia TV/The Douglas Cramer Company, 1974
THE HEALERS (TF)   Warner Bros. TV, 1974
BREAKOUT   Columbia, 1975
BREAKHEART PASS   United Artists, 1976
HELTER SKELTER (TF) ☆   Lorimar Productions, 1976
THE GREATEST   Columbia, 1977

D.W. GRIFFITH
(David (Lewelyn) Wark Griffith)
b. January 22, 1875 - La Grange, Kentucky
d. 1948

THE ADVENTURES OF DOLLIE   Biograph, 1908
THE FIGHT FOR FREEDOM   Biograph, 1908
THE REDMAN AND THE CHILD   Biograph, 1908

THE BANDIT'S WATERLOO   Biograph, 1908
A CALAMITOUS ELEPHANT   Biograph, 1908
THE GREASER'S GAUNTLET   Biograph, 1908
THE FATAL HOUR   Biograph, 1908
FOR LOVE OF GOLD   Biograph, 1908
BALKED AT THE ALTAR   Biograph, 1908
FOR A WIFE'S HONOR   Biograph, 1908
BETRAYED BY A HANDPRINT   Biograph, 1908
THE GIRL AND THE OUTLAW   Biograph, 1908
BEHIND THE SCENES: WHERE ALL IS NOT GOLD THAT GLITTERS   Biograph, 1908
THE RED GIRL   Biograph, 1908
THE HEART OF O YAMA   Biograph, 1908
WHERE THE BREAKERS ROAR   Biograph, 1908
A SMOKED HUSBAND   Biograph, 1908
THE STOLEN JEWELS   Biograph, 1908
THE DEVIL   Biograph, 1908
THE ZULU'S HEART   Biograph, 1908
FATHER GETS IN THE GAME   Biograph, 1908
THE BARBARIAN INGOMAR   Biograph, 1908
THE VAQUERO'S VOW   Biograph, 1908
THE PLANTER'S WIFE   Biograph, 1908
THE ROMANCE OF A JEWESS   Biograph, 1908
THE CALL OF THE WILD   Biograph, 1908
CONCEALING A BURGLAR   Biograph, 1908
AFTER MANY YEARS   Biograph, 1908
THE PIRATE'S GOLD   Biograph, 1908
THE TAMING OF THE SHREW   Biograph, 1908
THE GUERILLA   Biograph, 1908
THE SONG OF THE SHIRT   Biograph, 1908
THE INGRATE   Biograph, 1908
A WOMAN'S WAY   Biograph, 1908
THE CLUBMAN AND THE TRAMP   Biograph, 1908
THE VALET'S WIFE   Biograph, 1908
MONEY MAD   Biograph, 1908
THE FEUD AND THE TURKEY   Biograph, 1908
THE RECKONING   Biograph, 1908
THE TEST OF FRIENDSHIP   Biograph, 1908
AN AWFUL MOMENT   Biograph, 1908
THE CHRISTMAS BURGLARS   Biograph, 1908
MR. JONES AT THE BALL   Biograph, 1908
THE HELPING HAND   Biograph, 1908
ONE TOUCH OF NATURE   Biograph, 1909
THE MANIAC COOK   Biograph, 1909
MRS. JONES ENTERTAINS   Biograph, 1909
THE HONOR OF THIEVES   Biograph, 1909
LOVE FINDS A WAY   Biograph, 1909
A RURAL ELOPEMENT   Biograph, 1909
THE SACRIFICE   Biograph, 1909
THE CRIMINAL HYPNOTIST   Biograph, 1909
THOSE BOYS!   Biograph, 1909
MR. JONES HAS A CARD PARTY   Biograph, 1909
THE FASCINATING MRS. FRANCIS   Biograph, 1909
THE WELCOME BURGLAR   Biograph, 1909
THOSE AWFUL HATS   Biograph, 1909
THE CORD OF LIFE   Biograph, 1909
THE GIRLS AND DADDY   Biograph, 1909
THE BRAHMA DIAMOND   Biograph, 1909
A WREATH IN TIME   Biograph, 1909
EDGAR ALLAN POE   Biograph, 1909
TRAGIC LOVE   Biograph, 1909
THE CURTAIN POLE   Biograph, 1909
HIS WARD'S LOVE   Biograph, 1909
THE HINDOO DAGGER   Biograph, 1909
THE JONESES HAVE AMATEUR THEATRICALS   Biograph, 1909
THE POLITICIAN'S LOVE STORY   Biograph, 1909
THE GOLDEN LOUIS   Biograph, 1909
AT THE ALTAR   Biograph, 1909
HIS WIFE'S MOTHER   Biograph, 1909
THE PRUSSIAN SPY   Biograph, 1909

A FOOL'S REVENGE   Biograph, 1909
THE ROUE'S HEART   Biograph, 1909
THE WOODEN LEG   Biograph, 1909
THE SALVATION ARMY LASS   Biograph, 1909
THE LURE OF THE GOWN   Biograph, 1909
I DID IT MAMA   Biograph, 1909
THE VOICE OF THE VIOLIN   Biograph, 1909
THE DECEPTION   Biograph, 1909
AND A LITTLE CHILD SHALL LEAD THEM   Biograph,
   1909
A BURGLAR'S MISTAKE   Biograph, 1909
THE MEDICINE BOTTLE   Biograph, 1909
JONES AND HIS NEW NEIGHBORS   Biograph, 1909
A DRUNKARD'S REFORMATION   Biograph, 1909
THE ROAD TO THE HEART   Biograph, 1909
TRYING TO GET ARRESTED   Biograph, 1909
A RUDE HOSTESS   Biograph, 1909
SCHNEIDER'S ANTI-NOISE CRUSADE   Biograph, 1909
THE WINNING COAT   Biograph, 1909
A SOUND SLEEPER   Biograph, 1909
CONFIDENCE   Biograph, 1909
LADY HELEN'S ESCAPADE   Biograph, 1909
A TROUBLESOME SATCHEL   Biograph, 1909
THE DRIVE FOR A LIFE   Biograph, 1909
LUCKY JIM   Biograph, 1909
TWIN BROTHERS   Biograph, 1909
'TIS AN ILL WIND THAT BLOWS NO GOOD   Biograph,
   1909
THE EAVESDROPPER   Biograph, 1909
THE SUICIDE CLUB   Biograph, 1909
THE NOTE IN THE SHOE   Biograph, 1909
ONE BUSY HOUR   Biograph, 1909
JONES AND THE LADY BOOK AGENT   Biograph, 1909
THE FRENCH DUEL   Biograph, 1909
A BABY'S SHOE   Biograph, 1909
THE JILT   Biograph, 1909
RESURRECTION   Biograph, 1909
ELOPING WITH AUNTY   Biograph, 1909
TWO MEMORIES   Biograph, 1909
THE CRICKET ON THE HEARTH   Biograph, 1909
ERADICATING AUNTY   Biograph, 1909
HIS DUTY   co-director with Frank Powell, Biograph, 1909
WHAT DRINK DID   Biograph, 1909
THE VIOLIN MAKER OF CREMONA   Biograph, 1909
THE LONELY VILLA   Biograph, 1909
A NEW TRICK   Biograph, 1909
THE SON'S RETURN   Biograph, 1909
HER FIRST BISCUITS   Biograph, 1909
THE FADED LILIES   Biograph, 1909
WAS JUSTICE SERVED?   Biograph, 1909
THE PEACHBASKET HAT   Biograph, 1909
THE MEXICAN SWEETHEARTS   Biograph, 1909
THE WAY OF MAN   Biograph, 1909
THE NECKLACE   Biograph, 1909
THE MESSAGE   Biograph, 1909
THE COUNTRY DOCTOR   Biograph, 1909
THE CARDINAL'S CONSPIRACY   co-director with
   Frank Powell, Biograph, 1909
THE FRIEND OF THE FAMILY   Biograph, 1909
TENDER HEARTS   Biograph, 1909
THE RENUNCIATION   Biograph, 1909
SWEET AND TWENTY   Biograph, 1909
JEALOUSY AND THE MAN   Biograph, 1909
A CONVICT'S SACRIFICE   Biograph, 1909
THE SLAVE   Biograph, 1909
A STRANGE MEETING   Biograph, 1909
THE MENDED LUTE   Biograph, 1909
THEY WOULD ELOPE   Biograph, 1909
JONES' BURGLAR   Biograph, 1909
THE BETTER WAY   Biograph, 1909
WITH HER CARD   Biograph, 1909

HIS WIFE'S VISITOR   Biograph, 1909
MRS. JONES' LOVER   *I WANT MY HAT*   Biograph, 1909
THE INDIAN RUNNER'S ROMANCE   Biograph, 1909
OH UNCLE!   Biograph, 1909
THE SEVENTH DAY   Biograph, 1909
THE MILLS OF THE GODS   Biograph, 1909
THE LITTLE DARLING   Biograph, 1909
THE SEALED ROOM   Biograph, 1909
1776 *THE HESSIAN RENEGADES*   Biograph, 1909
COMATA THE SIOUX   Biograph, 1909
THE CHILDREN'S FRIEND   Biograph, 1909
GETTING EVEN   Biograph, 1909
THE BROKEN LOCKET   Biograph, 1909
IN OLD KENTUCKY   Biograph, 1909
A FAIR EXCHANGE   Biograph, 1909
LEATHER STOCKING   Biograph, 1909
THE AWAKENING   Biograph, 1909
WANTED - A CHILD   Biograph, 1909
PIPPA PASSES   *THE SONG OF CONSCIENCE*
   Biograph, 1909
FOOLS OF FATE   Biograph, 1909
THE LITTLE TEACHER   Biograph, 1909
A CHANGE OF HEART   Biograph, 1909
HIS LOST LOVE   Biograph, 1909
THE EXPIATION   Biograph, 1909
IN THE WATCHES OF THE NIGHT   Biograph, 1909
LINES OF WHITE ON A SULLEN SEA   Biograph, 1909
THE GIBSON GODDESS   Biograph, 1909
WHAT'S YOUR HURRY?   Biograph, 1909
NURSING A VIPER   Biograph, 1909
THE RESTORATION   Biograph, 1909
THE LIGHT THAT CAME   Biograph, 1909
TWO WOMEN AND A MAN   Biograph, 1909
A MIDNIGHT ADVENTURE   Biograph, 1909
SWEET REVENGE   Biograph, 1909
THE OPEN GATE   Biograph, 1909
THE MOUNTAINEER'S HONOR   Biograph, 1909
THE TRICK THAT FAILED   Biograph, 1909
IN THE WINDOW RECESS   Biograph, 1909
THE DEATH DISC   Biograph, 1909
THROUGH THE BREAKERS   Biograph, 1909
THE REDMAN'S VIEW   Biograph, 1909
A CORNER IN WHEAT   Biograph, 1909
IN A HEMPEN BAG   Biograph, 1909
THE TEST   Biograph, 1909
A TRAP FOR SANTA CLAUS   Biograph, 1909
IN LITTLE ITALY   Biograph, 1909
TO SAVE HER SOUL   Biograph, 1909
CHOOSING HER HUSBAND   Biograph, 1909
THE ROCKY ROAD   Biograph, 1910
THE DANCING GIRL OF BUTTE   Biograph, 1910
HER TERRIBLE ORDEAL   Biograph, 1910
ON THE REEF   Biograph, 1910
THE CALL   Biograph, 1910
THE HONOR OF HIS FAMILY   Biograph, 1910
THE LAST DEAL   Biograph, 1910
THE CLOISTER'S TOUCH   Biograph, 1910
THE WOMAN FROM MELLON'S   Biograph, 1910
THE COURSE OF TRUE LOVE   Biograph, 1910
THE DUKE'S PLAN   Biograph, 1910
ONE NIGHT AND THEN   Biograph, 1910
THE ENGLISHMAN AND THE GIRL   Biograph, 1910
HIS LAST BURGLARY   Biograph, 1910
TAMING A HUSBAND   Biograph, 1910
THE FINAL SETTLEMENT   Biograph, 1910
THE NEWLYWEDS   Biograph, 1910
THE THREAD OF DESTINY   Biograph, 1910
IN OLD CALIFORNIA   Biograph, 1910
THE CONVERTS   Biograph, 1910
THE MAN   Biograph, 1910
FAITHFUL   Biograph, 1910

THE TWISTED TRAIL   Biograph, 1910
GOLD IS NOT ALL   Biograph, 1910
AS IT IS IN LIFE   Biograph, 1910
A RICH REVENGE   Biograph, 1910
A ROMANCE OF THE WESTERN HILLS   Biograph,
   1910
THOU SHALT NOT   Biograph, 1910
THE WAY OF THE WORLD   Biograph, 1910
THE GOLD-SEEKERS   Biograph, 1910
THE UNCHANGING SEA   Biograph, 1910
LOVE AMONG THE ROSES   Biograph, 1910
OVER SILENT PATHS   Biograph, 1910
AN AFFAIR OF HEARTS   Biograph, 1910
RAMONA   Biograph, 1910
THE IMPALEMENT   Biograph, 1910
IN THE SEASON OF BUDS   Biograph, 1910
A CHILD OF THE GHETTO   Biograph, 1910
A VICTIM OF JEALOUSY   Biograph, 1910
IN THE BORDER STATES   Biograph, 1910
THE FACE AT THE WINDOW   Biograph, 1910
THE MARKED TIME-TABLE   Biograph, 1910
A CHILD'S IMPULSE   Biograph, 1910
MUGGSY'S FIRST SWEETHEART   Biograph, 1910
THE PURGATION   Biograph, 1910
A MIDNIGHT CUPID   Biograph, 1910
WHAT THE DAISY SAID   Biograph, 1910
A CHILD'S FAITH   Biograph, 1910
A FLASH OF LIGHT   Biograph, 1910
AS THE BELLS RANG OUT   Biograph, 1910
SERIOUS SIXTEEN   Biograph, 1910
THE CALL TO ARMS   Biograph, 1910
UNEXPECTED HELP   Biograph, 1910
AN ARCADIAN MAID   Biograph, 1910
HER FATHER'S PRIDE   Biograph, 1910
THE HOUSE WITH CLOSED SHUTTERS   Biograph, 1910
A SALUTARY LESSON   Biograph, 1910
THE USURER   Biograph, 1910
THE SORROWS OF THE UNFAITHFUL   Biograph, 1910
WILFUL PEGGY   Biograph, 1910
THE MODERN PRODIGAL   Biograph, 1910
A SUMMER IDYLL   Biograph, 1910
LITTLE ANGELS OF LUCK   Biograph, 1910
A MOHAWK'S WAY   Biograph, 1910
IN LIFE'S CYCLE   Biograph, 1910
THE OATH AND THE MAN   Biograph, 1910
ROSE O'SALEM-TOWN   Biograph, 1910
EXAMINATION DAY AT SCHOOL   Biograph, 1910
THE ICONOCLAST   Biograph, 1910
THE CHINK AT GOLDEN GULCH   Biograph, 1910
THE BROKEN DOLL   Biograph, 1910
THE MESSAGE OF THE VIOLIN   Biograph, 1910
TWO LITTLE WAIFS: A MODERN FAIRY TALE
   Biograph, 1910
WAITER NO. 5   Biograph, 1910
THE FUGITIVE   Biograph, 1910
SIMPLE CHARITY   Biograph, 1910
THE SONG OF THE WILDWOOD FLUTE   Biograph, 1910
A PLAIN SONG   Biograph, 1910
EFFECTING A CURE   Biograph, 1910
A CHILD'S STRATEGEM   Biograph, 1910
THE GOLDEN SUPPER   Biograph, 1910
THE LESSON   Biograph, 1910
WINNING BACK HIS LOVE   Biograph, 1910
THE TWO PATHS   Biograph, 1911
WHEN A MAN LOVES   Biograph, 1911
THE ITALIAN BARBER   Biograph, 1911
HIS TRUST   Biograph, 1911
HIS TRUST FULFILLED   Biograph, 1911
FATE'S TURNING   Biograph, 1911
THREE SISTERS   Biograph, 1911
HEART BEATS OF LONG AGO   Biograph, 1911

WHAT SHALL WE DO WITH OUR OLD   Biograph, 1911
FISHER FOLKS   Biograph, 1911
THE DIAMOND STAR   Biograph, 1911
HIS DAUGHTER   Biograph, 1911
THE LILY OF THE TENEMENTS   Biograph, 1911
THE HEART OF A SAVAGE   Biograph, 1911
A DECREE OF DESTINY   Biograph, 1911
CONSCIENCE   Biograph, 1911
WAS HE A COWARD?   Biograph, 1911
THE LONEDALE OPERATOR   Biograph, 1911
THE SPANISH GYPSY   Biograph, 1911
THE BROKEN CROSS   Biograph, 1911
THE CHIEF'S DAUGHTER   Biograph, 1911
MADAME REX   Biograph, 1911
A KNIGHT OF THE ROAD   Biograph, 1911
HIS MOTHER'S SCARF   Biograph, 1911
HOW SHE TRIUMPHED   Biograph, 1911
THE TWO SIDES   Biograph, 1911
IN THE DAYS OF '49   Biograph, 1911
THE NEW DRESS   Biograph, 1911
THE WHITE ROSE OF THE WILDS   Biograph, 1911
A ROMANY TRAGEDY   Biograph, 1911
A SMILE OF A CHILD   Biograph, 1911
ENOCH ARDEN PART I   Biograph, 1911
ENOCH ARDEN PART II   Biograph, 1911
THE PRIMAL CALL   Biograph, 1911
FIGHTING BLOOD   Biograph, 1911
THE THIEF AND THE GIRL   Biograph, 1911
BOBBY THE COWARD   Biograph, 1911
THE INDIAN BROTHERS   Biograph, 1911
THE LAST DROP OF WATER   Biograph, 1911
OUT FROM THE SHADOW   Biograph, 1911
THE RULING PASSION   Biograph, 1911
THE SORROWFUL EXAMPLE   Biograph, 1911
THE BLIND PRINCESS AND THE POET   Biograph,
   1911
THE ROSE OF KENTUCKY   Biograph, 1911
SWORDS AND HEARTS   Biograph, 1911
THE SQUAW'S LOVE   Biograph, 1911
DAN THE DANDY   Biograph, 1911
THE REVENUE MAN AND THE GIRL   Biograph, 1911
HER AWAKENING   Biograph, 1911
THE MAKING OF A MAN   Biograph, 1911
ITALIAN BLOOD   Biograph, 1911
THE UNVEILING   Biograph, 1911
THE ADVENTURES OF BILLY   Biograph, 1911
THE LONG ROAD   Biograph, 1911
LOVE IN THE HILLS   Biograph, 1911
THE BATTLE   Biograph, 1911
THE TRAIL OF BOOKS   Biograph, 1911
THROUGH DARKENED VALES   Biograph, 1911
THE MISER'S HEART   Biograph, 1911
SUNSHINE THROUGH THE DARK   Biograph, 1911
A WOMAN SCORNED   Biograph, 1911
THE FAILURE   Biograph, 1911
SAVED FROM HIMSELF   Biograph, 1911
AS IN A LOOKING GLASS   Biograph, 1911
A TERRIBLE DISCOVERY   Biograph, 1911
THE VOICE OF A CHILD   Biograph, 1911
A TALE OF THE WILDERNESS   Biograph, 1912
THE ETERNAL MOTHER   Biograph, 1912
THE OLD BOOKKEEPER   Biograph, 1912
FOR HIS SON   Biograph, 1912
A BLOT IN THE 'SCUTCHEON   Biograph, 1912
THE TRANSFORMATION OF MIKE   Biograph, 1912
BILLY'S STRATAGEM   Biograph, 1912
THE MENDER OF NETS   Biograph, 1912
UNDER BURNING SKIES   Biograph, 1912
THE SUNBEAM   Biograph, 1912
A SIREN OF IMPULSE   Biograph, 1912
A STRING OF PEARLS   Biograph, 1912

IOLA'S PROMISE   Biograph, 1912
THE ROOT OF EVIL   Biograph, 1912
THE GODDESS OF SAGEBRUSH GULCH
   Biograph, 1912
THE GIRL AND HER TRUST   Biograph, 1912
THE PUNISHMENT   Biograph, 1912
FATE'S INTERCEPTION   Biograph, 1912
THE FEMALE OF THE SPECIES   Biograph, 1912
JUST LIKE A WOMAN   Biograph, 1912
ONE IS BUSINESS, THE OTHER CRIME   Biograph,
   1912
THE LESSER EVIL   Biograph, 1912
THE OLD ACTOR   Biograph, 1912
A LODGING FOR THE NIGHT   Biograph, 1912
HIS LESSON   Biograph, 1912
WHEN KINGS WERE THE LAW   Biograph, 1912
A BEAST AT BAY   Biograph, 1912
AN OUTCAST AMONG THE OUTCASTS   Biograph,
   1912
HOME FOLKS   Biograph, 1912
A TEMPORARY TRUCE   Biograph, 1912
LENA AND THE GEESE   Biograph, 1912
THE SPIRIT AWAKENED   Biograph, 1912
THE SCHOOL TEACHER AND THE WAIF   Biograph,
   1912
MAN'S LUST FOR GOLD   Biograph, 1912
A MAN'S GENESIS   Biograph, 1912
THE SANDS OF DEE   Biograph, 1912
THE BLACK SHEEP   Biograph, 1912
THE NARROW ROAD   Biograph, 1912
A CHILD'S REMORSE   Biograph, 1912
THE INNER CIRCLE   Biograph, 1912
A CHANGE OF SPIRIT   Biograph, 1912
A PUEBLO LEGEND   Biograph, 1912
AN UNSEEN ENEMY   Biograph, 1912
TWO DAUGHTERS OF EVE   Biograph, 1912
FRIENDS   Biograph, 1912
SO NEAR, YET SO FAR   Biograph, 1912
A FEUD IN THE KENTUCKY HILLS   Biograph, 1912
IN THE AISLES OF THE WILD   Biograph, 1912
THE ONE SHE LOVED   Biograph, 1912
THE PAINTED LADY   Biograph, 1912
THE MUSKETEERS OF PIG ALLEY   Biograph, 1912
HEREDITY   Biograph, 1912
THE INFORMER   Biograph, 1912
BRUTALITY   Biograph, 1912
THE NEW YORK HAT   Biograph, 1912
THE BURGLAR'S DILEMMA   Biograph, 1912
A CRY FOR HELP   Biograph, 1912
THE GOD WITHIN   Biograph, 1912
THREE FRIENDS   Biograph, 1913
THE TELEPHONE GIRL AND THE LADY   Biograph,
   1913
AN ADVENTURE IN THE AUTUMN WOODS
   Biograph, 1913
OIL AND WATER   Biograph, 1913
BROKEN WAYS   Biograph, 1913
THE UNWELCOME GUEST   Biograph, 1913
FATE   co-director with Frank Powell, Biograph, 1913
THE SHERIFF'S BABY   Biograph, 1913
THE LITTLE TEASE   Biograph, 1913
A MISUNDERSTOOD BOY   Biograph, 1913
THE LADY AND THE MOUSE   Biograph, 1913
THE YAQUI CUR   Biograph, 1913
JUST GOLD   Biograph, 1913
HIS MOTHER'S SON   Biograph, 1913
DEATH'S MARATHON   Biograph, 1913
THE MOTHERING HEART   Biograph, 1913
THE MISTAKE   Biograph, 1913
THE REFORMERS OR THE LOST ART OF MINDING
   ONE'S BUSINESS   Biograph, 1913

TWO MEN OF THE DESERT   Biograph, 1913
THE MASSACRE   Biograph, 1914
THE BATTLE AT ELDERBUSH GULCH   Biograph,
   1914
JUDITH OF BETHULIA   Artcraft, 1914
BRUTE FORCE   Reliance-Majestic, 1914
THE BATTLE OF THE SEXES   *THE SINGLE
   STANDARD*   Mutual, 1914
THE ESCAPE   Mutual, 1914
HOME, SWEET, HOME   Mutual, 1914
THE AVENGING CONSCIENCE   Mutual, 1914
THE BIRTH OF A NATION   Mutual, 1915
INTOLERANCE   Triangle, 1916
HEARTS OF THE WORLD   Artcraft, 1918
THE GREAT LOVE   Artcraft, 1918
THE GREATEST THING IN LIFE   Artcraft, 1918
A ROMANCE OF HAPPY VALLEY   Artcraft, 1919
THE GIRL WHO STAYED AT HOME   Artcraft, 1919
BROKEN BLOSSOMS   United Artists, 1919
TRUE HEART SUSIE   Artcraft, 1919
SCARLET DAYS   Artcraft, 1919
THE GREATEST QUESTION   First National, 1919
THE IDOL DANCER   First National, 1920
THE LOVE FLOWER   First National, 1920
WAY DOWN EAST   United Artists, 1920
DREAM STREET   United Artists, 1921
ORPHANS OF THE STORM   United Artists, 1922
ONE EXCITING NIGHT   United Artists, 1922
THE WHITE ROSE   United Artists, 1923
AMERICA   United Artists, 1924
ISN'T LIFE WONDERFUL   United Artists, 1924
SALLY OF THE SAWDUST   Paramount, 1925
THAT ROYLE GIRL   Paramount, 1926
THE SORROWS OF SATAN   Paramount, 1926
DRUMS OF LOVE   United Artists, 1928
THE BATTLE OF THE SEXES   United Artists, 1928
LADY OF THE PAVEMENTS   United Artists, 1929
ABRAHAM LINCOLN   United Artists, 1930
THE STRUGGLE   United Artists, 1931

YILMAZ GUNEY
b. 1937 - Adana, Turkey
d. 1984

MY NAME IS KERIM   Sahinler Film, 1967, Turkish
NURI THE FLEA   co-director with Serif Gedik, Guney Film,
   1968, Turkish
BRIDE OF THE EARTH   Erman Film, 1968, Turkish
THE HUNGRY WOLVES   lale Film, 1969, Turkish
AN UGLY MAN   Guney Film, 1969, Turkish
HOPE   Guney Film, 1970, Turkish
THE FUGITIVES   Alfan Film, 1971, Turkish
THE WRONGDOERS   Guney Film, 1971, Turkish
TOMORROW IS THE FINAL DAY   Irfan Film, 1971,
   Turkish
THE HOPELESS ONES   Akin Film, 1971, Turkish
PAIN   Azleyis Film, 1971, Turkish
ELEGY   Guney Film, 1971, Turkish
THE FATHER   Akun Film, 1971, Turkish
THE FRIEND   Guney Film, 1974, Turkish
ANXIETY   co-director with Serif Goren, Guney Film, 1974,
   Turkish
THE POOR ONES   co-director with Atif Yilmaz, Guney
   Film, 1975, Turkish
YOL   directed by Serif Goren, supervised by Yilmaz
   Guney, Triumph/Columbia, 1982, Turkish-Swiss-
   West German
THE WALL   MK2/TF1, 1983, French

H

ALEXANDER HALL

b. 1894 - Boston, Massachusetts
d. 1968

SINNERS IN THE SUN   Paramount, 1932
MADAME RACKETEER   co-director with Harry Wagstaff
    Gribble, Paramount, 1932
THE GIRL IN 419   co-director with George Somnes,
    Paramount, 1933
MIDNIGHT CLUB   co-director with George Somnes,
    Paramount, 1933
TORCH SINGER   co-director with George Somnes,
    Paramount, 1933
MISS FANE'S BABY IS STOLEN   Paramount, 1934
LITTLE MISS MARKER   Paramount, 1934
THE PURSUIT OF HAPPINESS   Paramount, 1934
LIMEHOUSE BLUES   Paramount, 1934
GOIN' TO TOWN   Paramount, 1935
ANNAPOLIS FAREWELL   Paramount, 1935
GIVE US THIS NIGHT   Paramount, 1936
YOURS FOR THE ASKING   Paramount, 1936
EXCLUSIVE   Paramount, 1937
THERE'S ALWAYS A WOMAN   Columbia, 1938
I AM THE LAW   Columbia, 1938
THERE'S THAT WOMAN AGAIN   Columbia, 1938
THE LADY'S FROM KENTUCKY   Paramount, 1939
GOOD GIRLS GO TO PARIS   Columbia, 1939
THE AMAZING MR. WILLIAMS   Columbia, 1939
THE DOCTOR TAKES A WIFE   Columbia, 1940
HE STAYED FOR BREAKFAST   Columbia, 1940
THIS THING CALLED LOVE   Columbia, 1941
HERE COMES MR. JORDAN ★   Columbia, 1941
BEDTIME STORY   Columbia, 1941
THEY ALL KISSED THE BRIDE   Columbia, 1942
MY SISTER EILEEN   Columbia, 1942
THE HEAVENLY BODY   MGM, 1943
ONCE UPON A TIME   Columbia, 1944
SHE WOULDN'T SAY YES   Columbia, 1945
DOWN TO EARTH   Columbia, 1947
THE GREAT LOVER   Paramount, 1949
LOVE THAT BRUTE   20th Century-Fox, 1950
LOUISA   Universal, 1950
UP FRONT   Universal, 1951
BECAUSE YOU'RE MINE   MGM, 1952
LET'S DO IT AGAIN   Columbia, 1953
FOREVER DARLING   MGM, 1956

ROBERT HAMER

b. March 31, 1911 - Kidderminster, England
d. 1963

DEAD OF NIGHT   co-director with Alberto Cavalcanti,
    Basil Dearden & Charles Crichton, Universal, 1945,
    British
PINK STRING AND SEALING WAX   Eagle Lion, 1945,
    British
IT ALWAYS RAINS ON SUNDAY   General Film
    Distributors, 1947, British
KIND HEARTS AND CORONETS   General Film
    Distributors, 1949, British

THE SPIDER AND THE FLY   General Film Distributors,
    1949, British
HIS EXCELLENCY   General Film Distributors, 1952,
    British
THE LONG MEMORY   General Film Distributors, 1952,
    British
THE DETECTIVE   *FATHER BROWN*   Columbia, 1954,
    British
TO PARIS, WITH LOVE   General Film Distributors, 1955,
    British
THE SCAPEGOAT   MGM, 1959, British
SCHOOL FOR SCOUNDRELS   Warner Bros., 1960,
    British

HARVEY HART

b. 1928 - Toronto, Canada
d. 1989

BUS RILEY'S BACK IN TOWN   Universal, 1965
DARK INTRUDER   Universal, 1965
SULLIVAN'S EMPIRE   co-director with Thomas Carr,
    Universal, 1967
THE SWEET RIDE   20th Century-Fox, 1968
THE YOUNG LAWYERS (TF)   Paramount TV, 1969
FORTUNE AND MEN'S EYES   MGM, 1971, Canadian
MAHONEY'S ESTATE (TF)   Topaz Productions, 1972,
    Canadian
THE PYX   Cinerama Releasing Corporation, 1973,
    Canadian
CAN ELLEN BE SAVED? (TF)   ABC Circle Films, 1974
MURDER OR MERCY (TF)   QM Productions, 1974
PANIC ON THE 5:22 (TF)   QM Productions, 1974
SHOOT   Avco Embassy, 1976, Canadian
STREET KILLING (TF)   ABC Circle Films, 1976
THE CITY (TF)   QM Productions, 1977
GOLDENROD (TF)   Talent Associates/Film Funding Ltd. of
    Canada, 1977, U.S.-Canadian
THE PRINCE OF CENTRAL PARK (TF)   Lorimar Produc-
    tions, 1977
CAPTAINS COURAGEOUS (TF)   Norman Rosemont
    Productions, 1977
STANDING TALL (TF)   QM Productions, 1978
W.E.B. (TF)   NBC, 1978
LIKE NORMAL PEOPLE (TF)   Christiana Productions/20th
    Century-Fox TV, 1979
THE ALIENS ARE COMING (TF)   Woodruff Productions/QM
    Productions, 1980
JOHN STEINBECK'S EAST OF EDEN   *EAST OF EDEN*
    (MS)   Mace Neufeld Productions, 1981
THE HIGH COUNTRY   Crown International, 1981,
    Canadian
MASSARATI AND THE BRAIN (TF)   Aaron Spelling
    Productions, 1982
BORN BEAUTIFUL (TF)   Procter & Gamble Productions/
    Telecom Entertainment Inc., 1982
GETTING EVEN   New World, 1983, Canadian
MASTER OF THE GAME (MS)   co-director with Kevin
    Connor, Rosemont Productions, 1984
RECKLESS DISREGARD (CTF)   Telecom Entertainment/
    Polar Film Corporation/ Fremantle of Canada Ltd., 1985,
    U.S.-Canadian
BEVERLY HILLS MADAM (TF)   NLS Productions/Orion TV,
    1986
STONE FOX (TF)   Hanna-Barbera Productions/Allarcom
    Ltd./Taft Entertainment TV, 1987, U.S.-Canadian
MURDER SEES THE LIGHT (TF)   CBC, 1987, Canadian
PASSION AND PARADISE (TF)   Picturebase International/
    Primedia Productions/Leonard Hill Films, 1989, U.S.-
    Canadian
BLOOD SPORT   Comedia Entertainment/Radio Telefis
    Eirrean, 1989, Canadian-Irish

BYRON HASKIN

b. 1899 - Portland, Oregon
d. 1984

MATINEE LADIES 1927
IRISH HEARTS 1927
GINSBERG THE GREAT Warner Bros., 1927
THE SIREN Columbia, 1928
I WALK ALONE Paramount, 1947
MAN-EATER OF KUMAON Universal, 1948
TOO LATE FOR TEARS United Artists, 1949
TREASURE ISLAND RKO Radio, 1950, U.S.-British
TARZAN'S PERIL RKO Radio, 1951
WARPATH Paramount, 1951
SILVER CITY Paramount, 1951
THE DENVER AND RIO GRANDE Paramount, 1952
THE WAR OF THE WORLDS Paramount, 1953
HIS MAJESTY O'KEEFE Warner Bros., 1954
THE NAKED JUNGLE Paramount, 1954
LONG JOHN SILVER New Trends Associates, 1955,
    Australian
CONQUEST OF SPACE Paramount, 1955
THE FIRST TEXAN Allied Artists, 1956
THE BOSS United Artists, 1956
FROM THE EARTH TO THE MOON Warner Bros., 1958
THE LITTLE SAVAGE 20th Century-Fox, 1959
JET OVER THE ATLANTIC Intercontinental, 1959
SEPTEMBER STORM 20th Century-Fox, 1960
ARMORED COMMAND Allied Artists, 1961
CAPTAIN SINDBAD MGM, 1963
ROBINSON CRUSOE ON MARS Paramount, 1964
THE POWER MGM, 1968

HENRY HATHAWAY

b. March 13, 1898 - Sacramento, California
d. 1985

HERITAGE OF THE DESERT 1932
WILD HORSE MESA 1932
UNDER THE TONTO RIM 1933
SUNSET PASS 1933
MAN OF THE FOREST 1933
TO THE LAST MAN 1933
THE THUNDERING HERD 1933
THE LAST ROUND-UP 1934
COME ON MARINES! 1934
THE WITCHING HOUR Paramount, 1934
NOW AND FOREVER Paramount, 1934
THE LIVES OF A BENGAL LANCER ★ Paramount, 1935
PETER IBBETSON Paramount, 1935
THE TRAIL OF THE LONESOME PINE Paramount, 1936
GO WEST, YOUNG MAN Paramount, 1936
SOULS AT SEA Paramount, 1937
SPAWN OF THE NORTH Paramount, 1938
THE REAL GLORY United Artists, 1939
JOHNNY APOLLO 20th Century-Fox, 1940
BRIGHAM YOUNG, FRONTIERSMAN 20th Century-Fox,
    1940
THE SHEPHERD OF THE HILLS Paramount, 1941
SUNDOWN United Artists, 1941
TEN GENTLEMEN FROM WEST POINT 20th Century-
    Fox, 1942
CHINA GIRL 20th Century-Fox, 1942
HOME IN INDIANA 20th Century-Fox, 1944
WING AND A PRAYER 20th Century-Fox, 1944
NOB HILL 20th Century-Fox, 1945
THE HOUSE ON 92ND STREET 20th Century-Fox, 1945
THE DARK CORNER 20th Century-Fox, 1946
13 RUE MADELEINE 20th Century-Fox, 1947

KISS OF DEATH 20th Century-Fox, 1947
CALL NORTHSIDE 777 20th Century-Fox, 1948
DOWN TO THE SEA IN SHIPS 20th Century-Fox, 1949
THE BLACK ROSE 20th Century-Fox, 1950, British-U.S.
YOU'RE IN THE NAVY NOW 20th Century-Fox, 1951
FOURTEEN HOURS 20th Century-Fox, 1951
RAWHIDE 20th Century-Fox, 1951
THE DESERT FOX 20th Century-Fox, 1951
DIPLOMATIC COURIER 20th Century-Fox, 1952
O. HENRY'S FULL HOUSE co-director with Howard
    Hawks, Henry King, Henry Koster & Jean Negulesco,
    20th Century-Fox, 1952
NIAGARA 20th Century-Fox, 1953
WHITE WITCH DOCTOR 20th Century-Fox, 1953
PRINCE VALIANT 20th Century-Fox, 1954
GARDEN OF EVIL 20th Century-Fox, 1954
THE RACERS 20th Century-Fox, 1955
THE BOTTOM OF THE BOTTLE 20th Century-Fox, 1956
23 PACES TO BAKER STREET 20th Century-Fox, 1956,
    British-U.S.
LEGEND OF THE LOST United Artists, 1957
FROM HELL TO TEXAS 20th Century-Fox, 1958
WOMAN OBSESSED 20th Century-Fox, 1959
SEVEN THIEVES 20th Century-Fox, 1960
NORTH TO ALASKA 20th Century-Fox, 1960
HOW THE WEST WAS WON co-director with John Ford &
    George Marshall, MGM/Cinerama, 1962
CIRCUS WORLD Paramount, 1964
THE SONS OF KATIE ELDER Paramount, 1965
NEVADA SMITH Paramount, 1966
THE LAST SAFARI Paramount, 1967, British
5 CARD STUD Paramount, 1968
TRUE GRIT Paramount, 1969
RAIN ON ROMMEL Universal, 1971
SHOOT-OUT Universal, 1971
HANGUP *SUPER DUDE* Universal, 1974

HOWARD HAWKS

b. May 30, 1896 - Goshen, Indiana
d. 1977

THE ROAD TO GLORY Fox, 1926
FIG LEAVES Fox, 1926
THE CRADLE SNATCHERS Fox, 1927
PAID TO LOVE Fox, 1927
A GIRL IN EVERY PORT Fox, 1928
FAZIL Fox, 1928
THE AIR CIRCUS co-director with Lewis Seiler, Fox,
    1928
TRENT'S LAST CASE Fox, 1929
THE DAWN PATROL First National, 1930
THE CRIMINAL CODE Columbia, 1931
THE CROWD ROARS Warner Bros., 1932
SCARFACE *SCARFACE: SHAME OF A NATION*
    United Artists, 1932
TIGER SHARK First National, 1932
TODAY WE LIVE MGM, 1933
TWENTIETH CENTURY Columbia, 1934
BARBARY COAST United Artists, 1935
CEILING ZERO Warner Bros., 1935
THE ROAD TO GLORY 20th Century-Fox, 1936
COME AND GET IT co-director with William Wyler,
    United Artists, 1936
BRINGING UP BABY RKO Radio, 1938
ONLY ANGELS HAVE WINGS Columbia, 1939
HIS GIRL FRIDAY Columbia, 1940
SERGEANT YORK ★ Warner Bros., 1941
BALL OF FIRE RKO Radio, 1941
AIR FORCE Warner Bros., 1943

TO HAVE AND HAVE NOT   Warner Bros., 1944
THE BIG SLEEP   Warner Bros., 1946
RED RIVER   United Artists, 1948
A SONG IS BORN   RKO Radio, 1948
I WAS A MALE WAR BRIDE   20th Century-Fox, 1949
THE BIG SKY   RKO Radio, 1952
O. HENRY'S FULL HOUSE   co-director with Henry
   Hathaway, Henry King, Henry Koster & Jean Negulesco,
   20th Century-Fox, 1952
MONKEY BUSINESS   20th Century-Fox, 1952
GENTLEMEN PREFER BLONDES   20th Century-Fox,
   1953
LAND OF THE PHAROAHS   Warner Bros., 1955
RIO BRAVO   Warner Bros., 1959
HATARI!   Paramount, 1962
MAN'S FAVORITE SPORT?   Universal, 1964
RED LINE 7000   Paramount, 1965
EL DORADO   Paramount, 1967
RIO LOBO   National General, 1970

BEN HECHT

b. February 28, 1893 - New York, New York
d. 1964

CRIME WITHOUT PASSION   co-director with Charles
   MacArthur, Paramount, 1934
THE SCOUNDREL   co-director with Charles MacArthur,
   Paramount, 1935
ONCE IN A BLUE MOON   co-director with Charles
   MacArthur, Paramount, 1936
SOAK THE RICH   co-director with Charles MacArthur,
   Paramount, 1936
ANGELS OVER BROADWAY   co-director with Lee
   Garmes, Columbia, 1940
SPECTER OF THE ROSE   Republic, 1946
ACTORS AND SIN   United Artists, 1952

STUART HEISLER

b. 1894 - Los Angeles, California
d. 1979

STRAIGHT FROM THE SHOULDER   Paramount, 1936
THE BISCUIT EATER   Paramount, 1940
THE MONSTER AND THE GIRL   Paramount, 1941
AMONG THE LIVING   Paramount, 1941
THE REMARKABLE ANDREW   Paramount, 1942
THE GLASS KEY   Paramount, 1942
THE NEGRO SOLDIER (FD)   United States Army, 1944
ALONG CAME JONES   RKO Radio, 1945
BLUE SKIES   Paramount, 1946
SMASH-UP   SMASH-UP - THE STORY OF A WOMAN
   Universal, 1947
THE STORY OF A WOMAN   1947
TULSA   Eagle Lion, 1949
TOKYO JOE   Columbia, 1949
CHAIN LIGHTNING   Warner Bros., 1950
DALLAS   Warner Bros., 1950
STORM WARNING   Warner Bros., 1951
JOURNEY INTO LIGHT   20th Century-Fox, 1951
ISLAND OF DESIRE   SATURDAY ISLAND   United Artists,
   1952
THE STAR   20th Century-Fox, 1952
BEACHHEAD   United Artists, 1954
THIS IS MY LOVE   RKO Radio, 1954
I DIED A THOUSAND TIMES   Warner Bros., 1955
THE LONE RANGER   Warner Bros., 1956
THE BURNING HILLS   Warner Bros., 1956
HITLER   ALlied Artists, 1962

JIM HENSON

b. September 24, 1936 - Greenville, North Carolina
d. 1990

THE GREAT MUPPET CAPER   Universal/AFD,
   1981, British
THE DARK CRYSTAL   co-director with Frank Oz,
   Universal/AFD, 1982, British
LABYRINTH   Tri-Star, 1986, British

DOUGLAS HICKOX

b. London, England
d. 1988

IT'S ALL OVER TOWN   British Lion, 1963, British
DISK-O-TEK HOLIDAY   JUST FOR YOU   Columbia,
   1963, British
ENTERTAINING MR. SLOANE   Continental, 1970,
   British
SITTING TARGET   MGM, 1972, British
THEATRE OF BLOOD   United Artists, 1973, British
BRANNIGAN   United Artists, 1975, British
SKY RIDERS   20th Century-Fox, 1976
ZULU DAWN   American Cinema, 1979, British
THE PHOENIX (TF)   Mark Carliner Productions, 1981
THE HOUND OF THE BASKERVILLES   Mapleton
   Films Ltd., 1983, British
THE MASTER OF BALLANTRAE (TF)   Larry White-Hugh
   Benson Productions/HTV/Columbia TV, 1984,
   U.S.-British
MISTRAL'S DAUGHTER (MS)   co-director with Kevin
   Connor, Steve Krantz Productions/R.T.L. Productions/
   Antenne-2, 1984, U.S.-French
BLACKOUT (CTF)   HBO Premiere Films/Roger Gimbel
   Productions/Peregrine Entertainment Ltd./Lee Buck
   Industries/Alexander Smith & Parks, 1985, U.S.-
   Canadian
SINS (MS)   New World TV/The Greif-Dore Company/
   Collins-Holm Productions, 1986
I'LL TAKE MANHATTAN (MS)   co-director with Richard
   Michaels, Steve Krantz Productions, 1987

COLIN HIGGINS

b. July 28, 1941 - New Caledonia
d. 1988

FOUL PLAY   Paramount, 1978
NINE TO FIVE   20th Century-Fox, 1980
THE BEST LITTLE WHOREHOUSE IN TEXAS   Universal,
   1982

ALFRED HITCHCOCK

b. August 13, 1899 - London, England
d. 1980

NUMBER THIRTEEN   1922, British, unfinished
ALWAYS TELL YOUR WIFE   co-director with Seymour
   Hicks, 1922, British
THE PLEASURE GARDEN   Gainsborough-Emelka, 1925,
   British-German
THE MOUNTAIN EAGLE   FEAR O' GOD
   Gainsborough-Emelka, 1926, British-German
THE LODGER   Gainsborough, 1926, British
DOWNHILL   WHEN BOYS LEAVE HOME   Gainsborough,
   1927, British

EASY VIRTUE   Gainsborough, 1927, British
THE RING   British International Pictures, 1927, British
THE FARMER'S WIFE   British International Pictures, 1928,
   British
CHAMPAGNE   British International Pictures, 1928, British
HARMONY HEAVEN   co-director with Eddie Pola &
   Edward Brandt, 1929, British
THE MANXMAN   British International Pictures, 1929,
   British
BLACKMAIL   British International Pictures, 1929, British
ELSTREE CALLING   co-director with Andre Charlot, Jack
   Hulbert & Paul Murray, British International Pictures,
   1930, British
JUNO AND THE PAYCOCK   *THE SHAME OF MARY
   BOYLE*   British International Pictures, 1930, British
MURDER   British International Pictures, 1930, British
THE SKIN GAME   British International Pictures, 1931,
   British
RICH AND STRANGE   *EAST OF SHANGHAI*
   British International Pictures, 1932, British
NUMBER SEVENTEEN   British International Pictures,
   1932, British
WALTZES FROM VIENNA   *STRAUSS'S GREAT
   WALTZ*   Gaumont-British, 1933, British
THE MAN WHO KNEW TOO MUCH   Gaumont-British,
   1934, British
THE THIRTY-NINE STEPS   Gaumont-British, 1935,
   British
THE SECRET AGENT   Gaumont-British, 1936, British
SABOTAGE   *A WOMAN ALONE*   Gaumont-British, 1936,
   British
YOUNG AND INNOCENT   *THE GIRL WAS YOUNG*
   Gaumont-British, 1937, British
THE LADY VANISHES   United Artists, 1938, British
JAMAICA INN   Paramount, 1939, British
REBECCA ★   United Artists, 1940
FOREIGN CORRESPONDENT   United Artists, 1940
MR. AND MRS. SMITH   RKO Radio, 1941
SUSPICION   RKO Radio, 1941
SABOTEUR   Universal, 1942
SHADOW OF A DOUBT   Universal, 1943
LIFEBOAT ★   20th Century-Fox, 1944
BON VOYAGE (FD)   British Ministry of Information, 1944,
   British
SPELLBOUND ★   United Artists, 1945
NOTORIOUS   RKO Radio, 1946
THE PARADINE CASE   Selznick Releasing, 1947
ROPE   Warner Bros., 1948, U.S.-British
UNDER CAPRICORN   Warner Bros., 1949, British-U.S.
STAGE FRIGHT   Warner Bros., 1950
STRANGERS ON A TRAIN   Warner Bros., 1951
I CONFESS   Warner Bros., 1953
DIAL M FOR MURDER   Warner Bros., 1954
REAR WINDOW ★   Paramount, 1954
TO CATCH A THIEF   Paramount, 1955
THE TROUBLE WITH HARRY   Paramount, 1955
THE MAN WHO KNEW TOO MUCH   Paramount, 1956
THE WRONG MAN   Warner Bros., 1957
VERTIGO   Paramount, 1958
NORTH BY NORTHWEST   MGM, 1959
PSYCHO ★   Paramount, 1960
THE BIRDS   Universal, 1963
MARNIE   Universal, 1964
TORN CURTAIN   Universal, 1966
TOPAZ   Universal, 1969
FRENZY   Universal, 1972, British
FAMILY PLOT   Universal, 1976

SETH HOLT
b. 1923 - Palestine
d. 1971

NOWHERE TO GO   MGM, 1958, British
SCREAM OF FEAR   *TASTE OF FEAR*   Columbia, 1961,
   British
STATION SIX - SAHARA   Allied Artists, 1963, British-
   West German
THE NANNY   20th Century-Fox, 1965, British
DANGER ROUTE   United Artists, 1968, British
BLOOD FROM THE MUMMY'S TOMB   co-director with
   Michael Carreras, American International, 1971, British

JERRY HOPPER
b. July 29, 1907 - Guthrie, Oklahoma
d. 1988

THE ATOMIC CITY   Paramount, 1952
HURRICANE SMITH   Paramount, 1952
PONY EXPRESS   Paramount, 1953
ALASKA SEAS   Paramount, 1954
SECRET OF THE INCAS   Paramount, 1954
NAKED ALIBI   Universal, 1955
SMOKE SIGNAL   Universal, 1955
THE PRIVATE WAR OF MAJOR BENSON   Universal,
   1955
ONE DESIRE   Universal, 1955
THE SQUARE JUNGLE   Universal, 1956
NEVER SAY GOODBYE   Universal, 1956
TOY TIGER   Universal, 1956
THE MISSOURI TRAVELER   Buena Vista, 1958
BLUEPRINT FOR MURDER   Paramount, 1961
MADRON   Four Star-Excelsior, 1970, U.S.-Israeli

LESLIE HOWARD
(Leslie Stainer)
b. April 24, 1893 - London, England
d. 1943

PYGMALION   co-director with Anthony Asquith, MGM,
   1938, British
PIMPERNEL SMITH   *MISTER V*   Anglo-American,
   1941, British
SPITFIRE   *THE FIRST OF THE FEW*   RKO Radio, 1942,
   British
THE GENTLE SEX   co-director with Maurice Elvey, Two
   Cities, 1943, British

NOEL HOWARD
b. December 25, 1920
d. 1987

THE HAPPY ROAD   co-director with Gene Kelly, MGM,
   1957
MARCO THE MAGNIFICENT   co-director with Denys de la
   Patelliere, MGM, 1966, French-Afghanistani-Egyptian-
   Italian-Yugoslavian
D'OU VIENS TO JOHNNY   Hoche Productions, French
DON'T YOU HEAR THE DOGS BARK? (FD)   co-director
   with Francois Reichenbach, 1975, Mexican-French

HOWARD HUGHES
b. December 24, 1905 - Houston, Texas
d. 1976

HELL'S ANGELS   United Artists, 1930
THE OUTLAW   RKO Radio, 1943

H . B R U C E (L U C K Y) HUMBERSTONE
b. November 18, 1903 - Buffalo, New York
d. 1984

STRANGERS OF THE EVENING   Tiffany, 1932
THE CROOKED CIRCLE   Sono Art-World Wide, 1932
IF I HAD A MILLION   co-director, Paramount, 1932
KING OF THE JUNGLE   co-director with Max Marcin,
    Paramount, 1933
GOODBYE LOVE   RKO, 1933
THE MERRY WIVES OF RENO   Warner Bros., 1934
THE DRAGON MURDER CASE   First National, 1934
SILK HAT KID   Fox, 1935
LADIES LOVE DANGER   Fox, 1935
THREE LIVE GHOSTS   MGM, 1936
CHARLIE CHAN AT THE RACE TRACK   20th Century-Fox,
    1936
CHARLIE CHAN AT THE OPERA   20th Century-Fox, 1936
CHARLIE CHAN AT THE OLYMPICS   20th Century-Fox,
    1937
CHECKERS   20th Century-Fox, 1938
RASCALS   20th Century-Fox, 1938
TIME OUT FOR MURDER   20th Century-Fox, 1938
WHILE NEW YORK SLEEPS   20th Century-Fox, 1938
CHARLIE CHAN IN HONOLULU   20th Century-Fox, 1938
PACK UP YOUR TROUBLES   20th Century-Fox, 1939
LUCKY CISCO KID   20th Century-Fox, 1940
THE QUARTERBACK   Paramount, 1940
TALL, DARK AND HANDSOME   20th Century-Fox, 1941
SUN VALLEY SERENADE   20th Century-Fox, 1941
I WAKE UP SCREAMING   20th Century-Fox, 1941
TO THE SHORES OF TRIPOLI   20th Century-Fox, 1942

ICELAND   20th Century-Fox, 1942
HELLO, FRISCO, HELLO   20th Century-Fox, 1943
PIN-UP GIRL   20th Century-Fox, 1944
WONDER MAN   RKO Radio, 1945
WITHIN THESE WALLS   20th Century-Fox, 1946
THREE LITTLE GIRLS IN BLUE   20th Century-Fox, 1946
THE HOMESTRETCH   20th Century-Fox, 1947
FURY AT FURNACE CREEK   20th Century-Fox, 1948
SOUTH SEA SINNER   Universal, 1950
HAPPY GO LOVELY   RKO Radio, 1951, British
SHE'S WORKING HER WAY THROUGH COLLEGE
    Warner Bros., 1952
THE DESERT SONG   Warner Bros., 1953
THE PURPLE MASK   Universal, 1955
TEN WANTED MEN   Columbia, 1955
TARZAN AND THE LOST SAFARI   MGM, 1957,
    British-U.S.
TARZAN'S FIGHT FOR LIFE   MGM, 1958
TARZAN AND THE TRAPPERS (TF)   Warner Bros. TV,
    1958
MADISON AVENUE   20th Century-Fox, 1962

BRIAN DESMOND HURST
b. February 12, 1900 - Castle Reagh, Ireland
d. 1986

THE TELL-TALE HEART   BUCKET OF BLOOD
    Fox British, 1934, British

IRISH HEARTS   NORAH O'NEALE   MGM, 1934, Irish
RIDERS TO THE SEA   MGM, 1935, British
OURSELVES ALONE   RIVER OF UNREST   co-director
    with Walter Summers, Wardour, 1936, British
THE TENTH MAN   Wardour, 1936, British
SENSATION   Associated British Picture Corp., 1937,
    British
GLAMOROUS NIGHT   Associated British Picture Corp.,
    1937, British
PRISON WITHOUT BARS   United Artists, 1938, British
THE LION HAS WINGS   co-director with Michael Powell &
    Adrian Brunel, United Artists, 1939, British
ON THE NIGHT OF THE FIRE   THE FUGITIVE   General
    Film Distributors, 1939, British
SUICIDE SQUADRON   DANGEROUS MOONLIGHT
    RKO Radio, 1941, British
ALIBI   British Lion, 1942, British
THE HUNDRED POUND WINDOW   Warner Bros.-
    First National, 1944, British
HUNGRY HILL   Universal, 1947, British
MARK OF CAIN   Rank, 1948, British
THE GAY LADY   TROTTIE TRUE   Eagle Lion, 1949,
    British
A CHRISTMAS CAROL   SCROOGE   United Artists, 1951,
    British
THE MALTA STORY   Universal, 1953, British
SIMBA   Lippert, 1955, British
THE BLACK TENT   Rank, 1956, British
DANGEROUS EXILE   Rank, 1957, British
BEHIND THE MASK   Showcorporation, 1958, British
HIS AND HERS   Eros, 1961, British
THE PLAYBOY OF THE WESTERN WORLD   Janus,
    1962, Irish
MEN OF ARNHEM (FD)   Army Film Unit, 1944, British

JOHN HUSTON
b. August 5, 1906 - Nevada, Montana
d. 1987

THE MALTESE FALCON   Warner Bros., 1941
IN THIS OUR LIFE   Warner Bros., 1942
ACROSS THE PACIFIC   Warner Bros., 1942
THE TREASURE OF THE SIERRA MADRE ★★
    Warner Bros., 1948
KEY LARGO   Warner Bros., 1948
WE WERE STRANGERS   Columbia, 1949
THE ASPHALT JUNGLE ★   MGM, 1950
THE RED BADGE OF COURAGE   MGM, 1951
THE AFRICAN QUEEN ★   United Artists, 1952
MOULIN ROUGE ★   United Artists, 1952, British
BEAT THE DEVIL   United Artists, 1954, British
MOBY DICK   Warner Bros., 1956, British
HEAVEN KNOWS, MR. ALLISON   20th Century-Fox, 1957
THE BARBARIAN AND THE GEISHA   20th Century-Fox,
    1958
THE ROOTS OF HEAVEN   20th Century-Fox, 1958
THE UNFORGIVEN   United Artists, 1960
THE MISFITS   United Artists, 1961
FREUD   Universal, 1963
THE LIST OF ADRIAN MESSENGER   Universal, 1963
NIGHT OF THE IGUANA   MGM, 1964
THE BIBLE...IN THE BEGINNING   20th Century-Fox,
    1966, Italian
REFLECTIONS IN A GOLDEN EYE   Warner Bros., 1967
CASINO ROYALE   co-director with Val Guest, Ken Hughes,
    Joseph McGrath & Robert Parrish, Columbia, 1967,
    British
A WALK WITH LOVE AND DEATH   20th Century-Fox,
    1969, British
SINFUL DAVEY   United Artists, 1969, British

THE KREMLIN LETTER   20th Century-Fox, 1970
FAT CITY   Columbia, 1972
THE LIFE AND TIMES OF JUDGE ROY BEAN
    National General, 1973
THE MACKINTOSH MAN   Warner Bros., 1973, U.S.-
    British
THE MAN WHO WOULD BE KING   Allied Artists, 1975,
    British
WISE BLOOD   New Line Cinema, 1979
PHOBIA   Paramount, 1981, Canadian
VICTORY   Paramount, 1981
ANNIE   Columbia, 1982
UNDER THE VOLCANO   Universal, 1984
PRIZZI'S HONOR ★   20th Century Fox, 1985
THE DEAD   Vestron, 1987

I

HIROSHI INAGAKI

b. December 30, 1905 - Tokyo, Japan
d. ?

(The following is an incomplete list of Mr. Inagaki's credits)

PEACE ON EARTH   1928, Japanese
THE WANDERING GAMBLER   1928, Japanese
ELEGY OF HELL   1929, Japanese
A SAMURAI'S CAREER   1929, Japanese
THE IMAGE OF A MOTHER   1931, Japanese
A SWORD AND THE SUMO RING   1931, Japanese
TRAVELS UNDER THE BLUE SKY   1932, Japanese
CHUJI KUNISHADA   1933, Japanese, trilogy
BAD LUCK   1934, Japanese, trilogy
WHITE SNOWS OF FUJI   1935, Japanese
THE WHITE HOOD   1935, Japanese
JOURNEY OF A THOUSAND AND ONE NIGHTS   1936,
    Japanese
SPIRIT OF THE WILDERNESS   1937, Japanese
A GREAT WORLD POWER RISING   1938,
    Japanese
SHADOWS OF DARKNESS   1938, Japanese
MAZO   1939, Japanese
SAMURAI   *MUSASHI MIYAMOTO*   1940, Japanese,
    trilogy
THE LADY DAYS OF EDO   1941, Japanese
ONE-EYED DRAGON   1942, Japanese
THE LIFE OF MATSU THE UNTAMED   1943, Japanese
SIGNAL FIRES OF SHANGHAI   1944, Japanese
THE LAST ABDICATION   1945, Japanese
CHILDREN HAND IN HAND   1948, Japanese
FORGOTTEN CHILDREN   1949, Japanese
KOJIRO SASAKI   1951, Japanese, trilogy
PIRATES   1951, Japanese
SWORD FOR HIRE   1952, Japanese
SAMURAI, PART I: THE LEGEND OF MUSASHI
    MUSASHI MIYAMOTO   Fine Arts, 1954, Japanese
SAMURAI, PART II: MUSASHI AND KOJIRO
    MUSASHI MIYAMOTO   Toho, 1955, Japanese
SAMURAI, PART III: DUEL AT ICHIJOJI TEMPLE
    MUSASHI MIYAMOTO   Toho, 1956, Japanese
THE LONE JOURNEY   1955, Japanese
THE STORM   1956, Japanese
A GEISHA IN THE OLD CITY   1957, Japanese
SECRET SCROLLS, PART I   Toho, 1957, Japanese
SECRET SCROLLS, PART II   Toho, 1958, Japanese

THE RICKSHAW MAN   Toho, 1958, Japanese
NINJUTSU   1958, Japanese
SAMURAI SAGA   1959, Japanese
LIFE OF A COUNTRY DOCTOR   1960, Japanese
DAREDEVIL IN THE CASTLE   1961, Japanese
THE YOUTH AND HIS AMULET   1961, Japanese
BANDITS ON THE WIND   1961, Japanese
CHUSHINGURA   Toho, 1962, Japanese
TATSU   1962, Japanese
YOUNG SWORDSMAN   1963, Japanese
WHIRLWIND   1964, Japanese
THE RABBLE   1964, Japanese
RISE AGAINST THE SWORD   1966, Japanese
KOJIRO   1967, Japanese
SAMURAI BANNERS   *UNDER THE BANNER OF
    SAMURAI*   1969, Japanese
MACHIBUSE   *THE AMBUSH*   1970, Japanese

THOMAS H. INCE

b. November 6, 1882 - Newport, Rhode Island
d. 1924

LITTLE NELL'S TOBACCO   1910
THEIR FIRST MISUNDERSTANDING   co-director with
    George Loane Tucker, 1911
THE DREAM   co-director with George Loane Tucker, 1911
ARTFUL KATE   1911
BEHIND THE STOCKADE   co-director with George Loane
    Tucker, 1911
HER DARKEST HOUR   1911
A MANLY MAN   1911
IN OLD MADRID   1911
SWEET MEMORIES   1911
THE AGGRESSOR   co-director with George Loane Tucker,
    1911
THE INDIAN MASSACRE   1912
THE DESERTER   1912
THE WAR ON THE PLAINS   1912
THE CRISIS   1912
THE HIDDEN TRAIL   1912
ON THE FIRING LINE   1912
CUSTER'S LAST RAID   1912
THE COLONEL'S WARD   1912
THE BATTLE OF THE RED MEN   1912
WHEN LEE SURRENDERS   1912
THE INVADERS   co-director with Francis Ford, 1912
THE LAW OF THE WEST   1912
A DOUBLE REWARD   1912
A SHADOW OF THE PAST   1913
THE MOSAIC LAW   1913
WITH LEE IN VIRGINIA   1913
BREAD CAST UPON THE WATERS   1913
THE DRUMMER OF THE EIGHTH   1913
THE BOOMERANG   1913
THE SEAL OF SILENCE   1913
DAYS OF '49   1913
THE BATTLE OF GETTYSBURG   co-director with
    Charles Giblyn & Raymond B. West, Ince, 1914
LOVE'S SACRIFICE   co-director with William Clifford, 1914
A RELIC OF OLD JAPAN   1914
THE GOLDEN GOOSE   co-director with William Clifford,
    1914
ONE OF THE DISCARD   co-director with C. Gardner
    Sullivan, 1914
THE LAST OF THE LINE   1915
THE DEVIL   1915
THE ALIEN   1915
CIVILIZATION   co-director with Raymond B. West,
    Reginald Barker, Scott Sidney & J. Parker Read, Jr.,
    Ince, 1916

REX INGRAM
(Reginald Ingram Montgomery Hitchcock)
b. January 15, 1892 - Dublin, Ireland
d. 1950

THE GREAT PROBLEM   Universal, 1916
BROKEN FETTERS   Universal, 1916
THE CHALICE OF SORROWS   Universal, 1916
BLACK ORCHIDS   Universal, 1917
THE REWARD OF THE FAITHLESS   Universal, 1917
THE PULSE OF LIFE   Universal, 1917
THE FLOWER OF DOOM   Universal, 1917
THE LITTLE TERROR   Universal, 1917
HIS ROBE OF HONOR   Universal, 1918
HUMDRUM BROWN   Universal, 1918
THE DAY SHE PAID   Universal, 1919
UNDER CRIMSON SKIES   MGM, 1920
SHORE ACRES   MGM, 1920
HEARTS ARE TRUMPS   MGM, 1920
THE FOUR HORSEMEN OF THE APOCALYPSE
   MGM, 1921
THE CONQUERING POWER   MGM, 1921
TURN TO THE RIGHT   MGM, 1922
THE PRISONER OF ZENDA   MGM, 1922
TRIFLING WOMEN   MGM, 1922
WHERE THE PAVEMENT ENDS   MGM, 1923
SCARAMOUCHE   MGM, 1923
THE ARAB   MGM, 1924
MARE NOSTRUM   MGM, 1926
THE MAGICIAN   MGM, 1926
THE GARDEN OF ALLAH   MGM, 1927
THE THREE PASSIONS   MGM, 1929
BAROUD   *LOVE IN MOROCCO*   MGM, 1933

J

NUNNALLY JOHNSON
b. December 5, 1897 - Columbus, Georgia
d. 1977

NIGHT PEOPLE   20th Century-Fox, 1954
BLACK WIDOW   20th Century-Fox, 1954
HOW TO BE VERY, VERY POPULAR   20th Century-Fox,
   1955
THE MAN IN THE GRAY FLANNEL SUIT   20th
   Century-Fox, 1956
OH MEN! OH WOMEN!   20th Century-Fox, 1957
THE THREE FACES OF EVE   20th Century-Fox, 1957
THE MAN WHO UNDERSTOOD WOMEN   20th
   Century-Fox, 1959
THE ANGEL WORE RED   MGM, 1960, Italian-U.S.

RUPERT JULIAN
b. January 25, 1889 - Auckland, New Zealand
d. 1943

JEWEL   Universal, 1915
THE WATER CLUE   1915
THE TURN OF THE WHEEL   Universal, 1916
NAKED HEARTS   Universal, 1916
BETTINA LOVED A SOLDIER   Universal, 1916

THE BUGLER OF ALGIERS   Universal, 1916
THE EVIL WOMEN DO   Universal, 1916
THE RIGHT TO BE HAPPY   Universal, 1916
WE FRENCH   1916
THE GIFT GIRL   Universal, 1917
THE CIRCUS OF LIFE   Universal, 1917
THE MYSTERIOUS MR. TILLER   Bluebird, 1917
THE DESIRE OF THE MOTH   Bluebird, 1917
A KENTUCKY CINDERELLA   Universal, 1917
MOTHER O'MINE   Universal, 1917
THE DOOR BETWEEN   Bluebird, 1917
THE SAVAGE   Bluebird, 1917
THE KAISER - THE BEAST OF BERLIN   Universal, 1918
HUNGRY EYES   Bluebird, 1918
HANDS DOWN   Bluebird, 1918
MIDNIGHT MADNESS   Bluebird, 1918
CREAKING STAIRS   Universal, 1919
THE SLEEPING LION   Universal, 1919
THE FIRE FLINGERS   Universal, 1919
MILLIONAIRE PIRATE   Bluebird, 1919
THE HONEY BEE   Pathé, 1920
THE GIRL WHO RAN WILD   Universal, 1922
MERRY-GO-ROUND   co-director with Erich Von Stroheim,
   Universal-Jewel, 1923
LOVE AND GLORY   Universal-Jewel, 1924
HELL'S HIGHROAD   Producers Distributing Corp., 1925
THE PHANTOM OF THE OPERA   Universal-Jewel, 1925
THREE FACES EAST   Producers Distributing Corp., 1926
SILENCE   Producers Distributing Corp., 1926
THE YANKEE CLIPPER   Producers Distributing Corp.,
   1927
THE COUNTRY DOCTOR   Pathé, 1927
THE LEOPARD LADY   Pathé, 1928
WALKING BACK   Pathé, 1928
LOVE COMES ALONG   RKO, 1930
THE CAT CREEPS   Universal, 1930

CLAUDE JUTRA
b. March 11, 1930 - Montreal, Quebec, Canada
d. 1987

LES MAINS NETTES   NFB, 1958, Canadian
LE NIGER - JEUNE REPUBLIQUE (FD)   NFB, 1961,
   Canadian
A TOUT PRENDE   Lopert, 1963, Canadian
COMMENT SAVOIR   NFB, 1966, Canadian
WOW!   NFB, 1969, Canadian
MON ONCLE ANTOINE   NFB/Gendon Films Ltd., 1970,
   Canadian
KAMOURASKA   New Line Cinema, 1974, Canadian
POUR LE MEILLEUR ET POUR LE PIRE   1975,
   Canadian
DREAMSPEAKER (TF)   CBC, 1977, Canadian
ADA (TF)   CBC, 1977, Canadian
SURFACING   Arista, 1981, Canadian
BY DESIGN   Atlantic Releasing Corporation, 1982,
   Canadian
LA DAME EN COULEURS   Les Productions Pierre Lamy/
   NFB, 1985, Canadian
MY FATHER, MY RIVAL (CTF)   Scholastic Productions/
   Insight Productions, 1985

K

JAN KADAR
(Janos Kadar)
b. April 1, 1918 - Budapest, Hungary
d. 1979

KATYA   1950, Czechoslovakian
KIDNAPPED   co-director with Elmar Klos, 1952, Czechoslovakian
MUSIC FROM MARS   co-director with Elmar Klos, 1954, Czechoslovakian
YOUNG DAYS   co-director with Elmar Klos, 1956, Czechoslovakian
THE HOUSE AT THE TERMINUS   co-director with Elmar Klos, 1957, Czechoslovakian
THREE WISHES   co-director with Elmar Klos, 1958, Czechoslovakian
YOUTH (FD)   co-director with Elmar Klos, 1960, Czechoslovakian
THE SPARTAKIADE (FD)   co-director with Elmar Klos, 1960, Czechoslovakian
DEATH IS CALLED ENGELCHEN   co-director with Elmar Klos, 1963, Czechoslovakian
THE DEFENDANT   co-director with Elmar Klos, 1964, Czechoslovakian
THE SHOP ON MAIN STREET   co-director with Elmar Klos, Prominent Films, 1965, Czechoslovakian
ADRIFT   MPO Films, 1970, Czechoslovakian-U.S.
THE ANGEL LEVINE   United Artists, 1970
LIES MY FATHER TOLD ME   Columbia, 1975, Canadian
THE OTHER SIDE OF HELL (TF)   Aubrey-Lyon Productions, 1978
FREEDOM ROAD (TF)   Zev Braun Productions/Freedom Road Films, 1979

MIKHAIL KALATOZOV
(Mikhail Kalatozishvili)
b. December 23, 1903 - Tiflis, Georgia, Russia
d. 1973

BLIND   1930, Soviet
SALT FOR SVANETIA   1930, Soviet
A NAIL IN THE BOOT   1932, Soviet
MANHOOD   1939, Soviet
VALERI CHKALOV   1941, Soviet
INVINCIBLE   co-director with Sergei Gerasimov, 1943, Soviet
MOSCOW MUSIC-HALL   1945, Soviet
CONSPIRACY OF THE DOOMED   1950, Soviet
TRUE FRIENDS   1954, Soviet
THE FIRST ECHELON   1956, Soviet
THE HOSTILE WIND   1956, Soviet
WOMAN FROM WARSAW   1956, Soviet
THE CRANES ARE FLYING   Artkino, 1958, Soviet
THE LETTER THAT WAS NEVER SENT   1960, Soviet
I AM CUBA!   1966, Soviet-Cuban
THE RED TENT   Paramount, 1971, Italian-Soviet

PHIL KARLSON
(Philip Karlstein)
b. July 2, 1908 - Chicago, Illinois
d. 1986

A WAVE, A WAC AND A MARINE   Monogram, 1944
THERE GOES KELLY   Monogram, 1945
G.I. HONEYMOON   Monogram, 1945
THE SHANGHAI COBRA   Monogram, 1945
DARK ALIBI   Monogram, 1946
LIVE WIRES   Monogram, 1946
THE MISSING LADY   Monogram, 1946
SWING PARADE OF 1946   Monogram, 1946
BEHIND THE MASK   Monogram, 1946
BOWERY BOMBSHELL   Monogram, 1946
WIFE WANTED   Monogram, 1946
BLACK GOLD   Allied Artists, 1947
KILROY WAS HERE   Monogram, 1947
LOUISIANA   Monogram, 1947
ADVENTURES IN SILVERADO   Columbia, 1948
ROCKY   Monogram, 1948
THUNDERHOOF   Columbia, 1948
THE LADIES OF THE CHORUS   Columbia, 1948
DOWN MEMORY LANE   Eagle Lion, 1949
THE BIG CAT   Eagle Lion, 1949
THE IROQUOIS TRAIL   United Artists, 1950
LORNA DOONE   Columbia, 1951
THE TEXAS RANGERS   Columbia, 1951
MASK OF THE AVENGER   Columbia, 1951
SCANDAL SHEET   Columbia, 1952
KANSAS CITY CONFIDENTIAL   United Artists, 1952
THE BRIGAND   Columbia, 1952
99 RIVER STREET   United Artists, 1953
THEY RODE WEST   Columbia, 1954
HELL'S ISLAND   Paramount, 1955
TIGHT SPOT   Columbia, 1955
FIVE AGAINST THE HOUSE   Columbia, 1955
THE PHENIX CITY STORY   Allied Artists, 1955
THE BROTHERS RICO   Columbia, 1957
GUNMAN'S WALK   Columbia, 1958
HELL TO ETERNITY   Allied Artists, 1960
KEY WITNESS   MGM, 1960
THE SECRET WAYS   Universal, 1961
THE YOUNG DOCTORS   United Artists, 1961
THE SCARFACE MOB   Desilu, 1962
KID GALAHAD   United Artists, 1962
RAMPAGE   Warner Bros., 1963
THE SILENCERS   Columbia, 1966
A TIME FOR KILLING   Columbia, 1967
THE WRECKING CREW   Columbia, 1968
HORNET'S NEST   United Artists, 1970
BEN   Cinerama Releasing Corporation, 1972
WALKING TALL   Cinerama Releasing Corporation, 1973
FRAMED   Paramount, 1974

BUSTER KEATON
(Joseph Francis Keaton)
b. October 4, 1895 - Piqua, Kansas
d. 1966

ONE WEEK   co-director with Eddie Cline, 1920
CONVICT 13   co-director with Eddie Cline, 1920
THE SCARECROW   co-director with Eddie Cline, 1920
NEIGHBORS   co-director with Eddie Cline, 1920
THE HAUNTED HOUSE   co-director with Eddie Cline, 1921
HARD LUCK   co-director with Eddie Cline, 1921
THE HIGH SIGN   co-director with Eddie Cline, 1921
THE GOAT   co-director with Mal St. Clair, 1921

THE PLAYHOUSE   co-director with Eddie Cline, 1921
THE BOAT   co-director with Eddie Cline, 1921
THE PALEFACE   co-director with Eddie Cline, 1921
COPS   co-director with Eddie Cline, 1922
MY WIFE'S RELATIONS   co-director with Eddie Cline, 1922
THE BLACKSMITH   co-director with Mal St. Clair, 1922
THE FROZEN NORTH   co-director with Eddie Cline, 1922
DAY DREAMS   co-director with Eddie Cline, 1922
THE ELECTRIC HOUSE   co-director with Eddie Cline, 1922
THE BALLOONATIC   co-director with Eddie Cline, 1923
THE LOVE NEST   1923
THE THREE AGES   co-director with Eddie Cline, Metro, 1923
OUR HOSPITALITY   co-director with John G. Blystone, Metro, 1923
SHERLOCK, JR.   Metro, 1923
THE NAVIGATOR   co-director with Donald Crisp, Metro, 1924
SEVEN CHANCES   Metro, 1925
GO WEST   Metro, 1925
BATTLING BUTLER   Metro, 1925
THE GENERAL   co-director with Clyde Bruckman, United Artists, 1927
COLLEGE   1927
LIFE IN SOMETOWN, USA   1938
HOLLYWOOD HANDICAP   1938
STREAMLINED SWING   1938

WILLIAM KEIGHLEY

b. August 4, 1889
d. 1986

THE MATCH KING   co-director with Howard Bretherton, Warner Bros., 1933
LADIES THEY TALK ABOUT   co-director with Howard Bretherton, Warner Bros., 1933
EASY TO LOVE   Warner Bros., 1934
JOURNAL OF A CRIME   Warner Bros., 1934
DR. MONICA   Warner Bros., 1934
KANSAS CITY PRINCESS   Warner Bros., 1934
BIG HEARTED HERBERT   Warner Bros., 1934
BABBITT   Warner Bros., 1934
THE RIGHT TO LIVE   Warner Bros., 1935
G-MEN   Warner Bros., 1935
SPECIAL AGENT   Warner Bros., 1935
STARS OVER BROADWAY   Warner Bros., 1935
MARY JANE'S PA   Warner Bros., 1935
THE SINGING KID   Warner Bros., 1936
BULLETS OR BALLOTS   Warner Bros., 1936
THE GREEN PASTURES   co-director with Marc Connelly, Warner Bros., 1936
GOD'S COUNTRY AND THE WOMAN   Warner Bros., 1937
THE PRINCE AND THE PAUPER   Warner Bros., 1937
VARSITY SHOW   Warner Bros., 1937
THE ADVENTURES OF ROBIN HOOD   co-director with Michael Curtiz, Warner Bros., 1938
VALLEY OF THE GIANTS   Warner Bros., 1938
SECRETS OF AN ACTRESS   Warner Bros., 1938
BROTHER RAT   Warner Bros., 1938
YES, MY DARLING DAUGHTER   Warner Bros., 1939
EACH DAWN I DIE   Warner Bros., 1939
THE FIGHTING 69TH   Warner Bros., 1940
TORRID ZONE   Warner Bros., 1940
NO TIME FOR COMEDY   Warner Bros., 1940
FOUR MOTHERS   Warner Bros., 1941
THE BRIDE CAME C.O.D.   Warner Bros., 1941
THE MAN WHO CAME TO DINNER   Warner Bros., 1942

GEORGE WASHINGTON SLEPT HERE   Warner Bros., 1942
HONEYMOON   RKO Radio, 1947
THE STREET WITH NO NAME   20th Century-Fox, 1948
ROCKY MOUNTAIN   Warner Bros., 1950
CLOSE TO MY HEART   Warner Bros., 1951
THE MASTER OF BALLANTRAE   Warner Bros., 1953, British

HENRY KING

b. June 24, 1888 - Christiansburg, Virginia
d. 1982

WHO PAYS?   Pathé, 1915
THE BRAND OF MAN   1915
JOY AND THE DRAGON   Pathé, 1916
PAY DIRT   Pathé, 1916
THE STAINED PEARL   Pathé, 1916
LITTLE MARY SUNSHINE   Pathé, 1916
ONCE UPON A TIME   Pathé, 1916
THE CHILD OF M'SIEU   Triangle, 1916
TWIN KIDDIES   Pathé, 1917
THE CLIMBER   1917
TOLD AT TWILIGHT   Pathé, 1917
SUNSHINE AND GOLD   Pathé, 1917
SOULS IN PAWN   American Mutual, 1917
THE BRIDE'S SILENCE   American Mutual, 1917
THE UNAFRAID   1917
THE UPPER CRUST   1917
SCEPTER OF SUSPICION   *THE SPECTOR OF SUSPICION*   Mutual, 1917
THE MAINSPRING   Mutual, 1917
SOUTHERN PRIDE   Mutual, 1917
A GAME OF WITS   American Mutual, 1917
THE MATE OF SALLY ANN   American Mutual, 1917
KING SOCIAL BRIARS   1918
THE GHOST OF ROSY TAYLOR   1918
BEAUTY AND THE ROGUE   American Mutual, 1918

POWERS THAT PREY   American Mutual, 1918
THE LOCKED HEART   General, 1918
HEARTS AND DIAMONDS   *HEARTS OR DIAMONDS?*   Mutual, 1918
UP ROMANCE ROAD   1918
ALL THE WORLD TO NOTHING   Pathé, 1918
HOBBS IN A HURRY   Pathé, 1918
WHEN A MAN RIDES ALONE   Pathé, 1918
CUPID BY PROXY   Pathé, 1918
WHERE THE WEST BEGINS   Pathé, 1919
BRASS BUTTONS   Pathé, 1919
SOME LIAR   Pathé, 1919
A SPORTING CHANCE   Pathé, 1919
THIS HERO STUFF   Pathé, 1919
SIX FEET FOUR   Pathé, 1919
231/2 HOURS LEAVE   F.P.L., 1919
A FUGITIVE FROM MATRIMONY   Robertson-Cole, 1919
HAUNTING SHADOWS   Robertson-Cole, 1919
THE WHITE DOVE   Robertson-Cole, 1920
UNCHARTED CHANNELS   Robertson-Cole, 1920
ONE HOUR BEFORE DAWN   Pathé, 1920
DICE OF DESTINY   Pathé, 1920
HELP WANTED - MALE   Pathé, 1920
WHEN WE WERE 21   Pathé, 1921
THE MISTRESS OF SHENSTONE   Robertson-Cole, 1921
SALVAGE   Robertson-Cole, 1921
THE STING OF THE LASH   Robertson-Cole, 1921
TOL'ABLE DAVID   First National, 1921
THE SEVENTH DAY   First National, 1922
SONNY   First National, 1922
THE BOND BOY   First National, 1922

FURY   First National, 1923
THE WHITE SISTER   Metro, 1923
ROMOLA   Metro-Goldwyn, 1924
SACKCLOTH AND SCARLET   Paramount, 1925
ANY WOMAN   Paramount, 1925
STELLA DALLAS   United Artists, 1925
PARTNERS AGAIN   United Artists, 1926
THE WINNING OF BARBARA WORTH   United Artists, 1926
THE MAGIC FLAME   United Artists, 1927
THE WOMAN DISPUTED   co-director with Sam Taylor, United Artists, 1928
SHE GOES TO WAR   United Artists, 1929
HELL HARBOR   United Artists, 1930
THE EYES OF THE WORLD   Fox, 1930
LIGHTNIN'   Fox, 1930
MERELY MARY ANN   Fox, 1931
OVER THE HILL   Fox, 1931
THE WOMAN IN ROOM 13   Fox, 1932
STATE FAIR   Fox, 1933
I LOVED YOU WEDNESDAY   co-director with William Cameron Menzies, Fox, 1933
CAROLINA   Fox, 1934
MARIE GALANTE   Fox, 1934
ONE MORE SPRING   20th Century-Fox, 1935
WAY DOWN EAST   20th Century-Fox, 1935
THE COUNTRY DOCTOR   20th Century-Fox, 1936
RAMONA   20th Century-Fox, 1936
LLOYDS OF LONDON   20th Century-Fox, 1936
SEVENTH HEAVEN   20th Century-Fox, 1937
IN OLD CHICAGO   20th Century-Fox, 1938
ALEXANDER'S RAGTIME BAND   20th Century-Fox, 1938
JESSE JAMES   20th Century-Fox, 1939
STANLEY AND LIVINGSTONE   20th Century-Fox, 1939
LITTLE OLD NEW YORK   20th Century-Fox, 1940
MARYLAND   20th Century-Fox, 1940
CHAD HANNA   20th Century-Fox, 1940
A YANK IN THE R.A.F.   20th Century-Fox, 1941
REMEMBER THE DAY   20th Century-Fox, 1942
THE BLACK SWAN   20th Century-Fox, 1942
THE SONG OF BERNADETTE ★   20th Century-Fox, 1943
WILSON ★   20th Century-Fox, 1944
A BELL FOR ADANO   20th Century-Fox, 1945
MARGIE   20th Century-Fox, 1946
CAPTAIN FROM CASTILE   20th Century-Fox, 1947
DEEP WATERS   20th Century-Fox, 1948
PRINCE OF FOXES   20th Century-Fox, 1949
TWELVE O'CLOCK HIGH   20th Century-Fox, 1949
THE GUNFIGHTER   20th Century-Fox, 1950
I'D CLIMB THE HIGHEST MOUNTAIN   20th Century-Fox, 1951
WAIT 'TILL THE SUN SHINES, NELLIE   20th Century-Fox, 1952
THE SNOWS OF KILIMANJARO   20th Century-Fox, 1952
O. HENRY'S FULL HOUSE   co-director with Henry Hathaway, Howard Hawks, Henry Koster & Jean Negulesco, 20th Century-Fox, 1952
KING OF THE KHYBER RIFLES   20th Century-Fox, 1953
UNTAMED   20th Century-Fox, 1955
LOVE IS A MANY-SPLENDORED THING   20th Century-Fox, 1955
CAROUSEL   20th Century-Fox, 1956
THE SUN ALSO RISES   20th Century-Fox, 1957
THE BRAVADOS   20th Century-Fox, 1958
THIS EARTH IS MINE   20th Century-Fox, 1959
BELOVED INFIDEL   20th Century-Fox, 1959
TENDER IS THE NIGHT   20th Century-Fox, 1962

ALF KJELLIN
b. February 28, 1920 - Lund, Sweden
d. 1988

GIRL IN THE RAIN   1955, Swedish
SEVENTEEN YEARS OLD   1957, Swedish
ENCOUNTERS AT DUSK   1957, Swedish
SWINGING AT THE CASTLE   1959, Swedish
ONLY A WAITER   1960, Swedish
PLEASURE GARDEN   1961, Swedish
SISKA   1962, Swedish
MIDAS RUN   Cinerama Releasing Corporation, 1969
THE McMASTERS   Chevron, 1970
THE DEADLY DREAM (TF)   Universal TV, 1971
THE GIRLS OF HUNTINGTON HOUSE (TF)   Lorimar Productions, 1973

SIR ALEXANDER KORDA
(Sandor Laszlo Korda)
b. September 16, 1893 - Pusztaturpaszto, Hungary
d. 1956

A BECSAPOT UJSAGIRO   co-director with Gyula Zilahi, 1914, Hungarian
A TISZTI KARDBOJT   1915, Hungarian
TUTYU ES TOTYO   co-director with Gyula Zilahi, 1915, Hungarian
LYON LEA   co-director with Miklos M. Pasztory, 1915, Hungarian
FEHER EJSZAKAK   FEDORA   1916, Hungarian
CIKLAMEN   1916, Hungarian
THE OFFICER'S SWORD   1916, Hungarian
WHITE NIGHTS   1916, Hungarian
BATTLING HEARTS   1916, Hungarian
GRANDMOTHER   1916, Hungarian
A TYPEWRITER'S TALE   1916, Hungarian
A MILLION POUND NOTE   1916, Hungarian
MISKA THE GREAT   1917, Hungarian
A DOUBLE-HEARTED MAN   1917, Hungarian
THE ST. PETER'S UMBRELLA   1917, Hungarian
THE STORK CALIPH   1917, Hungarian
MAGIC   1917, Hungarian
THE FAUN   1917, Hungarian
HARRISON AND HARRISON   1917, Hungarian
THE WOMAN WITH TWO SOULS   1917, Hungarian
GOLDEN MAN   1918, Hungarian
MARY ANN   1918, Hungarian
NEITHER AT HOME NOR ABROAD   1918, Hungarian
AVE CAESAR!   1919, Hungarian
WHITE ROSES   1919, Hungarian
THE 111TH   1919, Hungarian
YAMATA   1919, Hungarian
SEINE MAJESTAT DES BETTLEKIND   THE PRINCE AND THE PAUPER   1920, Austrian
DIETRO LA MASCHERA   Italian, 1921
HERRIN DER MEERE   1922, Austrian
EINE VERSUNKENE WELT   1922, Austrian
SAMSON UND DALILA   1922, Austrian
DAS UNBEKANNTE MORGEN   1923, German
TRAGODIE IN HAUSE HAPSBURG   1924, German
JEDERMANNS FRAU   1924, German
DER TANZER MEINE FRAU   DANCE FEVER   1925, German
EINE DUBARRY VON HEUTE   A MODERN DUBARRY   1926, German
MADAME WUNSCHT KEINE KINDER   MADAME WANTS NO CHILDREN   1926, German

THE STOLEN BRIDE   First National, 1927
THE PRIVATE LIFE OF HELEN OF TROY   First National, 1927
THE YELLOW LILY   First National, 1928
THE NIGHT WATCH   First National, 1928
LOVE AND THE DEVIL   First National, 1929
THE SQUALL   First National, 1929
HER PRIVATE LIFE   First National, 1929
LILIES OF THE FIELD   First National, 1930
WOMEN EVERYWHERE   Fox, 1930
THE PRINCESS AND THE PLUMBER   Fox, 1930
RIVE GAUCHE   Paramount, 1931, French
DIE MANNER UM LUCIE   Paramount, 1931, German
MARIUS   1931, French
ZUM GOLDENEN AUKER   Paramount, 1931, German
RESERVED FOR LADIES   *SERVICE FOR LADIES* Paramount, 1932, British
WEDDING REHEARSAL   Ideal, 1932, British
LA DAME CHEZ MAXIM'S   1932, French
THE GIRL FROM MAXIM'S   1933, British
THE PRIVATE LIFE OF HENRY VIII   United Artists, 1933, British
THE PRIVATE LIFE OF DON JUAN   United Artists, 1934, British
REMBRANDT   United Artists, 1936, British
THAT HAMILTON WOMAN   *LADY HAMILTON* United Artists, 1941, British
VACATION FROM MARRIAGE   *PERFECT STRANGERS* MGM, 1945, British
AN IDEAL HUSBAND   20th Century-Fox, 1947, British

ZOLTAN KORDA
b. May 3, 1895 - Pusztaturpaszto, Hungary
d. 1961

DIE ELF TEUFEL   1927, German
CASH   1933, British
SANDERS OF THE RIVER   1935, British
FORGET ME NOT   1936, British
CONQUEST OF THE AIR (FD)   United Artists, 1936, British
ELEPHANT BOY   co-director with Robert J. Flaherty, United Artists, 1937, British
THE DRUM   United Artists, 1938, British
THE FOUR FEATHERS   United Artists, 1939, British
THE JUNGLE BOOK   United Artists, 1942
SAHARA   Columbia, 1943
COUNTER-ATTACK   Columbia, 1945
THE MACOMBER AFFAIR   United Artists, 1947
A WOMAN'S VENGEANCE   Universal, 1948
CRY, THE BELOVED COUNTRY   United Artists, 1951, British
STORM OVER THE NILE   co-director with Terence Young, Columbia, 1955, British

HENRY KOSTER
(Hermann Kosterlitz)
b. May 1, 1905 - Berlin, Germany
d. 1988

DAS ABENTEUER DER THEA ROLAND   1932, German
DAS HASSLICHE MADCHEN   1933, German
PETER   1934, Austrian-Hungarian
KLEINE MUTTI   1934, Austrian-Hungarian
KATHARINA DIE LETZTE   1935, Austrian
DAS TAGEBUCH DER GELIEBTEN   1936, Austrian-Italian
THREE SMART GIRLS   Universal, 1936
100 MEN AND A GIRL   Universal, 1937

THE RAGE OF PARIS   Universal, 1938
THREE SMART GIRLS GROW UP   Universal, 1939
FIRST LOVE   Universal, 1939
SPRING PARADE   Universal, 1940
IT STARTED WITH EVE   Universal, 1941
BETWEEN US GIRLS   Universal, 1942
MUSIC FOR MILLIONS   MGM, 1944
TWO SISTERS FROM BOSTON   MGM, 1946
THE UNFINISHED DANCE   MGM, 1947
THE BISHOP'S WIFE ★   RKO Radio, 1947
THE LUCK OF THE IRISH   20th Century-Fox, 1948
COME TO THE STABLE   20th Century-Fox, 1949
THE INSPECTOR GENERAL   Warner Bros., 1949
WABASH AVENUE   20th Century-Fox, 1950
MY BLUE HEAVEN   20th Century-Fox, 1950
HARVEY   Universal, 1950
NO HIGHWAY IN THE SKY   NO HIGHWAY   20th Century-Fox, 1951, British
MR. BELVEDERE RINGS THE BELL   20th Century-Fox, 1951
ELOPEMENT   20th Century-Fox, 1951
O. HENRY'S FULL HOUSE   co-director with Henry Hathaway, Howard Hawks, Henry King & Jean Negulesco, 20th Century-Fox, 1952
STARS AND STRIPES FOREVER   20th Century-Fox, 1953
MY COUSIN RACHEL   20th Century-Fox, 1953
THE ROBE   20th Century-Fox, 1953
DESIREE   20th Century-Fox, 1954
A MAN CALLED PETER   20th Century-Fox, 1955
THE VIRGIN QUEEN   20th Century-Fox, 1955
GOOD MORNING, MISS DOVE   20th Century-Fox, 1955
D-DAY, THE SIXTH OF JUNE   20th Century-Fox, 1956
THE POWER AND THE PRIZE   MGM, 1956
MY MAN GODFREY   Universal, 1957
FRAULEIN   20th Century-Fox, 1958
THE NAKED MAJA   United Artists, 1959
THE STORY OF RUTH   20th Century-Fox, 1960
FLOWER DRUM SONG   Universal, 1961
MR. HOBBS TAKES A VACATION   20th Century-Fox, 1962
TAKE HER, SHE'S MINE   20th Century-Fox, 1963
DEAR BRIGITTE   20th Century-Fox, 1965
THE SINGING NUN   MGM, 1966

GRIGORI KOZINTSEV
b. 1905 - Kiev, Russia
d. 1973

THE ADVENTURES OF OKTYABRINA   co-director with Leonid Trauberg, 1924, Soviet
MISHKA VERSUS YUDENICH   co-director with Leonid Trauberg, 1925, Soviet
THE DEVIL'S WHEEL   co-director with Leonid Trauberg, 1925, Soviet
THE OVERCOAT   co-director with Leonid Trauberg, 1926, Soviet
BRATISHK   co-director with Leonid Trauberg, 1926, Soviet
THE CLUB OF THE BIG DEED   co-director with Leonid Trauberg, 1927, Soviet
THE NEW BABYLON   co-director with Leonid Trauberg, 1929, Soviet
ALONE   co-director with Leonid Trauberg, 1931, Soviet
THE YOUTH OF MAXIM   co-director with Leonid Trauberg, 1935
THE RETURN OF MAXIM   co-director with Leonid Trauberg, 1937, Soviet
THE VYBORG SIDE   co-director with Loenid Trauberg, 1939, Soviet

PLAIN PEOPLE   co-director with Leonid Trauberg,
   1956, Soviet
PIROGOV   1947, Soviet
BELINSKI   1953, Soviet
DON QUIXOTE   MGM, 1957, Soviet
HAMLET   United Artists, 1964, Soviet
KING LEAR   Artkino, 1971, Soviet

L

GREGORY LA CAVA
b. March 10, 1892 - Towanda, Pennsylvania
d. 1952

HIS NIBS   Exceptional Pictures, 1921
RESTLESS WIVES   C.C. Burr, 1924
THE NEW SCHOOL TEACHER   C.C. Burr, 1924
WOMANHANDLED   Paramount, 1925
LET'S GET MARRIED   Paramount, 1926
SO'S YOUR OLD MAN   Paramount, 1926
SAY IT AGAIN   Paramount, 1926
PARADISE FOR TWO   Paramount, 1927
RUNNING WILD   Paramount, 1927
TELL IT TO SWEENEY   Paramount, 1927
THE GAY DEFENDER   Paramount, 1927
FEEL MY PULSE   Paramount, 1928
HALF A BRIDE   Paramount, 1928
SATURDAY'S CHILDREN   First National, 1929
BIG NEWS   Pathé, 1929
HIS FIRST COMMAND   Pathé, 1930
LAUGH AND GET RICH   RKO, 1931
SMART WOMAN   RKO, 1931
SYMPHONY OF SIX MILLION   RKO Radio, 1932
THE AGE OF CONSENT   RKO, 1932
THE HALF-NAKED TRUTH   RKO, 1932
GABRIEL OVER THE WHITE HOUSE   MGM, 1933
BED OF ROSES   RKO, 1933
GALLANT LADY   United Artists, 1934
THE AFFAIRS OF CELLINI   United Artists, 1934
WHAT EVERY WOMAN KNOWS   MGM, 1934
PRIVATE WORLDS   Paramount, 1935
SHE MARRIED HER BOSS   Columbia, 1935
MY MAN GODFREY ★   Universal, 1936
STAGE DOOR ★   RKO Radio, 1937
FIFTH AVENUE GIRL   RKO Radio, 1939
THE PRIMROSE PATH   RKO Radio, 1940
UNFINISHED BUSINESS   Universal, 1941
LADY IN A JAM   Universal, 1942
LIVING IN A BIG WAY   MGM, 1947

ALBERT LAMORISSE
b. January 13, 1922 - Paris, France
d. 1970

DJERBA   1947, French
BIM   1949, French
WHITE MANE   William Snyder, 1953, French
THE RED BALLOON   Lopert, 1956
STOWAWAY IN THE SKY   *LE VOYAGE EN BALLON*
   Lopert, 1960, French
FIFI LA PLUME   1965, French

VERSAILLES (FD)   1967, French
PARIS JAMAIS VE (FD)   1968, French
THE LOVERS' WIND (FD)   1968, French

LEW LANDERS
(Louis Friedlander)
b. January 2, 1901 - New York, New York
d. 1962

THE RED RIDER   Universal, 1934
TAILSPIN TOMMY   Universal, 1934
THE VANISHING SHADOW   Universal, 1934
THE CALL OF THE SAVAGE   Universal, 1935
RUSTLERS OF RED DOG   Universal, 1935
THE RAVEN   Universal, 1935
STORMY   Universal, 1935
PAROLE!   Universal, 1936
WITHOUT ORDERS   RKO, 1936
NIGHT WAITRESS   RKO, 1936
THEY WANTED TO MARRY   RKO, 1937
THE MAN WHO FOUND HIMSELF   RKO, 1937
YOU CAN'T BUY LUCK   RKO, 1937
BORDER CAFE   RKO, 1937
FLIGHT FROM GLORY   RKO, 1937
LIVING ON LOVE   RKO, 1937
DANGER PATROL   RKO, 1937
CRASHING HOLLYWOOD   RKO, 1938
DOUBLE DANGER   RKO, 1938
CONDEMNED WOMEN   RKO, 1938
LAW OF THE UNDERWORLD   RKO, 1938
BLIND ALIBI   RKO, 1938
SKY GIANT   RKO, 1938
SMASHING THE RACKETS   RKO, 1938
ANNABEL TAKES A TOUR   RKO, 1938
PACIFIC LINER   RKO, 1939
TWELVE CROWDED HOURS   RKO, 1939
FIXER DUGAN   RKO, 1939
THE GIRL AND THE GAMBLER   1939
BAD LANDS   RKO, 1939
CONSIPRACY   1939
HONEYMOON DEFERRED   Universal, 1940
ENEMY AGENT   Universal, 1940
SKI PATROL   Universal, 1940
LA CONGA NIGHTS   Universal, 1940
WAGONS WESTWARD   Republic, 1940
SING DANCE - PLENTY HOT   Republic, 1940
GIRL FROM HAVANA   Republic, 1940
SLIGHTLY TEMPTED   Republic, 1940
RIDIN' ON A RAINBOW   Republic, 1941
LUCKY DEVILS   Universal, 1941
BACK IN THE SADDLE   1941
THE SINGING HILL   Republic, 1941
I WAS A PRISONER ON DEVIL'S ISLAND   Columbia,
   1941
MYSTERY SHIP   Columbia, 1941
THE STORK PAYS OFF   Columbia, 1941
THE MAN WHO RETURNED TO LIFE   Columbia, 1942
ALIAS BOSTON BLACKIE   Columbia, 1942
CANAL ZONE   Columbia, 1942
HARVARD, HERE I COME   Columbia, 1942
NOT A LADIES' MAN   Columbia, 1942
SUBMARINE RAIDERS   Columbia, 1942
CADETS ON PARADE   Columbia, 1942
ATLANTIC CONVOY   Columbia, 1942
SABOTAGE SQUAD   Columbia, 1942
THE BOOGIE MAN WILL GET YOU   Columbia, 1942
SMITH OF MINNESOTA   Columbia, 1942
STAND BY ALL NETWORKS   Columbia, 1942
JUNIOR ARMY   Columbia, 1942

AFTER MIDNIGHT WITH BOSTON BLACKIE   Columbia, 1942
REDHEAD FROM MANHATTAN   Columbia, 1943
MURDER IN TIMES SQUARE   Columbia, 1943
POWER OF THE PRESS   Columbia, 1943
DOUGHBOYS IN IRELAND   Columbia, 1943
THE DEERSLAYER   Columbia, 1943
THE RETURN OF THE VAMPIRE   Columbia, 1944
COWBOY CANTEEN   Columbia, 1944
THE GHOST THAT WALKS ALONE   Columbia, 1944
TWO-MAN SUBMARINE   Columbia, 1944
STARS ON PARADE   Columbia, 1944
THE BLACK PARACHUTE   Columbia, 1944
U-BOAT PRISONER   Columbia, 1944
SWING IN THE SADDLE   Columbia, 1944
I'M FROM ARKANSAS   Columbia, 1944
CRIME, INC.   Columbia/Producers Releasing Corp., 1945
THE POWER OF THE WHISTLER   Columbia, 1945
TROUBLE CHASERS   1945
FOLLOW THAT WOMAN   Paramount, 1945
ARSON SQUAD   Producers Releasing Corp., 1945
SHADOW OF TERROR   Producers Releasing Corp., 1945
THE ENCHANTED FOREST   Producers Releasing Corp., 1945
TOKYO ROSE   Paramount, 1945
THE MASK OF DIJON   Producers Releasing Corp., 1946
A CLOSE CALL FOR BOSTON BLACKIE   Columbia, 1946
THE TRUTH ABOUT MURDER   RKO Radio, 1946
HOT CARGO   Paramount, 1946
SECRETS OF A SORORITY GIRL   Producers Releasing Corp., 1946
DEATH VALEY   Screen Guild, 1947
DANGER STREET   RKO, 1947
SEVEN KEYS TO BALDPATE   RKO Radio, 1947
UNDER THE TONTO RIM   RKO, 1947
THUNDER MOUNTAIN   RKO, 1947
THE SON OF RUSTY   Columbia, 1947
DEVIL SHIP   Columbia, 1947
MY DOG RUSTY   Columbia, 1948
ADVENTURES OF GALLANT BESS   Eagle Lion, 1948
INNER SANCTUM   Film Classics, 1948
STAGECOACH KID   RKO, 1949
LAW OF THE BARBARY COAST   Columbia, 1949
AIR HOSTESS   Columbia, 1949
BARBARY PIRATE   Columbia, 1949
DAVY CROCKETT, INDIAN SCOUT   United Artists, 1950
GIRLS' SCHOOL   Columbia, 1950
DYNAMITE PASS   Columbia, 1950
TYRANT OF THE SEA   Columbia, 1950
STATE PENITENTIARY   Columbia, 1950
BEAUTY ON PARADE   Columbia, 1950
CHAIN GANG   Columbia, 1950
LAST OF THE BUCCANEERS   Columubia, 1950
REVENUE AGENT   Columbia, 1950
BLUE BLOOD   Monogram, 1951
A YANK IN KOREA   Columbia, 1951
WHEN THE REDSKINS RODE   Columbia, 1951
THE BIG GUSHER   Columbia, 1951
HURRICANE ISLAND   Columbia, 1951
THE MAGIC CARPET   Columbia, 1951
JUNGLE MANHUNT   Columbia, 1951
ALADDIN AND HIS LAMP   Monogram, 1952
JUNGLE JIM IN THE FORBIDDEN LAND   Columbia, 1952
CALIFORNIA CONQUEST   Columbia, 1952
ARCTIC FLIGHT   Monogram, 1952
RIDERS OF CAPISTRANO   Revue-Exclusive, 1952
BAD MEN OF MARYSVILLE   Revue-Exclusive, 1952
THE RANGE MASTERS   Revue-Exclusive, 1952
THE NEON TORNADO   Revue-Exclusive, 1953
THE RETURN OF TRIGGER JOHNSON   Revue-Exclusive, 1953
ROARING CHALLENGE   Revue-Exclusive, 1953

TORPEDO ALLEY   Allied Artists, 1953
TANGIER INCIDENT   co-director with Paul Landres, Allied Artists, 1953
MAN IN THE DARK   Columbia, 1953
RUN FOR THE HILLS   Broder, 1953
CAPTAIN JOHN SMITH AND POCAHONTAS   United Artists, 1953
CAPTAIN KIDD AND THE SLAVE GIRL   United Artists, 1954
THE CRUEL TOWER   Allied Artists, 1956
HOT ROD GANG   American International, 1958
THE CHALLENGE OF RIN-TIN-TIN   Columbia, 1958
TERRIFIED!   Crown International, 1963

SIDNEY LANFIELD
b. April 20, 1898 - Chicago, Illinois
d. 1972

CHEER UP AND SMILE   Fox, 1930
THREE GIRLS LOST   Fox, 1931
HUSH MONEY   Fox, 1931
DANCE TEAM   Fox, 1931
SOCIETY GIRL   Fox, 1931
HAT CHECK GIRL   Fox, 1932
BROADWAY BAD   Fox, 1933
MOULIN ROUGE   Fox, 1934
THE LAST GENTLEMAN   Fox, 1934
HOLD 'EM YALE   20th Century-Fox, 1935
RED SALUTE   20th Century-century-Fox, 1936
KING OF BURLESQUE   20th Century-Fox, 1936
HALF ANGEL   20th Century-Fox, 1936
SING, BABY SING   20th Century-Fox, 1936
ONE IN A MILLION   20th Century-Fox, 1937
WAKE UP AND LIVE   20th Century-Fox, 1937
THIN ICE   20th Century-Fox, 1937
LOVE AND HISSES   20th Century-Fox, 1937
ALWAYS GOODBYE   20th Century-Fox, 1938
THE HOUND OF THE BASKERVILLES   20th Century-Fox, 1939
SECOND FIDDLE   20th Century-Fox, 1939
SWANEE RIVER   20th Century-Fox, 1939
YOU'LL NEVER GET RICH   Columbia, 1941
THE LADY HAS PLANS   Paramount, 1942
MY FAVORITE BLONDE   Paramount, 1942
THE MEANEST MAN IN THE WORLD   20th Century-Fox, 1943
LET'S FACE IT   Paramount, 1942
STANDING ROOM ONLY   Paramount, 1944
BRING ON THE GIRLS   Paramount, 1945
THE WELL-GROOMED BRIDE   Paramount, 1946
THE TROUBLE WITH WOMEN   Paramount, 1947
WHERE THERE'S LIFE   Paramount, 1947
STATION WEST   RKO Radio, 1948
SORROWFUL JONES   Paramount, 1949
THE LEMON DROP KID   Paramount, 1951
FOLLOW THE SUN   20th Century-Fox, 1951
SKIRTS AHOY!   MGM, 1952

FRITZ LANG
b. December 5, 1890 - Vienna, Austria
d. 1976

HALBBLUT   1919, German
DER HERR DER LIEBE   1919, German
DIE SPINNEN: DER GOLDENE SEE   1919, German
HARAKIRI   1919, German
DER SPINNEN: DAS BRILLANTENSCHIFF   1920, German
DAS WANDERNDE BILD   1920, German

VIER UM DIE FRAU   1920, German
DER MUDE TOD   1921, German
DR. MABUSE DER SPIELER: SPIELER AUS
   LEIDENSCHAFT   1922, German
DR. MABUSE DER SPIELER: INFERNO DES
   VERBRECHENS   1922, German
DIE NIBELUNGEN: SIEGFRIEDS TOD   UFA,
   1924, German
DIE NIBELUNGEN: KRIEMHILDS RACHE   UFA,
   1924, German
METROPOLIS   UFA, 1927, German
SPIES   MGM, 1928, German
BY ROCKET TO THE MOON   *DIE FRAU IM MOND*
   1929, German
M   Paramount, 1930, German
THE TESTAMENT OF DR. MABUSE   Janus, 1933,
   German
LILIOM   Fox-Europa, 1934, French
FURY   MGM, 1936
YOU ONLY LIVE ONCE   United Artists, 1937
YOU AND ME   Paramount, 1938
THE RETURN OF FRANK JAMES   20th Century-
   Fox, 1940
WESTERN UNION   20th Century-Fox, 1941
MAN HUNT   20th Century-Fox, 1941
HANGMEN ALSO DIE   United Artists, 1943
WOMAN IN THE WINDOW   RKO Radio, 1944
MINISTRY OF FEAR   Paramount, 1944
SCARLET STREET   Universal, 1945
CLOAK AND DAGGER   Warner Bros., 1945
SECRET BEYOND THE DOOR   Universal, 1948
HOUSE BY THE RIVER   Republic, 1950
AMERICAN GUERILLA IN THE PHILIPPINES
   20th Century-Fox, 1950
RANCHO NOTORIOUS   RKO Radio, 1952
CLASH BY NIGHT   RKO Radio, 1952
THE BLUE GARDENIA   Warner Bros., 1953
THE BIG HEAT   Columbia, 1953
HUMAN DESIRE   Columbia, 1954
MOONFLEET   MGM, 1955
WHILE THE CITY SLEEPS   RKO Radio, 1956
BEYOND A REASONABLE DOUBT   RKO Radio, 1956
DER TIGER VON ESCHNAPUR   *JOURNEY TO THE LOST
CITY*   American International, 1959, West German-
   French-Italian
DAS INDISCHE GRABMAL   *JOURNEY TO THE LOST
CITY*   American International, 1959, West German-
   French-Italian
THE 1000 EYES OF DR. MABUSE   Ajay Films, 1960,
   West German-French-Italian

WALTER LANG

b. August 10, 1898 - Memphis, Tennessee
d. 1972

RED KIMONO   Vital Exchange, 1925
THE CARNIVAL GIRL   Vitagraph, 1926
THE EARTH WOMAN   Associated Exhibitors, 1926
THE GOLDEN WEB   Lumas, 1926
MONEY TO BURN   Lumas, 1926
THE LADYBIRD   Chadwick, 1927
THE SATIN WOMAN   Lumas, 1927
SALLY IN OUR ALLEY   Columbia, 1927
BY WHOSE HAND?   Columbia, 1927
THE COLLEGE HERO   Columbia, 1927
THE NIGHT FLYER   Pathé, 1928
SHADOWS OF THE PAST   1928
THE DESERT BRIDE   Columbia, 1928
THE SPIRIT OF YOUTH   Tiffany, 1929
HELLO SISTER   World Wide, 1930
COCK O' THE WALK   co-director with Roy William Neill,
   World Wide, 1930

THE BIG FIGHT   World Wide, 1930
THE COSTELLO CASE   World Wide, 1930
BROTHERS   Columbia, 1930
COMMAND PERFORMANCE   1931
HELL BOUND   Tiffany, 1931
WOMEN GO ON FOREVER   1931
NO MORE ORCHIDS   Columbia, 1932
THE WARRIOR'S HUSBAND   Fox, 1933
MEET THE BARON   1933
THE PARTY'S OVER   1934
WHOM THE GODS DESTROY   1934
THE MIGHTY BARNUM   United Artists, 1934
CARNIVAL   Columbia, 1935
HOORAY FOR LOVE   1935
LOVE BEFORE BREAKFAST   Universal, 1936
WIFE, DOCTOR AND NURSE   20th Century-Fox, 1937
SECOND HONEYMOON   20th Century-Fox, 1937
THE BARONESS AND THE BUTLER   20th Century-Fox,
   1938
I'LL GIVE A MILLION   20th Century-Fox, 1938
THE LITTLE PRINCESS   20th Century-Fox, 1939
THE BLUE BIRD   20th Century-Fox, 1940
STAR DUST   20th Century-Fox, 1940
THE GREAT PROFILE   20th Century-Fox, 1940
TIN PAN ALLEY   20th Century-Fox, 1940
MOON OVER MIAMI   20th Century-Fox, 1941
WEEK-END IN HAVANA   20th Century-Fox, 1941
SONG OF THE ISLANDS   20th Century-Fox, 1942
THE MAGNIFICENT DOPE   20th Century-Fox, 1942
CONEY ISLAND   20th Century-Fox, 1943
GREENWICH VILLAGE   20th Century-Fox, 1944
STATE FAIR   20th Century-Fox, 1945
SENTIMENTAL JOURNEY   20th Century-Fox, 1946
CLAUDIA AND DAVID   20th Century-Fox, 1946
MOTHER WORE TIGHTS   20th Century-Fox, 1947
SITTING PRETTY   20th Century-Fox, 1947
WHEN MY BABY SMILES AT ME   20th Century-Fox,
   1948
YOU'RE MY EVERYTHING   20th Century-Fox, 1949

CHEAPER BY THE DOZEN   20th Century-Fox, 1950
THE JACKPOT   20th Century-Fox, 1950
ON THE RIVIERA   20th Century-Fox, 1951
WITH A SONG IN MY HEART   20th Century-Fox, 1952
CALL ME MADAM   20th Century-Fox, 1953
THERE'S NO BUSINESS LIKE SHOW BUSINESS
   20th Century-Fox, 1954
THE KING AND I ★   20th Century-Fox, 1956
THE DESK SET   20th Century-Fox, 1957
BUT NOT FOR ME   20th Century-Fox, 1959
CAN-CAN   20th Century-Fox, 1960
THE MARRIAGE-GO-ROUND   20th Century-Fox, 1961
SNOW WHITE AND THE THREE STOOGES   20th
   Century-Fox, 1961

CHARLES LAUGHTON

b. July 1, 1899 - Scarborough, England
d. 1962

THE NIGHT OF THE HUNTER   United Artists, 1955

WILFORD LEACH

d. 1988

THE WEDDING PARTY   co-director with Brian De Palma
   & Cynthia Munroe, Powell Productions Plus/Ondine,
   1969
THE PIRATES OF PENZANCE   Universal, 1983

PHILIP LEACOCK

b. October 8, 1917 - London, England
d. 1990

RIDERS OF THE NEW FOREST   Crown, 1946, British
THE BRAVE DON'T CRY   Mayer-Kingsley, 1952, British
ASSIGNMENT IN LONDON   Associated Artists,
    1953, British
THE LITTLE KIDNAPPERS   THE KIDNAPPERS   United
    Artists, 1954, British
ESCAPADE   DCA, 1955, British
THE SPANISH GARDENER   Rank, 1956, British
HIGH TIDE AT NOON   Rank, 1957, British
INNOCENT SINNERS   Rank, 1958, British
THE RABBIT TRAP   United Artists, 1959
LET NO MAN WRITE MY EPITAPH   Columbia, 1960
TAKE A GIANT STEP   United Artists, 1960
HAND IN HAND   Columbia, 1961, British
REACH FOR GLORY   Royal Films International,
    1962, British
13 WEST STREET   Columbia, 1962
THE WAR LOVER   Columbia, 1962, British
TAMAHINE   MGM, 1964, British
ADAM'S WOMAN   Warner Bros., 1970, Australian
THE BIRDMEN (TF)   Universal TV, 1971
WHEN MICHAEL CALLS (TF)   Palomar
    International, 1972
THE DAUGHTERS OF JOSHUA CABE (TF)   Spelling-
    Goldberg Productions, 1972
BAFFLED! (TF)   Arena Productions/ITC, 1973
THE GREAT MAN'S WHISKERS (TF)   Universal TV, 1973
DYING ROOM ONLY (TF)   Lorimar Productions, 1973
KEY WEST (TF)   Warner Bros. TV, 1973
KILLER ON BOARD (TF)   Lorimar Productions, 1977
WILD AND WOOLY (TF)   Aaron Spelling Productions, 1978
THE CURSE OF KING TUT'S TOMB (TF)   Stromberg-Kerby
    Productions/Columbia TV/HTV West, 1980
ANGEL CITY (TF)   Factor-Newland Productions, 1980
THE TWO LIVES OF CAROL LETNER (TF)   Penthouse
    One Presentations, 1981
THE WILD WOMEN OF CHASTITY GULCH (TF)   Aaron
    Spelling Productions, 1982
THREE SOVEREIGNS FOR SARAH (TF)   Night Owl
    Productions, 1985

REGINALD LE BORG

b. December 11, 1902 - Vienna, Austria
d. 1989

SHE'S FOR ME   Universal, 1943
CALLING DR. DEATH   Universal, 1943
ADVENTURE IN MUSIC   co-director, 1944
WEIRD WOMAN   Universal, 1944
THE MUMMY'S GHOST   Universal, 1944
JUNGLE WOMAN   Universal, 1944
SAN DIEGO - I LOVE YOU   Universal, 1944
DEAD MAN'S EYES   Universal, 1944
DESTINY   Universal, 1944
HONEYMOON AHEAD   Universal, 1945
JOE PALOOKA - CHAMP   Monogram, 1946
LITTLE IODINE   United Artists, 1946
SUSIE STEPS OUT   United Artists, 1946
FALL GUY   Monogram, 1947
THE ADVENTURES OF DON COYOTE   United Artists,
    1947
PHILO VANCE'S SECRET MISSION   Eagle-Lion, 1947
JOE PALOOKA IN THE KNOCKOUT   Monogram, 1947
PORT SAID   Columbia, 1948
JOE PALOOKA IN WINNER TAKE ALL   Monogram, 1948

FIGHTING MAD   Monogram, 1948
TROUBLE MAKERS   Monogram, 1948
FIGHTING FOOLS   Monogram, 1949
HOLD THAT BABY   Monogram, 1949
JOE PALOOKA IN THE COUNTERPUNCH   Monogram,
    1949
YOUNG DANIEL BOONE   Monogram, 1950
WYOMING MAIL   Universal, 1950
JOE PALOOKA IN THE SQUARED CIRCLE   Monogram,
    1950
G.I. JANE   Lippert, 1950
JOE PALOOKA IN TRIPLE CROSS   Monogram, 1950
MODELS, INC.   Mutual Pictures, 1951
BAD BLONDE   THE FLANAGAN BOY   Lippert, 1951,
    British
THE GREAT JESSE JAMES RAID   Lippert, 1953
SINS OF JEZEBEL   Lippert, 1953
THE WHITE ORCHID   United Artists, 1954
THE BLACK SHEEP   United Artists, 1956
VOODOO ISLAND   United Artists, 1957
THE DALTON GIRLS   United Artists, 1957
THE FLIGHT THAT DISAPPEARED   United Artists, 1961
DEADLY DUO   United Artists, 1962
DIARY OF A MADMAN   United Artists, 1963
THE EYES OF ANNIE JONES   20th Century-Fox, 1964,
    U.S.-British
SO EVIL MY SISTER   Zenith International, 1973

ROWLAND V. LEE

b. September 6, 1891 - Findlay, Ohio
d. 1975

THE CUP OF LIFE   Associated Producers, 1921
BLIND HEARTS   Associated Producers, 1921
CUPID'S BRAND   Arrow, 1921
THE SEA LION   Associated Producers, 1921
THE DUST FLOWER   Goldwyn, 1922
HIS BACK AGAINST THE WALL   Goldwyn, 1922
THE MEN OF ZANZIBAR   Fox, 1922
MIXED FACES   Fox, 1922
MONEY TO BURN   Fox, 1922
A SELF-MADE MAN   Fox, 1922
SHIRLEY OF THE CIRCUS   Fox, 1922
WHIMS OF THE GODS   Goldwyn, 1922
ALICE ADAMS   Associated Exhibitors, 1923
DESIRE   Metro, 1923
YOU CAN'T GET AWAY WITH IT   Fox, 1923
GENTLE JULIA   Fox, 1923
IN LOVE WITH LOVE   Fox, 1924
THE MAN WITHOUT A COUNTRY   Fox, 1925
HAVOC   Fox, 1925
THE OUTSIDER   Fox, 1926
THE SILVER TREASURE   Fox, 1926
THE WHIRLWIND OF YOUTH   Fox, 1927
BARBED WIRE   1927
THE SECRET HOUR   Paramount, 1928
DOOMSDAY   Paramount, 1928
THREE SINNERS   Paramount, 1928
THE FIRST KISS   Paramount, 1928
LOVES OF AN ACTRESS   Paramount, 1928
THE WOLF OF WALL STREET   Paramount, 1929
A DANGEROUS WOMAN   Paramount, 1929
THE MYSTERIOUS DR. FU MANCHU   Paramount,
    1929
PARAMOUNT ON PARADE   co-director, Paramount,
    1930
THE RETURN OF DR. FU MANCHU   Paramount, 1930
LADIES LOVE BRUTES   Paramount, 1930
A MAN FROM WYOMING   Paramount, 1930

Le

FILM
DIRECTORS
GUIDE

N
O
T
A
B
L
E

D
I
R
E
C
T
O
R
S

O
F

T
H
E

P
A
S
T

DERELICT   Paramount, 1930
UPPER UNDERWORLD   First National, 1931
THE RULING VOICE   First National, 1931
THE GUILTY GENERATION   Paramount, 1931
THAT NIGHT IN LONDON   *OVER NIGHT*   Paramount,
   1932, British
ZOO IN BUDAPEST   Fox, 1933
I AM SUZANNE   Fox, 1934
THE COUNT OF MONTE CRISTO   Universal, 1934
GAMBLING   Fox, 1934
CARDINAL RICHILIEU   United Artists, 1935
THE THREE MUSKETEERS   RKO Radio, 1935
ONE RAINY AFTERNOON   United Artists, 1936
LOVE FROM A STRANGER   United Artists, 1937, British
THE TOAST OF NEW YORK   RKO Radio, 1937
MOTHER CAREY'S CHICKENS   RKO Radio, 1938
SERVICE DE LUXE   Universal, 1938
THE SON OF FRANKENSTEIN   Universal, 1939
THE SUN NEVER SETS   Paramount, 1939
TOWER OF LONDON   Universal, 1939
THE SON OF MONTE CRISTO   United Artists, 1940
POWDER TOWN   RKO Radio, 1942
THE BRIDGE OF SAN LUIS REY   United Artists, 1944
CAPTAIN KIDD   United Artists, 1945

MITCHELL LEISEN
b. October 6, 1898 - Menominee, Michigan
d. 1972

CRADLE SONG   Paramount, 1933
DEATH TAKES A HOLIDAY   Paramount, 1934
MURDER AT THE VANITIES   Paramount, 1934
BEHOLD MY WIFE   Paramount, 1935
FOUR HOURS TO KILL   Paramount, 1935
HANDS ACROSS THE TABLE   Paramount, 1935
13 HOURS BY AIR   Paramount, 1936
THE BIG BROADCAST OF 1937   Paramount, 1936
SWING, HIGH, SWING LOW   Paramount, 1937
EASY LIVING   Paramount, 1937
THE BIG BROADCAST OF 1938   Paramount, 1938
ARTISTS AND MODELS ABROAD   Paramount, 1938
MIDNIGHT   Paramount, 1939
REMEMBER THE NIGHT   Paramount, 1940
ARISE, MY LOVE   Paramount, 1940
I WANTED WINGS   Paramount, 1941
HOLD BACK THE DAWN   Paramount, 1941
THE LADY IS WILLING   Columbia, 1942
TAKE A LETTER, DARLING   Paramount, 1942
NO TIME FOR LOVE   Paramount, 1943
LADY IN THE DARK   Paramount, 1944
FRENCHMAN'S CREEK   Paramount, 1944
PRACTICALLY YOURS   Paramount, 1944
KITTY   Paramount, 1945
MASQUERADE IN MEXICO   Paramount, 1945
TO EACH HIS OWN   Paramount, 1946
SUDDENLY IT'S SPRING   Paramount, 1947
GOLDEN EARRINGS   Paramount, 1947
DREAM GIRL   Paramount, 1948
BRIDE OF VENGEANCE   Paramount, 1949
SONG OF SURRENDER   Paramount, 1949
CAPTAIN CAREY, USA   Paramount, 1950
NO MAN OF HER OWN   Paramount, 1950
THE MATING SEASON   Paramount, 1951
DARLING, HOW COULD YOU!   Paramount, 1951
YOUNG MAN WITH IDEAS   MGM, 1952
TONIGHT WE SING   20th Century-Fox, 1953
BEDEVILLED   MGM, 1955
THE GIRL MOST LIKELY   Universal, 1958
SPREE (FD)   co-director with Walon Green, United
   Producers, 1967

ROBERT Z. LEONARD
(Robert Zigler Leonard)
b. October 7, 1889 - Chicago, Illinois
d. 1968

THE MASTER KEY   Universal, 1914
HERITAGE   Universal, 1915
THE SILENT COMMAND   Universal, 1915
JUDGE NOT   *THE WOMAN OF MONA DIGGINS*
   Universal, 1915
THE LOVE GIRL   Universal, 1916
THE CRIPPLED HAND   co-director with David Kirkland,
   1916, Universal
THE PLOW GIRL   Paramount, 1916
THE EAGLE'S WINGS   Universal, 1916
LITTLE EVA EGERTON   Universal, 1916
SECRET LOVE   Universal, 1916
THE LITTLE ORPHAN   Universal, 1917
AT FIRST SIGHT   Universal, 1917
THE PRIMROSE RING   Paramount, 1917
A MORMON MAID   Paramount, 1917
PRINCESS VIRTUE   Bluebird, 1917
FACE VALUE   Bluebird, 1917
THE BRIDE'S AWAKENING   Universal, 1918
HER BODY IN BOND   Murray, 1918
DANGER - GO SLOW   Universal, 1918
MODERN LOVE   Universal, 1918
THE DELICIOUS LITTLE DEVIL   Universal, 1919
THE BIG LITTLE PERSON   Universal, 1919
WHAT AM I BID?   Universal, 1919
THE SCARLET SHADOW   Universal, 1919
THE WAY OF A WOMAN   Selznick, 1919
MIRACLE OF LOVE   Paramount, 1919
APRIL FOLLY   Paramount, 1920
THE RESTLESS SEX   Paramount, 1920
THE GILDED LILY   Paramount, 1921
HEEDLESS MOTHS   Equity, 1921
PEACOCK ALLEY   Metro, 1921
FASCINATION   Metro, 1922
BROADWAY ROSE   Metro, 1922
JAZZMANIA   Metro, 1923
THE FRENCH DOLL   Metro, 1923
FASHION ROW   Metro, 1923
MADEMOISELLE MIDNIGHT   Metro-Goldwyn, 1924
CIRCE THE ENCHANTRESS   Metro, 1924
LOVE'S WILDERNESS   First National, 1924
CHEAPER TO MARRY   Metro-Goldwyn, 1925
BRIGHT LIGHTS   Metro-Goldwyn, 1925
TIME THE COMEDIAN   Metro-Goldwyn, 1925
DANCE MADNESS   MGM, 1926
MADEMOISELLE MODISTE   MGM, 1926
THE WANING SEX   MGM, 1926
A LITTLE JOURNEY   MGM, 1927
THE DEMI-BRIDE   MGM, 1927
ADAM AND EVIL   MGM, 1927
TEA FOR THREE   MGM, 1927
BABY MINE   MGM, 1928
THE CARDBOARD LOVER   MGM, 1928
A LADY OF CHANCE   MGM, 1928
MARIANNE   MGM, 1929
THE DIVORCEE ★   MGM, 1930
IN GAY MADRID   MGM, 1930
LET US BE GAY   MGM, 1930
THE BACHELOR FATHER   MGM, 1931
IT'S A WISE CHILD   MGM, 1931
FIVE AND TEN   MGM, 1931
SUSAN LENNOX: HER FALL AND RISE   MGM, 1931
LOVERS COURAGEOUS   MGM, 1932
STRANGE INTERLUDE   MGM, 1932
PEG O' MY HEART   MGM, 1933

DANCING LADY   MGM, 1933
OUTCAST LADY   MGM, 1934
AFTER OFFICE HOURS   MGM, 1935
ESCAPADE   MGM, 1935
THE GREAT ZIEGFELD ★   MGM, 1936
PICCADILLY JIM   MGM, 1936
MAYTIME   MGM, 1937
THE FIREFLY   MGM, 1937
THE GIRL OF THE GOLDEN WEST   MGM, 1938
BROADWAY SERENADE   MGM, 1939
NEW MOON   MGM, 1940
PRIDE AND PREJUDICE   MGM, 1940
THIRD FINGER, LEFT HAND   MGM, 1940
ZIEGFELD GIRL   MGM, 1941
WHEN LADIES MEET   MGM, 1941
WE WERE DANCING   MGM, 1942
STAND BY FOR ACTION   MGM, 1942
THE MAN FROM DOWN UNDER   MGM, 1943
MARRIAGE IS A PRIVATE AFFAIR   MGM, 1944
WEEK-END AT THE WALDORF   MGM, 1945
THE SECRET HEART   MGM, 1946
CYNTHIA   MGM, 1947
B.F.'S DAUGHTER   MGM, 1948
THE BRIBE   MGM, 1949
IN THE GOOD OLD SUMMERTIME   MGM, 1949
NANCY GOES TO RIO   MGM, 1950
DUCHESS OF IDAHO   MGM, 1950
GROUNDS FOR MARRIAGE   MGM, 1950
TOO YOUNG TO KISS   MGM, 1951
EVERYTHING I HAVE IS YOURS   MGM, 1952
THE CLOWN   MGM, 1953
THE GREAT DIAMOND ROBBERY   MGM, 1953
HER TWELVE MEN   MGM, 1954
THE KING'S THIEF   MGM, 1955
BEAUTIFUL BUT DANGEROUS   *LA DONNA PIU
   BELLA DEL MONDO*   20th Century-Fox, 1955,
   Italian
KELLY AND ME   Universal, 1957

IRVING LERNER
b. March 7, 1909 - New York, New York
d. 1976

C-MAN   Four Continents, 1949
SUICIDE ATTACK   1951
MAN CRAZY   20th Century-Fox, 1953
EDGE OF FURY   co-director with Robert Gurney, Jr.,
   United Artists, 1958
MURDER BY CONTRACT   Columbia, 1958
CITY OF FEAR   Columbia, 1959
STUDS LONIGAN   United Artists, 1960
CRY OF BATTLE   Allied Artists, 1963
THE ROYAL HUNT OF THE SUN   National General, 1968

MERVYN LeROY
b. October 15, 1900 - San Francisco, California
d. 1987

NO PLACE TO GO   First National, 1927
FLYING ROMEOS   First National, 1928
HAROLD TEEN   First National, 1928
OH KAY!   First National, 1928
NAUGHTY BABY   First National, 1929
HOT STUFF   First National, 1929
BROADWAY BABIES   First National, 1929
LITTLE JOHNNY JONES   First National, 1929
PLAYING AROUND   First National, 1929
SHOWGIRL IN HOLLYWOOD   First National, 1930
NUMBERED MEN   First National, 1930

TOP SPEED   First National, 1930
LITTLE CAESAR   First National, 1931
GENTLEMAN'S FATE   First National, 1931
TOO YOUNG TO MARRY   First National, 1931
BROAD MINDED   First National, 1931
FIVE STAR FINAL   First National, 1931
LOCAL BOY MAKES GOOD   First National, 1931
TONIGHT OR NEVER   United Artists, 1931
HIGH PRESSURE   Warner Bros., 1932
TWO SECONDS   First National, 1932
BIG CITY BLUES   Warner Bros., 1932
THREE ON A MATCH   First National, 1932
I AM A FUGITIVE FROM A CHAIN GANG   Warner Bros.,
   1932
HARD TO HANDLE   Warner Bros., 1933
ELMER THE GREAT   First National, 1933
GOLD DIGGERS OF 1933   Warner Bros., 1933
TUGBOAT ANNIE   MGM, 1933
THE WORLD CHANGES   First National, 1933
HI, NELLIE!   Warner Bros., 1934
HEAT LIGHTNING   Warner Bros., 1934
HAPPINESS AHEAD   First National, 1934
SWEET ADELINE   Warner Bros., 1935
OIL FOR THE LAMPS OF CHINA   Warner Bros., 1935
PAGE MISS GLORY   Warner Bros., 1935
I FOUND STELLA PARISH   First National, 1935
ANTHONY ADVERSE   Warner Bros., 1936
THREE MEN ON A HORSE   First National, 1936
THE KING AND THE CHORUS GIRL   Warner Bros., 1937
THEY WON'T FORGET   Warner Bros., 1937
FOOLS FOR SCANDAL   Warner Bros., 1938
WATERLOO BRIDGE   MGM, 1940
ESCAPE   MGM, 1940
BLOSSOMS IN THE DUST   MGM, 1941
UNHOLY PARTNERS   MGM, 1941
JOHNNY EAGER   MGM, 1941
RANDOM HARVEST ★   MGM, 1942
MADAME CURIE   MGM, 1943
THIRTY SECONDS OVER TOKYO   MGM, 1944
WITHOUT RESERVATIONS   RKO Radio, 1946
HOMECOMING   MGM, 1948
LITTLE WOMEN   MGM, 1949
ANY NUMBER CAN PLAY   MGM, 1949
EAST SIDE, WEST SIDE   MGM, 1950
QUO VADIS   MGM, 1951
LOVELY TO LOOK AT   MGM, 1952
MILLION DOLLAR MERMAID   MGM, 1952
LATIN LOVERS   MGM, 1953
ROSE MARIE   MGM, 1954
STRANGE LADY IN TOWN   Warner Bros., 1955
MISTER ROBERTS   co-director with John Ford,
   Warner Bros., 1955
THE BAD SEED   Warner Bros., 1956
TOWARD THE UNKNOWN   Warner Bros., 1956
NO TIME FOR SERGEANTS   Warner Bros., 1958
HOME BEFORE DARK   Warner Bros., 1958
THE FBI STORY   Warner Bros., 1959
WAKE ME WHEN IT'S OVER   20th Century-Fox, 1960
THE DEVIL AT 4 O'CLOCK   Columbia, 1961
A MAJORITY OF ONE   Warner Bros., 1962
GYPSY   Warner Bros., 1962
MARY, MARY   Warner Bros., 1963
MOMENT TO MOMENT   Universal, 1966

HENRY LEVIN
b. June 5, 1909 - Trenton, New Jersey
d. 1980

THE CRY OF THE WEREWOLF   Columbia, 1944
SERGEANT MIKE   Columbia, 1944
DANCING IN MANHATTAN   Columbia, 1944

I LOVE A MYSTERY   Columbia, 1945
THE FIGHTING GUARDSMAN   Columbia, 1945
THE BANDIT OF SHERWOOD FOREST   co-director with
    George Sherman, Columbia, 1946
NIGHT EDITOR   Columbia, 1946
THE UNKNOWN   Columbia, 1946
THE DEVIL'S MASK   Columbia, 1946
THE RETURN OF MONTE CRISTO   Columbia, 1946
THE GUILT OF JANET AMES   Columbia, 1948
THE CORPSE CAME C.O.D.   Columbia, 1948
THE MATING OF MILLIE   Columbia, 1948
GALLANT BLADE   Columbia, 1948
THE MAN FROM COLORADO   Columbia, 1948
MR. SOFT TOUCH   co-director with Gordon Douglas,
    Columbia, 1949
JOLSON SINGS AGAIN   Columbia, 1949
AND BABY MAKES THREE   Columbia, 1949
CONVICTED   Columbia, 1950
THE PETTY GIRL   Columbia, 1950
THE FLYING MISSILE   Columbia, 1951
TWO OF A KIND   Columbia, 1951
THE FAMILY SECRET   Columbia, 1951
BELLES ON THEIR TOES   20th Century-Fox, 1952
THE PRESIDENT'S LADY   20th Century-Fox, 1953
THE FARMER TAKES A WIFE   20th Century-Fox, 1953
MR. SCOUTMASTER   20th Century-Fox, 1953
THREE YOUNG TEXANS   20th Century-Fox, 1954
THE GAMBLER FROM NATCHEZ   20th Century-Fox,
    1954
THE WARRIORS   Allied Artists, 1955
THE LONELY MAN   Paramount, 1957
LET'S BE HAPPY   Allied Artists, 1957, British
BERNADINE   20th Century-Fox, 1957
APRIL LOVE   20th Century-Fox, 1957
A NICE LITTLE BANK THAT SHOULD BE ROBBED
    20th Century-Fox, 1958
THE REMARKABLE MR. PENNYPACKER   20th Century-
    Fox, 1958
HOLIDAY FOR LOVERS   20th Century-Fox, 1959
JOURNEY TO THE CENTER OF THE EARTH   20th
    Century-Fox, 1959
WHERE THE BOYS ARE   MGM, 1960
THE WONDERS OF ALADDIN   MGM, 1961, Italian-U.S.
THE WONDERFUL WORLD OF THE BROTHERS
    GRIMM   co-director with George Pal, MGM/Cinerama,
    1962
IF A MAN ANSWERS   Universal, 1962
COME FLY WITH ME   MGM, 1963
HONEYMOON HOTEL   MGM, 1964
GENGHIS KHAN   Columbia, 1965, U.S.-British-West
    German-Yugoslavian
MURDERERS' ROW   Columbia, 1966
KISS THE GIRLS AND MAKE THEM DIE   *SE TUTTE LE
    DONNE DEL MONDO/OPERAZIONE PARADISO*
    co-director with Dino Maiuri, Columbia, 1967,
    Italian-U.S.
THE AMBUSHERS   Columbia, 1967
THE DESPERADOS   Columbia, 1969
THAT MAN BOLT   co-director with David Lowell Rich,
    Universal, 1973
RUN FOR THE ROSES   *THE THOROUGHBREDS*
    Kodiak Films, 1978
SCOUT'S HONOR (TF)   Zephyr Productions, 1980

ALBERT   LEWIN
b. September 23, 1894 - Newark, New Jersey
d. 1968

THE MOON AND SIXPENCE   United Artists, 1942
THE PICTURE OF DORIAN GRAY   MGM, 1945

THE PRIVATE AFFAIRS OF BEL AMI   United Artists, 1947
PANDORA AND THE FLYING DUTCHMAN   MGM, 1951,
    British
SAADIA   MGM, 1954
THE LIVING IDOL   MGM, 1957

ANATOLE   LITVAK
(Michael Anatol Litwak)
b. May 10, 1902 - Kiev, Russia
d. 1974

TATIANA   1925, Russian
DOLLY MACHT KARRIERE   1930, German
NIE WIEDER LIEBE   1931, German
DAS LIED EINER NACHT   1932, German
COEUR DE LILAS   1932, French
LA CHANSON D'UNE NUIT   1932, German
TELL ME TONIGHT   *BE MINE TONIGHT*   1932, German
SLEEPING CAR   Gaumont-British, 1933, British
CETTE VIEILLE CANAILLE   1933, French
L'EQUIPAGE   *FLIGHT INTO DARKNESS*   1935, French
MADEMOISELLE DOCTEUR   co-director with G.W. Pabst,
    1935, French
MAYERLING   1936, French
THE WOMAN I LOVE   RKO Radio, 1937
TOVARICH   Warner Bros., 1937
THE AMAZING DR. CLITTERHOUSE   Warner Bros., 1938
THE SISTERS   Warner Bros., 1938
CONFESSIONS OF A NAZI SPY   Warner Bros., 1939
CASTLE ON THE HUDSON   Warner Bros., 1940
ALL THIS AND HEAVEN TOO   Warner Bros., 1940
CITY FOR CONQUEST   Warner Bros., 1940
OUT OF THE FOG   Warner Bros., 1941
BLUES IN THE NIGHT   Warner Bros., 1941
THIS ABOVE ALL   20th Century-Fox, 1942
THE NAZIS STRIKE (FD)   co-director with Frank Capra,
    U.S. Army, 1942
DIVIDE AND CONQUER (FD)   co-director with Frank
    Capra, U.S. Army, 1943
OPERATION TITANIC (FD)   U.S. Army, 1943
THE BATTLE OF RUSSIA (FD)   U.S. Army, 1943
THE BATTLE OF CHINA (FD)   co-director with Frank
    Capra, U.S. Army, 1944
WAR COMES TO AMERICA (FD)   U.S. Army, 1945
THE LONG NIGHT   RKO Radio, 1947
SORRY, WRONG NUMBER   Paramount, 1948
THE SNAKE PIT ★   20th Century-Fox, 1949
DECISION BEFORE DAWN   20th Century-Fox, 1949
ACT OF LOVE   United Artists, 1953, French-U.S.
THE DEEP, BLUE SEA   20th Century-Fox, 1955, British
ANASTASIA   20th Century-Fox, 1956
THE JOURNEY   MGM, 1959
GOODBYE AGAIN   *AIMEZ-VOUS BRAHMS?*   United
    Artists, 1961, French-U.S.
FIVE MILES TO MIDNIGHT   United Artists, 1963,
    U.S.-French-Italian
THE NIGHT OF THE GENERALS   Columbia, 1967,
    British-French
THE LADY IN THE CAR WITH GLASSES AND A GUN
    Columbia, 1970, French-U.S.

FRANK   LLOYD
b. February 2, 1888 - Glasgow, Scotland
d. 1960

JANE   Paramount, 1915
THE REFORM CANDIDATE   Paramount, 1915
FOR HIS SUPERIOR'S HONOR   1915
BILLIE'S BABY   1915

ELEVEN TO ONE   1915
FATE'S ALIBI   1915
FROM THE SHADOWS   1915
THE BAY OF SEVEN ISLANDS   1915
DR. MASON'S TEMPTATION   1915
A DOUBLE DEAL IN PORK   1915
AN ARRANGEMENT WITH FATE   1915
LITTLE MR. FIXER   1915
IN THE GRASP OF THE LAW   1915
HIS LAST TRICK   1915
THE LITTLE GIRL OF THE ATTIC   1915
THE PINCH   1915
THE PROPHET OF THE HILLS   1915
MARTIN LOWE - FIXER   1915
PATERNAL LOVE   1915
THEIR GOLDEN WEDDING   1915
10,000 DOLLARS   1915
THE TOLL OF YOUTH   1915
TRICKERY   1915
TO REDEEM AN OATH   1915
THE SOURCE OF HAPPINESS   1915
TO REDEEM A VALUE   1915
THE GENTLEMAN FROM INDIANA   Paramount, 1915
THE CALL OF THE CUMBERLANDS   Paramount, 1915
THE INTRIGUE   Paramount, 1915
THE TONGUES OF MEN   Paramount, 1916
MADAME PRESIDENT   Paramount, 1916
AN INTERNATIONAL MARRIAGE   Paramount, 1916
THE CODE OF MARCIA GRAY   Paramount, 1916
THE INTRIGUE   Paramount, 1915
THE MAKING OF MADDALENA   Paramount, 1916
SINS OF HER PARENTS   Fox, 1916
THE STRONGER LOVE   Paramount, 1916
DAVID GARRICK   Paramount, 1916
THE PRICE OF SILENCE   Fox, 1917
THE HEART OF A LION   Fox, 1917
AMERICAN METHODS   Fox, 1917
A TALE OF TWO CITIES   Fox, 1917
WHEN A MAN SEES RED   Fox, 1917
THE PLUNDERER   Fox, 1918
THE KINGDOM OF LOVE   Fox, 1919
LES MISERABLES   Fox, 1919
THE BLINDNESS OF DIVORCE   Fox, 1919
TRUE BLUE   Fox, 1919
FOR FREEDOM   Fox, 1919
THE RAINBOW TRAIL   Fox, 1919
THE RIDERS OF THE PURPLE SAGA   Fox, 1919
THE MAN HUNTER   Fox, 1919
PITFALLS OF A BIG CITY   Fox, 1919
THE WORLD AND ITS WOMEN   Goldwyn, 1919
THE LOVERS OF LETTY   Fox, 1920
THE SILVER HORDE   Goldwyn, 1920
THE WOMAN IN ROOM 13   Goldwyn, 1920
MADAME X   Goldwyn, 1920
THE GREAT LOVER   Goldwyn, 1920
A TALE OF TWO WORLDS   Goldwyn, 1921
ROADS TO DESTINY   ROADS OF DESTINY   Goldwyn,
   1921
A VOICE IN THE DARK   Goldwyn, 1921
THE INVISIBLE POWER   Goldwyn, 1921
THE MAN FROM LOST RIVER   Goldwyn, 1921
THE SIN FLOOD   Goldwyn, 1921
THE GRIM COMEDIAN   Goldwyn, 1922
THE ETERNAL FLAME   Associated First National, 1922
OLIVER TWIST   Associated First National, 1922
THE VOICE FROM THE MINARET   Associated First
   National, 1923
WITHIN THE LAW   Associated First National, 1923
ASHES OF VENGEANCE   Associated First National, 1923
BLACK OXEN   First National, 1924
THE SEA HAWK   First National, 1924
THE SILENT WATCHER   First National, 1924

WINDS OF CHANCE   First National, 1925
HER HUSBAND'S SECRET   First National, 1925
THE SPLENDID ROAD   First National, 1925
THE WISE GUY   First National, 1926
THE EAGLE OF THE SEA   Paramount, 1926
CHILDREN OF DIVORCE   Paramount, 1927
ADORATION   First National, 1928
WEARY RIVER ★★   First National, 1929
THE DIVINE LADY ★★   First National, 1929
DRAG ★★   First National, 1929
DARK STREETS   First National, 1929
YOUNG NOWHERES   First National, 1929
SON OF THE GODS   First National, 1930
THE WAY OF ALL MEN   First National, 1930
THE LASH   First National, 1930
EAST LYNNE   Fox, 1931
THE RIGHT OF WAY   First National, 1931
THE AGE FOR LOVE   United Artists, 1931
A PASSPORT TO HELL   Fox, 1932
CAVALCADE ★★   Fox, 1933
BERKELEY SQUARE   Fox, 1933
HOOPLA   Fox, 1933
SERVANTS' ENTRANCE   Fox, 1934
MUTINY ON THE BOUNTY ★   MGM, 1935
UNDER TWO FLAGS   20th Century-Fox, 1936
MAID OF SALEM   Paramount, 1937
WELLS FARGO   Paramount, 1937
IF I WERE KING   co-director, Paramount, 1938
RULERS OF THE SEA   Paramount, 1939
THE HOWARDS OF VIRGINIA   Columbia, 1940
THE LADY FROM CHEYENNE   Universal, 1941
THIS WOMAN IS MINE   Universal, 1941
FOREVER AND A DAY   co-director, RKO Radio, 1943
BLOOD ON THE SUN   United Artists, 1945
THE SHANGHAI STORY   Republic, 1954
THE LAST COMMAND   Republic, 1955

JOSHUA LOGAN

b. October 5, 1908 - Texarkana, Texas
d. 1988

I MET MY LOVE AGAIN   co-director with Arthur Ripley,
   United Artists, 1938
PICNIC ★   Columbia, 1956
BUS STOP   20th Century-Fox, 1956
SAYONARA ★   Warner Bros., 1957
SOUTH PACIFIC   Magna, 1958
TALL STORY   Warner Bros., 1960
FANNY   Warner Bros., 1961
ENSIGN PULVER   Warner Bros., 1964
CAMELOT   Warner Bros., 1967
PAINT YOUR WAGON   Paramount, 1969

JOSEPH LOSEY

b. January 14, 1909 - La Crosse, Wisconsin
d. 1984

THE BOY WITH GREEN HAIR   RKO Radio, 1948
THE LAWLESS   Paramount, 1950
M   Columbia, 1951
THE PROWLER   United Artists, 1951
THE BIG NIGHT   United Artists, 1951
STRANGER ON THE PROWL   directed under pseudonym
   of Andrea Forzano, United Artists, 1952, U.S.-Italian
THE SLEEPING TIGER   directed under pseudonym of
   Victor Hanbury, Astor, 1954, British
FINGER OF GUILT   THE INTIMATE STRANGER
   directed under pseudonym of Joseph Walton, RKO
   Radio, 1955, British

TIME WITHOUT PITY   Astor, 1956, British
THE GYPSY AND THE GENTLEMAN   Rank, 1958,
    British
CHANCE MEETING   *BLIND DATE*   Paramount, 1959,
    British
THE CONCRETE JUNGLE   *THE CRIMINAL*   Fanfare,
    1960, British
THESE ARE THE DAMNED   *THE DAMNED*   Columbia,
    1961, British
EVA   Times, 1962, French-Italian
THE SERVANT   Landau, 1964, British
KING AND COUNTRY   Allied Artists, 1965, British
MODESTY BLAISE   20th Century-Fox, 1966, British
ACCIDENT   Cinema 5, 1967, British
SECRET CEREMONY   Universal, 1968, British-U.S.
BOOM!   Universal, 1968, British-U.S.
FIGURES IN A LANDSCAPE   National General, 1971,
    British
THE GO-BETWEEN   Columbia, 1971, British
THE ASSASSINATION OF TROTSKY   Cinerama
    Releasing Corporation, 1972, French-Italian-British
A DOLL'S HOUSE   Tomorrow Entertainment, 1973,
    British-French
GALILEO   American Film Theatre, 1975, British-
    Canadian
THE ROMANTIC ENGLISHWOMAN   New World, 1975,
    British
MR. KLEIN   Quartet, 1977, French-Italian
LES ROUTES DU SUD   Parafrance, 1978, French
DON GIOVANNI   Gaumont/New Yorker, 1980, French
STEAMING   New World, 1984, British

DAVID R. LOXTON
d. 1989

THE PHANTOM OF THE OPEN HEARTH (TF)   co-director
    with Fred Barzyk, WNET-13 Television Laboratory/WGBH
    New Television Workshop, 1976
CHARLIE SMITH AND THE FRITTER TREE (TF)   co-
    director with Fred Barzyk, WNET-13 Television Labora-
    tory/WGBY New Television Workshop, 1978
THE LATHE OF HEAVEN (TF)   co-director with Fred
    Barzyk, WNET-13 Television Laboratory/Taurus Film,
    1980

ERNST LUBITSCH
b. January 28, 1892 - Berlin, Germany
d. 1947

FRAULEIN SEIFENSCHAUM   1914, German
BLINDE KUH   1915, German
AUF EIS GEFUHRT   1915, German
DAS SCHONSTE GESCHENK   1916, German
ZUCKER UND ZIMT   co-director with Ernst Matray,
    1915, German
LEUTNANT AUF BEFEHL   1916, German
WO IST MEIN SCHATZ?   1916, German
DER SCHWARZE MORITZ   1916, German
SCHUHPALAST PINKUS   1916, French
DER GEMISCHTE FRAUENCHOR   1916, German
DER G.M.B.H. TENOR   1916, German
DER ERSTE PATIENT   1916, German
DER KRAFTMEYER   1916, German
OSSIS TAGEBUCH   1917, German
DER BLUSEKONIG   1917, German

WENN VIER DASSELBE TUN   1917, German
EIN FIDELES GEFANGNIS   1917, German
DER LETZTE ANZUG   1917, German
PRINZ SAMI   1918, German
DER RODELKAVALIER   1918, German
DER FALL ROSENTOPF   1918, German
FUHRMANN HENSCHEL   1918, German
DAS MODEL VON BALLETT   1918, German
MARIONETTEN   1918, German
MEYER AUS BERLIN   1919, German
ICH MACHTE KEIN MANN SEIN   1919, German
DAS SCHWABENMADLE   1919, German
ROMEO UND JULIA IM SCHNEE   1916, German
ALS ICH TOT WAR   1916, German
DIE AUGEN DER MUMMIE MA   1918, German
CARMEN   *GYPSY BLOOD*   1918, German
MEINE FRAU DIE FILMSCHAUSPIELERIN   1919,
    German
DIE AUSTERNPRINZESSIN   1919, German
RAUSCH   1919, German
MADAME DUBARRY   *PASSION*   1919, German
DIE PUPPE   1919, German
KOHLHIESELS TOCHTER   1920, German
SUMURUN   *ONE ARABIAN NIGHT*   1920, German
ANNA BOLEYN   *DECEPTION*   1920, German
DIE BERGKATZE   1921, German
DAS WEIB DER PHARAO   *THE LOVES OF PHARAO*
    1922, German
DIE FLAMME   MONTMARTRE   1923, German
ROSITA   United Artists, 1923
THE MARRIAGE CIRCLE   Warner Bros., 1924
THREE WOMEN   Warner Bros., 1924
FORBIDDEN PARADISE   Paramount, 1924
KISS ME AGAIN   Warner Bros., 1925
LADY WINDERMERE'S FAN   Warner Bros., 1925
SO THIS IS PARIS   Warner Bros., 1926
THE STUDENT PRINCE   MGM, 1927
THE PATRIOT ★   Paramount, 1928
ETERNAL LOVE   United Artists, 1929
THE LOVE PARADE ★   Paramount, 1929
PARAMOUNT ON PARADE   co-director, Paramount,
    1930
MONTE CARLO   Paramount, 1930
THE SMILING LIEUTENANT   Paramount, 1931
BROKEN LULLABY   *THE MAN I KILLED*   Paramount,
    1932
ONE HOUR WITH YOU   Paramount, 1932
TROUBLE IN PARADISE   Paramount, 1932
IF I HAD A MILLION   co-director, Paramount, 1932
DESIGN FOR LIVING   Paramount, 1933
THE MERRY WIDOW   Paramount, 1933
ANGEL   Paramount, 1937
BLUEBEARD'S EIGHTH WIFE   Paramount, 1938
NINOTCHKA   MGM, 1939
THE SHOP AROUND THE CORNER   MGM, 1940
THAT UNCERTAIN FEELING   United Artists, 1941
TO BE OR NOT TO BE   United Artists, 1942
HEAVEN CAN WAIT ★   20th Century-Fox, 1943
CLUNY BROWN   20th Century-Fox, 1946
THAT LADY IN ERMINE   co-director with Otto Preminger,
    20th Century-Fox, 1948

M

CHARLES MacARTHUR
b. May 5, 1895 - Scranton, Pennsylvania
d. 1956

CRIME WITHOUT PASSION   co-director with Ben
    Hecht, Paramount, 1934
ONCE IN A BLUE MOON   co-director with Ben Hecht,
    Paramount, 1936
THE SCOUNDREL   co-director with Ben Hecht,
    Paramount, 1935
SOAK THE RICH   co-director with Ben Hecht, Paramount,
    1936

LEO McCAREY
b. October 3, 1898 - Los Angeles, California
d. 1969

ALL WET   1924
BAD BOY   1925
INNOCENT HUSBANDS   1926
WE FAW DOWN   1928
LIBERTY   1929
WRONG AGAIN   1929
SOCIETY SECRETS   Universal, 1921
THE SOPHOMORE   Pathé, 1929
RED HOT RHYTHM   Pathé, 1929
WILD COMPANY   Fox, 1930
LET'S GO NATIVE   Paramount, 1930
PART TIME WIFE   Fox, 1930
INDISCREET   United Artists, 1931
THE KID FROM SPAIN   United Artists, 1932
DUCK SOUP   Paramount, 1933
SIX OF A KIND   Paramount, 1934
BELLE OF THE NINETIES   Paramount, 1934
RUGGLES OF RED GAP   Paramount, 1935
THE MILKY WAY   Paramount, 1936
MAKE WAY FOR TOMORROW   Paramount, 1937
THE AWFUL TRUTH ★★   Columbia, 1937
LOVE AFFAIR   RKO Radio, 1939
ONCE UPON A HONEYMOON   RKO Radio, 1942
GOING MY WAY ★★   Paramount, 1944
THE BELLS OF ST. MARY'S ★   Paramount, 1945
GOOD SAM   RKO Radio, 1948
MY SON JOHN   Paramount, 1952
AN AFFAIR TO REMEMBER   20th Century-Fox, 1957
RALLY ROUND THE FLAG, BOYS!   20th Century-Fox,
    1958
SATAN NEVER SLEEPS   20th Century-Fox, 1962,
    U.S.-British

RANALD MacDOUGALL
b. March 10, 1915 - Schenectady, New York
d. 1973

QUEEN BEE   Columbia, 1955
MAN ON FIRE   MGM, 1957
THE WORLD, THE FLESH AND THE DEVIL   MGM, 1959
THE SUBTERRANEANS   MGM, 1960
GO NAKED IN THE WORLD   MGM, 1961

NORMAN Z. MacLEOD
(Norman Zenos MacLeod)
b. September 20, 1898 - Grayling, Michigan
d. 1964

TAKING A CHANCE   Fox, 1928
ALONG CAME YOUTH   co-director with Lloyd Corrigan,
    Paramount, 1930
FINN AND HATTIE   co-director with Norman Taurog,
    Paramount, 1931
MONKEY BUSINESS   Paramount, 1931
TOUCHDOWN   Paramount, 1931
THE MIRACLE MAN   Paramount, 1932
HORSE FEATHERS   Paramount, 1932
IF I HAD A MILLION   co-director, Paramount, 1932
A LADY'S PROFESSION   Paramount, 1933
MAMA LOVES PAPA   Paramount, 1933
ALICE IN WONDERLAND   Paramount, 1933
MELODY IN SPRING   Paramount, 1934
MANY HAPPY RETURNS   Paramount, 1934
IT'S A GIFT   Paramount, 1934
REDHEADS ON PARADE   Paramount, 1935
HERE COMES COOKIE   Paramount, 1935
CORONADO   Paramount, 1936
EARLY TO BED   Paramount, 1936
PENNIES FROM HEAVEN   Columbia, 1936
MIND YOUR OWN BUSINESS   Paramount, 1937
TOPPER   MGM, 1937
MERRILY WE LIVE   MGM, 1938
THERE GOES MY HEART   United Artists, 1938
TOPPER TAKES A TRIP   MGM, 1939
REMEMBER?   MGM, 1939
LITTLE MEN   RKO Radio, 1940
THE TRIAL OF MARY DUGAN   1941
LADY BE GOOD   MGM, 1941
JACKASS MAIL   MGM, 1942
PANAMA HATTIE   MGM, 1942
THE POWERS GIRL   United Artists, 1943
SWING SHIFT MAISIE   MGM, 1943
THE KID FROM BROOKLYN   RKO Radio, 1946
THE SECRET LIFE OF WALTER MITTY   RKO Radio,
    1947
THE ROAD TO RIO   Paramount, 1947
ISN'T IT ROMANTIC?   Paramount, 1948
THE PALEFACE   Paramount, 1948
LET'S DANCE   Paramount, 1950
MY FAVORITE SPY   Paramount, 1951
NEVER WAVE AT A WAC   RKO Radio, 1953
CASANOVA'S BIG NIGHT   Paramount, 1954
PUBLIC PIGEON NO. 1   Universal, 1957
ALIAS JESSE JAMES   United Artists, 1959

ROUBEN MAMOULIAN
b. October 8, 1897 - Tiflis, Georgia, Russia
d. 1987

APPLAUSE   Paramount, 1929
CITY STREETS   Paramount, 1931
DR. JEKYLL AND MR. HYDE   Paramount, 1932
LOVE ME TONIGHT   Paramount, 1932
SONG OF SONGS   Paramount, 1933
QUEEN CHRISTINA   MGM, 1933
WE LIVE AGAIN   United Artists, 1934
BECKY SHARP   RKO Radio, 1935
THE GAY DESPERADO   United Artists, 1936
HIGH, WIDE, AND HANDSOME   Paramount, 1937
GOLDEN BOY   Columbia, 1939
THE MARK OF ZORRO   20th Century-Fox, 1940
BLOOD AND SAND   20th Century-Fox, 1941

RINGS ON HER FINGERS 20th Century-Fox, 1942
SUMMER HOLIDAY MGM, 1948
SILK STOCKINGS MGM, 1957

ANTHONY MANN
(Emil Anton Bundmann)
b. June 30, 1906 - San Diego, California
d. 1967

DR. BROADWAY Paramount, 1942
MOONLIGHT IN HAVANA Universal, 1942
NOBODY'S DARLING Republic, 1943
MY BEST GAL Republic, 1944
STRANGERS IN THE NIGHT Republic, 1944
THE GREAT FLAMARION Republic, 1945
TWO O'CLOCK COURAGE RKO, 1945
SING YOUR WAY HOME RKO Radio, 1945
STRANGE IMPERSONATION Republic, 1946
THE BAMBOO BLONDE RKO, 1946
DESPERATE RKO Radio, 1947
RAILROADED Eagle Lion, 1947
T-MEN Eagle Lion, 1947
RAW DEAL Eagle Lion, 1948
REIGN OF TERROR *THE BLACK BOOK* Eagle Lion,
    1949
BORDER INCIDENT MGM, 1949
SIDE STREET MGM, 1950
WINCHESTER '73 Universal, 1950
THE FURIES Paramount, 1950
DEVIL'S DOORWAY MGM, 1950
THE TALL TARGET MGM, 1951
BEND OF THE RIVER Universal, 1952
THE NAKED SPUR MGM, 1953
THUNDER BAY Universal, 1953
THE GLENN MILLER STORY Universal, 1954
THE FAR COUNTRY Universal, 1954
STRATEGIC AIR COMMAND Paramount, 1955
THE MAN FROM LARAMIE Columbia, 1955
THE LAST FRONTIER Columbia, 1956
SERENADE Warner Bros., 1956
MEN IN WAR United Artists, 1957
THE TIN STAR Paramount, 1957
GOD'S LITTLE ACRE United Artists, 1958
MAN OF THE WEST United Artists, 1958
CIMARRON MGM, 1960
EL CID Allied Artists, 1961
THE FALL OF THE ROMAN EMPIRE Paramount, 1964
THE HEROES OF TELEMARK Columbia, 1965, British
A DANDY IN ASPIC Columbia, 1968, British

ALEX MARCH
d. 1989

THE DANGEROUS DAYS OF KIOWA JONES (TF) MGM
    TV, 1966
PAPER LION United Artists, 1968
THE BIG BOUNCE Warner Bros., 1969
FIREHOUSE (TF) Metromedia Productions/Stonehenge
    Productions, 1972
MASTERMIND Goldstone, 1977

EDWIN L. MARIN
b. February 21, 1899 - Jersey City, New Jersey
d. 1951

THE DEATH KISS World Wide, 1933
A STUDY IN SCARLET World Wide, 1933
THE AVENGER Monogram Pictures Corp., 1933
THE SWEETHEART OF SIGMA CHI Monogram, 1933

BOMBAY MAIL Universal, 1934
THE CROSBY CASE Universal, 1934
AFFAIRS OF A GENTLEMAN Universal, 1934
PARIS INTERLUDE MGM, 1934
THE CASINO MURDER CASE MGM, 1935
PURSUIT MGM, 1935
MOONLIGHT MURDER MGM, 1935
THE GARDEN MURDER CASE MGM, 1936
SPEED MGM, 1936
I'D GIVE MY LIFE MGM, 1936
SWORN ENEMY MGM, 1936
ALL AMERICAN CHUMP MGM, 1936
MAN OF THE PEOPLE MGM, 1937
MARRIED BEFORE BREAKFAST MGM, 1937
EVERYBODY SING MGM, 1938
HOLD THAT KISS MGM, 1938
THE CHASER MGM, 1938
LISTEN, DARLING MGM, 1938
A CHRISTMAS CAROL MGM, 1938
FAST AND LOOSE MGM, 1939
SOCIETY LAWYER MGM, 1939
MAISIE MGM, 1939
HENRY GOES ARIZONA MGM, 1939
FLORIAN MGM, 1940
GOLD RUSH MAISIE MGM, 1940
HULLABALOO MGM, 1940
MAISIE WAS A LADY MGM, 1941
RINGSIDE MAISIE MGM, 1941
PARIS CALLING Universal, 1942
A GENTLEMAN AFTER DARK United Artists, 1942
MISS ANNIE ROONEY United Artists, 1942
INVISIBLE AGENT Universal, 1942
TWO TICKETS TO LONDON Universal, 1943
SHOW BUSINESS RKO Radio, 1944
TALL IN THE SADDLE RKO Radio, 1944
JOHNNY ANGEL RKO Radio, 1945
ABILENE TOWN United Artists, 1946
YOUNG WIDOW United Artists, 1946
MR. ACE United Artists, 1946
LADY LUCK RKO Radio, 1946
NOCTURNE RKO Radio, 1946
CHRISTMAS EVE United Artists, 1947
INTRIGUE United Artists, 1947
RACE STREET RKO Radio, 1948
CANADIAN PACIFIC 20th Century-Fox, 1949
THE YOUNGER BROTHERS Warner Bros., 1949
FIGHTING MAN OF THE PLAINS 20th Century-Fox,
    1949
COLT .45 Warner Bros., 1950
THE CARIBOO TRAIL 20th Century-Fox, 1950
SUGARFOOT Warner Bros., 1951
RATON PASS Warner Bros., 1951
FORT WORTH Warner Bros., 1951

RICHARD MARQUAND
b. Wales
d. 1987

THE SEARCH FOR THE NILE (MS) BBC/Time-Life
    Productions, 1972, British
THE LEGACY Universal, 1979
BIRTH OF THE BEATLES (TF) Dick Clark Productions,
    1979, British-U.S.
EYE OF THE NEEDLE United Artists, 1981, U.S.-British
RETURN OF THE JEDI 20th Century-Fox, 1983
UNTIL SEPTEMBER MGM/UA, 1984
JAGGED EDGE Columbia, 1985
HEARTS OF FIRE Lorimar, 1987, U.S.-British

GEORGE MARSHALL
b. December 29, 1891 - Chicago, Illinois
d. 1975

LOVE'S LARIAT   Bluebird, 1916
THE MAN FROM MONTANA   Butterfly, 1917
THE EMBARRASSMENT OF RICHES   W. W. Hodkinson,
   1918
THE ADVENTURES OF RUTH   Pathé, 1919
RUTH OF THE ROCKIES   Pathé, 1920
PRAIRIE TRAILS   Fox, 1920
WHY TRUST YOUR HUSBAND?   Fox, 1921
HANDS OFF   Fox, 1921
A RIDIN' ROMEO   Fox, 1921
AFTER YOUR OWN HEART   Fox, 1921
THE LADY FROM LONGACRE   Fox, 1921
THE JOLT   1921
SMILES ARE TRUMPS   Fox, 1922
HAUNTED VALLEY   Pathé, 1923
DON QUICKSHOT OF THE RIO GRANDE   Universal,
   1923
MEN IN THE RAW   Universal, 1923
A TRIP TO CHINATOWN   Fox, 1926
THE GAY RETREAT   Fox, 1927
THE ADVENTURES OF RUTH   Pathé, 1929
PACK UP YOUR TROUBLES   co-director with Raymond
   McCarey, MGM, 1932
THEIR FIRST MISTAKE   1932
TOWED IN A HOLE   1932
EVER SINCE EVE   Warner Bros., 1934
WILD GOLD   Fox, 1934
SHE LEARNED ABOUT SAILORS   Fox, 1934
365 NIGHTS IN HOLLYWOOD   Fox, 1934
LIFE BEGINS AT 40   20th Century-Fox, 1935
TEN DOLLAR RAISE   20th Century-Fox, 1935
IN OLD KENTUCKY   20th Century-Fox, 1935
MUSIC IS MAGIC   20th Century-Fox, 1935
SHOW THEM NO MERCY   20th Century-Fox, 1935
A MESSAGE TO GARCIA   20th Century-Fox, 1936
THE CRIME OF DR. FORBES   20th Century-Fox, 1936
CAN THIS BE DIXIE?   20th Century-Fox, 1936
NANCY STEELE IS MISSING!   20th Century-Fox, 1937
LOVE UNDER FIRE   20th Century-Fox, 1937
THE GOLDWYN FOLLIES   United Artists, 1938
BATTLE OF BROADWAY   1938
HOLD THAT CO-ED   20th Century-Fox, 1938
YOU CAN'T CHEAT AN HONEST MAN   Universal, 1939
DESTRY RIDES AGAIN   Universal, 1939
THE GHOST BREAKERS   Paramount, 1940
WHEN THE DALTONS RODE   Universal, 1940
POT O'GOLD   United Artists, 1941
TEXAS   Columbia, 1941
VALLEY OF THE SUN   RKO Radio, 1942
THE FOREST RANGERS   Paramount, 1942
STAR SPANGLED RHYTHM   Paramount, 1942
TRUE TO LIFE   Paramount, 1943
RIDING HIGH   Paramount, 1943
AND THE ANGELS SING   Paramount, 1944
MURDER, HE SAYS   Paramount, 1945
INCENDIARY BLONDE   Paramount, 1945
HOLD THAT BLONDE   Paramount, 1945
THE BLUE DAHLIA   Paramount, 1946
MONSIEUR BEAUCAIRE   Paramount, 1946
THE PERILS OF PAULINE   Paramount, 1947
VARIETY GIRL   Paramount, 1947
HAZARD   Paramount, 1948
TAP ROOTS   Paramount, 1948
MY FRIEND IRMA   Paramount, 1949
FANCY PANTS   Paramount, 1950
NEVER A DULL MOMENT   RKO Radio, 1950
A MILLIONAIRE FOR CHRISTY   20th Century-Fox, 1951

THE SAVAGE   Paramount, 1952
OFF LIMITS   Paramount, 1953
SCARED STIFF   Paramount, 1953
HOUDINI   Paramount, 1953
MONEY FROM HOME   Paramount, 1954
RED GARTERS   Paramount, 1954
DUEL IN THE JUNGLE   Warner Bros., 1954
DESTRY   Universal, 1955
THE SECOND GREATEST SEX   Universal, 1955
PILLARS OF THE SKY   Universal, 1956
THE GUNS OF FORT PETTICOAT   Columbia, 1957
BEYOND MOMBASA   Columbia, 1956
THE SAD SACK   Paramount, 1957
THE SHEEPMAN   MGM, 1958
IMITATION GENERAL   MGM, 1958
THE MATING GAME   MGM, 1959
IT STARTED WITH A KISS   MGM, 1959
THE GAZEBO   MGM, 1960
CRY FOR HAPPY   Columbia, 1961
THE HAPPY THIEVES   United Artists, 1962
HOW THE WEST WAS WON   co-director with Henry
   Hathaway & John Ford, MGM/Cinerama, 1962
PAPA'S DELICATE CONDITION   Paramount, 1963
DARK PURPOSE   L'INTRIGO   Universal, 1964,
   Italian-French-U.S.
ADVANCE TO THE REAR   MGM, 1964
BOY, DID I GET A WRONG NUMBER!   United Artists,
   1966
EIGHT ON THE LAM   United Artists, 1967
THE WICKED DREAMS OF PAULA SCHULTZ
   United Artists, 1968
HOOK, LINE AND SINKER   Columbia, 1969

RUDOLPH MATE
(Rudolf Matheh)
b. January 21, 1898 - Cracow, Poland
d. 1964

IT HAD TO BE YOU   co-director with Don Hartman,
   Columbia, 1947
THE DARK PAST   Columbia, 1949
NO SAD SONGS FOR ME   Columbia, 1950
D.O.A.   United Artists, 1950
UNION STATION   Paramount, 1950
BRANDED   Paramount, 1951
THE PRINCE WHO WAS A THIEF   Universal, 1951
WHEN WORLDS COLLIDE   Paramount, 1951
THE GREEN GLOVE   United Artists, 1952
PAULA   Columbia, 1952
SALLY AND ST. ANNE   Universal, 1952
THE MISSISSIPPI GAMBLER   Universal, 1953
SECOND CHANCE   RKO Radio, 1953
FORBIDDEN   Universal, 1954
THE SIEGE AT RED RIVER   20th Century-Fox, 1954
THE BLACK SHIELD OF FALWORTH   Universal, 1954
THE VIOLENT MEN   Columbia, 1955
THE FAR HORIZONS   Paramount, 1955
MIRACLE IN THE RAIN   Warner Bros., 1956
THE RAWHIDE YEARS   Universal, 1956
PORT AFRIQUE   Columbia, 1956, British
THREE VIOLENT PEOPLE   Paramount, 1957
SERANADE EINER GROSSEN LIEBE   German, 1958
THE DEEP SIX   Warner Bros., 1958
FOR THE FIRST TIME   MGM, 1959, U.S.-West German-
   Italian
REVAK - LO SCHIAVO DI CARTAGINE   1960, Italian
THE IMMACULATE ROAD   20th Century-Fox, 1960
THE 300 SPARTANS   20th Century-Fox, 1962
SEVEN SEAS TO CALAIS   IL DOMINATORE DEI SETTE
   MARI   MGM, 1962, Italian
ALIKI   Funos-Aquarius, 1963, West German-U.S.

ARCHIE MAYO
(Archibald L. Mayo)
b. 1891 - New York, New York
d. 1968

MONEY TALKS   MGM, 1926
UNKNOWN TREASURES   Sterling, 1926
CHRISTINE OF THE BIG TOPS   Sterling, 1926
JOHNNY, GET YOUR HAIR CUT   co-director with
   B. Reaves Easton, MGM, 1927
QUARANTINED RIVALS   Lumas, 1927
DEARIE   Warner Bros., 1927
SLIGHTLY USED   Warner Bros., 1927
THE COLLEGE WIDOW   Warner Bros., 1927
BEWARE OF MARRIED MEN   Warner Bros., 1928
THE CRIMSON CITY   Warner Bros., 1928
STATE STREET SADIE   Warner Bros., 1928
ON TRIAL   Warner Bros., 1928
MY MAN   Warner Bros., 1928
SONNY BOY   Warner Bros., 1929
THE SAP   Warner Bros., 1929
IS EVERYBODY HAPPY?   Warner Bros., 1929
THE SACRED FLAME   Warner Bros., 1929
VENGEANCE   Columbia, 1930
WIDE OPEN   Warner Bros., 1930
COURAGE   Warner Bros., 1930
OH SAILOR, BEHAVE!   Warner Bros., 1930
THE DOORWAY TO HELL   Warner Bros., 1930
ILLICIT   Warner Bros., 1931
SVENGALI   Warner Bros., 1931
BOUGHT   Warner Bros., 1931
UNDER EIGHTEEN   Warner Bros., 1932
THE EXPERT   Warner Bros., 1932
STREET OF WOMEN   Warner Bros., 1932
TWO AGAINST THE WORLD   Warner Bros., 1932
NIGHT AFTER NIGHT   Warner Bros., 1932
THE LIFE OF JIMMY DOLAN   Warner Bros., 1933
THE MAYOR OF HELL   Warner Bros., 1933
EVER IN MY HEART   Warner Bros., 1933
CONVENTION CITY   Warner Bros., 1933
GAMBLING LADY   Warner Bros., 1934
THE MAN WITH TWO FACES   Warner Bros., 1934
DESIRABLE   Warner Bros., 1934
BORDERTOWN   Warner Bros., 1935
GO INTO YOUR DANCE   Warner Bros., 1935
THE CASE OF THE LUCKY LEGS   Warner Bros., 1935
THE PETRIFIED FOREST   Warner Bros., 1936
I MARRIED A DOCTOR   Warner Bros., 1936
GIVE ME YOUR HEART   Warner Bros., 1936
BLACK LEGION   Warner Bros., 1937
CALL IT A DAY   Warner Bros., 1937
IT'S LOVE I'M AFTER   Warner Bros., 1937
THE ADVENTURES OF MARCO POLO   United Artists,
   1938
YOUTH TAKES A FLING   Universal, 1938
THEY SHALL HAVE MUSIC   United Artists, 1939
THE HOUSE ACROSS THE BAY   United Artists, 1940
FOUR SONS   20th Century-Fox, 1940
THE GREAT AMERICAN BROADCAST   20th Century-Fox,
   1941
CHARLEY'S AUNT   20th Century-Fox, 1941
CONFIRM OR DENY   20th Century-Fox, 1941
MOONTIDE   20th Century-Fox, 1942
ORCHESTRA WIVES   20th Century-Fox, 1942
CRASH DIVE   20th Century-Fox, 1943
SWEET AND LOW-DOWN   20th Century-Fox, 1944
A NIGHT IN CASABLANCA   United Artists, 1946
ANGEL ON MY SHOULDER   United Artists, 1946

DAVID MAYSLES
b. January 10, 1932 - Brookline, Massachusetts
d. 1987

YOUTH IN POLAND (FD)   co-director with Albert Maysles,
   1957
SHOWMAN (FD)   co-director with Albert Maysles, 1962
WHAT'S HAPPENING: THE BEATLES IN THE USA (FD)
   co-director with Albert Maysles, 1964
MEET MARLON BRANDO (FD)   co-director with
   Albert Maysles, 1965
WITH LOVE FROM TRUMAN (FD)   co-director with
   Albert Maysles, 1966
SALESMAN (FD)   co-director with Albert Maysles
   & Charlotte Zwerin, Maysles Film, 1969
GIMME SHELTER (FD)   co-director with Albert Maysles &
   Charlotte Zwerin, Cinema 5, 1971
CHRISTO'S VALLEY CURTAIN (FD)   co-director with
   Albert Maysles & Ellen Giffard, 1972
GREY GARDENS (FD)   co-director with Albert Maysles &
   Ellen Hovde & Muffie Meyer, 1975
RUNNING FENCE (FD)   co-director with Albert Maysles &
   Charlotte Zwerin, 1977
VLADIMIR HOROWITZ: THE LAST ROMANTIC (TD) ☆
   co-director with Albert Maysles, Cami Video, 1985
ISLANDS (FD)   co-director with Albert Maysles &
   Charlotte Zwerin, Maysles Film, 1986
OZAWA (FD)   co-director with Albert Maysles, Deborah
   Dickson & Susan Froemke, Columbia Artists, 1986

GEORGES MELIES
b. December 8, 1861 - Paris, France
d. 1938

UNE PARTIE DE CARTES   Star Film, 1896, French
SEANCE DE PRESTIDIGITATION   Star Film, 1896,
   French
UN BON PETIT DIABLE   Star Film, 1896, French
LES CHEVAUX DU BOIS   Star Film, 1896, French
L'ARROSEUR   Star Film, 1896, French
ARRIVEE D'UN TRAIN GARE DE VINCENNES
   Star Film, 1896, French
PLACE DE L'OPERA   Star Film, 1896, French
BATEAU-MOUCHE SUR LA SEINE   Star Film, 1896,
   French
UNE NUIT TERRIBLE   Star Film, 1896, French
TRIBULATIONS D'UN CONCIERGE   Star Film, 1896,
   French
ENFANTS JOUANT SUR LA PLAGE   Star Film, 1896,
   French
DANSE SERPENTINE   Star Film, 1896, French
CORTEGE DU TSAR ALLANT A VERSAILLES
   Star Film, 1896, French
GRANDES MANOEUVRES   Star Film, 1896, French
ESCAMOTAGE D'UNE DAME CHEZ ROBERT-HOUDIN
   Star Film, 1896, French
LE FAKIR - MYSTERE INDIEN   Star Film, 1896, French
L'HOTEL EMPOISONNE   Star Film, 1896, French
CHICOT DENTISTE AMERICAIN   Star Film, 1897, French
COQUIN DE PRINTEMPS   Star Film, 1897, French
LE MALADE IMAGINAIRE   Star Film, 1897, French
L'HALLUCINATION DE L'ALCHIMESTE   Star Films, 1897,
   French
LE CHATEAU HANTE   Star Film, 1897, French
EPISODE DE GUERRE   Star Film, 1897, French
EXECUTION D'UN ESPION   Star Film, 1897, French
MASSACRES DE CRETE   Star Film, 1897, French
GUGUSSE ET L'AUTOMATE   Star Film, 1897, French
LA CIGALE ET LA FOURMI   Star Film, 1897, French

LE CABINET DE MEPHISTOPHELES   Star Film, 1897, French
FIGARO ET L'AUVERGNANT   Star Film, 1897, French
ARLEQUIN ET CHARBONNIER   Star Film, 1897, French
APRES LE BAL   Star Film, 1897, French
VENTE D'ESCLAVES AU HAREM   Star Film, 1897, French
FAUST ET MARGUERITE   Star Film, 1897, French
CARREFOUR DE L'OPERA   Star Film, 1898, French
MAGIE DIABOLIQUE   Star Film, 1898, French
LES RAYONS X   Star Film, 1898, French
VISITE DE L'EPAVE DU MAINE   Star Film, 1898, French
LE MAGICIEN   Star Film, 1898, French
ILLUSIONS FANTASMAGORIQUES   Star Film, 1898, French
PYGMALION ET GALATHEE   Star Film, 1898, French
DAMNATION DE FAUST   Star Film, 1898, French
GUILLAUME TELL ET LE CLOWN   Star Film, 1898, French
LA LUNE A UN METRE   Star Film, 1898, French
LA CAVERNE MAUDITE   Star Film, 1898, French
REVE D'ARTISTE   Star Film, 1898, French
L'HOMME DE TETES   Star Film, 1898, French
DEDOUBLEMENT CABALISTIQUE   Star Film, 1898, French
CREATIONS SPONTANEES   Star Film, 1898, French
CLEOPATRE   Star Film, 1899, French
RICHESSE ET MISERIE   Star Film, 1899, French
LE SPECTRE   Star Film, 1899, French
LE DIABLE AU COUVENT   Star Film, 1899, French
LA DANSE DU DEU   Star Film, 1899, French
LE PORTRAIT MYSTERIEUX   Star Film, 1899, French
LE MIROIR DE CAGLIOSTRO   Star Film, 1899, French
NEPTUNE ET AMPHITRITE   Star Film, 1899, French
LE CHRIST MARCHANT SUR LES FLOTS   Star Films, 1899, French
EVOCATION SPIRITE   Star Film, 1899, French
L'AFFAIRE DREYFUS   Star Film, 1899, French
L'ILE DU DIABLE   Star Film, 1899, French
CENDRILLON   Star Film, 1899, French
LE CHEVALIER MYSTERE   Star Film, 1899, French
TOM WHISKY OU L'ILLUSTRIONISTE TOQUE   Star Film, 1899, French
LES MIRACLES DU BRAHMINE   Star Film, 1899, French
EXPOSITION DE 1900   Star Film, 1900, French
L'HOMME-ORCHESTRE   Star Film, 1900, French
JEANNE D'ARC   Star Film, 1900, French
LES SEPT PECHES CAPITAUX   Star Film, 1900, French
LE REVE DU RADJAH   Star Film, 1900, French
LE FOU ASSASSIN   Star Film, 1900, French
LE LIVRE MAGIQUE   Star Film, 1900, French
SPIRITISME ABRACADABRANT   Star Film, 1900, French
L'ILLUSIONISTE DOUBLE ET LA TETE VIVANTE   Star Film, 1900, French
LE REVE DE NOEL   Star Film, 1900, French
COPPELIA   Star Film, 1900, French
GENS QUI PLEURENT ET GENS QUI RIENT   Star Film, 1900, French
LE DESHABILLAGE IMPOSSIBLE   Star Film, 1900, French
L'HOMME AUX CENT TRUCS   Star Film, 1900, French
LA MAISON TRANQUILLE   Star Film, 1900, French
MESAVENTURES D'UN AERONAUTE   Star Film, 1900, French
LA TOUR MAUDITE   Star Film, 1900, French
BOUQUET D'ILLUSIONS   Star Film, 1900, French
LE PETIT CHAPERON ROUGE   Star Film, 1901, French
CHEZ LA SORCIERE   Star Film, 1901, French
LE TEMPLE DE LA MAGIE   Star Film, 1901, French
LE CHARLATAN   Star Film, 1901, French

EXCELSIOR!   Star Film, 1901, French
LA FONTAINE SACREE   Star Film, 1901, French
BARBE-BLEUE   Star Film, 1901, French
LE PHRENOLOGIE BURLESQUE   Star Film, 1901, French
L'ECOLE INFERNALE   Star Film, 1901, French
LE REVE DU PARIA   Star Film, 1901, French
LE BATAILLON ELASTIQUE   Star Film, 1901, French
L'HOMME A LA TETE EN CAOUTCHOUC   Star Film, 1901, French
LE DIABLE GEANT   Star Film, 1901, French
L'OEUF DU SORCIER   Star Film, 1901, French
LA DANSEUSE MICROSCOPIQUE   Star Film, 1901, French
ERUPTION VOLCANIQUE A LA MARTINIQUE   Star Film, 1902, French
A TRIP TO THE MOON   Star Film, 1902, French
LA CLOWNESSE FANTOME   Star Film, 1902, French
LE SACRE D'EDOUARD VII   Star Film, 1902, French
LES TRESORS DE SATAN   Star Film, 1902, French
L'HOMME-MOUCHE   Star Film, 1902, French
LA FEMME VOLANTE   Star Film, 1902, French
L'EQUILIBRE IMPOSSIBLE   Star Film, 1902, French
LE POCHARD ET L'INVENTEUR   Star Film, 1902, French
LE VOYAGE DE GULLIVER A LILLIPUT ET CHEZ LES GEANTS   Star Film, 1902, French
LES AVENTURES DE ROBINSON CRUSOE   Star Film, 1902, French
LES FILLES DU DIABLE   Star Film, 1903, French
LE CAKE-WALK INFERNAL   Star Film, 1903, French
LES MOUSQUETAIRES DE LA REINE   Star Film, 1903, French
LA STATUE ANIMEE   Star Film, 1903, French
LA FLAMME MERVEUILLEUSE   Star Film, 1903, French
LE SORCIER   Star Film, 1903, French
L'ORACLE DE DELPHES   Star Film, 1903, French
LE MELOMANE   Star Film, 1903, French
LE MONSTRE   Star Film, 1903, French
LE ROYAUME DES FEES   Star Film, 1903, French
LE REVENANT   Star Film, 1903, French
LE TONNERRE DE JUPITER   Star Film, 1903, French
LA PARAPLUIE FANTASTIQUE   Star Film, 1903, French
TOM TIGHT ET DUM DUM   Star Film, 1903, French
LA LANTERNE MAGIQUE   Star Film, 1903, French
LE REVE DU MAITRE DE BALLET   Star Film, 1903, French
FAUST AUX ENFERS   Star Film, 1903, French
LES APACHES   Star Film, 1904, French
AU CLAIR DE LA LUNE   Star Film, 1904, French
LE COFFRE ENCHANTE   Star Film, 1904, French
LES APPARITIONS FUGITIVES   Star Film, 1904, French
LE ROI DU MAQUILLAGE   Star Film, 1904, French
LE REVE D'HORLOGER   Star Film, 1904, French
LES TRANSMUTATIONS IMPERCEPTIBLES   Star Film, 1904, French
UN MIRACLE SOUS L'INQUISITION   Star Film, 1904, French
BENVENUTO CELLINI   Star Film, 1904, French
DAMNATION DU DOCTEUR FAUST   Star Film, 1904, French
LE MERVEILLEUX EVENTAIL VIVANT   Star Film, 1904, French
LA SIRENE   Star Film, 1904, French
LE BARBIER DE SEVILLE   Star Film, 1904, French
LES COSTUMES ANIMES   Star Film, 1904, French
LA DAME FANTOME   Star Film, 1904, French
VOYAGE A TRAVERS L'IMPOSSIBLE   Star Film, 1904, French
LE JUIF ERRANT   Star Film, 1905, French
A PRESIDENT-ELECT ROOSEVELT   Star Film, 1905, French

LE CARTES VIVANTES   Star Film, 1905, French
LE DIABLE NOIR   Star Film, 1905, French
LE PHENIX   Star Film, 1905, French
LE BAQUET DE MESMER   Star Film, 1905, French
TABLEAU DIABOLIQUE   Star Film, 1905, French
LE MIROIR DE VENISE   Star Film, 1905, French
UNE MESAVENTURE DE SHYLOCK   Star Film, 1905,
   French
LES CHEVALIERS DU CHLOROFORME   Star Film,
   1905, French
LE PALAIS DES MILLE ET UNE NUITS   Star Film, 1905,
   French
LA TOUT DE LONDRES   Star Film, 1905, French
LA LEGENDE DE RIP VAN WINKLE   Star Film, 1905,
   French
LE DIRIGEABLE FANTASTIQUE   Star Film, 1906,
   French
JACK LE RAMONEUR   Star Film, 1906, French
LA MAGIE A TRAVERS LES AGES   Star Film, 1906,
   French
LES INCENDIAIRES   Star Film, 1906, French
L'ANARCHIE CHEZ GUIGNOL   Star Film, 1906, French
LE FANTOME D'ALGER   Star Film, 1906, French
LES QUATRE CENT FARCES DU DIABLE   Star Film,
   1906, French
L'ALCHIMESTE PARAFARAGARAMUS   Star Film, 1906,
   French
LE FEE CARABOSSE   Star Film, 1906, French
LE CARTON FANTASTIQUE   Star Film, 1907, French
LA DOUCE D'EAU BOUILLANTE   Star Film, 1907, French
VINGT MILLE LIEUES SOUS LES MERS   Star Films,
   1907, French
LE TUNNEL SOUS LA MANCHE   Star Film, 1907, French
LE DELIRIUM TREMENS   Star Film, 1907, French
L'ECLIPSE DE SOLEIL EN PLEIN LUNE   Star Film, 1907,
   French
LA MARCHE FUNEBRE DE CHOPIN   Star Film, 1907,
   French
HAMLET   Star Film, 1907, French
LA MORT DE JULES CESAR   Star Film, 1907, French
SATAN EN PRISON   Star Film, 1907, French
LA CUISINE DE L'OGRE   Star Film, 1908, French
LA CIVILISATION A TRAVERS LES AGES   Star Film,
   1908, French
TORCHES HUMAINES   Star Film, 1980, French
LE REVE D'UN FUMEUR D'OPIUM   Star Film, 1908,
   French
NUIT DE CARNAVAL   Star Film, 1908, French
LA PHOTOGRAPHIE ELECTRIQUE A DISTANCE
   Star Film, 1908, French
LA PROPHETESSE DE THEBES   Star Film, 1908, French
MARIAGE DE RAISON ET MARIAGE D'AMOUR
   Star Film, 1908, French
L'AVARE   Star Film, 1908, French
LE SERPENT DE LA RUE DE LA LUNE   Star Film, 1908,
   French
TARTARIN DE TARASCON   Star Film, 1908, French
LE RAID PARIS - NEW YORK EN AUTOMOBILE
   Star Film, 1908, French
AU PAYS DES JOUETS   Star Film, 1908, French
HALLUCINATION PHARMACEUTIQUE   Star Film, 1908,
   French
LA POUPEE VIVANTE   Star Film, 1908, French
LE FAKIR DE SINGAPOUR   Star Film, 1908, French
HYDROTHERAPIE FANTASTIQUE   Star Film, 1909,
   French
LES ILLUSIONS FANTAISISTES   Star Film, 1909, French
LA GIGUE MERVEILLEUSE   Star Film, 1909, French
LE PAPILLON FANTASTIQUE   Star Film, 1910, French
SI J'ETAIS ROI   Star Film, 1910, French
L'HOMME AUX MILLE INVENTIONS   Star Film, 1910,
   French

LE SECRET DU MEDECIN   Star Film, 1910, French
LES HALLUCINATIONS DU BARON DE MUNCHHAUSEN
   Pathé, 1911, French
A LA CONQUETE DU POLE   Pathé, 1912, French
CENDRILLON   Pathé, 1912, French
LE CHEVALIER DES NEIGES   Pathé, 1913, French
LE VOYAGE DE LA FAMILLE BOURRICHON   Pathé,
   1913, French

JEAN-PIERRE MELVILLE
(Jean-Pierre Grumbach)
b. October 20, 1917 - Paris, France
d. 1973

LE SILENCE DE LA MER   1949, French
LES ENFANTS TERRIBLES   *THE STRANGE ONES*
   Mayer-Kingsley, 1949, French
QUAND TU LIRAS CETTE LETTRE   1953, French
BOB LE FLAMBEUR   Samuel Goldwyn Company,
   1955, French
DEUX HOMMES DANS MANHATTAN   1959, French
LEON MORIN, PRETRE   1961, French-Italian
LE DOULOS   1962, French-Italian
L'AINE DES FERCHAUX   1962, French-Italian
LE DEUXIEME SOUFFLE   *SECOND BREATH*
   1966, French
LE SAMOURAI   1967, French-Italian
L'ARMEE DES OMBRES   1969, French-Italian
LE CERCLE ROUGE   1970, French-Italian
UN FLIC   *DIRTY MONEY*   1972, French

WILLIAM CAMERON MENZIES
b. July 29, 1896 - New Haven, Connecticut
d. 1957

THE SPIDER   co-director with Kenneth McKenna,
   Fox, 1931
ALWAYS GOODBYE   co-director with Kenneth
   McKenna, Fox, 1931
CHANDU THE MAGICIAN   co-director with Marcel
   Varnel, Fox, 1932
I LOVED YOU WEDNESDAY   co-director with Henry King,
   Fox, 1933
THE WHARF ANGEL   co-director with George Somnes,
   Paramount, 1934
THINGS TO COME   United Artists, 1936, British
THE GREEN COCKATOO   *FOUR DARK HOURS*
   1937, British
ADDRESS UNKNOWN   Columbia, 1944
DRUMS IN THE DEEP SOUTH   RKO Radio, 1951
THE WHIP HAND   RKO, 1951
INVADERS FROM MARS   20th Century-Fox, 1953
THE MAZE   Allied Artists, 1953

LEWIS MILESTONE
b. September 30, 1895 - Chisinau, Russia
d. 1980

SEVEN SINNERS   Warner Bros., 1925
THE CAVEMAN   Warner Bros., 1926
THE NEW KLONDIKE   Paramount, 1926
TWO ARABIAN KNIGHTS ★★   United Artists, 1927
THE GARDEN OF EDEN   United Artists, 1928
THE RACKET   Paramount, 1928
BETRAYAL   Paramount, 1929
NEW YORK NIGHTS   United Artists, 1929
ALL QUIET ON THE WESTERN FRONT ★★
   Universal, 1930

THE FRONT PAGE ★   United Artists, 1931
RAIN   United Artists, 1932
HALLELUJAH, I'M A BUM!   United Artists, 1933
THE CAPTAIN HATES THE SEA   Columbia, 1934
PARIS IN SPRING   Paramount, 1935
ANYTHING GOES *TOPS IS THE LIMIT*   Paramount, 1936
THE GENERAL DIED AT DAWN   Paramount, 1936
THE NIGHT OF NIGHTS   American Releasing, 1939
OF MICE AND MEN   United Artists, 1940
LUCKY PARTNERS   RKO Radio, 1940
MY LIFE WITH CAROLINE   RKO Radio, 1941
OUR RUSSIAN FRONT (FD)   co-director with Joris Ivens &
   Harry Rathner, 1942
EDGE OF DARKNESS   Warner Bros., 1943
THE NORTH STAR *ARMORED ATTACK*   RKO Radio, 1943
THE PURPLE HEART   20th Century-Fox, 1944
A WALK IN THE SUN   20th Century-Fox, 1946
THE STRANGE LOVE OF MARTHA IVERS   Paramount, 1946
THE ARCH OF TRIUMPH   United Artists, 1948
NO MINOR VICES   MGM, 1948
THE RED PONY   Republic, 1949
THE HALLS OF MONTEZUMA   20th Century-Fox, 1951
KANGAROO   20th Century-Fox, 1952
LES MISERABLES   20th Century-Fox, 1952
MELBA   United Artists, 1953, British
THEY WHO DARE   Allied Artists, 1953
THE WIDOW   DCA, 1955, Italian-French
PORK CHOP HILL   United Artists, 1959
OCEAN'S 11   Warner Bros., 1960
MUTINY ON THE BOUNTY   MGM, 1962

RAY MILLAND
(Reginald Truscott-Jones)
b. January 3, 1905 - Neath, Wales
d. 1986

A MAN ALONE   Republic, 1955
LISBON   Republic, 1956
THE SAFECRACKER   MGM, 1958, British
PANIC IN YEAR ZERO!   American International, 1962
HOSTILE WITNESS   1967, British

VINCENTE MINNELLI
b. February 28, 1910 - Chicago, Illinois
d. 1986

CABIN IN THE SKY   MGM, 1943
I DOOD IT   MGM, 1943
MEET ME IN ST. LOUIS   MGM, 1944
YOLANDA AND THE THIEF   MGM, 1945
THE CLOCK   MGM, 1945
ZIEGFELD FOLLIES   MGM, 1946
TILL THE CLOUDS ROLL BY   co-director with Richard
   Whorf, MGM, 1946
UNDERCURRENT   MGM, 1946
THE PIRATE   MGM, 1948
MADAME BOVARY   MGM, 1949
FATHER OF THE BRIDE   MGM, 1950
AN AMERICAN IN PARIS ★   MGM, 1951
FATHER'S LITTLE DIVIDEND   MGM, 1951
THE BAD AND THE BEAUTIFUL   MGM, 1952
THE STORY OF THREE LOVES   co-director with
   Gottfried Reinhardt, MGM, 1953
THE BAND WAGON   MGM, 1953
THE LONG, LONG TRAILER   MGM, 1954

BRIGADOON   MGM, 1954
THE COBWEB   MGM, 1955
KISMET   MGM, 1955
LUST FOR LIFE   MGM, 1956
TEA AND SYMPATHY   MGM, 1956
DESIGNING WOMAN   MGM, 1957
GIGI ★   MGM, 1958
THE RELUCTANT DEBUTANTE   MGM, 1958
SOME CAME RUNNING   MGM, 1959
HOME FROM THE HILL   MGM, 1960
BELLS ARE RINGING   MGM, 1960
THE FOUR HORSEMEN OF THE APOCALYPSE
   MGM, 1962
TWO WEEKS IN ANOTHER TOWN   MGM, 1962
THE COURTSHIP OF EDDIE'S FATHER   MGM, 1963
GOODBYE, CHARLIE   20th Century-Fox, 1964
THE SANDPIPER   MGM, 1965
ON A CLEAR DAY YOU CAN SEE FOREVER
   Paramount, 1970
A MATTER OF TIME   American International, 1976,
   U.S.-Italian

KENJI MIZOGUCHI
b. May 16, 1898 - Tokyo, Japan
d. 1956

RESURRECTION OF LOVE   1922, Japanese
FOGGY HARBOR   1923, Japanese
NATIVE COUNTRY   1923, Japanese
DREAMS OF YOUTH   1923, Japanese
BLOOD AND SOUL   1923, Japanese
AMONG THE RUINS   1923, Japanese
THE NIGHT   1923, Japanese
WOMAN OF PLEASURE   1924, Japanese
DEATH AT DAWN   1924, Japanese
WOMEN ARE STRONG   1924, Japanese
CHRONICLE OF THE MAY RAIN   1924, Japanese
THE MAN   1925, Japanese
THE SMILING EARTH   1925, Japanese
A PAPER DOLL'S WHISPER OF SPRING
   1926, Japanese
CHILDREN OF THE SEA   1926, Japanese
THE PASSION OF A WOMAN TEACHER   1926,
   Japanese
THE LIFE OF A MAN   1928, Japanese
TOKYO MARCH   1929, Japanese
METROPOLITAN SYMPHONY   1929, Japanese
HOMETOWN   1930, Japanese
AND YET THEY GO ON, PART I   1931, Japanese
AND YET THEY GO ON, PART II   1931, Japanese
THE WHITE THREADS OF THE WATERFALL
   1933, Japanese
GION FESTIVAL   1933, Japanese
THE PASSING OF LOVE AND HATE   1934,
   Japanese
THE VIRGIN FROM OYUKI   1935, Japanese
THE POPPIES   1935, Japanese
OSAKA ELEGY   1936, Japanese
SISTERS OF THE GION   1936, Japanese
THE STORY OF THE LAST CHRYSANTHEMUMS
   1939, Japanese
A WOMAN OF OSAKA   1940, Japanese
THE LIFE OF AN ARTIST   1941, Japanese
THE LOYAL 47 RONIN, PART I   1941, Japanese
THE LOYAL 47 RONIN, PART II   1942, Japanese
MUSASHI MIYAMOTO   1944, Japanese
WOMEN'S VICTORY   1946, Japanese
UTAMARO AND HIS FIVE WOMEN   1946, Japanese
THE LOVE OF ACTRESS SUMAKO   1947, Japanese
WOMEN OF THE NIGHT   1948, Japanese

FLAME OF MY LOVE   1949, Japanese
THE PICTURE OF MADAME YUKI   1950, Japanese
WOMAN OF MUSAHINO   1951, Japanese
THE LIFE OF OHARU   1952, Japanese
UGETSU   Harrison Pictures, 1953, Japanese
GION MUSIC   *A GEISHA*   1953, Japanese
SANSHO THE BAILIFF   1954, Japanese
THE WOMAN IN THE RUMOR   1954, Japanese
A STORY FROM CHIKAMATSU   1954, Japanese
YANG KWEI FEI   1955, Japanese
TALES OF THE TAIRA CLAN   1955, Japanese
STREET OF SHAME   1956, Japanese

ROBERT MONTGOMERY
(Henry Montgomery, Jr.)
b. May 21, 1904 - Beacon, New York
d. 1981

LADY IN THE LAKE   MGM, 1946
RIDE THE PINK HORSE   Universal, 1947
ONCE MORE, MY DARLING   Universal, 1949
EYE WITNESS   *YOUR WITNESS*   Eagle Lion, 1950,
   British
THE GALLANT HOURS   United Artists, 1960

ROBERT MOORE
b. August 17, 1927 - Detroit, Michigan
d. 1984

THURSDAY'S GAME (TF)   ABC Circle Films, 1974
MURDER BY DEATH   Columbia, 1976
THE CHEAP DETECTIVE   Columbia, 1978
CHAPTER TWO   Columbia, 1980

F.W. MURNAU
(Friedrich Wilhelm Plumpe)
b. December 28, 1888 - Bielefeld, Germany
d. 1931

DER KNABE IN BLAU   *DER TODESSMARAGD*
   1919, German
SATANAS   1920, German
SEHNSUCHT   *BAJAZZO*   1920, German
DER BUCKLIGE UND DIE TANZERIN   1920, German
DER JANUSKOPF   *SCHRECKEN*   1920, German
ABEND...NACHT...MORGEN   1920, German
DER GANG IN DIE NACHT   1920, German
SCHLOSS VOGELOD   1921, German
MARIZZA - GENNANT DIE SCHMUGGLERMADONNA
   1922, German
NOSFERATU THE VAMPIRE   *NOSFERATU - EINE
   SYMPHONIE DES GRAUENS*   Film Arts Guild, 1922,
   German
DER BRENNENDE ACKER   1922, German
PHANTOM   1922, German
DIE AUSTREIBUNG   1923, German
DIE FINANZEN DES GROSSHERZOGS   1924, German
THE LAST LAUGH   *DER LETZE MANN*   Universal,
   1924, German
TARTUFF   1926, German
FAUST   1926, German
SUNRISE - A STORY OF TWO HUMANS   Fox, 1927
FOUR DEVILS   Fox, 1928
OUR DAILY BREAD   *CITY GIRL*   Fox, 1930
TABU   co-director with Robert Flaherty, Paramount, 1931

N

MIKIO NARUSE
b. August 20, 1905 - Tokyo, Japan
d. 1969

MR. AND MRS. SWORDPLAY   1929, Japanese
PURE LOVE   1929, Japanese
WEEPING BLUE SKY   1931, Japanese
LOST SPRING   1932, Japanese
APART FROM YOU   1932, Japanese
EVERYNIGHT DREAMS   1933, Japanese
CARELESS   1933, Japanese
THREE SISTERS WITH MAIDEN HEARTS   1934,
   Japanese
THE ACTRESS AND THE POET   1934, Japanese
WIFE! BE LIKE A ROSE!   1935, Japanese
THE GIRL IN THE RUMOR   1935, Japanese
KIMIKO   1936, Japanese
NEW GRIEF   1937, Japanese
AVALANCHE   1937, Japanese
TSURUHACHI AND TSURUJIRO   1938, Japanese
SINCERITY   1939, Japanese
MOON OVER SHANGHAI   1941, Japanese
SONG OF THE LANTERN   1943, Japanese
THEATER   1944, Japanese
VICTORY IN THE SUN   1945, Japanese
SPRING AWAKENING   1947, Japanese
BAD DAUGHTER   1949, Japanese
REPAST   1951, Japanese
THE DANCER   1951, Japanese
MOTHER   1952, Japanese
LIGHTNING   1952, Japanese
HUSBAND AND WIFE   1953, Japanese
THE WIFE   1953, Japanese
OLDER BROTHER, YOUNGER SISTER   1953,
   Japanese
SOUNDS FROM THE MOUNTAINS   1954, Japanese
LATE CHRYSANTHEMUMS   1954, Japanese
FLOATING CLOUDS   1955, Japanese
FLOWING   1956, Japanese
A WIFE'S HEART   1956, Japanese
UNTAMED WOMAN   1957, Japanese
ANZUKKO   1958, Japanese
SUMMER CLOUDS   1958, Japanese
DAUGHTERS, WIVES AND MOTHERS   1960,
   Japanese
WHEN A WOMAN ASCENDS THE STAIRS
   East-West Classics, 1960, Japanese
THE LOVELORN GEISHA   1961, Japanese
THE OTHER WOMAN   1961, Japanese
A WOMAN'S PLACE   1962, Japanese
LONELY LANE   1962, Japanese
A WOMAN'S LIFE   1963, Japanese
YEARNING   1964, Japanese
THE THIN LINE   1966, Japanese
MOMENT OF TERROR   1966, Japanese
TWO IN THE SHADOW   1967, Japanese

JAMES NEILSON
b. 1910
d. 1979

NIGHT PASSAGE   Universal, 1957
THE COUNTRY HUSBAND   1958
MOON PILOT   Buena Vista, 1962
BON VOYAGE!   Buena Vista, 1962
DR. SYN, ALIAS THE SCARECROW   Buena Vista, 1964,
    British-U.S.
SUMMER MAGIC   Buena Vista, 1963
THE MOON-SPINNERS   Buena Vista, 1964, U.S.-British
THE ADVENTURES OF BULLWHIP GRIFFIN
    Buena Vista, 1967
GENTLE GIANT   Paramount, 1967
WHERE ANGELS GO...TROUBLE FOLLOWS!   Columbia,
    1968
THE FIRST TIME   United Artists, 1969
FLAREUP   MGM, 1969

RALPH NELSON
b. August 12, 1916 - New York, New York
d. 1987

REQUIEM FOR A HEAVYWEIGHT   Columbia, 1962
LILIES OF THE FIELD   United Artists, 1963
SOLDIER IN THE RAIN   Allied Artists, 1963
FATE IS THE HUNTER   20th Century-Fox, 1964
FATHER GOOSE   Universal, 1964
ONCE A THIEF   MGM, 1965
DUEL AT DIABLO   United Artists, 1966
COUNTERPOINT   Universal, 1968
CHARLY   Cinerama Releasing Corporation, 1968
...tick...tick...tick   MGM, 1970
SOLDIER BLUE   Avco Embassy, 1970
FLIGHT OF THE DOVES   Columbia, 1971, British
THE WRATH OF GOD   MGM, 1972
THE WILBY CONSPIRACY   United Artists, 1975, British
EMBRYO   Cine Artists, 1976
A HERO AIN'T NOTHIN' BUT A SANDWICH   New World,
    1977
LADY OF THE HOUSE (TF)   co-director with Vincent
    Sherman, Metromedia Productions, 1978
BECAUSE HE'S MY FRIEND (TF)   Australian
    Broadcasting Commission/Trans-Atlantic Enterprises,
    1979, Australian
CHRISTMAS LILIES OF THE FIELD (TF)
    Rainbow Productions/Osmond Productions, 1979
YOU CAN'T GO HOME AGAIN (TF)   CBS Entertainment,
    1979

KURT NEUMANN
b. April 5, 1906 - Nuremberg, Germany
d. 1958

THE KING OF JAZZ   Universal, 1930
FAST COMPANIONS   Universal, 1932
INFORMATION KID   Universal, 1932
MY PAL, THE KING   Universal, 1932
THE BIG CAGE   Universal, 1933
SECRETS OF THE BLUE ROOM   Universal, 1933
KING FOR A NIGHT   Universal, 1933
LET'S TALK IT OVER   Universal, 1934
HALF A SINNER   Universal, 1934
WAKE UP AND DREAM   1934
ALIAS MARY DOW   Universal, 1935
THE AFFAIR OF SUSAN   Universal, 1935
LET'S SING AGAIN   RKO, 1936
RAINBOW ON THE RIVER   RKO, 1936

ESPIONAGE   MGM, 1937
MAKE A WISH   RKO, 1937
HOLD 'EM NAVY   Paramount, 1937
WIDE OPEN FACES   Columbia, 1938
TOUCHDOWN ARMY   Paramount, 1938
AMBUSH   Paramount, 1939
UNMARRIED   Paramount, 1939
ISLAND OF LOST MEN   Paramount, 1939
ALL WOMEN HAVE SECRETS   Paramount, 1940
ELLERY QUEEN - MASTER DETECTIVE   Columbia, 1940
A NIGHT AT EARL CARROLL'S   Paramount, 1940
BROOKLYN ORCHID   United Artists, 1942
ABOUT FACE   United Artists, 1942
THE McGUERINS FROM BROOKLYN   United Artists,
    1942
FALL IN   United Artists, 1943
TAXI MISTER   United Artists, 1943
YANKS AHOY!   United Artists, 1943
THE UNKNOWN GUEST   Monogram, 1943
THE RETURN OF THE VAMPIRE   co-director with
    Lew Landers, Columbia, 1943
TARZAN AND THE AMAZONS   RKO Radio, 1945
TARZAN AND THE LEOPARD WOMAN   RKO Radio,
    1946
TARZAN AND THE HUNTRESS   RKO Radio, 1947
THE DUDE GOES WEST   Allied Artists, 1948
BAD MEN OF TOMBSTONE   Allied Artists, 1949
BAD BOY   Allied Artists, 1949
THE KID FROM TEXAS   Universal, 1950
ROCKETSHIP X-M   Lippert, 1950
CATTLE DRIVE   Universal, 1951
REUNION IN RENO   Universal, 1951
SON OF ALI BABA   Universal, 1952
THE RING   United Artists, 1952
HIAWATHA   Allied Artists, 1952
TARZAN AND THE SHE-DEVIL   RKO Radio, 1953
CARNIVAL STORY   RKO Radio, 1954
THEY WERE SO YOUNG   Lippert, 1955, U.S.-
    West German
MOHAWK   20th Century-Fox, 1956
THE DESPERADOES ARE IN TOWN   20th Century-Fox,
    1956
KRONOS   20th Century-Fox, 1957
THE SHE-DEVIL   20th Century-Fox, 1957
THE DEERSLAYER   20th Century-Fox, 1957
THE FLY   20th Century-Fox, 1958
CIRCUS OF LOVE   DCA, 1958, German
MACHETE   United Artists, 1958
WATUSI   MGM, 1959
COUNTERPLOT   United Artists, 1959

FRED NIBLO
(Federico Nobile)
b. January 6, 1874 - York, Nebraska
d. 1948

A DESERT WOOING   Paramount, 1918
THE MARRIAGE RING   Paramount, 1918
WHEN DO WE EAT?   Paramount, 1918
FUSS AND FEATHERS   Paramount, 1918
HAPPY THOUGH MARRIED   Paramount, 1919
THE HAUNTED BEDROOM   Paramount, 1919
THE LAW OF MEN   Paramount, 1919
PARTNERS THREE   Paramount, 1919
THE VIRTUOUS THIEF   Paramount, 1919
STEPPING OUT   Paramount, 1919
WHAT EVERY WOMAN LEARNS   Paramount, 1919
THE WOMAN IN THE SUITCASE   Paramount, 1920
DANGEROUS HOURS   Paramount, 1920
SEX   W.W. Hodkinson, 1920

THE FALSE ROAD   Paramount, 1920
HAIRPINS   Paramount, 1920
HER HUSBAND'S FRIEND   Paramount, 1920
THE MARK OF ZORRO   United Artists, 1920
SILK HOSIERY   Paramount, 1921
MOTHER O' MINE   Associated Producers, 1921
GREATER THAN LOVE   Associated Producers, 1921
THE THREE MUSKETEERS   United Artists, 1921
THE WOMAN HE MARRIED   First National, 1922
ROSE O' THE SEA   First National, 1922
BLOOD AND SAND   Paramount, 1922
THE FAMOUS MRS. FAIR   Metro, 1923
STRANGERS OF THE NIGHT   Metro, 1923
THY NAME IS WOMAN   Metro-Goldwyn, 1924
THE RED LILY   Metro-Goldwyn, 1924
BEN-HUR   MGM, 1926
THE TEMPTRESS   MGM, 1926
CAMILLE   First National, 1927
THE DEVIL DANCER   United Artists, 1927
THE ENEMY   MGM, 1928
TWO LOVERS   United Artists, 1928
THE MYSTERIOUS LADY   MGM, 1928
DREAM OF LOVE   MGM, 1928
REDEMPTION   MGM, 1930
WAY OUT WEST   MGM, 1930
YOUNG DONOVAN'S KID   MGM, 1931
THE BIG GAMBLE   Pathé, 1931
TWO WHITE ARMS   1932, British
DIAMOND CUT DIAMOND   co-director with Maurice Elvey,
    1932, British
BLAME THE WOMAN   1932

ELLIOTT NUGENT

b. September 20, 1899 - Dover, Ohio
d. 1980

THE MOUTHPIECE   co-director with James Flood,
    Warner Bros., 1932
LIFE BEGINS   co-director with James Flood, Warner Bros.,
    1932
WHISTLING IN THE DARK   MGM, 1933
THREE-CORNERED MOON   Paramount, 1933
IF I WERE FREE   Paramount, 1933
TWO ALONE   Paramount, 1934
STRICTLY DYNAMITE   Paramount, 1934
SHE LOVES ME NOT   Paramount, 1934
ENTER MADAME   Paramount, 1935
LOVE IN BLOOM   Paramount, 1935
COLLEGE SCANDAL   Paramount, 1935
SPLENDOR   United Artists, 1935
AND SO THEY WERE MARRIED   Columbia, 1936
WIVES NEVER KNOW   Paramount, 1936
IT'S ALL YOURS   Columbia, 1937
PROFESSOR BEWARE   Paramount, 1938
GIVE ME A SAILOR   Paramount, 1938
NEVER SAY DIE   Paramount, 1939
THE CAT AND THE CANARY   Paramount, 1939
NOTHING BUT THE TRUTH   Paramount, 1941
THE MALE ANIMAL   Warner Bros., 1942
THE CRYSTAL BALL   United Artists, 1943
UP IN ARMS   RKO Radio, 1944
MY FAVORITE BRUNETTE   Paramount, 1947
WELCOME STRANGER   Paramount, 1947
MY GIRL TISA   United Artists, 1948
MR. BELVEDERE GOES TO COLLEGE   20th Century-
    Fox, 1949
THE GREAT GATSBY   Paramount, 1949
THE SKIPPER SURPRISED HIS WIFE   MGM, 1950
MY OUTLAW BROTHER   Eagle Lion, 1951
JUST FOR YOU   Paramount, 1952

ARCH OBOLER

b. December 7, 1909 - Chicago, Illinois
d. 1987

BEWITCHED   MGM, 1945
STRANGE HOLIDAY   Producers Releasing Corporation,
    1946
THE ARNELO AFFAIR   MGM, 1947
FIVE   Columbia, 1951
BWANA DEVIL   United Artists, 1952
THE TWONKY   United Artists, 1953
ONE PLUS ONE: EXPLORING THE KINSEY REPORTS
    Selected Films, 1961, U.S.-Canadian
THE BUBBLE   Oboler Films, 1967
THE STEWARDESSES   directed under pseudonym of
    Alf Silliman, Sherpix, 1969
DOMO ARIGATO (FD)   Oboler Films, 1972

SIDNEY OLCOTT
(John S. Alcott)

b. September 20, 1873 - Toronto, Canada
d. 1949

BEN-HUR   co-director with Frank Oakes Rose, 1907
THE SLEIGH BELLS   1907
A FLORIDA FEUD   1909
ESCAPE FROM ANDERSONVILLE   1909
THE LAD FROM OLD IRELAND   1909
THE CONSPIRATORS   1909
THE DEACON'S DAUGHTER   1910
THE MISER'S CHILD   1910
THE FURTHER ADVENTURES OF A GIRL SPY
    1910
AN INDIAN SCOUT'S VENGEANCE   1910
SETH'S TEMPTATION   1910
THE GIRL SPY BEFORE VICKSBURG   1910
ARRAH-NA-POGUE   1911
THE COLLEEN BAWN   1911
THE FISHERMAN OF BALLYDAVID   1911
RORY O'MORE   1911
THE SHAUGHRAUN   1912
THE KERRY GOW   1912
IRELAND THE OPPRESSED   1913
FROM MANGER TO THE CROSS   Kalem, 1913
DAUGHTER OF THE CONFEDERACY   co-director
    with George Melford, 1913
THE PERILS OF THE SEA   co-director with George
    Melford, 1913
IN THE CLUTCHES OF THE KLU KLUX KLAN
    1913
THE VAMPIRE   co-director with Thomas Hayes Hunter,
    1913
THE OCTOROON   1913
A PASSOVER MIRACLE   1914
ALL FOR IRELAND   Lubin, 1915
BOLD EMMETT - IRELAND'S MARTYR   1915
NAN OF THE BACKWOODS   1915
MADAME BUTTERFLY   1915
THE SEVEN SISTERS   Paramount, 1915
THE MOTH AND THE FLAME   Paramount, 1916

MY LADY INCOGNITO   Paramount, 1916
POOR LITTLE PEPPINA   Paramount, 1916
DIPLOMACY   Paramount, 1916
THE INNOCENT LIE   Paramount, 1916
THE SMUGGLERS   Paramount, 1916
THE DAUGHTER OF MacGREGOR   Paramount, 1916
LESS THAN THE DUST   1916
THE BELGIAN   World, 1917
MARRIAGE FOR CONVENIENCE   Sherry, 1919
MOTHERS OF MEN   1920
SCRATCH MY BACK   Goldwyn, 1920
THE RIGHT WAY   Producers Security Corp., 1921
PARDON MY FRENCH   Goldwyn, 1921
GOD'S COUNTRY AND THE LAW   Arrow, 1921
TIMOTHY'S QUEST   American Releasing, 1922
THE GREEN GODDESS   Goldwyn, 1923
LITTLE OLD NEW YORK   Goldwyn, 1923
THE HUMMING BIRD   Paramount, 1924
MONSIEUR BEAUCAIRE   Paramount, 1924
THE ONLY WOMAN   First National, 1924
SALOME OF THE TENEMENTS   Paramount, 1925
THE CHARMER   Paramount, 1925
NOT SO LONG AGO   Paramount, 1925
THE BEST PEOPLE   Paramount, 1925
RANSON'S FOLLY   First National, 1926
THE AMATEUR GENTLEMAN   First National, 1926
THE WHITE BLACK SHEEP   First National, 1926
THE CLAW   Universal-Jewel, 1927

LAURENCE OLIVIER

b. May 22, 1907 - Dorking, England
d. 1989

HENRY V   Rank, 1945, British
HAMLET★   Universal, 1946, British
RICHARD III   Lopert, 1956, British
THE PRINCE AND THE SHOWGIRL   Warner Bros., 1957,
   U.S.-British
THREE SISTERS   American Film Theatre, 1970, British

MAX OPHULS
(Max Oppenheimer)
b. May 6, 1902 - Saarbrucken, Germany
d. 1957

DAS SCHON LIEBER LEBERTRAN   1930, German
DIE VERLIEBTE FIRMA   1932, German
DIE VERKAUFTE BRAUT   1932, German
DIE LACHENDE ERBEN   1933, German
LIEBELEI   1933, German
UNE HISTOIRE D'AMOUR   1933, French
ON A VOLE UN HOMME   1934, French
LA SIGNORA DI TUTTI   1934, Italian
DIVINE   1935, French
KOMEDIE OM GELD   1936, Dutch
AVE MARIA   1936, French
LA VALSE BRILLANTE   1936, French
LA TENDRE ENNEMIE   1936, French
YOSHIWARA   1937, French
LE ROMAN DE WERTHER   1938, French
SANS LENDEMAIN   1940, French
DE MAYERLING A SARAJEVO   1940, French
L'ECOLE DES FEMMES   1940, French, unfinished
THE EXILE   Universal, 1947
LETTER FROM AN UNKNOWN WOMAN   Universal,
   1948

CAUGHT   MGM, 1949
THE RECKLESS MOMENT   Columbia, 1949
LA RONDE   Commercial Pictures, 1950, French
LE PLAISIR   1952, French
THE EARRINGS OF MADAME DE...   *MADAME DE*
   Arian Pictures, 1953, French
LOLA MONTES   *THE SINS OF LOLA MONTES*
   Brandon, 1955, French-West German

GERD OSWALD

b. June 9, 1916 - Berlin, Germany
d. 1989

A KISS BEFORE DYING   United Artists, 1956
THE BRASS LEGEND   United Artists, 1956
CRIME OF PASSION   United Artists, 1957
FURY AT SHOWDOWN   United Artists, 1957
VALERIE   United Artists, 1957
PARIS HOLIDAY   United Artists, 1958
SCREAMING MIMI   Columbia, 1958
AM TAG ALS DER REGEN KAM   1959, West German
BRAINWASHED   Allied Artists, 1960, West German
TEMPESTA SU CEYLON   co-director with Giovanni
   Roccardi, FICIT/Rapid Film, 1963, Italian-French
AGENT FOR H.A.R.M.   Universal, 1966
80 STEPS TO JONAH   Warner Bros., 1969
BUNNY O'HARE   American International, 1971
BIS ZUR BITTEREN NEIGE   1975, West German-
   Australian

YASUJIRO OZU

b. December 15, 1903 - Tokyo, Japan
d. 1963

SWORD OF PENITENCE   1927, Japanese
DREAMS OF YOUTH   1928, Japanese
WIFE LOST   1928, Japanese
PUMPKIN   1928, Japanese
A COUPLE ON THE MOVE   1928, Japanese
BODY BEAUTIFUL   1928, Japanese
TREASURE MOUNTAIN   1929, Japanese
DAYS OF YOUTH   1929, Japanese
FIGHTING FRIENDS   1929, Japanese
I GRADUATED BUT...   1929, Japanese
THE LIFE OF AN OFFICE WORKER   1929, Japanese
A STRAIGHTFORWARD BOY   1929, Japanese
INTRODUCTION TO MARRIAGE   1930, Japanese
WALK CHEERFULLY   1930, Japanese
I FLUNKED BUT...   1930, Japanese
THAT NIGHT'S WIFE   1930, Japanese
THE REVENGEFUL SPIRIT OF EROS   1930, Japanese
LOST LUCK   1930, Japanese
YOUNG MISS   1930, Japanese
THE LADY AND THE BEARD   1931, Japanese
BEAUTY'S SORROWS   1931, Japanese
TOKYO CHORUS   1931, Japanese
I WAS BORN BUT...   1932, Japanese
WHERE ARE THE DREAMS OF YOUTH?   1932,
   Japanese
UNTIL THE DAY WE MEET AGAIN   1932, Japanese
WOMAN OF TOKYO   1933, Japanese
DRAGNET GIRL   1933, Japanese
PASSING FANCY   1933, Japanese
A MOTHER SHOULD BE LOVED   1934, Japanese
A STORY OF FLOATING WEEDS   1934, Japanese
AN INNOCENT MAID   1935, Japanese

TOKYO IS A NICE PLACE   1935, Japanese
AN INN IN TOKYO   1935, Japanese
COLLEGE IS A NICE PLACE   1936, Japanese
THE ONLY SON   1936, Japanese
WHAT DID THE LADY FORGET?   1937, Japanese
THE TODA BROTHERS AND SISTERS   1941,
    Japanese
THERE WAS A FATHER   1942, Japanese
THE RECORD OF A TENEMENT GENTLEMAN
    1947, Japanese
A HEN IN THE WIND   1948, Japanese
LATE SPRING   1949, Japanese
THE MUNEKATA SISTERS   1950, Japanese
EARLY SUMMER   New Yorker, 1951, Japanese
THE FLAVOR OF GREEN TEA OVER RICE   New
    Yorker, 1952, Japanese
TOKYO STORY   New Yorker, 1953, Japanese
EARLY SPRING   New Yorker, 1956, Japanese
TOKYO TWILIGHT   1957, Japanese
EQUINOX FLOWER   New Yorker, 1958, Japanese
OHAYO   1959, Japanese
FLOATING WEEDS   New Yorker, 1959, Japanese
LATE AUTUMN   New Yorker, 1960, Japanese
EARLY AUTUMN   New Yorker, 1961, Japanese
AN AUTUMN AFTERNOON   Toho, 1962, Japanese

P

G.W. PABST
(Georg Wilhelm Pabst)
b. August 27, 1885 - Raudnitz, Bohemia, Germany
d. 1967

DER SCHATZ   1923, German
GRAFIN DONELLI   1924, German
DIE FREUDLOSE GASSE   1925, German
GEHEIMNISSE EINER SEELE   1926, German
MAN SPIELT NICHT MIT DER LIEBE   1926, German
DIE LIEBE DER JEANNE NEY   1927, German
ABWEGE   1928, German
DIE BUCHSE DER PANDORA   1929, German
DIE WEISSE HOLLE VOM PIZ PALU   co-director with
    Arnold Fanck, 1929, German
DAS TAGEBUCH EINER VERLORENEN   1929, German
WESTFRONT 1918   1930, German
SKANDAL UM EVA   1930, German
THE THREEPENNY OPERA   Brandon, 1931, German
L'OPERA DE QUAT'SOUS   1931, German-French
KAMERADSCHAFT   1931, German
DIE HERRIN VON ATLANTIS   1932, German
LA TRAGÉDIE DE LA MINE   1932, German-French
L'ATLANTIDE   German, 1932
DON QUIXOTE   1933, British
DON QUICHOTTE   1933, French
DU HAUT EN BAS   1933, French
A MODERN HERO   Warner Bros., 1934
MADEMOISELLE DOCTEUR   SALONIQUE SHANGHAI
    1937, French
LE DRAME DE SHANGHAI   1938, French
JEUNES FILLES EN DETRESSE   1939, French
FEUERTAUFE   1940, German
KOMODIANTEN   1941, German
PARACELSUS   1943, German

MEINE VIER JUNGENS   German, 1944
DER FALL MOLANDER   1945, German
DER PROZESS   1948, Austrian
GEHEIMNISVOLLE TIEFEN   1949, Austrian
LA VOCE DEL SILENZIO   1952, Italian
COSE DA PAZZI   1953, Italian
DAS BEKENNTNIS DER INA KAHR   1954, West German
THE LAST TEN DAYS   Columbia, 1955, West German
ES GESCHAH AM 20   1955, West German
JULI   1955, West German
BALLERINA   ROSEN FUR BETTINA   Sam Baker
    Associates, 1956, West German
DURCH DIE WALDER, DURCH DIE AUEN   1956,
    West German

MARCEL PAGNOL
b. February 28, 1895 - Aubagne, France
d. 1974

DIRECT AU COEUR   co-director with Roger Lion, 1933,
    French
LA GENDRE DE MONSIEUR POIRIER   1933, French
LEOPOLD LE BIEN-AIME   1933, French
WAYS OF LOVE   JOFROI   1934, French
ANGELE   1934, French
LE VOYAGE DE MONSIEUR PERRICHON   1934, French
L'ARTICLE 330   1934, French
MERLUSSE   1935, French
CIGALON   1935, French
CESAR   1936, French
TOPAZE   1936, French
REGAIN   1937, French
LE SCHPOUNTZ   1938, French
THE BAKER'S WIFE   The Baker's Wife Inc., 1938,
    French
THE WELLDIGGER'S DAUGHTER   Siritzky International,
    1941, French
NAIS   French, 1946
LA BELLE MEUNIERE   1948, French
TOPAZE   1952, French
MANON DES SOURCES   French, 1952
LETTERS FROM MY WINDMILL   Tohan, 1954, French

GEORGE PAL
b. February 1, 1908 - Cegled, Hungary
d. 1980

tom thumb   MGM, 1958
THE TIME MACHINE   MGM, 1960, British
ATLANTIS, THE LOST CONTINENT   MGM, 1961
THE WONDERFUL WORLD OF THE BROTHERS
    GRIMM   co-director with Henry Levin, MGM/Cinerama,
    1962
THE SEVEN FACES OF DR. LAO   MGM, 1964

SERGEI PARADJANOV
b. 1924 - Georgia, U.S.S.R.
d. 1990

ANDRIESH   1954, Soviet
THE FIRST LAD   1958, Soviet
UKRAINIAN RHAPSODY   1961, Soviet
FLOWER ON THE STONE   1963, Soviet
THE BALLAD   1964, Soviet
SHADOWS OF OUR FORGOTTEN ANCESTORS
    1964, Soviet

SAYAT NOVAR   1968, Soviet
THE LEGEND OF SURAM FORTRESS   co-director
    with David Abachidze, International Film Exchange,
    1985, Soviet
ASHIK KERIB   co-director with David Abachidze,
    International Film Exchange, 1988, Soviet
THE GENTLE ONE   Gruziafilm, 1990, Soviet

JERRY PARIS

b. July 25, 1925 - San Francisco, California
d. 1986

DON'T RAISE THE BRIDGE - LOWER THE RIVER
    Columbia, 1968, British
NEVER A DULL MOMENT   Buena Vista, 1968
HOW SWEET IT IS!   Buena Vista, 1968
VIVA MAX!   Commonwealth United, 1969
THE GRASSHOPPER   National General, 1969
BUT I DON'T WANT TO GET MARRIED! (TF)
    Aaron Spelling Productions, 1970
THE FEMINIST AND THE FUZZ (TF)   Screen Gems/
    Columbia TV, 1970
TWO ON A BENCH (TF)   Universal TV, 1971
WHAT'S A NICE GIRL LIKE YOU...?   Universal TV, 1971
STAR SPANGLED GIRL   Paramount, 1971
CALL HER MOM (TF)   Screen Gems/Columbia TV, 1972
EVIL ROY SLADE (TF)   Universal TV, 1972
THE COUPLE TAKES A WIFE (TF)   Universal TV, 1972
EVERY MAN NEEDS ONE (TF)   ABC Circle Films, 1972
ONLY WITH MARRIED MEN (TF)   Spelling-Goldberg
    Productions, 1974
HOW TO BREAK UP A HAPPY DIVORCE (TF)
    Charles Fries Productions, 1976
MAKE ME AN OFFER (TF)   ABC Circle Films, 1980
LEO AND LOREE   United Artists, 1980
POLICE ACADEMY 2: THEIR FIRST ASSIGNMENT
    Warner Bros., 1985
POLICE ACADEMY 3: BACK IN TRAINING
    Warner Bros., 1986

GABRIEL PASCAL

b. June 4, 1894 - Arad, Transylvania
d. 1954

MAJOR BARBARA   United Artists, 1941, British
CAESAR AND CLEOPATRA   United Artists, 1945, British

PIER PAOLO PASOLINI

b. March 5, 1922 - Bologna, Italy
d. 1975

ACCATONE!   Brandon, 1961, Italian
MAMA ROMA   1962, Italian
ROGOPAG   co-director, 1962, Italian
LA RABBIA   co-director, 1963, Italian
SOPRALUOGHI IN PALESTINA (FD)   1964, Italian
THE GOSPEL ACCORDING TO ST. MATTHEW
    Continental, 1964, Italian
COMIZI D'AMORE (FD)   1965, Italian ·
THE HAWKS AND THE SPARROWS   Brandon, 1966,
    Italian
THE WITCHES   co-director, Lopert, 1967, Italian-French
OEDIPUS REX   Europix International, 1967, Italian
CAPRICCIO ALL'ITALIANA   co-director, 1968, Italian
TEOREMA   Continental, 1968, Italian

AMORE E RABBIA   co-director, 1969, Italian
PIGPEN   New Line Cinema, 1969, Italian-French
MEDEA   New Line Cinema, 1970, Italian-French-
    West German
THE DECAMERON   United Artists, 1971, Italian-French-
    West German
THE CANTERBURY TALES   United Artists, 1972, Italian
THE ARABIAN NIGHTS   IL FIORE DELL MILLE E
    UNA NOTTE   United Artists, 1974, Italian-French
SALO: THE LAST 120 DAYS OF SODOM   Zebra, 1975,
    Italian
ORESTIADE AFRICANO   1976, Italian
LA RICOTTA   1976, Italian

SAM PECKINPAH

b. February 21, 1925 - Fresno, California
d. 1984

THE DEADLY COMPANIONS   Pathé-American, 1961
RIDE THE HIGH COUNTRY   MGM, 1962
MAJOR DUNDEE   Columbia, 1965
THE WILD BUNCH   Warner Bros., 1969
THE BALLAD OF CABLE HOGUE   Warner Bros., 1970
STRAW DOGS   Cinerama Releasing Corporation, 1972,
    British
THE GETAWAY   National General, 1972
JUNIOR BONNER   Cinerama Releasing Corporation, 1973
PAT GARRETT & BILLY THE KID   MGM, 1973
BRING ME THE HEAD OF ALFREDO GARCIA
    United Artists, 1974
THE KILLER ELITE   United Artists, 1975
CROSS OF IRON   Avco Embassy, 1977, British-
    West German
CONVOY   United Artists, 1978
THE OSTERMAN WEEKEND   20th Century-Fox, 1983

ELIO PETRI

b. January 29, 1929 - Rome, Italy
d. 1982

THE ASSASSIN   THE LADY KILLER OF ROME
    Manson, 1961, Italian-French
I GIORNI CONTATI   1962, Italian
IL MAESTRO DI VIGEVANO   1963, Italian
HIGH INFIDELITY   co-director, Magna, 1964, Italian-
    French
THE TENTH VICTIM   Embassy, 1965, Italian
WE STILL KILL THE OLD WAY   A CIASCUNO IL SUO
    Lopert, 1967, Italian
A QUIET PLACE IN THE COUNTRY   United Artists, 1968,
    Italian-French
INVESTIGATION OF A CITIZEN ABOVE SUSPICION
    Columbia, 1970, Italian
LA CLASSE OPERAIA VA IN PARADISO   1971, Italian
LA PROPRIETA NON E PIU UN FURTO   1973, Italian
TODO MODO   1976, Italian

IRVING PICHEL

b. June 25, 1891 - Pittsburgh, Pennsylvania
d. 1954

THE MOST DANGEROUS GAME   co-director with
    Ernest B. Schoedsack, RKO Radio, 1932
BEFORE DAWN   RKO, 1933
SHE   co-director with Lansing C. Holden, RKO Radio,
    1935

THE GENTLEMAN FROM LOUISIANA   Republic, 1936
BEWARE OF LADIES   *LADIES BEWARE*   Republic, 1936
LARCENY ON THE AIR   Republic, 1937
THE SHEIK STEPS OUT   Republic, 1937
THE DUKE COMES BACK   Republic, 1937
EARTHBOUND   20th Century-Fox, 1940
THE MAN I MARRIED   20th Century-Fox, 1940
HUDSON'S BAY   20th Century-Fox, 1941
DANCE HALL   20th Century-Fox, 1941
THE GREAT COMMANDMENT   20th Century-Fox, 1941
SECRET AGENT OF JAPAN   20th Century-Fox, 1942
THE PIED PIPER   20th Century-Fox, 1942
LIFE BEGINS AT 8:30   20th Century-Fox, 1942
THE MOON IS DOWN   20th Century-Fox, 1943
THE HAPPY LAND   20th Century-Fox, 1943
AND NOW TOMORROW   Paramount, 1944
A MEDAL FOR BENNY   Paramount, 1945
COLONEL EFFINGHAM'S RAID   20th Century-Fox, 1945
TOMORROW IS FOREVER   RKO Radio, 1946
O.S.S.   Paramount, 1946
THE BRIDE WORE BOOTS   Paramount, 1946
TEMPTATION   Universal, 1946
THEY WON'T BELIEVE ME   RKO Radio, 1947
SOMETHING IN THE WIND   Universal, 1947
THE MIRACLE OF THE BELLS   RKO Radio, 1948
MR. PEABODY AND THE MERMAID   Universal, 1948
WITHOUT HONOR   United Artists, 1949
THE GREAT RUPERT   Eagle Lion, 1950
QUICKSAND   United Artists, 1950
DESTINATION MOON   Eagle Lion, 1950
SANTA FE   Columbia, 1951
MARTIN LUTHER   De Rochemont, 1953
DAY OF TRIUMPH   co-director with John T. Coyle,
    George J. Schaefer, 1954

EDWIN S. PORTER
(Edwin Stanton Porter)
b. April 21, 1869 - Cannellsville, Pennsylvania
d. 1941

THE AMERICA'S CUP RACE   Edison, 1899
WHY MRS. JONES GOT A DIVORCE   Edison, 1900
ANIMATED LUNCHEON   Edison, 1900
AN ARTIST'S DREAM   Edison, 1900
THE MYSTIC SWING   Edison, 1900
CHING LIN FOO OUTDONE   Edison, 1900
FAUST AND MARGUERITE   Edison, 1900
THE CLOWN AND THE ALCHEMIST   Edison, 1900
A WRINGING GOOD JOKE   Edison, 1900
THE ENCHANTED DRAWING   Edison, 1900
TERRIBLE TEDDY THE GRIZZLY KING   Edison, 1901
LOVE IN A HAMMOCK   Edison, 1901
A DAY AT THE CIRCUS   Edison, 1901
WHAT DEMORALIZED THE BARBER SHOP   Edison, 1901
THE FINISH OF BRIDGET McKEEN   Edison, 1901
HAPPY HOOLIGAN SURPRISED   Edison, 1901
MARTYRED PRESIDENTS   Edison, 1901
LOVE BY THE LIGHT OF THE MOON   Edison, 1901
CIRCULAR PANORAMA OF THE ELECTRIC TOWER
    Edison, 1901
PANORAMA OF THE ESPLANADE BY NIGHT
    Edison, 1901
THE MYSTERIOUS CAFE   Edison, 1901
UNCLE JOSH AT THE MOVING PICTURE SHOW
    Edison, 1902
CHARLESTON CHAIN GANG   Edison, 1902
BURLESQUE SUICIDE   Edison, 1902
ROCK OF AGES   Edison, 1902

JACK AND THE BEANSTALK   Edison, 1902
THE LIFE OF AN AMERICAN FIREMAN   Edison, 1903
THE STILL ALARM   Edison, 1903
ARABIAN JEWISH DANCE   Edison, 1903
RAZZLE DAZZLE   Edison, 1903
SEASHORE FROLICS   Edison, 1903
SCENES IN AN ORPHAN'S ASYLUM   Edison, 1903
THE GAY SHOE CLERK   Edison, 1903
THE BABY REVIEW   Edison, 1903
THE ANIMATED POSTER   Edison, 1903
THE OFFICE BOY'S REVENGE   Edison, 1903
UNCLE TOM'S CABIN   Edison, 1903
THE GREAT TRAIN ROBBERY   Edison, 1903
THE EX-CONVICT   Edison, 1904
COHEN'S ADVERTISING SCHEME   Edison, 1904
EUROPEAN REST CURE   Edison, 1904
PARSIFAL   Edison, 1904
THE KLEPTOMANIAC   Edison, 1905
STOLEN BY GYPSIES   Edison, 1905
HOW JONES LOST HIS ROLL   Edison, 1905
THE LITTLE TRAIN ROBBERY   Edison, 1905
THE WHITE CAPS   Edison, 1905
SEVEN AGES   Edison, 1905
THE LIFE OF A COWBOY   Edison, 1906
THREE AMERICAN BEAUTIES   Edison, 1906
KATHLEEN MAVOURNEEN   Edison, 1906
DANIEL BOONE   Edison, 1907
LOST IN THE ALPS   Edison, 1907
THE MIDNIGHT RIDE OF PAUL REVERE   Edison, 1907
LAUGHING GAS   Edison, 1907
RESCUED FROM AN EAGLE'S NEST   Edison, 1907
THE TEDDY BEARS   Edison, 1907
NERO AND THE BURNING OF ROME   Edison, 1908
THE PAINTER'S REVENGE   Edison, 1908
THE MERRY WIDOW WALTZ CRAZE   Edison, 1908
THE GENTLEMAN BURGLAR   Edison, 1908
HONESTY IS THE BEST POLICY   Edison, 1908
LOVE WILL FIND A WAY   Edison, 1908
SKINNY'S FINISH   Edison, 1908
THE FACE ON THE BARROOM FLOOR   Edison, 1908
THE BOSTON TEA PARTY   Edison, 1908
ROMANCE OF A WAR NURSE   Edison, 1908
A VOICE FROM THE DEAD   Edison, 1908
SAVED BY LOVE   Edison, 1908
SHE   Edison, 1908
LORD FEATHERTOP   Edison, 1908
THE ANGEL CHILD   Edison, 1908
MISS SHERLOCK HOLMES   Edison, 1908
AN UNEXPECTED SANTA CLAUS   Edison, 1908
THE ADVENTURES OF AN OLD FLIRT   Edison, 1909
A MIDNIGHT SUPPER   Edison, 1909
LOVE IS BLIND   Edison, 1909
A CRY FROM THE WILDERNESS   Edison, 1909
HARD TO BEAT   Edison, 1909
ON THE WESTERN FRONTIER   Edison, 1909
FUSS AND FEATHERS   Edison, 1909
PONY EXPRESS   Edison, 1909
ALL ON ACCOUNT OF A LAUNDRY MARK   Defender
    Pictures, 1910
RUSSIA - THE LAND OF OPPRESSION   Defender
    Pictures, 1910
TOO MANY GIRLS   Defender Pictures, 1910
ALMOST A HERO   Defender Pictures, 1910
THE TOYMAKER, THE DOLL AND THE DEVIL
    Defender Pictures, 1910
BY THE LIGHT OF THE MOON   Rex Film Company,
    1911
ON THE BRINK   Rex Film Company, 1911
THE WHITE RED MAN   Rex Film Company, 1911
SHERLOCK HOLMES, JR.   Rex Film Company, 1911
LOST ILLUSIONS   Rex Film Company, 1911

A SANE ASYLUM   Famous Players, 1912
EYES THAT SEE NOT   Famous Players, 1912
THE FINAL PARDON   Famous Players, 1912
TAMING MRS. SHREW   Famous Players, 1912
TESS OF THE D'URBERVILLES   co-director with
    J. Searle Dawley, Paramount, 1913
THE PRISONER OF ZENDA   co-director with Hugh
    Ford, Famous Players, 1913
HIS NEIGHBOR'S WIFE   Famous Players, 1913
THE COUNT OF MONTE CRISTO   co-director with
    Joseph Golden, Famous Players, 1913
IN THE BISHOP'S CARRIAGE   co-director with J. Searle
    Dawley, Famous Players, 1913
A GOOD LITTLE DEVIL   co-director with J. Searle
    Dawley, Famous Players, 1913
HEARTS ADRIFT   Paramount, Famous Players, 1914
TESS OF THE STORM COUNTRY   Famous Players,
    1914
SUCH A LITTLE QUEEN   co-director with Hugh Ford,
    Famous Players, 1914
THE ETERNAL CITY   co-director with Hugh Ford,
    Famous Players, 1914
THE SCALES OF JUSTICE   Paramount, 1914
A WOMAN'S TRIUMPH   Paramount, 1914
THE CRUCIBLE   Paramount, 1914
THE DICTATOR   Paramount, 1915
SOLD   Paramount, 1915
THE WHITE PEARL   Paramount, 1915
JIRM THE PENMAN   Paramount, 1915
ZAZA   co-director with Hugh Ford, Famous Players, 1915
SOLD   co-director with Hugh Ford, Famous Players,
    1915
THE PRINCE AND THE PAUPER   co-director with
    Hugh Ford, Famous Players, 1915
BELLA DONNA   co-director with Hugh Ford, Famous
    Players, 1915
LYDIA GILMORE   co-director with Hugh Ford, Famous
    Players, 1916

H.C. (HANK) POTTER
(Henry Codman Potter)
b. November 13, 1904 - New York, New York
d. 1977

BELOVED ENEMY   United Artists, 1936
WINGS OVER HONOLULU   Universal, 1937
ROMANCE IN THE DARK   Paramount, 1938
THE COWBOY AND THE LADY   United Artists, 1938
THE SHOPWORN ANGEL   MGM, 1938
THE STORY OF VERNON AND IRENE CASTLE
    RKO Radio, 1939
BLACKMAIL   MGM, 1939
CONGO MAISIE   MGM, 1940
SECOND CHORUS   Paramount, 1940
HELLZAPOPPIN!   Universal, 1941
VICTORY THROUGH AIR POWER (FD)   1943
MR. LUCKY   RKO Radio, 1943
THE FARMER'S DAUGHTER   RKO Radio, 1947
A LIKELY STORY   RKO Radio, 1947
MR. BLANDINGS BUILDS HIS DREAM HOUSE
    RKO Radio, 1948
THE TIME OF YOUR LIFE   United Artists, 1948
YOU GOTTA STAY HAPPY   Universal, 1948
THE MINIVER STORY   MGM, 1950
THREE FOR THE SHOW   Columbia, 1955
TOP SECRET AFFAIR   Warner Bros., 1957

DICK POWELL
(Richard E. Powell)
b. November 14, 1904 - Mountain View, Arkansas
d. 1963

SPLIT SECOND   RKO Radio, 1953
THE CONQUEROR   RKO Radio, 1956
YOU CAN'T RUN AWAY FROM IT   Columbia, 1956
THE ENEMY BELOW   20th Century-Fox, 1957
THE HUNTERS   20th Century-Fox, 1958

MICHAEL POWELL
b. September 30, 1905 - Canterbury, England
d. 1990

TWO CROWDED HOURS   Fox, 1931, British
MY FRIEND THE KING   Fox, 1931, British
RYNOX   Ideal, 1931, British
THE RASP   Fox, 1931, British
THE STAR REPORTER   Fox, 1931, British
HOTEL SPLENDIDE   Ideal, 1932, British
BORN LUCKY   MGM, 1932, British
C.O.D.   United Artists, 1932, British
HIS LORDSHIP   United Artists, 1932, British
THE FIRE RAISERS   Woolf & Freedman, 1933, British
THE NIGHT OF THE PARTY   Gaumont, 1934, British
RED ENSIGN   Gaumont, 1934, British
SOMETHING ALWAYS HAPPENS   Warner Bros., 1934,
    British
THE GIRL IN THE CROWD   First National, 1934, British
THE LOVE TEST   Fox British, 1935, British
LAZYBONES   Radio, 1935, British
SOME DAY   Warner Bros., 1935, British
HER LAST AFFAIRE   Producers Distributing Corporation,
    1935, British
THE PRICE OF A SONG   Fox British, 1935, British
THE PHANTOM LIGHT   Gaumont, 1935, British
THE BROWN WALLET   First National, 1936, British
CROWN VS. STEVENS   Warner Bros., 1936, British
THE MAN BEHIND THE MASK   MGM, 1936, British
THE EDGE OF THE WORLD   British Independent Exhib-
    itors' Distributors, 1937, British
U-BOAT 29   *THE SPY IN BLACK*   Columbia, 1939, British
THE LION HAS WINGS   co-director with Brian Desmond
    Hurst & Adrian Brunel, United Artists, 1939, British
THE THIEF OF BAGDAD   co-director with Ludwig Berger &
    Tom Whelan, United Artists, 1940, British
CONTRABAND   *BLACKOUT*   Anglo-American, 1940,
    British
THE FORTY-NINTH PARALLEL   *THE INVADERS*   Colum-
    bia, 1941, British
ONE OF OUR AIRCRAFT IS MISSING   co-director with
    Emeric Pressburger, United Artists, 1942, British
THE VOLUNTEER   co-director with Emeric Pressburger,
    Anglo, 1943, British
COLONEL BLIMP   *THE LIFE AND DEATH OF COLONEL
    BLIMP*   co- director with Emeric Pressburger, GFO,
    1943, British
A CANTERBURY TALE   co-director with Emeric
    Pressburger, Eagle-Lion, 1944, British
I KNOW WHERE I'M GOING   co-director with Emeric
    Pressburger, Universal, 1945, British
STAIRWAY TO HEAVEN   *A MATTER OF LIFE AND DEATH*
    co-director with Emeric Pressburger, Universal, 1946,
    British
BLACK NARCISSUS   co-director with Emeric Pressburger,
    Universal, 1947, British
THE RED SHOES   co-director with Emeric Pressburger,
    Eagle-Lion, 1948, British

THE SMALL BACK ROOM *HOUR OF GLORY* co-director with Emeric Pressburger, Snader Productions, 1948, British
THE WILD HEART *GONE TO EARTH* co-director with Emeric Pressburger, RKO Radio, 1950, British
THE ELUSIVE PIMPERNEL co-director with Emeric Pressburger, British Lion, 1950, British
THE TALES OF HOFFMAN co-director with Emeric Pressburger, Lopert, 1951, British
OH ROSALINDA! co-director with Emeric Pressburger, Associated British Picture Corporation, 1955, British
PURSUIT OF THE GRAF SPEE *THE BATTLE OF THE RIVER PLATE* co-director with Emeric Pressburger, Rank, 1956, British
NIGHT AMBUSH *ILL MET BY MOONLIGHT* co-director with Emeric Pressburger, Rank, 1957, British
HONEYMOON *LUNA DE MIEL* RKO Radio, 1958, Spanish
PEEPING TOM Astor, 1960, British
THE QUEEN'S GUARDS 20th Century-Fox, 1961, British
THEY'RE A WEIRD MOB Williamson/Powell, 1966, Australian
AGE OF CONSENT Columbia, 1970, Australian
THE TEMPEST 1974, Greek-British

OTTO PREMINGER
b. December 5, 1906 - Vienna, Austria
d. 1986

DIE GROSSE LIEBE 1931, Austrian-German
UNDER YOUR SPELL 20th Century-Fox, 1936
DANGER - LOVE AT WORK 20th Century-Fox, 1937
MARGIN FOR ERROR 20th Century-Fox, 1943
IN THE MEANTIME, DARLING 20th Century-Fox, 1944
LAURA ★ 20th Century-Fox, 1944
A ROYAL SCANDAL 20th Century-Fox, 1945
FALLEN ANGEL 20th Century-Fox, 1945
CENTENNIAL SUMMER 20th Century-Fox, 1946
FOREVER AMBER 20th Century-Fox, 1947
DAISY KENYON 20th Century-Fox, 1947
THE FAN 20th Century-Fox, 1949
WHIRLPOOL 20th Century-Fox, 1950
WHERE THE SIDEWALK ENDS 20th Century-Fox, 1950
THE 13TH LETTER 20th Century-Fox, 1951
ANGEL FACE RKO Radio, 1953
THE MOON IS BLUE United Artists, 1953
RIVER OF NO RETURN 20th Century-Fox, 1954
CARMEN JONES 20th Century-Fox, 1955
THE MAN WITH THE GOLDEN ARM United Artists, 1955
THE COURT-MARTIAL OF BILLY MITCHELL Warner Bros., 1955
SAINT JOAN United Artists, 1957
BONJOUR TRISTESSE Columbia, 1958
PORGY AND BESS Columbia, 1959
ANATOMY OF A MURDER Columbia, 1959
EXODUS United Artists, 1960
ADVISE AND CONSENT Columbia, 1962
THE CARDINAL ★ Columbia, 1963
IN HARM'S WAY Paramount, 1964
BUNNY LAKE IS MISSING Columbia, 1965, British
HURRY SUNDOWN Paramount, 1967
SKIDOO Paramount, 1968
TELL ME THAT YOU LOVE ME, JUNIE MOON Paramount, 1970
SUCH GOOD FRIENDS Paramount, 1971
ROSEBUD United Artists, 1975
THE HUMAN FACTOR United Artists, 1979, British

EMERIC PRESSBURGER
b. December 5, 1902 - Miskolc, Hungary
d. 1988

ONE OF OUR AIRCRAFT IS MISSING co-director with Michael Powell, United Artists, 1942, British
THE VOLUNTEER co-director with Michael Powell, Anglo, 1943, British
COLONEL BLIMP *THE LIFE AND DEATH OF COLONEL BLIMP* co-director with Michael Powell, GFO, 1943, British
A CANTERBURY TALE co-director with Michael Powell, Eagle-Lion, 1944, British
I KNOW WHERE I'M GOING co-director with Michael Powell, Universal, 1945, British
STAIRWAY TO HEAVEN *A MATTER OF LIFE AND DEATH* co-director with Michael Powell, Universal, 1946, British
BLACK NARCISSUS co-director with Michael Powell, Universal, 1947, British
THE RED SHOES co-director with Michael Powell, Eagle-Lion, 1948, British
THE SMALL BACK ROOM *HOUR OF GLORY* co-director with Michael Powell, Snader Productions, 1948, British
THE WILD HEART *GONE TO EARTH* co-director with Michael Powell, RKO Radio, 1950, British
THE ELUSIVE PIMPERNEL co-director with Michael Powell, British Lion, 1950, British
THE TALES OF HOFFMANN co-director with Michael Powell, Lopert, 1951, British
TWICE UPON A TIME 1953, British
OH ROSALINDA! co-director with Michael Powell, Associated British Picture Corporation, 1955, British
PURSUIT OF THE GRAF SPEE *THE BATTLE OF THE RIVER PLATE* co-director with Michael Powell, Rank, 1956, British
NIGHT AMBUSH *ILL MET BY MOONLIGHT* co-director with Michael Powell, Rank, 1957, British

VSEVOLOD PUDOVKIN
b. February 6, 1893 - Penza, Russia
d. 1953

HUNGER - HUNGER - HUNGER 1921, Soviet
CHESS FEVER co-director, 1925, Soviet
MOTHER Amkino, 1926, Soviet
MECHANICS OF THE BRAIN (FD) 1926, Soviet
THE END OF ST. PETERSBURG 1927, Soviet
STORM OVER ASIA *THE HEIR TO GENGHIS KHAN* 1928, Soviet
A SIMPLE CASE *LIFE IS BEAUTIFUL* 1932, Soviet
DESERTER 1933, Soviet
VICTORY *MOTHERS AND SONS* co-director with Mikhail Doller, 1938, Soviet
MININ AND POZHARSKY co-director with Mikhail Doller, 1939, Soviet
TWENTY YEARS OF CINEMA (FD) co-director with Esther Shub, 1940, Soviet
SUVOROV co-director with Mikhail Doller, 1941, Soviet
FEAST AT ZHIRMUNKA (FD) co-director, 1941, Soviet
THE MURDERERS ARE COMING co-director, 1942, Soviet
IN THE NAME OF THE FATHERLAND co-director with Dimitri Vasiliev, 1943, Soviet
ADMIRAL NAKHIMOV 1946, Soviet
THREE ENCOUNTERS co-director with Sergei Yutkevich & Alexander Ptushko, 1948, Soviet
ZHUKOVSKY co-director with Dimitri Vasiliev, 1951, Soviet
VASILI'S RETURN 1953, Soviet

IVAN PYRIEV

b. 1901 - Kamen, Russia
d. 1968

STRANGE WOMAN   1929, Soviet
THE FUNCTIONARY   1930, Soviet
CONVEYOR OF DEATH   1933, Soviet
THE PARTY CARD   1936, Soviet
THE RICH BRIDE   1938, Soviet
TRACTOR DRIVERS   1939, Soviet
THE LOVED ONE   1940, Soviet
SWINEHERD AND SHEPHERD   1941, Soviet
SECRETARY OF THE DISTRICT COMMITTEE
    1942, Soviet
AT 6 P.M. AFTER THE WAR   1944, Soviet
TALES OF THE SIBERIAN LAND   1947, Soviet
COSSACKS OF THE KUBAN   1949, Soviet
WE ARE ALL FOR PEACE (FD)   co-director with Joris
    Ivens, 1952, Soviet-East German
TEST OF FIDELITY   1954, Soviet
THE IDIOT   Artkino, 1958, Soviet
WHITE NIGHTS   1960, Soviet
OUR MUTUAL FRIEND   1961, Soviet
LIGHT OF A DISTANT STAR   1965, Soviet
THE BROTHERS KARAMAZOV   1968, Soviet

Q

RICHARD QUINE

b. November 12, 1920 - Detroit, Michigan
d. 1989

LEATHER GLOVES   co-director with William Asher,
    Columbia, 1948
SUNNY SIDE OF THE STREET   Columbia, 1951
PURPLE HEART DIARY   Columbia, 1951
SOUND OFF   Columbia, 1952
RAINBOW 'ROUND MY SHOULDER   Columbia, 1952
ALL ASHORE   Columbia, 1953
SIREN OF BAGDAD   Columbia, 1953
CRUISIN' DOWN THE RIVER   Columbia, 1953
DRIVE A CROOKED ROAD   Columbia, 1954
PUSHOVER   Columbia, 1954
SO THIS IS PARIS   Universal, 1955
MY SISTER EILEEN   Universal, 1955
THE SOLID GOLD CADILLAC   Columbia, 1956
FULL OF LIFE   1957
OPERATION MAD BALL   Columbia, 1957
BELL, BOOK AND CANDLE   Columbia, 1958
IT HAPPENED TO JANE   Columbia, 1959
STRANGERS WHEN WE MEET   Columbia, 1960
THE WORLD OF SUZIE WONG   Paramount, 1960
THE NOTORIOUS LANDLADY   Columbia, 1962
PARIS WHEN IT SIZZLES   Paramount, 1964
SEX AND THE SINGLE GIRL   Warner Bros., 1965
HOW TO MURDER YOUR WIFE   United Artists, 1965
SYNANON   Columbia, 1965
OH DAD, POOR DAD, MOMMA'S HUNG YOU IN THE
    CLOSET AND I'M FEELING SO SAD   Paramount, 1967
HOTEL   Warner Bros., 1967
A TALENT FOR LOVING   1969
THE MOONSHINE WAR   MGM, 1970
"W"   Cinerama Releasing Corporation, 1974, British
THE SPECIALISTS (TF)   Mark VII Ltd./Universal TV, 1975
THE PRISONER OF ZENDA   Universal, 1979

R

GREGORY RATOFF

b. April 20, 1897 - St. Petersburg, Russia
d. 1960

SINS OF MAN   co-director with Otto Brower, 20th Century-
Fox, 1936
THE LANCER SPY   20th Century-Fox, 1937
WIFE, HUSBAND AND FRIEND   20th Century-Fox, 1939
ROSE OF WASHINGTON SQUARE   20thCentury-Fox,
1939
HOTEL FOR WOMEN   20th Century-Fox, 1939
INTERMEZZO   United Artists, 1939
DAYTIME WIFE   20th Century-Fox, 1939
BARRICADE   20th Century-Fox, 1939
I WAS AN ADVENTURESS   20th Century-Fox, 1940
PUBLIC DEB NO. 1   20th Century-Fox, 1940
ADAM HAD FOUR SONS   Columbia, 1941
THE MEN IN HER LIFE   Columbia, 1941
THE CORSICAN BROTHERS   United Artists, 1941
TWO YANKS IN TRINIDAD   Columbia, 1942
FOOTLIGHT SERENADE   20th Century-Fox, 1942
SOMETHING TO SHOUT ABOUT   Columbia, 1943
THE HEAT'S ON   Columbia, 1943
SONG OF RUSSIA   MGM, 1943
IRISH EYES ARE SMILING   20th Century-Fox, 1944
WHERE DO WE GO FROM HERE?   20th Century-Fox,
    1945
PARIS UNDERGROUND   United Artists, 1945
DO YOU LOVE ME?   20th Century-Fox, 1946
CARNIVAL IN COSTA RICA   20th Century-Fox, 1947
MOSS ROSE   20th Century-Fox, 1947
BLACK MAGIC   United Artists, 1949
IF THIS BE SIN   *THAT DANGEROUS AGE*   United Artists,
    1950, British
OPERATION X   *MY DAUGHTER JOY*   Columbia, 1950
TAXI   20th Century-Fox, 1953
ABDULLAH'S HAREM   20th Century-Fox, 1956,
    Egyptian
OSCAR WILDE   Films Around the World, 1960, British

MAN RAY
(Emmanuel Rudnitsky)

b. August 17, 1890 - Philadelphia, Pennsylvania
d. 1976

LE RETOUR A LA RAISON   1923, French
EMAK BAKIA   1927, French
L'ETOILE DE MER   1928, French
LES MYSTERES DU CHATEAU DU DE   1929, French
DREAMS THAT MONEY CAN BUY   1946

NICHOLAS RAY
(Raymond Nicholas Kienzle)

b. August 7, 1911 - La Crosse, Wisconsin
d. 1979

THEY LIVE BY NIGHT   *THE TWISTED ROAD*
    RKO Radio, 1949
A WOMAN'S SECRET   RKO Radio, 1949

KNOCK ON ANY DOOR   Columbia, 1949
IN A LONELY PLACE   Columbia, 1950
BORN TO BE BAD   RKO Radio, 1950
FLYING LEATHERNECKS   RKO Radio, 1951
ON DANGEROUS GROUND   RKO Radio, 1952
THE LUSTY MEN   RKO Radio, 1952
JOHNNY GUITAR   Republic, 1954
RUN FOR COVER   Paramount, 1955
REBEL WITHOUT A CAUSE   Warner Bros., 1955
HOT BLOOD   Columbia, 1956
BIGGER THAN LIFE   20th Century-Fox, 1956
THE TRUE STORY OF JESSE JAMES   20th Century-Fox,
   1957
BITTER VICTORY   Columbia, 1957, U.S.-French
WIND ACROSS THE EVERGLADES   Warner Bros., 1958
PARTY GIRL   MGM, 1958
THE SAVAGE INNOCENTS   Paramount, 1960,
   Italian-French-British-U.S.
KING OF KINGS   MGM, 1961
55 DAYS AT PEKING   Allied Artists, 1963
YOU CAN'T GO HOME AGAIN   1976

SIR CAROL REED
b. December 30, 1906 - London, England
d. 1976

IT HAPPENED IN PARIS   co-director with Robert Wyler,
   Associated British Film Distributors, 1935, British
MIDSHIPMAN EASY   MEN OF THE SEA   Associated
   British Film Distributors, 1935, British
LABURNUM GROVE   Associated British Film Distributors,
   1936, British
TALK OF THE DEVIL   United Artists, 1937, British
WHO'S YOUR LADY FRIEND?   Associated British Film
   Distributors, 1937, British
THREE ON A WEEK-END   BANK HOLIDAY
   Gaumont-British, 1938, British
PENNY PARADISE   Associated British Film Distributors,
   1938, British
CLIMBING HIGH   MGM, 1939, British
A GIRL MUST LIVE   20th Century-Fox, 1939, British
THE STARS LOOK DOWN   MGM, 1939, British
NIGHT TRAIN   NIGHT TRAIN TO MUNICH   MGM,
   1940, British
THE GIRL IN THE NEWS   MGM, 1940, British
THE REMARKABLE MR. KIPPS   KIPPS   20th Century-
   Fox, 1941, British
THE YOUNG MR. PITT   20th Century-Fox, 1942, British
THE NEW LOT   Army Kinematograph Unit, 1943, British
THE WAY AHEAD   THE IMMORTAL BATTALION
   20th Century-Fox, 1944, British
THE TRUE GLORY (FD)   co-director with Garson Kanin,
   Columbia, 1945, British
ODD MAN OUT   General Film Distributors, 1947, British
THE FALLEN IDOL ★   Selznick Releasing, 1948, British
THE THIRD MAN ★   Selznick Releasing, 1949, British
OUTCAST OF THE ISLANDS   United Artists, 1951, British
THE MAN BETWEEN   United Artists, 1953, British
A KID FOR TWO FARTHINGS   Lopert, 1955, British
TRAPEZE   United Artists, 1956
THE KEY   Columbia, 1958, British
OUR MAN IN HAVANA   Columbia, 1959, British
THE RUNNING MAN   Columbia, 1963, British
THE AGONY AND THE ECSTASY   20th Century-Fox,
   1965
OLIVER! ★★   Columbia, 1968, British
FLAP   THE LAST WARRIOR   Warner Bros., 1970
FOLLOW ME!   Rank Film Distributors, 1971
THE PUBLIC EYE   Universal, 1972

MAX REINHARDT
(Maximilian Goldman)
b. September 8, 1873 - Baden, Austria
d. 1943

SUMURUN   1908, German
DAS MIRAKEL   1912, German
INSEL DER SELIGEN   1913, German
VENIZIANISCHE NACHT   1914, German
A MIDSUMMER NIGHT'S DREAM   co-director with
   William Dieterle, Warner Bros., 1935

IRVING REIS
b. May 7, 1906 - New York, New York
d. 1953

ONE CROWDED NIGHT   RKO Radio, 1940
I'M STILL ALIVE   RKO Radio, 1940
FOOTLIGHT FEVER   RKO Radio, 1941
THE GAY FALCON   RKO Radio, 1941
WEEKEND FOR THREE   RKO Radio, 1941
A DATE WITH THE FALCON   RKO Radio, 1941
THE FALCON TAKES OVER   RKO Radio, 1942
THE BIG STREET   RKO Radio, 1942
CRACK-UP   20th Century-Fox, 1946
THE BACHELOR AND THE BOBBY-SOXER   RKO Radio,
   1947
ALL MY SONS   Universal, 1948
ENCHANTMENT   RKO Radio, 1948
ROSEANNA McCOY   RKO Radio, 1949
DANCING IN THE DARK   20th Century-Fox, 1949
THREE HUSBANDS   United Artists, 1950
OF MEN AND MUSIC (FD)   co-director with Alex Hammid,
   20th Century-Fox, 1951
NEW MEXICO   United Artists, 1951
THE FOUR POSTER   Columbia, 1953

JEAN RENOIR
b. September 15, 1894 - Paris, France
d. 1979

LA FILLE DE L'EAU   1925, French
NANA   1926, French
CHARLESTON   1927, French
MARQUITTA   1927, French
LE PETITE MARCHANDE D'ALLUMETTES
   co-director with Jean Tedesco, 1928, French
TIRE-AU-FLANC   1929, French
LE TOURNOI   1928, French
LE BLED   1929, French
ON PURGE BEBE   1931, French
LA CHIENNE   1931, French
LA NUIT DE CAREFOUR   1932, French
BOUDOU SAVED FROM DROWNING   Pathé
   Contemporary, 1932, French
CHOTARD ET COMPAGNIE   1933, French
MADAME BOVARY   1934, French
TONI   1935, French
THE CRIME OF MONSIEUR LANGE   Brandon, 1936,
   French
LA VIE EST A NOUS   1936, French
A DAY IN THE COU NTRY   UNE PARTIE DE CAMPAGNE
   1936, French
LES BAS-FONDS   1936, French
GRAND ILLUSION   World Pictures, 1937, French
LA MARSEILLAISE   1938, French
LA BETE HUMAINE   1938, French
THE RULES OF THE GAME   Janus, 1983, French

LA TOSCA   co-director, 1940, Italian-French
SWAMP WATER   20th Century-Fox, 1941
THIS LAND IS MINE   RKO Radio, 1943
SALUTE TO FRANCE (FD)   co-director, 1944
THE SOUTHERNER ★   United Artists, 1945
THE DIARY OF A CHAMBERMAID   United Artists, 1946
THE WOMAN ON THE BEACH   RKO Radio, 1947
THE RIVER   United Artists, 1951, U.S.-Indian
THE GOLDEN COACH   Italian Films Export, 1952,
   Italian-French
FRENCH-CANCAN   ONLY THE FRENCH CAN   United
   Motion Picture Organization, 1954, French
PARIS DOES STRANGE THINGS   ELENA ET LES
   HOMMES   Warner Bros., 1957, French
PICNIC ON THE GRASS   Kingsley-Union, 1959, French
LE TESTAMENT DU DR. CORDELIER (TF)   1961, French
THE ELUSIVE CORPORAL   LE CAPORAL EPINGLE
   Pathé Contemporary, 1962, French
LA DIRECTION D'ACTEUR PAR JEAN RENOIR   1968,
   French
THE LITTLE THEATRE OF JEAN RENOIR (TF)   Phoenix
   Films, 1969, French-Italian-West German

JOHN S. ROBERTSON
b. June 14, 1878 - London, Ontario, Canada
d. 1964

BABY MINE   Goldwyn, 1917
INTRIGUE   Vitagraph, 1917
THE BOTTOM OF THE WELL   Vitagraph, 1917
THE MONEY MILL   Vitagraph, 1917
THE MENACE   Vitagraph, 1918
GIRL OF TODAY   Vitagraph, 1918
THE MAKE-BELIEVE WIFE   Paramount, 1918
HERE COMES THE BRIDE   Paramount, 1919
COME OUT OF THE KITCHEN   Paramount, 1919
THE MISLEADING WIDOW   Paramount, 1919
LITTLE MISS HOOVER   Paramount, 1919
THE TEST OF HONOR   Paramount, 1919
LET'S ELOPE   Paramount, 1919
ERSTWHILE SUSAN   Realart, 1919
SADIE LOVE   Paramount, 1919
THE BETTER HALF   Select, 1919
DR. JEKYLL AND MR. HYDE   Paramount, 1920
AWAY GOES PRUDENCE   Paramount, 1920
A DARK LANTERN   Realart, 1920
39 EAST   Realart, 1920
THE MAGIC CUP   Realart, 1921
SENTIMENTAL TOMMY   Paramount, 1921
FOOTLIGHTS   Paramount, 1921
LOVE'S BOOMERANG   Paramount, 1922
THE SPANISH JADE   Paramount, 1922
TESS OF THE STORM COUNTRY   United Artists, 1922
THE BRIGHT SHAWL   Associated First National, 1923
THE FIGHTING BLADE   Assoicated First National, 1923
TWENTY-ONE   Associated First National, 1923
THE ENCHANTED COTTAGE   First National, 1924
CLASSMATES   First National, 1924
NEW TOYS   First National, 1925
SOUL-FIRE   First National, 1925
SHORE LEAVE   First National, 1925
ANNIE LAURIE   First National, 1927
CAPTAIN SALVATION   MGM, 1927
THE ROAD TO ROMANCE   MGM, 1927
THE SINGLE STANDARD   MGM, 1929
SHANGHAI LADY   Universal, 1929
NIGHT RIDE   Universal, 1930
CAPTAIN OF THE GUARD   co-director with Paul Fejos,
   1930, Universal

MADONNA OF THE STREETS   Columbia, 1930
ONE MAN'S JOURNEY   RKO, 1933
THE CRIME DOCTOR   RKO, 1934
HIS GREATEST GAMBLE   RKO, 1934
WEDNESDAY'S CHILD   RKO, 1934
CAPTAIN HURRICANE   RKO, 1935
GRAND OLD GIRL   RKO, 1935
OUR LITTLE GIRL   Fox, 1935

MARK ROBSON
b. December 4, 1913 - Montreal, Canada
d. 1978

THE SEVENTH VICTIM   RKO Radio, 1943
THE GHOST SHIP   RKO Radio, 1943
YOUTH RUNS WILD   RKO Radio, 1944
ISLE OF THE DEAD   RKO Radio, 1945
BEDLAM   RKO Radio, 1946
CHAMPION   United Artists, 1949
HOME OF THE BRAVE   United Artists, 1949
ROUGHSHOD   RKO Radio, 1949
MY FOOLISH HEART   RKO Radio, 1949
EDGE OF DOOM   RKO Radio, 1950
BRIGHT VICTORY   Universal, 1951
I WANT YOU   RKO Radio, 1952
RETURN TO PARADISE   United Artists, 1953
HELL BELOW ZERO   MGM, 1954, British
PHFFFT   Columbia, 1954
THE BRIDGES AT TOKO-RI   Paramount, 1955
A PRIZE OF GOLD   Columbia, 1954
TRIAL   MGM, 1955
THE HARDER THEY FALL   Columbia, 1956
THE LITTLE HUT   MGM, 1957
PEYTON PLACE ★   20th Century-Fox, 1957
THE INN OF THE SIXTH HAPPINESS ★   20th
   Century-Fox, 1958, British
FROM THE TERRACE   20th Century-Fox, 1960
LISA   THE INSPECTOR   20th Century-Fox, 1962,
   British-U.S.
NINE HOURS TO RAMA   20th Century-Fox, 1963,
   British-U.S.
THE PRIZE   MGM, 1963
VON RYAN'S EXPRESS   20th Century-Fox, 1965
LOST COMMAND   Columbia, 1966
VALLEY OF THE DOLLS   20th Century-Fox, 1967
DADDY'S GONE A-HUNTING   National General, 1969
HAPPY BIRTHDAY, WANDA JUNE   Columbia, 1971
LIMBO   Universal, 1972
EARTHQUAKE   Universal, 1974
AVALANCHE EXPRESS   20th Century-Fox, 1979

GLAUBER ROCHA
b. 1938 - Victoria da Conquista, Bahia, Brazil
d. 1981

BARRAVENTO   1961, Brazilian
BLACK GOD - WHITE DEVIL   DEUS E O DIABO NA
   TERRA DEL SOL   1964, Brazilian
TERRA EM TRANSE   1967, Brazilian
ANTONIO DAS MORTES   O DRAGAO DA MALADE
   CONTRA O SANTO GUERREIRO   1969, Brazilian
THE LION HAS SEVEN HEADS   1970, African
CABEZAS CORTADAS   1970, African
CLARO   1975, Italian

ROBERTO ROSSELLINI
b. May 8, 1906 - Rome, Italy
d. 1977

LA NAVE BIANCA   1941, Italian
UNA PILOTA RITORNA   1942, Italian
I TRE AGUILLOTTI   co-director with Mario Mattoli, 1942, Italian
L'UOMO DELLA CROCE   1943, Italian
DESIDERIO   co-director with Marcello Pagliero, 1943, Italian
OPEN CITY   *ROMA, CITTA APERTA*   Mayer-Burstyn, 1945, Italian
PAISAN   Mayer-Burstyn, 1946, Italian
GERMANY YEAR ZERO   Superfilm, 1947, West German-French
L'AMORE   1948, Italian
LA MACCHINA AMMAZZACATTIVI   1948, Italian
STROMBOLI   RKO Radio, 1949, Italian
FRANCESCO - GIULLARE DI DIO   *FLOWERS OF ST. FRANCIS*   1950, Italian
THE SEVEN DEADLY SINS   co-director, Arian Pictures, 1952, French-Italian
THE GREATEST LOVE   *EUROPA '51*   Italian Films Export, 1952, Italian
DOV'E LA LIBERTA?   1953, Italian
STRANGERS   *VIAGGIO IN ITALIA*   Fine Arts, 1954, Italian
SIAMO DONNE   co-director, 1953, Italian
AMORI DI MEZZO SECOLO   co-director, 1954, Italian
GIOVANNA D'ARCO AL ROGO   1954, Italian
FEAR   *LA PAURA*   Astor, 1955, West German-Italian
LE PSYCHODRAME   1957, Italian
L'INDIA VISITA DA ROSSELLINI (TD)   1958, Italian
IL GENERALE DELLA ROVERE   Continental, 1959, Italian-French
ERA NOTTE A ROMA   1960, Italian
VIVA L'ITALIA   1960, Italian
VANINA VANINI   *THE BETRAYER*   1961, Italian
TORINO NEI CENTI'ANNI (TD)   1961, Italian T.V.
ANIMA NERA   1962, Italian
ROGOPAG   co-director, 1962, Italian
L'ETA DEL FERRO (TF)   1964, Italian T.V.
THE RISE OF LOUIS XIV   Brandon, 1966, French, originally made for television
IDEA DI UN'ISOLA (TD)   1967
GLI ATTI DEGLI APOSTOLI (TF)   1968, Italian
SOCRATES   New Yorker, 1969, Italian, originally made for television
LA LOTTA DELL'VORRO PER LE SOPRA VIVENZ (TF)   1970, Italian T.V.
AGOSTINO DI IPPONA   1972, Italian
PASCAL (TF)   1972, Italian T.V.
L'AMORA VANTI ANNI   1972, Italian-French
L'ETA DI COSIMO (TF)   1973, Italian T.V.
THE AGE OF THE MEDICIS (TF)   1973, Italian T.V.
CARTESIO (TF)   1974, Italian T.V.
ANNI CALDI (TF)   1974, Italian
BLAISE PASCAL (TF)   1975, Italian
ANNO UNO   1975, Italian
THE MESSIAH   1978, Italian

ROBERT ROSSEN
(Robert Rosen)
b. March 16, 1908 - New York, New York
d. 1966

JOHNNY O'CLOCK   Columbia, 1947
BODY AND SOUL   United Artists, 1947

ALL THE KING'S MEN ★   Columbia, 1949
THE BRAVE BULLS   Columbia, 1951
MAMBO   Paramount, 1954, U.S.-Italian
ALEXANDER THE GREAT   United Artists, 1956
ISLAND IN THE SUN   20th Century-Fox, 1957
THEY CAME TO CORDURA   Columbia, 1959
THE HUSTLER ★   20th Century-Fox, 1961
LILITH   Columbia, 1964

RUSSELL ROUSE
b. April 3, 1915 - New York, New York
d. 1987

THE WELL   co-director with Leo Popkins, United Artists, 1951
THE THIEF   United Artists, 1952
WICKED WOMAN   United Artists, 1954
NEW YORK CONFIDENTIAL   Warner Bros., 1955
THE FASTEST GUN ALIVE   MGM, 1956
HOUSE OF NUMBERS   Columbia, 1957
THUNDER IN THE SUN   Paramount, 1959
A HOUSE IS NOT A HOME   Embassy, 1964
THE OSCAR   Embassy, 1966
THE CAPER OF THE GOLDEN BULLS   Embassy, 1967

WESLEY RUGGLES
b. June 11, 1889 - Los Angeles, California
d. 1972

FOR FRANCE   Vitagraph, 1917
THE BLIND ADVENTURE   Vitagraph, 1918
THE WINCHESTER WOMAN   Vitagraph, 1919
PICCADILLY JIM   Select, 1920
SOONER OR LATER   1920
THE DESPERATE HERO   Selznick, 1920
THE LEOPARD WOMAN   Associated Producers, 1920
LOVE   Associated Producers, 1920
THE GREATER CLAIM   Metro, 1921
UNCHARTED SEAS   Metro, 1921
OVER THE WIRE   Metro, 1921
WILD HONEY   Universal, 1922
IF I WERE QUEEN   Film Booking Offices, 1922
SLIPPERY McGEE   First National, 1922
MR. BILLINGS SPENDS HIS DIME   Paramount, 1923
THE REMITTANCE WOMAN   Film Booking Offices, 1923
THE HEART RAIDER   Paramount, 1923
THE AGE OF INNOCENCE   Warner Bros., 1924
THE PLASTIC AGE   B.P. Schulberg, 1925
BROADWAY LADY   Film Booking Offices, 1925
THE KICK-OFF   Excellent, 1926
A MAN OF QUALITY   Excellent, 1926
BEWARE OF WIDOWS   Universal, 1927
SILK STOCKINGS   Universal, 1927
THE FOURFLUSHER   Universal, 1928
FINDERS KEEPERS   Universal, 1928
STREET GIRL   RKO, 1929
SCANDAL   Universal, 1929
CONDEMNED   United Artists, 1929
GIRL OVERBOARD   Universal, 1929
HONEY   Paramount, 1930
THE SEA BAT   MGM, 1930
CIMARRON ★   RKO Radio, 1931
ARE THESE OUR CHILDREN?   RKO, 1931
ROAR OF THE DRAGON   RKO, 1932
NO MAN OF HER OWN   Parmaount, 1932
THE MONKEY'S PAW   RKO, 1933
COLLEGE HUMOR   Paramount, 1933

I'M NO ANGEL   Paramount, 1933
BOLERO   Paramount, 1934
SHOOT THE WORKS   Paramount, 1934
THE GILDED LILY   Paramount, 1935
ACCENT ON YOUTH   Paramount, 1935
THE BRIDE COMES HOME   Paramount, 1935
VALIANT IS THE WORD FOR CARRIE
   Paramount, 1936
I MET HIM IN PARIS   Paramount, 1937
TRUE CONFESSION   Paramount, 1937
SING YOU SINNERS   Paramount, 1938
INVITATION TO HAPPINESS   Paramount, 1939
TOO MANY HUSBANDS   Columbia, 1940
ARIZONA   Columbia, 1940
YOU BELONG TO ME   Columbia, 1941
SOMEWHERE I'LL FIND YOU   MGM, 1942
SLIGHTLY DANGEROUS   MGM, 1943
SEE HERE, PRIVATE HARGROVE   MGM, 1944
LONDON TOWN   *MY HEART GOES CRAZY*
   Continental, 1946, British

S

BORIS SAGAL
b. 1923 - Dnepropettrovsk, Soviet Union
d. 1981

THE CRIMEBUSTER   MGM, 1961
DIME WITH A HALO   MGM, 1963
TWILIGHT OF HONOR   MGM, 1963
GIRL HAPPY   MGM, 1965
MADE IN PARIS   MGM, 1966
THE HELICOPTER SPIES   MGM, 1968
THE 1,000 PLANE RAID   United Artists, 1969
U.M.C.   *OPERATION HEARTBEAT*   (TF)
   MGM TV, 1969
DESTINY OF A SPY (TF)   Universal TV, 1969
NIGHT GALLERY (TF)   co-director with Barry Shear &
   Steven Spielberg, Universal TV, 1969
THE D.A.: MURDER ONE (TF)   Mark VII Ltd./
   Universal TV/Jack Webb Productions, 1969
MOSQUITO SQUADRON   United Artists, 1970
THE MOVIE MURDERER (TF)   Universal TV, 1970
HAUSER'S MEMORY (TF)   Universal TV, 1970
THE OMEGA MAN   Warner Bros., 1971
THE HARNESS (TF)   Universal TV, 1971
THE FAILING OF RAYMOND (TF)   Universal TV, 1971
HITCHED (TF)   Universal TV, 1973
DELIVER US FROM EVIL (TF)   Playboy
   Productions, 1973
INDICT AND CONVICT (TF)   Universal TV, 1974
A CASE OF RAPE (TF) ☆   Universal TV, 1974
THE GREATEST GIFT (TF)   Universal TV, 1974
THE DREAM MAKERS (TF)   MGM-TV, 1975
THE RUNAWAY BARGE (TF)   Lorimar Productions, 1975
MAN ON THE OUTSIDE (TF)   Universal TV, 1975
OREGON TRAIL (TF)   Universal TV, 1976
RICH MAN, POOR MAN (MS) ☆   co-director with David
   Greene, Universal TV, 1976
MALLORY: CIRCUMSTANTIAL EVIDENCE (TF)
   Universal TV/Crescendo Productions/R.B.
   Productions, 1976

SHERLOCK HOLMES IN NEW YORK (TF)   20th
   Century-Fox TV, 1976
ARTHUR HAILEY'S "THE MONKEYCHANGERS"
   THE MONKEYCHANGERS (MS)   Ross Hunter
   Productions/Paramount TV, 1976
ANGELA   1978, Canadian
THE AWAKENING LAND (MS)   Bensen-Kuhn-Sagal
   Productions/Warner Bros. TV, 1978
IKE (MS)   co-director with Melville Shavelson, ABC
   Circle Films, 1979
THE DIARY OF ANNE FRANK (TF)   Katz-Gallin/
   Half-Pint Productions/20th Century-Fox TV, 1980
WHEN THE CIRCUS CAME TO TOWN (TF)   Entheos
   Unlimited Productions/Meteor Films, 1981
MASADA (MS) ☆   Arnon Milchan Productions/
   Universal TV, 1981
DIAL M FOR MURDER (TF)   Freyda Rothstein
   Productions/Time Life TV, 1981

LUCIANO SALCE
b. September 22, 1922 - Italy
d. 1989

LE PILLOLE D'ERCOLE   Maxima Film/Dino De Laurentiis
   Cinematografica, 1960, Italian
IL FEDERALE   Dino De Laurentiis Cinematografica, 1961,
   Italian
CRAZY DESIRE   LA VOGLIA MATTA   Embassy, 1962,
   Italian
LA CUCCAGNA   CIRAC/Agliani Cinematografica, 1962,
   Italian
THE HOURS OF LOVE   Cinema 5, 1963, Italian
THE LITTLE NUNS   Embassy, 1963, Italian
HIGH INFIDELITY   co-director with Mario Monicelli, Franco
   Rossi & Elio Petri, Magna, 1964, Italian-French
KISS THE OTHER SHEIK   OGGI, DOMANI E DOPODO-
   MANI   co-director with Marco Ferreri & Eduardo de
   Filippo, MGM, 1965, Italian-French
SLALOM   Fair Film/Cocinor/Copro Film, 1965, Italian-
   French-British
EL GRECO   20th Century-Fox, 1966, Italian-French
THE QUEENS   LE FATE   co-director with Mario Monicelli,
   Mauro Bolognini, & Antonio Pietrangeli, Royal Films
   International, 1966, Italian-French
TI HO SPOSATO PER ALLEGRIA   Fair Film, 1967, Italian
LA PECORA NERA   Fair Film, 1969, Italian
COLPO DI STATO   Vides, 1969, Italian
IL PROF. DR. GUIDO TERSILLI, PRIMARIO DELLA CLINICA
   VILLA CELESTE, CONVENZIONATA CON LE MUTUE
   San Marco, 1969, Italian
BASTA GUARDARLA   Fair Film, 1971, Italian
IL PROVINCIALE   Fair Film, 1971, Italian
IO E LUI   Dino De Laurentiis Cinematografica, 1973, Italian
FANTOZZI   Cineriz, 1975, Italian
IL SECONDO TRAGICO FANTOZZI   Cineriz, 1976, Italian
LA PRESIDENTESSA   Gold Film, 1976, Italian
L'ANATRA ALL'ARANCIA   Cineriz, 1976, Italian
IL...BELPAESE   77 Cinematografica, 1977, Italian
DOVE VAI IN VACANZA?   co-director with Mauro Bolognini
   & Alberto Sordi, Cineriz, 1978, Italian
PROFESSOR KRANZ TEDESCO DI GERMANIA   Gold
   Film, 1979, Italian- Brazilian
RIAVANTI...MARSCH!   PAC, 1980, Italian
RAG. ARTURO DE FANTI BANCARIO PRECARIO   PAC,
   1980, Italian
THE INNOCENTS ABROAD (TF)   Nebraska ETV Network/
   The Great Amwell Company/WNET-13, 1983
VEDIAMOCI CHIARO   Adige Film 76, 1984, Italian
QUELLI DEL CASCO   Filmauro, 1988, Italian

MARK SANDRICH

b. August 26, 1900 - New York, New York
d. 1945

RUNAWAY GIRLS   Columbia, 1928
THE TALK OF HOLLYWOOD   Sono Art-World Wide, 1930
MELODY CRUISE   RKO, 1933
AGGIE APPLEBY - MAKER OF MEN   RKO, 1933
HIPS HIPS HOORAY   RKO, 1934
COCKEYED CAVALIERS   RKO, 1934
THE GAY DIVORCEE   RKO Radio, 1934
TOP HAT   RKO Radio, 1935
FOLLOW THE FLEET   RKO Radio, 1936
A WOMAN REBELS   RKO Radio, 1936
SHALL WE DANCE?   RKO Radio, 1937
CAREFREE   RKO Radio, 1938
MAN ABOUT TOWN   Paramount, 1939
BUCK BENNY RIDES AGAIN   Paramount, 1940
LOVE THY NEIGHBOR   Paramount, 1940
SKYLARK   Paramount, 1941
HOLIDAY INN   Paramount, 1941
SO PROUDLY WE HAIL!   Paramount, 1943
HERE COME THE WAVES   Paramount, 1944
I LOVE A SOLDIER   Paramount, 1944

ALFRED SANTELL

b. September 14, 1895 - San Francisco, California
d. 1981

MY VALET   1915
OUT OF THE BAG   1917
HOME JAMES   1918
VAMPING THE VAMP   1918
IT MIGHT HAPPEN TO YOU   1920
WILDCAT JORDAN   Phil Goldstone, 1922
LIGHTS OUT   Film Booking Offices, 1923
FOOLS IN THE DARK   FBO, 1924
EMPTY HEARTS   Banner, 1924
THE MAN WHO PLAYED SQUARE   Fox, 1924
THE MARRIAGE WHIRL   First National, 1925
PARISIAN NIGHTS   FBO, 1925
CLASSIFIED   First National, 1925
BLUEBEARD'S SEVEN WIVES   First National, 1926
THE DANCER OF PARIS   First National, 1926
SWEET DADDIES   First National, 1926
SUBWAY SADIE   First National, 1926
JUST ANOTHER BLONDE   First National, 1926
ORCHIDS AND ERMINE   First National, 1927
THE PATENT LEATHER KID   First National, 1927
THE GORILLA   First National, 1927
THE LITTLE SHEPHERD OF KINGDOM COME
     First National, 1928
WHEEL OF CHANCE   First National, 1928
SHOW GIRL   First National, 1928
THIS IS HEAVEN   United Artists, 1929
TWIN BEDS   First National, 1929
ROMANCE OF THE RIO GRANDE   Fox, 1929
THE ARIZONA KID   Fox, 1930
THE SEA WOLF   Fox, 1930
BODY AND SOUL   Fox, 1931
DADDY LONG LEGS   Fox, 1931
SOB SISTER   Fox, 1931
POLLY OF THE CIRCUS   Fox, 1932
REBECCA OF SUNNYBROOK FARM   Fox, 1932
TESS OF THE STORM COUNTRY   Fox, 1932
BONDAGE   Fox, 1933
THE RIGHT TO ROMANCE   RKO, 1933
THE LIFE OF VERGIE WINTERS   RKO, 1934
PEOPLE WILL TALK   Paramount, 1935

A FEATHER IN HER HAT   Columbia, 1935
WINTERSET   RKO, 1936
INTERNES CAN'T TAKE MONEY   Paramount, 1937
BREAKFAST FOR TWO   RKO Radio, 1937
COCONUT GROVE   Paramount, 1938
HAVING A WONDERFUL TIME   RKO Radio, 1938
THE ARKANSAS TRAVELER   Paramount, 1938
OUR LEADING CITIZEN   Paramount, 1939
ALOMA OF THE SOUTH SEAS   Paramount, 1941
BEYOND THE BLUE HORIZON   Paramount, 1942
JACK LONDON   United Artists, 1943
THE HAIRY APE   United Artists, 1944
MEXICANA   Republic, 1945
THAT BRENNAN GIRL   Republic, 1946

VICTOR SAVILLE

b. September 25 - Birmingham, England
d. 1979

CONQUEST OF OIL (FD)   1921, British
THE ARCADIANS   Gaumont-British, 1927, British
A WOMAN IN PAWN   co-director with Edwin Greenwood,
     1927, British
THE GLAD EYE   co-director with Maurice Elvey,
     Gaumont-British, 1927, British
TESHA   British International, 1928, British
KITTY   British International, 1929, British
WOMAN TO WOMAN   Gainsborough, 1929, British
THE W PLAN   Gaumont-British, 1930, British
A WARM CORNER   Gaumont-British, 1930, British
THE SPORT OF KINGS   Gaumont-British, 1931, British
THE CALENDAR   co-director with T. Hayes Hunter, 1931,
     British
SUNSHINE SUSIE   Gaumont-British, 1931, British
MICHAEL AND MARY   Gaumont-British, 1931, British
HINDLE WAKES   Gaumont-British, 1932, British
THE FAITHFUL HEART   Gaumont-British, 1932, British
LOVE ON WHEELS   Gaumont-British, 1932, British
THE GOOD COMPANIONS   Gaumont-British, 1933,
     British
I WAS A SPY   Gaumont-British, 1933, British
FRIDAY THE 13TH   Gaumont-British, 1933, British
EVENSONG   Gaumont-British, 1934, British
EVERGREEN   Gaumont-British, 1934, British
THE IRON DUKE   Gaumont-British, 1934, British
THE DICTATOR   *THE LOVE AFFAIR OF A DICTATOR/*
     LOVES OF A DICTATOR   1935, British
ME AND MARLBOROUGH   Gaumont-British, 1935,
     British
FIRST A GIRL   Gaumont-British, 1935, British
IT'S LOVE AGAIN   Gaumont-British, 1936, British
DARK JOURNEY   1937, British
STORM IN A TEACUP   co-director with Ian Dalrymple,
     1937, British
ACTION FOR SLANDER   co-director with Tim Whelan,
     1937, British
SOUTH RIDING   1938, British
FOREVER AND A DAY   co-director, RKO Radio, 1943
TONIGHT AND EVERY NIGHT   Columbia, 1945
THE GREEN YEARS   MGM, 1946
GREEN DOLPHIN STREET   MGM, 1947
IF WINTER COMES   MGM, 1948
CONSPIRATOR   MGM, 1949, British
KIM   MGM, 1950
CALLING BULLDOG DRUMMOND   MGM, 1951, British
AFFAIR IN MONTE CARLO   *24 HOURS IN A WOMAN'S*
     LIFE   Allied Artists, 1952, British
THE LONG WAIT   United Artists, 1954
THE SILVER CHALICE   Warner Bros., 1955

FRANKLIN J. SCHAFFNER
b. May 30, 1920 - Tokyo, Japan
d. 1989

THE STRIPPER   20th Century-Fox, 1962
THE BEST MAN   United Artists, 1964
THE WAR LORD   Universal, 1965
THE DOUBLE MAN   Warner Bros., 1968, British
PLANET OF THE APES   20th Century-Fox, 1968
PATTON★★   20th Century-Fox, 1970
NICHOLAS AND ALEXANDRA   Columbia, 1971, British
PAPILLON   Allied Artists, 1973
ISLANDS IN THE STREAM   Paramount, 1977
THE BOYS FROM BRAZIL   20th Century-Fox, 1978
SPHINX   Orion/Warner Bros., 1981
YES, GIORGIO   MGM/UA, 1982
LIONHEART   Orion, 1987
WELCOME HOME   Columbia, 1989

DORE SCHARY
b. August 31, 1905 - Newark, New Jersey
d. 1980

ACT ONE   Warner Bros., 1963

VICTOR SCHERTZINGER
b. April 8, 1880 - Mahanoy City, Pennsylvania
d. 1941

THE CLODHOPPER   Triangle, 1917
THE MILLIONAIRE VAGRANT   Triangle, 1917
THE PINCH HITTER   Triangle, 1917
SUDDEN JIM   Triangle, 1917
THE SON OF HIS FATHER   Paramount, 1917
HIS MOTHER'S BOY   Paramount, 1918
THE HIRED MAN   Paramount, 1918
THE FAMILY SKELETON   Ince-Triangle, 1918
PLAYING THE GAME   Paramount, 1918
HIS OWN HOME TOWN   Paramount, 1918
THE CLAWS OF THE HUN   Paramount, 1918
A NINE O'CLOCK TOWN   Ince-Triangle, 1918
STRING BEANS   Paramount, 1918
THE HOMEBREAKER   Paramount, 1919
HARD BOILED   Paramount, 1919
THE LADY OF RED BUTTE   Paramount, 1919
OTHER MEN'S WIVES   Paramount, 1919
THE SHERIFF'S SON   Paramount, 1919
QUICKSAND   Paramount, 1919
UPSTAIRS   Goldwyn, 1919
THE PEACE OF ROARING RIVER   Goldwyn, 1919
WHEN DOCTORS DISAGREE   Goldwyn, 1919
THE JINX   Goldwyn, 1919
PINTO   Goldwyn, 1920
THE BLOOMING ANGEL   Goldwyn, 1920
THE SLIM PRINCESS   Goldwyn, 1920
MADE IN HEAVEN   Goldwyn, 1921
THE CONCERT   Goldwyn, 1921
WHAT HAPPENED TO ROSA?   Goldwyn, 1921
BEATING THE GAME   Goldwyn, 1921
MR. BARNES OF NEW YORK   Goldwyn, 1921
HEAD OVER HEELS   Goldwyn, 1921
THE BOOTLEGGER'S DAUGHTER   Associated
   Exhibitors, 1921
THE KINGDOM WITHIN   WW. Hodkinson, 1921
SCANDALOUS TONGUES   Associated Exhibitors,
   1921
THE LONELY ROAD   First National, 1922

THE SCARLET LILY   First National, 1922
REFUGE   First National, 1923
DOLLAR DEVILS   W.W. Hodkinson, 1923
THE MAN NEXT DOOR   Vitagraph, 1923
LONG LIVE THE KING   Metro, 1923
THE MAN LIFE PASSED BY   Metro, 1923
CHASTITY   First National, 1923
A BOY OF FLANDERS   Metro-Goldwyn, 1924
BREAD   Metro-Goldwyn, 1924
FRIVOLOUS SAL   First National, 1925
MAN AND MAID   Metro-Goldwyn, 1925
THE WHEEL   Fox, 1925
THUNDER MOUNTAIN   Fox, 1925
THE GOLDEN STRAIN   First National, 1925
SIBERIA   Fox, 1926
THE LILY   Fox, 1926
THE RETURN OF PETER GRIMM   Fox, 1926
STAGE MADNESS   Fox, 1927
THE HEART OF SALOME   Fox, 1927
THE SECRET STUDIO   Fox, 1927
THE SHOWDOWN   Paramount, 1928
FORGOTTEN FACES   Paramount, 1928
MANHATTAN COCKTAIL   Paramount, 1928
REDSKIN   Paramount, 1929
FASHIONS IN LOVE   Paramount, 1929
THE WHEEL OF LIFE   Paramount, 1929
NOTHING BUT THE TRUTH   Paramount, 1929
THE LAUGHING LADY   Paramount, 1929
PARAMOUNT ON PARADE   co-director, Paramount,
   1930
SAFETY IN NUMBERS   Paramount, 1930
HEADS UP   Paramount, 1930
THE WOMAN BETWEEN   RKO, 1931
FRIENDS AND LOVERS   RKO, 1931
STRANGE JUSTICE   RKO, 1932
UPTOWN NEW YORK   SonoArt-World Wide, 1932
COCKTAIL HOUR   Columbia, 1933
THE CONSTANT WOMAN   World Wide, 1933
MY WOMAN   Columbia, 1933
BELOVED   Universal, 1934
ONE NIGHT OF LOVE ★   Columbia, 1934
LET'S LIVE TONIGHT   Columbia, 1935
LOVE ME FOREVER   Columbia, 1935
THE MUSIC GOES 'ROUND   Columbia, 1936
FOLLOW YOUR HEART   1936
SOMETHING TO SING ABOUT   Grand National, 1937
THE MIKADO   Universal, 1939, British
ROAD TO SINGAPORE   Paramount, 1940
RHYTHM ON THE RIVER   Paramount, 1940
ROAD TO ZANZIBAR   Paramount, 1941
KISS THE BOYS GOODBYE   Paramount, 1941
BIRTH OF THE BLUES   Paramount, 1941
THE FLEET'S IN   Paramount, 1942

ERNEST B. SCHOEDSACK
(Ernest Beaumont Schoedsack)
b. June 8, 1893 - Council Bluffs, Iowa
d. 1979

GRASS: A NATION'S BATTLE FOR LIFE   GRASS:
   THE EPIC OF A LOST TRIBE (FD)   co-director with
   Merian C. Cooper, Paramount, 1926
CHANG   co-director with Merian C. Cooper, Paramount,
   1927
THE FOUR FEATHERS   co-director with Merian C.
   Cooper & Lothar Mendes, United Artists, 1929
RANGE (FD)   Paramount, 1931
THE MOST DANGEROUS GAME   co-director with
   Irving Pichel, RKO Radio, 1932

KING KONG   co-director with Merian C. Cooper, RKO
    Radio, 1933
THE SON OF KONG   RKO Radio, 1933
BLIND ADVENTURE   RKO Radio, 1933
LONG LOST FATHER   RKO Radio, 1934
THE LAST DAYS OF POMPEII   RKO Radio, 1935
TROUBLE IN MOROCCO   Columbia, 1937
OUTLAWS OF THE ORIENT   Columbia, 1937
DR. CYCLOPS   Paramount, 1940
MIGHTY JOE YOUNG   RKO Radio, 1949

VICTOR SEASTROM
(See Victor SJOSTROM)

GEORGE SEATON
b. April 17, 1911 - South Bend, Indiana
d. 1979

BILLY ROSE'S DIAMOND HORSESHOE   20th Century-
    Fox, 1945
JUNIOR MISS   20th Century-Fox, 1945
THE SHOCKING MISS PILGRIM   20th Century-Fox, 1947
MIRACLE ON 34TH STREET   20th Century-Fox, 1947
APARTMENT FOR PEGGY   20th Century-Fox, 1948
CHICKEN EVERY SUNDAY   20th Century-Fox, 1949
THE BIG LIFT   20th Century-Fox, 1950
FOR HEAVEN'S SAKE   20th Century-Fox, 1950
ANYTHING CAN HAPPEN   Paramount, 1952
LITTLE BOY LOST   Paramount, 1953
THE COUNTRY GIRL ★   Paramount, 1954
THE PROUD AND THE PROFANE   Paramount, 1956
WILLIAMSBURG: THE STORY OF A PATRIOT (FD)
    1957
TEACHER'S PET   Paramount, 1958
THE PLEASURE OF HIS COMPANY   Paramount, 1961
THE COUNTERFEIT TRAITOR   Paramount, 1962
THE HOOK   MGM, 1963
36 HOURS   MGM, 1965
WHAT'S SO BAD ABOUT FEELING GOOD?   Universal,
    1968
AIRPORT   Universal, 1970
SHOWDOWN   Universal, 1973

LEWIS SEILER
b. 1891 - New York, New York
d. 1963

DARWIN WAS RIGHT   1924
NO MAN'S GOLD   1926
THE GREAT K&A TRAIN ROBBERY   1926
THE LAST TRAIL   1927
TUMBLING RIVER   1927
OUTLAWS OF RED RIVER   1927
WOLF FANGS   1927
SQUARE CROOKS   1928
THE AIR CIRCUS   co-director with Howard Hawks, Fox,
    1928
THE GHOST WALKS   1929
GIRLS GONE WILD   1929
A SONG OF KENTUCKY   1929
NO GREATER LOVE   1932
DECEPTION   1932
FRONTIER MARSHAL   1934
ASEGURE A SU MUJER   1935
CHARLIE CHAN IN PARIS   20th Century-Fox, 1935
GINGER   1935
PADDY O'DAY   1935

HERE COMES TROUBLE   1936
THE FIRST BABY   1936
STAR FOR A NIGHT   1936
CAREER WOMAN   1936
TURN OFF THE MOON   Paramount, 1937
HE COULDN'T SAY NO   1938
CRIME SCHOOL   Warner Bros., 1938
PENROD'S DOUBLE TROUBLE   Warner Bros., 1938
HEART OF THE NORTH   Warner Bros., 1938
KING OF THE UNDERWORLD   Warner Bros., 1939
YOU CAN'T GET AWAY WITH MURDER   Warner Bros.,
    1939
THE KID FROM KOKOMO   Warner Bros., 1939
HELL'S KITCHEN   co-director with E.A. Dupont,
    Warner Bros., 1939
DUST BE MY DESTINY   Warner Bros., 1939
IT ALL CAME TRUE   Warner Bros., 1940
FLIGHT ANGELS   Warner Bros., 1940
MURDER IN THE AIR   Warner Bros., 1940
TUGBOAT ANNIE SAILS AGAIN   Warner Bros., 1940
SOUTH OF SUEZ   Warner Bros., 1940
KISSES FOR BREAKFAST   Warner Bros., 1941
THE SMILING GHOST   Warner Bros., 1941
YOU'RE IN THE ARMY NOW   Warner Bros., 1941
THE BIG SHOT   Warner Bros., 1942
PITTSBURGH   Universal, 1942
GUADALCANAL DIARY   20th Century-Fox, 1943
SOMETHING FOR THE BOYS   20th Century-Fox, 1944
DOLL FACE   20th Century-Fox, 1945
MOLLY AND ME   20th Century-Fox, 1945
IF I'M LUCKY   20th Century-Fox, 1946
WHIPLASH   Warner Bros., 1949
BREAKTHROUGH   Warner Bros., 1950
THE TANKS ARE COMING   Warner Bros., 1951
THE WINNING TEAM   Warner Bros., 1952
OPERATION SECRET   Warner Bros., 1952
THE SYSTEM   Warner Bros., 1953
THE BAMBOO PRISON   Columbia, 1955
WOMEN'S PRISON   Columbia, 1955
BATTLE STATIONS   Columbia, 1956

WILLIAM A. SEITER
b. June 10, 1892 - New York, New York
d. 1964

TANGLED THREADS   1919
THE KENTUCKY COLONEL   W.W. Hodkinson, 1920
HEARTS AND MASKS   Film Booking Offices, 1921
PASSING THROUGH   Paramount, 1921
THE FOOLISH AGE   Robertson-Cole, 1921
EDEN AND RETURN   Robertson-Cole, 1921
BOY CRAZY   Robertson-Cole, 1922
GAY AND DEVILISH   Robertson-Cole, 1922
THE UNDERSTUDY   FBO, 1922
UP AND AT 'EM   FBO, 1922
WHEN LOVE COMES   FBO, 1922
THE BEAUTIFUL AND THE DAMNED   Warner Bros.,
    1922
BELL BOY 13   Associated First National, 1923
LITTLE CHURCH AROUND THE CORNER   Warner
    Bros., 1923
DADDIES   Warner Bros., 1924
THE WHITE SIN   FBO, 1924
HIS FORGOTTEN WIFE   FBO, 1924
LISTEN LESTER   Principal, 1924
HELEN'S BABIES   Principal, 1924
THE FAMILY SECRET   Universal-Jewel, 1924
THE FAST WORKER   Universal-Jewel, 1924
THE MAD WHIRL   Universal-Jewel, 1925
DANGEROUS INNOCENCE   Universal-Jewel, 1925

THE TEASER   Universal-Jewel, 1925
WHERE WAS I?   Universal-Jewel, 1925
WHAT HAPPENED TO JONES   Universal-Jewel, 1926
SKINNER'S DRESS SUIT   Universal-Jewel, 1926
ROLLING HOME   Universal, 1926
TAKE IT FROM ME   Universal-Jewel, 1926
THE CHEERFUL FRAUD   Universal, 1927
THE SMALL BACHELOR   Universal-Jewel, 1927
OUT ALL NIGHT   Universal-Jewel, 1927
THANKS FOR THE BUGGY RIDE   Universal-Jewel, 1928
GOOD MORNING JUDGE   Universal-Jewel, 1928
HAPPINESS AHEAD   First National, 1928
WATERFRONT   First National, 1928
OUTCAST   First National, 1928
SYNTHETIC WIFE   *SYNTHETIC SON*   First National, 1929
WHY BE GOOD?   First National, 1929
PRISONERS   First National, 1929
SMILING IRISH EYES   First National, 1929
FOOTLIGHTS AND FOOLS   First National, 1929
THE LOVE RACKET   First National, 1929
STRICTLY MODERN   First National, 1930
BACK PAY   First National, 1930
THE FLIRTING WIDOW   First National, 1930
THE TRUTH ABOUT YOUTH   First National, 1930
GOING WILD   First National, 1930
SUNNY   First National, 1930
KISS ME AGAIN   First National, 1931
BIG BUSINESS GIRL   First National, 1931
TOO MANY CROOKS   RKO, 1931
FULL OF NOTIONS   RKO, 1931
CAUGHT PLASTERED   RKO, 1931
PEACH O'RENO   RKO, 1931
WAY BACK HOME   RKO, 1932
GIRL CRAZY   RKO, 1932
YOUNG BRIDE   *LOVE STARVED*   RKO, 1932
IS MY FACE RED?   RKO, 1932
HOT SATURDAY   Paramount, 1932
IF I HAD A MILLION   co-director, Paramount, 1932
HELLO EVERYBODY!   Paramount, 1933
DIPLOMANIACS   RKO, 1933
PROFESSIONAL SWEETHEART   RKO, 1933
CHANCE AT HEAVEN   RKO, 1933
SONS OF THE DESERT   MGM, 1934
RAFTER ROMANCE   RKO, 1934
SING AND LIKE IT   RKO, 1934
LOVE BIRDS   Universal, 1934
WE'RE RICH AGAIN   RKO, 1934
THE RICHEST GIRL IN THE WORLD   RKO, 1934
ROBERTA   RKO Radio, 1935
THE DARING YOUNG MAN   Fox, 1935
ORCHIDS TO YOU   Fox, 1935
IN PERSON   RKO, 1935
IF YOU COULD ONLY COOK   Columbia, 1935
THE MOON'S OUR HOME   Paramount, 1936
THE CASE AGAINST MRS. AMES   Paramount, 1936
DIMPLES   20th Century-Fox, 1936
STOWAWAY   20th Century-Fox, 1936
THIS IS MY AFFAIR   20th Century-Fox, 1937
THE LIFE OF THE PARTY   20th Century-Fox, 1937
LIFE BEGINS IN COLLEGE   20th Century-Fox, 1937
SALLY, IRENE AND MARY   20th Century-Fox, 1938
THREE BLIND MICE   20th Century-Fox, 1938
ROOM SERVICE   RKO Radio, 1938
THANKS FOR EVERYTHING   20th Century-Fox, 1938
SUSANNAH OF THE MOUNTIES   20th Century-Fox, 1939
ALLEGHENY UPRISING   RKO Radio, 1940
IT'S A DATE   Universal, 1940
HIRED WIFE   Universal, 1940
NICE GIRL?   Universal, 1941

APPOINTMENT FOR LOVE   Universal, 1941
BROADWAY   Universal, 1942
YOU WERE NEVER LOVELIER   Columbia, 1942
DESTROYER   Columbia, 1943
A LADY TAKES A CHANCE   RKO Radio, 1943
FOUR JILLS IN A JEEP   20th Century-Fox, 1944
BELLE OF THE YUKON   RKO Radio, 1944
IT'S A PLEASURE   RKO Radio, 1945
THE AFFAIRS OF SUSAN   Paramount, 1945
THAT NIGHT WITH YOU   Universal, 1945
LITTLE GIANT   Universal, 1946
LOVER COME BACK   Universal, 1946
I'LL BE YOURS   Universal, 1947
UP IN CENTRAL PARK   Universal, 1948
ONE TOUCH OF VENUS   Universal, 1948
BORDERLINE   Universal, 1950
DEAR BRAT   Paramount, 1951
THE LADY WANTS MINK   Republic, 1953
CHAMP FOR A DAY   Republic, 1953
MAKE HASTE TO LIVE   Republic, 1954

GEORGE B. SEITZ
(George Brackett Seitz)
b. January 3, 1888 - Boston, Massachusetts
d. 1944

THE EXPLOITS OF ELAINE   co-director with Louis Gasnier, Pathé, 1914, serial
THE NEW EXPLOITS OF ELAINE   Pathé, 1915, serial
THE ROMANCE OF ELAINE   Pathé, 1915, serial
THE IRON CLAW   co-director with Edward Jose, 1916, serial
THE KING'S GAME   1916
THE LAST OF THE CARNABYS   Pathé, 1917
THE HUNTING OF THE HAWK   Pathé, 1917
NEW YORK NIGHTS   Pathé, 1917
THE FATAL RING   Pathé, 1917, serial
GETAWAY KATE   Pathé, 1918
THE HONEST THIEF   Pathé, 1918
THE HOUSE OF HATE   Pathé, 1918, serial
THE LIGHTNING RAIDER   Pathé, 1918, serial
THE BLACK SECRET   Pathé, 1919, serial
BOUND AND GAGGED   Pathé, 1919, serial
PIRATE GOLD   Pathé, 1920, serial
VELVET FINGERS   1920, serial
ROGUES AND ROMANCE   Pathé, 1920
THE SKY RANGER   Pathé, 1921, serial
HURRICANE HUTCH   Pathé, 1922, serial
SPEED   Pathé, 1922, serial
PLUNDER   Pathé, 1923, serial
THE WAY OF A MAN   Pathé, 1924, serial
LEATHERSTOCKING   Pathé, 1924, serial
THE 40TH DOOR   Pathé, 1924, serial
GALLOPING HOOFS   Pathé, 1924, serial
INTO THE NET   Pathé, 1924, serial
SUNKEN SILVER   *SUNKEN SAILOR*   Pathé, 1925, serial
WILD HORSE MESA   Paramount, 1925
THE VANISHING AMERICAN   Paramount, 1925
DESERT GOLD   Paramount, 1926
PALS IN PARADISE   Producers Distributing Corporation, 1926
THE ICE FLOOD   Universal, 1926
THE LAST FRONTIER   Producers Distributing Corporation, 1926
JIM THE CONQUEROR   Producers Distributing Corporation, 1927
THE GREAT MAIL ROBBERY   FBO, 1927
THE BLOOD SHIP   Columbia, 1927
THE TIGRESS   Columbia, 1927

THE ISLE OF FORGOTTEN WOMEN   Columbia, 1927
THE WARNING   Columbia, 1927
RANSOM   Columbia, 1928
BEWARE OF BLONDES   Columbia, 1928
COURT-MARTIAL   Columbia, 1928
THE CIRCUS KID   Columbia, 1928
BLOCKADE   RKO, 1928
HEY RUBE!   FBO, 1928
BLACK MAGIC   Fox, 1929
MURDER ON THE ROOF   Columbia, 1930
GUILTY?   Columbia, 1930
MIDNIGHT MYSTERY   RKO, 1930
DANGER LIGHTS   RKO, 1930
THE DRUMS OF JEOPARDY   Tiffany, 1931
THE LION AND THE LAMB   Columbia, 1931
ARIZONA *MEN ARE LIKE THAT*   Columbia, 1931
SHANGHAIED LOVE   Columbia, 1931
NIGHT BEAT   Action, 1931
SALLY OF THE SUBWAY   Mayfair, 1932
DOCKS OF SAN FRANCISCO   Mayfair, 1932
SIN'S PAY DAY   Mayfair, 1932
PASSPORT TO PARADISE   Mayfair, 1932
THE WIDOW IN SCARLET   Mayfair, 1932
TREASON   Columbia, 1933
THE THRILL HUNTER   Columbia, 1933
THE WOMAN IN HIS LIFE   MGM, 1933
LAZY RIVER   MGM, 1934
THE FIGHTING RANGER   Columbia, 1934
ONLY EIGHT HOURS   MGM, 1935
SOCIETY DOCTOR   1935
SHADOW OF DOUBT   MGM, 1935
TIMES SQUARE LADY   MGM, 1935
CALM YOURSELF   MGM, 1935
WOMAN WANTED   MGM, 1935
KIND LADY   MGM, 1935
EXCLUSIVE STORY   MGM, 1936
ABSOLUTE QUIET   1936
THE THREE WISE GUYS   MGM, 1936
THE LAST OF THE MOHICANS   United Artists, 1936
MAD HOLIDAY   MGM, 1936
UNDER COVER OF NIGHT   MGM, 1937
A FAMILY AFFAIR   MGM, 1937
THE 13TH CHAIR   MGM, 1937
MAMA STEPS OUT   MGM, 1937
BETWEEN TWO WOMEN   MGM, 1937
MY DEAR MISS ALDRICH   MGM, 1937
YOU'RE ONLY YOUNG ONCE   MGM, 1938
JUDGE HARDY'S CHILDREN   MGM, 1938
YELLOW JACK   MGM, 1938
LOVE FINDS ANDY HARDY   MGM, 1938
OUT WEST WITH THE HARDYS   MGM, 1938
THE HARDYS RIDE HIGH   MGM, 1939
SIX THOUSAND ENEMIES   MGM, 1939
THUNDER AFLOAT   MGM, 1939
JUDGE HARDY AND SON   MGM, 1939
ANDY HARDY MEETS DEBUTANTE   MGM, 1940
KIT CARSON   United Artists, 1940
SKY MURDER   MGM, 1940
GALLANT SONS   MGM, 1940
ANDY HARDY'S PRIVATE SECRETARY   MGM, 1941
LIFE BEGINS FOR ANDY HARDY   MGM, 1941
A YANK ON THE BURMA ROAD   MGM, 1942
THE COURTSHIP OF ANDY HARDY   MGM, 1942
PIERRE OF THE PLAINS   MGM, 1942
ANDY HARDY'S DOUBLE LIFE   MGM, 1942
ANDY HARDY'S BLONDE TROUBLE   MGM, 1944

STEVE SEKELY
(Istvan Szekely)
b. February 25, 1899 - Budapest, Hungary
d. 1979

RHAPSODIE DER LIEBE   1929, Austrian
DIE GROSSE SEHNSUCHT   1930, German
SEITENSPRUNGE   1930, German
ER UND SEIN DIENER   1931, German
EIN STEINREICHER MANN   1932, German
PIRI MINDONT TUD   1932, Hungarian
SCANDAL IN BUDAPEST   co-director with Geza von Bolvary, 1933, German-Hungarian
RAKOCZI MARSCH   1933, German-Hungarian
IDA REGENYE   1934, Hungarian
LILA AKAC   1934, Hungarian
BALL IM SAVOY   1934, Austrian-Hungarian
EMMY   1934, Hungarian
CAFE MOSZKVA   1936, Hungarian
SZENSACIO   co-director with Ladislao Vajda, 1936, Hungarian
AN AFFAIR OF HONOR   1936
TWO PRISONERS   1937, Hungarian
BEAUTY OF THE PUSZTA   1937, Hungarian
I MARRIED FOR LOVE   1937, Hungarian
HEART TO HEART   1938, Hungarian
A MIRACLE ON MAIN STREET   Columbia, 1940
BEHIND PRISON WALLS   Producers Releasing Corporation, 1941
REVENGE OF THE ZOMBIES   Monogram, 1943
WOMEN IN BONDAGE   Monogram, 1944
LADY IN THE DEATH HOUSE   Producers Releasing Corporation, 1944
WATERFRONT   Producers Releasing Corporation, 1944
MY BUDDY   Republic, 1944
LAKE PLACID SERENADE   Republic, 1944
THE FABULOUS SUZANNE   Republic, 1946
BLONDE SAVAGE   Eagle Lion, 1947
HOLLOW TRIUMPH *THE SCAR*   Eagle Lion, 1948
AMAZON QUEST   Film Classics, 1949
STRONGHOLD   Lippert, 1952
L'AVVENTURE DI CARTOUCHE   co-director with Gianni Vernuccio, 1954, Italian
THE DAY OF THE TRIFFIDS   Allied Artists, 1963, British
KENNER   MGM, 1969
THE GIRL WHO LIKED PURPLE FLOWERS   1973, Hungarian

LESLEY SELANDER
b. May 26, 1900 - Los Angeles, California
d. 1979

RIDE 'EM COWBOY   Universal, 1936
EMPTY SADDLES   Universal, 1936
THE BOSS RIDER OF GUN CREEK   Universal, 1936
SMOKE TREE RANGE   Universal, 1937
SANDFLOW   Universal, 1937
LEFT-HANDED LAW   Universal, 1937
THE BARRIER   Paramount, 1937
HOPALONG RIDES AGAIN   Paramount, 1937
BLACK ACES   1937
PARTNERS OF THE PLAINS   Paramount, 1938
BAR 20 JUSTICE   Paramount, 1938
HEART OF ARIZONA   Paramount, 1938
PRIDE OF THE WEST   Paramount, 1938
THE MYSTERIOUS RIDER   Paramount, 1938
SUNSET TRAIL   Paramount, 1938
THE FRONTIERSMAN   Paramount, 1938
SILVER ON THE SAGE   Paramount, 1939

THE RENEGADE TRAIL   Paramount, 1939
HERITAGE OF THE DESERT   Paramount, 1939
RANGE WAR   Paramount, 1939
SANTA FE MARSHAL   Paramount, 1939
THREE MEN FROM TEXAS   Paramount, 1940
KNIGHTS OF THE RANGE   Paramount, 1940
HIDDEN GOLD   Paramount, 1940
STAGECOACH WAR   Paramount, 1940
THE LIGHT OF THE WESTERN STARS   Mayer-
   Burstyn, 1940
CHEROKEE STRIP   Paramount, 1940
WIDE OPEN TOWN   Paramount, 1941
RIDERS OF THE TIMBERLINE   Paramount, 1941
STICK TO YOUR GUNS   Paramount, 1941
THE ROUNDUP   Paramount, 1941
DOOMED CARAVAN   Paramount, 1941
PIRATES ON HORSEBACK   Paramount, 1941
THUNDERING HOOFS   RKO, 1941
BANDIT RANGER   RKO, 1942
THE UNDERCOVER MAN   United Artists, 1942
LOST CANYON   United Artists, 1942
BAR 20   United Artists, 1943
RIDERS OF THE DEADLINE   United Artists, 1943
COMRADES   United Artists, 1943
BUCKSKIN FRONTIER   United Artists, 1943
BORDER PATROL   United Artists, 1943
COLT COMRADES   United Artists, 1943
RIDERS OF THE DEADLINE   Republic, 1944
BORDERLINE TRAIL   Republic, 1944
STAGECOACH TO MONTEREY   Republic, 1944
CHEYENNE WILDCAT   Republic, 1944
FIREBRANDS OF ARIZONA   Republic, 1944
SHERIFF OF LAS VEGAS   Republic, 1944
SHERIFF OF SUNDOWN   Republic, 1944
LUMBERJACK   United Artists, 1944
CALL OF THE ROCKIES   Republic, 1944
FORTY THIEVES   United Artists, 1944
THE GREAT STAGECOACH ROBBERY   Republic,
   1945
PHANTOM OF THE PLAINS   Republic, 1945
JUNGLE RAIDERS   Columbia, 1945, serial
THE TRAIL OF KIT CARSON   Republic, 1945
THE VAMPIRE'S GHOST   Republic, 1945
THE LAST FRONTIER UPRISING   Republic, 1946
THE CATMAN OF PARIS   Republic, 1946
PASSKEY TO DANGER   Republic, 1946
TRAFFIC IN CRIME   Republic, 1946
NIGHT TRAIN TO MEMPHIS   Republic, 1946
OUT CALIFORNIA WAY   Republic, 1946
SADDLE PALS   Republic, 1947
THE PILGRIM LADY   Republic, 1947
ROBIN HOOD OF TEXAS   Republic, 1947
BLACKMAIL   Republic, 1947
THE RED STALLION   Eagle Lion, 1947
STRIKE IT RICH   Allied Artists, 1948
PANHANDLE   Allied Artists, 1948
GUNS OF HATE   RKO Radio, 1948
BELLE STARR'S DAUGHTER   20th Century-Fox,
   1948
INDIAN AGENT   RKO, 1948
RUSTLERS   RKO, 1949
BROTHERS IN THE SADDLE   RKO, 1949
RIDERS OF THE RANGE   RKO, 1949
RIDER FROM TUCSON   RKO, 1950
RIO GRANDE PATROL   RKO, 1950
SHORT GRASS   Allied Artists, 1950
STAMPEDE   Monogram, 1949
SKY DRAGON   Monogram, 1949
MASKED RAIDERS   RKO, 1949
THE MYSTERIOUS DESPERADO   RKO, 1949
DAKOTA LIL   20th Century-Fox, 1950

STORM OVER WYOMING   RKO, 1950
THE KANGAROO KID   Eagle Lion, 1950
LAW OF THE BADLANDS   RKO, 1950
CAVALRY SCOUT   Monogram, 1951
I WAS AN AMERICAN SPY   Allied Artists, 1951
THE HIGHWAYMAN   Allied Artists, 1951
SADDLE LEGION   RKO, 1951
GUNPLAY   RKO, 1951
FLIGHT TO MARS   Monogram, 1951
PISTOL HARVEST   RKO, 1951
OVERLAND TELEGRAPH   RKO, 1951
TRAIL GUIDE   RKO, 1952
FORT OSAGE   Monogram, 1952
THE RIDING KID   United Artists, 1952
ROAD AGENT   RKO, 1952
DESERT PASSAGE   RKO, 1952
THE RAIDERS   Universal, 1952
BATTLE ZONE   Allied Artists, 1952
FLAT TOP   Allied Artists, 1952
COW COUNTRY   Allied Artists, 1953
FORT VENGEANCE   Allied Artists, 1953
WAR PAINT   United Artists, 1953
FORT ALGIERS   United Artists, 1953
THE ROYAL AFRICAN RIFLES   Allied Artists, 1953
FIGHTER ATTACK   Allied Artists, 1953
ARROW IN THE DUST   Allied Artists, 1954
RETURN FROM THE SEA   Allied Artists, 1954
THE YELLOW TOMAHAWK   United Artists, 1954
DRAGONFLY SQUADRON   Allied Artists, 1954
SHOTGUN   Allied Artists, 1955
TALL MAN RIDING   Warner Bros., 1955
DESERT SANDS   United Artists, 1955
FORT YUMA   United Artists, 1955
QUINCANNON, FRONTIER SCOUT   United Artists,
   1956
THE BROKEN STAR   United Artists, 1956
TAMING SUTTON'S GAL   Republic, 1957
THE WAYWARD GIRL   Republic, 1957
TOMAHAWK TRAIL   United Artists, 1957
REVOLT AT FORT LARAMIE   United Artists, 1957
OUTLAW'S SON   United Artists, 1957
THE LONE RANGER AND THE LOST CITY OF GOLD
   United Artists, 1958
FORT COURAGEOUS   20th Century-Fox, 1965
WAR PARTY   20th Century-Fox, 1965
CONVICT STAGE   20th Century-Fox, 1965
TOWN TAMER   Paramount, 1965
THE TEXICAN   Columbia, 1966
FORT UTAH   Paramount, 1967
ARIZONA BUSHWHACKERS   Paramount, 1968

LARRY SEMON
b. July 6, 1889 - West Point, Mississippi
d. 1928

THE MAN FROM EGYPT   Vitagraph, 1916
A VILLAINOUS VILLAIN   Vitagraph, 1916
LOVE AND LOOT   Vitagraph, 1916
FOOTLIGHTS AND FAKERS   Vitagraph, 1917
ROUGH TOUGHS AND ROOF TOPS   Vitagraph, 1917
BOASTS AND BOLDNESS   Vitagraph, 1917
SPOOKS AND SPASMS   Vitagraph, 1917
BABES AND BOOBS   Vitagraph, 1918
SPIES AND SPILLS   Vitagraph, 1918
PASSING THE BUCK   Vitagraph, 1919
THE SIMPLE LIFE   Vitagraph, 1919
THE STAGEHAND   co-director, Vitagraph, 1920
THE SUITOR   co-director, Vitagraph, 1920
THE SPORTSMAN   co-director, Vitagraph, 1921
THE FALL GUY   co-director, Vitagraph, 1921

THE SAWMILL   co-director, Vitagraph, 1922
THE SHOW   co-director, Vitagraph, 1922
THE SLEUTH   co-director, Vitagraph, 1922
NO WEDDING BELLS   1923
MIDNIGHT CABARET   1923
THE GIRL IN THE LIMOUSINE   1924
THE WIZARD OF OZ   1925
STOP, LOOK AND LISTEN   1926
SPUDS   1927

MACK SENNETT
(Mikall Sinnott)
b. January 17, 1880 - Danville, Quebec, Canada
d. 1960

THE LUCKY TOOTHACHE   Biograph, 1910
THE MASHER   Biograph, 1910
COMRADES   Biograph, 1911
CUPID'S JOKE   Biograph, 1911
THE COUNTRY LOVERS   Biograph, 1911
THE MANICURE LADY   Biograph, 1911
A DUTCH GOLD MINE   Biograph, 1911
THE WONDERFUL EYE   Biograph, 1911
THE GHOST   Biograph, 1911
THE BEAUTIFUL VOICE   Biograph, 1911
THE VILLAGE HERO   Biograph, 1911
TOO MANY BURGLARS   Biograph, 1911
THE INVENTOR'S SECRET   Biograph, 1911
THEIR FIRST DIVORCE   Biograph, 1911
RESOURCEFUL LOVERS   Biograph, 1911
CAUGHT WITH THE GOODS   Biograph, 1911
THE JOKE ON THE JOKER   Biograph, 1912
BRAVE AND BOLD   Biograph, 1912
PANTS AND PANSIES   Biograph, 1912
THE FATAL CHOCOLATE   Biograph, 1912
A SPANISH DILEMMA   Biograph, 1912
HOT STUFF   Biograph, 1912
OH THOSE EYES!   Biograph, 1912
THOSE HICKSVILLE BOYS   Biograph, 1912
THE LEADING MAN   Biograph , 1912
WHEN THE FIRE BELLS RANG   Biograph, 1912
NEIGHBORS   Biograph, 1912
THE NEW BABY   Biograph, 1912
ONE-ROUND O'BRIEN   Biograph, 1912
THE SPEED DEMON   Biograph, 1912
WILLIE BECOMES AN ARTIST   Biograph, 1912
THE TOURISTS   Biograph, 1912
COHEN COLLECTS A DEBT   Keystone, 1912
THE WATER NYMPH   Keystone, 1912
THE NEW NEIGHBOR   Keystone, 1912
PEDRO'S DILEMMA   Keystone, 1912
STOLEN GLORY   Keystone, 1912
THE AMBITIOUS BUTLER   Keystone, 1912
AT CONEY ISLAND   Keystone, 1912
MABEL'S LOVERS   Keystone, 1912
THE RIVALS   Keystone, 1912
MR. FIXIT   Keystone, 1912
BROWN'S SEANCE   Keystone, 1912
THE DRUMMER'S VACATION   Keystone, 1912
THE DUEL   Keystone, 1912
A DOUBLE WEDDING   Keystone, 1913
THE MISTAKEN MASHER   Keystone, 1913
THE ELITE BALL   Keystone, 1913
THE BATTLE OF WHO RUN   Keystone, 1913
A RED HOT ROMANCE   Keystone, 1913
THE SLEUTH'S LAST STAND   Keystone, 1913
A STRONG REVENGE   Keystone, 1913
AT TWELVE O'CLOCK   Keystone, 1913

HER NEW BEAU   Keystone, 1913
THOSE GOOD OLD DAYS   Keystone, 1913
A GAME OF POKER   Keystone, 1913
A LIFE IN THE BALANCE   Keystone, 1913
A FISHY AFFAIR   Keystone, 1913
THE BANGVILLE POLICE   Keystone, 1913
THE NEW CONDUCTOR   Keystone, 1913
THAT RAGTIME BAND   Keystone, 1913
ALGY ON THE FORCE   Keystone, 1913
HIS UPS AND DOWNS   Keystone, 1913
MABEL'S AWFUL MISTAKE   Keystone, 1913
THE FOREMAN OF THE JURY   Keystone, 1913
THE GANGSTERS   Keystone, 1913
BARNEY OLDFIELD'S RACE FOR A LIFE   Keystone,
    1913
THE HANSOM DRIVER   Keystone, 1913
THE SPEED QUEEN   Keystone, 1913
THE WAITERS' PICNIC   Keystone, 1913
THE TALE OF A BLACK EYE   Keystone, 1913
SAFE IN JAIL   Keystone, 1913
THE TELLTALE LIGHT   Keystone, 1913
A NOISE FROM THE DEEP   Keystone, 1913
COHEN'S OUTING   Keystone, 1913
THE FIREBUGS   Keystone, 1913
MABEL'S NEW HERO   Keystone, 1913
THE GYPSY QUEEN   Keystone, 1913
THE FAITHFUL TAXICAB   Keystone, 1913
SCHNITZ THE TAILOR   Keystone, 1913
A HEALTHY NEIGHBORHOOD   Keystone, 1913
TWO OLD TARS   Keystone, 1913
A QUIET LITTLE WEDDING   Keystone, 1913
THE SPEED KINGS   Keystone, 1913
LOVE SICKNESS AT SEA   Keystone, 1913
COHEN SAVES THE FLAG   Keystone, 1913
ZUZU THE BAND LEADER   Keystone, 1913
THE GUSHER   Keystone, 1913
A BAD GAME   Keystone, 1913
SOME NERVE   Keystone, 1913
LOVE AND DYNAMITE   Keystone, 1914
IN THE CLUTCHES OF THE GANG   co-director with
    George Nicholls, Keystone, 1914
TOO MANY BRIDES   Keystone, 1914
MABEL'S STRANGE PREDICAMENT   co-director with
    Henry "Pathé" Lehrman, Keystone, 1914
TANGO TANGLES   Keystone, 1914
MACK IT AGAIN   Keystone, 1914
A BATHING BEAUTY   Keystone, 1914
MABEL AT THE WHEEL   co-director with Mabel Normand,
    Keystone, 1914
TWENTY MINUTES OF LOVE   Keystone, 1914
THE FATAL FLIRTATION   Keystone, 1914
THE KNOCKOUT   Keystone, 1914
MABEL'S LATEST PRANK   Keystone, 1914
HE LOVED THE LADIES   Keystone, 1914
THE HIGH SPOTS ON BROADWAY   Keystone, 1914
STOUT HEART BUT WEAK KNEES   Keystone, 1914
TILLIE'S PUNCTURED ROMANCE   Keystone, 1914
A COLORED GIRL'S LOVE   Keystone, 1914
FOR BETTER - BUT WORSE   Triangle Film Corporation,
    1915
THOSE COLLEGE GIRLS   Triangle Film Corporation,
    1915
THE LITTLE TEACHER   Triangle Film Corporation, 1915
MY VALET   Triangle Film Corporation, 1915
A FAVORITE FOOL   Triangle Film Corporation, 1915
STOLEN MAGIC   Triangle Film Corporation, 1915
HOME TALENT   co-director with James E. Abbe, Mack
    Sennett Comedies, 1921
OH MABEL, BEHAVE   co-director with Ford Sterling,
    Mack Sennett Comedies, 1922
A FINISHED ACTOR   Pathé, 1928

THE LION'S ROAR   Pathé, 1928
THE BRIDE'S RELATIONS   Educational, 1929
WHIRLS AND GIRLS   Educational, 1929
THE BIG PALOOKA   Educational, 1929
GIRL CRAZY   Educational, 1929
JAZZ MAMAS   Educational, 1929
THE GOLFERS   Educational, 1929
A HOLLYWOOD STAR   Educational, 1929
CLANCY AT THE BAT   Educational, 1929
SCOTCH   Educational, 1930
SUGAR PLUM PAPA   Educational, 1930
BULLS AND BEARS   Educational, 1930
HONEYMOON ZEPPELIN   Educational, 1930
FAT WIVES FOR THIN   Educational, 1930
CAMPUS CRUSHERS   Educational, 1930
THE CHUMPS   Educational, 1930
GOODBYE LEGS   Educational, 1930
MIDNIGHT DADDIES   Educational, 1930
DIVORCED SWEETHEARTS   Educational, 1930
RACKET CHEERS   Educational, 1930
A POOR FISH   Educational, 1931
DANCE HALL MARGE   Educational, 1931
GHOST PARADE   Educational, 1931
MONKEY BUSINESS IN AFRICA   Educational, 1931
MOVIE TOWN   Educational, 1931
FAINTING LOVER   Educational, 1931
I SURRENDER DEAR   Educational, 1931
SPEED   Educational, 1931
ONE MORE CHANCE   Educational, 1931
HYPNOTIZED   Paramount, 1932
YE OLD SAW MILL   Educational, 1935
FLICKER FEVER   Educational, 1935
JUST ANOTHER MURDER   Educational, 1935
THE TIMID YOUNG MAN   Educational, 1935
WAY UP THAR   Educational, 1935

BARRY SHEAR
b. New York, New York
d. 1979

WILD IN THE STREETS   American International, 1968
NIGHT GALLERY (TF)   co-director with Boris Sagal &
    Steven Spielberg, Universal TV, 1969
THE TODD KILLINGS   National General, 1971
ELLERY QUEEN: YOU DON'T LOOK BEHIND YOU (TF)
    Universal TV, 1971
ACROSS 110TH STREET   United Artists, 1972
SHORT WALK TO DAYLIGHT (TF)   Universal TV, 1972
THE DEADLY TRACKERS   Warner Bros., 1973
JARRETT (TF)   Screen Gems/Columbia TV, 1973
PUNCH AND JODY (TF)   Metromedia Producers
    Corporation/Stonehenge Productions, 1974
STRIKE FORCE (TF)   D'Antoni-Weitz Television
    Productions, 1975
STARSKY AND HUTCH (TF)   Spelling-Goldberg
    Productions, 1975
THE SAN PEDRO BEACH BUMS (TF)   Aaron Spelling
    Productions, 1977
KEEFER (TF)   David Gerber Productions/Columbia TV,
    1978
CRASH (TF)   Charles Fries Productions, 1978
THE BILLION DOLLAR THREAT (TF)   David Gerber
    Productions/Columbia TV, 1979
UNDERCOVER WITH THE KKK (TF)   Columbia TV,
    1979
POWER (TF)   co-director with Virgil Vogel, David Gerber
    Company/Columbia TV, 1980

JACK SHER
b. March 16, 1913 - Minneapolis, Minnesota
d. 1988

FOUR GIRLS IN TOWN   Universal, 1957
KATHY O'   Universal, 1958
THE WILD AND THE INNOCENT   Universal, 1959
THE THREE WORLDS OF GULLIVER   Columbia, 1960,
    British
LOVE IN A GOLDFISH BOWL   Paramount, 1961

ROBERT SIODMAK
b. August 8, 1900 - Memphis, Tennessee
d. 1973

MENSCHEN AM SONNTAG (FD)   co-director with Edgar
    G. Ulmer, 1929, German
ABSCHIED SO SIND DIE MENSCHEN   1930, German
DER MANN DER SEINEN MORDER SUCHT   1931,
    German
VORUNTERSUCHUNG   1931, German
STURME DER LEIDENSCHAFT TEMPEST   1932,
    German
QUICK - KONIG DER CLOWNS   1932, German
BRENNENDES GEHEIMNIS THE BURNING SECRET
    1933, German
LE SEXE FAIBLE   1933, French
LA CRISE EST FINIE THE SLUMP IS OVER   1934,
    French
LA VIE PARISIENNE   1936, French
MISTER FLOW COMPLIMENTS OF MISTER FLOW
    1936, French
CARGAISON BLANCHE WOMAN RACKET   1937,
    French
MOLLENARD HATRED   1938, French
ULTIMATUM   co-director with Robert Wiene, 1938, French
PIEGES PERSONAL COLUMN   1939, French
WEST POINT WIDOW   Paramount, 1941
FLY BY NIGHT   Paramount, 1942
THE NIGHT BEFORE THE DIVORCE   20th Century-Fox,
    1942
MY HEART BELONGS TO DADDY   Paramount, 1942
SOMEONE TO REMEMBER   Republic, 1943
SON OF DRACULA   Universal, 1943
PHANTOM LADY   Universal, 1944
COBRA WOMAN   Universal, 1944
CHRISTMAS HOLIDAY   Universal, 1944
THE SUSPECT   Universal, 1945
CONFLICT   Warner Bros., 1945
UNCLE HARRY THE STRANGE AFFAIR OF UNCLE
    HARRY   Universal, 1945
THE SPIRAL STAIRCASE   RKO Radio, 1946
THE KILLERS ★   Universal, 1946
THE DARK MIRROR   Universal, 1946
TIME OUT OF MIND   Universal, 1947
CRY OF THE CITY   20th Century-Fox, 1948
CRISS CROSS   Universal, 1949
THE GREAT SINNER   MGM, 1949
THE FILE ON THELMA JORDAN   Paramount, 1949
DEPORTED   Universal, 1950
THE WHISTLE AT EATON FALLS   Columbia, 1951
THE CRIMSON PIRATE   Warner Bros., 1952,
    U.S.-British
FLESH AND THE WOMAN LE GRAND JEU   Dominant
    Pictures, 1954, French-Italian
DIE RATTEN   1955, West German
MEIN VATER DER SCHAUSPIELER   1956, West German

THE DEVIL STRIKES AT NIGHT *NACHTS, WENN DER TEUFEL KAM* Zenith International, 1957, West German
DOROTHEA ANGERMANN 1959, West German
PORTRAIT OF A SINNER *THE ROUGH AND THE SMOOTH* American International, 1959, British
MAGNIFICENT SINNER *UNE JEUNE FILLE, UN SEUL AMOUR/KATYA* Film-Mart, 1959, French
MEIN SCHULFREUND 1960, West German
L'AFFAIRE NINA B 1962, French-West German
ESCAPE FROM EAST BERLIN MGM, 1962, West German-U.S.
DER SCHUT 1964, West German
DER SCHATZ DER AZTEKEN 1965, West German-Italian-Spanish
DIE PYRAMIDE DES SONNENGOTTES 1965, West German-Italian-Spanish
CUSTER OF THE WEST Cinerama Releasing Corporation, 1968, U.S.-Spanish
DER KAMPF UM ROM 1969, West German-Italian

DOUGLAS SIRK
(Detlef Sierck/Claus Detlev Sierk)
b. April 26, 1900 - Skagen, Denmark
d. 1987

APRIL APRIL 1935, German
STUTZEN DER GESELLSCHAFT 1935, German
DAS MADCHEN VON MOORHOF 1935, German
DAS HOFKONZERT 1936, German
SCHLUSSAKKORD 1936, German
LA HABANERA 1937, German
LIEBLING DER MATROSEN 1937, German
ZU NEUEN UFERN 1937, German
DIE HEIMAT RUFT 1937, German
WILTON'S ZOO 1938, South African
HITLER'S MADMAN MGM, 1943
SUMMER DREAM United Artists, 1944
A SCANDAL IN PARIS United Artists, 1946
LURED Universal, 1947
SLEEP MY LOVE United Artists, 1948
SLIGHTLY FRENCH Columbia, 1949
SHOCKPROOF Columbia, 1949
MYSTERY SUBMARINE Universal, 1950
THE FIRST LEGION United Artists, 1951
THUNDER ON THE HILL Universal, 1951
THE LADY PAYS OFF Universal, 1951
WEEKEND WITH FATHER 1951
NO ROOM FOR THE GROOM Universal, 1952
HAS ANYBODY SEEN MY GAL? Universal, 1952
MEET ME AT THE FAIR Universal, 1953
TAKE ME TO TOWN Universal, 1953
ALL I DESIRE Universal, 1953
TAZA, SON OF COCHISE Universal, 1954
MAGNIFICENT OBSESSION Universal, 1954
SIGN OF THE PAGAN Universal, 1954
CAPTAIN LIGHTFOOT Universal, 1955
THERE'S ALWAYS TOMORROW Universal, 1956
ALL THAT HEAVEN ALLOWS Universal, 1956
WRITTEN ON THE WIND Universal, 1957
BATTLE HYMN Universal, 1957
INTERLUDE Universal, 1957
THE TARNISHED ANGELS Universal, 1958
A TIME TO LOVE AND A TIME TO DIE Universal, 1958
IMITATION OF LIFE Universal, 1959

ALF SJOBERG
b. June 21, 1903 - Stockholm, Sweden
d. 1980

THE STRONGEST 1929, Swedish
THEY STAKED THEIR LIVES 1940, Swedish
BLOSSOM TIME 1940, Swedish
HOME FROM BABYLON 1941, Swedish
HIMLASPELET 1942, Swedish
TORMENT Oxford Films, 1944, Swedish
THE ROYAL HUNT 1944, Swedish
JOURNEY OUT 1945, Swedish
IRIS AND THE LIEUTENANT 1946, Swedish
ONLY A MOTHER 1949, Swedish
MISS JULIE Trans-Global Pictures, 1951, Swedish
BARABBAS 1953, Swedish
KARIN, DAUGHTER OF MAN 1954, Swedish
WILD BIRDS 1955, Swedish
LAST PAIR OUT 1956, Swedish
THE JUDGE 1960, Swedish
THE ISLAND 1966, Swedish
THE FATHER 1969, Swedish

VICTOR SJOSTROM
(Victor Seastrom)
b. September 20, 1879 - Silbodal, Sweden
d. 1960

THE GARDENER 1912, Swedish
A SECRET MARRIAGE 1912, Swedish
A SUMMER TALE 1912, Swedish, unreleased
THE MARRIAGE BUREAU 1913, Swedish
SMILES AND TEARS 1913, Swedish
LADY MARION'S SUMMER FLIRTATION 1913, Swedish
THE VOICE OF BLOOD 1913, Swedish
INGEBORG HOLM 1913, Swedish
LIFE'S CONFLICTS 1913, Swedish
THE CLERGYMAN 1914, Swedish
LOVE STRONGER THAN HATE 1914, Swedish
HALF-BREED 1914, Swedish
THE MIRACLE 1914, Swedish
DO NOT JUDGE 1914, Swedish
A GOOD GIRL SHOULD SOLVE HER OWN PROBLEMS 1914, Swedish
CHILDREN OF THE STREET 1914, Swedish
DAUGHTER OF THE HIGH MOUNTAIN 1914, Swedish
HEARTS THAT MEET 1914, Swedish
THE STRIKE 1915, Swedish
ONE OUT OF MANY 1915, Swedish
EXPIATED GUILT 1915, Swedish
IT WAS IN MAY 1915, Swedish
KEEP TO YOUR TRADE 1915, Swedish
JUDAS MONEY 1915, Swedish
THE GOVERNOR'S DAUGHTERS 1916, Swedish
SEA VULTURES 1916, Swedish
AT THE MOMENT OF TRIAL 1916, Swedish
SHIPS THAT MEET 1916, Swedish
SHE WAS VICTORIOUS 1916, Swedish
THERESE 1916, Swedish
THE KISS OF DEATH 1917, Swedish
A MAN THERE WAS 1917, Swedish
THE OUTLAW AND HIS WIFE 1918, Swedish
THE SONS OF INGMAR, PART I 1919, Swedish
THE SONS OF INGMAR, PART II 1919, Swedish
A GIRL FROM THE MARSH CROFT 1919, Swedish
HIS GRACE'S WILL 1919, Swedish
THE MONASTERY OF SENDOMIR 1920, Swedish

KARIN, DAUGHTER OF INGMAR   1920, Swedish
THE EXECUTIONER   1920, Swedish
THE PHANTOM CARRIAGE   1921, Swedish
LOVE'S CRUCIBLE   1922, Swedish
THE SURROUNDED HOUSE   1922, Swedish
FIRE ON BOARD   1922, Swedish
NAME THE MAN   MGM, 1924
HE WHO GETS SLAPPED   MGM, 1924
CONFESSIONS OF A QUEEN   MGM, 1925
THE TOWER OF LIES   MGM, 1925
THE SCARLET LETTER   MGM, 1926
THE DIVINE WOMAN   MGM, 1928
THE WIND   MGM, 1928
MARKS OF THE DEVIL   MGM, 1928
A LADY TO LOVE   MGM, 1930
MARKURELLS I WADKOPING   1931, Swedish
UNDER THE RED ROBE   20th Century-Fox, 1937,
   British

R.G. (BUD) SPRINGSTEEN
b. September 8, 1904 - Tacoma, Washington
d. 1989

MARSHAL OF LAREDO   Republic, 1945
WAGON WHEELS WESTWARD   Republic, 1945
CALIFORNIA GOLD RUSH   Republic, 1946
HOME ON THE RANGE   Republic, 1946
CONQUEST OF CHEYENNE   Republic, 1946
SANTA FE UPRISING   Republic, 1946
STAGECOACH TO DENVER   Republic, 1946
MARSHAL OF CRIPPLE CREEK   Republic, 1947
ALONG THE OREGON TRAIL   Republic, 1947
UNDER COLORADO SKIES   Republic, 1947
THE MAIN STREET KID   Republic, 1948
HEART OF VIRGINIA   Republic, 1948
SECRET SERVICE INVESTIGATOR   Republic, 1948
OUT OF THE STORM   Republic, 1948
DEATH VALLEY GUNFIGHTERS   Republic, 1949
HELLFIRE   Republic, 1949
THE RED MENACE   Republic, 1949
FLAME OF YOUTH   Republic, 1949
SINGING GUNS   Republic, 1950
HARBOR OF MISSING MEN   Republic, 1950
THE ARIZONA COWBOY   Republic, 1950
HILLS OF OKLAHOMA   Republic, 1950
MILLION DOLLAR PURSUIT   Republic, 1951
HONEYCHILE   Republic, 1951
STREET BANDITS   Republic, 1951
THE FABULOUS SENORITA   Republic, 1952
OKLAHOMA ANNIE   Republic, 1952
GOBS AND GALS   Republic, 1952
TROPICAL HEAT WAVE   Republic, 1952
A PERILOUS JOURNEY   Republic, 1953
GERALDINE   Republic, 1954
I COVER THE UNDERWORLD   Republic, 1955
DOUBLE JEOPARDY   Republic, 1955
TRACK THE MAN DOWN   Republic, 1955, British
COME NEXT SPRING   Republic, 1956
WHEN GANGLAND STRIKES   Republic, 1956
AFFAIR IN RENO   Republic, 1957
COLE YOUNGER - GUNFIGHTER   Allied Artists, 1958
REVOLT IN THE BIG HOUSE   Allied Artists, 1958
BATTLE FLAME   Allied Artists, 1959
KING OF THE WILD STALLIONS   Allied Artists, 1959
OPERATION EICHMANN   Allied Artists, 1961
SHOWDOWN   Universal, 1963
HE RIDES TALL   Universal, 1964
BULLET FOR A BADMAN   Universal, 1964
TAGGART   Universal, 1965
BLACK SPURS   Paramount, 1965

APACHE UPRISING   Paramount, 1966
JOHNNY RENO   Paramount, 1966
WACO   Paramount, 1966
RED TOMAHAWK   Paramount, 1967
HOSTILE GUNS   Paramount, 1967
TIGER BY THE TAIL   1970

JOHN M. STAHL
b. January 21, 1886 - New York, New York
d. 1950

WIVES OF MEN   Pioneer, 1918
SUSPICION   H.H. Hoffman, 1918
HER CODE OF HONOR   Tribune-United, 1919
A WOMAN UNDER OATH   Tribune-United, 1919
GREATER THAN LOVE   American Cinema Association,
   1919
WOMEN MEN FORGET   United Pictures, 1920
THE WOMAN IN HIS HOUSE   Associated First
   National, 1920
THE CHILD THOU GAVEST ME   Associated First
   National, 1921
SOWING THE WIND   Associated First National, 1921
SUSPICIOUS WIVES   State Rights, 1921
THE SONG OF LIFE   Associated First National, 1922
ONE CLEAR CALL   Associated First National, 1922
THE DANGEROUS AGE   Associated First National, 1923
WHY MEN LEAVE HOME   First National, 1924
HUSBANDS AND LOVERS   First National, 1924
FINE CLOTHES   First National, 1925
MEMORY LANE   First National, 1926
THE GAY DECEIVER   MGM, 1926
LOVERS?   MGM, 1927
IN OLD KENTUCKY   MGM, 1927
A LADY SURRENDERS   Universal, 1930
SEED   Universal, 1931
STRICTLY DISHONORABLE   Universal, 1931
BACK STREET   Universal, 1932
ONLY YESTERDAY   Universal, 1933
IMITATION OF LIFE   Universal, 1934
MAGNIFICENT OBSESSION   Universal, 1935
PARNELL   MGM, 1937
LETTER OF INTRODUCTION   Universal, 1938
WHEN TOMORROW COMES   Universal, 1939
OUR WIFE   Columbia, 1941
THE IMMORTAL SERGEANT   20th Century-Fox, 1943
HOLY MATRIMONY   20th Century-Fox, 1943
THE EVE OF ST. MARK   20th Century-Fox, 1944
THE KEYS OF THE KINGDOM   20th Century-Fox, 1944
LEAVE HER TO HEAVEN   20th Century-Fox, 1945
THE FOXES OF HARROW   20th Century-Fox, 1947
THE WALLS OF JERICHO   20th Century-Fox, 1948
FATHER WAS A FULLBACK   20th Century-Fox, 1949
OH, YOU BEAUTIFUL DOLL   20th Century-Fox, 1949

JACK STARRETT
b. November 2, 1936 - Refugio, Texas
d. 1989

RUN, ANGEL, RUN!   Fanfare, 1969
THE LOSERS   Fanfare, 1970
CRY BLOOD, APACHE   Golden Eagle International, 1970
NIGHT CHASE (TF)   Cinema Center, 1970
THE STRANGE VENGEANCE OF ROSALIE   20th Century-
   Fox, 1972
SLAUGHTER   American International, 1972
CLEOPATRA JONES   Warner Bros., 1973
GRAVY TRAIN THE DION BROTHERS   Columbia, 1974
RACE WITH THE DEVIL   20th Century-Fox, 1975

A SMALL TOWN IN TEXAS   American International, 1976
FINAL CHAPTER - WALKING TALL   American International, 1977
ROGER & HARRY: THE MITERA TARGET (TF)   Bruce Lansbury Productions/ Columbia TV, 1977
NOWHERE TO HIDE (TF)   Mark Carliner Productions/ Viacom, 1977
THADDEUS ROSE AND EDDIE (TF)   CBS, Inc., 1978
BIG BOB JOHNSON AND HIS FANTASTIC SPEED CIRCUS (TF)   Playboy Productions/Paramount TV, 1978
MR. HORN (TF)   Lorimar Productions, 1979
SURVIVAL OF DANA (TF)   EMI TV, 1979
KISS MY GRITS   A TEXAS LEGEND/SUMMER HEAT   Ambassador, 1982

GEORGE STEVENS

b. December 18, 1904 - Oakland, California
d. 1975

THE COHENS AND KELLYS IN TROUBLE   RKO Radio, 1933
BACHELOR BAIT   RKO Radio, 1934
KENTUCKY KERNELS   RKO Radio, 1934
LADDIE   RKO Radio, 1935
THE NITWITS   RKO Radio, 1935
ALICE ADAMS   RKO Radio, 1935
ANNIE OAKLEY   RKO Radio, 1935
SWING TIME   RKO Radio, 1936
QUALITY STREET   RKO Radio, 1937
A DAMSEL IN DISTRESS   RKO Radio, 1937
VIVACIOUS LADY   RKO Radio, 1938
GUNGA DIN   RKO Radio, 1939
VIGIL IN THE NIGHT   RKO Radio, 1940
PENNY SERENADE   Columbia, 1941
WOMAN OF THE YEAR   MGM, 1942
THE TALK OF THE TOWN   Columbia, 1942
THE MORE THE MERRIER ★   Columbia, 1943
I REMEMBER MAMA   RKO Radio, 1948
A PLACE IN THE SUN ★★   Paramount, 1951
SOMETHING TO LIVE FOR   Paramount, 1952
SHANE ★   Paramount, 1953
GIANT ★★   Warner Bros., 1956
THE DIARY OF ANNE FRANK ★   20th Century-Fox, 1959
THE GREATEST STORY EVER TOLD   United Artists, 1965
THE ONLY GAME IN TOWN   20th Century-Fox, 1970

ROBERT STEVENSON

b. 1905 - London, England
d. 1986

HAPPILY EVER AFTER   Gaumont, 1932, British
FALLING FOR YOU   Woolf & Freedman, 1933, British
JACK OF ALL TRADES   Gaumont, 1936, British
NINE DAYS A QUEEN   TUDOR ROSE   Gaumont, 1936, British
THE MAN WHO LIVED AGAIN   THE MAN WHO CHANGED HIS MIND   Gaumont, 1936, British
KING SOLOMON'S MINES   Gaumont, 1937, British
NON-STOP NEW YORK   General Film Distributors, 1937, British
TO THE VICTOR   OWD BOB   Gaumont, 1938, British
THE WARE CASE   Associated British Film Distributors, 1939, British
A YOUNG MAN'S FANCY   Associated British Film Distributors, 1939, British
RETURN TO YESTERDAY   Associated British Film Distributors, 1939, British

TOM BROWN'S SCHOOLDAYS   RKO Radio, 1940
BACK STREET   Universal, 1941
JOAN OF PARIS   RKO Radio, 1942
FOREVER AND A DAY   co-director with Rene Clair, Edmund Goulding, Cedric Hardwicke, Frank Lloyd, Victor Saville & Herbert Wilcox, RKO Radio, 1943
JANE EYRE   RKO Radio, 1944
DISHONORED LADY   United Artists, 1947
TO THE ENDS OF THE EARTH   RKO Radio, 1948
THE WOMAN ON PIER 13   I MARRIED A COMMUNIST   RKO Radio, 1949
WALK SOFTLY, STRANGER   RKO Radio, 1950
MY FORBIDDEN PAST   RKO Radio, 1951
THE LAS VEGAS STORY   RKO Radio, 1952
JOHNNY TREMAIN   Buena Vista, 1957
OLD YELLER   Buena Vista, 1957
DARBY O'GILL AND THE LITTLE PEOPLE   Buena Vista, 1959
KIDNAPPED   Buena Vista, 1960, British-U.S.
THE ABSENT-MINDED PROFESSOR   Buena Vista, 1960
IN SEARCH OF THE CASTAWAYS   Buena Vista, 1962, British-U.S.
SON OF FLUBBER   Buena Vista, 1963
THE MISADVENTURES OF MERLIN JONES   Buena Vista, 1964
MARY POPPINS ★   Buena Vista, 1964
THE MONKEY'S UNCLE   Buena Vista, 1965
THAT DARN CAT   Buena Vista, 1965
THE GNOME-MOBILE   Buena Vista, 1967
BLACKBEARD'S GHOST   Buena Vista, 1968
THE LOVE BUG   Buena Vista, 1969
BEDKNOBS AND BROOMSTICKS   Buena Vista, 1971
HERBIE RIDES AGAIN   Buena Vista, 1974
THE ISLAND AT THE TOP OF THE WORLD   Buena Vista, 1974
ONE OF OUR DINOSAURS IS MISSING   Buena Vista, 1975, U.S.-British
THE SHAGGY D.A.   Buena Vista, 1976

MAURITZ STILLER
(Moshe Stiller)

b. July 17, 1883 - Helsinki, Finland
d. 1928

MOTHER AND DAUGHTER   1912, Swedish
THE BLACK MASKS   1912, Swedish
THE TYRANNICAL FIANCEE   1912, Swedish
THE VAMPIRE   1913, Swedish
WHEN LOVE KILLS   1913, Swedish
WHEN THE ALARM BELL RINGS   1913, Swedish
THE CHILD   1913, Swedish
THE UNKNOWN WOMAN   1913, Swedish
ON THE FATEFUL ROADS OF LIFE   1913, Swedish
THE MODERN SUFFRAGETTE   1913, Swedish
THE MODEL   1913, Swedish, unreleased
WHEN THE MOTHER-IN-LAW REIGNS   1914, Swedish
BROTHERS   1914, Swedish
PEOPLE OF THE BORDER   1914, Swedish
BECAUSE OF HER LOVE   1914, Swedish
THE CHAMBERLAIN   1914, Swedish
STORMY PETREL   1914, Swedish
THE SHOT   1914, Swedish
THE RED TOWER   1914, Swedish
WHEN ARTISTS LOVE   1915, Swedish
PLAYMATES   1915, Swedish
HIS WIFE'S PAST   1915, Swedish
ACE OF THIEVES   1915, Swedish
THE DAGGER   1915, Swedish

MADAME DE THEBES 1915, Swedish
THE AVENGER 1916, Swedish
THE MINE PILOT 1916, Swedish
HIS WEDDING NIGHT 1916, Swedish
THE LUCKY BROOCH 1916, Swedish
LOVE AND JOURNALISM 1916, Swedish
THE WINGS 1916, Swedish
THE FIGHT FOR HIS HEART 1916, Swedish
THE BALLET PRIMADONNA 1916, Swedish
THOMAS GRAAL'S BEST FILM 1917, Swedish
ALEXANDER THE GREAT 1917, Swedish
THOMAS GRAAL'S FIRST CHILD 1918, Swedish
SONG OF THE SCARLET FLOWER 191, Swedish
SIR ARNE'S TREASURE *THE THREE WHO WERE
    DOOMED* 1919, Swedish
THE FISHING VILLAGE 1920, Swedish
EROTIKON 1920, Swedish
JOHAN co-director with Arthur Nordeen, 1921,
    Swedish
THE EXILES 1921, Swedish
GUNNAR HEDE'S SAGA 1923, Swedish
THE STORY OF GOSTA BERLING 1924, Swedish
HOTEL IMPERIAL Paramount, 1927
THE WOMAN ON TRIAL Paramount, 1927
THE STREET OF SIN Paramount, 1928

PRESTON STURGES
(Edmund P. Biden)
b. August 29, 1898 - Chicago, Illinois
d. 1959

THE GREAT McGINTY Paramount, 1940
CHRISTMAS IN JULY Paramount, 1940
THE LADY EVE Paramount, 1941
SULLIVAN'S TRAVELS Paramount, 1941
THE PALM BEACH STORY Paramount, 1942
THE MIRACLE OF MORGAN'S CREEK
    Paramount, 1944
HAIL THE CONQUERING HERO Paramount, 1944
THE GREAT MOMENT Paramount, 1944
MAD WEDNESDAY *THE SIN OF HAROLD DIDDLEBOCK*
    RKO Radio, 1947
UNFAITHFULLY YOURS 20th Century-Fox, 1948
THE BEAUTIFUL BLONDE FROM BASHFUL BEND
    20th Century-Fox, 1949
THE FRENCH THEY ARE A FUNNY RACE *LES
    CARNETS DU MAJOR THOMPSON* Continental,
    1957, French

EDWARD SUTHERLAND
b. January 5, 1895 - London, England
d. 1974

COMING THROUGH Paramount, 1925
WILD WILD SUSAN Paramount, 1925
A REGULAR FELLOW Paramount, 1925
BEHIND THE FRONT Paramount, 1926
IT'S THE OLD ARMY GAME Paramount, 1926
WE'RE IN THE NAVY NOW Paramount, 1926
LOVE'S GREATEST MISTAKE Paramount, 1927
FIREMAN SAVE MY CHILD Paramount, 1927
FIGURES DON'T LIE Paramount, 1927
TILLIE'S PUNCTURED ROMANCE Paramount, 1928
THE BABY CYCLONE Paramount, 1928
WHAT A NIGHT! Paramount, 1928
CLOSE HARMONY co-director with John Cromwell,
    Paramount, 1929
THE DANCE OF LIFE co-director with John Cromwell,
    Paramount, 1929

FAST COMPANY Paramount, 1929
THE SATURDAY NIGHT KID Paramount, 1929
POINTED HEELS Paramount, 1929
PARAMOUNT ON PARADE co-director, Paramount,
    1930
BURNING UP Paramount, 1930
THE SOCIAL LION Paramount, 1930
THE SAP FROM SYRACUSE Paramount, 1930
THE GANG BUSTER Paramount, 1931
JUNE MOON Paramount, 1931
UP POPS THE DEVIL Paramount, 1931
PALMY DAYS United Artists, 1931
SKY DEVILS United Artists, 1932
MR. ROBINSON CRUSOE United Artists, 1932
SECRETS OF THE FRENCH POLICE RKO, 1932
MURDERS IN THE ZOO Paramount, 1933
INTERNATIONAL HOUSE Paramount, 1933
TOO MUCH HARMONY Paramount, 1933
MISSISSIPPI Paramount, 1935
DIAMOND JIM Universal, 1935
POPPY Paramount, 1936
CHAMPAGNE WALTZ Paramount, 1937
EVERY DAY'S A HOLIDAY Paramount, 1937
THE FLYING DEUCES RKO Radio, 1939
THE BOYS FROM SYRACUSE Universal, 1940
BEYOND TOMORROW RKO Radio, 1940
ONE NIGHT IN THE TROPICS Universal, 1940
THE INVISIBLE WOMAN Universal, 1941
NINE LIVES ARE NOT ENOUGH Warner Bros., 1941
STEEL AGAINST THE SKY Warner Bros., 1941
SING YOUR WORRIES AWAY RKO Radio, 1942
ARMY SURGEON RKO Radio, 1942
THE NAVY COME THROUGH RKO Radio, 1942
DIXIE Paramount, 1943
FOLLOW THE BOYS Universal, 1944
SECRET COMMAND Columbia, 1944
HAVING A WONDERFUL CRIME RKO Radio, 1945
ABIE'S IRISH ROSE United Artists, 1946
BERMUDA AFFAIR Columbia, 1956

T

FRED TAN
b. January 1, 1958
d. 1990

LOVERS Horizons Productions, 1984
STORM OF YOUTH Horizon Productions, 1986, Hong
    Kong
DARK NIGHT Goodyear Movie Company, 1986, Tai-
    wanese-Hong Kong
SPLIT OF THE SPIRIT Horizons Productions, 1987
ROUGE OF THE NORTH Central Motion Picture Corpora-
    tion, 1988, Taiwanese

ANDREI TARKOVSKY
b. April 4, 1932 - Zavrazhe, U.S.S.R.
d. 1986

THE ROLLER AND THE VIOLIN Mosfilm, 1906, Soviet
MY NAME IS IVAN Shore International, 1962, Soviet
ANDREI RUBLEV Columbia, 1968, Soviet
SOLARIS Mosfilm, 1972, Soviet

THE MIRROR   Mosfilm, 1974, Soviet
STALKER   New Yorker/Media Transactions Corporation, 1979, Soviet
NOSTALGHIA   Grange Communications, 1983, Italian-Soviet
THE SACRIFICE   Orion Classics, 1986, Swedish-French

FRANK TASHLIN
b. February 19, 1913
d. 1972

THE FIRST TIME   Columbia, 1952
SON OF PALEFACE   Paramount, 1952
MARRY ME AGAIN   RKO Radio, 1954
SUSAN SLEPT HERE   RKO Radio, 1954
ARTISTS AND MODELS   Paramount, 1955
THE LIEUTENANT WORE SKIRTS   20th Century-Fox, 1956
HOLLYWOOD OR BUST   Paramount, 1956
THE GIRL CAN'T HELP IT   20th Century-Fox, 1956
WILL SUCCESS SPOIL ROCK HUNTER?   20th Century-Fox, 1957
ROCK-A-BYE BABY   Paramount, 1958
THE GEISHA BOY   Paramount, 1958
SAY ONE FOR ME   20th Century-Fox, 1959
CINDERFELLA   Paramount, 1960
BACHELOR FLAT   20th Century-Fox, 1962
IT'S ONLY MONEY   Paramount, 1962
THE MAN FROM THE DINER'S CLUB   Columbia, 1963
WHO'S MINDING THE STORE?   Paramount, 1963
THE DISORDERLY ORDERLY   Paramount, 1964
THE ALPHABET MURDERS   *THE A.B.C. MURDERS* MGM, 1966, British
THE GLASS BOTTOM BOAT   MGM, 1966
CAPRICE   20th Century-Fox, 1967
THE PRIVATE NAVY OF SGT. O'FARRELL   United Artists, 1968

JACQUES TATI
(Jacques Tatischeff)
b. October 9, 1908 - Le Pecq, France
d. 1982

L'ECOLE DES FACTEURS   1947, French
JOUR DE FETE   Mayer-Kingsley, 1949, French
MR. HULOT'S HOLIDAY   G-B-D International, 1953, French
MY UNCLE, MR. HULOT   *MON ONCLE* Continental, 1956, French
PLAYTIME   Continental, 1968, French
TRAFFIC   Columbia, 1971, French
PARADE (TF)   1974, French

NORMAN TAUROG
b. February 23, 1899 - Chicago, Illinois
d. 1981

THE FARMER'S DAUGHTER   Fox, 1928
LUCKY BOY   co-director with Charles C. Wilson, Tiffany, 1929
TROOPERS THREE   co-director with Reeves Eason, Tiffany, 1930
SUNNY SKIES   Tiffany, 1930
HOT CURVES   Tiffany, 1930
FOLLOW THE LEADER   Paramount, 1930
FINN AND HATTIE   co-director with Norman Z. MacLeod, Paramount, 1931

SKIPPY ★★   Paramount, 1931
NEWLY RICH   Paramount, 1931
HUCKLEBERRY FINN   Paramount, 1931
SOOKY   Paramount, 1931
HOLD 'EM JAIL!   Paramount, 1932
THE PHANTOM PRESIDENT   Paramount, 1932
IF I HAD A MILLION   co-director, Paramount, 1932
A BEDTIME STORY   Paramount, 1933
THE WAY TO LOVE   Paramount, 1933
WE'RE NOT DRESSING   Paramount, 1934
MRS. WIGGS OF THE CABBAGE PATCH   Paramount, 1934
COLLEGE RHYTHM   Paramount, 1934
THE BIG BROADCAST OF 1936   Paramount, 1936
STRIKE ME PINK   United Artists, 1936
RHYTHM ON THE RANGE   Paramount, 1936
REUNION   20th Century-Fox, 1936
FIFTY ROADS TO TOWN   20th Century-Fox, 1937
YOU CAN'T HAVE EVERYTHING   20th Century-Fox, 1937
THE ADVENTURES OF TOM SAWYER   United Artists, 1938
MAD ABOUT MUSIC   Universal, 1938
BOYS TOWN ★   MGM, 1938
THE GIRL DOWNSTAIRS   MGM, 1938
LUCKY NIGHT   MGM, 1939
YOUNG TOM EDISON   MGM, 1940
BROADWAY MELODY OF 1940   MGM, 1940
LITTLE NELLIE KELLY   MGM, 1940
MEN OF BOYS TOWN   MGM, 1941
DESIGN FOR SCANDAL   MGM, 1941
ARE HUSBANDS NECESSARY?   Paramount, 1942
A YANK AT ETON   MGM, 1942
PRESENTING LILY MARS   MGM, 1943
GIRL CRAZY   MGM, 1943
THE HOODLUM SAINT   MGM, 1946
THE BEGINNING OR THE END   MGM, 1947
BIG CITY   MGM, 1948
THE BRIDE GOES WILD   MGM, 1948
WORDS AND MUSIC   MGM, 1948
THAT MIDNIGHT KISS   MGM, 1949
PLEASE BELIEVE ME   MGM, 1950
THE TOAST OF NEW ORLEANS   MGM, 1950
MRS. O'MALLEY AND MR. MALONE   MGM, 1950
RICH, YOUNG AND PRETTY   MGM, 1951
ROOM FOR ONE MORE   Warner Bros., 1952
JUMPING JACKS   Paramount, 1952
THE STOOGE   Paramount, 1953
THE STARS ARE SINGING   Paramount, 1953
THE CADDY   Paramount, 1953
LIVING IT UP   Paramount, 1954
YOU'RE NEVER TOO YOUNG   Paramount, 1955
THE BIRDS AND THE BEES   Paramount, 1956
PARDNERS   Paramount, 1956
BUNDLE OF JOY   RKO Radio, 1956
THE FUZZY PINK NIGHTGOWN   United Artists, 1957
ONIONHEAD   Warner Bros., 1958
DON'T GIVE UP THE SHIP   Paramount, 1959
VISIT TO A SMALL PLANET   Paramount, 1960
G.I. BLUES   Paramount, 1960
ALL HANDS ON DECK   20th Century-Fox, 1961
BLUE HAWAII   Paramount, 1961
GIRLS! GIRLS! GIRLS!   Paramount, 1962
IT HAPPENED AT THE WORLD'S FAIR   MGM, 1963
PALM SPRINGS WEEKEND   Warner Bros., 1963
TICKLE ME   Allied Artists, 1965
SERGEANT DEADHEAD   American International, 1965
DR. GOLDFOOT AND THE BIKINI MACHINE   American International, 1966
SPINOUT   MGM, 1966

DOUBLE TROUBLE   MGM, 1967
SPEEDWAY   MGM, 1968
C'MON, LET'S LIVE A LITTLE   Paramount, 1968
LIVE A LITTLE, LOVE A LITTLE   MGM, 1968

WILLIAM DESMOND TAYLOR
(William Cunningham Deane-Turner)
b. April 26, 1877 - Ireland
d. 1922

THE BEGGAR CHILD   1914
THE DIAMOND FROM THE SKY   co-director with
   Jacques Jaccard, American, 1915, serial
THE LAST CHAPTER   Reliance, 1915
THE HIGH HAND   Reliance, 1915
THE AMERICAN BEAUTY   Paramount, 1916
DAVY CROCKETT   Paramount, 1916
HE FELL IN LOVE WITH HIS WIFE   Paramount, 1916
BEN BLAIR   Paramount, 1916
HER FATHER'S SON   Paramount, 1916
THE HOUSE OF LIES   Paramount, 1916
PASQUALE   Paramount, 1916
THE PARSON OF PANAMINT   Paramount, 1916
THE REDEEMING LOVE   Paramount, 1917
THE HAPPINESS OF THREE WOMEN   Paramount,
   1917
THE VARMINT   Paramount, 1917
THE WORLD APART   Paramount, 1917
TOM SAWYER   Paramount, 1917
JACK AND JILL   Paramount, 1917
THE SPIRIT OF '17   Paramount, 1918
HUCK AND TOM   Paramount, 1918
UP THE ROAD WITH SALLY   Selznick, 1918
HIS MAJESTY BUNKER BEAN   Paramount, 1918
MILE-A-MINUTE KENDALL   Paramount, 1918
HOW COULD YOU, JEAN?   Artclass, 1918
JOHANNA ENLISTS   Artclass, 1918
CAPTAIN KIDD, JR.   Artclass, 1919
ANNE OF GREEN GABLES   Realart, 1919
JUDY OF ROGUE'S HARBOR   Realart, 1920
NURSE MARJORIE   Realart, 1920
JENNY BE GOOD   Realart, 1920
HUCKLEBERRY FINN   Paramount, 1920
THE SOUL OF YOUTH   Paramount, 1920
THE WITCHING HOUR   Paramount, 1921
SACRED AND PROFANE LOVE   Paramount, 1921
BEYOND   Paramount, 1921
WEALTH   Paramount, 1921
MORALS   Paramount, 1921
THE GREEN TEMPTATION   Paramount, 1922
THE TOP OF NEW YORK   Paramount, 1922

JACQUES TOURNEUR
b. November 12, 1904 - Paris, France
d. 1977

UN VIEUX GARCON   1931, French
TOUT CA NE VAUT PAS L'AMOUR   1931, French
LA FUSEE   1933, French
TOTO   1933, French
POUR ETRE AIMEE   1933, French
LES FILLES DE LA CONCIERGE   1934, French
THEY ALL CAME OUT   MGM, 1939
NICK CARTER - MASTER DETECTIVE   MGM, 1939
PHANTOM RAIDERS   MGM, 1940
DOCTORS DON'T TELL   MGM, 1941
CAT PEOPLE   RKO Radio, 1942
I WALKED WITH A ZOMBIE   RKO Radio, 1943

THE LEOPARD MAN   RKO Radio, 1943
DAYS OF GLORY   RKO Radio, 1944
EXPERIMENT PERILOUS   RKO Radio, 1944
CANYON PASSAGE   Universal, 1946
OUT OF THE PAST   RKO Radio, 1947
BERLIN EXPRESS   RKO Radio, 1948
EASY LIVING   RKO Radio, 1949
THE FLAME AND THE ARROW   Warner Bros., 1950
STARS IN MY CROWN   MGM, 1950
CIRCLE OF DANGER   Eagle Lion, 1951, British
ANNE OF THE INDIES   20th Century-Fox, 1951
WAY OF A GAUCHO   20th Century-Fox, 1952
APPOINTMENT IN HONDURAS   RKO Radio, 1953
STRANGER ON HORSEBACK   United Artists, 1955
WICHITA   Allied Artists, 1955
GREAT DAY IN THE MORNING   RKO Radio, 1956
NIGHTFALL   Columbia, 1957
CURSE OF THE DEMON   N*IGHT OF THE DEMON*
   Columbia, 1957, British
THE FEARMAKERS   United Artists, 1958
MISSION OF DANGER   co-director with George Waggner,
   MGM, 1959
TIMBUKTU   United Artists, 1959
FRONTIER RANGERS (TF)   co-director with George
   Waggner, MGM, 1959
FURY RIVER   co-director with George Waggner, MGM,
   1959
SAVAGE FRONTIER   MGM, 1960
THE GIANT OF MARATHON   *LA BATTAGLIA DI
   MARATONA*   MGM, 1960, Italian
THE COMEDY OF TERRORS   American International,
   1963
WAR-GODS OF THE DEEP   *THE CITY UNDER THE SEA*
   American International, 1965, British-U.S.

MAURICE TOURNEUR
(Maurice Thomas)
b. February 2, 1876 - Paris, France
d. 1961

LE FRIQUET   1912, French
JEAN LA POUDRE   1912, French
LE SYSTEME DU DOCTEUR GOUDRON ET DU
   PROFESSEUR PLUME   1912, French
FIGURES DE CIRE   1912, French
LE DERNIER PARDON   1913, French
LE PUITS MITOYEN   1913, French
LE CAMEE   1913, French
SOEURETTE   1913, French
LE CORSO ROUGE   1913, French
MADEMOISELLE 100 MILLIONS   1913, French
LES GAITES DE L'ESCADRON   1913, French
LA DAME DE MONTSOREAU   1913, French
MONSIEUR LECOCQ   1914, French
ROULETABILLE: LE MYSTERE DE LA CHAMBRE
   JAUNE   1914, French
ROULETABILLE: LA DERNIERE INCARNATION
   DE LARSAN   1914, French
THE MAN OF THE HOUR   World, 1914
MOTHER   World, 1914
THE WISHING RING   World, 1914
THE PIT   World, 1914
ALIAS JIMMY VALENTINE   World, 1915
THE CUB   World, 1915
THE IVORY SNUFF BOX   World, 1915
THE IRISH SNUFF BOX   World, 1915
TRILBY   World, 1915
THE BUTTERFLY ON THE WHEEL   World, 1915
HUMAN DRIFTWOOD   co-director with Emile Chautard,
   1916

THE PAWN OF FATE   World, 1916
THE HAND OF PERIL   Peerless-Brady-World, 1916
THE CLOSED ROAD   World, 1916
THE RAIL RIDER   Peerless-Brady-World, 1916
THE VELVET PAW   Peerless-Brady-World, 1916
A GIRL'S FOLLY   Peerless-Brady-World, 1917
THE WHIP   Paragon, 1917
THE UNDYING FLAME   Paramount, 1917
EXILE   Paramount, 1917
THE LAW OF THE LAND   Paramount, 1917
THE PRIDE OF THE CLAN   Artcraft, 1917
THE POOR LITTLE RICH GIRL   Artcraft, 1917
BARBARY SHEEP   Artcraft, 1917
THE RISE OF JENNY CUSHING   Artcraft, 1917
THE ROSE OF THE WORLD   Artcraft, 1918
A DOLL'S HOUSE   Artcraft, 1918
THE BLUE BIRD   Artcraft, 1918
PRUNELLA   Paramount, 1918
SPORTING LIFE   Hiller & Wilk, 1918
WOMAN   Hiller & Wilk, 1918
THE WHITE HEATHER   Hiller & Wilk, 1919
THE LIFE LINE   Paramount, 1919
THE BROKEN BUTTERFLY   Robertson-Cole, 1919
VICTORY   Paramount, 1919
THE COUNTY FAIR   co-director with Edward J. Mortimer,
   1920
MY LADY'S GARTER   Paramount, 1920
TREASURE ISLAND   Paramount, 1920
THE GREAT REDEEMER   co-director with Clarence
   Brown, Metro, 1920
THE WHITE CIRCLE   Paramount, 1920
DEEP WATERS   Paramount, 1920
THE LAST OF THE MOHICANS   co-director with
   Clarence Brown, Associated Producers, 1920
THE BAIT   Paramount, 1921
THE FOOLISH MATRONS   co-director with Clarence
   Brown, Associated Producers, 1921
LORNA DOONE   Associated First National, 1922
WHILE PARIS SLEEPS *THE GLORY OF LOVE*
   W.W. Hodkinson, 1923
THE CHRISTIAN   Goldwyn, 1923
THE ISLE OF LOST SHIPS   Associated First National,
   1923
THE BRASS BOTTLE   Associated First National, 1923
JEALOUS HUSBANDS   Associated First National, 1923
TORMENT   First National, 1924
THE WHITE MOTH   First National, 1924
SPORTING LIFE   Universal, 1925
NEVER THE TWAIN SHALL MEET   Metro-Goldwyn,
   1925
CLOTHES MAKE THE PIRATE   First National, 1925
OLD LOVES AND NEW   First National, 1926
ALOMA OF THE SOUTH SEAS   Paramount, 1926
L'EQUIPAGE   1927, French
DAS SCHIFF DER VERLORENE MENSCHEN
   1929, German
ACCUSEE - LEVEZ-VOUZ!   1930, French
MAISON DE DANSES   1931, French
PARTIR   1931, French
AU NOM DE LA LOI   1932, French
LES GAITES DE L'ESCADRON   1932, French
LIDOIRE   1932, French
LES DEUX ORPHELINES   1933, French
L'HOMME MYSTERIEUX   1933, French
LE VOLEUR   1934, French
JUSTIN DE MARSEILLES   1935, French
KOENIGSMARK   1936, French
SAMSON   1936, French
AVEC LE SOURIRE   1936, French
CRIMSON DYNASTY   1936, French
LE PATRIOTE   1938, French

KATIA   1938, French
VOLPONE   1941, French
PECHES DE JEUNESSE   1941, French
MAM'ZELLE BONAPARTE   1941, French
LA VAL D'ENFER   1943, French
LA MAIN DU DIABLE   1943, French
CECILE EST MORTE   1944, French
APRES L'AMOUR   1948, French
L'IMPASSE DES DEUX ANGES   1948, French

JOHN TRENT
d. 1983

THE BUSHBABY   MGM, 1970, British
HOMER   National General, 1970, Canadian
THE MAN WHO WANTED TO LIVE FOREVER (TF)
   Palomar Pictures International, 1970
JALNA (TF)   CBC/Thames TV, 1972, Canadian-British
SUNDAY IN THE COUNTRY   American International,
   1973, British
IT SEEMED LIKE A GOOD IDEA AT THE TIME
   Selective Cinema, 1974, Canadian
FIND THE LADY   Danton, 1975, Canadian
RIEL (TF)   CBC, 1977, Canadian
CROSSBAR (TF)   CBC, 1978, Canadian
MIDDLE AGE CRAZY   20th Century-Fox, 1980,
   Canadian-U.S.
BEST REVENGE   Lorimar Distribution International, 1983,
   Canadian

FRANÇOIS TRUFFAUT
b. February 6, 1932 - Paris, France
d. 1984

THE 400 BLOWS   Zenith, 1959, French
SHOOT THE PIANO PLAYER   Astor, 1960, French
JULES AND JIM   Janus, 1961, French
LOVE AT TWENTY   co-director with Renzo Rossellini,
   Shintaro Ishihara, Marcel Ophuls & Andrzej Wajda,
   Embassy, 1962, French-Italian-Japanese-Polish-
   West German
THE SOFT SKIN   Cinema 5, 1964, French
FAHRENHEIT 451   Universal, 1967, British
THE BRIDE WORE BLACK   Lopert, 1968, French-Italian
STOLEN KISSES   Lopert, 1969, French
MISSISSIPPI MERMAID   United Artists, 1970, French-
   Italian
THE WILD CHILD   United Artists, 1970, French-Italian
BED AND BOARD *DOMICILE CONJUGAL*
   Columbia, 1971, French
TWO ENGLISH GIRLS *LES DEUX ANGLAISES ET LE
   CONTINENT*   Janus, 1972, French
SUCH A GORGEOUS KID LIKE ME   Columbia, 1973,
   French
DAY FOR NIGHT *LA NUIT AMERICAINE* ★   Warner
   Bros., 1973, French-Italian
THE STORY OF ADELE H.   New World, 1975, French
SMALL CHANGE *L'ARGENT DE POCHE*   New World,
   1976, French
THE MAN WHO LOVED WOMEN   Cinema 5, 1977,
   French
THE GREEN ROOM   New World, 1978, French
LOVE ON THE RUN   New World, 1979, French
THE LAST METRO   United Artists Classics, 1980,
   French
THE WOMAN NEXT DOOR   United Artists Classics, 1981,
French
VIVEMENT DIMANCHE   Spectrafilm, 1983, French

U

EDGAR G. ULMER
b. September 17, 1904 - Vienna, Austria
d. 1972

MENSCHEN AM SONNTAG (FD)   co-director with
    Robert Siodmak, 1929, German
DAMAGED LIVES   Weidon, 1933
MR. BROADWAY   Broadway-Hollywood, 1933
THE BLACK CAT   Universal, 1934
THUNDER OVER TEXAS   directed under pseudonym of
    John Warner, 1934
FROM NINE TO NINE   directed under pseudonym of
    John Warner, 1935
NATALKA POLTAVKA   1937
GREEN FIELDS   co-director with Jacob Ben-Ami,
    Collective, 1937
THE SINGING BLACKSMITH   Collective, 1938
COSSACKS IN EXILE   Avramenko Films, 1939
THE LIGHT AHEAD   1939
FISHKE THE LAME   *FISHKE DER DRUME*   1939,
    German
MOON OVER HARLEM   Meteor, 1939
AMERICAN MATCHMAKER   1940
TOMORROW WE LIVE   Producers Releasing Corp., 1942
MY SON THE HERO   Producers Releasing Corp., 1943
GIRLS IN CHAINS   Producers Releasing Corp., 1943
ISLE OF FORGOTTEN SINS   *MONSOON*   Producers
    Releasing Corp., 1943
JIVE JUNCTION   Producers Releasing Corp., 1943
BLUEBEARD   Producers Releasing Corp., 1944
STRANGE ILLUSION   *OUT OF THE NIGHT*
    Producers Releasing Corp., 1945
CLUB HAVANA   Producers Releasing Corp., 1945
DETOUR   Producers Releasing Corp., 1946
THE WIFE OF MONTE CRISTO   Producers Releasing
    Corp., 1946
HER SISTER'S SECRET   Producers Releasing Corp.,
    1946
THE STRANGE WOMAN   United Artists, 1946
CARNEGIE HALL   United Artists, 1947
RUTHLESS   Eagle Lion, 1948
THE PIRATES OF CAPRI   *CAPTAIN SIROCCO*
    Film Classics, 1949, Italian
ST. BENNY THE DIP   United Artists, 1951
THE MAN FROM PLANET X   United Artists, 1951
BABES IN BAGDAD   United Artists, 1952
MURDER IS MY BEAT   Allied Artists, 1955
THE NAKED DAWN   Universal, 1955
THE DAUGHTER OF DR. JEKYLL   Allied Artists, 1957
HANNIBAL   Warner Bros., 1960, Italian
THE AMAZING TRANSPARENT MAN   American
    International, 1960
BEYOND THE TIME BARRIER   American International,
    1960
JOURNEY BENEATH THE DESERT   *ANTINEA,*
    L'AMANTE DELLA CITTA SEPOLTA   co-director with
    Giuseppe Masini, Embassy, 1961, Italian-French
THE CAVERN   *SETTE CONTRO LA MORTE*   20th
    Century-Fox, 1965, Italian-West German

V

W.S. ("WOODY")
VAN DYKE
(Woodbridge Strong Van Dyke II)
b. 1889 - Seattle, Washington
d. 1943

THE LAND OF LONG SHADOWS   Essanay, 1917
THE RANGE BOSS   Essanay, 1917
OPEN PLACES   Essanay, 1917
MEN OF THE DESERT   Essanay, 1917
GIFT O'GAB   Essanay, 1917
THE LADY OF THE DUGOUT   Jennings-Shipman, 1918
THE HAWK'S TRAIL   Burston, 1918, serial
DAREDEVIL JACK   Pathé, 1920, serial
DOUBLE ADVENTURE   Pathé, 1921, serial
THE AVENGING ARROW   co-director with William
    J. Bowman, Pathé, 1921, serial
WHITE EAGLE   Pathé, 1922, serial
ACCORDING TO HOYLE   Western, 1922
THE BOSS OF CAMP 4   Fox, 1922
FORGET-ME-NOT   Metro, 1922
THE LITTLE GIRL NEXT DOOR   Blair-Coan, 1923
YOU ARE IN DANGER   Blair-Coan, 1923
THE DESTROYING ANGEL   Associated Exhibitors, 1923
THE MIRACLE MAKERS   Associated Exhibitors, 1923
LOVING LIES   Allied Producers & Distributors, 1924
THE BEAUTIFUL SINNER   Perfection, 1924
HALF-A-DOLLAR BILL   Metro, 1924
WINNER TAKE ALL   Fox, 1924
THE BATTLING FOOL   C.B.C., 1924
GOLD HEELS   Fox, 1924
BARRIERS BURNED AWAY   Associated Exhibitors, 1925
HEARTS AND SPURS   Fox, 1925
THE TRAIL RIDER   Fox, 1925
RANGER OF THE BIG PINES   Fox, 1925
THE TIMBER WOLF   Fox, 1925
THE DESERT'S PRICE   Fox, 1925
THE GENTLE CYCLONE   Fox, 1926
WAR PAINT   MGM, 1926
WINNERS OF THE WILDERNESS   MGM, 1927
CALIFORNIA   Arrow, 1927
THE HEART OF THE YUKON   Pathé, 1927
EYES OF THE TOTEM   Pathé, 1927
SPOILERS OF THE WEST   MGM, 1927
FOREIGN DEVILS   MGM, 1927
WYOMING   MGM, 1928
UNDER THE BLACK EAGLE   MGM, 1928
WHITE SHADOWS OF THE SOUTH SEAS   co-director
    with Robert J. Flaherty, MGM, 1928
THE PAGAN   MGM, 1929
TRADER HORN   MGM, 1931
NEVER THE TWAIN SHALL MEET   MGM, 1931
GUILTY HANDS   MGM, 1931
THE CUBAN LOVE SONG   MGM, 1931
TARZAN, THE APE MAN   MGM, 1932
NIGHT COURT   MGM, 1932
PENTHOUSE   MGM, 1933
THE PRIZEFIGHTER AND THE LADY   MGM, 1933
ESKIMO   MGM, 1933
LAUGHING BOY   MGM, 1934
MANHATTAN MELODRAMA   MGM, 1934
THE THIN MAN ★   MGM, 1934

HIDE-OUT   MGM, 1934
FORSAKING ALL OTHERS   MGM, 1934
NAUGHTY MARIETTA   MGM, 1935
I LIFE MY LIFE   MGM, 1935
ROSE-MARIE   MGM, 1936
SAN FRANCISCO ★   MGM, 1936
HIS BROTHER'S WIFE   MGM, 1936
THE DEVIL IS A SISSY   MGM, 1936
LOVE ON THE RUN   MGM, 1936
AFTER THE THIN MAN   MGM, 1936
PERSONAL PROPERTY   MGM, 1937
THEY GAVE HIM A GUN   MGM, 1937
ROSALIE   MGM, 1937
MARIE ANTOINETTE   MGM, 1938
SWEETHEARTS   MGM, 1938
STAND UP AND FIGHT   MGM, 1939
IT'S A WONDERFUL WORLD   MGM, 1939
ANDY HARDY GETS SPRING FEVER   MGM, 1939
ANOTHER THIN MAN   MGM, 1939
I TAKE THIS WOMAN   MGM, 1940
I LOVE YOU AGAIN   MGM, 1940
BITTER SWEET   MGM, 1940
RAGE IN HEAVEN   MGM, 1941
SHADOW OF THE THIN MAN   MGM, 1941
THE FEMININE TOUCH   MGM, 1941
DR. KILDARE'S VICTORY   MGM, 1942
I MARRIED AN ANGEL   MGM, 1942
CAIRO   MGM, 1942
JOURNEY FOR MARGARET   MGM, 1942

DZIGA VERTOV
(Denis Arkadievitch Kaufman)
b. January 2, 1896 - Bialystok, Russia
d. 1954

ANNIVERSARY OF THE REVOLUTION (FD)   1919, Soviet
THE BATTLE OF TSARITSYN (FD)   1920, Soviet
KALININ - THE ELDER STATESMAN OF ALL RUSSIANS (FD)   1920, Soviet
THE EXHUMATION OF THE REMAINS OF SERGEI RADONEZHSKY (FD)   1920, Soviet
THE MIRONOV TRIAL (FD)   1920, Soviet
TRAIN OF THE CENTRAL COMMITTEE (FD)   1921, Soviet
HISTORY OF THE CIVIL WAR (FD)   1922, Soviet
THE EZEROV TRIAL (FD)   1922, Soviet
UNIVERMAG (FD)   1922, Soviet
OCTOBER CINEMA TRUTH (FD)   1923, Soviet
FIVE YEARS OF STRUGGLE AND VICTORY (FD)   1923, Soviet
TODAY (AF)   1924, Soviet
SOVIET PLAYTHINGS (AF)   1924, Soviet
KINO-GLAZ (FD)   1924, Soviet
STRIDE SOVIET! (FD)   1926, Soviet
A SIXTH OF THE WORLD (FD)   1926, Soviet
THE ELEVENTH YEAR (FD)   1928, Soviet
MAN WITH A MOVIE CAMERA (FD)   1929, Soviet
ENTHUSIASM (FD)   1931, Soviet
THREE SONGS ABOUT LENIN (FD)   1934, Soviet
LULLABY   1937, Soviet
SERGEI ORDZHONIKIDZE   1937, Soviet
THREE HEROINES   1938, Soviet
ELEVATION A   1941, Soviet
BLOOD FOR BLOOD - LIFE FOR LIFE   1941, Soviet
CAMERA REPORTERS ON THE LINE OF FIRE (FD)   1941, Soviet
ON TO THE FRONT! (FD)   1943, Soviet
ON THE MOUNTAINS OF ALA-TAU (FD)   1944, Soviet
THE OATH OF YOUTH   1947, Soviet

CHARLES VIDOR
b. July 27, 1900 - Budapest, Hungary
d. 1959

SENSATION HUNTERS   Monogram, 1934
DOUBLE DOOR   Paramount, 1934
STRANGERS ALL   RKO, 1935
THE ARIZONIAN   RKO, 1935
HIS FAMILY TREE   RKO, 1935
MUSS 'EM UP   RKO Radio, 1936
A DOCTOR'S DIARY   Paramount, 1937
THE GREAT GAMBINI   Paramount, 1937
SHE'S NO LADY   Paramount, 1937
ROMANCE OF THE REDWOODS   Columbia, 1939
BLIND ALLEY   Columbia, 1939
THOSE HIGH GREY WALLS   Columbia, 1939
MY SON, MY SON   Columbia, 1940
THE LADY IN QUESTION   Columbia, 1940
LADIES IN RETIREMENT   Columbia, 1941
NEW YORK TOWN   Paramount, 1941
THE TUTTLES OF TAHITI   RKO Radio, 1942
THE DESPERADOES   Columbia, 1942
COVER GIRL   Columbia, 1944
TOGETHER AGAIN   Columbia, 1944
A SONG TO REMEMBER   Columbia, 1945
OVER 21   Columbia, 1945
GILDA   Columbia, 1946
THE LOVES OF CARMEN   Columbia, 1948
IT'S A BIG COUNTRY   co-director, MGM, 1952
HANS CHRISTIAN ANDERSEN   RKO Radio, 1952
THUNDER IN THE EAST   Paramount, 1953
RHAPSODY   MGM, 1954
LOVE ME OR LEAVE ME   MGM, 1955
THE SWAN   MGM, 1956
THE JOKER IS WILD   *ALL THE WAY*   Paramount, 1957
A FAREWELL TO ARMS   20th Century-Fox, 1958
SONG WITHOUT END   co-director with George Cukor, Columbia, 1960

KING VIDOR
b. February 9, 1894 - Galveston, Texas
d. 1982

THE TURN IN THE ROAD   Robertson-Cole, 1919
BETTER TIMES   Brentwood-Mutual, 1919
THE OTHER HALF   Exclusive International, 1919
POOR RELATIONS   Robertson-Cole, 1919
THE FAMILY HONOR   Associated First National, 1920
THE JACK-KNIFE MAN   Associated First National, 1920
THE SKY PILOT   Associated First National, 1921
LOVE NEVER DIES   Associated First National, 1921
THE REAL ADVENTURE   Associated Exhibitors, 1922
DUSK TO DAWN   Associated Exhibitors, 1922
CONQUERING THE WOMAN   Associated Exhibitors, 1922
WILD ORANGES   Goldwyn, 1922
WOMAN, WAKE UP   Associated Exhibitors, 1922
ALICE ADAMS   Associated Exhibitors, 1923
PEG O' MY HEART   Metro, 1923
THE WOMAN OF BRONZE   Metro, 1923
THREE WISE FOOLS   Goldwyn, 1923
HAPPINESS   Metro, 1924
WINE OF YOUTH   Metro-Goldwyn, 1924
HIS HOUR   Metro-Goldwyn, 1924
WIFE OF THE CENTAUR   Metro-Goldwyn, 1924
PROUD FLESH   MGM, 1925
THE BIG PARADE   MGM, 1925
LA BOHEME   MGM, 1926
BARDELYS THE MAGNIFICENT   MGM, 1926

THE CROWD ★ MGM, 1927
THE PATSY MGM, 1928
SHOW PEOPLE MGM, 1928
HALLELUJAH! ★ MGM, 1929
NOT SO DUMB MGM, 1930
BILLY THE KID MGM, 1930
STREET SCENE United Artists, 1931
THE CHAMP ★ MGM, 1931
BIRD OF PARADISE RKO Radio, 1932
CYNARA United Artists, 1932
THE STRANGER'S RETURN MGM, 1933
OUR DAILY BREAD United Artists, 1934
THE WEDDING NIGHT United Artists, 1935
SO RED THE ROSE Paramount, 1935
THE TEXAS RANGERS Paramount, 1936
STELLA DALLAS United Artists, 1937
THE CITADEL ★ MGM, 1938
NORTHWEST PASSAGE MGM, 1940
COMRADE X MGM, 1940
H.M. PULHAM, ESQ. MGM, 1941
AN AMERICAN ROMANCE MGM, 1944
DUEL IN THE SUN Selznick Releasing, 1946
ON OUR MERRY WAY A MIRACLE CAN HAPPEN
    United Artists, 1948
THE FOUNTAINHEAD Warner Bros., 1949
BEYOND THE FOREST Warner Bros., 1949
LIGHTNING STRIKES TWICE Warner Bros., 1951
JAPANESE WAR BRIDE 20th Century-Fox, 1952
RUBY GENTRY 20th Century-Fox, 1953
MAN WITHOUT A STAR Universal, 1955
WAR AND PEACE ★ Paramount, 1956, Italian
SOLOMON AND SHEBA United Artists, 1959

JEAN VIGO
b. April 26, 1905 - Paris, France
d. 1934

A PROPOS DE NICE (FD) 1930, French
TARIS CHAMPION DE NATATION 1931, French
ZERO FOR CONDUCT Brandon, 1933, French
L'ATALANTE 1934, French

LUCHINO VISCONTI
(Count Don Luchino Visconti di Modrone)
b. November 2, 1906 - Milan, Italy
d. 1976

OSSESSIONE Brandon, 1942, Italian
GIORNI DI GLORIA (FD) co-director, 1945, Italian
LA TERRA TREMA Fleetwood Films, 1948, Italian
APPUNTI SU UN FATTO DI CRONACA (SD) 1951,
    Italian
BELLISSIMA Italian Films Export, 1951, Italian
OF LIFE AND LOVE SIAMO DONNE co-director, DCA,
    1953, Italian
SENSO THE WANTON CONTESSA Fleetwood Films,
    1955, Italian
WHITE NIGHTS LE NOTTI BIANCHE United Motion
    Picture Organization, 1957, Italian-French
ROCCO AND HIS BROTHERS Astor, 1960, Italian-
    French
BOCCACCIO '70 co-director with Federico Fellini &
    Vittorio De Sica, Embassy, 1962, Italian
THE LEOPARD 20th Century-Fox, 1963, Italian-French
VAGHE STELLE DELL'ORSA SANDRA 1965, Italian
THE WITCHES co-director, Lopert, 1967, Italian-French
THE STRANGER Paramount, 1967, Italian-French-
    Algerian

THE DAMNED LA CADUTA DEGLI DEI/
    GOTTERDAMERUNG Warner Bros., 1969, Italian-
    West German
DEATH IN VENICE Warner Bros., 1971, Italian-French
LUDWIG MGM, 1972, Italian-French-West German,
CONVERSATION PIECE GRUPPO DI FAMIGLIAIN UNO
    INTERNO New Line Cinema, 1975, Italian-French
THE INNOCENT 1976, Italian

JOSEF VON STERNBERG
(Josef Sternberg)
b. May 29, 1894 - Vienna, Austria
d. 1969

THE SALVATION HUNTERS United Artists, 1925
THE MASKED BRIDE co-director with Christy Cabanne,
    MGM, 1925
THE EXQUISITE SINNER co-director with Phil Rosen,
    MGM, 1926
A WOMAN OF THE SEA THE SEA GULL United Artists,
    1926
UNDERWORLD Paramount, 1927
THE LAST COMMAND Paramount, 1928
THE DRAGNET Paramount, 1928
THE DOCKS OF NEW ORLEANS Paramount, 1928
THE CASE OF LENA SMITH Paramount, 1929
THUNDERBOLT Paramount, 1929
THE BLUE ANGEL UFA, 1930, German
MOROCCO ★ Paramount, 1930
DISHONORED Paramount, 1931
AN AMERICAN TRAGEDY Paramount, 1931
SHANGHAI EXPRESS ★ Paramount, 1932
BLONDE VENUS Paramount, 1932
THE SCARLET EMPRESS Paramount, 1934
THE DEVIL IS A WOMAN Paramount, 1935
CRIME AND PUNISHMENT Columbia, 1935
THE KING STEPS OUT Columbia, 1936
I, CLAUDIUS 1937, unfinished
SERGEANT MADDEN MGM, 1939
THE SHANGHAI GESTURE United Artists, 1941
MACAO RKO Radio, 1952
THE SAGA OF ANATAHAN ANA-TA-HAN 1953,
    Japanese
JET PILOT Universal, 1957

ERICH VON STROHEIM
(Erich Oswald Stroheim)
b. September 22, 1885 - Vienna, Austria
d. 1957

BLIND HUSBANDS Universal, 1919
THE DEVIL'S PASS KEY Universal, 1920
FOOLISH WIVES Universal, 1922
MERRY-GO-ROUND co-director with Rupert Julian,
    Universal, 1923
GREED MGM, 1925
THE MERRY WIDOW MGM, 1925
THE WEDDING MARCH Paramount, 1928
QUEEN KELLY Paramount, 1928, unfinished
WALKING DOWN BROADWAY Paramount, 1932,
    unfinished

W

RAOUL WALSH
b. March 11, 1887 - New York, New York
d. 1980

THE LIFE OF GENERAL VILLA   co-director with Christy
    Cabanne, 1914
THE DOUBLE KNOT   1914
THE MYSTERY OF THE HINDU IMAGE   1914
THE FINAL VERDICT   1914
HIS RETURN   1915
THE GREASER   1915
THE FENCING MASTER   1915
A MAN FOR ALL THAT   1915
ELEVEN-THIRTY P.M.   1915
THE BURIED HAND   1915
THE CELESTIAL CODE   1915
A BAD MAN AND OTHERS   1915
THE REGENERATION   Fox, 1915
CARMEN   Fox, 1915
PILLARS OF SOCIETY   1916
THE SERPENT   Fox, 1916
BLUE BLOOD AND RED   Fox, 1916
THE HONOR SYSTEM   Fox, 1916
THE CONQUEROR   Fox, 1917
BETRAYED   Fox, 1917
THIS IS THE LIFE   Fox, 1917
THE PRIDE OF NEW YORK   Fox, 1917
THE SILENT LIE   Fox, 1917
THE INNOCENT SINNER   Fox, 1917
THE WOMAN AND THE LAW   Fox, 1918
THE PRUSSIAN CUR   Fox, 1918
ON THE JUMP   Fox, 1918
EVERY MOTHER'S SON   Fox, 1918
I'LL SAY SO   Fox, 1918
EVANGELINE   Fox, 1919
THE STRONGEST   Fox, 1919
SHOULD A HUSBAND FORGIVE?   Fox, 1919
FROM NOW ON   Fox, 1920
THE DEEP PURPLE   Realart, 1920
THE OATH   Mayflower, 1921
SERENADE   Associated First National, 1921
KINDRED OF THE DUST   Associated First National, 1922
LOST AND FOUND ON A SOUTH SEA ISLAND
    Goldwyn, 1923
THE THIEF OF BAGDAD   United Artists, 1924
EAST OF SUEZ   Paramount, 1925
THE SPANIARD   Paramount, 1925
THE WANDERER   Paramount, 1925
THE LUCKY LADY   Paramount, 1926
THE LADY OF THE HAREM   Paramount, 1926
WHAT PRICE GLORY   Fox, 1927
THE MONEY TALKS   Fox, 1927
THE LOVES OF CARMEN   Fox, 1927
SADIE THOMPSON   United Artists, 1928
THE RED DANCE   Fox, 1928
ME GANGSTER   Fox, 1928
IN OLD ARIZONA   co-director with Irving Cummings,
    Fox, 1929
THE COCK-EYED WORLD   Fox, 1929
HOT FOR PARIS   Fox, 1930
THE BIG TRAIL   Fox, 1930
THE MAN WHO CAME BACK   Fox, 1931
WOMEN OF ALL NATIONS   Fox, 1931

THE YELLOW TICKET   Fox, 1931
WILD GIRL   Fox, 1932
ME AND MY GAL   *PIER 13*   Fox, 1932
SAILOR'S LUCK   Fox, 1933
THE BOWERY   United Artists, 1933
GOING HOLLYWOOD   MGM, 1933
UNDER PRESSURE   Fox, 1935
BABY-FACE HARRINGTON   MGM, 1935
EVERY NIGHT AT EIGHT   Paramount, 1935
KLONDIKE ANNIE   Paramount, 1936
BIG BROWN EYES   Paramount, 1936
SPENDTHRIFT   Paramount, 1936
O.H.M.S.   *YOU'RE IN THE ARMY NOW*   Gaumont-British,
    1937, British
JUMP FOR GLORY   *WHEN THIEF MEETS THIEF*
    Criterion, 1937, British
ARTISTS AND MODELS   Paramount, 1937
HITTING A NEW HIGH   RKO Radio, 1937
COLLEGE SWING   Paramount, 1938
ST. LOUIS BLUES   Paramount, 1939
THE ROARING TWENTIES   Warner Bros., 1939
DARK COMMAND   Republic, 1940
THEY DRIVE BY NIGHT   Warner Bros., 1940
HIGH SIERRA   Warner Bros., 1941
THE STRAWBERRY BLONDE   Warner Bros., 1941
MANPOWER   Warner Bros., 1941
THEY DIED WITH THEIR BOOTS ON   Warner Bros.,
    1941
DESPERATE JOURNEY   Warner Bros., 1942
GENTLEMAN JIM   Warner Bros., 1942
BACKGROUND TO DANGER   Warner Bros., 1943
NORTHERN PURSUIT   Warner Bros., 1943
UNCERTAIN GLORY   Warner Bros., 1944
OBJECTIVE, BURMA!   Warner Bros., 1945
THE HORN BLOWS AT MIDNIGHT   Warner Bros., 1945
SALTY O'ROURKE   Paramount, 1945
THE MAN I LOVE   Warner Bros., 1947
PURSUED   Warner Bros., 1947
CHEYENNE   *THE WYOMING KID*   Warner Bros., 1947
SILVER RIVER   Warner Bros., 1948
FIGHTER SQUADRON   Warner Bros., 1948
ONE SUNDAY AFTERNOON   Warner Bros., 1948
COLORADO TERRITORY   Warner Bros., 1949
WHITE HEAT   Warner Bros., 1949
ALONG THE GREAT DIVIDE   Warner Bros., 1951
CAPTAIN HORATIO HORNBLOWER   Warner Bros.,
    1951
DISTANT DRUMS   Warner Bros., 1951
GLORY ALLEY   MGM, 1952
THE WORLD IN HIS ARMS   Universal, 1952
BLACKBEARD THE PIRATE   RKO Radio, 1952
THE LAWLESS BREED   Universal, 1953
SEA DEVILS   RKO Radio, 1953
A LION IS IN THE STREETS   Warner Bros., 1953
GUN FURY   Columbia, 1953
SASKATCHEWAN   Universal, 1954
BATTLE CRY   Warner Bros., 1955
THE TALL MEN   20th Century-Fox, 1955
THE REVOLT OF MAMIE STOVER   20th Century-Fox,
    1956
THE KING AND FOUR QUEENS   United Artists, 1956
BAND OF ANGELS   Warner Bros., 1957
THE NAKED AND THE DEAD   Warner Bros., 1958
THE SHERIFF OF FRACTURED JAW   20th Century-Fox,
    1958, British
A PRIVATE'S AFFAIR   20th Century-Fox, 1959
ESTHER AND THE KING   20th Century-Fox, 1960,
    Italian-U.S.
MARINES, LET'S GO!   20th Century-Fox, 1961
A DISTANT TRUMPET   Warner Bros., 1964

CHARLES WALTERS
b. November 17, 1911 - Brooklyn, New York
d. 1982

GOOD NEWS   MGM, 1947
EASTER PARADE   MGM, 1948
THE BARKLEYS OF BROADWAY   MGM, 1949
SUMMER STOCK   MGM, 1950
THREE GUYS NAMED MIKE   MGM, 1951
TEXAS CARNIVAL   MGM, 1951
THE BELLE OF NEW YORK   MGM, 1952
LILI ★   MGM, 1953
DANGEROUS WHEN WET   MGM, 1953
TORCH SONG   MGM, 1953
EASY TO LOVE   MGM, 1953
THE GLASS SLIPPER   MGM, 1955
THE TENDER TRAP   MGM, 1955
HIGH SOCIETY   MGM, 1956
DON'T GO NEAR THE WATER   MGM, 1957
ASK ANY GIRL   MGM, 1959
PLEASE DON'T EAT THE DAISIES   MGM, 1960
TWO LOVES   MGM, 1961
JUMBO   *BILLY ROSE'S JUMBO*   MGM, 1962
THE UNSINKABLE MOLLY BROWN   MGM, 1964
WALK, DON'T RUN   Columbia, 1966

ANDY WARHOL
(Andrew Warhola)
b. August 8, 1927 - Cleveland, Ohio
d. 1987

KISS   Film-Makers, 1963
EAT   Film-Makers, 1963
SLEEP   Film-Makers, 1963
HAIRCUT   Film-Makers, 1963
TARZAN AND JANE REGAINED...SORT OF
   co-director, Film-Makers, 1964
DANCE MOVIE   Film-Makers, 1964
BLOW JOB   Film-Makers, 1964
BATMAN DRACULA   Film-Makers, 1964
SALOME AND DELILAH   Film-Makers, 1964
SOAP OPERA   co-director, Film-Makers, 1964
COUCH   Film-Makers, 1964
13 MOST BEAUTIFUL WOMEN   Film-Makers, 1964
HARLOT   Film-Makers, 1964
THE LIFE OF JUANITA CASTRO   Film-Makers, 1965
EMPIRE   Film-Makers, 1965
POOR LITTLE RICH GIRL   Film-Makers, 1965
SCREEN TEST   Film-Makers, 1965
VINYL   Film-Makers, 1965
BEAUTY #2   Film-Makers, 1965
BITCH   Film-Makers, 1965
PRISON   Film-Makers, 1965
SPACE   Film-Makers, 1965
THE CLOSET   Film-Makers, 1965
HENRY GELDZAHLER   Film-Makers, 1965
TAYLOR MEAD'S ASS   Film-Makers, 1965
FACE   Film-Makers, 1965
MY HUSTLER   Film-Makers, 1965
CAMP   Film-Makers, 1965
SUICIDE   Film-Makers, 1965
DRUNK   Film-Makers, 1965
OUTER AND INNER SPACE   Film-Makers, 1966
HEDY   *HEDY THE SHOPLIFTER*   Film-Makers, 1966
PAUL SWAN   Film-Makers, 1966
MORE MILK, EVETTE   *LANA TURNER*   Film-Makers,
   1965
THE VELVET UNDERGROUND AND NICO   Film-Makers,
   1966

KITCHEN   Film-Makers, 1966
LUPE   Film-Makers, 1966
EATING TOO FAST   Film-Makers, 1966
THE CHELSEA GIRLS   Film-Makers, 1966
I, A MAN   Film-Makers, 1967
BIKE BOY   Film-Makers, 1967
NUDE RESTAURANT   Film-Makers, 1967
FOUR STARS   *24-HOUR MOVIE*   Film-Makers, 1967
IMITATION OF CHRIST   Film-Makers, 1967
THE LOVES OF ONDINE   Warhol, 1968
LONESOME COWBOYS   Sherpix, 1968
BLUE MOVIE   *FUCK*   Factory, 1969
WOMEN IN REVOLT   Warhol, 1972
L'AMOUR   co-director with Paul Morrissey, Altura, 1973

JOHN WAYNE
(Marion Michael Morrison)
b. May 26, 1907 - Winterset, Iowa
d. 1979

THE ALAMO   United Artists, 1960
THE GREEN BERETS   co-director with Ray Kellogg,
   Warner Bros., 1968

JACK WEBB
b. April 2, 1920 - Santa Monica, California
d. 1982

DRAGNET   Warner Bros., 1954
PETE KELLY'S BLUES   Warner Bros., 1955
THE D.I.   Warner Bros., 1957
-30-   Warner Bros., 1959
THE LAST TIME I SAW ARCHIE   United Artists, 1961
DRAGNET (TF)   Mark VII Ltd./Universal TV, 1969
O'HARA, UNITED STATES TREASURY:
   OPERATION COBRA (TF)   Mark VII Ltd./Universal TV,
   1971
EMERGENCY! (TF)   Mark VII Ltd./Universal TV, 1972
CHASE (TF)   Mark VII Ltd./Universal TV, 1973

LOIS WEBER
(Mrs. Phillips Smalley)
b. 1882 - Allegheny, Pennsylvania
d. 1939

THE TROUBADOUR'S TRIUMPH   1912
THE JEW'S CHRISTMAS   co-director with Phillips
   Smalley, 1913
THE FEMALE OF THE SPECIES   1913
THE MERCHANT OF VENICE   co-director with Phillips
   Smalley, Universal, 1914
A FOOL AND HIS MONEY   Universal, 1914
BEHIND THE VEIL   co-director with Phillips Smalley, 1914
FALSE COLORS   co-director with Phillips Smalley,
   Paramount, 1914
SUNSHINE MOLLY   co-director with Phillips Smalley,
   Paramount, 1915
SCANDAL   co-director with Phillips Smalley, Universal,
   1915
HYPOCRITES   co-director with Phillips Smalley,
   Bosworth, 1915
IT'S NO LAUGHING MATTER   Universal, 1915
A CIGARETTE, THAT'S ALL   Universal, 1915
HOP - THE DEVIL'S BREW   Universal, 1915
THE DUMB GIRL OF PORTICI   co-director with Phillips
   Smalley, Universal, 1916
SAVING THE FAMILY NAME   Universal, 1916

409

THE PEOPLE VS. JOHN DOE   Universal, 1916
IDLE WIVES   Universal, 1916
WHERE ARE MY CHILDREN?   co-director with Phillips
   Smalley, Universal, 1916
THE FLIRT   co-director with Phillips Smalley, Universal,
   1916
THE HAND THAT ROCKS THE CRADLE   Universal, 1917
EVEN AS YOU AND I   Peerless, 1917
THE PRICE OF A GOOD TIME   Universal-Jewel, 1917
THE MYSTERIOUS MRS. M   *THE MYSTERIOUS
   MRS. MUSSELWHITE*   Universal, 1917
FOR HUSBANDS ONLY   Weber-North, 1918
THE DOCTOR AND THE WOMAN   Universal, 1918
BORROWED CLOTHES   Universal, 1918
MARY REGAN   Associated First National, 1919
A MIDNIGHT ROMANCE   Associated First National, 1919
WHEN A GIRL LOVES   Universal, 1919
HOME   Universal, 1919
FORBIDDEN   Universal, 1920
TO PLEASE ONE WOMAN   Paramount, 1920
WHAT'S WORTH WHILE?   Paramount, 1921
TOO WISE WIVES   Paramount, 1921
THE BLOT   F.B. Warren, 1921
WHAT DO MEN WANT?   Wid Gunning, 1921
A CHAPTER IN HER LIFE   Universal-Jewel, 1923
THE MARRIAGE CLAUSE   Universal-Jewel, 1926
SENSATION SEEKERS   Universal-Jewel, 1927
THE ANGEL OF BROADWAY   Pathé, 1927
WHITE HEAT   Pinnacle, 1934

ORSON WELLES
(George Orson Welles)
b. May 6, 1915
d. 1985

THE HEARTS OF AGE   co-director with William Vance,
   1934
TOO MUCH JOHNSON   1938
CITIZEN KANE ★   RKO Radio, 1941
THE MAGNIFICENT AMBERSONS   RKO Radio, 1942
IT'S ALL TRUE   co-director with Norman Foster,
   RKO Radio, 1942, unfinished
THE STRANGER   RKO Radio, 1946
THE LADY FROM SHANGHAI   Columbia, 1948
MACBETH   Republic, 1948
OTHELLO   United Artists, 1952, U.S.-Italian
MR. ARKADIN   *CONFIDENTIAL REPORT*   Warner
   Bros., 1955, Spanish-Swiss
DON QUIXOTE   1955, Spanish, unfinished
TOUCH OF EVIL   Universal, 1958
THE TRIAL   Astor, 1962, French-Italian-West German
CHIMES AT MIDNIGHT   *FALSTAFF*   Peppercorn-
   Wormser, 1966, Spanish-Swiss
THE IMMORTAL STORY   Fleetwood Films, 1968,
   French, originally made for television
THE DEEP   1969, unfinished
THE OTHER SIDE OF THE WIND   1972, unfinished
F FOR FAKE   Specialty Films, 1974, French-Iranian-
   West German

WILLIAM A. WELLMAN
(William Augustus Wellman)
b. February 29, 1896 - Brookline, Massachusetts
d. 1975

THE MAN WHO WON   Fox, 1923
SECOND HAND LOVE   Fox, 1923
BIG DAN   Fox, 1923

CUPID'S FIREMAN   Fox, 1923
THE VAGABOND TRAIL   Fox, 1924
NOT A DRUM WAS HEARD   Fox, 1924
THE CIRCUS COWBOY   Fox, 1924
WHEN HUSBANDS FLIRT   Columbia, 1925
THE BOOB   MGM, 1926
THE CAT'S PAJAMAS   Paramount, 1926
YOU NEVER KNOW WOMEN   Paramount, 1926
WINGS   Paramount, 1929
THE LEGION OF THE CONDEMNED   Paramount, 1928
LADIES OF THE MOB   Paramount, 1928
BEGGARS OF LIFE   Paramount, 1928
CHINATOWN NIGHTS   Paramount, 1929
THE MAN I LOVE   Paramount, 1929
WOMAN TRAP   Paramount, 1929
DANGEROUS PARADISE   Paramount, 1930
YOUNG EAGLES   Paramount, 1930
MAYBE IT'S LOVE   Warner Bros., 1930
OTHER MEN'S WOMEN   *THE STEEL HIGHWAY*
   Warner Bros., 1931
THE PUBLIC ENEMY   Warner Bros., 1931
NIGHT NURSE   Warner Bros., 1931
THE STAR WITNESS   Warner Bros., 1931
SAFE IN HELL   First National, 1931
THE HATCHET MAN   First National, 1932
SO BIG   Warner Bros., 1932
LOVE IS A RACKET   First National, 1932
THE PURCHASE PRICE   Warner Bros., 1932
THE CONQUERORS   RKO, 1932
FRISCO JENNY   First National, 1933
CENTRAL AIRPORT   First National, 1933
LILLY TURNER   First National, 1933
MIDNIGHT MARY   MGM, 1933
HEROES FOR SALE   First National, 1933
WILD BOYS OF THE ROAD   First National, 1933
COLLEGE COACH   Warner Bros., 1933
LOOKING FOR TROUBLE   United Artists, 1934
STINGAREE   RKO Radio, 1934
THE PRESIDENT VANISHES   Paramount, 1935
CALL OF THE WILD   United Artists, 1935
THE ROBIN HOOD OF EL DORADO   MGM, 1936
SMALL TOWN GIRL   MGM, 1936
A STAR IS BORN ★   United Artists, 1937
NOTHING SACRED   United Artists, 1937
MEN WITH WINGS   Paramount, 1938
BEAU GESTE   Paramount, 1939
THE LIGHT THAT FAILED   Paramount, 1939
REACHING FOR THE SUN   Paramount, 1941
ROXIE HART   20th Century-Fox, 1942
THE GREAT MAN'S LADY   Paramount, 1942
THUNDER BIRDS   20th Century-Fox, 1942
THE OX-BOW INCIDENT   20th Century-Fox, 1943
LADY OF BURLESQUE   United Artists, 1943
BUFFALO BILL   20th Century-Fox, 1944
THIS MAN'S NAVY   MGM, 1945
THE STORY OF G.I. JOE   United Artists, 1945
GALLANT JOURNEY   Columbia, 1946
MAGIC TOWN   RKO Radio, 1947
THE IRON CURTAIN   20th Century-Fox, 1948
YELLOW SKY   20th Century-Fox, 1948
BATTLEGROUND ★   MGM, 1949
THE HAPPY YEARS   MGM, 1950
THE NEXT VOICE YOU HEAR   MGM, 1950
ACROSS THE WIDE MISSOURI   MGM, 1951
IT'S A BIG COUNTRY   co-director, MGM, 1952
WESTWARD THE WOMEN   MGM, 1952
MY MAN AND I   MGM, 1952
ISLAND IN THE SKY   Warner Bros., 1953
THE HIGH AND THE MIGHTY ★   Warner Bros., 1954
TRACK OF THE CAT   Warner Bros., 1954

BLOOD ALLEY   Warner Bros., 1955
GOODBYE, MY LADY   Warner Bros., 1956
DARBY'S RANGERS   Warner Bros., 1958
LAFAYETTE ESCADRILLE   Warner Bros., 1958

JAMES WHALE
b. July 22, 1896 - Dudley, England
d. 1957

JOURNEY'S END   Tiffany Productions, 1930
WATERLOO BRIDGE   Universal, 1931
FRANKENSTEIN   Universal, 1931
THE IMPATIENT MAIDEN   Universal, 1932
THE OLD DARK HOUSE   Universal, 1932
THE KISS BEFORE THE MIRROR   Universal, 1933
THE INVISIBLE MAN   Universal, 1933
BY CANDLELIGHT   Universal, 1933
ONE MORE RIVER   Universal, 1934
THE BRIDE OF FRANKENSTEIN   Universal, 1935
REMEMBER LAST NIGHT?   Universal, 1935
SHOW BOAT   Universal, 1936
THE ROAD BACK   Universal, 1937
THE GREAT GARRICK   Warner Bros., 1937
SINNERS IN PARADISE   Universal, 1938
WIVES *UNDER SUSPICION*   Universal, 1938
PORT OF SEVEN SEAS   MGM, 1938
THE MAN IN THE IRON MASK   United Artists, 1939
GREEN HELL   Universal, 1940
THEY DARE NOT LOVE   Columbia, 1941

RICHARD WHORF
b. June 4, 1906 - Winthrop, Massachusetts
d. 1966

BLONDE FEVER   MGM, 1944
THE HIDDEN EYE   MGM, 1945
THE SAILOR TAKES A WIFE   MGM, 1946
TILL THE CLOUDS ROLL BY   MGM, 1946
IT HAPPENED IN BROOKLYN   MGM, 1947
LOVE FROM A STRANGER   Eagle Lion, 1947
LUXURY LINER   MGM, 1948
CHAMPAGNE FOR CAESAR   Universal, 1950
THE GROOM WORE SPURS   Universal, 1951

ROBERT WIENE
b. 1881 - Sasku, Germany
d. 1938

ARME EVA   co-director with W.A. Berger, 1914,
   German
ER RECHTS SIE LINKS   1915, German
DIE KONSERVENBRAUT   1915, German
ER RECHTS, SIE LINKS   1915, German
DER SEKRETAR DER KONIGIN   1916, German
DIE LIEBESBRIEF DER KONIGIN   1916, German
DER SEKRETAR DER KONIGIN   1916, German
DER MANN IM SPIEGEL   1916, German
DIE RAUBERBRAUT   1916, German
DAS WANDERNDE LICHT   1916, German
THE CABINET OF DR. CALIGARI   Samuel Goldwyn,
   1919, German
DIE DREI TANZE DER MARY WILFORD   1920, German
GENUINE   1920, German
DIE NACHT DER KONIGIN ISABEAU   1920, German
DIE RAUCHE EINER FRAU   1920, German
HOLLISCHE NACHT   1921, German

DAS SPIEGEL MIT DEM FEUER   co-director with
   George Kroll, 1921, German
SALOME   1922, German
TRAGIKOMODIE   1922, German
I.N.R.I.   1923, German
DER PUPPENMACHER VON KIANG-NING   1923,
   German
RASKOLNIKOFF   *CRIME AND PUNISHMENT*
   1923, German
ORLACS HANDE   1925, Austrian
PENSION GROONEN   1925, German
DER GARDEOFFIZIER   1926, German
DIE KONIGIN VOM MOULIN-ROUGE   1926, German
DER ROSENKAVALIER   1926, German
DIE BERUHMTE FRAU   1927, German
DIE GELIEBTE   1927, German
DIE FRAU AUF DER FOLTER   1928, German
DIE GROSSE ABENTEURERIN   1928, German
LEONTINES EHEMANNER   1928, German
UNFUG DER LIEBE   1928, German
DER ANDERE   1930, German
PANIK IN CHIKAGO   1931, German
DER LIEBESEXPRESS   *ACHT TAGE GLUCK*
   1931, German
POLIZEIAKTE 909   1934, German
EINE NACHT IN VENEDIG   1934, German
ULTIMATUM   co-director with Robert Siodmak, 1938,
   French

HERBERT WILCOX
b. April 19, 1892 - Cork, Ireland
d. 1977

CHU CHIN CHOW   Graham-Wilcox, 1923, British
SOUTHERN LOVE *A WOMAN'S SECRET*   Graham-
   Wilcox, 1924, British
DECAMERON NIGHTS   Graham-Wilcox-Decla, 1924,
   British
THE ONLY WAY   First National, 1925, British
NELL GWYN   First National, 1926, British
LONDON *LIMEHOUSE*   Paramount, 1926, British
TIPTOES *TIP TOES*   Paramount, 1927, British
MADAME POMPADOUR   1927, British
MUMSIE   W&F, 1927, British
DAWN   W&F, 1928, British
THE BONDMAN   W&F, 1928, British
THE WOMAN IN WHITE   W&F, 1929, British
THE LOVES OF ROBERT BURNS   W&F, 1930, British
CHANCE OF A NIGHT-TIME   co-director with Ralph
   Lynn, W&F, 1931, British
CARNIVAL *VENETIAN NIGHTS*   W&F, 1931, British
THE BLUE DANUBE   W&F, 1932, British
GOODNIGHT VIENNA *MAGIC NIGHT*   W&F, 1932,
   British
YES, MR. BROWN   co-director with Jack Buchanan,
   W&F, 1933, British
THE KING'S CUP   co-director with Robert J. Cullen,
   Alan Cobham & Donald Macardie, W&F, 1933, British
BITTER SWEET   United Artists, 1933, British
THE LITTLE DAMOZEL   W&F, 1933, British
THE QUEEN'S AFFAIR *RUNAWAY QUEEN*   United
   Artists, 1934, British
NELL GWYN   United Artists, 1934, British
PEG OF OLD DRURY   United Artists, 1935, British
LIMELIGHT *BACKSTAGE*   GFD, 1936, British
THE THREE MAXIMS *THE SHOW GOES ON*   GFD,
   1936, British
THIS'LL MAKE YOU WHISTLE   GFD, 1936, British
LONDON MELODY *GIRLS IN THE STREET*   GFD,
   1937, British

OUR FIGHTING NAVY *TORPEDOED* 1937, British
VICTORIA THE GREAT RKO Radio, 1937, British
SIXTY GLORIOUS YEARS *QUEEN OF DESTINY*
    RKO Radio, 1938, British
NURSE EDITH CAVELL RKO Radio, 1939
IRENE RKO Radio, 1940
NO, NO, NANETTE RKO Radio, 1940
SUNNY RKO Radio, 1941
WINGS AND THE WOMAN *THEY FLEW ALONE*
    RKO Radio, 1942, British
FOREVER AND A DAY co-director, RKO Radio, 1943
YELLOW CANARY RKO Radio, 1943, British
A YANK IN LONDON *I LIVE IN GROSVENOR
    SQUARE* Pathé, 1945, British
PICCADILLY INCIDENT Pathé, 1946, British
THE COURTNEY AFFAIR *THE COURTNEYS OF
    CURZON STREET* British Lion, 1947, British
SPRING IN PARK LANE British Lion, 1948, British
ELIZABETH OF LADYMEAD British Lion, 1948,
    British
MAYTIME IN MAYFAIR British Lion, 1949, British
ODETTE British Lion, 1950, British
INTO THE BLUE *THE MAN IN THE DINGHY*
    British Lion, 1951, British
THE LADY WITH A LAMP British Lion, 1951, British
DERBY DAY *FOUR AGAINST FATE* Continental,
    1952, British
TRENT'S LAST CASE British Lion, 1952, British
LAUGHING ANNE Republic, 1953, British
TROUBLE IN THE GLEN Republic, 1953, British
LET'S MAKE UP *LILACS IN THE SPRING*
    Republic, 1954, British
KING'S RHAPSODY British Lion, 1955, British
TEENAGE BAD GIRL *MY TEENAGE DAUGHTER*
    British Lion, 1956, British
DANGEROUS YOUTH *THESE DANGEROUS
    YEARS* Warner Bros., 1957, British
THE MAN WHO WOULDN'T TALK British Lion,
    1958, British
WONDERFUL THINGS! ABP, 1958, British
THE LADY IS A SQUARE ABP, 1959, British
THE HEART OF A MAN RFD, 1959, British

CORNEL WILDE
b. October 13, 1915 - New York, New York
d. 1989

STORM FEAR United Artists, 1956
THE DEVIL'S HAIRPIN Paramount, 1957
MARACAIBO Paramount, 1958
THE SWORD OF LANCELOT *LANCELOT AND
    GUINEVERE* Universal, 1963, British
THE NAKED PREY Paramount, 1966, U.S.-South African
BEACH RED United Artists, 1967
NO BLADE OF GRASS MGM, 1970, British
SHARK'S TREASURE United Artists, 1975

EDWARD D. WOOD, JR.
b. 1924 - Poughkeepsie, New York
d. 1978

GLEN OR GLENDA *I CHANGED MY SEX/I LED TWO
    LIVES* Screen Classics, 1953
JAILBAIT Howco, 1955
BRIDE OF THE MONSTER *BRIDE OF THE ATOM*
    Banner, 1956
PLAN NINE FROM OUTER SPACE *GRAVE ROBBERS
    FROM OUTER SPACE* DCA, 1959

THE SINISTER URGE Headliner, 1961
NIGHT OF THE GHOULS *REVENGE OF THE DEAD*
    1981, filmed in 1959

SAM WOOD
(Samuel Grosvenor Wood)
b. July 18, 1883 - Philadelphia, Pennsylvania
d. 1949

DOUBLE SPEED Paramount, 1920
EXCUSE MY DUST Paramount, 1920
THE DANCIN' FOOL Paramount, 1920
SICK ABED *SICK-A-BED* Paramount, 1920
WHAT'S YOUR HURRY? Paramount, 1920
THE CITY SPARROW Paramount, 1920
HER BELOVED VILLAIN Realart, 1920
HER FIRST ELOPEMENT Realart, 1920
THE SNOB Realart, 1921
PECK'S BAD BOY First National, 1921
THE GREAT MOMENT Paramount, 1921
UNDER THE LASH Paramount, 1921
DON'T TELL EVERYTHING Paramount, 1921
HER HUSBAND'S TRADEMARK Paramount, 1922
BEYOND THE ROCKS Paramount, 1922
HER GILDED CAGE Paramount, 1922
THE IMPOSSIBLE MRS. BELLEW Paramount, 1922
MY AMERICAN WIFE Paramount, 1923
PRODIGAL DAUGHTERS Paramount, 1923
BLUEBEARD'S EIGHTH WIFE Paramount, 1923
HIS CHILDREN'S CHILDREN Paramount, 1923
THE NEXT CORNER Paramount, 1924
BLUFF Paramount, 1924
THE FEMALE First National, 1924
THE MINE WITH THE IRON DOOR Principal, 1924
THE RE-CREATION OF BRIAN KENT Principal, 1925
FASCINATING YOUTH Paramount, 1926
ONE MINUTE TO PLAY FBO, 1926
ROOKIES MGM, 1927
A RACING ROMEO FBO, 1927
THE FAIR CO-ED MGM, 1927
THE LATEST FROM PARIS MGM, 1928
TELLING THE WORLD MGM, 1928
SO THIS IS COLLEGE MGM, 1929
IT'S A GREAT LIFE MGM, 1929
THEY LEARNED ABOUT WOMEN co-director with
    Jack Conway, MGM, 1930
THE GIRL SAID NO MGM, 1930
SINS OF THE CHILDREN MGM, 1930
WAY FOR A SAILOR MGM, 1930
PAID MGM, 1930
A TAILOR-MADE MAN MGM, 1931
THE MAN IN POSSESSION MGM, 1931
GET-RICH-QUICK WALLINGFORD *NEW ADVENTURES
    OF GET-RICH-QUICK WALLINGFORD* MGM, 1931
HUDDLE MGM, 1932
PROSPERITY MGM, 1932
THE BARBARIAN MGM, 1933
HOLD YOUR MAN MGM, 1933
CHRISTOPHER BEAN MGM, 1933
STAMBOUL QUEST MGM, 1934
LET 'EM HAVE IT United Artists, 1935
A NIGHT AT THE OPERA MGM, 1935
WHIPSAW MGM, 1935
THE UNGUARDED HOUR MGM, 1936
A DAY AT THE RACES MGM, 1937
NAVY, BLUE AND GOLD MGM, 1937
MADAME X MGM, 1937
LORD JEFF MGM, 1938
STABLEMATES MGM, 1938

GOODBYE, MR. CHIPS ★   MGM, 1939
RAFFLES   United Artists, 1939
OUR TOWN   United Artists, 1940
RANGERS OF FORTUNE   Paramount, 1940
KITTY FOYLE ★   RKO Radio, 1940
THE DEVIL AND MISS JONES   RKO Radio, 1941
KINGS ROW ★   Warner Bros., 1942
THE PRIDE OF THE YANKEES   RKO Radio, 1942
FOR WHOM THE BELL TOLLS   Paramount, 1943
CASANOVA BROWN   RKO Radio, 1944
SARATOGA TRUNK   Warner Bros., 1945
GUEST WIFE   United Artists, 1945
HEARTBEAT   RKO Radio, 1946
IVY   Universal, 1947
COMMAND DECISION   MGM, 1948
THE STRATTON STORY   MGM, 1949
AMBUSH   MGM, 1950

WILLIAM WYLER

b. July 1, 1902 - Mulhouse, Alsace, Germany
d. 1981

CROOK BUSTERS   1925
LAZY LIGHTNING   Universal, 1926
THE STOLEN RANCH   Universal, 1926
BLAZING DAYS   Universal, 1927
HARD FISTS   Universal, 1927
STRAIGHT SHOOTIN'   *SHOOTING STRAIGHT/*
   RANGE RIDERS   Independent, 1927
THE BORDER CAVALIER   Universal, 1927
DESERT DUST   1927
THUNDER RIDERS   Universal, 1928
ANYBODY HERE SEEN KELLY?   Universal, 1928
THE SHAKEDOWN   Universal, 1929
THE LOVE TRAP   Universal, 1929
HELL'S HEROES   Universal, 1930
THE STORM   Universal, 1930
A HOUSE DIVIDED   Universal, 1932
TOM BROWN OF CULVER   Universal, 1932
HER FIRST MATE   Universal, 1933
COUNSELLOR-AT-LAW   Universal, 1933
GLAMOUR   Universal, 1934
THE GOOD FAIRY   Universal, 1935
THE GAY DECEPTION   20th Century-Fox, 1935
THESE THREE   United Artists, 1936
DODSWORTH ★   United Artists, 1936
COME AND GET IT   co-director with Howard Hawks,
   United Artists, 1936
DEAD END   United Artists, 1937
JEZEBEL   Warner Bros., 1938
WUTHERING HEIGHTS ★   United Artists, 1939
THE WESTERNER   United Artists, 1940
THE LETTER ★   Warner Bros., 1940
THE LITTLE FOXES ★   RKO Radio, 1941
MRS. MINIVER ★★   MGM, 1942
THE MEMPHIS BELLE (FD)   Paramount, 1944
THE FIGHTING LADY (FD)   20th Century-Fox,
   1944
THUNDERBOLT (FD)   co-director with John Sturges,
   Monogram, 1945
THE BEST YEARS OF OUR LIVES ★★   RKO Radio,
   1946
THE HEIRESS ★   Paramount, 1949
DETECTIVE STORY ★   Paramount, 1951
CARRIE   Paramount, 1952
ROMAN HOLIDAY ★   Paramount, 1953
THE DESPERATE HOURS   Paramount, 1955
FRIENDLY PERSUASION ★   Allied Artists, 1956
THE BIG COUNTRY   United Artists, 1958
BEN-HUR ★★   MGM, 1959

THE CHILDREN'S HOUR   United Artists, 1962
THE COLLECTOR ★   Columbia, 1965, U.S.-British
HOW TO STEAL A MILLION   Columbia, 1966
FUNNY GIRL   Columbia, 1968
THE LIBERATION OF L.B. JONES   Columbia, 1970

Y

SERGEI YUTKEVICH

b. September 15, 1904 - St. Petersburg, Russia
d. 1985

GIVE US RADIO!   co-director with S. Greenberg, 1925,
   Soviet
LACE   1928, Soviet
THE BLACK SAIL   1929, Soviet
GOLDEN MOUNTAINS   1931, Soviet
COUNTERPLAN   co-director with Friedrich Ermler, 1932,
   Soviet
ANKARA - HEART OF TURKEY (FD)   co-director with
   Lev Arnshtam, 1934, Soviet
THE MINERS   1937, Soviet
THE MAN WITH THE GUN   1938, Soviet
YAKOV SVERDLOV   1940, Soviet
THE NEW ADVENTURES OF SCHWEIK   1943,
   Russian
DIMITRI DONSKOI (FD)   1944, Soviet
FRANCE LIBERATED (FD)   1946, Soviet
HELLO MOSCOW! (FD)   1946, Soviet
OUR COUNTRY'S YOUTH (FD)   1946, Soviet
LIGHT OVER RUSSIA   1947, Soviet, unreleased
THREE ENCOUNTERS   co-director with Vsevolod
   Pudovkin & Alexander Ptushko, 1948, Russian
PRZHEVALSKY   1951, Soviet
SKANDERBEG   1954, Soviet-Albanian
OTHELLO   Universal, 1956, Soviet
STORIES ABOUT LENIN   1958, Soviet
ENCOUNTER WITH FRANCE (FD)   1960, Soviet
THE BATH HOUSE   co-director with Anatoly Karanovich,
   1962, Soviet
LENIN IN POLAND   PORTRAIT OF LENIN   1966,
   Russian-Polish
THEME FOR A SHORT STORY   1969, Soviet-French
MAYAKOVSKY LAUGHS   co-director with Anatoly
   Karanovich, 1976, Soviet

The Will Rogers Institute

Your Partner In Good Health.

"I never met a man I didn't like."

Words which typify the tradition upon which the Will Rogers Institute has prided itself for over 50 years.

Since 1936, the Institute has been caring for employees of the entertainment/communications industry by providing them with health services.

Our representatives can put you in touch with expert medical care and your first consultation with one of our nationwide pulmonary specialists is absolutely free.

Write or call - to learn more about the benefits we offer and you will see just how we embody the spirit of that great humanitarian and entertainer, Will Rogers.

National Headquarters
White Plains, NY 10605
(914) 761-5550

UCLA Medical Center
Los Angeles, CA 90024
(213) 206-6191

INDICES

**FILM TITLES·FOREIGN-BASED DIRECTORS
DIRECTORS GUILDS·AGENTS/MANAGERS·
FILM COMMISSIONS·ADVERTISERS**

This is one of the most powerful weapons in the fight for human rights.

It can help more innocent people get out of prison and free from torture than all the guns in the world. It's a guarantee to human rights everywhere on the globe. Everyday.

Amnesty International uses this weapon very effectively. Since 1961, A.I. has helped more than 25,000 women, men and children win their freedom from prison and torture. With simple, yet effective letters. Write today. It may be the most powerful letter you've ever written.

Write a letter, save a life.

Yes, I want to become a member of Amnesty International and make a difference.
Enclosed is my tax-deductible contribution for: ☐$25 ☐$35 ☐$50 ☐$75 ☐$100 ☐ Other $ _____
Minimum annual contribution is $25. $15 for students, senior citizens and limited income.

Name _____

Address _____

City _____ State _____ Zip Code _____

LE89

Amnesty International USA
322 Eighth Avenue, New York, New York 10001

INDEX OF FILM TITLES - FILM DIRECTORS

435

I
N
D
E
X

O
F

F
I
L
M

T
I
T
L
E
S

I
N
D
E
X

O
F

F
I
L
M

T
I
T
L
E
S

I
N
D
E
X

O
F

F
I
L
M

T
I
T
L
E
S

G

I
N
D
E
X

O
F

F
I
L
M

T
I
T
L
E
S

I
N
D
E
X

O
F

F
I
L
M

T
I
T
L
E
S

461

INDEX OF FILM TITLES

I
N
D
E
X

O
F

F
I
L
M

T
I
T
L
E
S

It-Jo

FILM
DIRECTORS
GUIDE

I N D E X   O F   F I L M   T I T L E S

467

K

Le-Li

FILM DIRECTORS GUIDE

I N D E X   O F   F I L M   T I T L E S

476

INDEX OF FILM TITLES

MONDO TOPLESS .... Russ Meyer
MONDO TRASHO .... John Waters
MONEY .... Steven Hilliard Stern
MONEY AND THREE BAD MEN .... Kon Ichikawa
MONEY CHANGERS, THE .... Jack Conway†
MONEY FROM HOME .... George Marshall†
MONEY MAD .... D.W. Griffith†
MONEY MASTER, THE .... George Fitzmaurice†
MONEY MILLV, THE .... John S. Robertson†
MONEY MONEY MONEY .... Claude Lelouch
MONEY MOVERS .... Bruce Beresford
MONEY ON THE SIDE (TF) .... Robert Collins
MONEY PIT, THE .... Richard Benjamin
MONEY TALKS .... Allen Funt
MONEY TALKS .... Kon Ichikawa
MONEY TALKS .... Archie Mayo†
MONEY TALKS, THE .... Raoul Walsh†
MONEY TO BURN .... Rowland V. Lee†
MONEY TO BURN .... Walter Lang†
MONEY TO BURN (TF) .... Robert M. Lewis
MONEY TRAP, THE .... Burt Kennedy
MONEY, POWER, MURDER (TF) .... Lee Philips
MONEY, MARBLES AND CHALK .... Ivan Nagy
MONEY, THE .... Carl (Chuck) Workman
MONEYCHANGERS, THE (MS) .... Boris Sagal†
MONGO'S BACK IN TOWN (TF) .... Marvin J. Chomsky
MONGOLS, THE .... Andre De Toth
MONIKA .... Ingmar Bergman
MONITORS, THE .... Jack Shea
MONJAS CORONADAS (FD) .... Paul Leduc
MONK, THE (TF) .... George McCowan
MONKEY BUSINESS .... Howard Hawks†
MONKEY BUSINESS .... Norman Z. MacLeod†
MONKEY BUSINESS IN AFRICA .... Mack Sennett†
MONKEY GRIP .... Ken Cameron
MONKEY HUSTLE, THE .... Arthur Marks
MONKEY IN WINTER, A .... Henri Verneuil
MONKEY ON MY BACK .... Andre De Toth
MONKEY SHINES .... George A. Romero
MONKEY'S PAW, THE .... Wesley Ruggles†
MONKEY'S UNCLE, THE .... Robert Stevenson†
MONKEYS, GO HOME! .... Andrew V. McLaglen
MONNAIRE DE SINGE .... Yves Robert
MONOCLED MUTINEER, THE (TF) .... Jim O'Brien
MONSIEUR BEAUCAIRE .... Sidney Olcott†
MONSIEUR BEAUCAIRE .... George Marshall†
MONSIEUR HIRE .... Patrice Leconte
MONSIEUR LECOCQ .... Maurice Tourneur†
MONSIEUR RIPOIS .... René Clement
MONSIEUR VERDOUX .... Charles (Charlie) Chaplin†
MONSIGNOR .... Frank Perry
MONSIGNOR QUIXOTE (TF) .... Rodney Bennett
MONSOON .... Rod Amateau
MONSOON .... Edgar G. Ulmer†
MONSTER A GO-GO .... Herschell Gordon Lewis
MONSTER AND THE GIRL, THE .... Stuart Heisler†
MONSTER CLUB, THE .... Roy Ward Baker
MONSTER IN THE CLOSET .... Bob Dahlin
MONSTER ON THE CAMPUS .... Jack Arnold
MONSTER SHARK .... Lamberto Bava
MONSTER SQUAD, THE .... Fred Dekker
MONSTER THAT CHALLENGED THE WORLD, THE .... Arnold Laven
MONTANA .... Ray Enright†
MONTANA (CTF) .... William A. Graham
MONTANA BELLE .... Allan Dwan†
MONTE CARLO .... Ernst Lubitsch†
MONTE CARLO (TF) .... Anthony Page
MONTE WALSH .... William A. Fraker
MONTECARLO GRAN CASINO' .... Carlo Vanzina
MONTENEGRO .... Dusan Makavejev
MONTENEGRO, OR PIGS AND PEARLS .... Dusan Makavejev
MONTEREY POP (FD) .... D.A. Pennebaker
MONTH IN THE COUNTRY, A .... Pat O'Connor
MONTREAL MAIN .... Allan Moyle
MONTY PYTHON AND THE HOLY GRAIL .... Terry Gilliam
MONTY PYTHON AND THE HOLY GRAIL .... Terry Jones
MONTY PYTHON LIVE AT THE HOLLYWOOD BOWL .... Terry Hughes
MONTY PYTHON'S LIFE OF BRIAN .... Terry Jones
MONTY PYTHON'S THE MEANING OF LIFE .... Terry Jones
MONUMENT OF TOTSUSEKI .... Kaneto Shindo
MOON 44 (INTRUDER) .... Roland Emmerich
MOON AND SIXPENCE, THE .... Albert Lewin†
MOON IN SCORPIO .... Gary Graver
MOON IN THE GUTTER, THE .... Jean-Jacques Beineix
MOON IS BLUE, THE .... Otto Preminger†
MOON IS DOWN, THE .... Irving Pichel†
MOON OF ISRAEL .... Michael Curtiz†
MOON OF THE WOLF (TF) .... Daniel Petrie
MOON OVER HARLEM .... Edgar G. Ulmer†
MOON OVER MIAMI .... Walter Lang†
MOON OVER MIAMI .... Edward Bianchi
MOON OVER PARADOR .... Paul Mazursky
MOON OVER SHANGHAI .... Mikio Naruse†
MOON PILOT .... James Neilson†
MOON ZERO TWO .... Roy Ward Baker
MOON'S OUR HOME, THE .... William A. Seiter†
MOON-SPINNERS, THE .... James Neilson†
MOONCHILD .... Alan Gadney
MOONFLEET .... Fritz Lang†
MOONLIGHT .... Alan Smithee
MOONLIGHT (TF) .... Jackie Cooper
MOONLIGHT (TF) .... Rod Holcomb
MOONLIGHT AND CACTUS .... Edward F. (Eddie) Cline†
MOONLIGHT AND PRETZELS .... Karl Freund†
MOONLIGHT IN HAVANA .... Anthony Mann†
MOONLIGHT MURDER .... Edwin L. Marin†
MOONLIGHTING .... Jerzy Skolimowski
MOONLIGHTING (TF) .... Robert Butler
MOONRAKER .... Lewis Gilbert
MOONRISE .... Frank Borzage†
MOONSHINE MOUNTAIN .... Herschell Gordon Lewis
MOONSHINE COUNTY EXPRESS .... Gus Trikonis
MOONSHINE VALLEY .... Herbert Brenon†
MOONSHINE WAR, THE .... Richard Quine†
MOONSTRUCK .... ★ Norman Jewison
MOONTIDE .... Archie Mayo†
MOONTRAP .... Robert Dyke
MOONWALKER .... Colin Chilvers
MOONWALKER .... Jerry Kramer
MORALS .... William Desmond Taylor†
MORD OHNE TATER .... E.A. Dupont†
MORDI E FUGGI .... Dino Risi
MORE .... Barbet Schroeder
MORE ABOUT THE CHILDREN OF BULLERBY VILLAGE .... Lasse Hallstrom
MORE AMERICAN GRAFFITI .... Bill L. Norton
MORE MILK, EVETTE .... Andy Warhol†
MORE THAN A MIRACLE .... Francesco Rosi
MORE THAN A SECRETARY .... Alfred E. Green†
MORE THAN FRIENDS (TF) .... James Burrows
MORE THE MERRIER, THE .... ★ George Stevens†
MORE WILD WILD WEST .... Burt Kennedy
MORGAN STEWART'S COMING HOME .... Alan Smithee
MORGAN STEWART'S COMING HOME .... Paul Aaron
MORGAN STEWART'S COMING HOME .... Terry Winsor
MORGAN THE PIRATE .... Andre De Toth
MORGAN! .... Karel Reisz
MORGAN: A SUITABLE CASE FOR TREATMENT .... Karel Reisz
MORIRAI A MEZZANOTTE .... Lamberto Bava
MORITURI .... Bernhard Wicki
MORMON MAID, A .... Robert Z. Leonard†
MORMON, THE .... Allan Dwan†
MORNING AFTER, THE .... Allan Dwan†
MORNING AFTER, THE .... Sidney Lumet
MORNING AFTER, THE (TF) .... Richard T. Heffron
MORNING BEFORE SLEEP, THE .... Dan Wolman
MORNING COMES .... Lionel Chetwynd
MORNING DEPARTURE .... Roy Ward Baker
MORO WITCH DOCTOR .... Eddie Romero
MOROCCO .... ★ Josef Von Sternberg†
MORONS FROM OUTER SPACE .... Mike Hodges
MOROS Y CRISTIANOS .... Luis Garcia Berlanga
MORTADELLA .... Mario Monicelli
MORTAL PASSIONS .... Andrew Lane
MORTAL STORM, THE .... Frank Borzage†
MORTAL THOUGHTS .... Alan Rudolph
MORTGAGE .... Bill Bennett
MORTUARY .... Howard (Hikmet) Avedis
MORTUARY ACADEMY .... Michael Schroeder
MOSAIC LAW, THE .... Thomas H. Ince†
MOSCA ADDIO .... Mauro Bolognini
MOSCOW MUSIC-HALL .... Mikhail Kalatozov†
MOSCOW NIGHTS .... Anthony Asquith†
MOSCOW ON THE HUDSON .... Paul Mazursky
MOSEDALE HORSESHOE, THE (TF) .... Michael Apted
MOSES .... Gianfranco Debosio
MOSES AND AARON .... Daniele Huillet
MOSES AND AARON .... Jean-Marie Straub
MOSES PENDLETON PRESENTS MOSES PENDLETON (FD) .... Robert Elfstrom
MOSES THE LAWGIVER (MS) .... Gianfranco Debosio
MOSQUITO COAST, THE .... Peter Weir
MOSQUITO SQUADRON .... Boris Sagal†
MOSS ROSE .... Gregory Ratoff†
MOST BEAUTIFUL, THE .... Akira Kurosawa
MOST DANGEROUS GAME, THE .... Ernest B. Schoedsack†
MOST DANGEROUS GAME, THE .... Irving Pichel†
MOST DANGEROUS MAN ALIVE .... Allan Dwan†
MOST DANGEROUS MAN IN THE WORLD, THE (TF) .... Gavin Millar
MOST WANTED (TF) .... Walter Grauman
MOST WANTED MAN IN THE WORLD, THE .... Henri Verneuil
MOTEL .... Luis Mandoki
MOTEL (FD) .... Christian Blackwood
MOTEL HELL .... Kevin Connor
MOTH AND THE FLAME, THE .... Sidney Olcott†
MOTHER .... Gleb Panfilov
MOTHER .... Kaneto Shindo
MOTHER .... Park Choi-Su
MOTHER .... Maurice Tourneur†
MOTHER .... Vsevelod Pudovkin†
MOTHER .... Mikio Naruse†
MOTHER AND DAUGHTER .... Marta Meszaros
MOTHER AND DAUGHTER .... Mauritz Stiller†
MOTHER AND DAUGHTER .... Robert Stevenson†
MOTHER AND DAUGHTER - THE LOVING WAR (TF) .... Burt Brinckerhoff
MOTHER AND THE WHORE, THE .... Jean Eustache†
MOTHER CAREY'S CHICKENS .... Rowland V. Lee†
MOTHER DEAR .... Lino Brocka
MOTHER IS A FRESHMAN .... Lloyd Bacon†
MOTHER KUSTERS GOES TO HEAVEN .... Rainer Werner Fassbinder†
MOTHER LODE .... Charlton Heston
MOTHER MACHREE .... John Ford†
MOTHER O' MINE .... Fred Niblo†
MOTHER O'MINE .... Rupert Julian†
MOTHER SHOULD BE LOVED, A .... Yasujiro Ozu†
MOTHER TERESA (FD) .... Ann Petrie
MOTHER TERESA (FD) .... Jeanette Petrie
MOTHER WORE TIGHTS .... Walter Lang†
MOTHER'S COURAGE: THE MARY THOMAS STORY, A (TF) .... John Patterson
MOTHER'S DAY .... Charles Kaufman
MOTHER'S DAY (CTF) .... Susan Rohrer
MOTHER'S DAY ON WALTON'S MOUNTAIN (TF) .... Gwen Arner
MOTHER, JUGS AND SPEED .... Peter Yates
MOTHERING HEART, THE .... D.W. Griffith†
MOTHERS AND SONS .... Vsevelod Pudovkin†
MOTHERS OF MEN .... Sidney Olcott†
MOTHERS, DAUGHTERS & LOVERS (TF) .... Matthew Robbins
MOTHRA .... Inoshiro Honda
MOTOR PSYCHO .... Russ Meyer
MOUCHETTE .... Robert Bresson
MOULIN ROUGE .... E.A. Dupont†
MOULIN ROUGE .... Sidney Lanfield†
MOULIN ROUGE .... ★ John Huston†
MOUNTAIN EAGLE, THE .... Alfred Hitchcock†
MOUNTAIN JUSTICE .... Michael Curtiz†
MOUNTAIN MAN .... David O'Malley
MOUNTAIN MEN, THE .... Richard Lang
MOUNTAIN MUSIC .... Robert Florey†
MOUNTAIN ROAD, THE .... Daniel Mann
MOUNTAIN, THE .... Markus Imhoof
MOUNTAIN, THE .... Edward Dmytryk
MOUNTAIN, THE (TF) .... Cedric Sundstrom
MOUNTAINEER'S HONOR, THE .... D.W. Griffith†
MOUNTAINS AT DUSK (TF) .... Krzysztof Zanussi
MOUNTAINS OF THE MOON .... Bob Rafelson
MOUNTAINTOP MOTEL MASSACRE .... Jim McCullough, Sr.
MOUSE AND HIS CHILD, THE (AF) .... Charles Swenson
MOUSE AND THE WOMAN, THE .... Karl Francis
MOUSE ON THE MOON, THE .... Richard Lester
MOUSE THAT ROARED, THE .... Jack Arnold
MOUSEY (TF) .... Daniel Petrie
MOUTH TO MOUTH .... John Duigan
MOUTHPIECE, THE .... Elliott Nugent†
MOVE .... Stuart Rosenberg
MOVE OVER, DARLING .... Michael Gordon
MOVERS & SHAKERS .... William Asher
MOVIE MOVIE .... Stanley Donen
MOVIE MURDERER, THE (TF) .... Boris Sagal†
MOVIE STAR AMERICAN STYLE OR LSD - I HATE YOU .... Albert Zugsmith
MOVIE TOWN .... Mack Sennett†
MOVING .... Alan Metter
MOVING OUT .... Michael Pattinson
MOVING PERSPECTIVES (FD) .... Mrinal Sen
MOVING SINGER, THE (TF) .... Roy Boulting
MOVING TARGET (TF) .... Chris Thomson

P

497

I
N
D
E
X

O
F

F
I
L
M

T
I
T
L
E
S

I
N
D
E
X

O
F

F
I
L
M

T
I
T
L
E
S

507

I
N
D
E
X

O
F

F
I
L
M

T
I
T
L
E
S

U

V

525

W

I
N
D
E
X

O
F

F
I
L
M

T
I
T
L
E
S

INDEX OF FILM TITLES

★★★

INDEX OF FOREIGN-BASED DIRECTORS

A

Tengiz Abuladze .... USSR
Jovan Acin .... Yugoslavia
David Acomba .... Canada/U.S.
Percy Adlon .... West Germany/U.S.
José Luis Garcia Agraz .... Mexico
Chantal Akerman .... Belgium
Luis Alcoriza .... Mexico
Nestor Almendros .... U.S./Spain/France
Pedro Almodovar .... Spain
Paul Almond .... Canada/U.S.
Denis Amar .... France
Suzana Amaral .... Brazil
Jon Amiel .... UK
Franco Amurri .... U.S./Italy
Torgny Anderberg .... Sweden
Lindsay Anderson .... UK/U.S.
Michael Anderson .... UK/Canada
Theo Angelopoulos .... Greece
Ken Annakin .... UK/U.S.
Jean-Jacques Annaud .... France
Michelangelo Antonioni .... Italy
Michael Apted .... U.S./UK
Alfonso Arau .... Mexico/U.S.
Dario Argento .... Italy
Adolfo Aristarain .... Argentina
Gillian Armstrong .... Australia/U.S.
Michael Armstrong .... U.S./UK
Manuel Gutierrez Aragon .... Spain
Isaac Artenstein .... U.S./Mexico
Olievier Assayas .... France
Richard Attenborough .... UK
Bille August .... Denmark
Igor Auzins .... Australia
Pupi Avati .... Italy
Gabriel Axel .... Denmark/France
Mario Azzopardi .... Canada

B

Hector Babenco .... Brazil/U.S.
Roy Ward Baker .... UK
Ferdinando Baldi .... Italy
Murray Ball .... New Zealand
Uri Barbash .... Israel
Barry Barclay .... New Zealand
Bruno Barreto .... Brazil
Lezli-An Barrett .... UK
Steve Barron .... U.S./UK
Zelda Barron .... U.S./UK
Jahnu Barua .... India
Michal Bat-Adam .... Israel
Roy Battersby .... UK
Giacomo Battiato .... Italy
Lamberto Bava .... Italy
Stephen Bayly .... UK
Michael Beckham .... UK
Terry Bedford .... U.S./UK
Jean-Jacques Beineix .... France
Marco Bellocchio .... Italy
Vera Belmont .... France
Maria Luisa Bemberg .... Argentina
Roberto Benigni .... Italy
Richard Benner .... Canada/U.S.
Bill Bennett .... Australia
Rodney Bennett .... UK
Jacques W. Benoit .... Canada
Bruce Beresford .... Australia/U.S.
Ingmar Bergman .... Sweden
Luis Garcia Berlanga .... Spain
Chris Bernard .... UK
Claude Berri .... France
John Berry .... France/U.S.
Bernardo Bertolucci .... Italy
Luc Besson .... France
Jean-Claude Biette .... France
Kevin Billington .... UK
Les Blair .... UK
Andrew Birkin .... UK
Alan Birkinshaw .... UK
Michael Blakemore .... UK
Bertrand Blier .... France
George Bloomfield .... Canada
Don Bluth .... U.S./Ireland
David Blyth .... New Zealand
Mauro Bolognini .... Italy
Ben Bolt .... U.S./UK
Robert Bolt .... UK
Timothy Bond .... Canada
Sergei Bondarchuk .... USSR
John Boorman .... UK
José Luis Borau .... U.S./Spain
Clay Borris .... U.S./Canada
Phillip Borsos .... Canada/U.S.
Roy Boulting .... UK
Serge Bourguignon .... France
Randy Bradshaw .... Canada
Kenneth Branagh .... UK
Klaus Maria Brandauer ..... West Germany
Charlotte Brandstrom .... France/U.S.
Gianni Bozzacchi .... Italy
Tinto Brass .... Italy
Robert Bresson .... France
Alan Bridges .... UK
Lino Brocka .... Philippines
Hugh Brody .... UK
Rex Bromfield .... Canada
Peter Brook .... UK
Bob Brooks .... UK
Nicholus Broomfield .... UK
Franco Brusti .... Italy
Bill Bryden .... UK
Colin Bucksey .... UK
Alan Bunce .... Canada
Juan Buñuel .... France
Derek Burbidge .... UK
Stuart Burge .... UK
Martyn Burke .... Canada
Geoff Burrowes .... Australia
Tim Burstall .... Australia

C

Michael Cacoyannis .... Greece
Ken Cameron .... Australia
Donald Cammell .... UK/France
Graeme Campbell .... Canada
Martin Campbell .... UK
Norman Campbell .... Canada
Jane Campion .... New Zealand/Australia
Mario Camus .... Spain
Bernt Capra .... Switzerland
Leos Carax .... France
Jack Cardiff .... UK
Gilles Carle .... Canada
Henning Carlsen .... Denmark
Marcel Carne .... France
Michael Carreras .... UK
Michael Caton-Jones .... UK/U.S.
Liliana Cavani .... Italy
Felipe Cazals .... Mexico
James Cellan-Jones .... UK
Claude Chabrol .... France
Don Chaffey .... U.S./UK
Jackie Chan .... Hong Kong
Bae Chang-Ho .... South Korea
Mehdi Charef .... France
Colin Chilvers .... Canada
Park Choi-Su .... South Korea
Mohamed Chouikh .... Algeria
Lionel Chetwynd .... U.S./Canada/UK
Elie Chouraqui .... France
Roger Christian .... UK
Vera Chytilova .... Czechoslovakia
Gerard Ciccoritti .... Canada
Souleymane Cissé .... Mali
Richard Ciupka .... Canada
Lawrence Gordon Clark .... UK
James Kenelm Clarke .... UK/U.S.
James Clavell .... Australia/UK
Jack Clayton .... UK/U.S.
Tom Clegg .... UK
Dick Clement .... UK/U.S.
René Clément .... France
Graeme Clifford .... U.S./Australia
Peter Clifton .... UK
Lewis Coates .... Italy
Annette Cohen .... Canada
Eli Cohen .... Israel
Harvey Cokliss .... U.S./UK
Luigi Comencini .... Italy
Kevin Connor .... UK/U.S.
Alan Cooke .... UK
Gerard Corbiau .... Belgium
Sergio Corbucci .... Italy
Rafael Corkidi .... Mexico
John Cornell .... Australia
Axel Corti .... Austria
Raoul Coutard .... France
Alex Cox .... UK/U.S.
Paul Cox .... Australia
Peter Crane .... U.S./UK
Charles Crichton .... UK
Donald Crombie .... Australia
David Cronenberg .... Canada

D

E

F

G

H

Ian Mune ....New Zealand
Fredi M. Murer ....Switzerland
Geoff Murphy ....New Zealand/U.S.

N

Mira Nair ......................................U.S./India
Leon Narbey ....New Zealand
Silvio Narizzano ....Canada
Ronald Neame ........................U.S./UK
Alberto Negrin.....................................Italy
Avi Nesher ....Israel/U.S.
Mike Newell ....UK
Anthony Newley ....UK
Paul Nicolas .............U.S./West Germany
Geoffrey Nottage ....Australia
Phillip Noyce ....Australia/U.S.
Trevor Nunn ....UK
Bruno Nuytten ....France
Peter Nydrle ....Czechoslovakia/U.S.

O

Jim O'Brien ....UK
Mike Ockrent ....UK
James O'Connolly ....UK
Pat O'Connor ....Ireland/U.S./UK
George Ogilvie ....Australia
Kohei Oguri ....Japan
Gerry O'Hara ....UK
Kihachi Okamoto ....Japan
Hector Olivera ....Argentina
Laurence Olivier ....UK
Ermanno Olmi ....Italy
Marcel Ophuls ....France
Stuart Orme ....UK
Peter Ormrod ....Ireland
Nagisa Oshima ....Japan
Thaddeus O'Sullivan ....Ireland/UK
Filippo Ottoni ....Italy
Idrissa Ouedraogo ....Burkina Faso
Gerard Oury ....France
Horace Ove ....UK
Cliff Owen ....UK
Don Owen ....Canada

P

Anthony Page ....UK/U.S.
Euzhan Palcy ....Martinique/U.S.
Tony Palmer ....UK
Gleb Panfilov ....USSR
Pekka Parikka ....Finland
Alan Parker ....UK/U.S.
Cary Parker ...............................U.S./UK
Larry Parr ....New Zealand
Goran Paskaljevic..................Yugoslavia
Ivan Passer .............U.S./Czechoslovakia
Michael Pate ....Australia
Sharad Patel ....UK
Willi Patterson ....UK
Michael Pattinson ....Australia
George Pavlou ....UK

Michael Pearce ....Australia
Ron Peck..UK
Clare Peploe ....UK
Étienne Perier ....France
Zoran Perisic ....UK
Wolfgang Petersen ....West Germany
Chris Petit ....UK
Daniel Petrie ........................U.S./Canada
Maurice Phillips ....UK
Maurice Pialat ....France
Sam Pillsbury ..............U.S./New Zealand
Harold Pinter ....UK
Roman Polanski.................Poland/France
Stephen Poliakoff ....UK
Gillo Pontecorvo ....Italy
Maurizio Ponzi ....Italy
Sally Potter ....UK
Gerald Potterton ....Canada
Michael Powell ....UK
Tristram Powell ....UK
Gaylene Preston ....New Zealand
Luis Puenzo ....Argentina/U.S.
Abraham Pulido ....Venezuela/U.S.

Q

John Quested ....UK/Ireland

R

Fons Rademakers ....Netherlands
Michael Radford ....UK
Michael Raeburn ....UK
Alvin Rakoff ....Canada/UK
Alexander Ramati ....Poland/Israel/Italy
Frederic Raphael...............................UK
Jean-Paul Rappaneau ....France
Harry Rasky ....Canada
Ousama Rawi ....Canada
Satyajit Ray ....India
Clive Rees ....UK
Geoffrey Reeve ....UK
François Reichenbach ....France
Alastair Reid ....UK
John Reid ....New Zealand
Karel Reisz ...............................U.S./UK
Barbara Rennie ....UK
Alain Resnais ....France
Peter Richardson ....UK
Tony Richardson ........................U.S./UK
Anthony Richmond ....UK/U.S.
Philip Ridley ....UK
Leni Riefenstahl ....West Germany
Wolf Rilla ....UK/France
Arturo Ripstein ....Mexico
Dino Risi ....Italy
Jacques Rivette ....France
Alain Robbe-Grillet ....France
Yves Robert ....France
Bruce Robinson ....UK
Franc Roddam ....UK/U.S.
Nicolas Roeg ....UK/U.S.
Eric Rohmer ....France
Eddie Romero ....Philippines
Darrell Roodt ....South Africa

Bernard Rose ....UK
Les Rose ....Canada
Martin Rosen ............................U.S./UK
Francesco Rosi ....Italy
Peter Rowe ....Canada
Patricia Rozema ....Canada
Michael Rubbo ....Canada
Raul Ruíz ....France/Chile/Portugal
Ken Russell ....UK/U.S.

S

Henri Safran ....Australia
Paul Saltzman ....Canada/U.S.
Glen Salzman ....Canada
Jimmy Sangster ....UK
Cirio H. Santiago ....Philippines
Michael Sarne ....UK
Peter Sasdy ....UK
Junya Sato ....Japan
Carlos Saura ....Spain
Claude Sautet ....France
Philip Saville ....UK
Joseph L. Scanlan ....Canada/U.S.
Hans Scheepsmaker ....Netherlands
Maximilian Schell ....Austria
Carl Schenkel ..........U.S./West Germany/
Switzerland
Fred Schepisi ....Australia/U.S.
Paul Schibli ....Canada
John Schlesinger ....UK/U.S.
Volker Schlondorff .....West Germany/U.S.
Oliver Schmitz ....South Africa
Renen Schorr ....Israel
Dale Schott ....Canada
Barbet Schroeder ....France/U.S.
Carl Schultz ....Australia/U.S.
Ettore Scola ....Italy
James Scott ....UK
Ridley Scott ....UK/U.S.
Tony Scott ....UK/U.S.
John Seale ....Australia
Arnaud Selignac ....France
Arna Selznick ....Canada
Ousmene Sembene ....Senegal
Mrinal Sen ....India
Michael Seresin ....UK/U.S.
Yahoo Serious ....Australia
Coline Serreau ....France
Alex Sessa ....Argentina
Philippe Setbon ....France
John Sexton ....Australia
Krishna Shah .............................U.S./India
Paul Shapiro ....Canada
Jim Sharman ....Australia
Don Sharp ....UK
Ian Sharp ....UK
Peter Shatalow ....Canada
Donald Shebib ....Canada
Riki Shelach ....Israel
Adrian Shergold ....UK
Jim Sheridan ....UK
John Sheppard ....Canada
Peter Shillingford ....UK/U.S.
Kaneto Shindo ....Japan
Masahiro Shinoda ....Japan
Slobodan Sijan ....Yugoslavia

Joel Silberg ....Israel/U.S.
Yves Simoneau .......................U.S./Israel
Anthony Simmons ....UK
Andrew Sinclair ....UK
Bernard Sinkel...................West Germany
Vilgot Sjoman ....Sweden
Jerzy Skolimowksi ............U.S./Poland/UK
John Smallcombe ....UK
Clive A. Smith ....Canada
Mel Smith ....UK
Alan Smithee ....International
Rainer Soehnlein ....West Germany
Fernando E. Solanas .....Argentina/France
Ola Solum ....Norway
Alberto Sordi ....Italy
Carlos Sorin ....Argentina
Robin Spry ....Canada
Terence Stamp .........................U.S./UK
Ringo Starr ....UK
David Steinberg ....Canada/U.S.
Martin Stellman ....UK
Sandor Stern .......................U.S./Canada
Steven Hilliard Stern ...........U.S./Canada
Jean-François Stevenin ....France
David Stevens ....Australia
Norman Stone ....UK
Jean-Marie Straub ....France/
                                           West Germany
Charles Sturridge ....UK
Eliseo Subiela ....Argentina
Kevin Sullivan ....Canada
Jeremy Summers ....UK
Shirley Sun ...........................U.S./China
Cedric Sundstrom ....England/U.S.
Bob Swaim .........................U.S./France
Hans-Jurgen Syberberg ... West Germany
Peter Sykes ....UK
Istvan Szabo ....Hungary

T

Jean-Charles Tacchella ....France
Tibor Takacs ....Canada/U.S.
Yojiro Takita ....Japan
Len Talan ....Israel
Alain Tanner ....Switzerland
Nadia Tass ....Australia
Bertrand Tavernier ....France
Paolo Taviani ....Italy
Vittorio Taviani.................................Italy
Baz Taylor ....UK
Julien Temple ....UK/U.S.
Conny Templeman ....UK
Hiroshi Teshigahara ....Japan
Dave Thomas ....Canada/U.S.
Gerald Thomas ....UK
Ralph Thomas ....UK
Ralph L. Thomas ....Canada
Chris Thomson ...................U.S./Australia
J. Lee Thompson ......................U.S./UK
Eric Till ....Canada
Augusto Tomayo ....Peru
Giuseppe Tornatore ....Italy

Ian Toynton ....UK
Jean-Claude Tramont ....France
Brian Trenchard -Smith ....Australia
Jan Troell ....Sweden
Massimo Troisi ....Italy
Fernando Trueba ....Spain
Michael Tuchner.........................U.S./UK
Sophia Turkiewicz ....Australia
Clive Turner ....UK

U

Liv Ullmann ....Norway/U.S./Sweden
Peter Ustinov ....UK/U.S.
Jamie Uys ....South Africa

V

Roger Vadim ......................U.S./France
Kees Van Oostrum ....Netherlands/U.S.
Carlo Vanzina...................................Italy
Agnes Varda ....France
Francis Veber ....France
Isela Vega ....Mexico
Carlo Verdone ....Italy
Paul Verhoeven ....Netherlands/U.S.
Henri Verneuil ....France
Daniel Vigne ....France
Marcela Fernandez Violante ....Mexico
Max Von Sydow ....Sweden
Margarethe von Trotta ...... West Germany

W

Daniel Wachsmann ....Israel
Andrzej Wajda ....Poland
Giles Walker ....Canada
Peter Walker ....British
Sam Wanamaker ........................U.S./UK
Peter Wang ....US/China
Wayne Wang ....US/Hong Kong
Vincent Ward ....New Zealand
Peter Watkins ....UK
Paul Watson ....UK
Al Waxman ....Canada/U.S.
Peter Webb ....UK
Stephen Weeks ....UK
Paul Weiland ....UK/U.S.
Peter Weir ....Australia/U.S.
Wim Wenders................... West Germany
Lina Wertmuller ....Italy
Tony Wharmby ....UK
Claude Whatham ....UK
David Wheatley ....UK
Anne Wheeler ....Canada
David Wickes ....UK
Bernhard Wicki .... West Germany
Bo Widerberg ....Sweden
Richard Williams ....UK/U.S.

Simon Wincer ....Australia/U.S.
Michael Winner ....UK/U.S.
Terry Winsor ....UK
Donovan Winter ....UK/U.S.
Franz Peter Wirth .... West Germany
Herbert Wise ....US/UK
Carol Wiseman ....UK
Stephen Withrow ....Canada
Carol Wiseman ....UK
Dan Wolman ....Israel
Casper Wrede ....UK

Y

Yoji Yamada ....Japan
Mitsuo Yanagimachi ....Japan
Edward Yang ....Taiwan
Peter Yates ....US/UK
Rebecca Yates ....Canada
Yegeny Yevtushenko ....USSR
Zhang Yimou ....China
Freddie Young ....UK
Robert William Young ....UK
Terence Young.........................UK/U.S.

Z

Krzysztof Zanussi ....Poland/West
                               Germany/France/UK
John Zaritsky .... Canada
Franco Zeffirelli ....Italy
Mai Zetterling ....Sweden
Rafal Zielinski ....Canada/U.S.
Marcos Zurinaga ....Puerto Rico

F
O
R
E
I
G
N

B
A
S
E
D

D
I
R
E
C
T
O
R
S

DIRECTORS GUILDS—U.S. & FOREIGN OFFICES

This is not a complete list of all national and international guilds/offices representing directors—just those which represent the majority of the directors listed in this book.

D
I
R
E
C
T
O
R
S

G
U
I
L
D
S

USA
Directors Guild of America--West
7920 Sunset Blvd.
Los Angeles, CA 90046
213/289-2000
FAX 213/289-2029

Directors Guild of America--East
110 W. 57th St.
New York, NY 10019
212/581-0370
FAX 212/581-1441

Directors Guild of America—Midwest
520 N. Michigan Avenue - Suite 1026
Chicago, IL 60611
312/644-5050

AUSTRALIA
Australian Screen Directors Association
Box 22
Trades Hall Four
Goulbern Street
Sydney, NSW 2000
AUSTRALIA
02/264-9986

CANADA
Directors Guild of Canada
3 Church St., Suite 500
Toronto, Ontario M5E1M2
CANADA
416/364-0122

Directors Guild of Canada
524 11th Avenue S.W.
Calgary, Alberta T2R 0X8
CANADA
403/237-0689

Directors Guild of Canada
163 West Hastings Street, Suite 339
Vancouver, British Columbia V6B 1H5
CANADA
604/688-2976

Directors Guild of Canada
2250 Guy Street, Suite 506
Montreal, Quebec H3H 2M3
CANADA
514/989-1714

FINLAND
Federation of Finnish Film
Directors
Mariankatu 15B
SF-00250 Helsinki, FINLAND
0/654-426

FRANCE
Association Professional Des
Realisateurs D'Oeurves Audio Visual
7 Rue Biscarnet
75012 Paris, FRANCE
4/730-4474

GREAT BRITAIN (UK)
Directors Guild of Great Britain
56 Whitfield St.
London W1, ENGLAND
71/880-9582

JAPAN
Directors Guild of Japan
Tsukada Building
8-33 Udagawa-cho, Shibuya-ku
Tokyo 150 JAPAN
3/461-4411

WEST GERMANY
German Film and Television Academy
Pommernallee 1
1 Berlin 19 WEST GERMANY
0311/302-6096

SPAIN
Ministry of Culture, Motion Picture Division
Avenida de Burgos 5,
28036 Madrid, SPAIN
91/202-5351

USSR
Union of Soviet Filmmakers
Vassilievskaya 13
Moscow, USSR
250-4114

YUGOSLAVIA
Yugoslavia Film, Knez Mihailova 19
11000 Belgrade, YUGOSLAVIA
011/625-860

A

ABRAMS ARTISTS & ASSOCIATES
9200 Sunset Blvd., Suite 625
Los Angeles, CA 90069
213/859-0625

ADDIS-WECHSLER & ASSOCIATES
8444 Wilshire Blvd.
Beverly Hills, CA 90211
213/653-8867

Mr. Keith Addis
Mr. Nick Wechsler

THE AGENCY
10351 Santa Monica Blvd.
Suite 211
Los Angeles, CA 90025
213/551-3000

AGENCY FOR THE PERFORMING ARTS, INC. (APA)
9000 Sunset Blvd., Suite 1200
Los Angeles, CA 90069
213/273-0744

888 Seventh Avenue
New York, NY 10016
212/582-1500

BUDDY ALTONI TALENT AGENCY
PO Box 1022
Newport Beach, CA 92660
714/851-1711

Mr. Buddy Altoni

CARLOS ALVARADO AGENCY
8820 Sunset Blvd., Suites A & B
Los Angeles, CA 90069
213/652-0272

Mr. Carlos Alvarado
Ms. Monalee Schilling

FRED AMSEL & ASSOCIATES, INC.
6310 San Vicente Blvd., Suite 407
Los Angeles, CA 90048
213/939-1188

Mr. Fred Amsel

THE ARTISTS AGENCY
10000 Santa Monica Blvd.
Suite 305
Los Angeles, CA 90067
213/277-7779

Mr. Mickey Freiberg
Ms. Merrily Kane

ARTISTS DIRECTIONS
9200 Sunset Blvd.
Penthouse 20
Los Angeles, CA 90069
213/273-0600

THE ARTISTS GROUP, LTD.
1930 Century Park West
Suite 403
Los Angeles, CA 90067
213/552-1100

Mr. Arnold Soloway
Mr. Hal Stalmaster

ASHER/KROST MANAGEMENT
644 North Doheny Drive
Los Angeles, CA 90069
213/273-9433

Mr. Peter Asher
Mr. Barry Krost

HOWARD J. ASKENASE
6217 Glen Airy Drive
Los Angeles, CA 90068
213/464-4114

ASSOCIATED MANAGEMENT, INC.
9200 Sunset Blvd.
Penthouse 20
Los Angeles, CA 90069
213/550-0570

Mr. Harold Cohen
Mr. Jerry Levy

ASSOCIATED TALENT AGENCY, INC.
9744 Wilshire Blvd., Suite 312
Beverly Hills, CA 90212
213/271-4662

B

BARRETT, BENSON, McCARTT & WETSON
2121 Avenue of the Stars
Suite 2450
Los Angeles, CA 90067

Mr. Christopher Barrett
Mr. Jeffrey A. Benson
Ms. Bettye McCartt
Mr. Richard A. Weston

THE BARSKIN AGENCY
120 South Victory Blvd.
Burbank, CA 91502
818/848-5536

Ms. Beverly Barskin

BAUER BENEDEK AGENCY
9255 Sunset Blvd., Suite 716
Los Angeles, CA 90069
213/275-2421

Mr. Marty Bauer
Mr. Peter Benedek
Mr. Dan Halsted

BAUMAN, HILLER & ASSOCIATES
5750 Wilshire Blvd., Suite 512
Los Angeles, CA 90036
213/857-6666

Mr. Richard Bauman
Mr. Walter Hiller

250 W. 57th Street
New York, NY 10019
212/757-0098

GEORGES BEAUME
3 Quai Malaquais
Paris, 75006 France
325-2837

Mr. Georges Beaume

HARRY BLOOM AGENCY, INC.
16272 Via Embeleso
San Diego, CA 92128
619/487-5531

**J. MICHAEL BLOOM &
ASSOCIATES**
233 Park Avenue South, Floor 10
New York, NY 10003
212/529-6500

Ms. Heidi Powers

9200 Sunset Blvd.
Suite 710
Los Angeles, CA 90069
213/275-6800

BRANDON & DWORSKI
9046 Sunset Blvd.
Los Angeles, CA 90069
213/273-6173

Mr. Paul Brandon
Mr. David Dworski

**BRESLER, KELLY &
KIPPERMAN**
15760 Ventura Blvd., Suite 1730
Encino, CA 91436
818/905-1155

111 West 57th Street, Suite 1409
New York, NY 10019
212/265-1980

Mr. Sandy Bresler
Mr. John Kelly
Mr. Perri Kipperman (NY)

THE BRILLSTEIN COMPANY
9200 Sunset Blvd., Suite 428
Los Angeles, CA 90069
213/275-6135

Mr. Bernie Brillstein

**BRODER-KURLAND-WEBB-
UFFNER AGENCY**
8439 Sunset Blvd., Suite 402
Los Angeles, CA 90069
213/656-9262

Mr. Bob Broder
Mr. Norman Kurland
Ms. Beth Uffner
Mr. Elliot Webb

NED BROWN AGENCY
407 North Maple Drive
Beverly Hills, CA 90210
213/276-1131

Mr. John Brown
Mr. Ned Brown

**DON BUCHWALD &
ASSOCIATES**
10 East 44th Street
New York, NY 10017
212/867-1070

Mr. Don Buchwald

C

BRETT CALDER AGENCY
17420 Ventura Blvd., Suite 4
Encino, CA 91316
818/906-2825

Mr. Maury Calder

CAMDEN ARTISTS, LTD.
2121 Avenue of the Stars
Suite 410
Los Angeles, CA 90067
213/556-2022

CAMERON'S MANAGEMENT
120 Victoria Street
Potts Point, NSW 2011
Australia

JUNE CANN MANAGEMENT
203 Alfred Street North
North Sydney, NSW 2060
Australia

CENTURY ARTISTS, LTD.
9744 Wilshire Blvd., Suite 308
Beverly Hills, CA 90212
213/273-4366

Mr. Louis Bershad

CHARTER MANAGEMENT
9000 Sunset Blvd., Suite 1112
Los Angeles, CA 90069
213/278-1690

THE CHASIN AGENCY
190 North Cañon Drive
Suite 201
Beverly Hills, CA 90210
213/278-7505

Ms. Laurie Apelian
Mr. Tom Chasin

CHATTO & LINNIT
Prince of Wales Theatre
Coventry Street
London W1, England

**CINEMA TALENT
INTERNATIONAL**
7906 Santa Monica Blvd.
Suite 212
Los Angeles, CA 90067
213/656-1937

Mr. George Rumanes

**KINGSLEY COLTON &
ASSOCIATES**
16661 Ventura Blvd., Suite 400
Encino, CA 91436
818/788-6043

Mr. Kingsley Colton

CONTEMPORARY ARTISTS, LTD.
132 Lasky Drive
Beverly Hills, CA 90212
213/278-8250

Mr. Ronald Leif

CONWAY & ASSOCIATES
12400 Wilshire Blvd., Suite 1240
Los Angeles, CA 90025
213/207-1145

Mr. Ben Conway
Mr. Scott Penney
Ms. Mary Rader

THE COOPER AGENCY
10100 Santa Monica Blvd.
Suite 310
Los Angeles, CA 90067
213/277-8422

Mr. Frank Cooper

**CREATIVE ARTISTS AGENCY
(CAA)**
1888 Century Park East, 14th Floor
Los Angeles, CA 90067
213/277-4545

PETER CROUCH & ASSOCIATES
59 Frith Street
London, W1 England
71/734-2167

CURTIS-BROWN, LTD.
Ten Astor Place
New York, NY 10003
212/473-5400

Mr. Timothy Knowlton

D

JUDY DAISH AGENCY
83 Eastbourne Mews
London W2 8LA, England
71/262-1101

LARRY DALZELL ASSOCIATES
Three Goodwin Court
St. Martin's Lane
London, W1 England
71/734-7311

DIAMOND ARTISTS, LTD.
9200 Sunset Blvd., Suite 909
Los Angeles, CA 90069
213/278-8146

Mr. Abby Greshler

D.R.M.
28 Charing Cross Road
London, WC2H 0DB England
71/836-3903

STEPHEN DUBRIDGE AGENCY
London, England
71/734/7311

E

ROBERT EISENBACH AGENCY
967 Hammond, Suite 1
Los Angeles, CA 90069
213/273-0801

Mr. Robert Eisenbach

EMERALD ARTISTS, INC.
6565 Sunset Blvd.
Suite 200
Los Angeles, CA 90028
213/465-2974

F

FILM ARTISTS ASSOCIATES
7080 Hollywood Blvd.
Suite 704
Hollywood, CA 90028
213/463-1010

Mr. Chris Dennis
Mr. Penn Dennis

KURT FRINGS AGENCY, INC.
139 S. Beverly Drive, Suite 328
Beverly Hills, CA 90210
213/227-1103

Mr. Kurt Frings

G

THE GAGE GROUP
9255 Sunset Blvd., Suite 515
Los Angeles, CA 90069
213/859-8777

1650 Broadway, Suite 406
New York, NY 10019
212/541-5250

Mr. Martin Gage

GALLIN-MOREY ASSOCIATES
8730 Sunset Blvd.
Penthouse West
Los Angeles, CA 90069
213/659-5593

Ms. Sandy Gallin
Mr. Jim Morey

GELFAND, RENNERT & FELDMAN
1880 Century Park East, Suite 900
Los Angeles, CA 90067
213/553-1707

GENERAL MANAGEMENT CORP.
9000 Sunset Blvd., Suite 400
Los Angeles, CA 90069
213/274-8805

Ms. Helen Kushnick

ROY GERBER & ASSOCIATES
9046 Sunset Blvd., Suite 208
Los Angeles, CA 90069
213/550-0100

Mr. Roy Gerber

THE GERSH AGENCY
232 North Cañon Drive
Beverly Hills, CA 90210
213/274-6611

Mr. Phil Gersh

J. CARTER GIBSON
9000 Sunset Blvd., Suite 801
Los Angeles, CA 90069
213/274-8813

J. Carter Gobson

PHILLIP B. GITTELMAN
1221 N. Kings Road
Penthouse 405
Los Angeles, CA 90059
213/656-9215

Mr. Phillip B. Gittelman

HARRY GOLD & ASSOCIATES
12725 Ventura Blvd., Suite E
Studio City, CA 91604
818/769-5003

Mr. Harry Gold

GOLDSTEIN & COMPANY, INC.
10100 Santa Monica Blvd.
Suite 200
Los Angeles, CA 90067
213/557-2507

Terry Goldstein

GORES/FIELDS AGENCY
10100 Santa Monica Blvd.
7th Floor
Los Angeles, CA 90067
213/277-4400

Mr. Jack Fields
Mr. Sam Gores

IVAN GREEN AGENCY
8383 Wilshire Blvd., Suite 1039
Beverly Hills, CA 90211
213/277-1541

HAROLD R. GREENE, INC.
8455 Beverly Blvd., Suite 309
Los Angeles, CA 90048
213/852-4959

Mr. Harold R. Greene

LARRY GROSSMAN & ASSOCIATES
211 South Beverly Drive, Suite 206
Beverly Hills, CA 90212
213/550-8127

Ms. Janet Grossman
Mr. Larry Grossman

REECE HALSEY AGENCY
8733 Sunset Blvd., Suite 101
Los Angeles, CA 90069
213/652-2409

Mr. Reece Halsey

**THE MITCHELL J. HAMILBURG
AGENCY**
292 South La Cienega Blvd.
Suite 312
Beverly Hills, CA 90211
213/657-1501

Mr. Michael Hamilburg

**HARRIS & GOLDBERG TALENT &
LITERARY AGENCY**
2121 Avenue of the Stars
Suite 950
Los Angeles, CA 90067
213/553-5200

Mr. Howard Goldberg
Mr. Scott Harris

HATTON & BAKER
18 Jermyn Street
London W1, England
71/439-2971

Mr. Terence Baker

JAMES HARPER
13063 Ventura Blvd., Suite 202
Studio City, CA 91604
818/788-8683

DUNCAN HEATH & ASSOCIATES
162 Wardour Street
London W1, England
71/439-1471

Mr. Duncan Heath

**HENDERSON/HOGAN
AGENCY**
405 West 44th Street
New York, NY 10036
212/765-5190

247 S. Beverly Drive, Suite 102
Beverly Hills, CA 90212
213/274-7815

Ms. Margaret Henderson
Mr. Jerry Hogan (NY)

NANCY HOTSON
605 North Cañon Drive
Beverly Hills, CA 90210
213/274-7141

**ROBERT G. HUSSONG
INTERNATIONAL FILMS**
721 N. La Brea Avenue, Suite 201
Los Angeles, CA 90038
213/652-2893

Mr. Robert Hussong

I

**MICHAEL IMISON
PLAYWRIGHTS**
71/354-3274 (London)
212/874-2671 (New York)

Mr. Alan Brodie (London)
Mr. Michael Imison (London)
Mr. Abbe Levin (NY)

**INTERNATIONAL CREATIVE
MANAGEMENT (ICM)**
8899 Beverly Blvd.
Los Angeles, CA 90048
213/550-4000

40 West 57th Street
New York, NY 10019
212/556-5600

38 Via Siacci
Rome, Italy
806-041

388-396 Oxford Street
London W1, England W1N 9HE
71/629-8080

INTERTALENT AGENCY
9200 Sunset Blvd., Penthouse 25
Los Angeles, CA 90069
213/271-0600

J

**JANKLOW & NESBITT
ASSOCIATES**
598 Madison Avenue
New York, NY 10022
212/421-1700

Mr. Morton Janklow
Ms. Lynn Nesbitt

MELINDA JASON COMPANY
Columbia Plaza
Producers Building 8
Room 209
Burbank, CA 91505
818/954-3472

Ms. Linda Clark
Ms. Melinda Jason

THE THOMAS JENNINGS AGENCY
427 N. Cañon Drive
Suite 205
Beverly Hills, CA 90210
213/274-5418

Mr. Tom Jennings

ANTHONY JONES
London, England
71/441/839-2556

K

THE KAPLAN-STAHLER AGENCY
8383 Wilshire Blvd.
Suite 923
Beverly Hills, CA 90211
213/653-4483

Mr. Mitchell Kaplan
Mr. Elliot Stahler

PATRICIA KARLAN AGENCY
4425 Riverside Drive
Suite 102
Bubank, CA 91505
818/846-8666

PAUL KOHNER, INC.
9169 Sunset Blvd.
Los Angeles, CA 90069
213/550-1060

Mr. Paul Kohner

KOPALOFF COMPANY
1930 Century Park West
Suite 403
Los Angeles, CA 90067
213/203-8430

Mr. Don Kopaloff

L

LAKE & DOUROUX
445 S. Beverly Drive, Suite 310
Beverly Hills, CA 90212
213/557-0700

Ms. Candace Lake
Mr. Michael Douroux

THE LANTZ OFFICE
9255 Sunset Blvd., Suite 505
Los Angeles, CA 90069
213/858-1144

888 Seventh Avenue, 25th Floor
New York, NY 10106
212/586-0200

Mr. Robert Lantz

IRVING PAUL LAZAR AGENCY
120 El Camino Drive, Suite 108
Beverly Hills, CA 90212
213/275-6153

One East 66th Street
New York, NY 10021
212/355-1177

Mr. Irving Paul Lazar

LEADING ARTISTS AGENCY
445 N. Bedford Drive, Penthouse
Beverly Hills, CA 90210
213/858-1999

**LEADING PLAYERS
MANAGEMENT**
29 Kings Road
London, SW3 England

JACK LENNY & ASSOCIATES
140 West 58th Street
New York, NY 10019
212/582-0270

9545 Wilshire Blvd, Suite 600
Beverly Hills, CA 90212
213/271-2174

Mr. Jim Lenny

THE LIBERTY AGENCY
10845 Lindbrook Drive, Suite 200
Los Angeles, CA 90024
213/824-7937

Ms. Glennis Liberty

**THE ROBERT LITTMAN
COMPANY, INC.**
409 North Camden Drive
Suite 105
Beverly Hills, CA 90210
213/278-1572

Mr. Robert Littman

LONDON MANAGEMENT
235/241 Regent Street
London W1, England
011/441/493-1610

STERLING LORD LITERISTIC
One Madison Avenue
New York, NY 10010
212/696-2800

Mr. Sterling Lord

M

CHRISTOPHER MANN, LTD.
39 Davies Street
London, W1 England
71/493-2810

Mr. Christopher Mann

SANDRA MARSH MANAGEMENT
14930 Ventura Blvd.
Suite 200
Sherman Oaks, CA 91403
818/905-6961

Ms. Sandra Marsh

KIRBY MC CAULEY
432 Park Avenue South
Suite 1509
New York, NY 10016
212/683-7561

JAMES McHUGH AGENCY
8150 Beverly Blvd.
Suite 303
Los Angeles, CA 90048
213/651-2770

Mr. James McHugh

HELEN MERRILL, LTD.
435 West 23rd Street
New York, NY 10011
212/591-5326

THE MILLER AGENCY
23560 Lyons Avenue
Suite 209
Santa Clarita, CA 91321
805/255-7173

Mr. Tom Miller

WILLIAM MORRIS AGENCY
151 S. El Camino Drive
Beverly Hills, CA 90212
213/274-7451

1350 Avenue of the Americas
New York, NY 10019
212/586-5100

2325 Crestmoore Road
Nashville, TN 37215
615/385-0310

31-32 Soho Square
London W12 5DG, England
71/434-2191

Via Giosue Carducci, 10
00187 Rome, Italy
48-6961

Lamonstrasse 9
Munich 80, West Germany
011/47/608-1234

THE MORTON AGENCY
1103-1/2 Glendon Avenue
Los Angeles, CA 90024
213/824-4089

Mr. Michael Werner

N

**CHRISTOPHER NASSIF &
ASSOCIATES**
1801 Avenue of the Stars
Suite 1250
Los Angeles, CA 90067
213/556-4343

Mr. Christopher Nassif

O

DICK ODGERS
London, England
71/262-1611

Mr. Peter Murphy
Mr. Dick Odgers

FIFI OSCARD AGENCY
19 West 44th Street
New York, NY 10036
212/764-1100

Ms. Fifi Oscard

THE DANIEL OSTROFF AGENCY
9200 Sunset Blvd., Suite 402
Los Angeles, CA 90069
213/278-2020

Mr. Daniel Ostroff

P

THE BARRY PERELMAN AGENCY
9200 Sunset Blvd., Suite 531
Los Angeles, CA 90069
213/274-5999

Mr. Douglas A. Brodax
Mr. Barry Perelman

PETERS, FRASER & DUNLOP
The Chambers, Chelsea Harbour
Lots Road
London SW10 OXF, England
71/376-7676

LYNN PLESHETTE AGENCY
2700 North Beachwood Drive
Los Angeles, CA 90068
213/465-0428

Ms. Lynn Pleshette

PREFERRED ARTISTS
16633 Ventura Blvd., Suite 1421
Encino, CA 91436
818/990-0305

JIM PREMINGER AGENCY
1650 Westwood Blvd., Suite 201
Los Angeles, CA 90024
213/475-9491

Mr. Jim Preminger

**PROGRESSIVE ARTISTS
AGENCY, INC.**
400 South Beverly Drive.
Suite 216
Beverly Hills, CA 90212
213/553-8561

R

DOUGLAS RAE MANAGEMENT
28 Charing Cross Road
London WC2, England
71/836-3903

Mr. Douglas Rae

MARGARET RAMSAY LTD.
14a Goodwin's Cout
St. Martin's Lane
London WC2, England
71/240-0691

JOHN REDWAY & ASSOCIATES
5 Denmark Street
LondonWC2H 8LP, England
71/836-2001

Mr. Derek Webster
Mr. David Booth

**THE RICHLAND/WUNSCH
AGENCY**
9220 Sunset Blvd., Suite 311
Los Angeles, CA 90069
213/278-1955

Mr. Dan Richland
Mr. Joe Richland
Mr. Bob Wunsch
Mr. Rafe Wunsch

**RISKY BUSINESS
MANAGEMENT**
10966 Le Conte Avenue, Suite A
Los Angeles, CA 90024
213/208-2335

THE ROBERTS COMPANY
427 N. Cañon Drive, Suite 215
Beverly Hills, CA 90210
213/275-9384

**ROBINSON, WEINTRAUB,
GROSS & ASSOCIATES, INC.**
8428 Melrose Place
Los Angeles, CA 90069
213/653-5802

Mr. Ken Gross
Mr. Stuart Robinson
Mr. Bernie Weintraub

**STEPHANIE ROGERS &
ASSOCIATES**
3855 Lankershim Blvd., Suite 218
North Hollywood, CA 91604
818/509-1010

Ms. Stephanie Rogers

**ROLLINS, MORRA & BREZNER,
INC.**
801 Westmount Drive
Los Angeles, CA 90069
213/657-5404

130 West 57th Street, Suite 11-D
New York, NY 10019
212/582-1940

Mr. Larry Brezner
Mr. Buddy Morra
Mr. Jack Rollins (NY)

JACK ROSE AGENCY
6430 Sunset Blvd., Suite 1203
Hollywood, CA 90028
213/463-7300

Mr. Jack Rose
Ms. Tanya Chasman

THE ROSEN/TURTLE GROUP
15010 Ventura Blvd., Suite 219
Sherman Oaks, CA 91403
818/907-9891

Mr. Michael Rosen
Ms. Cindy Turtle

ROSENSTONE/WENDER
Three East 48th Street
New York, NY 10017
212/832-8330

Mr. Howard Rosenstone
Ms. Phyllis Wender

S

SANFORD-BECKETT-SKOURAS
1015 Gayley Avenue
Suite 301
Los Angeles, CA 90024
213/208-2100

Ms. Brenda Beckett
Mr. Geoffrey Sanford
Ms. Brenda Beckett

**THE IRV SCHECHTER
COMPANY**
9300 Wilshire Blvd.
Suite 410
Beverly Hills, CA 90212
213/278-8070

Mr. Irv Schecter

**DON SCHWARTZ &
ASSOCIATES**
8749 Sunset Blvd., Suite 200
Los Angeles, CA 90069
213/657-8910

SELECTED ARTISTS AGENCY
13111 Ventura Blvd., Suite 204
Studio City, CA 91604
818/905-5744

Ms. Flo Joseph

DAVID SHAPIRA & ASSOCIATES
15301 Ventura Blvd., Suite 345
Sherman Oaks, CA 91403
818/906-0322

Mr. David Shapira

SHAPIRO-LICHTMAN, INC.
8827 Beverly Blvd.
Los Angeles, CA 90048
213/859-8877

Mr. Mark Lichtman
Mr. Martin Shapiro

SHAPIRO/WEST & ASSOCIATES
141 El Camino Drive, Suite 205
Beverly Hills, CA 90212
213/278-8896

Mr. George Shapiro
Mr. Howard West

SHARR ENTERPRISES, INC.
P.O. Box 69543
Los Angeles, CA 90069
213/278-1981

Ina Bernstein Sharr

LEW SHERRELL AGENCY, LTD.
7060 Hollywood Blvd., Suite 610
Los Angeles, CA 90028
213/461-9955

Lew Sherrell

SHORR/STILLE & ASSOCIATES
800 S. Robertson Blvd., Suite 6
Los Angeles, CA 90035
213/659-6160

Mr. Fred Shorr
Ms. Lucy Stille

SUSAN SHULMAN
454 West 44th Street
New York, NY 10036
212/713-1633

LINDA SIEFERT & ASSOCIATES
8A Brunswick Gardens
London W8 4AJ, England
71/229-5163

ERIC L'EPINE SMITH LTD.
10 Wyndham Place
London W1H 1AS, England
71/724-0739

SUSAN SMITH & ASSOCIATES
121 N. San Vicente Blvd.
Beverly Hills, CA 90211
213/852-4777

Ms. Susan Smith

**SMITH/GOSNELL/NICHOLSON &
ASSOCIATES**
P.O. Box 1166
1294 Calle de Sevilla
Pacific Palisades, CA 90272
213/459-0307

Mr. Creighton Smith
Mr. Ray Gosnell
Mr. Skip Nicholson

STE REPRESENTATION, LTD.
9301 Wilshire Blvd.
Suite 312
Beverly Hills, CA 90210
213/550-3982

888 Seventh Avenue
Suite 21-F
New York, NY 10106
212/246-1030

Mr. David Eidenberg
Mr. Clifford Stevens (NY)

**CHARLES H. STERN
AGENCY, INC.**
11755 Wilshire Blvd.
Suite 2320
Los Angeles, CA 90025
213/479-1788

Mr. Charles Stern

**STONE MANNERS
TALENT AGENCY**
9113 Sunset Blvd.
Los Angeles, CA 90069
213/275-9599

MR. Scott Manners
Mr. Tim Stone

THE SHIRLEY STRICK AGENCY
9220 Sunset Blvd.
Suite 204
Los Angeles, CA 90069
213/273-0919

Ms. Shirley Strick

H. N. SWANSON, INC. AGENCY
8523 Sunset Blvd.
Los Angeles, CA 90069
213/652-5385

H. N. Swanson

A
G
E
N
T
S

&

M
A
N
A
G
E
R
S

Tr-Zi T

FILM
DIRECTORS
GUIDE

TRIAD ARTISTS, INC.
10100 Santa Monica Blvd.
16th Floor
Los Angeles, CA 90067
213/556-2727

888 Seventh Avenue
Suite 1602
New York, NY 10106
212/489-8100

TWENTIETH CENTURY ARTISTS
3800 Barham Blvd., Suite 303
Los Angeles, CA 90068
213/850-5516

W

ELLIOT WAX & ASSOCIATES
9255 Sunset Blvd., Suite 612
Los Angeles, CA 90069
213/273-8217

Mr. Elliot Wax
Mr. Marc A. Wax

THE WELTMAN COMPANY
425 S. Beverly Drive
Beverly Hills, CA 90212
213/556-2801

Mr. Philip Weltman

PENNY WESSON
London, England
011/411/72266-7

STEVE WHITE AGENCY
260 South Beverly Drive, Suite 200
Beverly Hills, CA 90212
213/277-1638

MICHAEL WHITEHALL LTD.
125 Gloucester Road
London W7 4TE, England
71/244-8466

ALAN WILLIG & ASSOCIATES
47-A Horatio Street
New York, NY 10014
212/645-9400

WRITERS & ARTISTS AGENCY
11726 San Vicente Blvd., Suite 300
Los Angeles, CA 90049
213/820-2240

70 West 36th Street, Suite 501
New York, NY 10018
212/947-8765

Ms. Joan Scott

Z

ZIEGLER & ASSOCIATES
606 Wilshire Blvd., Suite 304
Santa Monica, CA 90401
213/278-0070

Mr. Martin Hurwitz

A CATERED CREATION

by

MARCI'A

Innovative Planning & Personalized Attention Given to Create the Perfect Party

Specializing in Exceptional Hors D'Oeuvres and Fine Foods from Around The World

Committed to Quality & Excellence in Food, Service & Style

Miracles Created to Accommodate Your Budget

Serving various industries for over 10 years, including:
Private parties & weddings for the entertainment industry
Lucasfilm, Ltd.
Warner Bros. Television

Consultations Available
213/453-0032

INDEX OF FILM COMMISSIONS

The following list does not include all city and province film commissions.
For further information, please refer to the main state or country listing.

UNITED STATES

ALABAMA
800/633-5898
FAX - 205/265-5078

ALASKA
907/562-4163
FAX - 907/563-3575

ARIZONA
602/542-5011
FAX - 602/280-1384

CALIFORNIA
213/736-2465
FAX - 213/736-3159

Oakland, CA
415/273-3109

San Francisco, CA
415/554-6144

COLORADO
303/866-2778
FAX - 303/866-2251

CONNECTICUT
203/258-4301
FAX - 203/563-4877

DELAWARE
302/736-4271
FAX - 203/736-5749

DISTRICT OF COLUMBIA
202/727-6600
FAX - 202/727-3787

FLORIDA
904/487-1100
FAX - 904/922-5943

Orlando, FL
407/422-7159

Tampa, FL
813/223-8419

GEORGIA
404/656-3951
FAX - 404/651-9063

HAWAII
808/548-4535
FAX - 808/548-2189

Hawaii County, HI
808/961-8366

IDAHO
800/942-8338
FAX - 208/234-2631

ILLINOIS
312/814-3600
FAX - 312/814-6732

INDIANA
317/232-8829
FAX - 317/232-4146

IOWA
800/779-3456
FAX - 525/281-7276

KANSAS
913/296-4927
FAX - 913/296-4927

KENTUCKY
502/564-3456
FAX - 502/564-7588

LOUISIANA
504/342-8150
FAX - 504/342-3207

MAINE
207/289-5710
FAX - 207/289-2861

MARYLAND
Prince George's County
301/386-3456

MASSACHUSETTS
617/973-8800

MICHIGAN
800/477-3456
FAX - 517/373-3872

MINNESOTA
612/332-6493

MISSISSIPPI
601/359-3297
FAX - 601/359-2832

MISSOURI
314/751-9050
FAX - 314/751-7384

MONTANA
800/548-3390
FAX - 406/444-2808

NEBRASKA
800/426-6505
FAX - 402/471-3778

NEVADA
702/486-7150
FAX - 702/486-7155

NEW HAMPSHIRE
603/271-2598
FAX - 603/271-2629

NEW JERSEY
201/648-6279
FAX - 201/648-7350

NEW MEXICO
800/545-9871
FAX - 505/827-8584

Albuquerque, NM
505/768-4512

NEW YORK
212/575-6570
FAX - 212/840-7149

NORTH CAROLINA
919/733-9900
FAX - 919/733-0110

NORTH DAKOTA
800/437-2077
FAX - 701/223-3081

OHIO
800/848-1300
FAX - 614/644-1789

OKLAHOMA
800/443-6552
FAX - 405/841-5199

OREGON
800/547-7842
FAX - 503/581-5115

PENNSYLVANIA
717/783-3456
FAX - 717/234-4560

PUERTO RICO
809/758-4747
FAX - 809/754-9640

RHODE ISLAND
401/277-3456
FAX - 401/277-6046

SOUTH CAROLINA
803/737-0400
FAX - 803/737-0418

SOUTH DAKOTA
800/843-8000
FAX - 605/773-3256

TENNESSEE
800/251-8594
FAX - 615/741-5829

TEXAS
512/469-9111
FAX - 512/473-2312

UTAH
800/453-8824
FAX - 801/538-8886

VERMONT
802/828-3236
FAX - 802/828-3233

U.S. VIRGIN ISLANDS
809/775-1444
FAX - 809/774-4390

VIRGINIA
804/371-8204
FAX - 804/786-1121

WASHINGTON STATE
206/464-7148
FAX - 206/464-5868

WEST VIRGINIA
800/225-5982
FAX - 304/348-0108

WISCONSIN
608/267-3456
FAX - 608/266-3403

WYOMING
800/458-6657

CANADA

ALBERTA
403/427-2005
FAX - 403/427-5924

BRITISH COLUMBIA
604/660-2732
FAX - 604/660-4790

THOMPSON-NICOLA
604/372-9336
FAX - 604/372-5048

NEW BRUNSWICK
506/453-2553
FAX - 506/453-2416

JOHN BYRNE
709/576-2800
FAX - 709/576-5936

FILM NOVA SCOTIA
902/422-3402
FAX - 902/424-0563

ONTARIO
416/965-8393
FAX - 416/965-0329

QUEBEC
514/873-7768
FAX - 514/873-4388

MONTREAL
514/872-2883
FAX - 514/872-1153

SASKATCHEWAN
306/347-3456
FAX - 306/565-2177

YUKON
403/667-5400
FAX - 403/667-2634

INTERNATIONAL

AUSTRALIA/VICTORIA
613/329-7033
FAX - 613/329-1950

AUSTRIA/L.A.
213/477-3322
FAX - 213/477-5141

BAHAMAS
809/326-0635
FAX - 809/328-0945

BARBADOS
212/986-6516
FAX - 212/573-9850

BERMUDA
809/292-0023
FAX - 809/292-7537

BRITISH VIRGIN ISLANDS
809/494-3134
FAX - 809/494-2506

CAYMAN ISLANDS
809/949-7999
FAX - 809/949-8487

CHILE
562/229-7212
FAX - 562-211-9826

COSTA RICA/L.A.
213/271-5858
FAX - 213/273-5566

ENGLAND/LIVERPOOL
051/225-5446
FAX - 051/207-1342

HOLLAND
213/399-1101

HONG KONG/L.A.
213/208-4582

ISRAEL/L.A.
213/658-7924
FAX - 213/651-0572

JAMAICA
809/924-9650
FAX - 809/926-7326

MEXICO
905/688-8864
FAX- 905/688-4211

NEW ZEALAND/L.A.
213/477-8241

PERU/HOLLYWOOD
213/465-8900

STANDING ORDERS?

Go ahead—make it easy on yourself.

Get on our standing order list
and receive your copy of
Michael Singer's
FILM DIRECTORS: A Complete Guide
hot off the press each year...
automatically.

Just send us a note on your letterhead
and we'll take care of the rest.

P.S. We can also put you on a standing order for
our other terrific annual directories, too:

- ★ **FILM WRITERS GUIDE**
- ★ **FILM PRODUCERS, STUDIOS, AGENTS & CASTING DIRECTORS GUIDE**
- ★ **CINEMATOGRAPHERS, PRODUCTION DESIGNERS,
  COSTUME DESIGNERS & EDITORS GUIDE**
- ★ **SPECIAL EFFECTS & STUNTS GUIDE**
- ★ **TELEVISION WRITERS GUIDE**

Forthcoming guides:
- ★ **TELEVISION DIRECTORS GUIDE**
- ★ **FILM COMPOSERS GUIDE**
- ★ **FILM ACTORS GUIDE**

LONE EAGLE PUBLISHING CO
9903 Santa Monica Blvd.
Beverly Hills, CA 90212
213/471-8066 or
1/800-FILMBKS (exept California)

CALLING ALL CREDITS!

The Ninth Annual International Edition of **Michael Singer's FILM DIRECTORS: A Complete Guide** is now in preparation. It will be published in Fall 1991. We update our records continuously. If you are a director and you qualify to be listed (please read the Introduction for qualifications), then send us your listing information **ASAP. Photocopy the form on the next page.**

Our editorial deadline is May 1, 1991.

(Please do not wait until then.)

Send all film directors listing information to:

**Michael Singer's
FILM DIRECTORS: A Complete Guide
2015 Vista Del Mar Avenue
Los Angeles, CA 90068
213/471-8066 or 1/800-FILMBKS**

If you are a writer (film or television), a television director, film actor, film composer, cinematographer, production designer, costume designer, editor, agent, producer or studio executive, special effects or stunts coordinator and want to find out about getting listed in our other directories, call **213/471-8066** or **1/800-FILMBKS** or write to:

**LONE EAGLE PUBLISHING CO
9903 Santa Monica Blvd. #204
Beverly Hills, CA 90212**

★★★

The
NINTH ANNUAL INTERNATIONAL EDITION
of
Michael Singer's
FILM DIRECTORS: A Complete Guide

DON'T BE LEFT OUT!!! Guarantee your *FREE* listing (for qualified directors)
by filling out and returning this form to us *IMMEDIATELY.*
(Photocopy as many times as necessary).

DIRECTOR'S INFORMATION

Name

Company

Address

City/State/Zip

Area Code/Phone

Birth Date & Place

Home ❑   Business ❑

PLEASE PRINT OR TYPE

REPRESENTATIVE'S INFORMATION

Agent ❑   Personal Manager ❑   Attorney ❑
Business Manager ❑   Other ❑   DGA ❑
(List as many representatives as you would like. Continue listing on reverse, if necessary.)

Name

Company

Address

City/State/Zip

Area Code/Telephone

PLEASE PRINT OR TYPE

List your credits as follows: Please note alternate (or foreign) titles in parentheses. "French," "British," etc., should be noted for foreign films. Also, please note Academy or Emmy nominations/awards for Best Director. If you need more space, please continue on reverse side.

FEATURES: CROSSED SWORDS (THE PRINCE AND THE PAUPER)   Warner Bros., 1978, British
TELEFEATURES: THE KAREN CARPENTER STORY (TF)   Weintraub Entertainment Group, 1989

Mail form *IMMEDIATELY* to:
Michael Singer's
FILM DIRECTORS:
A COMPLETE GUIDE (9th Edition)
2015 Vista Del Mar Avenue
Los Angeles, CA 90068

Questions ???
Problems ???
Call 213/471-8066

We couldn't have said it better ourselves...

If you ever get muddled on director's credits (who hasn't?), there's one book truly worthy of being called a "must," namely "Film Directors: A Complete Guide." It's an elephantine volume...compiled and edited by Michael Singer, and now out in its sixth annual edition, and best one so far. Like the earlier Singer deliveries, this one is a lulu, chock-full of screen credits of every working director from Paul Aaron to Edward Zwick, listed both by the director's name and by film title. Want to know who directed "Dynamite Chicken"? Want to know Oliver Stone's first film? It's all there, including, for the first time, a separate section with the full credits of 180 deceased directors, allowing one also a quick reference to the full body of screen work by everyone from the late Ernst Lubitsch (including his numerous German-made features) to Charles Laughton (who directed only one film, the excellent 1955 "The Night of the Hunter")... By Singer's own admission, "It's primarily aimed for industrites, including actors who might want to check out a director's credits before a reading or a meeting. But I think it also offers a lot of fun for anyone who's just crazy about the movies." Indeed it does. Singer's even included a full listing of all the screen credits of Alan Smithee (that's the pseudonym designed by the DGA for members who want to remove their real names from the credits of a film). And among other oddities there's the director, one of the best, who guided a 1973 Fox film under the pseudonym of "Bill Sampson"; that, of course, was the name of the fictional director in the Oscar-winning "all About Eve." Singer's book includes his real identity.

More on "Film Directors": A valuable thing about Michael singer's book is the fact it doesn't encompass just selected credits but each director's full portfolio, warts and all. This year's volume includes at leat 300 new additions as well as one major corrected omission from past volumes: Richard Thorpe, director of some 177 films in his heyday, and still very much alive. (Says Singer, who's also a publicist at Fox, "I'm embarrassed but I'd thought he was dead. But I talked to him on the phone and he's 92 now and sounds just as feisty as you'd expect the director of movies like 'Ivanhoe' and 'Jailhouse Rock' would be. He told me he didn't want to be interviewed anymore. He said, 'I'm too old to go over all that old stuff. I'll just let the work speak for itself.'") ...Singer's book, done with major help from Joan-Carrol Baron, also speaks for itself, and deserves a spot on anyone's bookshelf. As an invaluable reference, it's at the head of the class.

Robert Osborne
The Hollywood Reporter
August 1988

TO ORDER YOUR COPIES
Send **$59.95** plus $5.50 postage/handling (UPS) for first copy
and $3.00 for each additional copy.
Inquire for foreign shipping rates.
California residents must add $4.05 tax per book.

Use the handy post-paid order form in the front of the book,
or send order and payment to:

**LONE EAGLE PUBLISHING CO
9903 Santa Monica Blvd. #204
Beverly Hills, CA 90212
213/471-8066 or 1/800-FILMBKS (outside California)**

552

READ IT FIRST.

THE PRODUCTION MAGAZINE

8455 Beverly Boulevard, Suite 508, Los Angeles, California 90048 (213) 653-8053 Fax (213) 653-8190

Ask for *Lone Eagle* books at these fine bookstores.

AIVF
PUBLICATIONS

The
largest list of
books and tapes on
media production, for independents,
available by mail
or in person
in the U.S.

To receive a complete list, write or call us at 212 473 3400.
AIVF Publications, 625 Broadway, New York, NY 10012

The
DRAMA
BOOK SHOP,
Inc.

Specializing in Published Plays, Books on Film
and T.V. and Books on Every Aspect of the
Performing Arts.
Phone and Mail Orders Welcome.

Incorporated 1923

723 Seventh Ave., New York, NY
10019 Phone (212) 944-0595
Open 7 Days a Week.

When in **New York**, ask for **Lone Eagle books**
at these fine bookstores:
Applause, Coliseum Books, Barnes & Noble, **AIVF (*see advertisement*)**,
Drama Books (*see advertisement*),
and Shakespeare & Co.

Ask for *Lone Eagle* books at these fine bookstores.

Portrait Of A Bookstore

THEATRE, FILM
INTERNATIONAL BOOKS
SERVING THE
ENTERTAINMENT
INDUSTRY

**(818) 769-3853 10061 Riverside Drive
Toluca Lake, CA 91602**

"More reasons to love California."
Gentleman's Quarterly

**LARRY EDMUNDS
CINEMA & THEATRE BOOKSTORE**
6644 Hollywood Boulevard
LosAngeles, CA 90028 • 213/463-3273

SAMUEL FRENCH
THEATRE & FILM BOOKSHOPS

*PLAYS, and BOOKS on FILM, THEATRE
and the MOTION PICTURE INDUSTRY*

Business of Film
Screenplays
Screenwriting
Television
Video
Cinematography
Directing
Acting
Industry Directories
Animation
Special Effects
Biographies
Theory and History
and more

Samuel French, Inc.
*Play Publishers and
Authors Representatives*
Founded 1830 • Incorporated 1899

7623 Sunset Blvd.
(5 blks east of Fairfax)
Hollywood, CA 90046
(213) 876-0570

11963 Ventura Blvd.
(1 blk east of Laurel Cyn)
Studio City, CA 91604
(818) 762-0535

WORLDWIDE MAIL ORDER
(800) 8-ACT NOW (US)
(800) 7-ACT NOW (CA)
FAX (213) 876-8622

FILM BOOK CATALOGUE
(available on request)

If you would like information regarding
advertising in any of our Lone Eagle directories,
please contact:

Lori Copeland
Advertising Director
Lone Eagle Publishing Co.
Tel: 213/471-8066
Toll Free: 1/800-FILMBKS
FAX: 213/471-4969

BOOKS
For Film/TV
Now Over 350 Titles

• Pre-Production
• Animation
• Cinematography
• Production
• Video and TV
• Special Effects
• Directories
• Audio
• Writing, Directing
and Performing
• 14 categories

Write or call today for free #8 catalog:

ALAN GORDON ENTERPRISES, INC.
1430 Cahuenga Blvd., Hollywood, CA 90028
TEL: (213) 466-3561 • FAX: 213-871-2193

When in **the Los Angeles area**, ask for **Lone Eagle books**
at these fine bookstores:
Birns & Sawyer, Book Soup, Brentano's,
Crown Books (various locations including Westwood Village, Hollywood & Brentwood),
Dutton's (Valley), **Larry Edmunds** (*see advertisement*) , Elliott Katt Bookseller,
Samuel French (*see advertisement*), **Portrait of a Bookstore** (*see advertisement*),
Waldenbooks, and World Book & News.

NOTES

INDEX OF ADVERTISERS

A special thanks to our new and continued advertisers whose support makes it possible for us to bring you this *Eighth Annual International Edition* of **Michael Singer's FILM DIRECTORS: A Complete Guide.**

EDITOR/COMPILER

MICHAEL SINGER has worked in motion pictures for seventeen years as a writer, unit publicist, studio staff publicist, producer's aide, director's assistant, story analyst, researcher and journalist.

A native of New York City, he has resided in Los Angeles for 11 years...and is *still* breathing!